PC

INTERRUPTS

PC
INTERRUPTS

A PROGRAMMER'S REFERENCE TO
BIOS, DOS, AND THIRD-PARTY CALLS

RALF BROWN & JIM KYLE

Addison-Wesley Publishing Company, Inc.
Reading, Massachusetts   Menlo Park, California   New York
Don Mills, Ontario   Wokingham, England   Amsterdam   Bonn
Sydney   Singapore   Tokyo   Madrid   San Juan
Paris   Seoul   Mexico City   Taipei

Managing Editor: Amorette Pedersen
Set in 9-point Times-Roman by Benchmark Productions

1 2 3 4 5 6 7 8 9-HA-9594939291
First Printing, October 1991

ISBN: 0-201-57797-6

Table of Contents

Introduction

The IBM PC and compatibles form the largest portion of the computer market, and likely will continue to do so for the remainder of the decade. The MS-DOS operating system for IBM PCs is the most popular ever developed, and the large sales of the recently released MS-DOS 5.0 prove that it will remain so for some time. Because the architecture of the IBM PC allows programs to provide services to other programs via software interrupts, and MS-DOS provides a mechanism for retaining programs in memory in order to continue providing such services, hundreds of software vendors have extended the basic set of services in often incompatible ways. As more programs provide additional interrupt calls, the probability of conflict between different programs increases.

Over the years, literally dozens of books have been written which include reference sections detailing the ROM BIOS services built into IBM PCs, and the additional services provided by MS-DOS. Some also cover the Expanded Memory Specification (EMS) services, but few go beyond that.

Thus, programmers have been forced to accumulate information about additional interrupt services piecemeal—one document covering one specification, another a second, and an electronic bulletin-board message a third. With such a collection of sources, it can be quite difficult to determine that two programs are incompatible because they expect different services from the same interrupt call.

This book is a comprehensive collection of the varied calls which have been implemented by various programs over the years. It includes all calls for some 25 major application programming interfaces and dozens of resident utilities (including shareware programs and undocumented interfaces), as well as the usual coverage of BIOS and MS-DOS services. Because of the number of different calls covered (nearly 2800), there is no room for detailed discussions or sample code.

PC Interrupts is designed to be a reference, not a tutorial. It will form a companion to any texts covering MS-DOS or the IBM PC which you may already own. In addition to its main purpose as a programming reference, you may also find it valuable as a tool to help you track down undesirable interactions between various programs running on the same PC.

The material presupposes some familiarity with programming using software interrupts, although there is no need to know a particular programming language. Software interrupts may be invoked from most high-level languages for the IBM PC as well as assembler, and most books on those languages cover interrupts at least briefly.

Interrupts and the '86 CPU Family

While this book is intended as a reference rather than as a tutorial, so many different partial listings of interrupt usage have been published, each using its own vocabulary and assumptions, that it is necessary to take a few pages up front to present an overview of the subject. This section briefly describes the basic interrupt concept as implemented in the Intel 80x86 family of processor.

The Intel 80x86 family of processors all provide the capability of servicing a maximum of 256 distinct interrupt actions, by means of a table of 256 four-byte interrupt vectors. This table occupies the first 1024 bytes of the RAM address space. Each vector consists of a 32-bit address, in standard Segment:Offset format, of the routine that will be called automatically in response to the corresponding interrupt.

The interrupt request that triggers the calling of such a routine can be generated in any of three ways: it can be internally generated by the processor chip itself, it can be created by an external interrupt request signal (called INTR by Intel), or it can be the result of a software interrupt (INT) instruction.

The original members of this processor family, the 8086 and 8088, dedicated only the first five interrupt vectors (INT 00h through INT 04h) to serving internally generated interrupts, although Intel clearly warned all users of the chips that the remaining 27 of the first 32 interrupts were reserved for future use. IBM chose to ignore that warning in the design of the PC, and assigned INT 05h to the print-screen action, while using the upper 24 of the 32 reserved interrupts for communication with hardware devices and BIOS. Of these 24 vectors, the first eight were assigned to deal with external device interrupts (INT 08h through 0Fh, for IRQ0 through 7 respectively). The remaining 16 provided, via software INT requests, standardized interfaces to the BIOS routines.

When the next version of the processor, the 80186, appeared, problems ensued. Trade journals reported that the conflict between IBM's use of the reserved locations, and Intel's subsequent assignment of them, were the reason that no IBM machine used the 80186, but this was never publicly confirmed. However the following chip, the 80286, was more restrained in its assignment of interrupt actions. Subsequent designs have followed its lead; all of the first 32 locations now have internal actions assigned for at least some versions of the processor family, but all remain compatible with MS-DOS usage.

So far as the processor's actions are concerned, there is almost no difference between an interrupt caused by one of the sources and another caused by any other. The only significant difference is that external interrupts automatically disable response to additional external interrupt requests, while software interrupts do not.

Some Words of Caution

Much of the information in this book is undocumented, and has therefore been determined by tracing calls and by trial-and-error experiments. Such undocumented information may be inaccurate, incomplete, highly version-dependent, or have any mix of these attributes. You should take care when attempting to use any calls marked as "internal" or "undocumented", or containing a large amount of italicized text (signifying its questionable or incomplete nature). Further, you should use documented equivalents whenever possible, even if the undocumented call is simpler or faster.

Version information has been included in many function descriptions; note, however, that this information represents only the version limits that we (or our contributors) were able to verify. Especially in the case of third-party software, any function may well have been present but undetected in versions earlier than those listed. And open-ended items such as "Version 2.1+" (meaning "all versions equal to or newer than 2.1") may have a hidden upper limit imposed by changes not reported to us before this information went to press.

Sample Entry

To illustrate some of the aspects of the entries in this book which may not be self-explanatory, we present a mythical function followed by explanations of various parts of the entry.

INTERRUPT FFh - Function 0Fh
GET GONKULATOR SETTINGS

Purpose: Determine the current or default options for the gonkulator.

Available on: XYZZY models 17 and 23 only.

Restrictions: FROB.SYS must be installed.

Registers at call:

AH = 0Fh

AL = subfunction

   01h get default settings

   02h get current settings

ES:DI - > settings table (Table 99-1)

Return Registers:

CF clear if successful

   CX = number of times settings have been modified

   since startup

ES:DI buffer filled

CF set on error

   AX = error code (02h,FFh) (see Function 00h)

Details: The link farm directory is the location for the write-only memory, among other things.

Conflicts: DIDDLE.SYS (chapter 42)

See Also: Function 0Eh, DIDDLE.SYS INT FEh Function 02h (chapter 42)

Table 99-1. Format of Settings Table:

Offset	Size	Description
00h	WORD	heartbeat frequency in Hertz
02h	BYTE	feeper duration
03h	BYTE	feeper pitch

Table 99-1. Format of Settings Table (continued)

Offset	Size	Description
04h	DWORD	microfortnights between pings
08h	64 BYTEs	link farm directory name

Explanations

Following the heading which indicates the interrupt number, function number, and subfunction number (if applicable) along with the function name, each entry has a number of fields. **Available on** usually specifies the system or hardware which provides the call, but occasionally indicates the operating system or environment instead. Both **Registers at call** and **Return Registers** may have multiple mutually-exclusive cases, which are indicated by indentation. Thus, for this example, the call modifies CX and the user's buffer if the carry flag is clear on return, but modifies AX instead if the carry flag is set.

The cross-references for **Conflicts** and **See Also** indicate which chapter contains the referenced call, unless it is in the current chapter. Thus, the example has two references to chapter 42, and one to the current chapter. **Conflicts** specifies calls that use the same interrupt and function; you would look in chapter 99 for interrupt FFh Function 0Fh (or, in some cases, simply interrupt FFh) in the section for DIDDLE.SYS if the chapter is divided into sections. For **See Also**, the interrupt number is omitted if it is the same as the interrupt for the current entry; thus, you would look up interrupt FFh, function 0Eh in the current chapter.

In all sections, information which is known to be incomplete or of questionable accuracy is italicized. This generally occurs only for undocumented calls.

About The Authors

Ralf Brown

Ralf Brown is a Ph.D. candidate in the School of Computer Science at Carnegie Mellon University, specializing in natural language understanding. He has delved into the innards of MS-DOS and IBM PC compatibles since early 1984, and is well known in the on-line community for maintaining the MS-DOS Interrupt List and authoring a number of useful free programs. He coauthored *Undocumented DOS* (Addison-Wesley 1990).

Jim Kyle

Jim Kyle has been a professional writer since 1948, and has published more than a dozen books and hundreds of magazine articles, including coauthoring *Undocumented DOS* (Addison-Wesley 1990). Kyle has been disassembling operating systems as a hobby since 1970 or so, on mainframes and minicomputers as well as microcomputers. He has been Primary Forum Administrator of the Computer Language forum on CompuServe since 1985. Kyle is currently one-quarter of the graphics development staff at Norick Software, Inc.

Acknowledgements

The information in this book has been adapted from a large freely available electronic listing, known as the MS-DOS Interrupt List, maintained by Ralf Brown and updated several times per year. The Interrupt List is available in many places, including but not limited to:

> CompuServe (IBM Programming Forum [GO IBMPRO],
> > Download Library 6)
>
> Internet (SIMTEL20 and its mirror sites such as
> > wuarchive.wustl.edu, where it resides in
> > /mirrors/msdos/info)
>
> BITNET (any of the SIMTEL20 mailsavers, such as
> > LISTER@RPIECS in the United States or
> > TRICKLE@DTUZDV1 in Germany)
>
> Fidonet (bulletin boards belonging to the programmer's
> > Distribution Network, as well as others)

The list is distributed under the filenames INTERrrA and INTERrrB, where rr is the release number (26 for the June, 1991 version to which this edition corresponds). Unlike *PC Interrupts*, the electronic listing is in purely numerical order and does not contain an index or glossary.

Chapter ▪ 1

Reference Section Organization

This brief listing shows which chapters describe functions for each of the 256 possible interrupts. Those referenced as "Chapter 1" are not discussed in detail and are shown only to make the list complete. Those referenced for more than one chapter probably have conflicts under some conditions.

Two areas in particular have a high probability of conflicts. The first is the multiplex interrupt, 2Fh, and the second is the user interrupts, 60h to 66h.

Interrupt 2Fh is shared by many programs, with the value of AH on call specifying the program which is to handle the call. As more programs use the multiplex interrupt to provide an interface to resident code, the probability of conflicting multiplex numbers (the value in AH) increases. While there is a standardized method for determining whether a particular multiplex number is in use, there is no standardized approach to determine whether a specific program is using it. Thus, a program may be fooled into thinking that it is already installed if a different program happens to be using the same multiplex number. Table 1-2 lists programs we have identified as using the multiplex interrupt, but it is almost certainly incomplete despite our best efforts.

We recommend the following steps for automatically avoiding conflicts of multiplex numbers on Interrupt 2Fh:
1. choose a range of multiplex numbers to search
2. implement a two-level installation check as described below
3. search the chosen range for multiplex numbers which are not in use, and a multiplex number which answers as installed to the second level of the installation check.

The first level of the two-level installation check consists of the standard AL=00h call/AL=FFh response. However, if additional registers have specific flag values on call, additional registers will be modified on return. Thus, product WXYZ may have the following installation check:

Call:	AH = multiplex number	**Return:**
	AL = 00h	AL = FFh
Call:	AH = multiplex number	**Return:**
	AL = 00h	AL = FFh
	BX = 5758h ('WX')	BX = 4F4Bh ('OK')
	CX = 595Ah ('YZ')	ES:DI - entry point

The first form of the call allows other programs to detect that the multiplex number is already in use, while not destroying registers in a nonstandard way. The second form allows a program to determine who is using the multiplex number. For an example of such a two-level installation check, see Interrupt 2Fh, Function DEh in chapter 15. Due to the number of programs now chaining Interrupt 2Fh, it is advisable to provide an entry point that may be called directly, bypassing the interrupt chain.

The multiplex installation checks for a number of existing programs modify registers other than AL—even without the presence of flag values on entry. Thus, any program which searches a range of multiplex numbers must be prepared for all registers except SS:SP in order to be destroyed by an attempted installation check.

The user interrupts 60h to 66h do not have a standard installation-check call, and thus require a different approach. However, the user interrupts are rarely chained, so a check whether the vector is 0000h:0000h suffices to determine if a particular interrupt is available. To determine whether the vector is in use by the program making the installation check, the usual approach is to place a signature string immediately prior to (or occasionally after) the interrupt handler. Table 1-3 lists programs we have identified as using this group of interrupts, but, like Table 1-2, it is almost certain to be incomplete and, even had it included all such programs when this volume went to press, it could not include any added subsequently.

A final area of conflict needs to be mentioned here, as it is the reason so few programs use interrupts 86h through F0h. These are used by the BASIC interpreter in the ROM of genuine IBM machines to allow extensions and tracing. The BASIC.COM and BASICA.COM extensions of the ROM Cassette BASIC set these vectors to handlers inside themselves at startup, but never restore them. Thus, any resident programs which have hooked any of these interrupts will lose them if the user runs an interpreted BASIC program. Worse, the vectors will be pointing at whatever code or data happened to be loaded into those locations since BASIC terminated, virtually guaranteeing a system crash. GWBASIC (the version for those without an IBM ROM containing BASIC) on the other hand, only uses interrupts EFh and F0h, and restores those vectors on exit.

Table 1-1. Master Reference List

INT	Chap	Description
00	2	CPU-generated
01	2	CPU-generated
02	2	external hardware, HP 95LX
03	2	CPU-generated,
	36	Soft-ICE
04	2	CPU-generated
05	2	CPU-generated,
	3	Print Screen
06	2	CPU-generated,
	4	HP 95LX
07	2	CPU-generated
08	2	CPU-generated, IRQ0
09	2	CPU-generated, IRQ1
0A	2	CPU-generated, LPT2 (PC), Roland MPU MIDI interface, Tandy 1000 Hard Disk, Vertical Retrace Interrupt
0B	2	COM2, CPU-generated, HP 95LX
0C	2	COM1, CPU-generated,
	26	IBM System 36/38 Workstation Emulation
0D	2	CPU-generated, Fixed Disk (PC,XT), LPT2 (AT), Tandy 1000 60 Hz RAM Refresh, HP 95LX, reserved (PS/2)
0E	2	CPU-generated, Diskette Controller, HP 95LX
0F	2	Parallel Printer, HP 95LX
10	2	CPU-generated,
	5	BIOS Window Extension v1.1, DESQview Video, Direct Graphics Interface Standard (DGIS), EGA Register Interface Library, Everex Extended Video BIOS, FRIEZE, UltraVision, VESA SuperVGA BIOS, VIDEO, VUIMAGE Display Driver,
	9	GO32 DOS extender,
	15	TopView,
	18	Alloy 386/MultiWare,
	28	Carbon Copy Plus,
	36	FASTBUFF.COM, SCROLOCK.COM
11	2	CPU-generated,
	3	Get Equipment List,
	7	BNU FOSSIL,
	17	BACK&FORTH
12	3	Get Memory Size,
	17	BACK&FORTH

Table 1-1. Master Reference List (Continued)

INT	Chap	Description
13	6	Disk, ESDI Fixed Disk, Floppy Disk, Future Domain SCSI Controller, Hard Disk, HyperDisk, IBMCACHE.SYS, PC-CACHE, Priam EDVR.SYS, QCACHE, SWBIOS, Super PC Kwik
14	5	Video FOSSIL,
	7	3com BAPI Serial I/O, COURIERS.COM, FOSSIL (Fido/Opus/Seadog Standard Interface Level), IBM/Yale EBIOS Serial I/O, Interconnections Inc. TES, Serial I/O,
	16	MultiDOS Plus IODRV
	18	Alloy 386/MultiWare
15	3	Cassette, Joystick Support, OS Hooks, System functions, Wait functions,
	4	Amstrad PC1512, Compaq machines, EISA System ROM, Phoenix 386 BIOS,
	6	ESDI Formatting,
	8	PRINT.COM,
	9	DOS/16M,
	15	DESQview, TopView,
	16	MultiDOS Plus,
	17	Omniview Multitasker, VMiX
16	3	Keyboard,
	4	Compaq machines,
	5	Paint Tools,
	6	PC-Cache,
	14	MS Windows,
	27	Shamrock Software EMAIL,
	28	pcANYWHERE III,
	33	PC Tools BACKTALK, PC Tools DESKTOP, PC Tools PCShell, PC Tools PCRUN,
	36	FAKEY.COM, KBUF, MAKEY.COM, Microsoft Word, PC Magazine PUSHDIR.COM, TurboPower TSRs, WATCH.COM
17	3	Printer,
	18	Allow NTNX and 386/MultiWare,
	27	NorthNet Jetstream, Shamrock Software NET.24,
	36	FLASHUP.COM, INSET, PC Magazine PCSpool, SPEEDSCR.COM
18	3	Start Cassette BASIC
19	3	Bootstrap Loader
1A	3	PCjr, Time,
	4	AT&T 6300,
	36	Disk Spool II, Word Perfect,
1B	3	Control-Break Handler
1C	3	System Timer Tick
1D	5	Video Parameter Tables
1E	6	Diskette Parameters
1F	5	8x8 graphics font
20	8	DOS,
	36	Minix
21	6	NewSpace, PC Tools PC-CACHE, PCMag PCMANAGE/DCOMPRESS, Stacker, SMARTDRV.SYS
	8	MS-DOS, Concurrent DOS, DOS + Microsoft Networks, DR DOS, STARLITE architecture,

Table 1-1. Master Reference List (Continued)

INT	Chap	Description
21 (cont.)	9	OS/286, OS/386, OS/386 VMM, Phar Lap 386/DOS-Extender, Phar Lap 386/DOS-Extender VMM,
	15	DESQview,
	17	CTask, DoubleDOS,
	20	Novell NetWare,
	21	LANtastic Network,
	22	Banyan VINES,
	26	Attachmate Extra, IBM System 36/38 Workstation Emulation,
	27	LAN Manager Enhanced, LANstep, Network Driver Interface Specification, Topware Network Operating System,
	28	pcANYWHERE IV,
	34	F-DRIVER.SYS, miscellaneous viruses
	36	CED (Command EDitor), DOSED, ELRES, HIGHUMM.SYS, LASTBYTE.SYS, TAME, WCED, WILDUNIX.COM
22	8	DOS
23	8	DOS
24	8	DOS
25	6	Stacker
	8	DOS
26	8	DOS
27	8	DOS
28	8	DOS 2+
29	8	DOS 2+
2A	21	LANtastic Network,
	26	IBM PC 3270 Emulation Program,
	27	AT&T Starlan Extended NetBIOS, Microsoft Networks, NETBIOS
2B	8	DOS 2+
2C	8	DOS 2+, STARLITE architecture,
	14	MS Windows???
2D	8	DOS 2+
2E	8	Pass Command to Command Interpreter for Execution, 4DOS SHELL2E.COM
2F	5	SCRNSAV2.COM,
	6	AUTOPARK.COM, HyperDisk,
	7	AVATAR Serial Dispatcher,
	8	ANSI.SYS, APPEND, ASSIGN, COMMAND.COM, DISPLAY.SYS, DOS 3+ Critical Error Handler, DOS 3+ internal, DOS 5.0 kernel, DOSKEY, DOSSHELL, DRIVER.SYS support, EGA.SYS, GRAPHICS.COM, GRAFTABL.COM, IFSFUNC.EXE, KEYB.COM, NLSFUNC.COM, OS/2 compatibility box, PRINT.COM, SHARE, SHELLB.COM, Task Switcher, XMA2EMS.SYS
	9	Borland DOS extender, Ergo DOS extenders, Generic DOS extender installation check, Phar Lap DOS extenders,
	10	XMS,
	11	Borland DPMI Loader, DOS Protected-Mode Interface,
	14	MS WINDOWS, MS WINDOWS "WINOLDAP",
	15	DESQview 2.26 External Device Interface, Quarterdeck MANIFEST, Quarterdeck QEMM/QRAM, Quarterdeck VIDRAM,

Table 1-1. Master Reference List (Continued)

INT	Chap	Description
2F (cont.)	19	CDROM, MSCDEX (MS CD-ROM Extensions), Network Redirector, PC LAN Program REDIR.SYS, PC Network RECEIVER.COM,
	20	Novell NetWare, Novell ODI Link Support Layer (LSL.COM),
	21	LANtastic Network,
	22	Banyan VINES,
	26	IBM PC3270 Emulation Program,
	27	EASY-NET, LAN Manager Enhanced, Topware Network Operating System,
	28	LapLink Quick Connect, TeleReplica,
	29	Communicating Applications Specification,
	30	Intel Image Processing Interface,
	34	F-PROT, TBSCANX, ThunderByte,
	36	4DOS, ANARKEY, AVATAR.SYS, BMB Compuscience Canada Utilities Interface, GOLD.COM, InnerMission, MDEBUG, Norton Utilities, RAID, RESPLAY, SoftCom programs, SWELL.EXE, TRAP.COM, TesSeRact RAM-resident program interface, VIDCLOCK.COM, WHOA!.COM
30	8	(NOT A VECTOR!) FAR JMP instruction for CP/M-style calls
31	8	overwritten by CP/M jump instruction in 30,
	11	DOS Protected-Mode Interface
32	34	reportedly used by "Tiny" Viruses
33	13	Logitech Mouse, Microsoft Mouse, PCMOUSE Mouse
34	35	Borland/Microsoft languages, Floating Point emulation
35	35	Borland/Microsoft languages, Floating Point emulation
36	35	Borland/Microsoft languages, Floating Point emulation
37	35	Borland/Microsoft languages, Floating Point emulation
38	35	Borland/Microsoft languages, Floating Point emulation
39	35	Borland/Microsoft languages, Floating Point emulation
3A	35	Borland/Microsoft languages, Floating Point emulation
3B	35	Borland/Microsoft languages, Floating Point emulation
3C	35	Borland/Microsoft languages, Floating Point emulation
3D	35	Borland/Microsoft languages, Floating Point emulation
3E	35	Borland languages, Floating Point emulation "shortcut" call
3F	35	Microsoft Dynamic Link Library manager, Overlay manager interrupt
40	2	Z100 Master 8259,
	6	ROM BIOS Diskette Handler Relocated by Hard Disk BIOS
41	2	Z100 Master 8259,
	6	Hard Disk 0 Parameter Table
42	2	Z100 Master 8259,
	5	Video (EGA,VGA)
43	2	Z100 Master 8259,
	5	Video Character Table
44	2	Z100 Master 8259,
	5	PCjr BIOS Character Font,
	20	Novell NetWare High-Level Language API,
	26	IBM 3270-PC High Level Language API
45	2	Z100 Master 8259

Table 1-1. Master Reference List (Continued)

INT	Chap	Description
46	2	Z100 Master 8259,
	6	Hard Disk 1 Drive Parameter Table
47	2	Z100 Master 8259,
	36	SQL Base
48	2	Z100 Slave 8259,
	3	Keyboard (PCjr)
49	2	Z100 Slave 8259,
	3	Scan-Code Translation (PCjr),
	4	Texas Instruments PC Video
	36	MAGic
4A	2	Z100 Slave 8259,
	3	User Alarm Handler
4B	2	Z100 Slave 8259,
	6	Common Access Method SCSI interface, IBM SCSI interface,
	12	Virtual DMA Specification (VDS)
4C	2	Z100 Slave 8259
4D	2	Z100 Slave 8259
4E	2	Z100 Slave 8259,
	6	TI Professional PC - DISK I/O
4F	2	Z100 Slave 8259,
	6	Common Access Method SCSI interface
50	2	IRQ0 relocated by DESQview, IBM 3278 emulator, and OS/2
	27	TIL Xpert AIM (X.25)
51	2	IRQ1 relocated by DESQview, IBM 3278 emulator, and OS/2
52	2	IRQ2 relocated by DESQview, IBM 3278 emulator, and OS/2
53	2	IRQ3 relocated by DESQview, IBM 3278 emulator, and OS/2
54	2	IRQ4 relocated by DESQview, IBM 3278 emulator, and OS/2
55	2	IRQ5 relocated by DESQview, IBM 3278 emulator, and OS/2
56	2	IRQ6 relocated by DESQview, IBM 3278 emulator, and OS/2
57	2	IRQ7 relocated by DESQview, IBM 3278 emulator, and OS/2
58	2	IRQ0 relocated by DoubleDOS, IRQ8 relocated by DESQview 2.26+
59	2	IRQ1 relocated by DoubleDOS, IRQ9 relocated by DESQview 2.26+,
	5	GSS Computer Graphics Interface (GSS*CGI)
5A	2	IRQ10 relocated by DESQview 2.26+, IRQ2 relocated by DoubleDOS,
	27	Cluster adapter BIOS entry address
5B	2	IRQ11 relocated by DESQview 2.26+, IRQ3 relocated by DoubleDOS,
	18	Alloy NTNX,
	27	AT&T Starlan Extended NetBIOS, Microsoft Network Transport Layer Interface, cluster adapter
5C	2	IRQ12 relocated by DESQview 2.26+, IRQ4 relocated by DoubleDOS
	27	$25 LAN, ATALK.SYS, IBM 802.2 Interface (LLC), NetBIOS Interface, TOPS Interface
5D	2	IRQ13 relocated by DESQview 2.26+, IRQ5 relocated by DoubleDOS
5E	2	IRQ14 relocated by DESQview 2.26+, IRQ6 relocated by DoubleDOS
5F	2	IRQ15 relocated by DESQview 2.26+, IRQ7 relocated by DoubleDOS,
	4	HP 95LX

Table 1-1. Master Reference List (Continued)

INT	Chap	Description
60	1	reserved for user interrupt,
	4	Atari Portfolio, HP 95LX,
	6	Adaptec and OMTI controllers,
	22	Banyan VINES, 3com,
	23	10-NET,
	26	Tangram Arbiter,
	27	FTP Packet Driver,
	34	Zero Bug Virus,
	35	JPI TopSPEED Modula-2
	36	INTRSPY/CMDSPY API, MDEBUG, PC-IPC API, PC/370, SYS_PROF.EXE
61	1	reserved for user interrupt,
	4	Atari Portfolio, HP 95LX,
	6	Adaptec and OMTI controllers,
	22	Banyan VINES,
	26	Sangoma CCIP (CCPOP 3270 resident module) Interface,
	27	FTP Software PC/TCP
	35	JPI TopSPEED Modula-2
62	1	reserved for user interrupt,
	6	Adaptec and OMTI controllers,
	17	Cswitch,
	27	MS SQL Server/Sybase DBLIBRARY interface
63	1	reserved for user interrupt,
	6	4+Power Floppy Controller, Adaptec and OMTI controllers,
	9	Oracle SQL Protected Mode Executive
64	1	reserved for user interrupt, Data General DG10,
	6	Adaptec controllers,
	9	Oracle SQL Protected Mode Executive,
	20	Novell NetWare,
	36	Extended Batch Language v3.14+
65	1	reserved for user interrupt, Data General DG10,
	6	Adaptec controllers,
	27	FTP Software NDIS-Packet Driver adapter,
	36	Ad Lib SOUND.COM, SD.COM v6.2
66	1	reserved for user interrupt, Data General DG10,
	6	Adaptec controllers,
	36	The IBM Digitized Sound Package, MicroHelp Stay-Res/Stay-Res Plus
67	6	Adaptec controllers,
	10	EEMS, LIM EMS, Virtual Control Program Interface,
	18	Alloy NTNX (see PC-Net in chapter 27)
	26	Sangoma CCPOP 3270 resident module,
	27	PC-Net
68	25	APPC/PC,
	26	Sangoma CCPOP 3270 resident module
69	4	Zenith AT BIOS,
	24	DECnet DOS CTERM
6A	24	DECnet DOS Local Area Transport,
	36	OPTHELP.COM

Table 1-1. Master Reference List (Continued)

INT	Chap	Description
6B	20	Novell NASI/NACS,
	27	Ungermann-Bass Net One SERIAL I/O,
	34	"Saddam" virus,
	36	Tandy SCHOOLMATE PLUS
6C	3	system resume vector (Convertible),
	8	DOS 3.2 Realtime Clock update
6D	5	ATI VGA Wonder, VGA,
	24	DECnet DOS
6E	24	DECnet DOS
6F	4	HP ES-12 Extended BIOS,
	20	Novell NetWare,
	23	10-NET
	70	2 IRQ8 - CMOS Real-Time Clock,
	34	"stupid" virus
71	2	IRQ9 - Redirected to 0A by BIOS
72	2	IRQ10 - Reserved
73	2	IRQ11 - Reserved
74	2	IRQ12 - Pointing Device
75	2	IRQ13 - Math Coprocessor Exception
76	2	IRQ14 - Hard Disk Controller
77	2	IRQ15 - Power Conservation (Compaq),
	2	IRQ15 - RESERVED (AT,PS)
78	9	DBOS,
	36	TARGA.DEV
79	36	AVATAR.SYS
7A	20	Novell NetWare Low-Level API (IPX) Driver,
	26	IBM 3270 Workstation Program API, IBM Personal Communications/3270,
	27	Topware Network Operating System,
	36	AutoCAD Device Interface
7B	26	Eicon Access API (3270/5250 gateways),
	36	Btrieve API
7C	1	IBM REXX88PC command language
7D	1	not used
7E	1	DIP, Ltd. ROM Library
7F	5	Halo88, HDILOAD.EXE,
	17	MultiLink Advanced,
	18	Alloy 386/MultiWare, NTNX, and ANSK,
	26	HLLAPI (IBM 3270 High-Level Language API),
	27	Convergent Technologies ClusterShare CTOS Access Vector
80	1	reserved for BASIC,
	27	QPC Software PKTINT.COM,
	36	Q-PRO4, SoundBlaster SBFM
81	1	reserved for BASIC,
	27	IBM Token Ring Adapter
82	1	reserved for BASIC,
	27	IBM Token Ring Adapter

Table 1-1. Master Reference List (Continued)

INT	Chap	Description
83	1	reserved for BASIC
84	1	reserved for BASIC
85	1	reserved for BASIC
86	1	used by IBM ROM BASIC while in interpreter,
	27	NETBIOS - Original INT 18h,
	31	APL*PLUS/PC
87	1	used by IBM ROM BASIC while in interpreter,
	31	APL*PLUS/PC
88	1	used by IBM ROM BASIC while in interpreter,
	31	APL*PLUS/PC
89	1	used by IBM ROM BASIC while in interpreter
8A	1	used by IBM ROM BASIC while in interpreter,
	31	APL*PLUS/PC
8B	1	used by IBM ROM BASIC while in interpreter,
	31	APL*PLUS/PC
8C	1	used by IBM ROM BASIC while in interpreter,
	31	APL*PLUS/PC
8D	1	used by IBM ROM BASIC while in interpreter
8E	1	used by IBM ROM BASIC while in interpreter
8F	1	used by IBM ROM BASIC while in interpreter
90	1	used by IBM ROM BASIC while in interpreter,
	31	APL*PLUS/PC
91	1	used by IBM ROM BASIC while in interpreter,
	27	IBM TOKEN RING ADAPTER
92	1	used by IBM ROM BASIC while in interpreter,
	27	Sangoma X.25 Interface Program
93	1	used by IBM ROM BASIC while in interpreter,
	27	IBM Token Ring Adapter
94	1	used by IBM ROM BASIC while in interpreter
95	1	used by IBM ROM BASIC while in interpreter,
	31	APL*PLUS/PC
96	1	used by IBM ROM BASIC while in interpreter
97	1	used by IBM ROM BASIC while in interpreter
98	1	used by IBM ROM BASIC while in interpreter
99	1	used by IBM ROM BASIC while in interpreter
9A	1	used by IBM ROM BASIC while in interpreter
9B	1	used by IBM ROM BASIC while in interpreter
9C	1	used by IBM ROM BASIC while in interpreter
9D	1	used by IBM ROM BASIC while in interpreter
9E	1	used by IBM ROM BASIC while in interpreter
9F	1	used by IBM ROM BASIC while in interpreter
A0	1	used by IBM ROM BASIC while in interpreter,
	31	APL*PLUS/PC
A1	1	used by IBM ROM BASIC while in interpreter
A2	1	used by IBM ROM BASIC while in interpreter

Table 1-1. Master Reference List (Continued)

INT	Chap	Description
A3	1	used by IBM ROM BASIC while in interpreter
A4	1	used by IBM ROM BASIC while in interpreter,
	36	Right Hand Man API
A5	1	used by IBM ROM BASIC while in interpreter
A6	1	used by IBM ROM BASIC while in interpreter
A7	1	used by IBM ROM BASIC while in interpreter
A8	1	used by IBM ROM BASIC while in interpreter
A9	1	used by IBM ROM BASIC while in interpreter
AA	1	used by IBM ROM BASIC while in interpreter
AB	1	used by IBM ROM BASIC while in interpreter
AC	1	used by IBM ROM BASIC while in interpreter
AD	1	used by IBM ROM BASIC while in interpreter
AE	1	used by IBM ROM BASIC while in interpreter
AF	1	used by IBM ROM BASIC while in interpreter
B0	1	used by IBM ROM BASIC while in interpreter
B1	1	used by IBM ROM BASIC while in interpreter
B2	1	used by IBM ROM BASIC while in interpreter
B3	1	used by IBM ROM BASIC while in interpreter,
	32	ZIPKEY
B4	1	used by IBM ROM BASIC while in interpreter
B5	1	used by IBM ROM BASIC while in interpreter
B6	1	used by IBM ROM BASIC while in interpreter
B7	1	used by IBM ROM BASIC while in interpreter
B8	1	used by IBM ROM BASIC while in interpreter
B9	1	used by IBM ROM BASIC while in interpreter
BA	1	used by IBM ROM BASIC while in interpreter
BB	1	used by IBM ROM BASIC while in interpreter
BC	1	used by IBM ROM BASIC while in interpreter
BD	1	used by IBM ROM BASIC while in interpreter
BE	1	used by IBM ROM BASIC while in interpreter
BF	1	used by IBM ROM BASIC while in interpreter
C0	1	used by IBM ROM BASIC while in interpreter
C1	1	used by IBM ROM BASIC while in interpreter
C2	1	used by IBM ROM BASIC while in interpreter
C3	1	used by IBM ROM BASIC while in interpreter
C4	1	used by IBM ROM BASIC while in interpreter
C5	1	used by IBM ROM BASIC while in interpreter
C6	1	used by IBM ROM BASIC while in interpreter,
	31	APL*PLUS/PC
C7	1	used by IBM ROM BASIC while in interpreter,
	31	APL*PLUS/PC
C8	1	used by IBM ROM BASIC while in interpreter,
	31	APL*PLUS/PC

Table 1-1. Master Reference List (Continued)

INT	Chap	Description
C9	1	used by IBM ROM BASIC while in interpreter,
	31	APL*PLUS/PC
CA	1	used by IBM ROM BASIC while in interpreter,
	31	APL*PLUS/PC
CB	1	used by IBM ROM BASIC while in interpreter,
	31	APL*PLUS/PC
CC	1	used by IBM ROM BASIC while in interpreter,
	31	APL*PLUS/PC
CD	1	used by IBM ROM BASIC while in interpreter,
	31	APL*PLUS/PC
CE	1	used by IBM ROM BASIC while in interpreter,
	31	APL*PLUS/PC
CF	1	used by IBM ROM BASIC while in interpreter,
	31	APL*PLUS/PC
D0	1	used by IBM ROM BASIC while in interpreter,
	31	APL*PLUS/PC
D1	1	used by IBM ROM BASIC while in interpreter,
	31	APL*PLUS/PC
D2	1	used by IBM ROM BASIC while in interpreter,
	31	APL*PLUS/PC
D3	1	used by IBM ROM BASIC while in interpreter,
	31	APL*PLUS/PC
D4	1	used by IBM ROM BASIC while in interpreter, PC-MOS/386 API,
	31	APL*PLUS/PC
D5	1	used by IBM ROM BASIC while in interpreter,
	31	APL*PLUS/PC
D6	1	used by IBM ROM BASIC while in interpreter,
	31	APL*PLUS/PC
D7	1	used by IBM ROM BASIC while in interpreter,
	31	APL*PLUS/PC
D8	1	used by IBM ROM BASIC while in interpreter,
	31	APL*PLUS/PC
D9	1	used by IBM ROM BASIC while in interpreter,
	31	APL*PLUS/PC
DA	1	used by IBM ROM BASIC while in interpreter,
	31	APL*PLUS/PC
DB	1	used by IBM ROM BASIC while in interpreter,
	31	APL*PLUS/PC
DC	1	used by IBM ROM BASIC while in interpreter,
	31	APL*PLUS/PC,
	36	PC/370
DD	1	used by IBM ROM BASIC while in interpreter,
	31	APL*PLUS/PC
DE	1	used by IBM ROM BASIC while in interpreter,
	31	APL*PLUS/PC

Table 1-1. Master Reference List (Continued)

INT	Chap	Description
DF	1	used by IBM ROM BASIC while in interpreter,
	4	Victor 9000,
	31	APL*PLUS/PC
E0	1	used by IBM ROM BASIC while in interpreter,
	31	APL*PLUS/PC,
	34	"Micro-128" virus,
	36	CP/M-86 function calls
E1	1	used by IBM ROM BASIC while in interpreter, PC Cluster Disk Server Information
E2	1	used by IBM ROM BASIC while in interpreter, PC Cluster Program
E3	1	used by IBM ROM BASIC while in interpreter
E4	1	used by IBM ROM BASIC while in interpreter,
	35	Logitech Modula v2.0
E5	1	used by IBM ROM BASIC while in interpreter
E6	1	used by IBM ROM BASIC while in interpreter
E7	1	used by IBM ROM BASIC while in interpreter
E8	1	used by IBM ROM BASIC while in interpreter
E9	1	used by IBM ROM BASIC while in interpreter
EA	1	used by IBM ROM BASIC while in interpreter
EB	1	used by IBM ROM BASIC while in interpreter
EC	1	used by IBM ROM BASIC while in interpreter,
	18	Alloy NTNX,
	35	Exact Runtime Interface Multiplexor
ED	1	used by IBM ROM BASIC while in interpreter
EE	1	used by IBM ROM BASIC while in interpreter
EF	35	compiled BASIC, interpreted BASIC,
	36	GEM
F0	35	compiled BASIC, interpreted BASIC
F1	1	reserved for user interrupt,
	36	SPEECH.COM
F2	1	reserved for user interrupt
F3	1	reserved for user interrupt
F4	1	reserved for user interrupt,
	17	DoubleDOS
F5	1	reserved for user interrupt,
	17	DoubleDOS
F6	1	reserved for user interrupt,
	17	DoubleDOS
F7	1	reserved for user interrupt,
	17	DoubleDOS
F8	1	reserved for user interrupt,
	17	DoubleDOS
F9	1	reserved for user interrupt,
	17	DoubleDOS
FA	1	reserved for user interrupt,
	17	DoubleDOS

Table 1-1. Master Reference List (Continued)

INT	Chap	Description
FB	1	reserved for user interrupt,
	17	DoubleDOS
FC	1	reserved for user interrupt,
	17	DoubleDOS
FD	1	reserved for user interrupt,
	17	DoubleDOS
FE	1	destroyed by return to real mode on AT/XT286/PS50+,
	17	DoubleDOS
FF	1	destroyed by return to real mode on AT/XT286/PS50+,
	4	Z100 WARM BOOT

Table 1-2. Multiplex Interrupt Usage

Program	Low	Default	High	Selection
PRINT.COM	.	00h,01h	.	Fixed
PC LAN Program REDIR/REDIRIFS	.	02h	.	Fixed
DOS 3+ critical error messages	.	05h	.	Fixed
DOS 3+ ASSIGN	.	06h	.	Fixed
DOS 3+ DRIVER.SYS support	.	08h	.	Fixed
SHARE	.	10h	.	Fixed
Network redirector	.	11h	.	Fixed
MSCDEX	.	11h	.	Fixed
DOS 3+ internal utility functions	.	12h	.	Fixed
DOS 3.3+ disk interrupt handler	.	13h	.	Fixed
NLSFUNC	.	14h	.	Fixed
CDROM support	.	15h	.	Fixed
DOS 4.00 GRAPHICS.COM	.	15h	.	Fixed
MS Windows	.	16h	.	Fixed
MS Windows WINOLDAP	.	17h	.	Fixed
DOS 4.0x SHELLB.COM	.	19h	.	Fixed
DOS 4+ ANSI.SYS	.	1Ah	.	Fixed
AVATAR.SYS	.	1Ah	.	Fixed
DOS 4+ XMA2EMS.SYS	.	1Bh	.	Fixed
OS/2 compatibility box	.	40h	.	Fixed
LAN Manager 2.0 DOS Enhanced NETPOPUP	.	41h	.	Fixed
LAN Manager 2.0 DOS Enhanced MSRV	.	42h	.	Fixed
XMS	.	43h	.	Fixed
F-PROT utilities	.	46h	.	Fixed
MS Windows 3.0	.	46h	.	Fixed
DOS 5 HMA support	.	4Ah	.	Fixed
LAN Manager 2.0 DOS Enhanced NETWKSTA	.	4Bh	.	Fixed
DOS 5 task switchers	.	4Bh	.	Fixed
TesSeRact	.	54h	.	Fixed
DOS 5 COMMAND.COM interface	.	55h	.	Fixed
SCRNSAV2.COM	.	64h	.	Fixed
Novell NetWare IPX	.	7Ah	.	Fixed
PC/370	.	7Fh	.	Fixed
Easy-Net	.	80h	.	Fixed
RESPLAY	.	82h	.	Fixed
Whoa!.COM	.	89h	.	Fixed
RAID	.	90h	.	Fixed
InnerMission	.	93h	.	Fixed
Ergo DOS extenders	.	A1h	.	Fixed
VIDCLOCK.COM	.	AAh	.	Fixed
DOS 4.01+ GRAPHICS.COM	.	ACh	.	Fixed

Table 1-2. Multiplex Interrupt Usage (Continued)

Program	Low	Default	High	Selection
DISPLAY.SYS	.	ADh	.	Fixed
KEYB.COM	.	ADh	.	Fixed
DOS 3.3+ COMMAND.COM installable cmd	.	AEh	.	Fixed
GRAFTABL	.	B0h	.	Fixed
IBM PC3270 emulation program	.	B4h	.	Fixed
APPEND	.	B7h	.	Fixed
network	.	B8h	.	Fixed
PC Network RECEIVER.COM	.	B9h	.	Fixed
MS Windows 3.0 EGA.SYS	00h	BCh	FFh	Cmdline
PC LAN Program REDIRIFS	.	BFh	.	Fixed
Novell ODI Link Support Layer	C0h	C0h	FFh	Automatic
ThunderByte???	.	C9h	.	Fixed
TBSCANX	.	CAh	.	Fixed
Communicating Applications Spec	00h	CBh	FFh	Config
Intel Image Processing Interface	.	CDh	.	Fixed
SWELL	.	CDh	.	Fixed
MDEBUG display driver	C0h	D0h	FEh	Config,API
MDEBUG command driver	C1h	D1h	FFh	Config,API
Quarterdeck QEMM, QRAM, MFT	C0h	D2h	FFh	Automatic
TeleReplica	.	D3h	.	Fixed
LapLink Quick Connect	.	D3h	.	Fixed
4DOS	.	D4h	.	Fixed
Banyan VINES	.	D7h	.	Fixed
TRAP.COM	.	DAh	.	Fixed
GOLD.COM	.	DCh	.	Fixed
SoftCom programs	.	DDh	.	Fixed
DESQview External Device Interface	C0h	DEh	FFh	Automatic
HyperDisk v4.2+	.	DFh	.	Fixed
Anarkey	C0h	E3h	FFh	Cmdline
Phar Lap DOS extenders	.	EDh	.	Fixed
Generic DOS extender install check	.	F1h	.	Fixed
AUTOPARK.COM	.	F7h	.	Fixed
Borland International	.	FBh	.	Fixed
Norton Utilities	.	FEh	.	Fixed
Topware Network Operating System	.	FFh	.	Fixed
BMB Compuscience Canada utilities	00h	FFh	FFh	Automatic

Table 1-3. User Interrupt Usage

Program	60h	61h	62h	63h	64h	65h	66h	Selection
"Zero Bug" virus	D	.	.	.	.	.	.	Fixed
Atari Portfolio user interface	D	.	.	.	.	.	.	Fixed
SYS_PROF	D	.	.	.	.	.	.	Fixed
PC-IPC API	D	a	a	a	a	a	a	Cmdline
Tangram Arbiter API	D	a	a	a	a	a	a	Config
INTRSPY	D	a	a	a	a	a	a	Automatic
PC/370	D	a	a	a	a	a	a	Patch
FTP Packet Driver	D	a	a	a	a	a	a	Automatic
MDEBUG	D	a	a	a	a	a	a	Config
10-Net	D	.	.	.	.	.	.	Fixed
3com	D	.	.	.	.	.	.	Fixed
HP 95LX System Manager	D	D	.	.	.	.	.	Fixed
JPI TopSPEED Modula-2	D	D	.	.	.	.	.	Fixed
Atari Portfolio extended BIOS	.	D	.	.	.	.	.	Fixed
FTP Software TCP/IP	.	D	.	.	.	.	.	Fixed
Sangoma CCIP	.	D	.	.	.	.	.	Fixed
Banyan VINES	a	D	a	a	a	a	a	Config
MS SQL server	.	.	D	.	.	.	.	Fixed
Cswitch	.	.	D	.	.	.	.	Fixed
4+Power floppy controller	.	.	.	D	.	.	.	Fixed
Oracle SQL prot. mode executive	.	.	.	D	D	.	.	Fixed
Extended Batch Language	.	.	.	.	D	.	.	Fixed
FTP Software NDIS-Packet Driver	.	.	.	.	.	D	.	Fixed
SD.COM shareware version	.	.	.	.	.	D	.	Fixed
Ad Lib SOUND.COM	.	.	.	.	.	D	.	Fixed
DG10 MicroECLIPSE coproc i'face	.	.	.	.	.	D	D	Fixed
MicroHelp Stay-Res Plus	.	.	.	.	.	.	D	Fixed
IBM Digitized Sound Package	.	.	.	.	.	.	D	Fixed

Key: D = default interrupt
    a = alternate interrupt
    . = not usable by program

Chapter 2

Hardware Interrupts

This chapter describes hardware interrupts, including those generated internally by the CPU chip and those which arrive from external devices. Any interrupt signal described in this chapter may occur at any time.

INTERRUPT 00h
CPU-generated - DIVIDE ERROR

Purpose: Generated if the divisor of a DIV or IDIV instruction is zero or the quotient overflows the result register; DX and AX will be unchanged.

Available on: All machines.   **Restrictions:** none

Registers at call: n/a   **Return Registers:** n/a

Details: On an 8086/8088, the return address points to the instruction following the division instruction which caused the interrupt; on an 80286 or higher, the return address points to the beginning of the divide instruction (including any prefixes).

Conflicts: None known.

See Also: INT 04h

INTERRUPT 01h
CPU-generated - SINGLE STEP

Purpose: Used by debuggers for single-instruction execution tracing, such as MSDOS DEBUG's T command.

Available on: All machines.   **Restrictions:** none

Registers at call: n/a   **Return Registers:** n/a

Details: This interrupt is generated after each instruction if TF (trap flag) is set; TF is cleared on invoking the single-step interrupt handler. Interrupts are prioritized such that external interrupts are invoked after the INT 01h pushes CS:IP/FLAGS and clears TF, but before the first instruction of the handler executes.

Conflicts: None known.

See Also: INT 03h

INTERRUPT 01h
CPU-generated - DEBUGGING EXCEPTIONS

Purpose: Used by debuggers to halt program execution on any of a variety of conditions which may be detected by the CPU.

Available on: 80386 and above, when hardware   **Restrictions: none.**
                 debug registers are enabled.

Registers at call: n/a   **Return Registers: n/a**

Details: There are several different debugging traps:
  Instruction address breakpoint fault - will return to execute instruction
  Data address breakpoint trap - will return to the following instruction
  General detect fault, debug registers in use
  Task-switch breakpoint trap

Conflicts: None known.

See Also: INT 03h

INTERRUPT 02h
external hardware - NON-MASKABLE INTERRUPT

Purpose: Generated by the CPU when the input to the NMI pin is asserted.

Available on: All machines.   **Restrictions:** none.

Registers at call: n/a   **Return Registers:** n/a

Details: The return address for this interrupt points to the start of the interrupted instruction on the 80286 and higher. Although the Intel documentation states that this interrupt is typically used for power-failure procedures, it has many other uses on IBM-compatible machines:

> Memory parity error: all except Jr, CONV, and some machines without memory parity
> Breakout switch on hardware debuggers
> Coprocessor interrupt: all except PCjr and Convertible
> Keyboard interrupt: PCjr, Convertible
> I/O channel check: Convertible, PS models 50 and higher
> Disk-controller power-on request: Convertible
> System suspend: Convertible
> Real-time clock: Convertible
> System watch-dog timer, time-out interrupt: PS/2 models 50 and higher
> DMA timer time-out interrupt: PS/2 models 50 and higher
> Low battery: Hewlett-Packard HP 95LX
> Module pulled: HP 95LX

Conflicts: None known.

INTERRUPT 03h
CPU-generated - BREAKPOINT

Purpose: Generated by the one-byte breakpoint instruction (opcode CCh).

Available on: All machines.   **Restrictions:** none.

Registers at call: n/a   **Return Registers:** n/a

Details: Used by debuggers to implement breakpoints, such as MSDOS DEBUG's G command. The one-byte breakpoint instruction is also used by Turbo Pascal versions 1 through 3 when the $U+ compiler directive is specified. The return address points to the byte following the breakpoint instruction.

Conflicts: Soft-ICE Back Door commands (chapter 36).

See Also: INT 01h

INTERRUPT 04h
CPU-generated - INTO DETECTED OVERFLOW

Purpose: The INTO instruction will generate this interrupt if OF (Overflow Flag) is set; otherwise, INTO is effectively a NOP.

Available on: All machines.   **Restrictions:** none.

Registers at call: n/a   **Return Registers:** n/a

Details: May be used for convenient overflow testing (to prevent errors from propagating) instead of JO or a JNO/JMP combination.

See Also: INT 00h

INTERRUPT 05h
CPU-generated - BOUND RANGE EXCEEDED

Purpose: Generated by BOUND instruction when the value to be tested is less than the indicated lower bound or greater than the indicated upper bound.

Available on: 80186 and above.   **Restrictions:** none.

Registers at call: n/a   **Return Registers:** n/a

Details: Returning from this interrupt re-executes the failing BOUND instruction.

Conflicts: IBM PC BIOS Print Screen interrupt (Chapter 3).

INTERRUPT 06h
CPU-generated - INVALID OPCODE

Purpose: Generated when the CPU attempts to execute an invalid opcode (most protected-mode instructions are considered invalid in real mode). Generated on BOUND, LDS, LES, or LIDT instructions which specify a register rather than a memory address.

Available on: 80286 and above.　　　　　　　　　**Restrictions:** none.
Registers at call: n/a　　　　　　　　　　　　**Return Registers:** n/a
Details: Return address points to beginning of invalid instruction. With proper programming, this interrupt may be used to emulate instructions which do not exist; many 386 BIOSes emulate the 80286 undocumented LOADALL instruction which was removed from the 80386 and higher processors.
Conflicts: HP 95LX (chapter 4).
See Also: CPU-generated INT 0Ch, CPU-generated INT 0Dh

INTERRUPT 07h
CPU-generated - PROCESSOR EXTENSION NOT AVAILABLE

Purpose: Automatically called if a coprocessor instruction is encountered when no coprocessor is installed. Can be used to emulate a numeric coprocessor in software.

Available on: 80286 and above.　　　　　　　　　**Restrictions:** none.
Registers at call: n/a　　　　　　　　　　　　**Return Registers:** n/a
Conflicts: None known.
See Also: CPU-generated INT 09h

INTERRUPT 08h
CPU-generated - DOUBLE EXCEPTION DETECTED

Purpose: Called when multiple exceptions occur on one instruction, or an exception occurs in an exception handler. Called in protected mode if an interrupt above the defined limit of the interrupt vector table occurs.

Available on: 80286 and above.　　　　　　　　　**Restrictions:** none.
Registers at call: n/a　　　　　　　　　　　　**Return Registers:** n/a
Details: Return address points at beginning of instruction with errors or the beginning of the instruction which was about to execute when the external interrupt caused the exception. If an exception occurs in the double fault handler, the CPU goes into SHUTDOWN mode (which circuitry in the PC/AT converts to a reset); this "triple fault" is a faster way of returning to real mode on many 80286 machines than the standard keyboard controller reset.
Conflicts: BIOS System Timer, IRQ0.

INTERRUPT 08h
IRQ0 - SYSTEM TIMER

Purpose: Generated 18.2 times per second by channel 0 of the 8254 system timer, this interrupt is used to keep the time-of-day clock updated.

Available on: All machines.　　　　　　　　　　**Restrictions:** Bit 0 of I/O port 21h must be clear.
Registers at call: n/a　　　　　　　　　　　　**Return Registers:** n/a
Details: Programs which need to be invoked regularly should use INT 1Ch unless they need to reprogram the timer while still keeping the time-of-day clock running at the proper rate. The default handler is at F000h:FEA5h in IBM PC and 100%-compatible BIOSes.
Conflicts: DOUBLE EXCEPTION DETECTED.
See Also: INT 1Ch (chapter 3), User Alarm INT 4Ah (chapter 3), DESQview INT 50h, DoubleDOS INT 58h, INT 70h

INTERRUPT 09h
CPU-generated - PROCESSOR EXTENSION PROTECTION ERROR

Purpose: Called if the coprocessor attempts to access memory outside a segment boundary; it may occur at an arbitrary time after the coprocessor instruction was issued.

Available on: 80286 and 80386 in protected mode.　　　**Restrictions:** none.

Registers at call: n/a   **Return Registers:** n/a
Details: Until the condition is cleared or the coprocessor is reset, the only coprocessor instruction which may be used is FNINIT; WAIT or other coprocessor instructions will cause a deadlock because the coprocessor is still busy waiting for data.
Conflicts: BIOS Keyboard service routine (IRQ1).
See Also: CPU-generated INT 07h

INTERRUPT 09h
RESERVED BY Intel (80486 protected mode)

Purpose: Not used, to avoid conflicts.
Available on: 80486 operating in protected mode.   **Restrictions:** none.
Registers at call: n/a   **Return Registers:** n/a
Details: This exception has been moved to INT 0Dh on the 80486 because the math coprocessor is integrated into the CPU.
Conflicts: None known.
See Also: CPU-generated INT 09h, CPU-generated INT 0Dh

INTERRUPT 09h
IRQ1 - KEYBOARD DATA READY

Purpose: Generated when data is received from the keyboard.
Available on: All machines.   **Restrictions:** Bit 1 of I/O port 21h must be clear.
Registers at call: n/a   **Return Registers:** n/a
Details: The received data is normally a scan code, but may also be an ACK or NAK of a command on AT-class keyboards. If the BIOS supports an enhanced (101/102-key) keyboard, it calls INT 15h Function 4Fh after reading the scan code from the keyboard and before further processing.
    The interrupt handler performs the following actions for certain special keystrokes:
        Ctrl-Break   invoke INT 1Bh, set flag at 0040h:0071h
        SysRq invoke INT 15h Function 85h
        Ctrl-Numlock   place system in a tight wait loop
        Ctrl-Alt-Del   jump to BIOS startup code (either F000h:FFF0h or the destination of the jump at that address)
        Shift-PrtSc   invoke INT 05h
Conflicts: PROCESSOR EXTENSION PROTECTION ERROR fault on 80286 and 80386.
See Also: DESQview INT 51h, DoubleDOS INT 59h, Print Screen INT 05h (chapter 3), INT 15h Functions 4Fh and 85h (chapter 3), INT 16h (chapter 3), INT 1Bh (chapter 3)

INTERRUPT 0Ah
CPU-generated - INVALID TASK STATE SEGMENT

Purpose: Indicates task switching error.
Available on: 80286 and above.   **Restrictions:** Available only in protected mode.
Registers at call: n/a   **Return Registers:** n/a
Details: Automatically called during a task switch if the new TSS specified by the task gate is invalid for any of the following reasons:
        TSS limit is less than 43 (80286)
        LDT selector invalid or segment not present
        null SS selector, or SS selector outside LDT/GDT limit
        stack segment is read-only
        stack segment DPL differs from new CPL, or RPL <> CPL
        CS selector is outside LDT/GDT limit or not code
        non-conforming code segment's DPL differs from CPL
        conforming code segment's DPL > CPL
        DS/ES selectors outside LDT/GDT limit or not readable segments

The handler must use a task gate in order to have a valid TSS under which to execute; it must also reset the busy bit in the new TSS.
Conflicts: Roland MPU MIDI interface, Tandy hard disk, IRQ2.
See Also: CPU-generated INT 0Bh

INTERRUPT 0Ah
IRQ2 - VERTICAL RETRACE INTERRUPT

Purpose: Indicates occurrence of vertical retrace time.
Available on: EGA or VGA equipped systems.   **Restrictions:** none.
Registers at call: n/a   **Return Registers:** n/a
Details: The TOPS and PCnet adapters use this interrupt request line by default. DOS 3.2 revectors IRQ2 to a stack-switching routine. On ATs and above, the physical data line for IRQ2 is labeled IRQ9 and connects to the slave 8259. The BIOS redirects the interrupt for IRQ9 back here. Under DESQview, only the INT 15h vector and BASIC segment address (the word at 0000h:0510h) may be assumed to be valid for the handler's process.
Conflicts: CPU-generated INVALID TASK STATE SEGMENT, Roland MPU MIDI interface, Tandy hard disk, LPT2.
See Also: DESQview INT 52h, DoubleDOS INT 5Ah, INT 71h

INTERRUPT 0Ah
IRQ2 - LPT2

Purpose: Indicates that printer LPT2 needs attention.
Available on: Original PC only.   **Restrictions:** Will be preempted if EGA or VGA
                                                    video card is in system.
Registers at call: n/a   **Return Registers:** n/a
Details: Refer to IRQ2 for EGA/VGA.
Conflicts: CPU-generated INVALID TASK STATE SEGMENT, Roland MPU MIDI interface, Tandy hard disk.
See Also: DESQview INT 52h, DoubleDOS INT 5Ah, INT 71h

INTERRUPT 0Ah
IRQ2 - Tandy HARD DISK

Purpose: Indicates hard disk requires action.
Available on: Tandy 1000-series machines only.   **Restrictions:** none.
Registers at call: n/a   **Return Registers:** n/a
Details: May be masked by setting bit 2 on I/O port 21h
Conflicts: CPU-generated INVALID TASK STATE SEGMENT, Roland MPU MIDI interface, LPT2.
See Also: DESQview INT 52h, DoubleDOS INT 5Ah, INT 71h

INTERRUPT 0Ah
IRQ2 - ROLAND MPU MIDI INTERFACE

Purpose: Attention request from MIDI peripherals.
Available on: All machines.   **Restrictions:** Roland MIDI interface must be installed.
Registers at call: n/a   **Return Registers:** n/a
Details: Newer Roland cards and MIDI interfaces by other manufacturers use a jumper-selectable IRQ, but software and hardware generally defaults to IRQ2.
Conflicts: CPU-generated INVALID TASK STATE SEGMENT, Tandy hard disk, LPT2.
See Also: DESQview INT 52h, DoubleDOS INT 5Ah, INT 71h

INTERRUPT 0Bh
CPU-generated - SEGMENT NOT PRESENT

Purpose: Generated when loading a segment register if the segment descriptor indicates that the segment is not currently in memory, unless the segment is an LDT (see INT 0Ah) or stack segment (see INT 0Ch) needed by a task switch.
Available on: 80286 and above.   **Restrictions:** Available only in protected mode.

Registers at call: n/a   **Return Registers:** n/a
Details: May be used to implement virtual memory by loading in segments as they are accessed, clearing the "not present" bit after loading.
Conflicts: IRQ3.
See Also: CPU-generated INT 0Ah, CPU-generated INT 0Eh

INTERRUPT 0Bh
IRQ3 - SERIAL COMMUNICATIONS (COM2)

Purpose: Indicates service required by serial port COM2.
Available on: All machines.   **Restrictions:** Bit 3 of I/O port 21h must be clear.
Registers at call: n/a   **Return Registers:** n/a
Details: the TOPS and PCnet adapters use this interrupt request line as an alternate. On PS/2's, COM2 through COM8 share this interrupt; on many PC's, COM4 shares this interrupt.
Conflicts: CPU-generated SEGMENT NOT PRESENT, HP 95LX keyboard.
See Also: IRQ4 on INT 0Ch, DESQview INT 53h, DoubleDOS INT 5Bh

INTERRUPT 0Bh
LOW-LEVEL KEYBOARD HANDLER

Purpose: Called when a key is pressed. The handler debounces the key, places its scan code in I/O register 60h, and invokes INT 09h.
Available on: HP 95LX only.   **Restrictions:** none.
Registers at call: n/a   **Return Registers:** n/a
Conflicts: CPU-generated SEGMENT NOT PRESENT, COM2.
See Also: Keyboard INT 09h

INTERRUPT 0Ch
CPU-generated - STACK FAULT

Purpose: Generated on stack overflow/underflow in protected mode. Generated in protected mode if an inter-level transition or task switch references a stack segment marked "not present". Generated on accessing a word operand at SS:FFFFh in real mode.
Available on: 80286 and above.   **Restrictions:** none.
Registers at call: n/a   **Return Registers:** n/a
Details: The 80286 will shut down in real mode if SP=0001h before a push. On the PC AT and compatibles, external circuitry generates a reset on shutdown.
Conflicts: IRQ4, IBM System 36/38 workstation emulation (chapter 26).
See Also: CPU-generated INT 0Bh

INTERRUPT 0Ch
IRQ4 - SERIAL COMMUNICATIONS (COM1)

Purpose: Indicates serial port COM1 requires action.
Available on: All machines.   **Restrictions:** Bit 4 of I/O port 21h must be clear.
Registers at call: n/a   **Return Registers:** n/a
Details: On many PC's, COM3 shares this interrupt.
Conflicts: STACK FAULT, IBM System 36/38 workstation emulation (chapter 26).
See Also: IRQ3 on INT 0Bh, DESQview INT 54h, DoubleDOS INT 5Ch

INTERRUPT 0Dh
CPU-generated - GENERAL PROTECTION VIOLATION

Purpose: Traps any general protection fault; used for memory management.
Available on: 80286 and above.   **Restrictions:** none.
Registers at call: n/a   **Return Registers:** n/a
Details: Called in real mode when:
       (1) an instruction accesses a word operand located at offset FFFFh;

(2) a PUSH MEM or POP MEM instruction contains an invalid bit encoding in the second byte;

(3) an instruction exceeds the maximum length allowed (10 bytes for 80286, 15 bytes for 80386 and 80486);

(4) an instruction wraps from offset FFFFh to offset 0000h.

Called in protected mode on protection violations not covered by INT 06 through INT 0C, including:

(1) segment limit violations;

(2) write to read-only segments;

(3) accesses using null DS or ES selectors;

(4) accesses to segments with privilege greater than CPL;

(5) wrong descriptor type.

Called on 80486 protected-mode floating-point protection fault.

Conflicts: IRQ5, Tandy 1000 RAM refresh, HP 95LX infrared interrupt.
See Also: CPU-generated INT 09h, CPU-generated INT 0Ch

INTERRUPT 0Dh
IRQ5 - FIXED DISK (PC,XT), LPT2 (AT), reserved (PS/2)

Purpose: Indicates completion of fixed-disk activity, or need for attention at LPT2 printer.
Available on: All machines. **Restrictions:** none.
Registers at call: n/a **Return Registers:** n/a
Details: Under DESQview, only the INT 15h vector and BASIC segment address (the word at 0000h:0510h) may be assumed to be valid for the handler's process. May be masked by setting bit 5 on I/O port 21h.
Conflicts: General Protection Violation, Tandy 1000 RAM refresh, HP 95LX infrared interrupt.
See Also: IRQ6 on INT 0Eh, IRQ7 on INT 0Fh, DESQview INT 55h, DoubleDOS INT 5Dh

INTERRUPT 0Dh
IRQ5 - Tandy 1000 60 Hz RAM REFRESH

Purpose: Signals time to refresh dynamic RAM.
Available on: Tandy 1000 only. **Restrictions:** none.
Registers at call: n/a **Return Registers:** n/a
Conflicts: General Protection Violation, IRQ5, HP 95LX infrared interrupt.
See Also: DESQview INT 55h

INTERRUPT 0Dh
INFRARED INTERRUPT

Purpose: Indicates that the infrared data link needs attention.
Available on: HP 95LX only. **Restrictions:** none.
Registers at call: n/a **Return Registers:** n/a
Conflicts: General Protection Violation, IRQ5, Tandy 1000 RAM refresh.
See Also: DESQview INT 55h

INTERRUPT 0Eh
CPU-generated - PAGE FAULT

Purpose: Signals attempt to address memory location not currently in selector tables.
Available on: 80386 and above.

Restrictions: CPU must be operating in native mode or V86 mode.

Registers at call: n/a **Return Registers:** n/a
Details: Used to implement virtual memory.
Conflicts: IRQ6, HP 95LX external card interrupt.
See Also: CPU-generated INT 0Bh

INTERRUPT 0Eh
IRQ6 - DISKETTE CONTROLLER

Purpose: Generated by floppy disk controller on completion of an operation.
Available on: All machines.   **Restrictions:** Bit 6 of I/O port 21h must be clear.
Registers at call: n/a   **Return Registers:** n/a
Details: The default handler is at F000h:EF57h in IBM PC and 100%-compatible BIOSes.
Conflicts: Page Fault, HP 95LX external card interrupt.
See Also: IRQ5 on INT 0Dh, DESQview INT 56h, DoubleDOS INT 5Eh

INTERRUPT 0Eh
EXTERNAL CARD INTERRUPT

Purpose: Indicates that a peripheral card requires attention.
Available on: HP 95LX only.   **Restrictions:** none.
Registers at call: n/a   **Return Registers:** n/a
Conflicts: Page Fault, Diskette Controller.

INTERRUPT 0Fh
IRQ7 - PARALLEL PRINTER

Purpose: Generated by the LPT1 printer adapter when printer becomes ready.
Available on: All machines.   **Restrictions:** none.
Registers at call: n/a   **Return Registers:** n/a
Details: Most printer adapters do not reliably generate this interrupt. The 8259 interrupt controller generates an interrupt corresponding to IRQ7 when an error condition occurs.
Conflicts: HP 95LX real-time clock.
See Also: LPT2 INT 0Dh, DESQview INT 57h, DoubleDOS INT 5Fh

INTERRUPT 0Fh
REAL-TIME CLOCK

Purpose: Generated by the real-time clock in the HP 95LX.
Available on: HP 95LX only.   **Restrictions:** none.
Registers at call: n/a   **Return Registers:** n/a
Conflicts: IRQ7.
See Also: LPT2 INT 0Dh, DESQview INT 57h, DoubleDOS INT 5Fh

INTERRUPT 10h
CPU-generated - COPROCESSOR ERROR

Purpose: Generated by the CPU when the -ERROR pin is asserted by the coprocessor.
Available on: 80286 and above.   **Restrictions:** none.
Registers at call: n/a   **Return Registers:** n/a
Details: AT's and clones usually wire the coprocessor to use IRQ13, but not all get it right.
Conflicts: BIOS Video interface (chapter 5).
See Also: CPU-generated INT 09h, INT 75h

INTERRUPT 11h
CPU-generated - ALIGNMENT CHECK

Purpose: Traps reference to mis-aligned memory address.
Available on: 80486 and above.   **Restrictions:** Only available in privilege mode 3.
Registers at call: n/a   **Return Registers:** n/a
Details: Bit AC in the EFLAGS register enables this interrupt on a memory reference on a mis-aligned address when in privilege mode 3.
Conflicts: BIOS System Info (chapter 3).

INTERRUPT 40h
Z100 - Master 8259 - Parity error or S100 error

Purpose: Indicates error detected.
Available on: Heath-Zenith Z100 only.   **Restrictions:** none.
Registers at call: n/a   **Return Registers:** n/a
Conflicts: Relocated diskette handler (chapter 6)

INTERRUPT 41h
Z100 - Master 8259 - Processor Swap

Purpose: Requests swap to alternate processor.
Available on: Heath-Zenith Z100 only.   **Restrictions:** none.
Registers at call: n/a   **Return Registers:** n/a
Conflicts: Hard Disk Drive Parameter Table (chapter 6)

INTERRUPT 42h
Z100 - Master 8259 - Timer

Purpose: Indicates timer rundown.
Available on: Heath-Zenith Z100 only.   **Restrictions:** none.
Registers at call: n/a   **Return Registers:** n/a
Conflicts: Relocated default INT 10h (chapter 5)

INTERRUPT 43h
Z100 - Master 8259 - Slave 8259 input

Purpose: Chains slave PIC into master.
Available on: Heath-Zenith Z100 only.   **Restrictions:** none.
Registers at call: n/a   **Return Registers:** n/a
Details: Slave runs in a special fully-nested mode.
Conflicts: Video Character Table (chapter 5)

INTERRUPT 44h
Z100 - Master 8259 - Serial A

Purpose: Indicates that serial port A needs attention.
Available on: Heath-Zenith Z100 only.   **Restrictions:** none.
Registers at call: n/a   **Return Registers:** n/a
Conflicts: PCjr character font vector (chapter 5), IBM 3270-PC API (chapter 26), Novell Netware HLL API (chapter 20).

INTERRUPT 45h
Z100 - Master 8259 - Serial B

Purpose: Indicates that serial port B needs attention.
Available on: Heath-Zenith Z100 only.   **Restrictions:** none.
Registers at call: n/a   **Return Registers:** n/a
Conflicts: None known.

INTERRUPT 46h
Z100 - Master 8259 - Keyboard, Retrace, and Light Pen

Purpose: Indicates attention needed by keyboard or light pen.
Available on: Heath-Zenith Z100 only.   **Restrictions:** none.
Registers at call: n/a   **Return Registers:** n/a
Conflicts: Hard Disk Drive Parameter Table (chapter 6)

INTERRUPT 47h
Z100 - Master 8259 - Printer

Purpose: Indicates that the printer needs attention.
Available on: Heath-Zenith Z100 only.   **Restrictions:** none.
Registers at call: n/a   **Return Registers:** n/a
Conflicts: SQL Base API (chapter 36).

INTERRUPT 48h
Z100 - Slave 8259 - S100 vectored line 0

Purpose: Service request from S100 bus line 0.
Available on: Heath-Zenith Z100 only.   **Restrictions:** none.
Registers at call: n/a   **Return Registers:** n/a
Conflicts: None known.

INTERRUPT 49h
Z100 - Slave 8259 - S100 vectored line 1

Purpose: Service request from S100 bus line 1.
Available on: Heath-Zenith Z100 only.   **Restrictions:** none.
Registers at call: n/a   **Return Registers:** n/a
Conflicts: MAGic (chapter 36)

INTERRUPT 4Ah
Z100 - Slave 8259 - S100 vectored line 2

Purpose: Service request from S100 bus line 2.
Available on: Heath-Zenith Z100 only.   **Restrictions:** none.
Registers at call: n/a   **Return Registers:** n/a
Conflicts: Standard BIOS INT 4Ah (chapter 3)

INTERRUPT 4Bh
Z100 - Slave 8259 - S100 vectored line 3

Purpose: Service request from S100 bus line 3.
Available on: Heath-Zenith Z100 only.   **Restrictions:** none.
Registers at call: n/a   **Return Registers:** n/a
Conflicts: IBM SCSI Interface (chapter 6), Virtual DMA Specification (chapter 12)

INTERRUPT 4Ch
Z100 - Slave 8259 - S100 vectored line 4

Purpose: Service request from S100 bus line 4.
Available on: Heath-Zenith Z100 only.   **Restrictions:** none.
Registers at call: n/a   **Return Registers:** n/a
Conflicts: None known.

INTERRUPT 4Dh
Z100 - Slave 8259 - S100 vectored line 5

Purpose: Service request from S100 bus line 5.
Available on: Heath-Zenith Z100 only.   **Restrictions:** none.
Registers at call: n/a   **Return Registers:** n/a
Conflicts: None known.

INTERRUPT 4Eh
Z100 - Slave 8259 - S100 vectored line 6

Purpose: Service request from S100 bus line 6.

Available on: Heath-Zenith Z100 only.
Registers at call: n/a
Conflicts: None known.

Restrictions: none.
Return Registers: n/a

INTERRUPT 4Fh
Z100 - Slave 8259 - S100 vectored line 7

Purpose: Service request from S100 bus line 7.
Available on: Heath-Zenith Z100 only.
Registers at call: n/a
Conflicts: None known.

Restrictions: none.
Return Registers: n/a

INTERRUPT 50h
DESQview IRQ0

Purpose: IRQ0 relocated by DESQview.
Details: The vectors 50h to 57h listed here are the location used by older versions of DESQview. DESQview versions 2.26 and higher search for unused ranges of interrupts and use the lowest available range in the search list for relocating these IRQs and the next lowest for relocating IRQ8-IRQ15. A range of eight interrupts starting at a multiple of 8 is considered available for this use if all vectors are identical.

The list of ranges for v2.26 is 50h,58h,68h,78h,F8h; if none of these are available, F8h and then 50h are used anyway. The list of ranges for v2.31 is 68h,78h,88h-B8h,F8h; if none of these are available, F8h and then F0h are used anyway.
Conflicts: IBM 3278 emulator IRQ0, OS/2 IRQ0, TIL Expert AIM (chapter 27).
See Also: INT 08h

INTERRUPT 50h
IBM 3278 emulator IRQ0

Purpose: IRQ0 relocated by IBM 3278 emulation control program.
Conflicts: DESQview IRQ0, OS/2 IRQ0, TIL Expert AIM (chapter 27).
See Also: INT 08h

INTERRUPT 50h
OS/2 v1.x IRQ0

Purpose: IRQ0 relocated by OS/2 versions 1.x.
Conflicts: DESQview IRQ0, IBM 3278 IRQ0, TIL Expert AIM (chapter 27).
See Also: INT 08h

INTERRUPT 51h
DESQview IRQ1

Purpose: IRQ1 relocated by DESQview.
Conflicts: IBM 3278 emulator IRQ1, OS/2 IRQ1.
See Also: INT 09h, DESQview INT 50h

INTERRUPT 51h
IBM 3278 emulator IRQ1

Purpose: IRQ1 relocated by IBM 3278 emulation control program.
Conflicts: DESQview IRQ1, OS/2 IRQ1.
See Also: INT 09h

INTERRUPT 51h
OS/2 v1.x IRQ1

Purpose: IRQ1 relocated by OS/2 versions 1.x.
Conflicts: DESQview IRQ1, IBM 3278 emulator IRQ1.

See Also: INT 09h

INTERRUPT 52h
DESQview IRQ2

Purpose: IRQ2 relocated by DESQview.
Conflicts: IBM 3278 emulator IRQ2, OS/2 IRQ2.
See Also: INT 0Ah, DESQview INT 50h

INTERRUPT 52h
IBM 3278 emulator IRQ2

Purpose: IRQ2 relocated by IBM 3278 emulation control program.
Conflicts: DESQview IRQ2, OS/2 IRQ2.
See Also: INT 0Ah

INTERRUPT 52h
OS/2 v1.x IRQ2

Purpose: IRQ2 relocated by OS/2 versions 1.x.
Conflicts: DESQview IRQ2, IBM 3278 emulator IRQ2.
See Also: INT 0Ah

INTERRUPT 53h
DESQview IRQ3

Purpose: IRQ3 relocated by DESQview.
Conflicts: IBM 3278 emulator IRQ3, OS/2 IRQ3.
See Also: INT 0Bh, DESQview INT 50h

INTERRUPT 53h
IBM 3278 emulator IRQ3

Purpose: IRQ3 relocated by IBM 3278 emulation control program.
Conflicts: DESQview IRQ3, OS/2 IRQ3.
See Also: INT 0Bh

INTERRUPT 53h
OS/2 v1.x IRQ3

Purpose: IRQ3 relocated by OS/2 versions 1.x.
Conflicts: DESQview IRQ3, IBM 3278 emulator IRQ3.
See Also: INT 0Bh

INTERRUPT 54h
DESQview IRQ4

Purpose: IRQ4 relocated by DESQview.
Conflicts: IBM 3278 emulator IRQ4, OS/2 IRQ4.
See Also: INT 0Ch, DESQview INT 50h

INTERRUPT 54h
IBM 3278 emulator IRQ4

Purpose: IRQ4 relocated by IBM 3278 emulation control program.
Conflicts: DESQview IRQ4, OS/2 IRQ4.
See Also: INT 0Ch

INTERRUPT 54h
OS/2 v1.x IRQ4

Purpose: IRQ4 relocated by OS/2 versions 1.x.
Conflicts: DESQview IRQ4, IBM 3278 emulator IRQ4.
See Also: INT 0Ch

INTERRUPT 55h
DESQview IRQ5

Purpose: IRQ5 relocated by DESQview.
Conflicts: IBM 3278 emulator IRQ5, OS/2 IRQ5.
See Also: INT 0Dh, DESQview INT 50h

INTERRUPT 55h
IBM 3278 emulator IRQ5

Purpose: IRQ5 relocated by IBM 3278 emulation control program.
Conflicts: DESQview IRQ5, OS/2 IRQ5.
See Also: INT 0Dh

INTERRUPT 55h
OS/2 v1.x IRQ5

Purpose: IRQ5 relocated by OS/2 versions 1.x.
Conflicts: DESQview IRQ5, IBM 3278 emulator IRQ5.
See Also: INT 0Dh

INTERRUPT 56h
DESQview IRQ6

Purpose: IRQ6 relocated by DESQview.
Conflicts: IBM 3278 emulator IRQ6, OS/2 IRQ6.
See Also: INT 0Eh, DESQview INT 50h

INTERRUPT 56h
IBM 3278 emulator IRQ6

Purpose: IRQ6 relocated by IBM 3278 emulation control program.
Conflicts: DESQview IRQ6, OS/2 IRQ6.
See Also: INT 0Eh

INTERRUPT 56h
OS/2 v1.x IRQ6

Purpose: IRQ6 relocated by OS/2 versions 1.x.
Conflicts: DESQview IRQ6, IBM 3278 emulator IRQ6.
See Also: INT 0Eh

INTERRUPT 57h
DESQview IRQ7

Purpose: IRQ7 relocated by DESQview.
Conflicts: IBM 3278 emulator IRQ7, OS/2 IRQ7.
See Also: INT 0Fh, DESQview INT 50h

INTERRUPT 57h
IBM 3278 emulator IRQ7

Purpose: IRQ7 relocated by IBM 3278 emulation control program.
Conflicts: DESQview IRQ7, OS/2 IRQ7.

See Also: INT 0Fh

INTERRUPT 57h
OS/2 v1.x IRQ7

Purpose: IRQ7 relocated by OS/2 versions 1.x.
Conflicts: DESQview IRQ7, IBM 3278 emulator IRQ7.
See Also: INT 0Fh

INTERRUPT 58h
DoubleDOS IRQ0

Purpose: IRQ0 relocated by DoubleDOS
Conflicts: DESQview 2.26+ IRQ8
See Also: INT 08h

INTERRUPT 58h
DESQview IRQ8

Purpose: IRQ8 relocated by DESQview 2.26+
Conflicts: DoubleDOS IRQ0
See Also: INT 70h, DESQview INT 50h

INTERRUPT 59h
DoubleDOS IRQ1

Purpose: IRQ1 relocated by DoubleDOS
Conflicts: DESQview 2.26+ IRQ8, GSS*CGI (chapter 5)
See Also: INT 09h

INTERRUPT 59h
DESQview IRQ9

Purpose: IRQ9 relocated by DESQview 2.26+
Conflicts: DoubleDOS IRQ1, GSS*CGI (chapter 5)
See Also: INT 71h, DESQview INT 50h

INTERRUPT 5Ah
DoubleDOS IRQ2

Purpose: IRQ2 relocated by DoubleDOS
Conflicts: DESQview 2.26+ IRQ10, Cluster adapter BIOS (Chapter 27).
See Also: INT 0Ah

INTERRUPT 5Ah
DESQview IRQ10

Purpose: IRQ10 relocated by DESQview 2.26+
Conflicts: DoubleDOS IRQ2, Cluster adapter BIOS (Chapter 27).
See Also: INT 72h, DESQview INT 50h

INTERRUPT 5Bh
DoubleDOS IRQ3

Purpose: IRQ3 relocated by DoubleDOS.
Conflicts: DESQview IRQ11; AT&T Starlan Extended NetBIOS, Microsoft Network Transport Layer Interface, and cluster adapter (chapter 27).
See Also: INT 0Bh

INTERRUPT 5Bh
DESQview IRQ11

Purpose: IRQ11 relocated by DESQview 2.26+.
Conflicts: DoubleDOS IRQ3; AT&T Starlan Extended NetBIOS (chapter 27), Microsoft Network Transport Layer Interface (chapter 27), cluster adapter (chapter 27).
See Also: INT 73h, DESQview INT 50h

INTERRUPT 5Ch
DoubleDOS IRQ4

Purpose: IRQ4 relocated by DoubleDOS.
Conflicts: DESQview IRQ12; $25 LAN, ATALK.SYS, IBM 802.2 interface (LLC), NetBIOS interface, and TOPS interface (chapter 27).
See Also: INT 0Ch

INTERRUPT 5Ch
DESQview IRQ12

Purpose: IRQ12 relocated by DESQview 2.26+.
Conflicts: DoubleDOS IRQ4; $25 LAN, ATALK.SYS, IBM 802.2 interface (LLC), NetBIOS interface, and TOPS interface (chapter 27).
See Also: INT 74h, DESQview INT 50h

INTERRUPT 5Dh
DoubleDOS IRQ5

Purpose: IRQ5 relocated by DoubleDOS.
Conflicts: IRQ13 relocated by DESQview 2.26+.
See Also: INT 0Dh

INTERRUPT 5Dh
DESQview IRQ13

Purpose: IRQ13 relocated by DESQview 2.26+.
Conflicts: IRQ5 relocated by DoubleDOS.
See Also: INT 75h, DESQview INT 50h

INTERRUPT 5Eh
DoubleDOS IRQ6

Purpose: IRQ6 relocated by DoubleDOS.
Conflicts: IRQ14 relocated by DESQview 2.26+.
See Also: INT 0Eh

INTERRUPT 5Eh
DESQview IRQ14

Purpose: IRQ14 relocated by DESQview 2.26+.
Conflicts: IRQ6 relocated by DoubleDOS.
See Also: INT 76h, DESQview INT 50h

INTERRUPT 5Fh
DoubleDOS IRQ7

Purpose: IRQ7 relocated by DoubleDOS.
Conflicts: IRQ15 relocated by DESQview 2.26+, HP 95LX (chapter 4).
See Also: INT 0Fh

INTERRUPT 5Fh
DESQview IRQ15

Purpose: IRQ15 relocated by DESQview 2.26+.
Conflicts: IRQ7 relocated by DoubleDOS, HP 95LX (chapter 4).
See Also: INT 77h, DESQview INT 50h

INTERRUPT 70h
IRQ8 - CMOS REAL-TIME CLOCK

Purpose: This interrupt is called when the real-time clock chip generates an alarm or periodic interrupt, among others.
Available on: 80286 and above.   **Restrictions:** Only enabled if bit 0 of I/O port A1h is clear.
Registers at call: n/a   **Return Registers:** n/a
Details: The periodic interrupt occurs 1024 times per second, although many BIOSes turn it off in the INT 70h handler unless in an event wait (see INT 15h Functions 83h or 86h in chapter 3).
Conflicts: None known.
See Also: INT 08h, DESQview INT 58h, Amstrad INT 15h Function 01h (chapter 4), INT 15h Functions 83h and 86h (chapter 3), INT 1Ah Function 02h (chapter 3).

INTERRUPT 71h
IRQ9 - REDIRECTED TO INT 0A BY BIOS

Purpose: The default BIOS handler invokes INT 0A for compatibility, since the pin for IRQ2 on the PC expansion bus became the pin for IRQ9 on the AT expansion bus.
Available on: AT and later.   **Restrictions:** Only enabled if bit 1 of I/O port A1h is clear.
Registers at call: n/a   **Return Registers:** n/a
Details: Under DESQview, only the INT 15h vector and BASIC segment address (the word at 0000h:0510h) may be assumed to be valid for the handler's process.
Conflicts: None known.
See Also: INT 0Ah, DESQview INT 59h

INTERRUPT 72h
IRQ10 - RESERVED

Purpose: Reserved by IBM and not used on any current IBM models.
Available on: AT and later.   **Restrictions:** Only enabled if bit 2 of I/O port A1h is clear.
Registers at call: n/a   **Return Registers:** n/a
Conflicts: None known.
See Also: DESQview INT 5Ah

INTERRUPT 73h
IRQ11 - RESERVED

Purpose: Reserved by IBM and not used on any current IBM models.
Available on: AT and later.   **Restrictions:** Only enabled if bit 3 of I/O port A1h is clear.
Registers at call: n/a   **Return Registers:** n/a
Conflicts: None known.
See Also: DESQview INT 5Bh

INTERRUPT 74h
IRQ12 - POINTING DEVICE

Purpose: Attention request from mouse or other pointing device.

Available on: PS/2 series machines only.

Registers at call: n/a

Details: Under DESQview, only the INT 15h vector and BASIC segment address (the word at 0000h:0510h) may be assumed to be valid for the handler's process.

Conflicts: None known.

See Also: DESQview INT 5Ch, Mouse INT 33h (chapter 13)

Restrictions: Only enabled if bit 4 of I/O port A1h is clear.

Return Registers: n/a

INTERRUPT 75h
IRQ13 - MATH COPROCESSOR EXCEPTION

Purpose: Indicates math coprocessor error.

Available on: AT and later.

Registers at call: n/a

Details: Not all clones wire the coprocessor to generate this IRQ; some systems generate an NMI (see INT 02) or assert the -ERROR pin on the CPU (see INT 10h above).

The BIOS handler for this interrupt invokes INT 02h for compatibility with the PC. Under DESQview, only the INT 15h vector and BASIC segment address (the word at 0000h:0510h) may be assumed to be valid for the handler's process.

Conflicts: None known.

See Also: CPU-generated INT 10h, DESQview INT 5Dh

Restrictions: Only enabled if bit 5 of I/O port A1h is clear.

Return Registers: n/a

INTERRUPT 76h
IRQ14 - HARD DISK CONTROLLER

Purpose: Indicates completion of activity by HD controller.

Available on: AT and later.

Registers at call: n/a

Conflicts: None known.

See Also: Hard Disk IRQ6 on INT 0Eh, DESQview INT 5Eh

Restrictions: Only enabled if bit 6 of I/O port A1h is clear.

Return Registers: n/a

INTERRUPT 77h
IRQ15 - RESERVED (AT,PS)

Purpose: Reserved by IBM and not used on any current IBM models.

Available on: AT and PS lines only.

Registers at call: n/a

Conflicts: None known.

See Also: DESQview INT 5Fh

Restrictions: Only enabled if bit 7 of I/O port A1h is clear.

Return Registers: n/a

INTERRUPT 77h
IRQ15 - POWER CONSERVATION (Compaq SLT/286)

Purpose: Manage battery power by shutting down unused peripherals.

Available on: Compaq SLT/286 only.

Registers at call: n/a

Conflicts: None known.

See Also: Compaq INT 15h Function 46h Subfunction 00h (chapter 4), DESQview INT 5Fh

Restrictions: Only enabled if bit 7 of I/O port A1h is clear.

Return Registers: n/a

Chapter 3

ROM BIOS

This chapter deals primarily with the "standard" ROM-BIOS interfaces first established by the original IBM PC. It also includes several additional calls that appear to be more closely related to these interfaces than to any other functional area.

INTERRUPT 05h
PRINT SCREEN

Purpose: Transmits the current contents of the text screen to the printer (it may also dump graphics images if a special driver is loaded).

Available on: All machines.   **Restrictions:** none.

Registers at call: n/a   **Return Registers:** n/a

Details: This interrupt is normally invoked by the INT 09h handler when PrtSc key is pressed, but may be invoked directly by applications. The default handler is at F000h:FF54h in IBM PC and 100%-compatible BIOSes. Byte at 0050h:0000h contains status used by default handler:

00h	not active
01h	PrtSc in progress
FFh	last PrtSc encountered error

Conflicts: CPU-generated Bound Range Exceeded fault (chapter 2).

See Also: INT 10h Function 12h Subfunction 20h (chapter 5)

INTERRUPT 11h
GET EQUIPMENT LIST

Purpose: Determine system configuration.

Available on: All machines.   **Restrictions:** none.

Registers at call: n/a   **Return Registers:**
                                                    AX = BIOS equipment list word (Table 3-1)

Table 3-1. Format of BIOS Equipment List Word

Bits	Description
0	floppy disk(s) installed (see bits 6-7)
1	80x87 coprocessor installed
2,3	number of 16K banks of RAM on motherboard (PC only)
	number of 64K banks of RAM on motherboard (XT only)
2	pointing device installed (PS)
3	unused (PS)
4-5	initial video mode
	00 EGA, VGA, or PGA
	01 40x25 color
	10 80x25 color
	11 80x25 monochrome
6-7	number of floppies installed less 1 (if bit 0 set)
8	DMA support installed (PCjr, some Tandy 1000s, 1400LT)
9-11	number of serial ports installed
12	game port installed

Table 3-1. Format of BIOS Equipment List Word (continued)

Bits   Description
13   serial printer attached (PCjr)
            internal modem installed (PC/Convertible)
14-15   number of parallel ports installed

The following 32-bit extensions are used by Compaq and many other 386/486 machines:
EAX bit 23: page tables set so that Weitek coprocessor addressable in real mode
    bit 24: Weitek math coprocessor present

Compaq Systempro:
EAX bit 25: internal DMA parallel port available
    bit 26: IRQ for internal DMA parallel port (if bit 25 set)
            0 = IRQ5
            1 = IRQ7
    27,28: parallel port DMA channel
            00 = DMA channel 0
            01 = *DMA channel 0*
            10 = reserved
            11 = DMA channel 3

Conflicts: Alignment Check fault (chapter 2), Back&Forth (chapter 17).
See Also: INT 12h

INTERRUPT 12h
GET MEMORY SIZE

Purpose: Determine the amount of contiguous memory installed in the system.

Available on: All machines.	**Restrictions:** none.
Registers at call: n/a	**Return Registers:** AX = kilobytes of contiguous memory starting at absolute address 00000h.

Details: This call returns the contents of the word at 0040h:0013h; in PC and XT, this value is set from the switches on the motherboard.
Conflicts: Back&Forth (chapter 17).
See Also: INT 11h

INTERRUPT 15h - Function 00h
CASSETTE - TURN ON TAPE DRIVE MOTOR

Purpose: Turns tape cassette motor ON.

Available on: PC and PCjr only.	**Restrictions:** none.
Registers at call:	**Return Registers:**
AH = 00h	CF set on error
	AH = 86h no cassette present
	CF clear if successful

Conflicts: Amstrad PC1512 (chapter 4), MultiDOS Plus (chapter 16), VMiX (chapter 17).
See Also: Function 01h

INTERRUPT 15h - Function 01h
CASSETTE - TURN OFF TAPE DRIVE MOTOR

Purpose: Turns tape cassette motor OFF.

Available on: PC and PCjr only.	**Restrictions:** none.
Registers at call:	**Return Registers:**
AH = 01h	CF set on error
	AH = 86h no cassette present
	CF clear if successful

Conflicts: Amstrad PC1512 (chapter 4), MultiDOS Plus (chapter 16), VMiX (chapter 17).
See Also: Function 00h

INTERRUPT 15h - Function 02h
CASSETTE - READ DATA

Purpose: Read data from cassette.

Available on: PC and PCjr only.

Registers at call:

AH = 02h

CX = number of bytes to read

ES:BX -> buffer

Restrictions: none.

Return Registers:

CF clear if successful

    DX = number of bytes read

    ES:BX -> byte following last byte read

CF set on error

    AH = status

        00h successful

        01h CRC error

        02h bad tape signals

        04h no data

        80h invalid command

        86h no cassette present

Conflicts: Amstrad PC1512 (chapter 4), MultiDOS Plus (chapter 16), VMiX (chapter 17).

See Also: Functions 00h and 03h

INTERRUPT 15h - Function 03h
CASSETTE - WRITE DATA

Purpose: Writes data to cassette tape.

Available on: PC and PCjr only.

Registers at call:

AH = 03h

CX = number of bytes to write

ES:BX -> data buffer

Restrictions: none.

Return Registers:

CF clear if successful

    ES:BX -> byte following last byte written

CF set on error

    AH = status (see Function 02h)

    CX = 0000h

Conflicts: Amstrad PC1512 (chapter 4), MultiDOS Plus (chapter 16), VMiX (chapter 17).

See Also: Functions 00h and 02h

INTERRUPT 15h - Function 04h
SYSTEM - BUILD ABIOS SYSTEM PARAMETER TABLE

Purpose: Prepare for OS/2 operation using the Advanced BIOS.

Available on: PS models only.

Registers at call:

AH = 04h

ES:DI -> results buffer length 20h for System
    Parameter Table (Table 3-2)

DS = segment containing ABIOS RAM extensions
    (zero if none)

Restrictions: none.

Return Registers:

AH = 00h success: results at ES:DI

CF set on failure

Conflicts: Amstrad PC1512 (chapter 4), MultiDOS Plus (chapter 16), VMiX (chapter 17).

See Also: Functions 05h and C1h

Table 3-2. Format of ABIOS System Parameter Table

Offset	Size	Description
00h	DWORD	FAR address of ABIOS Common Start Routine
04h	DWORD	FAR address of ABIOS Interrupt Routine
08h	DWORD	FAR address of ABIOS Time-out Routine
0Ch	WORD	number of bytes of stack required by this ABIOS implementation
0Eh	16 BYTEs	reserved
1Eh	WORD	number of entries in initialization table

INTERRUPT 15h - Function 05h
SYSTEM - BUILD ABIOS INITIALIZATION TABLE

Purpose: Prepare for OS/2 operation using the Advanced BIOS.

Available on: PS/2 models only.

Registers at call:

AH = 05h

ES:DI -> results buffer length

    (18h * Number_of_Entries)

DS = segment containing ABIOS RAM extensions

    (zero if none)

Restrictions: none.

Return Registers:

AH = 00h success: results at ES:DI

CF set on failure

Conflicts: Amstrad PC1512 (chapter 4), MultiDOS Plus (chapter 16), VMiX (chapter 17).

See Also: Functions 04h and C1h

Table 3-3. Format of one entry of ABIOS Initialization Table

Offset	Size	Description
00h	WORD	device ID
02h	WORD	number of Logical IDs
04h	WORD	Device Block length (zero for ABIOS patch or extension)
06h	DWORD	Far pointer to init routine for Device Block and Function Transfer Table
0Ah	WORD	request block length
0Ch	WORD	Function Transfer Table length (zero for a patch)
0Eh	WORD	Data Pointers length (in Common Data Area)
10h	BYTE	secondary device ID (hardware level this ABIOS ver supports)
11h	BYTE	revision (device driver revision level this ABIOS supports)
12h	6 BYTEs	reserved

INTERRUPT 15h - Function 0Fh
SYSTEM - FORMAT UNIT PERIODIC INTERRUPT

Purpose: Called during ESDI drive formatting after each cylinder is completed to determine whether to continue.

Available on: PS/2 models with ESDI drives only.

Registers at call:

AH = 0Fh

AL = phase code

    00h reserved

    01h surface analysis

    02h formatting

Restrictions: none.

Return Registers:

CF clear if formatting should continue,

CF set if it should terminate.

Conflicts: MultiDOS Plus (chapter 16), VMiX (chapter 17).

See Also: ESDI Hard Disk INT 13h Function 1Ah (chapter 6)

INTERRUPT 15h - Function 20h, Subfunction 10h
OS HOOK - SETUP SYSREQ ROUTINE

Purpose: unknown.

Available on: DOS 3.0 and higher.

Registers at call:

AX = 2010h

other inputs, if any, unknown

Restrictions: none.

Return Registers: unknown

Conflicts: MultiDOS Plus (chapter 16).

See Also: Function 20h Subfunction 11h

INTERRUPT 15h - Function 20h, Subfunction 11h
OS HOOK - COMPLETION OF SYSREQ FUNCTION

Purpose: unknown.

Available on: AT, XT286, PS50+.

Restrictions: none.

Registers at call:
AX = 2011h
other inputs, if any, unknown
Conflicts: MultiDOS Plus (chapter 16).
See Also: Function 20h Subfunction 10h

Return Registers: unknown

INTERRUPT 15h - Function 21h
SYSTEM - POWER-ON SELF-TEST ERROR LOG

Purpose: Reads from or writes to Power On Self Test error log.
Available on: PS/2 Model 50 and above.
Registers at call:
AH = 21h
AL = subfunction:
    00h read POST log
    01h write POST log
BH = device ID
BL = error code

Restrictions: none.
Return Registers:
CF set on error
    AH = status
        00h OK
        01h list full
        80h invalid cmd
        86h unsupported
if function 00h:
    BX = number of error codes stored
    ES:DI -> error log

Details: The log is a series of words, the first byte of which identifies the error code and the second the device.
Conflicts: None known.

INTERRUPT 15h - Function 40h
SYSTEM - READ/MODIFY PROFILES

Purpose: Read from or write to system or modem profile words.
Available on: Convertible only.
Registers at call:
AH = 40h
AL = subfunction
    00h get system profile in CX and BX
    01h set system profile from CX and BX
    02h get internal modem profile in BX
    03h set internal modem profile from BX
Conflicts: Compaq SLT/286 or Portable 386 (chapter 4).

Restrictions: none.
Return Registers: n/a

INTERRUPT 15h - Function 41h
SYSTEM - WAIT ON EXTERNAL EVENT

Purpose: Pause execution of calling application until a specified event occurs.
Available on: Convertible only.
Registers at call:
AH = 41h
AL = condition type
    bits 0-2: condition to wait for
        0 any external event
        1 compare and return if equal
        2 compare and return if not equal
        3 test and return if not zero
        4 test and return if zero
    bit 3: reserved
    bit 4: 1=port address,
        0=user byte
    bits 5-7: reserved

Restrictions: none.
Return Registers: n/a

BH = condition compare or mask value
BL = timeout value times 55 milliseconds
    00h means no timeout
DX = I/O port address if AL bit 4 set
ES:DI -> user byte if AL bit 4 clear
Conflicts: None known.

INTERRUPT 15h - Function 42h
SYSTEM - REQUEST POWER OFF

Purpose: Turn off the system under software control.
Available on: Convertible only.   **Restrictions:** none.
Registers at call: **Return Registers:** n/a
AH = 42h
AL = 00h to use system profile
    01h to force suspend regardless of
        system profile
Conflicts: Compaq SLT/286 (chapter 4).
See Also: Function 44h

INTERRUPT 15h - Function 43h
SYSTEM - READ SYSTEM STATUS

Purpose: Determine state of power supply and which devices are currently turned on.
Available on: Convertible only.   **Restrictions:** none.
Registers at call: **Return Registers:**
AH = 43h   AL = status bits
                                                          bit 0: LCD detached
                                                          bit 1: reserved
    bit 2: RS232/parallel adapter powered on
    bit 3: internal modem powered on
    bit 4: power activated by alarm
    bit 5: standby power lost
    bit 6: external power in use
    bit 7: power low
Conflicts: None known.

INTERRUPT 15h - Function 44h
SYSTEM - (DE)ACTIVATE INTERNAL MODEM POWER

Purpose: Turn internal modem on or off under software control.
Available on: Convertible only.   **Restrictions:** none.
Registers at call: **Return Registers:** n/a
AH = 44h
AL = 00h to power off
    01h to power on
Conflicts: None known.
See Also: Function 42h

INTERRUPT 15h - Function 4Fh
OS HOOK - KEYBOARD INTERCEPT

Purpose: Permits an application or TSR to remap the keys on the keyboard before the BIOS decodes keypresses.
Available on: PC-AT models 3x9, XT2, XT286,   **Restrictions:** none.
                Convertible, PS/2 series.

Registers at call:
AH = 4Fh
AL = scan code
CF set

Return Registers:
CF set
    AL = scan code
CF clear
    scan code should be ignored

Details: Called by INT 09h handler to translate scan codes.
Conflicts: None known.
See Also: INT 09h (chapter 2)

INTERRUPT 15h - Function 80h
OS HOOK - DEVICE OPEN

Purpose: Notify the operating system that an application will be using a particular device.

Available on: AT and later.

Restrictions: none

Registers at call:
AH = 80h
BX = device ID
CX = process ID
CF clear

Return Registers:
CF clear if successful
    AH = 00h

CF set on error
    AH = status
        80h invalid command (PC, PCjr)
        86h function not supported (XT and later)

Details: This function should be hooked by a multitasker which wishes to keep track of device ownership; the default BIOS handler merely returns successfully.
Conflicts: None known.
See Also: Functions 81h and 82h

INTERRUPT 15h - Function 81h
OS HOOK - DEVICE CLOSE

Purpose: Notify the operating system that an application is finished with its use of a particular device.

Available on: AT and later.

Restrictions: none

Registers at call:
AH = 81h
BX = device ID
CX = process ID
CF clear

Return Registers:
CF clear if successful
    AH = 00h
CF set on error
    AH = status
        80h invalid command (PC, PCjr)
        86h function not supported (XT and later)

Details: This function should be hooked by a multitasker which wishes to keep track of device ownership; the default BIOS handler merely returns successfully.
Conflicts: None known.
See Also: Functions 80h and 82h

INTERRUPT 15h - Function 82h
OS HOOK - PROGRAM TERMINATION

Purpose: Closes all devices opened by the given process ID with function 80h.

Available on: AT and later.

Restrictions: none

Registers at call:
AH = 82h
BX = process ID
CF clear

Return Registers:
CF clear if successful
    AH = 00h

CF set on error

    AH = status

        80h invalid command (PC, PCjr)

        86h function not supported (XT and later)

Details: This function should be hooked by a multitasker which wishes to keep track of device ownership; the default BIOS handler merely returns successfully.

Conflicts: None known.

See Also: Functions 80h and 81h

INTERRUPT 15h - Function 83h
SET EVENT WAIT INTERVAL

Purpose: Establishes the duration of a wait period, at the end of which a user-specified flag is set.

Available on: PC-AT, PS/2 Model 50 and above.

Restrictions: none.

Registers at call:

AH = 83h

AL = subfunction

    00h set interval

        CX:DX = microseconds to delay

        ES:BX -> byte whose high bit is to
            be set at end of interval

    01h cancel wait interval

Return Registers:

CF set on error or function already busy

    AH = status

        80h invalid command (PC, PCjr)

        86h function not supported (XT and later)

CF clear if successful

Details: The resolution of the wait period is 977 microseconds on most systems because most BIOSes use the 1/1024 second fast interrupt from the AT real-time clock chip which is available on INT 70h.

Conflicts: None known.

See Also: Function 86h, IRQ8 on INT 70h (chapter 2)

INTERRUPT 15h - Function 84h
JOYSTICK SUPPORT

Purpose: Provides BIOS support for up to 2 joysticks.

Available on: XT with BIOS date after 11/8/82,
               PC-AT, XT286, and PS/2 models.

Restrictions: none.

Registers at call:

AH = 84h

DX = subfunction

    0000h read joystick switches

    0001h read positions of joysticks

Return Registers:

CF set on error

    AH = status

        80h invalid command (PC, PCjr)

        86h function not supported (other)

CF clear if successful

    AL bits 7-4 = switch settings for subfunction 0000

    AX = X position of joystick A for subfunction
        0001

    BX = Y position of joystick A

    CX = X position of joystick B

    DX = Y position of joystick B

Details: If no game port is installed, subfunction 0000h returns AL=00h (all switches open) and subfunction 0001h returns AX=BX=CX=DX=0000h. A 250kOhm joystick typically returns 0000h-01A0h.

INTERRUPT 15h - Function 85h
OS HOOK - SysRq KEY ACTIVITY

Purpose: Provides hook to monitor SysRq key.

Available on: PC-AT, PS/2.

Restrictions: none.

Registers at call:

AH = 85h

Return Registers:

CF clear if successful

    AH = 00h

AL = 00h SysRq key pressed
   = 01h SysRq key released
CF clear

CF set on error
   AH = status
      80h invalid command (PC, PCjr)
      86h function not supported (other)

Details: Called by keyboard decode routine. The default handler simply returns successfully; programs which wish to monitor the SysRq key must hook this call.
Conflicts: None known.
See Also: INT 09h (chapter 2)

INTERRUPT 15h - Function 86h
WAIT

Purpose: Delay execution for a specified period of time.
Available on: PC-AT, PS/2.
Restrictions: none.
Registers at call:
Return Registers:
AH = 86h
CF clear if successful (wait interval elapsed)
CX:DX = interval in microseconds
CF set on error
   AH = status
      80h invalid command (PC, PCjr)
      83h wait already in progress
      86h function not supported (other)

Details: The resolution of the wait period is 977 microseconds on most systems because most BIOSes use the 1/1024 second fast interrupt from the AT real-time clock chip which is available on INT 70h.
Conflicts: None known.
See Also: Function 83h, IRQ8 on INT 70h (chapter 2)

INTERRUPT 15h - Function 87h
SYSTEM - COPY EXTENDED MEMORY

Purpose: Copies a block of data via parameters passed in a global descriptor table.
Available on: PC-AT, PS/2.
Restrictions: none.
Registers at call:
Return Registers:
AH = 87h
CF set on error
CX = number of words to copy (max 8000h)
CF clear if successful
ES:SI -> global descriptor table (Table 3-4)
   AH = status
      00h source copied into destination
      01h parity error
      02h interrupt error
      03h address line 20 gating failed
      80h invalid command (PC, PCjr)
      86h unsupported function (XT, PS30)

Details: Copy is done in protected mode with interrupts disabled.
Conflicts: This function is incompatible with the OS/2 compatibility box.
See Also: Functions 88h and 89h

Table 3-4. Format of global descriptor table:

Offset	Size	Description
00h	16 BYTEs	zeros
10h	WORD	source segment length in bytes (2*CX-1 or greater)
12h	3 BYTEs	24-bit linear source address, low byte first
15h	BYTE	source segment access rights (93h)
16h	WORD	zero
18h	WORD	destination segment length in bytes (2*CX-1 or greater)
1Ah	3 BYTEs	24-bit linear destination address, low byte first

Table 3-4. Format of global descriptor table (continued)

Offset	Size	Description
1Dh	BYTE	destination segment access rights (93h)
1Eh	18 BYTEs	zeros

INTERRUPT 15h - Function 88h
SYSTEM - GET EXTENDED MEMORY SIZE

Purpose: Returns amount of extended memory available, in kilobytes.

Available on: PC-AT, XT286, PS/2 models with 80286 or above.

Restrictions: none.

Registers at call:
AH = 88h

Return Registers:
CF clear if successful
    AX = number of contiguous KB starting at absolute address 100000h
CF set on error
    AH = status
        80h invalid command (PC, PCjr)
        86h unsupported function (XT, PS30)

Details: TSRs which wish to allocate extended memory to themselves often hook this call, and return a reduced memory size. They are then free to use the memory between the new and old sizes at will.

Conflicts: None known.

See Also: Function 87h

INTERRUPT 15h - Function 89h
SYSTEM - SWITCH TO PROTECTED MODE

Purpose: Switches system into protected mode.

Available on: PC-AT, XT286, PS/2 models with 80286 or above.

Restrictions: none.

Registers at call:
AH = 89h
BL = interrupt number of IRQ0
    (IRQ1-7 use next 7 interrupts)
BH = interrupt number of IRQ8
    (IRQ9-F use next 7 interrupts)
ES:SI -> GDT for protected mode
  offset 0h null descriptor
      (initialize to zeros)
    08h GDT descriptor
    10h IDT descriptor
    18h DS
    20h ES
    28h SS
    30h CS
    38h uninitialized, used to build descriptor for BIOS CS
CX = offset into protected-mode CS to jump to

Return Registers:
CF set on error
    AH = FFh error enabling address line 20
CF clear if successful
    AH = 00h in protected mode at specified address

Details: BL and BH must be multiples of 8.

Conflicts: None known.

See Also: Functions 87h and 88h, VCPI INT 67h Function DEh Subfunction 0Ch (chapter 10)

INTERRUPT 15h - Function 90h
OS HOOK - DEVICE BUSY

Purpose: To permit other programs to run while waiting for a busy device to become available.

Available on: PC-AT, PS/2.
Registers at call:
AH = 90h
AL = device type
   00h disk
   01h diskette
   02h keyboard
   03h PS/2 pointing device
   21h waiting for keyboard input
      (Phoenix BIOS)
   80h network
   FCh disk reset (PS)
   FDh diskette motor start
   FEh printer
ES:BX -> request block for type codes 80h through
   BFh
CF clear

Restrictions: none.
Return Registers:
CF set if wait time satisfied
CF clear if driver must perform wait
   AH = 00h

Details: Type codes are allocated as follows:
        00h-7Fh non-reentrant devices; OS must arbitrate access.
        80h-BFh reentrant devices; ES:BX points to a unique control block.
        C0h-FFh wait-only calls, no complementary INT 15h Function 91h call.
   This function should be hooked by a multitasker to allow other tasks to execute while the BIOS is waiting for I/O completion; the default handler merely returns with AH=00h and CF clear.
Conflicts: None known.
See Also: Function 91h

INTERRUPT 15h - Function 91h
OS HOOK - DEVICE POST

Purpose: To permit other programs to run while waiting for a busy device to become available.
Available on: PC-AT, PS/2.
Registers at call:
AH = 91h
AL = device type (see Function 90h)
ES:BX -> request block for type codes 80h through
   BFh
CF clear

Restrictions: none.
Return Registers:
AH = 00h

Details: This function should be hooked by a multitasker to allow other tasks to execute while the BIOS is waiting for I/O completion; the default handler merely returns with AH=00h and CF clear.
Conflicts: None known.
See Also: Function 90h

INTERRUPT 15h - Function C0h
SYSTEM - GET CONFIGURATION

Purpose: Returns pointer to configuration table in ROM BIOS.
Available on: XT after 1/10/86, PC-AT models
       3x9, Convertible, XT286, PS/2
       models.

Restrictions: see notes at end of table.

Registers at call:
AH = C0h

Return Registers:
CF set if BIOS does not support call
CF clear on success
    ES:BX -> ROM table (Table 3-5)
AH = status
    00h successful
    86h unsupported function

Details: The 1/10/86 XT BIOS returns an incorrect value for the feature byte. The configuration table is at F000h:E6F5h in 100% compatible BIOSes.
Conflicts: None known.

Table 3-5. Format of ROM configuration table

Offset	Size	Description
00h	WORD	number of bytes following
02h	BYTE	model (see below)
03h	BYTE	submodel (see below)
04h	BYTE	BIOS revision: 0 for first release, 1 for second, etc.
05h	BYTE	features:
		bit 7 = DMA channel 3 used by hard disk BIOS
		bit 6 = 2nd 8259 installed
		bit 5 = Real-Time Clock installed
		bit 4 = INT 15h Func 4Fh called upon INT 9h
		bit 3 = wait for external event supported
		bit 2 = extended BIOS data area allocated (usually at top of RAM)
		bit 1 = bus is Micro Channel instead of ISA
		bit 0 reserved
06h	WORD	reserved (0)
08h	WORD	reserved (0)
--AWARD BIOS		
0Ah		AWARD copyright notice here
--Phoenix BIOS		
0Ah	BYTE	BIOS major version
0Bh	BYTE	BIOS minor version (BCD)
0Ch	4 BYTEs	ASCIZ "PTL" (Phoenix Technologies Ltd)

Table 3-6. Values for model/submodel/revision

Value 1	Value 2	Value 3	Date	Model
FFh	*	*	04/24/81	PC (original)
FFh	*	*	10/19/81	PC (some bugfixes)
FFh	*	*	10/27/82	PC (HD, 640K, EGA support)
FFh	46h	***	*unknown*	Olivetti M15
FEh	*	*	08/16/82	PC XT
FEh	*	*	11/08/82	PC XT and Portable
FEh	43h	***	*unknown*	Olivetti M240
FDh	*	*	06/01/83	PCjr
FCh	*	*	01/10/84	AT models 068,099 6 MHz 20MB
FCh	00h	01h	06/10/85	AT model 239 6 MHz 30MB
FCh	00h	<>01h	*unknown*	7531/2 Industrial AT
FCh	01h	00h	11/15/85	AT models 319,339 8 MHz, Enh Keyb, 3.5"

* This BIOS call is not implemented in these early versions. Read Model byte at F000h:FFFEh and BIOS date at F000h:FFF5h.

*** These Olivetti machines store the submodel in the byte at F000h:FFFDh.

Table 3-6. Values for model/submodel/revision (continued)

Value 1	Value 2	Value 3	Date	Model
FCh	01h	00h	01/15&88	Toshiba T5200/100
FCh	01h	00h	12/26*89	Toshiba T1200/XE
				(Those date characters are not typos)
FCh	01h	*unknown*	*unknown*	Compaq 286/386
FCh	02h	00h	04/21/86	PC XT-286
FCh	04h	00h	02/13/87	PS/2 Model 50**
FCh	04h	03h	04/18/88	PS/2 Model 50Z
FCh	05h	00h	02/13/87	PS/2 Model 60**
FCh	06h	*unknown*	*unknown*	7552 "Gearbox"
FCh	09h	02h	06/28/89	PS/2 Model 30-286
FCh	0Bh	00h	02/16/90	PS/1
FCh	42h	***	*unknown*	Olivetti M280
FCh	45h	***	*unknown*	Olivetti M380 (XP 1, XP 3, XP 5)
FCh	48h	***	*unknown*	Olivetti M290
FCh	4Fh	***	*unknown*	Olivetti M250
FCh	50h	***	*unknown*	Olivetti M380 (XP 7)
FCh	51h	***	*unknown*	Olivetti PCS286
FCh	52h	***	*unknown*	Olivetti M300
FCh	81h	00h	01/15/88	Phoenix 386 BIOS v1.10 10a
FBh	00h	01h	01/10/86	PC XT, Enh Keyb, 3.5" support
FBh	00h	02h	05/09/86	PC XT
FBh	4Ch	***	*unknown*	Olivetti M200
FAh	00h	00h	09/02/86	PS/2 Model 30
FAh	00h	01h	12/12/86	PS/2 Model 30
FAh	01h	00h	*unknown*	PS/2 Model 25
FAh	4Eh	***	*unknown*	Olivetti M111
F9h	00h	00h	09/13/85	PC Convertible
F8h	00h	00h	03/30/87	PS/2 Model 80 16MHz**
F8h	01h	00h	10/07/87	PS/2 Model 80 20MHz
F8h	04h	02h	04/11/88	PS/2 Model 70 20MHz, type 2 system brd
F8h	04h	03h	03/17/89	PS/2 Model 70 20MHz, type 2 system brd
F8h	09h	*unknown*	*unknown*	PS/2 Model 70 16MHz, type 1 system brd
F8h	09h	02h	04/11/88	PS/2 Model 70 some models
F8h	09h	03h	03/17/89	PS/2 Model 70 some models
F8h	0Bh	00h	01/18/89	PS/2 Model P70 (8573-121) typ 2 sys brd
F8h	0Bh	02h	12/16/89	*PS/2 Model P70*
F8h	0Ch	00h	11/02/88	PS/2 Model 55SX
F8h	0Dh	*unknown*	*unknown*	PS/2 Model 70 25MHz, type 3 system brd
F8h	11h	00h	10/01/90	PS/2, unknown model
F8h	13h	00h	10/01/90	PS/2, unknown model
F8h	14h	00h	10/01/90	PS/2 Model 90-AK9
F8h	16h	00h	10/01/90	PS/2 Model 90-AKD
F8h	1Bh	00h	10/02/89	PS/2 Model 70-486
F8h	1Ch	00h	02/08/90	PS/2 Model 65-121
F8h	1Eh	00h	02/08/90	PS/2, unknown model
F8h	50h	00h	*unknown*	PS/2 Model P70 (8573) 16 MHz
F8h	50h	01h	12/16/89	PS/2 Model P70 (8570-031)
F8h	61h	***	*unknown*	Olivetti P500
F8h	62h	***	*unknown*	Olivetti P800
F8h	80h	01h	11/21/89	PS/2 Model 80-A21
9Ah	*	*	*unknown*	Compaq XT/Compaq Plus
30h	*unknown*	*unknown*	*unknown*	Sperry PC
2Dh	*	*	*unknown*	Compaq PC/Compaq Deskpro

** These BIOS versions require the DASDDRVR.SYS patches.

INTERRUPT 15h - Function C1h
RETURN EXTENDED BIOS DATA-AREA SEGMENT ADDRESS

Purpose: Provides segment address (only) of extended BIOS data area; the offset portion of the address is always 0000h.

Available on: PS/2 models.

Registers at call:
AH = C1h

Restrictions: none.

Return Registers:
CF set on error
CF clear if successful
    ES = segment of data area

Conflicts: None known.
See Also: Function 04h

INTERRUPT 15h - Function C2h, Subfunction 00h
POINTING DEVICE BIOS INTERFACE - ENABLE/DISABLE

Purpose: To enable or disable pointing device.

Available on: PS/2 models.

Registers at call:
AX = C200h
BH = 00h disable
    01h enable

Restrictions: none.

Return Registers:
CF set on error
    AH = status
        00h successful
        01h invalid function
        02h invalid input
        03h interface error
        04h need to resend
        05h no device handler installed

Details: This function is called by the mouse driver's initialization code if applicable; it need not be called by applications.
Conflicts: None known.
See Also: Mouse INT 33h (chapter 13)

INTERRUPT 15h - Function C2h, Subfunction 01h
POINTING DEVICE BIOS INTERFACE - RESET

Purpose: Resets mouse or alternate pointing device.

Available on: PS/2 models.

Registers at call:
AX = C201h

Restrictions: none.

Return Registers:
CF set on error
    AH = status (see above)
CF clear if successful
    BH = device ID

Details: This function is called by the mouse driver if applicable; it need not be called by applications.
Conflicts: None known.
See Also: Mouse INT 33h Function 00h (chapter 13)

INTERRUPT 15h - Function C2h, Subfunction 02h
POINTING DEVICE BIOS INTERFACE - SET SAMPLING RATE

Purpose: Specifies the polling rate for the mouse or other pointing device.

Available on: PS/2 models.

Registers at call:
AX = C202h
BH = sampling rate
    00h 10/second
    01h 20/second

Restrictions: none.

Return Registers:
CF set on error
    AH = status
        00h successful
        01h invalid function

02h 40/second
03h 60/second
04h 80/second
05h 100/second
06h 200/second

02h invalid input
03h interface error
04h need to resend
05h no device handler installed

Details: This function is called by the mouse driver if applicable; it need not be called by applications.
Conflicts: None known.
See Also: Mouse INT 33h Function 1Ch (chapter 13)

INTERRUPT 15h - Function C2h, Subfunction 03h
POINTING DEVICE BIOS INTERFACE - SET RESOLUTION

Purpose: Specifies the sensitivity level of the mouse or alternate pointing device.
Available on: PS/2 models.
Registers at call:
AX = C203h
BH = resolution:
    00h one count per mm (25 dpi)
    01h two counts per mm (50 dpi)
    02h four counts per mm (100 dpi)
    03h eight counts per mm (200 dpi)

Restrictions: none.
Return Registers:
CF set on error
    AH = status (see above)
CF clear if successful

Details: This function is called by the mouse driver if applicable; it need not be called by applications.
Conflicts: None known.

INTERRUPT 15h - Function C2h, Subfunction 04h
POINTING DEVICE BIOS INTERFACE - GET TYPE

Purpose: Determine type of pointing device present.
Available on: PS/2 models.
Registers at call:
AX = C204h

Restrictions: none.
Return Registers:
CF set on error
    AH = status:
        00h successful
        01h invalid function
        02h invalid input
        03h interface error
        04h need to resend
        05h no device handler installed
CF clear if successful
    BH = device ID

Details: This function is called by the mouse driver if applicable; it need not be called by applications.
Conflicts: None known.

INTERRUPT 15h - Function C2h, Subfunction 05h
POINTING DEVICE BIOS INTERFACE - INITIALIZE

Purpose: Initializes BIOS interface to pointing device.
Available on: PS/2 models.
Registers at call:
AX = C205h
BH = data package size (1 - 8 bytes)

Restrictions: none.
Return Registers:
CF set on error
    AH = status (see above)
CF clear if successful

Details: This function is called by the mouse driver if applicable; it need not be called by applications.
Conflicts: None known.
See Also: Function C2h Subfunction 01h

INTERRUPT 15h - Function C2h, Subfunction 06h
POINTING DEVICE BIOS INTERFACE - GET/SET SCALING FACTOR

Purpose: Reads status of, or specifies scaling factor for, pointing device.

Available on: PS/2 models.	**Restrictions:** none.
Registers at call:	**Return Registers:**
AX = C206h	CF set on error
BH = subfunction:	AH = status:
00h return device status	00h successful
01h set scaling at 1:1	01h invalid function
02h set scaling at 2:1	02h invalid input
	03h interface error
	04h need to resend
	05h no device handler installed
	CF clear if successful
	If subfunction 00h:
	BL = status:
	bit 0: right button pressed
	bit 1: reserved
	bit 2: left button pressed
	bit 3: reserved
	bit 4: 0 if 1:1 scaling, 1 if 2:1 scaling
	bit 5: device enabled
	bit 6: 0 if stream mode, 1 if remote mode
	bit 7: reserved
	CL = resolution (see Function C2h Subfunction 03h)
	DL = sample rate (reports per second)

Details: This function is called by the mouse driver if applicable; it need not be called by applications.

Conflicts: None known.

INTERRUPT 15h - Function C2h, Subfunction 07h
POINTING DEVICE BIOS INTERFACE - SET DEVICE HANDLER ADDRESS

Purpose: Establishes address of pointing device handler routine.

Available on: PS/2 models.	**Restrictions:** none.
Registers at call:	**Return Registers:**
AX = C207h	CF set on error
ES:BX = user device handler	AH = status (see above)
	CF clear if successful

Details: This function is called by the mouse driver if applicable; it need not be called by applications.

Conflicts: None known.

See Also: Mouse INT 33h Function 0Ch (chapter 13)

INTERRUPT 15h - Function C3h
SYSTEM - ENABLE/DISABLE WATCHDOG TIMEOUT

Purpose: Enables or disables automatic watchdog timer.

Available on: PS/2 model 50 and above.	**Restrictions:** none.
Registers at call:	**Return Registers:**
AH = C3h	CF set on error
AL = 00h disable	CF clear if successful
01h enable	
BX = timer counter	

Details: The watchdog timer generates an NMI.

Conflicts: None known.

INTERRUPT 15h - Function C4h
SYSTEM - PROGRAMMABLE OPTION SELECT

Purpose: Modifies system's internal configuration registers.

Available on: PS/2 model 50 and above.

Registers at call:

AH = C4h

AL = 00h return base POS register address

    01h enable slot

        BL = slot number

    02h enable adapter

Restrictions: none.

Return Registers:

CF set on error

DX = base POS register address (if function 00h)

Details: This function can render a system inoperable and require total configuration via the reference diskette. It should be approached with extreme caution.

Conflicts: None known.

INTERRUPT 15h - Function C5h
Undocumented OS HOOK - ROM BIOS TRACING CALLOUT

Purpose: Allow a program to determine when and for which purpose various ROM BIOS interrupt handlers are invoked.

Available on: PS/2 models 30/286, 50Z, and 95.

Registers at call:

AH = C5h

AL = interrupt being invoked

    01h INT 19h

    02h INT 14h

    03h INT 16h

    04h INT 40h (floppy INT 13h)

    05h INT 17h

    06h INT 10h

    07h INT 12h

    08h INT 11h

    09h INT 1A

Return Registers:

all registers except AX must be preserved

Details: This call is made as the very first action of the indicated ROM BIOS interrupt handlers on newer models of the PS/2 line. The default handler does nothing and returns CF clear for the above subfunctions, CF set and AH=86h for all other subfunctions. The value of AX passed to the original interrupt handler is pushed on stack immediately prior to call, where the handler may inspect it, if desired.

Conflicts: None known.

INTERRUPT 15h - Functions C6h through CFh
Unknown Functions

Purpose: The purpose of these functions had not yet been determined at the time of writing.

Available on: PS/2 Model 95

Registers at call:

AH = C6h through CFh

other unknown.

Restrictions: unknown.

Return Registers: unknown.

Conflicts: None known.

INTERRUPT 16h - Function 00h
KEYBOARD - GET KEYSTROKE

Purpose: Waits for keyboard input.

Available on: All machines.

Registers at call:

AH = 00h

Restrictions: none.

Return Registers:

AH = scan code

AL = ASCII character

Details: On extended keyboards, this function discards all extended keystrokes, returning only when a non-extended keystroke is available.
Conflicts: None known.
See Also: Functions 01h, 05h, and 10h

INTERRUPT 16h - Function 01h
KEYBOARD - CHECK FOR KEYSTROKE

Purpose: Checks for availablity of keyboard input.
Available on: All machines.
Registers at call:
AH = 01h

Restrictions: none.
Return Registers:
ZF set if no keystroke available
ZF clear if keystroke available
    AH = scan code
    AL = ASCII character

Details: If a keystroke is present, it is not removed from the keyboard buffer; however, any extended keystrokes which are not compatible with 83/84-key keyboards are removed in the process of checking whether a non-extended keystroke is available.
Conflicts: None known.
See Also: Functions 00h and 11h

INTERRUPT 16h - Function 02h
KEYBOARD - GET SHIFT FLAGS

Purpose: Returns shift-flags byte maintained by BIOS.
Available on: All machines.
Registers at call:
AH = 02h

Restrictions: none.
Return Registers:
AL = shift flags:
    bit 7: Insert active
      6: CapsLock active
      5: NumLock active
      4: ScrollLock active
      3: Alt key pressed (either Alt on 101/102-key
        keyboards)
      2: Ctrl key pressed (either Ctrl on 101/102-key
        keyboards)
      1: left shift key pressed
      0: right shift key pressed

Conflicts: None known.
See Also: Function 12h

INTERRUPT 16h - Function 03h
KEYBOARD - SET TYPEMATIC RATE AND DELAY

Purpose: Adjust repeat rate of keyboard.
Available on: PCjr, PC-AT, PS/2.

Registers at call:
AH = 03h
AL = subfunction:
    00h (PCjr) set default delay and rate
    01h (PCjr) increase delay before repeat
    02h (PCjr) decrease repeat rate by factor
        of 2
    03h (PCjr) increase delay and decrease
        repeat rate

Restrictions: PCjr functions are totally unlike those for other systems.
Return Registers: n/a

04h (PCjr) turn off typematic repeat
05h (AT, PS/2) set repeat rate and delay
    BH = delay value
        (00h = 250ms to 03h = 1000ms)
    BL = repeat rate
        (00h=30/sec to 0Ch=10/sec
        [default] to 1Fh=2/sec)
Conflicts: None known.

INTERRUPT 16h - Function 04h
KEYBOARD - SET KEYCLICK

Purpose: Enables or disables keyclick sound action.

Available on: PCjr only.   **Restrictions:** none.
Registers at call: **Return Registers:** n/a
AH = 04h
AL = keyclick state:
    00h off
    01h on
Conflicts: None known.
See Also: Function 03h

INTERRUPT 16h - Function 05h
KEYBOARD - STORE KEYSTROKE IN KEYBOARD BUFFER

Purpose: Emulates entry of keystroke under program control.

Available on: AT or PS/2 with enhanced keyboard   **Restrictions:** none.
                support only.
Registers at call: **Return Registers:**
AH = 05h   AL = 00h if successful
CH = scan code   01h if keyboard buffer full
CL = ASCII character
Details: Under DESQview, the following "keystrokes" invoke the indicated actions when they are read from the keyboard buffer:

38FCh	pops up DESQview main menu.
38FEh	closes current window.
38FFh	pops up DESQview Learn menu.

Conflicts: None known.
See Also: Function 00h, FAKEY.COM Function 71h (chapter 36), DESQview INT 15h Function DEh Subfunction 10h (chapter 15)

INTERRUPT 16h - Function 10h
KEYBOARD - GET ENHANCED KEYSTROKE

Purpose: Wait for any keyboard input.

Available on: AT or PS/2 with enhanced keyboard   **Restrictions:** none.
                support only.
Registers at call: **Return Registers:**
AH = 10h   AH = scan code
                                                 AL = ASCII character
Details: If no keystroke is available, this function waits until one is placed in the keyboard buffer. Unlike Function 00h, this function does not discard extended keystrokes.
Conflicts: None known.
See Also: Functions 00h and 11h

INTERRUPT 16h - Function 11h
KEYBOARD - CHECK FOR ENHANCED KEYSTROKE

Purpose: Checks for availablity of any keyboard input.

Available on: AT or PS/2 with enhanced keyboard
      only.

Restrictions: none.

Registers at call:
AH = 11h

Return Registers:
ZF set if no keystroke available
ZF clear if keystroke available
    AH = scan code
    AL = ASCII character

Details: If a keystroke is available, it is not removed from the keyboard buffer. Unlike Function 01h, this function does not discard extended keystrokes.

Conflicts: None known.

See Also: Functions 01h and 10h

INTERRUPT 16h - Function 12h
KEYBOARD - GET EXTENDED SHIFT STATES

Purpose: Returns all shift-flags information from enhanced keyboards.

Available on: AT or PS/2 with enhanced keyboard
      only.

Restrictions: none.

Registers at call:
AH = 12h

Return Registers:
AL = shift flags 1 (same as returned by Function 02h):
    bit 7: Insert active
      6: CapsLock active
      5: NumLock active
      4: ScrollLock active
      3: Alt key pressed (either Alt on 101/102-key
        keyboards)
      2: Ctrl key pressed (either Ctrl on 101/102-key
        keyboards)
      1: left shift key pressed
      0: right shift key pressed
AH = shift flags 2:
    bit 7: SysRq key pressed
      6: CapsLock pressed
      5: NumLock pressed
      4: ScrollLock pressed
      3: right Alt key pressed
      2: right Ctrl key pressed
      1: left Alt key pressed
      0: left Ctrl key pressed

Details: AL bit 3 is set only for left Alt key on many machines. AH bits 7 through 4 are always clear on a Compaq SLT/286.

Conflicts: None known.

See Also: Function 02h

INTERRUPT 17h - Function 00h
PRINTER - WRITE CHARACTER

Purpose: Outputs one byte to printer.

Available on: All machines.

Restrictions: none.

Registers at call:
AH = 00h
AL = character to write
DX = printer number (00h-02h)

Return Registers:
AH = printer status:
bit 7: not busy
6: acknowledge
5: out of paper
4: selected
3: I/O error
2: unused
1: unused
0: timeout

Conflicts: None known.

INTERRUPT 17h - Function 01h
PRINTER - INITIALIZE PORT

Purpose: Resets printer port.
Available on: All machines.
Registers at call:
AH = 01h
DX = printer number (00h-02h)
Conflicts: None known.
See Also: Function 02h

Restrictions: none.
Return Registers:
AH = printer status (see above)

INTERRUPT 17h - Function 02h
PRINTER - GET STATUS

Purpose: Obtains status of printer.
Available on: All machines.
Registers at call:
AH = 02h
DX = printer number (00h-02h)
Conflicts: INSET (chapter 36).
See Also: Function 01h

Restrictions: none.
Return Registers:
AH = printer status: (see above)

INTERRUPT 18h
START CASSETTE BASIC

Purpose: Invoke ROM-based BASIC interpreter.
Available on: Genuine IBM machines only.
Registers at call: n/a

Restrictions: See "Details" below.
Return Registers: n/a

Details: Only PCs produced by IBM contain BASIC in ROM, so the action is unpredicatable on compatibles; this interrupt often reboots the system, and often has no effect at all.
Conflicts: None known.

INTERRUPT 19h
SYSTEM - BOOTSTRAP LOADER

Purpose: Reboots system without clearing memory or restoring interrupt vectors.
Available on: All machines.
Registers at call:
To accomplish a warm boot equivalent to Ctrl-Alt-Del, store 1234h in 0040h:0072h and jump to FFFFh:0000h. For a cold boot equivalent to a reset, store 0000h at 0040h:0072h before jumping.

Restrictions: none.
Return Registers:
never returns

Details: Because interrupt vectors are preserved, this interrupt usually causes a system hang if any TSRs have hooked vectors from 00h through 1Ch, particularly INT 08h.

Usually, the BIOS will try to read sector 1, head 0, track 0 from drive A: to 0000h:7C00h. If this fails, and a hard disk is installed, the BIOS will read sector 1, head 0, track 0 of the first hard disk. This sector should contain a master bootstrap loader and a partition table.

After loading the master boot sector at 0000h:7C00h, the master bootstrap loader is given control. It will scan the partition table for an active partition, and will then load the operating system's bootstrap loader (contained in the first sector of the active partition) and give it control. True IBM PCs issue an INT 18h if neither floppy nor hard disk have a valid boot sector.

VDISK.SYS hooks this interrupt to allow applications to find out how much extended memory has been used by VDISKs (the three bytes at offset 2Ch in the INT 19h handler's segment contain the linear address of the first free extended memory).

The default handler is at F000h:E6F2h for 100% compatible BIOSes.

Conflicts: None known.
See Also: INT 18h, FOSSIL INT 14h Function 17h (chapter 17)

Table 3-7. Format of hard disk master boot sector:

Offset	Size	Description
00h	446 BYTEs	Master bootstrap loader code
1BEh	16 BYTEs	partition record for partition 1 (see below)
1CEh	16 BYTEs	partition record for partition 2
1DEh	16 BYTEs	partition record for partition 3
1EEh	16 BYTEs	partition record for partition 4
1FEh	WORD	signature, AA55h indicates valid boot block

Table 3-8. Format of partition record:

Offset	Size	Description
00h	BYTE	boot indicator (80h = active partition)
01h	BYTE	partition start head
02h	BYTE	partition start sector (bits 0-5)
03h	BYTE	partition start track (bits 8,9 in bits 6,7 of sector)
04h	BYTE	operating system indicator (see below)
05h	BYTE	partition end head
06h	BYTE	partition end sector (bits 0-5)
07h	BYTE	partition end track (bits 8,9 in bits 6,7 of sector)
08h	DWORD	sectors preceding partition
0Ch	DWORD	length of partition in sectors

Table 3-9. Values for operating system indicator:

Value	System
00h	empty
01h	DOS 12-bit FAT
02h	XENIX file system
03h	XENIX /usr file system (obsolete)
04h	DOS 16-bit FAT
05h	DOS 3.3+ extended partition
06h	DOS Large File System
07h	QNX, OS/2 HPFS
08h	AIX bootable partition
09h	AIX data partition
51h	Disk Manager
52h	CP/M
56h	*GB*
61h	SpeedStor
63h	SysV/386
64h	Novell NetWare

Table 3-9. Values for operating system indicator (continued)

Value	System
75h	PC/IX
80h	Minix v1.3 and below
81h	Minix v1.5+
DBh	CP/M
E1h	SpeedStor 12-bit FAT extended partition
E4h	SpeedStor 16-bit FAT extended partition
FEh	LANstep
FFh	bad blocks

INTERRUPT 1Ah - Function 00h
TIME - GET SYSTEM TIME

Purpose: Reads BIOS real-time clock maintained in RAM.

Available on: All machines.

Restrictions: Destroys midnight flag without adjusting DOS calendar; this can cause system calendar to lose a day.

Registers at call:
AH = 00h

Return Registers:
CX:DX = number of clock ticks since midnight
AL = midnight flag, nonzero if midnight passed since time last read

Details: There are approximately 18.2 clock ticks per second, 1800B0h per 24 hrs. IBM and many clone BIOSes set the flag for AL rather than incrementing it, leading to loss of a day if two consecutive midnights pass without a request for the time (e.g. if the system is on but idle).

Conflicts: None known.

See Also: Functions 01h and 02h, DOS INT 21h Function 2Ch (chapter 8)

INTERRUPT 1Ah - Function 01h
TIME - SET SYSTEM TIME

Purpose: Sets BIOS real-time clock maintained in RAM.

Available on: All machines.

Restrictions: none.

Registers at call:
AH = 01h
CX:DX = number of clock ticks since midnight

Return Registers: n/a

Conflicts: None known.

See Also: Functions 00h and, DOS INT 21h Function 2Dh

INTERRUPT 1Ah - Function 02h
TIME - GET REAL-TIME CLOCK TIME

Purpose: Reads CMOS clock data.

Available on: PC-AT, XT286, PS/2.

Restrictions: none.

Registers at call:
AH = 02h

Return Registers:
CF clear if successful
    CH = hour (BCD)
    CL = minutes (BCD)
    DH = seconds (BCD)
    DL = daylight savings flag (00h standard time, 01h daylight time)
CF set on error (i.e. clock not running or in middle of update)

Conflicts: None known.

See Also: Function 00h

INTERRUPT 1Ah - Function 03h
TIME - SET REAL-TIME CLOCK TIME

Purpose: Sets CMOS clock.
Available on: PC-AT, XT286, PS/2.   **Restrictions:** none.
Registers at call: **Return Registers:** n/a
AH = 03h
CH = hour (BCD)
CL = minutes (BCD)
DH = seconds (BCD)
DL = daylight savings flag (00h standard time,
    01h daylight time)
Conflicts: None known.
See Also: Function 01h

INTERRUPT 1Ah - Function 04h
TIME - GET REAL-TIME CLOCK DATE

Purpose: Read date from CMOS calendar.
Available on: PC-AT, XT286, PS/2.   **Restrictions:** none.
Registers at call: **Return Registers:**
AH = 04h   CF clear if successful
          CH = century (BCD)
          CL = year (BCD)
          DH = month (BCD)
          DL = day (BCD)
     CF set on error

Conflicts: None known.
See Also: Functions 02h and 05h, DOS INT 21h Function 2Ah (chapter 8)

INTERRUPT 1Ah - Function 05h
TIME - SET REAL-TIME CLOCK DATE

Purpose: Sets CMOS calendar.
Available on: PC-AT, XT286, PS/2.   **Restrictions:** none.
Registers at call: **Return Registers:** n/a
AH = 05h
CH = century (BCD)
CL = year (BCD)
DH = month (BCD)
DL = day (BCD)
Conflicts: None known.
See Also: Function 04h, DOS INT 21h Function 2Bh (chapter 8)

INTERRUPT 1Ah - Function 06h
TIME - SET ALARM

Purpose: Sets alarm time in CMOS.
Available on: PC-AT, XT286, PS/2.   **Restrictions:** none.
Registers at call: **Return Registers:**
AH = 06h   CF set on error (alarm already set or clock stopped for
CH = hour (BCD)   update)
CL = minutes (BCD)   CF clear if successful
DH = seconds (BCD)
Details: The alarm occurs every 24 hours until turned off, invoking INT 4Ah each time.
Conflicts: None known.
See Also: Function 07h, INT 4Ah

INTERRUPT 1Ah - Function 07h
TIME - CANCEL ALARM

Purpose: Disables CMOS alarm.
Available on: PC-AT, XT286, PS/2.   **Restrictions:** none.
Registers at call: **Return Registers:** none.
AH = 07h
Details: Does not disable the real-time clock's IRQ
Conflicts: None known.
See Also: Function 06h, IRQ8 on INT 70h (chapter 2)

INTERRUPT 1Ah - Function 08h
TIME - SET RTC ACTIVATED POWER ON MODE

Purpose: Specify the time at which power will automatically be turned on.
Available on: Convertible only.   **Restrictions:** none.
Registers at call: **Return Registers:** n/a
AH = 08h
CH = hours in BCD
CL = minutes in BCD
DH = seconds in BCD
Conflicts: None known.
See Also: Function 09h

INTERRUPT 1Ah - Function 09h
TIME - READ RTC ALARM TIME AND STATUS

Purpose: Determine the status and time setting of the real-time-clock alarm.
Available on: Convertible, PS/2 model 30.   **Restrictions:** none.
Registers at call:
AH = 09h

Return Registers:
CH = hours in BCD
CL = minutes in BCD
DH = seconds in BCD
DL = alarm status
    00h alarm not enabled
    01h alarm enabled but will not power up system
    02h alarm will power up system

Conflicts: None known.
See Also: Function 08h

INTERRUPT 1Ah - Function 0Ah
TIME - READ SYSTEM-TIMER DAY COUNTER

Purpose: To determine setting of DOS calendar.
Available on: XT2, PS/2 models.   **Restrictions:** none.
Registers at call: **Return Registers:**
AH = 0Ah   CF set on error
                                             CF clear if successful
    CX = count of days since Jan. 1, 1980.

Conflicts: None known.
See Also: Functions 04h and 0Bh

INTERRUPT 1Ah - Function 0Bh
TIME - SET SYSTEM-TIMER DAY COUNTER

Purpose: To set DOS calendar.
Available on: XT2, PS/2 models.   **Restrictions:** none.
Registers at call: **Return Registers:**
AH = 0Bh   CF set on error
CX = count of days since Jan 1, 1980   CF clear if successful
Conflicts: None known.
See Also: Functions 05h and 0Ah

INTERRUPT 1Ah - Function 80h
PCjr - SET UP SOUND MULTIPLEXOR

Purpose: Controls sound multiplexor circuits.
Available on: PCjr only.   **Restrictions:** none.
Registers at call: AH = 80h   **Return Registers:** n/a
AL = 00h source is 8253 channel 2
    01h source is cassette input
    02h source is I/O channel "Audio IN"
    03h source is sound generator chip
Conflicts: None known.

INTERRUPT 1Bh
KEYBOARD - CONTROL-BREAK HANDLER

Purpose: Called when INT 09h determines that Control-Break has been pressed.
Available on: All machines.   **Restrictions:** none.
Registers at call: n/a   **Return Registers:** n/a
Details: Normally points to a short routine in DOS which sets the Ctrl-C flag, thus invoking INT 23h the next time DOS checks for Ctrl-C.
Conflicts: None known.
See Also: INT 23h

INTERRUPT 1Ch
TIME - SYSTEM TIMER TICK

Purpose: Called on each clock tick by the INT 08h handler.
Available on: All machines.   **Restrictions:** none.
Registers at call: n/a   **Return Registers:** n/a
Details: This is the preferred interrupt to chain when a program needs to be invoked regularly.
Conflicts: None known.
See Also: INT 08h (chapter 2)

INTERRUPT 48h
KEYBOARD - CORDLESS KEYBOARD TRANSLATION

Purpose: Initiates data translation from cordless keyboard.
Available on: PCjr only.   **Restrictions:** none.
Registers at call: n/a   **Return Registers:** n/a
Conflicts: None known.
See Also: INT 49h

INTERRUPT 49h
SYSTEM DATA - NON-KEYBOARD SCAN-CODE TRANSLATION TABLE

Purpose: Not an interrupt; this vector is a far pointer to the translation table described in Table 3-10.
Available on: PCjr only.   **Restrictions:** none.

Registers at call: n/a
Conflicts: None known.
See Also: INT 48h

Return Registers: n/a

Table 3-10. Format of translation table

Offset	Size	Description
00h	BYTE	number of non-keyboard scancodes in the table
01h	N WORDs	high byte 00h (NUL) byte scancode with low order byte representing the scancode mapped values relative to their input values within the range of 56h through 7Eh.

INTERRUPT 4Ah
SYSTEM - USER ALARM HANDLER

Purpose: Hook to user-supplied alarm function.
Available on: Systems which provide RTC alarm capability (PC-AT, XT2, Convertible, PS/2)

Restrictions: none.

Registers at call: n/a

Return Registers: n/a

Details: This interrupt is invoked by the BIOS when a real-time clock alarm occurs. An application may use it to perform an action at a predetermined time; however, this interrupt is called from within a hardware interrupt handler, so all usual precautions against reentering DOS must be taken.
Conflicts: None known.
See Also: INT 1Ah Function 06h, DOS 3.2 INT 6Ch (chapter 8)

System Resume Vector

Purpose: Provides hook that is called when system automatically resumes operation in response to an RTC alarm.
Available on: Convertible only.

Restrictions: none.

Registers at call: n/a

Return Registers: n/a

Conflicts: DOS 3.2 Realtime Clock update (chapter 8).
MSee Also: INT 4Ah

Chapter 4

Vendor-Specific ROM BIOS Extensions

This chapter describes ROM BIOS extensions that are unique to a single non-IBM vendor. The information is organized in alphabetic sequence by vendor name, and within each vendor's section, in numeric sequence by INT number, function, and subfunction.

Amstrad

INTERRUPT 15h - Function 00h

Amstrad PC1512 - GET AND RESET MOUSE COUNTS

Purpose: Reads mouse position and resets motion counters.

Available on: Amstrad PC1512 only.

Registers at call:

AH = 00h

Restrictions: none.

Return Registers:

CX = signed X count

DX = signed Y count

Conflicts: Cassette (chapter 3), MultiDOS Plus (chapter 16), VMiX (chapter 17).

INTERRUPT 15h - Function 01h

Amstrad PC1512 - WRITE DATA TO NON-VOLATILE RAM

Purpose: Writes one byte to CMOS RAM.

Available on: Amstrad PC1512 only.

Registers at call:

AH = 01h

AL = NVRAM location (00h to 3Fh)

BL = NVRAM data value

Restrictions: none.

Return Registers:

AH = return code

    00h OK

    01h address bad

    02h write error

Conflicts: None known.

See Also: Function 02h

Table 4-1. Format of Non-Volatile RAM

Offset	Size	Description
00h	BYTE	time of day: seconds
01h	BYTE	alarm time: seconds
02h	BYTE	time of day: minutes
03h	BYTE	alarm time: minutes
04h	BYTE	time of day: hours
05h	BYTE	alarm time: hours
06h	BYTE	day of week, 1 = Sunday
07h	BYTE	day of month
08h	BYTE	month
09h	BYTE	year mod 100
0Ah	BYTE	RTC status register A:
		bit 7: set if date/time being updated
		6-4: time base speed, default 010 = 32768 Hz
		3-0: interrupt rate selection, default 0110 = 1024 Hz

Table 4-1. Format of Non-Volatile RAM (continued)

Offset	Size	Description
0Bh	BYTE	RTC status register B:
		bit 7: clear if normal update, set if abort update
		6: periodic interrupt enable
		5: alarm interrupt enable
		4: update end interrupt enable
		3: square wave enable
		2: date mode (clear = BCD, set = binary)
		1: 24-hour format
		0: daylight saving time enable
0Ch	BYTE	RTC status register C (read-only):
		bit 7: IRQF flag
		6: PF flag
		5: AF flag
		4: UF flag
0Dh	BYTE	RTC status register D:
		bit 7: battery good
0Eh	6 BYTEs	time and date machine was last used
14h	BYTE	user RAM checksum
15h	WORD	Enter key scancode/ASCII code
17h	WORD	Forward delete key scancode/ASCII code
19h	WORD	Joystick fire button 1 scancode/ASCII code
1Bh	WORD	Joystick fire button 2 scancode/ASCII code
1Dh	WORD	mouse button 1 scancode/ASCII code
1Fh	WORD	mouse button 2 scancode/ASCII code
21h	BYTE	mouse X scaling factor
22h	BYTE	mouse Y scaling factor
23h	BYTE	initial VDU mode and drive count
24h	BYTE	initial VDU character attribute
25h	BYTE	size of RAM disk in 2K blocks
26h	BYTE	initial system UART setup byte
27h	BYTE	initial external UART setup byte
28h	24 BYTEs	available for user application

Details: Bytes 00h-0Dh are the same on the IBM AT since they are used/updated by the clock chip.
Conflicts: Cassette (chapter 3), MultiDOS Plus (chapter 16), VMiX (chapter 17).

INTERRUPT 15h - Function 02h
Amstrad PC1512 - READ DATA FROM NON-VOLATILE RAM

Purpose: To read data from NVRAM.
Available on: Amstrad PC1512 only.
Registers at call:
AH = 02h
AL = NVRAM location (00h to 3Fh)
    (see Table 4-1)

Restrictions: none.
Return Registers:
AH = return code:
    00h OK
    01h address bad
    02h checksum error
AL = NVRAM data value

Conflicts: Cassette (chapter 3), MultiDOS Plus (chapter 16), VMiX (chapter 17).
See Also: Function 01h

INTERRUPT 15h - Function 03h
Amstrad PC1512 - WRITE VDU COLOR PLANE WRITE REGISTER

Purpose: Sets video display unit plane(s) to be written.
Available on: Amstrad PC1512 only.

Restrictions: none.

Registers at call:
AH = 03h
AL = value (I,R,G,B bits)
Conflicts: Cassette (chapter 3), MultiDOS Plus (chapter 16), VMiX (chapter 17).
See Also: Function 04h

Return Registers: *unknown.*

INTERRUPT 15h - Function 04h
Amstrad PC1512 - WRITE VDU COLOR PLANE READ REGISTER

Purpose: Sets video display unit plane(s) to be read.
Available on: Amstrad PC1512 only.
Registers at call:
AH = 04h
AL = value (RDSEL1 and RDSEL0)
Conflicts: Build ABIOS System Parameter Table (chapter 3), MultiDOS Plus (chapter 16), VMiX (chapter 17).
See Also: Functions 03h and 05h

Restrictions: none.
Return Registers: *unknown.*

INTERRUPT 15h - Function 05h
Amstrad PC1512 - WRITE VDU GRAPHICS BORDER REGISTER

Purpose: Establishes border color for video display unit.
Available on: Amstrad PC1512 only.
Registers at call:
AH = 05h
AL = value (I,R,G,B bits)
Conflicts: Build ABIOS Initialisation Table (chapter 3), MultiDOS Plus (chapter 16), VMiX (chapter 17).
See Also: Function 04h

Restrictions: none.
Return Registers: *unknown.*

INTERRUPT 15h - Function 06h
Amstrad PC1512 - GET ROS VERSION NUMBER

Purpose: Determine ROM version number.
Available on: Amstrad PC1512 only.
Registers at call:
AH = 06h
Conflicts: MultiDOS Plus (chapter 16), VMiX (chapter 17).

Restrictions: none.
Return Registers:
BX = version number

AT&T 6300

INTERRUPT 1Ah - Function FEh
AT&T 6300 - READ TIME AND DATE

Purpose: Read both time and date for the system. Note that the day count starts four years later than the industry standard date.
Available on: AT&T 6300 systems only.
Registers at call:
AH = FEh

Restrictions: none.
Return Registers:
BX = day count (0 = Jan 1, 1984)
CH = hour
CL = minute
DL = hundredths

Conflicts: None known.
See Also: Function FFh, DOS INT 21h Functions 2Ah and 2Ch (chapter 8)

INTERRUPT 1Ah - Function FFh
AT&T 6300 - SET TIME AND DATE

Purpose: Set both time and date for the system. Note that the day count starts four years later than the industry standard date.

Available on: AT&T 6300 systems only.

Registers at call:

AH = FFh

BX = day count (0 = Jan 1, 1984)

CH = hour

CL = minute

DH = second

DL = hundredths

Conflicts: None known.

See Also: Function FEh, DOS INT 21h Functions 2Bh and 2Dh (chapter 8)

Restrictions: none.

Return Registers: *unknown.*

Atari Portfolio

The Portfolio is a "palmtop" computer.

INTERRUPT 60h
USER INTERFACE FUNCTIONS

Purpose: Provide functions for interacting with the user.

Available on: Atari Portfolio only.

Restrictions: none.

Details: This interrupt supplies a number of subfunctions which perform such functions as drawing boxes and menus, and provide input line editing.

Conflicts: see Table 1-3 in chapter 1.

See Also: INT 61h

INTERRUPT 61h
EXTENDED BIOS

Purpose: Access extended functions for controlling the system.

Available on: Atari Portfolio only.

Restrictions: none.

Details: This interrupt provides subfunctions such as turning off the machine, accessing internal variables, and mapping memory cards.

Conflicts: see Table 1-3 in chapter 1.

See Also: INT 60h

Compaq

INTERRUPT 15h - Function 40h, Subfunction 00h
Compaq SLT/286 or Portable 386 - READ LCD/PLASMA TIMEOUT

Purpose: Gets timeout value for display in minutes.

Available on: Compaq SLT/286 or Portable 386.

Registers at call:

AX = 4000h

Restrictions: none.

Return Registers:

AX = 4000h

CL = 00h timeout disabled
　　　else timeout in minutes

Conflicts: PC Convertible (chapter 3).

See Also: Function 40h Subfunction 01h, Function 46h Subfunction 00h

INTERRUPT 15h - Function 40h, Subfunction 01h
Compaq SLT/286 or Portable 386 - SET LCD/PLASMA TIMEOUT

Purpose: Sets timeout value for display in minutes.

Available on: Compaq SLT/286 or Portable 386.

Restrictions: none.

Registers at call:
AX = 4001h
CL = 00h timeout disabled
    else timeout in minutes

Return Registers:
AL = 00h timeout modified
    01h timeout cannot be modified
    40h timeout cannot be modified
CL = 00h timeout disabled
    else timeout in minutes

Conflicts: PC Convertible (chapter 3).
See Also: Function 40h Subfunction 00h, Function 46h Subfunction 01h

INTERRUPT 15h - Function 42h, Subfunction 80h
Compaq SLT/286 - ENTER STANDBY MODE

Purpose: Places system in power conservation (standby) mode.
Available on: Compaq SLT/286 only.
Registers at call:
AX = 4280h

Restrictions: none.
Return Registers:
AH = 42h
CF clear if successful
CF set if unable to enter standby

Conflicts: PC Convertible (chapter 3).
See Also: Function 46h Subfunction 00h

INTERRUPT 15h - Function 46h, Subfunction 00h
Compaq SLT/286 - READ POWER CONSERVATION/MODEM CONFIGURATION

Purpose: Determine current power conservation and modem configurations.
Available on: Compaq SLT/286 only.
Registers at call:
AX = 4600h

Restrictions: none.
Return Registers:
AH = modem configuration information:
    bit 0 powerup state
        0 off
        1 on
    1 modem installed
    2 IRQ line assignment
        0 IRQ 4
        1 IRQ 3
    3 COM port assignment
        0 = COM 2
        1 = COM 1
    4 modem state
        0 not assigned
        1 assigned
    5 modem is on
AL = power conservation status information:
    bit 0 power source (0 internal, 1 external)
    1-2 low battery state
        00 no low battery condition
        01 low battery 1
        10 reserved
        11 low battery 2
    3-4 power conservation mode
        00 automatic
        01 on
        10 off
        11 reserved
BH = default system inactivity timeout (1-21 minutes)

BL = current system inactivity timeout (1-21 minutes)
CH = default video display inactivity timeout
    (1-63 minutes)
CL = current video display inactivity timeout
    (1-63 minutes)
DH = default fixed disk drive inactivity timeout
    (1-21 minutes)
DL = current fixed disk drive inactivity timeout
    (1-21 minutes)

Conflicts: None known.
See Also: Function 42h Subfunction 80h, Function 46h Subfunction 01h, Compaq INT 77h (chapter 2)

INTERRUPT 15h - Function 46h, Subfunction 01h
Compaq SLT/286 - MODIFY POWER CONSERVATION/MODEM CONFIGURATION

Purpose: Set current power conservation and modem configurations.
Available on: Compaq SLT/286.　　　　　　**Restrictions:** none.
Registers at call:　　　　　　　　　　　　**Return Registers:**
AX = 4601h　　　　　　　　　　　　　　　　CF clear if successful
BL = system inactivity timeout (1-21 minutes)　　AH = 00h
　　FFh do not change　　　　　　　　　　　BL = current system inactivity timeout
CL = video display inactivity timeout (1-63　　　　　(1-21 minutes)
　　　minutes)　　　　　　　　　　　　　　CL = current video display inactivity timeout
　　FFh do not change　　　　　　　　　　　　　(1-63 minutes)
DL = current fixed disk drive inactivity timeout　DL = current fixed disk drive inactivity timeout
　　(1-21 minutes)　　　　　　　　　　　　　　(1-21 minutes)
　　FFh do not change　　　　　　　　　　　DH = FFh modem state unchanged
DH = 00h turn modem OFF　　　　　　　　　　　= 00h modem turned OFF
　　01h turn modem ON　　　　　　　　　　　　= 01h modem turned ON
　　FFh do not change modem state　　　　　CF set on error
　　　　　　　　　　　　　　　　　　　　　AH = 01h input is out of range
　　　　　　　　　　　　　　　　　　　　　　= 02h - No modem present

Conflicts: None known.
See Also: Function 46h Subfunction 00h, Compaq INT 77h (chapter 2)

INTERRUPT 15h - Function E0h, Subfunction 0Fh
Compaq Systempro - MULTIPROCESSOR DISPATCH

Purpose: Initiate a process on the other processor of a dual-processor system.
Available on: Compaq Systempro only.　　　**Restrictions:** none.
Registers at call:　　　　　　　　　　　　**Return Registers:**
AX = E00Fh　　　　　　　　　　　　　　　　AL = 0Fh successful
ES:BX -> start of 2nd processor's execution　　　00h failure
Conflicts: None known.
See Also: Function E1h Subfunction 0Eh, Function E2h Subfunction 00h

INTERRUPT 15h - Function E1h, Subfunction 0Eh
Compaq Systempro - MULTIPROCESSOR END-OF-DISPATCH

Purpose: Terminate the current activity on the other processor of a dual-processor system.
Available on: Compaq Systempro only.　　　**Restrictions:** none.
Registers at call:　　　　　　　　　　　　**Return Registers:**
AX = E10Eh　　　　　　　　　　　　　　　　AL = 0Fh successful (halted)
ES:BX -> start of 2nd processor's execution　　　00h failure (not halted)
Conflicts: None known.
See Also: Function E0h Subfunction 0Fh, Function E2h Subfunction 00h

INTERRUPT 15h - Function E2h, Subfunction 00h
Compaq Systempro - MULTIPROCESSOR AVAILABLE

Purpose: Determine whether the other processor of a dual-processor system is available for dispatching.

Available on: Compaq Systempro only.   **Restrictions:** none.

Registers at call: **Return Registers:**

AX = E200h   AX = 8000h if 2nd processor available

Conflicts: None known.

See Also: Function E0h Subfunction 0Fh, Function E1h Subfunction 0Eh

INTERRUPT 16h - Function F0h
Compaq 386 - SET CPU SPEED

Purpose: Set CPU speed for the system.

Available on: Compaq 386 models only.   **Restrictions:** none.

Registers at call: **Return Registers:** *unknown.*

AH = F0h

AL = speed:

   00h equivalent to 6 MHz 80286 (COMMON)

   01h equivalent to 8 MHz 80286 (FAST)

   02h full 16 MHz (HIGH)

   03h toggles between 8 MHz-equivalent and
      speed set by system-board switch (AUTO or
      HIGH)

   08h full 16 MHz except 8 MHz-equivalent
      during floppy-disk access

   09h specify speed directly

      CX = speed value, 1 (slowest) to 50 (full),
         3 is approximately 8088 speed

Conflicts: TurboPower TSRs Installation Check (chapter 36).

See Also: Functions F1h and F3h

INTERRUPT 16h - Function F1h
Compaq 386 - READ CURRENT CPU SPEED

Purpose: Obtain current speed setting.

Available on: Compaq 386 models only.   **Restrictions:** none.

Registers at call: **Return Registers:**

AH = F1h   AL = speed code (see Function F0h)

     CX = speed code if AL = 09h

Conflicts: None known.

See Also: Functions F0h and F3h

INTERRUPT 16h - Function F2h
Compaq 386 - DETERMINE ATTACHED KEYBOARD TYPE

Purpose: Determine whether the keyboard is PC or AT type.

Available on: Compaq 386 models only.   **Restrictions:** none.

Registers at call: **Return Registers:**

AH = F2h   AL = type:

        00h if 11-bit AT keyboard is in use

        01h if 9-bit PC keyboard is in use

Conflicts: None known.

INTERRUPT 16h - Function F3h
Compaq 80286s - SET CPU SPEED LIMIT (OVERRIDE JUMPER)

Purpose: Establish limit on CPU speed.
Available on: Compaq 80286 models only.   **Restrictions:** none.
Registers at call: **Return Registers:** *unknown.*
AH = F3h
AL = 00h limit is 6 Mhz
    01h limit is 8 Mhz/6 Mhz
Conflicts: None known.
See Also: Functions F0h and F1h

INTERRUPT 16h - Function F4h, Subfunction 00h
Compaq Systempro - CACHE CONTROLLER STATUS

Purpose: Determine whether memory is being cached.
Available on: Compaq Systempro only.   **Restrictions:** none.
Registers at call: **Return Registers:**
AX = F400h   AH = E2h
                                           AL = status
                                                00h no cache controller
                                                01h enabled
                                                02h disabled
Conflicts: None known.
See Also: Function F4h Subfunctions 01h and 02h
Compaq Systempro - ENABLE CACHE CONTROLLER

INTERRUPT 16h - Function F4h, Subfunction 01h

Purpose: Enable memory cache controller.
Available on: Compaq Systempro only.   **Restrictions:** none.
Registers at call: **Return Registers:**
AX = F401h   AX = E201h
Conflicts: None known.
See Also: Function F4h Subfunctions 00h and 02h

INTERRUPT 16h - Function F4h, Subfunction 02h
Compaq Systempro - DISABLE CACHE CONTROLLER

Purpose: Disable memory cache controller.
Available on: Compaq Systempro only.   **Restrictions:** none.
Registers at call: **Return Registers:**
AX = F402h   AX = E202h
Conflicts: None known.
See Also: Function F4h Subfunctions 00h and 01h

EISA System ROM

INTERRUPT 15h - Function D8h, Subfunction 00h
EISA SYSTEM ROM - READ SLOT CONFIGURATION INFORMATION

Purpose: Determine slot configuration.
Available on: EISA systems.   **Restrictions:** none.

Registers at call:
AX = D800h
CL = slot number (including embedded and virtual)

Return Registers:
CF clear if successful
    AH = 00h
CF set on error
    AH = error code
        80h invalid slot number
        82h EISA CMOS corrupt
        83h empty slot

        86h invalid BIOS-FW function call
        87h invalid system configuration
    AL bit flags
      bit 7: set if duplicate IDs
        6: set if product ID readable
        4,5: slot type (00=expansion, 01=embedded,
          10=virtual device)
        0-3: duplicate ID number if bit 7 set
    BH = major revision level of configuration utility
    BL = minor revision level of configuration utility
    CX = checksum of configuration file
    DH = number of device functions
    DL = combined function information byte
    SI:DI = 4-byte compressed ID (DI = bytes 0&1,
        SI = bytes 2&3)

Details: Call with AL=80h if using 32-bit CS addressing mode instead of 16-bit.
Conflicts: None known.
See Also: Function D8h Subfunctions 01h and 04h

INTERRUPT 15h - Function D8h, Subfunction 01h
EISA SYSTEM ROM - READ FUNCTION CONFIGURATION INFORMATION

Purpose: Determine function configuration.
Available on: EISA systems.
Registers at call:
AX = D801h
CH = function number to read
CL = slot number (including embedded and virtual)
DS:SI -> 320-byte buffer for standard configuration
    data block

Restrictions: none.
Return Registers:
CF clear if successful
    AH = 00h
    DS:SI buffer filled
CF set on error
    AH = error code:
        80h invalid slot number
        81h invalid function number
        82h EISA CMOS corrupt
        83h empty slot
        86h invalid BIOS-FW function call
        87h invalid system configuration
    BX destroyed

Details: Call with AL=81h if using 32-bit CS addressing mode instead of 16-bit.
Conflicts: None known.

INTERRUPT 15h - Function D8h, Subfunction 02h
EISA SYSTEM ROM - CLEAR NONVOLATILE MEMORY (EISA CMOS)

Purpose: Clear CMOS memory.
Available on: EISA systems.

Restrictions: none.

Registers at call:
AX = D802h
BH = EISA config utility major revision level
BL = EISA config utility minor revision level

Return Registers:
CF clear if successful
  AH = 00h
CF set on error
  AH = error code:
      84h error clearing CMOS
      86h invalid BIOS-FW function call
      88h config utility version not supported

Details: Call with AL=82h if using 32-bit CS addressing mode instead of 16-bit.
Conflicts: None known.
See Also: Function D8h Subfunction 03h

INTERRUPT 15h - Function D8h, Subfunction 03h
EISA SYSTEM ROM - WRITE NONVOLATILE MEMORY

Purpose: Write data to CMOS memory.
Available on: EISA systems.
Restrictions: none.

Registers at call:
AX = D803h
CX = length of data structure (0000h = empty slot)
    includes two bytes for config file checksum
DS:SI -> configuration data

Return Registers:
CF clear if successful
  AH = 00h
CF set on error
  AH = error code
      84h error clearing CMOS
      85h EISA CMOS is full
      86h invalid BIOS-FW function call

Details: Call with AL=83h if using 32-bit CS addressing mode instead of 16-bit.
Conflicts: None known.
See Also: Function D8h Subfunction 02h

INTERRUPT 15h - Function D8h, Subfunction 04h
EISA SYSTEM ROM - READ PHYSICAL SLOT

Purpose: Reads slot information.
Available on: EISA systems.
Restrictions: none.

Registers at call:
AX = D804h
CL = slot number (including embedded and virtual)

Return Registers:
CF clear if successful
  AH = 00h
CF set on error
  AH = error code
      80h invalid slot number
      83h empty slot
      86h invalid BIOS-FW function call
  SI:DI = 4-byte compressed ID
      (DI = bytes 0&1, SI = bytes 2&3)

Details: Call with AL=84h if using 32-bit CS addressing mode instead of 16-bit.
Conflicts: None known.
See Also: Function D8h Subfunction 00h

INTERRUPT 15h - Function D8h, Subfunctions 80h to 84h
EISA SYSTEM ROM - 32-bit CS ADDRESSING MODE CALLS

Purpose: Distinguish between 16-bit and 32-bit information.
Available on: EISA systems.
Restrictions: none.

Registers at call:
AH = D8h
AL = 80h to 84h
other registers as appropriate for AL=00h to 04h

Return Registers:
as appropriate for AL=00h to 04h

Details: These functions are identical to Function D8h Subfunctions 00h through 04h, except that they should be called when using 32-bit CS addressing mode (pointers use ESI rather than SI as offset) instead of 16-bit addressing mode.
Conflicts: None known.
See Also: Function D8h Subfunctions 00h through 04h

Hewlett-Packard

INTERRUPT 06h
HP 95LX - SLEEP/WAKEUP

Purpose: Called just before going into light or deep (shutdown) sleep and just after returning from a sleep.
Available on: HP 95LX only
Restrictions: none.
Registers at call: n/a
Return Registers: n/a
Conflicts: CPU-generated INVALID OPCODE (chapter 2).

INTERRUPT 5Fh
HP 95LX - GRAPHICS PRIMITIVES

Purpose: Provides a variety of useful graphics functions.
Available on: HP 95LX only
Restrictions: none.
Registers at call:
Return Registers: varies
AH = function number (00h-0Fh)
other registers vary
Conflicts: DESQview IRQ15 (chapter 2), DoubleDOS IRQ7 (chapter 2).
See Also: INT 60h

INTERRUPT 60h
HP 95LX SYSTEM MANAGER

Purpose: Provide access to the System Manager program.
Available on: HP 95LX only
Restrictions: none.
Conflicts: See Table 1-3 in chapter 1.
See Also: INT 5Fh, INT 61h

INTERRUPT 61h
HP 95LX SYSTEM MANAGER - LOAD DS

Purpose: Called by the System Manager program to determine where it should store its data.
Available on: HP 95LX only
Restrictions: none.
Conflicts: See Table 1-3 in chapter 1.
See Also: INT 5Fh, INT 60h

INTERRUPT 6Fh - Function 0012h, Subfunction 22h
HP ES-12 EXTENDED BIOS - READ CMOS MEMORY

Purpose: Read a byte from CMOS memory.
Available on: HP ES-12 Extended BIOS.
Restrictions: none.
Registers at call:
Return Registers:
BP = 0012h
AH = status
AH = 22h
AL = byte read
BL = address of CMOS byte to read
BP, DS destroyed
Conflicts: Novell NetWare PCOX API (chapter 20), 10-Net (chapter 23).
See Also: Function 0012h Subfunction 24h

INTERRUPT 6Fh - Function 0012h, Subfunction 24h
HP ES-12 EXTENDED BIOS - WRITE CMOS MEMORY

Purpose: Write a byte to CMOS memory.
Available on: HP ES-12 Extended BIOS.   **Restrictions:** none.
Registers at call: **Return Registers:**
BP = 0012h   AH = status
AH = 24h   BP, DS destroyed
BL = address of CMOS byte to write
AL = new value
Conflicts: Novell NetWare PCOX API (chapter 20), 10-Net (chapter 23).
See Also: Function 0012h Subfunction 22h

Phoenix BIOS

INTERRUPT 15h - Function BCh
DETERMINE CPU SPEED

Purpose: Determine CPU operating speed.
Available on: Systems using Phoenix 386 BIOS   **Restrictions:** none.
                 chips.
Registers at call: **Return Registers:**
AH = BCh   CF clear
                                                   BYTE 0040h:00B0h set to relative speed
                                                       (higher = faster CPU)
Details: The computed speed is affected by whether or not the BIOS is shadowed.
Conflicts: None known.

Texas Instruments

INTERRUPT 49h
Texas Instruments PC - VIDEO I/O

Purpose: Apparently provides direct video display on the TI Professional PC.
Available on: TI Professional PC only.   **Restrictions:** none.
Registers at call: *unknown.*   **Return Registers:** *unknown.*
Conflicts: None known.

Victor

INTERRUPT DFh
Victor 9000 SuperBIOS

Purpose: *unknown.*
Available on: Victor model 9000 only.   **Restrictions:** none.
Registers at call: *unknown.*   **Return Registers:** *unknown.*
Conflicts: None known.

Zenith

INTERRUPT 69h
Zenith AT BIOS - Unknown Function

Purpose: called by INT 09h handler.
Available on: Zenith 80286 models only.   **Restrictions:** none.
Registers at call: *unknown.*   **Return Registers:** *unknown.*
Conflicts: DECnet DOS CTERM (chapter 24).

INTERRUPT FFh
Z100 - WARM BOOT

Purpose: Re-boots the system.
Available on: Heath-Zenith Z-100 only.   **Restrictions:** none.
Registers at call: n/a   **Return Registers:** n/a.
Conflicts: AT/XT286/PS50+ return from protected mode (chapter 1).

Chapter 5

Video

Virtually all IBM and video-compatible systems use the BIOS interface at INT 10h to control video actions. Although this conflicts with the CPU-generated Coprocessor Error fault described in chapter 2, the conflict is not specifically mentioned in this chapter since it would apply to all uses of INT 10h for any interfacing purpose.

There are some additional calls related to video services in other chapters. TopView virtual screen support on INT 10h is covered in chapter 15, Alloy NTNX and 386/MultiWare screen-related calls are discussed in chapter 18, and MultiDOS screen-related calls on INT 15h are listed in chapter 16.

INTERRUPT 10h - Function 00h

SET VIDEO MODE

Purpose: Establishes CRT operating conditions.

Available on: All machines.

Registers at call:

AH = 00h
AL = mode (see Table 5-1)

Restrictions: none.

Return Registers:

AL = video mode flag (Phoenix BIOS):
    20h mode > 7
    30h modes <= 7 except mode 6
    3Fh mode 6
AL = CRT controller mode byte (Phoenix 386 BIOS v1.10)

Details: IBM standard modes do not clear the screen if the high bit of AL is set (EGA or higher only).

The Tseng ET-4000 chipset is used by the Orchid Prodesigner II, Diamond SpeedSTAR VGA, and Groundhog Graphics Shadow VGA.

Conflicts: None known other than those shown in table.

See Also: Function 00h Subfunctions 70h and 7Eh, Function 6Fh Subfunction 05h

Table 5-1. Values for Video Mode

TEXT/ GRPH	TEXT RESOL	PIXEL BOX	PIXEL RESOLTN	COLORS	DISPLY PAGES	SCRN ADDR	SYSTEM
00h = T	40x25	8x8		16gray	8	B800	CGA,PCjr
= T	40x25	8x14		16gray	8	B800	EGA
= T	40x25	8x16		16	8	B800	MCGA
= T	40x25	9x16		16	8	B800	VGA
01h = T	40x25	8x8		16	8	B800	CGA,PCjr
= T	40x25	8x14		16	8	B800	EGA
= T	40x25	8x16		16	8	B800	MCGA
= T	40x25	9x16		16	8	B800	VGA
02h = T	80x25	8x8		16gray	4	B800	CGA,PCjr
= T	80x25	8x14		16gray	4	B800	EGA
= T	80x25	8x16		16	4	B800	MCGA
= T	80x25	9x16		16	4	B800	VGA

Table 5-1. Values for Video Mode (continued)

TEXT/ GRPH	TEXT RESOL	PIXEL BOX	PIXEL RESOLTN	COLORS	DISPLAY PAGES	SCRN ADDR	SYSTEM
03h = T	80x25	8x8		16	4	B800	CGA,PCjr
= T	80x25	8x14		16	4	B800	EGA
= T	80x25	8x16		16	4	B800	MCGA
= T	80x25	9x16		16	4	B800	VGA
04h = G	40x25	8x8	320x200	4		B800	CGA, PCjr,EGA, MCGA, VGA
05h = G	40x25	8x8	320x200	4gray		B800	CGA, PCjr, EGA
= G	40x25	8x8	320x200	4		B800	MCGA, VGA
06h = G	80x25	8x8	640x200	2		B800	CGA, PCjr,EGA, MCGA, VGA
07h = T	80x25	9x14		mono	var	B000	MDA, Hercules, EGA
= T	80x25	9x16		mono		B000	VGA
08h = G	20x25	8x8	160x200	16			PCjr
= T	132x25	8x8		16		B800	ATI EGA/VGA Wonder **
= T	132x25	8x8		mono		B000	ATI EGA/VGA Wonder **
= G	90x43	8x8	720x352	mono		B000	Hercules +MSHERC.COM
09h = G	40x25	8x8	320x200	16			PCjr
0Ah = G	80x25	8x8	640x200	4			PCjr
0Bh = reserved (used internally by EGA BIOS)							
0Ch = reserved (used internally by EGA BIOS)							
0Dh = G	40x25	8x8	320x200	16	8	A000	EGA,VGA
0Eh = G	80x25	8x8	640x200	16	4	A000	EGA,VGA
0Fh = G	80x25	8x14	640x350	mono	2	A000	EGA,VGA
10h = G	80x25	8x14	640x350	4	2	A000	64k EGA
= G			640x350	16		A000	256k EGA,VGA
11h = G	80x30	8x16	640x480	mono		A000	VGA, MCGA, ATIEGA, ATI VIP
12h = G	80x30	8x16	640x480	16/256k		A000	VGA,ATI VIP
= G	80x30	8x16	640x480	16/64		A000	ATI EGA Wonder
= G			640x480	16			UltraVision+25KEGA
13h = G	40x25	8x8	320x200	256/256k		A000	VGA,MCGA,ATI VIP
14h = G	80x25	8x8	640x200				Lava Chrome II EGA
= G			640x400	16			Tecmar VGA/AD
15h = G	80x25	8x14	640x350				Lava Chrome IIEGA
16h = G	80x25	8x14	640x350				Lava Chrome II EGA
= G			800x600	16			Tecmar VGA/AD

** For ATI EGA Wonder, mode 08h is only valid if SMS.COM is loaded resident. SMS maps mode 08h to mode 27h if the byte at location 0040:0063 is 0B4h, otherwise to mode 23h, thus selecting the appropriate (monochrome or color) 132x25 character mode. For ATI VGA Wonder, mode 08h is the same, and only valid if VCONFIG loaded resident.

Table 5-1. Values for Video Mode (continued)

TEXT/ GRPH	TEXT RESOL	PIXEL BOX	PIXEL RESOLTN	COLORS	DISPLY PAGES	SCRN ADDR	SYSTEM
17h = G	80x34	8x14	640x480				Lava Chrome IIEGA
= T	132x25						Tecmar VGA/AD
18h = T	132x44	8x8		mono			Tseng Labs EVA
= T	132x44	8x8		16/256	2	B000	Tseng ET-4000 chipset
= G	80x34	8x14	640x480				Lava Chrome IIEGA
= G			1024x768		16		Tecmar VGA/AD
19h = T	132x25	8x14		mono			Tseng LabsEVA
= T	132x25	8x14		16/256	4	B000	Tseng ET-4000 chipset
1Ah = T	132x28	8x13		mono			Tseng Labs EVA
= T	132x28	8x13		16/256	4	B000	Tseng ET-4000 chipset
= G			640x350	256			Tecmar VGA/AD
1Bh = G			640x400	256			Tecmar VGA/AD
1Ch = G			640x480	256			Tecmar VGA/AD
1Dh = G			800x600	256			Tecmar VGA/AD
21h = G	80x43	8x8	720x348	mono		B000	DESQview 2.x + Hercules ***
22h = T	132x44	8x8					Tseng Labs EVA
= T	132x44	8x8		16/256	2	B800	Tseng ET-4000 chipset
= T	132x44	8x8					Ahead Systems EGA2001
= T	132x44	8x8		16	2	B800	Ahead B
= T	132x44				16		Orchid Prodesigner VGA
= T	132x43						Allstar Peacock (VGA)
= G	80x43	8x8	720x348	mono		B800	DESQview 2.x + Hercules ***
23h = T	132x25	6x14					Tseng Labs EVA
= T	132x25	8x14		16/256	4	B800	Tseng ET-4000 chipset
= T	132x25	8x14					Ahead Systems EGA2001
= T	132x25	8x14		16	4	B800	Ahead B
= T	132x25	8x8		16		B800	ATI EGA Wonder, ATI VIP
= T	132x28						Allstar Peacock (VGA)
= T	132x28			16			Orchid Prodesigner VGA
24h = T	132x28	6x13					Tseng LabsEVA
= T	132x28	8x13		16/256	4	B800	Tseng ET-4000 chipset
= T	132x28	8x12		16	1	B800	Ahead B
= T	132x25						Allstar Peacock (VGA)
= T	132x25			16			Orchid Prodesigner VGA
25h = G	80x60	8x8	640x480				Tseng Labs EVA
= G	80x60	8x8	640x480	16/256	1	A000	Tseng ET-4000 chipset
= G			640x480	16			VEGA VGA
= G	80x60	8x8	640x480	16		A000	Orchid Prodesigner VGA
= G	80x60	8x8	640x480	16	1	A000	Ahead B (same as 26h)

*** DESQview intercepts calls to change into these two modes (21h is page 0, 22h is page 1) even if there is no Hercules graphics board installed.

Table 5-1. Values for Video Mode (continued)

TEXT/ GRPH	TEXT RESOL	PIXEL BOX	PIXEL RESOLTN	COLORS	DISPLAY PAGES	SCRN ADDR	SYSTEM
26h = T	80x60	8x8					Tseng LabsEVA
= T	80x60	8x8		16/256	2	B800	Tseng ET-4000 chipset
= G	80x60	8x8	640x480				Ahead Systems EGA2001
= G	80x60	8x8	640x480	16	1	A000	Ahead B (same as 25h)
= T	80x60						Allstar Peacock (VGA)
= T	80x60			16			Orchid ProDesigner VGA
27h = G			720x512	16			VEGA VGA
= G			720x512	16			Genoa
= T	132x25	8x8		mono		B000	ATI EGA Wonder, ATI VIP
28h = T	???x???						VEGA VGA
29h = G			800x600	16			VEGA VGA
= G	100x37	8x16	800x600	16		A000	Orchid
= G			800x600	16		A000	STB, Genoa, Sigma
= G			800x600	16			Allstar Peacock (VGA)
= G	100x37	8x16	800x600	16/256	1	A000	Tseng ET-4000 chipset
2Ah = T	100x40						Allstar Peacock (VGA)
= T	100x40	8x16		16			Orchid Prodesigner VGA
= T	100x40	8x15		16/256	4	B800	Tseng ET-4000 chipset
2Dh = G			640x350	256			VEGA VGA
= G			640x350	256/256k		A000	Orchid, Genoa, STB
= G	80x25	8x14	640x350	256/256k	1	A000	Tseng ET-4000 chipset
2Eh = G			640x480	256			VEGA VGA
= G	80x30	8x16	640x480	256/256k		A000	Orchid
= G			640x480	256/256k		A000	STB, Genoa, Sigma
= G	80x30	8x16	640x480	256/256k	1	A000	Tseng ET-4000 chipset
2Fh = G			720x512	256			VEGA VGA
= G			720x512	256			Genoa
= G	80x25	8x16	640x400	256/256k	1	A000	Tseng ET-4000 chipset
= T	160x50	8x8	1280x400	16	4	A000	Ahead B (Wizard/3270)
30h = G			800x600	256			VEGA VGA
= G	100x37	8x16	800x600	256/256k		A000	Orchid
= G			800x600	256/256k		A000	STB, Genoa, Sigma
= G			720x350	2			3270 PC
= G			800x600	256			Cardinal
= G			???x???			B800	AT&T 6300
= G	100x37	8x16	800x600	256/256k	1	A000	Tseng ET-4000 chipset
32h = T	80x34	8x10		16	4	B800	Ahead B (Wizard/3270)
33h = T	132x44	8x8		16		B800	ATI EGA Wonder, ATI VIP
= T	80x34	8x8		16	4	B800	Ahead B (Wizard/3270)
34h = T	80x66	8x8		16	4	B800	Ahead B (Wizard/3270)
36h = G			960x720	16			VEGA VGA
= G			960x720	16			STB
37h = G			1024x768	16			VEGA VGA
= G	128x48	8x16	1024x768	16		A000	Orchid
= G			1024x768	16		A000	STB, Genoa, Sigma
= T	132x44	8x8		mono		B800	ATI EGA Wonder, ATI VIP

Table 5-1. Values for Video Mode (continued)

TEXT/ GRPH	TEXT RESOL	PIXEL BOX	PIXEL RESOLTN	COLORS	DISPLY PAGES	SCRN ADDR	SYSTEM
38h = G			1024x768	256			STB VGA/EM-16 Plus (1MB)
= G	128x48	8x16	1024x768	256/256k	1	A000	Tseng ET-4000 chipset
40h = G	80x25	8x16	640x400	2	1	B800	AT&T 6300, AT&T VDC600
= G	80x25	8x16	640x400	2	1	B800	Compaq Portable
= T	80x43						VEGA VGA, Tecmar VGA/AD
= T	80x43						Video7 V-RAM VGA
= T	80x43						Tatung VGA
41h = G			640x200	16	1		AT&T 6300
= T	132x25						VEGA VGA
= T	132x25						Tatung VGA
= T	132x25						Video7 V-RAM VGA
42h = G	80x25	8x16	640x400	16			AT&T 6300, AT&T VDC600
= T	132x43						VEGA VGA
= T	132x43						Tatung VGA
= T	132x43						Video7 V-RAM VGA
= T	80x34	9x10		4	4	B800	Ahead B(Wizard/3270)
43h = G			640x200 of 640x400 viewport AT&T 6300(unsupported)				
= T	80x60						VEGA VGA
= T	80x60						Tatung VGA
= T	80x60						Video7 V-RAM VGA
= T	80x45	9x8		4	4	B800	Ahead B (Wizard/3270)
44h =			disable VDC and DEB output AT&T 6300				
= T	100x60						VEGA VGA
= T	100x60						Tatung VGA
= T	100x60						Video7 V-RAM VGA
45h = T	132x28						Tatung VGA
= T	132x28						Video7 V-RAM VGA
46h = G	100x40	8x15	800x600	2			AT&T VDC600
47h = G	100x37	8x16	800x600	16			AT&T VDC600
48h = G	80x50	8x8	640x400	2		B800	AT&T 6300, AT&T VDC600
49h = G	80x30	8x16	640x480				Lava Chrome II EGA
4Dh = T	120x25						VEGA VGA
4Eh = T	120x43						VEGA VGA
4Fh = T	132x25						VEGA VGA
50h = G	80x30	8x16	640x480	16			Paradise EGA-480
= T	80x30	8x16		16/256k		B800	Trident TVGA 8800/8900
= T	80x34						Lava Chrome II EGA
= T	80x43			mono			VEGA VGA
= G			640x480	mono???			Taxan 565 EGA
= T	132x25	9x14		mono			Ahead Systems EGA2001
= T	132x25	9x14		4	4	B800	Ahead B
= T	132x25	8x14		16	8	B800	OAK Technologies VGA-16

Table 5-1. Values for Video Mode (continued)

TEXT/ GRPH	TEXT RESOL	PIXEL BOX	PIXEL RESOLTN	COLORS	DISPLY PAGES	SCRN ADDR	SYSTEM
51h = T	80x30	8x16					Paradise EGA-480
= T	80x30						Lava Chrome II EGA
= G	80x34	8x14	640x480	16			ATI EGA Wonder
= T	80x43	8x11		16/256k		B800	Trident TVGA 8800/8900
= T	132x25			mono			VEGA VGA
= T	132x43	8x8		16	5	B800	OAK Technologies VGA-16
= T	132x28	9x12		4	4	B800	Ahead B
52h = T	80x60						Lava Chrome II EGA
= T	80x60	8x8		16/256k		B800	Trident TVGA 8800/8900
= G	94x29	8x14	752x410	16			ATI EGA Wonder
= G	100x75	8x8	800x600	16	1	A000	OAK Technologies VGA-16
= T	132x43			mono			VEGA VGA
= T	132x44	9x8		mono			Ahead Systems EGA2001
= T	132x44	9x8		4	2	B800	Ahead B
53h = G	100x40	8x14	800x560	16			ATI EGA Wonder, ATI VIP
= T	132x25	8x14		16/256k		B800	Trident TVGA 8800/8900
= T	132x43						Lava Chrome II EGA
54h = G	100x42	8x14	800x600	16		A000	ATI EGA Wonder, VGA Wonder
= T	132x25						Lava Chrome II EGA
= T	132x30	8x16		16/256k		B800	Trident TVGA 8800/8900
= T	132x43	8x8					Paradise EGA-480
= T	132x43	7x9		16/256k		B800	Paradise VGA
= T	132x43	8x9		16/256k		B800	Paradise VGA on multisync
= T	132x43						Taxan 565 EGA
= T	132x43						AST VGA Plus
= T	132x43						Hewlett-Packard D1180A
= T	132x43	7x9		16			AT&T VDC600
55h = T	80x66	8x8		16/256k		A000	ATI VIP
= T	132x25	8x14					Paradise EGA-480
= T	132x25	7x16		16/256k		B800	Paradise VGA
= T	132x25	8x16		16/256k		B800	Paradise VGA on multisync
= T	132x25						Taxan 565 EGA
= T	132x25						AST VGA Plus
= T	132x25						Hewlett-Packard D1180A
= T	132x25	7x16		16			AT&T VDC600
= T	132x43	8x11		16/256k		B800	Trident TVGA 8800/8900
= G	94x29	8x14	752x410				Lava Chrome II EGA
= G	128x48	8x16	1024x768	16/256k		A000	ATI VGA Wonder v4+ *!
56h = T	132x43	8x8		3???	2	B000	NSI Smart EGA+
= T	132x43	7x9		4		B000	Paradise VGA
= T	132x43	8x9		4		B000	Paradise VGA on multisync
= T	132x43			mono			Taxan 565 EGA
= T	132x43	7x9		2			AT&T VDC600
= T	132x60	8x8		16/256k		B800	Trident TVGA 8800/8900

*! ATI BIOS v4-1.00 has a text-scrolling bug in this mode.

Table 5-1. Values for Video Mode (continued)

TEXT/ GRPH	TEXT RESOL	PIXEL BOX	PIXEL RESOLTN	COLORS	DISPLAY PAGES	SCRN ADDR	SYSTEM
57h = T	132x25	8x14		3???	4	B000	NSI Smart EGA+
= T	132x25	7x16		4		B000	Paradise VGA
= T	132x25	8x16		4		B000	Paradise VGA on multisync
= T	132x25			mono			Taxan 565 EGA
= T	132x25	7x16		2			AT&T VDC600
= T	132x25	9x14		16/256k		B800	Trident TVGA 8800/8900
58h = G	100x75	8x8	800x600	16/256k		A000	Paradise VGA
= G	100x75	8x8	800x600	16			AT&T VDC600
= T	80x33	8x14		16		B800	ATI EGA Wonder, ATI VIP
= G			800x600	16			AST VGA Plus, Compaq VGA
= G			800x600	16			Dell VGA
= G			800x600	16			Hewlett-Packard D1180A
= T	132x30	9x16		16/256k		B800	Trident TVGA 8800/8900
59h = G	100x75	8x8	800x600	2		A000	Paradise VGA
= G	100x75	8x8	800x600	2			AT&T VDC600
= T	80x66	8x8		16/256k		A000	ATI VIP
= G			800x600	2			AST VGA Plus, Compaq VGA
= G			800x600	2			Dell VGA
= G			800x600	2			Hewlett-Packard D1180A
= T	132x43	9x11		16/256k		B800	Trident TVGA 8800/8900
5Ah = T	132x60	9x8		16/256k		B800	Trident TVGA 8800/8900
5Bh = G			800x600	16			Maxxon, SEFCO TVGA, Imtec
= G			640x350	256			Genoa 6400
= T	80x30	8x16				B800	ATI VGA Wonder (undoc)
= G	100x75	8x8	800x600	16/256k		A000	Trident TVGA 8800/8900
5Ch = G			640x400	256			Logix, ATI Prism Elite
= G			640x400	256			Maxxon, SEFCO TVGA, Imtec
= G			640x400	256			Zymos Poach
= G	80x25	8x16	640x400	256		A000	Trident TVGA 8800/8900
= G			640x480	256			Genoa 6400
5Dh = G			640x480	256			Logix, ATI Prism Elite
= G			640x480	256			Maxxon, SEFCO TVGA, Imtec
= G			640x480	256			Zymos Poach
= G	80x30	8x16	640x480	256		A000	Trident TVGA 8800 (512K)
5Eh = G			640x400	256			Paradise VGA, VEGA VGA
= G			640x400	256			AST VGA Plus
= G			640x400	256			Compaq VGA, Dell VGA
= G	80x25	8x16	640x400	256			AT&T VDC600
= G			800x600	16			Logix, ATI Prism Elite
= G			800x600	256			Genoa 6400
= G			800x600	256			Zymos Poach, Trident 8900
5Fh = G			640x480	256			Paradise VGA
= G			640x480	256			AST VGA Plus
= G			640x480	256			Compaq VGA, Dell VGA
= G			640x480	256			Hewlett-Packard D1180A
= G	80x30	8x16	640x480	256			AT&T VDC600 (512K)
= G			1024x768	16			Logix, ATI Prism Elite
= G			1024x768	16			Maxxon, Genoa 6400, Imtec
= G			1024x768	16			Zymos Poach
= G	128x48	8x16	1024x768	16/256k		A000	Trident TVGA 8800/8900 512K

Table 5-1. Values for Video Mode (continued)

TEXT/ GRPH	TEXT RESOL	PIXEL BOX	PIXEL RESOLTN	COLORS	DISPLY PAGES	SCRN ADDR	SYSTEM
60h = G	80x???		???x400				Corona/Cordata BIOS 4.10+
= G			752x410				VEGA VGA
= G			752x410	16			Tatung VGA
= G			752x410	16			Video7 V-RAM VGA
= G	80x25	8x16	640x400	256	1	A000	Ahead B
= G	128x48	8x16	1024x768	4/256k		A000	Trident TVGA 8900
= T	132x25	8x14		16/64	8	B800	Quadram Ultra VGA
61h = G			???x400				Corona/Cordata BIOS 4.10+
= G			720x540				VEGA VGA
= G			720x540	16			Tatung VGA
= G			720x540	16			Video7 V-RAM VGA
= G	80x25	8x16	640x400	256		A000	ATI VGA Wonder
= G	80x30	8x16	640x480	256	1	A000	Ahead B
= G	96x64	8x16	768x1024	16/256k		A000	Trident TVGA 8800/8900 512K
= T	132x29	8x12		16/64	8	B800	Quadram Ultra VGA
62h = G			800x600				VEGA VGA
= G			800x600	16			Tatung VGA
= G			800x600	16			Video7 V-RAM VGA
= G	80x30	8x16	640x480	256		A000	ATI VGA Wonder
= G	100x75	8x8	800x600	256	1	A000	Ahead B (512K)
= G	128x48	8x16	1024x768	256/256k		A000	Trident TVGA 8900, Zymos
= T	132x32	8x11		/64	6	B800	Quadram Ultra VGA
63h = G			1024x768	2			Video7 V-RAM VGA
= G	100x42	8x14	800x600	256		A000	ATI VGA Wonder
= G	128x48	7x16	1024x768	256	1	A000	Ahead B (1MB)
= T	132x44	8x8		16/64	5	B800	Quadram Ultra VGA
64h = G			1024x768	4			Video7 V-RAM VGA
= G	128x48	8x16	1024x768	256		A000	ATI VGA Wonder Plus
65h = G			1024x768	16			Video7 V-RAM VGA
= G	128x48	8x16	1024x768	16		A000	ATI VGA Wonder
66h = G			640x400	256			Tatung VGA
= G			640x400	256			Video7 V-RAM VGA
67h = G			640x480	256			Video7 V-RAM VGA
= G	128x48	8x16	1024x768	4		A000	ATI VGA Wonder
69h = G			720x540	256			Video7 V-RAM VGA
6Ah = G			800x600	16		A000	VESA standard interface
= G			800x600	16			Genoa 6400
= G	100x75	8x8	800x600	16	1	A000	Ahead B (VESA) (see 71h)
= G			800x600	16			Zymos Poach
= G			800x600	16			Epson LT-386SX in CRT mode
= G			800x600	16			Compuadd 316SL in CRT mode
= G	100x42	8x14	800x600			A000	ATI VGA Wonder (undoc)
70h = G			800x600	16			Cardinal, C&T chipset
= G	90x28	8x14	720x392	16	1	A000	Ahead B
= T	40x25	8x8		16	8	B800	Quadram (CGA double scan)

70h with Everex Micro Enhancer EGA (see Func 00h Subfunc 70h)

Table 5-1. Values for video mode (continued)

TEXT/ GRPH	TEXT RESOL	PIXEL BOX	PIXEL RESOLTN	COLORS	DISPLY PAGES	SCRN ADDR	SYSTEM
71h = G	100x35	8x16	800x600	16/64		A000	NSI Smart EGA+
= G			960x720	16			Cardinal
= G	100x75	8x8	800x600	16	1	A000	Ahead B (same as 6Ah)
= T	80x25	8x8		16	8	B800	Quadram (CGA double scan)
72h = G			1024x768	16			Cardinal, C&T chipset
= T	80x60	8x8		16		B800	Quadram Ultra VGA
73h = G	80x60	8x8	640x480	16???		A000	Quadram Ultra VGA
74h = G			640x400	2		B800	Toshiba 3100 AT&T mode
= G	128x48	8x8	1024x768	16	1	A000	Ahead B (512K)
= T	80x66	8x8		16		B800	Quadram Ultra VGA
75h = G	128x48	8x16	1024x768	4	1	A000	Ahead B
= G	80x66		640x528	16???		A000	Quadram Ultra VGA
76h = G	128x48	8x16	1024x768	2	1	A000	Ahead B
= T	94x29	8x14		16		B800	Quadram Ultra VGA
77h = G	94x29		752x410	16???		A000	Quadram Ultra VGA
78h = G			640x400	256			STB VGA/EM-16 Plus
= G			640x400	256			Cardinal, C&T chipset
= T	100x75	8x8		16		B800	Quadram Ultra VGA
79h = G			640x480	256			Cardinal, C&T chipset
= G	100x75		800x600	16???		A000	Quadram Ultra VGA
7Ah = G			720x540	256			Cardinal
= T	114x60	8x8		16		B800	Quadram Ultra VGA
7Bh = G			800x600	256			Cardinal
= G	114x60		912x480	16???		A000	Quadram Ultra VGA
7Ch = G			512x512	16			Genoa
7Dh = G			512x512	256			Genoa

7Eh = special mode set (see Func 00h Subfunc 7Eh)   Paradise VGA, AT&T VDC600

7Fh = special function set (see Func 00h Subfunc 7Fh)   Paradise VGA, AT&T VDC600

82h = T	80x25			B&W			AT&T VDC overlay mode *
83h = T	80x25						AT&T VDC overlay mode *
86h = G			640x200	B&W			AT&T VDC overlay mode *
88h = G	90x43	8x8	720x352	mono		B800	Hercules + MSHERC.COM
C0h = G			640x400		2/prog pallet		AT&T VDC overlay mode *
C4h = disable output							AT&T VDC overlay mode *
D0h = G			640x400	2		B800	DEC VAXmate AT&T mode

* For AT&T VDC overlay modes, BL contains the DEB mode, which may be 06h, 40h, or 44h.

INTERRUPT 10h - Function 00h, Subfunction 70h
Everex Micro Enhancer EGA/Viewpoint VGA - EXTENDED MODE SET

Purpose: Select a non-standard Everex-specific video display mode.

Available on: Systems equipped with the   **Restrictions:** none.
applicable video cards listed below.

Registers at call:
AX = 0070h
BL = mode (see Table 5-2)
Conflicts: None known.
See Also: Function 00h, Function 6Fh Subfunction 05h

Table 5-2. Everex-specific Values for video mode

TEXT/ GRPH	TEXT RESOL	PIXEL BOX	PIXEL RESOLTN	COLORS	DISP PAGE	SCRN ADDR	MONITOR	ADAPTER
00h = G			640x480	16			multsync	EGA,VGA
01h = G			752x410	16			multsync	EGA,VGA
02h = G			800x600	16			multsync	EGA,VGA
03h = T	80x34						multsync	EGA,VGA
04h = T	80x60						multsync	EGA,VGA
05h = T	94x29						multsync	EGA only
06h = T	94x51						multsync	EGA only
07h = T	100x43	8x14		16				VGA only
08h = T	100x75	8x8		16				VGA only
09h = T	80x44						EGA	EGA only
0Ah = T	132x25						EGA	EGA, VGA
0Bh = T	132x44						EGA	EGA, VGA
0Ch = T	132x25						CGA	EGA only
0Dh = T	80x44						mono	EGA only
0Eh = T	132x25						mono	
0Fh = T	132x44						mono	
10h =reserved								
11h = G			1280x350	4				EGA only
12h = G			1280x600	4				EGA only
13h = G			640x350	256				EGA only
14h = G			640x400	256				
15h = G			512x480	256				
16h = T	80x30	8x16		256				VGA only
18h = T	100x27	8x16		16				VGA only
20h = G			1024x768	16				Everex 629, 678 only

Table 5-2. Everex-specific Values for video mode (continued)

TEXT/ GRPH	TEXT RESOL	PIXEL BOX	PIXEL RESOLTN	COLORS	DISP PAGE	SCRN ADDR	MONITOR	ADAPTER
21h = T	160x64	8x16	1280x1k	16				1MB VGA only
30h = G			640x480	256				Everex 629, 678 only
31h = G			800x600	256				Everex 629, 678 only
32h = G	128x48	8x16	1024x768	256				1MB VGA only
40h = T	132x30	8x16		16				VGA only
50h = T	132x32	8x16		mono				VGA only
62h = G	40x25	8x8	320x200	32K				Viewpoint TC (EV629)
70h = G	64x30	8x16	512x480	32K				Viewpoint TC
71h = G	80x30	8x16	640x480	32K				Viewpoint TC
76h = G	64x30	8x16	512x480	16M				Viewpoint TC
77h = G	80x30	8x16	640x480	16M				Viewpoint TC

INTERRUPT 10h - Function 00h, Subfunction 7Eh
SET SPECIAL VIDEO MODE

Purpose: Set special extended modes.

Available on: Paradise VGA, AT&T VDC600 only.

Registers at call:
AX = 007Eh
BX = The horizontal dimension of the mode desired
CX = The vertical dimension of the mode desired
    (both BX/CX in pixels for graphics
    modes, rows for alpha modes)
DX = The number of colors of the mode desired
    (use 0 for monochrome modes)

Conflicts: None known.

See Also: Function 00h, Function 00h Subfunctions 70h and 7Fh, Function 6Fh Subfunction 05h

Restrictions: none.

Return Registers:
BH = 7Eh if successful (Paradise VGA)
AL = 7Eh if successful (AT&T VDC600)

INTERRUPT 10h - Function 00h, Subfunction 7Fh
EXTENDED VIDEO MODE FUNCTIONS

Purpose: Provides extended control of video actions.

Available on: Paradise VGA, AT&T VDC600 only.

Registers at call:
AX = 007Fh
BH = 00h set VGA operation
    01h set non-VGA operation
        color modes (0, 1, 2, 3, 4, 5, 6) will
        set non-VGA CGA operation.
        monochrome mode 7 will set non-
        VGA MDA/Hercules operation.

Restrictions: none.

Return Registers:
AL = 7Fh if successful (AT&T VDC600)

02h query mode status

BL = 00h if operating in VGA mode,
   01h if non-VGA mode.
CH = total video RAM size in 64k byte units.
CL = video RAM used by the current mode.

03h lock current mode
   allows current mode (VGA or non-
   VGA) to survive re-boot.
04h enter CGA mode
   (AT&T VDC600 only)
05h enter MDA mode
   (AT&T VDC600 only)
0Ah, 0Bh, 0Ch, 0Dh, 0Eh, 0Fh WRITE
PARADISE REGISTERS 0, 1, 2, 3, 4, 5
   (port 03CEh indices 0Ah, 0Bh, 0Ch,
      0Dh, 0Eh, 0Fh)
   BL = value to set in the Paradise
      register.
1Ah, 1Bh, 1Ch, 1Dh, 1Eh, 1Fh READ
PARADISE REGISTERS 0, 1, 2, 3, 4, 5
   (port 03CEh indices 0Ah, 0Bh, 0Ch,
      0Dh, 0Eh, 0Fh)

BL = value of the Paradise register.
BH = 7Fh if successful.

Conflicts: None known.
See Also: Function 00h Subfunction 7Eh

INTERRUPT 10h - Function 01h
SET TEXT-MODE CURSOR SIZE

Purpose: Sets size of text-mode cursor.
Available on: All machines.
Registers at call:
AH = 01h
CH = bit 7   should be zero
   bits 6,5 cursor blink (00 = normal,
      01 = invisible, 10 = erratic,
      11 = slow)
      (00 = normal, other = invisible on
      EGA/VGA)
   bits 4-0 top scan line containing cursor
CL = bottom scan line containing cursor (bits 0-4)

Restrictions: none.
Return Registers: n/a.

Details: Buggy on EGA systems--the BIOS remaps the cursor shape in 43 line modes, but returns the unmapped cursor shape.

UltraVision scales the size to the current font height by assuming 14-line monochrome and 8-line color fonts; this call is not valid if cursor emulation has been disabled.

Applications which wish to change the cursor by programming the hardware directly on EGA or above should call INT 10h Function 11h Subfunction 30h or read 0040h:0085h first to determine the current font height.

BUG: AMI 386 BIOS and AST Premier 386 BIOS will lock up the system if AL is not equal to the current video mode.

Conflicts: None known.
See Also: Function 03h

INTERRUPT 10h - Function 02h
SET CURSOR POSITION

Purpose: Positions cursor on screen.
Available on: All machines.

Restrictions: none.

Registers at call:
AH = 02h
BH = page number
    0-3 in modes 2&3
    0-7 in modes 0&1
    0 in graphics modes
DH = row (00h is top)
DL = column (00h is left)
Conflicts: None known.
See Also: Functions 03h and 05h

Return Registers: n/a.

INTERRUPT 10h - Function 03h
GET CURSOR POSITION AND SIZE

Purpose: Reads current cursor position for a specific display page and the current cursor size.
Available on: All machines.

Restrictions: none.

Registers at call:
AH = 03h
BH = page number
    0-7 in modes 0 and 1
    0-3 in modes 2 and 3
    0 in graphics modes

Return Registers:
AX = 0000h (Phoenix BIOS)
CH = start scan line
CL = end scan line
DH = row (00h is top)
DL = column (00h is left)

Details: A separate cursor is maintained for each of up to 8 display pages.
Conflicts: None known.
See Also: Functions 01h and 02h

INTERRUPT 10h - Function 04h
READ LIGHT PEN POSITION

Purpose: Determines location of light pen on screen.
Available on: All machines.

Restrictions: Meaningful only if light-pen hardware installed or if mouse is emulating light pen.

Registers at call:
AH = 04h

Return Registers:
AH = light pen trigger flag: 00h not down/triggered
    01h down/triggered
DH,DL = row,column of character light pen is on
CH = pixel row (graphics modes 04h-06h)
CX = pixel row (graphics modes with >200 rows)
BX = pixel column

Details: On a CGA, returned column numbers are always multiples of 2 (320-column modes) or 4 (640-column modes). Returned row numbers are only accurate to two lines.
Conflicts: None known.

INTERRUPT 10h - Function 05h
SELECT ACTIVE DISPLAY PAGE

Purpose: Selects which display page is to be active (displayed).
Available on: All machines.

Restrictions: none.

Registers at call:
AH = 05h
AL = new page number
    (00h to number of pages - 1)
    (see Function 00h)

Return Registers: n/a.

Conflicts: PCjr page register manipulation, Corona/Cordata BIOS v4.10+ Graphics Bitmap Buffer.
See Also: Function 0Fh

INTERRUPT 10h - Function 05h, Subfunctions 80h to 83h
MANIPULATE CRT/CPU PAGE REGISTERS

Purpose: Controls video paging registers.

Available on: PCjr only.

Registers at call:

AH = 05h

AL = subfunction

    80h read CRT and CPU page registers

    81h set CPU page register
       BL = CPU page
    82h set CRT page register
       BH = CRT page
    83h set both CPU and CRT page registers
       BL = CPU pag
       BH = CRT page

Restrictions: none.

Return Registers:

BH = CRT page register
BL = CPU page register

Details: The CPU page determines which 16K block of the first 128K of physical memory will be mapped at B800h by the hardware. The CRT page determines the start address of the memory used by the video controller.

Conflicts: Select Active Display Page.

INTERRUPT 10h - Function 05h, Subfunctions 00h and 0Fh
GRAPHICS BITMAP BUFFER

Purpose: Establish location of graphics bitmap buffer.

Available on: Corona/Cordata BIOS v4.10+ only.

Registers at call:

AH = 05h

AL = 00h set address of graphics bitmap buffer
    (video modes 60h, 61h)
    BX = segment of buffer

AL = 0Fh get address of graphics bitmap buffer
    (video modes 60h, 61h)

Restrictions: none.

Return Registers:

DX = segment of graphics bitmap buffer

Conflicts: Select Active Display Page.

INTERRUPT 10h - Function 06h
SCROLL UP WINDOW

Purpose: Scrolls part or all of the screen up by the specified number of lines.

Available on: All machines.

Registers at call:

AH = 06h

AL = number of lines by which to scroll up
    (00h = clear entire window)

BH = attribute used to write blank lines at bottom of
    window

CH,CL = row,column of window's upper left corner

DH,DL = row,column of window's lower right
    corner

Restrictions: none.

Return Registers: n/a.

Details: Affects only the currently active page (see Function 05h).

Warning: Some implementations have a bug which destroys BP.

Conflicts: None known.

See Also: Functions 07h, 72h, and 73h

INTERRUPT 10h - Function 07h
SCROLL DOWN WINDOW

Purpose: Scrolls part or all of the screen down by the specified number of lines.

Available on: All machines.

Registers at call:

AH = 07h

AL = number of lines by which to scroll down
  (00h=clear entire window)

BH = attribute used to write blank lines at top of
  window

CH,CL = row,column of window's upper left corner

DH,DL = row,column of window's lower right
  corner

Restrictions: none.

Return Registers: n/a.

Details: Affects only the currently active page (see Function 05h).

Warning: Some implementations have a bug which destroys BP.

Conflicts: None known.

See Also: Functions 06h, 72h, and 73h

INTERRUPT 10h - Function 08h
READ CHARACTER AND ATTRIBUTE AT CURSOR POSITION

Purpose: Determines text character and attribute at current cursor location.

Available on: All machines.

Registers at call:

AH = 08h

BH = page number (00h to number of pages - 1)
  (see Function 00h)

Restrictions: none.

Return Registers:

AH = attribute:

  bit 7: blink

  bits 6-4: background color

    000 black

    001 blue

    010 green

    011 cyan

    100 red

    101 magenta

    110 brown

    111 white

  bits 3-0: foreground color

    0000 black 1000 dark gray

    0001 blue   1001 light blue

    0010 green 1010 light green

    0011 cyan   1011 light cyan

    0100 red   1100 light red

    0101 magenta   1101 light magenta

    0110 brown   1110 yellow

    0111 light gray 1111 white

AL = character

Details: For monochrome displays, a foreground of 1 with background 0 is underlined.

In graphics modes, the bitmap in the specified character cell must exactly match one of the bitmaps for the current mode's font, or the result is unpredictable.

The blink bit may be reprogrammed to enable intense background colors using Function 10h Subfunction 03h or by programming the CRT controller.

Conflicts: None known.

See Also: Function 09h, Function 10h Subfunction 03h

INTERRUPT 10h - Function 09h
WRITE CHARACTER AND ATTRIBUTE AT CURSOR POSITION

Purpose: Write specified character and attribute to display at current cursor location.

Available on: All machines.   **Restrictions:** none.

Registers at call: **Return Registers:** n/a.

AH = 09h

AL = character to display

BH = page number (00h to number of pages - 1)
   (see Function 00h)

BL = attribute (text mode) or color (graphics mode)
   if bit 7 set in graphics mode, character is
   xor'ed onto screen

CX = number of times to write character

Details: All characters are displayed, including CR, LF, and BS.

   The replication count in CX may produce an unpredictable result in graphics modes if it is greater than the number of positions remaining in the current row.

Conflicts: None known.

See Also: Functions 08h and 0Ah, INT 1Fh, INT 43h, INT 44h

INTERRUPT 10h - Function 0Ah
WRITE CHARACTER ONLY AT CURSOR POSITION

Purpose: Write specified character to display at current cursor location, leaving the current attribute intact.

Available on: All machines.   **Restrictions:** none.

Registers at call: **Return Registers:** n/a.

AH = 0Ah

AL = character to display

BH = page number (00h to number of pages - 1)
   (see Function 00h)

CX = number of times to write character

Details: All characters are displayed, including CR, LF, and BS.

   The replication count in CX may produce an unpredictable result in graphics modes if it is greater than the number of positions remaining in the current row.

Conflicts: None known.

See Also: Functions 08h and 09h, INT 1Fh, INT 43h, INT 44h

INTERRUPT 10h - Function 0Bh, Subfunction 00h
SET BACKGROUND/BORDER COLOR

Purpose: Sets background and border color value.

Available on: All machines.   **Restrictions:** none.

Registers at call: **Return Registers:** n/a.

AH = 0Bh

BH = 00h

BL = background/border color (border only in text
   modes)

Conflicts: None known.

See Also: Function 0Bh Subfunction 01h

INTERRUPT 10h - Function 0Bh, Subfunction 01h
SET COLOR PALETTE

Purpose: Establish CGA graphics palettes.

Available on: All machines.   **Restrictions:** Applies to CGA and CGA-emulation
                             only.

Registers at call:
AH = 0BH
BH = 01h
BL = palette ID
    00h background, green, red, and
        brown/yellow
    01h background, cyan, magenta, and
        white
Conflicts: None known.
See Also: Function 0Bh Subfunction 00h

Return Registers: n/a.

INTERRUPT 10h - Function 0Ch
WRITE GRAPHICS PIXEL

Purpose: Write single pixel to graphics display.
Available on: All machines.
Registers at call:
AH = 0Ch
BH = page number
AL = pixel color (if bit 7 set, value is xor'ed onto
    screen)
CX = column
DX = row
Details: BH is ignored if the current video mode supports only one page.
Conflicts: None known.
See Also: Functions 0Dh and 46h

Restrictions: Valid only in graphics modes.
Return Registers: n/a.

INTERRUPT 10h - Function 0Dh
READ GRAPHICS PIXEL

Purpose: Reads value of single pixel.
Available on: All machines.
Registers at call:
AH = 0Dh
BH = page number
CX = column
DX = row
Details: BH is ignored if the current video mode supports only one page.
Conflicts: None known.
See Also: Functions 0Ch and 47h

Restrictions: Valid only in graphics modes.
Return Registers:
AL = pixel color

INTERRUPT 10h - Function 0Eh
TELETYPE OUTPUT

Purpose: Provides simple text-mode output technique.
Available on: All machines.
Registers at call:
AH = 0Eh
AL = character to write
BH = page number
BL = foreground color (graphics modes only)
Details: Characters 07h (BEL), 08h (BS), 0Ah (LF), and 0Dh (CR) are interpreted and perform the expected actions. IBM PC ROMs dated 4/24/81 and 10/19/81 require that BH be the same as the current active page (see function 05h).
Conflicts: None known.
See Also: Functions 02h and 0Ah

Restrictions: none.
Return Registers: n/a.

INTERRUPT 10h - Function 0Fh
GET CURRENT VIDEO MODE

Purpose: Determine current video settings.
Available on: All machines.
Registers at call:
AH = 0Fh

Restrictions: none.
Return Registers:
AL = display mode (see Function 00h)
AH = number of character columns
BH = active page (see Function 05h)

Details: If mode was set with bit 7 set ("no blanking"), the returned mode will also have bit 7 set.
Conflicts: VUIMAGE Display Driver.
See Also: Functions 00h and 05h

INTERRUPT 10h - Function 0Fh, Subfunction 56h
VUIMAGE DISPLAY DRIVER (v2.20 and below)

Purpose: Special display driver for VUIMAGE graphics viewer program.
Available on: All machines.

Restrictions: Must have an appropriate VUIMAGE display driver loaded.

Registers at call:
AX = 0F56h
BX = 4756h
CX = 4944h
DL = function:
    01h installation check
    02h get first video mode's parameters

    03h get next video mode's parameters
    04h display line (?)
        ES:DI -> record (see Table 5-3)
        other registers unknown.
Conflicts: Standard video BIOS.

Return Registers:
AX = 5649h
BX = 4443h
CX = 5647h
DH = 01h

AX = BIOS mode number
BX = width in pixels
CX = height in pixels
DX = number of colors
as for DL=02h
unknown.

Table 5-3. Format of record for DL=04h:

Offset	Size	Description
00h	WORD	row number
02h	WORD	starting column???
04h	WORD	ending column???

INTERRUPT 10h - Function 10h
BIOS Window Extension v1.1 - SET WINDOW COORDINATES

Purpose: Establishes screen window area.
Available on: All machines.

Restrictions: Must have BIOS Window Extension TSR installed.

Registers at call:
AH = 10h
CH,CL = row,column of upper left corner of
    window
DH,DL = row,column of lower right corner of
    window

Return Registers:
AL = status
    00h successful
    01h failed
AH destroyed

Details: BWE is a TSR by John J. Seal published in the May 1986 issue of Dr. Dobb's Journal.

When a window has been set, all output via Function 0Eh is restricted to the specified window.
Conflicts: Standard PCjr, EGA, MCGA, and VGA video BIOS functions.
See Also: BIOS Window Extension Functions 11h and 12h

INTERRUPT 10h - Function 10h, Subfunction 00h
SET SINGLE PALETTE REGISTER

Purpose: Establish value for one palette register.
Available on: PCjr, EGA, MCGA, VGA.

Restrictions: On MCGA, only BX = 0712h is supported.
Return Registers: n/a.

Registers at call:
AX = 1000h
BL = palette register number (00h-0Fh)
    or attribute register number
    (undocumented)
        10h attribute mode control register
            (should let BIOS control this)
        11h overscan color register (see also
            Function 10h Subfunction 01h)
        12h color plane enable register (bits
            3-0 enable corresponding text
            attribute bit)
        13h horizontal PEL panning register
        14h color select register
BH = color
Details: Under UltraVision, the palette locking status (see function CDh, subfunction 01h) determines the outcome.
Conflicts: BIOS Windows Extension.
See Also: Function 10h Subfunctions 02h and 07h, Function CDh Subfunction 00h

INTERRUPT 10h - Function 10h, Subfunction 01h
SET BORDER (OVERSCAN) COLOR

Purpose: Establish color for overscan register.
Available on: PCjr, EGA, VGA.
Registers at call:
AX = 1001h
BH = border color

Restrictions: none.
Return Registers: n/a.

Details: Under UltraVision, the palette locking status (see function CDh, subfunction 01h) determines the outcome.
    BUG: The original IBM VGA BIOS incorrectly updates the parameter save area and places the border color at offset 11h of the palette table rather than offset 10h.
Conflicts: BIOS Windows Extension.
See Also: Function 10h Subfunctions 01h and 08h

INTERRUPT 10h - Function 10h, Subfunction 02h
SET ALL PALETTE REGISTERS

Purpose: Set all palette registers with one command.
Available on: PCjr, EGA, VGA.
Registers at call:
AX = 1002h
ES:DX -> palette register list (Table 5-4)

Restrictions: none.
Return Registers: n/a.

Details: Under UltraVision, the palette locking status (see function CDh, subfunction 01h) determines the outcome.
Conflicts: BIOS Windows Extension.
See Also: Function 10h Subfunctions 00h, 01h, and 09h

Table 5-4. Format of palette register list:

Offset	Size	Description
00h	16 Bytes	colors for palette registers 00h through 0Fh
10h	BYTE	border color

INTERRUPT 10h - Function 10h, Subfunction 03h
TOGGLE INTENSITY/BLINKING BIT

Purpose: Toggle between blinking characters or bright background color.

Available on: PCjr, PS, TANDY 1000, EGA, VGA.

Restrictions: none.

Registers at call:
AX = 1003h
BL = 00h enable background intensity
    01h enable blink

Return Registers: n/a.

Details: Although there is no function to get the current status, bit 5 of 0040h:0065h indicates the state.

Conflicts: BIOS Windows Extension.

See Also: Function 08h

INTERRUPT 10h - Function 10h, Subfunction 07h
GET INDIVIDUAL PALETTE REGISTER

Purpose: Read settings for single palette register.

Available on: VGA-equipped systems.

Restrictions: none.

Registers at call:
AX = 1007h
BL = palette or attribute (undocumented) register
    number (see subfunction 00h)

Return Registers:
BH = palette or attribute register value

Details: UltraVision v2+ supports this function even on color EGA systems in video modes 00h-03h, 10h, and 12h; direct programming of the palette registers will cause incorrect results because the EGA registers are write-only. To guard against older versions or unsupported video modes, programs which expect to use this function on EGA systems should set BH to FFh on entry.

Conflicts: BIOS Windows Extension.

See Also: Function 10h Subfunctions 00h and 09h

INTERRUPT 10h - Function 10h, Subfunction 08h\v
READ OVERSCAN (BORDER COLOR) REGISTER

Purpose: Read setting for overscan register.

Available on: VGA-equipped systems.

Restrictions: none.

Registers at call:
AX = 1008h

Return Registers:
BH = value

Details: UltraVision v2+ supports this function even on color EGA systems in video modes 00h-03h, 10h, and 12h; direct programming of the palette registers will cause incorrect results because the EGA registers are write-only. To guard against older versions or unsupported video modes, programs which expect to use this function on EGA systems should set BH to FFh on entry.

Conflicts: BIOS Windows Extension.

See Also: Function 10h Subfunction 01h

INTERRUPT 10h - Function 10h, Subfunction 09h
READ ALL PALETTE REGISTERS AND OVERSCAN REGISTER

Purpose: Obtain values for all registers with single command.

Available on: VGA-equipped systems.

Restrictions: none.

Registers at call:
AX = 1009h
ES:DX -> 17-byte buffer (Table 5-5)
Details: UltraVision v2+ supports this function even on color EGA systems in video modes 00h-03h, 10h, and 12h; direct programming of the palette registers will cause incorrect results because the EGA registers are write-only. To guard against older versions or unsupported video modes, programs which expect to use this function on EGA systems should set the ES:DX buffer to FFh before calling.
Conflicts: BIOS Windows Extension.
See Also: Function 10h Subfunctions 02h and 07h, Function CDh Subfunction 02h

Return Registers: n/a.

Table 5-5. Format of palette register list

Offset	Size	Description
00h	16 BYTEs	colors for palette registers 00h through 0Fh
10h	BYTE	border color

INTERRUPT 10h - Function 10h, Subfunction 10h
SET INDIVIDUAL DAC REGISTER

Purpose: Set RGB values for a single Digital-Analog Converter register.
Available on: VGA/MCGA-equipped systems.
Restrictions: none.
Registers at call:
AX = 1010h
BX = register number
CH = new value for green (0-63)
CL = new value for blue (0-63)
DH = new value for red (0-63)
Conflicts: BIOS Windows Extension.
See Also: Function 10h Subfunctions 12h and 15h

Return Registers: n/a.

INTERRUPT 10h - Function 10h, Subfunction 12h
SET BLOCK OF DAC REGISTERS

Purpose: Set multiple RGB values into Digital-Analog Converter with single command.
Available on: VGA/MCGA-equipped systems.
Restrictions: none.
Registers at call:
AX = 1012h
BX = starting color register
CX = number of registers to set
ES:DX -> table of 3*CX bytes where each 3 byte
    group represents one byte each of red,
    green and blue (0-63)
Conflicts: BIOS Windows Extension.
See Also: Function 10h Subfunctions 10h and 17h

Return Registers: n/a.

INTERRUPT 10h - Function 10h, Subfunction 13h
SELECT VIDEO DAC COLOR PAGE

Purpose: Select arrangement of DAC registers into blocks or the active block of registers.
Available on: VGA-equipped systems.
Restrictions: Not valid in mode 13h.
Registers at call:
AX = 1013h
BL = 00h Select paging mode
    BH = 00h Select 4 blocks of 64
    BH = 01h Select 16 blocks of 16

Return Registers: n/a.

BL = 01h Select Page
   BH = page number (00h to 03h) or (00h to 0Fh)
Conflicts: BIOS Windows Extension.
See Also: Function 10h Subfunction 1Ah

INTERRUPT 10h - Function 10h, Subfunction 15h
READ INDIVIDUAL DAC REGISTER

Purpose: Determine RGB settings for specified DAC register.
Available on: VGA/MCGA-equipped systems.   **Restrictions:** none.
Registers at call: **Return Registers:**
AX = 1015h   DH = red value
BL = palette register number   CH = green value
     CL = blue value

Conflicts: BIOS Windows Extension.
See Also: Function 10h Subfunctions 10h and 17h

INTERRUPT 10h - Function 10h, Subfunction 17h
READ BLOCK OF DAC REGISTERS

Purpose: Determine RGB settings for specified block of DAC registers.
Available on: VGA/MCGA-equipped systems.   **Restrictions:** none.
Registers at call: **Return Registers:**
AX = 1017h   buffer filled with red/green/blue triples.
BX = starting palette register
CX = number of palette registers to read
ES:DX -> buffer (3 * CX bytes in size) (see also
    Function 10h Subfunction 12h)
Conflicts: BIOS Windows Extension.
See Also: Function 10h Subfunctions 12h and 15h

INTERRUPT 10h - Function 10h, Subfunction 18h
Undocumented - SET PEL MASK

Purpose: Establishes new mask value.
Available on: VGA/MCGA-equipped systems.   **Restrictions:** none.
Registers at call: **Return Registers:** n/a.
AX = 1018h
BL = new PEL value
Conflicts: BIOS Windows Extension.
See Also: Function 10h Subfunction 19h

INTERRUPT 10h - Function 10h, Subfunction 19h
Undocumented - READ PEL MASK

Purpose: Determine current mask value.
Available on: VGA/MCGA-equipped systems.   **Restrictions:** none.
Registers at call: **Return Registers:**
AX = 1019h   BL = value read
Conflicts: BIOS Windows Extension.
See Also: Function 10h Subfunction 18h

INTERRUPT 10h - Function 10h, Subfunction 1Ah
GET VIDEO DAC COLOR-PAGE STATE

Purpose: Determine current setting of video paging mode and which block of color registers is active.
Available on: VGA-equipped systems.   **Restrictions:** none.

Registers at call:
AX = 101Ah

Return Registers:
BL = paging mode
    00h four pages of 64
    01h sixteen pages of 16
BH = current page

Conflicts: BIOS Windows Extension.
See Also: Function 10h Subfunction 13h

INTERRUPT 10h - Function 10h, Subfunction 1Bh
PERFORM GRAY-SCALE SUMMING

Purpose: Convert DAC registers from their current color to an equivalent gray-scale intensity level.
Available on: VGA/MCGA-equipped systems.   **Restrictions:** none.
Registers at call: **Return Registers:** n/a.
AX = 101Bh
BX = starting palette register
CX = number of registers to convert
Conflicts: BIOS Windows Extension.
See Also: Function 12h Subfunction 33h

INTERRUPT 10h - Function 10h, Subfunction F0h
Tseng ET-4000 BIOS - SET HiColor GRAPHICS MODE

Purpose: Select an extended graphics mode.
Available on: All machines.   **Restrictions:** Tseng ET-4000 BIOS must be present.
Registers at call: **Return Registers:**
AX = 10F0h   AX = 0000h if successful
BL = video mode (see also Function 00h):   other on error
    32768-color modes:
        13h = 320x200
        2Dh = 640x350
        2Eh = 640x480
        2Fh = 640x400
        30h = 800x600
Details: The Tseng HiColor BIOS extensions are supported by:
    Diamond Computer Systems   SpeedStar HiColor VGA
    Everex Systems   HC VGA
    Focus Information Systems   2theMax 4000
    Cardinal Technologies   VGA732
Conflicts: BIOS Windows Extension.
See Also: Function 10h Subfunction F1h

INTERRUPT 10h - Function 10h, Subfunction F1h
Tseng ET-4000 BIOS - GET DAC TYPE

Purpose: Determine type of Digital-Analog Converter installed in system.
Available on: All machines.   **Restrictions:** Tseng ET-4000 BIOS must be present.
Registers at call: **Return Registers:**
AX = 10F1h   BL = type of digital/analog converter:
        00h normal VGA DAC
        01h Sierra SC1148x HiColor DAC
        else other HiColor DAC

Conflicts: BIOS Windows Extension.
See Also: Function 10h Subfunction F0h

INTERRUPT 10h - Function 11h
BIOS Window Extension v1.1 - GET WINDOW COORDINATES

Purpose: Determine limits of currently active window.
Available on: All machines.

Registers at call:
AH = 11h

Details: BWE is a TSR by John J. Seal published in the May 1986 issue of Dr. Dobb's Journal.
Conflicts: Standard EGA/VGA video functions.
See Also: BIOS Window Extension Functions 10h and 12h

Restrictions: Must have BIOS Window Extension TSR installed.
Return Registers:
CH,CL = row,column of upper left corner
DH,DL = row,column of lower right corner

INTERRUPT 10h - Function 11h, Subfunctions 00h to 14h
TEXT-MODE CHARACTER GENERATOR FUNCTIONS

Purpose: Modifies text display fonts and sizes.
Available on: Systems equipped with EGA, VGA, or MCGA video.

Restrictions: The following functions will cause a mode set, completely resetting the video environment, but without clearing the video buffer.
Return Registers: n/a.

Registers at call:
AH = 11h
AL = 00h, 10h: load user-specified patterns
    ES:BP -> user table
    CX = count of patterns to store
    DX = character offset into map 2 block
    BL = block to load in map 2
    BH = number of bytes per character pattern
line
AL = 01h, 11h: load ROM monochrome patterns
  (8 by 14)
    BL = block to load
AL = 02h, 12h: load ROM 8 by 8 double-dot
  patterns
  BL = block to load
AL = 03h: set block specifier
  BL= block specifier
    (EGA/MCGA)
    bits 0,1 = block selected by chars with attribute bit 3=0
    bits 2,3 = block selected by chars with attribute bit 3=1
    (VGA)
    bits 0,1,4 = block selected by attribute bit 3=0
    bits 2,3,5 = block selected by attribute bit 3=1
AL = 04h, 14h: (VGA) load ROM 8x16 character set
The routines called with AL=1xh are designed to be called only immediately after a mode set and are similar to the routines called with AL=0xh, except that:
    Page 0 must be active.
    Bytes/character is recalculated.

Max character rows is recalculated.
CRT buffer length is recalculated.
CRTC registers are reprogrammed as follows:

> R09 = bytes/char-1 ; max scan line (mode 7 only)
> R0A = bytes/char-2 ; cursor start
> R0B = 0   ; cursor end
> R12 = ((rows+1)*(bytes/char))-1 ; vertical display end
> R14 = bytes/char   ; underline loc (*** BUG: should be 1 less ***)

Conflicts: BIOS Window Extension GET WINDOW COORDINATES.
See Also: Function CDh Subfunction 10h

INTERRUPT 10h - Function 11h, Subfunctions 20h to 29h
GRAPHICS-MODE CHARACTER GENERATOR FUNCTIONS

Purpose: Establishes font and display size for text characters in graphics modes.

Available on: Systems equipped with EGA, VGA, or MCGA video..

Restrictions: none.

Registers at call:

Return Registers: n/a.

AH = 11h
AL = 20h: set user 8 by 8 graphics characters
    (INT 1Fh)
    ES:BP -> user table
AL = 21h: set user graphics characters
    ES:BP -> user table
    CX = bytes per character
    BL = row specifier
        00h user set
            DL = number of rows
        01h 14 rows
        02h 25 rows
        03h 43 rows
AL = 22h: ROM 8 by 14 set
    BL = row specifier
        00h user set
            DL = number of rows
        01h 14 rows
        02h 25 rows
        03h 43 rows
AL = 23h: ROM 8 by 8 double dot
    BL = row specifier
        00h user set
            DL = number of rows
        01h 14 rows
        02h 25 rows
        03h 43 rows
AL = 24h: load 8x16 graphics characters
  (VGA/MCGA)
    BL = row specifier
        00h user set
            DL = number of rows
        01h 14 rows
        02h 25 rows
        03h 43 rows

AL = 29h: load 8x16 graphics characters
(Compaq Systempro)
    BL = row specifier
        00h user set
            DL = number of rows
        01h 14 rows
        02h 25 rows
        03h 43 rows
Details: These functions are meant to be called only after a mode set.
    UltraVision v2+ sets INT 43h to the appropriate font for AL=22h, 23h, 24h, and 29h.
Conflicts: BIOS Window Extension GET WINDOW COORDINATES.
See Also: INT 1Fh, INT 43h

INTERRUPT 10h - Function 11h, Subfunction 30h
GET FONT INFORMATION

Purpose: Returns pointer to specified font table.
Available on: Systems equipped with EGA, VGA, or MCGA video.

Restrictions: none.

Registers at call:
AX = 1130h
BH = pointer specifier
    00h INT 1Fh pointer
    01h INT 43h pointer
    02h ROM 8 by 14 character font pointer
    03h ROM 8 by 8 double dot font pointer
    04h ROM 8 by 8 DD font (top half)
    05h ROM alpha alternate (9 by 14)
        pointer
    06h ROM 8 by 16 font (VGA,MCGA
        only)
    07h ROM alternate 9 by 16 font (VGA
        only)
    11h (UltraVision v2+) 8x20 font (VGA)
        or 8x19 font (autosync EGA)
    12h (UltraVision v2+) 8x10 font (VGA)
        or 8x11 font (autosync EGA)

Return Registers:
ES:BP = specified pointer
CX = bytes/character
DL = character rows on screen

Details: For UltraVision v2+, the 9xN alternate fonts follow the corresponding 8xN font at ES:BP+256N.
Conflicts: BIOS Window Extension GET WINDOW COORDINATES.
See Also: Function 11h Subfunctions 00h and 20h, INT 1Fh, INT 43h

INTERRUPT 10h - Function 12h
BIOS Window Extension v1.1 - GET BLANKING ATTRIBUTE

Purpose: Determine attribute which will be used on blanked lines when scrolling.
Available on: All machines.

Restrictions: Must have BIOS Window Extension TSR installed.

Registers at call:
AH = 12h

Return Registers:
BH = attribute

Details: BWE is a TSR by John J. Seal published in the May 1986 issue of Dr. Dobb's Journal.
Conflicts: Normal EGA/VGA video functions.
See Also: BIOS Window Extension Functions 10h and 11h

INTERRUPT 10h - Function 12h, Subfunction 10h
ALTERNATE FUNCTION SELECT - GET EGA INFO

Purpose: Determine video system characteristics.

Available on: Systems equipped with EGA, VGA, or MCGA video.

Restrictions: none.

Registers at call:
AH = 12h
BL = 10h

Return Registers:
BH = 00h color mode in effect (I/O port 3Dxh)
     01h mono mode in effect (I/O port 3Bxh)
BL = 00h 64k bytes memory installed
     01h 128k bytes memory installed
     02h 192k bytes memory installed
     03h 256k bytes memory installed
CH = feature bits
CL = switch settings

Conflicts: BIOS Window Extension GET BLANKING ATTRIBUTE.

INTERRUPT 10h - Function 12h, Subfunction 20h
ALTERNATE FUNCTION SELECT - ALTERNATE PRTSC

Purpose: Selects alternate PrtScr routine.

Available on: Systems equipped with EGA, VGA, or MCGA video.

Restrictions: none.

Registers at call:
AH = 12h
BL = 20h select alternate print screen routine

Return Registers: n/a.

Details: Installs a PrtSc routine from the video card's BIOS to replace the default PrtSc handler from the ROM BIOS, which usually does not understand screen heights other than 25 lines. Some adapters disable print-screen instead of enhancing it.

Conflicts: BIOS Window Extension GET BLANKING ATTRIBUTE.

See Also: INT 05h (chapter 2)

INTERRUPT 10h - Function 12h, Subfunction 30h
ALTERNATE FUNCTION SELECT - SELECT VERTICAL RESOLUTION

Purpose: Sets number of scanlines; permits switching between 25- and 28-character modes, or 43- and 50-character modes, when used following INT 10h Function 11h.

Available on: VGA-equipped systems.

Restrictions: none.

Registers at call:
AH = 12h
BL = 30h
AL = vertical resolution
    00h 200 scan lines
    01h 350 scan lines
    02h 400 scan lines

Return Registers:
AL = 12h if function supported

See Also: Character Generator Functions under Function 11h

Conflicts: BIOS Window Extension GET BLANKING ATTRIBUTE.

INTERRUPT 10h - Function 12h, Subfunction 31h
ALTERNATE FUNCTION SELECT - PALETTE LOADING

Purpose: Control loading of default palette.

Available on: VGA/MCGA-equipped systems.

Restrictions: none.

Registers at call:
AH = 12h
BL = 31h
AL = 00h enable default palette loading
   01h disable default palette loading
Conflicts: BIOS Window Extension GET BLANKING ATTRIBUTE.

Return Registers:
AL = 12h if function supported.

INTERRUPT 10h - Function 12h, Subfunction 32h
ALTERNATE FUNCTION SELECT - VIDEO ADDRESSING

Purpose: Control CPU access to video memory.
Available on: VGA/MCGA-equipped systems.
Registers at call:
AH = 12h
BL = 32h
AL = 00h enable video addressing
   01h disable video addressing
Conflicts: BIOS Window Extension GET BLANKING ATTRIBUTE.

Restrictions: none.
Return Registers:
AL = 12h if function supported.

INTERRUPT 10h - Function 12h, Subfunction 33h
ALTERNATE FUNCTION SELECT - GRAY-SCALE SUMMING

Purpose: Controls usability of gray-scale summing function.
Available on: VGA/MCGA-equipped systems.
Registers at call:
AH = 12h
BL = 33h
AL = 00h enable gray scale summing
   01h disable gray scale summing
Conflicts: BIOS Window Extension GET BLANKING ATTRIBUTE.
See Also: Function 10h Subfunction 1Bh

Restrictions: none.
Return Registers:
AL = 12h if function supported.

INTERRUPT 10h - Function 12h, Subfunction 34h
ALTERNATE FUNCTION SELECT - CURSOR EMULATION

Purpose: Enable/disable cursor emulation.
Available on: VGA-equipped systems.
Registers at call:
AH = 12h
BL = 34h
AL = 00h enable alphanumeric cursor emulation
   01h disable alphanumeric cursor
     emulation
Conflicts: BIOS Window Extension GET BLANKING ATTRIBUTE.

Restrictions: none.
Return Registers:
AL = 12h if function supported.

INTERRUPT 10h - Function 12h, Subfunction 35h
ALTERNATE FUNCTION SELECT - DISPLAY-SWITCH INTERFACE

Purpose: Switches between two video displays.
Available on: VGA/MCGA-equipped systems.
Registers at call:
AH = 12h
BL = 35h
AL = 00h initial adapter video off
   01h initial planar video on
   02h switch active video off
   03h switch inactive video on

Restrictions: none.
Return Registers:
AL = 12h if function supported.

80h (undocumented) set system board
video active flag
ES:DX -> buffer
   (128 byte save area if AL = 0, 2 or 3)
Conflicts: BIOS Window Extension GET BLANKING ATTRIBUTE.

INTERRUPT 10h - Function 12h, Subfunction 36h
ALTERNATE FUNCTION SELECT - VIDEO REFRESH CONTROL

Purpose: Enable/disable video refresh.
Available on: VGA/MCGA-equipped systems.
Registers at call:
AH = 12h
BL = 36h
AL = 00h enable refresh
   01h disable refresh

Restrictions: none.
Return Registers:
AL = 12h if function supported

Details: Display is blanked when video refresh is disabled.
Conflicts: BIOS Window Extension GET BLANKING ATTRIBUTE.

INTERRUPT 10h - Function 12h, Subfunction 55h
ALTERNATE FUNCTION SELECT - ENHANCED FEATURES

Purpose: Provides advanced features.
Available on: ATI, Tatung, Taxan video cards
        only.
Registers at call:
AH = 12h
BH = 55h
BL = subfunction:
   00h disabled enhanced features
   01h enable enhanced features
   02h get status

Restrictions: none.

Return Registers: n/a.

AL = status flags
     bit 3: set if enhanced features enabled
     bits 7-5 monitor type
        000 PS/2 mono
        001 PS/2 color
        010 multi-sync
        011 Taxan 650 25kHz
        100 RGB
        101 mono
        110 EGA
        111 Compaq internal

   03h disable register trapping
     (CGA emulation)
   04h enable register trapping
   05h program mode described by table
     at ES:BP (Table 5-6)
   06h get mode table (Table 5-6)
     AL = video mode

ES:BP -> table suitable for mode AL (and
     subfunction BL=05h)
BP = FFFFh on error

Conflicts: BIOS Window Extension GET BLANKING ATTRIBUTE.

Table 5-6. Format of ATI VGA Wonder video mode table:

Offset	Size	Description
00h	BYTE	number of columns
01h	BYTE	maximum row (number of rows - 1)
02h	BYTE	scan lines per row
03h	WORD	video buffer size in bytes
05h	4 Bytes	values for Sequencer registers 1-4
09h	BYTE	value for Miscellaneous Output register
0Ah	25 BYTEs	values for CRTC registers 00h-18h:

> 00h horizontal total size (chars)
> 01h horizontal displayed (chars)
> 02h horizontal sync position (chars)
> 03h horizontal sync width (chars)
> 04h vertical total size (char rows)
> 05h vertical total adjust (scan lines)
> 06h vertical displayed (char rows)
> 07h vertical sync position (char rows)
> 08h interlace mode
> 09h max scan par in row
> 0Ah cursor start scan line
> 0Bh cursor end scan line
> 0Ch screen memory start (high)
> 0Dh screen memory start (low)
> 0Eh cursor address (high)
> 0Fh cursor address (low)
> 10h light pen (high)
> 11h light pen (low)

Offset	Size	Description
23h	20 BYTEs	default palette (values for AttributeController registers 00h-13h)
37h	9 BYTEs	values for Graphics Controller registers 00h-08h

INTERRUPT 10h - Function 13h
WRITE STRING

Purpose: Displays string on CRT.

Available on: All AT and later systems, plus all systems with EGA or later video card.

Restrictions: none.

Registers at call:
AH = 13h
AL = write mode:
> bit 0: update cursor position after writing
> 1: string contains alternating characters and attributes

BH = page number
BL = attribute if string contains only characters
CX = number of characters in string
DH,DL = row,column at which to start writing
ES:BP -> string to write

Return Registers: n/a.

Details: Recognizes CR, LF, BS, and bell.
Conflicts: None known.
See Also: Functions 09h and 0Ah

INTERRUPT 10h - Function 14h, Subfunction 00h
LOAD USER-SPECIFIED LCD CHARACTER FONT

Purpose: Changes character font.

Available on: IBM Convertible, Compaq Portable
    386.
Registers at call:
AX = 1400h
ES:DI -> character font
BH = number of bytes per character: 08h or 10h
    (Compaq)
BL = 00h load main font (block 0)
    01h load alternate font (block 1)
CX = number of characters to store
DX = character offset into RAM font area
Conflicts: None known.
See Also: Function 11h, Function 14h Subfunction 01h

Restrictions: none.

Return Registers: n/a.

INTERRUPT 10h - Function 14h, Subfunction 01h
LOAD SYSTEM ROM DEFAULT LCD CHARACTER FONT

Purpose: Loads default character font.
Available on: IBM Convertible, Compaq Portable
    386.
Registers at call:
AX = 1401h
BL = 00h load main font (block 0)
    01h load alternate font (block 1)
Conflicts: None known.
See Also: Function 11h, Function 14h Subfunction 00h

Restrictions: none.

Return Registers: n/a.

INTERRUPT 10h - Function 14h, Subfunction 02h
SET MAPPING OF LCD HIGH INTENSITY ATTRIBUTES

Purpose: Modifies display of high-intensity attribute.
Available on: IBM Convertible, Compaq Portable
    386.
Registers at call:
AX = 1402h
BL = 00h ignore high intensity attribute
    01h map high intensity to underscore
    02h map high intensity to reverse video
    03h map high intensity to selected
        alternate font
    B0h half intensity (Compaq)
    B1h toggle active intensity bit
        interpretation (Compaq Portable 386)

Restrictions: none.

Return Registers: n/a.

INTERRUPT 10h - Function 15h
GET PHYSICAL DISPLAY PARAMETERS

Purpose: Obtains physical display information.
Available on: IBM Convertible.
Registers at call:
AH = 15h

Restrictions: none.
Return Registers:
AX = alternate display adapter type:
    0000h none
    5140h LCD
    5153h CGA
    5151h mono
ES:DI -> parameter table (see Table 5-7)

Conflicts: Set Superimpose Mode (Sperry PC).
See Also: Function 1Bh

Table 5-7. Format of display parameter table:

Offset	Size	Description
00h	WORD	monitor model number
02h	WORD	vertical pixels per meter
04h	WORD	horizontal pixels per meter
06h	WORD	total vertical pixels
08h	WORD	total horizontal pixels
0Ah	WORD	horizontal pixel separation in micrometers
0Ch	WORD	vertical pixel separation in micrometers

INTERRUPT 10h - Function 15h
SET SUPERIMPOSE MODE

Purpose: Permit simultaneous text and graphics display.
Available on: Sperry PC only.   **Restrictions:** none.
Registers at call: **Return Registers:** n/a.
AH = 15h
AL = superimpose mode
   00h show graphics screen
   01h show text screen
   02h text superimposed on graphics screen
Conflicts: Get Physical Display Parameters.

INTERRUPT 10h - Function 1Ah
DISPLAY COMBINATION

Purpose: Determine video card and monitor characteristics.
Available on: VGA/MCGA-equipped systems.   **Restrictions:** none.
Registers at call: **Return Registers:**
AH = 1Ah   AL = 1Ah if function was supported
AL = 00h read display combination code   BL = active display code (see below)
   01h set display combination code   BH = alternate display code

BL = active display code (see Table 5-8)
BH = alternate display code
Conflicts: None known.

Table 5-8. Values for display combination codes

Value	Display Combination
00h	no display
01h	monochrome adapter with monochrome display
02h	CGA with color display
03h	reserved
04h	EGA with color display
05h	EGA with monochrome display
06h	PGA with color display
07h	VGA with monochrome analog display
08h	VGA with color analog display
09h	reserved
0Ah	MCGA with digital color display
0Bh	MCGA with monochrome analog display
0Ch	MCGA with color analog display
FFh	unknown display type

INTERRUPT 10h - Function 1Bh
FUNCTIONALITY/STATE INFORMATION

Purpose: Obtain full details of video setup.

Available on: VGA/MCGA-equipped systems.

Registers at call:

AH = 1Bh

BX = implementation type
    0000h return functionality/state
        information

ES:DI -> 64 byte buffer for state information
    (see Table 5-9)

Conflicts: None known.

See Also: Function 15h

Restrictions: none.

Return Registers:

AL = 1Bh if function supported

ES:DI buffer filled with state information

Table 5-9. Format of state information

Offset	Size	Description
00h	DWORD	address of static functionality table (see Table 5-10)
04h	BYTE	video mode in effect
05h	WORD	number of columns
07h	WORD	length of regen buffer in bytes
09h	WORD	starting address of regen buffer
0Bh	WORD	cursor position for page 0
0Dh	WORD	cursor position for page 1
0Fh	WORD	cursor position for page 2
11h	WORD	cursor position for page 3
13h	WORD	cursor position for page 4
15h	WORD	cursor position for page 5
17h	WORD	cursor position for page 6
19h	WORD	cursor position for page 7
1Bh	WORD	cursor type
1Dh	BYTE	active display page
1Eh	WORD	CRTC port address
20h	BYTE	current setting of register (3?8)
21h	BYTE	current setting of register (3?9)
22h	BYTE	number of rows
23h	WORD	bytes/character
25h	BYTE	DCC of active display
26h	BYTE	DCC of alternate display
27h	WORD	number of colors supported in current mode
29h	WORD	number of pages supported in current mode
2Ah	BYTE	number of scan lines active:
		0 = 200
		1 = 350
		2 = 400
		3 = 480
2Bh	BYTE	primary character block
2Ch	BYTE	secondary character block
2Dh	BYTE	miscellaneous flags:
		bit 0 all modes on all displays on
		1 gray summing on
		2 monochrome display attached
		3 default palette loading disabled
		4 cursor emulation enabled
		5 0 = intensity; 1 = blinking
		6 PS/2 P70 plasma display (without 9-dot widefont) active
		7 reserved

Table 5-9. Format of state information (continued)

Offset	Size	Description
2Eh	3 BYTEs	reserved
31h	BYTE	video memory available:
		00h = 64K,
		01h = 128K,
		02h = 192K,
		03h = 256K
32h	BYTE	save pointer state flags:
		bit 0 512 character set active
		1 dynamic save area present
		2 alpha font override active
		3 graphics font override active
		4 palette override active
		5 DCC override active
		6 reserved
		7 reserved
33h	13 BYTEs	reserved

Table 5-10. Format of Static Functionality Table

Offset	Size	Description
00h	BYTE	modes supported #1:
		bit 0 to bit 7 = 1 modes 0, 1, 2, 3, 4, 5, 6 supported
01h	BYTE	modes supported #2:
		bit 0 to bit 7 = 1 modes 8, 9, 0Ah, 0Bh, 0Ch, 0Dh, 0Eh, 0Fh supported
02h	BYTE	modes supported #3:
		bit 0 to bit 3 = 1 modes 10h, 11h, 12h, 13h supported
		bit 4 to bit 7 reserved
03h	4 BYTEs	reserved
07h	BYTE	scan lines supported:
		bit 0 to bit 2 = 1 if scan lines 200,350,400 supported
08h	BYTE	total number of character blocks available in text modes
09h	BYTE	maximum number of active character blocks in text modes
0Ah	BYTE	miscellaneous function flags #1:
		bit 0 all modes on all displays function supported
		1 gray summing function supported
		2 character font loading function supported
		3 default palette loading enable/disablesupported
		4 cursor emulation function supported
		5 EGA palette present
		6 color palette present
		7 color paging function supported
0Bh	BYTE	miscellaneous function flags #2:
		bit 0 light pen supported
		1 save/restore state function 1Ch supported
		2 intensity blinking function supported
		3 Display Combination Code supported
		4-7 reserved
0Ch	WORD	reserved

Table 5-10. Format of Static Functionality Table (continued)

Offset	Size	Description
0Eh	BYTE	save pointer function flags:

bit 0 512 character set supported
    1 dynamic save area supported
    2 alpha font override supported
    3 graphics font override supported
    4 palette override supported
    5 DCC extension supported
    6 reserved
    7 reserved

Offset	Size	Description
0Fh	BYTE	reserved

INTERRUPT 10h - Function 1Ch
SAVE/RESTORE VIDEO STATE

Purpose: Saves or restores video state.
Available on: VGA-equipped systems.
Registers at call:
AH = 1Ch
AL = 00h return state buffer size
    01h save video state
        ES:BX -> buffer for video state
    02h restore video state
        ES:BX -> buffer containing
            previously saved state
        CX = requested states:
            bit 0 video hardware
            1 BIOS data areas
            2 color registers and DAC state
            3-15 reserved
Conflicts: None known.

Restrictions: none.
Return Registers:
AL = 1Ch if function supported.
BX = number of 64-byte blocks needed

INTERRUPT 10h - Function 30h, Subfunction 00h
LOCATE 3270PC CONFIGURATION TABLE

Purpose: Determines whether 3270PC program is active and if so, returns pointer to configuration table.
Available on: 3270PC only.
Registers at call:
AX = 3000h
CX = 0000h
DX = 0000h
Conflicts: None known.

Restrictions: none.
Return Registers:
CX:DX -> 3270PC configuration table (Table 5-11)
CX:DX = 0000h:0000h if 3270PC Control Program
    not active

Table 5-11. Format of 3270 PC configuration table

Offset	Size	Description
00h	BYTE	aspect ratio X
01h	BYTE	aspect ratio Y

Table 5-11. Format of 3270 PC configuration table (continued)

Offset	Size	Description
02h	BYTE	monitor type:
		00h = 5151 (mono) or 5272 (color)
		01h = 3295
		02h = 5151 or 5272 with XGA (???) graphics adapter
		03h = 5279 with 3270PC G adapter
		04h = 5379 model C01 with 3270PC GX adapter
		05h = 5379 model M01 with 3270PC GX adapter
		07h = non-3270PC with 3270 Workstation Program
		FFh = 3270PC Control Program not loaded
03h	BYTE	reserved
04h	BYTE	adapter ID:
		00h = 5151/5272 adapter
		04h = 5151/5272 with XGA adapter
		30h = 3295 or 3270PC G/GX adapter
05h	BYTE	reserved
06h	BYTE	function flags 1:
		bit 1: 720x350 eight-color graphics
		2: 360x350 four-color graphics
		3: 720x350 two-color graphics
		4: CGA color graphics
		5: color text, 4 pages
		6: color text, 1 page
		7: mono text, 1 page
07h	BYTE	function flags 2:
		bit 6: GPI graphics supported
08h	WORD	segment address of Control Program Level table (see Table 5-12)
0Ah	10 BYTEs	reserved

Table 5-12. Format of Control Program Level table:

Offset	Size	Description
00h	WORD	program version: 02xxh = 3270PC Control Program v2.xx
		03xxh = 3270PC Control Program v3.xx
		04xxh = 3270 Workstation Program v1.xx
02h	BYTE	Control Program ID (00h)
03h	27 BYTEs	Control Program Descriptor ("IBM 3270 PC CONTROL PROGRAM")

INTERRUPT 10h - Function 40h
SET GRAPHICS MODE

Purpose: Places system into graphics mode.
Available on: Hercules-equipped systems.
Registers at call:
AH = 40h
Conflicts: None known.
See Also: Function 41h

Restrictions: Must have GRAFIX software installed.
Return Registers: n/a.

INTERRUPT 10h - Function 41h
SET TEXT MODE

Purpose: Places system into text mode.
Available on: Hercules-equipped systems.
Registers at call:
AH = 41h
Conflicts: None known.
See Also: Function 40h

Restrictions: Must have GRAFIX software installed.
Return Registers: n/a.

INTERRUPT 10h - Function 42h
CLEAR CURRENT PAGE

Purpose: Erases all data on current display page.
Available on: Hercules-equipped systems.
Registers at call:
AH = 42h
Conflicts: None known.
See Also: Function 45h

Restrictions: Must have GRAFIX software installed.
Return Registers: n/a.

INTERRUPT 10h - Function 43h
SELECT DRAWING PAGE

Purpose: Specifies page to be drawn on.
Available on: Hercules-equipped systems.
Registers at call:
AH = 43h
AL = page number (0 or 1)
Conflicts: None known.
See Also: Functions 44h and 45h

Restrictions: Must have GRAFIX software installed.
Return Registers: n/a.

INTERRUPT 10h - Function 44h
SELECT DRAWING FUNCTION

Purpose: Specifies function to be used when drawing.
Available on: Hercules-equipped systems.
Registers at call:
AH = 44h
AL =   00h clear pixels
      01h set pixels
      02h invert pixels
Conflicts: None known.
See Also: Functions 44h, 46h, 4Ch, and 4Dh

Restrictions: Must have GRAFIX software installed.
Return Registers: n/a.

INTERRUPT 10h - Function 45h
SELECT PAGE TO DISPLAY

Purpose: Specifies which page to display.
Available on: Hercules-equipped systems.
Registers at call:
AH = 45h
AL = page number (0,1)
Conflicts: None known.
See Also: Functions 42h and 43h

Restrictions: Must have GRAFIX software installed.
Return Registers: n/a.

INTERRUPT 10h - Function 46h
DRAW ONE PIXEL

Purpose: Draws one pixel at specified location using operation and page already set by other functions.
Available on: Hercules-equipped systems.
Registers at call:
AH = 46h
DI = x (0-720)
BP = y (0-347)
Details: Function 44h determines operation and function 43h which page to use for drawing.
Conflicts: None known.
See Also: Functions 0Ch, 47h,49h, 4Ch, and 4Dh

Restrictions: Must have GRAFIX software installed.
Return Registers: n/a.

INTERRUPT 10h - Function 47h
FIND PIXEL VALUE

Purpose: Reads one pixel at specified location from page already set by other functions.

Available on: Hercules-equipped systems.   **Restrictions:** Must have GRAFIX software installed.

Registers at call: **Return Registers:**

AH = 47h   AL = 00h pixel clear

DI = x (0-720)   AL = 01h pixel set

BP = y (0-347)

Details: Function 43h specifies which page is used.

Conflicts: None known.

See Also: Functions 0Dh and 46h

INTERRUPT 10h - Function 48h
MOVE TO POINT

Purpose: Moves current position to specified location.

Available on: Hercules-equipped systems.   **Restrictions:** Must have GRAFIX software installed.

Registers at call: **Return Registers:** n/a.

AH = 48h

DI = x (0-720)

BP = y (0-347)

Conflicts: None known.

See Also: Function 49h

INTERRUPT 10h - Function 49h
DRAW TO POINT

Purpose: Draws line from current position to specified location and sets that location as new current position.

Available on: Hercules-equipped systems.   **Restrictions:** Must have GRAFIX software installed.

Registers at call: **Return Registers:** n/a.

AH = 49h

DI = x (0-720)

BP = y (0-347)

Details: Prior call to function 48h or 49h specify first point, 44h specifies operation and 43h specifies page on which to draw.

Conflicts: None known.

See Also: Functions 43h, 44h, 48h, 4Ch, and 4Dh

INTERRUPT 10h - Function 4Ah
BLOCK FILL

Purpose: Draws a solid rectangle.

Available on: Hercules-equipped systems.   **Restrictions:** Must have GRAFIX software installed.

Registers at call: **Return Registers:** n/a.

AH = 4Ah

DI = x coordinate of lower left corner

BP = y coordinate of lower left corner

BX = height in pixels

CX = width in pixels

Conflicts: None known.

See Also: Function 4Eh

INTERRUPT 10h - Function 4Bh
DISPLAY CHARACTER

Purpose: Displays character at specified location.

Available on: Hercules-equipped systems.
Registers at call:
AH = 4Bh
AL = character to display
DI = x (0-720)
BP = y (0-347)
Details: Unlike the other BIOS character functions, character position is specified in pixels rather than rows and columns.
Conflicts: FRIEZE v7+ API.
See Also: Functions 09h and 0Ah

Restrictions: Must have GRAFIX software installed.
Return Registers: n/a.

INTERRUPT 10h - Function 4Bh
FRIEZE v7+ API

Purpose: Provides interface between Frieze graphics printing system and application programs.
Available on: All machines.

Restrictions: Frieze software (part of ZSoft's Paintbrush systems) must be installed.

Registers at call:
AH = 4Bh
CL = function
   00h reserved
   01h load window
      ES:BX -> ASCIIZ filename from
        which to read
   02h save window
      ES:BX -> ASCIIZ filename to which
        to write
   07h set window size
      ES:BX -> four- WORD structure
        with Xmin, Ymin, Xmax, Ymax
   09h set patterns
      ES:BX -> 16-BYTE vector of
        screen-> printer color-
        correspondences
   0Ah get patterns
      ES:BX -> 16-BYTE buffer for color
        correspondences
   0Bh set mode
      AL = mode
   0Fh get window
      ES:BX -> four- WORD buffer for
        Xmin, Ymin, Xmax, Ymax
   10h set print options
      ES:BX -> printer options in same
        format as FRIEZE cmdline
   14h get version

   15h set parameters
      ES:BX -> parameter table
        (Table 5-13)
   16h get parameters
      ES:BX -> buffer for parameter table
        (Table 5-13)

Return Registers:
AX = status:
   00h successful
   01h user aborted printout with ESC
   02h reserved
   03h file read error
   04h file write error
   05h file not found
   06h invalid header (not an image or wrong screen
      mode)
   07h file close error
   08h disk error
   09h printer error
   0Ah invalid function
   0Bh can't create file
   0Ch wrong video mode

AH = major version (00h if FRIEZE version before 7)
AL = minor version

17h get printer resolution
  ES:BX -> 12-WORD table for six
    horizontal/vertical resol pairs
18h reserved (v8.0 only)
Conflicts: Hercules GRAFIX Display Character function.

Table 5-13. Format of Frieze parameter table

Offset	Size	Description
00h	WORD	top margin (1/100 inch)
02h	WORD	left margin (1/100 inch)
04h	WORD	horizontal size (1/100 inch)
06h	WORD	vertical size (1/100 inch)
08h	WORD	quality/draft mode:
		00h draft mode
		01h quality mode
		02h use horizontal/vertical resolution for output resolution
0Ah	WORD	printer horizontal resolution (dots per inch)
0Ch	WORD	printer vertical resolution (dots per inch)
0Eh	WORD	reserved (FFFFh)

Details: Any field which should remain unchanged may be filled with FFFFh.

INTERRUPT 10h - Function 4Ch
DRAW ARC

Purpose: Draws specified arc on current page.
Available on: Hercules-equipped systems.
Registers at call:
AH = 4Ch
AL = quadrant (1 = upper right, 2 = upper left, etc)
DI = x coordinate of center
BP = y coordinate of center
BX = radius
Conflicts: None known.
See Also: Functions 49h and 4Dh

Restrictions: Must have GRAFIX software installed.
Return Registers: n/a.

INTERRUPT 10h - Function 4Dh
DRAW CIRCLE

Purpose: Draws specified circle on current page.
Available on: Hercules-equipped systems.
Registers at call:
AH = 4Dh
DI = x of center
BP = y of center
BX = radius
Conflicts: None known.
See Also: Functions 49h and 4Ch

Restrictions: Must have GRAFIX software installed.
Return Registers: n/a.

INTERRUPT 10h - Function 4Eh
FILL AREA

Purpose: Fills any convex polygonal area.
Available on: Hercules-equipped systems.

Restrictions: Must have GRAFIX software installed.

Registers at call:
AH = 4Eh
DI = x coordinate of an interior point
BP = y coordinate of an interior point

Return Registers: n/a.

Details: The first fill makes the figure solid, the second erases it.
Conflicts: None known.
See Also: Function 4Ah

INTERRUPT 10h - Function 4Fh, Subfunction 00h
VESA SuperVGA BIOS - GET SuperVGA INFORMATION

Purpose: Determine whether SuperVGA BIOS is present and if so, obtain information about its setup.

Available on: All machines.

Restrictions: VESA SuperVGA BIOS must be present.

Registers at call:
AX = 4F00h
ES:DI -> 256-byte buffer for SuperVGA
    information (Table 5-14)

Return Registers:
AL = 4Fh function supported
AH = status
    00h successful
    01h failed

Conflicts: None known.
See Also: Function 4Fh Subfunction 01h

Table 5-14. Format of SuperVGA information:

Offset	Size	Description
00h	4 BYTEs	signature ('VESA')
04h	WORD	VESA version number
06h	DWORD	pointer to OEM name
0Ah	4 BYTEs	capabilities
0Eh	DWORD	pointer to list of supported VESA and OEM video modes
12h	238 BYTEs	reserved

INTERRUPT 10h - Function 4Fh, Subfunction 01h
GET VESA SuperVGA MODE INFORMATION

Purpose: Determine operating mode of SuperVGA BIOS.

Available on: Systems equipped with VESA SuperVGA BIOS.

Restrictions: none.

Registers at call:
AX = 4F01h = SuperVGA video mode
ES:DI -> 256-byte buffer mode information
    (Table 5-15)

Return Registers:
AL = 4Fh function supported
AH = status:
    00h successful
    01h failed

Conflicts: None known.
See Also: Function 4Fh Subfunctions 00h and 02h

Table 5-15. Format of mode information

Offset	Size	Description
00h	WORD	mode attributes: bit 0: mode supported bit 1: optional information available bit 2: BIOS output supported bit 3: set if color, clear if monochrome bit 4: set if graphics mode, clear if text mode

Table 5-15. Format of mode information (continued)

Offset	Size	Description
02h	BYTE	window A attributes: bit 0: exists bit 1: readable bit 2: writable bits 3-7 reserved
03h	BYTE	window B attributes (as for window A)
04h	WORD	window granularity (smallest KB increment by which window can be moved)
06h	WORD	window size in K
08h	WORD	start segment of window A
0Ah	WORD	start segment of window B
0Ch	DWORD	-> FAR window positioning function (equivalent to Function 4Fh Subfunction 05h)
10h	WORD	bytes per scan line

---remainder is optional for VESA modes, needed for OEM modes---

Offset	Size	Description
12h	WORD	width in pixels
14h	WORD	height in pixels
16h	BYTE	width of character cell in pixels
17h	BYTE	height if character cell in pixels
18h	BYTE	number of memory planes
19h	BYTE	number of bits per pixel
1Ah	BYTE	number of banks
1Bh	BYTE	memory model type
1Ch	BYTE	size of bank in K

INTERRUPT 10h - Function 4Fh, Subfunction 02h
SET VESA SuperVGA VIDEO MODE

Purpose: Select a video display mode defined by the VESA committee.

Available on: Systems equipped with VESA SuperVGA BIOS.

Restrictions: none.

Registers at call:
AX = 4F02h
BX = mode:

100h	640x400x256
101h	640x480x256
102h	800x600x16
103h	800x600x256
104h	1024x768x16
105h	1024x768x256
106h	1280x1024x16
107h	1280x1024x256
108h	80x60 text
109h	132x25 text
10Ah	132x43 text
10Bh	132x50 text
10Ch	132x60 text

bit 15 set means don't clear video memory

Return Registers:
AL = 4Fh function supported
AH = status
    00h successful
    01h failed

Details: Video modes less than 100h are defined to be identical to the non-VESA video mode set with INT 10h Function 00h and are thus vendor-specific.

Conflicts: None known.

See Also: Function 4Fh Subfunctions 01h and 03h

INTERRUPT 10h - Function 4Fh, Subfunction 03h
GET CURRENT VESA SuperVGA VIDEO MODE

Purpose: Determines current video mode.

Available on: Systems equipped with VESA
SuperVGA BIOS.

Registers at call:
AX = 4F03h

Restrictions: none.

Return Registers:
AL = 4Fh function supported
AH = status:
   00h successful
   01h failed
BX = video mode:
   100h   640x400x256
   101h   640x480x256
   102h   800x600x16
   103h   800x600x256
   104h   1024x768x16
   105h   1024x768x256
   106h   1280x1024x16
   107h   1280x1024x256
   108h   80x60 text
   109h   132x25 text
   10Ah   132x43 text
   10Bh   132x50 text
   10Ch   132x60 text

Details: Video modes less than 100h are defined to be identical to the non-VESA video mode set with INT 10h Function 00h and are thus vendor-specific.

Conflicts: None known.

See Also: Function 4Fh Subfunction 02h

INTERRUPT 10h - Function 4Fh, Subfunction 04h
SAVE/RESTORE VESA SuperVGA VIDEO STATE

Purpose: Saves or restores specified states of video BIOS.

Available on: Systems equipped with VESA
SuperVGA BIOS.

Registers at call:
AX = 4F04h
DL = subfunction:

   00h get state buffer size
   01h save video states
      ES:BX -> buffer
   02h restore video states
      ES:BX -> buffer
      CX = flags for states to save/restore
         bit 0: video hardware state
         bit 1: video BIOS data state
         bit 2: video DAC state
         bit 3: SuperVGA state

Restrictions: none.

Return Registers:
AL = 4Fh function supported
AH = status
   00h successful
   01h failed
BX = number of 64-byte blocks needed

Conflicts: None known.

INTERRUPT 10h - Function 4Fh, Subfunction 05h
VESA SuperVGA CPU VIDEO MEMORY CONTROL

Purpose: Controls access to video RAM.

Available on: Systems equipped with VESA
SuperVGA BIOS.

Restrictions: none.

Registers at call:
AX = 4F05h
BH = subfunction:
    00h select video memory window
        DX = window address in video
           memory (in granularity units)
    01h get video memory window

Return Registers:
AL = 4Fh function supported
AH = status:
    00h successful
    01h failed

DX = window address in video memory (in
      granularity units)
BL = window number:
    00h window A
    01h window B

Conflicts: None known.
See Also: Function 4Fh Subfunctions 06h and 07h

INTERRUPT 10h - Function 4Fh, Subfunction 06h
GET/SET SuperVGA LOGICAL SCAN LINE LENGTH

Purpose: Reads current logical line length, or sets new value.
Available on: Systems equipped with VESA
        SuperVGA BIOS v1.1 or higher.

Restrictions: none.

Registers at call:
AX = 4F06h
BL = 00h set scan line length
CX = desired width in pixels
BL = 01h get scan line length

Return Registers:
AL = 4Fh if function supported
AH = status:
    00h successful
    01h failed
BX = bytes per scan line
CX = number of pixels per scan line
DX = maximum number of scan lines

Details: If the desired width is not achievable, the next larger width will be set. The scan line may be wider than the visible area of the screen. This function is valid in text modes, provided that values are multiplied by the character cell width/height.
Conflicts: None known.
See Also: Function 4Fh Subfunctions 01h, 05h, and 07h

INTERRUPT 10h - Function 4Fh, Subfunction 07h
GET/SET SuperVGA DISPLAY START

Purpose: Reads or sets pixel address of leftmost pixel in scan line.
Available on: Systems equipped with VESA
        SuperVGA BIOS v1.1 or higher.

Restrictions: none.

Registers at call:
AX = 4F07h
BH = 00h (reserved)
BL = 00h set display start
    CX = leftmost displayed pixel in scan line
    DX = first displayed scan line
BL = 01h get display start

Return Registers:
AL = 4Fh if function supported
AH = status:
    00h successful
    01h failed

BH = 00h
CX = leftmost displayed pixel in scan line
DX = first displayed scan line

Details: This function is valid in text modes, provided that values aremultiplied by the character cell width/height.
Conflicts: None known.
See Also: Function 4Fh Subfunctions 01h, 05h, and 06h

INTERRUPT 10h - Function 55h, Subfunction 55h
ATI EGA/VGA Wonder Super Switch - INSTALLATION CHECK

Purpose: Determine whether Super Switch program is present.

Available on: Systems equipped with ATI EGA or VGA Wonder video card.

Restrictions: Super Switch (SMS.COM) or VCONFIG must be installed.

Registers at call:
AX = 5555h

Return Registers:
AX = AAAAh if installed
BX:CX -> *unknown data or routine in SMS.COM resident portion*
-> data area in VCONFIG (Table 5-16)

Details: Super Switch (SMS.COM) is a video mode switch program supplied with the ATI EGA Wonder. It also maps video mode 08h to 27h or 23h.

Conflicts: None known.

See Also: INT 10h Function 00h

Table 5-16. Format of data area:

Offset	Size	Description
00h	DWORD	original INT 09h vector
04h	DWORD	original INT 10h vector
08h	DWORD	original INT 1Ch vector
0Ch	WORD	screen saver state, 0=off, 1=on
0Eh	WORD	blanking interval in clock ticks

INTERRUPT 10h - Function 6Ah, Subfunction 00h
Direct Graphics Interface Standard - INQUIRE AVAILABLE DEVICES

Purpose: To determine what DGIS-compatible devices, if any, are present.

Available on: Systems with DGIS software installed.

Restrictions: none.

Registers at call:
AX = 6A00h
BX = 0000h
CX = 0000h
DX = buffer length (may be 0)
ES:DI -> buffer

Return Registers:
BX = number of bytes stored in buffer
CX = bytes required for all descriptions (0 if no DGIS)

Details: Buffer contains descriptions and addresses of DGIS-compatible display(s) and printer(s).

Conflicts: None known.

See Also: Function 6Ah Subfunction 02h

INTERRUPT 10h - Function 6Ah, Subfunction 01h
DGIS - REDIRECT CHARACTER OUTPUT

Purpose: Changes destination of all output sent via INT 10h.

Available on: Systems with DGIS software installed.

Restrictions: none.

Registers at call:
AX = 6A01h
CX = 0000h
ES:DI = address of device to get INT 10h output

Return Registers:
CX = 0000h output could not be redirected
else INT 10h output now routed to requested display

Conflicts: None known.

See Also: Function 6Ah Subfunction 02h

INTERRUPT 10h - Function 6Ah, Subfunction 02h
DGIS - INQUIRE INT 10h OUTPUT DEVICE

Purpose: Determine currently active destination for INT 10h output.

Available on: Systems with DGIS software installed.

Restrictions: none.

Registers at call:
AX = 6A02h
ES:DI = 0000h:0000h

Conflicts: None known.

See Also: Function 6Ah Subfunctions 00h and 01h

Return Registers:
ES:DI = 0000h:0000h if current display is non-DGIS
else address of the current DGIS INT 10h display

INTERRUPT 10h - Function 6Fh, Subfunction 00h
Video7/VEGA VGA INSTALLATION CHECK

Purpose: To determine whether Video7 VGA, or VEGA VGA, BIOS extensions are present.

Available on: Systems equipped with Video7 VGA or VEGA VGA card.

Restrictions: none.

Registers at call:
AX = 6F00h

Return Registers:
BX = 5637h ('V7') indicates Video7 VGA/VEGA VGA extensions are present

Conflicts: None known.

INTERRUPT 10h - Function 6Fh, Subfunction 01h
Video7/VEGA VGA - GET MONITOR INFO

Purpose: Obtains video and CRT information.

Available on: Systems equipped with Video7 VGA or VEGA VGA card.

Restrictions: none.

Registers at call:
AX = 6F01h

Return Registers:
AL = monitor type code (VEGA VGA only)
AH = status register information:
    bit 0 = display enable
        0 = display enabled
        1 = vertical or horizontal retrace in progress
    bit 1 = light pen flip flop set
    bit 2 = light pen switch activated
    bit 3 = vertical sync
    bit 4 = monitor resolution
        0 = high resolution (>200 lines)
        1 = low resolution (<=200 lines)
    bit 5 = display type
        0 = color
        1 = monochrome
    bits 6, 7 = diagnostic bits

Details: Bits 0-3 are the same as the EGA/VGA status register bits 0-3.

Conflicts: None known.

INTERRUPT 10h - Function 6Fh, Subfunction 04h
GET VIDEO MODE AND SCREEN RESOLUTION

Purpose: Returns current video mode and display size.

Available on: Systems equipped with Video7 VGA or VEGA VGA card.

Restrictions: none.

Registers at call:
AX = 6F04h

Return Registers:
AL = current video mode (see Function 6Fh
    Subfunction 05h)
BX = horizontal columns (text) or pixels (graphics)
CX = vertical columns (text) or pixels (graphics)

Conflicts: None known.
See Also: Function 6Fh Subfunction 05h

INTERRUPT 10h - Function 6Fh, Subfunction 05h
SET VIDEO MODE

Purpose: Select a nonstandard Video7-specific display mode.
Available on: Systems equipped with Video7 VGA   **Restrictions:** none.
             or VEGA VGA card.
Registers at call: **Return Registers:** n/a.
AX = 6F05h
BL = mode (see Table 5-17)
Conflicts: None known.
See Also: Function 00h, Function 00h Subfunctions 70h and 7Eh, Function 6Fh Subfunction 04h

Table 5-17. Values for Video7-specific video modes

TEXT/ GRPH	TEXT RESOL	PIXEL BOX	PIXEL RESOLTN	COLORS	DISP PAGE	SCRN ADDR	SYSTEM
00h-13h = standard IBM modes (see Function 00h)							
40h = T	80x43	8x8					Video7/VEGA VGA
41h = T	132x25	8x14					Video7/VEGA VGA
42h = T	132x43	8x8					Video7/VEGA VGA
43h = T	80x60	8x8					Video7/VEGA VGA
44h = T	100x60	8x8					Video7/VEGA VGA
45h = T	132x28	8x8					Video7/VEGA VGA
60h = G			752x410	16			Video7 VGA, VEGA VGA
61h = G			720x540	16			Video7 VGA, VEGA VGA
= G			720x540	16			Northgate
62h = G			800x600	16			Video7 VGA,VEGA Ext EGA
63h = G			1024x768	2			Video7 VGA
64h = G			1024x768	4			Video7 VGA
65h = G			1024x768	16			Video7 VGA, VEGA Ext EGA
66h = G			640x400	256			Video7 VGA, VEGA Ext VGA
= G			640x400	256			Northgate
67h = G			640x480	256			Video7 VGA,VEGA Ext VGA
68h = G			720x540	256			Video7 VGA, VEGA Ext VGA
69h = G			800x600	256			Video7 VGA, VEGA Ext VGA
70h = G			752x410	16gray			Video7 VGA, VEGA VGA
71h = G			720x540	16gray			Video7 VGA, VEGA VGA

Table 5-17. Values for Video7-specific video modes (continued)

TEXT/ GRPH	TEXT RESOL	PIXEL BOX	PIXEL RESOLTN	COLORS	DISP PAGE	SCRN ADDR	SYSTEM
72h = G			800x600	16gray			Video7 VGA
73h = G			1024x768	2gray			Video7 VGA
74h = G			1024x768	4gray			Video7 VGA
75h = G			1024x768	16gray			Video7 VGA
76h = G			640x400	256gray			Video7 VGA
77h = G			640x480	256gray			Video7 VGA
78h = G			720x540	256gray			Video7 VGA
79h = G			800x600	256gray			(future)

INTERRUPT 10h - Function 6Fh, Subfunction 06h
SELECT AUTOSWITCH MODE

Purpose: Sets type of video-mode autoswitching.

Available on: Systems equipped with Video7 VGA or VEGA VGA card.

Restrictions: none.

Registers at call:
AX = 6F06h
BL = Autoswitch mode select:
    00h select EGA/VGA- only modes
    01h select Autoswitched VGA/ EGA/
        CGA/ MGA modes
    02h select 'bootup' CGA/MGA modes
BH = enable/disable (00h enable,
    01h = disable selection)
Conflicts: None known.

Return Registers: n/a.

INTERRUPT 10h - Function 6Fh, Subfunction 07h
GET VIDEO MEMORY CONFIGURATION

Purpose: Determine size and type of video RAM present.

Available on: Systems equipped with Video7 VGA or VEGA VGA card.

Restrictions: none.

Registers at call:
AX = 6F07h

Return Registers:
AL = 6Fh
AH = bits 0-6 = number of 256K blocks of video
        memory
    bit 7 = DRAM/VRAM (0: DRAM, 1: VRAM)
BH = chip revision (SR8F) (S/C Chip in VEGA VGA)
BL = chip revision (SR8E) (G/A Chip in VEGA VGA)
CX = 0000h

Conflicts: None known.
See Also: Function 12h Subfunction 10h

INTERRUPT 10h - Function 70h
GET ADDRESS OF VIDEO RAM

Purpose: Determine where the three color planes of video RAM are located.

Available on: Tandy 2000 only.

Restrictions: none.

Registers at call:
AH = 70h

Return Registers:
AX:BX -> word containing green plane's offset
AX:CX -> word containing green plane's segment
AX:DX -> word containing segment of red (offset 0)
and blue (offset 4000) planes

Conflicts: Everex Extended Video BIOS
See Also: Function 71h

INTERRUPT 10h - Function 7000h, Subfunction 0000h
Everex Extended Video BIOS - RETURN EMULATION STATUS

Purpose: Determine video operating setup.
Available on: Systems equipped with Everex
Extended Video BIOS.

Restrictions: none.

Registers at call:
AX = 7000h
BX = 0000h

Return Registers:
CL = monitor type:
00h mono
01h CGA
02h EGA
03h digital multifrequency
04h IBM PS/2
05h IBM 8514
06h SuperVGA
07h analog multifrequency
08h super multifrequency
CH = feature bits:
bits 7,6: 00 = 256K memory
01 = 512K memory
10 = 1024K
11 = 2048K memory
bit 5: special oscillator present
bit 4: VGA protect enabled
bit 0: 6845 emulation
DX = video board info:
bits 4-15: board ID model
bits 0-3: board ID revision
DI = BCD BIOS version number

Conflicts: Get Video RAM Address (Tandy 1000).

INTERRUPT 10h - Function 7000h, Subfunction 0004h
GET PAGING FUNCTION POINTER FOR CURRENT MODE

Purpose: Obtains pointer to function selecting which page of video memory is to be mapped into the CPU's address space.
Available on: Systems equipped with Everex
Extended Video BIOS.

Restrictions: none.

Registers at call:
AX = 7000h
BX = 0004h

Return Registers:
ES:DI -> FAR paging function (call with DL = page to set)

Details: The word preceding ES:DI is the length of the function in bytes, and the last byte of the function is a FAR return instruction.
Conflicts: Get Video RAM Address (Tandy 1000).
See Also: Function 7000h Subfunctions 0000h and 0005h

INTERRUPT 10h - Function 7000h, Subfunction 0005h
Everex Extended Video BIOS - GET SUPPORTED MODE INFO

Purpose: Determine information about supported video mode(s).

Available on: Systems equipped with Everex Extended Video BIOS.

Restrictions: none.

Registers at call:
AX = 7000h
BX = 0005h
CL = maximum number of modes for which to get info
CH = mode type to get info for:
    00h all modes
    01h monochrome text modes
    02h color text modes
    03h four-color CGA graphics modes
    04h two-color CGA graphics modes
    05h 16-color graphics modes
    06h 256-color graphics modes
DL = monitor type to get info for
ES:DI -> buffer for mode info (Table 5-18)

Return Registers:
CL = total number of modes fitting criteria
CH = size of each info record

Conflicts: Get Video RAM Address (Tandy 1000).

See Also: Function 7000h Subfunctions 0000h and 0004h

Table 5-18. Format of mode information record:

Offset	Size	Description
00h	BYTE	mode number (bit 7 set if extended mode)
01h	BYTE	mode type (see above)
02h	BYTE	info bits:
		bits 7,6 reserved
		5 monochrome mode
		4 interlaced display
		3 requires special oscillator
		2,1 memory required:
		00 = 256K
		01 = 512K
		10 = 1024K
		11 = 2048K
		0 reserved
03h	BYTE	font height
04h	BYTE	text columns on screen
05h	BYTE	text rows on screen
06h	WORD	number of scan lines
08h	BYTE	color information:
		bits 7-4 reserved
		3-0 bits per pixel

INTERRUPT 10h - Function 71h
GET ADDRESS OF INCRAM

Purpose: Determine where INCRAM is located.

Available on: Tandy 2000 only.

Registers at call:
AH = 71h

Restrictions: none.

Return Registers:
AX:BX -> word containing INCRAM segment
AX:CX -> word containing INCRAM offset

Conflicts: None known.
See Also: Function 70h

INTERRUPT 10h - Function 72h
RIGHT SCROLL

Purpose: Scroll part of all of the display to the right.
Available on: Tandy 2000 only.
Registers at call:
AH = 72h
AL = number of columns by which to shift
   00h = blank scroll area
BH = atttribute for blanked columns at left
CH = topmost row in scroll area
CL = leftmost column in scroll area
DH = bottommost row in scroll area
DL = rightmost column in scroll area
Conflicts: None known.
See Also: Functions 06h, 07h, and 73h

Restrictions: none.
Return Registers: n/a

INTERRUPT 10h - Function 73h
LEFT SCROLL

Purpose: Scroll part or all of the display to the left.
Available on: Tandy 2000 only.
Registers at call:
AH = 73h
AL = number of columns by which to shift
   00h = blank scroll area
BH = atttribute for blanked columns at right
CH = topmost row in scroll area
CL = leftmost column in scroll area
DH = bottommost row in scroll area
DL = rightmost column in scroll area
Conflicts: None known.
See Also: Functions 06h, 07h, and 72h

Restrictions: none.
Return Registers: n/a

INTERRUPT 10h - Function 80h
Undocumented - SET unknown HANDLER

Purpose: *unknown.*
Available on: All machines.
Registers at call:
AH = 80h
DX = 4456h ('DV')
ES:DI -> FAR subroutine to be called on
   unknown event.

Restrictions: DESQview 2.0x must be operating.
Return Registers:
DS = segment of DESQview data structure for video
   buffer

Details: This function is probably meant for internal use only, due to the magic value required in DX. The subroutine seems to be called when the DESQview menu is accessed; on entry, AL = 03h or 04h.
Conflicts: None known.

INTERRUPT 10h - Function 81h
Undocumented - GET unknown DATA STRUCTURE

Purpose: Return the address of an internal data structure related to the program's DESQview window.
Available on: All machines.

Restrictions: DESQview 2.0x must be operating.

Registers at call:
AH = 81h
DX = 4456h ('DV')

Return Registers:
ES = segment of DESQview data structure for video
    buffer
BYTE ES:[0] = current window number in DV 2.0x

Details: This function is probably meant for internal use only, due to the magic value required in DX.
Conflicts: None known.
See Also: Function 82h

INTERRUPT 10h - Function 82h
Undocumented - GET CURRENT WINDOW INFO

Purpose: *unknown.*
Available on: All machines.
Registers at call:
AH = 82h
DX = 4456h ('DV')

Restrictions: DESQview 2.0x must be operating.
Return Registers:
DS = segment in DESQview for data
    structure in DV 2.00,
        BYTE DS:[0] = window number
        WORD DS:[1] = segment of other data structure
        WORD DS:[3] = segment of window's object
            handle
ES = segment of DESQview data structure for video
    buffer
AL = current window number
AH = *unknown.*
BL = direct screen writes:
    00h program does not do direct writes
    01h program does direct writes, so shadow buffer
        not usable
BH = *unknown.*
CL = current video mode

CH = *unknown.*

Details: This function is probably meant for internal use only, due to the magic value required in DX.
Conflicts: None known.
See Also: Function 81h

INTERRUPT 10h - Function BFh, Subfunction 00h
SELECT EXTERNAL MONITOR

Purpose: Switches to external monitor.
Available on: Compaq Portable only.
Registers at call:
AX = BF00h

Restrictions: none.
Return Registers: n/a.

Details: All registers are preserved and the internal monitor is blanked. The external monitor becomes the active monitor.
Conflicts: None known.
See Also: Function BFh Subfunction 01h

INTERRUPT 10h - Function BFh, Subfunction 01h
SELECT INTERNAL MONITOR

Purpose: Switches to internal monitor.
Available on: Compaq Portable only.
Registers at call:
AX = BF01h

Restrictions: none.
Return Registers: n/a.

Details: All registers are preserved and the external monitor is blanked. The internal monitor becomes the active monitor.
Conflicts: None known.
See Also: Function BFh Subfunction 00h

INTERRUPT 10h - Function BFh, Subfunction 02h
SET MASTER MODE OF CURRENT VIDEO CONTROLLER

Purpose: Selects emulation mode for video controller.
Available on: Compaq Portable only.
Registers at call:
AX = BF02h
BH = master mode:
    04h CGA
    05h EGA
    07h MDA
Conflicts: None known.
See Also: Function BFh Subfunction 03h

Restrictions: none.
Return Registers: n/a.

INTERRUPT 10h - Function BFh, Subfunction 03h
GET VIDEO ENVIRONMENT

Purpose: Determine video operating environment in effect.
Available on: Compaq Portable and Systempro only.
Registers at call:
AX = BF03h
BX = 0000h

Restrictions: none.

Return Registers:
BH = active monitor:
    00h = external
    01h = internal
BL = master mode:
    00h = switchable VDU not present
    04h = CGA
    05h = EGA
    07h = MDA
    08h = switchable LCD controller present
CH = 00h (reserved)
CL = switchable VDU mode supported:
    bit 0 = CGA supported
    bits 1,2 = reserved (1)
    bit 3 = MDA supported
    bits 4-7 = reserved (1)
DH = internal monitor type:
    00h = none
    01h = Dual-mode monitor
    02h = 5153 RGB monitor
    03h = Compaq Color monitor
    04h = 640x400 flat panel
    07h = LCD VGA
DL = external monitor type:
    00h = none
    01h = dual-mode monitor
    02h = 5153 RGB monitor
    03h = Compaq Color monitor

04h = 640x400 flat panel
05h = VGC monochrome
06h = VGC color

Conflicts: None known.
See Also: Function 1Ah, Function BFh Subfunctions 00h-02h

INTERRUPT 10h - Function BFh, Subfunction 04h
SET MODE SWITCH DELAY

Purpose: Control delay when switching video modes.
Available on: Compaq Portable only.
Registers at call:
AX = BF04h
BH = 00h enable delay
    01h disable delay
Conflicts: None known.
See Also: Function BFh Subfunction 05h

Restrictions: none.
Return Registers: n/a.

INTERRUPT 10h - Function BFh, Subfunction 05h
ENABLE/DISABLE DISPLAY

Purpose: Turn video off/on.
Available on: Compaq Systempro only.
Registers at call:
AX = BF05h
BH = 00h video off
    01h video on
Conflicts: None known.
See Also: Function BFh Subfunction 04h

Restrictions: none.
Return Registers: n/a.

INTERRUPT 10h - Function BFh, Subfunction 06h
READ GRAY SCALE TABLE

Purpose: Obtain value of specified gray scale table entry.
Available on: Compaq SLT/286 only.
Registers at call:
AX = BF06h
CL = address to be read from gray scale table
Conflicts: None known.
See Also: Function 12h Subfunction 33h, Function BFh Subfunction 07h

Restrictions: none.
Return Registers:
AL = bit 3-0 - Value read from gray scale table
CL = address to be read from gray scale table

INTERRUPT 10h - Function BFh, Subfunction 07h
WRITE GRAY SCALE TABLE

Purpose: Set value of specified gray scale table entry.
Available on: Compaq SLT/286 only.
Registers at call:
AX = BF07h
CH = value to write to gray scale table
CL = address to be written to gray scale table
Conflicts: None known.
See Also: Function BFh Subfunction 06h

Restrictions: none.
Return Registers: n/a.

INTERRUPT 10h - Function BFh, Subfunction 08h
WRITE COLOR MIX REGISTERS

Purpose: Establish color weights for gray scale conversion.
Available on: Compaq SLT/286 only.

Restrictions: none.

Registers at call:
AX = BF08h
CH = bits 7-4 - Green weight
    bits 3-0 - Blue weight
CL = bits 7-4 - unused
    bits 3-0 - Red weight
Conflicts: None known.

Return Registers: n/a.

INTERRUPT 10h - Function CCh, Subfunction 00h
GET ULTRAVISION STATUS

Purpose: Determines whether UltraVision is active, and if so, details of its setup.
Available on: EGA and VGA systems.

Restrictions: UltraVision, a video-BIOS extender program from Personics, Inc., must be loaded.

Registers at call:
AX = CC00h
SI = 0000h (if checking version)

Return Registers:
CX = ABCDh
AL = Ultravision extensions
    00h enabled
    FFh disabled
AH = card designator
BX:00F0h -> palette values (for compatibility with NEWFONT)
DX = support for high resolution modes
    00h not active
    01h active
SI = UltraVision version number (v1.2 or higher): high byte=major, low byte=minor
    unchanged for versions below 1.2

Conflicts: None known.
See Also: Function CCh Subfunctions 01h and 02h

INTERRUPT 10h - Function CCh, Subfunction 01h
DISABLE ULTRAVISION EXTENSIONS

Purpose: Returns video action to non-UltraVision operation without unloading program.
Available on: EGA and VGA systems.

Restrictions: UltraVision, a video-BIOS extender program from Personics, Inc., must be loaded.

Registers at call:
AX = CC01h

Return Registers: n/a

Details: Subsequent BIOS calls will be passed through to previous handler. Should be followed immediately by mode set to restore normal EGA/VGA state.
Conflicts: None known.
See Also: Function CCh Subfunction 02h

INTERRUPT 10h - Function CCh, Subfunction 02h
ENABLE ULTRAVISION EXTENSIONS

Purpose: Allow UltraVision to modify video operations.
Available on: EGA and VGA systems.

Restrictions: UltraVision, a video-BIOS extender program from Personics, Inc., must be loaded.

Registers at call:
AX = CC02h

Return Registers: n/a

Details: Should be followed immediately by mode set to restore previous UltraVision state.

Conflicts: None known.
See Also: Function CCh Subfunction 01h

INTERRUPT 10h - Function CDh, Subfunction 00h
LOAD ULTRAVISION PALETTE

Purpose: Change color palette.
Available on: Color EGA and VGA systems.

Restrictions: UltraVision, a video-BIOS extender program from Personics, Inc., must be loaded.
Return Registers: n/a.

Registers at call:
AX = CD00h
CL = palette table number (01h-07h for v1.x,
    01h-0Fh for v2+)
DS:DX -> 16-byte palette register list
    (colors for registers 00h-0Fh)

Details: If palette locking is in effect for the current mode, the new colors will be displayed immediately; otherwise, the system reverts to the default palette. Palette table 0 is reserved for the default palette and cannot be set.
    UltraVision always sets the border color to black.
Conflicts: None known.
See Also: Function CDh Subfunctions 01h and 02h

INTERRUPT 10h - Function CDh, Subfunction 01h
SET PALETTE LOCKING STATUS

Purpose: Controls palette locking action.
Available on: Color EGA and VGA systems.

Restrictions: UltraVision, a video-BIOS extender program from Personics, Inc., must be loaded.
Return Registers: n/a.

Registers at call:
AX = CD01h
CL = palette locking value:
    00h none
    01h text modes only (02h,03h)
    FFh all modes (all standard color text and
        graphics modes)

Details: Intended for video modes with 16 or fewer colors.
Conflicts: None known.
See Also: Function 10h Subfunctions 00h and 02h, Function CDh Subfunction 03h

INTERRUPT 10h - Function CDh, Subfunction 02h
GET ULTRAVISION PALETTE

Purpose: Determine current palette.
Available on: EGA and VGA systems.

Restrictions: UltraVision, a video-BIOS extender program from Personics, Inc., must be loaded.

Registers at call:
AX = CD02h

Return Registers:
CL = palette table number
DS:DX -> 17-byte palette register list (Table 5-19)
DS:SI -> current font names table (Tables 5-20, 5-21))

Details: Only the font names are valid on monochrome EGA systems.
Conflicts: None known.
See Also: Function 10h Subfunction 09h, Function CDh Subfunction 00h

Table 5-19. Format of palette register list:

Offset	Size	Description
00h	16 BYTEs	colors for palette registers 00h through 0Fh
10h	BYTE	border color

Table 5-20. Format of current font names table (v2+):

Offset	Size	Generic EGA	Generic VGA	Super VGA
00h	8 BYTEs	N/A	F19 font	F20 font
08h	8 BYTEs	F14 font	F14 font	F14 font
10h	8 BYTEs	N/A	F11 font	F10 font
18h	8 BYTEs	F8 font	F8 font	F8 font

Table 5-21. Format of current font names table (v1.x):

Offset	Size	Description
00h	8 BYTEs	F19/F14 font
08h	8 BYTEs	F11/F8 font

INTERRUPT 10h - Function CDh, Subfunction 03h
GET PALETTE LOCKING STATUS

Purpose: Read current status of palette locking feature.
Available on: Color EGA and VGA systems.

Registers at call:
AX = CD03h

Conflicts: None known.
See Also: Function CDh Subfunction 01h

Restrictions: UltraVision, a video-BIOS extender program from Personics, Inc., must be loaded.

Return Registers:
CL = palette locking value:
    00h none
    01h text modes only
    FFh all modes

INTERRUPT 10h - Function CDh, Subfunction 04h
GET UltraVision TEXT MODE

Purpose: Determine current text mode display format.
Available on: EGA and VGA systems.

Registers at call:
AX = CD04h

Restrictions: UltraVision, a video-BIOS extender program from Personics, Inc., must be loaded.

Return Registers:
AL = mode number: see below.

UltraVision mode numbers:

11h 80x25
12h 80x43, 80x50
13h 80x34, 80x36
14h 80x60, 80x63
19h 94x25
1Ah 94x43, 94x50
1Bh 94x36

1Ch 94x63
21h 108x25
22h 108x43, 108x50
23h 107x34, 108x36
24h 108x60, 108x63
31h 120x25
32h 120x43, 120x50

UltraVision mode numbers (continued):

33h 132x25
34h 132x44, 132x50
39h 120x36

3Ah 120x63
3Bh 132x36
3Ch 132x60

Conflicts: None known.
See Also: Function 0Fh, Function CCh Subfunction 00h, Function CDh Subfunctions 11h+

INTERRUPT 10h - Function CDh, Subfunction 05h
SET CURSOR TYPE

Purpose: Establish cursor style.
Available on: EGA and VGA systems.

Registers at call:
AX = CD05h
CL =   00h line cursor
     FFh box cursor
Details: Sets default cursor type for text-based programs.
Conflicts: None known.
See Also: Function 01h, Function CDh Subfunction 06h

Restrictions: UltraVision, a video-BIOS extender program from Personics, Inc., must be loaded.
Return Registers: n/a.

INTERRUPT 10h - Function CDh, Subfunction 06h
GET CURSOR TYPE

Purpose: Determine current cursor style.
Available on: EGA and VGA systems.

Registers at call:
AX = CD06h

Conflicts: None known.
See Also: Function 03h, Function CDh Subfunction 05h

Restrictions: UltraVision, a video-BIOS extender program from Personics, Inc., must be loaded.
Return Registers:
CL = 00h line cursor
     FFh box cursor

INTERRUPT 10h - Function CDh, Subfunction 07h
SET UNDERLINE STATUS

Purpose: Controls underline feature.
Available on: EGA and VGA systems.

Registers at call:
AX = CD07h
CL = hardware underline status:
     00h off (color systems only)
     01h underline below characters
     02h strike through characters
BL = foreground color for normal text
     (FFh = current)
BH = foreground color for bright text
     (FFh = current)

Restrictions: Version 1.2 or higher of UltraVision, a video-BIOS extender program from Personics, Inc., must be loaded.
Return Registers:
CL = hardware underline status
BL = current foreground color for normal text
BH = current foreground color for bright text

Details: When underline or strikeout is enabled in color text modes, the specified colors will be assigned temporarily to colors 01h and 09h, allowing affected text to match non-underlined text. The color remapping uses values from the current onscreen palette regardless of the palette locking status (see Function CDh Subfunction 01h).

Specify the standard colors (BL=01h,BH=09h) to enable underline or strikeout without color remapping.

Conflicts: None known.
See Also: Function CDh Subfunction 08h

INTERRUPT 10h - Function CDh, Subfunction 08h
GET UNDERLINE STATUS

Purpose: Determines current setting of hardware underline support.
Available on: EGA and VGA systems.

Restrictions: Version 1.2 or higher of UltraVision, a video-BIOS extender program from Personics, Inc., must be loaded.

Registers at call:
AX = CD08h

Return Registers:
CL = hardware underline status (see Function CDh Subfunction 07h)
BL = foreground color for normal text
BH = foreground color for bright text

Details: Only CL is valid on monochrome EGA systems.
Conflicts: None known.
See Also: Function CDh Subfunction 07h

INTERRUPT 10h - Function CDh, Subfunction 10h
LOAD USER FONT

Purpose: Loads user-supplied font.
Available on: EGA and VGA systems.

Restrictions: UltraVision, a video-BIOS extender program from Personics, Inc., must be loaded.

Registers at call:
AX = CD10h
BH = bytes per character (08h, 0Ah, 0Bh, 0Eh, 13h, 14h)
CX = ABCDh load 9xN alternate font (v2+)
   else number of characters to load
DX = character offset into font table
DS:SI -> 8-byte ASCII font name
ES:BP -> font definitions

Return Registers:
AX = FFFFh if invalid font parameters

Details: Loads the designated characters into UltraVision's resident font area. Should be followed by a video mode set to reload character generator.
Conflicts: None known.
See Also: Function 11h Subfunction 00h

INTERRUPT 10h - Function CDh, Subfunctions 11h-FFh
SET ULTRAVISION TEXT MODE

Purpose: Select text display format.
Available on: EGA and VGA systems.

Restrictions: UltraVision, a video-BIOS extender program from Personics, Inc., must be loaded.

Registers at call:
AH = CDh
AL = text mode number: see below.

Return Registers:
AX = CDCDh if invalid mode

UltraVision mode numbers:

11h 80x25
12h 80x43, 80x50
13h 80x34, 80x36

14h 80x60, 80x63
19h 94x25
1Ah 94x43, 94x50

UltraVision mode numbers (continued):

1Bh 94x36	33h 132x25
1Ch 94x63	34h 132x44, 132x50
21h 108x25	39h 120x36
22h 108x43, 108x50	3Ah 120x63
23h 107x34, 108x36	3Bh 132x36
24h 108x60, 108x63	3Ch 132x60
31h 120x25	
32h 120x43, 120x50	

Conflicts: None known.
See Also: Function CDh Subfunction 04h

INTERRUPT 10h - Function EFh
MSHERC.COM INSTALLATION CHECK???

Purpose: Extend capabilities of Hercules-equipped systems.
Available on: Systems equipped with a Hercules graphics card or equivalent.

Restrictions: MSHERC.COM must be loaded.

Registers at call:
AH = EFh

Return Registers:
DL = video adapter type:
  00h original Hercules
  01h *unknown.* \ one is probably Hercules Plus,
  02h *unknown.* / the other Hercules InColor
  FFh non-Hercules
DH = video memory mode byte
  01h "half" (one page)
  03h "full" (two pages)

Details: MSHERC.COM is a support program for the Microsoft Quick languages which makes their graphics libraries compatible with a Hercules card by adding video modes 08h and 88h, and supporting text in the new graphics modes. While in mode 08h or 88h, INT 10h supports the Hercules card much like a CGA.
Conflicts: None known.

INTERRUPT 10h - Function F0h
EGA Register Interface Library - READ ONE REGISTER

Purpose: Determine the current state of one EGA registers as stored by the RIL.
Available on: EGA-equipped systems.

Restrictions: RIL must be loaded.

Registers at call:
AH = F0h
BL = register number
BH = 00h
DX = group index (see table)

Return Registers:
BL = data

RIL Group Index Codes

Pointer/data chips
00h CRT Controller (25 reg) 3B4h mono modes,
  3D4h color modes
08h Sequencer (5 registers) 3C4h
10h Graphics Controller (9 registers) 3CEh
18h Attribute Controller (20 registers) 3C0h

Single registers
20h Miscellaneous Output register 3C2h
28h Feature Control register (3BAh mono modes,
  3DAh color modes)
30h Graphics 1 Position register 3CCh
38h Graphics 2 Position register 3CAh

Details: The RIL is provided by the Microsoft Mouse driver, OS/2 compatibility box, and others; it provides a means for restoring the state of the EGA even though the EGA's registers are write-only.
Conflicts: None known.
See Also: Functions F1h and F2h

INTERRUPT 10h - Function F1h
EGA Register Interface Library - WRITE ONE REGISTER

Purpose: Set an EGA register and update the RIL record of that register.
Available on: EGA-equipped systems.   **Restrictions:** RIL must be loaded.
Registers at call: **Return Registers:**
AH = F1h   BL = data
DX = group index (see Function F0h)
     if single register:
         BL = value to write
     otherwise
         BL = register number
         BH = value to write
Details: The RIL is provided by the Microsoft Mouse driver, OS/2 compatibility box, and others; it provides a means for restoring the state of the EGA even though the EGA's registers are write-only.
Conflicts: None known.
See Also: Functions F0h and F3h

INTERRUPT 10h - Function F2h
EGA Register Interface Library - READ REGISTER RANGE

Purpose: Determine the values of a contiguous range of EGA registers.
Available on: EGA-equipped systems.   **Restrictions:** RIL must be loaded.
Registers at call: **Return Registers:** n/a.
AH = F2h
CH = starting register number
CL = Number of registers (>1)
DX = group index
     00h CRTC (3B4h mono modes,
         3D4h color modes)
     08h Sequencer 3C4h
     10h Graphics Controller 3CEh
     18h Attribute Controller 3C0h
ES:BX -> buffer, CL bytes
Details: The RIL is provided by the Microsoft Mouse driver, OS/2 compatibility box, and others; it provides a means for restoring the state of the EGA even though the EGA's registers are write-only.
Conflicts: None known.
See Also: Functions F0h and F3h

INTERRUPT 10h - Function F3h
EGA Register Interface Library - WRITE REGISTER RANGE

Purpose: Set a contiguous range of EGA registers, recording the new values.
Available on: EGA-equipped systems.   **Restrictions:** RIL must be loaded.
Registers at call: **Return Registers:** n/a.
AH = F3h
CH = starting register
CL = number of registers (>1)
DX = group index (see Function F2h)
ES:BX -> buffer, CL bytes
Details: The RIL is provided by the Microsoft Mouse driver, OS/2 compatibility box, and others; it provides a means for restoring the state of the EGA even though the EGA's registers are write-only.
Conflicts: None known.
See Also: Functions F1h and F2h

INTERRUPT 10h - Function F4h
EGA Register Interface Library - READ REGISTER SET

Purpose: Determine the values of multiple non-contiguous EGA registers.

Available on: EGA-equipped systems.

Restrictions: RIL must be loaded.

Registers at call:

Return Registers:

AH = F4h

register values in table filled in

CX = number of registers to read (>1)

ES:BX -> table of records (Table 5-22)

Details: The RIL is provided by the Microsoft Mouse driver, OS/2 compatibility box, and others; it provides a means for restoring the state of the EGA even though the EGA's registers are write-only.

Conflicts: None known.

See Also: Functions F0h, F2h, and F5h

Table 5-22. Format of entries in table of register records:

Offset	Size	Description
00h	WORD	group index
		Pointer/data chips
		00h CRTC (3B4h mono modes, 3D4h color modes)
		08h Sequencer 3C4h
		10h Graphics Controller 3CEh
		18h Attribute Controller 3C0h
		Single registers
		20h Miscellaneous Output register 3C2h
		28h Feature Control register (3BAh mono modes, 3DAhcolor)
		30h Graphics 1 Position register 3CCh
		38h Graphics 2 Position register 3CAh
02h	BYTE	register number (0 for single registers)
03h	BYTE	register value

INTERRUPT 10h - Function F5h
EGA Register Interface Library - WRITE REGISTER SET

Purpose: Set multiple non-contiguous EGA registers, recording the new values.

Available on: EGA-equipped systems.

Restrictions: RIL must be loaded.

Registers at call:

Return Registers: n/a.

AH = F5h

CX = number of registers to write (>1)

ES:BX -> table of records (see Function F4h)

Details: The RIL is provided by the Microsoft Mouse driver, OS/2 compatibility box, and others; it provides a means for restoring the state of the EGA even though the EGA's registers are write-only.

Conflicts: None known.

See Also: Functions F1h, F3h, and F4h

INTERRUPT 10h - Function F6h
EGA Register Interface Library - REVERT TO DEFAULT REGISTERS

Purpose: Set all EGA registers to previously-specified default values.

Available on: EGA-equipped systems.

Restrictions: RIL must be loaded.

Registers at call:

Return Registers: n/a.

AH = F6h

Details: The RIL is provided by the Microsoft Mouse driver, OS/2 compatibility box, and others; it provides a means for restoring the state of the EGA even though the EGA's registers are write-only.

Conflicts: None known.

See Also: Function F7h

INTERRUPT 10h - Function F7h
EGA Register Interface Library - DEFINE DEFAULT REGISTER TABLE

Purpose: Specify the default values to be used by Function F6h.
Available on: EGA-equipped systems.
Registers at call:
AH = F7h
DX = port number (see Group Index table)
ES:BX -> table of one-byte entries, one byte to be
    written to each register

Restrictions: RIL must be loaded.
Return Registers: n/a.

RIL Group Index Codes

Pointer/data chips
00h CRT Controller (25 reg) 3B4h mono modes,
    3D4h color modes
08h Sequencer (5 registers) 3C4h
10h Graphics Controller (9 registers) 3CEh
18h Attribute Controller (20 registers) 3C0h

Single registers
20h Miscellaneous Output register 3C2h
28h Feature Control register (3BAh mono modes,
    3DAh color modes)
30h Graphics 1 Position register 3CCh
38h Graphics 2 Position register 3CAh

Details: The RIL is provided by the Microsoft Mouse driver, OS/2 compatibility box, and others; it provides a means for restoring the state of the EGA even though the EGA's registers are write-only.
Conflicts: None known.
See Also: Function F6h

INTERRUPT 10h - Function FAh
EGA Register Interface Library - INTERROGATE DRIVER

Purpose: Determine whether a Register Interface Library provider is loaded.
Available on: EGA-equipped systems.
Registers at call:
AH = FAh
BX = 0000h

Restrictions: none.
Return Registers:
BX = 0000h if mouse driver not present
ES:BX -> EGA Register Interface version number, if
    present:
    byte 0 = major release number
    byte 1 = minor release number

Details: The RIL is provided by the Microsoft Mouse driver, OS/2 compatibility box, and others; it provides a means for restoring the state of the EGA even though the EGA's registers are write-only.
Conflicts: FASTBUFF Installation Check (chapter 36).
See Also: Function F6h

INTERRUPT 10h - Function FFh
DJ GO32.EXE 80386+ DOS extender VIDEO EXTENSIONS

Purpose: Allow simplified video mode setting
Available on: 80386 and higher.

Restrictions: Must be executing under DJ GO32.EXE
    DOS extender.

Registers at call:
AH = FFh
AL = video mode:
    00h 80x25 text
    01h default text
    02h CXxDX text
    03h biggest text
    04h 320x200 graphics
    05h default graphics
    06h CXxDX graphics
    07h biggest non-interlaced graphics
    08h biggest graphics

Return Registers: n/a

Conflicts: TopView (chapter 15), Carbon Copy Plus (chapter 28).
See Also: Function 00h, GO32.EXE INT 21h Function FFh (chapter 8)

INTERRUPT 14h - Function 81h, Subfunction 00h
RETURN VIDEO FOSSIL INFORMATION

Purpose: To determine configuration of Video FOSSIL when present.
Available on: All machines.
Registers at call:
AX = 8100h
ES:DI -> buffer for VFOSSIL information
    (Table 5-23)

Restrictions: Video FOSSIL must be installed.
Return Registers:
AX = 1954h if installed

Details: The Video FOSSIL is an appendage which may be installed in any standard FOSSIL driver. It supports a subset of the OS/2 video functions, permitting porting between the VFOSSIL and OS/2 with minimal changes.
Conflicts: COURIERS.COM (chapter 7).
See Also: Function 81h Subfunction 01h, FOSSIL Function 7Eh (chapter7)

Table 5-23. Format of VFOSSIL information:

Offset	Size	Description
00h	WORD	size of information in bytes, including this field
02h	WORD	VFOSSIL major version
04h	WORD	VFOSSIL revision level
06h	WORD	highest VFOSSIL application function supported

INTERRUPT 14h - Function 81h, Subfunction 01h
OPEN VIDEO FOSSIL

Purpose: Initializes Video FOSSIL and returns pointers to the   functions which it provides.
Available on: All machines.
Registers at call:
AX = 8101h
ES:DI -> buffer for application function table
    (Table 5-24)
CX = length of buffer in bytes

Restrictions: Video FOSSIL must be installed.
Return Registers:
AX = 1954h if installed
BH = highest VFOSSIL application function supported

Details: The number of initialized pointers in the application function table will never exceed CX/4; if the buffer is large enough, BH+1 pointers will be initialized. All functions of Video FOSSIL are called indirectly through the far pointers in the application function table, with parameters passed on the stack as described in the following paragraphs.

The Video FOSSIL is an appendage which may be installed in any standard FOSSIL driver. It supports a subset of the OS/2 video functions, permitting porting between the VFOSSIL and OS/2 with minimalchanges.
Conflicts: COURIERS.COM (chapter 7).
See Also: Function 81h Subfunction 02h

Table 5-24. Format of application function table:

Offset	Size	Description
00h	DWORD	far pointer to VioGetMode function (query current video mode)
04h	DWORD	far pointer to VioSetMode function (set video mode)
08h	DWORD	far pointer to VioGetConfig function (query hardware config)
0Ch	DWORD	far pointer to VioWrtTTY function (write data in TTY mode)
10h	DWORD	far pointer to VioGetANSI function (get current ANSI state)
14h	DWORD	far pointer to VioSetANSI function (set new ANSI state)
18h	DWORD	far pointer to VioGetCurPos function (get cursor position)
1Ch	DWORD	far pointer to VioSetCurPos function (set cursor position)
20h	DWORD	far pointer to VioGetCurType function (get cursor shape)
24h	DWORD	far pointer to VioSetCurType function (set cursor shape)
28h	DWORD	far pointer to VioScrollUp function (scroll screen up)
2Ch	DWORD	far pointer to VioScrollDn function (scroll screen down)
30h	DWORD	far pointer to VioReadCellStr function (read cell string from screen)
34h	DWORD	far pointer to VioReadCharStr function (read charstring from screen)
38h	DWORD	far pointer to VioWrtCellStr function (write a cell string)
3Ch	DWORD	far pointer to VioWrtCharStr function (write char string, leaving attr)
40h	DWORD	far pointer to VioWrtCharStrAttr function (write charstring, const attr)
44h	DWORD	far pointer to VioWrtNAttr function (replicate an attribute)
48h	DWORD	far pointer to VioWrtNCell function (replicate a cell)
4Ch	DWORD	far pointer to VioWrtNChar function (replicate a character)

Call VioGetMode with:

> STACK: WORD   VIO handle (must be 00h)
> DWORD   pointer to video mode data structure (Table 5-25).

Returns with:

> AX = error code:
> 0000h successful
> 0074h internal VIO failure
> 017Eh buffer too small
> 01B4h invalid VIO handle

Table 5-25. Format of video mode data structure:

Offset	Size	Description
00h	WORD	length of structure including this field
02h	BYTE	mode characteristics:
		bit 0: clear if MDA, set otherwise
		bit 1: graphics mode
		bit 2: color disabled (black-and-white)
03h	BYTE	number of colors supported (1=2 colors, 4=16 colors,etc)
04h	WORD	number of text columns
06h	WORD	number of text rows
08h	WORD	reserved
0Ah	WORD	reserved
0Ch	DWORD	reserved

Call VioSetMode with:

> STACK: WORD   VIO handle (must be 00h)
> DWORD   pointer to video mode data structure (Table 5-25)

Returns with:

> AX = error code:
> 0000h successful
> 0074h internal VIO failure
> 0163h unsupported mode

017Eh buffer too small
01A5h invalid VIO parameter
01B4h invalid VIO handle

Call VioGetConfig with:
STACK: WORD   VIO handle (must be 00h)
          DWORD   pointer to video configuration data buffer (Table 5-26).

Returns with:
AX = error code:
    0000h successful
    0074h internal VIO failure
    017Eh buffer too small
    01B4h invalid VIO handle

Table 5-26. Format of video configuration data:

Offset	Size	Description
00h	WORD	structure length including this field
02h	WORD	adapter type:
		00h monochrome/printer
		01h CGA
		02h EGA
		03h VGA
		07h 8514/A
04h	WORD	display type:
		00h monochrome
		01h color
		02h enhanced color
		09h 8514
06h	DWORD	adapter memory size

Call VioWrtTTY with:
STACK: WORD   VIO handle (must be 00h)
          WORD   length of string
          DWORD   pointer to character string to be written to screen

Returns with:
AX = error code:
    0000h successful
    0074h internal VIO failure
    01B4h invalid VIO handle

Details: Write wraps at end of line and terminates if it reaches end of screen. In ANSI mode, ANSI control sequences are interpreted, and this function is not required to be reentrant; in non-ANSI mode, the function is reentrant and may be called from within an MS-DOS function call.

Call VioGetANSI with:
STACK: WORD   VIO handle (must be 00h)
          DWORD   pointer to WORD which will be set to 00h if ANSI is off or 01h if ANSI is on

Returns with:
AX = error code:
    0000h successful
    0074h internal VIO failure
    01B4h invalid VIO handle

Call VioSetANSI with:
STACK: WORD   VIO handle (must be 00h)
          DWORD   pointer to WORD indicating new state of ANSI
                00h off
                01h on

Returns with:
    AX = error code:
                0000h successful
                0074h internal VIO failure
                0163h unsupported mode
                0166h invalid row value
                0167h invalid column value
                017Eh buffer too small
                01A5h invalid VIO parameter
                01B4h invalid VIO handle

Call VioGetCurPos with:
    STACK: WORD   VIO handle (must be 00h)
                DWORD   pointer to WORD to hold current cursor column (0-based)
                DWORD   pointer to WORD to hold current cursor row (0-based)

Returns with:
    AX = error code:
                0000h successful
                0074h internal VIO failure
                01B4h invalid VIO handle

Call VioSetCurPos with:
    STACK: WORD   VIO handle (must be 00h)
                WORD   cursor column
                WORD   cursor row

Returns with:
    AX = error code:
                0000h successful
                0074h internal VIO failure
                0166h invalid row value
                0167h invalid column value
                01B4h invalid VIO handle
Details: If either coordinate is invalid, the cursor is not moved.

Call VioGetCurType with:
    STACK: WORD   VIO handle (must be 00h)
                DWORD   pointer to cursor type record (Table 5-27).

Returns with:
    AX = error code:
                0000h successful
                0074h internal VIO failure
                01B4h invalid VIO handle

Table 5-27. Format of cursor type record:

Offset	Size	Description
00h	WORD	cursor start line
02h	WORD	cursor end line
04h	WORD	cursor width (always 01h)
06h	WORD	cursor attribute (FFFFh = hidden)

Call VioSetCurType with:
    STACK: WORD   VIO handle (must be 00h)
                DWORD   pointer to cursor type record (see above)

Returns with:
    AX = error code:
                0000h successful
                0074h internal VIO failure

01A5h invalid VIO parameter
01B4h invalid VIO handle

Call VioScrollUp with:
STACK: WORD   VIO handle (must be 00h)
        DWORD pointer to char/attr cell for filling emptied rows
        WORD   number or rows to scroll (FFFFh = clear area)
        WORD   right column of scroll area
        WORD   bottom row of scroll area
        WORD   left column of scroll area
        WORD   top row of scroll area

Returns with:
AX = error code:
        0000h successful
        0074h internal VIO failure
        0166h invalid row value
        0167h invalid column value
        01B4h invalid VIO handle

Call VioScrollDn with:
STACK: WORD   VIO handle (must be 00h)
        DWORD pointer to char/attr cell for filling emptied rows
        WORD   number or rows to scroll (FFFFh = clear area)
        WORD   right column of scroll area
        WORD   bottom row of scroll area
        WORD   left column of scroll area
        WORD   top row of scroll area

Returns with:
AX = error code:
        0000h successful
        0074h internal VIO failure
        0166h invalid row value
        0167h invalid column value
        01B4h invalid VIO handle

Call VioReadCellStr with:
STACK: WORD   VIO handle (must be 00h)
        WORD   column at which to start reading
        WORD   row at which to start reading
        DWORD pointer to WORD containing length of buffer in bytes;
                     on return, WORD contains number of bytes actually read
        DWORD pointer to buffer for cell string

Returns with:
AX = error code:
        0000h successful
        0074h internal VIO failure
        0166h invalid row value
        0167h invalid column value
        01B4h invalid VIO handle

Call VioReadCharStr with:
STACK: WORD   VIO handle (must be 00h)
        WORD   column at which to start reading
        WORD   row at which to start reading
        DWORD pointer to WORD containing length of buffer in bytes
                     on return, WORD contains number of bytes actually read
        DWORD pointer to buffer for character string

Returns with:
    AX = error code:
               0000h successful
               0074h internal VIO failure
               0166h invalid row value
               0167h invalid column value
               01B4h invalid VIO handle

Call VioWrtCellStr with:

STACK:	WORD	VIO handle (must be 00h)
	WORD	column at which to start writing
	WORD	row at which to start writing
	WORD	length of cell string in bytes
	DWORD	pointer to cell string to write

Returns with:
    AX = error code:
               0000h successful
               0074h internal VIO failure
               0166h invalid row value
               0167h invalid column value
               01B4h invalid VIO handle

Details: Write wraps at end of line and terminates if it reaches the end of the screen.

Call VioWrtCharStr with:

STACK:	WORD	VIO handle (must be 00h)
	WORD	column at which to start writing
	WORD	row at which to start writing
	WORD	length of character string
	DWORD	pointer to character string to write

Returns with:
    AX = error code:
               0000h successful
               0074h internal VIO failure
               0166h invalid row value
               0167h invalid column value
               01B4h invalid VIO handle

Details: Write wraps at end of line and terminates if it reaches the end of the screen.

Call VioWrtCharStrAttr with:

STACK:	WORD	VIO handle (must be 00h)
	DWORD	pointer to attribute to be applied to each character
	WORD	column at which to start writing
	WORD	row at which to start writing
	WORD	length of character string
	DWORD	pointer to character string to write

Returns with:
    AX = error code:
               0000h successful
               0074h internal VIO failure
               0166h invalid row value
               0167h invalid column value
               01B4h invalid VIO handle

Details: Write wraps at end of line and terminates if it reaches the end of the screen.

Call VioWrtNAttr with:

STACK:	WORD	VIO handle (must be 00h)
	WORD	column at which to start writing
	WORD	row at which to start writing

	WORD	number of times to write attribute
	DWORD	pointer to display attribute to replicate

Returns with:
    AX = error code:
        0000h successful
        0074h internal VIO failure
        0166h invalid row value
        0167h invalid column value
        01B4h invalid VIO handle

Details: Write wraps at end of line and terminates if it reaches the end of the screen.

Call VioWrtNCell with:

STACK:	WORD	VIO handle (must be 00h)
	WORD	column at which to start writing
	WORD	row at which to start writing
	WORD	number of times to write cell
	DWORD	pointer to cell to replicate

Returns with:
    AX = error code:
        0000h successful
        0074h internal VIO failure
        0166h invalid row value
        0167h invalid column value
        01B4h invalid VIO handle

Details: Write wraps at end of line and terminates if it reaches the end of the screen.

Call VioWrtNChar with:

STACK:	WORD	VIO handle (must be 00h)
	WORD	column at which to start writing
	WORD	row at which to start writing
	WORD	number of times to write character
	DWORD	pointer to character to replicate

Returns with:
    AX = error code:
        0000h successful
        0074h internal VIO failure
        0166h invalid row value
        0167h invalid column value
        01B4h invalid VIO handle

Details: Write wraps at end of line and terminates if it reaches the end of the screen.

INTERRUPT 14h - Function 81h, Subfunction 02h
CLOSE VIDEO FOSSIL

Purpose: Terminates operation of the Video FOSSIL.

Available on: All machines.   **Restrictions:** Video FOSSIL must be installed.

Registers at call: **Return Registers:**

AX = 8102h   AX = 1954h

Details: Terminates all operations; after this call, the video FOSSIL may be either removed from memory or reinitialized.

Conflicts: COURIERS.COM (chapter 7).

See Also: Function 81h Subfunctions 01h and 03h

INTERRUPT 14h - Function 81h, Subfunction 03h
UNINSTALL VIDEO FOSSIL

Purpose: Removes the Video FOSSIL routines from memory.

Available on: All machines.   **Restrictions:** Video FOSSIL must be installed.

Registers at call:
AX = 8103h

Return Registers:
AX = 1954h

Details: This is an extension to the VFOSSIL spec by Bob Hartman's VFOS_IBM.
Conflicts: COURIERS.COM (chapter 7).

INTERRUPT 16h - Function AAh
CALL GATE FOR Paint Tools GRAPHICS

Purpose: Paint Tools is a graphics library for Turbo Pascal, Modula 2 and others from DataBiten in Sweden. The Library is installed as a memory resident driver.

Available on: All machines.

Restrictions: PTxxx.COM (xxx = CGA, EGA, VGA, HER, ...) must be installed.

Registers at call:
AH = AAh
Various registers set up by high level language.

Return Registers:
Graphics performed.

Conflicts: None known.

INTERRUPT 1Dh
VIDEO PARAMETER TABLES

Purpose: This is not an interrupt; the vector contains the address of the currently active video parameter table.

Available on: All machines.

Restrictions: none.

Registers at call: n/a

Return Registers: n/a.

Details: Default video parameter table (Table 5-28) is located at F000h:F0A4h for 100% compatible BIOSes.
Conflicts: None known.
See Also: INT 10h Function 00h

Table 5-28. Format of video parameter table:

Offset	Size	Description
00h	16 BYTEs	6845 register values for modes 00h and 01h
10h	16 BYTEs	6845 register values for modes 02h and 03h
20h	16 BYTEs	6845 register values for modes 04h and 05h
30h	16 BYTEs	6845 register values for modes 06h and 07h
40h	WORD	bytes in video buffer for modes 00h and 01h
42h	WORD	bytes in video buffer for modes 02h and 03h
44h	WORD	bytes in video buffer for modes 04h and 05h
46h	WORD	bytes in video buffer for modes 06h and 07h
48h	8 BYTEs	columns on screen for each of modes 00h through 07h
50h	8 BYTEs	CRT controller mode bytes for each of modes 00h through 07h

INTERRUPT 1Fh
8x8 GRAPHICS FONT

Purpose: This is not an interrupt; the vector contains the address of a 1024-byte table of bitmap data, 8 bytes for each character 80h-FFh, which provides the 8x8 character font used in graphics modes.

Available on: All machines.

Restrictions: Used in graphics modes only.

Registers at call: n/a

Return Registers: n/a.

Details: Graphics data for characters 00h-7Fh is stored at F000h:FA6Eh in 100% compatible BIOSes.
See Also: INT 43h, INT 44h

INTERRUPT 2Fh - Function 64h, Subfunction 00h
Multiplex - SCRNSAV2.COM INSTALLATION CHECK

Purpose: Determine whether SCRNSAV2.COM screen-saver TSR is installed.

Available on: All machines.

Restrictions: none.

Registers at call:
AX = 6400h

Return Registers:
AL = 00h not installed
= FFh installed

Details: SCRNSAV2.COM is a screen saver for PS/2's with VGA by Alan Ballard.

INTERRUPT 42h
RELOCATED DEFAULT INT 10h VIDEO SERVICES

Purpose: Replaces INT 10h for default video services when INT 10h is re-routed to video card's ROM.

Available on: Systems equipped with EGA or VGA.

Restrictions: none.

See Also: INT 10h

INTERRUPT 43h
CHARACTER TABLE

Purpose: This is not an interrupt; the vector contains the address of graphics data for characters 00h-7Fh of the current font.

Available on: Systems equipped with EGA, MCGA, or VGA.

Restrictions: none.

Registers at call: n/a

Return Registers: n/a.

Conflicts: Z100 (chapter 2)
See Also: INT 1Fh, INT 44h

INTERRUPT 44h
ROM BIOS CHARACTER FONT, CHARACTERS 00h-7Fh

Purpose: This is not an interrupt; the vector contains the address of graphics data for the current character font.

Available on: PCjr only.

Restrictions: none.

Registers at call: n/a

Return Registers: n/a.

Conflicts: Z100 (chapter 2), Novell NetWare (chapter 20).
See Also: INT 1Fh, INT 43h

INTERRUPT 59h
GSS Computer Graphics Interface (GSS*CGI)

Purpose: INT 59h is the means by which GSS*CGI language bindings communicate with GSS*CGI device drivers and the GSS*CGI device driver controller. Also used by the IBM Graphic Development Toolkit.

Available on: All machines.

Restrictions: Appropriate device drivers must be installed.

Registers at call:
DS:DX -> block of 5 array pointers

Return Registers:
CF set on error
AX = error code
CF clear if successful
AX = return code

Conflicts: DESQview 2.26+ IRQ8 (chapter 2), DoubleDOS IRQ1 (chapter 2).

INTERRUPT 6Dh
ATI VGA Wonder - VIDEO BIOS ENTRY POINT

Purpose: Called internally by ATI VGA Wonder video BIOS. Points at the original INT 10h entry point set up by the ATI BIOS.

Available on: Systems equipped with an ATI VGA Wonder video card.

Restrictions: none.

Registers at call:
See INT 10h.

Return Registers: n/a.

Conflicts: VGA internal, DECnet DOS CTERM (chapter 24).
See Also: INT 10h

INTERRUPT 6Dh
VGA - internal

Purpose: *unknown.*
Available on: All machines.

Restrictions: Specific video BIOS using this must be present.

Details: Used by IBM, Paradise, Video7, and NCR.
Conflicts: ATI VGA Wonder, DECnet DOS CTERM (chapter 24).

INTERRUPT 7Fh
Halo88 API

Purpose: Halo88 is a suite of graphics routines.
Available on: All machines.
Registers at call:
BX = function code (Table 5-29)

Restrictions: none.
Return Registers: *unknown.*

Table 5-29. HALO Function Codes

64h arc	89h movefrom
65h bar	8Ah moveto
66h box	8Bh pie
67h circle	8Ch polylnabs
68h clr	8Dh polylnrel
69h default hatch style	8Eh ptabs
6Ah default line style	8Fh ptrel
6Bh delhcur	91h setasp
6Ch delln / deltcur	92h set color
6Dh ellipse	93h set font
6Eh fill	94h set hatch style
6Fh flood	95h set line style
70h flood2	97h settext
71h init graphics	98h set text color
72h init hcur	99h btext
73h init marker	9Ah setseg
74h init tcur	9Bh display
75h inqarc	9Ch setscreen
76h inqbknd	9Eh close graphics
77h inqclr	9Fh ftinit
78h inqerr	A0h ftlocate
79h inqgcur	A1h ftext
7Ah inqhcur	A5h set viewport
7Bh inqmarker	A6h set window
7Dh inqtcur	A7h set world
7Eh inqtext	AAh ftcolor
7Fh lnabs	ACh initlp
80h lnrel	ADh inqasp
81h markerabs	AEh inqdev
82h markerrel	AFh inqdisplay
83h moveabs	B0h inqft
84h movehcurabs	B1h inqftcolor
85h movehcurrel	B2h inqinterlace
86h moverel	B3h inqlpa
87h movetcurabs	B4h inqlpg
88h movetcurrel	B5h inqmode

Table 5-29. HALO Function Codes (continued)

B6h inqscreen	F4h inqdrange
B7h inqversion	F5h inqstang
B8h roam	F6h orglocator
B9h scroll	F7h inqlocator
BAh setieee	F8h inqarea
BBh set interlace	F9h setpal
BCh shift	FAh setborder
BDh start graphics	FBh inqcrange
BEh vpan	FEh setclip
CBh gwrite	FFh fcir
CCh gread	100h setcrange
CDh setxor	101h setdrange
CEh rbox	102h setlattr
CFh rcir	103h polycabs
D0h rlnabs	104h polycrel
D1h rlnrel	108h memcom
D2h delbox	109h memexp
D3h delcir	10Ah memmov
D5h setseg2	10Eh movefx
DCh worldoff	10Fh movetx
DDh mapwtod	110h inqrgb
DEh mapdtow	111h save image
DFh mapwton	112h restore image
E0h mapntow	113h setapal
E1h mapdton	114h setxpal
E2h mapntod	118h inqtsize
E3h inqworld	12Eh gprint
E4h inqviewport	130h setprn
E5h set line width	131h setpattr
E6h lnjoint	133h setbattr
E7h set locator	135h pexpand
E8h read locator	136h ptnorm
E9h setdev	137h pfnorm
EBh setstext	13Bh inqprn
ECh setstclr	13Ch lopen
EDh setstang	13Dh lclose
EEh stext	13Eh lappend
EFh inqstext	13Fh lrecord
F0h setdegree	140h lswitch
F1h inqstsize	142h inqfun
F2h polyfabs	15Dh lsetup
F3h polyfrel	15Eh lrest
	15Fh lsave

Additional parameters on stack.

Details: According to Stuart Kemp, the code appears to make no provisions for chaining.

Conflicts: Alloy NTNX and MW386 (chapter 18), ClusterShare access (chapter 27).

INTERRUPT 7Fh - Function 01h, Subfunction 05h
HDILOAD.EXE - 8514/A VIDEO CONTROLLER INTERFACE

Purpose: Determine the addresses to call in order to manipulate the 8514/A display.

Available on: Systems equipped with 8514/A display adapter.

Restrictions: HDILOAD.EXE must be installed.

Registers at call:
AX = 0105h

Return Registers:
CF set on error
CF clear if successful
   CX:DX -> array of FAR pointers to entry points

Details: Most 8514/A functions are invoked by pushing the DWORD parameter block pointer and then performing a FAR call via the appropriate vector of the entry point array.

Conflicts: Halo88 (chapter 5), Alloy 386/MultiWare and NTNX (chapter 18), Convergent Technologies ClusterShare (chapter 27).

Function numbers: (do FAR call via entry_points + 4 * function)

08h	HOPEN	1Dh	HQMODE
10h	HINT	22h	HCLOSE
13h	HLDPAL	30h	HINIT
15h	HBBW	31h	HSYNC
17h	HBBR	39h	HSPAL
18h	HBBCHN	3Ah	HRPAL

Chapter 6

Low-Level Disk I/O

This chapter discusses the interrupt functions that provide low-level disk input/output capability. Since disk systems usually funnel all I/O operations through these functions, many add-on and third-party products hook into them and relocate the original functions to other vectors. We have separated the listings into six major subdivisions to help you locate specific functions: General-Usage functions are those which normally remain unchanged; Floppies are those functions used only for floppy-disk operation and which are often relocated when a system contains both floppy and fixed disk drives; Hard Disks describes the functions used only with fixed or hard disks; Special Controllers includes those functions used with ESDI, SCSI, and other advanced interfaces; Disk Caches includes the functions that support cache programs; and Disk Compression includes functions supported by programs which automatically compress data written to the disk.

Within each of these subdivisions, functions are listed by numeric sequence of interrupt number, function, and subfunction; potential conflicts with other functions are noted. When no chapter reference appears for a listed conflict, the conflicting function is also described in this chapter.

General-Usage Functions

The functions described in this section are used by all standard disk interfacing routines, whether dealing with floppy disks or fixed drives.

INTERRUPT 13h - Function 00h
RESET DISK SYSTEM

Purpose: Restores disk system conditions to power-up state.

Available on: All machines.	**Restrictions:** none.
Registers at call:	**Return Registers:**
AH = 00h	AH = status (Table 6-1)

DL = drive (if bit 7 is set both hard disks and floppy
    disks are reset)

Details: Forces controller to recalibrate drive heads (seek to track 0).

Conflicts: None known.

See Also: Functions 0Dh and 11h, INT 21h Function 0Dh (chapter 8)

INTERRUPT 13h - Function 01h
GET STATUS OF LAST OPERATION

Purpose: Determine status resulting from previous disk operation.

Available on: All machines.	**Restrictions:** none.
Registers at call:	**Return Registers:**
AH = 01h	AH = status of previous operation

DL = drive (bit 7 set for hard disk)

Details: The PS/2 Model 30/286 returns the status in both AH and AL.

Conflicts: None known.

Table 6-1. Values of Disk Status Codes

00h successful completion
01h invalid function in AH or invalid parameter
02h address mark not found
03h disk write-protected (floppy)
04h sector not found
05h reset failed (hard disk)
06h disk changed (floppy)
07h drive parameter activity failed (hard disk)
08h DMA overrun
09h attempted DMA across 64K boundary
0Ah bad sector detected (hard disk)
0Bh bad track detected (hard disk)
0Ch unsupported track or invalid media

0Dh invalid number of sectors on format (hard disk)
0Eh control data address mark detected (hard disk)
0Fh DMA arbitration level out of range (hard disk)
10h uncorrectable CRC or ECC error on read
11h data ECC corrected (hard disk)
20h controller failure
40h seek failed
80h timeout (not ready)
AAh drive not ready (hard disk)
BBh undefined error (hard disk)
CCh write fault (hard disk)
E0h status register error (hard disk)
FFh sense operation failed (hard disk)

INTERRUPT 13h - Function 02h
READ SECTOR(S) INTO MEMORY

Purpose: Read data from disk using absolute cylinder, head, and sector addresses.
Available on: All machines.   **Restrictions:** none.
Registers at call: **Return Registers:**
AH = 02h   CF set on error
AL = number of sectors to read (must be nonzero)   CF clear if successful
CH = low eight bits of cylinder number   AH = status (Table 6-1)
CL = sector number (bits 0-5)   if AH = 11h (corrected ECC error),
    high two bits of cylinder   AL = burst length
      (bits 6-7, hard disk only)   AL = number of sectors transferred
DH = head number
DL = drive number (bit 7 set for hard disk)
ES:BX -> data buffer
Details: Errors on a floppy may be due to the motor failing to spin up quickly enough; the read should be retried at least three times, resetting the disk with Function 00h between attempts. DOS does this automatically.

The AWARD AT BIOS has been extended to handle more than 1024 cylinders by placing bits 10 and 11 of the cylinder number into bits 6 and 7 of DH. The AMI BIOS apparently also follows this convention.
Conflicts: None known.
See Also: Function 03h, Hard Disk Function 0Ah

INTERRUPT 13h - Function 03h
WRITE DISK SECTOR(S)

Purpose: Write data to disk using absolute cylinder, head, and sector addresses.
Available on: All machines.   **Restrictions:** none.
Registers at call: **Return Registers:**
AH = 03h   CF set on error
AL = number of sectors to write (must be nonzero) CF clear if successful
CH = low eight bits of cylinder number   AH = status (Table 6-1)
CL = sector number (bits 0-5)   AL = number of sectors transferred
    high two bits of cylinder
      (bits 6-7, hard disk only)
DH = head number
DL = drive number (bit 7 set for hard disk)
ES:BX -> data buffer
Details: Errors on a floppy may be due to the motor failing to spin up quickly enough; the write should be retried at least three times, resetting the disk with Function 00h between attempts. DOS does so automatically.

The AWARD AT BIOS has been extended to handle more than 1024 cylinders by placing bits 10 and 11 of the cylinder number into bits 6 and 7 of DH. The AMI BIOS apparently also follows this convention.
Conflicts: None known.
See Also: Function 02h, Hard Disk Function 0Bh

INTERRUPT 13h - Function 04h
VERIFY DISK SECTOR(S)

Purpose: Check whether one or more sectors were correctly written to disk by comparing the data in the sector against the CRC stored on the disk.

Available on: All machines.

Registers at call:
AH = 03h
AL = number of sectors to verify (must be nonzero)
CH = low eight bits of cylinder number
CL = sector number (bits 0-5)
    high two bits of cylinder
        (bits 6-7, hard disk only)
DH = head number
DL = drive number (bit 7 set for hard disk)
ES:BX -> data buffer (PC, XT, AT with BIOS prior
    to 11/15/85)

Restrictions: none.

Return Registers:
CF set on error
CF clear if successful
AH = status (Table 6-1)
AL = number of sectors verified

Details: Errors on a floppy may be due to the motor failing to spin up quickly enough; the write should be retried at least three times, resetting the disk with Function 00h between attempts.

The AWARD AT BIOS has been extended to handle more than 1024 cylinders by placing bits 10 and 11 of the cylinder number into bits 6 and 7 of DH. The AMI BIOS apparently also follows this convention.
Conflicts: None known.
See Also: Function 02h

INTERRUPT 13h - Function 08h
GET DRIVE PARAMETERS

Purpose: Obtain parameters for the specified drive, either floppy or fixed.

Available on: PC, XT286, Convertible, and PS/2
          models.

Registers at call:
AH = 08h
DL = drive (bit 7 set for hard disk)

Restrictions: none.

Return Registers:
CF set on error
    AH = status (07h) (Table 6-1)
CF clear if successful
    AH = 00h
    BL = drive type (see function 17h)
        (AT/PS2 floppies only)
    CH = low eight bits of maximum cylinder number
    CL = maximum sector number (bits 5-0)
        high two bits of maximum cylinder number
            (bits 7-6)
    DH = maximum head number
    DL = number of drives
    ES:DI -> drive parameter table (floppies only)

Details: This function may return successfully even though the specified drive number is greater than the number of attached drives of that type (floppy or hard). The calling program should check DL to ensure validity.
Conflicts: None known.
See Also: Floppy INT 1Eh, Hard Disk INT 41h

INTERRUPT 13h - Function 15h
GET DISK TYPE

Purpose: Determine the type of the specified drive.

Available on: XT with BIOS dated 01/10/86 or later, XT286, AT, and PS/2 machines.

Restrictions: none.

Registers at call:
AH = 15h
DL = drive number (bit 7 set for hard disk)

Return Registers:
CF clear if successful
    AH = type code:
        00h no such drive
        01h floppy without change-line support
        02h floppy with change-line support
        03h hard disk
            CX:DX = number of 512-byte sectors
CF set on error
    AH = status (Table 6-1)

Conflicts: None known.
See Also: Functions 16h and 17h, SCSI Function 19h

INTERRUPT 13h - Function 18h
SET MEDIA TYPE FOR FORMAT

Purpose: Specify drive parameters to be used when formatting a disk.

Available on: AT model 3x9, XT2, XT286, PS/2 machines.

Restrictions: none.

Registers at call:
AH = 18h
DL = drive number
CH = lower 8 bits of number of tracks
CL = sectors per track (bits 0-5)
    top 2 bits of number of tracks (bits 6,7)

Return Registers:
AH = status
    00h requested combination supported
    01h function not available
    0Ch not supported or drive type unknown
    80h there is no disk in the drive
ES:DI -> 11-byte parameter table

Conflicts: Future Domain SCSI Controller.
See Also: Functions 05h, 07h, and 17h

INTERRUPT 13h - Function 20h
Western Digital "Super BIOS" - UNKNOWN FUNCTION

Purpose: *unknown.* No information is available on this call.

Available on: Systems equipped with appropriate Western Digital controllers.

Restrictions: *unknown.*

Registers at call:
AH = 20h
other registers, if any, unknown.

Return Registers: *unknown.*

Details: Seems to return some kind of status.
Conflicts: QCACHE - Dismount.

INTERRUPT 4Eh
TI Professional PC - DISK I/O

Purpose: Used instead of INT 13h on the TI Professional PC.
Available on: TI Professional PC only.
Registers at call: Same as INT 13h.
Conflicts: None known.
See Also: INT 13h

Restrictions: none.
Return Registers: Same as INT 13h.

Floppies

The functions described in this section are used by floppy disk operations only.

INTERRUPT 13h - Function 05h
Floppy Diskette: FORMAT TRACK

Purpose: Prepare a floppy diskette for data storage.

Available on: All machines.

Restrictions: On AT or later, function 17h must be called first.

Registers at call:
AH = 05h
AL = number of sectors to format
CH = track number
DH = head number
DL = drive number
ES:BX -> address field buffer (Table 6-2)

Return Registers:
CF set on error
CF clear if successful
AH = status (Table 6-1)

Details: The number of sectors per track is read from the Diskette Parameter Table pointed at by INT 1Eh.

Conflicts: Fixed Disk - Format Track.

See Also: Hard Disk Function 05h, Functions 17h and 18h, INT 1Eh

Table 6-2. Format of address field buffer entry (one per sector in track):

Offset	Size	Description
00h	BYTE	track number
01h	BYTE	head number (0-based)
02h	BYTE	sector number
03h	BYTE	sector size:

00h 128 bytes
01h 256 bytes
02h 512
03h 1024

INTERRUPT 13h - Function 16h
DETECT DISK CHANGE

Purpose: Determine whether a removable diskette has been changed.

Available on: XT with BIOS dated 01/10/86 or later, XT286, AT, and PS/2 machines.

Restrictions: none.

Registers at call:
AH = 16h
DL = drive number

Return Registers:
CF clear if change line inactive
　　AH = 00h (disk not changed)
CF set if change line active
　　AH = 06h change line active or not supported
　　　　80h drive not ready or not present

Details: Function 15h should be called first to determine whether the desired drive supports a change line.

Conflicts: None known.

INTERRUPT 13h - Function 17h
SET DISK TYPE FOR FORMAT

Purpose: Prepare to format floppy diskette.

Available on: AT and PS/2 machines.

Restrictions: none.

Registers at call:
AH = 17h
AL = format type:
    01h = 320/360K disk in 360K drive
    02h = 320/360K disk in 1.2M drive
    03h = 1.2M disk in 1.2M drive
    04h = 720K disk in 720K drive
DL = drive number

Return Registers:
CF set on error
CF clear if successful
AH = status (Table 6-1)

Details: This function does not handle 1.44M drives; function 18h should be used instead when formatting diskettes in a 1.44M drive.
Conflicts: None known.
See Also: Functions 15h and 18h

INTERRUPT 1Eh
SYSTEM DATA - DISKETTE PARAMETERS

Purpose: Not an interrupt. This vector points to the default floppy disk parameter table (Table 6-3), which is located at F000h:EFC7h for 100 percent compatible BIOSes.
Available on: All machines.
Registers at call: n/a
Conflicts: None known.
See Also: INT 13h Function 0Fh, Hard Disk INT 41h

Restrictions: none.
Return Registers: n/a

Table 6-3. Format of diskette parameter table:

Offset	Size	Description
00h	BYTE	first specify byte
		bits 7-4: step rate
		3-0: head unload time (0Fh = 240 ms)
01h	BYTE	second specify byte
		bits 7-1: head load time (01h = 4 ms)
		0: non-DMA mode (always 0)
02h	BYTE	delay until motor turned off (in clock ticks)
03h	BYTE	bytes per sector:
		00h = 128
		01h = 256
		02h = 512
		03h = 1024
04h	BYTE	sectors per track
05h	BYTE	length of gap between sectors (2Ah for 5.25", 1Bh for 3.5")
06h	BYTE	data length (ignored if bytes-per-sector field is nonzero)
07h	BYTE	gap length when formatting (50h for 5.25", 6Ch for 3.5")
08h	BYTE	format filler byte (default F6h)
09h	BYTE	head settle time in milliseconds
0Ah	BYTE	motor start time in 1/8 seconds

INTERRUPT 40h
ROM BIOS DISKETTE HANDLER RELOCATED BY HARD DISK BIOS

Purpose: Permit floppy disk support to be hooked independently of fixed disk support.
Available on: All machines.
Registers at call: Same as INT 13h.

Restrictions: Hard disk must be installed.
Return Registers: Same as INT 13h.

Details: INT 40h was originally used to allow the hard disk BIOS on an IBM PC or XT hard disk controller to chain to the floppy disk code in the system's ROM BIOS. Although IBM ATs and later support hard disks in the ROM BIOS, the INT 40h functionality was kept for backward compatibility.
Conflicts: None known.
See Also: INT 13h, 4+Power INT 63h

INTERRUPT 63h
4+Power FLOPPY CONTROLLER - ORIGINAL INT 13h/INT 40h

Purpose: The "4+Power" quad floppy controller BIOS hooks INT 13h (or INT 40h if INT 13h has been moved there) and places the old value here.

Available on: All machines.

Restrictions: 4+Power floppy controller must be installed.

Registers at call: See INT 13h.

Return Registers: See INT 13h.

Conflicts: Adaptec and OMTI controllers - DRIVE 0 DATA, Oracle SQL Protected Mode Executive (chapter 9).

Hard Disks

The functions described in this section are used by fixed/hard disk operations only.

INTERRUPT 13h - Function 05h
Fixed Disk: FORMAT TRACK

Purpose: Prepare a fixed disk for data storage.

Available on: All machines with fixed disk installed.

Restrictions: For XT-type controllers on on AT or later, Function 0Fh should be called first.

Registers at call:
AH = 05h
AL = interleave value (XT-type controllers only)
ES:BX = 512-byte format buffer:
    The first 2*(sectors/ track) bytes contain
        F,N for each sector:
        F = 00h for good sector,
            80h for bad sector
        N = sector number
CH = cylinder number (bits 8,9 in high bits of CL)
CL = high bits of cylinder number (bits 7,6)
DH = head
DL = drive

Return Registers:
AH = status code (Table 6-1)

Details: The AWARD AT BIOS has been extended to handle more than 1024 cylinders by placing bits 10 and 11 of the cylinder number into bits 6 and 7 of DH. The AMI BIOS apparently also follows this convention.

Conflicts: Floppy - Format Track.

See Also: Functions 06h, 07h, 0Fh, 18h, and 1Ah

INTERRUPT 13h - Function 06h
Fixed Disk: FORMAT TRACK AND SET BAD SECTOR FLAGS

Purpose: Prepare a fixed disk for data storage and note "bad sector" information.

Available on: XT and Portable only.

Restrictions: none.

Registers at call:
AH = 06h
AL = interleave value
CH = cylinder number (bits 8,9 in high bits of CL)
CL = sector number
DH = head
DL = drive

Return Registers:
AH = status code (Table 6-1)

Details: The AWARD AT BIOS has been extended to handle more than 1024 cylinders by placing bits 10 and 11 of the cylinder number into bits 6 and 7 of DH. The AMI BIOS apparently also follows this convention.

Conflicts: None known.

INTERRUPT 13h - Function 07h
Fixed Disk: FORMAT DRIVE STARTING AT GIVEN TRACK

Purpose: Prepare only part of a fixed disk for data storage.
Available on: XT and Portable only.
Registers at call:
AH = 07h
AL = interleave value (XT only)
ES:BX = 512-byte format buffer (see Function 05h)
CH = cylinder number (bits 8,9 in high bits of CL)
CL = sector number
DH = head
DL = drive

Restrictions: none.
Return Registers:
AH = status code (Table 6-1)

Details: The AWARD AT BIOS has been extended to handle more than 1024 cylinders by placing bits 10 and 11 of the cylinder number into bits 6 and 7 of DH. The AMI BIOS apparently also follows this convention.
Conflicts: None known.
See Also: Function 1Ah

INTERRUPT 13h - Function 09h
INITIALIZE CONTROLLER WITH DRIVE PARAMETERS

Purpose: Re-initialize fixed disk controller.
Available on: AT and PS/2 models.
Registers at call:
AH = 09h
DL = drive (80h for first, 81h for second)

Restrictions: none.
Return Registers:
CF clear if successful
CF set on error
AH = status (Table 6-1)

Details: On the PC and XT, this function uses the parameter table pointed at by INT 41h. On the AT and later, this function uses the parameter table pointed at by INT 41h if DL=80h, and the parameter table pointed at by INT 46h if DL=81h.
Conflicts: None known.
See Also: INT 41h, INT 46h

INTERRUPT 13h - Function 0Ah
READ LONG SECTOR(S)

Purpose: This function reads in four to seven bytes of error-correcting code along with each sector's worth of information.
Available on: AT and later.
Registers at call:
AH = 0Ah
AL = number of sectors
CH = low eight bits of cylinder number
CL = sector number (bits 5-0)
  high two bits of cylinder number
    (bits 7-6)
DH = head number
DL = drive number (80h = first, 81h = second)
ES:BX -> data buffer

Restrictions: none.
Return Registers:
CF clear if successful
CF set on error
AH = status (Table 6-1)
AL = number of sectors transferred

Details: Data errors are not automatically corrected, and the read is aborted after the first sector with an ECC error. Used for diagnostics only on PS/2 systems.
Conflicts: None known.
See Also: Function 0Bh, general Function 02h

INTERRUPT 13h - Function 0Bh
WRITE LONG SECTOR(S)

Purpose: Write one or more sectors together with explicit error-correcting information. Used for diagnostics only on PS/2 systems.

Available on: AT and later.

Registers at call:
AH = 0Ah
AL = number of sectors
CH = low eight bits of cylinder number
CL = sector number (bits 5-0)
   high two bits of cylinder number
       (bits 7-6)
DH = head number
DL = drive number (80h = first, 81h = second)
ES:BX -> data buffer

Restrictions: none.

Return Registers:
CF clear if successful
CF set on error
AH = status (Table 6-1)
AL = number of sectors transferred

Details: Each sector's worth of data must be followed by four to seven bytes of error-correction information.

Conflicts: None known.

See Also: Function 0Ah, general Function 03h

INTERRUPT 13h - Function 0Ch
SEEK TO CYLINDER

Purpose: Position fixed disk to specified cylinder.

Available on: All machines.

Registers at call:
AH = 0Ch
CH = low eight bits of cylinder number
CL = sector number (bits 5-0)
   high two bits of cylinder number
       (bits 7-6)
DH = head number
DL = drive number (80h = first, 81h = second)

Restrictions: none.

Return Registers:
CF set on error
CF clear if successful
AH = status (Table 6-1)

Conflicts: None known.

See Also: Function 0Ah, general Functions 00h and 02h

INTERRUPT 13h - Function 0Dh
RESET HARD DISKS

Purpose: Reinitializes the hard disk controller, resets the specified drive's parameters, and recalibrates the drive's heads (seek to track 0).

Available on: All machines with fixed disks.

Registers at call:
AH = 0Dh
DL = drive number (80h = first, 81h = second)

Restrictions: Not for PS/2 ESDI drives.

Return Registers:
CF set on error
CF clear if successful
AH = status (Table 6-1)

Conflicts: None known.

See Also: Function 00h, INT 21h Function 0Dh (chapter 8)

INTERRUPT 13h - Function 0Eh
READ SECTOR BUFFER

Purpose: Transfers controller's sector buffer. No data is read from the drive.

Available on: XT only.

Restrictions: none.

Registers at call:
AH = 0Eh
DL = drive number (80h = first, 81h = second)
ES:BX -> buffer
Details: Used for diagnostics only on PS/2 systems.
Conflicts: None known.
See Also: Function 0Ah

Return Registers:
CF set on error
CF clear if successful
AH = status code (Table 6-1)

INTERRUPT 13h - Function 0Fh
WRITE SECTOR BUFFER

Purpose: Initializes controller's sector buffer. Does not write data to the drive.
Available on: XT only.   **Restrictions:** none.
Registers at call: **Return Registers:**
AH = 0Fh   CF set on error
DL = drive number (80h = first, 81h = second) CF clear if successful
ES:BX -> buffer   AH = status code (Table 6-1)
Details: Should be called before formatting to initialize an XT-type controller's sector buffer. Used for diagnostics only on PS/2 systems.
Conflicts: None known.
See Also: Function 0Bh

INTERRUPT 13h - Function 10h
CHECK IF DRIVE READY

Purpose: Determine whether fixed disk is ready for operation.
Available on: All machines with fixed disk.   **Restrictions:** none.
Registers at call: **Return Registers:**
AH = 10h   CF set on error
DL = drive number (80h = first, 81h = second)   CF clear if successful
                                                    AH = status (Table 6-1)
Conflicts: None known.

INTERRUPT 13h - Function 11h
RECALIBRATE DRIVE

Purpose: Cause hard disk controller to seek the specified drive to cylinder 0.
Available on: All machines with fixed disk.   **Restrictions:** none.
Registers at call: **Return Registers:**
AH = 11h   CF set on error
DL = drive number (80h = first, 81h = second)   CF clear if successful
                                                    AH = status (Table 6-1)
Conflicts: None known.
See Also: Functions 00h, 0Ch, and 19h

INTERRUPT 13h - Function 12h
CONTROLLER RAM DIAGNOSTIC

Purpose: Perform built-in RAM diagnostics of hard disk controller.
Available on: XT and PS/2 models.   **Restrictions:** none.
Registers at call: **Return Registers:**
AH = 12h   CF set on error
DL = drive number (80h = first, 81h = second)   CF clear if successful
                                                    AH = status code (Table 6-1)
Conflicts: Future Domain SCSI Controller.
See Also: Functions 13h and 14h

INTERRUPT 13h - Function 13h
DRIVE DIAGNOSTIC

Purpose: Perform built-in diagnostics of hard disk controller.

Available on: XT and PS/2 models.

Registers at call:
AH = 13h
DL = drive number (80h = first, 81h = second)

Restrictions: none.

Return Registers:
CF set on error
CF clear if successful
AH = status code (Table 6-1)

Conflicts: None known.
See Also: Functions 12h and 14h

INTERRUPT 13h - Function 14h
CONTROLLER INTERNAL DIAGNOSTIC

Purpose: Perform built-in internal diagnostics of hard disk controller.

Available on: All machines.

Registers at call:
AH = 14h

Restrictions: none.

Return Registers:
CF set on error
CF clear if successful
AH = status code (Table 6-1)

Conflicts: None known.
See Also: Functions 12h and 13h

INTERRUPT 13h - Function 19h
PARK HEADS

Purpose: Move the drive heads to a safe position for powerdown and transport. On many drives, the heads are automatically locked in place on seeking to the parking position.

Available on: XT286 and PS/2 machines.

Registers at call:
AH = 19h
DL = drive

Restrictions: none.

Return Registers:
CF set on error
AH = status (Table 6-1)

Conflicts: Future Domain SCSI Controller.
See Also: Function 11h

INTERRUPT 2Fh - Function F7h, Subfunction 00h
Multiplex - AUTOPARK.COM - INSTALLATION CHECK

Purpose: Determine whether AUTOPARK TSR has been installed. AUTOPARK.COM is a resident hard disk parker by Alan D. Jones.

Available on: All machines.

Restrictions: DOS versions prior to 3.0 must verify that interrupt vector is not 0000:0000 before using INT 2Fh.

Registers at call:
AX = F700h

Return Registers:
AL = 00h not installed
FFh installed

Conflicts: None known.

INTERRUPT 2Fh - Function F7h, Subfunction 01h
Multiplex - AUTOPARK.COM - SET PARKING DELAY

Purpose: Establish timeout interval before disk parking is done automatically.

Available on: All machines.

Registers at call:
AX = F701h
BX:CX = 32-bit count of 55ms timer ticks

Restrictions: AUTOPARK TSR must be installed.

Return Registers: n/a

Conflicts: None known.

INTERRUPT 41h
SYSTEM DATA - HARD DISK 0 PARAMETER TABLE

Purpose: Not a procedure; this vector contains a far pointer to the parameter table (Table 6-4) for Hard Disk 0.
Available on: All machines.   **Restrictions:** none.
Details: The default parameter table array is located at F000h:E401h in 100 percent compatible BIOSes.
Conflicts: None known.
See Also: INT 13h Function 09h, INT 46h, Diskette INT 1Eh

Table 6-4. Format of fixed disk parameters:

Offset	Size	Description
00h	WORD	number of cylinders
02h	BYTE	number of heads
03h	WORD	starting reduced write current cylinder (XT only, 0 for others)
05h	WORD	starting write precompensation cylinder number
07h	BYTE	maximum ECC burst length (XT only)
08h	BYTE	control byte:
		bits 0-2: drive option (XT only, 0 for others)
		bit 3: set if more than 8 heads (AT and later only)
		bit 4: always 0
		bit 5: set if manufacturer's defect map on max cylinder+1
		(AT and later only)
		bit 6: disable ECC retries
		bit 7: disable access retries
09h	BYTE	standard timeout (XT only, 0 for others)
0Ah	BYTE	formatting timeout (XT only, 0 for others)
0Bh	BYTE	timeout for checking drive (XT only, 0 for others)
0Ch	WORD	cylinder number of landing zone (AT and later only)
0Eh	BYTE	number of sectors per track (AT and later only)
0Fh	BYTE	reserved

INTERRUPT 46h
SYSTEM DATA - HARD DISK 1 DRIVE PARAMETER TABLE

Purpose: Not a procedure; this vector contains a far pointer to the parameter table (Table 6-4) for Hard Disk 1.
Available on: All machines.   **Restrictions:** none.
Conflicts: None known.
See Also: INT 13h Function 09h, INT 41h

Special Controllers
The functions described in this section include those used by EDSI, SCSI, and other advanced interfaces.

INTERRUPT 13h - Function 12h
Future Domain - STOP SCSI DISK

Purpose: Terminate disk operation ("park disk").
Available on: Machines with Future Domain SCSI   **Restrictions:** none.
        controller present.

Registers at call:	**Return Registers:**
AH = 12h	CF set on error
DL = hard drive ID	AH = status code (Table 6-1)

Details: Available on at least the TMC-870 8-bit SCSI controller BIOS v6.0A. If the given drive is a SCSI device, the SCSI Stop Unit command is sent and either "Disk prepared for shipping" or "Disk Stop command failed" is displayed.
Conflicts: Hard Disk - Controller RAM Diagnostic.

INTERRUPT 13h - Function 18h
Future Domain - GET SCSI CONTROLLER INFORMATION

Purpose: Obtain information about specified SCSI drive.

Available on: Machines with Future Domain SCSI controller present.

Restrictions: none.

Registers at call:
AH = 18h
DL = hard drive ID

Return Registers:
CF set on error
    AH = status code (Table 6-1)
CF clear if successful
    AX = 4321h (*magic number???*)
    BH = number of SCSI drives connected
    BL = SCSI device number for specified drive
    CX = 040Ah (*magic number???*)

Details: This call also sets an internal flag (non-resettable) which prevents some controller messages from being displayed and allows writes to removable devices.

Conflicts: Disk - Set Media Type for Format.

See Also: Future Domain Function 1Bh

INTERRUPT 13h - Function 19h
Future Domain - REINITIALIZE SCSI DRIVE

Purpose: Reinitializes specified SCSI drive.

Available on: Machines with Future Domain SCSI controller present.

Restrictions: none.

Registers at call:
AH = 19h
DL = hard drive ID

Return Registers:
CF set on error
    AH = status code (Table 6-1)
CF clear if successful
    AH = disk type (03h = fixed disk)
    CX:DX = number of 512-byte sectors

Details: Sends a SCSI Read Capacity command to get the number of logical blocks and adjusts the result for 512-byte sectors. Displays either "Error in Read Capacity Command" or "nnn Bytes per sector" (nnn=256 or 512, the only sizes supported in the translation code). This function should probably be called when a removable device has its media changed. Returns the same values as Function 15h.

Conflicts: Fixed Disk - Park Heads.

See Also: Future Domain Function 1Ah, general Function 15h

INTERRUPT 13h - Function 1Ah
ESDI FORMAT UNIT

Purpose: Prepare ESDI fixed disk for data storage.

Available on: PS/2 machines.

Registers at call:
AH = 1Ah
AL = defect table count
CL = format modifiers:
    bit 4: generate periodic interrupt
    bit 3: perform surface analysis
    bit 2: update secondary defect map
    bit 1: ignore secondary defect map
    bit 0: ignore primary defect map
DL = drive
ES:BX -> defect table

Restrictions: none.

Return Registers:
CF set on error
    AH = status (Table 6-1)

Details: If periodic interrupt is selected, INT 15h Function 0Fh is called after each cylinder is formatted.

Conflicts: Future Domain SCSI Controller.
See Also: Function 07h, INT 15h Function 0Fh

INTERRUPT 13h - Function 1Ah
Future Domain - GET SCSI PARTIAL MEDIUM CAPACITY

Purpose: Determine media capacity for SCSI drive.

Available on: Machines with Future Domain SCSI controller present.

Registers at call:
AH = 1Ah
CH = track (bits 8, 9 in high bits of CL)
CL = sector (01h to number of sectors/track for drive)
DH = head
DL = hard drive ID

Restrictions: none.

Return Registers:
CF set on error
AH = status code (Table 6-1)
CX:DX = logical block number of last quickly-accessible block after given block

Details: Sends SCSI Read Capacity command with the PMI bit set to obtain the logical block address of the last block after which a substantial delay in data transfer will be encountered (usually the last block on the current cylinder). No translation to 512 byte sectors is performed on the result if data is stored on the disk in other than 512 byte sectors.

Conflicts: ESDI Fixed Disk.

See Also: Function 15h, Future Domain Function 19h

INTERRUPT 13h - Function 1Bh
GET ESDI MANUFACTURING HEADER

Purpose: Get list of manufacturing defects for the specified drive.

Available on: Systems with ESDI fixed disk.

Registers at call:
AH = 1Bh
AL = number of record
DL = drive
ES:BX -> buffer for manufacturing header (defect list)

Restrictions: none.

Return Registers:
CF set on error
AH = status

Details: The manufacturing header format (Defect Map Record format) can be found in the IBM 70MB, 115MB Fixed Disk Drives Technical Reference.

Conflicts: Future Domain SCSI Controller.

INTERRUPT 13h - Function 1Bh
Future Domain - GET POINTER TO SCSI DISK INFO BLOCK

Purpose: Return pointer to SCSI information block.

Available on: Machines with Future Domain SCSI controller present.

Registers at call:
AH = 1Bh
DL = hard drive ID

Restrictions: none.

Return Registers:
CF set on error
  AH = status code (Table 6-1)
CF clear if successful
    ES:BX -> SCSI disk information block
    (Table 6-5)

Details: Also sets a non-resettable flag which prevents some controller messages from being displayed.

Conflicts: Get ESDI Manufacturing Header.

See Also: Future Domain Functions 18h and 1Ch

Table 6-5. Format of SCSI disk information block:

Offset	Size	Description
00h	BYTE	drive physical information:
		bit 0: *unknown*.
		bit 1: device uses parity
		bit 2: 256 bytes per sector instead of 512
		bit 3: don't have capacity yet???
		bit 4: disk is removable
		bit 5: logical unit number is not present
01h	WORD	translated number of cylinders
03h	BYTE	translated number of heads
04h	BYTE	translated number of sectors per track (17, 34, or 63)
05h	BYTE	drive address:
		bits 0-2: logical unit number
		bits 3-5: device number
06h	BYTE	01h at initialization
07h	BYTE	sense code byte 00h, or extended sense code byte 0Ch
08h	BYTE	00h
09h	BYTE	00h or extended sense code byte 02h (sense key)
0Ah	BYTE	00h
0Bh	10 BYTEs	copy of Command Descriptor Block (CDB)
15h	DWORD	translated number of sectors on device

INTERRUPT 13h - Function 1Ch
Future Domain - GET POINTER TO FREE SCSI CONTROLLER RAM

Purpose: Obtain address of first byte of free RAM in controller.

Available on: Machines with Future Domain SCSI controller present.

Restrictions: none.

Registers at call:
AH = 1Ch
DL = hard drive ID (any valid SCSI hard disk)

Return Registers:
CF set on error
   AH = status code (Table 6-1)
CF clear if successful
   ES:BX -> first byte of free RAM on controller

Details: The Future Domain TMC-870 contains 1024 bytes of RAM at offsets 1800h to 1BFFh on-board the controller for storing drive information and controller status; ES:BX points to the first byte available for other uses. ES contains the segment at which the controller resides; the controller's two memory-mapped I/O ports are at offsets 1C00h and 1E00h.

Conflicts: ESDI Fixed Disk.

See Also: Future Domain Function 1Bh

INTERRUPT 13h - Function 1Ch, Subfunction 0Ah
GET ESDI DEVICE CONFIGURATION

Purpose: Determine configuration of ESDI fixed disk.

Available on: PS/2 systems with ESDI fixed disk.

Registers at call:
AX = 1C0Ah
DL = drive
ES:BX -> buffer for device configuration
   (drive physical parameters)

Restrictions: none.
Return Registers:
CF set on error
AH = status

Details: The device configuration format can be found in the IBM ESDI Fixed Disk Drive Adapter/A Technical Reference.

Conflicts: Future Domain - Get Pointer to Free SCSI Controller RAM.

INTERRUPT 13h - Function 1Ch, Subfunction 0Bh
GET ESDI ADAPTER CONFIGURATION

Purpose: Read adapter configuration into buffer.
Available on: PS/2 systems with ESDI fixed disk.   **Restrictions:** none.
Registers at call: **Return Registers:**
AX = 1C0Bh   CF set on error
ES:BX -> buffer for adapter configuration   AH = status
Conflicts: Future Domain - Get Pointer to Free SCSI Controller RAM.
See Also: Function 1C0Ch

INTERRUPT 13h - Function 1Ch, Subfunction 0Ch
GET ESDI POS INFORMATION

Purpose: Read Programmable Option Select information into buffer.
Available on: PS/2 systems with ESDI fixed disk.   **Restrictions:** none.
Registers at call: **Return Registers:**
AX = 1C0Ch   CF set on error
ES:BX -> POS information   AH = status
Conflicts: Future Domain - Get Pointer to Free SCSI Controller RAM.
See Also: ESDI Function 1Ch Subfunction 0Bh

INTERRUPT 13h - Function 1Ch, Subfunction 0Eh
ESDI - TRANSLATE RBA TO ABA

Purpose: Convert relative block address format to absolute block address format.
Available on: PS/2 systems with ESDI fixed disk.   **Restrictions:** none.
Registers at call: **Return Registers:**
AX = 1C0Eh   CF set on error
CH = low 8 bits of cylinder number   AH = status
CL = sector number, high two bits of cylinder
    number in bits 6 and 7
DH = head number
DL = drive number
ES:BX -> ABA number
Details: ABA (absolute block address) format can be found in IBM ESDI Adapter Technical Reference by using its Device Configuration Status Block.
Conflicts: Future Domain - Get Pointer to Free SCSI Controller RAM.

INTERRUPT 13h - Function 70h
Priam EDVR.SYS DISK PARTITIONING SOFTWARE

Purpose: *unknown.*
Available on: All machines using Priam software.   **Restrictions:** none.
Registers at call: **Return Registers:** *unknown.*
AH = 70h
Others, if any, unknown.
Details: Priam's EDISK.EXE (FDISK replacement) and EFMT.EXE (low-level formatting program) make this call, presumably to EDVR.SYS (the partitioning driver).
Conflicts: None known.
See Also: Function ADh

INTERRUPT 13h - Function ADh
Priam HARD DISK CONTROLLER

Purpose: *unknown.*
Available on: All machines using Priam controller.   **Restrictions:** none.

Registers at call:
AH = ADh
Others, if any, unknown.
Return Registers: *unknown.*
Details: This call is made from Priam's EFMT.EXE (low-level formatter), probably to check the ROM type on the controller for their hard disk kits.
Conflicts: None known.
See Also: Function 70h

INTERRUPT 13h - Function EEh
SWBIOS - SET 1024 CYLINDER FLAG

Purpose: Sets flag so that the following INT 13h call will interpret the desired cylinder number as 1024 more than the specified cylinder. The flag is cleared by all INT 13h calls except this one.
Available on: All machines using SWBIOS.
Restrictions: none.
Registers at call:
AH = EEh
DL = drive number (80h, 81h)
Return Registers:
CF clear
AH = 00h
Details: SWBIOS is a TSR by Ontrack Computer Systems; Disk Manager, HyperDisk v4.01+, and PC-Cache v6.0 also support this call.
Conflicts: HyperDisk 4.01.
See Also: SWBIOS Functions F9h and FEh

INTERRUPT 13h - Function F9h
SWBIOS - INSTALLATION CHECK

Purpose: Determines whether SWBIOS is present in system. SWBIOS is a TSR by Ontrack Computer Systems.
Available on: All machines.
Restrictions: none.
Registers at call:
AH = F9h
DL = drive number (80h, 81h)
Return Registers:
CF clear
    DX = configuration word
        bit 15 set if other SWBIOS extensions
           available
CF set on error

Details: Disk Manager also supports these calls.
Conflicts: None known.
See Also: SWBIOS Function EEh

INTERRUPT 13h - Function FEh
SWBIOS - GET EXTENDED CYLINDER COUNT

Purpose: Read size of drive larger than 1024 cylinders.
Available on: All machines with SWBIOS installed.
Restrictions: none.
Registers at call:
AH = FEh
DL = drive number (80h, 81h)
Return Registers:
CF clear
DX = number of cylinders beyond 1024 on drive
Details: SWBIOS is a TSR by Ontrack Computer Systems; Disk Manager also supports these calls.
    Standard INT 13h Function 08h will return a cylinder count truncated to 1024. BIOS without this extension would return count modulo 1024.
Conflicts: None known.
See Also: SWBIOS Function EEh

INTERRUPT 4Bh
Common Access Method SCSI interface (draft revision 1.9)

Purpose: Standardize methods for communicating with SCSI devices.
Available on: All machines.
Restrictions: CAM SCSI interface must be present.

Details: The CAM committee moved the interface to INT 4Fh after revision 1.9 to avoid conflicting with the IBM SCSI interface and the Virtual DMA specification. It is not known whether any drivers actually implemented this interface on INT 4Bh instead of INT 4Fh.

The installation check for the driver is the string "SCSI_CAM" eight bytes past the INT 4Bh handler.

Conflicts: IBM SCSI interface, Virtual DMA (chapter 12).

See Also: INT 4Fh

INTERRUPT 4Bh - Function 80h
IBM SCSI interface

Purpose: Permit access to IBM SCSI disks.

Available on: IBM PS/2 models with IBM SCSI controllers.

Restrictions: none.

Registers at call:
AH = 80h
additional registers unknown.

Return Registers: *unknown.*

Conflicts: Common Access Method revision 1.9

INTERRUPT 4Fh - Function 8100h
Common Access Method SCSI interface - SEND CCB TO XPT/SIM

Purpose: Execute commands on SCSI devices in a vendor-independent manner.

Available on: Machines equipped with a SCSI host adaptor

Restrictions: SCSI interface conforming to CAM revision 2.3 or higher must be installed

Registers at call:
AX = 8100h
ES:BX -> CAM Control Block (Table 6-6)

Return Registers:
AH = status
  00h successful
  01h invalid CCB address (0000h:0000h)

Details: The SCSI Interface Module (SIM) may complete the requested function and invoke the completion callback function before this call returns.

Conflicts: Z100 Slave 8259 (chapter 2)

See Also: Function 8200h, INT 4Bh

Table 6-6. Format of CAM Control Block:

Offset	Size	Description
00h	DWORD	physical address of this CCB
04h	WORD	CAM control block length
06h	BYTE	function code (Table 6-7)
07h	BYTE	CAM status (Table 6-8)
08h	BYTE	SCSI status
09h	BYTE	path ID (FFh = XPT)
0Ah	BYTE	target ID
0Bh	BYTE	logical unit number
0Ch	BYTE	CAM flags

        bits 7-6: direction
           00 reserved
           01 in
           10 out
           11 no data transfer
      bit 5: disable autosense
      bit 4: scatter/gather
      bit 3: disable callback on completion
      bit 2: linked CDB
      bit 1: tagged queue action enable
      bit 0: CDB is a pointer

Table 6-6. Format of CAM Control Block (continued)

Offset	Size	Description
0Dh	BYTE	CAM flags

      bit 7: disable disconnect
      bit 6: initiate synchronous transfers mutually
      bit 5: disable synchronous transfers   /exclusive
      bit 4: SIM queue priority
            1 head insertion
            0 tail insertion (normal)
      bit 3: SIM queue freeze
      bit 2: engine synchronize
      bits 1-0: reserved

Offset	Size	Description
0Eh	BYTE	CAM address flags

      bit 7: SG list/data (0 = host, 1 = engine)
      bit 6: CDB pointer   (bits 6-1: 0=virtual addr,1=phys addr)
      bit 5: SG list/data
      bit 4: sense buffer
      bit 3: message buffer
      bit 2: next CCB
      bit 1: callback on completion
      bit 0: reserved

Offset	Size	Description
0Fh	BYTE	target-mode flags

      bit 7: data buffer valid
      bit 6: status valid
      bit 5: message buffer valid
      bit 4: reserved
      bit 3: phase-cognizant mode
      bit 2: target CCB available
      bit 1: disable autodisconnect
      bit 0: disable autosave/restore

---function 02h

Offset	Size	Description
10h	DWORD	pointer to 36-byte buffer for inquiry data or 0000h:0000h
14h	BYTE	peripheral device type of target logical unit number

---function 03h

Offset	Size	Description
10h	BYTE	version number (00h-07h prior to rev 1.7, 08h = rev 1.7, 09h-FFh = rev no, i.e. 23h = rev 2.3
11h	BYTE	SCSI capabilities

      bit 7: modify data pointers
      bit 6: wide bus (32 bits)
      bit 5: wide bus (16 bits)
      bit 4: synchronous transfers
      bit 3: linked commands
      bit 2: reserved
      bit 1: tagged queueing
      bit 0: soft reset

Offset	Size	Description
12h	BYTE	target mode support

      bit 7: processor mode
      bit 6: phase-cognizant mode
      bits 5-0: reserved

Offset	Size	Description
13h	BYTE	miscellaneous flags

      bit 7: scanned high to low instead of low to high
      bit 6: removables not included in scan
      bit 5: inquiry data not kept by XPT
      bit 4-0: reserved

Offset	Size	Description
14h	WORD	engine count
16h	14 BYTEs	vendor-specific data

Table 6-6. Format of CAM Control Block (continued)

24h	DWORD	size of private data area
28h	DWORD	asynchronous event capabilities
		bits 31-24: vendor-specific
		bits 23-8: reserved
		bit 7: new devices found during rescan
		bit 6: SIM module deregistered
		bit 5: SIM module registered
		bit 4: sent bus device reset to target
		bit 3: SCSI AEN
		bit 2: reserved
		bit 1: unsolicited reselection
		bit 0: unsolicited SCSI bus reset
2Ch	BYTE	highest path ID assigned
2Dh	BYTE	SCSI device ID of initiator
2Eh	2 BYTEs	reserved
30h	16 BYTEs	SIM vendor ID
40h	16 BYTEs	HBA (host bus adaptor) vendor ID
50h	4 BYTEs	operating-system dependant usage

---functions 00h,04h,11h,12h
no additional fields

---function 05h

10h	DWORD	asynchronous event enables (see function 03h)
14h	DWORD	pointer to asynchronous callback routine
18h	DWORD	pointer to peripheral driver buffer
1Ch	BYTE	size of peripheral buffer

---function 06h

10h	BYTE	peripheral device type of target

---functions 10h,13h

10h	DWORD	pointer to CCB to be aborted

---function 20h

10h	WORD	engine number
12h	BYTE	engine type
		00h buffer memory
		01h lossless compression
		02h lossy compression
		03h encryption
13h	BYTE	engine algorithm ID
		00h vendor-unique
		01h LZ1 variation 1 (STAC)
		02h LZ2 variation 1 (HP DCZL)
		03h LZ2 variation 2 (Infochip)
14h	DWORD	engine memory size

---function 21h

10h	DWORD	pointer to peripheral driver
14h	4 BYTEs	reserved
18h	DWORD	OS-dependent request-mapping info
1Ch	DWORD	address of completion callback routine
20h	DWORD	pointer to scatter/gather list or data buffer
24h	DWORD	length of data transfer
28h	DWORD	pointer to engine buffer data
2Ch	2 BYTEs	reserved
2Eh	WORD	number of scatter/gather entries
30h	DWORD	maximum destination data length
34h	DWORD	length of destination data
38h	DWORD	source residual length

Table 6-6. Format of CAM Control Block (continued)

Offset	Size	Description
---function 21h *(continued)*		
3Ch	12 BYTEs	reserved
48h	DWORD	OS-dependent timeout value
4Ch	4 BYTEs	reserved
50h	WORD	engine number
52h	WORD	vendor-unique flags
54h	4 BYTEs	reserved
58h	N BYTEs	private data area for SIM
---function 30h		
10h	WORD	group 6 vendor-unique CDB length
12h	WORD	group 7 vendor-unique CDB length
14h	DWORD	pointer to target CCB list
18h	WORD	number of target CCBs
---other functions		
10h	DWORD	pointer to peripheral driver
14h	DWORD	pointer to next CCB
18h	DWORD	OS-dependent request mapping information
1Ch	DWORD	address of completion callback routine
20h	DWORD	pointer to scatter/gather list or data buffer
24h	DWORD	length of data transfer
28h	DWORD	pointer to sense info buffer
2Ch	BYTE	length of sense info buffer
2Dh	BYTE	CDB length
2Eh	WORD	number of scatter/gather entries
30h	4 BYTEs	reserved
34h	BYTE	SCSI status
35h	3 BYTEs	reserved
38h	DWORD	residual length
40h	12 BYTEs	Command Descriptor Block (CDB)
44h	DWORD	OS-dependent timeout value
48h	DWORD	pointer to message buffer
4Ch	WORD	length of message buffer
4Eh	WORD	vendor-unique flags
50h	BYTE	tag queue action
51h	3 BYTEs	reserved
54h	N BYTEs	private data area for SIM

Table 6-7. Values for CAM function code:

Value	Meaning	Value	Meaning
00h	NOP	12h	reset SCSI device
01h	execute SCSI I/O	13h	terminate I/O process
02h	get device type	14h-1Fh	reserved
03h	path inquiry	20h	engine inquiry
04h	release SIM queue	21h	execute engine request
05h	set async callback	22h-2Fh	reserved
06h	set device type	30h	enable logical unit number
07h-0Fh	reserved	31h	execute target I/O
10h	abort SCSI command	32h-7Fh	reserved
11h	reset SCSI bus	80h-FFh	vendor-specific functions

Table 6-8. Values for CAM status:

Value	Meaning	Value	Meaning
00h	request in progress	11h	no HBA detected
01h	request successful	12h	data over/underrun
02h	host aborted request	13h	bus freed unexpectedly
03h	unable to abort request	14h	target bus phase sequence failure
04h	request completed with error	15h	CCB too small
05h	CAM is busy	16h	requested capability not available
06h	invalid request	17h	sent bus device reset
07h	invalid path ID	18h	terminate I/O process
08h	no such SCSI device	38h	invalid LUN
09h	unable to terminate I/O process	39h	invalid target ID
0Ah	timeout on target selection	3Ah	unimplemented function
0Bh	timeout on command	3Bh	nexus not established
0Dh	receive message rejection	3Ch	invalid initiator ID
0Eh	sent/received SCSI bus reset	3Dh	received SCSI Command Descriptor Block
0Fh	detected uncorrectable parity error	3Eh	LUN already enabled
10h	Autosense request failed	3Fh	SCSI bus busy

Note: bit 6 of the status is set to indicate a frozen SIM queue; bit 7 is set to indicate valid autosense

Completion callback function called with:
> interrupts disabled
> ES:BX -> completed CCB

Asynchronous callback function called with:
> AH = opcode
> AL = path ID generating callback
> DH = target ID causing event
> DL = LUN causing event
> CX = data byte count (if applicable)
> ES:BX -> data buffer (if applicable)

Return with: all registers preserved

INTERRUPT 4Fh - Function 8200h
Common Access Method rev 2.3 - INSTALLATION CHECK

Purpose: Determine whether a driver conforming to the CAM SCSI interface specification (revision 2.3 or higher) is installed.

Available on: Machines equipped with a SCSI host adaptor

Restrictions: none.

Registers at call:
AX = 8200h
CX = 8765h
DX = CBA9h

Return Registers:
AH = 00h if installed
> CX = 9ABCh
> DX = 5678h
> ES:DI -> "SCSI_CAM"

Conflicts: Z100 Slave 8259 (chapter 2)
See Also: Function 8100h, INT 4Bh

INTERRUPTS 60h to 63h
Adaptec and OMTI controllers - DRIVE 0 DATA

Purpose: These interrupts do not contain any addresses; rather, they store the actual hard disk parameter table pointed at by INT 41h.

Available on: Machines with Adaptec and OMTI hard-disk controllers.

Restrictions: none.

Details: Adaptec controllers which use these interrupts for data storage provide a small device driver which relocates the data into the device driver, protecting it from corruption and allowing the use of these interrupts for actual vectors.

Conflicts: 4+Power Floppy Controller Original INT 13h/INT 40h, Oracle SQL Protected Mode Executive (chapter 9). Also see Table 1-3 in Chapter 1.

See Also: Adaptec INT 64h

INTERRUPTS 64h to 67h
Adaptec controllers - DRIVE 1 DATA

Purpose: These interrupts do not contain any addresses; rather, they store the actual hard disk parameter table pointed at by INT 46h.

Available on: Machines with Adaptec hard-disk controllers.   **Restrictions:** none.

Details: Adaptec controllers which use these interrupts for data storage provide a small device driver which relocates the data into the device driver, protecting it from corruption and allowing the use of these interrupts for actual vectors.

Conflicts: EMS (chapter 10). Also see Table 1-3 in Chapter 1.

See Also: Adaptec/OMTI INT 60h

INTERRUPT 78h - Function 00h
TARGA.DEV - SET I/O PORT

Purpose: Specify at which location in the I/O address space the SCSI controller may be accessed.

Available on: All machines.   **Restrictions:** TARGA.DEV must be installed.

Registers at call: **Return Registers:**

AH = 00h   CF set on error

DX = interface board I/O port

　　　　　AL = error code

　　　　　　　00h illegal command given to SCSI code

　　　　　　　01h invalid I/O port specified (must be from 100H to 3F8H, and must be on an 8-port boundary)

　　　　　　　02h invalid DMA channel specified (must be from 1 to 3)

　　　　　　　03h invalid SCSI board number specified (must be from 0 to 7)

　　　　　　　04h error from data register during self-test

　　　　　　　05h SCSI input signals not all 0 when SCSI RST activated

　　　　　　　06h SCSI input signals not all 0 before selecting a SCSI device

　　　　　　　07h BSY signal is active; SCSI bus is busy

　　　　　　　08h SCSI board not selected, BSY signal did not come on in response to raising SEL

　　　　　　　09h time-out waiting for status state, signifying end of DMA transfer

Details: TARGA.DEV is a CMC International SCSI device driver. If this routine is not called, the port is the driver's default (usually 0280h or 0300h). An installation check is performed by TARGA.DEV upon initialization by checking for the string "SCSI" at offset 03h into the interrupt handler.

Conflicts: DBOS (chapter 9).

See Also: Functions 01h and 02h

INTERRUPT 78h - Function 01h
TARGA.DEV - GET I/O PORT

Purpose: Determine at which location in the I/O address space the SCSI controller may be accessed.

Available on: All machines.
Registers at call:
AH = 01h
Details: TARGA.DEV is a CMC International SCSI device driver.
Conflicts: DBOS (chapter 9).
See Also: Functions 00h and 03h

Restrictions: TARGA.DEV must be installed.
Return Registers:
DX = current interface board I/O port

INTERRUPT 78h - Function 02h
TARGA.DEV - SET DMA CHANNEL

Purpose: Specify which DMA channel the SCSI controller should use for data transfers.
Available on: All machines.
Registers at call:
AH = 02h
AL = interface board DMA channel

Restrictions: TARGA.DEV must be installed.
Return Registers:
CF set on error
 AL = error code (see Function 00h)

Details: TARGA.DEV is a CMC International SCSI device driver. If this routine is not called, the DMA channel used will be the driver's default (usually 3).
Conflicts: DBOS (chapter 9).
See Also: Functions 00h and 03h

INTERRUPT 78h - Function 03h
TARGA.DEV - GET DMA CHANNEL

Purpose: Determine which DMA channel the SCSI controller is using for data transfers.
Available on: All machines.
Registers at call:
AH = 03h

Restrictions: TARGA.DEV must be installed.
Return Registers:
AL = current interface board DMA channel

Details: TARGA.DEV is a CMC International SCSI device driver.
Conflicts: DBOS (chapter 9).
See Also: Functions 01h and 02h

INTERRUPT 78h - Function 04h
TARGA.DEV - SET SCSI DEVICE NUMBER

Purpose: Specify the logical device number for the SCSI controller.
Available on: All machines.
Registers at call:
AH = 04h
AL = SCSI device number

Restrictions: TARGA.DEV must be installed.
Return Registers:
CF set on error
 AL = error code (see AH=00h)

Details: If this routine is not called, the device number used will be the driver's default (usually 0)
Conflicts: DBOS (chapter 9).
See Also: Functions 02h and 05h

INTERRUPT 78h - Function 05h
TARGA.DEV - GET SCSI DEVICE NUMBER

Purpose: Determine the current logical device number of the SCSI controller.
Available on: All machines.
Registers at call:
AH = 05h

Restrictions: TARGA.DEV must be installed.
Return Registers:
AL = current SCSI device number

Details: TARGA.DEV is a CMC International SCSI device driver.
Conflicts: DBOS (chapter 9).
See Also: Functions 03h and 04h

INTERRUPT 78h - Function 06h
TARGA.DEV - SET/CLEAR EARLY RETURN MODE

Purpose: Specify whether a SCSI command function call may return before the command completes.

Available on: All machines.
Registers at call:
AH = 06h
AL = 00h clear early return mode
   = 01h set early return mode

Restrictions: TARGA.DEV must be installed.
Return Registers: n/a

Details: If early return mode is set then SCSI will return with no errors when the last DMA transfer is started in a call to Functions 13h or 14h. Early return mode is cleared until this function is called.
Conflicts: DBOS (chapter 9).
See Also: Functions 13h, 14h, and 15h

INTERRUPT 78h - Function 08h
TARGA.DEV - INTERFACE BOARD SELF-TEST

Purpose: Perform diagnostics on the SCSI controller.
Available on: All machines.
Registers at call:
AH = 08h

Restrictions: TARGA.DEV must be installed.
Return Registers:
CF set on error
   AL = error code (see Function 00h)

Details: This function also resets the SCSI bus.
Conflicts: DBOS (chapter 9).
See Also: Function 09h

INTERRUPT 78h - Function 09h
TARGA.DEV - RESET SCSI BUS

Purpose: Reset the SCSI bus.
Available on: All machines.
Registers at call:
AH = 09h

Restrictions: TARGA.DEV must be installed.
Return Registers:
CF set on error
   AL = error code (see Function 00h)

Details: TARGA.DEV is a CMC International SCSI device driver.
Conflicts: DBOS (chapter 9).
See Also: Function 08h

INTERRUPT 78h - Function 10h
TARGA.DEV - SEND SCSI COMMAND

Purpose: Transmit a requets to the SCSI controller which does not involve a data transfer.
Available on: All machines.
Registers at call:
AH = 10h
DS:SI -> command bytes (Table 6-9)

Restrictions: TARGA.DEV must be installed.
Return Registers:
AH = SCSI status byte
CF clear if successful
   AL = SCSI message byte
CF set on error
   AL = error code (see Function 00h)

Details: TARGA.DEV is a CMC International SCSI device driver.
Conflicts: DBOS (chapter 9).
See Also: Function 11h

Table 6-9. Format of SCSI Command:

Offset	Size	Description
00h	BYTE	length of command
01h	variable	command bytes

INTERRUPT 78h - Function 11h
TARGA.DEV - SEND SCSI COMMAND, RECEIVE DATA (PROGRAMMED I/O)

Purpose: Transmit a request to read data from a device on the SCSI bus.

Available on: All machines.

Registers at call:
AH = 11h
DS:SI -> command bytes (Table 6-9)
ES:BX -> data storage area
CX = number of data bytes to transfer

Restrictions: TARGA.DEV must be installed.

Return Registers:
AH = SCSI status byte
CF clear if successful
    AL = SCSI message byte
CF set on error
    AL = error code (see AH=00h)

Details: This command receives data internally one byte at a time, using the CPU to receive each byte.

Conflicts: DBOS (chapter 9).

See Also: Functions 10h and 13h

INTERRUPT 78h - Function 12h
TARGA.DEV - SEND SCSI COMMAND AND DATA (PROGRAMMED I/O)

Purpose: Transmit a request to write data to a device on the SCSI bus.

Available on: All machines.

Registers at call:
AH = 12h
DS:SI -> command bytes (Table 6-9)
ES:BX -> data storage area
CX = number of data bytes to transfer

Restrictions: TARGA.DEV must be installed.

Return Registers:
AH = SCSI status byte
CF clear if successful
    AL = SCSI message byte
CF set on error
    AL = error code (see AH=00h)

Details: This command sends data internally one byte at a time, using the CPU to send each byte.

Conflicts: DBOS (chapter 9).

See Also: Function 14h

INTERRUPT 78h - Function 13h
TARGA.DEV - SEND SCSI COMMAND, RECEIVE DATA (DMA)

Purpose: Transmit a request to read data from a device on the SCSI bus.

Available on: All machines.

Registers at call:
AH = 13h
DS:SI -> command bytes (Table 6-9)
ES:BX -> data storage area
DX:CX = number of data bytes to transfer

Restrictions: TARGA.DEV must be installed.

Return Registers:
AH = SCSI status byte (if early return mode is clear)
CF clear if successful
    AL = SCSI message byte (if early return mode is
      clear)
CF set on error
    AL = error code (see AH=00h)

Details: This command receives data using DMA transfers.

Conflicts: DBOS (chapter 9).

See Also: Functions 11h and 12h

INTERRUPT 78h - Function 14h
TARGA.DEV - SEND SCSI COMMAND AND DATA (DMA)

Purpose: Transmit a request to write data to a device on the SCSI bus.

Available on: All machines.

Restrictions: TARGA.DEV must be installed.

Registers at call:
AH = 14h
DS:SI -> command bytes (Table 6-9)
ES:BX -> data storage area
DX:CX = number of data bytes to transfer

Return Registers:
AH = SCSI status byte (if early return mode is clear)
CF clear if successful
    AL = SCSI message byte (if early return mode is clear)
CF set on error
    AL = error code (see Function 00h)

Details: This command sends data using DMA transfers.
Conflicts: DBOS (chapter 9).
See Also: Functions 12h and 13h

INTERRUPT 78h - Function 15h
TARGA.DEV - FINISH DATA TRANSFER (DMA)

Purpose: Wait until the last SCSI command completes.
Available on: All machines.
Registers at call:
AH = 15h

Restrictions: TARGA.DEV must be installed.
Return Registers:
AH = SCSI status byte
CF clear if successful
    AL = SCSI message byte
CF set on error
    AL = error code (see Function 00h)

Details: If Function 06h was previously called to set the early return mode, this function terminates a command started by Function 13h or 14h which returned before the last DMA transfer was completed.
Conflicts: DBOS (chapter 9).
See Also: Functions 06h, 13h, and 14h

Disk Caches
The functions described in this section are used by disk cache programs.

INTERRUPT 13h - Function 1Dh
IBMCACHE.SYS - CACHE STATUS

Purpose: Determine or update cache status.
Available on: All machines.
Registers at call:
AH = 1Dh
AL = subfunction:
    01h get status record:
        DL = *drive*

        02h set cache status:
        ES:BX -> status record (Table 6-10)
    DL = *drive*
Conflicts: None known.

Restrictions: IBMCACHE.SYS must be installed.
Return Registers:

ES:BX -> status record (Table 6-10)
CF set on error
    AH = error code
CF set on error

Table 6-10. Format of status record:

Offset	Size	Description
00h	DWORD	total number of read requests
04h	DWORD	total number of hits
08h	DWORD	number of physical disk reads
0Ch	DWORD	total number of sectors requested by physical disk reads
10h	6 BYTEs	*unknown.*
16h	DWORD	pointer to start of error list (Table 6-11)
1Ah	DWORD	pointer to end of error list

Table 6-10. Format of status record (continued)

Offset	Size	Description
1Eh	WORD	*unknown.*
20h	BYTE	using extended memory if nonzero
21h	BYTE	*unknown.*
22h	4 BYTEs	ASCII version number
26h	WORD	cache size in K
28h	WORD	sectors per page

Table 6-11. Format of error list entry:

Offset	Size	Description
00h	DWORD	relative block address of bad page
04h	BYTE	drive
05h	BYTE	sector bit-map
06h	WORD	next error

INTERRUPT 13h - Function 20h, Subfunction FFh
QCACHE - DISMOUNT

Purpose: Apparently used to remove QCACHE from system.

Available on: All machines.

Registers at call:
AX = 20FFh

Conflicts: Western Digital "Super BIOS"

Restrictions: QCACHE must be installed.

Return Registers: *unknown.*

INTERRUPT 13h - Function 21h
QCACHE - FLUSH CACHE

Purpose: Write cache content to disk and invalidate cache buffers.

Available on: All machines.

Registers at call:
AH = 21h

Conflicts: None known.

See Also: QCACHE Functions 25h and 2Eh

Restrictions: QCACHE must be installed.

Return Registers: *unknown.*

INTERRUPT 13h - Function 22h
QCACHE - ENABLE/DISABLE CACHE

Purpose: Control QCACHE operation.

Available on: All machines.

Registers at call:
AH = 22h
AL = 00h disable cache
      01h enable cache

Conflicts: None known.

Restrictions: QCACHE must be installed.

Return Registers: *unknown.*

INTERRUPT 13h - Function 24h
QCACHE - SET SECTORS

Purpose: *unknown.*

Available on: All machines.

Registers at call:
AH = 24h
BX = number of sectors

Conflicts: None known.

Restrictions: QCACHE must be installed.

Return Registers: *unknown.*

INTERRUPT 13h - Function 25h
QCACHE - SET FLUSH INTERVAL

Purpose: Establish interval for automatic cache flushing.
Available on: All machines.
Registers at call:
AH = 25h
BX = interval
Conflicts: None known.
See Also: QCACHE Functions 21h and 2Eh

Restrictions: QCACHE must be installed.
Return Registers: *unknown.*

INTERRUPT 13h - Function 27h
QCACHE - INSTALLATION CHECK

Purpose: Determine whether QCACHE is present.
Available on: All machines.
Registers at call:
AH = 27h
BX = 0000h
Conflicts: None known.

Restrictions: none.
Return Registers:
BX nonzero if installed.

INTERRUPT 13h - Function 2Ah
QCACHE - SET BUFFER SIZE

Purpose: Establish size of buffer for cache.
Available on: All machines.
Registers at call:
AH = 2Ah
AL = buffer size
Conflicts: None known.

Restrictions: QCACHE must be installed.
Return Registers: *unknown.*

INTERRUPT 13h - Function 2Ch
QCACHE - SET BUFFERED WRITES

Purpose: Control whether cache will buffer disk writes.
Available on: All machines.
Registers at call:
AH = 2Ch
AL =   00h disable buffered writes
        01h enable buffered writes
Conflicts: None known.
See Also: QCACHE Function 2Dh

Restrictions: QCACHE must be installed.
Return Registers: *unknown.*

INTERRUPT 13h - Function 2Dh
QCACHE - SET BUFFERED READ

Purpose: Control whether cache will buffer disk reads.
Available on: All machines.
Registers at call:
AH = 2Dh
AL =   00h disable buffered reads
        01h enable buffered reads
Conflicts: None known.
See Also: QCACHE Function 2Ch

Restrictions: QCACHE must be installed.
Return Registers: *unknown.*

INTERRUPT 13h - Function 2Eh
QCACHE - SET FLUSH COUNT

Purpose: *unknown.*
Available on: All machines.
Registers at call:
AH = 2Eh
BX = flush count
Conflicts: None known.
See Also: QCACHE Functions 21h and 25h

Restrictions: QCACHE must be installed.
Return Registers: *unknown.*

INTERRUPT 13h - Function 30h
QCACHE - GET INFO

Purpose: Determine cache operating conditions.
Available on: All machines.
Registers at call:
AH = 30h
AL = what to get:
    00h system info
    01h drive info
DS:DX -> buffer for info
Conflicts: None known.

Restrictions: QCACHE must be installed.
Return Registers: *unknown.*

INTERRUPT 13h - Function 75h
Unknown Function

Purpose: *unknown.*
Available on: All machines.
Registers at call:
AH = 75h
addtional registers, if any, unknown
Details: This function is intercepted by PC-Cache (v5.1 only), but no further information is known about it.

Restrictions: none.
Return Registers: *unknown*

INTERRUPT 13h - Function 76h
Unknown Function

Purpose: *unknown.*
Available on: All machines.
Registers at call:
AH = 76h
addtional registers, if any, unknown
Details: This function is intercepted by PC-Cache (v5.1 only), but no further information is known about it.

Restrictions: none.
Return Registers: *unknown*

INTERRUPT 13h - Function 81h
Super PC Kwik/PC-Cache 5.x - Unknown Function

Purpose: *unknown.*
Available on: All machines.

Restrictions: Super PC Kwik or PC-Cache v5.x must
be loaded.
Return Registers: *unknown.*

Registers at call:
AH = 81h
SI = 4358h
Other registers, if any, unknown.
Details: PC Tools PC-Cache v5.x is an OEM version of Super PC Kwik, and thus supports this call. However, PC-Cache does nothing and returns immediately.
Conflicts: None known.

INTERRUPT 13h - Function 82h
Super PC Kwik/PC-Cache 5.x - Unknown Function

Purpose: *unknown.*
Available on: All machines.

Restrictions: Super PC Kwik or PC-Cache v5.x must be loaded.

Registers at call:
AH = 82h
SI = 4358h
Other registers, if any, unknown.

Return Registers:
AL = *unknown*
additional return values, if any, unknown.

Details: PC Tools PC-Cache v5.x is an OEM version of Super PC Kwik, and thus supports this call.
Conflicts: None known.
See Also: Function 84h

INTERRUPT 13h - Function 83h
Super PC Kwik/PC-Cache 5.x - Unknown Function

Purpose: *unknown.*
Available on: All machines.

Restrictions: Super PC Kwik or PC-Cache v5.x must be loaded.

Registers at call:
AH = 83h
SI = 4358h
AL = *unknown*
ES:BX -> *unknown*
other registers, if any, unknown.

Return Registers: *unknown.*

Details: PC Tools PC-Cache v5.x is an OEM version of Super PC Kwik, and thus supports this call.
Conflicts: None known.
See Also: Function 85h

INTERRUPT 13h - Function 84h
Super PC Kwik/PC-Cache 5.x - Unknown Function

Purpose: *unknown.*
Available on: All machines.

Restrictions: Super PC Kwik or PC-Cache v5.x must be loaded.

Registers at call:
AH = 84h
SI = 4358h
AL = *unknown*
other registers, if any, unknown.

Return Registers:
AL = *unknown*
additional return values, if any, unknown.

Details: PC Tools PC-Cache v5.x is an OEM version of Super PC Kwik, and thus supports this call.
Conflicts: None known.
See Also: Function 82h

INTERRUPT 13h - Function 85h
Super PC Kwik/PC-Cache 5.x - Unknown Function

Purpose: *unknown.*
Available on: All machines.

Restrictions: Super PC Kwik or PC-Cache v5.x must be loaded.

Registers at call:
AH = 85h
SI = 4358h
AL = *unknown*
DL = *unknown*
other registers, if any, unknown.
Details: PC Tools PC-Cache v5.x is an OEM version of Super PC Kwik, and thus supports this call.
Conflicts: None known.
See Also: Function 83h

Return Registers: *unknown.*

INTERRUPT 13h - Function 8Eh, Subfunction EDh
HyperDisk - Unknown Function

Purpose: *unknown.*
Available on: All machines.

Restrictions: HyperDisk cache version 4.01 or higher must be installed.

Registers at call:
AX = 8EEDh
other registers, if any, unknown.
Details: HyperDisk is a shareware disk cache by Roger Cross.
Conflicts: None known.
See Also: Function 8Eh Subfunctions EEh and EFh, Function EEh

Return Registers: *unknown.*

INTERRUPT 13h - Function 8Eh, Subfunction EEh
HyperDisk - Unknown Function

Purpose: *unknown.*
Available on: All machines.

Restrictions: HyperDisk cache version 4.01 or higher must be installed.

Registers at call:
AX = 8EEEh

Return Registers:
CF set
AX = CS of HyperDisk resident code
other return values, if any, unknown.

Conflicts: None known.
See Also: Function 8Eh Subfunctions EDh and EFh, Function EEh

INTERRUPT 13h - Function 8Eh, Subfunction EFh
HyperDisk - Unknown Function

Purpose: *unknown.*
Available on: All machines.

Restrictions: HyperDisk cache version 4.01 or higher must be installed.

Registers at call:
AX = 8EEFh unknown.

Return Registers:
CF set
AX = CS of HyperDisk resident code
other return values, if any, unknown.

Conflicts: None known.
See Also: Function 8Eh Subfunction EDh and EEh, Function EEh

INTERRUPT 13h - Function A0h
Super PC Kwik - GET RESIDENT CODE SEGMENT

Purpose: Determine address at which cache TSR was loaded in order to access internal data.
Available on: All machines.

Restrictions: Super PC Kwik or PC-Cache v5.x must be loaded.

Registers at call:
AH = A0h
SI = 4358h

Return Registers:
AX = segment of resident code

Details: PC Tools PC-Cache v5.x is an OEM version of Super PC Kwik, and thus supports this call.
Conflicts: None known.
See Also: INT 16h Function FFA5h Subfunction 1111h

INTERRUPT 13h - Function A1h
Super PC Kwik - FLUSH CACHE

Purpose: Write any modified cache buffers to disk immediately, and invalidate all cache buffers.
Available on: All machines.

Restrictions: Super PC Kwik or PC-Cache v5.x must be loaded.

Registers at call:
AH = A1h
SI = 4358h

Return Registers: *unknown.*

Details: PC Tools PC-Cache v5.x is an OEM version of Super PC Kwik, and thus supports this call.
Conflicts: None known.
See Also: INT 16h Function FFA5h Subfunction FFFFh

INTERRUPT 13h - Function A2h
Super PC Kwik - Unknown Function

Purpose: *unknown.*
Available on: All machines.

Restrictions: Super PC Kwik or PC-Cache v5.x must be loaded.

Registers at call:
AH = A2h
SI = 4358h
other registers, if any, unknown.

Return Registers: *unknown.*

Details: PC Tools PC-Cache v5.x is an OEM version of Super PC Kwik, and thus supports this call.
Conflicts: None known.

INTERRUPT 13h - Function B0h
Super PC Kwik - Unknown Function

Purpose: *unknown.*
Available on: All machines.

Restrictions: Super PC Kwik or PC-Cache v5.x must be loaded.

Registers at call:
AH = B0h
SI = 4358h
other registers, if any, unknown.

Return Registers: *unknown.*

Details: PC Tools PC-Cache v5.x is an OEM version of Super PC Kwik, and thus supports this call.
Conflicts: None known.

INTERRUPT 13h - Function EEh
HyperDisk, PC-Cache - SWBIOS COMPATIBILITY

Purpose: Permit access to cylinders beyond the first 1024 supported directly by the ROM BIOS.
Available on: All machines.

Restrictions: HyperDisk (version 4.01 or higher) or PC-Cache (version 5.5 or higher) must be installed.

Registers at call:
AH = EEh
DL = drive number (80h, 81h)

Return Registers:
CF clear
AH = 00h

Details: Recent versions of HyperDisk and PC-Cache support this call in order to properly cache large disks which use SWBIOS to access more than 1024 cylinders.
Conflicts: None known.
See Also: Function 8Eh Subfunction EDh, EEh, and EFh, SWBIOS Function EEh

INTERRUPT 16h - Function FFA5h, Subfunction 1111h
PC-Cache - INSTALLATION CHECK

Purpose: Determine whether PC-Cache is loaded.
Available on: All machines.

Registers at call:
AX = FFA5h
CX = 1111h

Restrictions: Only valid for PC-Cache version 6.0 or higher.
Return Registers:
CH = 00h if installed
    ES:DI -> internal data (Table 6-12)
    CL = cache state
    01h enabled
    02h disabled

Conflicts: None known.
See Also: INT 13h Function A0h, INT 21h Function 2Bh

Table 6-12. Format of PC-Cache internal data:

Offset	Size	Description
-1Ch	20 BYTEs	cached drive list, one byte per drive A: to T: each byte is either blank (20h) or drive letter(41h-54h)
-8	BYTE	*unknown.*
-7	WORD	number of physical transfers (scaled down to 0000h-7FFFh)
-5	WORD	number of saved transfers (scaled down to 0000h-7FFFh)
-3	3 BYTEs	*unknown.*

INTERRUPT 16h - Function FFA5h, Subfunction AAAAh
PC-Cache - ENABLE DELAYED WRITES

Purpose: Allow cache to return to caller before disk writes complete.
Available on: All machines.

Registers at call:
AX = FFA5h
CX = AAAAh

Restrictions: PC-Cache version 6.0 or higher must be installed.
Return Registers:
AX = *apparently either 0000h or sectors_in_cache - 5*

Conflicts: None known.
See Also: Function FFA5h Subfunction CCCCh

INTERRUPT 16h - Function FFA5h, Subfunction CCCCh
PC-Cache - FLUSH CACHE AND DISABLE DELAYED WRITES

Purpose: Write all modified cache buffers to disk and then set cache into write-through mode.
Available on: All machines.

Registers at call:
AX = FFA5h
CX = CCCCh

Restrictions: PC-Cache version 6.0 or higher must be installed.
Return Registers:
AX = *apparently either 0000h or sectors_in_cache - 5*

Details: Delayed writes are automatically disabled on executing a program named either WIN.CO? or DV.E??; however, delayed writes are not automatically reenabled upon the program's termination in version 6.
Conflicts: None known.
See Also: Function FFA5h Subfunctions AAAAh and FFFFh

INTERRUPT 16h - Function FFA5h, Subfunction DDDDh
PC-Cache - FLUSH AND DISABLE CACHE

Purpose: Write all modified cache buffers to disk and then turn off the caching function.
Available on: All machines.   **Restrictions:** PC-Cache version 6.0 or higher must be installed.

Return Registers: n/a

Registers at call:
AX = FFA5h
CX = DDDDh
Details: After executing this function, all I/O requests will be passed directly to the disks.
Conflicts: None known.
See Also: Function FFA5h Subfunction EEEEh and FFFFh

INTERRUPT 16h - Function FFA5h, Subfunction EEEEh
PC-Cache - ENABLE CACHE

Purpose: Turn on the caching function.
Available on: All machines.   **Restrictions:** PC-Cache version 6.0 or higher must be installed.

Return Registers: n/a

Registers at call:
AX = FFA5h
CX = EEEEh
Conflicts: None known.
See Also: Function FFA5h Subfunction DDDDh

INTERRUPT 16h - Function FFA5h, Subfunction FFFFh
PC-Cache - FLUSH CACHE

Purpose: Force all modified buffers in cache to be written to disk immediately.
Available on: All machines.   **Restrictions:** PC-Cache version 6.0 or higher must be installed.

Return Registers: n/a

Registers at call:
AX = FFA5h
CX = FFFFh
Conflicts: None known.
See Also: Function FFA5h Subfunctions CCCCh and DDDDh

INTERRUPT 21h - Function 2Bh
PC Tools v5.x PC-Cache - INSTALLATION CHECK

Purpose: Determine whether PC Tools PC-Cache is present in system.
Available on: All machines.   **Restrictions:** Valid only for PC-Cache versions 5.x.
Registers at call: **Return Registers:**
AH = 2Bh   AL = FFh if PC-Cache not installed
CX = 4358h ('CX')   AL = 00h if installed
                    CX = 6378h ('cx')
                    BX = *unknown.*
                    DX = *unknown.*

Conflicts: DOS 1+ - Set System Date (chapter 8), DESQview - Installation Check (chapter 15), ELRES v1.1 (chapter 36).
See Also: INT 16h Function FFA5h Subfunction 1111h

INTERRUPT 25h - Function FFh
PC-CACHE.SYS - INSTALLATION CHECK

Purpose: Determine whether the PC-CACHE.SYS driver is loaded in support of PC-Cache v5.x.
Available on: All machines.   **Restrictions:** none.

Registers at call:
AL = FFh
SI = 4358h

Return Registers:
SI = 6378h if installed
   CX = segment of device driver
   DX = driver version (major in DH, minor in DL)

Details: PC-CACHE.SYS is a small device driver used by PC-Cache v5.x to obtain access to certain drivers for devices such as Bernoulli drives.
Conflicts: DOS Absolute Disk Read (chapter 8).

INTERRUPT 2Fh - Function DFh
Multiplex - HyperDisk v4.20+ - INSTALLATION CHECK

Purpose: Determine whether HyperDisk cache is installed. HyperDisk is a shareware disk cache by HyperWare (Roger Cross).
Available on: All machines.

Restrictions: DOS versions prior to 3.0 must verify that the interrupt vector is not 0000h:0000h before using INT 2Fh.

Registers at call:
AH = DFh
BX = 4448h ('DH')

Return Registers:
AL = 00h not installed
   FFh installed
      CX = 5948h ('YH')
      BX:DX -> ??? in resident portion if BX=4448h
on entry

Conflicts: See table 1-3 in chapter 1.
See Also: INT 13h Function 8Eh Subfunction EDh

INTERRUPT 21h - Function 44h, Subfunction 02h
SMARTDRV.SYS - GET CACHE STATUS

Purpose: Determine cache settings and caching statistics.
Available on: All machines.
Registers at call:
AX = 4402h
BX = file handle for device "SMARTAAR"
CX = number of bytes to read (min 28h)
DS:DX -> buffer for status record (Table 6-13)

Restrictions: SMARTDRV.SYS must be installed.
Return Registers:
CF clear if successful
   AX = number of bytes actually read
CF set on error
   AX = error code (01h, 05h, 06h, 0Dh)
      (see DOS Function 59h, chapter 8)

Conflicts: DOS IOCTL (chapter 8)
See Also: Function 44h Subfunction 03h

Table 6-13. Format of SMARTDRV status record:

Offset	Size	Description
00h	BYTE	write-through flag (always 01h)
01h	BYTE	writes should be buffered (always 00h)
02h	BYTE	cache enabled if 01h
03h	BYTE	driver type
04h	WORD	clock ticks between cache flushes (currently unused)
06h	BYTE	cache locked if nonzero
07h	BYTE	flush cache on reboot if nonzero
08h	BYTE	cache full track writes if nonzero
09h	BYTE	double buffering state (00h off, 01h on, 02h dynamic)
0Ah	DWORD	original INT 13 vector
0Eh	BYTE	minor version number
0Fh	BYTE	major version number
10h	WORD	unused
12h	WORD	sectors read \
14h	WORD	sectors already in cache > may be scaled rather than

Table 6-13. Format of SMARTDRV status record:

Offset	Size	Description
16h	WORD	sectors already in track buffer / absolute counts
18h	BYTE	cache hit rate in percent
19h	BYTE	track buffer hit rate in percent
1Ah	WORD	total tracks in cache
1Ch	WORD	number of tracks in use
1Eh	WORD	number of locked tracks
20h	WORD	number of dirty tracks
22h	WORD	current cache size in 16K pages
24h	WORD	original cache size in 16K pages
26h	WORD	minimum cache size in 16K pages
28h	DWORD	pointer to byte flag to increment for locking cache contents

INTERRRUPT 21h - Function 44h, Subfunction 03h
SMARTDRV.SYS - CACHE CONTROL

Purpose: Control operation of cache.
Available on: All machines.
Registers at call:
AX = 4403h
BX = handle for device "SMARTAAR"
CX = number of bytes to write
DS:DX -> SMARTDRV control block (Table 6-14)

Restrictions: SMARTDRV.SYS must be installed.
Return Registers:
CF clear if successful
    AX = number of bytes actually written
CF set on error
    AX = error code (01h, 05h, 06h, 0Dh)
        (see DOS Function 59h, chapter 8)

Conflicts: DOS IOCTL (chapter 8)
See Also: Function 44h Subfunction 02h

Table 6-14. Format of SMARTDRV control block:

Offset	Size	Description
00h	BYTE	function code
		00h flush cache
		01h flush and discard cache
		02h disable caching
		03h enable caching
		05h set flushing tick count
		06h lock cache contents
		07h unlock cache contents
		08h set flush-on-reboot flag
		0Bh reduce cache size
		0Ch increase cache size
		0Dh set INT 13 chain address

---function 08h
Offset	Size	Description
01h	BYTE	new flush-on-reboot flag (00h off, 01h on)

---functions 0Bh,0Ch
Offset	Size	Description
01h	WORD	number of 16K pages by which to increase/reduce cache size

---function 0Dh
Offset	Size	Description
01h	DWORD	new address to which to chain on INT 13 **Note:** the previous address is not preserved

Disk Compression

The functions listed in this section affect the operation of programs which increase disk capacity by compressing all data written to the disk or automatically decompressing files when they are accessed.

INTERRUPT 21h - Function 44h, Subfunction 04h
Stacker - GET DEVICE DRIVER ADDRESS AND SET VOLUME NUMBER

Purpose: Determine the address at which the Stacker device driver has been loaded, and set an internal variable indicating the current volume number.

Available on: All machines.

Registers at call:
AX = 4404h
BL = drive number (00h = default, 01h = A:, etc)
CX = 0004h
DS:DX -> DWORD buffer to receive device driver address

Restrictions: Stacker driver must be installed.

Return Registers: n/a

Details: In addition to returning the address of the Stacker device driver, this call also sets the volume number at offset 3Eh in the device driver (see INT 25h Function CDh Subfunction CDh).

See Also: INT 25h Function CDh Subfunction CDh

INTERRUPT 21h - Function 44h, Subfunction 10h
ENABLE NewSpace DRIVER

Purpose: Permit NewSpace to compress all data written to the disk and expand any compressed data which is read from the disk.

Available on: All machines.

Registers at call:
AX = 4410h
BX = FFFFh

Restrictions: NewSpace driver must be installed.

Return Registers: *unknown.*

Details: NewSpace is a TSR by Isogon Corporation which automatically compresses all files as they are written and decompresses them as they are read; compressed files are not accessible unless the driver is enabled.

Conflicts: DOS Generic IOCTL Capabilities (chapter 8)

See Also: Function 44h Subfunction 11h

INTERRUPT 21h - Function 44h, Subfunction 11h
DISABLE NewSpace DRIVER

Purpose: Prohibit NewSpace from compressing data which is written to the disk.

Available on: All machines.

Registers at call:
AX = 4411h
BX = FFFFh

Restrictions: NewSpace driver must be installed.

Return Registers: *unknown.*

Details: NewSpace is a TSR by Isogon Corporation which automatically compresses all files as they are written and decompresses them as they are read; compressed files are not accessible unless the driver is enabled

Conflicts: DOS Generic IOCTL Capabilities (chapter 8)

See Also: Function 44h Subfunction 10h

INTERRUPT 21h - Function 44h, Subfunction 12h
NewSpace INSTALLATION CHECK

Purpose: Apparently used to determine whether NewSpace is installed; also returns the address of the resident driver.

Available on: All machines.

Registers at call:
AX = 4412h
BX = FFFFh

Restrictions: none.

Return Registers:
AX = PSP segment of NewRes (resident
    driver for NewSpace)
BX:DX -> *unknown data or code*
CX = *unknown*

See Also: Function 44h Subfunction 11h

INTERRUPT 21h - Function 44h, Subfunction 13h
NewSpace - GET UNKNOWN INFORMATION

Purpose: *unknown.*
Available on: All machines.
Registers at call:
AX = 4413h
BX = FFFFh

Restrictions: NewSpace driver must be installed.
Return Registers:
AX = code segment of NewRes (resident driver for NewSpace)
BX = *offset of unknown data or code*

See Also: Function 44h Subfunction 12h

INTERRUPT 21h - Function 44h, Subfunction 14h
NewSpace DEBUGGING DUMP

Purpose: Store the complete internal state of NewSpace in a disk file for debugging purposes.
Available on: All machines.
Registers at call:
AX = 4414h
BX = FFFFh
See Also: Function 44h Subfunctions 13h and FFh

Restrictions: NewSpace driver must be installed.
Return Registers:
debugging dump written to NEWSPACE.SMP on current drive

INTERRUPT 21h - Function 44h, Subfunction FFh
NewSpace - Unknown Function

Purpose: *unknown.*
Available on: All machines.
Registers at call:
AX = 44FFh
BX = FFFFh
DX = *unknown.*
See Also: Function 44h Subfunction 14h

Restrictions: NewSpace driver must be installed.
Return Registers: *unknown.*

INTERRUPT 21h - Function DCh
PCMANAGE/DCOMPRES - TURN ON OR OFF

Purpose: Enable/disable automatic decompression of previously-compressed files.
Available on: All machines.

Registers at call:
AH = DCh
DX = 0000h turn on
    0001h turn off
Conflicts: Novell NetWare (chapter 20).
See Also: Function FEh Subfunction DCh

Restrictions: PC Magazine DCOMPRES must be installed.
Return Registers: *unknown.*

INTERRUPT 21h - Function FEh, Subfunction DCh
PCMANAGE/DCOMPRES - INSTALLATION CHECK

Purpose: Determine whether the DCOMPRES resident driver for PC Magazine's automatic file compression system is installed.
Available on: All machines.
Registers at call:
AX = FEDCh
Conflicts: DoubleDOS (chapter 17), "Black Monday" virus (chapter 34).
See Also: Function DCh

Restrictions: none.
Return Registers:
AX = CDEFh if installed

INTERRUPT 25h - Function CDh, Subfunction CDh
Stacker - GET DEVICE DRIVER ADDRESS

Purpose: Determine whether the Stacker device driver is loaded and the address at which it was loaded.

Available on: All machines.

Registers at call:
AX = CDCDh
DS:BX -> buffer for address (Table 6-15)
CX = 0001h
DX = 0000h

Conflicts: DOS Absolute Disk Read (chapter 8).

See Also: INT 21h Function 44h, Subfunction 04h

Restrictions: none.

Return Registers:
AX = CDCDh if installed
DS:BX buffer filled

Table 6-15. Format of device driver address buffer:

Offset	Size	Description
00h	WORD	signature CDCDh
02h	WORD	*unknown* (apparently always 0001h)
04h	DWORD	pointer to start of Stacker device driver (Table 6-16)

Table 6-16. Format of Stacker device driver:

Offset	Size	Description
00h	WORD	signature A55Ah
02h	WORD	Stacker version * 64h
04h	WORD	offset of volume-specific information offset table (list of WORDs, one per drive, containing offsets to various information)
06h	56 BYTEs	n/a
3Eh	BYTE	volume number, set after INT 21/AX=4404h (use to index into volume-specific info offset table)
3Fh	19 BYTEs	n/a
52h	4 BYTEs	ASCII string "SWAP"
56h	26 BYTEs	drive mapping table (one byte for each drive A: through Z:)

Table 6-17. Format of Stacker boot record:

Offset	Size	Description
1F0h	8 BYTEs	Stacker signature (first byte is CDh)
1F8h	DWORD	pointer to start of Stacker device driver
1FCh	WORD	Stacker volume number
1FEh	WORD	*unknown*

Chapter 7

Serial I/O

This chapter lists the interrupts involved with serial input/output. Since the original PC BIOS provided inadequate support for data communications, many third-party routines have been developed to fill the resulting need. This has led to more redundancy and conflict in this area than in any other single group of interrupts.

Within this chapter, interrupts are divided into two major groups: those furnished as original equipment within the BIOS that comes with a system, and those furnished as third-party add-on packages. The "standard" group is listed by interrupt service first and then by function and subfunction, all in numeric sequence. The add-on packages are listed in alphabetic sequence by name, with each package then listed by interrupt, function, and subfunction.

In addition to the calls here, there are some network calls which are related to serial I/O; those are discussed as part of the network software in the appropriate chapters (18 through 27).

Standard BIOS Interface

This group of functions includes those supplied with all machines, and those that are furnished only with specific models. It excludes the services that are available only as third-party add-ons.

INTERRUPT 14h - Function 00h
INITIALIZE PORT

Purpose: Establish operating parameters for the specified serial port.

Available on: All machines.　　　　　　　　　　　**Restrictions:** none.

Registers at call:　　　　　　　　　　　　　　　**Return Registers:**

AH = 00hAH = line status (see Table 7-2)

AL = port parameters (see Table 7-1)　　　　　　　AL = modem status (see Table 7-2)

DX = port number (00h-03h)

Details: The default handler is at F000h:E739h in IBM PC and 100% compatible BIOSes. Since the PCjr supports a maximum of 4800 bps, attempting to set 9600 bps will result in 4800 bps.

Conflicts: FOSSIL Initialize, which effectively replaces this function.

See Also: Function 04h, Function 05h, MultiDOS Function 04h (chapter 16), COURIERS.COM Function 82h, COURIERS.COM Function 8Ch

INTERRUPT 14h - Function 01h
WRITE CHARACTER TO PORT

Purpose: Output one character to the specified serial port.

Available on: All machines.　　　　　　　　　　　**Restrictions:** none.

Registers at call:　　　　　　　　　　　　　　　**Return Registers:**

AH = 01hAH bit 7 clear if successful　　　　　　　AH bit 7 set on error

AL = character to write　　　　　　　　　　　　　　AH bits 6-0 = port status (see Table 7-2)

DX = port number (00h-03h)

Conflicts: None known.

See Also: Function 02h, FOSSIL Function 0Bh, COURIERS.COM Function 89h

Table 7-1. Serial Port Initialization Parameters

-BAUD RATE- 7 - 6 - 5	PARITY BITS 4 - 3	STOP LENGTH 2	WORD 1 - 0
000: 110*	00: none	0: 1	00: 5
001: 150**	01: odd	1: 2	01: 6
010: 300	10: none***		10: 7
011: 600	11: even		11: 8
100: 1200			
101: 2400			
110: 4800			
111: 9600 (4800 on PCjr)			

Table 7-2. Serial Port Status Returns

Reg	Bit 7	Bit 6	Bit 5	Bit 4	Bit 3	Bit 2	Bit 1	Bit 0
AH	Timeout	Transmit Shift Register Empty	Transmit Holding Register Empty	Break Detected	Framing Error	Parity Error	Overrun Error	Receive Data Ready
AL	Carrier Detect (CD)	Ring Indicator (RI)	Data Set Ready (DSR)	Clear to Send (CTS)	Delta Carrier Detect	Trailing Edge of Ring	Delta Data Set Ready	Delta Clear to Send

INTERRUPT 14h - Function 02h
READ CHARACTER FROM PORT

Purpose: Read one character from the specified port, waiting if necessary.

Available on: All machines.

Restrictions: none.

Registers at call:

AH = 02h

DX = port number (00h-03h)

Return Registers:

AH = line status (see Table 7-2)

AL = received character if AH bit 7 clear

Details: Will timeout if DSR is not asserted, even if function 03h returns data ready.

Conflicts: FOSSIL - Receive Character With Wait.

See Also: Function 01h, COURIERS.COM Function 84h, IBM/Yale EBIOS Function FCh, FOSSIL Function 02h

INTERRUPT 14h - Function 03h
GET PORT STATUS

Purpose: Read the status of the specified serial port.

Available on: All machines.

Restrictions: none.

Registers at call:

AH = 03h

DX = port number (00h-03h)

Return Registers:

AH = line status (see Table 7-2)

AL = modem status (see Table 7-2)

Conflicts: None known.

See Also: Function 00h, MultiDOS Function 07h (chapter 16), COURIERS.COM Function 81h, IBM/Yale EBIOS Function FDh Subfunction 02h

---

* Standard BIOS only, 19,200 BPS for FOSSIL initialization.

** Standard BIOS only, 38,400 BPS for FOSSIL initialization.

*** Standard BIOS only, not defined for FOSSIL initialization.

INTERRUPT 14h - Function 04h
EXTENDED INITIALIZE

Purpose: Establish operating conditions for the specified serial port.

Available on: IBM Convertible and PS/2 models only.

Restrictions: none.

Registers at call:
AH = 04h
AL = break status:
  00h if break
  01h if no break
BH = parity:
  00h no parity
  01h odd parity
  02h even parity
  03h stick parity odd
  04h stick parity even
BL = number of stop bits:
  00h one stop bit
  01h two stop bits (1.5 if 5 bit word length)
CH = word length:
  00h 5 bits
  01h 6 bits
  02h 7 bits
  03h 8 bits
CL = bps rate:
  00h 110
  01h 150
  02h 300
  03h 600
  04h 1200
  05h 2400
  06h 4800
  07h 9600
  08h 19200
DX = port number

Return Registers:
AX = port status code (see Table 7-2)

Conflicts: FOSSIL - Initialize Driver, MultiDOS Plus IODRV - Initialize Port (chapter 16).

See Also: Function 00h, FOSSIL Function 1Eh

INTERRUPT 14h - Function 05h
EXTENDED COMMUNICATION PORT CONTROL

Purpose: Determine or establish additional operating conditions for the specified serial port.

Available on: IBM Convertible and PS/2 models only.

Restrictions: none.

Registers at call:
AH = 05h
DX = port number
AL = function:
  00h read modem control register

Return Registers:
vary with function:

BL = modem control register (see below)
AH = status (see Table 7-2)

01h write modem control register
    BL = modem control register: AX = status (see Table 7-2)
       bit 0: data terminal ready
       bit 1: request to send
       bit 2: OUT1
       bit 3: OUT2
       bit 4: LOOP
       bits 5-7 reserved

Conflicts: FOSSIL - Deinitialize Driver, MultiDOS Plus IODRV - Read Character from Port (chapter 16).
See Also: Function 00h, FOSSIL Function 1Fh

Third-Party BIOS-like Systems

This group of functions includes all serial I/O functions other than those included within the "standard" group. In several cases, specific subfunctions listed here essentially duplicate the matching subfunctions of the standard group, but are listed here with the rest of the package in which they are supplied.

3com BAPI SERIAL I/O

INTERRUPT 14h - Function A0h
CONNECT TO PORT

Purpose: Request a session on a serial port and establish a connection for that session.
Available on: All machines.   **Restrictions:** 3com BAPI must be installed.
Registers at call: **Return Registers:** *unknown.*
AH = A0h
others *unknown.*
Conflicts: Interconnections Inc. TES.
See Also: 3com BAPI Function A1h

INTERRUPT 14h - Function A1h
DISCONNECT FROM PORT

Purpose: Terminate a connection and free the serial port corresponding to that session.
Available on: All machines.   **Restrictions:** 3com BAPI must be installed.
Registers at call: **Return Registers:** *unknown.*
AH = A1h
others unknown.
Conflicts: Interconnections Inc. TES.
See Also: 3com BAPI Function A0h

INTERRUPT 14h - Function A4h
WRITE BLOCK

Purpose: Send one or more characters through the serial port corresponding to the specified connection.
Available on: All machines.   **Restrictions:** 3com BAPI must be installed.
Registers at call: **Return Registers:**
AH = A4h   CX = number of bytes sent
CX = length
DH = session number (00h)
ES:BX -> buffer
Conflicts: Interconnections Inc. TES.
See Also: FOSSIL Function 19h, COURIERS.COM Function 86h, 3com BAPI Function A5h

INTERRUPT 14h - Function A5h
READ BLOCK

Purpose: Read characters from the serial port corresponding to the specified connection.

Available on: All machines.
Registers at call:
AH = A5h
CX = length
DH = session number (00h)
ES:BX -> buffer
Conflicts: Interconnections Inc. TES.
See Also: FOSSIL Function 18h, COURIERS.COM Function 83h, 3com BAPI Function A4h, IBM/Yale EBIOS Function FFh Subfunction 02h

Restrictions: 3com BAPI must be installed.
Return Registers:
CX = number of bytes read

INTERRUPT 14h - Function A6h
SEND SHORT BREAK

Purpose: Transmit a short (less than 0.5s) break character on the serial port for the specified session.
Available on: All machines.
Registers at call:
AH = A6h
DH = session number (00h)
Conflicts: Interconnections Inc. TES.
See Also: FOSSIL Function 1Ah, COURIERS.COM Function 8Ah, IBM/Yale EBIOS Function FAh

Restrictions: 3com BAPI must be installed.
Return Registers: n/a

INTERRUPT 14h - Function A7h
READ STATUS

Purpose: Determine status.
Available on: All machines.
Registers at call:
AH = A7h
others unknown.
Conflicts: Interconnections Inc. TES.

Restrictions: 3com BAPI must be installed.
Return Registers: *unknown.*

INTERRUPT 14h - Function AFh, Subfunction 00h
INSTALLATION CHECK

Purpose: Determine whether 3com BAPI Serial I/O software is installed.
Available on: All machines.
Registers at call:
AX = AF00h
BX = AAAAh
Conflicts: None known.

Restrictions: None.
Return Registers:
AX = AF01h if installed

INTERRUPT 14h - Function B0h
ENABLE/DISABLE "ENTER COMMAND MODE" CHARACTER

Purpose: Specify whether the control character that switches to command mode is honored.
Available on: All machines.
Registers at call:
AH = B0h
AL =   00h disable
       01h enable
Conflicts: None known.

Restrictions: 3com BAPI must be installed.
Return Registers: n/a

INTERRUPT 14h - Function B1h
ENTER COMMAND MODE

Purpose: Switch to command mode.
Available on: All machines.

Restrictions: 3com BAPI must be installed.

Registers at call: **Return Registers:** n/a
AH = B1h
Conflicts: None known.

AVATAR Serial Dispatcher

The AVATAR Serial Dispatcher is a small module within AVATAR.SYS which allows multiple programs to share an interrupt request line, allowing the use of multiple serial ports on one IRQ. AVATAR.SYS (chapter 36) is a CON replacement by George Adam Stanislav which interprets AVATAR command codes in the same way that ANSI.SYS interprets ANSI command codes.

INTERRUPT 2Fh - Function 1Ah, Subfunction 42h
INSTALL IRQ3 HANDLER

Purpose: Add a routine to the chain of interrupt handlers for IRQ3.
Available on: All machines.   **Restrictions:** AVATAR driver must be installed.
Registers at call: **Return Registers:**
AX = 1A42h   AX = 1A42h if ASD not installed
BX = 4156h ('AV')   0000h if no more room
ES:DI -> FAR handler for serial port using IRQ3   else handle to use when uninstalling
DS = data segment needed by handler
Details: The handler need not save/restore registers or signal EOI to the interrupt controller. It should return AX=0000h if the interrupt was meant for it, and either leave AX unchanged or return a non-zero value otherwise.
     The most recently installed handler will be called first, continuing to earlier handlers until one returns AX=0000h.
Conflicts: None known.
See Also: Function 1Ah Subfunction 43h, Function 1Ah Subfunction 62h

INTERRUPT 2Fh - Function 1Ah, Subfunction 43h
INSTALL IRQ4 HANDLER

Purpose: Add a routine to the chain of interrupt handlers for IRQ4.
Available on: All machines.   **Restrictions:** AVATAR driver must be installed.
Registers at call: **Return Registers:**
AX = 1A43h   AX = 1A43h if ASD not installed
BX = 4156h ('AV')   0000h if no more room
ES:DI -> FAR handler for serial port using IRQ4   else handle to use when uninstalling
DS = data segment needed by handler
Details: The handler need not save/restore registers or signal EOI to the interrupt controller. It should return AX=0000h if the interrupt was meant for it, and either leave AX unchanged or return a non-zero value otherwise.
     The most recently installed handler will be called first, continuing to earlier handlers until one returns AX=0000h.
Conflicts: None known.
See Also: Function 1Ah Subfunction 42h, Function 1Ah Subfunction 63h

INTERRUPT 2Fh - Function 1Ah, Subfunction 62h
UNINSTALL IRQ3 HANDLER

Purpose: Remove a routine from the chain of interrupt handlers for IRQ3.
Available on: All machines.   **Restrictions:** AVATAR driver must be installed.
Registers at call: **Return Registers:** n/a
AX = 1A62h
BX = 4156h ('AV')
CX = handle for IRQ routine returned by
     Subfunction 42h
Conflicts: None known.
See Also: Function 1Ah Subfunction 42h, Function 1Ah Subfunction 63h

INTERRUPT 2Fh - Function 1Ah, Subfunction 63h
UNINSTALL IRQ4 HANDLER

Purpose: Remove a routine from the chain of interrupt handlers for IRQ4.
Available on: All machines.   **Restrictions:** AVATAR driver must be installed.
Registers at call: **Return Registers:** n/a
AX = 1A63h
BX = 4156h ('AV')
CX = handle for IRQ routine returned by
    Subfunction 43h
Conflicts: None known.
See Also: Function 1Ah Subfunction 43h, Function 1Ah Subfunction 62h

COURIERS.COM
COURIERS is a TSR by PC Magazine, published in Volume 8 Number 19 (November 14, 1989). It provides serial
port services for the 1STCLASS program to send binary files via MCI which was published in the same issue.

INTERRUPT 14h - Function 80h
INSTALLATION CHECK

Purpose: Determine whether COURIERS is installed.
Available on: All machines.   **Restrictions:** none.
Registers at call: **Return Registers:**
AH = 80h   AH = E8h if loaded
Conflicts: Communications FOSSIL (see FOSSIL Function 7Eh).

INTERRUPT 14h - Function 81h
CHECK IF PORT BUSY

Purpose: Determine port status.
Available on: All machines.   **Restrictions:** COURIERS.COM must be installed.
Registers at call: **Return Registers:**
AH = 81h   AH = 00h port available
AL = port number (1-4)   01h port exists but already in use
                                                   02h port nonexistent

Details: COURIERS is a TSR utility by PC Magazine
Conflicts: Video FOSSIL (chapter 5).
See Also: Function 83h, Function 8Dh

INTERRUPT 14h - Function 82h
CONFIGURE PORT

Purpose: Establish operating conditions for the specified serial port.
Available on: All machines.   **Restrictions:** COURIERS.COM must be installed.
Registers at call: **Return Registers:** n/a
AH = 82h
AL = port number (1-4)
BX = speed (bps)
CX = bit flags:
    bit 0: enable input flow control
    bit 1: enable output flow control
    bit 2: use X.PC protocol (not
        yet implemented)
Conflicts: Keyboard FOSSIL (see FOSSIL Function 7Eh).
See Also: Function 8Ch, Standard BIOS Function 00h

INTERRUPT 14h - Function 83h
START INPUT

Purpose: Set up input buffers.
Available on: All machines.
Registers at call:
AH = 83h
ES:BX -> circular input buffer
CX = length of buffer (should be at least 128 bytes
   if input flow control enabled)
Conflicts: System FOSSIL (see FOSSIL Function 7Eh).
See Also: Function 87h, Function 8Dh, FOSSIL Function 18h, 3com BAPI Function A5h

Restrictions: COURIERS.COM must be installed.
Return Registers: n/a

INTERRUPT 14h - Function 84h
READ CHARACTER

Purpose: Read one character from the specified port, waiting if necessary.
Available on: All machines.
Registers at call:
AH = 84h

Restrictions: COURIERS.COM must be installed.
Return Registers:
ZF set if no characters available
ZF clear
    AL = character
    AH = modem status bits:
        bit 7: set on input buffer overflow

Conflicts: None known.
See Also: Function 86h, Function 89h, Standard BIOS Function 02h

INTERRUPT 14h - Function 85h
FLUSH PENDING INPUT

Purpose: Discard all pending input.
Available on: All machines.
Registers at call:
AH = 85h
Conflicts: None known.
See Also: Function 88h, FOSSIL Function 0Ah

Restrictions: COURIERS.COM must be installed.
Return Registers: n/a

INTERRUPT 14h - Function 86h
START OUTPUT

Purpose: Set up output buffering.
Available on: All machines.
Registers at call:
AH = 86h
ES:BX -> output buffer
CX = length of output buffer
Conflicts: None known.
See Also: Function 83h, FOSSIL Function 19h, 3com BAPI Function A4h

Restrictions: COURIERS.COM must be installed.
Return Registers: n/a

INTERRUPT 14h - Function 87h
OUTPUT STATUS

Purpose: Check output status.
Available on: All machines.
Registers at call:
AH = 87h
Conflicts: None known.

Restrictions: COURIERS.COM must be installed.
Return Registers:
AX = number of unsent characters

INTERRUPT 14h - Function 88h
ABORT OUTPUT

Purpose: Halt output.
Available on: All machines.
Registers at call:
AH = 88h
Conflicts: None known.
See Also: Function 85h, FOSSIL Function 09h

Restrictions: COURIERS.COM must be installed.
Return Registers: n/a

INTERRUPT 14h - Function 89h
SEND SINGLE CHARACTER

Purpose: Send one character to the specified port.
Available on: All machines.
Registers at call:
AH = 89h
CL = character to send
Conflicts: None known.
See Also: Function 84h, Standard BIOS Function 01h

Restrictions: COURIERS.COM must be installed.
Return Registers: n/a

INTERRUPT 14h - Function 8Ah
SEND BREAK

Purpose: Send BREAK character to the specified port.
Available on: All machines.
Registers at call:
AH = 8Ah
Conflicts: None known.
See Also: Function 89h, IBM/Yale EBIOS Function FAh

Restrictions: COURIERS.COM must be installed.
Return Registers: n/a

INTERRUPT 14h - Function 8Ch
SET SPEED

Purpose: Establish port speed.
Available on: All machines.
Registers at call:
AH = 8Ch
BX = speed in bps
Conflicts: None known.
See Also: Function 82h, Standard BIOS Function 00h

Restrictions: COURIERS.COM must be installed.
Return Registers: n/a

INTERRUPT 14h - Function 8Dh
DECONFIGURE PORT

Purpose: Turn off all interrupts and modem control signals for the specified port.
Available on: All machines.
Registers at call:
AH = 8Dh
Conflicts: None known.
See Also: Function 82h

Restrictions: COURIERS.COM must be installed.
Return Registers: n/a

FOSSIL (Fido/Opus/Seadog Standard Interface Level)

FOSSIL is a driver which allows hardware-independent access to serial ports and (through extensions which a FOSSIL allows to be loaded) other hardware, permitting software to run unchanged on MSDOS machines which are not 100% IBM-compatible. The FOSSIL specification grew out of the Generic Fido(tm) driver when the authors of the Seadog and Opus systems adopted and extended the set of calls supported by the drivers.

INTERRUPT 11h - Function BCh
BNU - INSTALLATION CHECK

Purpose: Determine whether the BNU implementation of FOSSIL is installed.

Available on: All machines.
Registers at call:
AH = BCh
DX = 1954h
Conflicts: None known.

Restrictions: none.
Return Registers:
AX = 1954h
ES:DX -> entry point of driver (instead of INT 14)

INTERRUPT 14h - Function 00h
INITIALIZE

Purpose: Establish operating conditions for the specified serial port.

Available on: All machines.
Registers at call:
AH = 00h
AL = initializing parameters (see Table 7-1)
DX = port number (0-3 or FFh if only performing
   non-I/O setup)

Restrictions: FOSSIL software must be installed.
Return Registers:
AH = RS-232 status code bits:
   0: RDA - input data is available in buffer
   1: OVRN - data has been lost
   5: THRE - room is available in output buffer
   6: TSRE - output buffer empty
AL = modem status bits:
   3: always 1
   7: DCD - carrier detect

Conflicts: None known.
See Also: Function 05h, COURIERS.COM Function 82h

INTERRUPT 14h - Function 02h
RECEIVE CHARACTER WITH WAIT

Purpose: Read one character from the specified port, waiting if necessary.

Available on: All machines.
Registers at call:
AH = 02h
DX = port number (0-3)
Conflicts: SERIAL - Read Character From Port.
See Also: Standard BIOS Function 01h

Restrictions: FOSSIL software must be installed.
Return Registers:
AL = character received
AH = 00h

INTERRUPT 14h - Function 04h
INITIALIZE DRIVER

Purpose: Prepare the specified serial port for use.

Available on: All machines.
Registers at call:
AH = 04h
DX = port number
optionally BX = 4F50h
      ES:CX -> byte to be set upon ^C

Restrictions: FOSSIL software must be installed.
Return Registers:
AX = 1954h (if successful)
BL = maximum function number supported (excluding
      7Eh and above)
BH = revision of FOSSIL specification supported
DTR is raised

Details: The word at offset 6 in the interrupt handler contains 1954h, and the following byte contains the maximum function number supported.
Conflicts: Standard BIOS - Extended Initialize, MultiDOS Plus IODRV - Initialize Port (chapter 16).
See Also: Function 05h, Function 1Ch

INTERRUPT 14h - Function 05h
DEINITIALIZE DRIVER

Purpose: Deactivate FOSSIL driver for the specified port and perform cleanup, such as unhooking interrupt vectors.

Available on: All machines.

Registers at call:

AH = 05h

DX = port number

Restrictions: FOSSIL software must be installed.

Return Registers: none

Details: DTR is not affected.

Conflicts: Standard BIOS Extended Communication Port Control, MultiDOS Plus IODRV Read Character from Port (chapter 16).

See Also: Function 00h, Function 04h, Function 1Dh, COURIERS.COM Function 8Dh

INTERRUPT 14h - Function 06h
RAISE/LOWER DTR

Purpose: Control level of the Data Terminal Ready control signal.

Available on: All machines.

Registers at call:

AH = 06h

DX = port

AL =   00h = lower DTR

   01h = raise DTR

Restrictions: FOSSIL software must be installed.

Return Registers: n/a

Conflicts: MultiDOS Plus IODRV - Write Character to Port (chapter 16).

See Also: Function 1Ah

INTERRUPT 14h - Function 07h
RETURN TIMER TICK PARAMETERS

Purpose: Determine information about tick-timer settings.

Available on: All machines.

Registers at call:

AH = 07h

Restrictions: FOSSIL software must be installed.

Return Registers:

AL = timer tick interrupt number

AH = ticks per second on interrupt number in AL

DX = approximate number of milliseconds per tick

Conflicts: MultiDOS Plus IODRV - Get Port Status (chapter 16).

See Also: Function 16h

INTERRUPT 14h - Function 08h
FLUSH OUTPUT BUFFER WAITING TILL ALL OUTPUT IS DONE

Purpose: Empty all pending output data to the specified port.

Available on: All machines.

Registers at call:

AH = 08h

DX = port number

Restrictions: FOSSIL software must be installed.

Return Registers: n/a

Conflicts: MultiDOS Plus 4.0 IODRV - Get and Reset Port Line Status (chapter 16).

See Also: Function 09h

INTERRUPT 14h - Function 09h
PURGE OUTPUT BUFFER THROWING AWAY ALL PENDING OUTPUT

Purpose: Discard all pending output for the specified port.

Available on: All machines.

Registers at call:

AH = 09h

DX = port number

Restrictions: FOSSIL software must be installed.

Return Registers: n/a

Conflicts: MultiDOS Plus IODRV - Reset Port Status (chapter 16).
See Also: Function 08h, Function 0Ah, COURIERS.COM Function 88h

INTERRUPT 14h - Function 0Ah
PURGE INPUT BUFFER THROWING AWAY ALL PENDING INPUT

Purpose: Discard all pending input for the specified port.
Available on: All machines.   **Restrictions:** FOSSIL software must be installed.
Registers at call: **Return Registers:** n/a
AH = 0Ah
DX = port number
Conflicts: None known.
See Also: Function 09h, COURIERS.COM Function 85h

INTERRUPT 14h - Function 0Bh
TRANSMIT NO WAIT

Purpose: Start transmitting a character out the specified port, without waiting for its transmission to complete.
Available on: All machines.   **Restrictions:** FOSSIL software must be installed.
Registers at call: **Return Registers:**
AH = 0Bh   AX = 0000h character not accepted
AL = character   0001h character accepted
DX = port number
Conflicts: None known.
See Also: Standard BIOS Function 01h

INTERRUPT 14h - Function 0Ch
NON-DESTRUCTIVE READ AHEAD

Purpose: Peek at next input character without removing it from the input buffer.
Available on: All machines.   **Restrictions:** FOSSIL software must be installed.
Registers at call: **Return Registers:**
AH = 0Ch   AX = FFFFh character not available
DX = port number   00xxh character xx available
Conflicts: None known.
See Also: Function 20h

INTERRUPT 14h - Function 0Dh
KEYBOARD READ WITHOUT WAIT

Purpose: Obtain keyboard input, if available (similar to INT 16h function).
Available on: All machines.   **Restrictions:** FOSSIL software must be installed.
Registers at call: **Return Registers:**
AH = 0Dh   AX = FFFFh character not available
                                                               xxyyh standard IBM-style scan code

Conflicts: None known.
See Also: Function 0Eh, INT 16h Function 01h (chapter 2)

INTERRUPT 14h - Function 0Eh
KEYBOARD READ WITH WAIT

Purpose: Obtain keyboard input, waiting until a keystroke is available if necessary (similar to INT 16h function).
Available on: All machines.   **Restrictions:** FOSSIL software must be installed.
Registers at call: **Return Registers:**
AH = 0Eh   AX = xxyyh standard IBM-style scan code
Conflicts: None known.
See Also: Function 0Dh, INT 16h Function 00h (chapter 2)

INTERRUPT 14h - Function 0Fh
ENABLE/DISABLE FLOW CONTROL

Purpose: Set flow control protocol to use, if any, on the specified port.

Available on: All machines.

Registers at call:

AH = 0Fh

AL = bit mask describing flow control requested:

    0: xon/xoff on transmit (watch for xoff
       while sending)

    1: CTS/RTS (CTS on transmit/RTS on
       receive)

    2: reserved

    3: xon/xoff on receive (send xoff when
       buffer near full)

    4-7: all 1

DX = port number

Restrictions: FOSSIL software must be installed.

Return Registers: n/a

Conflicts: None known.

See Also: Function 10h

INTERRUPT 14h - Function 10h
EXTENDED ^C/^K CHECKING AND TRANSMIT ON/OFF

Purpose: Control user-interrupt checking actions for the specified port.

Available on: All machines.

Registers at call:

AH = 10h

AL = bit mask:

    0: enable/disable ^C/^K checking

    1: enable/disable the transmitter

DX = port number

Restrictions: FOSSIL software must be installed.

Return Registers: n/a

Conflicts: None known.

See Also: Function 0Fh

INTERRUPT 14h - Function 11h
SET CURRENT CURSOR LOCATION

Purpose: Establish cursor position (similar to INT 10h function).

Available on: All machines.

Registers at call:

AH = 11h

DH = row

DL = column

Restrictions: FOSSIL software must be installed.

Return Registers: n/a

Details: This is the same as INT 10h Function 02h (chapter 5).

Conflicts: None known.

See Also: Function 12h

INTERRUPT 14h - Function 12h
READ CURRENT CURSOR LOCATION

Purpose: Determine cursor position (similar to INT 10h function).

Available on: All machines.

Registers at call:

AH = 12h

Restrictions: FOSSIL software must be installed.

Return Registers:

DH = row

DL = column

Details: This is the same as INT 10h Function 03h (chapter 5).

Conflicts: None known.
See Also: Function 11h

INTERRUPT 14h - Function 13h
SINGLE CHARACTER ANSI WRITE TO SCREEN

Purpose: Writes character at current cursor position.
Available on: All machines.   **Restrictions:** FOSSIL software must be installed.
Registers at call: **Return Registers:** n/a
AH = 13h
AL = character
Details: This function should not be called at times when it is unsafe to call DOS.
Conflicts: None known.
See Also: Function 15h

INTERRUPT 14h - Function 14h
ENABLE OR DISABLE WATCHDOG PROCESSING

Purpose: Control watchdog timer actions for the specified port.
Available on: All machines.   **Restrictions:** FOSSIL software must be installed.
Registers at call: **Return Registers:** n/a
AH = 14h
AL = 01h enable watchdog
    00h disable watchdog
DX = port number
Conflicts: None known.

INTERRUPT 14h - Function 15h
WRITE CHARACTER TO SCREEN USING BIOS SUPPORT ROUTINES

Purpose: Write a character at the current cursor position (similar to INT 10h function).
Available on: All machines.   **Restrictions:** FOSSIL software must be installed.
Registers at call: **Return Registers:** n/a
AH = 15h
AL = character
Conflicts: None known.
See Also: Function 13h

INTERRUPT 14h - Function 16h
INSERT/DELETE FUNCTION FROM TIMER TICK CHAIN

Purpose: Add a function to, or remove a function from, the interrupt chain for the system timer.
Available on: All machines.   **Restrictions:** FOSSIL software must be installed.
Registers at call: **Return Registers:**
AH = 16h   AX = status:
AL =   00h = delete function   0000h successful
    01h = add function   0001h unsuccessful
        ES:DX -> routine to call
Conflicts: None known.
See Also: Function 07h

INTERRUPT 14h - Function 17h
REBOOT SYSTEM

Purpose: Reboot the system, performing either a cold boot (with self-test) or a warm boot.
Available on: All machines.   **Restrictions:** FOSSIL software must be installed.

Registers at call:
AH = 17h
AL =   00h = cold boot
    01h = warm boot
Conflicts: None known.
See Also: INT 19h (chapter 2)

Return Registers: n/a

INTERRUPT 14h - Function 18h
READ BLOCK

Purpose: Read a block of characters from the specified port, waiting if necessary.
Available on: All machines.   **Restrictions:** FOSSIL software must be installed.
Registers at call: **Return Registers:**
AH = 18h   AX = number of characters transferred
CX = maximum number of characters to transfer
DX = port number
ES:DI -> user buffer
Conflicts: None known.
See Also: Function 19h, COURIERS.COM Function 83h, IBM/Yale EBIOS Function FFh Subfunction 02h, Novell NASI Function 01h

INTERRUPT 14h - Function 19h
WRITE BLOCK

Purpose: Write a block of characters to the specified port.
Available on: All machines.   **Restrictions:** FOSSIL software must be installed.
Registers at call: **Return Registers:**
AH = 19h   AX = number of characters transferred
CX = maximum number of characters to transfer
DX = port number
ES:DI -> user buffer
Conflicts: None known.
See Also: Function 18h, COURIERS.COM Function 86h, Novell NASI Function 00h

INTERRUPT 14h - Function 1Ah
BREAK BEGIN OR END

Purpose: Start or stop sending a BREAK signal on the specified port.
Available on: All machines.   **Restrictions:** FOSSIL software must be installed.
Registers at call: **Return Registers:** n/a
AH = 1Ah
AL =   00h stop sending 'break'
    01h start sending 'break'
DX = port number
Conflicts: None known.
See Also: Function 06h, COURIERS.COM Function 8Ah, IBM/Yale EBIOS Function FAh

INTERRUPT 14h - Function 1Bh
RETURN INFORMATION ABOUT THE DRIVER

Purpose: Obtain driver information.
Available on: All machines.   **Restrictions:** FOSSIL software must be installed.
Registers at call: **Return Registers:**
AH = 1Bh   AX = number of characters transferred
DX = port number   CX = 3058h ("0X") (X00 FOSSIL only)
CX = size of user buffer   DX = 2030h (" 0") (X00 FOSSIL only)
ES:DI -> user buffer for driver info (Table 7-3)

Conflicts: None known.

Table 7-3. Format of driver info:

Offset	Size	Description
00h	WORD	size of structure in bytes
02h	BYTE	FOSSIL spec to which driver conforms
03h	BYTE	revision level of this specific driver
04h	DWORD	pointer to ASCIZ identification string
08h	WORD	size of the input buffer
0Ah	WORD	number of bytes left in buffer
0Ch	WORD	size of the output buffer
0Eh	WORD	number of bytes left in buffer
10h	BYTE	width of screen
11h	BYTE	length of screen
12h	BYTE	actual baud rate, computer to modem

INTERRUPT 14h - Function 1Ch
X00 - ACTIVATE PORT

Purpose: Establish operating conditions for the specified serial port.

Available on: All machines.

Restrictions: The X00 implementation of the FOSSIL software must be installed.

Registers at call:
AH = 1Ch
DX = port number

Return Registers:
AX = 1954h if successful
BL = maximum function number supported (not including 7Eh and above)
BH = revision of FOSSIL specification supported

Details: This is a duplicate of function 04h, so that that function may be made compatible with the PS/2 BIOS in a future release.

Conflicts: None known.

See Also: Function 04h, Function 1Dh

INTERRUPT 14h - Function 1Dh
X00 - DEACTIVATE PORT

Purpose: Deactivate FOSSIL driver for the specified port and perform any necessary cleanup, such as unhooking interrupt vectors.

Available on: All machines.

Restrictions: The X00 implementation of the FOSSIL software must be installed.

Registers at call:
AH = 1Dh
DX = port number

Return Registers: n/a

Details: This is a duplicate of Function 05h, so that that function may be made compatible with the PS/2 BIOS in a future release. Ignored if the port was never activated with Function 04h or Function 1Ch.

Conflicts: None known.

See Also: Function 05h, Function 1Ch

INTERRUPT 14h - Function 1Eh
X00 - EXTENDED LINE CONTROL INITIALIZATION

Purpose: Establish operating conditions for the specified serial port.

Available on: All machines.

Restrictions: The X00 implementation of the FOSSIL software must be installed.

Registers at call:
AH = 1Eh

Return Registers:
AX = port status code (see Table 7-2)

AL = break status:
  00h if break
  01h if no breakBH = parity:
  00h no parity
  01h odd parity
  02h even parity
  03h stick parity odd
  04h stick parity even
BL = number of stop bits:
  00h one stop bit
  01h two stop bits (1.5 if 5 bit word length)
CH = word length:
  00h 5 bits
  01h 6 bits
  02h 7 bits
  03h 8 bits
CL = bps rate:
  00h 110
  01h 150
  02h 300
  03h 600
  04h 1200
  05h 2400
  06h 4800
  07h 9600
  08h 19200
DX = port number

Details: This function is intended to exactly emulate the PS/2 BIOS Function 04h call. If the port was locked at X00 load time, the appropriate parameters are ignored.
Conflicts: None known.
See Also: Function 00h, Standard BIOS Function 04h

INTERRUPT 14h - Function 1Fh
X00 - EXTENDED SERIAL PORT STATUS/CONTROL

Purpose: Establish additional operating conditions for the specified serial port.
Available on: All machines.   **Restrictions:** The X00 implementation of the FOSSIL software must be installed.

Registers at call: **Return Registers:**
AH = 1Fh   vary with function
AL = function:
  00h read modem control register: BL = modem control register (see below)
                                          AH = status
  01h write modem control register: AX = status
    BL = modem control register: DX = port number
    bit 0: data terminal ready
    bit 1: request to send
    bit 2: OUT1
    bit 3: OUT2 (interrupts) enabled
    bit 4: LOOP
    bits 5-7 reserved

Details: This function is intended to exactly emulate the PS/2 BIOS Function 05h call. X00 forces BL bit 3 set (interrupts cannot be disabled).
Conflicts: None known.

See Also: Function 00h, Standard BIOS Function 05h

INTERRUPT 14h - Function 20h
X00 - DESTRUCTIVE READ WITH NO WAIT

Purpose: Read one character, if available, from the specified port; does not wait for character to arrive.

Available on: All machines.

Restrictions: The X00 implementation of the FOSSIL software must be installed.

Registers at call:
AH = 20h
DX = port number

Return Registers:
AH = 00h if character was available
AL = next character (removed from receive buffer)
AX = FFFFh if no character available

Conflicts: MultiDOS Plus - Initialize Port (chapter 16), Alloy MW386 (chapter 18).
See Also: Function 0Ch, Function 21h

INTERRUPT 14h - Function 21h
X00 - STUFF RECEIVE BUFFER

Purpose: Insert the specified character at end of receive buffer as if it had just arrived from the serial port; all normal receive processing (XON/XOFF, ^C/^K) is performed on the character.

Available on: All machines.

Restrictions: The X00 implementation of the FOSSIL software must be installed.

Registers at call:
AH = 21h
AL = character
DX = port number

Return Registers: n/a

Details: This function is fully re-entrant.
Conflicts: Alloy MW386 (chapter 18), MultiDOS Plus - Transmit Character (chapter 16).
See Also: Function 20h

INTERRUPT 14h - Function 7Eh
INSTALL AN EXTERNAL APPLICATION FUNCTION

Purpose: Installs extended capabilities of FOSSIL.

Available on: All machines.

Restrictions: FOSSIL software must be installed.

Registers at call:
AH = 7Eh
AL = code for external application (80h-BFh):
    80h reserved for communications FOSSIL
    81h video FOSSIL
    82h reserved for keyboard FOSSIL
    83h reserved for system FOSSIL
    ES:DX -> entry point

Return Registers:
AX = 1954h
BL = code assigned to application (same as input AL)
DH = 00h failed
    01h successful

Conflicts: None known.
See Also: Function 7Fh, Function 81h Subfunction 00h (chapter 5)

INTERRUPT 14h - Function 7Fh
REMOVE AN EXTERNAL APPLICATION FUNCTION

Purpose: De-installs specified extended capability of FOSSIL.

Available on: All machines.

Restrictions: FOSSIL software must be installed.

Registers at call:
AH = 7Fh
AL = code assigned to external application
    (see Function 7Eh)
        ES:DX -> entry point

Return Registers:
AX = 1954h
BL = code assigned to application (same as input AL)
DH = 00h failed
    01h successful

Conflicts: None known.

See Also: Function 7Eh

IBM/Yale EBIOS SERIAL I/O

INTERRUPT 14h - Function F4h, Subfunction FFh
INSTALLATION CHECK

Purpose: Determine whether EBIOS has been installed.
Available on: All machines.
Registers at call:
AX = F4FFh
DX = port (00h-03h)

Restrictions: none.
Return Registers:
CF clear if present
  AX = 0000h
CF set if not present
  AX <> 0000h

Conflicts: None known.

INTERRUPT 14h - Function F9h
REGAIN CONTROL

Purpose: Recapture the interrupt vector (if hooked by another application) and perform any other actions needed to begin I/O processing on the specified serial port.
Available on: All machines.
Registers at call:
AH = F9h
DX = port (00h-03h)
Conflicts: None known.

Restrictions: EBIOS must be installed.
Return Registers: n/a

INTERRUPT 14h - Function FAh
SEND BREAK

Purpose: Send BREAK character on the specified serial port.
Available on: All machines.
Registers at call:
AH = FAh
DX = port (00h-03h)
Conflicts: None known.
See Also: FOSSIL Function 1Ah, COURIERS.COM Function 8Ah

Restrictions: EBIOS must be installed.
Return Registers: n/a

INTERRUPT 14h - Function FBh
SET OUTGOING MODEM SIGNALS

Purpose: Establish levels of modem control signals for the specified port.
Available on: All machines.
Registers at call:
AH = FBh
AL = modem control register:
    bit 0: data terminal ready
       1: request to send
       2: OUT1
       3: OUT2
       4: loopback
    bits 5-7 unused
DX = port (00h-03h)
Conflicts: None known.

Restrictions: EBIOS must be installed.
Return Registers: n/a

INTERRUPT 14h - Function FCh
READ CHARACTER, NO WAIT

Purpose: Obtain a character, if available, from the specified port; will not wait if no character available.

Available on: All machines.

Restrictions: EBIOS must be installed.

Registers at call:
AH = FCh
DX = port (00h-03h)

Return Registers:
AH = RS232 status bits (see Table 7-2)
AL = character

Conflicts: None known.

See Also: Function FFh Subfunction 02h, Standard BIOS Function 02h, FOSSIL Function 0Ch

INTERRUPT 14h - Function FDh, Subfunction 02h
READ STATUS

Purpose: Determine how many characters are available in the input buffer.

Available on: All machines.

Restrictions: EBIOS must be installed.

Registers at call:
AX = FD02h

Return Registers:
CX = number of characters available

Conflicts: None known.

INTERRUPT 14h - Function FFh, Subfunction 02h
BUFFERED READ

Purpose: Read all available characters up to the specified limit.

Available on: All machines.

Restrictions: EBIOS must be installed.

Registers at call:
AX = FF02h
CX = length
DX = port (00h-03h)
ES:BX -> buffer

Return Registers:
CX = number of characters read

Conflicts: None known.

See Also: Function FCh, FOSSIL Function 18h, COURIERS.COM Function 83h, 3com BAPI Function A5h

Interconnections Inc. TES

TES is a network serial port emulation program by Interconnections, Inc.

INTERRUPT 14h - Function A0h
INSTALLATION CHECK/STATUS REPORT

Purpose: Determine whether TES is installed.

Available on: All machines.

Restrictions: Status report is only valid if TES is installed.

Registers at call:
AH = A0h
CX = FFFFh

Return Registers:
CF clear if successful
    AX = 5445h ('TE')
    CX <> FFFFh
    DX = port number
CF set on error

Conflicts: 3com BAPI SERIAL I/O.

See Also: Function A1h

INTERRUPT 14h - Function A1h
GET LIST OF SESSIONS WITH STATUS

Purpose: Determine the currently-active sessions and the status of each.

Available on: All machines.

Restrictions: TES must be installed.

Registers at call:
AH = A1h

Return Registers:
CX = number of active sessions
ES:SI -> status array (Table 7-4)

Table 7-4. Format of status array entry:

Offset	Size	Description
00h	BYTE	status
01h	WORD	offset of name

Conflicts: 3com BAPI SERIAL I/O.
See Also: Function A2h, Function A3h

INTERRUPT 14h - Function A2h
GET LIST OF SERVER NAMES

Purpose: Determine the names of the servers TES is using.
Available on: All machines.
Registers at call:
AH = A2h

Restrictions: TES must be installed.
Return Registers:
CX = number of servers
ES:SI -> array of offsets from ES for server names

Conflicts: None known.
See Also: Function A1h

INTERRUPT 14h - Function A3h
START A NEW SESSION

Purpose: Create a new connection.
Available on: All machines.
Registers at call:
AH = A3h
ES:SI -> unknown, probably a data structure.

Restrictions: TES must be installed.
Return Registers:
CF clear if successful
    AX = 5445h ('TE')
    CX <> FFFFh
    DX = port number
CF set on error

Conflicts: None known.
See Also: Function A1h, Function A4h, Function A6h

INTERRUPT 14h - Function A4h
HOLD CURRENTLY ACTIVE SESSION

Purpose: Temporarily suspend a session.
Available on: All machines.
Registers at call:
AH = A4h unknown.

Restrictions: TES must be installed.
Return Registers: *unknown.*

Conflicts: 3com BAPI SERIAL I/O.
See Also: Function A3h, Function A5h

INTERRUPT 14h - Function A5h
RESUME A SESSION

Purpose: Restart a session which was previously suspended.
Available on: All machines.
Registers at call:
AH = A5h
AL = session number

Restrictions: TES must be installed.
Return Registers: *unknown.*

Conflicts: 3com BAPI SERIAL I/O.
See Also: Function A4h, Function A6h

INTERRUPT 14h - Function A6h
DROP A SESSION

Purpose: Terminate a connection.
Available on: All machines.
Registers at call:
AH = A6h
AL = session number

Restrictions: TES must be installed.
Return Registers:
AH = status:
   00h successful
   else error

Conflicts: 3com BAPI SERIAL I/O.
See Also: Function A3h, Function A5h

INTERRUPT 14h - Function A7h
SWITCH TO NEXT ACTIVE SESSION

Purpose: Select a different connection to be the current connection on which commands and I/O are performed.
Available on: All machines.
Registers at call:
AH = A7h
others *unknown*.

Restrictions: TES must be installed.
Return Registers: *unknown*.

Conflicts: 3com BAPI SERIAL I/O.
See Also: Function A3h, Function A5h

INTERRUPT 14h - Function A8h
SEND STRING TO COMMAND INTERPRETER

Purpose: Interpret a command string as if it had been typed by the user.
Available on: All machines.
Registers at call:
AH = A8h
AL = 00h no visible response
ES:SI -> ASCIZ command

Restrictions: TES must be installed.
Return Registers: *unknown*.

Conflicts: None known.

Novell NASI/NACS and Ungermann-Bass Net One
Novell NASI, Novell NACS, and Ungermann-Bass Net One provide network serial port emulation through INT 6Bh. The functions described in this section are sometimes referred to as the "generic INT 6Bh interface".

INTERRUPT 6Bh - Function 00h
BUFFERED WRITE

Purpose: Write one or more characters to the emulated serial port.
Available on: All machines.

Restrictions: Novell NASI/NACS or Ungermann-Bass Net One must be installed.

Registers at call:
AX = 0000h
CX = length
ES:BX -> buffer

Return Registers:
CX = number of bytes written

Conflicts: "Saddam" virus (chapter 34)
See Also: Function 01h, FOSSIL Function 19h

INTERRUPT 6Bh - Function 01h
BUFFERED READ

Purpose: Read one or more characters from the emulated serial port.
Available on: All machines.

Restrictions: Novell NASI/NACS or Ungermann-Bass Net One must be installed.

Registers at call:
AX = 0100h
CX = length of buffer
ES:BX -> buffer
Conflicts: "Saddam" virus (chapter 34)
See Also: Function 00h, FOSSIL Function 18h, IBM/Yale EBIOS Function FFh Subfunction 02h

Return Registers:
CX = number of bytes read

INTERRUPT 6Bh - Function 02h
INSTALLATION CHECK

Purpose: Determine whether Novell NASI/NACS or Ungermann-Bass Net One is installed.
Available on: All machines.   **Restrictions:** none.
Registers at call: **Return Registers:**
AH = 02h   AL = 00h if present and OK
AL nonzero
Conflicts: "Saddam" virus (chapter 34)
See Also: Function 07h

INTERRUPT 6Bh - Function 06h
CONTROL

Purpose: Execute a control action on a connection, such as sending a break signal or disconnecting.
Available on: All machines.   **Restrictions:** Novell NASI/NACS or Ungermann-Bass
                                                   Net One must be installed.
Registers at call: **Return Registers:**n/a
AX = 0600h
CX = command
   02h send break
   04h disconnect
   06h hold
Conflicts: "Saddam" virus (chapter 34)

INTERRUPT 6Bh - Function 07h
GET STATUS

Purpose: Determine whether a connection is presently active.
Available on: All machines.   **Restrictions:** Novell NASI/NACS or Ungermann-Bass
                                                   Net One must be installed.
Registers at call: **Return Registers:**
AX = 0700h   CH <> 00h if connection active
Conflicts: "Saddam" virus (chapter 34)
See Also: Function 02h

Chapter 8

MS-DOS and Compatibles

This chapter tabulates the interrupts used by MS-DOS since version 1.0; since most of these routines have been widely documented elsewhere, discussion of their use is kept to a minimum.

The chapter is divided into three sections. Within each section or subsection, functions are listed by numeric sequence of the interrupt first, then by function number within each interrupt, and by subfunction within each function. In the few cases in which multiple versions of the same subfunction exist, they are listed in alphabetic sequence by identifier.

The first section contains the functions provided by the MS-DOS kernel, except for those on interrupt 2Fh (the multiplex interrupt). The second section contains the multiplex interrupt functions provided by both the kernel and various DOS utilities, as well as two non-multiplex calls provided by PRINT.COM. This section is divided into subsections by the program providing the services. Finally, the third section details calls provided by various MS-DOS-compatible operating systems.

INTERRUPT 20h
TERMINATE PROGRAM

Purpose: Ends current process and returns to parent (usually the command interpreter).
Available on: All versions of DOS.   **Restrictions:** none.
Registers at call: **Return Registers:** never returns
CS = PSP segment
Details: Microsoft recommends using INT 21h Function 4Ch for DOS 2.0 and higher. Execution continues at the address stored in INT 22h after DOS performs whatever cleanup is necessary (closing files, etc). If the PSP is its own parent, the process's memory is not freed; if INT 22h additionally points into the terminating program, the process is effectively not terminated. This feature is used by COMMAND.COM.
Conflicts: Minix Send/Receive Message (chapter 36).
See Also: INT 21h Functions 00h and 4Ch

INTERRUPT 21h - Function 00h
TERMINATE PROGRAM

Purpose: Ends current process and returns to parent (usually command interpreter).
Available on: All versions of DOS.

                                           Restrictions: Not supported by MS Windows **3.0**
                                           DOSX.EXE DOS extender.
Registers at call: **Return Registers:** n/a
AH = 00h
CS = PSP segment
Details: Microsoft recommends using INT 21h Function 4Ch for DOS 2.0 and higher. Execution continues at the address stored in INT 22h after DOS performs whatever cleanup may be necessary (closing files, etc). If the PSP is its own parent, the process's memory is not freed; if INT 22h additionally points into the terminating program, the process is effectively not terminated.
Conflicts: None known.
See Also: Functions 26h, 31h, and 4Ch, INT 20h, INT 22h

INTERRUPT 21h - Function 01h
READ CHARACTER FROM STANDARD INPUT, WITH ECHO

Purpose: Reads one character from standard input, and echoes the character to standard output.

Available on: All versions of DOS.   **Restrictions:** none.

Registers at call: **Return Registers:**

AH = 01h   AL = character read

Details: Control-C and Control-Break are checked, and INT 23h is executed if either was pressed. The character is echoed to standard output. Standard input is always the keyboard and standard output the screen under DOS 1.x, but they may be redirected under DOS 2.0 and higher.

Conflicts: None known.

See Also: Functions 06h, 07h, 08h, and 0Ah

INTERRUPT 21h - Function 02h
WRITE CHARACTER TO STANDARD OUTPUT

Purpose: Writes one character to standard output.

Available on: All versions of DOS.   **Restrictions:** none.

Registers at call: **Return Registers:** n/a

AH = 02h

DL = character to write

Details: Control-C and Control-Break are checked, and INT 23h is executed if either was pressed. Standard output is always the screen under DOS 1.x, but may be redirected under DOS 2+.

Conflicts: None known.

See Also: Function 06h, Function 09h

INTERRUPT 21h - Function 03h
READ CHARACTER FROM STDAUX

Purpose: Reads one character from the predefined STDAUX handle, waiting for it if none is available. Not often used.

Available on: All versions of DOS.   **Restrictions:** none.

Registers at call: **Return Registers:**

AH = 03h   AL = character read

Details: The keyboard is checked for Control-C or Control-Break, and INT 23h is executed if either is detected.

The STDAUX handle usually refers to the AUX device, which is the first serial port, but it may be redirected under DOS 2.0 or higher.

Conflicts: None known.

See Also: Function 04h, INT 14h Function 02h (chapter 7)

INTERRUPT 21h - Function 04h
WRITE CHARACTER TO STDAUX

Purpose: Writes one character to the predefined STDAUX handle. Not often used.

Available on: All versions of DOS.   **Restrictions:** none.

Registers at call: **Return Registers:** n/a

AH = 04h

DL = character to write

Details: The keyboard is checked for Control-C or Control-Break, and INT 23h is executed if either is detected.

If STDAUX is busy, this function will wait until it becomes free.

The STDAUX handle usually refers to the AUX device, which is the first serial port, but it may be redirected under DOS 2.0 and higher.

Conflicts: None known.

See Also: Function 03h, INT 14h Function 01h (chapter 7)

INTERRUPT 21h - Function 05h
WRITE CHARACTER TO PRINTER

Purpose: Write one character to the predefined STDPRN handle.

Available on: All versions of DOS.

Restrictions: none.

Registers at call:

Return Registers: n/a

AH = 05h

DL = character to print

Details: The keyboard is checked for Control-C or Control-Break, and INT 23h is executed if either is detected.

The STDPRN handle normally refers to the PRN device (the first parallel port), but it may be redirected under DOS 2.0 and higher. If the printer is busy, this function will wait.

Conflicts: None known.

See Also: INT 17h Function 00h (chapter 3)

INTERRUPT 21h - Function 06h
DIRECT CONSOLE OUTPUT

Purpose: Write one character to the predefined STDOUT handle.

Available on: All versions of DOS.

Restrictions: none.

Registers at call:

Return Registers: n/a

AH = 06h

DL = character (except FFh)

Details: This call does not check for Control-C or Control-Break.

Conflicts: None known.

See Also: Functions 02h and 09h

INTERRUPT 21h - Function 06h, Subfunction FFh
DIRECT CONSOLE INPUT

Purpose: Reads one character, if available, from the predefined STDIN handle; if no character is available, it returns immediately.

Available on: All versions of DOS.

Restrictions: none.

Registers at call:

Return Registers:

AH = 06h

ZF set if no character available

DL = FFh

ZF clear if character available

   AL = character read

Details: Does not check for Control-C or Control-Break.

If the returned character is 00h, the user pressed a key with an extended keycode, which will be returned by the next call of this function.

Conflicts: None known.

See Also: Function 0Bh

INTERRUPT 21h - Function 07h
DIRECT CHARACTER INPUT WITHOUT ECHO

Purpose: Reads one character from the predefined STDIN handle; if no character is available, it waits for the next keystroke.

Available on: All versions of DOS.

Restrictions: none.

Registers at call:

Return Registers:

AH = 07h

AL = character read from standard input

Details: This function does not check for Control-C or Control-Break, and does not echo the returned character to STDOUT.

If the interim console flag is set (see Function 63h Subfunction 01h), partially-formed double-byte characters may be returned.

Conflicts: None known.

See Also: Functions 01h, 06h, 08h, and 0Ah

INTERRUPT 21h - Function 08h
CHARACTER INPUT WITHOUT ECHO

Purpose: Reads one character from the predefined STDIN handle; if no character is available, it waits for the next keystroke.

Available on: All versions of DOS.   **Restrictions:** none.

Registers at call: **Return Registers:**

AH = 08h   AL = character read from standard input

Details: Control-C and Control-Break are checked, and INT 23h is executed if either was pressed.

If the interim console flag is set (see Function 63h Subfunction 01h), partially-formed double-byte characters may be returned.

Conflicts: None known.

See Also: Function 01h, Function 06h, Function 07h, Function 0Ah, Function 64h

INTERRUPT 21h - Function 09h
WRITE STRING TO STANDARD OUTPUT

Purpose: Writes '$'-terminated string to STDOUT.

Available on: All versions of DOS.   **Restrictions:** none.

Registers at call: **Return Registers:** n/a

AH = 09h

DS:DX -> '$'-terminated string

Details: Control-C and Control-Break are checked, and INT 23h is called if either was pressed.

Conflicts: None known.

See Also: Function 02h, Function 06h for output

INTERRUPT 21h - Function 0Ah
BUFFERED INPUT

Purpose: Obtains keyboard input from STDIN.

Available on: All versions of DOS.   **Restrictions:** none.

Registers at call: **Return Registers:**

AH = 0Ah   buffer filled with user input

DS:DX -> buffer (Table 8-1)

Details: Control-C and Control-Break are checked, and INT 23h is called if either is detected.

If the maximum buffer size (Table 8-1) is set to 00h, this call returns immediately without reading any input.

Conflicts: WCED v1.6 Installation Check (chapter 36).

See Also: Function 0Ch

Table 8-1. Format of input buffer:

Offset	Size	Description
00h	BYTE	maximum characters buffer can hold
01h	BYTE	(input) number of chars from last input which may be recalled
		(return) number of characters actually read, excluding CR
02h	N BYTEs	actual characters read, including the final carriage return

INTERRUPT 21h - Function 0Bh
GET STDIN STATUS

Purpose: Determine whether a keystroke is available for input from STDIN.

Available on: All versions of DOS.   **Restrictions:** none.

Registers at call: **Return Registers:**

AH = 0Bh   AL = 00h if no character available

                                                              = FFh if character is available

Details: Control-C and Control-Break are checked, and INT 23h is called if either was pressed.

If the interim console flag is set (see Function 63h Subfunction 01h), this function returns AL=FFh if a partially-formed double-byte character is available.

Conflicts: "G" Virus (chapter 34).
See Also: Function 06h for input, Function 44h Subfunction 06h

INTERRUPT 21h - Function 0Ch
FLUSH BUFFER AND READ STANDARD INPUT

Purpose: Discard all keystrokes in the typeahead buffer, then perform keyboard input action as specified.

Available on: All versions of DOS.	**Restrictions:** none.
Registers at call:	**Return Registers:**
AH = 0Ch	as appropriate for the specified input function

AL = function to execute after flushing buffer
other registers as appropriate for the input function
Details: If AL is not one of 01h, 06h, 07h, 08h, or 0Ah, the buffer is flushed but no input is attempted.
Conflicts: None known.
See Also: Function 06h for input, Functions 01h, 07h, 08h, and 0Ah

INTERRUPT 21h - Function 0Dh
DISK RESET

Purpose: Write all modified disk buffers to disk immediately.

Available on: All versions of DOS.	**Restrictions:** none.
Registers at call:	**Return Registers:** n/a
AH = 0Dh	

Details: This function does not update directory information (that is only done when files are closed or a SYNC call is issued).
Conflicts: None known.
See Also: Function 5Dh Subfunction 01h, INT 13h Function 00h (chapter 6), INT 2Fh Function 11h Subfunction 20h (chapter 19)

INTERRUPT 21h - Function 0Eh
SELECT DEFAULT DRIVE

Purpose: Log onto specified drive and return the number of available drives.

Available on: All versions of DOS.	**Restrictions:** none.
Registers at call:	**Return Registers:**
AH = 0Eh	AL = number of potentially valid drive letters

AL = new default drive
   00h = A:, 01h = B:, etc.
Details: Under Novell NetWare, the return value is always 32, the number of drives that NetWare supports. Under DOS 3+, the return value is the greatest of 5, the value of LASTDRIVE= in CONFIG.SYS, and the number of drives actually present. On a DOS 1.x/2.x single-floppy system, AL returns 2 since the floppy may be accessed as either A: or B:. Otherwise, the return value is the highest drive actually present.

    DOS 1.x supports a maximum of 16 drives, 2.x a maximum of 63 drives, and 3+ a maximum of 26 drives.
Conflicts: None known.
See Also: Functions 19h and 3Bh, NetWare Function DBh (chapter 20)

INTERRUPT 21h - Function 0Fh
OPEN FILE USING FCB

Purpose: Make file available for access using the original FCB method (now obsolete).

Available on: All versions of DOS.	**Restrictions:** none.
Registers at call:	**Return Registers:**
AH = 0Fh	AL = status:
DS:DX -> unopened File Control Block (Table 8-2)	00h successful
	FFh file not found or access denied

Details: DOS 3.1+ opens the file for read/write in compatibility mode.

An unopened FCB has the drive, filename, and extension fields filled in and all other bytes cleared.

This call is not supported by the MS Windows 3.0 DOSX.EXE DOS extender.

Conflicts: None known.

See Also: Functions 10h, 16h, and 3Dh

Table 8-2. Format of File Control Block:

Offset	Size	Description
-7	BYTE	extended FCB if FFh
-6	5 BYTEs	reserved
-1	BYTE	file attribute if extended FCB
00h	BYTE	drive number (0 = default, 1 = A, etc)
01h	8 BYTEs	blank-padded file name
09h	3 BYTEs	blank-padded file extension
0Ch	WORD	current block number
0Eh	WORD	logical record size
10h	DWORD	file size
14h	WORD	date of last write (see Function 57h Subfunction 00h)
16h	WORD	(DOS 1.1+) time of last write (see Function 57h Subfunction 00h)
18h	8 BYTEs	reserved (Tables 8-3 thru 8-6)
20h	BYTE	record within current block
21h	DWORD	random access record number (if record size is > 64 bytes, high byte is omitted)

Note: To use an extended FCB, you must specify the address of the FFh flag at offset -7, rather than the address of the drive number field.

Table 8-3. Format of reserved field for DOS 1.0:

Offset	Size	Description
16h	WORD	location in directory (if high byte = FFh, low byte is device ID)
18h	WORD	number of first cluster in file
1Ah	WORD	last cluster number accessed (absolute)
1Ch	WORD	relative current cluster number
1Eh	BYTE	dirty flag (00h = not dirty)
1Fh	BYTE	unused

Table 8-4. Format of reserved field for DOS 1.10-1.25:

Offset	Size	Description
18h	BYTE	bit 7: set if logical device
		bit 6: not dirty
		bits 5-0: disk number or logical device ID
19h	WORD	starting cluster number
1Bh	WORD	absolute current cluster number
1Dh	WORD	relative current cluster number
1Fh	BYTE	unused

Table 8-5. Format of reserved field for DOS 2.x:

Offset	Size	Description
18h	BYTE	bit 7: set if logical device
		bit 6: set if open
		bits 5-0: *unknown.*
19h	WORD	starting cluster number
1Bh	WORD	*unknown.*
1Dh	BYTE	*unknown.*
1Eh	BYTE	*unknown.*
1Fh	BYTE	*unknown.*

Table 8-6. Format of reserved field for DOS 3.x:

Offset	Size	Description
18h	BYTE	number of system file table entry for file
19h	BYTE	attributes:
		bits 7,6: 00 = SHARE.EXE not loaded, disk file
		01 = SHARE.EXE not loaded, character device
		10 = SHARE.EXE loaded, remote file
		11 = SHARE.EXE loaded, local file
		bits 5-0: low six bits of device attribute word

---SHARE.EXE loaded, local file

1Ah	WORD	starting cluster of file
1Ch	WORD	offset within SHARE of sharing record (see Function 52h)
1Eh	BYTE	file attribute
1Fh	BYTE	unknown.

---SHARE.EXE loaded, remote file

1Ah	WORD	number of sector containing directory entry
1Ch	WORD	relative cluster within file of last cluster accessed
1Eh	BYTE	absolute cluster number of last cluster accessed
1Fh	BYTE	unknown.

---SHARE.EXE not loaded

1Ah	BYTE	(low byte of device attribute word AND 0Ch) OR open mode
1Bh	WORD	starting cluster of file
1Dh	WORD	number of sector containing directory entry
1Fh	BYTE	number of directory entry within sector

Note: If an FCB is opened on a character device, the dword at 1Ah is set to the address of the device driver header, then the byte at 1Ah is overwritten.

INTERRUPT 21h - Function 10h
CLOSE FILE USING FCB

Purpose: Flush all buffers for file to disk and update directory information (obsolete method).

Available on: All versions of DOS.   **Restrictions:** none.

Registers at call: **Return Registers:**

AH = 10h   AL = status:

DS:DX -> File Control Block (see Table 8-2)   00h successful

          FFh failed

Details: A successful close forces all disk buffers used by the file to be written and the directory entry to be updated.

This call is not supported by the MS Windows 3.0 DOSX.EXE DOS extender.

Conflicts: None known.

See Also: Functions 0Fh, 16h, and 3Eh

INTERRUPT 21h - Function 11h
FIND FIRST MATCHING FILE USING FCB

Purpose: Locate first file in current directory that matches FCB (now obsolete).

Available on: All versions of DOS.   **Restrictions:** none.

Registers at call: **Return Registers:**

AH = 11h   AL = status:

DS:DX -> unopened FCB (see Table 8-2), may   00h successful

    contain '?' wildcards   [DTA] = unopened FCB for first matching file

          FFh no matching filename, or bad FCB

Details: DOS 3+ also allows the '*' wildcard.

The type of the returned FCB depends on whether the input FCB was a normal or an extended FCB. The search FCB must not be modified if Function 12h will be used to continue searching; DOS 3.3 has set the following parts of the FCB:

Table 8-7. Values set into FCB by DOS 3.3:

Offset	Size	Description
0Ch	BYTE	*unknown.*
0Dh	WORD	directory entry number of matching file
0Fh	WORD	cluster number of current directory
11h	4 BYTEs	*unknown.*
15h	BYTE	drive number (1=A:)

Note: At least for DOS 3.3, the unopened FCB in the DTA is actually the drive number followed by the file's directory entry.

Conflicts: None known.

See Also: Functions 12h, 1Ah, and 4Eh, INT 2Fh Function 11h Subfunction 1Bh (chapter 19)

INTERRUPT 21h - Function 12h
FIND NEXT MATCHING FILE USING FCB

Purpose: Locate next file that matches FCB (now obsolete).

Available on: All versions of DOS.

Restrictions: Function 11h must have been called previously.

Registers at call:
AH = 12h
DS:DX -> unopened FCB (Table 8-2)

Return Registers:
AL = status:
    00h successful
        [DTA] = unopened FCB
    FFh no more matching filenames

Details: Assumes that a successful FindFirst (see Function 11h) was executed on the search FCB before the call.

Conflicts: None known.

See Also: Functions 1Ah and 4Fh, INT 2Fh Function 11h Subfunction 1Ch (chapter 19)

INTERRUPT 21h - Function 13h
DELETE FILE USING FCB

Purpose: Delete all files that match FCB (now obsolete).

Available on: All versions of DOS.

Restrictions: none.

Registers at call:
AH = 13h
DS:DX -> unopened FCB (see Table 8-2)
    filename filled with template for deletion
    ('?' wildcards allowed)

Return Registers:
AL = status:
    00h one or more files successfully deleted
    FFh no matching files or all were read-only or
        locked

Details: DOS 1.25+ deletes everything in the current directory (including subdirectories) and sets the first byte of the name to 00h (entry never used) instead of E5h if called on an extended FCB with filename '???????????' and bits 0-4 of the attribute set (bits 1 and 2 for DOS 1). This may have originally been an optimization to minimize directory searching after a mass deletion, but can corrupt the filesystem under DOS 2+ because subdirectories are removed without deleting the files they contain.

Currently-open files should not be deleted.

Conflicts: None known.

See Also: Function 41h, INT 2Fh Function 11h Subfunction 13h (chapter 19)

INTERRUPT 21h - Function 14h
SEQUENTIAL READ FROM FCB FILE

Purpose: Read one record (usually 128 bytes) from the specified FCB-opened file into the Disk Transfer Area.

Available on: All versions of DOS.

Restrictions: none.

Registers at call:
AH = 14h
DS:DX -> opened FCB (see Table 8-2)

Return Registers:
AL = status:
  00h successful
  01h end of file (no data)
  02h segment wrap in DTA
  03h end of file, partial record read
[DTA] = record read from file

Details: Reads a record of the size specified in the FCB beginning at the current file position, then updates the current block and current record fields in the FCB. If a partial record was read, it is zero-padded to the full size.

This call is not supported by the MS Windows 3.0 DOSX.EXE DOS extender.

Conflicts: None known.

See Also: Functions 0Fh, 15h, 1Ah, and 3Fh, INT 2Fh Function 11h Subfunction 08h (chapter 19)

INTERRUPT 21h - Function 15h
SEQUENTIAL WRITE TO FCB FILE

Purpose: Write one record (usually 128 bytes) to the specified FCB-opened file from the Disk Transfer Area.

Available on: All versions of DOS.

Restrictions: none.

Registers at call:
AH = 15h
DS:DX -> opened FCB (see Table 8-2)
[DTA] = record to write

Return Registers:
AL = status:
  00h successful
  01h disk full
  02h segment wrap in DTA

Details: Writes a record of the size specified in the FCB beginning at the current file position, then updates the current block and current record fields in the FCB. If less than a full disk sector is written, the data is placed in a DOS buffer to be written out at a later time.

This call is not supported by the MS Windows 3.0 DOSX.EXE DOS extender.

Conflicts: None known.

See Also: Functions 0Fh, 14h, 1Ah, and 40h, INT 2Fh Function 11h Subfunction 09h (chapter 19)

INTERRUPT 21h - Function 16h
CREATE OR TRUNCATE FILE USING FCB

Purpose: Create empty file using FCB (now obsolete).

Available on: All versions of DOS.

Restrictions: none.

Registers at call:
AH = 16h
DS:DX -> unopened FCB (see Table 8-2),
    wildcards not allowed

Return Registers:
AL = status:
  00h successful
  FFh directory full or file exists and is read-only or
      locked

Details: If the file already exists, it is truncated to zero length. If an extended FCB is used, the file is given the attribute in the FCB.

This call is not supported by the MS Windows 3.0 DOSX.EXE DOS extender.

Conflicts: None known.

See Also: Functions 0Fh, 10h, and 3Ch

INTERRUPT 21h - Function 17h
RENAME FILE USING FCB

Purpose: Change name of file using FCB (now obsolete).

Available on: All versions of DOS.

Restrictions: none.

Registers at call:
AH = 17h
DS:DX -> modified FCB (see Table 8-2). The old
    filename ('?' wildcards OK) is in the
    standard location, while the new filename
    ('?' wildcards OK) is stored in the 11 bytes
    beginning at offset 11h

Return Registers:
AL = status:
    00h successfully renamed
    FFh no matching files, file is read-only, or new
        name already exists

Details: Subdirectories may be renamed using an extended FCB with the appropriate attribute.
Conflicts: None known.
See Also: Functions 0Fh, 13h, and 56h, INT 2Fh Function 11h Subfunction 11h (chapter 19)

INTERRUPT 21h - Function 18h
NULL FUNCTION FOR CP/M COMPATIBILITY

Purpose: This function does nothing; it corresponds to a CP/M BDOS function which is meaningless under MSDOS.

Available on: All versions of DOS.
Registers at call:
AH = 18h
Conflicts: None known.
See Also: Functions 1Dh, 1Eh, and 20h

Restrictions: none.
Return Registers:
AL = 00h

INTERRUPT 21h - Function 19h
GET CURRENT DEFAULT DRIVE

Purpose: Determine number of "current" drive.
Available on: All versions of DOS.
Registers at call:
AH = 19h
Conflicts: None known.
See Also: Functions 0Eh and 47h

Restrictions: none.
Return Registers:
AL = drive (00h = A:, 01h = B:, etc)

INTERRUPT 21h - Function 1Ah
SET DISK TRANSFER AREA ADDRESS

Purpose: Establish address of buffer to use for disk I/O and directory searches.
Available on: All versions of DOS.
Registers at call:
AH = 1Ah
DS:DX -> Disk Transfer Area (DTA)

Restrictions: none.
Return Registers: n/a

Details: The DTA is set to PSP:0080h when a program is started.
Conflicts: None known.
See Also: Functions 11h, 12h, 2Fh, 4Eh, and 4Fh

INTERRUPT 21h - Function 1Bh
GET ALLOCATION INFORMATION FOR DEFAULT DRIVE

Purpose: Determine size of current default drive.
Available on: All versions of DOS.
Registers at call:
AH = 1Bh

Restrictions: none.
Return Registers:
AL = sectors per cluster (allocation unit)
CX = bytes per sector
DX = total number of clusters
DS:BX -> media ID byte (Table 8-8)

Details: Under DOS 1.x, DS:BX points at an actual copy of the first FAT sector; later versions return a pointer to a copy of the FAT's ID byte.
Conflicts: None known.

See Also: Functions 1Ch and 36h

Table 8-8. Values for ID byte (not always accurate):

Byte	Media	Description
FFh	floppy	double-sided, 8 sectors per track (320K)
FEh	floppy	single-sided, 8 sectors per track (160K)
FDh	floppy	double-sided, 9 sectors per track (360K)
FCh	floppy	single-sided, 9 sectors per track (180K)
F9h	floppy	double-sided, 15 sectors per track (1.2M)
F8h	hard disk	
F0h	other	

INTERRUPT 21h - Function 1Ch
GET ALLOCATION INFORMATION FOR SPECIFIC DRIVE

Purpose: Determine size of specified drive.

Available on: All versions of DOS.　　　　　　　**Restrictions:** none.

Registers at call:
AH = 1Ch
DL = drive (00h = default, 01h = A:, etc)

Return Registers:
AL = sectors per cluster (allocation unit)
CX = bytes per sector
DX = total number of clusters
DS:BX -> media ID byte (see Function 1Bh)

Details: Under DOS 1.x, DS:BX points at an actual copy of the first FAT sector; later versions return a pointer to a copy of the FAT's ID byte.

Conflicts: None known.

See Also: Functions 1Bh and 36h

INTERRUPT 21h - Function 1Dh
NULL FUNCTION FOR CP/M COMPATIBILITY

Purpose: This function does nothing; it corresponds to a CP/M BDOS function which is meaningless under MSDOS.

Available on: All versions of DOS.　　　　　　**Restrictions:** none.

Registers at call:　　　　　　　　　　　　　　　**Return Registers:**
AH = 1Dh　　　　　　　　　　　　　　　　　　　　　AL = 00h

Conflicts: None known.

See Also: Functions 18h, 1Eh, and 20h

INTERRUPT 21h - Function 1Eh
NULL FUNCTION FOR CP/M COMPATIBILITY

Purpose: This function does nothing; it corresponds to a CP/M BDOS function which is meaningless under MSDOS.

Available on: All versions of DOS.　　　　　　**Restrictions:** none.

Registers at call:　　　　　　　　　　　　　　　**Return Registers:**
AH = 1Eh　　　　　　　　　　　　　　　　　　　　　AL = 00h

Conflicts: None known.

See Also: Function 18h, Function 1Dh, Function 20h

INTERRUPT 21h - Function 1Fh
GET DRIVE PARAMETER BLOCK FOR DEFAULT DRIVE

Purpose: Obtain details of disk parameters for the current drive.

Available on: All versions of DOS.　　　　　　**Restrictions:** none.

Registers at call:
AH = 1Fh

Return Registers:
AL = status:
    00h successful
        DS:BX -> Drive Parameter Block (DPB)
        (see Table 8-9 for DOS 1.x,
        Function 32h for DOS 2+)
    FFh invalid drive

Details: This function has been newly documented for DOS 5.0; it was undocumented in prior versions.
Conflicts: None known.
See Also: Function 32h

Table 8-9. Format of DOS 1.1 and MSDOS 1.25 drive parameter block:

Offset	Size	Description
00h	BYTE	entry number
01h	BYTE	physical drive number
02h	WORD	bytes per sector
04h	BYTE	highest sector number within a cluster
05h	BYTE	shift count to convert clusters to sectors
06h	WORD	starting sector number of first FAT
08h	BYTE	number of copies of FAT
09h	WORD	number of directory entries
0Bh	WORD	number of first data sector
0Dh	WORD	highest cluster number (number of data clusters + 1)
0Fh	BYTE	sectors per FAT
10h	WORD	starting sector of (root) directory
12h	WORD	address of allocation table

    Note: The DOS 1.0 parameter block is the same except that it omits the first and last fields.

INTERRUPT 21h - Function 20h
NULL FUNCTION FOR CP/M COMPATIBILITY

Purpose: This function does nothing; it corresponds to a CP/M BDOS function which is meaningless under MSDOS.
Available on: All versions of DOS.
Registers at call:
AH = 20h
Conflicts: None known.
See Also: Functions 18h, 1Dh, and 1Eh

Restrictions: none.
Return Registers:
AL = 00h

INTERRUPT 21h - Function 21h
READ RANDOM RECORD FROM FCB FILE

Purpose: Read specified record from file using FCB (now obsolete).
Available on: All versions of DOS.
Registers at call:
AH = 21h
DS:DX -> opened FCB (see Table 8-2)

Restrictions: none.
Return Registers:
AL = status:
    00h successful
    01h end of file, no data read
    02h segment wrap in DTA, no data read
    03h end of file, partial record read
    [DTA] = record read from file

Details: The record is read from the current file position as specified by the random record and record size fields of the FCB. The file position is not updated after reading the record. If a partial record is read, it is zero-padded to the full size.
    This call is not supported by the MS Windows 3.0 DOSX.EXE DOS extender.
Conflicts: None known.

See Also: Functions 14h, 22h, 27h, and 3Fh

INTERRUPT 21h - Function 22h
WRITE RANDOM RECORD TO FCB FILE

Purpose: Write specified record to file using FCB (now obsolete).

Available on: All versions of DOS.

Restrictions: none.

Registers at call:
AH = 22h
DS:DX -> opened FCB (see Table 8-2)
[DTA] = record to write

Return Registers:
AL = status:
  00h successful
  01h disk full
  02h segment wrap in DTA

Details: The record is written to the current file position as specified by the random record and record size fields of the FCB. The file position is not updated after writing the record.

If the record is located beyond the end of the file, the file is extended but the intervening data remains uninitialized. If the record only partially fills a disk sector, it is copied to a DOS disk buffer to be written out to disk at a later time.

This call is not supported by the MS Windows 3.0 DOSX.EXE DOS extender.

Conflicts: None known.

See Also: Functions 15h, 21h, 28h, and 40h

INTERRUPT 21h - Function 23h
GET FILE SIZE FOR FCB

Purpose: Get size of file into its FCB (now obsolete).

Available on: All versions of DOS.

Restrictions: none.

Registers at call:
AH = 23h
DS:DX -> unopened FCB (see Function 0Fh),
    wildcards not allowed

Return Registers:
AL = status:
  00h successful (matching file found) FCB random
      record field filled with size in records,
      rounded up to the next full record
  FFh failed (no matching file found)

Details: This call is not supported by the MS Windows 3.0 DOSX.EXE DOS extender.

Conflicts: None known.

See Also: Function 42h

INTERRUPT 21h - Function 24h
SET RANDOM RECORD NUMBER FOR FCB

Purpose: Specify record to be read/written by Functions 21h/22h.

Available on: All versions of DOS.

Restrictions: none.

Registers at call:
AH = 24h
DS:DX -> opened FCB (see Function 0Fh)

Return Registers: n/a

Details: Computes the random record number corresponding to the current record number and record size, then stores the result in the FCB. Normally used when switching from sequential to random access.

This call is not supported by the MS Windows 3.0 DOSX.EXE DOS extender.

Conflicts: None known.

See Also: Functions 21h, 27h, and 42h

INTERRUPT 21h - Function 25h
SET INTERRUPT VECTOR

Purpose: Modify address of routine to service specified interrupt.

Available on: All versions of DOS.

Restrictions: none.

Registers at call: **Return Registers:** n/a
AH = 25h
AL = interrupt number
DS:DX -> new interrupt handler
Details: This function is preferred over direct modification of the interrupt vector table.
Conflicts: Phar Lap 386/DOS-Extender (chapter 9).
See Also: Function 35h

INTERRUPT 21h - Function 26h
CREATE NEW PROGRAM SEGMENT PREFIX

Purpose: Create Program Segment Prefix (PSP); now obsolete, as the same action is performed as part of Function 4Bh.
Available on: All versions of DOS.   **Restrictions:** none.
Registers at call: **Return Registers:** n/a
AH = 26h
DX = segment at which to create PSP (Table 8-10)
Details: The new PSP is updated with memory size information; INTs 22h, 23h, 24h are taken from interrupt vector table. DOS 2+ assumes that the caller's CS is the segment of the PSP to copy.

In DOS versions 3.0 and up, the limit on simultaneously open files may be increased by allocating memory for a new open file table, filling it with FFh, copying the first 20 bytes from the default table, and adjusting the pointer and count at 34h and 32h. However, DOS versions through at least 3.30 will only copy the first 20 file handles into a child PSP (including the one created on EXEC). Network redirectors based on the original MS-Net implementation use values of 80h-FEh in the open file table to indicate remote files.
Conflicts: None known.
See Also: Functions 4Bh, 50h, 51h, 55h, 62h, and 67h

Table 8-10. Format of PSP:

Offset	Size	Description
00h	2 BYTEs	INT 20h instruction for CP/M CALL 0 program termination
02h	WORD	segment of first byte beyond memory allocated to program
04h	BYTE	unused filler
05h	BYTE	CP/M CALL 5 service request (FAR JMP to 000C0h)
		BUG: (DOS 2+) PSPs created by INT 21h Function 4Bh point at 000BEh
06h	WORD	CP/M compatibility--size of first segment for .COM files
08h	2 BYTEs	remainder of FAR JMP at 05h
0Ah	DWORD	stored INT 22h termination address
0Eh	DWORD	stored INT 23h control-Break handler address
12h	DWORD	stored INT 24h critical error handler address (DOS 1.1+)
16h	WORD	segment of parent PSP
18h	20 BYTEs	DOS 2+ Job File Table, one byte per file handle, FFh = closed
2Ch	WORD	DOS 2+ segment of environment block (Table 8-11) for process
2Eh	DWORD	DOS 2+ process's SS:SP on entry to last INT 21h call
32h	WORD	DOS 3+ number of entries in JFT (default 20)
34h	DWORD	DOS 3+ pointer to JFT (default PSP:0018h)
38h	DWORD	DOS 3+ pointer to previous PSP (default FFFFFFFFh in 3.x) used by SHARE in DOS 3.3
3Ch	4 BYTEs	unused by DOS versions <= 5.00
40h	2 BYTEs	DOS 5.0 version to return on INT 21h Function 30h
42h	14 BYTEs	unused by DOS versions <= 5.00
50h	3 BYTEs	DOS 2+ service request (INT 21h/RETF instructions)
53h	9 BYTEs	unused in DOS versions <= 5.00
5Ch	16 BYTEs	first default FCB, filled in from first commandline argument
		overwrites second FCB if opened
6Ch	16 BYTEs	second default FCB, filled in from second commandline argument
		overwrites beginning of commandline if opened
7Ch	4 BYTEs	unused

Table 8-10. Format of PSP (continued)

Offset	Size	Description
80h	128 BYTEs	commandline / default DTA. Command tail is BYTE for length of tail, N BYTEs for the tail, followed by a BYTE containing 0Dh

Table 8-11. Format of environment block:

Offset	Size	Description
00h	N BYTEs	first environment variable, ASCIZ string of form "var=value"
	N BYTEs	second environment variable, ASCIZ string
	...	
	N BYTEs	last environment variable, ASCIZ string of form "var=value"
	BYTE	00h

---DOS 3+

	WORD	number of strings following environment (normally 1)
	N BYTEs	ASCIZ pathname of program owning this environment; other strings may follow

INTERRUPT 21h - Function 27h
RANDOM BLOCK READ FROM FCB FILE

Purpose: Read multiple records from FCB (obsolete), starting with specified record.

Available on: All versions of DOS.

Restrictions: none.

Registers at call:

AH = 27h

CX = number of records to read

DS:DX -> opened FCB (see Table 8-2)

Return Registers:

AL = status:

    00h successful, all records read

    01h end of file, no data read

    02h segment wrap in DTA, no data read

    03h end of file, partial read

[DTA] = records read from file

CX = number of records read (status 00h or 03h)

Details: The read begins at the current file position as specified in FCB; the file position is updated after reading.

    This call is not supported by the MS Windows 3.0 DOSX.EXE DOS extender.

Conflicts: None known.

See Also: Functions 21h, 28h, and 3Fh

INTERRUPT 21h - Function 28h
RANDOM BLOCK WRITE TO FCB FILE

Purpose: Write multiple records from FCB (obsolete), starting with specified record.

Available on: All versions of DOS.

Restrictions: none.

Registers at call:

AH = 28h

CX = number of records to write

DS:DX -> opened FCB (see Table 8-2)

[DTA] = records to write

Return Registers:

AL = status:

    00h successful

    01h disk full or file read-only

    02h segment wrap in DTA

CX = number of records written

Details: The write begins at the current file position as specified in FCB; the file position is updated after writing. If CX = 0000h on entry, no data is written; instead the file size is adjusted to be the same as the file position specified by the random record and record size fields of the FCB. If the data to be written is less than a disk sector, it is copied into a DOS disk buffer, to be written out to disk at a later time.

    This call is not supported by the MS Windows 3.0 DOSX.EXE DOS extender.

Conflicts: None known.

See Also: Functions 22h, 27h, 40h, and 59h

INTERRUPT 21h - Function 29h
PARSE FILENAME INTO FCB

Purpose: Analyze a filename and copy the appropriate portions into an FCB; obsolete except when using obsolete FCB calls or spawning a child program.

Available on: All versions of DOS.

Registers at call:
AH = 29h
AL = parsing options:
    bit 0: skip leading separators
    bit 1: use existing drive number in FCB if
        no drive is specified, instead of
        setting field to zero
    bit 2: use existing filename in FCB if no
        base name is specified, instead of
        filling field with blanks
    bit 3: use existing extension in FCB if no
        extension is specified, instead of
        filling field with blanks
    bits 4-7: reserved (0)
DS:SI -> filename string (both '*' and '?' wildcards
    OK)
ES:DI -> buffer for unopened FCB

Restrictions: none.

Return Registers:
AL = result code:
    00h successful parse, no wildcards encountered
    01h successful parse, wildcards present
    FFh invalid drive specifier
DS:SI -> first unparsed character
ES:DI buffer filled with unopened FCB
    (see Table 8-2)

Details: Asterisks are expanded to question marks in the FCB. All processing stops when a filename terminator is encountered. Cannot be used with filespecs which include a path (DOS 2+). Can be used to determine whether a specified drive exists, without generating a DOS critical error if it does not.

Conflicts: None known.

See Also: Functions 0Fh, 16h, and 26h

INTERRUPT 21h - Function 2Ah
GET SYSTEM DATE

Purpose: Read date from system internal calendar.

Available on: All versions of DOS.

Registers at call:
AH = 2Ah

Restrictions: none.

Return Registers:
CX = year (1980-2099)
DH = month
DL = day
AL = (DOS 1.10+) day of week (00h=Sunday)

Conflicts: None known.

See Also: Functions 2Bh-2Dh, NetWare Function E7h (chapter 20), INT 1Ah Function 04h (chapter 3)

INTERRUPT 21h - Function 2Bh
SET SYSTEM DATE

Purpose: Change date as shown on system internal calendar.

Available on: All versions of DOS.

Registers at call:
AH = 2Bh
CX = year (1980-2099)
DH = month
DL = day

Restrictions: none.

Return Registers:
AL = status:
    00h successful
    FFh invalid date, system date unchanged

Details: DOS 3.3+ also sets the CMOS real-time clock.

Conflicts: PC Tools v5.1 PC-CACHE (chapter 6), DESQview Installation Check (chapter 15), pcANYWHERE IV (chapter 28), ELRES v1.1 (chapter 36), TAME (chapter 36).

See Also: Functions 2Ah and 2Dh, INT 1Ah Function 05h (chapter 3)

INTERRUPT 21h - Function 2Ch
GET SYSTEM TIME

Purpose: Read time as shown on system internal clock.

Available on: All versions of DOS.   **Restrictions:** none.

Registers at call: **Return Registers:**

AH = 2Ch

CH = hour

CL = minute

DH = second

DL = 1/100 seconds

Details: On most systems, the resolution of the system clock is about 5/100sec, so returned times generally do not increment by 1. On some systems, DL may always return 00h.

Conflicts: None known.

See Also: Functions 2Ah and 2Dh, NetWare Function E7h (chapter 20), INT 1Ah Functions 00h and 02h (chapter 3), INT 1Ah Function FEh (chapter 4)

INTERRUPT 21h - Function 2Dh
SET SYSTEM TIME

Purpose: Change time as shown on system internal clock.

Available on: All versions of DOS.   **Restrictions:** none.

Registers at call: **Return Registers:**

AH = 2Dh   AL = result:

CH = hour   00h successful

CL = minute   FFh invalid time, system time unchanged

DH = second

DL = 1/100 seconds

Details: DOS 3.3+ also sets the CMOS real-time clock.

Conflicts: None known.

See Also: Functions 2Ah-2Ch, INT 1Ah Functions 01h and 03h (chapter 3), INT 1Ah Function FFh (chapter 4)

INTERRUPT 21h - Function 2Eh
SET VERIFY FLAG

Purpose: Control the state of the disk-write verification flag.

Available on: All versions of DOS.   **Restrictions:** none.

Registers at call: **Return Registers:** n/a

AH = 2Eh

DL = 00h (DOS 1.x/2.x only)

AL =   00h verify flag off

      01h verify flag on

Details: The default state at system boot is OFF. When ON, all disk writes are verified provided the device driver supports read-after-write verification. Many drivers, including those supplied with MS-DOS, only perform CRC checking as "verification".

Conflicts: None known.

See Also: Function 54h

INTERRUPT 21h - Function 2Fh
GET DISK TRANSFER AREA ADDRESS

Purpose: Determine the address of the current disk I/O buffer.

Available on: DOS 2.0 or higher.   **Restrictions:** none.

Registers at call: **Return Registers:**

AH = 2Fh   ES:BX -> current DTA

Conflicts: None known.

See Also: Function 1Ah

INTERRUPT 21h - Function 30h
GET DOS VERSION

Purpose: Determine which version of MS-DOS is in use.

Available on: DOS 2.0 or higher.

Registers at call:
AH = 30h
AL = what to return in BH (DOS 5+ only)
   00h OEM number
   01h version flag

Restrictions: none.

Return Registers:
AL = major version number (00h if DOS 1.x)
AH = minor version number
BL:CX = 24-bit user serial number (most versions do
   not use this)
BH = OEM number:
   00h IBM
   16h DEC
   99h STARLITE architecture (OEM DOS,
        NETWORK DOS, SMP DOS)
   FFh   Phoenix
BH = version flag (DOS 5.0 only):
   08h DOS is in ROM
   10h DOS is in HMA

Details: The OS/2 v1.x Compatibility Box returns major version 0Ah, while the OS/2 v2.x Compatibility Box returns major version 14h. DOS 4.01 and 4.02 identify themselves as version 4.00.

The version returned under DOS 4.0x may be modified by entries in the special program list (see AH=52h). The version returned under DOS 5+ may be modified by SETVER; use Function 33h Subfunction 06h to get the true version number.

Conflicts: Phar Lap 386/DOS-Extender (chapter 9), CTask 2.0+ (chapter 17), "Dutch-555" virus (chapter 34).

See Also: Function 33h Subfunction 06h, INT 2Fh Function 12h Subfunction 2Fh

INTERRUPT 21h - Function 31h
TERMINATE AND STAY RESIDENT

Purpose: Terminate process without releasing resources allocated to it; these resources include environment space, memory, and file handles.

Available on: DOS 2.0 or higher.

Registers at call:
AH = 31h
AL = return code
DX = number of paragraphs to keep resident

Restrictions: none.

Return Registers:
never returns

Details: The value in DX only affects the memory block containing the PSP; additional memory allocated via Function 48h is not affected. Most TSRs can save some memory by releasing their environment block before terminating (see Functions 26h and 49h).

Conflicts: None known.

See Also: Functions 00h, 4Ch, and 4Dh, INT 20h, INT 22h, INT 27h

INTERRUPT 21h - Function 32h
GET DOS DRIVE PARAMETER BLOCK FOR SPECIFIC DRIVE

Purpose: Obtain details of disk parameters for specified drive.

Available on: DOS 2.0 or higher.

Registers at call:
AH = 32h
DL = drive number (00h = default, 01h = A:, etc)

Restrictions: none.

Return Registers:
AL = status:
   00h successful
      DS:BX -> Drive Parameter Block (DPB) for
         specified drive (Table 8-12)
   FFh invalid drive

Details: The OS/2 compatibility box supports the DOS 3.3 version of this call except for the DWORD at offset 12h. This function has been newly documented for DOS 5.0; it was undocumented in prior versions.
Conflicts: None known.
See Also: Function 1Fh

Table 8-12. Format of DOS Drive Parameter Block:

Offset	Size	Description
00h	BYTE	drive number (00h = A:, 01h = B:, etc)
01h	BYTE	unit number within device driver
02h	WORD	bytes per sector
04h	BYTE	highest sector number within a cluster
05h	BYTE	shift count to convert clusters into sectors
06h	WORD	number of reserved sectors at beginning of drive
08h	BYTE	number of FATs
09h	WORD	number of root directory entries
0Bh	WORD	number of first sector containing user data
0Dh	WORD	highest cluster number (number of data clusters + 1)

---*DOS 2.x-3.x*

0Fh	BYTE	number of sectors per FAT
10h	WORD	sector number of first directory sector
12h	DWORD	address of device driver header
16h	BYTE	media ID byte
17h	BYTE	00h if disk accessed, FFh if not
18h	DWORD	pointer to next DPB

---*DOS 2.x*

1Ch	WORD	cluster containing start of current directory, 0000h=root, FFFFh = not known
1Eh	64 BYTEs	ASCIZ pathname of current directory for drive

---*DOS 3.x*

1Ch	WORD	cluster at which to start search for free space when writing
1Eh	WORD	number of free clusters on drive, FFFFh = not known

---*DOS 4.0-5.0*

0Fh	WORD	number of sectors per FAT
11h	WORD	sector number of first directory sector
13h	DWORD	address of device driver header
17h	BYTE	media ID byte
18h	BYTE	00h if disk accessed, FFh if not
19h	DWORD	pointer to next DPB
1Dh	WORD	cluster at which to start search for free space when writing
1Fh	WORD	number of free clusters on drive, FFFFh = not known

INTERRUPT 21h - Function 33h, Subfunctions 00h and 01h
EXTENDED BREAK CHECKING

Purpose: Determine the state of the control-BREAK check flag.

Available on: DOS 2.0 or higher.	**Restrictions:** none.
Registers at call:	**Return Registers:**
AH = 33h	DL = current state, 00h = off, 01h = on
AL = 00h get current extended break state	AL = 01h set state of extended Control-C and Control-Break checking:
	DL = 00h off, check only on character I/O functions
	01h on, check on all DOS functions

Details: Under DOS 3.1+, this function does not use any of the DOS-internal stacks and is thus fully reentrant.
Conflicts: None known.
See Also: Function 33h Subfunction 02h

INTERRUPT 21h - Function 33h, Subfunction 02h
GET AND SET EXTENDED CONTROL-BREAK CHECKING STATE

Purpose: Determine and update the state of the control-BREAK flag in a single operation.

Available on: DOS 3.0 or higher.

Restrictions: This call is not documented and therefore subject to change.

Registers at call:
AX = 3302h
DL =   00h checking OFF
       01h checking ON

Return Registers:
DL = old state of extended BREAK checking

Details: This function does not use any of the DOS-internal stacks and is thus fully reentrant.

Conflicts: None known.

See Also: Function 33h Subfunction 01h

INTERRUPT 21h - Function 33h, Subfunction 05h
GET BOOT DRIVE

Purpose: Determine drive from which the system was booted.

Available on: DOS 4.0 or higher.

Restrictions: none.

Registers at call:
AX = 3305h

Return Registers:
DL = boot drive (1=A:,...)

Conflicts: None known.

INTERRUPT 21h - Function 33h, Subfunction 06h
GET TRUE VERSION NUMBER

Purpose: Determine the actual version of MSDOS in use even if SETVER has changed the version that Function 30h returns.

Available on: DOS 5.0 or higher.

Registers at call:
AX = 3306h

Restrictions: none.

Return Registers:
BL = major version
BH = minor version
DL = revision
DH = version flags
   bit 3: DOS is in ROM
   bit 4: DOS in in HMA

Conflicts: None known.

See Also: Function 30h

INTERRUPT 21h - Function 34h
GET ADDRESS OF INDOS FLAG

Purpose: Determine the address of the InDOS indicator flag. The value of InDOS is incremented whenever an INT 21h function begins and decremented whenever one completes.

Available on: DOS 2.0 or higher.

Restrictions: none.

Registers at call:
AH = 34h

Return Registers:
ES:BX -> one-byte InDOS flag

Details: During an INT 28h call, it is safe to call some INT 21h functions even though InDOS may be 01h instead of zero. InDOS alone is not sufficient for determining when it is safe to enter DOS, as the critical error handling decrements InDOS and increments the critical error flag for the duration of the critical error. Thus, it is possible for InDOS to be zero even if DOS is busy.

The critical error flag is the byte immediately following InDOS in DOS 2.x, and the byte **before** the InDOS flag in DOS 3+ (except COMPAQ DOS 3.0, where the critical error flag is located 1AAh bytes **before** the critical section flag). For DOS 3.1+, an undocumented call exists to get the address of the critical error flag (see Function 5Dh Subfunction 06h).

Conflicts: None known.

See Also: Function 5Dh Subfunctions 06h and 0Bh, INT 28h

INTERRUPT 21h - Function 35h
GET INTERRUPT VECTOR

Purpose: Determine address of service routine for specified interrupt.

Available on: DOS 2.0 or higher.

Registers at call:
AH = 35h
AL = interrupt number

Conflicts: "Agiplan" virus (chapter 34).

See Also: Function 25h

Restrictions: none.

Return Registers:
ES:BX -> current interrupt handler

INTERRUPT 21h - Function 36h
GET FREE DISK SPACE

Purpose: Determine the amount of space available on the specified drive.

Available on: DOS 2.0 or higher.

Registers at call:
AH = 36h
DL = drive number (00h = default, 01h = A:, etc)

Restrictions: none.

Return Registers:
AX = FFFFh if invalid drive
else
      AX = sectors per cluster
      BX = number of free clusters
      CX = bytes per sector
      DX = total clusters on drive

Details: Free space on drive in bytes is AX * BX * CX; total space on drive in bytes is AX * CX * DX. "Lost clusters" are considered to be in use. The value in DX is reportedly incorrect for non-default drives after ASSIGN is run on some versions of DOS.

Conflicts: None known.

See Also: Functions 1Bh and 1Ch

INTERRUPT 21h - Function 37h, Subfunction 00h
"SWITCHAR" - GET SWITCH CHARACTER

Purpose: Determine whether '/' or '-' is used as "switch" indicator in command lines.

Available on: DOS 2.0 or higher.

Registers at call:
AX = 3700h

Restrictions: none.

Return Registers:
AL = status:
    00h successful
        DL = current switch character
          (always '/' in DOS 5)
    FFh unsupported subfunction

Details: Documented in some OEM versions of some releases of DOS. Supported by OS/2 compatibility box.

Conflicts: None known.

See Also: Function 37h Subfunction 01h

INTERRUPT 21h - Function 37h, Subfunction 01h
"SWITCHAR" - SET SWITCH CHARACTER

Purpose: Determines whether '/' or '-' is used as "switch" indicator in command lines. Not all DOS utility programs pay attention, however.

Available on: DOS 2.0 or higher.

Registers at call:
AX = 3701h
DL = new switch character

Restrictions: none.

Return Registers:
AL = status:
    00h successful
    FFh unsupported subfunction

Details: Documented in some OEM versions of some releases of DOS. Supported by OS/2 compatibility box. DOS 5 returns 00h but does not change character.
Conflicts: None known.
See Also: Function 37h Subfunction 00h

INTERRUPT 21h - Function 37h, Subfunctions 02h and 03h
"AVAILDEV" - SPECIFY PREFIX USE

Purpose: Control use of "\DEV\" prefix on device names.

Available on: DOS 2.x and DOS 3.3 or higher only.	**Restrictions:** none.
Registers at call:	**Return Registers:**
AH = 37h	AL = status:
	00h successful
	FFh unsupported subfunction
AL = subfunction:	
02h get availdev flag	DL = 00h must precede character device names
	nonzero is optional
03h set availdev flag	
DL = 00h is mandatory	
nonzero is optional	

Details: All versions of DOS from 2.00 allow "\DEV\" to be prepended to device names without generating an error even if the directory does not actually exist (other paths generate an error if they do not exist). Although DOS 3.3+ accepts these calls, they have no effect, and AL=02h always returns DL=FFh.
Conflicts: None known.

INTERRUPT 21h - Function 38h
GET COUNTRY-SPECIFIC INFORMATION

Purpose: Obtain certain information that varies with country.

Available on: DOS 2.0 or higher.	**Restrictions:** none.
Registers at call: (DOS 2.x)	**Return Registers:**
AH = 38h	CF set on error
AL = 00h get current-country info	AX = error code (02h)
DS:DX -> buffer for returned info (Table 8-13)	CF clear if successful
	AX = country code (MSDOS 2.11 only)
	buffer at DS:DX filled
Registers at call: (DOS 3+)	**Return Registers:**
AH = 38h	CF set on error
AL = 00h for current country	AX = error code (02h)
AL = 01h thru 0FEh for specific country with	CF clear if successful
code <255	BX = country code
AL = 0FFh for specific country with code >= 255	DS:DX buffer filled
BX = 16-bit country code	
DS:DX -> buffer for returned info (Table 8-14)	

Conflicts: None known.
See Also: Function 65h, INT 2Fh Function 11h Subfunction 0Ch (chapter 19), INT 2Fh Function 14h Subfunction 04h

Table 8-13. Format of PCDOS 2.x country info:

Offset	Size	Description		
00h	WORD	date format:	0 = USA	mm dd yy
			1 = Europe	dd mm yy
			2 = Japan	yy mm dd
02h	BYTE	currency symbol		

Table 8-13. Format of PCDOS 2.x country info:

Offset	Size	Description
03h	BYTE	00h
04h	BYTE	thousands separator char
05h	BYTE	00h
06h	BYTE	decimal separator char
07h	BYTE	00h
08h	24 BYTEs	reserved

Table 8-14. Format of MSDOS 2.x,DOS 3+ country info:

Offset	Size	Description
00h	WORD	date format (see above)
02h	5 BYTEs	ASCIZ currency symbol string
07h	BYTE	thousands separator char
08h	BYTE	00h
09h	BYTE	decimal separator char
0Ah	BYTE	00h
0Bh	BYTE	date separator char
0Ch	BYTE	00h
0Dh	BYTE	time separator char
0Eh	BYTE	00h
0Fh	BYTE	currency format:
		bit 2 = set if currency symbol replaces decimal point
		bit 1 = number of spaces between value and currency symbol
		bit 0 = 0 if currency symbol precedes value
		1 if currency symbol follows value
10h	BYTE	number of digits after decimal in currency
11h	BYTE	time format:
		bit 0 = 0 if 12-hour clock
		1 if 24-hour clock
12h	DWORD	address of case map routine (FAR CALL, AL = char to map to upper case [>= 80h])
16h	BYTE	data-list separator char
17h	BYTE	00h
18h	10 BYTEs	reserved

INTERRUPT 21h - Function 38h, Subfunction FFFFh
SET COUNTRY CODE

Purpose: Establish current "country code" to control country-specific information.

Available on: DOS 3.0 or higher.   **Restrictions:** none.

Registers at call: **Return Registers:**

AH = 38h   CF set on error

AL = 01h thru 0FEh for specific country with   AX = error code (see Function 59h)
   code <255   CF clear if successful

AL = FFh for specific country with code >= 255

BX = 16-bit country code

DX = FFFFh

Conflicts: None known.

See Also: INT 2Fh Function 14h Subfunction 03h

INTERRUPT 21h - Function 39h
"MKDIR" - CREATE SUBDIRECTORY

Purpose: Create a new subdirectory in the current directory tree.

Available on: DOS 2.0 or higher.   **Restrictions:** none.

Registers at call:
AH = 39h
DS:DX -> ASCIZ pathname

Return Registers:
CF clear if successful
   AX destroyed
CF set on error
   AX = error code (03h,05h) (see Function 59h)

Details: All directories in the given path except the last must exist. The call fails if the parent directory is the root and is full.
Conflicts: None known.
See Also: Functions 3Ah and 3Bh, INT 2Fh Function 11h Subfunction 03h (chapter 19)

INTERRUPT 21h - Function 3Ah
"RMDIR" - REMOVE SUBDIRECTORY

Purpose: Destroy a subdirectory.
Available on: DOS 2.0 or higher.
Registers at call:
AH = 3Ah
DS:DX -> ASCIZ pathname of directory to be
   removed

Restrictions: none.
Return Registers:
CF clear if successful
   AX destroyed
CF set on error
   AX = error code (03h,05h,06h,10h) (Function 59h)

Details: The directory must be empty (contain only '.' and '..' entries), or this call will fail.
Conflicts: None known.
See Also: Functions 39h and 3Bh, INT 2Fh Function 11h Subfunction 01h (chapter 19)

INTERRUPT 21h - Function 3Bh
"CHDIR" - SET CURRENT DIRECTORY

Purpose: Changes "current" directory to that specified.
Available on: DOS 2.0 or higher.
Registers at call:
AH = 3Bh
DS:DX -> ASCIZ pathname to become current
   directory (max 64 bytes)

Restrictions: none.
Return Registers:
CF clear if successful
   AX destroyed
CF set on error
   AX = error code (03h) (see Function 59h)

Details: If the new directory name includes a drive letter, the default drive is not changed, only the current directory on that drive. Changing the current directory also changes the directory in which FCB file calls operate.
Conflicts: None known.
See Also: Function 47h, INT 2Fh Function 11h Subfunction 05h (chapter 19)

INTERRUPT 21h - Function 3Ch
"CREAT" - CREATE OR TRUNCATE FILE

Purpose: Create an empty file for writing.
Available on: DOS 2.0 or higher.
Registers at call:
AH = 3CH
CX = file attribute:
   bit 0: read-only
      1: hidden
      2: system
      3: volume label (ignored)
      4: reserved, must be zero (directory)
      5: archive bit
      7: if set, file is shareable under Novell
         NetWare
DS:DX -> ASCIZ filename

Restrictions: none.
Return Registers:
CF clear if successful
   AX = file handle
CF set on error
   AX = error code (03h,04h,05h) (see Function 59h)

Details: If a file with the given name exists, it is truncated to zero length.
Conflicts: None known.
See Also: Functions 16h, 3Dh, 5Ah, and 5Bh

INTERRUPT 21h - Function 3Dh
"OPEN" - OPEN EXISTING FILE

Purpose: Open file for reading, writing, or appending.
Available on: DOS 2.0 or higher.
Registers at call:
AH = 3Dh
AL = access and sharing modes:
    bits 2-0: access mode:
        000 read only
        001 write only
        010 read/write
    bit 3: reserved (0)
    bits 6-4: sharing mode (DOS 3+):
        000 compatibility mode
        001 "DENYALL" prohibit both read and
            write access by others
        010 "DENYWRITE" prohibit write access
            by others
        011 "DENYREAD" prohibit read access
            by others
        100 "DENYNONE" allow full access by
            others
    bit 7: inheritance:
        if set, the file is private to the current
            process and will not be inherited by
            child processes
DS:DX -> ASCIZ filename
CL = attribute mask for file (server call only), file
    will not be opened if it has any attributes
    other than the specified ones, read-only,
    or archive set.

Restrictions: none.
Return Registers:
CF clear if successful
    AX = file handle
CF set on error
    AX = error code (01h,02h,03h,04h,05h,0Ch) (see
Function 59h)

Details: The file pointer is set to the start of the file. File handles which are inherited from a parent also inherit sharing and access restrictions. Files may be opened even if given the hidden or system attributes.
Conflicts: None known.
See Also: Functions 0Fh and 3Ch, Function 5Dh Subfunction 00h, INT 2Fh Function 12h Subfunction 26h

Table 8-15. File sharing behavior

First Opened as:		Compat R W RW	Deny All R W RW	Deny Write R W RW	Deny Read R W RW	Deny None R W RW
Compat	R	Y Y Y	N N N	1 N N	N N N	1 N N
	W	Y Y Y	N N N	N N N	N N N	N N N
	RW	Y Y Y	N N N	N N N	N N N	N N N
Deny All	R	C C C	N N N	N N N	N N N	N N N
	W	C C C	N N N	N N N	N N N	N N N
	RW	C C C	N N N	N N N	N N N	N N N
Deny Write	R	2 C C	N N N	Y N N	N N N	Y N N
	W	C C C	N N N	N N N	Y N N	Y N N
	RW	C C C	N N N	N N N	N N N	Y N N
Deny Read	R	C C C	N N N	N Y N	N N N	N Y N
	W	C C C	N N N	N N N	N Y N	N Y N
	RW	C C C	N N N	N N N	N N N	N Y N
Deny none	R	2 C C	N N N	Y Y Y	N N N	Y Y Y
	W	C C C	N N N	N N N	Y Y Y	Y Y Y
	RW	C C C	N N N	N N N	N N N	Y Y Y

Legend: Y = open succeeds
          N = open fails with error code 05h
          C = open fails, INT 24h generated
          1 = open succeeds if file read-only, else fails with error code
          2 = open succeeds if file read-only, else fails with INT 24h

INTERRUPT 21h - Function 3Eh
"CLOSE" - CLOSE FILE

Purpose: Force all buffers to be flushed and directory information updated, then invalidate the file handle.

Available on: DOS 2.0 or higher.

Restrictions: none.

Registers at call:
AH = 3Eh
BX = file handle

Return Registers:
CF clear if successful
   AX destroyed
CF set on error
   AX = error code (06h) (see Function 59h)

Details: If the file was written to, any pending disk writes are performed, the time and date stamps are set to the current time, and the directory entry is updated.

Conflicts: None known.

See Also: Functions 10h, 3Ch, and 3Dh, INT 2Fh Function 11h Subfunction 06h (chapter 19), INT 2Fh Function 12h Subfunction 27h

INTERRUPT 21h - Function 3Fh
"READ" - READ FROM FILE OR DEVICE

Purpose: Read data to the specified buffer from a file or device.

Available on: DOS 2.0 or higher.

Restrictions: none.

Registers at call:
AH = 3Fh
BX = file handle
CX = number of bytes to read
DS:DX -> buffer for data

Return Registers:
CF clear if successful
    AX = number of bytes actually read (0 if at EOF
      before call)
CF set on error
    AX = error code (05h,06h) (see Function 59h)

Details: Data is read beginning at the current file position, and the file position is updated after a successful read. The returned AX may be smaller than the request in CX if a partial read occurred. If reading from CON, read stops at first CR.
Conflicts: None known.
See Also: Functions 27h and 40h, INT 2Fh Function 11h Subfunction 08h (chapter 19), INT 2Fh Function 12h Subfunction 29h

INTERRUPT 21h - Function 40h
"WRITE" - WRITE TO FILE OR DEVICE

Purpose: Write data from specified buffer to file or device.
Available on: DOS 2.0 or higher.   **Restrictions:** none.
Registers at call: **Return Registers:**
AH = 40h   CF clear if successful
BX = file handle   AX = number of bytes actually written
CX = number of bytes to write   CF set on error
DS:DX -> data to write   AX = error code (05h,06h) (see Function 59h)

Details: If CX is zero, no data is written, and the file is truncated or extended to the current position. Data is written beginning at the current file position, and the file position is updated after a successful write. The usual cause for AX < CX on return is a full disk.
Conflicts: None known.
See Also: Functions 28h and 3Fh, INT 2Fh Function 11h Subfunction 09h (chapter 19)

INTERRUPT 21h - Function 41h
"UNLINK" - DELETE FILE

Purpose: Destroy the specified file.
Available on: DOS 2.0 or higher.   **Restrictions:** none.
Registers at call: **Return Registers:**
AH = 41h   CF clear if successful
DS:DX -> ASCIZ filename (no wildcards, but see   AX destroyed (DOS 3.3), AL seems to be drive of
  below)   deleted file
CL = attribute mask (server call only, see below)   CF set on error
                                              AX = error code (02h,03h,05h) (see Function
                                                  59h)

Details: DOS 3.1+ allows wildcards if this function is invoked via Function 5Dh Subfunction 00h, in which case the filespec must be canonical (as returned by Function 60h), and only files matching the attribute mask in CL are deleted.
    DOS does not erase the file's data; it merely becomes inaccessible because the FAT chain for the file is cleared. Deleting a file which is currently open may lead to filesystem corruption. Unless SHARE is loaded, DOS does not close the handles referencing the deleted file, thus allowing writes to a nonexistant file.
Conflicts: None known.
See Also: Functions 13h and 60h, Function 5Dh Subfunction 00h, INT 2Fh Function 11h Subfunction 13h (chapter 19)

INTERRUPT 21h - Function 42h
"LSEEK" - SET CURRENT FILE POSITION

Purpose: Position to specified location in file.
Available on: DOS 2.0 or higher.   **Restrictions:** none.

Registers at call:
AH = 42h
AL = origin of move:
   00h start of file
   01h current file position
   02h end of file
BX = file handle
CX:DX = offset from origin of new file position

Return Registers:
CF clear if successful
   DX:AX = new file position in bytes from start of file
CF set on error
   AX = error code (01h,06h) (see Function 59h)

Details: For origins 01h and 02h, the pointer may be positioned before the start of the file; no error is returned in that case, but subsequent attempts at I/O will produce errors. If the new position is beyond the current end of file, the file will be extended by the next write (see Function 40h).
Conflicts: "Shake" virus (chapter 34), "Invader" virus (chapter 34).
See Also: Function 24h, INT 2Fh Function 12h Subfunction 28h

INTERRUPT 21h - Function 43h, Subfunction 00h
GET FILE ATTRIBUTES

Purpose: Determine control attributes for the specified file.
Available on: DOS 2.0 or higher.
Registers at call:
AX = 4300h
DS:DX -> ASCIZ filename

Restrictions: none.
Return Registers:
CF clear if successful
   CX = attributes:
      bit 8: shareable (Novell NetWare)
        7: unused
        6: unused
        5: archive
        4: directory
        3: volume label
        2: system
        1: hidden
        0: read-only
CF set on error
   AX = error code (01h,02h,03h,05h) (see Function 59h)

Conflicts: None known.
See Also: Function 43h Subfunction 01h, Function B6h, INT 2Fh Function 11h Subfunction 0Fh (chapter 19)

INTERRUPT 21h - Function 43h, Subfunction 01h
"CHMOD" - SET FILE ATTRIBUTES

Purpose: Sets control attributes for the specified file.
Available on: DOS 2.0 or higher.
Registers at call:
AX = 4301h
CX = new attributes:
   bit 8: shareable (Novell NetWare)
      7: unused
      6: unused
      5: archive
      4: directory (ignored)
      3: volume label (ignored)
      2: system
      1: hidden
      0: read-only
DS:DX -> ASCIZ filename

Restrictions: none.
Return Registers:
CF clear if successful
   AX destroyed
CF set on error
   AX = error code (01h,02h,03h,05h) (see Function 59h)

Details: This function will not change the volume label or directory attributes.
Conflicts: None known.
See Also: Function 43h Subfunction 00h, INT 2Fh Function 11h Subfunction 0Eh (chapter 19)

INTERRUPT 21h - Function 44h, Subfunction 00h
IOCTL - GET DEVICE INFORMATION

Purpose: Determine characteristics of specified file or device.
Available on: DOS 2.0 or higher.
Registers at call:
AX = 4400h
BX = handle

Restrictions: none.
Return Registers:
CF clear if successful
  DX = device information word:
  character device if bit 7 set:
    14: device driver can process IOCTL requests
      (see Function 44h Subfunction 02h)
    13: output until busy supported
    11: driver supports OPEN/CLOSE calls
     7: set (indicates device)
     6: EOF on input
     5: raw (binary) mode
     4: device is special (uses INT 29h)
     3: clock device
     2: NUL device
     1: standard output
     0: standard input
  disk file if bit 7 clear:
    15: file is remote (DOS 3+)
    14: don't set file date/time on closing (DOS 3+)
    11: media not removable
     8: (DOS 4+) generate INT 24 if no disk space
      on write
     7: clear (indicates file)
     6: file has not been written
    5-0: drive number (0 = A:)
CF set on error
  AX = error code (01h,05h,06h) (see Function
    59h)

Details: The value in DH corresponds to the high byte of the device driver's attribute word if the handle refers to a character device.
Conflicts: None known.
See Also: Function 44h Subfunction 01h, INT 2Fh Function 12h Subfunction 2Bh

INTERRUPT 21h - Function 44h, Subfunction 01h
IOCTL - SET DEVICE INFORMATION

Purpose: Set the changeable characteristics of the specified character device.
Available on: DOS 2.0 or higher.
Registers at call:
AX = 4401h
BX = handle (must refer to character device)
DX = device information word (see Function 44h
    Subfunction 00h) (DH must be zero)
Conflicts: None known.
See Also: Function 44h Subfunction 00h, INT 2Fh Function 12h Subfunction 2Bh

Restrictions: none.
Return Registers:
CF clear if successful
CF set on error
  AX = error code (01h,05h,06h,0Dh) (see Function
    59h)

INTERRUPT 21h - Function 44h, Subfunction 02h
IOCTL - READ FROM CHARACTER DEVICE CONTROL CHANNEL

Purpose: Read data from the control channel of the specified device.

Available on: DOS 2.0 or higher.

Restrictions: Device driver must support the IOCTL call.

Registers at call:
AX = 4402h
BX = file handle referencing character device
CX = number of bytes to read
DS:DX -> buffer

Return Registers:
CF clear if successful
   AX = number of bytes actually read
CF set on error
   AX = error code (01h,05h,06h,0Dh) (see Function 59h)

Details: The format of the data is driver-specific.

Conflicts: SMARTDRV (chapter 6), Network Driver Interface Specification (chapter 27), IBM System 36/38 Workstation Emulation (chapter 26), HIGHUMM.SYS IOCTL (chapter 36), LASTBYTE.SYS (chapter 36).

See Also: Function 44h Subfunctions 00h, 03h, and 04h, INT 2Fh Function 12h Subfunction 2Bh

INTERRUPT 21h - Function 44h, Subfunction 03h
IOCTL - WRITE TO CHARACTER DEVICE CONTROL CHANNEL

Purpose: Write data to the control channel of the specified device.

Available on: DOS 2.0 or higher.

Restrictions: Device driver must support the IOCTL call.

Registers at call:
AX = 4403h
BX = file handle referencing character device
CX = number of bytes to write
DS:DX -> data to write

Return Registers:
CF clear if successful
   AX = number of bytes actually written
CF set on error
   AX = error code (01h,05h,06h,0Dh) (see Function 59h)

Details: The format of the data is driver-specific. If the file handle refers to "4DOSSTAK" (or "NDOSSTAK"), the 4DOS (or NDOS) KEYSTACK.SYS driver will push the specified characters on the keyboard stack.

Conflicts: SMARTDRV (chapter 6).

See Also: Function 44h Subfunctions 00h, 02h, and 05h, INT 2Fh Function 12h Subfunction 2Bh, INT 2Fh Function D4h Subfunction 4Dh

INTERRUPT 21h - Function 44h, Subfunction 04h
IOCTL - READ FROM BLOCK DEVICE CONTROL CHANNEL

Purpose: Read data from the control channel of the specified device.

Available on: DOS 2.0 or higher.

Restrictions: Device driver must support the IOCTL call.

Registers at call:
AX = 4404h
BL = drive number (00h = default, 01h = A:, etc)
CX = number of bytes to read
DS:DX -> buffer

Return Registers:
CF clear if successful
   AX = number of bytes actually read
CF set on error
   AX = error code (01h,05h,06h,0Dh) (see Function 59h)

Details: The format of the data is driver-specific.

Conflicts: None known.

See Also: Function 44h Subfunctions 02h and 05h, INT 2Fh Function 12h Subfunction 2Bh

INTERRUPT 21h - Function 44h, Subfunction 05h
IOCTL - WRITE TO BLOCK DEVICE CONTROL CHANNEL

Purpose: Write data to the control channel of the specified device.

Available on: DOS 2.0 or higher.

Registers at call:
AX = 4405h
BL = drive number (00h = default, 01h = A:, etc)
CX = number of bytes to write
DS:DX -> data to write

Details: The format of the data is driver-specific.
Conflicts: None known.
See Also: Function 44h Subfunctions 03h and 04h, INT 2Fh Function 12h Subfunction 2Bh

Restrictions: Device driver must support the IOCTL call.
Return Registers:
CF clear if successful
    AX = number of bytes actually written
CF set on error
    AX = error code (01h,05h,06h,0Dh) (see Function 59h)

INTERRUPT 21h - Function 44h, Subfunction 06h
IOCTL - GET INPUT STATUS

Purpose: Get input status of specified device.
Available on: DOS 2.0 or higher.
Registers at call:
AX = 4406h
BX = file handle

Restrictions: none.
Return Registers:
CF clear if successful
    AL = input status:
        00h not ready (device) or at EOF (file)
        FFh ready
CF set on error
    AX = error code (01h,05h,06h,0Dh) (see Function 59h)

Details: Files may not register as being at EOF if positioned there by Function 42h.
Conflicts: None known.
See Also: Function 44h Subfunction 07h, INT 2Fh Function 12h Subfunction 2Bh

INTERRUPT 21h - Function 44h, Subfunction 07h
IOCTL - GET OUTPUT STATUS

Purpose: Get output status of specified device.
Available on: DOS 2.0 or higher.
Registers at call:
AX = 4407h
BX = file handle

Restrictions: none.
Return Registers:
CF clear if successful
    AL = input status:
        00h not ready
        FFh ready
CF set on error
    AX = error code (01h,05h,06h,0Dh) (see Function 59h)

Details: For DOS 2+, files are always ready for output.
Conflicts: None known.
See Also: Function 44h Subfunction 06h, INT 2Fh Function 12h Subfunction 2Bh

INTERRUPT 21h - Function 44h, Subfunction 08h
IOCTL - CHECK IF BLOCK DEVICE REMOVABLE

Purpose: Determine whether the specified device has removeable media.
Available on: DOS 3.0 or higher.
Restrictions: none.

Registers at call:
AX = 4408h
BL = drive number (00h = default, 01h = A:, etc)

Return Registers:
CF clear if successful
    AX = 0000h if removable
           0001h if fixed
CF set on error
    AX = error code (01h,0Fh) (see Function 59h)

Conflicts: None known.
See Also: Function 44h Subfunctions 00h and 09h, INT 2Fh Function 12h Subfunction 2Bh

INTERRUPT 21h - Function 44h, Subfunction 09h
IOCTL - CHECK IF BLOCK DEVICE REMOTE

Purpose: Determine whether the specified device is local or remote.
Available on: DOS 3.1 or higher.
Restrictions: none.
Registers at call:
AX = 4409h
BL = drive number (00h = default, 01h = A:, etc)

Return Registers:
CF clear if successful
    DX = device attribute word:
        bit 15: drive is SUBSTituted
        bit 12: drive is remote
        bit 9: direct I/O not allowed
CF set on error
    AX = error code (01h,0Fh) (see Function 59h)

Details: On local drives, DX bits not listed above are the attribute word from the device driver header (see Function 52h); for remote drives, the other bits appear to be undefined.
Conflicts: None known.
See Also: Function 44h Subfunctions 00h, 08h, and 0Ah, INT 2Fh Function 12h Subfunction 2Bh

INTERRUPT 21h - Function 44h, Subfunction 0Ah
IOCTL - CHECK IF HANDLE IS REMOTE

Purpose: Determine whether the specified handle refers to a file on a remote device.
Available on: DOS 3.1 or higher.
Restrictions: none.
Registers at call:
AX = 440Ah
BX = handle

Return Registers:
CF clear if successful
    DX = attribute word (as stored in SFT)
        bit 15: set if remote
CF set on error
    AX = error code (01h,06h) (see Function 59h)

Details: If the file is remote, Novell Advanced NetWare 2.0 returns the number of the file server on which the handle is located in CX.
Conflicts: None known.
See Also: Function 44h Subfunctions 00h and 09h, Function 52h, INT 2Fh Function 12h Subfunction 2Bh

INTERRUPT 21h - Function 44h, Subfunction 0Bh
IOCTL - SET SHARING RETRY COUNT

Purpose: Establish the number of retries to be used in case of a SHARE failure on opening or locking a file.
Available on: DOS 3.1 or higher.
Restrictions: none.
Registers at call:
AX = 440Bh
CX = pause between retries (default 1)
DX = number of retries (default 3)

Return Registers:
CF clear if successful
CF set on error
    AX = error code (01h) (see Function 59h)

Details: The delay is dependent on the processor's speed (the value in CX specifies the number of 64K-iteration empty loops to execute). If DX=0000h on entry, the retry count is left unchanged.
Conflicts: None known.

See Also: Function 52h, INT 2Fh Function 12h Subfunctions 24h and 2Bh

INTERRUPT 21h - Function 44h, Subfunction 0Ch
IOCTL - GENERIC CHARACTER DEVICE REQUEST

Purpose: Miscellaneous requests to character device drivers.

Available on: DOS 3.2 or higher.

Registers at call:
AX = 440Ch
BX = device handle
CH = category code:
    00h unknown (DOS 3.3+)
    01h COMn: (DOS 3.3+)
    03h CON (DOS 3.3+)
    05h LPTn:
    9Eh Media Access Control driver
       (STARLITE)
CL = function:
    00h MAC driver Bind (STARLITE)
    45h set iteration count
    4Ah select code page
    4Ch start code-page preparation
    4Dh end code-page preparation
    5Fh set display information (DOS 4.0)
    65h get iteration count
    6Ah query selected code page
    6Bh query prepare list
    7Fh get display information (DOS 4.0)
DS:DX -> (DOS) parameter block (Tables 8-16
    thru 8-22)
SI:DI -> (OS/2 comp box) parameter block
    (Tables 8-16 thru 8-22)

Restrictions: none.

Return Registers:
CF set on error
    AX = error code (see Function 59h)
CF clear if successful
    DS:DX -> iteration count if CL=65h
DS:DX -> (OS/2 comp box) data block

Conflicts: None known.

See Also: Function 44h Subfunctions 0Dh and 10h, INT 2Fh Function 08h Subfunction 02h, INT 2Fh Function 12h Subfunction 2Bh, INT 2Fh Function 1Ah Subfunction 01h

Table 8-16. Format of parameter block for function 00h:

Offset	Size	Description
00h	8 BYTEs	ASCIZ signature "STARMAC"
08h	WORD	version
0Ah	WORD	flags:
		bit 0: media requires connect or listen request before use
		bit 1: network is a LAN (broadcast/multicast supported)
		bit 2: point-to-point network
0Ch	WORD	handle for use with MAC driver's private interface (filled in by MAC driver)
0Eh	WORD	context
10h	WORD	approximate speed in KB/sec (filled in by MAC driver)
12h	WORD	approximate cost in cents per hour (filled in by MAC driver)
14h	WORD	maximum packet size in bytes (filled in by MAC driver)
16h	WORD	addressing format (filled in by MAC driver)
		0000h general addressing
		0001h Ethernet addressing
		0002h Token Ring addressing
		0003h Token Bus addressing
18h	DWORD	Send entry point (filled in by MAC driver)

Table 8-16. Format of parameter block for function 00h (continued)

Offset	Size	Description
1Ch	DWORD	RegisterEventHandler entry point (filled in by MAC driver)
20h	DWORD	SetPacketFilter entry point (filled in by MAC driver)
24h	DWORD	UnBind entry point (filled in by MAC driver)

Table 8-17. Format of parameter block for function 45h:

Offset	Size	Description
00h	WORD	number of times output is attempted before driver assumes device is busy

Table 8-18. Format of parameter block for functions 4Ah and 6Ah:

Offset	Size	Description
00h	WORD	length of data
02h	WORD	code page ID
04h	2N BYTEs	DCBS (double byte character set) lead byte range start/end for each of N ranges (DOS 4.0)
	WORD	0000h end of data (DOS 4.0)

Table 8-19. Format of parameter block for function 4Ch:

Offset	Size	Description
00h	WORD	flags:
		DISPLAY.SYS = 0000h
		PRINTER.SYS bit 0 clear to prepare downloaded font, set to prepare cartridge selection
02h	WORD	length of remainder of parameter block
04h	WORD	number of code pages following
06h	N WORDs	code page 1,...,N

Table 8-20. Format of parameter block for function 4Dh:

Offset	Size	Description
00h	WORD	length of data
02h	WORD	code page ID

Table 8-21. Format of parameter block for functions 5Fh and 7Fh:

Offset	Size	Description
00h	BYTE	level (0 for DOS 4.x and 5.0)
01h	BYTE	reserved (0)
02h	WORD	length of following data (14)
04h	WORD	control flags:
		bit 0 set for blink, clear for intensity
		bits 1 to 15 reserved
06h	BYTE	mode type (1=text, 2=graphics)
07h	BYTE	reserved (0)
08h	WORD	colors:
		0 = monochrome
		else N bits per pixel
0Ah	WORD	pixel columns
0Ch	WORD	pixel rows
0Eh	WORD	character columns
10h	WORD	character rows

Table 8-22. Format of parameter block for function 6Bh:

Offset	Size	Description
00h	WORD	length of following data
02h	WORD	number of hardware code pages
04h	N WORDs	hardware code pages 1,...,N
	WORD	number of prepared code pages
	N WORDs	prepared code pages 1,...,N

INTERRUPT 21h - Function 44h, Subfunction 0Dh
IOCTL - GENERIC BLOCK DEVICE REQUEST

Purpose: Miscellaneous requests to block device drivers.

Available on: DOS 3.2 or higher.

Registers at call:

AX = 440Dh

BL = drive number (00h=default,01h=A:,etc)

CH = category code:

    08h disk drive

CL = function:

    40h set device parameters

    41h write logical device track

    42h format and verify logical device track

    46h (DOS 4.0) set volume serial number

      (see also Function 69h)

    47h (DOS 4.0) set access flag

    60h get device parameters

    61h read logical device track

    62h verify logical device track

    66h (DOS 4.0) get volume serial number

      (see also Function 69h)

    67h (DOS 4.0) get access flag

DS:DX -> (DOS) parameter block

    (Tables 8-23 thru 8-27)

SI:DI -> (OS/2 comp box) parameter block

    (Tables 8-23 thru 8-27)

Restrictions: none.

Return Registers:

CF set on error

    AX = error code (see Function 59h)

CF clear if successful

    DS:DX -> data block if CL=60h or CL=61h

Details: DOS 4.01 seems to ignore the high byte of the number of directory entries in the BPB for diskettes.

Function codes 46h and 66h were undocumented in DOS 4.x, but are documented for DOS 5.0.

Conflicts: None known.

See Also: Function 44h Subfunctions 0Ch and 11h, Function 69h, INT 2Fh Function 08h Subfunction 02h, INT 2Fh Function 12h Subfunction 2Bh

Table 8-23. Format of parameter block for functions 40h, 60h:

Offset	Size	Description
00h	BYTE	special functions:

    bit 0 set if function to use current BPB, clear if Device BIOS Parameter Block field

          contains new default BPB

    bit 1 set if function to use track layout fields only must be clear if CL=60h

    bit 2 set if all sectors in track same size (should be set)

    bits 3-7 reserved

Table 8-23. Format of parameter block for functions 40h, 60h (continued)

Offset	Size	Description
01h	BYTE	device type:
		00h 320K/360K disk
		01h 1.2M disk
		02h 720K disk
		03h single-density 8-inch disk
		04h double-density 8-inch disk
		05h fixed disk
		06h tape drive
		07h 1.44M disk
		08h other type of block device
02h	WORD	device attributes:
		bit 0 set if nonremovable medium
		bit 1 set if door lock supported
		bits 2-15 reserved
04h	WORD	number of cylinders
06h	BYTE	media type:
		for 1.2M drive:
		00h 1.2M disk (default)
		01h 320K/360K disk
		always 00h for other drive types
07h	31 BYTEs	device BPB (see Function 53h), bytes after BPB offset 1Eh omitted
26h	WORD	number of sectors per track (start of track layout field) not used by function 60h
28h	N word	pairs: number,size of each sector in track

Table 8-24. Format of parameter block for functions 41h, 61h:

Offset	Size	Description
00h	BYTE	special functions (reserved, must be zero)
01h	WORD	number of disk head
03h	WORD	number of disk cylinder
05h	WORD	number of first sector to read/write
07h	WORD	number of sectors
09h	DWORD	transfer address

Table 8-25. Format of parameter block for functions 42h, 62h:

Offset	Size	Description
00h	BYTE	reserved, must be zero (DOS <3.2)
		bit 0=0: format/verify track
		1: format status call (DOS 3.2+)
		bits 1-7 reserved, must be zero on return (DOS 4.0):
		bit 0: set if specified tracks, sectors/track supported
		bit 1: set if function not supported by BIOS
		bit 2: set if specified tracks, sectors/track not supported
		bit 3: set if no disk in drive
01h	WORD	number of disk head
03h	WORD	number of disk cylinder

Table 8-26. Format of parameter block for functions 46h, 66h:

Offset	Size	Description
00h	WORD	info level (00h)
02h	DWORD	disk serial number (binary)
06h	11 BYTEs	volume label or "NO NAME "
11h	8 BYTEs	filesystem type "FAT12 " or "FAT16 " (CL=66h only)

Table 8-27. Format of parameter block for functions 47h, 67h:

Offset	Size	Description
00h	BYTE	special-function field (must be zero)
01h	BYTE	disk-access flag, nonzero if access allowed by driver

INTERRUPT 21h - Function 44h, Subfunction 0Eh
IOCTL - GET LOGICAL DRIVE MAP

Purpose: Determine last letter used to reference the specified drive.
Available on: DOS 3.2 or higher.
Registers at call:
AX = 440Eh
BL = drive number (00h=default, 01h=A:, etc)

Restrictions: none.
Return Registers:
CF set on error
    AX = error code (01h,0Fh) (see Function 59h)
CF clear if successful
    AL = 00h block device has only one logical drive
        assigned
        1..26 the last letter used to reference the
           drive (1=A:,etc)

Conflicts: None known.
See Also: Function 44h Subfunction 0Fh, INT 2Fh Function 12h Subfunction 2Bh

INTERRUPT 21h - Function 44h, Subfunction 0Fh
IOCTL - SET LOGICAL DRIVE MAP

Purpose: Maps logical drives to physical drives, similar to DOS's treatment of a single physical floppy drive as both A: and B:.
Available on: DOS 3.2 or higher.
Registers at call:
AX = 440Fh
BL = physical drive number (00h=default, 01h=A:, etc)

Restrictions: none.
Return Registers:
CF set on error
    AX = error code (01h,0Fh) (see Function 59h)
CF clear if successful
    drive now responds to next logical drive number

Conflicts: None known.
See Also: Function 44h Subfunction 0Eh, INT 2Fh Function 12h Subfunction 2Bh

INTERRUPT 21h - Function 44h, Subfunction 10h
IOCTL - QUERY GENERIC IOCTL CAPABILITY (HANDLE)

Purpose: Determine whether a character device supports a particular generic IOCTL call.
Available on: DOS 5.0 or higher.

Restrictions: device driver must support Generic IOCTL Check call.

Registers at call:
AX = 4410h
BX = handle for device
CH = category code (see Function 44h Subfunction 0Ch)
CL = function code

Return Registers:
CF clear if successful
    AX = 0000h   specified IOCTL function is
        supported
CF set on error
    AL = 01h IOCTL capability not available

Details: A program which wishes to use Generic IOCTL calls beyond the basic set of calls defined for DOS 3.2 may use this call to verify whether a particular call is supported by the driver.
Conflicts: NewSpace (chapter 6)
See Also: Function 44h Subfunctions 0Ch and 11h

INTERRUPT 21h - Function 44h, Subfunction 11h
IOCTL - QUERY GENERIC IOCTL CAPABILITY (DRIVE)

Purpose: Determine whether a block device supports a particular generic IOCTL call.

Available on: DOS 5.0 or higher.

Restrictions: device driver must support Generic IOCTL Check call.

Registers at call:
AX = 4411h
BL = drive number
CH = category code (see Function 44h Subfunction 0Dh)
CL = function code

Return Registers:
CF clear if successful
   AX = 0000h   specified IOCTL function is supported
CF set on error
   AL = 01h IOCTL capability not available

Details: A program which wishes to use Generic IOCTL calls beyond the basic set of calls defined for DOS 3.2 may use this call to verify whether a particular call is supported by the driver.

Conflicts: NewSpace (chapter 6)

See Also: Function 44h Subfunctions 0Dh and 10h

INTERRUPT 21h - Function 45h
"DUP" - DUPLICATE FILE HANDLE

Purpose: Creates new file handle that references the specified file or device via the same System File Table entry.

Available on: DOS 2.0 or higher.

Restrictions: none.

Registers at call:
AH = 45h
BX = file handle

Return Registers:
CF clear if successful
   AX = new handle
CF set on error
   AX = error code (04h,06h) (see Function 59h)

Details: Moving the file pointer for either handle will also move it for the other, because both refer to the same system file table. For DOS versions prior to 3.3, file writes may be forced to disk by duplicating the file handle and closing the duplicate; DOS 3.3 and up provide a function for that purpose.

Conflicts: None known.

See Also: Functions 3Dh and 46h

INTERRUPT 21h - Function 46h
"DUP2", "FORCEDUP" - FORCE DUPLICATE FILE HANDLE

Purpose: Forces a particular handle to become a duplicate of the specified handle.

Available on: DOS 2.0 or higher.

Restrictions: none.

Registers at call:
AH = 46h
BX = file handle
CX = file handle to become duplicate of first handle

Return Registers:
CF clear if successful
CF set on error
   AX = error code (04h,06h) (see Function 59h)

Details: Closes file with handle BX if it is still open. DOS 3.30 hangs if BX=CX on entry. Moving the file pointer for either handle will also move it for the other, because both will refer to the same system file table.

Conflicts: None known.

See Also: Functions 3Dh and 45h

INTERRUPT 21h - Function 47h
"CWD" - GET CURRENT DIRECTORY

Purpose: Determine current working directory.

Available on: DOS 2.0 or higher.

Restrictions: none.

Registers at call:
AH = 47h
DL = drive number (00h = default, 01h = A:, etc)
DS:SI -> 64-byte buffer for ASCIZ pathname

Return Registers:
CF clear if successful
   AX = 0100h (undocumented)
CF set on error
   AX = error code (0Fh) (see Function 59h)

Details: The returned path does not include a drive or the initial backslash. Many Microsoft products for Windows rely on AX being 0100h on success.
Conflicts: None known.
See Also: Functions 19h and 3Bh

INTERRUPT 21h - Function 48h
ALLOCATE MEMORY

Purpose: Assigns memory for program use, if available.
Available on: DOS 2.0 or higher.
Registers at call:
AH = 48h
BX = number of paragraphs to allocate

Restrictions: none.
Return Registers:
CF clear if successful
   AX = segment of allocated block
CF set on error
   AX = error code (07h,08h) (see Function 59h)
   BX = size of largest available block

Details: DOS 3.30 coalesces free blocks while scanning for a block to allocate.
   COM-format programs are initially allocated the largest available memory block, and should free some memory with Function 49h before attempting any allocations. EXE-format programs are initially allocated memory as specified in their headers (most compilers set the allocation such that the program is given the largest available memory block).
Conflicts: None known.
See Also: Functions 49h, 4Ah, and 58h

INTERRUPT 21h - Function 49h
FREE MEMORY

Purpose: Releases allocated memory blocks.
Available on: DOS 2.0 or higher.
Registers at call:
AH = 49h
ES = segment of block to free

Restrictions: none.
Return Registers:
CF clear if successful
CF set on error
   AX = error code (07h,09h) (see Function 59h)

Details: Apparently never returns an error 07h, despite official documentation; DOS 3.30 code contains only an error 09h exit. DOS 3.30 does not coalesce adjacent free blocks when a block is freed, only when a block is allocated or resized,
Conflicts: None known.
See Also: Function 48h and 4Ah

INTERRUPT 21h - Function 4Ah
RESIZE MEMORY BLOCK

Purpose: Changes the size of a previously-allocated memory block, if possible.
Available on: DOS 2.0 or higher.
Registers at call:
AH = 4Ah
BX = new size in paragraphs
ES = segment of block to resize

Restrictions: none.
Return Registers:
CF clear if successful
CF set on error
   AX = error code (07h,08h,09h) (see Function 59h)
   BX = maximum paragraphs available for specified memory block

Details: Under PCDOS 2.1 and 3.1 and MSDOS 3.2 and 3.3, if there is insufficient memory to expand the block as much as requested, the block will be made as large as possible. DOS 3.30 coalesces any free blocks immediately following the block to be resized.

Conflicts: None known.

See Also: Function 48h and 49h

INTERRUPT 21h - Function 4Bh, Subfunctions 00h-04h
"EXEC" - LOAD AND/OR EXECUTE PROGRAM

Purpose: Dispatch a child process, or optionally load a program without dispatching it.

Available on: DOS 2.0 or higher.

Registers at call:

AH = 4Bh

AL = type of load:

00h load and execute

01h load but do not execute

03h load overlay

04h load and execute in background (European
   OEM MSDOS 4.00 only)

DS:DX -> ASCIZ program name (must include
  extension)

ES:BX -> parameter block (Tables 8-28, 8-29)

Restrictions: none.

Return Registers:

CF clear if successful

  BX,DX destroyed

  If subfunction 01h, the current process ID
    is set to the new program's PSP; get it with
    INT 21h Function 62h

CF set on error

  AX = error code (01h,02h,05h,08h,0Ah,0Bh) (see
    Function 59h)

Details: DOS 2.x destroys all registers, including SS:SP. For functions 00h, 01h, and 04h, the calling process must ensure that there is enough unallocated memory available; if necessary, by releasing memory with Function 49h or Function 4Ah. For function 03h, DOS assumes that the overlay is being loaded into memory allocated by the caller.

    Function 01h has been documented for DOS 5.0, but was undocumented in prior versions.

BUG: DOS 2.00 assumes that DS points at the current program's PSP.

Conflicts: ELRES V1.0 (chapter 36), "MG" virus (chapter 34), "699" virus (chapter 34), "Plastique" virus (chapter 34), "Murphy-2" virus (chapter 34), "Plastique-2576" virus (chapter 34), "Murphy-1" virus (chapter 34), "Nomenklatura" virus (chapter 34), "948" virus, "Magnitogorsk" virus (chapter 34), "Lozinsky" virus (chapter 34), F-DRIVER.SYS v1.14+ (chapter 34), "707" virus, "Justice" virus (chapter 34).

See Also: Functions 4Ch and 4Dh, INT 2Eh

Table 8-28. Format of EXEC parameter block for AL=00h, 01h, 04h:

Offset	Size	Description
00h	WORD	segment of environment to copy for child process (copy caller's environment if 0000h)
02h	DWORD	pointer to command tail to be copied into child's PSP
06h	DWORD	pointer to first FCB to be copied into child's PSP
0Ah	DWORD	pointer to second FCB to be copied into child's PSP
0Eh	DWORD	(AL=01h) will hold subprogram's initial SS:SP on return
12h	DWORD	(AL=01h) will hold entry point (CS:IP) on return

Table 8-29. Format of EXEC parameter block for AL=03h:

Offset	Size	Description
00h	WORD	segment at which to load overlay
02h	WORD	relocation factor to apply to overlay if in .EXE format

Table 8-30. Format of .EXE file header:

Offset	Size	Description
00h	2 BYTEs	.EXE signature, either "MZ" or "ZM" (5A4Dh or 4D5Ah)
02h	WORD	number of bytes in last 512-byte page of executable
04h	WORD	total number of 512-byte pages in executable (includes any partial last page)
06h	WORD	number of relocation entries

Table 8-30. Format of .EXE file header (continued)

Offset	Size	Description
08h	WORD	header size in paragraphs
0Ah	WORD	minimum paragraphs of memory to allocation (in addition to executable's size)
0Ch	WORD	maximum paragraphs to allocate (in addition to executable's size)
0Eh	WORD	initial SS relative to start of executable
10h	WORD	initial SP
12h	WORD	checksum (one's complement of sum of all words in the executable)
14h	DWORD	initial CS:IP relative to start of executable
18h	WORD	offset within header of relocation table
1Ah	WORD	overlay number (normally 0000h = main program)

---*Borland TLINK*

Offset	Size	Description
1Ch	2 BYTEs	*unknown*. (apparently always 01h 00h)
1Eh	BYTE	signature FBh
1Fh	BYTE	TLINK version (major in high nybble, minor in low nybble)
20h	2 BYTEs	*unknown*. (v2.0 apparently always 72h 6Ah, v3.0 seems always 6Ah 72h)

---*other linkers*

Offset	Size	Description
1Ch	var	optional information

N	N DWORDs	relocation items

Details: If the word at offset 02h is 4, it should be treated as 00h, since pre-1.10 versions of the MS linker set it that way. If both minimum and maximum allocation (offsets 0Ah/0Ch) are zero, the program is loaded as high in memory as possible. The maximum allocation is set to FFFFh paragraphs by default.

Table 8-31. Format of new executable header:

Offset	Size	Description
00h	2 BYTEs	"NE" (4Eh 45h) signature
02h	2 BYTEs	linker version (major, then minor)
04h	WORD	offset to entry table
06h	WORD	length of entry table in bytes
08h	DWORD	file load CRC (0 in Borland's TPW)
0Ch	BYTE	program flags
		bits 0-1 DGROUP type
		0 = none
		1 = single shared
		2 = multiple (unshared)
		3 = (null)
		bit 2: global initialization
		bit 3: protected mode only
		bit 4: 8086 instructions
		bit 5: 80286 instructions
		bit 6: 80386 instructions
		bit 7: 80x87 instructions
0Dh	BYTE	application flags
		bits 0-1: API awareness
		01 full screen (not aware of Windows/P.M. API)
		10 compatible with Windows/P.M. API
		11 uses Windows/P.M. API
		bit 5: errors in image
		bit 7: DLL
0Eh	WORD	auto data segment index
10h	WORD	initial local heap size
12h	WORD	initial stack size
14h	DWORD	program entry point (CS:IP)
18h	DWORD	initial stack pointer (SS:SP)
1Ch	WORD	segment count

Table 8-31. Format of new executable header (continued)

Offset	Size	Description
1Eh	WORD	module reference count
20h	WORD	length of nonresident names table
22h	WORD	offset to segment table (see below)
24h	WORD	offset to resource table
26h	WORD	offset to resident names table
28h	WORD	offset to module reference table
2Ah	WORD	offset to imported names table
2Ch	DWORD	offset to nonresident names table
30h	WORD	moveable entry point count
32h	BYTE	file alignment shift size
33h	3 BYTEs	*unknown.*
36h	BYTE	operating system
		01h OS/2
		02h Windows
37h	BYTE	other EXE flags
		bit 0: supports long filenames
		bit 1: 2.X protected mode
		bit 2: 2.X proportional font
		bit 3: gangload area
38h	WORD	offset to return thunks or start of gangload area
3Ah	WORD	offset to segment reference thunks or length of gangload area
3Ch	WORD	minimum code swap area size
3Eh	2 BYTEs	expected Windows version (minor version first)

Table 8-32. Format of segment table record:

Offset	Size	Description
00h	WORD	offset in file (shifted right by alignment shift)
02h	WORD	length of image in file
04h	WORD	attributes
		bit 0,1,2: DATA segment flags
		bit 3: iterated
		bit 4: movable
		bit 5: sharable
		bit 6: preloaded
		bit 7: execute-only
		bit 8: relocations (directly following code for this segment)
		bit 9: debug info
		bits 10,11: 80286 DPL bits
		bit 12: discardable
		bits 13-15: discard priority
06h	WORD	size to allocate

INTERRRUPT 21h - Function 4Bh, Subfunction 05h
SET EXECUTION STATE

Purpose: May be used by programs which wish to bypass the normal EXEC function.

Available on: DOS 5.0 or higher.   **Restrictions:** none.

Registers at call: **Return Registers:**

AX = 4B05h   CF clear if successful

DS:DX -> execution state structure (Table 8-33)   AX = 0000h

                                                CF set on error

                                                    AX = error code (see Function 59h)

Details: Used by programs which intercept Function 4Bh Subfunction 00h to prepare new programs for execution (including setting the DOS version number). No DOS, BIOS or other software interrupts may be called after return from this call before commencement of the child process. If DOS is running in the HMA, A20 is turned off on return from this call.

Conflicts: None known.
See Also: Function 4Bh Subfunctions 00h-04h

Table 8-33. Format of execution state structure:

Offset	Size	Description
00h	WORD	reserved (00h)
02h	WORD	type flags
		bit 0: program is an .EXE
		1: program is an overlay
04h	DWORD	pointer to ASCIZ name of program file
08h	WORD	PSP segment of new program
0Ah	DWORD	starting CS:IP of new program
0Eh	DWORD	program size including PSP

INTERRUPT 21h - Function 4Ch
"EXIT" - TERMINATE WITH RETURN CODE

Purpose: Ends current process and returns to parent (usually command interpreter), passing exit code to indicate completion status.

Available on: DOS 2.0 or higher.

Restrictions: none.

Registers at call:
AH = 4Ch
AL = return code

Return Registers:
never returns

Details: Unless the process is its own parent (see Function 26h, offset 16h in PSP), all open files are closed and all memory belonging to the process is freed. All network file locks should be removed before calling this function.

Conflicts: None known.
See Also: Functions 00h, 26h, 4Bh, and 4Dh, INT 20h, INT 22h

INTERRUPT 21h - Function 4Dh
GET RETURN CODE

Purpose: Reads exit code returned by Function 31h or 4Ch.

Available on: DOS 2.0 or higher.

Restrictions: none.

Registers at call:
AH = 4Dh

Return Registers:
AH = termination type:
>00h normal (INT 20h, INT 21h
>>Function 00h, or INT 21h Function 4Ch)
>01h control-C abort
>02h critical error abort
>03h terminate and stay resident (INT 21h
>>Function 31h or INT 27h)

AL = return code

Details: The word in which DOS stores the return code is cleared after being read by this function, so the return code can be retrieved only once.

Conflicts: None known.
See Also: Function 4Bh and 4Ch

INTERRUPT 21h - Function 4Eh
"FINDFIRST" - FIND FIRST MATCHING FILE

Purpose: Locates the first file matching a specified pathspec and supplies information about it.

Available on: DOS 2.0 or higher.

Restrictions: none.

Registers at call:
AH = 4Eh
CX = file attribute mask (see Function 43h
    Subfunction 01h) (bits 0 and 5 ignored)
DS:DX -> ASCIZ file specification (may include
    path and wildcards)

Return Registers:
CF clear if successful
    [DTA] = FindFirst data block (Table 8-34)
CF set on error
    AX = error code (02h,03h,12h) (see Function
        59h)

Details: For search attributes other than 08h, all files with at **most** the specified combination of hidden, system, and directory attributes will be returned. Under DOS 2.x, searching for attribute 08h (volume label) will also return normal files, while under DOS 3+ only the volume label (if any) will be returned.

This call also returns successfully if given the name of a character device without wildcards. DOS 2.x returns attribute 00h, size 0, and the current date and time. DOS 3+ returns attribute 40h and the current date and time.

Under LANtastic, this call may be used to obtain a list of a server's shared resources by searching for "\SERVER.*"; a list of printer resources may be obtained by searching for "\SERVER*.*".

BUG: Under DOS 3.x and 4.x, the second and subsequent calls to this function with a character device name (no wildcards) and search attributes which include the volume-label bit (08h) will fail unless there is an intervening DOS call which implicitly or explicity performs a directory search without the volume-label bit. Such implicit searches are performed by CREATE (Function 3Ch), OPEN (Function 3Dh), UNLINK (Function 41h), and RENAME (Function 56h).

Conflicts: WILDUNIX.COM Installation Check (chapter 36).

See Also: Functions 11h and 4Fh, Function 43h Subfunction 01h, INT 2Fh Function 11h Subfunction 1Bh (chapter 19)

Table 8-34. Format of FindFirst data block:

Offset	Size	Description
---PCDOS 3.10, PCDOS 4.01, MSDOS 3.2/3.3/5.0		
00h	BYTE	drive letter
01h	11 BYTEs	search template
0Ch	BYTE	search attributes
---DOS 2.x (and some DOS 3.x)		
00h	BYTE	search attributes
01h	BYTE	drive letter
02h	11 BYTEs	search template
---WILDUNIX.COM		
00h	12 BYTEs	15-character wildcard search pattern and drive letter (packed)
0Ch	BYTE	search attributes
---DOS 2.x and most 3.x		
0Dh	WORD	entry count within directory
0Fh	DWORD	*pointer to DTA*
13h	WORD	cluster number of start of parent directory
---PCDOS 4.01, MSDOS 3.2/3.3/5.0		
0Dh	WORD	entry count within directory
0Fh	WORD	cluster number of start of parent directory
11h	4 BYTEs	reserved
---all versions, documented fields		
15h	BYTE	attribute of file found
16h	WORD	file time:
		bits 11-15: hour
		bits 5-10: minute
		bits 0-4: seconds/2
18h	WORD	file date:
		bits 9-15: year-1980
		bits 5-8: month
		bits 0-4: day

Table 8-34. Format of FindFirst data block (continued)

Offset	Size	Description
1Ah	DWORD	file size
1Eh	13 BYTEs	ASCIZ filename+extension

INTERRUPT 21h - Function 4Fh
"FINDNEXT" - FIND NEXT MATCHING FILE

Purpose: Locates the next file matching the pathspec which was supplied to a previous invocation of Function 4Eh.

Available on: DOS 2.0 or higher.

Restrictions: Function 4Eh (FindFirst) must have been executed previously to set up the DTA.

Registers at call:
AH = 4Fh
[DTA] = data block from previous FindFirst or
    FindNext call

Return Registers:
CF clear if successful
CF set on error
    AX = error code (12h) (see Function 59h)

Conflicts: None known.

See Also: Functions 12h and 4Eh

INTERRUPT 21h - Function 50h
SET CURRENT PROCESS ID (SET PSP ADDRESS)

Purpose: Sets supplied PID value into "current process" variable used by MS-DOS internal code.

Available on: DOS 2.0 or higher.

Restrictions: none.

Registers at call:
AH = 50h
BX = segment of PSP for new process

Return Registers: n/a

Details: DOS uses the current PSP address to determine which processes own files and memory; it corresponds to process identifiers used by other operating systems.

    Under DOS 2.x, this function cannot be invoked inside an INT 28h handler without setting the Critical Error flag. Under DOS 3+, this function does not use any of the DOS-internal stacks and is thus fully reentrant.

    This call is supported by the OS/2 compatibility box. It is not documented for DOS 2.0 through 4.0x, but has been documented for DOS 5.0.

Conflicts: None known.

See Also: Functions 26h, 51h, and 62h

INTERRUPT 21h - Function 51h
GET CURRENT PROCESS ID (GET PSP ADDRESS)

Purpose: Reads "current process" variable used by MS-DOS internal code.

Available on: DOS 2.0 or higher.

Restrictions: none.

Registers at call:
AH = 51h

Return Registers:
BX = segment of PSP for current process

Details: DOS uses the current PSP address to determine which processes own files and memory; it corresponds to process identifiers used by other OSs.

    Under DOS 2.x, this function cannot be invoked inside an INT 28h handler without setting the Critical Error flag. Under DOS 3+, this function does not use any of the DOS-internal stacks and is thus fully reentrant.

    This call is supported by the OS/2 compatibility box. It is identical to the documented Function 62h, and has finally been documented for DOS 5.0.

Conflicts: None known.

See Also: Functions 26h, 50h, and 62h

INTERRUPT 21h - Function 52h
"SYSVARS" - GET LIST OF LISTS

Purpose: Obtain pointer to most DOS internal information.

Available on: DOS 2.0 or higher.

Restrictions: This call is not documented and therefore subject to change.

Registers at call:
AH = 52h

Return Registers:
ES:BX -> DOS list of lists (Table 8-35)

Details: The list of lists is partially supported by the OS/2 v1.1+ compatibility box (however, most pointers are FFFFh:FFFFh, LASTDRIVE is FFh, and the NUL header "next" pointer is FFFFh:FFFFh).

Conflicts: "516" virus installation check (chapter 34).

Table 8-35. Format of List of Lists:

Offset	Size	Description
-12	WORD	(DOS 3.1-5.0) sharing retry count (see Function 44h Subfunction 0Bh)
-10	WORD	(DOS 3.1-5.0) sharing retry delay (see Function 44h Subfunction 0Bh)
-8	DWORD	(DOS 3.x) pointer to current disk buffer
-4	WORD	(DOS 3.x) pointer in DOS code segment of unread CON input. When CON is read via a handle, DOS reads an entire line, and returns the requested portion, buffering the rest for the next read. 0000h indicates no unread input
-2	WORD	segment of first memory control block (Tables 8-36 thru 8-38)
00h	DWORD	pointer to first Drive Parameter Block (see Function 32h)
04h	DWORD	pointer to first System File Table (Tables 8-45 thru 8-48)
08h	DWORD	pointer to active CLOCK$ device's header
0Ch	DWORD	pointer to active CON device's header

---DOS 2.x

Offset	Size	Description
10h	BYTE	number of logical drives in system
11h	WORD	maximum bytes/block of any block device
13h	DWORD	pointer to first disk buffer (Table 8-52)
17h	18 BYTEs	actual NUL device driver header (not a pointer!). NUL is always the first device on DOS's linked list of device drivers. (see Table 8-50 for format)

---DOS 3.0

Offset	Size	Description
10h	BYTE	number of block devices
11h	WORD	maximum bytes/block of any block device
13h	DWORD	pointer to first disk buffer (Table 8-53)
17h	DWORD	pointer to array of current directory structures (Table 8-49)
1Bh	BYTE	value of LASTDRIVE command in CONFIG.SYS (default 5)
1Ch	DWORD	pointer to STRING= workspace area
20h	WORD	size of STRING area (the x in STRING=x from CONFIG.SYS)
22h	DWORD	pointer to FCB table
26h	WORD	the y in FCBS=x,y from CONFIG.SYS
28h	18 BYTEs	actual NUL device driver header (not a pointer!). NUL is always the first device on DOS's linked list of device drivers. (see Table 8-50 for format)

---DOS 3.1-3.3

Offset	Size	Description
10h	WORD	maximum bytes per sector of any block device
12h	DWORD	pointer to first disk buffer in buffer chain (Table 8-53)
16h	DWORD	pointer to array of current directory structures (Table 8-49)
1Ah	DWORD	pointer to system FCB tables (see below)
1Eh	WORD	number of protected FCBs (the y in the CONFIG.SYS FCBS=x,y)
20h	BYTE	number of block devices installed
21h	BYTE	number of available drive letters (largest of 5, installed block devices, and CONFIG.SYS LASTDRIVE=). Also indicates size of current directory structure array.
22h	18 BYTEs	actual NUL device driver header (not a pointer!). NUL is always the first device on DOS's linked list of device drivers. (see below for format)
34h	BYTE	number of JOIN'ed drives

---DOS 4.x

Offset	Size	Description
10h	WORD	maximum bytes per sector of any block device
12h	DWORD	pointer to disk buffer info record (Tables 8-54 and 8-55)
16h	DWORD	pointer to array of current directory structures (Table 8-49)

Table 8-35. Format of List of Lists (continued)

Offset	Size	Description
1Ah	DWORD	pointer to system FCB tables (see below)
1Eh	WORD	number of protected FCBs (the y in the CONFIG.SYS FCBS=x,y; always zero for DOS 5.0)
20h	BYTE	number of block devices installed
21h	BYTE	number of available drive letters (largest of 5, installed block devices, and CONFIG.SYS LASTDRIVE=). Also indicates size of current directory structure array.
22h	18 BYTEs	actual NUL device driver header (not a pointer!). NUL is always the first device on DOS's linked list of device drivers. (see below for format)
34h	BYTE	*number of JOIN'ed drives*
35h	WORD	pointer within IBMDOS code segment to list of special program names (see below; always zero for DOS 5.0)
37h	DWORD	pointer to FAR routine for resident IFS utility functions (see below). May be called by any IFS driver which does not wish to service functions 20h or 24h-28h itself
3Bh	DWORD	pointer to chain of IFS (installable file system) drivers
3Fh	WORD	the x in BUFFERS x,y (rounded up to multiple of 30 if in EMS)
41h	WORD	the y in BUFFERS x,y
43h	BYTE	boot drive (1=A:)
44h	BYTE	apparently 01h if 80386+, 00h otherwise
45h	WORD	extended memory size in K
---DOS 5.0		
10h	39 BYTEs	as for DOS 4.x (see above)
37h	DWORD	pointer to SETVER program list or 0000h:0000h
3Bh	WORD	*pointer to unknown function in DOS CS*
3Dh	WORD	*apparently 0000h if DOS loaded low, PSP of most-recently EXECed program if DOS in HMA*
3Fh	8 BYTEs	as for DOS 4.x (see above)

Table 8-36. Format of memory control block (see also Tables 8-37 and 8-38):

Offset	Size	Description
00h	BYTE	block type: 5Ah if last block in chain, otherwise 4Dh
01h	WORD	PSP segment of owner, 0000h if free, 0008h if belongs to DOS
03h	WORD	size of memory block in paragraphs
05h	3 BYTEs	unused
---DOS 2.x,3.x		
08h	8 BYTEs	unused
---DOS 4+		
08h	8 BYTEs	ASCII program name if PSP memory block, else garbage null-terminated if less than 8 characters

Details: Under DOS 3.1+, the first memory block is the DOS data segment, containing installable drivers, buffers, etc. Under DOS 4.x it is divided into subsegments, each with its own memory control block (see below), the first of which is at offset 0000h.

For DOS 5.0, blocks owned by DOS may have either "SC" or "SD" in bytes 08h and 09h. "SC" is system code or locked-out inter-UMB memory, "SD" is system data, device drivers, etc.

Table 8-37. Format of DOS 5.0 UMB control block:

Offset	Size	Description
00h	BYTE	type: 5Ah if last block in chain, 4Dh otherwise
01h	WORD	first available paragraph in UMB if control block is at start of UMB, 000Ah if control block is at end of UMB.
03h	WORD	length in paragraphs of following UMB or locked-out region
05h	3 BYTEs	unused
08h	8 BYTEs	block type name: "UMB" if start block, "SM" if end block in UMB.

Table 8-38. Format of STARLITE memory control block:

Offset	Size	Description
00h	BYTE	block type: 5Ah if last block in chain, otherwise 4Dh
01h	WORD	PSP segment of owner, 0000h if free, 0008h if belongs to DOS
03h	WORD	size of memory block in paragraphs
05h	BYTE	unused
06h	WORD	segment address of next memory control block (0000h if last)
08h	WORD	segment address of previous memory control block or 0000h
0Ah	6 BYTEs	reserved

Table 8-39. Format of DOS 4.x data segment subsegment control blocks:

Offset	Size	Description
00h	BYTE	subsegment type (blocks typically appear in this order)
		"D" device driver
		"E" device driver appendage
		"I" IFS (Installable File System) driver
		"F" FILES= control block storage area (for FILES>5)
		"X" FCBS= control block storage area, if present
		"C" BUFFERS EMS workspace area (if BUFFERS /X option used)
		"B" BUFFERS= storage area
		"L" LASTDRIVE= current directory structure array storage area
		"S" STACKS= code and data area, if present (Table 8-40)
01h	WORD	paragraph of subsegment start (usually the next paragraph)
03h	WORD	size of subsegment in paragraphs
05h	3 BYTEs	unused
08h	8 BYTEs	for types "D" and "I", base name of file from which the driver was loaded (unused for other types)

Table 8-40. Format of data at start of STACKS code segment (if present):

Offset	Size	Description
00h	WORD	*unknown.*
02h	WORD	number of stacks (the x in STACKS=x,y)
04h	WORD	size of stack control block array (should be 8*x)
06h	WORD	size of each stack (the y in STACKS=x,y)
08h	DWORD	ptr to STACKS data segment
0Ch	WORD	offset in STACKS data segment of stack control block array
0Eh	WORD	offset in STACKS data segment of last element of that array
10h	WORD	offset in STACKS data segment of the entry in that array for the next stack to be allocated (initially same as value in 0Eh and works its way down in steps of 8 to the value in 0Ch as hardware interrupts pre-empt each other)

Details: The STACKS code segment data may, if present, be located as follows:

DOS 3.2: The code segment data is at a paragraph boundary fairly early in the IBMBIO segment (seen at 0070:0190h).

DOS 3.3: The code segment is at a paragraph boundary in the DOS data segment, which may be determined by inspecting the segment pointers of the vectors for those of interrupts 02h, 08h-0Eh, 70h, 72-77h which have not been redirected by device drivers or TSRs.

DOS 4.x: Identified by sub-segment control block type "S" within the DOS data segment.

Table 8-41. Format of array elements in STACKS data segment:

Offset	Size	Description
00h	BYTE	status:
		00h = free,
		01h = in use,
		03h = corrupted by overflow of higher stack.

Table 8-41. Format of array elements in STACKS data segment (continued)

Offset	Size	Description
01h	BYTE	not used
02h	WORD	previous SP
04h	WORD	previous SS
06h	WORD	ptr to word at top of stack (new value for SP). The word at the top of the stack is preset to point back to this control block.

Table 8-42. Format of SHARE.EXE hooks (DOS 3.1-4.01) (offsets from first SFT--pointed at by ListOfLists+04h):

Offset	Size	Description
-3Ch	DWORD	pointer to *unknown FAR routine*

Note: not called by MSDOS 3.3,
set to 0000h:0000h by SHARE 3.3

-38h	DWORD	pointer to FAR routine called on opening file

on call, internal DOS location points at filename (see Function 5Dh Subfunction 06h)
  Return: CF clear if successful
     CF set on error
      AX = DOS error code (24h) (see Function 59h)
  Note: SHARE assumes DS=SS=DOS DS and directly accesses DOS
internals to get name of file just opened

-34h	DWORD	pointer to FAR routine called on closing file

ES:DI -> system file table
  Note: SHARE assumes SS=DOS DS, directly accesses DOS internals. It
performs an unknown action on every lock record for the file.

-30h	DWORD	pointer to FAR routine to close all files for given computer

(called by Function 5Dh Subfunction 03h)
  Note: SHARE assumes SS=DOS DS, directly accesses DOS internals

-2Ch	DWORD	pointer to FAR routine to close all files for a given

process (called by Function 5Dh Subfunction 04h)
  Note: SHARE assumes SS=DOS DS, directly accesses DOS internals

-28h	DWORD	pointer to FAR routine to close file by name

(called by Function 5Dh Subfunction 02h)
DS:SI -> DOS parameter list (see Function 5Dh Subfunction 00h)
 DPL's DS:DX -> name of file to close
  Return: CF clear if successful
     CF set on error
      AX = DOS error code (03h) (see Function 59h)
  Note: SHARE assumes SS=DOS DS, directly accesses DOS internals

-24h	DWORD	pointer to FAR routine to lock region of file

call with BX = file handle
    CX:DX = starting offset
    SI:AX = size
  Return: CF set on error
    AL = DOS error code (21h) (see Function 59h)
  Note: only called if file is marked as remote; SHARE assumes SS=DOS
DS, directly accesses DOS internals

-20h	DWORD	pointer to FAR routine to unlock region of file

call with BX = file handle
    CX:DX = starting offset
    SI:AX = size
  Return: CF set on error
    AL = DOS error code (21h) (see Function 59h)
  Note: only called if file is marked as remote; SHARE assumes SS=DOS
DS, directly accesses DOS internals

Table 8-42. Format of SHARE.EXE hooks (DOS 3.1-4.01) (continued)

Offset	Size	Description
-1Ch	DWORD	pointer to FAR routine to check if file region is locked

call with ES:DI -> system file table entry for file
  CX = length of region from current position in
   file
Return: CF set if any portion of region locked
  AX = 0021h
Note: SHARE assumes SS=DOS DS, directly accesses DOS internals

-18h	DWORD	pointer to FAR routine to get open file list entry

(called by Function 5Dh Subfunction 05h)
call with DS:SI -> DOS parameter list (see Function 5Dh Subfunction 00h)
  DPL's BX = index of sharing record
  DPL's CX = index of SFT in SFT chain of sharing
   rec
Return: CF set on error or not loaded
  AX = DOS error code (12h) (see Function 59h)
  CF clear if successful
   ES:DI -> filename
   CX = number of locks owned by specified SFT
   BX = network machine number
   DX destroyed
Note: SHARE assumes SS=DOS DS, directly accesses DOS internals

-14h	DWORD	pointer to FAR routine for *updating FCB from SFT*

call with DS:SI -> unopened FCB
  ES:DI -> system file table entry
Return: *BL = C0h*
Note: copies the following fields from SFT to FCB:
 starting cluster of file: 0Bh 1Ah
 sharing record offset: 33h 1Ch
 file attribute: 04h 1Eh

-10h	DWORD	pointer to FAR routine to *get first cluster of FCB file*

call with ES:DI -> system file table entry
  DS:SI -> FCB
Return: CF set if SFT closed or sharing record offsets mismatched
  CF clear if successful
   BX = starting cluster number from FCB

-0Ch	DWORD	pointer to FAR routine to close file if duplicate for process

DS:SI -> system file table
Return: AX = number of handle in JFT which already uses SFT
Notes: called during open/create of a file; SHARE assumes SS=DOS
DS, directly accesses DOS internals.

If the SFT was opened with inheritance enabled and sharing mode 111,
does something to all other SFTs owned by same process which have the same
file open
mode and sharing record

-08h	DWORD	pointer to *unknown FAR routine*

Note: SHARE assumes SS=DS=DOS DS, direct-accesses DOS
internals; it closes various handles referring to the file most-recently
opened

-04h	DWORD	pointer to FAR routine to update directory info in related SFT entries

call with ES:DI -> system file table entry for file (see below)
  AX = subfunction (apply to each related SFT)
    00h: update time stamp (offset 0Dh) and
     date stamp (offset 0Fh)

Table 8-42. Format of SHARE.EXE hooks (DOS 3.1-4.01) (continued)

Offset	Size	Description
-40h	(continued)	AX = subfunction

> 01h: update file size (offset 11h) and
> starting cluster (offset 0Bh).
> Sets last-accessed cluster fields
> to start of file if file never
> accessed
> 02h: as function 01h, but last-accessed
> fields always changed
> 03h: do both functions 00h and 02h

Note: follows ptr at offset 2Bh in system file table entries; this call is a NOP if the file was opened with no-inherit or via FCB

Table 8-43. Format of sharing record:

Offset	Size	Description
00h	BYTE	flag:
		00h free block
		01h allocated block
		FFh end marker
01h	WORD	size of block
03h	BYTE	checksum of pathname (including NUL)
		if sum of ASCII values is N, checksum is (N/256 + N%256)
04h	WORD	offset in SHARE's DS of lock record (see below)
06h	DWORD	pointer to start of system file table chain for file
0Ah	WORD	unique sequence number
0Ch	var	ASCIZ full pathname

Table 8-44. Format of SHARE.EXE lock record:

Offset	Size	Description
00h	WORD	offset in SHARE's DS of next lock table in list
02h	DWORD	offset in file of start of locked region
06h	DWORD	offset in file of end of locked region
0Ah	DWORD	pointer to System File Table entry for this file
0Eh	WORD	PSP segment of lock's owner

Table 8-45. Format of DOS 2.x system file tables:

Offset	Size	Description
00h	DWORD	pointer to next file table
04h	WORD	number of files in this table
06h	28h bytes	per file in following format:

Offset	Size	Description
00h	BYTE	number of file handles referring to this file
01h	BYTE	file open mode (see Function 3Dh)
02h	BYTE	file attribute
03h	BYTE	drive (0 = character device, 1 = A, 2 = B, etc)
04h	11 BYTEs	filename in FCB format (no path,no period,blank-padded)
0Fh	WORD	*unknown.*
11h	WORD	*unknown.*
13h	DWORD	*file size*
17h	WORD	file date in packed format (see Function 57h Subfunction 00h)
19h	WORD	file time in packed format (see Function 57h Subfunction 00h)
1Bh	BYTE	device attribute (see Function 44h Subfunction 00h)

Table 8-45. Format of DOS 2.x system file tables (continued):

Offset	Size	Description
---character device---		
1Ch	DWORD	pointer to device driver
---block device---		
1Ch	WORD	starting cluster of file
1Eh	WORD	relative cluster in file of last cluster accessed

20h	WORD	absolute cluster number of current cluster
22h	WORD	*unknown.*
24h	DWORD	*current file position*

Table 8-46. Format of DOS 3.0 system file tables and FCB tables:

Offset	Size	Description
00h	DWORD	pointer to next file table
04h	WORD	number of files in this table

Offset	Size	Description
00h-1Eh		as for DOS 3.1+ (see Table 8-47)
1Fh	WORD	byte offset of directory entry within sector
21h	11 BYTEs	filename in FCB format (no path/period, blank-padded)
2Ch	DWORD	(SHARE.EXE) pointer to previous SFT sharing same file
30h	WORD	(SHARE.EXE) *network machine number*
32h	WORD	PSP segment of file's owner
34h	WORD	(SHARE.EXE) offset in SHARE code seg of share record
36h	WORD	*apparently always 0000h*

Table 8-47. Format of DOS 3.1-3.3x system file tables and FCB tables:

Offset	Size	Description
00h	DWORD	pointer to next file table
04h	WORD	number of files in this table
06h	35h bytes	per file:

Offset	Size	Description
00h	WORD	number of file handles referring to this file
02h	WORD	file open mode (see Function 3Dh); bit 15 set if this file opened via FCB
04h	BYTE	file attribute (see Function 43h Subfunction 01h)
05h	WORD	device info word (see Function 44h Subfunction 00h) bit 15 set if remote file bit 14 set means do not set file date/time on closing
07h	DWORD	pointer to device driver header if character device, else pointer to DOS Drive Parameter Block (see Function 32h)
0Bh	WORD	starting cluster of file
0Dh	WORD	file time in packed format (see Function 57h Subfunction 00h)
0Fh	WORD	file date in packed format (see Function 57h Subfunction 00h)
11h	DWORD	file size
15h	DWORD	current offset in file (may be larger than size of file; INT 21h Function 42h does not check the new position)
19h	WORD	relative cluster within file of last cluster accessed
1Bh	WORD	absolute cluster number of last cluster accessed, *0000h if file never read or written*
1Dh	WORD	number of sector containing directory entry
1Fh	BYTE	number of dir entry within sector (byte offset/32)
20h	11 BYTEs	filename in FCB format (no path/period, blank-padded)
2Bh	DWORD	(SHARE.EXE) pointer to previous SFT sharing same file
2Fh	WORD	(SHARE.EXE) network machine number which opened file
31h	WORD	PSP segment of file's owner (see Function 26h)

Table 8-47. Format of DOS 3.1-3.3x system file tables and FCB tables (continued):

Offset	Size	Description
33h	WORD	offset within SHARE.EXE code segment of sharing record (see below) 0000h = none

Table 8-48. Format of DOS 4.0-5.0 system file tables and FCB tables:

Offset	Size	Description
00h	DWORD	pointer to next file table
04h	WORD	number of files in this table
06h		3Bh Bytes per file:

Offset	Size	Description
00h	WORD	number of file handles referring to this file
02h	WORD	file open mode (see Function 3Dh)
		bit 15 set if this file opened via FCB
04h	BYTE	file attribute (see Function 43h Subfunction 01h)
05h	WORD	device info word (see Function 44h Subfunction 00h)
		bit 15 set if remote file
		bit 14 set means do not set file date/time on closing
07h	DWORD	pointer to device driver header if character device
		else pointer to DOS Drive Parameter Block (see Function 32h) or REDIR data
0Bh	WORD	starting cluster of file
0Dh	WORD	file time in packed format (see Function 57h Subfunction 00h)
0Fh	WORD	file date in packed format (see Function 57h Subfunction 00h)
11h	DWORD	file size
15h	DWORD	current offset in file

---local file

Offset	Size	Description
19h	WORD	relative cluster within file of last cluster accessed
1Bh	DWORD	number of sector containing directory entry
1Fh	BYTE	number of dir entry within sector (byte offset/32)

---network redirector

Offset	Size	Description
19h	DWORD	pointer to REDIRIFS record

Offset	Size	Description
1Dh	3 BYTEs	*unknown.*
20h	11 BYTEs	filename in FCB format (no path/period, blank-padded)
2Bh	DWORD	(SHARE.EXE) pointer to previous SFT sharing same file
2Fh	WORD	(SHARE.EXE) network machine number which opened file
31h	WORD	PSP segment of file's owner (see Function 26h)
33h	WORD	offset within SHARE.EXE code segment of sharing record (see below) 0000h = none
35h	WORD	(local) absolute cluster number of last cluster accessed (redirector) *unknown.*
37h	DWORD	pointer to IFS driver for file, 0000000h if native DOS

Table 8-49. Format of current directory structure (array, 51h bytes [58h for DOS 4.0-5.0] per drive):

Offset	Size	Description
00h	67 BYTEs	ASCIZ path in form X: (local) or \MACH (network)
		Note: This is the true path that would be needed if not under SUBST or JOIN.
43h	WORD	drive attributes:
		bit 15: uses network redirector
		14: physical drive
		Note: drive invalid if 15/14 = 00, installable file system if 11
		13: JOIN'ed
		12: SUBST'ed
45h	DWORD	pointer to Drive Parameter Block for drive (see Function 32h)

Table 8-49. Format of current directory structure (continued):

Offset	Size	Description
---*local drives*		
49h	WORD	starting cluster of current directory
		0000h = root, FFFFh = never accessed
4Bh	WORD	*unknown*. seems to be FFFFh always
4Dh	WORD	*unknown*. seems to be FFFFh always
---*network drives*		
49h	DWORD	pointer to redirector or REDIRIFS record, or FFFFh:FFFFh
4Dh	WORD	*stored user data from INT 21h Function 5Fh Subfunction 03h*

4Fh	WORD	offset in current directory path of backslash corresponding to root directory for drive. This value specifies how many characters to hide from the "CHDIR" and "GETDIR" calls; normally set to 2 to hide the drive letter and colon. SUBST, JOIN, and networks change it so that only the appropriate portion of the true path is visible to the user.
---*DOS 4.x*		
51h	BYTE	*unknown*. used by network
52h	DWORD	pointer to IFS driver for this drive, 00000000h if native DOS
56h	WORD	*unknown*.

Table 8-50. Format of device driver header:

Offset	Size	Description
00h	DWORD	pointer to next driver, offset=FFFFh if last driver
04h	WORD	device attributes:

Character device:
   bit 15 set
   bit 14 IOCTL supported (see Function 44h)
   bit 13 (DOS 3+) output until busy supported
   bit 12 reserved
   bit 11 (DOS 3+) OPEN/CLOSE/RemMedia calls supported
   bits 10-8 reserved
   bit 7 (DOS 5.0) Generic IOCTL Check call supported (command 19h) (see Function 44h Subfunction 10h)
   bit 6 (DOS 3.2+) Generic IOCTL call supported (command 13h) (see Function 44h Subfunction 0Ch, Function 44h Subfunction 0Dh)
   bit 5 reserved
   bit 4 device is special (supports INT 29h "fast console output")
   bit 3 device is CLOCK$ (all reads/writes use transfer record described below)
   bit 2 device is NUL
   bit 1 device is standard output
   bit 0 device is standard input

Block device:
   bit 15 clear
   bit 14 IOCTL supported
   bit 13 non-IBM format
   bit 12 reserved
   bit 11 (DOS 3+) OPEN/CLOSE/RemMedia calls supported
   bit 10 reserved
   bit 9 *direct I/O not allowed* (set by DOS 3.3 DRIVER.SYS for "new" drives)
   bit 8 *unknown*, set by DOS 3.3 DRIVER.SYS for "new" drives
   bit 7 (DOS 5.0) Generic IOCTL Check call supported (command 19h) (see Function 44h Subfunction 11h)
   bit 6 (DOS 3.2+) Generic IOCTL call supported (command 13h) implies support for commands 17h and 18h (see Function 44h Subfunctions 0Ch-0Fh)

Table 8-50. Format of device driver header (continued)

Offset	Size	Description
		bits 5-2 reserved
		bit 1 driver supports 32-bit sector addressing
		bit 0 reserved
06h	WORD	device strategy entry point, call with ES:BX -> request header (see INT 2Fh Function 08h Subfunction 02h)
08h	WORD	device interrupt entry point
---*character device*		
0Ah	8 BYTEs	blank-padded character device name
---*block device*		
0Ah	BYTE	number of subunits (drives) supported by driver
0Bh	7 BYTEs	unused

12h	WORD	(CD-ROM driver) reserved, must be 0000h
14h	BYTE	(CD-ROM driver) drive letter (must initially be 00h)
15h	BYTE	(CD-ROM driver) number of units
16h	6 BYTEs	(CD-ROM driver) signature 'MSCDnn' where 'nn' is version (currently '00')

Table 8-51. Format of CLOCK$ transfer record:

Offset	Size	Description
00h	WORD	number of days since 1-Jan-1980
02h	BYTE	minutes
03h	BYTE	hours
04h	BYTE	hundredths of second
05h	BYTE	seconds

Table 8-52. Format of DOS 2.x disk buffer:

Offset	Size	Description
00h	DWORD	pointer to next disk buffer, offset = FFFFh if last least-recently used buffer is first in chain
04h	BYTE	drive (0=A, 1=B, etc), FFh if not in use
05h	3 BYTEs	*unused (seems always to be 00h 00h 01h)*
08h	WORD	logical sector number
0Ah	BYTE	number of copies to write (1 for non-FAT sectors)
0Bh	BYTE	sector offset between copies if multiple copies to be written
0Ch	DWORD	pointer to DOS Drive Parameter Block (see Function 32h)
10h		buffered data

Table 8-53. Format of DOS 3.x disk buffer:

Offset	Size	Description
00h	DWORD	pointer to next disk buffer, offset = FFFFh if last least-recently used buffer is first in chain
04h	BYTE	drive (0=A,1=B, etc), FFh if not in use
05h	BYTE	flags:
		bit 7: *unknown*.
		bit 6: buffer dirty
		bit 5: buffer has been referenced
		bit 4: *unknown*.
		bit 3: sector in data area
		bit 2: sector in a directory, either root or subdirectory
		bit 1: sector in FAT
		bit 0: *boot sector*
06h	WORD	logical sector number
08h	BYTE	number of copies to write (1 for non-FAT sectors)
09h	BYTE	sector offset between copies if multiple copies to be written

Table 8-53. Format of DOS 3.x disk buffer (continued)

Offset	Size	Description
0Ah	DWORD	pointer to DOS Drive Parameter Block (see Function 32h)
0Eh	WORD	*unused* (almost always 0)
10h		buffered data

Table 8-54. Format of DOS 4.00 (pre UR 25066) disk buffer info:

Offset	Size	Description
00h	DWORD	pointer to array of disk buffer hash chain heads (Table 8-56)
04h	WORD	number of disk buffer hash chains (referred to as NDBCH below)
06h	DWORD	pointer to lookahead buffer, zero if not present
0Ah	WORD	number of lookahead sectors, else zero (the y in BUFFERS=x,y)
0Ch	BYTE	00h if buffers in EMS (/X), FFh if not
0Dh	WORD	EMS handle for buffers, zero if not in EMS
0Fh	WORD	EMS physical page number used for buffers (usually 255)
11h	WORD	*unknown.* seems always to be 0001h
13h	WORD	segment of EMS physical page frame
15h	WORD	*apparently always zero*
17h	4 WORDs	*EMS partial page mapping information*

Table 8-55. Format of DOS 4.01 (from UR 25066 Corrective Services Disk on) disk buffer info:

Offset	Size	Description
00h	DWORD	pointer to array of disk buffer hash chain heads (Table 8-56)
04h	WORD	number of disk buffer hash chains (referred to as NDBCH below)
06h	DWORD	pointer to lookahead buffer, zero if not present
0Ah	WORD	number of lookahead sectors, else zero (the y in BUFFERS=x,y)
0Ch	BYTE	01h, possibly to distinguish from pre-UR 25066 format
0Dh	WORD	*EMS segment for BUFFERS* (only with /XD)
0Fh	WORD	*EMS physical page number of EMS seg above* (only with /XD)
11h	WORD	*unknown EMS segment* (only with /XD)
13h	WORD	*EMS physical page number of above* (only with /XD)
15h	BYTE	*number of EMS page frames present* (only with /XD)
16h	WORD	segment of one-sector workspace buffer allocated in main memory if BUFFERS/XS or /XD options in effect, possibly to avoid DMA into EMS
18h	WORD	EMS handle for buffers, zero if not in EMS
1Ah	WORD	EMS physical page number used for buffers (usually 255)
1Ch	WORD	*unknown.* appears always to be 0001h
1Eh	WORD	segment of EMS physical page frame
20h	WORD	*unknown.* appears always to be zero
22h	BYTE	00h if /XS, 01h if /XD, FFh if BUFFERS not in EMS

Table 8-56. Format of DOS 4.x disk buffer hash chain head (array, one entry per chain):

Offset	Size	Description
00h	WORD	EMS logical page number in which chain is resident, -1 if not in EMS
02h	DWORD	pointer to least recently used buffer header. All buffers on this chain are in the same segment.
06h	BYTE	number of dirty buffers on this chain
07h	BYTE	reserved (00h)

Details: Buffered disk sectors are assigned to chain N where N is the sector's address modulo NDBCH, 0 <= N <= NDBCH-1. Each chain resides completely within one EMS page. This structure is in main memory even if buffers are in EMS.

Table 8-57. Format of DOS 4.0-5.0 disk buffer:

Offset	Size	Description
00h	WORD	forward ptr, offset only, to next least recently used buffer
02h	WORD	backward ptr, offset only
04h	BYTE	drive (0=A,1=B, etc), FFh if not in use
05h	BYTE	flags:
		bit 7: remote buffer
		bit 6: buffer dirty
		bit 5: buffer has been referenced
		bit 4: search data buffer (only valid if remote buffer)
		bit 3: sector in data area
		bit 2: sector in a directory, either root or subdirectory
		bit 1: sector in FAT
		bit 0: reserved
06h	DWORD	logical sector number
0Ah	BYTE	number of copies to write: for FAT sectors, same as number of FATs for data and directory sectors, usually 1
0Bh	WORD	offset in sectors between copies to write for FAT sectors
0Dh	DWORD	pointer to DOS Drive Parameter Block (see Function 32h)
11h	WORD	buffer use count if remote buffer (see flags above)
13h	BYTE	reserved
14h		buffered data

Details: All buffered sectors which have the same hash value (computed as the sum of high and low words of the logical sector number divided by NDBCH) are on the same doubly-linked circular chain; for DOS 5.0, only a single chain exists. The links consist of offset addresses only, the segment being the same for all buffers in the chain.

Table 8-58. Format of DOS 5.0 disk buffer info:

Offset	Size	Description
00h	DWORD	pointer to least-recently-used buffer header (may be in HMA) (see above)
04h	WORD	0000h *number of disk buffer hash chains* (DOS 5 does not hash the buffers)
06h	DWORD	pointer to lookahead buffer, zero if not present
0Ah	WORD	number of lookahead sectors, else zero (the y in BUFFERS=x,y)
0Ch	BYTE	buffer location
		00h base memory, no workspace buffer
		01h HMA, workspace buffer is in base memory
0Dh	DWORD	pointer to one-segment workspace buffer in base memory
11h	3 BYTEs	*unknown.*
14h	WORD	*unknown*
16h	BYTE	*unknown*
17h	BYTE	*unknown*
18h	BYTE	*unknown*
19h	BYTE	*unknown*
1Ah	WORD	*unknown*
1Ch	BYTE	bit 0 set if UMB memory chain linked to normal MCB chain
1Dh	WORD	*unknown*
1Fh	WORD	segment of first memory control block in upper memory blocks or FFFFh if DOS memory chain in base 640K only
21h	WORD	paragraph of start of most recent MCB chain search

Table 8-59. Format of IFS driver list:

Offset	Size	Description
00h	DWORD	pointer to next driver header
04h	8 BYTEs	IFS driver name (blank padded), as used by FILESYS command
0Ch	4 BYTEs	*unknown.*

Table 8-59. Format of IFS driver list (continued):

Offset	Size	Description
10h	DWORD	pointer to IFS utility function entry point (see Table 8-60) call with ES:BX -> IFS request (see Table 8-61)
14h	WORD	offset in header's segment of driver entry point *unknown.*

Table 8-60. Use of IFS utility function entry point

Call IFS utility function entry point with:

AH = 20h miscellaneous functions

    AL = 00h get date

        Return: CX = year

                DH = month

                DL = day

    AL = 01h get process ID and computer ID

        Return: BX = current PSP segment

                DX = active network machine number

    AL = 05h get file system info

        ES:DI -> 16-byte info buffer

        Return: buffer filled as follows:

Offset	Size	Description
00h	2 BYTEs	unused
02h	WORD	number of SFTs (actually counts only the first two file table arrays)
04h	WORD	number of FCB table entries
06h	WORD	number of proctected FCBs
08h	6 BYTEs	unused
0Eh	WORD	largest sector size supported

    AL = 06h get machine name

        ES:DI -> 18-byte buffer for name

        Return: buffer filled with name starting at offset 02h

    AL = 08h get sharing retry count

        Return: BX = sharing retry count

    AL = other

        Return: CF set

AH = 21h get redirection state

        BH = type (03h disk, 04h printer)

        Return: BH = state (00h off, 01h on)

AH = 22h unknown. some sort of time calculation

    AL = 00h *unknown*

        nonzero *unknown*

AH = 23h *appears to be a time calculation*

AH = 24h compare filenames

  DS:SI -> first ASCIZ filename

  ES:DI -> second ASCIZ filename

  Return: ZF set if filenames are same ignoring case

AH = 25h normalize filename

  DS:SI -> ASCIZ filename

  ES:DI -> buffer for result

  Return: filename uppercased, forward slashes changed to backslashes

AH = 26h get DOS stack

    Return: DS:SI -> top of stack

            CX = size of stack in bytes

AH = 27h increment InDOS flag

Table 8-60. Use of IFS utility function entry point (continued)

AH = 28h decrement InDOS flag

Details: IFS drivers which do not wish to implement functions 20h or 24h-28h may pass them on to the default handler pointed at by [ListOfLists+37h].

Table 8-61. Format of IFS request block:

Offset	Size	Description
00h	WORD	total size in bytes of request
02h	BYTE	class of request:
		02h *unknown.*
		03h redirection
		04h *unknown.*
		05h file access
		06h convert error code to string
		07h *unknown.*
03h	WORD	returned DOS error code
05h	BYTE	IFS driver exit status:
		00h success
		01h *unknown.*
		02h *unknown.*
		03h *unknown.*
		04h *unknown.*
		FFh internal failure
06h	16 BYTEs	*unknown.*

---*request class 02h*

16h	BYTE	function code
		04h *unknown.*
17h	BYTE	*apparently unused*
18h	DWORD	pointer to *unknown.*
1Ch	DWORD	pointer to *unknown.*
20h	2 BYTEs	*unknown.*

---*request class 03h*

16h	BYTE	function code
17h	BYTE	*unknown.*
18h	DWORD	pointer to *unknown.*
1Ch	DWORD	pointer to *unknown.*
22h	WORD	returned *unknown.*
24h	WORD	returned *unknown.*
26h	WORD	returned *unknown.*
28h	BYTE	returned *unknown.*
29h	BYTE	*apparently unused.*

---*request class 04h*

16h	DWORD	pointer to *unknown.*
1Ah	DWORD	pointer to *unknown.*

---*request class 05h*

16h	BYTE	function code:

01h flush disk buffers	0Bh read from file
02h get disk space	0Ch write to file
03h MKDIR	0Dh lock region of file
04h RMDIR	0Eh commit/close file
05h CHDIR	0Fh get/set file attributes
06h delete file	10h printer control
07h rename file	11h *unknown.*
08h search directory	12h process termination
09h file open/create	13h *unknown.*
0Ah LSEEK	

Table 8-61. Format of IFS request block (continued)

Offset	Size	Description
---class 05h function 01h		
17h	7 BYTEs	*unknown.*
1Eh	DWORD	pointer to *unknown.*
22h	4 BYTEs	*unknown.*
26h	BYTE	*unknown.*
27h	BYTE	*unknown.*
---class 05h function 02h		
17h	7 BYTEs	*unknown.*
1Eh	DWORD	pointer to *unknown.*
22h	4 BYTEs	*unknown.*
26h	WORD	returned total clusters
28h	WORD	returned sectors per cluster
2Ah	WORD	returned bytes per sector
2Ch	WORD	returned available clusters
2Eh	BYTE	returned *unknown.*
2Fh	BYTE	*unknown.*
---class 05h functions 03h,04h,05h		
17h	7 BYTEs	*unknown.*
1Eh	DWORD	pointer to *unknown.*
22h	4 BYTEs	*unknown.*
26h	DWORD	pointer to directory name
---class 05h function 06h		
17h	7 BYTEs	*unknown.*
1Eh	DWORD	pointer to *unknown.*
22h	4 BYTEs	*unknown.*
26h	WORD	attribute mask
28h	DWORD	pointer to filename
---class 05h function 07h		
17h	7 BYTEs	*unknown.*
1Eh	DWORD	pointer to *unknown.*
22h	4 BYTEs	*unknown.*
26h	WORD	attribute mask
28h	DWORD	pointer to source filespec
2Ch	DWORD	pointer to destination filespec
---class 05h function 08h		
17h	7 BYTEs	*unknown.*
1Eh	DWORD	pointer to *unknown.*
22h	4 BYTEs	*unknown.*
26h	BYTE	00h FINDFIRST
		01h FINDNEXT
28h	DWORD	pointer to FindFirst search data + 01h if FINDNEXT
2Ch	WORD	search attribute if FINDFIRST
2Eh	DWORD	pointer to filespec if FINDFIRST
---class 05h function 09h		
17h	7 BYTEs	*unknown.*
1Eh	DWORD	pointer to *unknown.*
22h	DWORD	pointer to IFS open file structure (see below)
26h	WORD	*unknown.* together, specify open vs. create, whether
28h	WORD	*unknown.* / or not to truncate
2Ah	4 BYTEs	*unknown.*
2Eh	DWORD	pointer to filename
32h	4 BYTEs	*unknown.*
36h	WORD	file attributes on call
		returned *unknown.*

Table 8-61. Format of IFS request block (continued)

Offset	Size	Description
38h	WORD	returned *unknown*.

---class 05h function 0Ah

Offset	Size	Description
17h	7 BYTEs	*unknown*.
1Eh	DWORD	pointer to *unknown*.
22h	DWORD	pointer to IFS open file structure (see below)
26h	BYTE	seek type (02h = from end)
28h	DWORD	offset on call
		returned new absolute position

---class 05h functions 0Bh,0Ch

Offset	Size	Description
17h	7 BYTEs	*unknown*.
1Eh	DWORD	pointer to *unknown*.
22h	DWORD	pointer to IFS open file structure (see below)
28h	WORD	number of bytes to transfer
		returned bytes actually transferred
2Ah	DWORD	transfer address

---class 05h function 0Dh

Offset	Size	Description
17h	7 BYTEs	*unknown*.
1Eh	DWORD	pointer to *unknown*.
22h	DWORD	pointer to IFS open file structure (see below)
26h	BYTE	*file handle*
27h	BYTE	*apparently unused*
28h	WORD	*unknown*.
2Ah	WORD	*unknown*.
2Ch	WORD	*unknown*.
2Eh	WORD	*unknown*.

---class 05h function 0Eh

Offset	Size	Description
17h	7 BYTEs	*unknown*.
1Eh	DWORD	pointer to *unknown*.
22h	DWORD	pointer to IFS open file structure (see below)
26h	BYTE	00h commit file
		01h close file
27h	BYTE	*apparently unused*

---class 05h function 0Fh

Offset	Size	Description
17h	7 BYTEs	*unknown*.
1Eh	DWORD	pointer to *unknown*.
22h	4 BYTEs	*unknown*.
26h	BYTE	02h GET attributes
		03h PUT attributes
27h	BYTE	*apparently unused*
28h	12 BYTEs	*unknown*.
34h	WORD	*search attributes*
36h	DWORD	pointer to filename
3Ah	WORD	(GET) returned *unknown*.
3Ch	WORD	(GET) returned *unknown*.
3Eh	WORD	(GET) returned *unknown*.
40h	WORD	(GET) returned *unknown*.
42h	WORD	(PUT) new attributes
		(GET) returned attributes

---class 05h function 10h

Offset	Size	Description
17h	7 BYTEs	*unknown*.
1Eh	DWORD	pointer to *unknown*.
22h	DWORD	pointer to IFS open file structure (see below)
26h	WORD	*unknown*.
28h	DWORD	pointer to *unknown*.

Table 8-61. Format of IFS request block (continued)

Offset	Size	Description
---*class 05h function 10h (continued)*		
2Ch	WORD	*unknown.*
2Eh	BYTE	*unknown.*
2Fh	BYTE	subfunction:
		01h get printer setup
		03h *unknown.*
		04h *unknown.*
		05h *unknown.*
		06h *unknown.*
		07h *unknown.*
		21h set printer setup
---*class 05h function 11h*		
17h	7 BYTEs	*unknown.*
1Eh	DWORD	pointer to *unknown.*
22h	DWORD	pointer to IFS open file structure (see below)
26h	BYTE	subfunction
27h	BYTE	*apparently unused*
28h	WORD	*unknown.*
2Ah	WORD	*unknown.*
2Ch	WORD	*unknown.*
2Eh	BYTE	*unknown.*
2Fh	BYTE	*unknown.*
---*class 05h function 12h*		
17h	15 BYTEs	*apparently unused*
26h	WORD	PSP segment
28h	BYTE	type of process termination
29h	BYTE	*apparently unused*
---*class 05h function 13h*		
17h	15 BYTEs	*apparently unused*
26h	WORD	PSP segment
---*request class 06h*		
16h	DWORD	returned pointer to string corresponding to error code at 03h
1Ah	BYTE	returned *unknown.*
1Bh	BYTE	unused
---*request class 07h*		
16h	DWORD	pointer to IFS open file structure (see below)
1Ah	BYTE	*unknown.*
1Bh	BYTE	*apparently unused*

Table 8-62. Format of IFS open file structure:

Offset	Size	Description
00h	WORD	*unknown.*
02h	WORD	device info word
04h	WORD	file open mode
06h	WORD	*unknown.*
08h	WORD	file attributes
0Ah	WORD	owner's network machine number
0Ch	WORD	owner's PSP segment
0Eh	DWORD	file size
12h	DWORD	current offset in file
16h	WORD	file time
18h	WORD	file date
1Ah	11 BYTEs	filename in FCB format

Table 8-62. Format of IFS open file structure (continued)

Offset	Size	Description
25h	WORD	*unknown.*
27h	WORD	hash value of SFT address (low word of linear address + segment&F000h)
29h	3 WORDs	network info from SFT
2Fh	WORD	*unknown.*

Table 8-63. Format of one item in DOS 4+ list of special program names:

Offset	Size	Description
00h	BYTE	length of name (00h = end of list)
01h	N BYTEs	name in format name.ext
N	2 BYTES	DOS version to return for program (major, minor) (see Function 30h, INT 2Fh Function 12h Subfunction 2Fh)
N+2	BYTE	(DOS 4.x only) number of times to return fake version number (FFh = always)

Details: If the name of the executable for the program making the DOS "get version" call matches one of the names in this list, DOS returns the specified version rather than the true version number.

INTERRUPT 21h - Function 53h
TRANSLATE BIOS PARAMETER BLOCK TO DRIVE PARAMETER BLOCK

Purpose: Converts drive parameter information from the format stored on disk to that used by DOS routines.
Available on: DOS 2.0 or higher.　　　　　　　**Restrictions:** This call is not documented and is therefore subject to change.

Registers at call:
AH = 53h
DS:SI -> BIOS Parameter Block (Table 8-64)
ES:BP -> buffer for Drive Parameter Block (see
　　Function 32h for format)

Return Registers:
ES:BP buffer filled

Details: For DOS 3+, the cluster at which to start searching is set to 0000h and the number of free clusters is set to FFFFh (not known).
Conflicts: None known.

Table 8-64. Format of BIOS Parameter Block:

Offset	Size	Description
00h	WORD	number of bytes per sector
02h	BYTE	number of sectors per cluster
03h	WORD	number of reserved sectors at start of disk
05h	BYTE	number of FATs
06h	WORD	number of entries in root directory
08h	WORD	total number of sectors; For DOS 4.0, set to zero if partition >32M, then set DWORD at 15h to actual number of sectors
0Ah	BYTE	media ID byte
0Bh	WORD	number of sectors per FAT
---DOS 3+		
0Dh	WORD	number of sectors per track
0Fh	WORD	number of heads
11h	DWORD	number of hidden sectors
15h	11 BYTEs	reserved
---DOS 4+		
15h	DWORD	total number of sectors if word at 08h contains zero
19h	6 BYTEs	*unknown.*
1Fh	WORD	number of cylinders
21h	BYTE	device type
22h	WORD	device attributes (removable or not, etc)

INTERRUPT 21h - Function 54h
GET VERIFY FLAG

Purpose: Reads MS-DOS "verify" flag value.
Available on: DOS 2.0 or higher.
Registers at call:
AH = 54h

Restrictions: none.
Return Registers:
AL = verify flag:
    00h off
    01h on (all disk writes verified after writing)

Conflicts: None known.
See Also: Function 2Eh

INTERRUPT 21h - Function 55h
CREATE CHILD PSP

Purpose: Creates PSP for use by child process (obsolete, function now performed by Function 4Bh).
Available on: DOS 2.0 or higher.

Restrictions: This call is not documented and is therefore subject to change.

Registers at call:
AH = 55h
DX = segment at which to create new PSP
SI = (DOS 3+) value to place in memory size field
    at DX:[0002h]

Return Registers:
CF clear if successful

Details: Creates a "child" PSP rather than making an exact copy of the current PSP; the new PSP's parent pointer is set to the current PSP and the reference count for each inherited file is incremented. The current PSP is set to DX. DOS 3+ marks "no inherit" file handles as closed in the child PSP.
Conflicts: None known.
See Also: Functions 26h and 50h

INTERRUPT 21h - Function 56h
"RENAME" - RENAME FILE

Purpose: Changes the name of a file as specified; can move a file from one directory to another so long as both are on the same logical volume.
Available on: DOS 2.0 or higher.
Registers at call:
AH = 56h
DS:DX -> ASCIZ filename of existing file (no
    wildcards, but see below)
ES:BX -> ASCIZ new filename (may include path,
    but not wildcards)
CL = file attribute mask (server call only, see
    below)

Restrictions: none.
Return Registers:
CF clear if successful
CF set on error
    AX = error code (02h,03h,05h,11h) (see Function
    59h)

Details: Renaming does not set the archive attribute (see Function 43h Subfunction 00h), which results in incremental backups not backing up the file under its new name. Open files should not be renamed. DOS 3.0 and higher allow renaming of directories, but not moving.

    Wildcards are allowed under DOS 3.1+ if this call is invoked via Function 5Dh Subfunction 00h, in which case error 12h (no more files) is returned on success, and both source and destination specifications must be canonical (as returned by Function 60h); only files matching the specified attribute mask will be renamed. Wildcards in the destination are replaced by the corresponding character of each source file being renamed. Under DOS 3.x, the call will fail if the destination wildcard is *.* or equivalent.
Conflicts: None known.
See Also: Functions 17h and 60h, Function 5Dh Subfunction 00h

INTERRUPT 21h - Function 57h, Subfunction 00h
GET FILE'S DATE AND TIME

Purpose: Reads date and time a file was last modified, as contained in the file's directory information.

Available on: DOS 2.0 or higher.

Registers at call:
AX = 5700h
BX = file handle

Restrictions: none.

Return Registers:
CF clear if successful
    CX = file's time:
        bits 15-11: hours (0-23)
            10-5: minutes
            4-0: seconds/2
    DX = file's date:
        bits 15-9: year - 1980
           8-5: month
           4-0: day
CF set on error
    AX = error code (01h,06h) (see Function 59h)

Conflicts: None known.
See Also: Function 57h Subfunction 01h

INTERRUPT 21h - Function 57h, Subfunction 01h
SET FILE'S DATE AND TIME

Purpose: Changes file's last-modified date and time information to the specified values.

Available on: DOS 2.0 or higher.

Registers at call:
AX = 5701h
BX = file handle
CX = new time (see Function 57h Subfunction 00h)
DX = new date (see Function 57h Subfunction 00h)

Restrictions: none.

Return Registers:
CF clear if successful
CF set on error
    AX = error code (01h,06h) (see Function 59h)

Conflicts: None known.
See Also: Function 57h Subfunction 00h

INTERRUPT 21h - Function 57h, Subfunction 02h
GET unknown value

Purpose: unknown.

Available on: DOS 4.x only.

Registers at call:
AX = 5702h
BX = *unknown.* (0000h through 0004h)
DS:SI -> *unknown.*
ES:DI -> result buffer
CX = size of result buffer

Restrictions: none.

Return Registers:
CX = size of returned data

Conflicts: None known.
See Also: Function 57h Subfunctions 03h and 04h

INTERRUPT 21h - Function 57h, Subfunction 03h
GET unknown value

Purpose: unknown.

Available on: DOS 4.x only.

Restrictions: none.

Registers at call:
AX = 5703h
BX = file handle (only 0000h through 0004h valid)
DS:SI -> *unknown*. passed through to INT 2Fh
    Function 11h Subfunction 2Dh
ES:DI -> result buffer
CX = size of result buffer
Conflicts: None known.
See Also: Function 57h Subfunctions 02h and 04h, INT 2Fh Function 11h Subfunction 2Dh (chapter 19)

Return Registers:
CX = size of returned data
ES:DI -> zero word (DOS 4.0) if CX >= 2 on entry

INTERRUPT 21h - Function 57h, Subfunction 04h
TRUNCATE OPEN FILE TO ZERO LENGTH

Purpose: Discard the contents of the file corresponding to one of the five standard file handles (if redirected over the network).
Available on: DOS 4.x only.

Registers at call:
AX = 5704h
BX = file handle (only 0000h through 0004h valid)
DS:SI -> *unknown*. passed through to INT 2Fh
    Function 11h Subfunction 2Dh
ES:DI -> result buffer
CX = size of result buffer
Conflicts: None known.
See Also: Function 57h Subfunctions 02h and 03h, INT 2Fh Function 11h Subfunction 2Dh (chapter 19)

Restrictions: none.
Return Registers:
CX = size of returned data
ES:DI buffer filled with zero word (DOS 4.0)
    if CX >= 2 on entry

INTERRUPT 21h - Function 58h
GET OR SET MEMORY ALLOCATION STRATEGY

Purpose: Read or write memory allocation strategy control byte used by MS-DOS.
Available on: DOS 3.0 or higher.

Registers at call:
AH = 58h
AL = subfunction:

    00h get allocation strategy

Restrictions: none.
Return Registers:
CF set on error
    AX = error code (01h) (see Function 59h)
CF clear if successful

AX = current strategy:
    00h low memory first fit
    01h low memory best fit
    02h low memory last fit
    ---DOS 5+
    40h high memory first fit
    41h high memory best fit
    42h high memory last fit
    80h first fit, try high then low memory
    81h best fit, try high then low memory
    82h last fit, try high then low memory

    01h set allocation strategy:
        BL = new allocation strategy
          (see above)
        BH = 00h (DOS 5.0)

    02h (DOS 5+) get UMB link state:

AL = 00h UMBs not part of DOS memory chain
   = 01h UMBs in DOS memory chain

03h (DOS 5+) set UMB link state:
  BX = 0000h remove UMBs from
           DOS memory chain
      = 0001h add UMBs to memory chain

Details: The Set subfunction accepts any value in BL for DOS 2 through DOS 4.x; a value of 2 or greater means last fit. The Get subfunction returns the last value set.

A program which changes the allocation strategy should restore it before terminating.

Conflicts: None known.

See Also: Functions 48h, 49h, and 4Ah

INTERRUPT 21h - Function 59h
GET EXTENDED ERROR INFORMATION

Purpose: Translate and expand on error codes returned by DOS.

Available on: DOS 3.0 or higher.

Restrictions: none.

Registers at call:
AH = 59h
BX = 0000h

Return Registers:
AX = extended error code (Table 8-68)
BH = error class (Table 8-65)
BL = recommended action (Table 8-66)
CH = error locus (Table 8-67)
CL, DX, SI, DI, BP, DS, and ES destroyed

Details: Functions available under DOS 2.x map the true DOS 3+ error code into one supported under DOS 2.x. You should call this function to retrieve the true error code when an FCB or DOS 2.x call returns an error.

Conflicts: None known.

See Also: Function 5Dh Subfunction 0Ah, INT 2Fh Function 12h Subfunction 2Dh

Table 8-65. Values for Error Class:

Value	Meaning	Value	Meaning
01h	out of resource (storage space or I/O channels)	07h	application program error
		08h	not found
02h	temporary situation (file or record lock)	09h	bad format
03h	authorization (denied access)	0Ah	locked
04h	internal (system software bug)	0Bh	media error
05h	hardware failure	0Ch	already exists
06h	system failure (configuration file missing or incorrect)	0Dh	unknown

Table 8-66. Values for Suggested Action:

Value	Meaning	Value	Meaning
01h	retry	04h	abort after cleanup
02h	delayed retry	05h	immediate abort
03h	prompt user to reenter input	06h	ignore
		07h	retry after user intervention

Table 8-67. Values for Error Locus:

Value	Meaning	Value	Meaning
01h	unknown or not appropriate	03h	network related
02h	block device (disk error)	04h	serial device (timeout)
		05h	memory related

Table 8-68. Values for extended error code:

Value	Meaning	Value	Meaning
00h	no error	32h	network request not supported
01h	function number invalid	33h	remote computer not listening
02h	file not found	34h	duplicate name on network
03h	path not found	35h	network name not found
04h	too many open files (no handles available)	36h	network busy
05h	access denied	37h	network device no longer exists
06h	invalid handle	38h	network BIOS command limit exceeded
07h	memory control block destroyed	39h	network adapter hardware error
08h	insufficient memory	3Ah	incorrect response from network
09h	memory block address invalid	3Bh	unexpected network error
0Ah	environment invalid (usually >32K in length)	3Ch	incompatible remote adapter
		3Dh	print queue full
0Bh	format invalid	3Eh	queue not full
0Ch	access code invalid	3Fh	not enough space to print file
0Dh	data invalid	40h	network name was deleted
0Eh	reserved	41h	network: Access denied
0Fh	invalid drive	42h	network device type incorrect
10h	attempted to remove current directory	43h	network name not found
11h	not same device	44h	network name limit exceeded
12h	no more files	45h	network BIOS session limit exceeded
---DOS 3+		46h	temporarily paused
13h	disk write-protected	47h	network request not accepted
14h	unknown unit	48h	network print/disk redirection paused
15h	drive not ready	49h	(LANtastic) invalid network version
16h	unknown command	4Ah	(LANtastic) account expired
17h	data error (CRC)	4Bh	(LANtastic) password expired
18h	bad request structure length	4Ch	(LANtastic) login attempt invalid at this time
19h	seek error	4Dh	(LANtastic v3+) disk limit exceeded on network node
1Ah	unknown media type (non-DOS disk)	4Eh	(LANtastic v3+) not logged in to network node
1Bh	sector not found	4Fh	reserved
1Ch	printer out of paper	50h	file exists
1Dh	write fault	51h	reserved
1Eh	read fault	52h	cannot make directory
1Fh	general failure	53h	fail on INT 24h
20h	sharing violation	**---DOS 3.3+**	
21h	lock violation	54h	too many redirections
22h	disk change invalid: ES:DI -> ASCIZ volume label of required disk	55h	duplicate redirection
		56h	invalid password
23h	FCB unavailable	57h	invalid parameter
24h	sharing buffer overflow	58h	network write fault
25h	(DOS 4+) code page mismatch	**---DOS 4+**	
26h	(DOS 4+) cannot complete file operation (out of input)	59h	function not supported on network
27h	(DOS 4+) insufficient disk space	5Ah	required system component not installed
28h-31h	reserved		

INTERRUPT 21h - Function 5Ah
CREATE TEMPORARY FILE

Purpose: Creates a file with a unique name which must be explicitly deleted.
Available on: DOS 3.0 or higher.   **Restrictions:** none.

Registers at call:
AH = 5Ah
CX = file attribute (see Function 43h Subfunction 01h)
DS:DX -> ASCIZ path ending with at least 13 zero bytes to receive the generated filename

Return Registers:
CF clear if successful
    AX = file handle opened for read/write in compatibility mode
    DS:DX pathname extended with generated name for temporary file
CF set on error
    AX = error code (03h,04h,05h) (Table 8-68)

Details: COMPAQ DOS 3.31 hangs if the pathname is at XXXXh:0000h; it apparently wraps around to the end of the segment.
Conflicts: None known.
See Also: Functions 3Ch and 5Bh

INTERRUPT 21h - Function 5Bh
CREATE NEW FILE

Purpose: Same as Function 3Ch except that this function will fail with an error code if the requested file already exists.
Available on: DOS 3.0 or higher.

Registers at call:
AH = 5Bh
CX = file attribute (see Function 43h Subfunction 01h)
DS:DX -> ASCIZ filename

Restrictions: none.
Return Registers:
CF clear if successful
    AX = file handle opened for read/write in compatibility mode
CF set on error
    AX = error code (03h,04h,05h,50h) (Table 8-68)

Details: Unlike Function 3Ch, this function will fail if the specified file exists rather than truncating it; this permits its use in creating semaphore files because it is an atomic "test and set" operation.
Conflicts: None known.
See Also: Function 3Ch, Function 5Ah

INTERRUPT 21h - Function 5Ch
"FLOCK" - RECORD LOCKING

Purpose: Prevent multiple users from accessing the same area of the specified file.
Available on: DOS 3.0 or higher.

Registers at call:
AH = 5Ch
AL = subfunction:
    00h lock region of file
    01h unlock region of file
BX = file handle
CX:DX = start offset of region within file
SI:DI = length of region in bytes

Restrictions: SHARE or network must be installed.
Return Registers:
CF clear if successful
CF set on error
    AX = error code (01h,06h,21h,24h) (Table 8-68)

Details: An unlock call must specify the same region as some prior lock call. Locked regions become entirely inaccessible to other processes. Duplicate handles created with Functions 45h or 46h inherit locks, but handles inherited by child processes (see Function 4Bh) do not.
Conflicts: None known.
See Also: Function 44h Subfunction 0Bh, INT 2Fh Function 11h Subfunctions 0Ah and 0Bh

INTERRUPT 21h - Function 5Dh, Subfunction 00h
SERVER FUNCTION CALL

Purpose: Allows network server to execute DOS calls originating on another machine.
Available on: DOS 3.1 or higher.
Restrictions: This call is not documented and therefore subject to change.

Registers at call:
AX = 5D00h
DS:DX -> DOS parameter list (Table 8-69); DPL
    contains all register values for a call to
    INT 21h

Return Registers:
As appropriate for function being called.

Details: This call does not check AH; out of range values will crash the system. Executes using the specified computer ID and process ID. Sharing delay loops are skipped, and a special sharing mode is enabled. Wildcards are enabled for DELETE (Function 41h) and RENAME (Function 56h), and an extra file attribute parameter is enabled for those two functions and OPEN (Function 3Dh). Functions which take filenames require canonical names (as returned by Function 60h); this is apparently to prevent multi-hop file forwarding.
Conflicts: None known.
See Also: Function 60h

Table 8-69. Format of DOS parameter list:

Offset	Size	Description
00h	WORD	AX
02h	WORD	BX
04h	WORD	CX
06h	WORD	DX
08h	WORD	SI
0Ah	WORD	DI
0Ch	WORD	DS
0Eh	WORD	ES
10h	WORD	reserved (0)
12h	WORD	computer ID (0 = current system)
14h	WORD	process ID (PSP segment on specified computer)

INTERRUPT 21h - Function 5Dh, Subfunction 01h
COMMIT ALL FILES FOR SPECIFIED COMPUTER/PROCESS

Purpose: Flushes buffers and updates directory entries for each file which has been modified; if remote file, calls INT 2Fh Function 11h Subfunction 07h.
Available on: DOS 3.1 or higher.

Restrictions: This function is not documented and therefore subject to change.

Registers at call:
AX = 5D01h
DS:DX -> DOS parameter list (Table 8-69), only
    computer ID and process ID fields used

Return Registers:
CF set on error
    AX = error code (see Function 59h)
CF clear if successful

Details: The computer ID and process ID are stored but ignored under DOS 3.3.
Conflicts: None known.
See Also: Functions 0Dh and 68h, INT 2Fh Function 11h Subfunction 07h

INTERRUPT 21h - Function 5Dh, Subfunction 02h
internal - CLOSE FILE BY NAME

Purpose: Closes the named file.
Available on: DOS 3.1 or higher.

Restrictions: SHARE must be loaded.

Registers at call:
AX = 5D02h
DS:DX -> DOS parameter list (Table 8-69), only
    fields DX, DS, computer ID, and process ID
    used
DPL's DS:DX -> ASCIZ name of file to close

Return Registers:
CF set on error
    AX = error code (see Function 59h)
CF clear if successful

Details: Error unless SHARE is loaded (calls [SysFileTable-28h]) (see Function 52h). Name must be canonical fully-qualified, such as returned by Function 60h.
Conflicts: None known.
See Also: Function 5Dh Subfunctions 03h and 04h, Functions 3Eh and 60h

INTERRUPT 21h - Function 5Dh, Subfunction 03h
internal - CLOSE ALL FILES FOR GIVEN COMPUTER

Purpose: Closes all files for the specified computer.
Available on: DOS 3.1 or higher.

Restrictions: SHARE must be loaded (calls [SysFileTable-30h]).

Registers at call:
AX = 5D03h
DS:DX -> DOS parameter list (Table 8-69), only
    computer ID used
Conflicts: None known.
See Also: Function 5Dh Subfunctions 02h and 04h

Return Registers:
CF set on error
    AX = error code (see Function 59h)
CF clear if successful

INTERRUPT 21h - Function 5Dh, Subfunction 04h
internal - CLOSE ALL FILES FOR GIVEN PROCESS

Purpose: Close all files currently open for the specified process.
Available on: DOS 3.1 or higher.
Registers at call:
AX = 5D04h
DS:DX -> DOS parameter list (Table 8-69), only
    computer ID and process ID fields used
Conflicts: None known.
See Also: Function 5Dh Subfunctions 02h and 03h

Restrictions: SHARE must be loaded.
Return Registers:
CF set on error
    AX = error code (see Function 59h)
CF clear if successful

INTERRUPT 21h - Function 5Dh, Subfunction 05h
internal - GET OPEN FILE LIST ENTRY

Purpose: Return the name of an open file, given a system file table index for that file.
Available on: DOS 3.1 or higher.
Registers at call:
AX = 5D05h
DS:DX -> DOS parameter list (Table 8-69)
DPL's BX = index of sharing record
DPL's CX = index of SFT in sharing record's SFT
    list

Restrictions: SHARE must be loaded.
Return Registers:
CF clear if successful
    ES:DI -> ASCIZ filename
    BX = network machine number of SFT's owner
    CX = number of locks held by SFT's owner
CF set if either index out of range
    AX = 0012h (no more files)

Details: Names are always canonical fully-qualified, such as returned by Function 60h.
Conflicts: None known.
See Also: Functions 5Ch and 60h

INTERRUPT 21h - Function 5Dh, Subfunction 06h
GET ADDRESS OF DOS SWAPPABLE DATA AREA

Purpose: Determine address of swappable data area.
Available on: DOS 3.0 or higher.

Restrictions: This function is not documented and therefore subject to change.

Registers at call:
AX = 5D06h

Return Registers:
CF set on error
    AX = error code (see Function 59h)
CF clear if successful
    DS:SI -> nonreentrant data area, including all three
        DOS stacks (critical error flag is first byte)
    CX = size in bytes of area which must be swapped
        while in DOS
    DX = size in bytes of area which must always be
        swapped

Details: The Critical Error flag is used in conjunction with the InDOS flag (see Function 34h) to determine when it is safe to enter DOS from a TSR. Setting the Critical Error flag allows use of functions 50h/51h from INT 28h under DOS 2.x by forcing use of the correct stack.

Swapping the data area allows reentering DOS unless DOS is in a critical section delimited by INT 2Ah Function 80h and INT 2Ah Functions 81h/82h. Under DOS 4.0, Function 5Dh Subfunction 0Bh should be used instead of this function.

Table 8-70 describes what has been identified in the swappable data areas for DOS 3.10 thru 3.30.

Conflicts: None known.

See Also: Function 5Dh Subfunction 0Bh, INT 2Ah Functions 80h-82h

Table 8-70. Format of DOS 3.10-3.30 Swappable Data Area:

Offset	Size	Description
00h	BYTE	critical error flag
01h	BYTE	InDOS flag (count of active INT 21h calls)
02h	BYTE	drive on which current critical error occurred, or FFh
03h	BYTE	locus of last error
04h	WORD	extended error code of last error
06h	BYTE	suggested action for last error
07h	BYTE	class of last error
08h	DWORD	ES:DI pointer for last error
0Ch	DWORD	current DTA
10h	WORD	current PSP
12h	WORD	stores SP across an INT 23h
14h	WORD	return code from last process termination (zeroed after reading with Function 4Dh)
16h	BYTE	current drive
17h	BYTE	extended break flag

---remainder need only be swapped if in DOS

Offset	Size	Description
18h	WORD	value of AX on call to INT 21h
1Ah	WORD	PSP segment for sharing/network
1Ch	WORD	network machine number for sharing/network (0000h = us)
1Eh	WORD	first usable memory block found when allocating memory
20h	WORD	best usable memory block found when allocating memory
22h	WORD	last usable memory block found when allocating memory
24h	WORD	memory size in paragraphs (used only during initialization)
26h	WORD	*unknown.*
28h	BYTE	INT 24h returned Fail
29h	BYTE	bit flags for allowable actions on INT 24h
2Ah	BYTE	*unknown flag.*
2Bh	BYTE	FFh if Ctrl-Break termination, 00h otherwise
2Ch	BYTE	*unknown flag.*
2Dh	BYTE	*unknown.* apparently not referenced by kernel
2Eh	BYTE	day of month
2Fh	BYTE	month
30h	WORD	year - 1980
32h	WORD	number of days since 1-1-1980
34h	BYTE	day of week (0 = Sunday)

Table 8-70. Format of DOS 3.10-3.30 Swappable Data Area (continued)

Offset	Size	Description
35h	BYTE	*working SFT pointer at SDA+2AAh is valid*
36h	BYTE	safe to call INT 28h if nonzero
37h	BYTE	flag: if nonzero, INT 24h abort turned into INT 24h fail (set only during process termination)
38h	26 BYTEs	device driver request header
52h	DWORD	pointer to device driver entry point (used in calling driver)
56h	22 BYTEs	device driver request header
6Ch	22 BYTEs	device driver request header
82h	BYTE	type of PSP copy: 00h = simple for INT 21h Function 26h FFh = make child
83h	BYTE	*unknown.* apparently not referenced by kernel
84h	3 BYTEs	24-bit user number (see Function 30h)
87h	BYTE	OEM number (see Function 30h)
88h	2 BYTEs	*unknown.*
8Ah	6 BYTEs	CLOCK$ transfer record (see Function 52h)
90h	BYTE	*apparently buffer for single-byte I/O functions*
91h	BYTE	*apparently not referenced by kernel*
92h	128 BYTEs	buffer for filename
112h	128 BYTEs	buffer for filename
192h	21 BYTEs	findfirst/findnext search data block (see Function 4Eh)
1A7h	32 BYTEs	directory entry for found file
1C7h	81 BYTEs	copy of current directory structure for drive being accessed
218h	11 BYTEs	FCB-format filename for device name comparison
223h	BYTE	*apparently unused*
224h	11 BYTEs	wildcard destination specification for rename (FCB format)
22Fh	2 BYTEs	*unknown.*
231h	WORD	*unknown.*
233h	5 BYTEs	*unknown.*
238h	BYTE	extended FCB file attribute
239h	BYTE	type of FCB (00h regular, FFh extended)
23Ah	BYTE	directory search attributes
23Bh	BYTE	*file open mode*
23Ch	BYTE	*unknown flags, bits 0 and 4.*
23Dh	BYTE	*unknown flag or counter.*
23Eh	BYTE	*unknown flag.*
23Fh	BYTE	flag indicating how DOS function was invoked (00h = direct INT 20h/INT 21h, FFh = server call Function 5Dh Subfunction 00h)
240h	BYTE	*unknown.*
241h	BYTE	*unknown flag.*
242h	BYTE	flag: 00h if read, 01h if write
243h	BYTE	*unknown drive number.*
244h	BYTE	*unknown.*
245h	BYTE	*unknown flag or counter.*
246h	BYTE	line edit (Function 0Ah) insert mode flag (nonzero = on)
247h	BYTE	canonicalized filename referred to existing file or directory if FFh
248h	BYTE	*unknown flag or counter.*
249h	BYTE	type of process termination (00h-03h) (see Function 4Dh)
24Ah	BYTE	*unknown flag.*
24Bh	BYTE	value with which to replace first byte of deleted file's name (normally E5h, but 00h as described under INT 21h Function 13h)
24Ch	DWORD	pointer to Drive Parameter Block for critical error invocation
250h	DWORD	pointer to stack frame containing user registers on INT 21h
254h	WORD	stores SP across INT 24h
256h	DWORD	pointer to *unknown DOS Drive Parameter Block*
25Ah	WORD	*unknown.*
25Ch	WORD	*unknown temporary storage.*

Table 8-70. Format of DOS 3.10-3.30 Swappable Data Area (continued)

Offset	Size	Description
25Eh	WORD	*unknown flag.* only low byte referenced
260h	WORD	*unknown temporary storage.*
262h	BYTE	Media ID byte returned by Functions 1Bh/1Ch
263h	BYTE	*unknown.* apparently not referenced by kernel
264h	DWORD	*unknown pointer to device header*
268h	DWORD	pointer to current SFT
26Ch	DWORD	pointer to current directory structure for drive being accessed
270h	DWORD	pointer to caller's FCB
274h	WORD	number of SFT to which file being opened will refer
276h	WORD	temporary storage for file handle
278h	DWORD	pointer to a JFT entry in process handle table (see Function 26h)
27Ch	WORD	offset in DOS DS of first filename argument
27Eh	WORD	offset in DOS DS of second filename argument
280h	WORD	offset of last component in filename or FFFFh.
282h	WORD	*unknown offset.*
284h	WORD	*relative cluster within file being accessed*
286h	WORD	*absolute cluster number being accessed*
288h	WORD	*current sector number.*
28Ah	WORD	*current cluster number.*
28Ch	WORD	*current relative sector number within file.*
28Eh	2 BYTEs	*unknown.*
290h	WORD	*byte offset within current sector.*
292h	DWORD	current offset in file
296h	6 WORDs	*unknown.*
2A2h	DWORD	number of bytes appended to file
2A6h	DWORD	pointer to *unknown disk buffer*
2AAh	DWORD	pointer to working SFT
2AEh	WORD	used by INT 21h dispatcher to store caller's BX
2B0h	WORD	used by INT 21h dispatcher to store caller's DS
2B2h	WORD	temporary storage while saving/restoring caller's registers
2B4h	DWORD	pointer to previous call frame (offset 250h) if INT 21h reentered; also switched to for duration of INT 24h
2B8h	21 BYTEs	FindFirst search data for source file(s) of a rename operation (see Function 4Eh)
2CDh	32 BYTEs	directory entry for file being renamed
2EDh	331 BYTEs	critical error stack (a scratch SFT is located from 403h-437h)
438h	384 BYTEs	disk stack (functions greater than 0Ch, INT 25h, INT 26h)
5B8h	384 BYTEs	character I/O stack (functions 01h through 0Ch)

---DOS 3.2,3.3 only

Offset	Size	Description
738h	BYTE	device driver lookahead flag (see Function 64h)
739h	BYTE	*unknown drive number*
73Ah	BYTE	*unknown flag.*
73Ah	BYTE	*unknown.*

INTERRUPT 21h - Function 5Dh, Subfunction 07h
GET REDIRECTED PRINTER MODE

Purpose: Gets current printer redirection mode.

Available on: DOS 3.1 or higher.

Restrictions: Network software must be installed.

Registers at call:
AX = 5D07h

Return Registers:
DL = mode:
    00h redirected output is combined
    01h redirected output in separate print jobs

Conflicts: None known.

See Also: Function 5Dh Subfunctions 08h and 09h, INT 2Fh Function 11h Subfunction 25h (chapter 19)

INTERRUPT 21h - Function 5Dh, Subfunction 08h
SET REDIRECTED PRINTER MODE

Purpose: Sets printer redirection mode.
Available on: DOS 3.1 or higher.
Registers at call:
AX = 5D08h
DL = mode:
    00h redirected output is combined
    01h redirected output placed in separate
        jobs, start new print job now

Restrictions: Network software must be installed.
Return Registers: n/a

Conflicts: None known.
See Also: Function 5Dh Subfunctions 07h and 09h, INT 2Fh Function 11h Subfunction 25h (chapter 19)

INTERRUPT 21h - Function 5Dh, Subfunction 09h
FLUSH REDIRECTED PRINTER OUTPUT

Purpose: Forces redirected printer output to be printed, and starts a new print job.
Available on: DOS 3.1 or higher.
Registers at call:
AX = 5D09h

Restrictions: Network software must be installed.
Return Registers: n/a

Conflicts: None known.
See Also: Function 5Dh Subfunction 07h, Function 5Dh Subfunction 08h, INT 2Fh Function 11h Subfunction 25h
(chapter 19)

INTERRUPT 21h - Function 5Dh, Subfunction 0Ah
SET EXTENDED ERROR INFORMATION

Purpose: Modifies extended error information returned by Function 59h.
Available on: DOS 3.1 or higher.
Registers at call:
AX = 5D0Ah
DS:DX -> 11-word DOS parameter list (see
    Function 5Dh Subfunction 00h)

Restrictions: none.
Return Registers: n/a

Details: The next call to Function 59h will return values from fields AX, BX, CX, DX, DI, and ES in the corresponding registers. This function has been documented for DOS 5.0, but was undocumented in prior versions.
Conflicts: None known.
See Also: Function 59h

INTERRUPT 21h - Function 5Dh, Subfunction 0Bh
GET DOS SWAPPABLE DATA AREAS

Purpose: Obtain pointer to list of swappable data areas.
Available on: DOS 4.x only.
Registers at call:
AX = 5D0Bh

Restrictions: This call is undocumented.
Return Registers:
CF set on error
    AX = error code (see Function 59h)
CF clear if successful
    DS:SI -> swappable data area list (Table 8-71)

Details: Copying and restoring the swappable data areas allows DOS to be reentered unless it is in a critical section delimited by calls to INT 2Ah Function 80h and INT 2Ah Functions 81h/82h.
Conflicts: None known.
See Also: Function 5Dh Subfunction 06h, INT 2Ah Functions 80h-82h

Table 8-71. Format of swappable data area list:

Offset	Size	Description
00h	WORD	count of data areas
02h	N BYTEs	"count" copies of data area record:

Offset	Size	Description
00h	DWORD	address
04h	WORD	length and type:
		bit 15 set if swap always, clear if swap in DOS
		bits 14-0: length in bytes

Table 8-72. Format of DOS 4.0-5.0 swappable data area:

Offset	Size	Description
00h	BYTE	critical error flag
01h	BYTE	InDOS flag (count of active INT 21h calls)
02h	BYTE	drive on which current critical error occurred, or FFh
03h	BYTE	locus of last error
04h	WORD	extended error code of last error
06h	BYTE	suggested action for last error
07h	BYTE	class of last error
08h	DWORD	ES:DI pointer for last error
0Ch	DWORD	current DTA
10h	WORD	current PSP
12h	WORD	stores SP across an INT 23h
14h	WORD	return code from last process termination (zerod after reading with Function 4Dh)
16h	BYTE	current drive
17h	BYTE	extended break flag
18h	2 BYTEs	*unknown.*

---remainder need only be swapped if in DOS

Offset	Size	Description
1Ah	WORD	value of AX on call to INT 21h
1Ch	WORD	PSP segment for sharing/network
1Eh	WORD	network machine number for sharing/network (0000h = us)
20h	WORD	first usable memory block found when allocating memory
22h	WORD	best usable memory block found when allocating memory
24h	WORD	last usable memory block found when allocating memory
26h	WORD	memory size in paragraphs (not referenced after initialization)
28h	WORD	*unknown.*
2Ah	5 BYTEs	*unknown.*
2Fh	BYTE	*unknown.* apparently not referenced by kernel
30h	BYTE	day of month
31h	BYTE	month
32h	WORD	year - 1980
34h	WORD	number of days since 1-1-1980
36h	BYTE	day of week (0 = Sunday)
37h	3 BYTEs	*unknown.*
38h	30 BYTEs	device driver request header
58h	DWORD	pointer to device driver entry point (used in calling driver)
5Ch	22 BYTEs	device driver request header
72h	30 BYTEs	device driver request header
90h	6 BYTEs	*unknown.*
96h	6 BYTEs	CLOCK$ transfer record (see Function 52h)
9Ch	2 BYTEs	*unknown.*
9Eh	128 BYTEs	buffer for filename
11Eh	128 BYTEs	buffer for filename
19Eh	21 BYTEs	findfirst/findnext search data block (see Function 4Eh)
1B3h	32 BYTEs	directory entry for found file

Table 8-72. Format of DOS 4.0-5.0 swappable data area (continued)

Offset	Size	Description
1D3h	88 BYTEs	copy of current directory structure for drive being accessed
22Bh	11 BYTEs	FCB-format filename for device name comparison
236h	BYTE	*unknown.*
237h	11 BYTEs	wildcard destination specification for rename (FCB format)
242h	2 BYTEs	*unknown.*
244h	WORD	*unknown.*
246h	5 BYTEs	*unknown.*
24Bh	BYTE	extended FCB file attributes
24Ch	BYTE	type of FCB (00h regular, FFh extended)
24Dh	BYTE	attribute mask for directory search
24Eh	BYTE	file open attribute
24Fh	BYTE	*unknown flag bits.*
250h	BYTE	*unknown flag or counter.*
251h	BYTE	*unknown.*
252h	BYTE	flag indicating how DOS function was invoked: (00h = direct INT 20h/INT 21h, FFh = server call Function 5Dh Subfunction 00h)
253h	7 BYTEs	*unknown.*
25Ah	BYTE	canonicalized filename referred to existing file or directory if FFh
25Bh	BYTE	*unknown.*
25Ch	BYTE	type of process termination (00h-03h)
25Dh	3 BYTEs	*unknown.*
260h	DWORD	pointer to Drive Parameter Block for critical error invocation
264h	DWORD	pointer to stack frame containing user registers on INT 21h
268h	WORD	*apparently stores SP*
26Ah	DWORD	pointer to *unknown DOS Drive Parameter Block*
26Eh	WORD	segment of disk buffer
270h	4 WORDs	*unknown.*
278h	BYTE	Media ID byte returned by Functions 1Bh/1Ch
279h	BYTE	*unknown.* (apparently not referenced by kernel)
27Ah	DWORD	pointer to *unknown.*
27Eh	DWORD	pointer to current SFT
282h	DWORD	pointer to current directory structure for drive being accessed
286h	DWORD	pointer to caller's FCB
28Ah	WORD	number of SFT to which file being opened will refer
28Ch	WORD	temporary storage for file handle
28Eh	DWORD	pointer to a JFT entry in process handle table (see Function 26h)
292h	WORD	offset in DOS DS of first filename argument
294h	WORD	offset in DOS DS of second filename argument
296h	6 WORDs	*unknown.*
2A2h	WORD	*unknown.* Possibly *directory cluster number*
2A4h	DWORD	*unknown.*
2A8h	DWORD	*unknown.*
2ACh	WORD	*unknown.*
2AEh	DWORD	*offset in file*
2B2h	WORD	*unknown.*
2B4h	WORD	bytes in partial sector
2B6h	WORD	number of sectors
2B8h	3 WORDs	*unknown.*
2BEh	DWORD	number of bytes appended to file
2C2h	DWORD	pointer to *unknown disk buffer*
2C6h	DWORD	pointer to *unknown SFT*
2CAh	WORD	used by INT 21h dispatcher to store caller's BX
2CCh	WORD	used by INT 21h dispatcher to store caller's DS
2CEh	WORD	temporary storage while saving/restoring caller's registers
2D0h	DWORD	pointer to previous call frame (offset 264h) if INT 21h reentered; also switched to for duration of INT 24h
2D4h	WORD	open mode/action for INT 21h Function 6Ch

Table 8-72. Format of DOS 4.0-5.0 swappable data area (continued)

Offset	Size	Description
2D6h	BYTE	*unknown.* (set to 00h by INT 21h dispatcher, 02h when a read is performed, and 01h or 03h by INT 21h Function 6Ch)
2D7h	WORD	*unknown.*
2D9h	DWORD	stored ES:DI for INT 21h Function 6Ch
2DDh	WORD	extended file open action code (see Function 6Ch Subfunction 00h)
2DFh	WORD	extended file open attributes (see Function 6Ch Subfunction 00h)
2E1h	WORD	extended file open file mode (see Function 6Ch Subfunction 00h)
2E3h	DWORD	pointer to name of file to open (see Function 6Ch Subfunction 00h)
2E7h	2 WORDs	*unknown.*
2EBh	BYTE	*unknown.*
2ECh	WORD	stores DS during call to IFS utility functions at [List-of-Lists + 37h]
2EEh	WORD	*unknown.*
2F0h	BYTE	*unknown.*
2F1h	WORD	*unknown bit flags.*
2F3h	DWORD	pointer to user-supplied filename
2F7h	DWORD	pointer to *unknown.*
2FBh	WORD	stores SS during call to [List-of-Lists + 37h]
2FDh	WORD	stores SP during call to [List-of-Lists + 37h]
2FFh	BYTE	flag, nonzero if stack switched in calling [List-of-Lists+37h]
300h	21 BYTEs	FindFirst search data for source file(s) of a rename operation (see Function 4Eh)
315h	32 BYTEs	directory entry for file being renamed
335h	331 BYTEs	critical error stack
480h	384 BYTEs	disk stack (functions greater than 0Ch, INT 25h, INT 26h)
600h	384 BYTEs	character I/O stack (functions 01h through 0Ch)
780h	BYTE	device driver lookahead flag (see Function 64h)
781h	BYTE	*unknown drive number*
782h	BYTE	*unknown flag.*
783h	BYTE	*unknown.*
784h	WORD	*unknown.*
786h	WORD	*unknown.*
788h	WORD	*unknown.*
78Ah	WORD	*unknown.*

INTERRUPT 21h - Function 5Eh, Subfunction 00h
GET MACHINE NAME

Purpose: Determine machine name used by network software.

Available on: DOS 3.1 or higher.

Restrictions: Result is only meaningful if network is installed.

Registers at call:
AX = 5E00h
DS:DX -> 16-byte buffer for ASCIZ machine name

Return Registers:
CF clear if successful
   CH = validity
      00h name invalid
      nonzero valid
   CL = NetBIOS number for machine name
   DS:DX buffer filled with blank-paded name
CF set on error
   AX = error code (01h) (see Function 59h)

Details: Supported by OS/2 v1.3+ compatibility box.
Conflicts: None known.
See Also: Function 5Eh Subfunction 01h

INTERRUPT 21h - Function 5Eh, Subfunction 01h
SET MACHINE NAME

Purpose: Establish machine name used by network software.

Available on: DOS 3.1 or higher.

Registers at call:
AX = 5E01h
CH = 00h undefine name (make it invalid)
   nonzero   define name
CL = name number
DS:DX -> 15-character blank-padded ASCIZ
   name
Conflicts: None known.
See Also: Function 5Eh Subfunction 00h

Restrictions: The specified name is only meaningful if
                 network is installed.
Return Registers: n/a

INTERRUPT 21h - Function 5Eh, Subfunction 02h
SET NETWORK PRINTER SETUP STRING

Purpose: Establish the printer setup string to be used by the network printer.
Available on: DOS 3.1 or higher.
Registers at call:
AX = 5E02h
BX = redirection list index (see Function 5Fh
   Subfunction 02h)
CX = length of setup string
DS:SI -> setup string
Conflicts: None known.
See Also: Function 5Eh Subfunction 03h, INT 2Fh Function 11h Subfunction 1Fh (chapter 19)

Restrictions: Network software must be installed.
Return Registers:
CF clear if successful
CF set on error
   AX = error code (01h) (see Function 59h)

INTERRUPT 21h - Function 5Eh, Subfunction 03h
GET NETWORK PRINTER SETUP STRING

Purpose: Read printer setup string used by network printer.
Available on: DOS 3.1 or higher.
Registers at call:
AX = 5E03h
BX = redirection list index (see Function 5Fh
   Subfunction 02h)
ES:DI -> 64-byte buffer for setup string

Conflicts: None known.
See Also: Function 5Eh Subfunction 02h, INT 2Fh Function 11h Subfunction 1Fh (chapter 19)

Restrictions: Network software must be installed.
Return Registers:
CF clear if successful
   CX = length of setup string
   ES:DI buffer filled
CF set on error
   AX = error code (01h) (see Function 59h)

INTERRUPT 21h - Function 5Eh, Subfunction 04h
SET PRINTER MODE

Purpose: Specify whether the network printer should operation in text or binary mode.
Available on: DOS 3.1 or higher.
Registers at call:
AX = 5E04h
BX = redirection list index (see Function 5Fh
   Subfunction 02h)
DX = mode:
   bit 0: set if binary, clear if text (tabs
      expanded to blanks)
Details: Calls INT 2Fh Function 11h Subfunction 1Fh with 5E04h on stack.
Conflicts: None known.
See Also: Function 5Eh Subfunction 05h, INT 2Fh Function 11h Subfunction 1Fh (chapter 19)

Restrictions: Network software must be installed.
Return Registers:
CF set on error
   AX = error code (see Function 59h)
CF clear if successful

INTERRUPT 21h - Function 5Eh, Subfunction 05h
GET PRINTER MODE

Purpose: Read current printer mode.

Available on: DOS 3.1 or higher.

Registers at call:
AX = 5E05h
BX = redirection list index (see Function 5Fh
   Subfunction 02h)

Restrictions: Network software must be installed.

Return Registers:
CF set on error
   AX = error code (see Function 59h)
CF clear if successful
   DX = printer mode (see Function 5Eh
      Subfunction 04h)

Details: Calls INT 2Fh Function 11h Subfunction 1Fh with 5E05h on stack.

Conflicts: None known.

See Also: Function 5Eh Subfunction 04h, INT 2Fh Function 11h Subfunction 1Fh (chapter 19)

INTERRUPT 21h - Function 5Fh, Subfunction 00h
GET REDIRECTION MODE

Purpose: Determine current redirection mode (printer/disk).

Available on: DOS 3.1 or higher.

Registers at call:
AX = 5F00h
BL = redirection type:
   03h printer
   04h disk drive

Restrictions: Network software must be installed.

Return Registers:
CF set on error
   AX = error code (see Function 59h)
CF clear if successful
   BH = redirection state (00h off, 01h on)

Conflicts: None known.

See Also: Function 5Fh Subfunction 01h

INTERRUPT 21h - Function 5Fh, Subfunction 01h
SET REDIRECTION MODE

Purpose: Set current redirection mode (printer/disk).

Available on: DOS 3.1 or higher.

Registers at call:
AX = 5F01h
BL = redirection type:
   03h printer
   04h disk drive
BH = redirection state (00h off, 01h on)

Restrictions: Network software must be installed.

Return Registers:
CF set on error
   AX = error code (see Function 59h)
CF clear if successful

Details: When redirection is off, the local device (if any) rather than the remote device is used.

Conflicts: None known.

See Also: Function 5Fh Subfunction 00h, INT 2Fh Function 11h Subfunction 1Eh (chapter 19)

INTERRUPT 21h - Function 5Fh, Subfunction 02h
GET REDIRECTION LIST ENTRY

Purpose: Obtain redirection list entry for specified device.

Available on: DOS 3.1 or higher.

Restrictions: Network software (MS Networks, Banyan VINES) must be installed.

Registers at call:
AX = 5F02h
BX = redirection list index
DS:SI -> 16-byte buffer for ASCIZ device name
ES:DI -> 128-byte buffer for ASCIZ network name

Return Registers:
CF clear if successful
BH = device status (00h valid, 01h invalid)
BL = device type (03h printer, 04h disk drive)
CX = user data previously set by Subfunction 03h
DS:SI and ES:DI buffers filled
DX,BP destroyed
CF set on error
AX = error code (01h,12h) (see Function 59h)

Details: This function is passed through to INT 2Fh Function 11h Subfunction 1Eh. Error code 12h is returned if BX is greater than the size of the list.
Conflicts: None known.
See Also: Function 5Fh Subfunction 03h, INT 2Fh Function 11h Subfunction 1Eh (chapter 19)

INTERRUPT 21h - Function 5Fh, Subfunction 03h
REDIRECT DEVICE

Purpose: Cause specified device to be redirected to specified network name.
Available on: DOS 3.1 or higher.

Restrictions: Network software (MS Networks, Banyan VINES) must be installed.

Registers at call:
AX = 5F03h
BL = device type (03h printer, 04h disk drive)
CX = user data to save
DS:SI -> ASCIZ local device name (16 bytes max)
ES:DI -> ASCIZ network name + ASCIZ password
(128 bytes max total)

Return Registers:
CF clear if successful
CF set on error
AX = error code (01h,03h,05h,08h,0Fh,12h) (see Function 59h)

Details: If the device type is disk drive, DS:SI must point at either a null string or a string consisting of the drive letter followed by a colon; if a null string, the network attempts to access the destination without redirecting a local drive.
Conflicts: None known.
See Also: Function 5Fh Subfunction 02h, Function 5Fh Subfunction 04h, INT 2Fh Function 11h Subfunction 1Eh (chapter 19)

INTERRUPT 21h - Function 5Fh, Subfunction 04h
CANCEL REDIRECTION

Purpose: Cancel redirection for the specified device.
Available on: DOS 3.1 or higher.

Restrictions: Network software (MS Networks, Banyan VINES) must be installed.

Registers at call:
AX = 5F04h
DS:SI -> ASCIZ device name or path

Return Registers:
CF clear if successful
CF set on error
AX = error code (01h,03h,05h,08h,0Fh,12h) (see Function 59h)

Details: The DS:SI string must be either a local device name, a drive letter followed by a colon, or a network directory beginning with two backslashes.
Conflicts: None known.
See Also: Function 5Fh Subfunction 03h, INT 2Fh Function 11h Subfunction 1Eh

INTERRUPT 21h - Function 5Fh, Subfunction 05h
GET REDIRECTION LIST EXTENDED ENTRY

Purpose: Obtain the redirection list entry for the specified device.
Available on: DOS 4.0 or higher.

Restrictions: Network software (i.e. MS Networks) must be installed.

Registers at call:
AX = 5F05h
BX = redirection list index
DS:SI -> buffer for ASCIZ source device name
ES:DI -> buffer for destination ASCIZ network path

Return Registers:
CF clear if successful
    BH = device status flag (bit 0 clear if valid)
    BL = device type (03h if printer, 04h if drive)
    CX = stored parameter value (user data)
    BP = NETBIOS local session number
    DS:SI buffer filled
    ES:DI buffer filled
CF set on error
    AX = error code (see Function 59h)

Details: The local session number allows sharing the redirector's session number; however, if an error is caused on the NETBIOS LSN, the redirector may be unable to correctly recover from errors.
Conflicts: STARLITE architecture.
See Also: Function 5Fh Subfunction 06h, Network redirector INT 2Fh Function 11h Subfunction 1Eh (chapter 19)

INTERRUPT 21h - Function 5Fh, Subfunction 06h
GET REDIRECTION LIST

Purpose: *Appears to be similar to subfunctions 02h and 05h.*
Available on: DOS 4.0 or higher.

Restrictions: Network software (i.e. MS Networks) must be installed.

Registers at call:
AX = 5F06h
other *unknown.*

Return Registers: *unknown.*

Conflicts: STARLITE architecture.
See Also: Function 5Fh Subfunctions 02h and 05h

INTERRUPT 21h - Function 5Fh, Subfunction 07h
ENABLE DRIVE

Purpose: Make a logical drive valid after previously disabling it.
Available on: DOS 5.0.

Restrictions: none.

Registers at call:
AX = 5F07h
DL = drive number (0=A:)

Return Registers:
CF clear if successful
CF set on error
    AX = error code (0Fh) (see Function 59h)

Details: This function merely sets the "valid" bit in the current directory structure for the specified drive.
Conflicts: STARLITE architecture.
See Also: Function 5Fh Subfunction 08h

INTERRUPT 21h - Function 5Fh, Subfunction 08h
DISABLE DRIVE

Purpose: Temporarily make a logical drive invalid.
Available on: DOS 5.0.

Restrictions: none.

Registers at call:
AX = 5F08h
DL = drive number (0=A:)

Return Registers:
CF clear if successful
CF set on error
    AX = error code (0Fh) (see Function 59h)

Details: This function merely clears the "valid" bit in the current directory structure for the specified drive.
Conflicts: STARLITE architecture.
See Also: Function 5Fh Subfunction 07h

INTERRUPT 21h - Function 60h
CANONICALIZE FILENAME OR PATH

Purpose: Translate the specified pathname to canonical form.

Available on: DOS 3.0 or higher.
Registers at call:
AH = 60h
DS:SI -> ASCIZ filename or path
ES:DI -> 128-byte buffer for canonicalized name

Restrictions: none.
Return Registers:
CF set on error
    AX = error code:
        02h invalid component in directory path or
           drive letter only
        03h malformed path or invalid drive letter
    ES:DI buffer unchanged
CF clear if successful
    AH = 00h
    AL = destroyed (00h or 5Ch or last character of
        current directory on drive)
    buffer filled with qualified name of the form
        D:.EXT or \MACHINE.EXT

Details: The input path need not actually exist. Letters are uppercased, forward slashes converted to backslashes, asterisks converted to the appropriate number of question marks, and file and directory names are truncated to 8.3 if necessary. '.' and '..' in the path are resolved. Filespecs on local drives always start with "d:", those on network drives always start with "\".

If the path string is on a JOINed drive, the returned name is the one that would be needed if the drive were not JOINed; similarly for a SUBSTed, ASSIGNed, or network drive letter. For this reason, it is possible to get a qualified name that is not legal under the current combination of SUBSTs, ASSIGNs, JOINs, and network redirections.

Functions which take pathnames require canonical paths if invoked via INT 21h Function 5Dh Subfunction 00h. This function is used to form the full pathname of an invoked program which is stored after the end of its environment.

This function is supported by the OS/2 v1.1 compatibility box.

For DOS 3.3, the input and output buffers may be the same, as the canonicalized name is built in an internal buffer and copied to the specified output buffer as the very last step

Under DOS 3.3 to 5.0, a device name is translated differently if the device name does not have an explicit directory or the directory is \DEV\ (relative directory DEV from the root directory works correctly). In these cases, the returned string consists of the unchanged device name and extension appended to the string X:/ (forward slash instead of backward slash as in all other cases) where X is the default or explicit drive letter.

The input and output buffers may be the same, as this function uses an internal buffer and does not modify the output buffer until after completing the canonicalization, at which time it copies the result into the output buffer.
Conflicts: None known.
See Also: INT 2Fh Function 11h Subfunction 23h, INT 2Fh Function 12h Subfunction 21h

INTERRUPT 21h - Function 61h
UNUSED FUNCTION

Purpose: None.
Available on: DOS 3.0 or higher.
Registers at call:
AH = 61h

Restrictions: none.
Return Registers:
AL = 00h

Details: This function does nothing and returns immediately.
Conflicts: None known.

INTERRUPT 21h - Function 62h
GET CURRENT PSP ADDRESS

Purpose: Get "current process" identifier from MS-DOS.
Available on: DOS 3.0 or higher.
Registers at call:
AH = 62h

Restrictions: none.
Return Registers:
BX = segment of PSP for current process

Details: Under DOS 3+, this function does not use any of the DOS-internal stacks and is thus fully reentrant. The current PSP is not necessarily the caller's PSP. Identical to the undocumented Function 51h.
Conflicts: None known.
See Also: Functions 50h and 51h

INTERRUPT 21h - Function 63h, Subfunction 00h
GET LEAD BYTE TABLE ADDRESS

Purpose: Get address of lead byte table. Applies only to extended (2-byte) character sets.

Available on: DOS 2.25 only.	**Restrictions:** none.
Registers at call:	**Return Registers:**
AX = 6300h	CF clear if successful
	DS:SI -> lead byte table (Table 8-73)
	CF set on error
	AX = error code (01h) (see Function 59h)

Details: Does not preserve any registers other than SS:SP. The US version of MSDOS 3.30 treats this as an unused function, setting AL=00h and returning immediately.
Conflicts: Asian DOS 3.2+.
See Also: Function 63h Subfunction 01h, Function 07h, Function 08h, Function 0Bh

Table 8-73. Format of lead byte table entry:

Offset	Size	Description
00h	2 BYTEs	low/high ends of a range of leading byte of double-byte chars
02h	2 BYTEs	low/high ends of a range of leading byte of double-byte chars
	...	
N	2 BYTEs	00h,00h end flag

INTERRUPT 21h - Function 63h, Subfunction 00h
GET DOUBLE BYTE CHARACTER SET LEAD TABLE

Purpose: Get address of lead byte table. Applies only to extended (2-byte) character sets.

Available on: Asian DOS 3.2 or higher only.	**Restrictions:** none.
Registers at call:	**Return Registers:**
AX = 6300h	AL = error code:
	00h successful
	DS:SI -> DBCS table (Table 8-74)
	all other registers except CS:IP and SS:SP
	destroyed
	FFh not supported

Details: Probably identical to DOS 2.25 Function 63h Subfunction 00h. The US version of MSDOS 3.30 treats this as an unused function, setting AL=00h and returning immediately. The US version of DOS 4.0+ accepts this function, but returns an empty list.
Conflicts: DOS 2.25.
See Also: DOS 2.25 Function 63h Subfunction 00h

Table 8-74. Format of DBCS table:

Offset	Size	Description
00h	2 BYTEs	low/high ends of a range of leading byte of double-byte chars
02h	2 BYTEs	low/high ends of a range of leading byte of double-byte chars
	...	
N	2 BYTEs	00h,00h end flag

INTERRUPT 21h - Function 63h, Subfunction 01h
SET KOREAN (HONGEUL) INPUT MODE

Purpose: Establishes Hongeul input mode, which determines whether partially-formed double-byte characters may be read.

Available on: DOS 2.25 and Asian DOS 3.2 or higher only.

Restrictions: none.

Registers at call:
AX = 6301h
DL = new mode:
   00h return only full characters on DOS
     keyboard input functions
   01h return partially-formed characters
     also

Return Registers:
AL = status:
   00h successful
   FFh invalid mode

Conflicts: None known.
See Also: Functions 07h, 08h, 0Bh, and 63h, Function 63h Subfunction 02h

INTERRUPT 21h - Function 63h, Subfunction 02h
GET KOREAN (HONGEUL) INPUT MODE

Purpose: Determine whether Hongeul input mode is active.

Available on: DOS 2.25 and Asian DOS 3.2 or higher only.

Restrictions: none.

Registers at call:
AX = 6302h

Return Registers:
AL = status:
   00h successful
      DL = current input mode:
         00h return only full characters
         01h return partial characters
   FFh not supported

Conflicts: None known.
See Also: Functions 07h, 08h, 0Bh, and 63h, Function 63h Subfunction 01h

INTERRUPT 21h - Function 64h
SET DEVICE DRIVER LOOKAHEAD FLAG

Purpose: Determine whether DOS should check for the availability of input prior to requesting input on console input functions.

Available on: DOS 3.2 or higher.

Restrictions: This call is not documented and therefore subject to change.

Registers at call:
AH = 64h
AL = lookahead flag:
   00h (default) call device driver function 5
     (non-destructive read) before
     Functions 01h, 08h, and 0Ah
   nonzero don't call driver function 5

Return Registers: n/a

Details: Called by DOS 3.3+ PRINT.COM. This function does not use any of the DOS-internal stacks and is thus fully reentrant.
Conflicts: None known.
See Also: Functions 01h, 08h, and 0Ah

INTERRUPT 21h - Function 65h, Subfunctions 01-07h
GET EXTENDED COUNTRY INFORMATION

Purpose: Obtain extended country-dependent information.

Available on: DOS 3.3 or higher.
Registers at call:
AH = 65h
AL = info ID:
   01h get general internationalization info
   02h get pointer to uppercase table
   04h get pointer to filename uppercase table
   05h (DOS 3.3+) get pointer to filename
      terminator table
   06h get pointer to collating sequence table
   07h (DOS 4+) get pointer to Double-Byte
      Character Set table
BX = code page (-1=global code page)
DX = country ID (-1=current country)
ES:DI -> country information buffer (see below)
CX = size of buffer (>= 5)

Restrictions: none.
Return Registers:
CF set on error
   AX = error code (see Function 59h)
CF clear if succesful
   CX = size of country information returned
   ES:DI -> country information (Table 8-75)

Details: Subfunction 05h appears to return the same information for all countries and codepages; it was undocumented in DOS 3.3 through 4.x, but has been partially documented for DOS 5.0. NLSFUNC must be installed to get information for countries other than the default.
Conflicts: None known.
See Also: Function 38h, INT 2Fh Function 14h Subfunctions 01h and 02h

Table 8-75. Format of country information:

Offset	Size	Description
00h	BYTE	info ID
---if info ID = 01h		
01h	WORD	size
03h	WORD	country ID
05h	WORD	code page
07h	34 BYTEs	country-dependent info (see Function 38h)
---if info ID = 02h		
01h	DWORD	pointer to uppercase table (see Table 8-76)
---if info ID = 04h		
01h	DWORD	pointer to filename uppercase table (see Table 8-79)
---if info ID = 05h		
01h	DWORD	pointer to filename character table (see Table 8-78)
---if info ID = 06h		
01h	DWORD	pointer to collating table (see Table 8-77)
---if info ID = 07h (DOS 4.x)		
01h	DWORD	pointer to DBCS lead byte table (see Table 8-80)

Table 8-76. Format of uppercase table:

Offset	Size	Description
00h	WORD	table size
02h	128 BYTEs	uppercase equivalents (if any) of chars 80h to FFh

Table 8-77. Format of collating table:

Offset	Size	Description
00h	WORD	table size
02h	256 BYTEs	values used to sort characters 00h to FFh

Table 8-78. Format of filename terminator table:

Offset	Size	Description
00h	WORD	table size
02h	BYTE	*unknown* (01h for MSDOS 3.30-5.00)
03h	BYTE	lowest permissible character value for filename
04h	BYTE	highest permissible character value for filename
05h	BYTE	*unknown* (00h for MSDOS 3.30-5.00)
06h	BYTE	first excluded character in illegal range
07h	BYTE	last excluded character in illegal range
08h	BYTE	*unknown* (02h for MSDOS 3.30-5.00)
09h	BYTE	length of filename terminator list
0Ah	N BYTEs	characters which terminate a filename: ."/]:|<>+=;,

Table 8-79. Format of filename uppercase table:

Offset	Size	Description
00h	WORD	table size
02h	128 BYTEs	uppercase equivalents (if any) of chars 80h to FFh

Table 8-80. Format of DBCS lead byte table:

Offset	Size	Description
00h	WORD	length
02h	2N BYTEs	start/end for N lead byte ranges
	WORD	0000h (end of table)

INTERRUPT 21h - Function 65h, Subfunctions 20h-22h
COUNTRY-DEPENDENT CHARACTER CAPITALIZATION

Purpose: Capitalize text in a country-dependent fashion.
Available on: DOS 4.0 or higher.
Registers at call:
AH = 65h
AL = function:
    20h capitalize character:
        DL = character to capitalize
        Return: DL = capitalized character
    21h capitalize string:
        DS:DX -> string to capitalize
        CX = length of string
    22h capitalize ASCIZ string:
        DS:DX -> ASCIZ string to capitalize

Restrictions: none.
Return Registers:
CF set on error
    AX = error code (see Function 59h)
CF clear if successful

Details: These calls have been documented for DOS 5.0, but were undocumented in DOS 4.x.
Conflicts: None known.

INTERRUPT 21h - Function 65h, Subfunction 23h
DETERMINE IF CHARACTER REPRESENTS YES/NO RESPONSE

Purpose: Translate "yes/no" responses for current country.
Available on: DOS 4.0 or higher.

Restrictions: This call is not documented and therefore subject to change.

Registers at call:
AX = 6523h
DL = character
DH = second character of double-byte character (if
applicable)

Return Registers:
CF set on error
CF clear if successful
AX = type:
00h no
01h yes
02h neither yes nor no

Conflicts: None known.

INTERRUPT 21h - Function 65h, Subfunctions A0h-A2h
COUNTRY-DEPENDENT FILENAME CAPITALIZATION

Purpose: Perform capitalization of filenames properly for country.
Available on: DOS 4.0 or higher.

Restrictions: This call is not documented and
therefore subject to change.

Registers at call:
AH = 65h
AL = function:
A0h capitalize filename character
DL = character to capitalize
Return: DL = capitalized character
A1h capitalize counted filename string
DS:DX -> filename string to capitalize
CX = length of string
A2h capitalize ASCIZ filename
DS:DX -> ASCIZ filename to capitalize

Return Registers:
CF set on error
AX = error code (see Function 59h)
CF clear if successful

Details: Nonfunctional in DOS 4.00 through 5.00 due to a bug (the code sets a pointer depending on whether the high bit of AL is set, but doesn't clear the bit before branching by function number).
Conflicts: None known.

INTERRUPT 21h - Function 66h, Subfunction 01h
GET GLOBAL CODE PAGE TABLE

Purpose: Determine current code-page table.
Available on: DOS 3.3 or higher.
Registers at call:
AX = 6601h

Restrictions: none.
Return Registers:
CF set on error
AX = error code (see Function 59h)
CF clear if successful
BX = active code page (see Function 66h
Subfunction 02h)
DX = system code page

Conflicts: None known.
See Also: Function 66h Subfunction 02h

INTERRUPT 21h - Function 66h, Subfunction 02h
SET GLOBAL CODE PAGE TABLE

Purpose: Establish code-page table to use.
Available on: DOS 3.3 or higher.

Restrictions: none.

Registers at call:
AX = 6602h
BX = active code page:
   437 US
   850 Multilingual
   852 Slavic (DOS 5+)
   860 Portugal
   861 Iceland
   863 Canada (French)
   865 Norway/Denmark
DX = system code page (active page at boot time)
Conflicts: None known.
See Also: Function 66h Subfunction 01h

Return Registers:
CF set on error
   AX = error code (see Function 59h)
CF clear if successful

INTERRUPT 21h - Function 67h
SET HANDLE COUNT

Purpose: Change maximum number of handles available to the calling program.
Available on: DOS 3.3 or higher.
Registers at call:
AH = 67h
BX = size of new file handle table for process

Restrictions: none.
Return Registers:
CF clear if successful
CF set on error
   AX = error code (see Function 59h)

Details: If BX <= 20, no action is taken if the handle limit has not yet been increased, and the table is copied back into the PSP if the limit is currently greater than 20 handles. For file handle tables of more than 20 handles, DOS 3.30 never reuses the same memory block, even if the limit is being reduced; this can lead to memory fragmentation as a new block is allocated and the existing one freed.

Only the first 20 handles are copied to child processes in DOS 3.3.
BUG: The original release of DOS 3.30 allocates a full 64K for the handle table on requests for an even number of handles.
Conflicts: None known.
See Also: Function 26h

INTERRUPT 21h - Function 68h
"FFLUSH" - COMMIT FILE

Purpose: Forces a file to be updated on the disk. All data still in DOS disk buffers is written to disk immediately, and the file's directory entry is updated.
Available on: DOS 3.3 or higher.
Registers at call:
AH = 68h
BX = file handle

Restrictions: none.
Return Registers:
CF clear if successful
CF set on error
   AX = error code (see Function 59h)

Conflicts: None known.
See Also: Function 5Dh Subfunction 01h, INT 2Fh Function 11h Subfunction 07h (chapter 19)

INTERRUPT 21h - Function 69h
GET/SET DISK SERIAL NUMBER

Purpose: Read or write volume label and serial number for the specified disk.
Available on: DOS 4.0 or higher.

Restrictions: This call is not documented and therefore subject to change.

Registers at call:	Return Registers:
AH = 69h	CF set on error
AL = subfunction:	AX = error code (see Function 59h)
00h get serial number	CF clear if successful
01h set serial number	AX destroyed
BL = drive (0=default, 1=A, 2=B, etc)	(AL = 00h) buffer filled with appropriate
DS:DX -> disk serial number info (Table 8-81)	values from extended BPB
	(AL = 01h) extended BPB on disk set to values
	from buffer

Details: Does not generate a critical error; all errors are returned in AX. Error 0005h is returned if there is no extended BPB on the disk. This call does not work on network drives (error 0001h). The buffer after the first two bytes is an exact copy of bytes 27h thru 3Dh of the extended BPB on the disk.
Conflicts: None known.
See Also: Function 44h Subfunction 0Dh

Table 8-81. Format of disk serial number info:

Offset	Size	Description
00h	WORD	info level (zero)
02h	DWORD	disk serial number (binary)
06h	11 BYTEs	volume label or "NO NAME " if none present
11h	8 BYTEs	(AL=00h only) filesystem type--string "FAT12 " or "FAT16 "

INTERRUPT 21h - Function 6Ah
Unknown Function

Purpose: unknown.
Available on: DOS 4.0 or higher.

Restrictions: This call is not documented and therefore subject to change.

Registers at call:	Return Registers: *unknown.*
AH = 6Ah	
other *unknown.*	

Details: This function may be equivalent to INT 21h Function 48h.

INTERRUPT 21h - Function 6Bh
Unknown Function

Purpose: unknown.
Available on: DOS 4.0 only.

Restrictions: This call is not documented.

Registers at call:	Return Registers:
AH = 6Bh	CF set on error
AL = subfunction:	AX = error code (see INT 21h Function 59h)
00h unknown.	CF clear if successful
DS:SI -> *Current Directory Structure*	
CL = drive (1=A:)	
01h unknown.	
DS:SI -> unknown.	
CL = *file handle*	
02h unknown.	
DS:SI -> *Current Directory Structure*	
DI = unknown.	
CX = drive (1=A:)	

Others, if any, unknown.
Details: This call is passed through to INT 2Fh Function 11h Subfunction 2Fh with AX on top of the stack.
Conflicts: None known.
See Also: INT 2Fh Function 11h Subfunction 2Fh (chapter 19)

INTERRUPT 21h - Function 6Bh
Null Function

Purpose: This function does nothing and returns immediately.

Available on: DOS 5.0.　　　　　　　**Restrictions:** none.

Registers at call:　　　　　　　　**Return Registers:**

AH = 6Bh　　　　　　　　　　　　　AL = 00h

Conflicts: None known.

INTERRUPT 21h - Function 6Ch, Subfunction 00h
EXTENDED OPEN/CREATE

Purpose: Combines functions of all older "open" and "create" functions into a single common function.

Available on: DOS 4.0 or higher.　　　**Restrictions:** none.

Registers at call:　　　　　　　　**Return Registers:**

AX = 6C00h　　　　　　　　　　　　CF set on error

BL = open mode as in AL for normal open (INT　　　　AX = error code (see Function 59h)

　　21h Function 3Dh):　　　　　　CF clear if successful

　　bit 7: inheritance　　　　　　　　AX = file handle

　　bits 4-6: sharing mode　　　　　CX =　1 file opened

　　bit 3 reserved　　　　　　　　　　　2 file created

　　bits 0-2: access mode　　　　　　　　3 file replaced

BH = flags:

　　bit 6 = auto commit on write

　　bit 5 = return error rather than doing INT 24h

CX = create attribute:

　　bits 6-15 reserved

　　bit 5: archive

　　bit 4: reserved

　　bit 3: volume label

　　bit 2: system

　　bit 1: hidden

　　bit 0: readonly

DL = action if file exists/does not exists:

　　bits 7-4 action if file does not exist

　　　　(0000 fail, 0001 create)

　　bits 3-0 action if file exists

　　　　(0000 fail, 0001 open, 0010 replace/open)

DH = 00h (reserved)

DS:SI -> ASCIZ file name

Details: The PC LAN Program only supports DL=01h, DL=10h/sharing=compatibility, and DL=12h.

Conflicts: None known.

See Also: Functions 3Ch and 3Dh

INTERRUPT 21h - Function 80h
EXECUTE PROGRAM IN BACKGROUND

Purpose: Load and begin executing a background program which does not require interactive input.

Available on: European DOS 4.00 only.　　**Restrictions:** *unknown*

Registers at call:　　　　　　　　**Return Registers:**

AH = 80h　　　　　　　　　　　　　CF clear if successful

DS:DX -> ASCIZ full program name　　　　AX = *CSID*

ES:BX -> parameter block (see Function 4Bh　　CF set on error

Subfunction 00h)　　　　　　　　　　AX = error code (see Function 59h)

Details: This function is equivalent to Function 4Bh Subfunction 04h.

See Also: Function 4Bh Subfunction 04h

INTERRUPT 21h - Function 87h, Subfunction 00h
GET PID

Purpose: Determine Process Identifier, which indicates whether the calling program is foreground or the background program.

Available on: European DOS 4.00 only.   **Restrictions:** *unknown*

Registers at call: **Return Registers:**

AX = 8700h   AX = PID if AL nonzero

Details: Called by MS C v5.1 getpid() function.

Conflicts: None known.

See Also: Function 62h

INTERRUPT 21h - Function 89h
Unknown Function

Purpose: *unknown*.

Available on: European DOS 4.00 only   **Restrictions:** *unknown*

Registers at call: **Return Registers:** n/a

AH = 89h

other *unknown*.

Details: This function is reportedly called by the Microsoft C 4.0 startup code.

Conflicts: None known.

INTERRUPT 22h
PROGRAM TERMINATION ADDRESS

Purpose: Specifies the address of the routine which is to be given control after a program is terminated; this interrupt should never be called directly, since it does not point at an interrupt handler.

Available on: All versions of DOS.   **Restrictions:** none.

Details: This vector is restored from the DWORD at offset 0Ah in the PSP during termination, and then a far jump is performed to the address in INT 22h. It normally points at the instruction immediately following the INT 21h Function 4Bh call which loaded the current program.

Conflicts: None known.

See Also: INT 20h, INT 21h Functions 00h, 31h, and 4Ch

INTERRUPT 23h
CONTROL-C/CONTROL-BREAK HANDLER

Purpose: Invoked by DOS whenever it detects a Control-C or Control-Break; should never be called directly.

Available on: All versions of DOS.   **Restrictions:** none.

Registers at call: n/a   **Return Registers: (DOS 1.x)**

         AH = 00h abort program

            if all registers preserved, restart DOS call

         Return Registers: (DOS 2+)

            return via RETF or RETF 2 with CF set

               DOS will abort program with errorlevel 0

         else

               interrupted DOS call continues if all registers

                   preserved

Details: MSDOS 1.25 also invokes INT 23h on a divide overflow (INT 00h). Any DOS call may safely be made from within the INT 23h handler, although the handler will need to check for a recursive invocation if it does call DOS.

Conflicts: None known.

See Also: INT 1Bh (chapter 3)

INTERRUPT 24h
CRITICAL ERROR HANDLER

Purpose: Invoked when a critical (usually hardware) error is encountered; should never be called directly.

Available on: All versions of DOS.

Restrictions: none.

Registers at call: (supplied by DOS)

Handler must return:

AH = type and processing flags:

    bit 7 clear = disk I/O error

      set = if block device,

           bad FAT image in memory

      if char device, error code in DI

    bit 6 unused

    bit 5 = 1 if Ignore allowed, 0 if not

      (DOS 3+)

    bit 4 = 1 if Retry allowed, 0 if not

      (DOS 3+)

    bit 3 = 1 if Fail allowed, 0 if not (DOS 3+)

    bit 2 disk area of error 00 = DOS area

    bit 1 /   01 = FAT

                      10 = root dir

                      11 = data area

    bit 0 = 1 if write, 0 if read

AL = drive number if AH bit 7 clear

BP:SI -> device driver header (BP:[SI+4] bit

    15 set if char device)

DI low byte contains error code

      if AH bit 7 set:

  00h write-protection violation attempted

  01h unknown unit for driver

  02h drive not ready

  03h unknown command given to driver

  04h data error (bad CRC)

  05h bad device driver request structure

      length

  06h seek error

  07h unknown media type

  08h sector not found

  09h printer out of paper

  0Ah write fault

  0Bh read fault

  0Ch general failure

  0Dh (DOS 3+) sharing violation

  0Eh (DOS 3+) lock violation

  0Fh invalid disk change

  10h (DOS 3+) FCB unavailable

  11h (DOS 3+) sharing buffer overflow

  12h (DOS 4+) code page mismatch

  13h (DOS 4+) out of input

  14h (DOS 4+) insufficient disk space

AL = action code:

    00h ignore error and continue processing request

    01h retry operation

    02h terminate program through INT 23h

    03h fail system call in progress

SS,SP,DS,ES,BX,CX,DX preserved

STACK:
DWORD		return address for INT 24h call
WORD		flags pushed by INT 24h
WORD		original AX on entry to INT 21h
WORD	BX	
WORD	CX	
WORD	DX	
WORD	SI	
WORD	DI	
WORD	BP	
WORD	DS	
WORD	ES	
DWORD		return address for INT 21h call
WORD		flags pushed by INT 21h

Details: The only DOS calls the handler may make are INT 21h Functions 01h-0Ch, 30h, and 59h. If the handler returns to the application by popping the stack, DOS will be in an unstable state until the first call with AH > 0Ch.

For DOS 3.1+, IGNORE (AL=00h) is turned into FAIL (AL=03h) on network critical errors. If IGNORE is specified but not allowed, it is turned into FAIL. If RETRY is specified but not allowed, it is turned into FAIL. If FAIL is specified but not allowed, it is turned into ABORT. For DOS 3+, if a critical error occurs inside the critical error handler, the DOS call is automatically failed.

Conflicts: None known.

INTERRUPT 25h
ABSOLUTE DISK READ (small partitions)

Purpose: Read disk by logical sector number.
Available on: All versions of DOS.

Registers at call:
AL = drive number (00h = A:, 01h = B:, etc)
CX = number of sectors to read
DX = starting logical sector number (0000h to highest sector on drive)
DS:BX -> buffer for data

Restrictions: Only valid for disks and partitions up to 32 MB.

Return Registers:
CF clear if successful
CF set on error
    AH = status
        80h device failed to respond (timeout)
        40h seek operation failed
        20h controller failed
        10h data error (bad CRC)
        08h DMA failure
        04h requested sector not found
        03h write-protected disk (INT 26h only)
        02h bad address mark
        01h bad command
    AL = error code (same as passed to INT 24h in DI)
May destroy all other registers except segment registers

Details: The original flags are left on the stack, and must be popped by the caller. This call bypasses the DOS filesystem.
BUG: DOS 3.1 through 3.3 set the word at ES:[BP+1Eh] to FFFFh if AL is an invalid drive number.
Conflicts: None known.
See Also: INT 13h Function 02h, INT 26h

INTERRUPT 25h - Function FFFFh
ABSOLUTE DISK READ (large hard-disk partition)

Purpose: Read disk from volume >32 Mb.

Available on: DOS 3.31 or higher, some OEM versions of DOS 3.30.

Restrictions: Drive must be larger than 32 MB.

Registers at call:
AL = drive number (0=A, 1=B, etc)
CX = FFFFh
DS:BX -> disk read packet (Table 8-82)

Return Registers: same as above.

Details: Partition is potentially greater than 32M (and requires this form of the call) if bit 1 of the device driver's attribute word is set. The original flags are left on the stack, and must be removed by the caller. This call bypasses the DOS filesystem.

Conflicts: None known.

See Also: INT 13h Function 02h, INT 26h

Table 8-82. Format of disk read packet:

Offset	Size	Description
00h	DWORD	sector number
04h	WORD	number of sectors to read
06h	DWORD	transfer address

INTERRUPT 26h
ABSOLUTE DISK WRITE (small partitions)

Purpose: Absolute address write via Logical Sector Number.

Available on: All versions of DOS.

Restrictions: Only valid for disks and partitions up to 32MB.

Registers at call:
AL = drive number (00h = A:, 01h = B:, etc)
CX = number of sectors to write
DX = starting logical sector number (0000h to highest sector on drive)
DS:BX -> data to write

Return Registers:
CF clear if successful
CF set on error
    AH = status:
        80h device failed to respond (timeout)
        40h seek operation failed
        20h controller failed
        10h data error (bad CRC)
        08h DMA failure
        04h requested sector not found
        03h write-protected disk (INT 26h only)
        02h bad address mark
        01h bad command
    AL = error code (same as passed to INT 24h in DI)
May destroy all other registers except segment registers

Details: The original flags are left on the stack, and must be popped by the caller. This call bypasses the DOS filesystem.

BUG: DOS 3.1 through 3.3 set the word at ES:[BP+1Eh] to FFFFh if AL is an invalid drive number.

Conflicts: None known.

See Also: INT 13h Function 03h, INT 25h

INTERRUPT 26h - Function FFFFh
ABSOLUTE DISK WRITE (large hard-disk partition)

Purpose: Absolute address write via Logical Sector Number.

Available on: DOS 3.31 or higher, some OEM versions of DOS 3.30.

Restrictions: Drive must be larger than 32 MB.

Registers at call: **Return Registers:** same as above
AL = drive number (0=A, 1=B, etc)
CX = FFFFh
DS:BX -> disk write packet (Table 8-83)
Details: Partition is potentially greater than 32M (and requires this form of the call) if bit 1 of the device driver's attribute word is set. The original flags are left on the stack, and must be removed by the caller. This call bypasses the DOS filesystem.
Conflicts: None known.
See Also: INT 13h Function 03h, INT 25h

Table 8-83. Format of disk write packet:

Offset	Size	Description
00h	DWORD	sector number
04h	WORD	number of sectors to read
06h	DWORD	transfer address

INTERRUPT 27h
TERMINATE AND STAY RESIDENT

Purpose: Terminate process without releasing the resources allocated to it; these resources include environment space, other memory, and file handles.
Available on: All versions of DOS.   **Restrictions:** none.
Registers at call: **Return Registers:** never returns
DX = number of bytes to keep resident
   (max FFF0h)
CS = segment of PSP
Details: This is an obsolete call; use INT 21h Function 31h instead for DOS 2.0 or higher. INT 22h, INT 23h, and INT 24h are restored from the PSP.
Conflicts: None known.
See Also: INT 21h Function 31h

INTERRUPT 28h
DOS IDLE INTERRUPT

Purpose: Invoked each time one of the DOS character input functions loops while waiting for input. Since a DOS call is in progress even though DOS is actually idle during such input waits, hooking this function is necessary to allow a TSR to perform DOS calls while the foreground program is waiting for user input.
Available on: DOS 2.0 or higher.   **Restrictions:** The INT 28h handler may invoke any
                                                          INT 21h function except functions 00h
                                                          through 0Ch.
Details: Under DOS 2.x, the critical error flag (the byte immediately after the InDOS flag) must be set in order to call DOS functions 50h/51h without destroying the DOS stacks. Calls to INT 21h Functions 3Fh/40h may not use a handle which refers to CON.
   At the time of the call, the InDOS flag (see INT 21h Function 34h) is normally set to 01h; if larger, DOS is truly busy and should not be reentered.
   The default handler is an IRET instruction. This call is supported by the OS/2 compatibility box.
Conflicts: None known.
See Also: INT 21h Function 34h, INT 2Ah Function 84h

INTERRUPT 29h
FAST CONSOLE OUTPUT

Purpose: Provides a simpler and faster means of displaying a single character than the normal device driver invocation of the CON device.

Available on: DOS 2.0 or higher.

Registers at call:
AL = character to display

Restrictions: Current console driver must have attribute bit 4 set.

Return Registers: nothing

Details: COMMAND.COM v3.2 and v3.3 compare the INT 29h vector against the INT 20h vector and assume that ANSI.SYS is installed if the segment of INT 29h is larger.

The default INT 29h handler under DOS 2.x and 3.x simply calls INT 10h Function 0Eh (chapter 5), while the default handler under DESQview 2.2 understands the "<Esc>[2J" screen-clearing sequence but calls INT 10h Function 0Eh for all others.

See Also: AVATAR.SYS INT 79h (chapter 36)

INTERRUPT 2Bh
RESERVED

Purpose: This interrupt is not currently in use, but has been reserved for possible future use.

Available on: DOS 2.0 or higher.

Registers at call: n/a

Restrictions: none.

Return Registers: n/a

Details: This vector is not used in DOS versions through 5.00, and points at an IRET.

Conflicts: None known.

INTERRUPT 2Ch
RESERVED

Purpose: This interrupt is not currently in use, but has been reserved for possible future use.

Available on: DOS 2.0 or higher.

Registers at call: n/a

Restrictions: none.

Return Registers: n/a

Details: This vector is not used in DOS versions through 5.00, and points at an IRET.

Conflicts: STARLITE architecture Kernel API, MS Windows (chapter 14).

INTERRUPT 2Dh
RESERVED

Purpose: This interrupt is not currently in use, but has been reserved for possible future use.

Available on: DOS 2.0 or higher.

Registers at call: n/a

Restrictions: none.

Return Registers: n/a

Details: This vector is not used in DOS versions through 5.00, and points at an IRET.

Conflicts: None known.

INTERRUPT 2Eh
PASS COMMAND TO COMMAND INTERPRETER FOR EXECUTION

Purpose: This call allows execution of arbitrary commands (including COMMAND.COM internal commands) without loading another copy of COMMAND.COM.

Available on: DOS 2.0 or higher.

Registers at call:
DS:SI -> commandline to execute (Table 8-84)

Restrictions: COMMAND.COM must be installed.

Return Registers:
All registers except CS:IP destroyed

Details: If COMMAND.COM is the user's command interpreter, the primary copy executes the command; this allows the master environment to be modified by issuing a "SET" command, but changes in the master environment will not become effective until all programs descended from the primary COMMAND.COM terminate.

Since COMMAND.COM processes the string as if typed from the keyboard, the transient portion needs to be present, and the calling program must ensure that sufficient memory to load the transient portion can be allocated by DOS if necessary.

Results are unpredictable if invoked by a program run from a batch file because this call is not reentrant and COMMAND.COM uses the same internal variables when processing a batch file.

Hooked but ignored by the 4DOS v3.0 COMMAND.COM replacement unless SHELL2E has been loaded.

Conflicts: 4DOS SHELL2E.COM TSR (Chapter 36).

Table 8-84. Format of COMMAND.COM commandline:

Offset	Size	Description
00h	BYTE	length of command string, not counting trailing CR
01h	var	command string
N	BYTE	0Dh (CR)

INTERRUPT 30h
FAR JMP instruction for CP/M-style calls

Purpose: Used for CP/M compatible calls only; now obsolete. The CALL 5 entry point does a far jump to here.
Available on: All versions of DOS.   **Restrictions:** none.
BUG: Under DOS 2+, the instruction at PSP:0005 points two bytes too low in memory.
Conflicts: None known.
See Also: INT 21h Function 26h

INTERRUPT 31h

Purpose: This vector is overwritten by the CP/M jump instruction in INT 30h.
Available on: All versions of DOS.   **Restrictions:** none.
Conflicts: DOS Protected-Mode Interface (DPMI) API (chapter 11).

INTERRUPT 6Ch
Realtime Clock update

Purpose: unknown.
Available on: DOS 3.2.   **Restrictions:** none.
Registers at call: *unknown.*   **Return Registers:** *unknown.*
Conflicts: System Resume Vector (chapter 3).

Multiplex Interrupt

The multiplex interrupt, 2Fh, is shared by many programs, with the value of AH on call specifying the program which is to handle the call. A (probably incomplete) table of programs using this interrupt service appears in Chapter 1; MS-DOS itself was the original user of the multiplex capability, and still accounts for a significant portion of activity in this area. The remainder of this chapter lists and describes the Multiplex functions that have been included in various versions of the operating system.

In this section, the functions are listed alphabetically by name, rather than in numeric sequence by function. Within each named area, functions appear in numeric order by function and subfunction numbers.

ANSI.SYS

INTERRUPT 2Fh - Function 1Ah, Subfunction 00h
INSTALLATION CHECK

Purpose: Determine whether ANSI.SYS is installed.
Available on: DOS 4.0 or higher.   **Restrictions:** none.
Registers at call: **Return Registers:**
AX = 1A00h   AL = FFh if installed
Details: AVATAR.SYS also responds to this call. This function was undocumented in DOS 4.x, but has been documented for DOS 5.0.
Conflicts: AVATAR.SYS (chapter 36).

INTERRUPT 2Fh - Function 1Ah, Subfunction 01h
internal - GET/SET DISPLAY INFORMATION

Purpose: Control display information.
Available on: DOS 4.0 or higher.   **Restrictions:** ANSI.SYS must be installed.

Registers at call:
AX = 1A01h
CL = 7Fh for GET
   = 5Fh for SET
DS:DX -> parm block as for INT 21h Function 44h
   Subfunction 0Ch, CX=037Fh/035Fh
   respectively

Return Registers:
CF set on error
   AX = error code (many non-standard)
CF clear if successful
   AX destroyed

Details: This is presumably the DOS IOCTL interface to ANSI.SYS.
Conflicts: None known.
See Also: Function 1Ah Subfunction 02h, INT 21h Function 44h Subfunction 0Ch

INTERRUPT 2Fh - Function 1Ah, Subfunction 02h
internal - MISCELLANEOUS REQUESTS

Purpose: Control interlocks.
Available on: DOS 4.0 or higher.
Registers at call:
AX = 1A02h
DS:DX -> parameter block (Table 8-85)
Conflicts: None known.
See Also: Function 1Ah Subfunction 01h

Restrictions: ANSI.SYS must be installed.

Table 8-85. Format of parameter block:

Offset	Size	Description
00h	BYTE	subfunction
		00h set/reset interlock
		01h get /L flag
01h	BYTE	interlock state: 00h=reset, 01h=set
		This interlock prevents some of the ANSI.SYS post-processing in its hook onto INT 10h
		Function 00h mode set
02h	BYTE	(returned)
		00h if /L not in effect
		01h if /L in effect

APPEND

INTERRUPT 2Fh - Function B7h, Subfunction 00h
INSTALLATION CHECK

Purpose: Determine whether APPEND is installed.
Available on: All machines.
Registers at call:
AX = B700h

Restrictions: none.
Return Registers:
AL = status:
   00h not installed
   FFh installed

Details: MSDOS 3.30 APPEND refuses to install itself when run inside TopView or a TopView-compatible environment.

INTERRUPT 2Fh - Function B7h, Subfunction 01h
Unknown Function

Purpose: *unknown.*
Available on: All machines.
Registers at call:
AX = B701h
other *unknown.*

Restrictions: APPEND must be installed.
Return Registers: *unknown.*

Details: MSDOS 3.30 APPEND displays "Incorrect APPEND Version" and aborts caller.

INTERRUPT 2Fh - Function B7h, Subfunction 02h
APPEND VERSION CHECK

Purpose: Determine which version of APPEND is installed.
Available on: All machines.
Registers at call:
AX = B702h

Restrictions: APPEND must be installed.
Return Registers:
AX = FFFFh if not DOS 4.0 APPEND (also if
    DOS 5.0 APPEND);
AL = major version number
AH = minor version number, otherwise

Conflicts: None known.
See Also: Function B7h Subfunction 10h

INTERRUPT 2Fh - Function B7h, Subfunction 03h
HOOK INT 21h

Purpose: Each invocation of this function toggles a flag which APPEND uses to determine whether to chain to the user handler or the original INT 21h.
Available on: DOS 3.3 and 5.0.
Registers at call:
AX = B703h
ES:DI -> INT 21h handler to which APPEND
    should chain

Restrictions: APPEND must be installed.
Return Registers:
ES:DI -> APPEND's INT 21h handler

Conflicts: None known.

INTERRUPT 2Fh - Function B7h, Subfunction 04h
GET APPEND PATH

Purpose: Determine the currently active APPEND path.
Available on: DOS 3.3 or higher.
Registers at call:
AX = B704h

Restrictions: APPEND must be installed.
Return Registers:
ES:DI -> active APPEND path (128 bytes max)

Conflicts: None known.

INTERRUPT 2Fh - Function B7h, Subfunction 06h
GET APPEND FUNCTION STATE

Purpose: Determine current state of APPEND.
Available on: DOS 4.0 or higher.
Registers at call:
AX = B706h

Restrictions: APPEND must be installed.
Return Registers:
BX = APPEND state:
    bit 0: set if APPEND enabled
    bits 1-11 reserved
    bit 12: (DOS 5) set if APPEND applies directory
        search even if a drive has been specified
    bit 13: set if /PATH flag active
    bit 14: set if /E flag active (environment var
        APPEND exists)
    bit 15: set if /X flag active

Conflicts: None known.

INTERRUPT 2Fh - Function B7h, Subfunction 07h
SET APPEND FUNCTION STATE

Purpose: Sets state of APPEND.
Available on: DOS 4.0 or higher.

Restrictions: APPEND must be installed.

Registers at call:
AX = B707h
BX = APPEND state bits (see Subfunction 06h)
Conflicts: None known.

Return Registers: n/a

INTERRUPT 2Fh - Function B7h, Subfunction 10h
GET VERSION INFO

Purpose: Obtain version of APPEND.
Available on: DOS 3.3 or higher.
Registers at call:
AX = B710h

Restrictions: APPEND must be installed.
Return Registers:
AX = *unknown.*
BX = *unknown.* (0000h in MSDOS 3.30 and 5.00)
CX = *unknown.* (0000h in MSDOS 3.30 and 5.00)
DL = major version
DH = minor version

Conflicts: None known.
See Also: Function B7h Subfunction 02h

INTERRUPT 2Fh - Function B7h, Subfunction 11h
SET RETURN FOUND NAME STATE

Purpose: If the next INT 21h call (and ONLY the next) is function 3Dh, 43h, or 6Ch, the fully qualified filename is written over top of the filename passed to the INT 21h call. The application must provide a sufficiently large buffer. This state is reset after next INT 21h call processed by APPEND.
Available on: DOS 4.0 or higher.
Registers at call:
AX = B711h
Conflicts: None known.

Restrictions: APPEND must be installed.
Return Registers: n/a

ASSIGN

INTERRUPT 2Fh - Function 06h, Subfunction 00h
INSTALLATION CHECK

Purpose: Determine whether ASSIGN installed.
Available on: DOS 3.0 or higher.
Registers at call:
AX = 0600h

Restrictions: none.
Return Registers:
AL = status:
    00h not installed
    01h not installed, but not OK to install
    FFh installed

Conflicts: None known.
See Also: Function 06h Subfunction 01h

INTERRUPT 2Fh - Function 06h, Subfunction 01h
GET DRIVE ASSIGNMENT TABLE

Purpose: Determine drive assignments.
Available on: DOS 3.0 or higher.
Registers at call:
AX = 0601h

Restrictions: ASSIGN must be installed.
Return Registers:
ES = segment of ASSIGN work area and assignment
    table

Details: The 26 bytes starting at ES:0103h specify which drive each of A: to Z: is mapped to. Initially set to 01h 02h 03h ... 1Ah.
Conflicts: None known.
See Also: Function 06h Subfunction 00h

COMMAND.COM

INTERRUPT 2Fh - Function 55h, Subfunction 00h
COMMAND.COM INTERFACE

Purpose: Determine the addresses of various routines which may be shared between copies of COMMAND.COM.

Available on: DOS 5.0 or higher.　　　　**Restrictions:** COMMAND.COM must be the shell.

Registers at call:　　　　**Return Registers:**

AX = 5500h　　　　AX = 0000h if COMMAND.COM present

　　　　DS:SI -> entry point table

Details: The entry point table is used to access the shareable portion of COMMAND.COM, which may have been moved into the HMA; only the primary COMMAND.COM retains this portion. The procedures pointed at by the table are called from a dispatcher in COMMAND's resident portion; most assume that the segment address of the resident portion is on the stack and are thus not of general use.

Conflicts: None known.

CRITICAL ERROR HANDLER

INTERRUPT 2Fh - Function 05h, Subfunction 00h
CRITICAL ERROR HANDLER - INSTALLATION CHECK

Purpose: Determine whether Critical Error message handler is installed.

Available on: DOS 3.0 or higher.　　　　**Restrictions:** none.

Registers at call:　　　　**Return Registers:**

AX = 0500h　　　　AL = 00h not installed, OK to install

　　　　　　01h not installed, can't install

　　　　　　FFh installed

Details: This set of functions allows a user program to partially or completely override the default critical error handler in COMMAND.COM.

Conflicts: None known.

See Also: Function 12h Subfunction 2Eh, INT 24h

INTERRUPT 2Fh - Function 05h, Subfunctions 01h-FFh
CRITICAL ERROR HANDLER - EXPAND ERROR INTO STRING

Purpose: Called at start of COMMAND.COM's default critical error handler if installed by a user program, allowing partial or complete overriding of the default error message.

Available on: DOS 3.0 or higher.　　　　**Restrictions:** Critical Error Handler must be installed.

Registers at call:　　　　**Return Registers:**

---DOS 3.x　　　　CF clear if successful

AH = 05h　　　　　　ES:DI -> ASCIZ error message (read-only)

AL = extended error code (not zero)　　　　　　AL = *unknown*.

---DOS 4.x　　　　CF set if error code can't be converted to string

AH = 05h

AL = error type:

　　01h DOS extended error code

　　02h parameter error

BX = error code

Details: Subfunction 02h is called by many DOS 4 external programs.

Conflicts: None known.

See Also: Function 12h Subfunction 2Eh, INT 24h

DISPLAY.SYS

INTERRUPT 2Fh - Function ADh, Subfunction 00h
internal - INSTALLATION CHECK

Purpose: Determine whether the DISPLAY.SYS driver is installed.
Available on: DOS 3.3 or higher.
Registers at call:
AX = AD00h

Restrictions: none.
Return Registers:
AL = FFh if installed
BX = *unknown*. (0100h in MS-DOS 3.30, PCDOS 4.01)

Conflicts: None known.

INTERRUPT 2Fh - Function ADh, Subfunction 01h
internal - SET unknown value

Purpose: unknown.
Available on: DOS 3.3 or higher.
Registers at call:
AX = AD01h
BX = *unknown*.
Conflicts: None known.

Restrictions: DISPLAY.SYS driver must be installed.
Return Registers:
CF set on error
other *unknown*.

INTERRUPT 2Fh - Function ADh, Subfunction 02h
internal - GET unknown value

Purpose: unknown.
Available on: DOS 3.3 or higher.
Registers at call:
AX = AD02h
Conflicts: None known.

Restrictions: DISPLAY.SYS driver must be installed.
Return Registers:
BX = *unknown*. (value set with Subfunction 01h)

INTERRUPT 2Fh - Function ADh, Subfunction 03h
internal - GET unknown value

Purpose: unknown.
Available on: DOS 3.3 or higher.
Registers at call:
AX = AD03h
ES:DI -> user buffer
CX = size of buffer
Conflicts: None known.

Restrictions: DISPLAY.SYS driver must be installed.
Return Registers:
CF set if buffer too small
CF clear if successful

INTERRUPT 2Fh - Function ADh, Subfunction 04h
internal - Unknown Function

Purpose: unknown.
Available on: DOS 4.x only.
Registers at call:
AX = AD04h
other *unknown*.

Restrictions: DISPLAY.SYS driver must be installed.
Return Registers: *unknown*.

INTERRUPT 2Fh - Function ADh, Subfunction 10h
internal - INSTALLATION CHECK

Purpose: unknown.
Available on: DOS 4.0 or higher.

Restrictions: DISPLAY.SYS driver must be installed.

Registers at call:
AX = AD10h
other *unknown.*

Return Registers:
AX = FFFFh
BX = *unknown.* (0100h in PCDOS 4.01)

DOS DISK ACCESS

INTERRUPT 2Fh - Function 13h
SET DISK INTERRUPT HANDLER

Purpose: Specify which routines DOS's built-in disk device drivers call.
Available on: DOS 3.30 or higher.
Registers at call:
AH = 13h
DS:DX -> interrupt handler disk driver calls on
     read/write
ES:BX = address to restore INT 13 to on system
     halt (exit from root shell) or warm boot
     (INT 19)

Restrictions: none.
Return Registers:
DS:DX from previous invocation of this function
ES:BX from previous invocation of this function

Details: IO.SYS hooks INT 13h and inserts one or more filters ahead of the original INT 13h handler. The first is for disk change detection on floppy drives, the second is for tracking formatting calls and correcting DMA boundary errors, the third is for working around problems in a particular version of IBM's ROM BIOS.

Before the first call, ES:BX points at the original BIOS INT 13; DS:DX also points there unless IO.SYS has installed a special filter for hard disk reads (on systems with model byte FCh and BIOS date "01/10/84" only), in which case it points at the special filter.

Most DOS 3.3+ disk access is via the vector in DS:DX, although a few functions are still invoked via an INT 13 instruction. This is a dangerous security loophole for any virus-monitoring software which does not trap this call (at least two viruses are known to use it to get the original ROM entry point).
See Also: INT 13h Function 01h (chapter 6), INT 19h (chapter 3)

DOS INTERNAL

Beginning with version 3.0, DOS provides a number of utility functions for use by SHARE, network redirectors, and similar software. Several of these functions assume that an INT 21h call is in progress; most of the remainder assume that the active stack is one of the internal DOS stacks, making them effectively only available from within an INT 21h call.

DOS version 5.0 adds additional calls on other multiplex numbers; these are included here in numerical order.

INTERRUPT 2Fh - Function 12h, Subfunction 00h
internal - INSTALLATION CHECK

Purpose: Determine whether DOS internal functions API is present.
Available on: DOS 3.0 or higher.
Registers at call:
AX = 1200h

Restrictions: none.
Return Registers:
AL = FFh (for compatibility with other INT 2Fh
     functions)

Conflicts: None known.

INTERRUPT 2Fh - Function 12h, Subfunction 01h
internal - CLOSE CURRENT FILE

Purpose: Closes current file.
Available on: DOS 3.0 or higher.
Registers at call:
AX = 1201h
SS = DOS DS
SDA current SFT pointer -> SFT of file to close

Restrictions: none.
Return Registers:
CF set on error
BX *unknown.*
CX = new reference count of SFT
ES:DI -> SFT for file

Conflicts: None known.
See Also: Function 11h Subfunction 06h (chapter 19), Function 12h Subfunction 27h, INT 21h Function 3Eh

INTERRUPT 2Fh - Function 12h, Subfunction 02h
internal - GET INTERRUPT ADDRESS

Purpose: Similar to INT 21h Function 25h but does not use INT 21h dispatcher code and returns the address of the DWORD storing the interrupt vector rather than the contents of the vector.

Available on: DOS 3.0 or higher.

Registers at call:
AX = 1202h
STACK: WORD vector number

Conflicts: None known.

Restrictions: none.

Return Registers:
ES:BX -> interrupt vector
STACK unchanged

INTERRUPT 2Fh - Function 12h, Subfunction 03h
internal - GET DOS DATA SEGMENT

Purpose: Determine segment address of data area in the DOS kernel.

Available on: DOS 3.0 or higher.

Registers at call:
AX = 1203h

Conflicts: None known.

Restrictions: none.

Return Registers:
DS = segment of IBMDOS.COM/MSDOS.SYS data

INTERRUPT 2Fh - Function 12h, Subfunction 04h
internal - NORMALIZE PATH SEPARATOR

Purpose: Identify whether the specified character separates directories in a path specification, and turn it into the standard backslash if so.

Available on: DOS 3.0 or higher.

Registers at call:
AX = 1204h
STACK: WORD character to normalize

Restrictions: none.

Return Registers:
AL = normalized character
    (forward slash turned to backslash, all others
        unchanged)
ZF set if character is a path separator
STACK unchanged

Details: Characters returned by this call may not be recognized by all programs.
Conflicts: None known.

INTERRUPT 2Fh - Function 12h, Subfunction 05h
internal - OUTPUT CHARACTER TO STANDARD OUTPUT

Purpose: Sends one character to the predefined STDOUT handle.

Available on: DOS 3.0 or higher.

Registers at call:
AX = 1205h
STACK: WORD character to output

Conflicts: None known.

Restrictions: Can be called only from within DOS.

Return Registers:
STACK unchanged

INTERRUPT 2Fh - Function 12h, Subfunction 06h
internal - INVOKE CRITICAL ERROR

Purpose: Calls critical error handler.

Available on: DOS 3.0 or higher.

Restrictions: none.

Registers at call:
AX = 1206h
DI = error code
BP:SI -> device driver header
SS = DOS DS
STACK: WORD value to be passed to INT 24h in
    AX
Conflicts: None known.
See Also: INT 24h

Return Registers:
AL = 0-3 for Abort, Retry, Ignore, Fail
STACK unchanged

INTERRUPT 2Fh - Function 12h, Subfunction 07h
internal - MAKE DISK BUFFER MOST-RECENTLY USED

Purpose: Moves buffer to the end of the buffer list (least-recently used is first).
Available on: DOS 3.0 or higher.
Registers at call:
AX = 1207h
DS:DI -> disk buffer
Conflicts: None known.
See Also: Function 12h Subfunction 0Fh

Restrictions: Can be called only from within DOS.
Return Registers: n/a

INTERRUPT 2Fh - Function 12h, Subfunction 08h
internal - DECREMENT SFT REFERENCE COUNT

Purpose: Reduce use-count of a System File Table entry; used when closing a file.
Available on: DOS 3.0 or higher.
Registers at call:
AX = 1208h
ES:DI -> SFT

Restrictions: none.
Return Registers:
AX = original value of reference count

Details: If the reference count was 1, it is set to FFFFh (since 0 indicates that the SFT is not in use). It is the caller's responsibility to set the reference count to zero after cleaning up.
Conflicts: None known.

INTERRUPT 2Fh - Function 12h, Subfunction 09h
internal - FLUSH AND FREE DISK BUFFER

Purpose: Mark disk buffer as unused, and write contents to disk if buffer is dirty.
Available on: DOS 3.0 or higher.
Registers at call:
AX = 1209h
DS:DI -> disk buffer
Conflicts: None known.
See Also: Function 12h Subfunctions 0Eh and 15h

Restrictions: Can be called only from within DOS.
Return Registers: n/a

INTERRUPT 2Fh - Function 12h, Subfunction 0Ah
internal - PERFORM CRITICAL ERROR INTERRUPT

Purpose: Calls critical error handler from DOS.
Available on: DOS 3.0 or higher.

Restrictions: Can only be called during a DOS function call, as it uses various fields in the SDA to set up the registers for the INT 24h.

Registers at call:
AX = 120Ah
DS = SS = DOS DS
STACK: WORD extended error code

Return Registers:
AL = user response (0=ignore, 1=retry, 2=abort, 3=fail)
CF clear if retry, set otherwise
STACK unchanged

Details: Reportedly sets current DPB's first root directory sector to 1.
Conflicts: None known.
See Also: INT 24h

INTERRUPT 2Fh - Function 12h, Subfunction 0Bh
internal - SIGNAL SHARING VIOLATION TO USER

Purpose: Notify user that sharing rules have been violated.
Available on: DOS 3.0 or higher.

Restrictions: Can only be called during a DOS function call.

Registers at call:
AX = 120Bh
ES:DI -> system file table entry for previous open
   of file
STACK: WORD extended error code (should be
20h--sharing violation)

Return Registers:
CF clear if operation should be retried
CF set if operation should not be retried
   AX = error code (20h) (see Function 59h)
STACK unchanged

Details: Should only be called if an attempt was made to open an already-open file contrary to the sharing rules. Invokes INT 24h if SFT file opened via FCB or in compatibility mode with inheritance allowed.
Conflicts: None known.

INTERRUPT 2Fh - Function 12h, Subfunction 0Ch
internal - OPEN DEVICE AND SET SFT OWNER

Purpose: Changes owner of last-accessed SFT to calling process if it was opened via an FCB call. Called by network redirectors.
Available on: DOS 3.0 or higher.

Restrictions: none.

Registers at call:
AX = 120Ch
SDA current SFT pointer -> SFT for file
DS = SS = DOS DS

Return Registers:
ES, DI, AX destroyed

Details: This call invokes the "device open" function of the SFT's device driver.
Conflicts: None known.

INTERRUPT 2Fh - Function 12h, Subfunction 0Dh
internal - GET DATE AND TIME

Purpose: Get system date and time in file directory format.
Available on: DOS 3.0 or higher.

Restrictions: none.

Registers at call:
AX = 120Dh
SS = DOS DS

Return Registers:
AX = current date in packed format (see INT 21h
   Function 57h Subfunction 00h)
DX = current time in packed format (see INT 21h
   Function 57h Subfunction 00h)

Conflicts: None known.
See Also: INT 21h Functions 2Ah and 2Ch

INTERRUPT 2Fh - Function 12h, Subfunction 0Eh
internal - MARK ALL DISK BUFFERS UNREFERENCED

Purpose: Clears "referenced" flag on all disk buffers.
Available on: DOS 3.0 or higher.

Restrictions: none.
Return Registers:
DS:DI -> first disk buffer

Registers at call:
AX = 120Eh
SS = DOS DS
Conflicts: None known.
See Also: Function 12h Subfunctions 09h and 10h, INT 21h Function 0Dh

INTERRUPT 2Fh - Function 12h, Subfunction 0Fh
internal - MAKE BUFFER MOST RECENTLY USED

Purpose: The indicated disk buffer is moved to end of the buffer chain, which is ordered by decreasing time since last use.

Available on: DOS 3.0 or higher.

Registers at call:
AX = 120Fh
DS:DI -> disk buffer
SS = DOS DS

Conflicts: None known.

See Also: Function 12h Subfunction 07h

Restrictions: none.

Return Registers:
DS:DI -> next buffer in buffer list

INTERRUPT 2Fh - Function 12h, Subfunction 10h
internal - FIND UNREFERENCED DISK BUFFER

Purpose: Locate an unreferenced disk buffer.

Available on: DOS 3.0 or higher.

Registers at call:
AX = 1210h
DS:DI -> first disk buffer to check

Conflicts: None known.

See Also: Function 12h Subfunction 0Eh

Restrictions: none.

Return Registers:
ZF clear if found
    DS:DI -> first unreferenced disk buffer
ZF set if not found

INTERRUPT 2Fh - Function 12h, Subfunction 11h
internal - NORMALIZE ASCIZ FILENAME

Purpose: Fills destination buffer with uppercase filename, converting slashes to backslashes.

Available on: DOS 3.0 or higher.

Registers at call:
AX = 1211h
DS:SI -> ASCIZ filename to normalize
ES:DI -> buffer for normalized filename

Conflicts: None known.

See Also: Function 12h Subfunctions 1Eh and 21h

Restrictions: none.

Return Registers:
ES:DI buffer filled with normalized filename

INTERRUPT 2Fh - Function 12h, Subfunction 12h
internal - GET LENGTH OF ASCIZ STRING

Purpose: Count number of characters in null-terminated string.

Available on: DOS 3.0 or higher.

Registers at call:
AX = 1212h
ES:DI -> ASCIZ string

Conflicts: None known.

See Also: Function 12h Subfunction 25h

Restrictions: none.

Return Registers:
CX = length of string

INTERRUPT 2Fh - Function 12h, Subfunction 13h
internal - UPPERCASE CHARACTER

Purpose: Convert a character to uppercase.

Available on: DOS 3.0 or higher.

Registers at call:
AX = 1213h
STACK: WORD character to convert to uppercase

Conflicts: None known.

Restrictions: none.

Return Registers:
AL = uppercase character
STACK unchanged

INTERRUPT 2Fh - Function 12h, Subfunction 14h
internal - COMPARE FAR POINTERS

Purpose: Compare two far pointers for identity.

Available on: DOS 3.0 or higher.

Registers at call:
AX = 1214h
DS:SI = first pointer
ES:DI = second pointer

Restrictions: none.

Return Registers:
ZF set if pointers are equal, ZF clear if not equal.

Details: No assumptions or normalizations are made; if the pointers are not bit-for-bit identical, the function returns "not equal".

Conflicts: None known.

INTERRUPT 2Fh - Function 12h, Subfunction 15h
internal - FLUSH BUFFER

Purpose: Force buffer to be written to disk if it has been modified.

Available on: DOS 3.0 or higher.

Registers at call:
AX = 1215h
DS:DI -> disk buffer
SS = DOS DS
STACK:
    WORD drives for which to skip buffer; ignore
       buffer if drive same as high byte, or bytes
       differ and the buffer is for a drive OTHER
       than that given in low byte

Restrictions: Can be called only from within DOS.

Return Registers:
STACK unchanged

Conflicts: None known.

See Also: Function 12h Subfunction 09h

INTERRUPT 2Fh - Function 12h, Subfunction 16h
internal - GET ADDRESS OF SYSTEM FILE TABLE

Purpose: Obtain a far pointer to the specified SFT entry.

Available on: DOS 3.0 or higher.

Registers at call:
AX = 1216h
BX = system file table entry number

Restrictions: none.

Return Registers:
CF clear if successful
    ES:DI -> system file table entry
CF set if BX greater than FILES=

Conflicts: None known.

See Also: Function 12h Subfunction 20h

INTERRUPT 2Fh - Function 12h, Subfunction 17h
internal - SET WORKING DRIVE

Purpose: Establish current default drive.

Available on: DOS 3.0 or higher.

Registers at call:
AX = 1217h
SS = DOS DS
STACK: WORD drive (0 = A:, 1 = B:, etc)

Restrictions: none.

Return Registers:
CF set on error
    (drive > LASTDRIVE)
CF clear if successful
    DS:SI -> current directory structure for specified
       drive
STACK unchanged

Conflicts: None known.

See Also: Function 12h Subfunction 19h

INTERRUPT 2Fh - Function 12h, Subfunction 18h
internal - GET CALLER'S REGISTERS

Purpose: Obtain far pointer to DOS register-save locations.
Available on: DOS 3.0 or higher.
Registers at call:
AX = 1218h

Restrictions: Only valid while within a DOS call.
Return Registers:
DS:SI -> saved caller's AX, BX, CX, DX, SI, DI, BP, DS, ES (on stack)

Conflicts: None known.

INTERRUPT 2Fh - Function 12h, Subfunction 19h
internal - SET DRIVE

Purpose: unknown.
Available on: DOS 3.0 or higher.
Registers at call:
AX = 1219h
SS = DOS DS
STACK: WORD drive (0 = default, 1 = A:, etc)

Restrictions: none.
Return Registers:
STACK unchanged

Details: Calls Function 12h Subfunction 17h. Builds a current directory structure if inside server call (INT 21h Function 5Dh Subfunction 00h).
Conflicts: None known.
See Also: Function 12h Subfunctions 17h and 1Fh

INTERRUPT 2Fh - Function 12h, Subfunction 1Ah
internal - GET FILE'S DRIVE

Purpose: Separate drive and path in pathspec.
Available on: DOS 3.0 or higher.
Registers at call:
AX = 121Ah
DS:SI -> filename
Conflicts: None known.
See Also: INT 21h Functions 19h and 60h

Restrictions: none.
Return Registers:
AL = drive (0 = default, 1 = A:, etc, FFh = invalid)
DS:SI -> filename without leading "X:" (if present)

INTERRUPT 2Fh - Function 12h, Subfunction 1Bh
internal - SET YEAR AND LENGTH OF FEBRUARY

Purpose: Modify DOS month table for leap years.
Available on: DOS 3.0 or higher.

Registers at call:
AX = 121Bh
CL = year - 1980
Conflicts: None known.
See Also: INT 21h Function 2Bh

Restrictions: Requires DS to be set to the DOS data segment.
Return Registers:
AL = number of days in February

INTERRUPT 2Fh - Function 12h, Subfunction 1Ch
internal - CHECKSUM MEMORY

Purpose: Tally days from month table to determine day count; also useful to redirectors as a general checksum function.
Available on: DOS 3.0 or higher.
Registers at call:
AX = 121Ch
DS:SI -> start of memory to checksum
CX = number of bytes

Restrictions: none.
Return Registers:
AX, CX destroyed
DX = checksum
DS:SI -> first byte after checksummed range

DX = initial checksum
SS = DOS DS
Details: Used by DOS to determine day count since 1/1/80 given a date.
Conflicts: None known.
See Also: Function 12h Subfunction 1Dh

INTERRUPT 2Fh - Function 12h, Subfunction 1Dh
internal - SUM MEMORY

Purpose: Used by DOS to determine year or month given the count of days since 1/1/80.

Available on: DOS 3.0 or higher.	**Restrictions:** none.
Registers at call:	**Return Registers:**
AX = 121Dh	AL = byte which exceeded limit
DS:SI -> memory to add up	CX = number of bytes before limit exceeded
CX = 0000h	DX = remainder after adding first CX bytes
DX = limit	DS:SI -> byte beyond the one which exceeded the limit

Conflicts: None known.
See Also: Function 12h Subfunction 1Ch

INTERRUPT 2Fh - Function 12h, Subfunction 1Eh
internal - COMPARE FILENAMES

Purpose: Determine whether two filenames are equivalent when ignoring case and forward/backslash differences.

Available on: DOS 3.0 or higher.	**Restrictions:** none.
Registers at call:	**Return Registers:**
AX = 121Eh	ZF set if filenames equivalent, ZF clear if not
DS:SI -> first ASCIZ filename	
ES:DI -> second ASCIZ filename	

Conflicts: None known.
See Also: Function 12h Subfunction 11h, Function 12h Subfunction 21h

INTERRUPT 2Fh - Function 12h, Subfunction 1Fh
internal - BUILD CURRENT DIRECTORY STRUCTURE

Purpose: Creates a current directory structure for the given drive in a temporary buffer.

Available on: DOS 3.0 or higher.	**Restrictions:** none.
Registers at call:	**Return Registers:**
AX = 121Fh	ES:DI -> current directory structure (will be
SS = DOS DS	overwritten by next call)
STACK: WORD drive letter	STACK unchanged

Conflicts: None known.

INTERRUPT 2Fh - Function 12h, Subfunction 20h
internal - GET JOB FILE TABLE ENTRY

Purpose: Convert "file handle" to SFT index number using job's handle table.

Available on: DOS 3.0 or higher.	**Restrictions:** none.
Registers at call:	**Return Registers:**
AX = 1220h	CF set on error
BX = file handle	AL = 6 (invalid file handle)
	CF clear if successful
	ES:DI -> JFT entry for file handle in current
	process

Details: The byte pointed at by ES:DI contains the number of the SFT for the file handle, or FFh if the handle is not open.
Conflicts: None known.
See Also: Function 12h Subfunctions 16h and 29h

INTERRUPT 2Fh - Function 12h, Subfunction 21h
internal - CANONICALIZE FILE NAME

Purpose: Identical to INT 21h Function 60h.

Available on: DOS 3.0 or higher.

Registers at call:
AX = 1221h
DS:SI -> file name to be fully qualified
ES:DI -> 128-byte buffer for resulting canonical file
    name
SS = DOS DS

Conflicts: None known.

See Also: Function 11h Subfunction 23h, INT 21h Function 60h

Restrictions: none.

Return Registers: (see INT 21h Function 60h)

INTERRUPT 2Fh - Function 12h, Subfunction 22h
internal - SET EXTENDED ERROR INFO

Purpose: Modify tables used by INT21h Function 59h.

Available on: DOS 3.0 or higher.

Registers at call:
AX = 1222h
SS = DOS data segment
SS:SI -> 4-byte records
    BYTE error code, FFh = last record
    BYTE error class, FFh = don't change
    BYTE suggested action, FFh = don't change
    BYTE error locus, FFh = don't change
SDA error code field set

Conflicts: None known.

See Also: Function 12h Subfunction 2Dh, INT 21h Function 59h

Restrictions: Can be called only from within DOS.

Return Registers:
SI destroyed
SDA error class, error locus, and suggested action
    fields set

INTERRUPT 2Fh - Function 12h, Subfunction 23h
internal - CHECK IF CHARACTER DEVICE

Purpose: Determine whether the supplied name is a character device.

Available on: DOS 3.0 or higher.

Registers at call:
AX = 1223h
SDA+218h (DOS 3.10-3.30) = eight-character
    blank-padded name
SDA+22Bh (DOS 4.0x) = eight-character blank-
    padded name

Conflicts: None known.

See Also: INT 21h Function 5Dh Subfunction 06h, INT 21h Function 5Dh Subfunction 0Bh

Restrictions: Can only be called from within DOS
    (assumes DS=SS=DOS DS).

Return Registers:
CF set if no character device by that name found
CF clear if found
    BH = low byte of device attribute word

INTERRUPT 2Fh - Function 12h, Subfunction 24h
internal - DELAY

Purpose: Initiate a time delay, unless in a server call (INT 21h Function 5Dh Subfunction 00h), in order to wait before retrying a failed SHARE operation.

Available on: DOS 3.0 or higher.

Registers at call:
AX = 1224h
SS = DOS DS

Restrictions: none.

Return Registers: n/a

Details: The delay is dependent on the processor speed, and is skipped entirely if inside a server call.

Conflicts: None known.
See Also: INT 21h Function 44h Subfunction 0Bh, INT 21h Function 52h

INTERRUPT 2Fh - Function 12h, Subfunction 25h
internal - GET LENGTH OF ASCIZ STRING

Purpose: Determine the length of a null-terminated string.
Available on: DOS 3.0 or higher.   **Restrictions:** none.
Registers at call: **Return Registers:**
AX = 1225h   CX = length of string
DS:SI -> ASCIZ string
Conflicts: None known.
See Also: Function 12h Subfunction 12h

INTERRUPT 2Fh - Function 12h, Subfunction 26h
internal - OPEN FILE

Purpose: Open the specified file without going through the INT 21h dispatch routine.
Available on: DOS 3.3 or higher.   **Restrictions:** Can only be called from within DOS
                                                              (assumes SS=DOS DS).

Registers at call: **Return Registers:**
AX = 1226h   CF set on error
CL = access mode   AL = error code (see INT 21h Function 59h)
DS:DX -> ASCIZ filename   CF clear if successful
                                                    AX = file handle

Details: Equivalent to INT 21h Function 3Dh.
Conflicts: None known.
See Also: Function 12h Subfunction 27h, INT 21h Function 3Dh

INTERRUPT 2Fh - Function 12h, Subfunction 27h
internal - CLOSE FILE

Purpose: Close the specified file without going through the INT 21h dispatch routine.
Available on: DOS 3.3 or higher.   **Restrictions:** Can only be called from within DOS
                                                              (assumes SS=DOS DS).

Registers at call: **Return Registers:**
AX = 1227h   CF set on error
BX = file handle   AL = 06h invalid file handle
                                                 CF clear if successful

Details: Equivalent to INT 21h Function 3Eh.
Conflicts: None known.
See Also: Function 11h Subfunction 06h, Function 12h Subfunctions 01h and 26h, INT 21h Function 3Eh

INTERRUPT 2Fh - Function 12h, Subfunction 28h
internal - MOVE FILE POINTER

Purpose: Change position within a file without going through the INT 21h dispatch routine.
Available on: DOS 3.3 or higher.   **Restrictions:** May only be called from inside a DOS
                                                              function call.
Registers at call: **Return Registers:** as for INT 21h Function 42h
AX = 1228h
BP = 4200h, 4201h, 4202h (see INT 21h Function
    42h)
BX = file handle
CX:DX = offset in bytes
SS = DOS DS

Details: Equivalent to INT 21h Function 42h. Sets user stack frame pointer to dummy buffer, moves BP to AX, performs LSEEK, and restores frame pointer.
Conflicts: None known.
See Also: INT 21h Function 42h

INTERRUPT 2Fh - Function 12h, Subfunction 29h
internal - READ FROM FILE

Purpose: Read from the specified file without going through the INT 21h dispatch routine.
Available on: DOS 3.3 or higher.

Restrictions: May only be called when already inside a DOS function call.
Return Registers: as for INT 21h Function 3Fh

Registers at call:
AX = 1229h
BX = file handle
CX = number of bytes to read
DS:DX -> buffer
SS = DOS DS
Details: Equivalent to INT 21h Function 3Fh.
Conflicts: None known.
See Also: Function 12h Subfunction 26h, INT 21h Function 3Fh

INTERRUPT 2Fh - Function 12h, Subfunction 2Ah
internal - SET FASTOPEN ENTRY POINT

Purpose: Sets entry point for FASTOPEN routines.
Available on: DOS 3.3 or higher.
Registers at call:
AX = 122Ah
BX = entry point to set (0001h or 0002h)
S:SI -> FASTOPEN entry point (entry point not set
   if SI = FFFFh for DOS 4+)

Restrictions: none.
Return Registers:
CF set if specified entry point already set

Details: The entry point in BX is ignored under DOS 3.30. Both entry points are set to the same handler by DOS 4.01 FASTOPEN.
Conflicts: None known.

> **DOS 3.30 FASTOPEN is called with:**
> AL = 01h unknown.
> > CX = *unknown.* seems to be an offset
> > DI = *unknown.* seems to be an offset
> > SI = offset in DOS DS of filename
> AL = 02h *unknown.*
> AL = 03h *open file* (calls function 01h first)
> > SI = offset in DOS DS of filename
> AL = 04h unknown.
> AH = subfunction (00h, 01h, 02h)
> ES:DI -> *unknown.*
> CX = *unknown.* (subfunctions 01h and 02h only)

> **Return Registers:**
> CF set on error or not installed

> **PCDOS 4.01 FASTOPEN is additionally called with:**
> AL = 04h unknown.
> > AH = 03h unknown.
> AL = 05h unknown.
> AL = 0Bh unknown.
> AL = 0Ch unknown.
> AL = 0Dh unknown.
> AL = 0Eh unknown.

AL = 0Fh unknown.
AL = 10h unknown.

INTERRUPT 2Fh - Function 12h, Subfunction 2Bh
internal - IOCTL

Purpose: Perform IOCTL driver actions without going through INT 21h dispatch routine.
Available on: DOS 3.3 or higher.   **Restrictions:** May only be called when already inside
                                                        a DOS function call.
                                                        Return Registers: as for INT 21h Function 44h
Registers at call:
AX = 122Bh
BP = 44xxh
SS = DOS DS
additional registers as appropriate for INT 21h
    Function 44h
Details: Equivalent to INT 21h Function 44h. Sets user stack frame pointer to dummy buffer, moves BP to AX,
performs IOCTL, and restores frame pointer.
Conflicts: None known.
See Also: INT 21h Function 44h

INTERRUPT 2Fh - Function 12h, Subfunction 2Ch
internal - GET DEVICE DRIVER CHAIN

Purpose: Locate first non-NUL device driver.
Available on: DOS 3.3 or higher.   **Restrictions:** none.
Registers at call: **Return Registers:**
AX = 122Ch   BX:AX -> header of second device driver (NUL is the
                                                            first) in driver chain

Conflicts: None known.
See Also: INT 21h Function 52h

INTERRUPT 2Fh - Function 12h, Subfunction 2Dh
internal - GET EXTENDED ERROR CODE

Purpose: Obtain most recent extended error code.
Available on: DOS 3.3 or higher.   **Restrictions:** none.
Registers at call: **Return Registers:**
AX = 122Dh   AX = current extended error code
Conflicts: None known.
See Also: Function 12h Subfunction 22h, INT 21h Function 59h

INTERRUPT 2Fh - Function 12h, Subfunction 2Eh
internal - GET OR SET ERROR TABLE ADDRESSES

Purpose: Retrieve or replace various error tables.
Available on: DOS 4.0 or higher.   **Restrictions:** none.
Registers at call: **Return Registers:**
AX = 122Eh
DL = subfunction:
    00h get standard DOS error table   ES:DI -> error table (Tables 8-86 thru 8-88)
        (errors 00h-12h,50h-5Bh)
    01h set standard DOS error table
        ES:DI -> error table
    02h get parameter error table (errors 00h-0Ah)   ES:DI -> error table
    03h set parameter error table
        ES:DI -> error table

04h get critical/SHARE error table	ES:DI -> error table
(errors 13h-2Bh)	
05h set critical/SHARE error table	
ES:DI -> error table	
06h get *unknown error table*	ES:DI -> error table
07h set *unknown error table*	
ES:DI -> error table	
08h get error retrieval function	ES:DI -> FAR retrieval function
09h set unknown error table	
ES:DI -> error table	

Details: If the returned segment on a "get" is 0001h, then the offset specifies the offset of the error message table within COMMAND.COM, and the routine returned by subfunction 08h should be called to get the address of the error message.

DOS 5.0 COMMAND.COM does not allow setting any of the addresses; they are always returned with segment 0001h.

Conflicts: None known.

See Also: INT 2Fh Function 05h Subfunction 00h, INT 21h Function 59h

Table 8-86. Format of DOS 4.x error table:

Offset	Size	Description
00h	BYTE	FFh
01h	2 BYTEs	04h,00h (*possibly DOS version*)
03h	BYTE	number of error headers following
04h	2N WORDs	table of all error headers for table

Table 8-87. Format of each header:

Offset	Size	Description
00h	WORD	error message number
02h	WORD	offset of error message from start of header; error messages consist of a count byte followed by actual message text

Table 8-88. Format of DOS 5.0 error table:

Offset	Size	Description
00h	N WORDs	array of words (one per error number) containing either the offset of a counted string or 0000h (invalid error number).

Call error retrieval function with:
    AX = error number
    DI = offset of error table

Return:
    ES:DI -> error message (counted string)

Note: This function needs to access COMMAND.COM if the messages were not loaded into memory permanently with the /MSG switch; the caller should assume that the returned message will be overwritten by the next call to the retrieval function.

INTERRUPT 2Fh - Function 12h, Subfunction 2Fh
internal - SET DOS VERSION NUMBER TO RETURN

Purpose: Permits DOS to lie about version, for compatibility with older programs.

Available on: DOS 4.0 or higher.   **Restrictions:** none.

Registers at call:
AX = 122Fh
DX = DOS version number
　　(0000h = return true DOS version)
Conflicts: None known.

Return Registers: n/a

INTERRUPT 2Fh - Function 46h, Subfunction 01h
internal - Unknown Function

Purpose: *unknown.*
Available on: DOS 5.0 or higher.
Registers at call:
AX = 4601h

Restrictions: *unknown.*
Return Registers: *unknown.*

Details: This functions appears to copy the MCB following the caller's PSP memory block into the DOS data segment.
Conflicts: None known.
See Also: Function 46h Subfunction 02h

INTERRUPT 2Fh - Function 46h, Subfunction 02h
internal - Unknown Function

Purpose: *unknown.*
Available on: DOS 5.0 or higher.
Registers at call:
AX = 4602h

Restrictions: *unknown.*
Return Registers: *unknown.*

Details: Appears to copy a previously saved MCB from the DOS data segment into the MCB following the caller's PSP memory block.
Conflicts: None known.
See Also: Function 46h Subfunction 01h

DOSKEY
DOS 5.0 introduced a commandline recall and editing utility as a separate program. Unlike the similar utilities which have been available from third parties for years, DOSKEY does not replace INT 21h Function 0Ah, and thus works only which programs which are aware of its existence.

INTERRUPT 2Fh - Function 48h, Subfunction 00h
INSTALLATION CHECK

Purpose: Determine whether DOSKEY is installed.
Available on: DOS 5.0 or higher.
Registers at call:
AX = 4800h
Conflicts: None known.
See Also: Function 48h Subfunction 10h

Restrictions: none.
Return Registers:
AL = nonzero if installed

INTERRUPT 2Fh - Function 48h, Subfunction 10h
READ INPUT LINE FROM CONSOLE

Purpose: Get a line of input from the user, who may recall and edit previously-input lines.
Available on: DOS 5.0 or higher.
Registers at call:
AX = 4810h
DS:DX -> line buffer (see INT 21/AH=0Ah)

Restrictions: DOSKEY must be installed.
Return Registers:
AX = 0000h if successful

Details: The first byte (length) of the buffer MUST be 80h, or DOSKEY chains to the previous handler.
If the user's input is a macro name, no text is placed in the buffer even though AX=0000h on return; the program must immediately issue this call again to retrieve the expansion of the macro. Similarly, if the user enters a special

parameter such as $*, this call must be repeated to retrieve the expansion; on the second call, DOSKEY overwrites the macro name on the screen with its expansion.

Conflicts: None known.

See Also: Function 48h Subfunction 00h, INT 21h Function 0Ah

DOSSHELL

DOSSHELL is the text-mode/graphics shell included with MSDOS version 5.0. In addition to the call shown here, DOSSHELL implements the task switcher interface, which is listed in a separate section below.

The shell of the same name included with DOS 4.x does not provide an API itself, although one of its components, SHELLB, does; SHELLB is described in a separate section below.

INTERRUPT 2Fh - Function 4Ah, Subfunction 05h
Unknown Function

Purpose: Access a number of unknown functions within the shell.

Available on: DOS 5.0 or higher.   **Restrictions:** DOSSHELL must be active.

Registers at call: **Return Registers:** *unknown.*
AX = 4A05h
SI = function
   0000h *reset*

   0001h *unknown.*

   0002h *unknown.*

   0003h *unknown.*

   0004h *unknown.*
     BL = *unknown.*

   0005h *unknown.*

   0006h get *unknown* value   ES:DI -> *unknown.*

   0007h get *unknown* value   AX = *unknown.*

   0008h get *unknown* value   DX:AX -> *unknown.*

   0009h get *unknown* value

   000Ah *unknown.*
     BL = *unknown.*
     ES:DI -> *unknown.*

   000Bh get *unknown* value   AX = *unknown.*

   000Ch *unknown.*   DX:AX -> *unknown.*
     BL = *unknown.*

Details: DOSSHELL chains to the previous handler if SI is not one of the values listed above.

Conflicts: None known.

See Also: Function 4Bh Subfunction 02h

DRIVER.SYS SUPPORT
DOS version 3.3 introduced the DRIVER.SYS driver to allow the use of nonstandard disk formats. To support this driver, the hardware-dependent portion of MSDOS (IO.SYS/IBMBIO.COM) provides a number of services on multiplex number 08h.

INTERRUPT 2Fh - Function 08h, Subfunction 00h
INSTALLATION CHECK

Purpose: Determine whether DRIVER.SYS support is available.

Available on: DOS 3.3 or higher.

Registers at call:
AX = 0800h

Restrictions: none.

Return Registers:
AL = 00h not installed, OK to install
01h not installed, not OK to install
FFh installed

Conflicts: None known.

INTERRUPT 2Fh - Function 08h, Subfunction 01h
ADD NEW BLOCK DEVICE

Purpose: Moves down internal list of drive data tables, copying and modifying the drive description flags word for tables referencing same physical drive.

Available on: DOS 3.3 or higher.

Registers at call:
AX = 0801h
DS:DI -> drive data table (see Subfunction 03h)
Details: Data table appended to chain of tables.
Conflicts: None known.
See Also: Function 08h Subfunction 03h

Restrictions: none.

Return Registers: n/a

INTERRUPT 2Fh - Function 08h, Subfunction 02h
EXECUTE DEVICE DRIVER REQUEST

Purpose: Pass driver request packet to driver.

Available on: DOS 3.3 or higher.

Registers at call:
AX = 0802h
ES:BX -> device driver request header (Table 8-89)
Conflicts: None known.

Restrictions: none.

Return Registers:
request header updated as per requested operation

Table 8-89. Format of device driver request header:

Offset	Size	Description
00h	BYTE	length of request header
01h	BYTE	subunit within device driver
02h	BYTE	command code (see Table 8-90)
03h	WORD	status (filled in by device driver):
		bit 15: error
		bits 14-10: reserved
		bit 9: busy
		bit 8: done
		bits 7-0: error code if bit 15 set (see Table 8-91)

---*DOS*
| 05h | 8 BYTEs | reserved (unused in DOS 2.x and 3.x) |

---*STARLITE architecture*
| 05h | DWORD | pointer to next request header |
| 09h | 4 BYTEs | reserved |

Table 8-89. Format of device driver request header (continued)

Offset	Size	Description
---command code 00h		
0Dh	BYTE	number of units (set by driver)
0Eh	DWORD	address of first free byte following driver (set by driver)
12h	DWORD	pointer to BPB array (set by block drivers only)
16h	BYTE	(DOS 3+) drive number for first unit of block driver (0=A)
---command code 01h		
0Dh	BYTE	media descriptor
0Eh	BYTE	returned status:
		00h don't know
		01h media has not changed
		FFh media has been changed
0Fh	DWORD	(DOS 3+) pointer to previous volume ID if OPEN/ CLOSE/ RM bit in device header set and disk changed (set by driver)
---command code 02h		
0Dh	BYTE	media descriptor
0Eh	DWORD	transfer address
		-> scratch sector if NON-IBM FORMAT bit in device header set
		-> first FAT sector otherwise
12h	DWORD	pointer to BPB (set by driver)
---command codes 03h,0Ch		
0Dh	BYTE	media descriptor (block devices only)
0Eh	DWORD	transfer address
12h	WORD	byte count (character devices) or sector count (block devices)
14h	WORD	starting sector number (block devices only)
---command codes 04h,08h,09h		
0Dh	BYTE	media descriptor (block devices only)
0Eh	DWORD	transfer address
12h	WORD	byte count (character devices) or sector count (block devices)
14h	WORD	starting sector number (block devices only)
16h	DWORD	(DOS 3+) pointer to volume ID if error 0Fh returned
1Ah	DWORD	(DOS 4+) 32-bit starting sector number (block devices with attribute bit 1 set only) (see INT 21h Function 52h)
---command code 05h		
0Dh	BYTE	byte read from device if BUSY bit clear on return
---command codes 06h,07h,0Ah,0Bh,0Dh,0Eh,0Fh		
		no further fields
---command code 10h		
0Dh	BYTE	unused
0Eh	DWORD	transfer address
12h	WORD	byte count
---command code 13h		
0Dh	BYTE	category code:
		00h unknown
		01h COMn:
		03h CON
		05h LPTn:
		08h disk
		9Eh (STARLITE) Media Access Control driver
0Eh	BYTE	function code:
		00h (STARLITE) MAC Bind request
0Fh	WORD	copy of DS at time of IOCTL call (apparently unused in DOS 3.3)
11h	WORD	offset of device driver header
13h	DWORD	pointer to parameter block from INT 21h Function 44h Subfunction 0Dh

Table 8-90. Values for command code:

Value	Command	Value	Command
00h	INIT	11h	unused
01h	MEDIA CHECK (block devices)	12h	unused
02h	BUILD BPB (block devices)	13h	(DOS 3.2+) GENERIC IOCTL
03h	IOCTL INPUT	14h	unused
04h	INPUT	15h	unused
05h	NONDESTRUCTIVE INPUT, NO WAIT	16h	unused
	(character devices)	17h	(DOS 3.2+) GET LOGICAL DEVICE
06h	INPUT STATUS (character devices)	18h	(DOS 3.2+) SET LOGICAL DEVICE
07h	INPUT FLUSH (character devices)	19h	(DOS 5+) GENERIC IOCTL CHECK
08h	OUTPUT	80h	(CD-ROM) READ LONG
09h	OUTPUT WITH VERIFY	81h	(CD-ROM) reserved
0Ah	OUTPUT STATUS (character devices)	82h	(CD-ROM) READ LONG PREFETCH
0Bh	OUTPUT FLUSH (character devices)	83h	(CD-ROM) SEEK
0Ch	IOCTL OUTPUT	84h	(CD-ROM) PLAY AUDIO
0Dh	(DOS 3+) DEVICE OPEN	85h	(CD-ROM) STOP AUDIO
0Eh	(DOS 3+) DEVICE CLOSE	86h	(CD-ROM) WRITE LONG
0Fh	(DOS 3+) REMOVABLE MEDIA	87h	(CD-ROM) WRITE LONG VERIFY
	(block devices)	88h	(CD-ROM) RESUME AUDIO
10h	(DOS 3+) OUTPUT UNTIL BUSY		
	(character devices)		

Table 8-91. Values for error code:

Value	Error	Value	Error
00h	write-protect violation	08h	sector not found
01h	unknown unit	09h	printer out of paper
02h	drive not ready	0Ah	write fault
03h	unknown command	0Bh	read fault
04h	CRC error	0Ch	general failure
05h	bad drive request structure length	0Dh	reserved
06h	seek error	0Eh	reserved
07h	unknown media	0Fh	invalid disk change

INTERRUPT 2Fh - Function 08h, Subfunction 03h
GET DRIVE DATA TABLE LIST

Purpose: Obtain far pointer to first drive data table.

Available on: DOS 4.0 or higher.

Registers at call:

AX = 0803h

Conflicts: None known.

See Also: Function 08h Subfunction 01h

Restrictions: none.

Return Registers:

DS:DI -> first drive data table (Table 8-92) in list

Table 8-92. Format of DOS 3.30 drive data table:

Offset	Size	Description
00h	DWORD	pointer to next table
04h	BYTE	physical unit number (for INT 13h)
05h	BYTE	logical drive number
06h	19 BYTEs	BIOS Parameter Block (see also INT 21h Function 53h)
19h	BYTE	flags
		bit 6: 16-bit FAT instead of 12-bit FAT
1Ah	WORD	number of DEVICE OPEN calls without corresponding DEVICE CLOSE
1Ch	11 BYTEs	volume label or "NO NAME " if none (always "NO NAME" for fixed media)
27h	BYTE	*terminating null for volume label*
28h	BYTE	device type (see INT 21h Function 44h Subfunction 0Dh)

Table 8-92. Format of DOS 3.30 drive data table (continued)

Offset	Size	Description
29h	WORD	bit flags describing drive:
		bit 0: fixed media
		bit 1: door lock supported
		bit 2: *unknown*. (used in determining BPB to set for INT 21h Function 44h Subfunction 0Dh)
		bit 3: all sectors in a track are the same size
		bit 4: physical drive has multiple logical units
		bit 5: current logical drive for physical drive
		bit 6: *unknown*.
		bit 7: *unknown*.
		bit 8: *unknown*. (related to disk change detection)
2Bh	WORD	number of cylinders
2Dh	19 BYTEs	BIOS Parameter Block for highest capacity supported
40h	3 BYTEs	*unknown*.
43h	9 BYTEs	*filesystem type*, default = "NO NAME " (apparently only MSDOS 3.30 fixed media, nulls for removable media and PCDOS 3.30)
4Ch	BYTE	least-significant byte of last-accessed cylinder number

---removable media

Offset	Size	Description
4Dh	DWORD	time of last access in clock ticks (FFFFFFFFh if never)

---fixed media

Offset	Size	Description
4Dh	WORD	partition (FFFFh = primary, 0001h = extended)
4Fh	WORD	absolute cylinder number of partition's start on physical drive (always FFFFh if primary partition)

Table 8-93. Format of BIOS Parameter Block for DOS 3.30:

Offset	Size	Description
00h	WORD	bytes per sector
02h	BYTE	sectors per cluster, FFh if unknown
03h	WORD	number of reserved sectors
05h	BYTE	number of FATs
06h	WORD	number of root dir entries
08h	WORD	total sectors
0Ah	BYTE	media descriptor, 00h if unknown
0Bh	WORD	sectors per FAT
0Dh	WORD	sectors per track
0Fh	WORD	number of heads
11h	WORD	number of hidden sectors

Table 8-94. Format of COMPAQ DOS 3.31 drive data table:

Offset	Size	Description
00h	DWORD	pointer to next table
04h	BYTE	physical unit number (for INT 13h)
05h	BYTE	logical drive number
06h	25 BYTEs	BIOS Parameter Block (see DOS 4.01 drive data, Table 8-95)
1Fh	6 BYTEs	*unknown*. apparently always zeros
25h	BYTE	flags:
		bit 6: 16-bit FAT instead of 12-bit FAT
		5: *large volume*
26h	WORD	*device-open count*
28h	11 BYTEs	volume label or "NO NAME " if none (always "NO NAME" for fixed media)
33h	BYTE	terminating null for volume label
34h	BYTE	device type (see INT 21h Function 44h Subfunction 0Dh)
35h	WORD	bit flags describing drive

Table 8-94. Format of COMPAQ DOS 3.31 drive data table (continued)

Offset	Size	Description
37h	WORD	number of cylinders
39h	25 BYTEs	BIOS parameter block for highest capacity drive supports
52h	6 BYTEs	*unknown.* apparently always zeros
58h	BYTE	least-significant byte of last-accessed cylinder number

---removable media

Offset	Size	Description
59h	DWORD	time of last access in clock ticks (FFFFFFFFh if never)

---fixed media

Offset	Size	Description
59h	WORD	partition (FFFFh = primary, 0001h = extended)
5Bh	WORD	absolute cylinder number of partition's start on physical drive (always FFFFh if primary partition)

Table 8-95. Format of DOS 4.0-5.0 drive data table:

Offset	Size	Description
00h	DWORD	pointer to next table
04h	BYTE	physical unit number (for INT 13h)
05h	BYTE	logical drive number
06h	25 BYTEs	BIOS Parameter Block (see also INT 21h Function 53h)
1Fh	BYTE	flags:
		bit 6: 16-bit FAT instead of 12-bit
20h	2 BYTEs	*unknown.*
22h	BYTE	device type (see INT 21h Function 44h Subfunction 0Dh)
23h	WORD	bit flags describing drive:
		bit 0: fixed media
		bit 1: door lock supported
		bit 2: *unknown.*
		bit 3: all sectors in a track are the same size
		bit 4: physical drive has multiple logical units
		bit 5: current logical drive for physical drive
		bit 6: *unknown.*
		bit 7: *unknown.*
		bit 8: *unknown.*
25h	WORD	number of cylinders
27h	25 BYTEs	BIOS Parameter Block for highest capacity supported
40h	7 BYTEs	*unknown.*
47h	DWORD	time of last access in clock ticks (FFFFFFFFh if never)
4Bh	11 BYTEs	volume label or "NO NAME " if none
56h	BYTE	*terminating null for volume label*
57h	DWORD	serial number
5Bh	8 BYTEs	filesystem type ("FAT12 " or "FAT16 ")
63h	BYTE	*terminating null for filesystem type*

Table 8-96. Format of BIOS Parameter Block for DOS 4.0-5.0:

Offset	Size	Description
00h	WORD	bytes per sector
02h	BYTE	sectors per cluster, FFh if unknown
03h	WORD	number of reserved sectors
05h	BYTE	number of FATs
06h	WORD	number of root dir entries
08h	WORD	total sectors (see offset 15h if zero)
0Ah	BYTE	media descriptor, 00h if unknown
0Bh	WORD	sectors per FAT
0Dh	WORD	sectors per track
0Fh	WORD	number of heads

Table 8-96. Format of BIOS Parameter Block for DOS 4.0-5.0 (continued)

Offset	Size	Description
11h	DWORD	number of hidden sectors
15h	DWORD	total sectors if WORD at 08h is zero

EGA.SYS

One limitation of the EGA in task-swapping and multitasking environments is its write-only registers. The EGA Register Interface Library described in chapter 5 provides a fairly standard method for programs to program the EGA's registers while still allowing the swapper or multitasker to maintain separate states for each program. EGA.SYS is one particular implementation of the Register Interface Library.

INTERRUPT 2Fh - Function BCh, Subfunction 00h
INSTALLATION CHECK

Purpose: Determine whether the EGA.SYS driver for Windows 3.0 or DOS 5.0 is installed.

Available on: All machines.

Registers at call:
AX = BC00h

Restrictions: none.

Return Registers:
AL = 00h not installed, OK to install
= 01h not installed, not OK to install
= FFh installed
BX = 5456h ("TV")

Details: BCh is the default multiplex number, which may be changed by a command line parameter to any value between 80h and FFh.

Conflicts: None known.

See Also: Function BCh Subfunction 06h, EGA Register Interface Library INT 10h Function FAh (chapter 5)

INTERRUPT 2Fh - Function BCh, Subfunction 06h
GET VERSION INFORMATION

Purpose: Determine which version of EGA.SYS is installed.

Available on: All machines.

Registers at call:
AX = BC06h

Restrictions: Windows 3.0 or DOS 5.0 EGA.SYS must be installed.

Return Registers:
BX = 5456h ("TV")
CH = major version
CL = minor version
DL = revision

Conflicts: None known.

See Also: Function BCh Subfunction 00h, EGA Register Interface Library INT 10h Function FAh (chapter 5)

GRAFTABL.COM

INTERRUPT 2Fh - Function B0h, Subfunction 00h
INSTALLATION CHECK

Purpose: Determine whether GRAFTABL is installed.

Available on: DOS 3.3 or higher.

Registers at call:
AX = B000h

Restrictions: none.

Return Registers:
AL = 00h not installed, OK to install
= 01h not installed, not OK to install
= FFh installed

Details: Called by DISPLAY.SYS.

Conflicts: None known.

INTERRUPT 2Fh - Function B0h, Subfunction 01h
GET ADDRESS OF GRAPHICS FONT TABLE

Purpose: unknown.

Available on: DOS 3.3 or higher.

Registers at call:
AX = B001h
DS:DX -> DWORD buffer for address of 8x8 font
  table

Restrictions: GRAFTABL must be installed.

Return Registers:
buffer filled
AL = FFh

Conflicts: None known.

GRAPHICS.COM

INTERRUPT 2Fh - Function 15h, Subfunction 00h
INSTALLATION CHECK

Purpose: Determine whether GRAPHICS.COM is installed.

Available on: DOS 4.00 only.

Registers at call:
AX = 1500h

Restrictions: none.

Return Registers:
AX = FFFFh
ES:DI -> *unknown.* (possibly *graphics data*)

Details: This installation check conflicts with the CDROM Extensions installation check; moved to Function ACh Subfunction 00h in later versions.

Conflicts: CDROM Installation Check (chapter 19).

See Also: Function ACh Subfunction 00h

INTERRUPT 2Fh - Function ACh, Subfunction 00h
INSTALLATION CHECK

Purpose: Determine whether GRAPHICS.COM is installed.

Available on: DOS 4.01 or higher.

Registers at call:
AX = AC00h

Restrictions: none.

Return Registers:
AX = FFFFh
ES:DI -> *unknown.* (possibly *graphics data*)

Details: This installation check was moved here to avoid the conflict with the CDROM extensions that occurred in DOS 4.00.

Conflicts: None known.

See Also: GRAPHICS.COM Function 15h Subfunction 00h

HMA

The High Memory Area is an unusual 64K-16 bytes of memory available on 80286 and higher processors. While technically extended memory because it lies beyond the 1 megabyte limit of the 8086's address space, it is still accessible from real mode. Chapter 10 includes more calls related to the HMA under the Extended Memory Specification (XMS).

INTERRUPT 2Fh - Function 4Ah, Subfunction 01h
QUERY FREE HMA SPACE

Purpose: Determine how much, if any, space in the high memory area at segment FFFFh is still unused.

Available on: DOS 5.0 or higher.

Registers at call:
AX = 4A01h

Restrictions: none.

Return Registers:
BX = number of bytes available in HMA (0000h if
  DOS not using HMA)
ES:DI -> start of available HMA area (FFFFh:FFFFh if
  not using HMA)

Conflicts: None known.

See Also: Function 4Ah Subfunction 02h, XMS Function 43h Subfunction 10h (chapter 10)

INTERRUPT 2Fh - Function 4Ah, Subfunction 02h
ALLOCATE HMA SPACE

Purpose: Reserve a portion of the High Memory Area.

Available on: DOS 5.0 or higher.

Restrictions: DOS must be loaded into the HMA (DOS=HIGH).

Registers at call:
AX = 4A02h
BX = number of bytes

Return Registers:
ES:DI -> start of allocated HMA block or
    FFFFh:FFFFh
BX destroyed

Conflicts: None known.
See Also: Function 4Ah Subfunction 01h

IFSFUNC.EXE

Although included on the DOS system disk, IFSFUNC is described separately, in chapter 19, as it implements the network redirector. IFSFUNC was included with DOS 4.x in an attempt to allow network vendors to provide version-independent redirectors; however, IFSFUNC suffered from performance problems due to the additional layer of software, and has been dropped with MSDOS version 5. The DOS 5 kernel still uses the same calls, but they are now once again implemented by version-dependent network redirectors.

INSTALLABLE COMMAND

INTERRUPT 2Fh - Function AEh, Subfunction 00h
internal - INSTALLABLE COMMAND - INSTALL CHECK

Purpose: Determine whether code for a particular installable command is present.

Available on: DOS 3.3 or higher.

Restrictions: none.

Registers at call:
AX = AE00h
DX = FFFFh
DS:BX -> command line (Table 8-97)

Return Registers:
AL = FFh if this command is a TSR extension to
    COMMAND.COM
AL = 00h if the command should be executed as usual

Details: This call provides a mechanism for TSRs to install permanent extensions to the command repertoire of COMMAND.COM. It appears that COMMAND.COM makes this call before executing the current command line, and does not execute it itself if the return is FFh. APPEND hooks this call, to allow subsequent APPEND commands to execute without re-running APPEND. CH appears to be set to FFh on the first call and 00h on the second.

Conflicts: None known.

Table 8-97. Format of command line:

Offset	Size	Description
00h	BYTE	max length of command line, as in INT 21h Function 0Ah
01h	BYTE	count of bytes to follow
	N BYTEs	command line text, terminated by 0Dh

INTERRUPT 2Fh - Function AEh, Subfunction 01h
internal - INSTALLABLE COMMAND - EXECUTE

Purpose: Requests execution of the command which a previous call to Function AEh Subfunction 00h indicated was resident.

Available on: DOS 3.3 or higher.

Restrictions: Installable Command routines must be installed.

Registers at call:
AX = AE01h
DX = FFFFh
DS:SI -> buffer

Return Registers:
Buffer at DS:SI filled with a length byte followed by the uppercase internal command to execute (if length not 0).

Details: APPEND hooks this call. If the buffer is filled with a nonempty string, COMMAND.COM will attempt to execute it as an internal command.
Conflicts: None known.

KEYB.COM

INTERRUPT 2Fh - Function ADh, Subfunction 80h
INSTALLATION CHECK

Purpose: Determine whether KEYB.COM is installed.
Available on: DOS 3.3 or higher.

Restrictions: none.

Registers at call:
AX = AD80h

Return Registers:
AL = FFh if installed
BX = version (BH = major, BL = minor)
ES:DI -> internal data (Table 8-98)

Details: Newly documented for DOS 5.0 although present since 3.3.
Conflicts: None known.
See Also: Function ADh Subfunction 81h

Table 8-98. Format of KEYB internal data:

Offset	Size	Description
00h	DWORD	original INT 09h
04h	DWORD	original INT 2Fh
08h	6 BYTEs	*unknown.*
0Eh	WORD	flags
10h	BYTE	*unknown.*
11h	BYTE	*unknown.*
12h	4 BYTEs	*unknown.*
16h	2 BYTEs	country ID letters
18h	WORD	current code page
---DOS 3.3		
1Ah	WORD	pointer to *first item in list of code page tables* (Table 8-99)
1Ch	WORD	pointer to *unknown* item in list of code page tables (Table 8-99)
1Eh	2 BYTEs	*unknown.*
20h	WORD	pointer to key translation data (Table 8-100)
22h	WORD	pointer to last item in code page table list (Table 8-99)
24h	9 BYTEs	*unknown.*
---DOS 4.01		
1Ah	2 BYTEs	*unknown.*
1Ch	WORD	pointer to first item in list of code page tables (Table 8-99)
1Eh	WORD	pointer to *unknown* item in list of code page tables (Table 8-99)
20h	2 BYTEs	*unknown.*
22h	WORD	pointer to key translation data (Table 8-100)
24h	WORD	pointer to last item in code page table list (Table 8-99)
26h	9 BYTEs	*unknown.*

Table 8-99. Format of code page table list entries:

Offset	Size	Description
00h	WORD	pointer to next item, FFFFh = last
02h	WORD	code page
04h	2 BYTEs	*unknown.*

Table 8-100. Format of translation data:

Offset	Size	Description
00h	WORD	size of data in bytes, including this word
02h	N-2 BYTEs	*unknown.*

INTERRUPT 2Fh - Function ADh, Subfunction 81h
SET KEYBOARD CODE PAGE

Purpose: Establish translation set for keyboard.

Available on: DOS 3.3 or higher.　　**Restrictions:** KEYB.COM must be installed.

Registers at call:　　**Return Registers:**

AX = AD81h　　CF set on error

BX = code page　　　　AX = 0001h (code page not available)

　　CF clear if successful

Details: Called by DISPLAY.SYS. Newly documented for DOS 5.0 although present since 3.3.

Conflicts: None known.

See Also: Function ADh Subfunction 82h

INTERRUPT 2Fh - Function ADh, Subfunction 82h
SET KEYBOARD MAPPING

Purpose: Establish keyboard mapping.

Available on: DOS 3.3 or higher.　　**Restrictions:** KEYB.COM must be installed.

Registers at call:　　**Return Registers:**

AX = AD82h　　CF set on error (BL not 00h or FFh)

BL = 00h US keyboard (Control-Alt-F1)　　CF clear if successful

　= FFh foreign keyboard (Control-Alt-F2)

Details: Newly documented for DOS 5.0 although present since 3.3.

Conflicts: None known.

See Also: Function ADh Subfunctions 81h and 83h

INTERRUPT 2Fh - Function ADh, Subfunction 83h
GET KEYBOARD MAPPING

Purpose: Determine current keyboard mapping.

Available on: DOS 5.0.　　**Restrictions:** KEYB.COM must be installed.

Registers at call:　　**Return Registers:**

AX = AD83h　　BL = 00h US keyboard (Control-Alt-F1)

　　　= FFh foreign keyboard (Control-Alt-F2)

Conflicts: None known.

See Also: Function ADh Subfunction 82h

NLSFUNC.COM

INTERRUPT 2Fh - Function 14h, Subfunction 00h
INSTALLATION CHECK

Purpose: Determine whether NLSFUNC.COM is installed.

Available on: DOS 3.3 or higher.　　**Restrictions:** none.

Registers at call:　　**Return Registers:**

AX = 1400h　　AL = status

　　　00h not installed, OK to install

　　　01h not installed, not OK

　　　FFh installed

Details: Called by DOS v3.3+ kernel. Supported by OS/2 v1.3+ compatibility box, which always returns AL=FFh. This function has been documented for DOS 5.0, but was undocumented in prior versions.

Conflicts: None known.

INTERRUPT 2Fh - Function 14h, Subfunction 01h
CHANGE CODE PAGE

Purpose: Changes code page used by INT 21h Function 65h.

Available on: DOS 3.3 or higher.   **Restrictions:** NLSFUNC.COM must be installed.

Registers at call: **Return Registers:**
AX = 1401h   AL = status
DS:SI -> internal code page structure (Table 8-101)   00h successful
BX = new code page   else DOS error code
DX = *country code*

Details: Called by DOS v3.3+ kernel.

Conflicts: None known.

See Also: INT 21h Function 66h

Table 8-101. Format of DOS 3.30 internal code page structure:

Offset	Size	Description
00h	8 BYTEs	*unknown.*
08h	64 BYTEs	name of country information file
48h	WORD	system code page
4Ah	WORD	number of supported subfunctions
4Ch	5 BYTEs	data to return for INT 21h Function 65h Subfunction 02h
51h	5 BYTEs	data to return for INT 21h Function 65h Subfunction 04h
56h	5 BYTEs	data to return for INT 21h Function 65h Subfunction 05h
5Bh	5 BYTEs	data to return for INT 21h Function 65h Subfunction 06h
60h	41 BYTEs	data to return for INT 21h Function 65h Subfunction 01h

INTERRUPT 2Fh - Function 14h, Subfunction 02h
GET COUNTRY INFORMATION

Purpose: Obtain country information from code page.

Available on: DOS 3.3 or higher.   **Restrictions:** NLSFUNC.COM must be installed.

Registers at call: **Return Registers:**
AX = 1402h   AL = status
BP = subfunction (same as AL for INT 21h   00h successful
    Function 65h)   else DOS error code
BX = code page
DX = country code
DS:SI -> internal code page structure (see Function
    14h Subfunction 01h)
ES:DI -> user buffer
CX = size of user buffer

Details: Called by DOS v3.3+ kernel on INT 21h Function 65h. The code page structure is apparently only needed for the COUNTRY.SYS pathname.

Conflicts: None known.

See Also: Function 14h Subfunction 03h, Function 14h Subfunction 04h, INT 21h Function 65h

INTERRUPT 2Fh - Function 14h, Subfunction 03h
SET COUNTRY INFORMATION

Purpose: Sets country information into code page.

Available on: DOS 3.3 or higher.   **Restrictions:** NLSFUNC.COM must be installed.

Registers at call:
AX = 1403h
DS:SI -> internal code page structure (see Function
    14h Subfunction 01h)
BX = code page
DX = country code

Return Registers:
AL = status
    values unknown.

Details: Called by DOS v3.3+ kernel on INT 21h Function 38h.
Conflicts: None known.
See Also: Function 14h Subfunction 02h, Function 14h Subfunction 04h, INT 21h Function 38h"SET"

INTERRUPT 2Fh - Function 14h, Subfunction 04h
GET COUNTRY INFORMATION

Purpose: Obtain country information from code page.
Available on: DOS 3.3 or higher.
Restrictions: NLSFUNC.COM must be installed.
Registers at call:
AX = 1404h
BX = code page
DX = country code
DS:SI -> internal code page structure (see Function
    14h Subfunction 01h)
ES:DI -> user buffer

Return Registers:
AL = status
other return values unknown.

Details: Called by DOS v3.3+ kernel on INT 21h Function 38h. The code page structure is apparently only needed for the COUNTRY.SYS pathname.
Conflicts: None known.
See Also: Function 14h Subfunction 02h, Function 14h Subfunction 03h, INT 21h Function 38h"GET"

PRINT.COM

INTERRUPT 15h - Function 20h, Subfunction 00h
DISABLE PRINT.COM CRITICAL REGION FLAG

Purpose: Stop updating a user flag which indicates whether PRINT is currently making a DOS call.
Available on: DOS 3.0 or higher.
Restrictions: PRINT must be installed.
Registers at call:
AX = 2000h
Return Registers: n/a
Conflicts: None known.
See Also: Function 20h Subfunction 01h

INTERRUPT 15h - Function 20h, Subfunction 01h
ENABLE PRINT.COM CRITICAL REGION FLAG

Purpose: Begin updating a user flag whenever PRINT enters or leaves a DOS call.
Available on: DOS 3.0 or higher.
Restrictions: PRINT must be installed.
Registers at call:
AX = 2001h
ES:BX -> byte which is to be incremented while in
    a DOS call
Return Registers: n/a
Conflicts: None known.
See Also: Function 20h Subfunction 00h

INTERRUPT 2Fh - Function 00h
Unknown Function

Purpose: *unknown.*
Available on: DOS 2.x only.
Restrictions: PRINT must be installed.

Registers at call:
AH = 00h
other *unknown*.

Return Registers: *unknown*.

Details: DOS 2.x PRINT does not chain to previous INT 2Fh handler. Values in AH other than 00h or 01h cause PRINT to return the number of files in the queue in AH.
Conflicts: None known.
See Also: Function 01h

INTERRUPT 2Fh - Function 00h, Subfunction 80h
GIVE PRINT A TIME SLICE

Purpose: Forces time slice for PRINT.
Available on: DOS 3.1 or higher.
Registers at call:
AX = 0080h
Details: Returns after PRINT executes.

Restrictions: PRINT must be installed.
Return Registers: n/a

INTERRUPT 2Fh - Function 01h
Unknown Function

Purpose: *unknown*.
Available on: DOS 2.x only.
Registers at call:
AH = 01h
other *unknown*.

Restrictions: PRINT must be installed.
Return Registers: *unknown*.

Details: DOS 2.x PRINT does not chain to previous INT 2Fh handler. Values in AH other than 00h or 01h cause PRINT to return the number of files in the queue in AH.
Conflicts: None known.
See Also: Function 00h

INTERRUPT 2Fh - Function 01h, Subfunction 00h
INSTALLATION CHECK

Purpose: Determine whether PRINT is installed.
Available on: DOS 3.0 or higher.
Registers at call:
AX = 0100h

Restrictions: none.
Return Registers:
AL = status:
    00h not installed
    01h not installed, but not OK to install
    FFh installed

Conflicts: None known.
See Also: Function 01h Subfunction 01h

INTERRUPT 2Fh - Function 01h, Subfunction 01h
SUBMIT FILE FOR PRINTING

Purpose: Place a file on the queue of files to be printed.
Available on: DOS 3.0 or higher.

Restrictions: PRINT must be installed.

Registers at call:
AX = 0101h
DS:DX -> submit packet (Table 8-102)

Return Registers:
CF clear if successful
    AL = 01h added to queue
        9Eh now printing
CF set on error
    AX = error code (see also INT 21h Function 59h):
        01h invalid function
        02h file not found
        03h path not found
        04h out of file handles
        05h access denied
        08h print queue full
        09h spooler busy
        0Ch name too long
        0Fh invalid drive

Conflicts: None known.
See Also: Function 01h Subfunction 02h

Table 8-102. Format of submit packet:

Offset	Size	Description
00h	BYTE	level (must be 00h)
01h	DWORD	pointer to ASCIZ filename (no wildcards)

INTERRUPT 2Fh - Function 01h, Subfunction 02h
REMOVE FILE FROM PRINT QUEUE

Purpose: Cancel the pending printing of a file.
Available on: DOS 3.0 or higher.
Registers at call:
AX = 0102h
DS:DX -> ASCIZ filename (wildcards allowed)

Restrictions: PRINT must be installed.
Return Registers:
CF clear if successful
CF set on error
    AX = error code (see Function 01h Subfunction
        01h)

Conflicts: None known.
See Also: Function 01h Subfunctions 01h and 03h

INTERRUPT 2Fh - Function 01h, Subfunction 03h
CANCEL ALL FILES IN PRINT QUEUE

Purpose: Stop printing the current file and forget all other queued files.
Available on: DOS 3.0 or higher.
Registers at call:
AX = 0103h

Restrictions: PRINT must be installed.
Return Registers:
CF clear if successful
CF set on error
    AX = error code (see Function 01h Subfunction
01h)

Conflicts: None known.
See Also: Function 01h Subfunction 02h

INTERRUPT 2Fh - Function 01h, Subfunction 04h
FREEZE PRINT QUEUE TO READ JOB STATUS

Purpose: Stop printing momentarily so that the print queue does not change during a status check.
Available on: DOS 3.0 or higher.
Restrictions: PRINT must be installed.

Registers at call:
AX = 0104h

Return Registers:
CF clear if successful
    DX = error count
    DS:SI -> print queue
CF set on error
    AX = error code (see Function 01h Subfunction
        01h)

Details: The print queue is an array of 64-byte ASCIZ filenames terminated by an empty filename; the first name is the file currently being printed. Printing is stopped until Function 01h Subfunction 05h is called to prevent the queue from changing while the filenames are being read.
Conflicts: None known.
See Also: Function 01h Subfunction 01h, Function 01h Subfunction 05h

INTERRUPT 2Fh - Function 01h, Subfunction 05h
RESTART PRINT QUEUE AFTER STATUS READ

Purpose: Resume printing after a temporary stop to prevent status changes.
Available on: DOS 3.0 or higher.
Registers at call:
AX = 0105h

Restrictions: PRINT must be installed.
Return Registers:
CF clear if successful
CF set on error
    AX = error code (see Function 01h Subfunction
        01h)

Conflicts: None known.
See Also: Function 01h Subfunction 04h

INTERRUPT 2Fh - Function 01h, Subfunction 06h
GET PRINTER DEVICE

Purpose: Determine whether there are any files in PRINT's queue, and if so, which device is being used for output.
Available on: DOS 3.3 or higher.
Registers at call:
AX = 0106h

Restrictions: PRINT must be installed.
Return Registers:
CF set if files in print queue
    AX = error code 0008h (queue full)
    DS:SI -> device driver header
CF clear if print queue empty
    AX = 0000h

Details: This call has been documented for DOS 5.0, but was undocumented in prior versions.
Conflicts: None known.
See Also: Function 01h Subfunction 04h

SHARE

INTERRUPT 2Fh - Function 10h, Subfunction 00h
INSTALLATION CHECK

Purpose: Determine whether SHARE.EXE is installed.
Available on: DOS 3.0 or higher.
Registers at call:
AX = 1000h

Restrictions: none.
Return Registers:
AL = status
    00h not installed, OK to install
    01h not installed, not OK to install
    FFh installed

Details: Supported by OS/2 v1.3+ compatibility box, which always returns AL=FFh.
BUGS: Values of AL other than 00h put DOS 3.x SHARE into an infinite loop (08E9: OR AL, AL 08EB: JNZ 08EB) <- the buggy instruction (DOS 3.3). Values of AL other than described here put PCDOS 4.00 into the same

loop (the buggy instructions are the same); DOS 5.0 fixes the bug so that SHARE chains to the previous handler if AL is nonzero on entry.

If DOS 4.01 SHARE was automatically loaded, file sharing is in an inactive state until this call is made.
Conflicts: None known.
See Also: INT 21h Function 52h

INTERRUPT 2Fh - Function 10h, Subfunction 40h
internal - Unknown Function

Purpose: *unknown.*
Available on: DOS 4.x only.
Registers at call:
AX = 1040h
other *unknown.*

Restrictions: SHARE.EXE must be installed.
Return Registers: *unknown.*

INTERRUPT 2Fh - Function 10h, Subfunction 80h
internal - TURN ON FILE SHARING CHECKS

Purpose: Enable enforcement of file sharing rules.
Available on: DOS 4.x only.
Registers at call:
AX = 1080h

Restrictions: SHARE.EXE must be installed.
Return Registers:
AL = status
    F0h successful
    FFh checking was already on

Details: DOS 4.x SHARE has two functions: FCB support for large (over 32 MB) media and file sharing checks. If SHARE is automatically loaded for FCB support, the file sharing checks are initially turned off; they may also be turned off with the undocumented /NC commandline switch.
See Also: Function 10h Subfunctions 00h and 81h

INTERRUPT 2Fh - Function 10h, Subfunction 81h
internal - TURN OFF FILE SHARING CHECKS

Purpose: Disable enforcement of file sharing rules.
Available on: DOS 4.x only.
Registers at call:
AX = 1081h

Restrictions: SHARE.EXE must be installed.
Return Registers:
AL = status
    F0h successful
    FFh checking was already off

See Also: Function 10h Subfunctions 00h and 80h

SHELLB.COM (DOS V4 only)

INTERRUPT 2Fh - Function 19h, Subfunction 00h
SHELLB.COM - INSTALLATION CHECK

Purpose: Determine whether SHELLB.COM is installed.
Available on: DOS 4.x only.
Registers at call:
AX = 1900h

Restrictions: none.
Return Registers:
AL = status
    00h not installed
    FFh installed

INTERRUPT 2Fh - Function 19h, Subfunction 01h
SHELLB.COM - SHELLC.EXE INTERFACE

Purpose: Interfaces to SHELLC.
Available on: DOS 4.x only.

Restrictions: SHELLB.COM must be installed.

Registers at call:
AX = 1901h
BL = 00h if SHELLC transient
　= 01h if SHELLC resident
DS:DX -> far call entry point for resident
SHELLC.EXE

Return Registers:
ES:DI -> SHELLC.EXE workspace within
SHELLB.COM

Details: SHELLB.COM and SHELLC.EXE are parts of the DOS 4.x shell

INTERRUPT 2Fh - Function 19h, Subfunction 02h
SHELLB.COM - COMMAND.COM INTERFACE

Purpose: Interfaces to COMMAND.COM.
Available on: DOS 4.x only.
Registers at call:
AX = 1902h
ES:DI -> ASCIZ full filename of current batch file,
　with at least the final filename element
　uppercased
DS:DX -> buffer for results

Restrictions: SHELLB.COM must be installed.
Return Registers:
AL = 00h failed, either
　(a) final filename element quoted at ES:DI does
　　not match identity of shell batch file quoted as
　　parameter of most recent call of SHELLB
　　command, or
　(b) no more Program Start Commands available.
AL= FFh success, then memory at DS:[DX+1]
　onwards filled as:

DX+1:	BYTE	count of bytes of PSC
DX+2:	N BYTEs	Program Start Command text
	BYTE	0Dh terminator

Details: COMMAND.COM executes the result of this call in preference to reading a command from a batch file. Thus the batch file does not advance in execution for so long as SHELLB provides Program Start Commands from its workspace. The PSCs are planted in the SHELLB workspace by SHELLC, the user menu interface. The final PSC of a sequence is finished with a GOTO COMMON, which causes a loop back in the batch file which called SHELLC so as to execute SHELLC again. The check on batch file name permits PSCs to CALL nested batch files while PSCs are still stacked up for subsequent execution.

INTERRUPT 2Fh - Function 19h, Subfunction 03h
SHELLB.COM - COMMAND.COM interface

Purpose: Interface to COMMAND.COM.
Available on: DOS 4.x only.
Registers at call:
AX = 1903h
ES:DI -> ASCIZ batch file name as for Function
　19h Subfunction 02h

Restrictions: SHELLB.COM must be installed.
Return Registers:
AL = FFh if quoted batch file name matches last
　SHELLB parameter

AL = 00h if it does not

INTERRUPT 2Fh - Function 19h, Subfunction 04h
SHELLB.COM - SHELLB transient to TSR interface

Purpose: Allows the transient portion of SHELLB to communicate with the resident portion.
Available on: DOS 4.x only.
Registers at call:
AX = 1904h

Restrictions: SHELLB.COM must be installed.
Return Registers:
ES:DI -> name of current shell batch file:

WORD	number of bytes of name following
N BYTEs	(8 bytes max) uppercase name of shell batch file

TASK SWITCHER
With the release of DOS 5.0, Microsoft documented the DOSSHELL task switcher interface. This interface has been designed with sufficient generality to allow other task switchers to use the same interface, or even let multiple task switchers coexist in memory at once.

INTERRUPT 2Fh - Function 4Bh, Subfunction 01h
BUILD TASK SWITCHER CALLOUT CHAIN

Purpose: Called by task switcher to permit clients to request notification on task switcher state changes.

Available on: All machines.	**Restrictions:** none.
Registers at call:	**Return Registers:**
AX = 4B01h	ES:BX -> callback info structure (Table 8-103)
CX:DX -> task switcher entry point	or 0000h:0000h
(see Function 4Bh Subfunction 02h)	
ES:BX = 0000h:0000h	

Details: This function should be hooked by clients which require notification of task switcher activities; the call must first be passed on to the prior handler with registers unchanged using a simulated interrupt. On return, the client must build a callback info structure and store the returned ES:BX in the "next" field, then return the address of its own callback info structure.

A client program must add itself to the notification chain if it provides services to other programs; before terminating, it must remove itself from the chain by calling the task switcher's entry point with AX=0005h (see Function 4Bh Subfunction 02h).

The task switcher entry point should not be saved, as it is subject to change and will be provided on any notification call.

Conflicts: LAN Manager 2.0 (chapter 27).

See Also: Function 4Bh Subfunction 02h

Offset	Size	Description
00h	DWORD	pointer to next callback info structure
04h	DWORD	pointer to notification function (see below)
08h	DWORD	reserved
0Ch	DWORD	address of zero-terminated list of API info structures
		(see Function 4Bh Subfunction 02h)

Notification function called with:	**Function should return:**
AX = function	
0000h switcher initialization	AX = 0000h if OK to load
	= nonzero to abort task switcher
0001h query suspend	AX = 0000h if OK to switch session
BX = session ID	= 0001h if not
0002h suspend session	AX = 0000h if OK to switch session
BX = session ID	= 0001h if not
interrupts disabled	
0003h activate session	AX = 0000h
BX = session ID	
CX = session status flags	
bit 0: set if first activation of session	
bits 1-15: reserved (0)	
interrupts disabled	
0004h session active	AX = 0000h
BX = session ID	
CX = session status flags	
bit 0: set if first activation of session	
bits 1-15: reserved (0)	

0005h create session
  BX = session ID

AX = 0000h if OK to create session
  = 0001h if not

0006h destroy session
  BX = session ID

AX = 0000h

0007h switcher termination
  BX = flags
    bit 0: set if calling switcher is the
    only switcher loaded
    bits 1-15: reserved (0)

AX = 0000h
ES:DI -> task switcher entry point
  (see Function 4Bh Subfunction 02h)

Details: Function 0000h is generally called by the program which controls or invokes the task switcher, rather than by the task switcher itself; the entry point supplied to this function is not necessarily the entry point to the task switcher itself, and may be 0000h:0000h. If any client indicates that loading is not possible, all clients will be called with function 0007h; thus it is possible for a client to receive a termination notice without a corresponding initialization notice.

Except for functions 0002h and 0003h, the notification handler is called with interrupts enabled and may make any INT 21h function call; interrupts must not be enabled in functions 0002h and 0003h, nor may any MSDOS function calls be made.

Function 0007h may be called with ES:DI = 0000h:0000h if the entry point is no longer valid.

INTERRUPT 2Fh - Function 4Bh, Subfunction 02h
INSTALLATION CHECK

Purpose: Determine whether a task switcher is installed.
Available on: All machines.
Registers at call:
AX = 4B02h
BX = 0000h
ES:DI = 0000h:0000h

Restrictions: none.
Return Registers:
ES:DI = 0000h:0000h if task switcher not loaded
ES:DI -> task switcher entry point (see below)
    if loaded
    AX = 0000h

Details: The returned entry point is that for the most-recently loaded task switcher; the entry points for prior task switchers may be determined with the "get version" call (see below).
Conflicts: LAN Manager 2.0 (chapter 27).
See Also: Function 4Ah Subfunction 05h, Function 4Bh Subfunction 03h

Call task switcher entry point with:
AX = 0000h get version

Task Switcher Returns:
CF clear if successful
  AX = 0000h
  ES:BX -> task switcher version structure
    (Table 8-104)
CF set if unsupported function

AX = 0001h test memory region
ES:DI -> first byte to be tested
CX = size of region to test

CF clear if successful
  AX = memory type of tested region
    0000h global
    0001h global and local
    0002h local (replaced on session switch)
CF set if unsupported function

AX = 0002h suspend switcher
ES:DI -> new task switcher's entry point

CF clear if successful
    AX = state
        0000h switcher has been suspended
        0001h switcher not suspended, new switcher
            must abort
        0002h switcher not suspended, but new
            switcher may run anyway
CF set if unsupported function

AX = 0003h resume switcher
ES:DI -> new task switcher's entry point

CF clear if successful
    AX = 0000h
CF set if unsupported function

AX = 0004h hook notification chain
ES:DI -> callback info structure to be added to
    chain (see Function 4Bh Subfunction 01h)

CF clear if successful
    AX = 0000h
CF set if unsupported function

AX = 0005h unhook notification chain
ES:DI -> callback info structure to be removed from
    chain (see Function 4Bh Subfunction 01h)

CF clear if successful
    AX = 0000h
CF set if unsupported function

AX = 0006h query API support
BX = asynchronous API identifier

CF clear if successful
    AX = 0000h
    ES:BX -> API info structure (Table 8-105) for the
        client which provides the highest level of
        support
CF set if unsupported function

Table 8-104. Format of task switcher version structure:

Offset	Size	Description
00h	WORD	major version of supported protocol (current protocol is 1.0)
02h	WORD	minor version of supported protocol
04h	WORD	major version of task switcher
06h	WORD	minor version of task switcher
08h	WORD	task switcher ID (see Function 4Bh Subfunction 03h)
0Ah	WORD	operation flags
		bit 0: set if task switcher disabled
		bits 1-15: reserved (0)
0Ch	DWORD	pointer to ASCIZ task switcher name
		("MS-DOS Shell Task Switcher" for DOSSHELL task switcher)
10h	DWORD	pointer to previous task switcher's entry point or 0000h:0000h

Table 8-105. Format of API info structure:

Offset	Size	Description
00h	WORD	size of structure in bytes (000Ah)
02h	WORD	API identifier
		0001h NetBIOS
		0002h 802.2
		0003h TCP/IP
		0004h LAN Manager named pipes
		0005h Novell NetWare IPX
04h	WORD	major version of highest version of API for which the support
06h	WORD	minor version / level specified in the next field is provided

Table 8-105. Format of API info structure (continued)

Offset	Size	Description
08h	WORD	support level
		0001h minimal support
		0002h API-level support
		0003h switcher compatibility
		0004h seamless compatibility

INTERRUPT 2Fh - Function 4Bh, Subfunction 03h
ALLOCATE TASK SWITCHER ID

Purpose: Request a new task switcher identifier to ensure unique session identifiers.

Available on: All machines.　　　　　　　　　　**Restrictions:** Task switcher must be loaded.

Registers at call:　　　　　　　　　　　　　　**Return Registers:**

AX = 4B03h　　　　　　　　　　　　　　　　　　AX = 0000h

ES:DI -> task switcher entry point　　　　　　　　BX = switcher ID (0001h-000Fh), or 0000h if no more
　　(see Function 4Bh Subfunction 02h)　　　　　　available

Details: If a task switcher has determined that it is the first to be loaded, it must allocate an identifier for itself and provide this function to all subsequent task switchers; if it is not the first to be loaded, it must call this function to allocate an ID. The switcher ID is used as the high four bits of all session identifiers to ensure unique session IDs.

　　If no more switcher IDs are available, the new task switcher making the call must terminate or disable itself. The task switcher providing the identifiers may call the new task switcher's entry point as needed.

Conflicts: LAN Manager 2.0 (chapter 27).

See Also: Function 4Bh Subfunctions 02h and 04h

INTERRUPT 2Fh - Function 4Bh, Subfunction 04h
FREE TASK SWITCHER ID

Purpose: Deallocate a previously allocated task switcher identifier.

Available on: All machines.　　　　　　　　　　**Restrictions:** Task switcher must be loaded.

Registers at call:　　　　　　　　　　　　　　**Return Registers:**

AX = 4B04h　　　　　　　　　　　　　　　　　　AX = 0000h

BX = switcher ID　　　　　　　　　　　　　　　　BX = status

ES:DI -> task switcher entry point　　　　　　　　　0000h successful
　　(see Function 4Bh Subfunction 02h)　　　　　　other error (invalid ID or ID not allocated)

Details: This function is called by a task switcher when it exits, unless it was the first loaded and is providing the support for Subfunctions 03h and 04h. The task switcher providing the identifiers may call the terminating task switcher's entry point as needed.

　　This call is available from within DOSSHELL even if the task switcher is not installed.

Conflicts: LAN Manager 2.0 (chapter 27).

See Also: Function 4Bh Subfunctions 02h and 03h

INTERRUPT 2Fh - Function 4Bh, Subfunction 05h
IDENTIFY INSTANCE DATA

Purpose: Called by task switchers to allow clients to identify data which must be duplicated for each session.

Available on: All machines.　　　　　　　　　　**Restrictions:** none.

Registers at call:　　　　　　　　　　　　　　**Return Registers:**

AX = 4B05h　　　　　　　　　　　　　　　　　　ES:BX -> startup info structure (Table 8-106) or

ES:BX = 0000h:0000h　　　　　　　　　　　　　　0000h:0000h

CX:DX -> task switcher entry point
　　(see Function 4Bh Subfunction 02h)

Details: Clients with instance data should hook this call, pass it through to the previous handler with unchanged registers using a simulated interrupt. On return, the client should create a startup info structure (Table 8-106), store the returned ES:BX in the "next" field, and return the address of the created structure in ES:BX.

　　All MSDOS function calls are available from within this call.

Conflicts: LAN Manager 2.0 (chapter 27).
See Also: Function 4Bh Subfunction 02h, Windows Function 16h Subfunction 05h (chapter 14)

Table 8-106. Format of startup info structure:

Offset	Size	Description
00h	2 BYTEs	major, minor version of info structure (03h,00h)
02h	DWORD	pointer to next startup info structure or 0000h:0000h
06h	DWORD	0000h:0000h (ignored)
0Ah	DWORD	ignored
0Eh	DWORD	pointer to instance data records (Table 8-107)

Table 8-107. Format of one instance data record in array:

Offset	Size	Description
00h	DWORD	address of instance data (end of array if 0000h:0000h)
04h	WORD	size of instance data

XMA2EMS.SYS

INTERRUPT 2Fh - Function 1Bh, Subfunction 00h
internal - INSTALLATION CHECK

Purpose: Determine whether XMA2EMS.SYS is installed.
Available on: DOS 4.0 or higher.   **Restrictions:** none.
Registers at call: **Return Registers:**
AX = 1B00h   AL = FFh if installed
Details: The XMA2EMS.SYS extension is only installed if DOS has page frames to hide. This extension hooks onto INT 67h Function 58h and returns from that call data which excludes the physical pages being used by DOS.
Conflicts: None known.
See Also: Function 1Bh Subfunction 01h

INTERRUPT 2Fh - Function 1Bh, Subfunctions 01h-FFh
internal - GET HIDDEN FRAME INFO

Purpose: Determine which page frames XMA2EMS has hidden from normal EMS calls.
Available on: DOS 4.0 or higher.   **Restrictions:** XMA2EMS.SYS must be installed.
Registers at call: **Return Registers:**
AH = 1Bh   AX = FFFFh if failed (no such hidden page)
AL nonzero   AX = 0000h if OK, then
DI = hidden physical page number   ES = segment of page frame
    DI = physical page number
Details: This corresponds to the data edited out of the INT 67h Function 58h call.
Conflicts: None known.
See Also: Function 1Bh Subfunction 00h

Compatible and Semi-Compatible Systems
The functions described in this section are used by operating systems which are at least somewhat compatible with MS-DOS, though not necessarily completely so. In this section, functions are listed in numeric sequence.

INTERRUPT 21h - Function 44h, Subfunction 51h
Concurrent DOS - INSTALLATION CHECK

Purpose: Determine whether Digital Research's Concurrent DOS v3.2 or higher is installed.
Available on: All machines.   **Restrictions:** none.

Registers at call:
AX = 4451h

Return Registers:
CF set if not Concurrent DOS
  AX = error code (see DOS Function 59h)
CF clear if successful
  AH = 14h
  AL = version (high nybble = major version
    low nybble = minor version)

Conflicts: NewSpace (chapter 6).
See Also: Function 44h Subfunctions 52h and 59h

INTERRUPT 21h - Function 44h, Subfunction 52h
DR DOS 3.41-5.0 - IOCTL - DETERMINE DOS TYPE

Purpose: Determine DOS type present.
Available on: All machines.

Restrictions: DR DOS rather than MS-DOS must be installed.

Registers at call:
AX = 4452h
CF set

Return Registers:
CF set if not DR DOS
  AX = error code (see Function 59h)
CF clear if DR DOS

Details: The DR DOS version is stored in the environment variable VER. Digital Research indicates that this call may change in future versions, making the installation check unreliable. DR DOS 3.41+ is supposedly sufficiently compatible with MSDOS that programs need not decide which of the two they are running under.
Conflicts: None known.
See Also: Function 44h Subfunctions 51h and 59h

INTERRUPT 21h - Function 44h, Subfunction 59h
DR MultiUser DOS 5.0 - API

Purpose: Alternate, mostly-compatible, operating system.
Available on: Digital Research DOS 5.0.

Restrictions: none.
Return Registers: n/a

Registers at call:
AX = 4459h
CL = function (Table 8-108)
DS,DX = parameters
Conflicts: None known.
See Also: Function 44h Subfunction 52h

Table 8-108. Values for Digital Research DOS 5.0 function number:

Value	Function
00h	terminate calling process
02h	write character to default console (see Function 02h)
03h	read character from default AUX (see Function 03h)
05h	write character to default list device (see Function 05h)
06h	perform raw I/O on default console
07h	return default AUX input status
08h	return default AUX output status
09h	write string to default console (see Function 09h)
0Ah	read string from default console (see Function 0Ah)
0Bh	return default console input status (see Function 0Bh)
0Ch	get BDOS release ID
0Dh	reset all disk drives (see Function 0Dh)
0Eh	set default drive (see Function 0Eh)
0Fh	open file via FCB (see Function 0Fh)
10h	close file via FCB (see Function 10h)
11h	search for first matching file with FCB (see Function 11h)

Table 8-108. Values for Digital Research DOS 5.0 function number (continued)

Value	Function
12h	search for next matching file with FCB (see Function 12h)
13h	delete file via FCB (see Function 13h)
14h	sequential read via FCB (see Function 14h)
15h	sequential write via FCB (see Function 15h)
16h	create file via FCB (see Function 16h)
17h	rename file via FCB (see Function 17h)
18h	get bit map of logged drives
19h	get default drive (see Function 19h)
1Ah	set DMA address offset
1Bh	get default disk allocation vector (see Function 1Bh)
1Ch	set default drive to read-only
1Dh	get bit map of read-only drives
1Eh	set file attributes via FCB
1Fh	get address of disk parameter block (see Function 1Fh)
20h	get/set default user number
21h	read random record via FCB (see Function 21h)
22h	write random record via FCB (see Function 22h)
23h	compute file size with FCB (see Function 23h)
24h	get FCB random record number (see Function 24h)
25h	reset specified drives
26h	access specified drives
27h	free specified drives
28h	write random with FCB, zero fill (see also Function 28h)
2Ah	lock records in FCB file (see Function 5Ch)
2Bh	unlock records in FCB file (see Function 5Ch)
2Ch	set BDOS multisector count
2Dh	set BDOS error mode
2Eh	get free space on disk
2Fh	load, initialize, and jump to process
30h	flush write-deferred buffers
32h	call BIOS character routine
33h	set DMA address segment
34h	get DMA buffer address
35h	CP/M-86 allocate maximum memory
36h	allocate maximum memory segment absoute
37h	CP/M-86 allocate memory segment
38h	allocate memory segment absolute
39h	CP/M-86 free specified memory segment
3Ah	CP/M-86 free all memory
3Bh	load .CMD file into memory
40h	(DR-NET) log on a server
41h	(DR-NET) log off a server
42h	(DR-NET) send a message
43h	(DR-NET) receive a message
44h	(DR-NET) get network status
45h	(DR-NET) get requestor configuration table
46h	(DR-NET) set compatibility attributes
47h	(DR-NET) get server configuration table
48h	(DR-NET) set network error mode
49h	(DR-NET) attach network
4Ah	(DR-NET) detach network
4Bh	(DR-NET) set default password
4Ch	(DR-NET) get-set long timeout
4Dh	(DR-NET) get parameter table
50h	(DR-NET) get network information
53h	get current time
54h	set current time

Table 8-108. Values for Digital Research DOS 5.0 function number (continued)

Value	Function
55h	get binary system date
56h	set system date
57h	allocate system flag
58h	deallocate system flag
59h	reserve memory in global area
5Ah	lock physical drive
5Bh	unlock physical drive
5Ch	search path for executable file
5Dh	load and execute command (see Function 4Bh)
5Eh	get/set process exit code
5Fh	set country information
60h	get country information
63h	truncate FCB file (see Function 28h)
64h	create/update directory label
65h	get directory label
66h	get FCB date stamp and password mode
67h	write extended FCB
68h	set system date and time
69h	get system date and time in binary
6Ah	establish password for file access
6Bh	get OS serial number
6Dh	get/set console mode
6Eh	get/set string delimiter
6Fh	write block to default console
70h	write block to default list device
71h	execute DOS-compatible function
74h	set FCB time and date stamps
80h	allocate memory
82h	deallocate memory
83h	poll I/O device
84h	wait on system flag
85h	set system flag
86h	create message queue
87h	open message queue
88h	delete message queue
89h	read from message queue
8Ah	conditionally read from message queue
8Bh	write to message queue
8Ch	conditionally write to message queue
8Dh	delay calling process
8Eh	call process dispatcher
8Fh	terminate calling process
90h	create a process
91h	set calling process' priority
92h	attach to default console
93h	detach from default console
95h	assign default console to process
96h	interpret and execute commandline
97h	resident procedure library
98h	parse ASCII string into FCB (see Function 29h)
99h	return default console
9Ah	get address of system data
9Bh	get system time and date
9Ch	return calling process' descriptor
9Dh	terminate process by name or PD address

Table 8-108. Values for Digital Research DOS 5.0 function number (continued)

Value	Function
9Eh	attach to default list device
9Fh	detach from default list device
A0h	select default list device
A1h	conditionally attach to default list device
A2h	conditionally attach to default console
A3h	get OS version number
A4h	get default list device
A5h	attach to default AUX
A6h	detach from default AUX
A7h	conditionally attach to default AUX
A8h	set default AUX
A9h	return default AUX
ACh	read block from default AUX
B0h	configure default AUX
B1h	get/set device control parameters
B2h	send Break through default AUX
B3h	allocate physical memory
B4h	free physical memory
B5h	map physical memory
B6h	nondestructive message queue read
B7h	timed wait on system flag
B8h	get/set I/O port mapping
B9h	set list device timeout
BAh	set AUX timeout value
BBh	execute XIOS service
FFh	return 80386 to native mode

INTERRUPT 21h - Function 5Fh, Subfunction 05h
STARLITE architecture - MAP LOCAL DRIVE LETTER TO REMOTE FILE SYSTEM

Purpose: Map local drive letter to remote file system.
Available on: STARLITE architecture only.
Registers at call:
AX = 5F05h
DL = drive number (0=A:)
DS:SI -> ASCIZ name of the object to map the
    drive to

Restrictions: none.
Return Registers:
CF set on error
    AX = error code (see Function 59h)
CF clear if successful

Conflicts: DOS 4.x + Microsoft Networks.
See Also: STARLITE Function 5Fh Subfunction 06h

INTERRUPT 21h - Function 5Fh, Subfunction 06h
STARLITE architecture - UNMAP DRIVE LETTER

Purpose: Removes drive letter mapping.
Available on: STARLITE architecture only.
Registers at call:
AX = 5F06h
DL = drive to be unmapped (0=A:)

Restrictions: none.
Return Registers:
CF set on error
    AX = error code (see Function 59h)
CF clear if successful

Conflicts: DOS 4.x + Microsoft Networks.
See Also: STARLITE Function 5Fh Subfunction 05h

INTERRUPT 21h - Function 5Fh, Subfunction 07h
STARLITE architecture - MAKE NAMED OBJECT AVAILABLE ON NETWORK

Purpose: Makes specified object available to network.

Available on: STARLITE architecture only.
Registers at call:
AX = 5F07h
DS:SI -> ASCIZ name of object to offer to network
ES:DI -> ASCIZ name under which object will be
    known on the network MUST begin with three
    slashes
Conflicts: DOS 5.0.
See Also: Function 5Fh Subfunction 08h

Restrictions: none.
Return Registers:
CF set on error
    AX = error code (see Function 59h)
CF clear if successful

INTERRUPT 21h - Function 5Fh, Subfunction 08h
STARLITE architecture - REMOVE GLOBAL NETWORK NAME OF OBJECT

Purpose: Cancels specified network name, making the object inaccessible from the network.
Available on: STARLITE architecture only.
Registers at call:
AX = 5F08h
DS:SI -> ASCIZ network name (not local name) of
    object to unshare
Conflicts: DOS 5.0.
See Also: Function 5Fh Subfunction 07h

Restrictions: none.
Return Registers:
CF set on error
    AX = error code (see Function 59h)
CF clear if successful

INTERRUPT 21h - Function 5Fh, Subfunction 09h
STARLITE architecture - BIND TO NETWORK DEVICE

Purpose: Attach to specified network.
Available on: STARLITE architecture only.
Registers at call:
AX = 5F09h
DS:DX -> ASCIZ name of the device driver to
    which to attach

Restrictions: none.
Return Registers:
CF set on error
    AX = error code (see Function 59h)
CF clear if successful

Details: The STARLITE distributed file system can attach to multiple networks simultaneously.
Conflicts: None known.
See Also: Function 5Fh Subfunction 0Ah

INTERRUPT 21h - Function 5Fh, Subfunction 0Ah
STARLITE architecture - DETACH FROM NETWORK DEVICE

Purpose: Detach from specified network.
Available on: STARLITE architecture only.
Registers at call:
AX = 5F0Ah
DS:DX -> ASCIZ name of device driver to detach
    from
Conflicts: None known.
See Also: Function 5Fh Subfunction 09h

Restrictions: none.
Return Registers:
CF set on error
    AX = error code (see Function 59h)
CF clear if successful

INTERRUPT 2Ch
STARLITE architecture - KERNEL API

Purpose: STARLITE is an architecture by General Software for a series of MS-DOS compatible operating systems (OEM DOS, NETWORK DOS, and SMP DOS) to be released in 1991.
Available on: STARLITE architecture only.
Registers at call: *unknown.*
Details: The interrupt number is subject to change before the actual release.
Conflicts: DOS reserved, MS Windows (chapter 14).

Restrictions: none.
Return Registers: *unknown.*

OS/2 compatibility box

INTERRUPT 2Fh - Function 40h, Subfunction 01h
OS/2 compatibility box - SWITCHING DOS TO BACKGROUND

Purpose: Called by OS/2 when the DOS box is about to be placed in the background; the intent is to allow graphics programs to save their state until the DOS box is placed in the foreground again.

Available on: OS/2 systems.   **Restrictions:** none.
Registers at call: **Return Registers:** n/a
AX = 4001h
Conflicts: None known.
See Also: Function 40h Subfunction 02h

INTERRUPT 2Fh - Function 40h, Subfunction 02h
OS/2 compatibility box - SWITCHING DOS TO FOREGROUND

Purpose: Called by OS/2 when the DOS box is about to be switched to foreground operation.

Available on: OS/2 systems.   **Restrictions:** none.
Registers at call: **Return Registers:** n/a
AX = 4002h
Conflicts: None known.
See Also: Function 40h Subfunction 01h

Unknown

INTERRUPT 2Fh - Function ADh, Subfunction 40h
Unknown Function

Purpose: *unknown.*
Available on: DOS 4.0.   **Restrictions:** *unknown.*
Registers at call: **Return Registers:** *unknown.*
AX = AD40h
DX = *unknown.*
other *unknown.*
Details: The only information known about this call is that it is invoked by the PCDOS 4.01 PRINT.COM.

Chapter 9

DOS Extenders

As programs on the IBM PC and compatibles became ever larger, the "640K barrier" of real-mode operation became an increasing problem. In response, DOS extenders were created to provide nearly-transparent access to DOS (running in real mode) from protected mode. With a DOS extender, programs can be recompiled (with minimal changes) to permit access to a full 16 megabytes on 80286s and up to 4 gigabytes of memory on the 80386 and later processors. The DOS extender handles all the details of switching to real mode on DOS calls and copying data which is beyond the 1-megabyte mark so that DOS can access it, while the program continues operating essentially unchanged.

This chapter is organized by interrupt and function number. This results in the following sequence of sections: Rational Systems DOS/16M, Phar Lap 386/DOS-Extender, OS/286 and OS/386, GO32.EXE, Ergo DOS extenders installation check, Phar Lap DOS extenders installation check, Generic installation check, Borland DOS extender (TKERNEL), Oracle SQL Protected Mode Executive, and University of Salford DBOS.

Rational Systems DOS/16M

DOS/16M is one of the oldest DOS extenders available, and is used in numerous commercial programs, such as Lotus 1-2-3 version 3.0.

INTERRUPT 15h - Function BFh
DOS/16M - INSTALLATION CHECK

Purpose: Determine whether DOS/16M software is installed.
Available on: All machines.
Registers at call:
AX = BF02h
DX = 0000h
Conflicts: None known.
See Also: INT 2Fh Function A1h, INT 2Fh Function FBA1h

Restrictions: none.
Return Registers:
DX = nonzero if installed
DS:SI - XBRK structure

Phar Lap 386/DOS-Extender

Phar Lap uses INT 21h Function 25h as the entry point for all 386/DOS-Extender system calls; the DOS real-mode Set Interrupt Vector (see chapter 8) which it conflicts with is meaningless in protected mode. These calls are only available when directly using 386/DOS-Extender, or when using a product that was created with 386-DOS/Extender.

INTERRUPT 21h - Function 25h, Subfunction 01h
RESET 386/DOS-EXTENDER DATA STRUCTURES

Purpose: Return the DOS extender to a known initial state.
Available on: 80386 or higher in protected mode.

Registers at call:
AX = 2501h
Conflicts: DOS Set Interrupt Vector (chapter 8).

Restrictions: Phar Lap 386/DOS-extender must be installed.
Return Registers:
CF clear

INTERRUPT 21h - Function 25h, Subfunction 02h
GET PROTECTED-MODE INTERRUPT VECTOR

Purpose: Determine which procedure gains control when a specified interrupt occurs in protected mode.

Available on: 80386 or higher in protected mode.

Restrictions: Phar Lap 386/DOS-extender must be installed.

Registers at call:
AX = 2502h
CL = interrupt number

Return Registers:
ES:EBX -> 48-bit address of protected-mode
    interrupt handler
CF clear

Conflicts: DOS Set Interrupt Vector (chapter 8).
See Also: Function 25h Subfunctions 03h and 04h, DPMI INT 31h Function 02h Subfunction 04h (Chapter 11)

INTERRUPT 21h - Function 25h, Subfunction 03h
GET REAL-MODE INTERRUPT VECTOR

Purpose: Determine which procedure gains control when a specified interrupt occurs in real mode.

Available on: 80386 or higher in protected mode.

Restrictions: Phar Lap 386/DOS-extender must be installed.

Registers at call:
AX = 2503h
CL = interrupt number

Return Registers:
EBX = 32-bit address of real-mode interrupt handler
CF clear

Conflicts: DOS Set Interrupt Vector (chapter 8).
See Also: Function 25h Subfunctions 02h and 04h, DPMI INT 31h Function 02h Subfunction 00h (Chapter 11)

INTERRUPT 21h - Function 25h, Subfunction 04h
SET PROTECTED-MODE INTERRUPT VECTOR

Purpose: Specify which procedure gains control when a specified interrupt occurs in protected mode.

Available on: 80386 or higher in protected mode.

Restrictions: Phar Lap 386/DOS-extender must be installed.

Registers at call:
AX = 2504h
CL = interrupt number
DS:EDX -> 48-bit address of protected-mode
    interrupt handler

Return Registers:
CF clear

Conflicts: DOS Set Interrupt Vector (chapter 8).
See Also: Function 25h Subfunctions 02h and 05h, DPMI INT 31h Function 02h Subfunction 05h (Chapter 11)

INTERRUPT 21h - Function 25h, Subfunction 05h
SET REAL-MODE INTERRUPT VECTOR

Purpose: Specify which procedure gains control when a specified interrupt occurs in real mode.

Available on: 80386 or higher in protected mode.

Restrictions: Phar Lap 386/DOS-extender must be installed.

Registers at call:
AX = 2505h
CL = interrupt number
EBX = 32-bit address of real- mode interrupt
    handler

Return Registers:
CF clear

Conflicts: DOS Set Interrupt Vector (chapter 8).
See Also: Function 25h Subfunctions 03h and 04h, DPMI INT 31h Function 02h Subfunction 01h (Chapter 11)

INTERRUPT 21h - Function 25h, Subfunction 06h
SET INTERRUPT TO ALWAYS GAIN CONTRL IN PROTECTED MODE

Purpose: Specify that a particular real-mode interrupt will switch to protected mode to invoke the interrupt handler.

Available on: 80386 or higher in protected mode.

Restrictions: Phar Lap 386/DOS-extender must be installed.

Registers at call:
AX = 2506h
CL = interrupt number
DS:EDX -> 48-bit address of protected-mode
    interrupt handler

Return Registers:
CF clear

Details: This function modifies both the real-mode low-memory interrupt vector table and the protected-mode Interrupt Descriptor Table (IDT). Interrupts occurring in real mode are resignaled in protected mode.
Conflicts: DOS Set Interrupt Vector (chapter 8).

INTERRUPT 21h - Function 25h, Subfunction 07h
SET REAL- & PROTECTED-MODE INT VECTORS

Purpose: Specify the procedures which gain control when an interrupt occurs depending on which mode the processor is in at the time of the interrupt.

Available on: 80386 or higher in protected mode.

Restrictions: Phar Lap 386/DOS-extender must be installed.

Registers at call:
AX = 2507h
CL = interrupt number
DS:EDX -> 48-bit address of protected-mode
    interrupt handler
EBX = 32-bit address of real-mode interrupt handler

Return Registers:
CF clear

Details: Interrupts are disabled until both vectors have been modified.
Conflicts: DOS Set Interrupt Vector (chapter 8).
See Also: Function 25h Subfunctions 04h and 05h

INTERRUPT 21h - Function 25h, Subfunction 08h
GET SEGMENT LINEAR BASE ADDRESS

Purpose: Determine the physical address at which a segment is located.

Available on: 80386 or higher in protected mode.

Restrictions: Phar Lap 386/DOS-extender must be installed.

Registers at call:
AX = 2508h
BX = segment selector

Return Registers:
CF clear if successful
    ECX = linear base address of segment
CF set if invalid segment selector

Conflicts: DOS Set Interrupt Vector (chapter 8).

INTERRUPT 21h - Function 25h, Subfunction 09h
CONVERT LINEAR TO PHYSICAL ADDRESS

Purpose: Determine the physical memory address corresponding to the specified logical address.

Available on: 80386 or higher in protected mode.

Restrictions: Phar Lap 386/DOS-extender must be installed.

Registers at call:
AX = 2509h
EBX = linear address to convert

Return Registers:
CF clear if successful
    ECX = physical address (carry flag clear)
CF set if linear address not mapped in page tables

Conflicts: DOS Set Interrupt Vector (chapter 8).

INTERRUPT 21h - Function 25h, Subfunction 0Ah
MAP PHYSICAL MEMORY AT END OF SEGMENT

Purpose: Associate physical memory with a range of addesses within a segment.

Available on: 80386 or higher in protected mode.

Registers at call:
AX = 250Ah
ES = segment selector in the Local Descriptor Table
(LDT) of segment to modify
EBX = physical base address of memory to map
(multiple of 4K)
ECX = number of physical 4K pages to map

Restrictions: Phar Lap 386/DOS-extender must be
installed.
Return Registers:
CF clear if successful:
EAX = 32-bit offset in segment of mapped
memory
CF set on error
EAX = error code:
08h insufficient memory to create page tables
09h invalid segment selector

Conflicts: DOS Set Interrupt Vector (chapter 8).
See Also: DPMI INT 31h Function 08h Subfunction 00h (Chapter 11)

INTERRUPT 21h - Function 25h, Subfunction 0Ch
GET HARDWARE INTERRUPT VECTORS

Purpose: Determine the mapping from interrupt request lines to interrupt numbers.
Available on: 80386 or higher in protected mode.

Registers at call:
AX = 250Ch

Restrictions: Phar Lap 386/DOS-extender must be
installed.
Return Registers:
CF clear
AL = base interrupt vector for IRQ0-IRQ7
AH = base interrupt vector for IRQ8-IRQ15
BL = interrupt vector for BIOS print screen function

Conflicts: DOS Set Interrupt Vector (chapter 8).
See Also: DPMI INT 31h Function 04h Subfunction 00h (Chapter 11)

INTERRUPT 21h - Function 25h, Subfunction 0Dh
GET REAL-MODE LINK INFORMATION

Purpose: Determine the addresses of procedures and data structures used in switching from real mode to protected mode.
Available on: 80386 or higher in protected mode.

Registers at call:
AX = 250Dh

Restrictions: Phar Lap 386/DOS-extender must be
installed.
Return Registers:
CF clear
EAX = 32-bit address of real-mode 386/DOS-Extender
proc that will call through from real mode to a
protected- mode routine
EBX = 32-bit real-mode address of intermode call data
buffer
ECX = size in bytes of intermode call data buffer
ES:EDX -> protected-mode address of intermode call
data buffer

Conflicts: DOS Set Interrupt Vector (chapter 8).

INTERRUPT 21h - Function 25h, Subfunction 0Eh
CALL REAL-MODE PROCEDURE

Purpose: Invoke a procedure which is running in real mode.
Available on: 80386 or higher in protected mode.

Restrictions: Phar Lap 386/DOS-extender must be
installed.

Registers at call:
AX = 250Eh
EBX = 32-bit address of real-mode procedure to
call
ECX = number of two-byte words to copy from
protected-mode stack to real-mode stack

Return Registers:
CF clear if successful
all segment registers unchanged
all general registers contain values set by real-
mode procedure
all other flags set as they were left by real-
mode procedure
CF set on error
EAX = error code
01h not enough real-mode stack space

Conflicts: DOS Set Interrupt Vector (chapter 8).
See Also: OS/286 Function E1h, DPMI INT 31h Function 03h Subfunction 01h (Chapter 11)

INTERRUPT 21h - Function 25h, Subfunction 0Fh
CONVERT PROTECTED-MODE ADDRESS TO MS-DOS

Purpose: Determine a real-mode physical address corresponding to the specified logical address.
Available on: 80386 or higher in protected mode.

Restrictions: Phar Lap 386/DOS-extender must be installed.

Registers at call:
AX = 250Fh
ES:EBX -> 48-bit protected-mode address to
convert
ECX = length of data, in bytes
Conflicts: DOS Set Interrupt Vector (chapter 8).
See Also: Function 25h Subfunction 10h

Return Registers:
CF clear if successful
ECX = 32-bit MS-DOS address
CF set on error
ECX destroyed

INTERRUPT 21h - Function 25h, Subfunction 10h
CALL REAL-MODE PROCEDURE, REGISTERS

Purpose: Invoke a procedure running in real mode with the specified values in the processor registers.
Available on: 80386 or higher in protected mode.

Restrictions: Phar Lap 386/DOS-extender must be installed.

Registers at call:
AX = 2510h
EBX = 32-bit address of real-mode procedure to
call
ECX = number of two-byte words to copy to
protected-mode stack to real-mode stack
DS:EDX -> pointer to parameter block (Table 9-1)

Return Registers:
CF clear if successful
all segment registers unchanged, EDX unchanged
all other general registers contain values set by
real-mode proc
all other flags are set as they were left by real-
mode procedure
real-mode register values are returned in the
parameter block
CF set on error
EAX = error code
01h not enough real-mode stack space

Conflicts: DOS Set Interrupt Vector (chapter 8).
See Also: Function 25h Subfunction 0Fh

Table 9-1. Format of parameter block:

Offset	Size	Description
00h	WORD	real-mode DS value
02h	WORD	real-mode ES value
04h	WORD	real-mode FS value
06h	WORD	real-mode GS value
08h	DWORD	real-mode EAX value

Table 9-1. Format of parameter block (continued)

Offset	Size	Description
0Ch	DWORD	real-mode EBX value
10h	DWORD	real-mode ECX value
14h	DWORD	real-mode EDX value

INTERRUPT 21h - Function 25h, Subfunction 11h
ISSUE REAL-MODE INTERRUPT

Purpose: Invoke an interrupt handler which is running in real mode.

Available on: 80386 or higher in protected mode.

Restrictions: Phar Lap 386/DOS-extender must be installed.

Registers at call:
AX = 2511h
DS:EDX -> pointer to parameter block (Table 9-2)

Return Registers:
All segment registers unchanged
EDX unchanged
All other registers contain values set by the real- mode int handler
The flags are set as they were left by the real- mode interrupt handler
Real-mode register values are returned in the parameter block

Details: All other real-mode values set from protected-mode registers.

Conflicts: DOS Set Interrupt Vector (chapter 8).

See Also: Function 25h Subfunctions 03h and 05h, DPMI Function 03h Subfunction 00h (Chapter 11)

Table 9-2. Format of parameter block:

Offset	Size	Description
00h	WORD	interrupt number
02h	WORD	real-mode DS value
04h	WORD	real-mode ES value
06h	WORD	real-mode FS value
08h	WORD	real-mode GS value
0Ah	DWORD	real-mode EAX value
0Eh	DWORD	real-mode EDX value

INTERRUPT 21h - Function 25h, Subfunction 12h
LOAD PROGRAM FOR DEBUGGING

Purpose: Read a program into memory but do not start executing it.

Available on: 80386 or higher in protected mode.

Restrictions: Phar Lap 386/DOS-extender must be installed.

Registers at call:
AX = 2512h
DS:EDX -> pointer to ASCIIZ program name
ES:EBX -> pointer to parameter block (Table 9-3)
ECX = size in bytes of LDT buffer

Return Registers:
CF clear if successful
    EAX = number of segment descriptors in LDT
CF set on error
    EAX = error code
        02h file not found or path invalid
        05h access denied
        08h insufficient memory
        0Ah environment invalid
        0Bh invalid file format
        80h LDT too small

Conflicts: DOS Set Interrupt Vector (chapter 8).

Table 9-3. Format of parameter block:

Offset	Size	Description
Input:		
00h	DWORD	32-bit offset of environment string
04h	WORD	segment of environment string
06h	DWORD	32-bit offset of command-tail string
0Ah	WORD	segment of command-tail string
0Ch	DWORD	32-bit offset of LDT buffer (size in ECX)
10h	WORD	segment of LDT buffer
Output:		
12h	WORD	real-mode paragraph address of PSP (see also INT 21h Function 26h [chapter 8])
14h	WORD	real/protected mode flag
		0000h real mode
		0001h protected mode
16h	DWORD	initial EIP value
1Ah	WORD	initial CS value
1Ch	DWORD	initial ESP value
20h	WORD	initial SS value
22h	WORD	initial DS value
24h	WORD	initial ES value
26h	WORD	initial FS value
28h	WORD	initial GS value

INTERRUPT 21h - Function 25h, Subfunction 13h
ALIAS SEGMENT DESCRIPTOR

Purpose: Create a new segment selector which refers to the same memory as the specified selector.

Available on: 80386 or higher in protected mode.

Restrictions: Phar Lap 386/DOS-extender must be installed.

Registers at call:
AX = 2513h
BX = segment selector of descriptor in GDT or LDT
CL = access-rights byte for alias descriptor
CH = use-type bit (USE16 or USE32) for alias descriptor

Conflicts: DOS Set Interrupt Vector (chapter 8).

Return Registers:
CF clear if successful
AX = segment selector for created alias
CF set on error
EAX = error code
08h insufficient memory (can't grow LDT)
09h invalid segment selector in BX

INTERRUPT 21h - Function 25h, Subfunction 14h
CHANGE SEGMENT ATTRIBUTES

Purpose: Specify the segment type for the given selector.

Available on: 80386 or higher in protected mode.

Restrictions: Phar Lap 386/DOS-extender must be installed.

Registers at call:
AX = 2514h
BX = segment selector of descriptor in GDT or LDT
CL = new access-rights byte
CH = new use-type bit (USE16 or USE32)

Conflicts: DOS Set Interrupt Vector (chapter 8).

See Also: Function 25h Subfunction 15h, DPMI Function 00h Subfunction 09h (Chapter 11)

Return Registers:
CF clear if successful
CF set on error
EAX = error code
09h invalid selector in BX

INTERRUPT 21h - Function 25h, Subfunction 15h
GET SEGMENT ATTRIBUTES

Purpose: Determine the type of segment for the specified selector.

Available on: 80386 or higher in protected mode.

Registers at call:
AX = 2515h
BX = segment selector of descriptor in GDT or
    LDT

Restrictions: Phar Lap 386/DOS-extender must be installed.

Return Registers:
CF clear if successful
    CL = access-rights byte for segment
    CH = use-type bit (USE16 or USE32)
    ECX<16-31> destroyed
CF set on error
    EAX = error code
        09h invalid segment selector in BX

Conflicts: DOS Set Interrupt Vector (chapter 8).
See Also: Function 25h Subfunction 14h

INTERRUPT 21h - Function 25h, Subfunction 16h
FREE ALL MEMORY OWNED BY LDT

Purpose: Release the memory allocated to each descriptor within the specified Local Descriptor Table.

Available on: 80386 or higher in protected mode.

Registers at call:
AX = 2516h
others *unknown*.

Restrictions: Phar Lap 386/DOS-extender must be installed.

Return Registers: *unknown*.

Conflicts: DOS Set Interrupt Vector (chapter 8).

INTERRUPT 21h - Function 25h, Subfunction 17h
GET INFO ON DOS DATA BUFFER

Purpose: Determine the size and location of the real-mode buffer used in making DOS function calls from protected mode.

Available on: 80386 or higher in protected mode.

Registers at call:
AX = 2517h
others *unknown*.

Restrictions: Phar Lap 386/DOS-extender must be installed.

Return Registers: *unknown*.

Conflicts: DOS Set Interrupt Vector (chapter 8).

INTERRUPT 21h - Function 25h, Subfunction 18h
SPECIFY HANDLER FOR MOVED SEGMENTS

Purpose: *Indicate which procedure is to be called when a memory segment is moved.*

Available on: 80386 or higher in protected mode.

Registers at call:
AX = 2518h
others *unknown*.

Restrictions: Phar Lap 386/DOS-extender must be installed.

Return Registers: *unknown*.

Conflicts: DOS Set Interrupt Vector (chapter 8).

INTERRUPT 21h - Function 25h, Subfunction 19h
VMM - GET ADDITIONAL MEMORY ERROR INFO

Purpose: Retrieve more detailed information on the previous memory-related error.

Available on: 80386 or higher in protected mode.

Restrictions: Phar Lap 386/DOS-extender Virtual Memory Manager must be installed.

Registers at call:
AX = 2519h

Return Registers:
CF clear
    EAX = error code:
        0000h no error
        0001h out of physical memory
        0002h out of swap space (unable to grow swap file)
        0003h out of LDT entries and unable to grow LDT
        0004h unable to change extended memory allocation mark
        FFFFFFFFh   paging disabled

Details: VMM is the Virtual Memory Manager option.
Conflicts: DOS Set Interrupt Vector (chapter 8).

INTERRUPT 21h - Function 25h, Subfunction 1Ah
VMM - LOCK PAGES IN MEMORY

Purpose: Prevent a range of pages from being swapped out of memory when demand for memory exceeds the available physical memory.
Available on: 80386 or higher in protected mode.

Restrictions: Phar Lap 386/DOS-extender Virtual Memory Manager must be installed.

Registers at call:
AX = 251Ah
EDX = number of 4k pages to lock
if BL = 00h
    ECX = linear address of first page to lock
if BL = 01h
    ES:ECX -> pointer to first page to lock

Return Registers:
CF clear if successful
CF set on error
    EAX = error code
        08h insufficient memory
        09h invalid address range

Conflicts: DOS Set Interrupt Vector (chapter 8).
See Also: Function 25h Subfunction 1Bh, OS/386 Function EBh Subfunction 06h, DPMI INT 31h Function 06h Subfunction 00h (Chapter 11)

INTERRUPT 21h - Function 25h, Subfunction 1Bh
VMM - UNLOCK PAGES

Purpose: Allow a range of memory pages to be swapped out when demand for memory exceeds the available physical memory.
Available on: 80386 or higher in protected mode.

Restrictions: Phar Lap 386/DOS-extender Virtual Memory Manager must be installed.

Registers at call: AX = 251Bh
EDX = number of pages to unlock
if BL = 00h
    ECX = linear address of first page to unlock
if BL = 01h
    ES:ECX -> pointer to first page to unlock

Return Registers:
CF clear if successful
CF set on error
    EAX = error code
        09h invalid address range

Conflicts: DOS Set Interrupt Vector (chapter 8).
See Also: Function 25h Subfunction 1Ah, OS/386 Function EBh Subfunction 07h, DPMI INT 31h Function 06h Subfunction 01h (Chapter 11)

INTERRUPT 21h - Function 25h, Subfunction 1Dh
VMM - READ PAGE-TABLE ENTRY

Purpose: Determine the attributes and physical location of a 4K memory page.
Available on: 80386 or higher in protected mode.

Restrictions: Phar Lap 386/DOS-extender Virtual Memory Manager must be installed.

Registers at call:	**Return Registers:** *unknown.*
AX = 251Dh	
Others *unknown.*	

Conflicts: DOS Set Interrupt Vector (chapter 8).
See Also: Function 25h Subfunction 1Eh, OS/386 Function EBh Subfunction 00h, DPMI INT 31h Function 05h Subfunction 06h (Chapter 11)

INTERRUPT 21h - Function 25h, Subfunction 1Eh
VMM - WRITE PAGE-TABLE ENTRY

Purpose: Specify the attributes and physical location of a 4K memory page.

Available on: 80386 or higher in protected mode.	**Restrictions:** Phar Lap 386/DOS-extender Virtual Memory Manager must be installed.
Registers at call:	**Return Registers:** *unknown.*
AX = 251Eh	
Others *unknown.*	

Conflicts: DOS Set Interrupt Vector (chapter 8).
See Also: Function 25h Subfunction 1Dh, DPMI INT 31h Function 05h Subfunction 07h (Chapter 11)

INTERRUPT 21h - Function 25h, Subfunction 1Fh
VMM - EXHANGE TWO PAGE-TABLE ENTRIES

Purpose: Swap the physical location and attributes of two 4K memory pages.

Available on: 80386 or higher in protected mode.	**Restrictions:** Phar Lap 386/DOS-extender Virtual Memory Manager must be installed.
Registers at call:	**Return Registers:** *unknown.*
AX = 251Fh	
Others *unknown.*	

Conflicts: DOS Set Interrupt Vector (chapter 8).
See Also: Function 25h Subfunctions 1Dh and 1Eh

INTERRUPT 21h - Function 25h, Subfunction 20h
VMM - GET MEMORY STATISTICS

Purpose: Retrieve detailed information about memory use and availability.

Available on: 80386 or higher in protected mode.	**Restrictions:** Phar Lap 386/DOS-extender Virtual Memory Manager must be installed.
Registers at call:	**Return Registers:**
AX = 2520h	carry flag clear
DS:EDX -> pointer to buffer at least 100 bytes in size (Table 9-4)	
BL = 0 (don't reset VM stats), 1 (reset VM stats)	

Conflicts: DOS Set Interrupt Vector (chapter 8).

Table 9-4. Format of VM statistics buffer:

Offset	Size	Description
00h	DWORD	VM status
		0001h VM subsystem is present
		0000h VM not present
04h	DWORD	"nconvpg" number of conventional memory pages available
08h	DWORD	"nbimpg" number of Compaq built-in memory pages available
0Ch	DWORD	"nextpg" total number of extended memory pages
10h	DWORD	"extlim" extender memory pages limit
14h	DWORD	"aphyspg" number of physical memory pages allocated to appl
18h	DWORD	"alockpg" number of locked pages owned by application
1Ch	DWORD	"sysphyspg" number physical memory pages allocated to system

Table 9-4. Format of VM statistics buffer (continued)

Offset	Size	Description
20h	DWORD	"nfreepg" number of free physical pages; approx if EMS VCPI
24h	DWORD	linear address of beginning of application address space
28h	DWORD	linear address of end of application address space
2Ch	DWORD	number of seconds since last time VM stats were reset
30h	DWORD	number of page faults since last time
34h	DWORD	number of pages written to swap file since last time
38h	DWORD	number of reclaimed pages (page faults on swapped pages)
3Ch	DWORD	number of virtual pages allocated to the application
40h	DWORD	size in pages of swap file
44h	DWORD	number of system pages allocated with EMS calls
48h	DWORD	minimum number of conventional memory pages
4Ch	DWORD	maximum size in bytes to which swap file can be increased
50h	DWORD	"vmflags" bit 0 = 1 if page fault in progress
54h	16 BYTEs	reserved for future expansion (set to zero)

INTERRUPT 21h - Function 25h, Subfunction 21h
VMM - LIMIT PROGRAM'S EXTENDED MEMORY USAGE

Purpose: Specify the maximum amount of protected-mode memory a program may allocate.

Available on: 80386 or higher in protected mode.

Restrictions: Phar Lap 386/DOS-extender Virtual Memory Manager must be installed.

Registers at call:
AX = 2521h
EBX = max 4k pages of physical extended memory
   which program may use

Return Registers:
CF clear if successful
   EBX = maximum limit in pages
   ECX = minimum limit in pages
CF set on error
   EAX = error code
      08h insufficient memory or - nopage switch
        used

Conflicts: DOS Set Interrupt Vector (chapter 8).
See Also: Function 25h Subfunction 22h

INTERRUPT 21h - Function 25h, Subfunction 22h
VMM - SPECIFY ALTERNATE PAGE-FAULT HANDLER

Purpose: Indicate which routine is to be given control when a program accesses a page of memory which is currently swapped out.

Available on: 80386 or higher in protected mode.

Restrictions: Phar Lap 386/DOS-extender Virtual Memory Manager must be installed.

Registers at call:
AX =2522h
Others *unknown.*

Return Registers: *unknown.*

Conflicts: DOS Set Interrupt Vector (chapter 8).
See Also: Function 25h Subfunction 23h

INTERRUPT 21h - Function 25h, Subfunction 23h
VMM - SPECIFY OUT-OF-SWAP-SPACE HANDLER

Purpose: Indicate which routine is to be given control when virtual memory use exceeds the available swapping space.

Available on: 80386 or higher in protected mode.

Restrictions: Phar Lap 386/DOS-extender Virtual Memory Manager must be installed.

Registers at call:
AX = 2523h
Others *unknown.*

Return Registers: *unknown.*

Conflicts: DOS Set Interrupt Vector (chapter 8).
See Also: Function 25h Subfunction 22h

INTERRUPT 21h - Function 25h, Subfunction 24h
VMM - INSTALL PAGE-REPLACEMENT HANDLERS

Purpose: Specify routines to be called in order to determine which page(s) to swap out when memory demands exceed the available physical memory.
Available on: 80386 or higher in protected mode.

Restrictions: Phar Lap 386/DOS-extender Virtual Memory Manager must be installed.

Registers at call:
AX = 2524h
Others *unknown*.
Conflicts: DOS Set Interrupt Vector (chapter 8).

Return Registers: *unknown*.

INTERRUPT 21h - Function 25h, Subfunction 25h
VMM - LIMIT PROGRAM'S CONVENTIONAL MEMORY USAGE

Purpose: Specify the maximum amount of real-mode memory a program may allocate.
Available on: 80386 or higher in protected mode.

Restrictions: Phar Lap 386/DOS-extender Virtual Memory Manager must be installed.

Registers at call:
AX = 2525h
EBX = limit in 4k pages of physical conventional
   memory which program may use

Return Registers:
CF clear if successful
   EBX = maximum limit in pages
   ECX = minimum limit in pages
CF set on error
   EAX = error code
      08h insufficient memory or - nopage switch
         used

Conflicts: DOS Set Interrupt Vector (chapter 8).
See Also: Function 25h Subfunction 21h

INTERRUPT 21h - Function 25h, Subfunction 26h
GET CONFIGURATION INFORMATION

Purpose: Retrieve detailed information on the system's configuration.
Available on: 80386 or higher in protected mode.

Restrictions: Phar Lap 386/DOS-extender must be installed.

Registers at call:
AX = 2526h
others *unknown*.
Conflicts: DOS Set Interrupt Vector (chapter 8).

Return Registers: *unknown*.

INTERRUPT 21h - Function 25h, Subfunction C0h
ALLOCATE MS-DOS MEMORY BLOCK

Purpose: Request a block of real-mode memory from MSDOS.
Available on: 80386 or higher in protected mode.

Restrictions: Phar Lap 386/DOS-extender must be installed.

Registers at call:
AX = 25C0h
BX = number of 16-byte paragraphs of MS-DOS
   memory requested

Return Registers:
CF clear if successful
   AX = real-mode paragraph address of memory
CF set on error
   AX = error code
      07h MS-DOS memory control blocks
         destroyed

08h insufficient memory
BX = size in paragraphs of largest available
memory block

Conflicts: DOS Set Interrupt Vector (chapter 8).
See Also: Function 25h Subfunctions C1h and C2h

INTERRUPT 21h - Function 25h, Subfunction C1h
RELEASE MS-DOS MEMORY BLOCK

Purpose: Return a block of real-mode memory to MSDOS.
Available on: 80386 or higher in protected mode.

Registers at call:
AX = 25C1h
CX = real-mode paragraph address of memory
    block to free

Restrictions: Phar Lap 386/DOS-extender must be
    installed.

Return Registers:
CF clear if successful
    EAX destroyed
CF set on error
    AX = error code
        07h MS-DOS memory control blocks
            destroyed
        09h invalid memory block address in CX

Conflicts: DOS Set Interrupt Vector (chapter 8).
See Also: Function 25h Subfunctions C0h and C2h

INTERRUPT 21h - Function 25h, Subfunction C2h
MODIFY MS-DOS MEMORY BLOCK

Purpose: Change the size of a previously allocated real-mode memory block.
Available on: 80386 or higher in protected mode.

Registers at call:
AX = 25C2h
BX = new requested block size in paragraphs
CX = real-mode paragraph address of memory
    block to modify

Restrictions: Phar Lap 386/DOS-extender must be
    installed.

Return Registers:
CF clear if successful
    EAX destroyed
CF set on error
    AX = error code
        07h MS-DOS memory control blocks
            destroyed
        08h insufficient memory
        09h invalid memory block address in CX
    BX = size in paragraphs of largest available
        memory block

Conflicts: DOS Set Interrupt Vector (chapter 8).
See Also: Function 25h Subfunctions C0h and C1h

INTERRUPT 21h - Function 25h, Subfunction C3h
EXECUTE PROGRAM

Purpose: Start running the specified program with the given command line and environment.
Available on: 80386 or higher in protected mode.

Registers at call:
AX = 25C3h
ES:EBX -> pointer to parameter block (Table 9-5)
DS:EDX -> pointer to ASCIIZ program filename

Restrictions: Phar Lap 386/DOS-extender must be
    installed.

Return Registers:
CF clear if successful
    all registers unchanged
CF set on error
    EAX = error code:
        01h *function code in AL is invalid*

02h file not found or path invalid
05h access denied
08h insufficient memory to load program
0Ah environment invalid
0Bh invalid file format

Conflicts: DOS Set Interrupt Vector (chapter 8).

Table 9-5. Format of parameter block:

Offset	Size	Description
00h	DWORD	32-bit offset of environment string
04h	WORD	segment selector of environment string
06h	DWORD	32-bit offset of command-tail string
0Ah	WORD	segment selector of command-tail string

INTERRUPT 21h - Function 30h
GET DOS-EXTENDER VERSION

Purpose: Determine which version of the Phar Lap DOS extender is installed.

Available on: 80386 or higher in protected mode.

Restrictions: Phar Lap 386/DOS-extender must be installed.

Registers at call:
AH = 30h
EBX = 50484152h ("PHAR")

Return Registers: *unknown.*

Conflicts: DOS 2+ Get DOS Version (chapter 8), CTask 2.0+ (chapter 17), "Dutch-555" virus (chapter 34).

OS/286 and OS/386

OS/286 and OS/386 are 80286- and 80386-specific DOS extenders, respectively. Originally by AI Architects, they are now being marketed and further developed by Ergo Computing.

INTERRUPT 21h - Function E0h
INITIALIZE REAL PROCEDURE

Purpose: Prepare for calling a procedure running in real mode.

Available on: 80286 or higher.

Restrictions: OS/286 or OS/386 must be installed.

Registers at call:
AH = E0h
others *unknown.*

Return Registers: *unknown.*

Conflicts: DoubleDOS (chapter 17), Alloy NTNX (chapter 18), Novell NetWare 4.0 (chapter 20), "Jerusalem" and "Armagedon" viruses (chapter 34), "8-tunes" virus (chapter 34).

See Also: Functions E1h and E2h

INTERRUPT 21h - Function E1h
ISSUE REAL PROCEDURE CALL

Purpose: Call a procedure which runs in real mode.

Available on: 80286 or higher.

Restrictions: OS/286 or OS/386 must be installed.

Registers at call:
AH = E1h
others *unknown.*

Return Registers: *unknown.*

Details: This function is presumably available in protected mode only.

Conflicts: DoubleDOS (chapter 17), Novell NetWare 4.0 (chapter 20), "Mendoza", "Fu Manchu" viruses (chapter 34).

See Also: Functions E0h, E2h, and E3h, Phar Lap Function 25h Subfunction 0Eh DPMI INT 31h Function 03h Subfunction 01h (chapter 11)

INTERRUPT 21h - Function E2h
SET REAL PROCEDURE SIGNAL HANDLER

Purpose: Specify the real-mode function to receive control when a signal is issued.

Available on: 80286 or higher.　　　　　　　　　**Restrictions:** OS/286 or OS/386 must be installed.

Registers at call:　　　　　　　　　　　　　　**Return Registers:** *unknown.*

AH = E2h

others *unknown.*

Conflicts: DoubleDOS (chapter 17), Alloy NTNX (chapter 18), Novell NetWare 4.0 (chapter 20).

See Also: Functions E0h, E1h, and E6h

INTERRUPT 21h - Function E3h
ISSUE REAL INTERRUPT

Purpose: Invoke an interrupt handler running in real mode.

Available on: 80286 or higher.　　　　　　　　　**Restrictions:** OS/286 or OS/386 must be installed.

Registers at call:　　　　　　　　　　　　　　**Return Registers:** *unknown.*

AH = E3h

AL = interrupt number

others *unknown.*

Details: This function is presumably available in protected mode only.

Conflicts: None known.

See Also: Function E1h, Phar Lap Function 25h Subfunction 11h, DPMI INT 31h Function 03h Subfunction 00h (chapter 11)

INTERRUPT 21h - Function E4h, Subfunction 00h
CHAIN TO REAL-MODE HANDLER

Purpose: Pass an interrupt down to a chained handler running in real mode.

Available on: 80286 or higher.　　　　　　　　　**Restrictions:** OS/286 or OS/386 must be installed.

Registers at call:　　　　　　　　　　　　　　**Return Registers:** *unknown.*

AX = E400h

others *unknown.*

Details: This function is presumably available in protected mode only.

Conflicts: None known.

INTERRUPT 21h - Function E4h, Subfunction 02h
SET PROTECTED-MODE TASK GATE

Purpose: Specify a task gate *for calls between processes.*

Available on: 80286 or higher.　　　　　　　　　**Restrictions:** OS/286 or OS/386 must be installed.

Registers at call:　　　　　　　　　　　　　　**Return Registers:** *unknown.*

AX = E402h

others *unknown.*

Details: This function is presumably available in protected mode only.

Conflicts: None known.

See Also: Function E4h Subfunction 03h

INTERRUPT 21h - Function E4h, Subfunction 03h
REMOVE PROTECTED-MODE TASK GATE

Purpose: Delete a previously-created task gate.

Available on: 80286 or higher.　　　　　　　　　**Restrictions:** OS/286 or OS/386 must be installed.

Registers at call:　　　　　　　　　　　　　　**Return Registers:** *unknown.*

AX = E403h

others *unknown.*

Details: This function is presumably available in protected mode only.

Conflicts: None known.
See Also: Function E4h Subfunction 02h

INTERRUPT 21h - Function E5h, Subfunction 00h
HEAP MANAGEMENT STRATEGY

Purpose: Determine the manner in which the heap of allocatable memory is managed.
Available on: 80286 or higher.   **Restrictions:** OS/286 or OS/386 must be installed.
Registers at call: **Return Registers:** *unknown.*
AX = E500h
others *unknown.*
Conflicts: None known.
See Also: Function E5h Subfunction 01h

INTERRUPT 21h - Function E5h, Subfunction 01h
FORCE HEAP COMPACTION

Purpose: Consolidate free areas of memory.
Available on: 80286 or higher.   **Restrictions:** OS/286 or OS/386 must be installed.
Registers at call: **Return Registers:** *unknown.*
AX = E501h
others *unknown.*
Conflicts: None known.
See Also: Function E5h Subfunction 00h

INTERRUPT 21h - Function E6h
ISSUE REAL PROCEDURE SIGNAL FROM PROTECTED MODE

Purpose: Send a signal which will invoke a previously-defined function in real mode.
Available on: 80286 or higher.   **Restrictions:** OS/286 or OS/386 must be installed.
Registers at call: **Return Registers:** *unknown.*
AH = E6h
others *unknown.*
Details: This function is presumably available in protected mode only.
Conflicts: None known.
See Also: Function E2h

INTERRUPT 21h - Function E7h
CREATE CODE SEGMENT

Purpose: Create a new segment descriptor for a code segment and return its selector.
Available on: 80286 or higher.   **Restrictions:** OS/286 or OS/386 must be installed.
Registers at call: **Return Registers:** *unknown.*
AH = E7h
others *unknown.*
Conflicts: None known.
See Also: Functions E8h, E9h and EAh

INTERRUPT 21h - Function E8h
SEGMENT CREATION

Purpose: Create a new segment descriptor of a specified type and return its selector.
Available on: 80286 or higher.   **Restrictions:** OS/286 or OS/386 must be installed.
Registers at call: **Return Registers:** *unknown.*
AH = E8h
AL = type
   00h data segment
   01h data window/alias

02h real segment
03h real window/alias
06h shareable segment
others *unknown*.
Conflicts: None known.
See Also: Functions E7h, E9h and EAh

INTERRUPT 21h - Function E9h
CHANGE SEGMENTS

Purpose: Modify the descriptor corresponding to a segment selector.
Available on: 80286 or higher.   **Restrictions:** OS/286 or OS/386 must be installed.
Registers at call: **Return Registers:** *unknown*.
AH = E9h
AL = function:
    01h change code segment parameters
    02h change data segment parameters
    05h adjust segment limit
    06h change segment base address
others *unknown*.
Details: This function is presumably available in protected mode only.
Conflicts: None known.
See Also: Functions E7h, E8h, EAh, and EDh, DPMI INT 31h Function 00h Subfunctions 07h-09h (chapter 11)

INTERRUPT 21h - Function EAh
ALLOCATE HUGE SEGMENT

Purpose: Allocate a block of memory larger than 64K.
Available on: 80286 or higher.   **Restrictions:** OS/286 or OS/386 must be installed.
Registers at call: **Return Registers:** *unknown*.
AH = EAh
others *unknown*.
Details: This function is presumably available in protected mode only.
Conflicts: None known.
See Also: Functions E7h, E8h and E9h

INTERRUPT 21h - Function EBh, Subfunction 00h
VMM - GET A PAGE TABLE ENTRY BY LINEAR ADDRESS

Purpose: Determine the attributes and physical location of a 4K memory page.
Available on: 80386 or higher.   **Restrictions:** OS/386 Virtual Memory Manager must
                                                             be installed.
Registers at call: **Return Registers:** *unknown*.
AX = EB00h
others *unknown*.
Details: This function is presumably available in protected mode only.
Conflicts: None known.
See Also: Function EBh Subfunctions 02h and 04h, Phar Lap Function 25h Subfunction 1Dh, DPMI INT 31h Function 05h Subfunction 06h (Chapter 11)

INTERRUPT 21h - Function EBh, Subfunction 02h
VMM - GET A PAGE TABLE ENTRY BY 16-BIT SEGMENT:OFFSET

Purpose: Determine the attributes and physical location of a 4K memory page.
Available on: 80386 or higher.   **Restrictions:** OS/386 Virtual Memory Manager must
                                                             be installed.

Registers at call: **Return Registers:** *unknown*.
AX = EB02h
others *unknown*.
Details: This function is presumably available in protected mode only.
Conflicts: None known.
See Also: Function EBh Subfunctions 00h and 04h

INTERRUPT 21h - Function EBh, Subfunction 03h
VMM - FREE MAPPED PAGES

Purpose: Remove the association between a range of logical addresses and physical memory.
Available on: 80386 or higher.   **Restrictions:** OS/386 Virtual Memory Manager must
                                                 be installed.

Registers at call: **Return Registers:** *unknown*.
AX = EB03h
others *unknown*.
Details: This function is presumably available in protected mode only.
Conflicts: None known.
See Also: Function EBh Subfunction 05h, DPMI INT 31h Function 08h Subfunction 01h (Chapter 11)

INTERRUPT 21h - Function EBh, Subfunction 04h
VMM - GET A PAGE TABLE ENTRY BY 32-BIT SEGMENT:OFFSET

Purpose: Determine the attributes and physical location of a 4K memory page.
Available on: 80386 or higher.   **Restrictions:** OS/386 Virtual Memory Manager must
                                                 be installed.

Registers at call: **Return Registers:** *unknown*.
AX = EB04h
others *unknown*.
Details: This function is presumably available in protected mode only.
Conflicts: None known.
See Also: Function EBh Subfunctions 00h and 02h

INTERRUPT 21h - Function EBh, Subfunction 05h
VMM - MAP PAGES

Purpose: Associate physical memory with a range of logical addresses.
Available on: 80386 or higher.   **Restrictions:** OS/386 Virtual Memory Manager must
                                                 be installed.

Registers at call: **Return Registers:** *unknown*.
AX = EB05h
others *unknown*.
Details: This function is presumably available in protected mode only.
Conflicts: None known.
See Also: Function EBh Subfunction 03h, DPMI INT 31h Function 08h Subfunction 00h (Chapter 11)

INTERRUPT 21h - Function EBh, Subfunction 06h
VMM - LOCK PAGES IN MEMORY

Purpose: Prevent a range of pages from being swapped out of memory when demand for memory exceeds the available physical memory.
Available on: 80386 or higher.   **Restrictions:** OS/386 Virtual Memory Manager must
                                                 be installed.

Registers at call: **Return Registers:** *unknown*.
AX = EB06h
others *unknown*.
Details: This function is presumably available in protected mode only.

Conflicts: None known.
See Also: Function EBh Subfunction 07h, Phar Lap Function 25h Subfunction 1Ah, DPMI INT 31h Function 06h Subfunction 00h (Chapter 11)

INTERRUPT 21h - Function EBh, Subfunction 07h
VMM - UNLOCK MEMORY PAGES

Purpose: Allow a range of memory pages to be swapped out when demand for memory exceeds the available physical memory.

Available on: 80386 or higher.

Restrictions: OS/386 Virtual Memory Manager must be installed.

Registers at call:
AX = EB07h
others *unknown.*

Return Registers: *unknown.*

Details: This function is presumably available in protected mode only.
Conflicts: None known.
See Also: Function EBh Subfunction 06h, Phar Lap Function 25h Subfunction 1Bh, DPMI INT 31h Function 06h Subfunction 01h (Chapter 11)

INTERRUPT 21h - Function ECh
BLOCK TRANSFER

Purpose: Copy a section of memory.

Available on: 80286 or higher.

Restrictions: OS/286 or OS/386 must be installed.

Registers at call:
AH =ECh
others *unknown.*

Return Registers: *unknown.*

Conflicts: None known.

INTERRUPT 21h - Function EDh
GET SEGMENT OR WINDOW DESCRIPTOR

Purpose: Determine the location, size, and attributes of a memory segment.

Available on: 80286 or higher.

Restrictions: OS/286 or OS/386 must be installed.

Registers at call:
AH = EDh
others *unknown.*

Return Registers: *unknown.*

Details: This function is presumably available in protected mode only.
Conflicts: None known.
See Also: Function E9h

GO32.EXE
GO32 is a DOS extender written to support an 80386 port of the Free Software Foundation's GNU C and C++ compilers made by DJ Delorie.

INTERRUPT 21h - Function FFh, Subfunctions 01h to 07h
DOS EXTENSIONS

Purpose: Simplify access to certain frequently-used MSDOS functions from protected mode.

Available on: 80386 or higher.

Restrictions: Must be operating under DJ Delorie's GO32 DOS extender.

Registers at call:
AH = FFh
AL = subfunction
  01h create file
  02h open file
  03h get file statistics

Return Registers: varies by function

04h get time of day
05h set time of day
06h stat
07h system
other varies by function
Conflicts: Topware Network Operating System (chapter 27), "Sunday", "PSQR/1720", and "Ontario" viruses (chapter 34), CED (chapter 36), DOSED (chapter 36).
See Also: INT 10h Function FFh (chapter 5).

Ergo DOS Extenders

Ergo Computing produces a number of DOS extenders; the following call is a general installation check for its extenders.

INTERRUPT 2Fh - Function A1h
Ergo DOS extenders - INSTALLATION CHECK

Purpose: Determine whether one of the DOS extenders produced by Ergo Computing is installed.
Available on: 80286 or higher.   **Restrictions:** none.
Registers at call: **Return Registers:**
AH = A1h   If installed, first four bytes of ES:DI buffer are "IABH"
AL = which:
  FEh OS/286,OS/386
  FFh HummingBoard DOS extender
BX = 0081h
ES:DI -> 16-byte buffer
Conflicts: None known, but see Table 1-3 in chapter 1.
See Also: Function FBA1h, INT 15h Function BFh Subfunction 02h

Phar Lap DOS Extenders

Recent versions of Phar Lap's DOS extenders have added the following call, which is a general installation check for its extenders.

INTERRUPT 2Fh - Function EDh, Subfunction 00h
DOS EXTENDER INSTALLATION CHECK

Purpose: Determine whether a recent version of one of Phar Lap's DOS extenders is installed.
Available on: 80286 or higher.   **Restrictions:** none.
Registers at call: **Return Registers:**
AX = ED00h   AL = status
BL = DOS extender   00h not installed
  01h 286dosx v1.3+ (Software Development Kit)   FFh installed
  02h 286dosx v1.3+ (Run-Time Kit)   SI = 5048h ("PH")
  03h 386dosx v4.0+ (SDK)   DI = 4152h ("AR")
  04h 386dosx v4.0+ (RTK)   CH = major version number
                                                     CL = minor version number
                                                     DX = flags
                                                       bit 0: running under DPMI
                                                       bit 1: running under Phar Lap VMM
Conflicts: None known.
See Also: Function A1h, Function F1h Subfunction 00h, Function FBA1h

Generic DOS extender installation check

A number of DOS-extender vendors have agreed upon the following installation check, which will indicate whether a DOS extender is present, though not which one. To determine which DOS extender is present, a program must still query each installation check individually.

INTERRUPT 2Fh - Function F1h
DOS EXTENDER INSTALLATION CHECK

Purpose: Determine whether a DOS extender is present.

Available on: 80286 or higher.

Registers at call:
AX = F100h

Restrictions: none.

Return Registers:
AL = FFh if DOS extender present
SI = 444Fh ("DO")
DI = 5358h ("SX")

Details: This function is supported or soon to be supported by DOS extenders from Phar Lap, Rational Systems, Ergo Computing, and IGC.

Conflicts: None known.

See Also: Function A1h, Function EDh Subfunction 00h, Function FBh Subfunction A1h, INT 15h Function BFh Subfunction 02h

Borland DOS Extender

With the introduction of Turbo Pascal version 6 and Borland C++ in February 1991, Borland International added a DOS extender to permit its compilers to compile files too large to be compiled in real mode. The protected-mode versions of the compilers will automatically load the extender, but the TKERNEL program may also be installed as a TSR to speed up the loading of the compiler.

INTERRUPT 2Fh - Function FBA1h, Subfunction 0081h
TKERNEL - INSTALLATION CHECK

Purpose: Determine whether TKERNEL is installed.

Available on: All machines.

Registers at call:
AX = FBA1h
BX = 0081h
ES:DI -> 16-byte buffer

Restrictions: none.

Return Registers:
If installed, first four bytes of ES:DI buffer are "IABH"

Conflicts: None known, but see Table 1-3 in chapter 1.

See Also: Function A1h, Function FBA1h Subfunctions 0082h and 0084h, INT 15h Function BFh Subfunction 02h

INTERRUPT 2Fh - Function FBA1h, Subfunction 0082h
TKERNEL - GET ENTRY POINT

Purpose: Determine the address to call for the TKERNEL API.

Available on: All machines.

Registers at call:
AX = FBA1h
BX = 0082h
ES:DI -> response buffer (Table 9-6)

Restrictions: TKERNEL must be installed.

Return Registers:
ES:DI buffer filled

Conflicts: None known, but see Table 1-3 in chapter 1.

See Also: Function FBA1h Subfunctions 0081h and 0084h

Table 9-6. Format of response buffer:

Offset	Size	Description
00h	4 BYTEs	signature "IABH"
04h	DWORD	pointer to FAR extender entry point

Call entry point with:
AX = function number
　　　　0000h to 0026h *unknown.*
　　　　FFFFh *unknown.*
BX:SI -> *unknown.*

CX:DI -> *unknown*.
other

Returns with:
AX = 0001h

INTERRUPT 2Fh - Function FBA1h, Subfunction 0084h
TKERNEL - UNINSTALL

Purpose: Remove TKERNEL from memory.
Available on: All machines.
Registers at call:
AX = FBA1h
BX = 0084h
ES:DI -> response buffer (Table 9-7)
Conflicts: None known, but see Table 1-3 in chapter 1.
See Also: Function FBA1h Subfunctions 0081h and 0084h

Restrictions: TKERNEL must be installed.
Return Registers:
ES:DI buffer filled

Table 9-7. Format of response buffer:

Offset	Size	Description
00h	4 BYTEs	signature "IABH"
04h	WORD	success indicator:
		0001h failed (INT 2Fh hooked by another program
		unchanged if successful

Oracle SQL Protected Mode Executive

INTERRUPT 63h
Oracle SQL Protected Mode Executive - Unknown Function

Purpose: *unknown*.
Available on: 80286 or higher.

Restrictions: Oracle SQL Protected Mode Executive must be active.

Registers at call: *unknown*.
Return Registers: *unknown*.
Conflicts: Adaptec and OMTI controllers - DRIVE 0 DATA (chapter 7), 4+Power FLOPPY CONTROLLER (chapter 7). Also see table 1-2 in chapter 1.

INTERRUPT 64h
Oracle SQL Protected Mode Executive - Unknown Function

Purpose: *unknown*.
Available on: 80286 or higher.

Restrictions: Oracle SQL Protected Mode Executive must be active.

Registers at call: *unknown*.
Return Registers: *unknown*.
Conflicts: Adaptec controllers - DRIVE 1 DATA (chapter 7). Also see table 1-2 in chapter 1.

DBOS
DBOS is a DOS extender written at the University of Salford in England.

INTERRUPT 78h - Function 03h
SWITCH TO PROTECTED MODE

Purpose: Begin execution in protected mode.
Available on: 80286 or higher.

Restrictions: University of Salford DBOS DOS extender must be active.

Registers at call:
AH = 03h
other *unknown.*

Return Registers: *unknown.*

Details: DBOS supports functions 00h through 50h, but no information was available on the functions not listed here at the time of writing.
Conflicts: TARGA.DEV
See Also: Functions 1Eh and 22h, INT 15h Function 89h (chapter 3)

INTERRUPT 78h - Function 1Eh
SET REAL-MODE MEMORY SIZE

Purpose: Specify how much real-mode memory to leave free when running FTN77 programs.
Available on: 80286 or higher.

Restrictions: University of Salford DBOS DOS extender must be active.
Return Registers: *unknown.*

Registers at call:
AH = 1Eh
other *unknown.*

Details: DBOS supports functions 00h through 50h, but no information was available on the functions not listed here at the time of writing.
Conflicts: None known.
See Also: Functions 03h and 22h

INTERRUPT 78h - Function 22h
UNINSTALL

Purpose: Remove DBOS from memory.
Available on: 80286 or higher.

Restrictions: University of Salford DBOS DOS extender must be active.
Return Registers: *unknown.*

Registers at call:
AH = 22h
other *unknown.*

Details: DBOS supports functions 00h through 50h, but no information was available on the functions not listed here at the time of writing.
Conflicts: None known.
See Also: Functions 03h and 1Eh

Chapter 10

EMS, XMS, and VCPI

In chapter 9, DOS extenders were presented as a means of using more memory than is ordinarily available to real-mode DOS programs. This chapter covers three additional ways to access additional memory.

Because of the numerical ordering of the interrupts, the three sections of this chapter are arranged in the order XMS, EMS, and VCPI.

XMS

The Extended Memory Specification gives access to extended memory and noncontiguous, non-EMS memory above the 640K point. It provides controlled access to extended memory, unlike BIOS INT 15h Functions 87h and 88h, thus permitting applications to share extended memory without conflicts. XMS is provided by Microsoft's HIMEM.SYS and most 386 memory managers (such as 386^{MAX} or QEMM-386).

INTERRUPT 2Fh - Function 43h, Subfunction 00h
INSTALLATION CHECK

Purpose: Determine whether XMS high-memory management software is present.

Available on: All machines.

Registers at call:
AX = 4300h

Restrictions: none.

Return Registers:
AL = 80h XMS driver installed
AL<>80h no driver

Details: This installation check does not follow the format used by other software.
Conflicts: None known.
See Also: Function 43h Subfunction 10h

INTERRUPT 2Fh - Function 43h, Subfunction 10h
GET XMS DRIVER ADDRESS

Purpose: Obtain address of XMS driver in order to use its functions.

Available on: 80286 and up systems only.

Registers at call:
AX = 4310h

Restrictions: XMS software must be installed.

Return Registers:
ES:BX - > driver entry point

Details: HIMEM.SYS requires at least 256 bytes of free stack space. Perform a FAR call to the driver entry point with AH set to the function code.

Code/Function/Regs:

00h Get XMS version number

01h Request High Memory Area (1M to 1M + 64K)
DX = memory in bytes (for TSR or device drivers)
    FFFFh if application program

Returns:

AX = XMS version (in BCD)
BX = internal revision number
DX = 0001h if HMA (1M to 1M + 64K) exists
      0000h if HMA does not exist
AX = 0001h success
      0000h failure
BL = error code (Table 10-1)

02h Release High Memory Area

AX = 0001h success
    0000h failure
        BL = error code (Table 10-1)

03h Global enable A20, for using the HMA

AX = 0001h success
    0000h failure
        BL = error code (see below)

04h Global disable A20

AX = 0001h success
    0000h failure
        BL = error code (see below)

05h Local enable A20, for direct access to
     extended memory

AX = 0001h success
    0000h failure
        BL = error code (see below)

06h Local disable A20

AX = 0001h success
    0000h failure
        BL = error code (see below)

07h Query A20 state

AX = 0001h enabled
    0000h disabled
        BL = error code (0 = successful)

08h Query free extended memory, not counting
     HMA

AX = size of largest extended memory block in K
DX = total extended memory in K
BL = error code (see below)

09h Allocate extended memory block
    DX = Kbytes needed

AX = 0001h success
        DX = handle for memory block
    0000h failure
        BL = error code (see below)

0Ah Free extended memory block
    DX = handle of block to free

AX = 0001h success
    0000h failure
BL = error code (see below)

0Bh Move extended memory block
    DS:SI -> EMM structure (Table 10-2). **Note:** if
    either handle is 0000h, the corresponding
    offset is considered to be an absolute
    segment:offset address in directly
    addressable memory

AX = 0001h success
    0000h failure
BL = error code (see below)

0Ch Lock extended memory block
    DX = handle of block to lock

AX = 0001h success
        DX:BX = 32-bit linear address of locked
        block
    0000h failure
        BL = error code (see below)

0Dh Unlock extended memory block
    DX = handle of block to unlock

AX = 0001h success
    0000h failure
BL = error code (see below)

0Eh Get handle information
     DX = handle for which to get
          info

AX = 0001h success
            BH = block's lock count
            BL = number of free handles left
            DX = block size in K
      0000h failure
            BL = error code (see below)

0Fh Reallocate extended memory block
     DX = handle of block
     BX = new size of block in K

AX = 0001h success
      0000h failure
BL = error code (see below)

10h Request upper memory block (nonEMS
          memory above 640K)
     DX = size of block in paragraphs

AX = 0001h success
            BX = segment address of UMB
            DX = actual size of block
      0000h failure
            BL = error code (see below)
            DX = largest available block

11h Release upper memory block
     DX = segment address of UMB to release

AX = 0001h success
      0000h failure
BL = error code (see below)

Conflicts: None known.
See Also: Function 43h Subfunction 00h

Table 10-1. Values of error codes returned in BL:

80h	Function not implemented	A3h	Source handle is invalid
81h	Vdisk was detected	A4h	Source offset is invalid
82h	An A20 error occurred	A5h	Destination handle is invalid
8Eh	a general driver error	A6h	Destination offset is invalid
8Fh	unrecoverable driver error	A7h	Length is invalid
90h	HMA does not exist	A8h	Move has an invalid overlap
91h	HMA is already in use	A9h	Parity error occurred
92h	DX is less than the /HMAMIN= parameter	AAh	Block is not locked
93h	HMA is not allocated	ABh	Block is locked
94h	A20 line still enabled	ACh	Block lock count overflowed
A0h	all extended memory is allocated	ADh	Lock failed
A1h	all available extended memory handles are allocated	B0h	Only a smaller UMB is available
		B1h	No UMB's are available
A2h	Invalid handle	B2h	UMB segment number is invalid

Table 10-2. Format of EMM structure:

Offset	Size	Description
00h	DWORD	number of bytes to move (must be even)
04h	WORD	source handle
06h	DWORD	offset into source block
0Ah	WORD	destination handle
0Ch	DWORD	offset into destination block

LIM EMS

The Lotus/Intel/Microsoft Expanded Memory Specification 3.2 is the original interface to bank-switched memory allowing programs to use more memory than is addressable in real mode. Two additional variants of the specification (EEMS and LIM EMS 4.0) were later created to address shortcomings in the original standard. The calls in this section are supported by all three extant variants of EMS; the following sections cover additional calls supported by EEMS and EMS 4.0.

INTERRUPT 67h - Function 40h
GET MANAGER STATUS

Purpose: Determine whether the expanded memory hardware is functioning properly.

Available on: All machines.

Restrictions: This call can only be used after establishing that the EMS driver is in fact present.

Registers at call:
AH = 40h

Return Registers:
AH = status
   00h successful
   80h internal error
   81h hardware malfunction
   84h undefined function requested by application

Conflicts: None known.

INTERRUPT 67h - Function 41h
GET PAGE FRAME SEGMENT

Purpose: Determine the segment address at which the first four 16K physical pages are located.

Available on: All machines.

Restrictions: LIM EMS driver must be installed.

Registers at call:
AH = 41h

Return Registers:
AH = 00h function successful
   BX = segment of page frame
AH = error code (see Function 40h)

Details: EEMS and LIM EMS 4 may provide additional physical pages into which EMS may be mapped; these additional pages need not be contiguous or even located at a higher address than the page frame.

Conflicts: None known.

See Also: EEMS Function 68h, LIM EMS 4 Function 58h

INTERRUPT 67h - Function 42h
GET NUMBER OF PAGES

Purpose: Determine how many 16K pages of memory are available for allocation, and the total number of pages present in the system.

Available on: All machines.

Restrictions: LIM EMS driver must be installed.

Registers at call:
AH = 42h

Return Registers:
AH = 00h function successful
   BX = number of unallocated pages
   DX = total number of pages
AH = error code (see Function 40h)

Conflicts: None known.

INTERRUPT 67h - Function 43h
GET HANDLE AND ALLOCATE MEMORY

Purpose: Request a number of 16K logical pages and associate them with a unique identifier which will later be used to manipulate those pages.

Available on: All machines.

Restrictions: LIM EMS driver must be installed.

Registers at call:
AH = 43h
BX = number of logical pages to allocate

Return Registers:
AH = status
    00h function successful
        DX = handle
    80h internal error
    81h hardware malfunction
    84h undefined function requested
    85h no more handles available
    87h more pages requested than physically exist
    88h more pages requested than currently available
    89h zero pages requested

Conflicts: None known.
See Also: Function 45h

INTERRUPT 67h - Function 44h
MAP MEMORY

Purpose: Specify an association between a physical page of addresses and a logical page of expanded memory.
Available on: All machines.   **Restrictions:** LIM EMS driver must be installed.
Registers at call: **Return Registers:**
AH = 44h   AH = status
AL = physical page number (0-3)   00h function successful
BX = logical page number   80h internal error
DX = handle   81h hardware malfunction
                                                      83h invalid handle
                                                      84h undefined function requested
                                                      8Ah invalid logical page number
                                                      8Bh illegal physical-page number

Conflicts: None known.
See Also: Function 69h

INTERRUPT 67h - Function 45h
RELEASE HANDLE AND MEMORY

Purpose: Deallocate pages previously associated with an expanded memory identifier and invalidate the identifier.
Available on: All machines.   **Restrictions:** LIM EMS driver must be installed.
Registers at call: **Return Registers:**
AH = 45h   AH = status
DX = EMM handle   00h successful
                                                      80h internal error
                                                      81h hardware malfunction
                                                      83h invalid handle
                                                      84h undefined function requested
                                                      86h error in save or restore of mapping context

Conflicts: None known.
See Also: Function 43h

INTERRUPT 67h - Function 46h
GET EMM VERSION

Purpose: Determine which version of the memory management software is installed.
Available on: All machines.   **Restrictions:** LIM EMS driver must be installed.

Registers at call:
AH = 46h

Return Registers:
AH = status
  00h successful
    AL = EMM version number (high
      nybble=major, low nybble=minor)
  80h internal error
  81h hardware malfunction
  84h undefined function requested

Conflicts: None known.

INTERRUPT 67h - Function 47h
SAVE MAPPING CONTEXT

Purpose: Save the current set of associations between physical and logical pages for later restoration.

Available on: All machines.

Registers at call:
AH = 47h
DX = handle

Restrictions: LIM EMS driver must be installed.

Return Registers:
AH = status
  00h successful
  80h internal error
  81h hardware malfunction
  83h invalid handle
  84h undefined function requested
  8Ch page-mapping hardware state save area is full
  8Dh save of mapping context failed

Conflicts: None known.
See Also: Function 47h

INTERRUPT 67h - Function 48h
RESTORE MAPPING CONTEXT

Purpose: Restore the most recently saved set of associations between physical and logical pages.

Available on: All machines.

Registers at call:
AH = 48h
DX = handle

Restrictions: LIM EMS driver must be installed.
AH = status
  00h successful
  80h internal error
  81h hardware malfunction
  83h invalid handle
  84h undefined function requested
  8Eh restore of mapping context failed

Conflicts: None known.
See Also: Function 47h

INTERRUPT 67h - Function 49h
reserved - GET I/O PORT ADDRESSES

Purpose: This function has been removed from the specification.

Available on: All machines.

Registers at call:
AH = 49h

Restrictions: LIM EMS driver must be installed.
Return Registers: n/a

Details: This function was defined in EMS 3.0, but became undocumented in EMS 3.2.
Conflicts: None known.

INTERRUPT 67h - Function 4Ah
reserved - GET TRANSLATION ARRAY

Purpose: This function has been removed from the specification.

Available on: All machines.

Restrictions: LIM EMS driver must be installed.

Registers at call: **Return Registers:** n/a
AH = 4Ah
Details: This function was defined in EMS 3.0, but became undocumented in EMS 3.2.
Conflicts: None known.

INTERRUPT 67h - Function 4Bh
GET NUMBER OF EMM HANDLES

Purpose: Determine how many expanded memory handles are currently in use.
Available on: All machines.   **Restrictions:** LIM EMS driver must be installed.
Registers at call: **Return Registers:**
AH = 4Bh   AH = status
          00h successful
               BX = number of EMM handles
          80h internal error
          81h hardware malfunction
          83h invalid handle
          84h undefined function requested

Conflicts: None known.

INTERRUPT 67h - Function 4Ch
GET PAGES OWNED BY HANDLE

Purpose: Determine how many pages of memory are allocated to the specified expanded memory handle.
Available on: All machines.   **Restrictions:** LIM EMS driver must be installed.
Registers at call: **Return Registers:**
AH = 4Ch   AH = status
DX = EMM handle

          00h successful
               BX = number of logical pages
          80h internal error
          81h hardware malfunction
          83h invalid handle
          84h undefined function requested

Conflicts: None known.
See Also: Function 4Dh

INTERRUPT 67h - Function 4Dh
GET PAGES FOR ALL HANDLES

Purpose: Determine all active expanded memory handles and how many pages of memory are allocated to each.
Available on: All machines.   **Restrictions:** LIM EMS driver must be installed.
Registers at call: **Return Registers:**
AH = 4Dh   AH = status
ES:DI -> array to receive information   00h successful
               BX = number of active EMM handles
                  array filled with 2-word entries, consisting
                  of a handle and the number of pages
                  allocated to that handle
          80h internal error
          81h hardware malfunction
          84h undefined function requested

Conflicts: None known.
See Also: Function 4Ch

INTERRUPT 67h - Function 4Eh
GET OR SET PAGE MAP

Purpose: Save or restore the current set of associations between physical and logical pages using an application-provided data area.

Available on: All machines.

Registers at call:

AH = 4Eh

AL = 00h if getting mapping registers
   01h if setting mapping registers
   02h if getting and setting mapping registers at
     once
   03h if getting size of page-mapping array
        DS:SI -> array holding information
        (AL=01/02)
        ES:DI -> array to receive information
        (AL=00/02)

Restrictions: LIM EMS driver must be installed.

Return Registers:

AH = status
   00h successful
     array pointed to by ES:DI receives mapping
      info (AL=00h/02h)
     AL = bytes in page-mapping array (AL=03h
      only)
   80h internal error
   81h hardware malfunction
   84h undefined function requested
   8Fh undefined subfunction parameter
   A3h contents of source array corrupted (EMS 4.0?)

Details: This function was designed to be used by multitasking operating systems and should not ordinarily be used by appplication software.

Conflicts: None known.

See Also: Function 4Fh

LIM EMS 4.0

EMS version 4.0 is the third variant of the Expanded Memory Specification to be defined. It adds most of the capabilities of EEMS to the basic EMS 3.2 function calls, then extends the command set even further. The functions in this section are only available with drivers conforming to version 4.0 of the specification. It should be noted, however, that drivers can conform to EMS 4.0 without having the extra hardware mandated by EEMS; this creates confusion when attempting to select an expanded memory board, since some programs such as multitaskers require more than four mappable pages.

INTERRUPT 67h - Function 4Fh
GET/SET PARTIAL PAGE MAP

Purpose: Save or restore the current associations between physical and logical pages, using an application-provided data area, for a subset of all physical pages.

Available on: All machines.

Registers at call:

AH = 4Fh

AL = subfunction:

00h get partial page map
   DS:SI -> structure containing list of segments
     whose mapping contexts are to be saved
   ES:DI -> array to receive page map

01h set partial page map
   DS:SI -> structure containing saved partial page
     map

02h get size of partial page map
   BX = number of mappable segments in the
     partial map to be saved

Conflicts: None known.

Restrictions: LIM 4.0 EMS driver must be installed.

Return Registers:

AH = status
   00h successful
   80h internal error
   81h hardware malfunction
   84h undefined function requested
   8Bh one of specified segments is not mappable
   8Fh undefined subfunction parameter
   A3h contents of partial page map corrupted or
      count of mappable segments exceeds total
      number of mappable segments in system
AL = size of partial page map for subfunction 02h

See Also: Function 4Eh

INTERRUPT 67h - Function 50h
MAP/UNMAP MULTIPLE HANDLE PAGES

Purpose: Create or remove associations between a set of physical and logical pages.

Available on: All machines.

Registers at call:
AH = 50h
AL = subfunction
    00h use physical page numbers
    01h use segment adresses
DX = handle
CX = number of entries in array
DS:SI -> mapping array

Restrictions: LIM 4.0 EMS driver must be installed.

Return Registers:
AH = status
    00h successful
    80h internal error
    81h hardware malfunction
    83h invalid handle
    84h undefined function requested
    8Ah one or more logical pages are invalid
    8Bh one or more physical pages are invalid
    8Fh invalid subfunction

Conflicts: None known.
See Also: Function 40h

INTERRUPT 67h - Function 51h
REALLOCATE PAGES

Purpose: Modify the number of logical pages assigned to an expanded memory handle.

Available on: All machines.

Registers at call:
AH = 51h
DX = handle
BX = number of pages to be allocated to handle

Restrictions: LIM 4.0 EMS driver must be installed.

Return Registers:
BX = actual number of pages allocated to handle
AH = status
    00h successful
    80h internal error
    81h hardware malfunction
    83h invalid handle
    84h undefined function requested
    87h more pages requested than present in system
    88h more pages requested than currently available

Conflicts: None known.

INTERRUPT 67h - Function 52h
GET/SET HANDLE ATTRIBUTES

Purpose: Determine or change the attribute associated with an expanded memory handle.

Available on: All machines.

Registers at call:
AH = 52h
DX = handle
AL = subfunction:

Restrictions: LIM 4.0 EMS driver must be installed.

Return Registers:
AH = status
    00h successful
    80h internal error
    81h hardware malfunction
    83h invalid handle
    84h undefined function requested
    8Fh undefined subfunction
    90h undefined attribute type
    91h feature not supported

00h get handle attributes

AL = attribute
    00h handle is volatile
    01h handle is nonvolatile

01h set handle attributes
    BL = new attribute:
        00h handle is volatile
        01h handle is nonvolatile
02h get attribute capability

        AL = attribute capability
            00h only volatile handles supported
            01h both volatile and non-volatile supported

Conflicts: None known.
See Also: Function 53h

INTERRUPT 67h - Function 53h
GET/SET HANDLE NAME

Purpose: Determine or set the eight-character name which may be used to identify the specified expanded memory handle.

Available on: All machines.

Restrictions: LIM 4.0 EMS driver must be installed.

Registers at call:
AH = 53h
DX = handle
AL = subfunction:
    00h get handle name
        ES:DI -> 8-byte handle name array
    01h set handle name
        DS:SI -> 8-byte handle name

Return Registers:
AH = status
    00h successful
    80h internal error
    81h hardware malfunction
    83h invalid handle
    84h undefined function requested
    8Fh undefined subfunction
    A1h duplicate handle name

Conflicts: None known.
See Also: Function 52h

INTERRUPT 67h - Function 54h
GET HANDLE DIRECTORY

Purpose: Get a list of active expanded memory handles and the names which have been assigned to them.

Available on: All machines.

Restrictions: LIM 4.0 EMS driver must be installed.

Registers at call:
AH = 54h
AL = subfunction:

Return Registers:
AH = status
    00h successful
    80h internal error
    81h hardware malfunction
    84h undefined function requested
    8Fh undefined subfunction
    A0h no such handle name
    A1h a handle found had no name

00h get handle directory
    ES:DI -> buffer for handle directory
        (Table 10-3)

AL = number of entries in handle directory

01h search for named handle
    DS:SI -> 8-byte name

DX = value of named handle

02h get total number of handles

BX = total number of handles

Conflicts: None known.

Table 10-3. Format of handle directory entry:

Offset	Size	Description
00h	WORD	expanded memory handle
02h	8 BYTEs	name assigned to handle

INTERRUPT 67h - Function 55h
ALTER PAGE MAP AND JUMP

Purpose: Change the association between specified physical pages and logical pages, then perform a far jump to the given address.

Available on: All machines.

Registers at call:
AH = 55h
AL = subfunction:

    00h physical page numbers provided by caller

    01h segment addresses provided by caller
DX = handle
DS:SI -> structure containing map and jump address

Conflicts: None known.
See Also: Function 56h

Restrictions: LIM 4.0 EMS driver must be installed.

Return Registers: (at target address unless error)
AH = status
    00h successful
    80h internal error
    81h hardware failure
    83h invalid handle
    84h undefined function requested
    8Ah invalid logical page number encountered
    8Bh invalid physical page number encountered
    8Fh invalid subfunction

INTERRUPT 67h - Function 56h
ALTER PAGE MAP AND CALL

Purpose: Change the association between specified physical pages and logical pages for the duration of a far call to the given address.

Available on: All machines.

Registers at call:
AH = 56h
AL = subfunction:

00h physical page numbers provided by caller
    DX = handle
    DS:SI -> structure containing page map and call
        address
01h segment addresses provided by caller
    DX = handle
    DS:SI -> structure containing page map and call
        address
02h get page map stack space required
Conflicts: None known.
See Also: Function 55h

Restrictions: LIM 4.0 EMS driver must be installed.

Return Registers: (if successful, the target address is called. Use a RETF to return and restore mapping context)
AH = status (see Function 55h)

BX = stack space required

INTERRUPT 67h - Function 57h
MOVE/EXCHANGE MEMORY REGION

Purpose: Copy or swap the contents of a region of memory; the source and destination may both be either conventional or expanded memory.

Available on: All machines.

Registers at call:
AH = 57h
AL = subfunction
00h move memory region

Restrictions: LIM 4.0 EMS driver must be installed.

Return Registers:
AH = status
    00h successful
    80h internal error
    81h hardware failure

01h exchange memory region
     DS:SI -> structure describing source and
          destination (Table 10-4)

83h invalid handle
84h undefined function requested
8Ah invalid logical page number encountered
8Fh undefined subfunction
92h successful, but a portion of the source region
     has been overwritten
93h length of source or destination region exceeds
     length of region allocated to either source or
     destination handle
94h conventional and expanded memory regions
     overlap
95h offset within logical page exceeds size of
     logical page
96h region length exceeds 1M
97h source and destination EMS regions have same
     handle and overlap
98h memory source or destination type undefined
A2h attempted to wrap around 1M conventional
     address space

Details: The source and destination of a move may overlap, in which case the copy direction is chosen such that the destination receives an intact copy of the source region.
Conflicts: None known.

Table 10-4. Format of EMS copy data:

Offset	Size	Description
00h	DWORD	region length in bytes
04h	BYTE	source memory type

Table 10-4. Format of EMS copy data (continued)

Offset	Size	Description
		00h conventional
		01h expanded
05h	WORD	source handle (0000h if conventional memory)
07h	WORD	source initial offset (within page if EMS, segment if convent)
09h	WORD	source initial segment (conv mem) or logical page (EMS)
0Bh	BYTE	destination memory type
		00h conventional
		01h expanded
0Ch	WORD	destination handle
0Eh	WORD	destination initial offset
10h	WORD	destination initial segment or page

INTERRUPT 67h - Function 58h
GET MAPPABLE PHYSICAL ADDRESS ARRAY

Purpose: Determine the segment and physical page number of each mappable 16K physical page in the system.
Available on: All machines.   **Restrictions:** LIM 4.0 EMS driver must be installed.

Registers at call:
AH = 58h
AL = subfunction:

00h get mappable physical address array
    ES:DI -> buffer to be filled with array

01h get number of entries in m.p.a. array

Return Registers:
CX = number of entries (Table 10-5) in array
AH = status
    00h successful
    80h internal error
    81h hardware failure
    84h undefined function requested
    8Fh undefined subfunction

Details: The returned array for subfunction 00h is filled in physical segment address order.
Conflicts: None known.
See Also: EEMS Function 68h

Table 10-5. Format of mappable physical address entry:

Offset	Size	Description
00h	WORD	physical page segment
02h	WORD	physical page number

INTERRUPT 67h - Function 59h
GET EXPANDED MEMORY HARDWARE INFORMATION

Purpose: Determine the expanded memory hardware's capabilities.
Available on: All machines.   **Restrictions:** LIM 4.0 EMS driver must be installed.

Registers at call:
AH = 59h
DX = total raw pages
AL = subfunction:

00h get hardware configuration array
    ES:DI -> buffer to be filled with array
        (Table 10-6)

01h get unallocated raw page count

Return Registers:
AH = status
    00h successful
    80h internal error
    81h hardware failure
    84h undefined function requested
    8Fh undefined subfunction
    A4h access denied by operating system

BX = unallocated raw pages

Details: Subfunction 00h is for use by operating systems only, and can be enabled or disabled at any time by the operating system.
Conflicts: None known.

Table 10-6. Format of hardware configuration array:

Offset	Size	Description
00h	WORD	size of raw EMM pages in paragraphs
02h	WORD	number of alternate register sets
04h	WORD	size of mapping-context save area in bytes
06h	WORD	number of register sets assignable to DMA
08h	WORD	DMA operation type:
		0000h DMA with alternate register sets
		0001h only one DMA register set

INTERRUPT 67h - Function 5Ah
ALLOCATE STANDARD/RAW PAGES

Purpose: Reserve a specified number of pages (possibly of a nonstandard size) and associate them with a unique expanded memory handle.
Available on: All machines.   **Restrictions:** LIM 4.0 EMS driver must be installed.

Registers at call:
AH = 5Ah
AL = subfunction:
  00h allocate standard pages

  01h allocate raw pages
BX = number of pages to allocate

Return Registers:
DX = handle
AH = status
  00h successful
  80h internal error
  81h hardware failure
  84h undefined function requested
  85h no more handles available
  87h insufficient memory pages in system
  88h insufficient memory pages available
  8Fh undefined subfunction

Conflicts: None known.

INTERRUPT 67h - Function 5Bh
ALTERNATE MAP REGISTER SET

Purpose: Use or simulate multiple sets of hardware mapping registers.
Available on: All machines.   **Restrictions:** LIM 4.0 EMS driver must be installed.
Registers at call: **Return Registers:**
AH = 5Bh   AH = status
AL = subfunction: 00h successful
                                             80h internal error
                                             81h hardware malfunction
                                             84h undefined function requested
                                             8Fh undefined subfunction
                                             9Ah specified alternate map register set not
                                                 supported
                                             9Bh all alternate map register sets currently
                                                 allocated
                                             9Ch alternate map register sets not supported
                                             9Dh undefined or unallocated alternate map
                                                 register set
                                             A3h source array corrupted
                                             A4h operating system denied access

  00h get alternate map register set   BL = current active alternate map register set
                                                 number
                                           ES:DI -> map register context save area if BL=00h

  01h set alternate map register set
    BL = new alternate map register set number
    ES:DI -> map register context save area if
        BL=0
  02h get alternate map save array size   DX = array size in bytes

  03h allocate alternate map register set BL = number of map register set; 00h = not supported

  04h deallocate alternate map register set
    BL = number of alternate map register set
Details: This function is for use by operating systems only, and can be enabled or disabled at any time by the operating system.
Conflicts: None known.

INTERRUPT 67h - Function 5Bh
ALTERNATE MAP REGISTER SET - DMA REGISTERS

Purpose: Manage the use of mapping registers with direct memory accesses by other hardware.

Available on: All machines.

Restrictions: LIM 4.0 EMS driver must be installed.

Registers at call:

AH = 5Bh
AL = subfunction:
05h allocate DMA register set
06h enable DMA on alternate map register set
    BL = DMA register set number
    DL = DMA channel number
07h disable DMA on alternate map register set
    BL = DMA register set number
08h deallocate DMA register set
    BL = DMA register set number

Return Registers:

AH = status
    00h successful
    80h internal error
    81h hardware malfunction
    84h undefined function requested
    8Fh undefined subfunction
    9Ah specified DMA register set not supported
    9Bh all DMA register sets currently allocated
    9Ch alternate DMA sets not supported
    9Dh undefined or unallocated DMA register set
    9Eh dedicated DMA channels not supported
    9Fh specified dedicated DMA channel not
        supported
    A3h source array corrupted
    A4h operating system denied access
BL = DMA register set number (subfunction 05h
only),
        00h if not supported

Details: This function is for use by operating systems only, and can be enabled or disabled at any time by the operating system.

Conflicts: None known.

INTERRUPT 67h - Function 5Ch
PREPARE EXPANDED MEMORY HARDWARE FOR WARM BOOT

Purpose: Place the expanded memory hardware into readiness for an impending warm boot.

Available on: All machines.

Restrictions: LIM 4.0 EMS driver must be installed.

Registers at call:

AH = 5Ch

Return Registers:

AH = status
    00h successful
    80h internal error
    81h hardware malfunction
    84h undefined function requested

Conflicts: None known.

INTERRUPT 67h - Function 5Dh
ENABLE/DISABLE OS FUNCTION SET FUNCTIONS

Purpose: Specify whether applications may use LIM EMS 4.0 functions designed for use by the operating system.

Available on: All machines.

Restrictions: LIM 4.0 EMS driver must be installed.

Registers at call:
AH = 5Dh
AL = subfunction:
00h enable OS Function Set

01h disable OS Function Set

02h return access key (resets memory manager,
     returns access key at next invocation)
    BX,CX = access key returned by first
     invocation
Conflicts: None known.

Return Registers:
BX,CX = access key, returned only on first invocation
    of function
AH = status
    00h successful
    80h internal error
    81h hardware malfunction
    84h undefined function requested
    8Fh undefined subfunction
    A4h operating system denied access

EEMS

The Enhanced Expanded Memory Specification by Ashton-Tate, Quarterdeck, and AST addresses some of the perceived deficiences in version 3.2 of the Expanded Memory Specification. The additional capabilities of EEMS were later added to EMS version 4.0, but using different calls.

INTERRUPT 67h - Function 60h
GET PHYSICAL WINDOW ARRAY

Purpose: Determine where in memory pages are mapped.
Available on: All machines.
Registers at call:
AH = 60h
ES:DI -> buffer

Restrictions: EEMS driver must be installed.
Return Registers:
AH = status
AL = number of entries
buffer at ES:DI filled

Conflicts: None known.

INTERRUPT 67h - Function 61h
GENERIC ACCELERATOR CARD SUPPORT

Purpose: Can be used by an accelarator card manufacturer to flush a RAM cache, ensuring that the cache accurately reflects what the processor would see without the cache.
Available on: All machines.
Registers at call:
AH = 61h
Others *unknown.*
Conflicts: None known.

Restrictions: EEMS driver must be installed.
Return Registers: *unknown.*

INTERRUPT 67h - Function 68h
GET ADDRESSES OF ALL PAGE FRAMES IN SYSTEM

Purpose: Determine where in memory pages may be mapped.
Available on: All machines.
Registers at call:
AH = 68h
ES:DI -> buffer

Restrictions: EEMS driver must be installed.
Return Registers:
AH = status
AL = number of entries
buffer at ES:DI filled

Conflicts: None known.
See Also: LIM EMS 4 Function 58h

INTERRUPT 67h - Function 69h
MAP PAGE INTO FRAME

Purpose: Make a logical page of memory addressable as real memory at a specified location.
Available on: All machines.

Restrictions: EEMS driver must be installed.

Registers at call:
AH = 69h
AL = frame number
BX = page number
DX = handle
Details: Similar to EMS function 44h.
Conflicts: None known.
See Also: Functions 44h, 50h, and 6Ah

Return Registers:
AH = status

INTERRUPT 67h - Function 6Ah
PAGE MAPPING

Purpose: Save or restore the associations between a set of physical addresses and logical addresses.
Available on: All machines.   **Restrictions:** EEMS driver must be installed.
Registers at call: **Return Registers:**
AH = 6Ah   AH = status
AL = subfunction:
00h save partial page map
    CH = first page frame
    CL = number of frames
    ES:DI -> buffer which is to be filled
01h restore partial page map
    CH = first page frame
    CL = number of frames
    DI:SI -> previously saved page map
02h save and restore partial
    page map
    CH = first page frame
    CL = number of frames
    ES:DI = buffer for
    current page map
    DI:SI = new page map
03h get size of save array   AL = size of array in bytes
    CH = first page frame
    CL = number of frames
04h switch to standard map register setting
05h switch to alternate map register setting
06h deallocate pages mapped to frames in
      conventional memory
    CH = first page frame
    CL = number of frames
Details: Similar to LIM EMS function 4Eh, except that a subrange of pages can be specified.
Conflicts: None known.
See Also:

Virtual Control Program Interface
VCPI was created out of the need to have multiplex 386 protected-mode supervisors (such as a multitasker and a DOS extender) coexist. It provides rudimentary services which will allow a master supervisor program to stay in control of the system while still permitting other programs access to protected mode.

The VCPI specification contains only a small set of services; for a more complete set, see the DOS Protected-Mode Interface in chapter 11. DPMI is unfortunately incompatible with VCPI.

INTERRUPT 67h - Function DEh, Subfunction 00h
INSTALLATION CHECK

Purpose: Determine whether a Virtual Control Program Interface (VCPI) master program is installed.

Available on: All machines.

Registers at call:
AX = DE00h

Restrictions: none.

Return Registers:
AH = 00h   VCPI is present
    BH = major version number
    BL = minor version number
AH nonzero   VCPI not present

Conflicts: None known.

INTERRUPT 67h - Function DEh, Subfunction 01h
GET PROTECTED MODE INTERFACE

Purpose: Determine the entry point for accessing VCPI services in protected mode.

Available on: 80386 or higher.

Registers at call:
AX = DE01h
ES:DI -> 4K page table buffer
DS:SI -> three descriptor table entries in GDT: first
    becomes code segment descriptor, other two for
    use by main control program.

Restrictions: VCPI must be installed.

Return Registers:
AH = 00h successful
    DI -> first unused page table entry in buffer
    EBX -> protected mode entry point in code
      segment
AH = nonzero failed

Conflicts: None known.

INTERRUPT 67h - Function DEh, Subfunction 02h
GET MAXIMUM PHYSICAL MEMORY ADDRESS

Purpose: Determine highest page which could be allocated in order to initialize memory management structures.

Available on: 80386 or higher.

Registers at call:
AX = DE02h

Restrictions: VCPI must be installed.

Return Registers:
AH = 00h successful
    EDX = physical address of highest 4K memory
      page
AH nonzero: failed

Conflicts: None known.

INTERRUPT 67h - Function DEh, Subfunction 03h
GET NUMBER OF FREE 4K PAGES

Purpose: Determine how much memory is still available for allocation.

Available on: 80386 or higher.

Registers at call:
AX = DE03h

Restrictions: VCPI must be installed.

Return Registers:
AH = 00h successful
    EDX = number of free 4K pages
AH nonzero: failed

Details: Returns total number of pages available to ALL tasks in system. Also available in protected mode by calling the protected-mode VCPI entry point.

Conflicts: None known.

See Also: Function DEh Subfunction 04h

INTERRUPT 67h - Function DEh, Subfunction 04h
ALLOCATE A 4K PAGE

Purpose: Reserve a single page of memory.

Available on: 80386 or higher.

Restrictions: VCPI must be installed.

Registers at call:
AX = DE04h

Return Registers:
AH = 00h successful
    EDX = physical address of allocated page
AH nonzero: failed

Details: The client program is responsible for freeing all memory allocated with this call before terminating. Also available in protected mode by calling the protected-mode VCPI entry point.
Conflicts: None known.
See Also: Function DEh Subfunctions 03h and 05h

INTERRUPT 67h - Function DEh, Subfunction 05h
FREE 4K PAGE

Purpose: Return the specified page of memory to the system.
Available on: 80386 or higher.   **Restrictions:** VCPI must be installed.
Registers at call: **Return Registers:**
AX = DE05h   AH = 00h successful
EDX = physical address of 4K page   AH nonzero: failed
Details: Also available in protected mode by calling the protected-mode VCPI entry point.
Conflicts: None known.
See Also: Function DEh Subfunction 04h

INTERRUPT 67h - Function DEh, Subfunction 06h
GET PHYSICAL ADDRESS OF PAGE IN FIRST MB

Purpose: Determine the physical address of a logical page within the one-megabyte Virtual-86 mode address space.
Available on: 80386 or higher.   **Restrictions:** VCPI must be installed.
Registers at call   **Return Registers:**
AX = DE06h   AH = 00h successful
CX = page number (linear address shifted right 12   EDX = physical address of page
    bits)   AH nonzero: invalid page number (AH = 8Bh
                                     recommended)

Conflicts: None known.

INTERRUPT 67h - Function DEh, Subfunction 07h
READ CR0

Purpose: Determine value of CPU Control Register 0; in Virtual-86 mode this register is normally inaccessible.
Available on: 80386 or higher.   **Restrictions:** VCPI must be installed.
Registers at call: **Return Registers:**
AX = DE07h   AH = 00h
                                     EBX = value of Control Register 0

Conflicts: None known.
See Also: Function DEh Subfunction 07h

INTERRUPT 67h - Function DEh, Subfunction 08h
READ DEBUG REGISTERS

Purpose: Determine the current contents of the CPU's debugging registers.
Available on: 80386 or higher.   **Restrictions:** VCPI must be installed.
Registers at call: **Return Registers:**
AX = DE08h   AH = 00h
ES:DI -> array of 8 DWORDs   buffer filled with DR0 first, DR7 last, DR4 and DR5
                                     unused

Conflicts: None known.
See Also: Function DEh Subfunction 09h

INTERRUPT 67h - Function DEh, Subfunction 09h
SET DEBUG REGISTERS

Purpose: Specify new contents for the CPU's debugging registers.

Available on: 80386 or higher.   **Restrictions:** VCPI must be installed.

Registers at call: **Return Registers:**

AX = DE09h   AH = 00h

ES:DI -> array of 8 DWORDs holding new values
  of debug registers

Details: Values for DR4 and DR5 ignored.

Conflicts: None known.

See Also: Function DEh Subfunction 08h

INTERRUPT 67h - Function DEh, Subfunction 0Ah
GET 8259 INTERRUPT VECTOR MAPPINGS

Purpose: Determine the interrupt numbers corresponding to the hardware interrutp request lines.

Available on: 80386 or higher.   **Restrictions:** VCPI must be installed.

Registers at call: **Return Registers:**

AX = DE0Ah   AH = 00h successful

               BX = first vector used by master 8259 (IRQ0)

               CX = first vector used by slave 8259 (IRQ8)

           AH nonzero: failed

Details: CX is undefined in systems without a slave 8259.

Conflicts: None known.

See Also: Function DEh Subfunction 0Bh

INTERRUPT 67h - Function DEh, Subfunction 0Bh
SET 8259 INTERRUPT VECTOR MAPPINGS

Purpose: Specify which interrupt numbers should correspond to the hardware interrupt request lines.

Available on: 80386 or higher.   **Restrictions:** VCPI must be installed.

Registers at call: **Return Registers:**

AX = DE0Bh   AH = 00h successful

BX = first vector used by master 8259 AH nonzero: failed

CX = first vector used by slave 8259

interrupts disabled

Details: This call merely informs the server that the client has changed the interrupt mappings. The client may not change the mappings if they have already been changed by the server or another client, and is responsible for restoring the original mappings before terminating.

Conflicts: None known.

See Also: Function DEh Subfunction 0Ah

INTERRUPT 67h - Function DEh, Subfunction 0Ch
SWITCH TO PROTECTED MODE

Purpose: Begin executing in protected mode rather than Virtual-86 mode.

Available on: 80386 or higher.   **Restrictions:** VCPI must be installed.

Registers at call: **Return Registers:**

AX = DE0Ch   interrupts disabled

ESI = linear address in first megabyte of values for GDTR, IDTR, LDTR, TR loaded

  system registers (Table 10-7)   SS:ESP must have at least 16 bytes space, and entry

interrupts disabled   point must set up new stack before enabling interrupts

              EAX, ESI, DS, ES, FS, GS destroyed

Details: In protected mode, calling the protected-mode VCPI entry point with:
    AX = DE0Ch

DS = segment selector from function DE01h
SS:ESP in first megabyte of linear memory
STACK: QWORD return address from FAR call to 32-bit segment
            DWORD EIP
            DWORD CS
            DWORD reserved for EFLAGS
            DWORD ESP
            DWORD SS
            DWORD ES
            DWORD DS
            DWORD FS
            DWORD GS

and interrupts disabled, will switch to virtual86 mode with interrupts disabled, all segment registers loaded, and EAX destroyed.

Conflicts: None known.

See Also: INT 15h Function 89h (chapter 3)

Table 10-7. Format of system register values for switch to protected mode:

Offset	Size	Description
00h	DWORD	value for CR3
04h	DWORD	linear address in first megabyte of value for GDTR
08h	DWORD	linear address in first megabyte of value for IDTR
0Ch	WORD	value for LDTR
0Eh	WORD	value for TR
10h	PWORD	CS:EIP of protected mode entry-point

Chapter 11

DOS Protected-Mode Interface

DPMI is the intended successor to VCPI (Virtual Control Program Interface, see chapter 10). It allows DOS programs to use the protected-mode features of the 80286 and later processors without compromising built-in system protections.

Although not itself a DOS extender, DPMI provides all the primitives necessary to implement one. As a result, there are numerous cross-references from this chapter to chapter 9.

Borland DPMI LOADER

INTERRUPT 2Fh - Function FBh, Subfunction 42h
Borland DPMI LOADER (DPMILOAD.EXE)

Purpose: Load Turbo Assembler (TASM) into extended memory under DPMI.

Available on: 80286 or higher with DPMI.	**Restrictions:** DPMILOAD must be installed.
Registers at call:	**Return Registers:**
AX = FB42h	AX = 0001h
BX = 0001h *unknown.*	ES:BX - >u*nknown.*
	CX = *unknown.*
	DX = *unknown.*
BX = 0002h *unknown.*	AX = *unknown.*
Call: ES,SI,DI	
BX = 0003h get free memory.	DX:AX = free memory
BX = 0004h *unknown.*	CX = *unknown.*
BX = 0005h *unknown.*	DX = *unknown.*
BX = 0006h *unknown.*	DX = *unknown.*
CX = *unknown.*	
DX = *unknown.*	
BX = 0007h *unknown.*	*unknown.*
CX = *unknown.*	
BX = 0008h *unknown.*	DX = *unknown.*
CX = *unknown.*	
DX = *unknown.*	

else calls DPMI INT 31h Function 09h
Subfunction 00h
Conflicts: None known.

DOS Protected-Mode Interface
Note: All INT 31h calls listed in this chapter are available in protected mode only. Where a version of DPMI is referenced, the meaning is any DPMI host conforming to the stated version of the specification.

INTERRUPT 2Fh - Function 16h, Subfunction 86h
DETECT PROCESSOR MODE
Purpose: Determine current operating mode of CPU under DPMI.

Available on: All machines.	**Restrictions:** DPMI must be installed.

Registers at call:
AX = 1686h

Return Registers:
AX = 0000h if operating in protected mode under
    DPMI (INT 31 available)
AX nonzero if in real/V86 mode or no DPMI
    (INT 31 not available)

Conflicts: None known.
See Also: Function 16h Subfunction 87h

INTERRUPT 2Fh - Function 16h, Subfunction 87h
DPMI INSTALLATION CHECK

Purpose: Determine whether DPMI installed.
Available on: All machines.

Registers at call:
AX = 1687h

Restrictions: none.
Return Registers:
AX = 0000h if installed
BX = flags
    bit 0: 32-bit programs supported
CL = processor type
    (02h=80286, 03h=80386, 04h=80486)
DH = DPMI major version
DL = two-digit DPMI minor version
SI = number of paragraphs of DOS extender
    private data
ES:DI -> DPMI mode-switch entry point

Details: Mode Switch routine changes from real to protected mode.
Conflicts: None known.
See Also: Function 16h Subfunction 86h

    Call Mode Switch entry point with:
        AX = flags
          bit 0: set if 32-bit program
        ES = real mode segment of buffer for DPMI private data (ignored if SI was zero)
Note: This entry point is only called for the initial switch to protected mode.

    Mode Switch routine returns with:
        CF set on error, program still in real mode
        CF clear if successful, program now in protected mode, registers:
                CS = 16-bit selector corresponding to real-mode CS
                SS = selector corresponding to real-mode SS (64K limit)
                DS = selector corresponding to real-mode DS (64K limit)
                ES = selector to program's PSP (100h byte limit)
                FS = GS = 0
                high word of ESP = 0 if 32-bit program

INTERRUPT 2Fh - Function 16h, Subfunction 8Ah
GET VENDOR-SPECIFIC API ENTRY POINT

Purpose: Determine the address to call for vendor-specific extensions to the DPMI specification.
Available on: 80286 or higher in protected mode.

Registers at call:
AX = 168Ah
DS:(E)SI = selector:offset of ASCIZ vendor name

Restrictions: DPMI version 0.9 or higher must be
                    installed.
Return Registers:
AL = status
  00h successful
    ES:(E)DI -> extended API entry point
  8Ah unsuccessful

Details: The vendor name is used to determine which entry point to return; it is case-sensitive. 32-bit applications use ESI and EDI, 16-bit applications use SI and DI. Although not documented until version 1.0 of the DPMI specification, this call is available in version 0.9 implementations.
Conflicts: None known.
See Also: INT 31h Function 0Ah Subfunction 00h

INTERRUPT 31h - Function 00h, Subfunction 00h
ALLOCATE LDT DESCRIPTORS

Purpose: Allocate a specified number of contiguous descriptor's in the calling task's Local Descriptor Table.
Available on: 80286 or higher in protected mode.

Restrictions: DPMI version 0.9 or higher must be installed.

Registers at call:
AX = 0000h
CX = number of descriptors to allocate

Return Registers:
CF clear if successful
   AX = base selector
CF set on error
   AX = error code (DPMI 1.0+)

Table 11-1. DPMI Version 1.0 Error Codes

0000h-7FFFh DOS error passed through by DPMI
8001h unsupported function
8002h object in wrong state for function
8003h system integrity would be endangered
8004h deadlock detected
8005h pending serialization request cancelled
8010h out of DPMI internal resources
8011h descriptor unavailable
8012h linear memory unavailable
8013h physical memory unavailable
8014h backing store unavailable
8015h callback unavailable

8016h handle unavailable
8017h maximum lock count exceeded
8018h shared memory already serialized exclusively
   by another
8019h shared memory already serialized shared by
   another client
8021h invalid value for numeric or flag parameter
8022h invalid segment selector
8023h invalid handle
8024h invalid callback
8025h invalid linear address
8026h request not supported by hardware

Details: The base and limit of the returned descriptors will be 0, and the type will be "data". Add the value returned by INT 31h Function 00h Subfunction 03h to move to subsequent descriptors if multiple descriptors were allocated. This function is not supported by MS Windows 3.0 in Standard mode.
Conflicts: None known.
See Also: Function 00h Subfunctions 01h and 0Dh

INTERRUPT 31h - Function 00h, Subfunction 01h
FREE LDT DESCRIPTOR

Purpose: Release a Local Descriptor Table segment descriptor.
Available on: 80286 or higher in protected mode.

Restrictions: DPMI version 0.9 or higher must be installed.

Registers at call:
AX = 0001h
BX = selector to free

Return Registers:
CF clear if successful
CF set on error
   AX = error code (DPMI 1.0+) (8022h) (see
Function
   00h Subfunction 00h)

Details: Only one descriptor is freed per call. The program's initial CS, DS, and SS descriptors may be freed; any segment registers containing the selector will be set to zero.
   This function is not supported by MS Windows 3.0 in Standard mode.
Conflicts: None known.
See Also: Function 00h Subfunctions 00h, 0Ah, and 0Dh

INTERRUPT 31h - Function 00h, Subfunction 02h
SEGMENT TO DESCRIPTOR

Purpose: Create an LDT descritor referencing the specified real-mode segment.

Available on: 80286 or higher in protected mode.

Restrictions: DPMI version 0.9 or higher must be installed.

Registers at call:
AX = 0002h
BX = real mode segment

Return Registers:
CF clear if successful
   AX = selector corresponding to real mode segment (64K limit)
CF set on error
   AX = error code (DPMI 1.0+) (8011h) (see Function 00h Subfunction 00h)

Details: Multiple calls for the same real mode segment return the same selector. The returned descriptor can never be modified or freed.

This function is not supported by MS Windows 3.0 in Standard mode.

Conflicts: None known.

INTERRUPT 31h - Function 00h, Subfunction 03h
GET NEXT SELECTOR INCREMENT VALUE

Purpose: Determine the numerical difference between adjacent descriptors returned by any call which can allocate multiple descriptors.

Available on: 80286 or higher in protected mode.

Restrictions: DPMI version 0.9 or higher must be installed.

Registers at call:
AX = 0003h

Return Registers:
CF clear
   AX = value to add to get next sequential selector

Details: The increment will be a power of two.

This function is not supported by MS Windows 3.0 in Standard mode.

Conflicts: None known.

See Also: Function 00h Subfunction 00h

INTERRUPT 31h - Function 00h, Subfunction 04h
RESERVED FOR HISTORICAL REASONS

Purpose: This function was originally defined, but has been dropped from publicly-released versions of the specification. It should never be called.

Available on: 80286 or higher in protected mode.

Restrictions: DPMI must be installed.

Registers at call: AX = 0004h

Return Registers: n/a

Conflicts: None known.

INTERRUPT 31h - Function 00h, Subfunction 05h
RESERVED FOR HISTORICAL REASONS

Purpose: This function was originally defined, but has been dropped from publicly-released versions of the specification. It should never be called.

Available on: 80286 or higher in protected mode.

Restrictions: DPMI version 0.9 or higher must be installed.

Registers at call: AX = 0005h

Return Registers: n/a

Conflicts: None known.

INTERRUPT 31h - Function 00h, Subfunction 06h
GET SEGMENT BASE ADDRESS

Purpose: Determine the starting linear address of the specified LDT descriptor.

Available on: 80286 or higher in protected mode.

Registers at call:
AX = 0006h
BX = selector

Restrictions: DPMI version 0.9 or higher must be installed.

Return Registers:
CF clear if successful
    CX:DX = linear base address of segment
CF set on error
    AX = error code (DPMI 1.0+) (8022h) (see Function 00h Subfunction 00h)

Details: This function is not supported by MS Windows 3.0 in Standard mode.
Conflicts: None known.
See Also: Function 00h Subfunction 07h

INTERRUPT 31h - Function 00h, Subfunction 07h
SET SEGMENT BASE ADDRESS

Purpose: Specify the linear starting address for the indicated LDT descriptor.
Available on: 80286 or higher in protected mode.

Registers at call:
AX = 0007h
BX = selector
CX:DX = linear base address

Restrictions: DPMI version 0.9 or higher must be installed.

Return Registers:
CF clear if successful
CF set on error
    AX = error code (DPMI 1.0+) (8022h, 8025h) (see Function 00h Subfunction 00h)

Details: Only modify descriptors allocated with INT 31h Function 00h Subfunction 00h. Only the low 24 bits of the address will be used by 16-bit DPMI implementations even on a 386 or higher. DPMI 1.0+ automatically reloads any segment registers containing the selector being modified.
This function is not supported by MS Windows 3.0 in Standard mode.
Conflicts: None known.
See Also: Function 00h Subfunctions 06h, 08h, 09h, and 0Ch, OS/286 INT 21h Function E9h (chapter 9)

INTERRUPT 31h - Function 00h, Subfunction 08h
SET SEGMENT LIMIT

Purpose: Specify the highest offset within the segment for the indicated LDT descriptor.
Available on: 80286 or higher in protected mode.

Registers at call:
AX = 0008h
BX = selector
CX:DX = segment limit

Restrictions: DPMI version 0.9 or higher must be installed.

Return Registers:
CF clear if successful
CF set on error
    AX = error code (DPMI 1.0+) (8021h, 8022h, 8025h) (see Function 00h Subfunction 00h)

Details: CX must be zero for 16-bit DPMI implementations. Limits greater than 1MB must be page aligned (low 12 bits set). Only modify descriptors allocated with INT 31h Function 00h Subfunction 00h. DPMI 1.0+ automatically reloads any segment registers containing the selector being modified.
    This function is not supported by MS Windows 3.0 in Standard mode.
Conflicts: None known.
See Also: Function 00h Subfunctions 07h, 09h, and 0Ch, OS/286 INT 21h Function E9h (chapter 9)

INTERRUPT 31h - Function 00h, Subfunction 09h
SET DESCRIPTOR ACCESS RIGHTS

Purpose: Specify the type of segment and manner in which it may be accessed for the indicated LDT descriptor.
Available on: 80286 or higher in protected mode.

Registers at call:
AX = 0009h

Restrictions: DPMI version 0.9 or higher must be installed.

Return Registers:
CF clear if successful

BX = selector
CL = access rights/type byte
CH = 80386 extended rights/ type byte (32-bit
  DPMI implementations only)

CF set on error
  AX = error code (DPMI 1.0+) (8021h, 8022h,
    8025h) (see Function 00h Subfunction 00h)

Details: If the Present bit is clear, CL bits 0-3 may have any value. DPMI 1.0+ automatically reloads any segment registers containing the selector being modified.
  This function is not supported by MS Windows 3.0 in Standard mode.
Conflicts: None known.
See Also: Function 00h Subfunctions 07h, 08h, and 0Ch, Phar Lap INT 21h Function 25h Subfunction 14h

INTERRUPT 31h - Function 00h, Subfunction 0Ah
CREATE ALIAS DESCRIPTOR

Purpose: Make a new LDT descriptor which references the same memory as the specified descriptor.
Available on: 80286 or higher in protected mode.   **Restrictions:** DPMI version 0.9 or higher must be
                                                                                 installed.

Registers at call: **Return Registers:**
AX = 000Ah   CF clear if successful
BX = selector   AX = new data selector
                                                          CF set on error
                                                            AX = error code (DPMI 1.0+) (8011h, 8022h) (see
                                                              Function 00h Subfunction 00h)

Details: Fails if selector in BX is not a code segment or is invalid. Use INT 31h Function 00h Subfunction 01h to free new selector. Future changes to the original selector will not be reflected in the returned alias selector.
  This function is not supported by MS Windows 3.0 in Standard mode.
Conflicts: None known.
See Also: Function 00h Subfunction 01h

INTERRUPT 31h - Function 00h, Subfunction 0Bh
GET DESCRIPTOR

Purpose: Copy the specified entry in the local descriptor table into a caller-provided buffer.
Available on: 80286 or higher in protected mode.   **Restrictions:** DPMI version 0.9 or higher must be
                                                                                 installed.

Registers at call: **Return Registers:**
AX = 000Bh   CF clear if successful
BX = LDT selector   buffer filled
ES:(E)DI -> 8-byte buffer for copy of descriptor   CF set on error
                                                            AX = error code (DPMI 1.0+) (8022h) (see
                                                              Function 00h Subfunction 00h)

Details: 16-bit programs use ES:DI as pointer, 32-bit must use ES:EDI.
  This function is not supported by MS Windows 3.0 in Standard mode.
Conflicts: None known.
See Also: Function 00h Subfunction 0Ch

INTERRUPT 31h - Function 00h, Subfunction 0Ch
SET DESCRIPTOR

Purpose: Copy a caller-provided buffer into the specified entry in the local descriptor table, thus changing the memory referenced by that particular selector.
Available on: 80286 or higher in protected mode.   **Restrictions:** DPMI version 0.9 or higher must be
                                                                                 installed.

Registers at call: **Return Registers:**
AX = 000Ch   CF clear if successful

BX = LDT selector
ES:(E)DI -> 8-byte buffer containing descriptor

CF set on error
    AX = error code (DPMI 1.0+) (8021h, 8022h,
        8025h) (see Function 00h Subfunction 00h)

Details: 16-bit programs use ES:DI as pointer, 32-bit must use ES:EDI. Only modify descriptors allocated with INT 31h Function 00h Subfunction 00h. DPMI 1.0+ automatically reloads any segment registers containing the selector being modified.
    This function is not supported by MS Windows 3.0 in Standard mode.
Conflicts: None known.
See Also: Function 00h Subfunction 0Bh

INTERRUPT 31h - Function 00h, Subfunction 0Dh
ALLOCATE SPECIFIC LDT DESCRIPTOR

Purpose: Reserve a Local Descriptor Table entry by number.
Available on: 80286 or higher in protected mode.

Restrictions: DPMI version 0.9 or higher must be installed.

Registers at call:
AX = 000Dh
BX = LDT selector

Return Registers:
CF clear if successful
    descriptor allocated
CF set on error
    AX = error code (DPMI 1.0+) (8011h, 8022h) (see
        Function 00h Subfunction 00h)

Details: Free descriptor with INT 31h Function 00h Subfunction 01h. The first 16 descriptors (04h-7Ch) are reserved for this function, but some may already be in use by other applications under DPMI 0.9; DPMI 1.0 guarantees 16 descriptors per client.
    This function is not supported by MS Windows 3.0 in Standard mode.
Conflicts: None known.
See Also: Function 00h Subfunctions 00h and 01h

INTERRUPT 31h - Function 00h, Subfunction 0Eh
GET MULTIPLE DESCRIPTORS

Purpose: Copy one or more entries from the Local Descriptor Table into a caller-provided data buffer.
Available on: 80286 or higher in protected mode.

Restrictions: DPMI version 1.0 or higher must be installed.

Registers at call:
AX = 000Eh
CX = number of descriptors to copy
ES:(E)DI -> descriptor buffer (see Table 11-2)

Return Registers:
CF clear if successful
    descriptors copied
CF set on error
    AX = error code (8022h) (see Function 00h
        Subfunction 00h)
    CX = number of descriptors successfully copied

Details: 16-bit programs use ES:DI as pointer, 32-bit must use ES:EDI. If the function fails, the first CX descriptors are valid; the remainder are not modified.
Conflicts: None known.
See Also: Function 00h Subfunctions 0Bh and 0Fh

Table 11-2. Format of descriptor buffer entry (one per descriptor to get):

Offset	Size	Description
00h	WORD	selector (set by client)
02h	QWORD	descriptor (set by host)

INTERRUPT 31h - Function 00h, Subfunction 0Fh
SET MULTIPLE DESCRIPTORS

Purpose: Copy one or more descriptors into the Local Descriptor Table from a caller-provided data buffer, thus modifying the segments corresponding to those selectors.

Available on: 80286 or higher in protected mode.

Restrictions: DPMI version 1.0 or higher must be installed.

Registers at call:
AX = 000Fh
CX = number of descriptors to copy
ES:(E)DI -> descriptor buffer (Table 11-3)

Return Registers:
CF clear if successful
    descriptors copied
CF set on error
    AX = error code (8021h,8022h,8025h) (see Function 00h Subfunction 00h)
    CX = number of descriptors successfully copied

Details: 16-bit programs use ES:DI as pointer, 32-bit must use ES:EDI. If the function fails, the first CX descriptors are valid; the remainder are not modified. DPMI 1.0+ automatically reloads any segment registers containing a selector being modified.

Conflicts: None known.

See Also: Function 00h Subfunctions 0Ch and 0Eh

Table 11-3. Format of descriptor buffer entry (one per descriptor to set):

Offset	Size	Description
00h	WORD	selector
02h	QWORD	descriptor

INTERRUPT 31h - Function 01h, Subfunction 00h
ALLOCATE DOS MEMORY BLOCK

Purpose: Requests a block of real-mode memory from DOS and creates segment selectors which may be used to reference that block.

Available on: 80286 or higher in protected mode.

Restrictions: DPMI version 0.9 or higher must be installed.

Registers at call:
AX = 0100h
BX = number of paragraphs to allocate

Return Registers:
CF clear if successful
    AX = real mode segment of allocated block
    DX = first selector for allocated block
CF set on error
    (DPMI 0.9) AX = DOS error code (07h, 08h) (see INT 21/AH=59h)
    (DPMI 1.0+) AX = DPMI error code (8011h) (see Function 00h Subfunction 00h)
    BX = size (in paragraphs) of largest available block

Details: Multiple contiguous selectors are allocated for blocks of more than 64K if the caller is a 16-bit program. Never modify or deallocate returned descriptors.

This function is not supported by MS Windows 3.0 in Standard mode.

Conflicts: None known.

See Also: Function 01h Subfunction 01h, Function 05h Subfunction 01h, DOS INT 21h Function 48h (chapter 8)

INTERRUPT 31h - Function 01h, Subfunction 01h
FREE DOS MEMORY BLOCK

Purpose: Returns a block of real-mode memory to DOS and frees the descriptors which were created to reference that block.

Available on: 80286 or higher in protected mode.

Registers at call:
AX = 0101h
DX = selector of block

Restrictions: DPMI version 0.9 or higher must be installed.

Return Registers:
CF set if successful
CF set on error
    AX = DOS error code (07h,09h) (see INT 21/AH=59h)

Details: All descriptors allocated for the block are automatically freed. DPMI 1.0+ automatically zeros any segment registers containing a selector freed by this function.

This function is not supported by MS Windows 3.0 in Standard mode.

Conflicts: None known.

See Also: Function 01h Subfunctions 00h and 02h, Function 05h Subfunction 02h, DOS INT 21h Function 49h (chapter 8)

INTERRUPT 31h - Function 01h, Subfunction 02h
RESIZE DOS MEMORY BLOCK

Purpose: Modifies the size of a real-mode block of memory which was previously allocated, and creates or frees descriptors referencing that block as needed.

Available on: 80286 or higher in protected mode.

Registers at call:
AX = 0102h
BX = new block size in paragraphs
DX = selector of block

Restrictions: DPMI version 0.9 or higher must be installed.

Return Registers:
CF clear if successful
CF set on error
    AX = DOS error code (07h,08h,09h) (see INT 21/AH=59h)
    (DPMI 1.0+) DPMI error code (8011h,8022h) (see Function 00h Subfunction 00h)
    BX = maximum block size (in paragraphs) possible

Details: Increasing the size of a block past a 64K boundary will fail if the next descriptor in the LDT is already in use. Shrinking a block past a 64K boundary will cause some selectors to be freed; DPMI 1.0+ automatically zeros any segment registers containing a selector freed by this function.

This function is not supported by MS Windows 3.0 in Standard mode.

Conflicts: None known.

See Also: Function 01h Subfunction 00h, DOS INT 21h Function 4Ah (chapter 8)

INTERRUPT 31h - Function 02h, Subfunction 00h
GET REAL MODE INTERRUPT VECTOR

Purpose: Determine which procedure currently handles the specified interrupt in real mode for the current virtual machine.

Available on: 80286 or higher in protected mode.

Registers at call:
AX = 0200h
BL = interrupt number

Restrictions: DPMI version 0.9 or higher must be installed.

Return Registers:
CF clear
CX:DX = segment:offset of real mode interrupt handler

Details: The DPMI implementation is required to support all 256 vectors.

Conflicts: None known.

See Also: Function 02h Subfunctions 01h and 04h, Phar Lap INT 21h Function 25h Subfunction 03h (chapter 9)

INTERRUPT 31h - Function 02h, Subfunction 01h
SET REAL MODE INTERRUPT VECTOR

Purpose: Specify which procedure will handle the indicated interrupt in real mode for the current virtual machine.

Available on: 80286 or higher in protected mode.

Registers at call:
AX = 0201h
BL = interrupt number
CX:DX = segment:offset of real mode handler

Details: All memory that may be touched by a hardware interrupt handler must be locked down with INT 31h Function 06h Subfunction 00h.

Conflicts: None known.

See Also: Function 02h Subfunctions 00h and 05h, Function 06h Subfunction 00h, Phar Lap INT 21h Function 25h Subfunction 05h (chapter 9)

Restrictions: DPMI version 0.9 or higher must be installed.

Return Registers:
CF clear

INTERRUPT 31h - Function 02h, Subfunction 02h
GET PROCESSOR EXCEPTION HANDLER VECTOR

Purpose: Determine which procedure currently handles processor exceptions.

Available on: 80286 or higher in protected mode.

Registers at call:
AX = 0202h
BL = exception number (00h-1Fh)

Restrictions: DPMI version 0.9 or higher must be installed.

Return Registers:
CF clear if successful
    CX:(E)DX = selector:offset of handler
CF set on error
    AX = error code (DPMI 1.0+) (8021h) (see Function 00h Subfunction 00h)

Details: 16-bit programs receive the pointer in CX:DX, 32-bit programs in CX:EDX. DPMI 1.0+ supports this function only for backward compatibility; use Function 02h Subfunctions 10h or 11h instead.

This function is not supported by MS Windows 3.0 in Standard mode.

Conflicts: None known.

See Also: Function 02h Subfunctions 03h, 10h and 11h

INTERRUPT 31h - Function 02h, Subfunction 03h
SET PROCESSOR EXCEPTION HANDLER VECTOR

Purpose: Specify which procedure will handle processor exceptions.

Available on: 80286 or higher in protected mode.

Registers at call:
AX = 0203h
BL = exception number (00h-1Fh)
CX:(E)DX = selector:offset of handler

Restrictions: DPMI version 0.9 or higher must be installed.

Return Registers:
CF clear if successful
CF set on error
    AX = error code (DPMI 1.0+) (8021h, 8022h) (see Function 00h Subfunction 00h)

Details: 32-bit programs must supply an offset in EDX and use a 32-bit interrupt stack frame on chaining to the next exception handler. The handler should return using a FAR return. All fault stack frames contain an error code, but it is only valid for exceptions 08h and 0Ah-0Eh. Handlers will only be called if the exception occurs in protected mode, and the DPMI host does not transparently handle the exception. The handler may change certain values on the stack frame (see Tables 11-4 and 11-5). DPMI 1.0+ supports this function only for backward compatibility; use Function 02h Subfunctions 12h or 13h instead.

This function is not supported by MS Windows 3.0 in Standard mode.

Conflicts: None known.

See Also: Function 02h Subfunctions 02h, 12h, and 13h

Table 11-4. Format of stack frame for 16-bit programs: (offset from SS:SP)

Offset	Size	Description
00h	DWORD	return CS:IP (do not change)
04h	WORD	error code

Table 11-4. Format of stack frame for 16-bit programs (continued)

Offset	Size	Description
06h	DWORD	CS:IP of exception
0Ah	WORD	flags
0Ch	DWORD	SS:SP

Table 11-5. Format of stack frame for 32-bit programs: (offset from SS:ESP)

Offset	Size	Description
00h	DWORD	return EIP (do not change)
04h	WORD	return CS selector (do not change)
06h	WORD	reserved (do not change)
08h	DWORD	error code
0Ch	DWORD	EIP of exception
10h	WORD	CS selector of exception
12h	WORD	reserved (do not change)
14h	DWORD	EFLAGS
18h	DWORD	ESP
1Ch	WORD	SS
1Eh	WORD	reserved (do not change)

INTERRUPT 31h - Function 02h, Subfunction 04h
GET PROTECTED MODE INTERRUPT VECTOR

Purpose: Determine which procedure currently handles the specified interrupt in protected mode.

Available on: 80286 or higher in protected mode.

Restrictions: DPMI version 0.9 or higher must be installed.

Registers at call:
AX = 0204h
BL = interrupt number

Return Registers:
CF clear
CX:(E)DX = selector:offset of handler

Details: 16-bit programs use CX:DX, 32-bit programs use CX:EDX. DPMI implementations are required to support all 256 vectors.

This function is not supported by MS Windows 3.0 in Standard mode.

Conflicts: None known.

See Also: Function 02h Subfunctions 00h and 05h, Phar Lap INT 21h Function 25h Subfunction 02h (chapter 9)

INTERRUPT 31h - Function 02h, Subfunction 05h
SET PROTECTED MODE INTERRUPT VECTOR

Purpose: Specify which procedure will handle the indicated interrupt in protected mode.

Available on: 80286 or higher in protected mode.

Restrictions: DPMI version 0.9 or higher must be installed.

Registers at call:
AX = 0205h
BL = interrupt number
CX:(E)DX = selector:offset of handler

Return Registers:
CF clear if successful
CF set on error
AX = error code (DPMI 1.0+) (8022h) (see Function 00h Subfunction 00h)

Details: 16-bit programs use CX:DX, 32-bit programs use CX:EDX. 32-bit programs must use a 32-bit interrupt stack frame when chaining to the next handler. DPMI implementations are required to support all 256 vectors. Hardware interrupts are reflected to the virtual machine's primary client, software interrupts to the current client.

This function is not supported by MS Windows 3.0 in Standard mode.

Conflicts: None known.

See Also: Function 02h Subfunctions 01h and 04h, Phar Lap INT 21h Function 25h Subfunction 04h (chapter 9)

INTERRUPT 31h - Function 02h, Subfunction 10h
GET PROTECTED MODE EXTENDED PROCESSOR EXCEPTION HANDLER

Purpose: Determine which procedure currently handles the specified protected mode processor exception.

Available on: 80286 or higher in protected mode.

Restrictions: DPMI version 1.0 or higher must be installed.

Registers at call:
AX = 0210h
BL = exception number (00h-1Fh)

Return Registers:
CF clear if successful
    CX:(EDX) = selector:offset of exception handler
CF set on error
    AX = error code (8021h) (see Function 00h
      Subfunction 00h)

Details: DPMI host reflects exception to current client's handler.
Conflicts: None known.
See Also: Function 02h Subfunctions 02h, 11h, and 12h

INTERRUPT 31h - Function 02h, Subfunction 11h
GET REALMODE EXTENDED PROCESSOR EXCEPTION HANDLER

Purpose: Determine which protected-mode procedure currently handles the specified real-mode processor exception.

Available on: 80286 or higher in protected mode.

Restrictions: DPMI version 1.0 or higher must be installed.

Registers at call:
AX = 0211h
BL = exception number (00h-1Fh)

Return Registers:
CF clear if successful
    CX:(EDX) = selector:offset of exception handler
CF set on error
    AX = error code (8021h) (see Function 00h
      Subfunction 00h)

Details: Returns address of protected-mode handler for real-mode exception. DPMI host performs a switch to protected mode, reflects the exception to the virtual machine's primary client, and returns to real mode on the handler's completion.
Conflicts: None known.
See Also: Function 02h Subfunctions 02h, 10h, and 13h

INTERRUPT 31h - Function 02h, Subfunction 12h
SET PROTECTED MODE EXTENDED PROCESSOR EXCEPTION HANDLER

Purpose: Specify which procedure will handle the indicated protected mode processor exception.

Available on: 80286 or higher in protected mode.

Restrictions: DPMI version 1.0 or higher must be installed.

Registers at call:
AX = 0212h
BL = exception or fault number (00h-1Fh)
CX:(E)DX = exception handler selector:offset

Return Registers:
CF clear if successful
CF set on error
    AX = error code (8021h,8022h) (see Function 00h
      Subfunction 00h)

Details: DPMI host sends exception to current client's handler.
Conflicts: None known.
See Also: Function 02h Subfunction 03h, 10h, and 13h

INTERRUPT 31h - Function 02h, Subfunction 13h
SET REALMODE EXTENDED PROCESSOR EXCEPTION HANDLER

Purpose: Specify which protected-mode procedure will handle the indicated real-mode processor exception.

Available on: 80286 or higher in protected mode.

Restrictions: DPMI version 1.0 or higher must be installed.

Registers at call:
AX = 0213h
BL = exception or fault number (00h-1Fh)
CX:(E)DX = exception handler selector:offset

Return Registers:
CF clear if successful
CF set on error
    AX = error code (8021h, 8022h) (see Function 00h
      Subfunction 00h)

Details: Specifies address of protected-mode handler for real-mode exception. DPMI host performs a switch to protected mode, reflects the exception to the virtual machine's primary client, and returns to real mode on the handler's completion.
Conflicts: None known.
See Also: Function 02h Subfunction 03h, 11h, and 12h

INTERRUPT 31h - Function 03h, Subfunction 00h
SIMULATE REAL MODE INTERRUPT

Purpose: Executes a real-mode interrupt handler.
Available on: 80286 or higher in protected mode.

Restrictions: DPMI version 0.9 or higher must be installed.

Registers at call:
AX = 0300h
BL = interrupt number
BH = flags:
    bit 0: reset the interrupt controller and A20 line
      (DPMI 0.9)
        reserved, must be 0 (DPMI 1.0+)
    others must be 0
CX = number of words to copy from protected
    mode to real mode stack
ES:(E)DI = selector:offset of real mode call
    structure (see Table 11-6)

Return Registers:
CF clear if successful
    real mode call structure modified (all fields except
      SS:SP, CS:IP filled with return values from
      real mode interrupt)

CF set on error
    AX = error code (DPMI 1.0+) (8012h, 8013h,
      8014h, 8021h) (see Function 00h Subfunction
      00h)
protected mode stack unchanged

Details: 16-bit programs use ES:DI as pointer, 32-bit programs use ES:EDI. CS:IP in the real mode call structure is ignored for this call, instead, the indicated interrupt vector is used for the address. The flags in the call structure are pushed on the real mode stack to form an interrupt stack frame, and the trace and interrupt flags are clear on entry to the handler. DPMI will provide a small (30 words) real mode stack if SS:SP is zero. The real mode handler must return with the stack in the same state as it was on being called.
Conflicts: None known.
See Also: Function 03h Subfunction 02h, Phar Lap INT 21h Function 25h Subfunction 11h (chapter 9), OS/286 INT 21h Function E3h (chapter 9).

Table 11-6. Format of real mode call structure:

Offset	Size	Description
00h	DWORD	EDI
04h	DWORD	ESI
08h	DWORD	EBP
0Ch	DWORD	reserved (00h)
10h	DWORD	EBX
14h	DWORD	EDX
18h	DWORD	ECX
1Ch	DWORD	EAX
20h	WORD	flags
22h	WORD	ES
24h	WORD	DS
26h	WORD	FS
28h	WORD	GS
2Ah	WORD	IP
2Ch	WORD	CS

Table 11-6. Format of real mode call structure (continued)

Offset	Size	Description
2Eh	WORD	SP
30h	WORD	SS

INTERRUPT 31h - Function 03h, Subfunction 01h
CALL REAL MODE PROCEDURE WITH FAR RETURN FRAME

Purpose: Executes a subroutine in real mode.
Available on: 80286 or higher in protected mode.

Restrictions: DPMI version 0.9 or higher must be installed.

Registers at call:
AX = 0301h
BH = flags
    bit 0: reset the interrupt controller and A20
        line (DPMI 0.9)
        reserved, must be 0 (DPMI 1.0+)
    others must be 0
CX = number of words to copy from protected
    mode to real mode stack
ES:DI/ES:EDI = selector:offset of real mode call
    structure (see INT 31h Function 03h
    Subfunction 00h)

Return Registers:
CF clear if successful
    real mode call structure modified (all fields except
        SS:SP, CS:IP filled with return values from
        real mode interrupt)
CF set on error
    AX = error code (DPMI 1.0+) (8012h, 8013h,
        8014h, 8021h) (see Function 00h Subfunction
        00h)
protected mode stack unchanged

Details: 16-bit programs use ES:DI as pointer, 32-bit programs use ES:EDI. The real mode procedure must exit with a FAR return. DPMI will provide a small (30 words) real mode stack if SS:SP is zero. The real mode handler must return with the stack in the same state as it was on being called.
Conflicts: None known.
See Also: Function 03h Subfunctions 00h and 02h, Phar Lap INT 21h Function 25h Subfunction 0Eh (chapter 9), OS/286 INT 21h Function E3h (chapter 9)

INTERRUPT 31h - Function 03h, Subfunction 02h
CALL REAL MODE PROCEDURE WITH IRET FRAME

Purpose: Executes a subroutine in real mode.
Available on: 80286 or higher in protected mode.

Restrictions: DPMI version 0.9 or higher must be installed.

Registers at call:
AX = 0302h
BH = flags
    bit 0: reset the interrupt controller and A20 line
        (DPMI 0.9)
        reserved, must be 0 (DPMI 1.0+)
    others must be 0
CX = number of words to copy from protected
    mode to real mode stack
ES:DI/ES:EDI = selector:offset of real mode call
    structure (see INT 31h Function 03h
    Subfunction 00h)

Return Registers:
CF clear if successful
    real mode call structure modified (all fields except
        SS:SP, CS:IP filled with return values from
        real mode interrupt)
CF set on error
    AX = error code (DPMI 1.0+) (8012h, 8013h,
        8014h, 8021h) (see Function 00h Subfunction
        00h)
protected mode stack unchanged

Details: 16-bit programs use ES:DI as pointer, 32-bit programs use ES:EDI. The flags in the call structure are pushed on the real mode stack to form an interrupt stack frame, and the trace and interrupt flags are clear on entry to the handler. The real mode procedure must exit with an IRET. DPMI will provide a small (30 words) real mode stack if SS:SP is zero; the real mode handler must return with the stack in the same state as it was on being called.
Conflicts: None known.
See Also: Function 03h Subfunction 00h

INTERRUPT 31h - Function 03h, Subfunction 03h
ALLOCATE REAL MODE CALLBACK ADDRESS

Purpose: Reserve a unique real mode address which may be called to transfer control from a real-mode procedure or interrupt handler to a protected-mode subroutine.

Available on: 80286 or higher in protected mode.

Restrictions: DPMI version 0.9 or higher must be installed.

Registers at call:
AX = 0303h
DS:SI/DS:ESI = selector:offset of procedure to call
ES:DI/ES:EDI = selector:offset of real mode call
   structure (see Function 03h Subfunction 00h)

Return Registers:
CF clear if successful
   CX:DX = segment:offset of real mode call address
CF set on error
   AX = error code (DPMI 1.0+) (8015h) (see
     Function 00h Subfunction 00h)

Details: The real mode call structure is static, causing reentrancy problems; its contents are only valid at the time of a callback. The called procedure must modify the real mode CS:IP before returning. Values are returned to real mode by modifying the real mode call structure. DPMI hosts must provide at least 16 callbacks per client.

Conflicts: None known.

See Also: Function 03h Subfunction 04h, Function 0Ch Subfunction 00h

Table 11-7. Values callback procedure called with:
DS:SI / DS:ESI = selector:offset of real mode SS:SP
ES:DI / ES:EDI = selector:offset of real mode call structure
SS:SP / SS:ESP = locked protected mode API stack
interrupts disabled

   Returns (with IRET):
      ES:DI / ES:EDI = selector:offset of real mode call structure to restore

INTERRUPT 31h - Function 03h, Subfunction 04h
FREE REAL MODE CALLBACK ADDRESS

Purpose: Release a previously reserved callback.

Available on: 80286 or higher in protected mode.

Restrictions: DPMI version 0.9 or higher must be installed.

Registers at call:
AX = 0304h
CX:DX = real mode callback address

Return Registers:
CF clear if successful
CF set on error
   AX = error code (DPMI 1.0+) (8024h) (see
     Function 00h Subfunction 00h)

Conflicts: None known.
See Also: Function 03h Subfunction 03h

INTERRUPT 31h - Function 03h, Subfunction 05h
GET STATE SAVE/RESTORE ADDRESSES

Purpose: Determine which procedures to call for saving and restoring the current task's registers in the currently inactive processor mode.

Available on: 80286 or higher in protected mode.

Restrictions: DPMI version 0.9 or higher must be installed.

Registers at call:
AX = 0305h

Return Registers:
CF clear
   AX = size in bytes of state buffer
   BX:CX = real mode address of procedure to
     save/restore state

SI:DI / SI:EDI = protected mode procedure to
save/restore state

Details: The buffer size will be zero if it is not necessary to preserve state. 16-bit programs should call SI:DI, 32-bit programs should call SI:EDI. This function is only needed if using the raw mode switch service.

Conflicts: None known.

See Also: Function 03h Subfunction 06h

Table 11-8. Values to call state-save procedures with:

> AL = direction
> > 00h save state
> > 01h restore state
> ES:DI / ES:EDI -> state buffer

Returns all registers preserved.

INTERRUPT 31h - Function 03h, Subfunction 06h
GET RAW MODE SWITCH ADDRESSES

Purpose: Determine low-level procedures which may be used to switch from protected to real mode and real mode to protected mode.

Available on: 80286 or higher in protected mode.

Restrictions: DPMI version 0.9 or higher must be installed.

Registers at call:
AX = 0306h

Return Registers:
CF clear
> BX:CX -> procedure to switch from real to
> protected mode
> SI:DI / SI:EDI -> procedure to switch from
> protected to real mode

Details: 16-bit programs should jump to SI:DI, 32-bit programs should use SI:EDI. The caller must save and restore the state of the task with Function 03h Subfunction 05h.

This function is not supported by MS Windows 3.0 in Standard mode.

Conflicts: None known.

See Also: Function 03h Subfunction 05h

Table 11-9. Values to JUMP at mode-switch procedures with:

> AX = new DS
> CX = new ES
> DX = new SS
> BX/EBX = new SP/ESP
> SI = new CS
> DI/EDI = new IP/EIP

BP/EBP is preserved across the call, but AX/EAX, BX/EBX, CX/ECX, DX/EDX, SI/ESI, and DI/EDI will be undefined; FS and GS will be 0000h. Interrupts will stay disabled during the entire mode switch if they are disabled on entry to the mode-switch procedure.

INTERRUPT 31h - Function 04h, Subfunction 00h
GET DPMI VERSION

Purpose: Determine the version of the DPMI specification supported by the host and which options are available.

Available on: 80286 or higher in protected mode.

Restrictions: DPMI version 0.9 or higher must be installed.

Registers at call: AX = 0400h

Return Registers:
CF clear
> AH = major version of DPMI spec supported
> AL = two-digit minor version of DPMI spec
> supported

BX = flags
> bit 0: running under an 80386 (32-bit)
>   implementation
> bit 1: processor returns to real mode for
>   reflected interrupts instead of V86 mode
> bit 2: virtual memory supported
> bit 3: reserved (undefined)
> others reserved (zero)

CL = processor type (02h = 80286, 03h = 80386,
04h = 80486)

DH = curr value of virtual master interrupt
controller base interrupt

DL = curr value of virtual slave interrupt controller
base interrupt

Conflicts: None known.
See Also: Function 04h Subfunction 01h, Phar Lap INT 21h Function 25h Subfunction 0Ch (chapter 9)

INTERRUPT 31h - Function 04h, Subfunction 01h
GET DPMI CAPABILITIES

Purpose: Determine the capabilities supported by the installed DPMI host.

Available on: 80286 or higher in protected mode.

Restrictions: DPMI version 1.0 or higher must be installed.

Registers at call:
AX = 0401h
ES:(E)DI -> 128-byte host version buffer
(see Table 11-10)

Return Registers:
CF clear if successful
> AX = capabilities
> > bit 0: page accessed/dirty supported (see
> >   Function 05h Subfunctions 06h or 07h)
> > 1: exceptions restartability supported
> > 2: device mapping supported (see Function 05h
> >   Subfunction 08h)
> > 3: conventional memory mapping supported
> >   (see Function 05h Subfunction 09h)
> > 4: demand zero-fill supported
> > 5: write-protect client capability supported
> > 6: write-protect host capability supported
> > 7-15: reserved
> CX = reserved (00h)
> DX = reserved (00h)
> buffer filled
CF set on error (DPMI 0.9 only)

Conflicts: None known.
See Also: Function 04h Subfunction 00h

Table 11-10. Format of host version buffer:

Offset	Size	Description
00h	BYTE	host major version number
01h	BYTE	host minor version number
02h	126 Bytes	ASCIZ host vendor name

INTERRUPT 31h - Function 05h, Subfunction 00h
GET FREE MEMORY INFORMATION

Purpose: Determine total and available memory amounts.

Available on: 80286 or higher in protected mode.

Registers at call:
AX = 0500h
ES:DI / ES:EDI -> buffer for memory information
    (see Table 11-11)

Restrictions: DPMI version 0.9 or higher must be installed.

Return Registers:
CF clear

Details: 16-bit programs use ES:DI, 32-bit programs use ES:EDI. This function must be considered advisory because other applications may affect the results at any time after the call. Fields not supported by the DPMI implementation are filled with FFFFFFFFh. DPMI 1.0+ supports this function solely for backward compatibility; use Function 05h Subfunction 0Bh instead.

Conflicts: None known.

See Also: Function 05h Subfunction 01h, Function 06h Subfunction 04h

Table 11-11. Format of memory information:

Offset	Size	Description
00h	DWORD	largest available block in bytes
04h	DWORD	maximum unlocked page allocation
08h	DWORD	maximum locked page allocation
0Ch	DWORD	total linear address space in pages
10h	DWORD	total unlocked pages
14h	DWORD	free pages
18h	DWORD	total physical pages
1Ch	DWORD	free linear address space in pages
20h	DWORD	size of paging file/partition in pages
24h	12 Bytes	reserved

INTERRUPT 31h - Function 05h, Subfunction 01h
ALLOCATE MEMORY BLOCK

Purpose: Request a block of committed (physical or virtual with backing store) memory.

Available on: 80286 or higher in protected mode.

Registers at call:
AX = 0501h
BX:CX = size in bytes

Restrictions: DPMI version 0.9 or higher must be installed.

Return Registers:
CF clear if successful
    BX:CX = linear address of block
    SI:DI = memory block handle for resizing and
        freeing block
CF set on error
    AX = error code (DPMI 1.0+) (8012h-8014h,
        8016h, 8021h) (see Function 00h Subfunction
        00h)

Details: No selectors are allocated. The memory block is allocated unlocked (can be locked with Function 06h Subfunction 00h). Allocations are often page granular (see Function 06h Subfunction 04h).

Conflicts: None known.

See Also: Function 00h Subfunction 00h, Function 01h Subfunction 00h, Function 05h Subfunctions 00h and 02h-04h, Function 0Dh Subfunction 00h

INTERRUPT 31h - Function 05h, Subfunction 02h
FREE MEMORY BLOCK

Purpose: Release a previously allocated block of memory.

Available on: 80286 or higher in protected mode.

Restrictions: DPMI version 0.9 or higher must be installed.

Registers at call:
AX = 0502h
SI:DI = handle of memory block

Return Registers:
CF clear if successful
CF set on error
    AX = error code (DPMI 1.0+) (8023h) (see
        Function 00h Subfunction 00h)

Details: Any selectors allocated for the memory block must also be freed, preferably before freeing the memory block.
Conflicts: None known.
See Also: Function 00h Subfunction 01h, Function 01h Subfunction 01h, Function 05h Subfunction 01h, Function 0Dh Subfunction 01h

INTERRUPT 31h - Function 05h, Subfunction 03h
RESIZE MEMORY BLOCK

Purpose: Change the size of a previously allocated block of memory.
Available on: 80286 or higher in protected mode.

Restrictions: DPMI version 0.9 or higher must be installed.

Registers at call:
AX = 0503h
BX:CX = new size in bytes (nonzero)
SI:DI = handle of memory block

Return Registers:
CF clear if successful
    BX:CX = new linear address
    SI:DI = new handle of memory block
CF set on error
    AX = error code (DPMI 1.0+) (8012h-8014h,
        8016h, 8021h, 8023h) (see Function 00h
        Subfunction 00h)

Details: Any selectors pointing at the block must be updated. The previous memory block handle becomes invalid. An error is returned if the new size is 0.
Conflicts: None known.
See Also: Function 01h Subfunction 02h, Function 05h Subfunctions 01h and 05h

INTERRUPT 31h - Function 05h, Subfunction 04h
ALLOCATE LINEAR MEMORY BLOCK

Purpose: Reserve a page-aligned block of the linear address space.
Available on: 80386 or higher in protected mode.

Restrictions: DPMI version 1.0 or higher must be installed.

Registers at call:
AX = 0504h
EBX = page-aligned linear address of memory
    block (00000000h if any address is acceptable)
ECX = size in bytes (nonzero)
EDX = flags
    bit 0: set to create committed pages instead of
        uncommitted pages
    bits 1-31: reserved (0)

Return Registers:
CF clear if successful
    EBX = linear address of memory block
    ESI = memory block handle
CF set on error
    AX = error code (8001h, 8012h-8014h, 8016h,
        8021h, 8025h) (see Function 00h Subfunction
        00h)

Details: Only supported by 32-bit DPMI hosts, but may be used by 16-bit clients.
Conflicts: None known.
See Also: Function 05h Subfunctions 01h and 05h

INTERRUPT 31h - Function 05h, Subfunction 05h
RESIZE LINEAR MEMORY BLOCK

Purpose: Modify the size of a previously allocated page-aligned block of linear address space.
Available on: 80386 or higher in protected mode.

Restrictions: DPMI version 1.0 or higher must be installed.

Registers at call:
AX = 0505h
ESI = memory block handle
ECX = new size in bytes (nonzero)
EDX = flags
    bit 0: create committed pages rather than
        uncommitted pages
    bit 1: segment descriptor update required
        ES:EBX -> buffer containing array of
            WORDs with selectors
        EDI = number of selectors in array
    bits 2-31: reserved (0)

Return Registers:
CF clear if successful
    EBX = new linear base address
    ESI = new memory block handle
CF set on error
    AX = error code (8001h, 8012h-8014h, 8016h,
        8021h, 8023h) (see Function 00h Subfunction
        00h)

Details: Only supported by 32-bit DPMI hosts, but may be used by 16-bit clients. The old memory block handle becomes invalid. If EDX bit 1 set and the block's base address is changed, DPMI updates all descriptors for selectors in the update buffer which fall within the memory block.
Conflicts: None known.
See Also: Function 05h Subfunctions 03h and 04h

INTERRUPT 31h - Function 05h, Subfunction 06h
GET PAGE ATTRIBUTES

Purpose: Determine the type and status of one or more pages of memory within a previously allocated block of memory.
Available on: 80386 or higher in protected mode.

Restrictions: DPMI version 1.0 or higher must be installed.

Registers at call:
AX = 0506h
ESI = memory block handle
EBX = offset in memory block of first page
ECX = number of pages
ES:EDX -> array of WORDs to hold page attributes
   (see Table 11-12)

Return Registers:
CF clear if successful
   buffer filled
CF set on error
    AX = error code (8001h, 8023h, 8025h) (see
        Function 00h Subfunction 00h)

Details: Only supported by 32-bit DPMI hosts, but may be used by 16-bit clients. If EBX is not page-aligned, it will be rounded down.
Conflicts: None known.
See Also: Function 05h Subfunctions 04h and 07h, Phar Lap INT 21h Function 25h Subfunction 1Dh (chapter 9), OS/386 INT 21h Function EBh Subfunction 00h (chapter 9)

Table 11-12. Format of page attribute words:

Bits	Meaning
0-2	page type
	000 uncommitted
	001 committed
	010 mapped (see Function 05h Subfunctions 08h or 09h)
	other currently unused
3	page is read/write rather than read-only
4	accessed/dirty bits supplied in bits 5 and 6
5	page has been accessed (only valid if bit 4 set)
6	page has been written (only valid if bit 4 set)
7-15	reserved (0)

INTERRUPT 31h - Function 05h, Subfunction 07h
MODIFY PAGE ATTRIBUTES

Purpose: Specify the type and status of one or more memory pages within a previously allocated block of memory.

Available on: 80386 or higher in protected mode.

Registers at call:
AX = 0507h
ESI = memory block handle
EBX = offset in memory block of first page
ECX = number of pages
ES:EDX -> array of WORDs with new page
   attributes (see Function 05h Subfunction 06h)

Restrictions: DPMI version 1.0 or higher must be
   installed.

Return Registers:
CF clear if successful
CF set on error
   AX = error code (8001h, 8002h, 8013h, 8014h,
      8021h, 8023h, 8025h) (see Function 00h
      Subfunction 00h)
   ECX = number of pages which have been set

Details: Only supported by 32-bit DPMI hosts, but may be used by 16-bit clients. If EBX is not page-aligned, it will
be rounded down.
Conflicts: None known.
See Also: Function 05h Subfunctions 04h and 06h, Phar Lap INT 21h Function 25h Subfunction 1Eh (chapter 9)

INTERRUPT 31h - Function 05h, Subfunction 08h
MAP DEVICE IN MEMORY BLOCK

Purpose: Make a memory-mapped physical device visible in the specified previously-allocated block of memory.
Available on: 80386 or higher in protected mode.

Registers at call:
AX = 0508h
ESI = memory block handle
EBX = page-aligned offset within memory block of
   page(s) to be mapped
ECX = number of pages to map
EDX = page-aligned physical address of device

Restrictions: DPMI version 1.0 or higher must be
   installed.

Return Registers:
CF clear if successful
CF set on error
   AX = error code (8001h, 8003h, 8023h, 8025h)
      (see Function 00h Subfunction 00h)

Details: Only supported by 32-bit DPMI hosts, but may be used by 16-bit clients. Support of this function is
optional; hosts are also allowed to support the function for some devices but not others.
Conflicts: None known.
See Also: Function 05h Subfunctions 04h and 09h, Function 08h Subfunctions 00h and 01h

INTERRUPT 31h - Function 05h, Subfunction 09h
MAP CONVENTIONAL MEMORY IN MEMORY BLOCK

Purpose: Make a portion of the one megabyte real-mode address space visible in the specified previously-allocated
block of memory.
Available on: 80386 or higher in protected mode.

Registers at call:
AX = 0509h
ESI = memory block handle
EBX = page-aligned offset within memory block of
   page(s) to map
ECX = number of pages to map
EDX = page-aligned linear address of conventional
   (below 1M) memory

Restrictions: DPMI version 1.0 or higher must be
   installed.

Return Registers:
CF clear if successful
CF set on error
   AX = error code (8001h, 8003h, 8023h, 8025h)
      (see Function 00h Subfunction 00h)

Details: Only supported by 32-bit DPMI hosts, but may be used by 16-bit clients. Support of this function is
optional.
Conflicts: None known.
See Also: Function 05h Subfunctions 04h and 08h, Function 08h Subfunction 01h

INTERRUPT 31h - Function 05h, Subfunction 0Ah
GET MEMORY BLOCK SIZE AND BASE

Purpose: Determine the size and physical address of a previously allocated block of memory.

Available on: 80286 or higher in protected mode.

Registers at call:
AX = 050AH
SI:DI = memory block handle

Restrictions: DPMI version 1.0 or higher must be installed.

Return Registers:
CF clear if successful
    SI:DI = size in bytes
    BX:CX = base address
CF set on error
    AX = error code (8023h) (see Function 00h Subfunction 00h)

Conflicts: None known.
See Also: Function 05h Subfunctions 01h and 04h

INTERRUPT 31h - Function 05h, Subfunction 0Bh
GET MEMORY INFORMATION

Purpose: Determine the available physical and virtual memory.
Available on: 80286 or higher in protected mode.

Registers at call:
AX = 050Bh
ES:(E)DI -> 128-byte buffer for memory
    information (see below)

Restrictions: DPMI version 1.0 or higher must be installed.

Return Registers:
CF clear if successful
CF set on error (DPMI 0.9 only)

Details: 16-bit programs use ES:DI, 32-bit programs must use ES:EDI.
Conflicts: None known.
See Also: Function 05h Subfunction 00h

Table 11-13. Format of memory information:

Offset	Size	Description
00h	DWORD	total allocated bytes of physical memory controlled by host
04h	DWORD	total allocated bytes of virtual memory controlled by host
08h	DWORD	total available bytes of virtual memory controlled by host
0Ch	DWORD	total allocated bytes of virtual memory for curr virtual mach
10h	DWORD	total available bytes of virtual memory for curr virtual mach
14h	DWORD	total allocated bytes of virtual memory for current client
18h	DWORD	total available bytes of virtual memory for current client
1Ch	DWORD	total locked bytes for current client
20h	DWORD	maximum locked bytes for current client
24h	DWORD	highest linear address available to current client
28h	DWORD	largest available memory block in bytes
2Ch	DWORD	minimum allocation unit in bytes
30h	DWORD	allocation alignment unit size in bytes
34h	76 BYTEs	reserved (00h)

INTERRUPT 31h - Function 06h, Subfunction 00h
LOCK LINEAR REGION

Purpose: Prevent a specified portion of the program's address space from being paged out if memory demands exceed the total physical memory.
Available on: 80386 or higher in protected mode.

Restrictions: DPMI version 0.9 or higher must be installed.

Registers at call:
AX = 0600h
BX:CX = starting linear address
SI:DI = size of region in bytes

Return Registers:
CF clear if successful
CF set on error
   none of the memory is locked
   AX = error code (DPMI 1.0+) (8013h, 8017h,
      8025h) (see Function 00h Subfunction 00h)

Details: Pages at beginning and end will be locked if the region overlaps them. May be called multiple times for a given page; the DPMI host keeps a lock count for each page.
Conflicts: None known.
See Also: Function 06h Subfunction 01h, Phar Lap INT 21h Function 25h Subfunction 1Ah (chapter 9), OS/386 INT 21h Function EBh Subfunction 06h (chapter 9)

INTERRUPT 31h - Function 06h, Subfunction 01h
UNLOCK LINEAR REGION

Purpose: Permit a specified portion of the program's address space to be paged out if memory demands exceed the total physical memory.
Available on: 80386 or higher in protected mode.

Restrictions: DPMI version 0.9 or higher must be installed.

Registers at call:
AX = 0601h
BX:CX = starting linear address
SI:DI = size of region in bytes

Return Registers:
CF clear if successful
CF set on error
   none of the memory is unlocked
   AX = error code (DPMI 1.0+) (8002h, 8025h) (see
      Function 00h Subfunction 00h)

Details: Pages at beginning and end will be unlocked if the region overlaps them. Any memory whose lock count has not reached zero remains locked.
Conflicts: None known.
See Also: Function 06h Subfunction 00h, Phar Lap INT 21h Function 25h Subfunction 1Bh (chapter 9), OS/386 INT 21h Function EBh Subfunction 07h (chapter 9)

INTERRUPT 31h - Function 06h, Subfunction 02h
MARK REAL MODE REGION AS PAGEABLE

Purpose: Prevent a specified portion of the real-mode one megabyte address space from being paged out if memory demands exceed the total physical memory.
Available on: 80386 or higher in protected mode.

Restrictions: DPMI version 0.9 or higher must be installed.

Registers at call:
AX = 0602h
BX:CX = starting linear address
SI:DI = size of region in bytes

Return Registers:
CF clear if successful
CF set on error
   none of the memory is made pageable
   AX = error code (DPMI 1.0+) (8002h, 8025h) (see
      Function 00h Subfunction 00h)

Details: Must relock all unlocked real mode memory before terminating process for DPMI 0.9; DPMI 1.0+ automatically relocks real mode memory. Pages at beginning and end will be unlocked if the region overlaps them. Pageability of real mode pages is binary, not a count.
Conflicts: None known.
See Also: Function 06h Subfunctions 00h and 03h

INTERRUPT 31h - Function 06h, Subfunction 03h
RELOCK REAL MODE REGION

Purpose: Permit a specified portion of the real-mode one megabyte to be paged out if memory demands exceed the total physical memory.

Available on: 80386 or higher in protected mode.

Registers at call:
AX = 0603h
BX:CX = starting linear address
SI:DI = size of region in bytes

Restrictions: DPMI version 0.9 or higher must be installed.
Return Registers:
CF clear if successful
CF set on error
    none of the memory is relocked
      AX = error code (DPMI 1.0+) (8002h, 8013h, 8025h) (see Function 00h Subfunction 00h)

Details: Pages at beginning and end will be relocked if the region overlaps them. Pageability of real mode pages is binary, not a count.
Conflicts: None known.
See Also: Function 06h Subfunction 02h

INTERRUPT 31h - Function 06h, Subfunction 04h
GET PAGE SIZE

Purpose: Determine the size of a single page of memory.
Available on: 80386 or higher in protected mode.

Registers at call:
AX = 0604h

Restrictions: DPMI version 0.9 or higher must be installed.
Return Registers:
CF clear if successful
    BX:CX = page size in bytes
CF set on error
    AX = error code (DPMI 1.0+)
      8001h unsupported, 16-bit host

Conflicts: None known.

INTERRUPT 31h - Function 07h, Subfunction 00h
RESERVED FOR HISTORICAL REASONS

Purpose: This function was originally defined, but has been dropped from publicly-released versions of the specification; it should never be called.
Available on: 80286 or higher in protected mode.
Registers at call:
AX = 0700h
Conflicts: None known.

Restrictions: DPMI must be installed.
Return Registers: n/a

INTERRUPT 31h - Function 07h, Subfunction 01h
RESERVED FOR HISTORICAL REASONS

Purpose: This function was originally defined, but has been dropped from publicly-released versions of the specification; it should never be called.
Available on: 80286 or higher in protected mode.
Registers at call:
AX = 0701h
Conflicts: None known.

Restrictions: DPMI must be installed.
Return Registers: n/a

INTERRUPT 31h - Function 07h, Subfunction 02h
MARK PAGE AS DEMAND PAGING CANDIDATE

Purpose: Indicate that the specified page or pages should be among the first to be paged out if memory demands exceed the total physical memory. This function may be used to improve system performance when the pages will not be accessed for a long period of time.
Available on: 80386 or higher in protected mode.

Registers at call:
AX = 0702h

Restrictions: DPMI version 0.9 or higher must be installed.
Return Registers:
CF clear if successful

BX:CX = starting linear address
SI:DI = number of bytes to mark as paging
   candidates

CF set on error
   AX = error code (DPMI 1.0+) (8025h) (see
      Function 00h Subfunction 00h)

Details: This function is advisory, and does not force immediate paging. Partial pages will not be discarded.
Conflicts: None known.
See Also: Function 07h Subfunction 03h

INTERRUPT 31h - Function 07h, Subfunction 03h
DISCARD PAGE CONTENTS

Purpose: Indicate that the contents of a region of memory are no longer needed and may be discarded rather than written to disk.
Available on: 80386 or higher in protected mode.

Restrictions: DPMI version 0.9 or higher must be installed.

Registers at call:
AX = 0703h
BX:CX = starting linear address
SI:DI = number of bytes to mark as discarded

Return Registers:
CF clear if successful
CF set on error
   AX = error code (DPMI 1.0+) (8025h) (see
      Function 00h Subfunction 00h)

Details: This function is advisory, and may be ignored by DPMI implementations. Partial or locked pages will not be discarded.
Conflicts: None known.
See Also: Function 07h Subfunction 02h

INTERRUPT 31h - Function 08h, Subfunction 00h
PHYSICAL ADDRESS MAPPING

Purpose: Make a physical address above the one-megabyte real-mode address space visible within the caller's linear address space.
Available on: 80286 or higher in protected mode.

Restrictions: DPMI version 0.9 or higher must be installed.

Registers at call:
AX = 0800h
BX:CX = physical address (should be above 1 MB)
SI:DI = size in bytes

Return Registers:
CF clear if successful
   BX:CX = linear address which maps the requested
      physical memory
CF set on error
   AX = error code (DPMI 1.0+) (8003h, 8021h) (see
      Function 00h Subfunction 00h)

Details: Implementations may refuse this call because it can circumvent protects. The caller must build an appropriate selector for the memory. Do not use for memory mapped in the first megabyte.
Conflicts: None known.
See Also: Function 00h Subfunction 02h, Function 05h Subfunctions 08h and 09h, Function 08h Subfunction 01h, Phar Lap INT 21h Function 25h Subfunction 0Ah (chapter 9), OS/386 INT 21h Function EBh Subfunction 05h (chapter 9)

INTERRUPT 31h - Function 08h, Subfunction 01h
FREE PHYSICAL ADDRESS MAPPING

Purpose: Release a previously-created mapping from a physical address to the caller's linear address space.
Available on: 80286 or higher in protected mode.

Restrictions: DPMI version 1.0 or higher must be installed.

Registers at call:
AX = 0801h
BX:CX = linear address returned by Function 08h
   Subfunction 00h

Return Registers:
CF clear if successful
CF set on error
   AX = error code (8025h) (see Function 00h
      Subfunction 00h)

Details: Should be called at end of access to device mapped with Function 08h Subfunction 00h.
Conflicts: None known.
See Also: Function 05h Subfunctions 08h and 09h, Function 08h Subfunction 00h, OS/386 INT 21h Function EBh Subfunction 03h (chapter 9)

INTERRUPT 31h - Function 09h, Subfunction 00h
GET AND DISABLE VIRTUAL INTERRUPT STATE

Purpose: Determine the current state of the virtual interrupt flag and clear it.
Available on: 80286 or higher in protected mode.   **Restrictions:** DPMI version 0.9 or higher must be installed.

Registers at call: **Return Registers:**
AX = 0900h   CF clear
                                          virtual interrupts disabled
                                          AL = 00h if previously disabled
                                             = 01h if previously enabled
                                          AH preserved

Details: The previous state may be restored simply by executing another INT 31. A CLI instruction may be used if the previous state is unimportant, but should be assumed to be very slow due to trapping by the host.
Conflicts: None known.
See Also: Function 09h Subfunctions 01h and 02h

INTERRUPT 31h - Function 09h, Subfunction 01h
GET AND ENABLE VIRTUAL INTERRUPT STATE

Purpose: Determine the current state of the virtual interrupt flag and set it.
Available on: 80286 or higher in protected mode.   **Restrictions:** DPMI version 0.9 or higher must be installed.

Registers at call: **Return Registers:**
AX = 0901h   CF clear
                                          virtual interrupts enabled
                                          AL = 00h if previously disabled
                                             = 01h if previously enabled
                                          AH preserved

Details: The previous state may be restored simply by executing another INT 31. A STI instruction may be used if the previous state is unimportant, but should be assumed to be very slow due to trapping by the host.
Conflicts: None known.
See Also: Function 09h Subfunctions 00h and 02h

INTERRUPT 31h - Function 09h, Subfunction 02h
GET VIRTUAL INTERRUPT STATE

Purpose: Determine the current state of the virtual interrupt flag.
Available on: 80286 or higher in protected mode.   **Restrictions:** DPMI version 0.9 or higher must be installed.

Registers at call: **Return Registers:**
AX = 0902h   CF clear
                                          AL = 00h if disabled
                                             = 01h if enabled

Details: Should be used rather than PUSHF because that instruction yields the physical interrupt state rather than the per-client virtualized interrupt flag.
Conflicts: None known.
See Also: Function 09h Subfunctions 00h and 01h

INTERRUPT 31h - Function 0Ah, Subfunction 00h
GET VENDOR SPECIFIC API ENTRY POINT

Purpose: Determine the address to call for vendor-specific extensions to the DPMI specification.

Available on: 80286 or higher in protected mode.

Restrictions: DPMI version 0.9 or higher must be installed.

Registers at call:
AX = 0A00h
DS:SI/DS:ESI -> case-sensitive ASCIZ vendor
   name or identifier

Return Registers:
CF clear if successful
   ES:DI/ES:EDI -> FAR extended API entry point
   DS, FS, GS, EAX, EBX, ECX, EDX, ESI, EBP
     destroyed
CF set on error
   AX = error code (DPMI 1.0+) (8001h) (see
     Function 00h Subfunction 00h)

Details: Extended API parameters are vendor-specific. DPMI 1.0+ supports this function solely for backward compatibility; use INT 2Fh Function 16h Subfunction 8Ah instead.

Conflicts: None known.

See Also: INT 2Fh Function 16h Subfunction 8Ah

INTERRUPT 31h - Function 0Bh, Subfunction 00h
SET DEBUG WATCHPOINT

Purpose: Set a breakpoint at the specified linear address.

Available on: 80286 or higher in protected mode.

Restrictions: DPMI version 0.9 or higher must be installed.

Registers at call:
AX = 0B00h
BX:CX = linear address
DL = size (1,2,4 bytes)
DH = type (00h execute, 01h write, 02h read/write)

Return Registers:
CF clear if successful
   BX = watchpoint handle
CF set on error
   AX = error code (DPMI 1.0+) (8016h, 8021h,
     8025h) (see Function 00h Subfunction 00h)

Conflicts: None known.

See Also: Function 02h Subfunction 12h, Function 06h Subfunction 01h

INTERRUPT 31h - Function 0Bh, Subfunction 01h
CLEAR DEBUG WATCHPOINT

Purpose: Remove a previously set debugging breakpoint.

Available on: 80286 or higher in protected mode.

Restrictions: DPMI version 0.9 or higher must be installed.

Registers at call:
AX = 0B01h
BX = watchpoint handle

Return Registers:
CF clear if successful
CF set on error
   AX = error code (DPMI 1.0+) (8023h) (see
     Function 00h Subfunction 00h)

Details: The watchpoint handle is freed.

Conflicts: None known.

See Also: Function 0Bh Subfunction 00h

INTERRUPT 31h - Function 0Bh, Subfunction 02h
GET STATE OF DEBUG WATCHPOINT

Purpose: Determine whether the specified breakpoint has been encountered.

Available on: 80286 or higher in protected mode.

Restrictions: DPMI version 0.9 or higher must be installed.

Registers at call:
AX = 0B02h
BX = watchpoint handle.

Return Registers:
CF clear if successful
    AX = status flags
        bit 0: watch point has been executed since
            Function 0Bh Subfunctions 00h or 03h
CF set on error
    AX = error code (DPMI 1.0+) (8023h) (see
        Function 00h Subfunction 00h)

Conflicts: None known.
See Also: Function 0Bh Subfunctions 00h and 03h

INTERRUPT 31h - Function 0Bh, Subfunction 03h
RESET DEBUG WATCHPOINT

Purpose: Clear the specified breakpoint's activation flag.
Available on: 80286 or higher in protected mode.

Restrictions: DPMI version 0.9 or higher must be
    installed.

Registers at call:
AX = 0B03h
BX = watchpoint handle

Return Registers:
CF clear if successful
CF set on error
    AX = error code (DPMI 1.0+) (8023h) (see
        Function 00h Subfunction 00h)

Conflicts: None known.
See Also: Function 0Bh Subfunction 02h

INTERRUPT 31h - Function 0Ch, Subfunction 00h
INSTALL RESIDENT HANDLER INITIALIZATION CALLBACK

Purpose: Request notification of loading or termination of other DPMI programs within the same virtual machine.
Available on: 80286 or higher in protected mode.

Restrictions: DPMI version 1.0 or higher must be
    installed.

Registers at call:
AX = 0C00h
ES:(E)DI -> resident service provider structure (see
    Table 11-14)

Return Registers:
CF clear if successful
CF set on error
    AX = error code (8015h,8021h,8025h) (see
        Function 00h Subfunction 00h)

Details: Calling this function declares an intent to provide resident protected mode services after terminating with Function 0Ch Subfunction 01h.
Conflicts: None known.
See Also: Function 03h Subfunction 03h, AX=0C01h

Table 11-14. Format of resident service provider structure:

Offset	Size	Description
00h	QWORD	descriptor for 16-bit data segment
08h	QWORD	descriptor for 16-bit code segment (zeros if not supported)
10h	WORD	offset of 16-bit callback procedure
12h	2 BYTEs	reserved
14h	QWORD	descriptor for 32-bit data segment
1Ch	QWORD	descriptor for 32-bit code segment (zeros if not supported)
24h	DWORD	offset of 32-bit callback procedure

INTERRUPT 31h - Function 0Ch, Subfunction 01h
TERMINATE AND STAY RESIDENT

Purpose: End execution but do not free the program's resources (such as memory).

Available on: 80286 or higher in protected mode.

Registers at call:
AX = 0C01h
BL = return code
DX = number of paragraphs of DOS memory to
    reserve (0 or >= 6)

Restrictions: DPMI version 1.0 or higher must be
    installed.

Return Registers: never

Details: Should only be used if the program will only provide services to other DPMI programs. Any protected mode memory remains allocated to the program unless explicitly freed before this call. Must first call Function 0Ch Subfunction 00h or program will simply be terminated.

Conflicts: None known.

See Also: Function 0Ch Subfunction 00h, DOS INT 21h Function 31h (chapter 8)

INTERRUPT 31h - Function 0Dh, Subfunction 00h
ALLOCATE SHARED MEMORY

Purpose: Request a block of memory which may be visible at the same address to other DPMI programs in the same virtual machine.

Available on: 80286 or higher in protected mode.

Registers at call:
AX = 0D00h
ES:(E)DI -> shared memory allocation request
    structure (see Table 11-15)

Restrictions: DPMI version 1.0 or higher must be
    installed.

Return Registers:
CF clear if successful
    request structure updated
CF set on error
    AX = error code (8012h, 8013h, 8014h, 8016h,
        8021h) (see Function 00h Subfunction 00h)

Details: First 16 bytes of memory block will be initialized to zeros on the first allocation.

Conflicts: None known.

See Also: Function 05h Subfunction 01h, Function 0Dh Subfunctions 01h and 02h

Table 11-15. Format of shared memory allocation request structure:

00h	DWORD	requested length of shared memory block in bytes
04h	DWORD	(return) allocated length of block
08h	DWORD	(return) shared memory handle
0Ch	DWORD	(return) linear address of memory block
10h	6 BYTEs	selector:offset32 of ASCIZ name for memory block (name max 128 bytes)
16h	2 BYTEs	reserved
18h	4 BYTEs	reserved (00h)

INTERRUPT 31h - Function 0Dh, Subfunction 01h
FREE SHARED MEMORY

Purpose: Release a previously-allocated block of shared memory; the block itself continues to exist until all programs which allocated it have released it.

Available on: 80286 or higher in protected mode.

Registers at call:
AX = 0D01h
SI:DI = shared memory block handle

Restrictions: DPMI version 1.0 or higher must be
    installed.

Return Registers:
CF clear if successful
CF set on error
    AX = error code (8023h) (see Function 00h
        Subfunction 00h)

Details: Handle becomes invalid after this call. DPMI maintains separate global and virtual machine use counts for each shared memory block; when the global use counts reaches zero, the block is finally destroyed.

Conflicts: None known.

See Also: Function 05h Subfunction 02h, Function 0Dh Subfunction 00h

INTERRUPT 31h - Function 0Dh, Subfunction 02h
SERIALIZE SHARED MEMORY

Purpose: Request either an exclusive or a shared lock on a block of shared memory to prevent conflicting accesses to that block.

Available on: 80286 or higher in protected mode.

Restrictions: DPMI version 1.0 or higher must be installed.

Registers at call:
AX = 0D02h
SI:DI = shared memory block handle
DX = flags
    bit 0: return immediately rather than suspending
    if serialization unavailable
    1: shared rather than exclusive serialization
    2-15: reserved (0)

Return Registers:
CF clear if successful
CF set on error
    AX = error code (8004h, 8005h, 8017h- 8019h,
    8023h) (see Function 00h Subfunction 00h)

Details: An exclusive serialization blocks any other serialization attempts for the same block by another virtual machine; a shared serialization blocks attempts at exclusive serialization by another virtual machine. Hosts are not required to detect deadlock. A client's interrupt handler can cancel a serialization call which caused it to block by calling Function 0Dh Subfunction 03h.

Conflicts: None known.

See Also: Function 0Dh Subfunctions 00h and 03h

INTERRUPT 31h - Function 0Dh, Subfunction 03h
FREE SERIALIZATION ON SHARED MEMORY

Purpose: Release a previously-granted lock on a block of shared memory.

Available on: 80286 or higher in protected mode.

Restrictions: DPMI version 1.0 or higher must be installed.

Registers at call:
AX = 0D03h
SI:DI = shared memory block handle
DX = flags
    bit 0: release shared serialization rather than
      exclusive serialization
    bit 1: free pending serialization
    bits 2-15: reserved (0)

Return Registers:
CF clear if successful
CF set on error
    AX = error code (8002h, 8023h) (see Function 00h
    Subfunction 00h)

Conflicts: None known.

See Also: Function 0Dh Subfunctions 00h and 02h

INTERRUPT 31h - Function 0Eh, Subfunction 00h
GET COPROCESSOR STATUS

Purpose: Determine whether a coprocessor exists or is being emulated.

Available on: 80286 or higher in protected mode.

Restrictions: DPMI version 1.0 or higher must be installed.

Registers at call:
AX = 0E00h

Return Registers:
CF clear
    AX = coprocessor status
      bit 0: numeric coprocessor enabled for current
        client
      bit 1: client is emulating coprocessor
      bit 2: numeric coprocessor is present
      bit 3: host is emulating coprocessor
        instructions

bits 4-7: coprocessor type
  0000 none
  0010 80287
  0011 80387
  0100 80486 with numeric coprocessor
  other reserved
bits 8-15: not used

Conflicts: None known.
See Also: Function 0Eh Subfunction 01h

INTERRUPT 31h - Function 0Eh, Subfunction 01h
SET COPROCESSOR EMULATION

Purpose: Specify whether to enable or emulate the coprocessor.

Available on: 80286 or higher in protected mode.

Restrictions: DPMI version 1.0 or higher must be installed.

Registers at call:
AX = 0E01h
BX = coprocessor flag bits
  bit 0: enable numeric coprocessor for current client
  bit 1: client will emulate coprocessor
  bits 2-15: not used

Return Registers:
CF clear if successful
CF set on error
  AX = error code (8026h) (see Function 00h Subfunction 00h)

Conflicts: None known.
See Also: Function 0Eh Subfunction 00h

Chapter 12

Virtual DMA Specification

The Virtual DMA Specification was introduced with the Micro Channel models of the PS/2 series to address problems inherent in protected mode use of DMA and the presence of multiple bus masters independently performing DMA operations. It contains, among others, functions to allocate buffers at fixed physical addresses and to lock address ranges to prevent multiple DMA operations on the same memory.

INTERRUPT 4Bh - Function 81h, Subfunction 02h
GET VERSION

Purpose: Determine the version of Virtual DMA software installed.

Available on: All machines.   **Restrictions:** none.

Registers at call:	**Return Registers:**
AX = 8102h	CF clear if successful
DX = 0000h	AH = major version number (currently 01h)

CF clear if successful
    AH = major version number (currently 01h)
    AL = minor version number (currently 00h)
    BX = product number
    CX = product revision number
    SI:DI = maximum DMA buffer size in bytes
    DX = flags:
        bit 0: PC/XT bus (DMA in first megabyte only)
        1: physical buffer/remap region is in the first megabyte
        2: automatic remap is enabled
        3: all memory is physically contiguous
        4-15: reserved (zero)
CF set on error
    AL = error code (see Table 12-1)

Details: Bit 5 of 0040h:007Bh is supposed to be set if VDS is supported; this is apparently not always the case. QEMM-386 returns product number 5145h ("QE").

    Bits 1-11 of the page table entries in Extended DMA Descriptor structures should be zero; bit 0 set if page is present and locked.

Conflicts: Z100 S100 vectored line 3 (chapter 2), Common Access Method SCSI interface, draft revision 1.9 (chapter 6).

See Also: INT 31

Table 12-1. DMA Error Codes

01h	region not in contiguous memory	07h	invalid memory region
02h	region crossed a physical alignment boundary	08h	region was not locked
03h	unable to lock pages	09h	number of physical pages greater than table length
04h	no buffer available		
05h	region too large for buffer	0Ah	invalid buffer ID
06h	buffer currently in use	0Bh	copy out of buffer range
		0Ch	invalid DMA channel number

Table 12-1. DMA Error Codes (continued)

0Dh	disable count overflow		0Fh	function not supported
0Eh	disable count underflow		10h	reserved flag bits set in DX

Table 12-2. Format of DMA descriptor structure (DDS):

Offset	Size	Description
00h	DWORD	region size
04h	DWORD	offset
08h	WORD	segment/selector
0Ah	WORD	buffer ID
0Ch	DWORD	physical address

Table 12-3. Format of Extended DMA descriptor structure (EDDS):

Offset	Size	Description
00h	DWORD	region size
04h	DWORD	offset
08h	WORD	segment/selector
0Ah	WORD	reserved
0Ch	WORD	number available
0Eh	WORD	number used
10h	DWORD	region 0 physical address
14h	DWORD	region 0 size in bytes
18h	DWORD	region 1 physical address
1Ch	DWORD	region 1 size in bytes
		...

Table 12-4. Format of Extended DMA descriptor structure (EDDS) with page table entries:

Offset	Size	Description
00h	DWORD	region size
04h	DWORD	offset
08h	WORD	segment/selector
0Ah	WORD	reserved
0Ch	WORD	number available
0Eh	WORD	number used
10h	DWORD	page table entry 0 (same as 80386 page table entry)
14h	DWORD	page table entry 1
		...

INTERRUPT 4Bh - Function 81h, Subfunction 03h
LOCK DMA REGION

Purpose: Prevent conflict or address remapping of DMA region during asynchronous operations.

Available on: All machines.

Restrictions: Virtual DMA software must be installed.

Registers at call:

Return Registers:

AX = 8103h

DX = flags

   bit 0: reserved (zero)

     1: data should be copied into buffer (ignored if bit 2 set)

     2: buffer should not be allocated if region is noncontiguous or crosses a physical alignment boundary specified by bits 4-5

CF clear if successful

   DDS physical address field filled in

   DDS buffer ID field filled (0000h if no buffer allocated)

CF set on error

   AL = error code (see Table 12-1)

3: don't attempt automatic remap
4: region must not cross 64K physical alignment boundary
5: region must not cross 128K physical alignment boundary
6-15: reserved (zero)
DS:SI -> DMA descriptor structure (see Function 81h Subfunction 02h)

DDS region size field filled with maximum contiguous length in bytes

Conflicts: Z100 S100 vectored line 3 (chapter 2), Common Access Method SCSI interface, draft revision 1.9 (chapter 6).
See Also: Function 81h Subfunctions 04h and 05h

INTERRUPT 4Bh - Function 81h, Subfunction 04h
UNLOCK DMA REGION

Purpose: Remove lock on DMA region installed by Subfunction 03h.
Available on: All machines.
Registers at call:
AX = 8104h
DX = flags
  bit 0: reserved (zero)
  1: data should be copied out of buffer
  2-15: reserved (zero)
ES:DI -> DMA descriptor structure (see Function 81h Subfunction 02h) with region size, physical address, and buffer ID fields set

Restrictions: Virtual DMA software must be installed.
Return Registers:
CF clear if successful
  DDS physical address field set
  DDS buffer ID field set (0000h if no buffer allocated)
CF set on error
  AL = error code (see Table 12-1)
  DDS region size field filled with maximum contiguous length in bytes

Conflicts: Z100 S100 vectored line 3 (chapter 2), Common Access Method SCSI interface, draft revision 1.9 (chapter 6).
See Also: Function 81h Subfunctions 03h and 06h

INTERRUPT 4Bh - Function 81h, Subfunction 05h
SCATTER/GATHER LOCK REGION

Purpose: Prevent remapping of multiple discontinuous regions of memory used by a scatter-read or gather-write operation.
Available on: All machines.
Registers at call:
AX = 8105h
DX = flags
  bits 0-5: reserved (zero)
  6: EDDS should be returned with page table entries
  7: only present pages should be locked (not-present pages receive entry of 0000h)
  8-15: reserved (zero)
ES:DI -> Extended DMA descriptor structure (see Table 12-1) region size, linear segment, linear offset, and number available fields set

Restrictions: Virtual DMA software must be installed.
Return Registers:
CF clear if successful
  EDDS number used field set
  if DX bit 6 set, lower 12 bits of BX = offset in first page
CF set on error
  AL = error code (see Table 12-1)
  EDDS region size field filled with max length in bytes that can be locked and described in the EDDS table

Conflicts: Z100 S100 vectored line 3 (chapter 2), Common Access Method SCSI interface, draft revision 1.9 (chapter 6).
See Also: Function 81h Subfunctions 03h and 06h

INTERRUPT 4Bh - Function 81h, Subfunction 06h
SCATTER/GATHER UNLOCK REGION

Purpose: Permit remapping of multiple previously locked regions of memory after a scatter-read or gather-write operation.

Available on: All machines.

Registers at call:

AX = 8106h

DX = flags

       bits 0-5: reserved (zero)

       6: EDDS contains page table entries

       7: EDDS may contain not-present pages

         (entry = 0000h)

       8-15: reserved (zero)

ES:DI -> Extended DMA descriptor structure (see
    Function 81h Subfunction 02h) returned by
    Function 81h Subfunction 05h

Restrictions: Virtual DMA software must be installed.

Return Registers:

CF clear if successful

CF set on error

    AL = error code (see Table 12-1)

Conflicts: Z100 S100 vectored line 3 (chapter 2), Common Access Method SCSI interface, draft revision 1.9 (chapter 6).

See Also: Function 81h Subfunctions 04h and 05h

INTERRUPT 4Bh - Function 81h, Subfunction 07h
REQUEST DMA BUFFER

Purpose: Allocate a region of memory which will not be remapped and may thus be used without explicit locking for each DMA operation.

Available on: All machines.

Registers at call:

AX = 8107h

DX = flags

       bit 0: reserved (zero)

       1: data should be copied into buffer

       2-15: reserved (zero)

ES:DI -> DMA descriptor structure (see Function
    81h Subfunction 02h) with region size set (also
    region offset and region segment if DX bit 1
    set)

Restrictions: Virtual DMA software must be installed.

Return Registers:

CF clear if successful

    DDS physical address and buffer ID set

    DDS region size filled with length of buffer

CF set on error

    AL = error code (see Table 12-1)

Conflicts: Z100 S100 vectored line 3 (chapter 2), Common Access Method SCSI interface, draft revision 1.9 (chapter 6).

See Also: Function 81h Subfunction 08h

INTERRUPT 4Bh - Function 81h, Subfunction 08h
RELEASE DMA BUFFFER

Purpose: Free a previously allocated buffer used for DMA operations.

Available on: All machines.

Registers at call:

AX = 8108h

DX = flags

       bit 0: reserved (zero)

Restrictions: Virtual DMA software must be installed.

Return Registers:

CF clear if successful

CF set on error

    AL = error code (see Table 12-1)

1: data should be copied out of buffer

2-15: reserved (zero)

ES:DI -> DMA descriptor structure (see Function
    81h Subfunction 02h) with buffer ID set (also
    region size, region offset, and segment if DX bit
    1 is set)

Conflicts: Z100 S100 vectored line 3 (chapter 2), Common Access Method SCSI interface, draft revision 1.9
(chapter 6).

See Also: Function 81h Subfunction 07h

INTERRUPT 4Bh - Function 81h, Subfunction 09h
COPY INTO DMA BUFFER

Purpose: Place the specified information into a previously allocated buffer in preparation for a DMA write
operation.

Available on: All machines.

Registers at call:

AX = 8109h

DX = 0000h

ES:DI -> DMA descriptor structure (see Function
    81h Subfunction 02h) with buffer ID, region
    segment/offset, and region size fields set

BX:CX = starting offset into DMA buffer

Restrictions: Virtual DMA software must be installed.

Return Registers:

CF clear if successful

CF set on error

    AL = error code (see Table 12-1)

Conflicts: Z100 S100 vectored line 3 (chapter 2), Common Access Method SCSI interface, draft revision 1.9
(chapter 6).

See Also: Function 81h Subfunction 0Ah

INTERRUPT 4Bh - Function 81h, Subfunction 0Ah
COPY OUT OF DMA BUFFER

Purpose: Retrieve the contents of a previously allocated buffer after a DMA read operation.

Available on: All machines.

Registers at call:

AX = 810Ah

DX = 0000h

ES:DI -> DMA descriptor structure (see Function
    81h Subfunction 02h) with buffer ID, region
    segment/offset, and region size fields set

BX:CX = starting offset into DMA buffer

Restrictions: Virtual DMA software must be installed.

Return Registers:

CF clear if successful

CF set on error

    AL = error code (see Table 12-1)

Conflicts: Z100 S100 vectored line 3 (chapter 2), Common Access Method SCSI interface, draft revision 1.9
(chapter 6).

See Also: Function 81h Subfunction 09h

INTERRUPT 4Bh - Function 81h, Subfunction 0Bh
DISABLE DMA TRANSLATION

Purpose: Turn off the translation of addresses used by DMA operations.

Available on: All machines.

Registers at call:

AX = 810Bh

BX = DMA channel number

DX = 0000h

Restrictions: Virtual DMA software must be installed.

Return Registers:

CF clear if successful

CF set on error

    AL = error code (see Table 12-1)

Conflicts: Z100 S100 vectored line 3 (chapter 2), Common Access Method SCSI interface, draft revision 1.9
(chapter 6).

See Also: Function 81h Subfunction 0Ch

INTERRUPT 4Bh - Function 81h, Subfunction 0Ch
ENABLE DMA TRANSLATION

Purpose: Permit the translation of addresses used by DMA operations.

Available on: All machines.

Restrictions: Virtual DMA software must be installed.

Registers at call:
AX = 810Ch
BX = DMA channel number
DX = 0000h

Return Registers:
CF clear if successful
   ZF set if disable count decremented to zero
CF set on error
   AL = error code (see Table 12-1)

Conflicts: Z100 S100 vectored line 3 (chapter 2), Common Access Method SCSI interface, draft revision 1.9 (chapter 6).

See Also: Function 81h Subfunction 0Bh

Chapter 13

Mouse Support

Mouse Support

In recent years, the mouse has taken a place almost equal to that of the keyboard itself as an input device. Part of the reason for its rise in popularity has been the relative ease of using it, since virtually all mice (regardless of manufacturer) make use of the "standard" INT 33h interface established by Microsoft with its first mouse driver. This chapter describes that interface.

Some non-Microsoft drivers provide additional capabilities beyond the ones provided by Microsoft drivers. Those calls are described under the Logitech and Mouse Systems headings following the general Microsoft calls.

Microsoft Mouse

Microsoft MouseThe Microsoft mouse driver (at version 8.0 as this chapter is being written) is the acknowledged standard of the MS-DOS world, and is used by nearly all programs as the interface to the rodent. Note that versions prior to 6.24 may not fully support video displays having more than 25 lines of text, or high-resolution video graphics modes. Neither do all "Microsoft compatible" drivers from other vendors necessarily support all functions listed here.

INTERRUPT 10h - Functions F0h thru FAh
EGA REGISTER INTERFACE LIBRARY

Purpose: Facilitate support of mouse cursor with EGA video cards.
Available on: All machines.   **Restrictions:** Microsoft or fully compatible mouse
                                        driver or EGA.SYS must be installed.

Details: Support of the mouse pointer requires the ability to modify the video display as the mouse moves, which in turn makes it necessary for the mouse driver software to determine the video mode at the instant mouse motion is detected. The write-only registers of the EGA card make it impossible to get this information directly from the card, so the Microsoft mouse drivers include these functions for register interfacing which trap out all BIOS calls that modify the EGA registers, and record the register content so that the mouse driver itself can later read the register content when required.

Although these functions are physically included within the mouse driver software, they affect video operation, and therefore are described in Chapter 5.

INTERRUPT 33h - Function 0000h
RESET DRIVER AND READ STATUS

Purpose: Determine the type of mouse present and reset both software and hardware for it.
Available on: All machines.   **Restrictions:** Vector for INT 33h must not be NULL
                                        (DOS V3.0+ initializes it, earlier
                                        versions do not).

Registers at call: **Return Registers:**
AX = 0000h   AX = status
                                               0000h hardware/driver not installed
                                               FFFh hardware/driver installed
                                          BX = number of buttons
                                               FFFFh two buttons
                                               0000h other than two
                                               0003h Mouse Systems/Logitech mouse

Details: To use mouse on a Hercules-compatible monographics card in graphics mode, you must first set 0040h:0049h to 6 for page 0 or 5 for page 1, and then call this function. The Logitech mouse driver contains the signature string "LOGITECH".
Conflicts: None known.
See Also: Function 0021h, INT 74h (chapter 2)

INTERRUPT 33h - Function 0001h
SHOW MOUSE CURSOR

Purpose: Make the mouse cursor/pointer visible.
Available on: All machines.

Restrictions: Microsoft or fully compatible mouse driver software must be installed.

Registers at call:
AX = 0001h

Return Registers: n/a

Details: To avoid leaving "mouse droppings" on the screen, the cursor should always be hidden before any action which changes the video display.
Conflicts: None known.
See Also: Functions 0002h and 0010h, PC Tools INT 16h Function FFh Subfunction FEh (chapter 33)

INTERRUPT 33h - Function 0002h
HIDE MOUSE CURSOR

Purpose: Make the mouse cursor/pointer invisible on the screen.
Available on: All machines.

Restrictions: Microsoft or fully compatible mouse driver software must be installed.

Registers at call:
AX = 0002h

Return Registers: n/a

Details: Multiple calls to hide the cursor require multiple calls to Function 0001h to unhide it, as the driver maintains a count of the number of times the mouse cursor has been hidden.
Conflicts: None known.
See Also: Functions 0001h and 0010h, PC Tools INT 16h Function FFh Subfunction FFh (chapter 33)

INTERRUPT 33h - Function 0003h
RETURN POSITION AND BUTTON STATUS

Purpose: Determine the current location and button status of the mouse.
Available on: All machines.

Restrictions: Microsoft or fully compatible mouse driver software must be installed.

Registers at call:
AX = 0003h

Return Registers:
BX = button status
  bit 0 left button pressed if 1
  bit 1 right button pressed if 1
  bit 2 middle button pressed if 1 (Mouse
       Systems/Logitech mouse)
CX = column
DX = row

Conflicts: None known.
See Also: Functions 0004h and 000Bh

INTERRUPT 33h - Function 0004h
POSITION MOUSE CURSOR

Purpose: Move the mouse cursor to the specified position.
Available on: All machines.

Restrictions: Microsoft or fully compatible mouse driver software must be installed.

Registers at call:
AX = 0004h
CX = column
DX = row

Return Registers: n/a

Details: The row and column are truncated to the next lower multiple of the cell size; however, some versions of the Microsoft documentation incorrectly state that the coordinates are rounded.
Conflicts: None known.
See Also: Function 0003h

INTERRUPT 33h - Function 0005h
RETURN BUTTON PRESS DATA

Purpose: Determine button status, click count, and the location where a button was last pressed.
Available on: All machines.

Restrictions: Microsoft or fully compatible mouse driver software must be installed.

Registers at call:
AX = 0005h
BX = button
    0000h left
    0001h right
    0002h middle (Mouse Systems/Logitech
        mouse)

Return Registers:
AX = button states
    bit 0 left button pressed if 1
    bit 1 right button pressed if 1
    bit 2 middle button pressed if 1 (Mouse
        Systems/Logitech mouse)
BX = number of times specified button has been
    pressed since last call
CX = column at time specified button was last pressed
DX = row at time specified button was last pressed

Conflicts: None known.
See Also: Function 0006h

INTERRUPT 33h - Function 0006h
RETURN BUTTON RELEASE DATA

Purpose: Determine button status, click count, and the location where a button was last released.
Available on: All machines.

Restrictions: Microsoft or fully compatible mouse driver software must be installed.

Registers at call:
AX = 0006h
BX = button
    0000h left
    0001h right
    0002h middle (Mouse Systems/Logitech
        mouse)

Return Registers:
AX = button states
    bit 0 left button pressed if 1
    bit 1 right button pressed if 1
    bit 2 middle button pressed if 1 (Mouse
        Systems/Logitech mouse)
BX = number of times specified button has been
    released since last call
CX = column at time specified button was last released
DX = row at time specified button was last released

Conflicts: None known.
See Also: Function 0005h

INTERRUPT 33h - Function 0007h
DEFINE HORIZONTAL CURSOR RANGE

Purpose: Establish limits on the horizontal motion of the mouse cursor/pointer.
Available on: All machines.

Restrictions: Microsoft or fully compatible mouse driver software must be installed.

Registers at call:
AX = 0007h

Return Registers: n/a

CX = minimum column
DX = maximum column
Conflicts: None known.
See Also: Functions 0008h and 0010h

INTERRUPT 33h - Function 0008h
DEFINE VERTICAL CURSOR RANGE

Purpose: Establish limits on the vertical motion of the mouse cursor/pointer.
Available on: All machines.

Restrictions: Microsoft or fully compatible mouse driver software must be installed.

Registers at call:
AX = 0008h
CX = minimum row
DX = maximum row

Return Registers: n/a

Conflicts: None known.
See Also: Functions 0007h and 0010h

INTERRUPT 33h - Function 0009h
DEFINE GRAPHICS CURSOR

Purpose: Specify the bitmap of the mouse pointer for graphics modes.
Available on: All machines.

Restrictions: Microsoft or fully compatible mouse driver software must be installed.

Registers at call:
AX = 0009h
BX = column of cursor hot spot in bitmap (-16 to 16)
CX = row of cursor hot spot (-16 to 16)
ES:DX -> bitmap
   16 words screen mask
   16 words cursor mask
      each word defines the sixteen pixels of a
      row, low bit rightmost

Return Registers: n/a

Conflicts: None known.
See Also: Functions 000Ah and 0012h

INTERRUPT 33h - Function 000Ah
DEFINE TEXT CURSOR

Purpose: Specify the shape and attribute of the mouse cursor/pointer for text modes.
Available on: All machines.

Restrictions: Microsoft or fully compatible mouse driver software must be installed.

Registers at call:
AX = 000Ah
BX = hardware/software text cursor
   0000h software
      CX = screen mask
      DX = cursor mask
  0001h hardware
      CX = start scan line
      DX = end scan line

Return Registers: n/a

Details: When the software cursor is selected, the char/attribute data at the current screen position is ANDed with the screen mask and then XORed with the cursor mask.
Conflicts: None known.
See Also: Function 0009h

INTERRUPT 33h - Function 000Bh
READ MOTION COUNTERS

Purpose: Determine the distances the mouse has moved since its position was last read.

Available on: All machines.

Restrictions: Microsoft or fully compatible mouse driver software must be installed.

Registers at call:
AX = 000Bh

Return Registers:
CX = number of mickeys mouse moved horizontally since last call
DX = number of mickeys mouse moved vertically

Details: A mickey is the smallest increment of motion the mouse can sense, typically equal to 1/8 mm or approximately 1/200 inch. Positive values indicate down/right.

Conflicts: None known.

See Also: Functions 0003h and 001Bh

INTERRUPT 33h - Function 000Ch
DEFINE INTERRUPT SUBROUTINE PARAMETERS

Purpose: Specify the actions to be performed at each mouse event.

Available on: All machines.

Restrictions: Microsoft or fully compatible mouse driver software must be installed.

Registers at call:
AX = 000Ch
CX = call mask (see Table 13-1)
ES:DX -> FAR pointer to Mouse Service Routine

Return Registers: n/a

Details: When the subroutine is called, it is passed the following values:

AX = condition mask (same bit assignments as call mask)
BX = button state
CX = cursor column
DX = cursor row
SI = horizontal mickey count
DI = vertical mickey count

Some versions of the Microsoft documentation incorrectly state that CX bit 0 requests invocation if the mouse cursor moves, and swap the meanings of SI and DI.

Conflicts: None known.

See Also: Functions 0018h

Table 13-1. Mouse Service Routine Call Mask Codes

Bit	Significance
0	call if mouse moves
1	call if left button pressed
2	call if left button released
3	call if right button pressed
4	call if right button released
5	call if middle button pressed (Mouse Systems/Logitech mouse)
6	call if middle button released (Mouse Sys/Logitech mouse)

INTERRUPT 33h - Function 000Dh
LIGHT PEN EMULATION ON

Purpose: Make the mouse emulate a light pen.

Available on: All machines.

Restrictions: Microsoft or fully compatible mouse driver software must be installed.

Registers at call:
AX = 000Dh

Return Registers: n/a

Conflicts: None known.
See Also: Function 000Eh

INTERRUPT 33h - Function 000Eh
LIGHT PEN EMULATION OFF

Purpose: End light pen emulation.
Available on: All machines.

Registers at call:
AX = 000Eh
Conflicts: None known.
See Also: Function 000Dh

Restrictions: Microsoft or fully compatible mouse driver software must be installed.
Return Registers: n/a

INTERRUPT 33h - Function 000Fh
DEFINE MICKEY/PIXEL RATIO

Purpose: Change mouse's sensitivity to movement.
Available on: All machines.

Registers at call:
AX = 000Fh
CX = number of mickeys per 8 pixels horizontally
   (default 8)
DX = number of mickeys per 8 pixels vertically
   (default 16)
Conflicts: None known.
See Also: Functions 0013h and 001Ah

Restrictions: Microsoft or fully compatible mouse driver software must be installed.
Return Registers: n/a

INTERRUPT 33h - Function 0010h
DEFINE SCREEN REGION FOR UPDATING

Purpose: Indicate to the mouse driver that the specified portion of the display is about to be modified, and the mouse cursor should not appear within that area.
Available on: All machines.

Registers at call:
AX = 0010h
CX,DX = X,Y coordinates of upper left corner
SI,DI = X,Y coordinates of lower right corner
Details: The mouse cursor is hidden during updating, and must be explicitly turned on again.
Conflicts: None known.
See Also: Functions 0001h 0002h, and 0007h

Restrictions: Microsoft or fully compatible mouse driver software must be installed.
Return Registers: n/a

INTERRUPT 33h - Function 0012h
SET LARGE GRAPHICS CURSOR BLOCK

Purpose: Define a graphics-mode mouse cursor of arbitrary (up to an implementation-dependent limit) size; this is a superset of Function 0009h.
Available on: All machines.

Registers at call:
AX = 0012h
BH = cursor width in words
CH = rows in cursor
BL = horizontal hot spot (-16 to 16)

Restrictions: Microsoft or fully compatible mouse driver software must be installed.
Return Registers:
AX = FFFFh if successful

CL = vertical hot spot (-16 to 16)
ES:DX -> bit map of screen and cursor maps
Conflicts: None known.
See Also: Function 0009h

INTERRUPT 33h - Function 0013h
DEFINE DOUBLE-SPEED THRESHOLD

Purpose: Permit rapid movement of the mouse pointer when the mouse is moved quickly.

Available on: All machines.

Restrictions: Microsoft or fully compatible mouse driver software must be installed.

Registers at call:
AX = 0013h
DX = threshold speed in mickeys/second,
    0000h = default of 64/second

Return Registers: n/a

Details: If the mouse's speed exceeds the given threshold, the cursor's on-screen motion is doubled.
Conflicts: None known.
See Also: Functions 000Fh, 001Bh, and 002Ch

INTERRUPT 33h - Function 0014h
EXCHANGE INTERRUPT SUBROUTINES

Purpose: Temporarily replace a mouse service routine (see Function 000Ch). The original routine is returned to allow later restoration.

Available on: All machines.

Restrictions: Microsoft or fully compatible mouse driver software must be installed.

Registers at call:
AX = 0014h
CX = call mask (see Table 13-1)
ES:DX -> FAR routine
Conflicts: None known.
See Also: Function 0018h

Return Registers:
CX = call mask of previous interrupt routine
ES:DX = FAR address of previous interrupt routine

INTERRUPT 33h - Function 0015h
RETURN DRIVER STORAGE REQUIREMENTS

Purpose: Determine the space required to save the mouse driver's state.

Available on: All machines.

Restrictions: Microsoft or fully compatible mouse driver software must be installed.

Registers at call:
AX = 0015h
Conflicts: None known.
See Also: Functions 0016h and 0017h, Mouse Systems Function 0042h

Return Registers:
BX = size of buffer needed to store driver state

INTERRUPT 33h - Function 0016h
SAVE DRIVER STATE

Purpose: Copy the mouse driver's state to a user-supplied save buffer.

Available on: All machines.

Restrictions: Microsoft or fully compatible mouse driver software must be installed.

Registers at call:
AX = 0016h
BX = size of buffer (see Function 0015h)
ES:DX -> buffer for driver state

Return Registers: n/a

Details: Although not documented, many drivers appear to require BX on input.
Conflicts: None known.
See Also: Functions 0015h and 0017h, Mouse Systems Function 0050h

INTERRUPT 33h - Function 0017h
RESTORE DRIVER STATE

Purpose: Copy the saved mouse driver state from the user's save buffer back to the driver.

Available on: All machines.

Restrictions: Microsoft or fully compatible mouse driver software must be installed.

Registers at call:
AX = 0017h
BX = size of buffer (see Function 0015h)
ES:DX -> buffer containing saved state

Return Registers: n/a

Details: Although not documented, many drivers appear to require BX on input. Some mouse drivers range-check the values in the saved state based on the current video mode; thus, the video mode should be restored before the mouse driver's state is restored.

Conflicts: None known.

See Also: Functions 0015h and 0016h

INTERRUPT 33h - Function 0018h
SET ALTERNATE MOUSE USER HANDLER

Purpose: Provide enhanced mouse capabilities using shift, Alt, and Ctrl keys.

Available on: All machines.

Restrictions: Microsoft or fully compatible mouse driver software must be installed.

Registers at call:
AX = 0018h
CX = call mask (see Table 13-2)
ES:DX = address of FAR routine

Return Registers:
AX = 0018h if successful
    FFFFh on error

Details: When the subroutine is called, it is passed the following values:

         AX = condition mask (same bit assignments as call mask)
         BX = button state
         CX = cursor column
         DX = cursor row
         DI = horizontal mickey count
         SI = vertical mickey count

Up to three handlers can be defined by separate calls to this function.

Conflicts: None known.

See Also: Functions 0014h and 0019h

Table 13-2. Bit Assignments for Alternate User Handler

Bit	Significance
0	call if alt key pressed during event
1	call if ctrl key pressed during event
2	call if shift button pressed during event
3	call if right button released
4	call if right button pressed
5	call if left button released
6	call if left button pressed
7	call if mouse moves

INTERRUPT 33h - Function 0019h
RETURN USER ALTERNATE INTERRUPT VECTOR

Purpose: Determine the location of the specified alternate interrupt service routine.

Available on: All machines.

Restrictions: Microsoft or fully compatible mouse driver software must be installed.

Registers at call:
AX = 0019h
CX = call mask (see Table 13-2)

Return Registers:
BX:DX = user interrupt vector
CX = call mask (0 if not found)

Details: This function attempts to find a user event handler (defined by Function 0018h) whose call mask matches CX.
Conflicts: None known.
See Also: Function 0018h

INTERRUPT 33h - Function 001Ah
SET MOUSE SENSITIVITY

Purpose: Combines older functions that set the sensitivity and threshold separately.
Available on: All machines.

Registers at call:
AX = 001Ah
BX = horizontal speed \
CX = vertical speed   / (see Function 000Fh)
DX = double speed threshold (see Function 0013h)
Conflicts: None known.
See Also: Functions 0013h and 001Bh

Restrictions: Microsoft or fully compatible mouse driver software must be installed.
Return Registers: n/a

INTERRUPT 33h - Function 001Bh
RETURN MOUSE SENSITIVITY

Purpose: Determine the current sensitivity settings.
Available on: All machines.

Registers at call:
AX = 001Bh

Restrictions: Microsoft or fully compatible mouse driver software must be installed.
Return Registers:
BX = horizontal speed
CX = vertical speed
DX = double speed threshold

Conflicts: None known.
See Also: Functions 000Bh and 001Ah

INTERRUPT 33h - Function 001Ch
SET INTERRUPT RATE

Purpose: Adjust the interrupt rate of the InPort mouse.
Available on: Machines with InPort mouse installed.
Registers at call:
AX = 001Ch
BX = rate
    00h no interrupts allowed
    01h 30 per second
    02h 50 per second
    03h 100 per second
    04h 200 per second

Restrictions: Microsoft or fully compatible mouse driver software must be installed.
Return Registers: n/a

Details: This function is only available on the InPort mouse. Values greater than 4 may cause unpredictable driver behavior.
Conflicts: None known.

INTERRUPT 33h - Function 001Dh
DEFINE DISPLAY PAGE NUMBER

Purpose: Control on which video page the mouse pointer is displayed.

Available on: All machines.

Registers at call:
AX = 001Dh
BX = display page number
Details: The cursor will be displayed on the specified page.
Conflicts: None known.
See Also: Function 001Eh

Restrictions: Microsoft or fully compatible mouse driver software must be installed.
Return Registers: n/a

INTERRUPT 33h - Function 001Eh
RETURN DISPLAY PAGE NUMBER

Purpose: Determine the current display page used by the mouse pointer.
Available on: All machines.

Restrictions: Microsoft or fully compatible mouse driver software must be installed.

Registers at call:
AX = 001Eh
Conflicts: None known.
See Also: Function 001Dh

Return Registers:
BX = display page number

INTERRUPT 33h - Function 001Fh
DISABLE MOUSE DRIVER

Purpose: Halt operation of the mouse driver.
Available on: All machines.

Restrictions: Microsoft or fully compatible mouse driver software must be installed.

Registers at call:
AX = 001Fh

Return Registers:
AX = 001Fh successful
    FFFFh unsuccessful
ES:BX = vector for INT 33h before mouse driver was first installed

Details: Restores vectors for INT 10h and INT 71h (8086) or INT 74h (286/386). If you restore INT 33h to the values returned in ES:BX, driver will be completely disabled.
Conflicts: None known.
See Also: Function 0020h

INTERRUPT 33h - Function 0020h
ENABLE MOUSE DRIVER

Purpose: Restore operation of the mouse driver after a halt.
Available on: All machines.

Restrictions: Microsoft or fully compatible mouse driver software must be installed.

Registers at call:
AX = 0020h
Details: Restores vectors for INT 10h and INT 71h (8086) or INT 74h (286/386) which were removed by Function 001Fh.
Conflicts: None known.
See Also: Function 001Fh

Return Registers: n/a

INTERRUPT 33h - Function 0021h
SOFTWARE RESET

Purpose: Resets mouse driver software without affecting the hardware.
Available on: All machines.

Restrictions: Microsoft or fully compatible mouse driver software must be installed.

Registers at call:
AX = 0021h

Return Registers:
AX = FFFFh if mouse driver installed
      0021h if mouse driver not installed
BX = 2 if mouse driver is installed

Details: Identical to Function 0000h, but does not reset the mouse.
Conflicts: None known.
See Also: Function 0000h

INTERRUPT 33h - Function 0022h
SET LANGUAGE FOR MESSAGES

Purpose: Specify the language in which messages from the mouse software are displayed.
Available on: All machines.

Restrictions: International version of Microsoft or fully compatible mouse driver software must be installed.

Registers at call:
AX = 0022h
BX = language
    00h English
    01h French
    02h Dutch
    03h German
    04h Swedish
    05h Finnish
    06h Spanish
    07h Portugese
    08h Italian

Return Registers: n/a

Details: Only available on international versions of the driver; US versions ignore this call.
Conflicts: None known.
See Also: Function 0023h

INTERRUPT 33h - Function 0023h
GET LANGUAGE FOR MESSAGES

Purpose: Determine the message language set by Function 0022h.
Available on: All machines.

Restrictions: International version of Microsoft or fully compatible mouse driver software must be installed.

Registers at call:
AX = 0023h

Return Registers:
BX = language (see Function 0022h)

Details: The US version of the driver always returns zero.
Conflicts: None known.
See Also: Function 0022h

INTERRUPT 33h - Function 0024h
GET SOFTWARE VERSION AND MOUSE TYPE

Purpose: Determine the current driver version and the type of mouse present.
Available on: All machines.

Restrictions: Microsoft or fully compatible mouse driver software must be installed.

Registers at call:
AX = 0024h

Return Registers:
AX = FFFFh on errorotherwise,
    BH = major version
    BL = minor version

CH = type (1=bus, 2=serial, 3=InPort, 4=PS/2, 5=HP)
CL = interrupt (0=PS/2, 2=IRQ2, 3=IRQ3,...,7=IRQ7)

Conflicts: None known.
See Also: Function 004Dh

INTERRUPT 33h - Function 0026h
Unknown Function

Purpose: *unknown.*
Available on: All machines.

Registers at call:
AX = 0026h
Details: Called by the newest Microsoft applications.
Conflicts: None known.

Restrictions: Microsoft or fully compatible mouse driver software must be installed.
Return Registers: *unknown.*

INTERRUPT 33h - Function 002Ch
SET ACCELERATION PROFILES

Purpose: Define one or more relations between the actual mouse speed and the speed of the mouse cursor. The older double-speed threshold is a special case of an acceleration profile.
Available on: All machines.

Restrictions: Microsoft or fully compatible mouse driver software must be installed.
Return Registers: n/a

Registers at call:
AX = 002Ch
ES:DX -> name of file containing profiles
Details: The mouse software includes an example set of acceleration profiles in the file MOUSEPRO.FIL.
Conflicts: None known.
See Also: Functions 0013h and 002Dh

INTERRUPT 33h - Function 002Dh
SELECT ACCELERATION PROFILE

Purpose: Begin using a previously defined relation between the actual mouse speed and the speed of the mouse cursor.
Available on: All machines.

Restrictions: Microsoft or fully compatible mouse driver software must be installed.
Return Registers: n/a

Registers at call:
AX = 002Dh
BX = acceleration level (01h to 04h)
Details: An acceleration of FFFFh appears to be legal as well, since it is used by the MS Control Panel v7.04.
Conflicts: None known.
See Also: Functions 0013h and 002Ch

INTERRUPT 33h - Function 004Dh
MS MOUSE, LOGITECH - RETURN POINTER TO COPYRIGHT STRING

Purpose: Determine the address of the copyright statement embedded within the mouse driver.
Available on: All machines.

Registers at call:
AX = 004Dh

Conflicts: None known.
See Also: Functions 0024h and 006Dh

Restrictions: Microsoft or fully compatible mouse driver software must be installed.
Return Registers:
ES:DI -> copyright message "Copyright 1983 Microsoft ***"

INTERRUPT 33h - Function 006Dh
MS MOUSE, LOGITECH - GET VERSION STRING

Purpose: Determine the version of the Microsoft driver to which the mouse software corresponds.

Available on: All machines.

Restrictions: Microsoft or fully compatible mouse driver software must be installed.

Registers at call:
AX = 006Dh
Conflicts: None known.
See Also: Function 004Dh

Return Registers:
ES:DI -> Microsoft version number of resident driver

Logitech Mouse

Most Logitech mice have three buttons as opposed to the Microsoft mouse, which has two buttons. As a result, some of the functions in the Microsoft section above indicate extra bits for the three-button mice.

INTERRUPT 33h - Function 1D6Ch
GET COMPASS PARAMETER

Purpose: Determine the current relation between the direction of mouse movement and the direction of the mouse cursor's movement.

Available on: All machines.

Restrictions: Logitech mouse driver software must be installed.

Registers at call:
AX = 1D6Ch
Conflicts: None known.
See Also: Function 1E6Ch

Return Registers:
BX = direction (0=north, 1=south, 2=east, 3=west)

INTERRUPT 33h - Function 1E6Ch
SET COMPASS PARAMETER

Purpose: Specify the relation between the direction of mouse movement and the direction of the mouse cursor's movement.

Available on: All machines.

Restrictions: Logitech mouse driver software must be installed.

Registers at call:
AX = 1E6Ch
BX = direction (0=north, 1=south, 2=east, 3=west)
Conflicts: None known.
See Also: Function 1D6Ch

Return Registers: n/a

INTERRUPT 33h - Function 1F6Ch
GET BALLISTICS INFORMATION

Purpose: Determine how much the mouse cursor's speed increases as the mouse's speed increases.

Available on: All machines.

Restrictions: Logitech mouse driver software must be installed.

Registers at call:
AX = 1F6Ch

Conflicts: None known.
See Also: Functions 002Ch and 236Ch

Return Registers:
BX = 0=off, 1=on
CX = 1=low, 2=high

INTERRUPT 33h - Function 206Ch
SET LEFT OR RIGHT PARAMETER

Purpose: Specify whether the mouse is left-handed or right-handed.

Available on: All machines.

Registers at call:
AX = 206Ch
BX = parameter (00h = right, FFh = left)
Conflicts: None known.
See Also: Function 216Ch

Restrictions: Logitech mouse driver software must be installed.
Return Registers: n/a

INTERRUPT 33h - Function 216Ch
GET LEFT OR RIGHT PARAMETER

Purpose: Determine whether the mouse is currently left-handed or right-handed.
Available on: All machines.

Registers at call:
AX = 216Ch
Conflicts: None known.
See Also: Function 206Ch

Restrictions: Logitech mouse driver software must be installed.
Return Registers:
BX = parameter (00h = right, FFh = left)

INTERRUPT 33h - Function 226Ch
REMOVE DRIVER FROM MEMORY

Purpose: Free the memory used by the mouse driver.
Available on: All machines.

Registers at call:
AX = 226Ch
Details: This only frees memory; it does not restore hooked interrupts.
Conflicts: None known.

Restrictions: Logitech mouse driver software must be installed.
Return Registers: n/a

INTERRUPT 33h - Function 236Ch
SET BALLISTICS INFORMATION

Purpose: Specify how much the mouse cursor's speed increases as the mouse's speed increases.
Available on: All machines.

Registers at call:
AX = 236Ch
BX = 0=off, 1=on
CX = 1=low, 2=high
Conflicts: None known.
See Also: Functions 002Ch and 1F6Ch

Restrictions: Logitech mouse driver software must be installed.
Return Registers: n/a

INTERRUPT 33h - Function 246Ch
GET PARAMETERS AND RESET SERIAL MOUSE

Purpose: Determine the current settings for the mouse hardware and place the mouse port in a known initial state.
Available on: All machines.

Registers at call:
AX = 246Ch
ES:DX -> parameter table buffer (Table 13-3)
Conflicts: None known.
See Also: Function 256Ch and Microsoft Function 0000h

Restrictions: Logitech mouse driver software must be installed.
Return Registers:
AX = FFFFh if driver installed for serial mouse

Table 13-3. Format of parameter table:

Offset	Size	Description
00h	WORD	baud rate divided by 100 (serial mouse only)
02h	WORD	emulation (serial mouse only)
04h	WORD	report rate (serial mouse only)
06h	WORD	firmware revision (serial mouse only)
08h	WORD	0 (serial mouse only)
0Ah	WORD	port (serial mouse only)
0Ch	WORD	physical buttons
0Eh	WORD	logical buttons

INTERRUPT 33h - Function 256Ch
SET PARAMETERS

Purpose: Specify new settings for the mouse hardware.
Available on: All machines.

Registers at call:
AX = 256Ch
BX = 00h set baud rate (serial mouse only)
      CX = rate (0=1200, 1=2400, 2=4800,
      3=9600)
BX = 01h set emulation (serial mouse only)
      CX = emulation
      0 = 5 byte packed binary
      1 = 3 byte packed binary
      2 = hexadecimal
      3 = relative bit pad
      4 = not supported
      5 = MM Series
      6 = not supported
      7 = Microsoft
BX = 02h set report rate (serial mouse only)
      CX = rate (0=10, 1=20, 2=35, 3=50, 4=70,
      5=100, 6=150)
BX = 03h set port (serial mouse only)
      CX = port (1, 2)
BX = 04h set mouse logical buttons
      CX = buttons (2, 3)
Conflicts: None known.
See Also: Function 246Ch

Restrictions: Logitech mouse driver software must be
installed.
Return Registers:
AX = FFFFh if driver installed for serial mouse

INTERRUPT 33h - Function 266Ch
GET VERSION

Purpose: Determine which version of the Logitech mouse software is loaded.
Available on: All machines.

Registers at call:
AX = 266Ch

Restrictions: Logitech mouse driver software must be
installed.
Return Registers:
BX = 'SS'
CH = major version number (ASCII digit)
CL = minor version number (ASCII digit)

Conflicts: None known.
See Also: Microsoft Mouse Function 006Dh

INTERRUPT 33h - Function 276Ch
Unknown Function

Purpose: This function apparently tries to set the mouse to emulate an MM Series mouse at 2400 bps.

Available on: All machines.

Restrictions: Logitech mouse driver software must be installed.

Registers at call:
AX = 276Ch

Return Registers: n/a

Conflicts: None known.

Mouse Systems PCMOUSE

As with Logitech, most Mouse Systems mice have three buttons, and thus make use of an additional bit for many of the functions listed in the Microsoft section. In addition to the standard INT 33h functions, the PCMOUSE provides its own functions for saving and restoring the driver's state; these presumably predate the Microsoft equivalents.

INTERRUPT 33h - Function 0042h
GET MSMOUSE STORAGE REQUIREMENTS

Purpose: Determine how much space is needed to store the driver's state.

Available on: All machines.

Restrictions: Mouse Systems mouse software must be installed.

Registers at call:
AX = 0042h

Return Registers:
AX = FFFFh if successful
BX = buffer size in bytes for functions 50h and 52h
   = 0000h MSMOUSE not installed
   = 0042h Functions 42h, 50h, and 52h are not
      supported

Conflicts: None known.
See Also: Function 0050h, Microsoft Mouse Function 0015h

INTERRUPT 33h - Function 0050h
SAVE MSMOUSE STATE

Purpose: Copy the driver's current state into a user-provided buffer.

Available on: All machines.

Restrictions: Mouse Systems mouse software must be installed.

Registers at call:
AX = 0050h
BX = buffer size
ES:DX -> buffer

Return Registers:
AX = FFFFh if successful

Conflicts: None known.
See Also: Functions 0042h and 0052h, Microsoft Mouse Function 0016h

INTERRUPT 33h - Function 0052h
RESTORE MSMOUSE STATE

Purpose: Copy a previously-stored state from the specified buffer back into the mouse driver.

Available on: All machines.

Restrictions: Mouse Systems mouse software must be installed.

Registers at call:
AX = 0052h
BX = buffer size
ES:DX -> buffer

Return Registers:
AX = FFFFh if successful

Conflicts: None known.
See Also: Function 0050h, Microsoft Mouse Function 0017h

Chapter 14

Microsoft Windows

Microsoft Windows is currently the most popular graphical user interface for the IBM PC family. In addition to its graphical interface, it has some multitasking abilities, though only specially-written programs can be multitasked unless running on a 386 or higher processor. Other multitaskers will be covered in chapters 15 through 18.

In addition to the calls listed here, the EGA.SYS driver uses INT 2Fh Function BCh. It is covered in chapter 8 because EGA.SYS is now included with DOS 5.0 as well as Windows.

MS WINDOWS

The calls in this section are provided by Windows itself. INT 2Fh Function 16h comprises an API for non-Windows programs (DOS device drivers, TSRs, and applications) to cooperate with multitasking under Windows/386 2.x and Windows 3.0 and higher enhanced mode. Some of those calls are also supported by the Microsoft 80286 DOS extender in Windows standard mode.

INTERRUPT 16h - Function 6Fh, Subfunction 00h
Unknown Function

Purpose: *unknown.*
Available on: All machines.
Registers at call:
AX = 6F00h
BX = 0000h
other unknown.

Restrictions: *unknown.*
Return Registers:
BX = 4850h
 other *unknown.*

Details: This function is called by recent Microsoft Mouse drivers.
Conflicts: None known.

INTERRUPT 2Fh - Function 16h, Subfunction 00h
MS WINDOWS ENHANCED MODE INSTALLATION CHECK

Purpose: Determine whether MS Windows/386 version 2.x or MS Windows 3.x in enhanced mode is running.
Available on: All machines.
Registers at call:
AX = 1600h

Restrictions: none.
Return Registers:
AL = 00h if Windows 3.x enhanced mode or
  Windows/386 2.x not running
AL = 80h if Windows 3.x enhanced mode or
  Windows/386 2.x not running
AL = 01h if Windows/386 2.x running
AL = FFh if Windows/386 2.x running
AL = anything else
  AL = Windows major version number> = 3
  AH = Windows minor version number

Conflicts: None known.
See Also: Function 46h Subfunction 80h

INTERRUPT 2Fh - Function 16h, Subfunction 02h
GET API ENTRY POINT

Purpose: Determine address to call to invoke Windows/386 functions.

Available on: All machines.

Restrictions: MS Windows/386 version 2.x must be running.

Registers at call:
AX = 1602h

Return Registers:
ES:DI -> Windows/386 2.x API procedure entry point

Details: This interface is supported in Windows 3.x only for 2.x compatibility to get the current virtual machine (VM) ID in Windows/386 2.x:

>   AX = 0000h
>   ES:DI -> return address
>   JUMP to address returned from INT 2Fh Function 16h Subfunction 02h

After JUMP, at return address:

>   BX = current VM ID.

INTERRUPT 2Fh - Function 16h, Subfunction 05h
WINDOWS ENHANCED MODE & 286 DOSX INIT BROADCAST

Purpose: Called by Windows to allow programs to perform any preparations necessary for compatibility with Windows execution, or prevent Windows from starting up if any incompatible programs are loaded.

Available on: All machines.

Restrictions: MS Windows 3.0 or higher must be running in standard or enhanced mode.

Registers at call:
AX = 1605h
ES:BX = 0000h:0000h
DS:SI = 0000h:0000h
CX = 0000h
DX = flags
  bit 0 = 0 if Windows enhanced-mode
      initialization
  bit 0 = 1 if Microsoft 286 DOS extender
      initialization
  bits 1-15 reserved (undefined)
DI = version number (major in upper byte, minor in
  lower)

Return Registers:
CX = 0000h if okay for Windows to load
CX <> 0 if Windows should not load
ES:BX -> startup info structure (Table 14-1)
DS:SI -> virtual86 mode enable/disable callback or
  0000h:0000h

Details: The Windows enhanced mode loader and Microsoft 286 DOS extender will broadcast an INT 2Fh Function 16h Subfunction 05h call when initializing. Any DOS device driver or TSR can watch for this broadcast and return the appropriate values. If the driver or TSR returns CX nonzero, it is also its responsibility to display an error message. Each handler must first chain to the prior INT 2F handler with registers unchanged before processing the call.

  If the handler requires local data on a per-VM basis, it must store the returned ES:BX in the "next" field of a startup info structure and return a pointer to that structure in ES:BX. A single TSR may set the V86 mode enable/disable callback; if DS:SI is already nonzero, the TSR must fail the initialization by setting CX nonzero.

Conflicts: None known.

See Also: Function 16h Subfunctions 06h and 08h

Table 14-1. Format of Startup Information Structure:

Offset	Size	Description
00h	2 BYTEs	major, minor version of info structure
02h	DWORD	pointer to next startup info structure
06h	DWORD	pointer to ASCIZ name of virtual device file or 0000h:0000h
0Ah	DWORD	virtual device reference data (only used if above nonzero)
0Eh	DWORD	pointer to instance data records (Table 14-2) or 0000h:0000h

Table 14-2. Format of One Instance Item in Array:

Offset	Size	Description
00h	DWORD	address of instance data (end of array if 0000h:0000h)
04h	WORD	size of instance data

Virtual mode enable/disable procedure called with:
AX = 0000h disable V86 mode
AX = 0001h enable V86 mode
interrupts disabled

Return Registers:
CF set on error
CF clear if successful
interrupts disabled

INTERRUPT 2Fh - Function 16h, Subfunction 06h
WINDOWS ENHANCED MODE & 286 DOSX EXIT BROADCAST

Purpose: Called by Windows to allow programs to perform any cleanup necessary for resuming standard DOS operation.

Available on: All machines.

Restrictions: MS Windows 3.0 or higher must be running in standard or enhanced mode.

Registers at call:
AX = 1606h
DX = flags
   bit 0 = 0 if Windows enhanced-mode exit
   bit 0 = 1 if Microsoft 286 DOS extender exit
   bits 1-15 reserved (undefined)

Return Registers: n/a

Details: If the init broadcast fails (Function 16h Subfunction 05h returned CX <> 0), then this broadcast will be issued immediately. This call will be issued in real mode.

Conflicts: None known.

See Also: Function 16h Subfunctions 05h and 09h

INTERRUPT 2Fh - Function 16h, Subfunction 07h
VIRTUAL DEVICE CALL OUT API

Purpose: Called by Windows virtual devices to communicate with DOS device drivers.

Available on: All machines.

Restrictions: MS Windows 3.0 or higher must be running.

Registers at call:
AX = 1607h
BX = virtual device ID (see INT 2Fh Function 16h
   Subfunction 84h)

Return Registers: device-dependent

Details: More of a convention than an API, this call specifies a standard mechanism for Windows enhanced-mode virtual devices (VxD's) to talk to DOS device drivers and TSRs.

Conflicts: None known.

See Also: Function 16h Subfunctions 05h and 84h

INTERRUPT 2Fh - Function 16h, Subfunction 08h
WINDOWS ENHANCED MODE INIT COMPLETE BROADCAST

Purpose: Called by Windows to inform programs that Windows is fully operational.

Available on: All machines.

Restrictions: MS Windows 3.0 or higher must be running.

Registers at call:
AX = 1608h

Return Registers: n/a

Details: Called after all installable devices have been initialized. Real-mode software may be called between the Windows enhanced-mode init call (Function 16h Subfunction 05h) and this call; the software must detect this situation.

Conflicts: None known.
See Also: Function 16h Subfunctions 05h and 09h

INTERRUPT 2Fh - Function 16h, Subfunction 09h
WINDOWS ENHANCED MODE BEGIN EXIT BROADCAST

Purpose: Called by Windows to inform programs that it is about to terminate.

Available on: All machines.

Restrictions: MS Windows 3.0 or higher must be running.

Registers at call:
AX = 1609h

Return Registers: n/a

Details: Called at the beginning of a normal exit sequence; not made in the event of a fatal system crash.
Conflicts: None known.
See Also: Function 16h Subfunctions 06h and 08h

INTERRUPT 2Fh - Function 16h, Subfunction 80h
RELEASE CURRENT VIRTUAL MACHINE TIME-SLICE

Purpose: Inform Windows (or OS/2, DOS 5, or DPMI hosts) that the caller is idle and does not need the rest of its time slice.

Available on: All machines.

Restrictions: MS Windows 3.0+, OS/2 v2.0+, DPMI v1.0+, or DOS 5.0+ must be running.

Registers at call:
AX = 1680h

Return Registers:
AL = 00h if the call is supported
AL = 80h (unchanged) if the call is not supported

Details: Programs can use this function even when not running under Windows in 386 enhanced mode, because OS/2 can use the call to detect idleness even though it does not support the complete Windows enhanced-mode API. This call is supported by the DPMI specification version 1.0, will be supported in OS/2 2.0 for multitasking DOS applications, and is reportedly supported by DOS 5.0. This call does not block the program; it merely gives up the remainder of the time slice and must thus be called repeatedly as long as the program remains idle. It should only be used by non-Windows programs.
Conflicts: None known.
See Also: TopView INT 15h Function 10h Subfunction 00h (chapter 15)

INTERRUPT 2Fh - Function 16h, Subfunction 81h
BEGIN CRITICAL SECTION

Purpose: Inform Windows that it should temporarily halt task-switching while the calling program performs nonreentrant actions.

Available on: All machines.

Restrictions: MS Windows version 3+ must be running.

Registers at call:
AX = 1681h

Return Registers: n/a

Details: Used to prevent a task switch from occurring. Should be followed by a call to Function 16h Subfunction 82h as soon as possible. Nested calls are allowed, and must be followed by an appropriate number of "end critical section" calls. Not supported in Windows/386 2.x. Get INDOS flag with INT 21h Function 34h and increment by hand.
Conflicts: None known.
See Also: Function 16h Subfunction 82h, TopView INT 15h Function 10h Subfunction 1Bh (chapter 15), DOS INT 21h Function 34h (chapter 8)

INTERRUPT 2Fh - Function 16h, Subfunction 82h
END CRITICAL SECTION

Purpose: Inform Windows that it may resume task-switching.

Available on: All machines.

Restrictions: MS Windows version 3+ must be running.

Registers at call: **Return Registers:** n/a
AX = 1682h
Details: Not supported in Windows/386 2.x. Get InDOS flag with INT 21h Function 34h and decrement by hand, taking care not to decrement InDOS flag through zero.
Conflicts: None known.
See Also: Function 16h Subfunction 81h, TopView INT 15h Function 10h Subfunction 1Ch (chapter 15), DOS INT 21h Function 34h (chapter 8)

INTERRUPT 2Fh - Function 16h, Subfunction 83h
GET CURRENT VIRTUAL MACHINE ID

Purpose: Determine the number identifying the virtual machine in which the caller is running.
Available on: All machines.   **Restrictions:** MS Windows version 3+ must be
                                                                                        running.

Registers at call: **Return Registers:**
AX = 1683h   BX = current virtual machine (VM) ID
Details: Windows itself currently runs in VM 1, but this can't be relied upon. VM IDs are reused when VMs are destroyed. An ID of 0 will never be returned.
Conflicts: None known.
See Also: Function 16h Subfunctions 84h and 85h

INTERRUPT 2Fh - Function 16h, Subfunction 84h
GET DEVICE API ENTRY POINT

Purpose: Determine the address to call in order to communicate with a virtual device.
Available on: All machines.   **Restrictions:** MS Windows version 3+ must be
                                                                                        running.

Registers at call: **Return Registers:**
AX = 1684h   ES:DI -> VxD API entry point, or 0:0 if the VxD does
BX = virtual device (VxD) ID (Table 14-3)   not support an API
ES:DI = 0000h:0000h
Details: Some Windows enhanced-mode virtual devices provide services that applications can access. For example, the Virtual Display Device (VDD) provides an API used in turn by WINOLDAP.
Conflicts: None known.
See Also: Function 16h Subfunction 83h

Table 14-3. Values for VxD ID:

01h	VMM	Virtual Machine Manager
02h	Debug	
03h	VPICD	Virtual Prog. Interrupt Controller (PIC) Device
04h	VDMAD	Virtual Direct Memory Access (DMA) Device
05h	VTD	Virtual Timer Device
06h	V86MMGR	Virtual 8086 Mode Device
07h	PAGESWAP	Paging Device
08h	Parity	
09h	Reboot	
0Ah	VDD	Virtual Display Device (GRABBER)
0Bh	VSD	Virtual Sound Device
0Ch	VMD	Virtual Mouse Device
0Dh	VKD	Virtual Keyboard Device
0Eh	VCD	Virtual COMM Device
0Fh	VPD	Virtual Printer Device
10h	VHD	Virtual Hard Disk Device
11h	VMCPD	
12h	EBIOS	Reserve EBIOS page (e.g., on PS/2)
13h	BIOSXLAT	Map ROM BIOS API between prot & V86 mode
14h	VNETBIOS	Virtual NetBIOS Device

Table 14-3. Values for VxD ID (continued):

15h	DOSMGR	
16h	WINLOAD	
17h	SHELL	
18h	VMPoll	
19h	VPROD	
1Ah	DOSNET	assures network integrity across VMs
1Bh	VFD	Virtual Floppy Device
1Ch	VDD2	Secondary display adapter
1Dh	WINDEBUG	
1Eh	TSRLoad	TSR instance utility

Details: The high bit of the VxD ID is reserved for future use. The next 10 bits are the OEM number which is assigned by Microsoft. The low 5 bits are the device number.

INTERRUPT 2Fh - Function 16h, Subfunction 85h
SWITCH VMs AND CALLBACK

Purpose: Force execution of a subroutine in a specific virtual machine.

Available on: All machines.

Restrictions: MS Windows version 3+ must be running.

Registers at call:
AX = 1685h
BX = VM ID of virtual machine to switch to
CX = flags
    bit 0 wait until interrupts enabled
    bit 1 wait until critical section unowned
    bits 2-15 reserved (zero)
DX:SI = priority boost (see VMM.INC)
ES:DI -> FAR procedure to callback

Return Registers:
CF set on error
    AX = error code
        01h invalid VM ID
        02h invalid priority boost
        03h invalid flags
CF clear if successful
    event will be or has been called

Details: Some DOS devices, such as networks, need to call functions in a specific VM. This call forces the appropriate VM to be installed. The callback procedure must preserve all registers and return with IRET.

Conflicts: None known.

See Also: Function 16h Subfunction 83h, DESQview INT 15h Function 11h Subfunction 17h (chapter 15)

INTERRUPT 2Fh - Function 46h, Subfunction 80h
INSTALLATION CHECK

Purpose: Determine whether Microsoft Windows 3.0 is running in real or standard mode.

Available on: All machines.

Restrictions: none.

Registers at call:
AX = 4680h

Return Registers:
AX = 0000h if MS Windows 3.0 is running in real or
    standard mode
    nonzero if Windows 3.0 running in enhanced
        mode, Windows prior to 3.0 is running, or
        Windows is not present.

Details: This function is not officially documented. Microsoft has indicated that future versions will provide an installation check which works in all modes.

Conflicts: None known.

See Also: Function 16h Subfunction 00h

MS WINDOWS "WINOLDAP"

WinOldAp (WINOLDAP.MOD) is a Microsoft Windows extension supporting "old" (character-mode) application access to Dynamic Data Exchange, menus, and the Windows clipboard.

INTERRUPT 2Fh - Function 17h, Subfunction 00h
IDENTIFY WinOldAp VERSION

Purpose: Determine which version of WinOldAP is installed.
Available on: All machines.

Registers at call:
AX = 1700h

Restrictions: MS Windows version 3.0+ WINOLDAP
       must be running.
Return Registers:
AX = 1700h if this version of WINOLDAP does not
    support the clipboard
AX <> 1700h
    AL = WINOLDAP major version
    AH = WINOLDAP minor version

Details: This installation check DOES NOT follow the format used by other software.
Conflicts: None known.

INTERRUPT 2Fh - Function 17h, Subfunction 01h
OPEN CLIPBOARD

Purpose: Prepare to manipulate the clipboard.
Available on: All machines.

Registers at call:
AX = 1701h

Restrictions: MS Windows version 3.0+ WINOLDAP
       must be running.
Return Registe rs:
AX = 0000h   clipboard is already open
AX nonzero   successful

Conflicts: None known.

INTERRUPT 2Fh - Function 17h, Subfunction 02h
EMPTY CLIPBOARD

Purpose: Delete the entire contents of the clipboard.
Available on: All machines.

Registers at call:
AX = 1702h

Restrictions: MS Windows version 3.0+ WINOLDAP
       must be running.
Return Registers:
AX = 0000h   failure
AX nonzero   clipboard has been emptied

Conflicts: None known.

INTERRUPT 2Fh - Function 17h, Subfunction 03h
SET CLIPBOARD DATA

Purpose: Specify the data to be stored in the clipboard and its type.
Available on: All machines.

Restrictions: MS Windows version 3.0+ WINOLDAP
       must be running.

Registers at call:
AX = 1703h
DX = clipboard format supported by WinOldAp:
   01h text
   02h bitmap
   03h metafile picture
   04h SYLK
   05h DIF
   06h TIFF
   07h OEM text
ES:BX -> data (Tables 14-4 and 14-5)
SI:CX = size of data
Conflicts: None known.
See Also: Function 17h Subfunctions 04h and 05h

Return Registers:
AX = 0000h failure
AX nonzero data copied into the clipboard

Table 14-4. Format of Bitmap:

Offset	Size	Description
00h	WORD	type (0000h)
02h	WORD	width of bitmap in pixels
04h	WORD	height of bitmap in pixels
06h	WORD	bytes per line
08h	BYTE	number of color planes
09h	BYTE	number of adjacent color bits in pixel
0Ah	DWORD	pointer to start of data
0Eh	WORD	width in 0.1mm units
10h	WORD	height in 0.1mm units
12h	N BYTEs	bitmap data

Table 14-5. Format of Metafile Picture:

Offset	Size	Description
00h	WORD	mapping mode
02h	WORD	X extent
04h	WORD	Y extent
06h	WORD	picture data

INTERRUPT 2Fh - Function 17h, Subfunction 04h
GET CLIPBOARD DATA SIZE

Purpose: Determine the amount of data of a particular type stored in the clipboard.
Available on: All machines.
Restrictions: MS Windows version 3.0+ WINOLDAP must be running.

Registers at call:
AX = 1704h
DX = clipboard format supported by WinOldAp
   (see Function 17h Subfunction 03h)
Conflicts: None known.
See Also: Function 17h Subfunctions 03h and 05h

Return Registers:
DX:AX = size of data in bytes, including any headers
DX:AX = 0 no data of the specified format in the clipboard

INTERRUPT 2Fh - Function 17h, Subfunction 05h
GET CLIPBOARD DATA

Purpose: Retrieve the data of a particular type stored in the clipboard.
Available on: All machines.
Restrictions: MS Windows version 3.0+ WINOLDAP must be running.

Registers at call:
AX = 1705h
DX = clipboard format supported by WinOldAp
   (see Function 17h Subfunction 03h)
ES:BX -> buffer
Conflicts: None known.
See Also: Function 17h Subfunction 04h

Return Registers:
AX = 0000h   error, or no data of the specified format
   in clipboard
AX nonzero   success

INTERRUPT 2Fh - Function 17h, Subfunction 08h
CLOSE CLIPBOARD

Purpose: Indicate that clipboard manipulation is complete.
Available on: All machines.

Restrictions: MS Windows version 3.0+ WINOLDAP
              must be running.

Registers at call:
AX = 1708h

Return Registers:
AX = 0000h failure
AX nonzero success

Conflicts: None known.

INTERRUPT 2Fh - Function 17h, Subfunction 09h
COMPACT CLIPBOARD

Purpose: Combine any unused spaces in the clipboard into a single region.
Available on: All machines.

Restrictions: MS Windows version 3.0+ WINOLDAP
              must be running.

Registers at call:
AX = 1709h
SI:CX = desired size in bytes

Return Registers:
DX:AX = number of bytes in largest block of free
   memory

Details: WinOldAp is responsible for including the size of any headers.
Conflicts: None known.

INTERRUPT 2Fh - Function 17h, Subfunction 0Ah
GET DEVICE CAPABILITIES

Purpose: Determine the parameters of the specified device or what types of operations it supports.
Available on: All machines.

Restrictions: MS Windows version 3.0+ WINOLDAP
              must be running.

Registers at call:
AX = 170Ah
DX = GDI information index
   (see Table)

Return Registers:
AX = integer value of the desired item
   (see Table)

Details: This function returns the device-capability bits for the given display
Conflicts: None known.

Chapter 15

TopView and DESQview/QEMM

The first multiple-application system introduced for MS-DOS systems was IBM's TopView package. The first such system to gain wide acceptance, however, was a TopView-compatible multitasker called DESQview, from Quarterdeck Office Systems.

While it is almost impossible to find a TopView application in use today, DESQview is very much alive and well. This chapter describes the functions used by both systems; those which apply to both are identified primarily as TopView functions, while those available only under DESQview are so noted. The few functions that were available for TopView, but which are not available under DESQview are noted. The names given in this chapter reflect those used by DESQview; the TopView nomenclature may differ.

Although not specifically stated here, most of the TopView functions are also available under TaskView (and its follow-on OmniView) by Sunny Hill Software. See chapter 17 for additional calls that are unique to OmniView.

This chapter is divided into four sections: TopView calls, DESQview calls, the DESQview External Device Interface, and Quarterdeck Programs (QEMM, QRAM, Manifest, and VIDRAM).

TopView
INTERRUPT 10h - Function FEh
GET SHADOW BUFFER

Purpose: Determine the address of a virtual screen to use instead of the physical display memory.
Available on: All machines.   **Restrictions:** none.
Registers at call: **Return Registers:**
AH = FEh   ES:DI - > actual video buffer for calling process
ES:DI -> assumed video buffer (B800h:0000h
   color, B000h:0000h mono)
Details: If no multitasker is installed, ES:DI is returned unchanged. TopView requires a call to Function FFh to notify if that the screen has changed; DESQview will check for changes itself until the first call to Function FFh.
See Also: Function FFh, INT 15h Function 10h Subfunction 24h, DESQview INT 21h Function 2Bh

INTERRUPT 10h - Function FFh

UPDATE SCREEN FROM SHADOW BUFFER
Purpose: Indicate which portion of the virtual screen has been modified and needs to be updated on the physical display.
Available on: All machines.   **Restrictions:** TopView or compatible must be
                                                           running.
Registers at call: **Retirn Registers:** n/a
AH = FFh
CX = number of consecutive changed characters
ES:DI - first changed character in shadow buffer
Details: Avoid CX=0000h. DESQview will discontinue the automatic screen updating initiated by Function FEh after this call.
Conflicts: GO32 DOS Extender (chapter 9), Carbon Copy Plus (chapter 28).

See Also: Function FEh

INTERRUPT 15h - Function 10h, Subfunction 00h
"PAUSE" - GIVE UP CPU TIME

Purpose: Indicate that the calling program is idle and that other programs may be given the remainder of the current time slice.

Available on: All machines.

Restrictions: TopView or compatible must be running.

Registers at call:
AX = 1000h

Return Registers:
return after other processes run

Details: Under DESQview, if the process issuing this call has hooked INT 08h, the current time-slice is set to expire at the next clock tick rather than immediately.

Conflicts: MultiDOS Plus (chapter 16), VMiX (chapter 17).

See Also: MultiDOS Function 00h (chapter 16), DoubleDOS INT 21h Function EEh (chapter 17), Windows INT 2Fh Function 16h Subfunction 80h (chapter 14)

INTERRUPT 15h - Function 10h, Subfunction 01h
"GETMEM" - ALLOCATE "SYSTEM" MEMORY

Purpose: Request a portion of the per-process pool of reserved memory.

Available on: All machines.

Restrictions: TopView or compatible must be running.

Registers at call:
AX = 1001h
BX = number of bytes to allocate

Return Registers:
ES:DI -> block of memory or 0000h:0000h (DV 2.26+)

Details: Use SETERROR (DESQview Function DEh Subfunction 15h) to avoid a user prompt if there is insufficient system memory.

Conflicts: MultiDOS Plus (chapter 16), VMiX (chapter 17).

See Also: Function 10h Subfunction 02h, DESQview Function DEh Subfunctions 0Ch and 15h

INTERRUPT 15h - Function 10h, Subfunction 02h
"PUTMEM" - DEALLOCATE "SYSTEM" MEMORY

Purpose: Free a previously allocated block of the per-process pool of reserved memory.

Available on: All machines.

Restrictions: TopView or compatible must be running.

Registers at call:
AX = 1002h
ES:DI -> previously allocated block

Return Registers:
block freed

Conflicts: MultiDOS Plus (chapter 16), VMiX (chapter 17).

See Also: Function 10h Subfunction 01h, DESQview Function DEh Subfunction 0Dh

INTERRUPT 15h - Function 10h, Subfunction 03h
"PRINTC" - DISPLAY CHARACTER/ATTRIBUTE ON SCREEN

Purpose: Output a single character with the specified attribute to the indicated window.

Available on: All machines.

Restrictions: TopView or compatible must be running.

Registers at call:
AX = 1003h
BH = attribute
BL = character
DX = segment of object handle for window

Return Registers: n/a

Details: BX=0000h does not display anything, it only positions the hardware cursor.

Conflicts: None known.

INTERRUPT 15h - Function 10h, Subfunction 13h
"GETBIT" - DEFINE A 2ND-LEVEL INTERRUPT HANDLER

Purpose: Specify a handler which will perform actions which a hardware interrupt handler is not allowed to perform under TopView or DESQview.

Available on: All machines.

Restrictions: TopView or compatible must be running.

Registers at call:
AX = 1013h
ES:DI -> FAR service routine

Return Registers:
BX = bit mask indicating which bit was allocated
 0000h if no more bits available

Details: Only a few TopView/DESQview API calls are allowed during a hardware interrupt; if other calls need to be made, the interrupt handler must schedule a 2nd-level interrupt with "SETBIT" (Function 10h Subfunction 15h).

Conflicts: MultiDOS Plus (chapter 16), VMiX (chapter 17).

See Also: Function 10h Subfunctions 14h and 15h

INTERRUPT 15h - Function 10h, Subfunction 14h
"FREEBIT" - UNDEFINE A 2ND-LEVEL INTERRUPT HANDLER

Purpose: Release a previously defined handler so that another program may define a handler.

Available on: All machines.

Restrictions: TopView or compatible must be running.

Registers at call:
AX = 1014h
BX = bit mask from INT 15h Function 10h
 Subfunction 13h

Return Registers: n/a

Conflicts: MultiDOS Plus (chapter 16), VMiX (chapter 17).

See Also: Function 10h Subfunctions 13h and 15h

INTERRUPT 15h - Function 10h, Subfunction 15h
"SETBIT" - SCHEDULE ONE OR MORE 2ND-LEVEL INTERRUPTS

Purpose: Set a flag which requests that the indicated handlers should be invoked as soon as it is safe for them to make arbitrary API calls.

Available on: All machines.

Restrictions: TopView or compatible must be running.

Registers at call:
AX = 1015h
BX = bit mask for interrupts to post

Return Registers:
indicated routines will be called:
 (DV 2.0x) at next task switch
 (DV 2.2x) immediately

Details: This is one of the few TopView calls which are allowed from a hardware interrupt handler. The handler will be called with ES containing the segment of the handle of the next task to be executed; on return, ES must be the segment of a task handle.

Conflicts: MultiDOS Plus (chapter 16), VMiX (chapter 17).

See Also: Function 10h Subfunctions 13h and 14h

INTERRUPT 15h - Function 10h, Subfunction 16h
"ISOBJ" - VERIFY OBJECT HANDLE

Purpose: Determine whether the indicated value is a valid reference to a TopView or DESQview object.

Available on: All machines.

Restrictions: TopView or compatible must be running.

Registers at call:
AX = 1016h
ES:DI = possible object handle

Return Registers:
BX = FFFFh if ES:DI is a valid object handle
 0000h if ES:DI is not

Conflicts: MultiDOS Plus (chapter 16), VMiX (chapter 17).

See Also: DESQview Function DEh Subfunction 14h

INTERRUPT 15h - Function 10h, Subfunction 18h
"LOCATE" - FIND WINDOW AT A GIVEN SCREEN LOCATION

Purpose: Determine which window is visible at the specified location on the screen, or would be visible if the indicated window were moved.

Available on: All machines.

Registers at call:
AX = 1018h
BH = column
BL = row
ES = segment of object handle for window below
     which to search
    0000h = start search with topmost window

Conflicts: MultiDOS Plus (chapter 16), VMiX (chapter 17).

See Also: Function 10h Subfunctions 23h and 24h

Restrictions: TopView or compatible must be running.

Return Registers:
ES = segment of object handle for window which is
    visible at the indicated position, or covered by
    indicated window;
   = 0000h no window.

INTERRUPT 15h - Function 10h, Subfunction 19h
"SOUND" - MAKE TONE

Purpose: Turn on the speaker at the specified frequency for the indicated duration.

Available on: All machines.

Registers at call:
AX = 1019h
BX = frequency in Hertz (0000h = silence)
CX = duration in clock ticks (18.2 ticks/sec)

Restrictions: TopView or compatible must be running.

Return Registers:
immediately, tone continues to completion

Details: If another tone is already playing, the new tone does not start until completion of the previous one. Up to 32 tones may be queued before the process is blocked until a note completes. In DV 2.00, the lowest tone allowed is 20 Hz. If CX = 0, the current note is cancelled; if BX = 0 as well, all queued notes are also cancelled.

Conflicts: MultiDOS Plus (chapter 16), VMiX (chapter 17).

See Also: FAKEY INT 16h Function 73h (chapter 36)

INTERRUPT 15h - Function 10h, Subfunction 1Ah
"OSTACK" - SWITCH TO TASK'S INTERNAL STACK

Purpose: Change from the user's stack to a per-task private stack in preparation for making TopView API calls.

Available on: All machines.

Registers at call:
AX = 101Ah

Restrictions: TopView or compatible must be running.

Return Registers:
stack switched

Details: This call may not be nested; a second call must be preceded by a call to "USTACK" (Function 10h Subfunction 25h). While TopView requires many API calls to be executed while on the task's internal stack, DESQview allows those calls to be executed regardless of the current stack.

Conflicts: MultiDOS Plus (chapter 16), VMiX (chapter 17).

See Also: Function 10h Subfunction 25h

INTERRUPT 15h - Function 10h, Subfunction 1Bh
"BEGINC" - BEGIN CRITICAL REGION

Purpose: Indicate that the calling program is about to perform uninterruptible or nonreentrant operations and that task switching should be temporarily suspended.

Available on: All machines.

Registers at call:
AX = 101Bh

Restrictions: TopView or compatible must be running.

Return Registers:
task-switching temporarily disabled

Details: Will not task-switch until "ENDC" (AX = 101Ch) called unless task voluntarily releases the CPU (upon regaining the CPU, task-switching will again be disabled). Suspends the caller until DOS is free.
Conflicts: MultiDOS Plus (chapter 16), VMiX (chapter 17).
See Also: Function 10h Subfunction 1Ch, DESQview Function DEh Subfunctions 13h and 1Ch, MultiDOS Function 0Dh (chapter 16), MS Windows INT 2Fh Function 16h Subfunction 81h (chapter 14)

INTERRUPT 15h - Function 10h, Subfunction 1Ch
"ENDC" - END CRITICAL REGION

Purpose: Indicate that the program has completed its nonreentrant operations and that task switching may resume.
Available on: All machines.

Restrictions: TopView or compatible must be running.

Registers at call:
AX = 101Ch

Return Registers:
Task-switching enabled

Details: This API call may be made from within a hardware interrupt handler.
Conflicts: MultiDOS Plus (chapter 16), VMiX (chapter 17).
See Also: Function 10h Subfunction 1Bh, DESQview Function DEh Subfunctions 13h and 1Bh, MS Windows INT 2Fh Function 16h Subfunction 82h (chapter 14)

INTERRUPT 15h - Function 10h, Subfunction 1Dh
"STOP" - STOP TASK

Purpose: Request that the indicated task not receive any more time slices until explicitly restarted.
Available on: All machines.

Restrictions: TopView or compatible must be running.

Registers at call:
AX = 101Dh
ES = segment of object handle for task to be
   stopped (== handle of main window for that
   task)

Return Registers:
Indicated task will not get any CPU time until restarted
   with Function 10h Subfunction 1Eh

Details: Once a task has been stopped, additional "STOP"s are ignored.
BUG: In DV 2.00, this function is ignored unless the indicated task is the current task.
Conflicts: MultiDOS Plus (chapter 16), VMiX (chapter 17).
See Also: Function 10h Subfunctions 1Eh and 2Bh, VMix Function 12h (chapter 17)

INTERRUPT 15h - Function 10h, Subfunction 1Eh
"START" - START TASK

Purpose: Request that the indicated task be restarted and begin receiving time slices again.
Available on: All machines.

Restrictions: TopView or compatible must be running.

Registers at call:
AX = 101Eh
ES = segment of object handle for task to be started
   (== handle of main window for that task)

Return Registers:
Indicated task is started up again

Details: Once a task has been started, additional "START"s are ignored.
Conflicts: MultiDOS Plus (chapter 16), VMiX (chapter 17).
See Also: Function 10h Subfunctions 1Dh and 2Bh

INTERRUPT 15h - Function 10h, Subfunction 1Fh
"DISPEROR" - POP-UP ERROR WINDOW

Purpose: Display a standardized error window, and specify which actions the user may take to acknowledge it.
Available on: All machines.

Restrictions: TopView or compatible must be running.

Registers at call:
AX = 101Fh

Return Registers:
BX = status:

BX = bit fields
  bits 0-12: number of characters to display

  bits 13,14: which mouse button may be pressed
        to remove window
    00 = either
    01 = left
    10 = right
    11 = either
  bit 15: beep if 1
DS:DI -> text of message
CH = width of error window (0 = default)
CL = height of error window (0 = default)
DX = segment of object handle

1 = left button,
2 = right,
27 = ESC pressed

Details: The window remains on-screen until ESC or indicated mouse button is pressed.
Conflicts: None known.

INTERRUPT 15h - Function 10h, Subfunction 21h
"PGMINT" - INTERRUPT ANOTHER TASK

Purpose: Force another task to execute the specified subroutine regardless of what it is currently executing.
Available on: All machines.

Restrictions: TopView or compatible must be running.

Return Registers: n/a

Registers at call:
AX = 1021h
BX = segment of object handle for task to interrupt
  (not self)
DX:CX -> FAR routine to jump to next time task is
  run

Details: The FAR routine is entered with the current ES, DS, SI, DI, and BP values, using the task's internal stack (see Function 10h Subfunction 1Ah); only SS:SP needs to be preserved. Multiple PGMINTs to a single task are processed last-in first-out. If the other task is in a DOS or DV API call, the interruption will occur on return from that call.
Conflicts: None known.

INTERRUPT 15h - Function 10h, Subfunction 22h
"GETVER" - GET VERSION

Purpose: Determine whether TopView or a compatible is running, and if so the TopView version number.
Available on: All machines.

Restrictions: none.

Registers at call:
AX = 1022h
BX = 0000h

Return Registers:
BX nonzero if TopView or compatible loaded (BL = major version, BH = minor version)

Details: TaskView returns BX = 0001h, DESQview 2.0+ returns BX = 0A01h
Conflicts: None known.

INTERRUPT 15h - Function 10h, Subfunction 23h
"POSWIN" - POSITION WINDOW

Purpose: Specify a new location for the indicated window, possibly in relation to another window on the screen.
Available on: All machines.

Restrictions: TopView or compatible must be running.

Return Registers: n/a

Registers at call:
AX = 1023h

BX = segment of object handle for parent window within which to position the window (0 = full screen)
ES = segment of object handle for window to be positioned
DL = bit flags
    bits 0,1: horizontal position
        00 = current
        01 = center
        10 = left
        11 = right
    bits 2,3: vertical position
        00 = current
        01 = center
        10 = top
        11 = bottom
    bit 4: don't redraw screen if set
    bits 5-7 not used
CH = number of columns to offset from position specified by DL
CL = number of rows to offset from position specified by DL
Conflicts: None known.

INTERRUPT 15h - Function 10h, Subfunction 24h
"GETBUF" - GET VIRTUAL SCREEN INFO

Purpose: Determine the address, size, and type of the virtual screen buffer for the specified window.

Available on: All machines.

Restrictions: TopView or compatible must be running.

Registers at call:
AX = 1024h
BX = segment of object handle for window (0 = use default)

Return Registers:
ES:DI -> virtual screen
CX = size of virtual screen in bytes
DL = 00h text screen
    01h graphics screen

Conflicts: MultiDOS Plus (chapter 16), VMiX (chapter 17).
See Also: INT 10h Function FEh

INTERRUPT 15h - Function 10h, Subfunction 25h
"USTACK" - SWITCH BACK TO USER'S STACK

Purpose: Change back to the user stack after operating on the per-task private stack while making TopView API calls.

Available on: All machines.

Restrictions: TopView or compatible must be running.

Registers at call:
AX = 1025h

Return Registers:
stack switched back

Details: Call only after having switched to internal stack with Function 10h Subfunction 1Ah. While TopView requires many API calls to be executed while on the task's private stack, DESQview allows those calls to be executed regardless of the current stack.
Conflicts: MultiDOS Plus (chapter 16), VMiX (chapter 17).
See Also: Function 10h Subfunction 1Ah

INTERRUPT 15h - Function 10h, Subfunction 2Bh
"POSTTASK" - AWAKEN TASK

Purpose: Force a task which is waiting on its OBJECTQ to continue by placing the handle for the task on the OBJECTQ.

Available on: All machines.

Restrictions: DESQview version 2.00 or higher (or possibly TopView) must be running.

Registers at call:
AX = 102Bh
BX = segment of object handle for task
Conflicts: MultiDOS Plus (chapter 16), VMiX (chapter 17).
See Also: Function 10h Subfunctions 1Dh and 1Eh

Return Registers: n/a

INTERRUPT 15h - Function 10h, Subfunction 2Ch
START NEW APPLICATION IN NEW PROCESS

Purpose: Start up a new program as if the user had started it manually from the "Open Window" menu; this call is not limited to programs on that menu, however.

Available on: All machines.

Restrictions: DESQview version 2.00 or higher (or possibly TopView) must be running.

Registers at call:
AX = 102Ch
ES:DI -> contents of .PIF/ .DVP file (Table 15-1)
BX = size of .PIF/.DVP info
Conflicts: MultiDOS Plus (chapter 16), VMiX (chapter 17).

Return Registers:
BX = segment of object handle for new task 0000h on error

Table 15-1. Format of .PIF/.DVP File:

Offset	Size	Description
00h	WORD	reserved (0)
02h	30 BYTEs	blank-padded program title
20h	WORD	maximum memory to allocate to partition in K
22h	WORD	minimum memory required in K
24h	64 BYTEs	ASCIZ program pathname
64h	BYTE	default drive letter ('A',...)
65h	64 BYTEs	ASCIZ default directory name
A5h	64 BYTEs	ASCIZ program parameters
E5h	BYTE	initial screen mode (0-7) (see also offset 189h)
E6h	BYTE	number of text pages used
E7h	BYTE	number of first interrupt to save
E8h	BYTE	number of last interrupt to save
E9h	BYTE	rows in virtual screen buffer
EAh	BYTE	columns in virtual screen buffer
EBh	BYTE	initial window position, row
ECh	BYTE	initial window position, column
EDh	WORD	system memory in K
EFh	64 BYTEs	ASCIZ shared program name
12Fh	64 BYTEs	ASCIZ shared program data file
16Fh	BYTE	flags1
		bit 7: writes text directly to screen
		bit 6: runs in foreground only
		bit 5: uses math coprocessor
		bit 4: accesses system keyboard buffer directly
		bits 3-1: reserved (0)
		bit 0: swappable
170h	BYTE	flags2
		bit 6: uses command-line parameters in field at A5h

Table 15-1. Format of .PIF/.DVP File (continued)

Offset	Size	Description
		bit 5: swaps interrupt vectors

---information unique to .DVP files

Offset	Size	Description
171h	2 BYTEs	keys to use on open menu
173h	WORD	size of script buffer in bytes
175h	WORD	automatically give up CPU after this many tests for keyboard input in one clock tick (default 0 = never)
177h	BYTE	nonzero = "uses own colors"
178h	BYTE	nonzero if application swappable
179h	3 BYTEs	reserved (0)
17Ch	BYTE	nonzero to automatically close on exit
17Dh	BYTE	nonzero if copy-protect floppy is required

---information unique to DESQview 2.0 and higher

Offset	Size	Description
17Eh	BYTE	.DVP version number
		00h DESQview 1.2+
		01h DESQview 2.0+
		02h DESQview 2.2+
17Fh	BYTE	reserved (0)
180h	BYTE	initial number of rows in physical window
181h	BYTE	initial number of columns in physical window
182h	WORD	maximum expanded memory to allow, in K
184h	BYTE	flags3
		bit 7: automatically assign window position
		bit 5: maximum memory value has been specified
		bit 4: disallow "Close" command
		bit 3: foreground-only when doing graphics
		bit 2: don't virtualize
185h	BYTE	keyboard conflict level (0-4 for DV<2.26, 00h-0Fh for DV2.26+)
186h	BYTE	number of graphics pages used
187h	WORD	extra system memory size
189h	BYTE	initial screen mode (FFh = default) (overrides offset E5h)

---information unique to DESQview 2.2+

Offset	Size	Description
18Ah	BYTE	serial port usage
		FFh uses all serial ports
		00h no serial ports
		01h only COM1
		02h only COM2
18Bh	BYTE	flags4
		bit 7: automatically close application on exit if .COM or .EXE specified
		bit 6: swappable if not using serial ports
		bit 5: start program with window hidden (v2.26+)
		bit 4: start program in background (v2.26+)
		bit 3: virtualize text
		bit 2: virtualize graphics
		bit 1: share CPU when foreground
		bit 0: share EGA when foreground and zoomed
18Ch	BYTE	protection level for 386 machines
18Dh	19 BYTEs	reserved (0)

INTERRUPT 15h - Function 10h, Subfunction 2Dh
"KMOUSE" - KEYBOARD MOUSE CONTROL

Purpose: Determine whether the keyboard mouse emulation is currently on, or force the emulation on or off.

Available on: All machines.　　　　　　　　**Restrictions:** DESQview version 2.00 or higher must be running.

Registers at call:
AX = 102Dh
BL = subfunction:
   00h determine whether using keyboard mouse
   01h turn keyboard mouse on
   02h turn keyboard mouse off
Conflicts: MultiDOS Plus (chapter 16), VMiX (chapter 17).

Return Registers:
BL = 00h using real mouse
     01h using keyboard mouse

INTERRUPT 15h - Function 11h
TopView commands

Purpose: Additional TopView API calls; these are discussed under Function DEh in the DESQview section.
Available on: All machines.

Restrictions: TopView or compatible must be running.

Registers at call:
AH = 11h
AL = various (except 17h)

Return Registers: varies

Details: In DESQview 2.x, subfunctions 00h through 0Ah are identical to the same-numbered subfunctions of Function DEh.
Conflicts: MultiDOS Plus (chapter 16), VMiX (chapter 17).
See Also: DESQview Function DEh

INTERRUPT 15h - Function 11h, Subfunction 17h
"ASSERTMAP" - GET/SET MAPPING CONTEXT

Purpose: Force a specified EMS mapping register set into activity, to ensure addressability of a particular program's code or data.
Available on: All machines.

Restrictions: DESQview version 2.20 or higher must be running.

Registers at call:
AX = 1117h
BX = 0000h   get current mapping context without setting
   nonzero   set new mapping context

Return Registers:
BX = mapping context in effect before call
interrupts enabled

Details: Unlike all other subfunctions, this call differs from AX = DE17h for DESQview v2.20 through 2.25. Mapping contexts determine conventional-memory addressability; setting a mapping context ensures that the associated program and data areas are in memory for access. Usable by drivers, TSRs and shared programs. Caller need not be running under DESQview, but must ensure that the stack in use will not be mapped out by the call.
Conflicts: MultiDOS Plus (chapter 16), VMiX (chapter 17).
See Also: DESQview Function DEh Subfunction 17h, MS Windows INT 2Fh Function 16h Subfunction 85h (chapter 14)

INTERRUPT 15h - Function 12h, Subfunction 00h
SEND MESSAGE "HANDLE" - RETURN OBJECT HANDLE

Purpose: Determine the handle of the specified object.
Available on: All machines.

Restrictions: TopView or compatible must be running.

Registers at call:
AH = 12h
BH = 00h

BL = which handle to return
   00h handle in DWORD on top of stack
   01h current task's window handle

Return Registers:
DWORD on top of stack is object handle

02h given task's mailbox handle (task's handle
    on stack)
03h current task's mailbox handle
04h given task's keyboard handle (task's handle
    on stack)
05h current task's keyboard object handle
06h given task's OBJECTQ handle (task's
handle on stack)
07h current task's OBJECTQ handle
08h \
  thru > return 0000:0000 under DV prior to
10h /   2.26
0Ch (DESQview 2.26+) task owning object
    with handle in DWORD on top of stack
0Dh (DESQview 2.26+) task handle of owner
    (parent) of current task
Details: BL=0Ch,0Dh returns 00000000h if the object is not open (keyboard, mailbox, panel, pointer, and timer objects) or is an orphan (task, window).
Conflicts: MultiDOS Plus (chapter 16), VMiX (chapter 17).

INTERRUPT 15h - Function 12h, Subfunction 01h
SEND MESSAGE "NEW" - CREATE NEW OBJECT

Purpose: Allocate resources for a new object of the specified type, and return a handle by which it may be referenced.
Available on: All machines.

Restrictions: TopView or compatible must be running.

Registers at call:
AH = 12h
BH = 01h
BL = object type to create
    00h (DV 2.0x only) handle is DWORD on top
      of stack
    01h (DV 2.0x only) use task's window handle
    02h (DV 2.0x only) given task's mailbox (task's
      handle on stack)
    03h (DV 2.0x only) current task's mailbox
    04h (DV 2.0x only) given task's keyboard
      (task's handle on stack)
    05h (DV 2.0x only) current task's keyboard
      object
    08h WINDOW class
    09h MAILBOX class
    0Ah KEYBOARD class
    0Bh TIMER object (counts down 32-bit time in
      10ms increments)
    0Fh POINTER object
    10h PANEL object
STACK: (if window object or WINDOW class)
    DWORD address to jump to (no new task if
      high word == 0)
    DWORD (reserved)
      0 = non-task window,
      FFFFh = task window

Return Registers:
DWORD on top of stack is new object handle
all input stack arguments have been popped

DWORD bytes for task's private stack
   (FFFFh == default of 0100h)
DWORD bytes system memory for input buffer
   for READ/READN (0 == none, -1 ==
   default--same as logical window size)
DWORD window size, columns
DWORD window size, rows
DWORD length of window title
DWORD address of window title

Details: If a new task is created, it is started with:
   AX = BX = SI = DI = BP = 0
   DX:CX = handle of parent task
   DS = ES = SS = segment of private stack (and new task's handle)

New windows are orphans, inherit the colors/hidden status of the creating task's window, and are placed in the upper left hand corner of the screen but not automatically redrawn. New keyboards are closed, and have all object bits cleared except for the hardware cursor bit.

Conflicts: MultiDOS Plus (chapter 16), VMiX (chapter 17).

See Also: Function 12h Subfunction 02h

INTERRUPT 15h - Function 12h, Subfunction 02h
SEND MESSAGE "FREE" - FREE AN OBJECT

Purpose: Release the specified objects and the resources it is using.

Available on: All machines.

Restrictions: TopView or compatible must be running.

Registers at call:
AH = 12h
BH = 02h
BL = object
   00h handle in DWORD on top of stack
      window: close window and free
      timer: free timer
      panel: free panel object
      pointer: free pointer
   01h task's window handle - kills task, never
      returns
   02h given task's mailbox (task's handle on top
      of stack)
   03h current task's mailbox
   04h given task's keyboard (task's handle on top
      of stack)
   05h current task's keyboard object

Return Registers: n/a

Details: When a window is freed, its keyboard and pointer objects are freed; task windows also free any mailbox, objectq, and panel objects held by the task and any child tasks. If the keyboard being freed is the default keyboard for a task, this call is equivalent to CLOSE. Panel and pointer objects are automatically closed if open.

Conflicts: MultiDOS Plus (chapter 16), VMiX (chapter 17).

See Also: Function 12h Subfunction 01h, Function 12h Subfunction 0Dh

INTERRUPT 15h - Function 12h, Subfunction 03h
SEND MESSAGE "ADDR" - GET HANDLE OF MESSAGE SENDER

Purpose: Determine which task sent the last message read from the given mailbox.

Available on: All machines.

Restrictions: TopView or compatible must be running.

Registers at call:
AH = 12h
BH = 03h
BL = object
    00h mailbox handle in DWORD on top of stack
    02h sender of last msg read from mailbox
        (task's handle on stack)
    03h sender of last msg read from current task's
        mailbox
Conflicts: MultiDOS Plus (chapter 16), VMiX (chapter 17).
See Also: Function 12h Subfunction 00h

Return Registers:
DWORD on stack is task handle of message sender

INTERRUPT 15h - Function 12h, Subfunction 03h
SEND MESSAGE "CONNECT" - CONNECT TWO WINDOWS

Purpose: Attach the specified window to another so that both will always move in unison.
Available on: All machines.

Restrictions: DESQview version 2.26 or higher must be running.

Registers at call:
AH = 12h
BH = 03h
BL = window to be connected
    00h handle of window to be attached is in
        DWORD on top of the stack
    01h attach current task's main window
STACK: DWORD handle of attaching window (if
        passed on stack)
    DWORD handle of window to attach to or
        00000000h to detach

Return Registers:
STACK arguments popped

Details: Multiple windows may be attached to a single window, but each window may only be attached to one window at a time.
Conflicts: MultiDOS Plus (chapter 16), VMiX (chapter 17).

INTERRUPT 15h - Function 12h, Subfunction 03h
SEND MESSAGE "DIR" - GET PANEL FILE DIRECTORY

Purpose: Determine the names and locations of the panels contained in a panel file (Table 15-2).
Available on: All machines.

Restrictions: TopView or compatible must be running.

Registers at call:
AH = 12h
BX = 0300h
STACK: DWORD handle of panel object
Details: A null string is returned if the object is not open.
Conflicts: MultiDOS Plus (chapter 16), VMiX (chapter 17).

Return Registers:
STACK: DWORD length of directory (always multiple of 14 bytes)
    DWORD address of directory

Table 15-2. Format of TopView panel file:

Offset	Size	Description
00h	2 BYTEs	C0h C3h
02h	BYTE	number of panels in file
03h		for each panel in file:
	8 BYTEs	blank-padded panel name
	DWORD	panel offset in file

Table 15-2. Format of TopView Panel File (continued)

Offset	Size	Description
	WORD	panel length
		data for panels (each consists of one or more window/query/manager streams). First byte of each panel must be 1Bh, fifth byte must be E5h

INTERRUPT 15h - Function 12h, Subfunction 04h
SEND MESSAGE "READ" - READ NEXT LOGICAL LINE OF WINDOW

Purpose: Retrieve a line's worth of characters or attributes from the specified window.

Available on: All machines.

Restrictions: TopView or compatible must be running.

Registers at call:
AH = 12h
BH = 04h
BL = window to read from
    00h handle is DWORD on top of stack
    01h use calling task's default window
    0Ch (DV 2.26+) default window of task owning
        handle on top of stack
    0Dh (DV 2.26+) default window of parent task
        of current task

Return Registers:
STACK: DWORD number of bytes read
       DWORD address of buffer

Details: Reading starts at the current logical cursor position; the cursor is updated to point at the character following the last one read. Any translucent blanks (FFh) which are visible on screen are changed to the character which is seen through them. The string produced by the read is placed in an input buffer which may be reused by the next READ or READN of a window. Window stream opcodes D8h and D9h determine whether the read returns characters or attributes.

Conflicts: MultiDOS Plus (chapter 16), VMiX (chapter 17).

See Also: Function 12h Subfunctions 05h and 12h

INTERRUPT 15h - Function 12h, Subfunction 04h
SEND MESSAGE "READ" - GET NEXT RECORD FROM OBJECT

Purpose: Get the next unit of input from the specified object; the unit returned depends upon the type of the object.

Available on: All machines.

Restrictions: TopView or compatible must be running.

Registers at call:
AH = 12h
BH = 04h

BL = object
    00h handle is DWORD on top of stack
      mailbox: wait for and get next message
      keyboard: wait for and get pointer to next input
        buffer
      pointer: wait for and get
        next message
    02h get next message from mailbox (task's handle
        on top of stack)
    03h get next message from current task's mailbox
    04h get the next input from keyboard (handle on
        top of stack)
    05h get the next input from task's default
        keyboard

Return Registers:
STACK: (if objectq) DWORD handle of object with
      input

    (otherwise) DWORD number of bytes
        DWORD address

06h wait for input from any object in
   OBJECTQ (handle on stack)
07h wait for input from any object in task's
   default OBJECTQ

Details: For a keyboard in keystroke mode, the input buffer is a single byte containing the character code as returned by the BIOS; the BIOS scan code is available via the STATUS call if the character is zero. For a keyboard in field mode, the input buffer format is determined by the field table header for the window to which the keyboard is attached. Keyboard input buffers and mailbox message buffers may be invalidated by the next READ, ERASE, CLOSE, or FREE message to the same object.

Conflicts: MultiDOS Plus (chapter 16), VMiX (chapter 17).

See Also: Function 12h Subfunction 05h

Table 15-3. Format of pointer message:

Offset	Size	Description
00h	WORD	row
02h	WORD	column
04h	BYTE	status
		bit 6: set when press/release mode active and button released
		bits 7-2: number of clicks-1 if multiple-click mode active
		bits 1,0: button pressed (00=none,01=button1,10=button2)
05h	BYTE	field number or zero (APILEVEL >= 2.00 only)

INTERRUPT 15h - Function 12h, Subfunction 04h
SEND MESSAGE "READ" - WAIT FOR TIMER TO EXPIRE

Purpose: Suspend calling program until the expiration of the specified timer object.

Available on: All machines.

Restrictions: TopView or compatible must be running.

Registers at call:
AH = 12h
BX = 0400h
STACK: DWORD timer's handle

Return Registers:
after timer expires
STACK: DWORD time in 1/100 sec after midnight
   when timer expired

Conflicts: MultiDOS Plus (chapter 16), VMiX (chapter 17).

INTERRUPT 15h - Function 12h, Subfunction 04h
SEND MESSAGE "APPLY" - WRITE PANEL TO WINDOW

Purpose: Display all of the fields of the specified panel to the indicated window, then create an object which may be read to retrieve the user's input if the panel defines any input fields.

Available on: All machines.

Restrictions: TopView or compatible must be running.

Registers at call:
AH = 12h
BX = 0400h
STACK: DWORD handle of panel object
DWORD window's handle (or 0 for current task's window)
DWORD length of panel name
DWORD pointer to panel name

Return Registers:
STACK: DWORD handle of keyboard or 0
DWORD handle of window which was used

Details: The status of the APPLY may be checked with the STATUS message. The panel MUST have the following format:
   first byte must be 1Bh (i.e. must start with a stream)
   the first opcode in the stream must be E5h
      single byte arg of opcode is interpreted thus:
      bits 7,6   11 means create new window

10 means create new field table for existing window

01 means use existing window and field table

bit 5 if set, panel contains a field table (creates a new keyboard and puts it in field mode)

bit 4 if set, panel contains input fields

bit 3 if set, panel contains select fields but no input fields

If the panel contains input or select fields, a keyboard handle is returned; either the window's current open keyboard or a newly-created keyboard object. The caller should read that keyboard to obtain input from the panel.

Conflicts: MultiDOS Plus (chapter 16), VMiX (chapter 17).

INTERRUPT 15h - Function 12h, Subfunction 05h
SEND MESSAGE "WRITE" - WRITE TO OBJECT

Purpose: Send information to the specified object; the action taken is dependent upon the type of object.

Available on: All machines.

Restrictions: TopView or compatible must be running.

Registers at call:
AH = 12h
BH = 05h
BL = object

00h handle is DWORD on top of stack

timer: start timer to end at a specified time

keyboard: add input buffer to queue

pointer: move pointer icon to specified position

02h send message by value/ status = 0 to mbox (task's handle on stack)

03h send message by value/ status = 0 to current task's mailbox

04h add input buffer to KEYBOARD queue (handle on top of stack)

05h add input buffer to task's default KEYBOARD queue

06h add an object to OBJECTQ (handle on top of stack)

07h add an object to task's default OBJECTQ

STACK:

(if mailbox)

DWORD length

DWORD address

(if keyboard)

DWORD status (scan code in keystroke mode)

DWORD length (should be 1 in keystroke mode)

DWORD address

(if objectq)

DWORD handle of object to add

(if timer)

DWORD 1/100ths seconds since midnight (actually only accurate to 1/18 sec)

(if pointer)

DWORD column relative to origin of window

DWORD row relative to origin of window

Return Registers:
STACK arguments popped
CF set on error

Details: Under DESQview version 2.20 or higher, failed mailbox writes may return CF set (see Function DEh Subfunction 15h) rather than aborting the calling program. The data and status written to a keyboard object must match the format returned by the keyboard object in the current mode. The pointer position is scaled according to the current scaling factors.

Conflicts: MultiDOS Plus (chapter 16), VMiX (chapter 17).

See Also: Function 12h Subfunction 04h

INTERRUPT 15h - Function 12h, Subfunction 05h
SEND MESSAGE "WRITE" - WRITE STRING TO WINDOW

Purpose: Output the specified string, which may contain TopView/DESQview control sequences.

Available on: All machines.

Restrictions: TopView or compatible must be running.

Registers at call:

AH = 12h

BH = 05h

BL = window to write to

    00h DWORD on top of stack is window handle

    01h write string to task's default window

    0Ch (DV 2.26+) default window of task owning
        handle on top of the stack

    0Dh (DV 2.26+) default window of parent of
        current task

STACK: DWORD object handle if handle passed
    on stack

    DWORD total length of string (high word == 0)

    DWORD address of string to display

Return Registers:

indicated actions performed

STACK: DWORD handle of new window if the string
    contains a window stream (see below) with
    opcode E6h

else nothing

Details: Non-control characters are displayed (opcodes DEh and DFh control whether the attributes are left as is or changed to the current attribute); CR/LF/BS/Tab cause the usual cursor movement; and ESC starts a data structure with additional commands if the following byte is less than 20h; otherwise, the ESC character is written to the window

Conflicts: MultiDOS Plus (chapter 16), VMiX (chapter 17).

Table 15-4. Format of TopView Data Structure:

      MAGIC DB 1Bh

      MODE DB ? ; 00h, 01h, 10h, 14h-1Fh legal

      LENGTH DW ? ; length of remainder in bytes

      var-length fields follow, each an OPCODE followed by
         zero or more args

MODE 00h (set or display values) "WINDOW STREAM"

  Opcodes:arguments

      00h display 20h blanks with the default attribute

      01h-1Fh display OPCODE blanks with the default attribute

      20h display char with default attribute 20h times
        BYTE char to repeat

      21h-3Fh display char with default attribute OPCODE-20h times
        BYTE char to repeat

      40h display 20h blanks with specified attribute
        BYTE attribute of blanks

      41h-5Fh display OPCODE-40h blanks with specified attribute
        BYTE attribute of blanks

      60h display next 20h characters
        20h BYTEs characters to display

      61h-7Fh display next OPCODE-60h characters
        N BYTEs characters to display

Table 15-4. Format of TopView Data Structure (continued)

80h-87h display N blanks with default attribute
　　BYTE low 8 bits of 11-bit count (high 3 in low 3 bits of OPCODE)
　　　　　[000h means 800h]
88h-8Fh display N copies of the character
　　BYTE low 8 bits of 11-bit count (high 3 in low 3 bits of OPCODE)
　　　　　[000h means 800h]
　　BYTE character to repeat
90h-97h display N blanks with specified attribute
　　BYTE low 8 bits of 11-bit length (high 3 in low 3 bits of OPCODE)
　　　　　[000h means 800h]
　　BYTE attribute
98h-9FH display string at logical cursor pos
　　BYTE low 8 bits of 11-bit length (high 3 in low 3 bits of OPCODE)
　　　　　[000h means 800h]
　　N BYTEs string to display
A0h set logical cursor row
　　BYTE row number (0 is top)
A1h set logical cursor column
　　BYTE column number (0 is leftmost)
A2h set top edge of scrolling region
　　BYTE row
A3h set left edge of scrolling region
　　BYTE column
A4h set row of physical window position
　　BYTE line
A5h set column of physical window position
　　BYTE column
A6h set height of physical window
　　BYTE #rows
A7h set width of physical window
　　BYTE #columns
A8h set viewport row
　　BYTE row
A9h set viewport column
　　BYTE column
AAh set virtual screen height [contents of window unpredictable after]
　　BYTE rows
ABh set virtual screen width [contents of window unpredictable after]
　　BYTE columns
ACh-AEh unused
AFh set compatible/preferred video modes
　　BYTE compatibility/preference mask
　　　　　bit 7　　compatible with monochrome
　　　　　bit 6　　compatible with color text, EGA/VGA graphics
　　　　　bit 5　　compatible with medium-resolution CGA graphics
　　　　　bit 4　　compatible with high-resolution CGA graphics
　　　　　bit 3　　prefer monochrome
　　　　　bit 2　　prefer color text, EGA/VGA graphics
　　　　　bit 1　　prefer medium-resolution CGA graphics
　　　　　bit 0　　prefer high-resolution CGA graphics

Table 15-4. Format of TopView Data Structure (continued)

B0h move logical cursor down
 BYTE #rows (signed, negative values move up)
      [if #rows=0 and hardware cursor owner, update hw crsr]
B1h move logical cursor right
 BYTE #cols (signed, negative values move left)
      [if #cols=0 and hardware cursor owner, update hw crsr]
B2h shift top edge of scrolling region
 BYTE #rows (signed)
B3h shift left edge of scrolling region
 BYTE #cols (signed)
B4h shift physical window down
 BYTE #lines (signed)
B5h shift physical window right
 BYTE #columns (signed)
B6h expand physical window vertically
 BYTE #lines (signed)
B7h expand physical window horizontally
 BYTE #columns (signed)
B8h adjust viewport row
 BYTE #rows (signed)
B9h adjust viewport column
 BYTE #columns (signed)
BAh adjust virtual screen height [contents of window unpredictable after]
 BYTE #rows to increase (signed)
BBh adjust virtual screen width [contents of window unpredictable after]
 BYTE #cols to increase (signed)
BCh-BFh reserved (currently unused)
C0h set logical cursor position
 BYTE row number (0 is top border)
 BYTE column number (0 is left border)
C1h set top left corner of scrolling region
 BYTE row
 BYTE column
C2h set physical window pos
 BYTE upper left row (no top border if 0)
 BYTE upper left column (no left border if 0)
C3h set current window size
 BYTE #rows
 BYTE #cols
C4h set upper left corner of viewport (portion of virtual screen
 displayed in window)
 BYTE row
 BYTE column
C5h set size of virtual screen [contents unpredictable afterwards]
 BYTE #rows
 BYTE #cols
C6h unused
C7h unused

Table 15-4. Format of TopView Data Structure (continued)

 C8h set logical cursor relative to current position
   BYTE number of rows to move down (signed)
   BYTE number of columns to move right (signed)
      [if #rows=#cols=0 and hardware cursor owner, update hw cursr]
 C9h shift top left corner of scrolling region
   BYTE #rows (signed)
   BYTE #cols (signed)
 CAh set window pos relative to current position
   BYTE number of rows to shift down (signed)
   BYTE number of columns to shift right (signed)
 CBh set window size relative to current size
   BYTE number of rows to expand (signed)
   BYTE number of cols to expand (signed)
 CCh shift viewport relative to current position
   BYTE rows to shift (signed)
   BYTE cols to shift (signed)
 CDh resize virtual screen
   BYTE #rows to expand (signed)
   BYTE #cols to expand (signed)
 CEh scroll text when using E8h-EBh/F8h-FBh opcodes (default)
 CFh scroll attributes when using E8h-EBh/F8h-FBh opcodes
 D0h allow window frame to extend beyond screen
 D1h always display a complete frame, even if window extends beyond
   edge of screen
 D2h allow DV to change logical colors on video mode switch (default)
 D3h application changes logical attributes
 D4h window is visible [must redraw to actually make visible]
 D5h window is hidden [must redraw to actually remove]
 D6h window has frame (default)
 D7h window unframed [must redraw to actually remove frame]
 D8h READ/READN will read characters from window (default)
 D9h READ/READN will read attributes from window
 DAh use logical attributes, which may be remapped attributes
     1 normal text
     2 highlighted normal text
     3 help text
     4 highlighted help text
     5 error message
     6 highlighted error message
     7 emphasized text
     8 marked text
     9-16 are reverse video versions of 1-8
 DBh use physical attributes for characters
 DCh enable special actions for control characters (default)
 DDh disable special control char handling, all chars displayable by
   BIOS TTY call
 DEh write both character and attribute (default)
 DFh write character only, leave attribute untouched
 E0h repeat following commands through E1h opcode
   BYTE number of times to repeat (00h means 256 times)
 E1h end of commands to repeat, start repeating them

Table 15-4. Format of TopView Data Structure (continued)

E2h set current output color
   BYTE color
E3h clear virtual screen from scroll origin to end using current color
E4h redraw window
E5h select menu style
   BYTE style (normally 18h)
      bits 5,4 = 01 use two-letter menu entries for remainder of this stream
E5h (panel file only)
   BYTE modifier
      bits 7,6 = 11 panel stream creates new window
            = 10 panel defines new field table for existing window
            = 01 panel stream uses existing window & field table
      bit 5 = 1 stream contains a field table (create kyboard object)
      bit 4 = 1 stream defines input fields (create keyboard object)
      bit 3 = 1 stream defines select fields but not input fields
      bit 2 = 1 stream defines exclusive input window (DV 2.2)
      bit 1 reserved
      bit 0 reserved
E6h create new window and perform rest of manipulations in new window
   BYTE number of rows
   BYTE number of columns
   Return: DWORD object handle of new window returned on stack at end
E7h no operation
E8h scroll area up (top left corner defined by opcode C1h)
   BYTE height
   BYTE width
E9h scroll area down (top left corner defined by opcode C1h)
   BYTE height
   BYTE width
EAh scroll area left (top left corner defined by opcode C1h)
   BYTE height
   BYTE width
EBh scroll area right (top left corner defined by opcode C1h)
   BYTE height
   BYTE width
ECh set logical attributes for window contents
   BYTE video modes command applies to
      bit 7   monochrome
      bit 6   color text, EGA/VGA graphics
      bit 5   medium-resolution CGA graphics
      bit 4   high-resolution CGA graphics
   BYTE which attributes to set
      bit 7 if set, copy single following byte to indicated attributes
      bits 4-6 # of first attribute to change - 1
      bits 0-3 # of consecutive attributes to change
   N BYTEs new attributes
EDh set logical attributes for window frame
   BYTE video modes command applies to (see opcode ECh)
   BYTE which attributes to set
      bit 7 if set, copy single following byte to indicated attributes
      bits 4-6 # of first attribute to change - 1
      bits 0-3 # of consecutive attributes to change

Table 15-4. Format of TopView Data Structure (continued)

```
        N BYTEs new attributes
                attributes
                        1 = top left corner
                        2 = top right corner
                        3 = bottom left corner
                        4 = bottom right corner
                        5 = top edge
                        6 = bottom edge
                        7 = left edge
                        8 = right edge
EEh  set characters for window frame
    BYTE video modes command applies to (see opcode ECh)
    BYTE which characters to set
            bit 7  if set, copy single following byte to indicated chars
            bits 4-6  # of first char to change - 1
            bits 0-3  # of consecutive chars to change
        N BYTEs new chars (same relative position as attributes above)
EFh  set window name
    BYTE length of name (should be in range 0 to logical screen width)
    N BYTEs name
F0h  clear input field to blanks
    BYTE field number
F1h  fill input field with character
    BYTE field number
    BYTE char
F2h  set color of input field
    BYTE field number (1-N)
    BYTE attribute
F3h  set initial contents of input field
    BYTE field number (1-N)
    N BYTEs enough chars to exactly fill field as defined by op FFh
F4h  position cursor to start of specific input field
    BYTE field number (1-N)
F5h  change field table entry
    BYTE field number
    7-8 BYTEs field table entry (see opcode FFh below)
F6h  set field type
    BYTE field number
    BYTE type
                        00h inactive
                        40h output field
                        80h input field
                        C0h deselected field
                        C2h selected field
F7h  "broadcast write"          write data to fields with program output bit set
            in field table entry, in field number order
        N BYTEs (total length of all program output fields)
F8h  scroll field up a line
    BYTE field number
F9h  scroll field down a line
    BYTE field number
```

Table 15-4. Format of TopView Data Structure (continued)

FAh scroll field left
    BYTE field number
FBh scroll field right
    BYTE field number
FCh set field table header
    BYTE number of fields (must be <= existing number of fields)
    BYTE screen behavior bits
        bit 7 reserved
        bit 6 set if menu items may be selected via keyboard
        bit 5 set if left mouse button may terminate entry
        bit 4 set if right mouse button may terminate entry
        bit 3 if set, select fields return contents or blanks rather than 'Y' or 'N'
        bit 2 if set, modified bits reset on return to application
        bits 0,1 = 00 no data returned on read of keyboard
                01 data returned as array of chars containing all fields packed together, with no field numbers
                10 data returned as numbered variable-length records for all fields
                11 data returned as numbered variable-length records for the fields which were modified
    BYTE current input field (updated by DESQview)
    BYTE current select field (updated by DESQview)
    BYTE attribute for select fields when they are pointed at
    BYTE attribute for select fields which have been selected
FDh reset modified bit for all fields
FEh reset selected and modified bits for all fields
FFh set up input fields
    6 BYTEs field table header (see opcode FCh above)
    the field table entries, one for each field
        BYTE start row   \
        BYTE start column \ if menu selection and start is to
        BYTE end row   / right or below end, select from kbd only
        BYTE end column /
        BYTE field type
          bits 7,6 = 00 inactive (non-entry) field
                  01 echos keystrokes input to make menu selection
                  10 fill-in field
                  11 select field
          bit 5 field can be filled by broadcast write (F7h opcode)
          bit 4 reserved
          bit 3 reserved
          bit 2 reserved
          bit 1 set if field selected
          bit 0 set if field modified
        BYTE modifier
          if type is fill-in, then bit flags to determine behavior
                bit 7 if set, automatically enter CR when field full
                bit 6 move to next field when current field is full
                bit 5 if set, enter text from right end (for numbers)
                bit 4 if set, force input to uppercase
                bit 3 if set, clear old contents on first keystroke

Table 15-4. Format of TopView Data Structure (continued)

bit 2 if set, input returned when cursor moves out of modified field (API level 2.02+)

bit 1 reserved

bit 0 reserved

if select field, first key to press to activate

00h if have to point-&-click or is an extended-ASCII keystroke (only if two-key menus enabled)

BYTE (select field only) normal color of field

BYTE second key for select field. This byte is present if two-letter menu entries selected with opcode E5h, and in that case is present regardless of field type

Note: DESQview uses and updates the actual copy of the information which is contained in the stream. Thus this info must remain intact until after the data entry is complete.

MODE 01h "QUERY STREAM" (valid only for those opcodes listed here)

A0h return logical cursor row in next byte

A1h return logical cursor column in next byte

A2h return top row of scrolling region in next byte

A3h return left column of scrolling region in next byte

A4h return row of physical window origin in next byte

A5h return column of physical window origin in next byte

A6h return height of physcial window in next byte

A7h return width of physical window in next byte

A8h return row of viewport origin in next byte

A9h return column of viewport origin in next byte

AAh return height of virtual screen in next byte

ABh return width of virtual screen in next byte

AFh return current video mode in next byte

C0h return current logical cursor position in next two bytes

C1h return top left corner of scrolling region in next two bytes

C2h return current window position in next two bytes

C3h return current window size in next two bytes

C4h return current viewport origin in next two bytes

C5h return current virtual screen size in next two bytes

D0h \ overwritten with D0h if frames may fall off screen edge

D1h /   D1h if frames always displayed entirely

D2h \ overwritten with D2h if DESQview controls color palette

D3h /   D3h if application changes color palette

D4h \ overwritten with D4h if window visible

D5h /   D5h if window hidden

D6h \ overwritten with D6h if window has frame

D7h /   D7h if window unframed

D8h \ overwritten with D8h if reading characters from window

D9h /   D9h if reading attributes from window

DAh \ overwritten with DAh if using logical attributes

DBh /   DBh if using physical attributes

DCh \ overwritten with DCh if TTY control char interpretation on

DDh /   DDh if TTY control char interpretation off

DEh \ overwritten with DEh if writing both characters and attributes

DFh /   DFh if leaving attributes untouched

E2h return current color in next byte

ECh get logical attributes for window contents

BYTE execute call if currently in specified video mode

bit 7   monochrome

bit 6   color text, EGA/VGA graphics

Table 15-4. Format of TopView Data Structure (continued)

        bit 5   medium-resolution CGA graphics

        bit 4   high-resolution CGA graphics

    BYTE which attributes to get

        bit 7 unused

        bits 4-6 first attribute to get - 1

        bits 0-3 # consecutive attributes

    N BYTEs buffer to hold attributes

EDh get logical attributes for window frame

    BYTE execute call if currently in video mode (see opcode ECh)

    BYTE which attributes to get

        bit 7 unused

        bits 4-6 first attribute to get - 1

        bits 0-3 # consecutive attributes

    N BYTEs buffer to hold attributes

EEh get characters for window frame

    BYTE execute call if currently in video mode (see opcode ECh)

    BYTE which attributes to get

        bit 7 unused

        bits 4-6 first char to get - 1

        bits 0-3 # consecutive chars

    N BYTEs buffer to hold chars

EFh return first N characters of current window name

    BYTE   max length of returned name

    N BYTEs buffer to hold window name

F3h return contents of specified field

    BYTE field number

    N BYTEs buffer to hold field contents (size exactly equal to field

          size)

F5h get field table entry

    BYTE field number

    7-8 BYTEs buffer to hold field table entry

      Notes: DV < 2.26 always returns 7 bytes

             DV 2.26+ w/ APILEVEL < 2.26 returns 8 bytes if and only if field

               table is using 8-byte entries and eighth byte after

               F5h is E7h (NOP); otherwise, 7 bytes are returned

             DV 2.26+ w/ APILEVEL > 2.26 returns 7 or 8 bytes

               depending on the field table entry size

F6h get type of a field

    BYTE field number

    BYTE type

FCh get field table header

    6 BYTEs buffer to store header

MODE 10h "MANAGER STREAM" (valid only for opcodes listed here)

    00h allow window to be moved horizontally

    01h allow window to be moved vertically

    02h allow window to change width

    03h allow window to change height

    04h allow window to be scrolled horizontally

    05h allow window to be scrolled vertically

    06h allow "Close Window" menu selection for application

    07h allow "Hide Window" menu selection for application

    08h allow application to be suspended ("Rearrange/Freeze")

Table 15-4. Format of TopView Data Structure (continued)

0Eh allow "Scissors" menu
10h allow DESQview main menu to be popped up
11h allow "Switch Windows" menu
12h allow "Open Window" menu
13h allow "Quit" menu selection
20h-33h opposite of 00h-13h, disallow specified action
40h notify if horizontal position of window changes
41h notify if vertical position of window changes
42h notify if width of window changes
43h notify if height of window changes
44h notify if window scrolled horizontally
45h notify if window scrolled vertically
46h notify if window is closed--program has to clean up and exit itself
47h notify if window is hidden
48h notify if "?" on main menu selected
49h notify if pointer message sent to window
4Ah notify if window is placed in foreground
4Bh notify if window is placed in background
4Ch notify if video mode changes
4Dh notify if "Scissors" menu "Cut" option selected
4Eh notify if "Scissors" menu "Copy" option selected
4Fh notify if "Scissors" menu "Paste" option selected
50h notify if DESQview main menu about to pop up
51h notify if DESQview main menu popped down
60h-71h opposite of 40h-51h: don't notify on specified event
84h attach window to parent task's window (both move together)
85h detach window from parent task's window (may move independently)
86h disable background operation for application
87h enable running in background
88h set minimum size of physical window
    BYTE rows
    BYTE columns
89h set maximum size of physical window
    BYTE rows
    BYTE cols
8Ah set primary asynchronous notification routine
    DWORD address of routine, 0000h:0000h means none (see also below)
8Bh set asynchronous notification parameter
    DWORD 32-bit value passed to 8Ah async routine in DS:SI
ACh (DV2.2+) perform regular select field attribute processing
ADh (DV2.2+) protect attributes in selected field from being lost
AEh make window default notify window for owning app (API level 2.00+)
AFh set selected field marker character
    BYTE character to display at left edge of selected fields
BCh set standard field processing mode
BDh set alternate field processing mode (enables cursor pad for menus)
BEh disables changing reverse logical attributes with ECh opcode
BFh enables changing reverse logical attributes with ECh opcode
C0h make current window topmost in system
C1h force current process into foreground
C2h make current window topmost in process

Table 15-4. Format of TopView Data Structure (continued)

      C3h position mouse pointer relative to origin of current field
         BYTE rows below upper left corner of field
         BYTE columns to right of upper left corner of field
      C4h position mouse pointer relative to origin of given field
         BYTE field number
         BYTE rows below upper left corner of field
         BYTE columns to right of upper left corner of field
      C5h orphan current window (also hides it)
              Note: must be last in stream; all subsequent commands ignored
      C6h show all windows for this process
      C7h hide all windows for this process
      C8h suspend process and hide all its windows
      C9h force current process into background
      CAh make current window bottom-most in process
      CBh cancel current window manager operation, remove DV menu, give
         control to topmost application
      CCh orphan window and give it to the system for use as paste data
      CEh reorder windows
         DWORD pointer to null-terminated list of words; each word is the segment of the object handle for a
            window
      FFh no operation

MODES 14h to 1Fh "USER STREAMS"

      normally NOPs, but may be defined by SETESC message to invoke FAR
      routines, one for each mode number
       on entry to handler,
           DS:SI -> first byte of actual stream (not header)
           CX = #bytes in stream
           ES:DI = window's handle

Asynchronous notification routine defined by manager stream 8Ah is called with:

      ES:DI = handle of window
      DS:SI is 32-bit value set by 8Bh manager stream opcode
       mailbox contains message indicating event
       Opcode   Arguments (if any)
       40h horizontal movement
           DWORD object handle of window
           BYTE new row
           BYTE new col
       41h vertical movement
           DWORD object handle of window
           BYTE new row
           BYTE new col
       42h horizontal size change
           DWORD object handle of window
           BYTE new rows
           BYTE new cols
       43h vertical size change
           DWORD object handle of window
           BYTE new rows
           BYTE new cols
       44h scrolled horizontally
           DWORD object handle of window
           BYTE mouse row within window

Table 15-4. Format of TopView Data Structure (continued)

           BYTE mouse column within window
           BYTE field mouse is on, 0 if none
           BYTE amount moved: >0 right, <0 left, 0 done
45h scrolled vertically
           DWORD object hande of window
           BYTE mouse row within window
           BYTE mouse column within window
           BYTE field mouse is on, 0 if none
           BYTE amount moved: >0 down, <0 up, 0 done
46h window close request
           DWORD object handle of window
           BYTE mouse pointer row
           BYTE mouse pointer column
           BYTE field mouse is on, 0 if none
47h application's windows hidden
48h Help for Program selected
           DWORD object handle of window
           BYTE mouse pointer row
           BYTE mouse pointer column
           BYTE field mouse is on, 0 if none
49h pointer message sent to window
           DWORD pointer handle which received message
4Ah switched to window from another ("raise")
4Bh switched away from the window ("lower")
4Ch video mode changed
           BYTE new BIOS video mode
4Dh Scissors/cUt selected
           DWORD object handle of window
           BYTE row of upper left corner
           BYTE column of upper left corner
           BYTE field number ul corner is in, 0=none
           DWORD handle of orphaned window created with
                    copy of data from specified region
           BYTE height of region
           BYTE width of region
4Eh Scissors/Copy selected
           DWORD object handle of window
           BYTE row of upper left corner
           BYTE column of upper left corner
           BYTE field number ul corner is in, 0=none
           DWORD handle of orphaned window created with
                    copy of data from specified region
           BYTE height of region
           BYTE width of region
4Fh Scissors/Paste selected
           DWORD object handle of window
           BYTE row of upper left corner
           BYTE column of upper left corner
           BYTE field number ul corner is in, 0=none

Table 15-4. Format of TopView Data Structure (continued)

> DWORD handle of orphaned window with data
> BYTE height of region
> BYTE width of region
> > **Note:** the orphaned data window should be
> > adopted or freed when done
>
> 50h main menu about to pop up
> 51h main menu popped down

Return Registers:
> all registers unchanged

INTERRUPT 15h - Function 12h, Subfunction 06h
SEND MESSAGE "SETPRI" - SET PRIORITY WITHIN OBJECTQ

Purpose: Specify the relative order in which events for the given object will be retrieved from the task's OBJECTQ. Higher-priority objects will receive attention first even if a lower-priority object is already waiting for attention.

Available on: All machines.

Restrictions: DESQview version 2.20 or higher must be running.

Registers at call:
AH = 12h
BH = 06h
BL = object
> 00h object handle is in DWORD on top of stack
> > (mailbox, keyboard, pointer, or timer)
> 04h given task's keyboard (task's handle on top
> > of stack)
> 05h current task's default keyboard
> STACK: DWORD object handle if passed on
top of
> > stack
> DWORD new priority of object in task's
> > OBJECTQ

Return Registers:
all registers unchanged,
STACK arguments popped

Details: Initially all objects have the same default value. The program should only make relative adjustments to this default value, as the default value is not guaranteed to be constant from version to version. When changing priorities, all objects already on the objectq are reordered.

Conflicts: MultiDOS Plus (chapter 16), VMiX (chapter 17).

See Also: Function 12h Subfunction 07h

INTERRUPT 15h - Function 12h, Subfunction 07h
SEND MESSAGE "GETPRI" - GET PRIORITY WITHIN OBJECTQ

Purpose: Determine the relative order in which events for the given object will be retrieved from the task's OBJECTQ.

Available on: All machines.

Restrictions: DESQview version 2.20 or higher must be running.

Registers at call:
AH = 12h
BH = 07h
BL = object
    00h object handle in DWORD on top of stack
        mailbox, keyboard, pointer, or timer
    04h given task's keyboard (task's handle on top
        of stack)
    05h current task's default keyboard

Return Registers:
STACK: DWORD object priority

Details: Initially all objects have the same default value. The program should only make relative adjustments to this default value, as the default value is not guaranteed to be constant from version to version.
Conflicts: MultiDOS Plus (chapter 16), VMiX (chapter 17).
See Also: Function 12h Subfunction 06h

INTERRUPT 15h - Function 12h, Subfunction 08h
SEND MESSAGE "SIZEOF" - GET OBJECT SIZE

Purpose: Determine the logical size of an object; the units in which the size is measured depend on the type of the object.
Available on: All machines.

Restrictions: TopView or compatible must be running.

Registers at call:
AH = 12h
BH = 08h
BL = object
    00h handle in DWORD on top of stack
        window: total character positions in window
        timer: elapsed time since timer started
        pointer: number of messages queued to
            pointer object
        panel: number of panels in panel file
        keyboard: number of input buffers queued
    01h total chars in current task's default window
    02h number of messages in task's mailbox
        (task's handle on stack)
    03h number of messages in current task's
        mailbox
    04h number of input buffers queued in task's
        kbd (handle on stack)
    05h number of input buffers queued for current
        task's default kbd
    06h number of objects queued in OBJECTQ
        (task's handle on stack)
    07h number of objects queued in current task's
        OBJECTQ
    0Ch (DV 2.26+) total chars in window owning
        handle on top of stack
    0Dh (DV 2.26+) total chars in parent task's
        window

Return Registers:
DWORD on top of stack is result

Details: For panel objects, a count of zero is returned if no panel file is open for the object.
Conflicts: MultiDOS Plus (chapter 16), VMiX (chapter 17).
See Also: Function 12h Subfunctions 04h and 09h

INTERRUPT 15h - Function 12h, Subfunction 09h
SEND MESSAGE "LEN" - GET OBJECT LENGTH

Purpose: Determine the length of a window's line or the length of time remaining on a timer object.

Available on: All machines.

Restrictions: TopView or compatible must be running.

Registers at call:
AH = 12h
BH = 09h
BL = object
  00h handle in DWORD on top of stack
    window: get chars/line
    timer: get 1/100 seconds remaining before timer
      expires
  01h get number of chars/line in current task's
    default window
  0Ch (DV 2.26+) get chars/line in window owning
    handle on top of stk
  0Dh (DV 2.26+) get chars/line in parent task's
    window

Return Registers:
DWORD on top of stack is length

Conflicts: MultiDOS Plus (chapter 16), VMiX (chapter 17).

See Also: Function 12h Subfunction 08h

INTERRUPT 15h - Function 12h, Subfunction 0Ah
SEND MESSAGE "ADDTO" - WRITE CHARACTERS AND ATTRIBUTES TO WINDOW

Purpose: Output matched strings of characters and attributes as a single stream of alternating characters and attributes to the specified window.

Available on: All machines.

Restrictions: TopView or compatible must be running.

Registers at call:
AH = 12h
BH = 0Ah
BL = window to write to
  00h window handle is DWORD on top of stack
  01h current task's default window
  0Ch (DV 2.26+) default window of task owning
    handle on top of stack
  0Dh (DV 2.26+) default window of parent of
    current task
    STACK: DWORD window/task handle if
      passed on top of stack
    DWORD count of attributes
    DWORD address of attribute string
    DWORD count of characters
    DWORD address of character string

Return Registers:
STACK arguments popped

Details: If one string is longer than the other, the shorter one will be reused until the longer one is exhausted. The cursor is left just after the last character written.

Conflicts: MultiDOS Plus (chapter 16), VMiX (chapter 17).

See Also: Function 12h Subfunction 0Bh

INTERRUPT 15h - Function 12h, Subfunction 0Ah
SEND MESSAGE "ADDTO" - SEND MAILBOX MESSAGE/STATUS BY VALUE

Purpose: Store a message and associated status byte in the specified mailbox by making an actual copy of the message in a system-internal buffer.

Available on: All machines.

Restrictions: TopView or compatible must be running.

Registers at call:
AH = 12h
BH = 0Ah
BL = mailbox to write to
   00h handle is DWORD on top of stack
   02h default mailbox of task whose handle is on
       top of stack
   03h current task's default mailbox
     STACK: DWORD mailbox/task handle if passed on
        top of stack
   DWORD status (in low byte)
   DWORD length of message
   DWORD address of message

Return Registers:
STACK arguments popped
CF set on error

Details: The message is copied into either system or common memory. Insufficient memory normally causes the process to be aborted; under DESQview 2.2+, failed writes may return CF set instead (see Function DEh Subfunction 15h).

Conflicts: MultiDOS Plus (chapter 16), VMiX (chapter 17).

See Also: Function 12h Subfunction 0Bh

INTERRUPT 15h - Function 12h, Subfunction 0Ah
SEND MESSAGE "ADDTO" - SET OBJECT BITS

Purpose: Turn on the specified control flags for the indicated object; the meaning of the flag bits depends on the type of the object.

Available on: All machines.

Restrictions: TopView or compatible must be running.

Registers at call:
AH = 12h
BH = 0Ah
BL = object
   00h handle is DWORD on top of stack
      timer: start timer for specified interval
      pointer: set control flags (Table 15-5)
      keyboard: set control flags (Table 15-6)
   04h set control flags on KEYBOARD object
      (handle on top of stack)
   05h set control flags on task's default
      KEYBOARD object
STACK:
(if timer)
   DWORD duration in 1/100 seconds
(otherwise)
   DWORD bits to set

Return Registers:
STACK argument popped

Conflicts: MultiDOS Plus (chapter 16), VMiX (chapter 17).

See Also: Function 12h Subfunction 0Bh

Table 15-5. Pointer Objects, Bit Significance:

Bit	Significance
15	reserved, can't be set
14-8	unused
7	mouse pointer is hidden while in window
6	get messages even if window not topmost
5	get messages even if window not foreground
4	multiple clicks separated by less than 1/3 second are counted and returned in a single message
3	pointer position is relative to screen origin, not window origin
2	send message on button release as well as button press
1	(DV 2.23+) send message with row=FFFFh and col=FFFFh whenever pointer leaves the window
0	send message only on button activity, not movement (DV-specific, and Function DEh Subfunction 0Fh must have been called first)

Table 15-6. Keyboard Objects, Bit Significance:

Bit	Significance
15	reserved, can't be set
14	unused
13	reserved, can't be set
12-6	unused
5	(DV 2.2+) exclusive input
4	filter all keys (used with handler established by SETESC) if 0, only keys that would normally be displayed are filtered
3	program continues executing while input in progress
2	insert mode active for field mode
1	hardware cursor displayed when task is hardware cursor owner must be set if keyboard in field mode and field table includes input fields
0	keyboard is in field mode rather than keystroke mode

INTERRUPT 15h - Function 12h, Subfunction 0Bh
SEND MESSAGE "SUBFROM" - WRITE ATTRIBUTES TO WINDOW

Purpose: Output a string of display attributes to the specified window, preserving the characters currently in the locations where the attributes are written.

Available on: All machines.

Restrictions: TopView or compatible must be running.

Registers at call:
AH = 12h
BH = 0Bh
BL = window to write attributes to
    00h handle is DWORD on top of stack (pushed after other parameters)
    01h current task's default window
    0Ch (DV 2.26+) default window of task owning handle on top of stack
    0Dh (DV 2.26+) default window of parent of current task
    STACK: DWORD number of attributes to write
    DWORD address of attributes

Return Registers:
STACK arguments popped

Details: The specified attributes are written starting at the current cursor position; the cursor is left just after the last position written.

Conflicts: MultiDOS Plus (chapter 16), VMiX (chapter 17).

See Also: Function 12h Subfunction 0Ah

INTERRUPT 15h - Function 12h, Subfunction 0Bh
SEND MESSAGE "SUBFROM" - SEND MAILBOX MESSAGE/STATUS BY REFERENCE

Purpose: Store a message and associated status byte in the specified mailbox, only placing a pointer to the message in the mailbox rather than the actual message.

Available on: All machines.

Restrictions: TopView or compatible must be running.

Registers at call:
AH = 12h
BH = 0Bh
BL = mailbox to write to
    00h handle is DWORD on top of stack
    02h default mailbox of task whose handle is on
        top of stack
    03h current task's default mailbox
STACK: DWORD status (low byte)
    DWORD   length of message
    DWORD   address of message

Return Registers:
STACK arguments popped
CF set on error

Details: Even though only a pointer to the message is stored, the write may still fail due to insufficient memory. Under DV 2.2+, failed mailbox writes may return CF set (see Function DEh Subfunction 15h); prior versions always terminated the program.

Conflicts: MultiDOS Plus (chapter 16), VMiX (chapter 17).

See Also: Function 12h Subfunction 0Ah

INTERRUPT 15h - Function 12h, Subfunction 0Bh
SEND MESSAGE "SUBFROM" - REMOVE OBJECT FROM OBJECTQ

Purpose: Indicate that an object no longer needs attention, either because it has been serviced or because it no longer exists.

Available on: All machines.

Restrictions: TopView or compatible must be running.

Registers at call:
AH = 12h
BH = 0Bh
BL = OBJECTQ from which to remove all copies of
       a particular object
    06h OBJECTQ of task whose handle is on top
       of the stack
    07h task's default OBJECTQ
STACK: DWORD task handle if passed on stack
    DWORD   handle of object to remove

Return Registers:
STACK arguments popped

Details: This message should be sent whenever an object is erased or closed, so that a subsequent read of the OBJECTQ does not return an object handle which no longer requires attention.

Conflicts: MultiDOS Plus (chapter 16), VMiX (chapter 17).

INTERRUPT 15h - Function 12h, Subfunction 0Bh
SEND MESSAGE "SUBFROM" - RESET OBJECT BITS

Purpose: Turn off the specified control flags for the indicated object; the meaning of the flag bits depends on the type of the object.

Available on: All machines.

Restrictions: TopView or compatible must be running.

Registers at call:
AH = 12h

Return Registers:
STACK arguments popped

BH = 0Bh
BL = object
    00h handle is DWORD on top of stack
        pointer: reset control flags
        keyboard: reset control flags
    04h clear control flags on KEYBOARD object
        (handle on top of stack)
    05h clear control flags on task's default
        KEYBOARD object
STACK: DWORD object handle if passed on top of
        the stack
    DWORD which bits to clear (see Function 12h
        Subfunction 0Ah "SET OBJECT BITS"
        above)

Details: The attributes are written starting at the current cursor position; the cursor is left just after the last position written.

Conflicts: MultiDOS Plus (chapter 16), VMiX (chapter 17).

See Also: Function 12h Subfunction 0Ah

INTERRUPT 15h - Function 12h, Subfunction 0Ch
SEND MESSAGE "OPEN" - OPEN OBJECT

Purpose: Prepare of I/O or other manipulation of the specified object.

Available on: All machines.

Restrictions: TopView or compatible must be running.

Registers at call:
AH = 12h
BH = 0Ch
BL = object
    00h handle is DWORD on top of stack
        window: fill with given character from
            scroll origin to end
        keyboard: attach to a window
        timer: open
        pointer: start taking input for window
        panel: associate with a panel file
    01h fill task's default window with given char
        from scrl org to end
    02h open given task's mailbox for input (task's
        handle on stack)
    03h open current task's mailbox
    04h attach a KEYBOARD to a window (handle
        on top of stack)
    05h attach task's default KEYBOARD to a
        window

    06h open a task's OBJECTQ (task's handle on
        top of stack)
    07h open current task's OBJECTQ
    0Ch (DV 2.26+) fill def window of task owning
        handle on top of stck
    0Dh (DV 2.26+) fill default window of parent
        of current task

Return Registers:
STACK arguments popped

STACK:
(if window)
    DWORD character to fill with
(if keyboard or pointer)
    DWORD handle of window to attach to
(if panel)
    DWORD length of filename or resident panel
    DWORD address of filename or resident panel
(otherwise)
    nothing

Details: If first byte of panel file name is 1Bh, then the "name" IS a panel. If first two bytes of panel file "name" are C0hC3h, then the "name" IS the panel file. Result code of open may be retrieved with STATUS message. Logical cursor is left at scroll origin after filling window. The task opening a mailbox becomes its owner, and the only task allowed to read the mailbox. Messages are only sent to a pointer object when the mouse is positioned in the window to which the pointer has been attached. There is no need to explicitly open a timer object, as ADDTO and WRITE messages automatically open the timer.

Conflicts: MultiDOS Plus (chapter 16), VMiX (chapter 17).

See Also: Function 12h Subfunctions 0Dh and 14h

INTERRUPT 15h - Function 12h, Subfunction 0Dh
SEND MESSAGE "CLOSE" - CLOSE OBJECT

Purpose: Indicate that the specified object no longer needs to be manipulated.

Available on: All machines.

Restrictions: TopView or compatible must be running.

Registers at call:
AH = 12h
BH = 0Dh
BL = object
    00h handle is DWORD on top of stack
        timer: close
        keyboard: detach from window and discard
            queued input
        pointer: stop taking input
        panel: close
        mailbox: close, unlock, and discard any
            pending messages
    02h close given task's mailbox (task's handle on
        top of stack)
    03h close task's default mailbox
    04h close KEYBOARD object (handle on top of
        stack)
    05h close task's default KEYBOARD
    06h close given task's OBJECTQ (task's handle
        on top of stack)
    07h close current task's OBJECTQ

Return Registers: n/a

Details: When an OBJECTQ is closed, each object in the OBJECTQ is sent an ERASE message (Function 12h Subfunction 0Eh). When a panel object is closed, the panel file and any panels currently in use are freed; window and keyboard objects created by APPLY are not affected, but field mode input ceases. Open but idle timer objects consume a small amount of CPU time.

Conflicts: MultiDOS Plus (chapter 16), VMiX (chapter 17).

See Also: Function 12h Subfunctions 0Ch, 0Eh, and 14h

INTERRUPT 15h - Function 12h, Subfunction 0Eh
SEND MESSAGE "ERASE" - ERASE OBJECT

Purpose: Discard all pending I/O for the object, or otherwise clear it; the action taken depends upon the type of the object.

Available on: All machines.

Registers at call:
AH = 12h
BH = 0Eh
BL = object
    00h handle is DWORD on top of stack
        window: clear from scroll origin to end of
            window
        keyboard: discard input timer: cancel
            current interval
        pointer: discard all pending messages
        mailbox: discard all pending messages
    01h clear task's default window from scroll
        origin to end
    02h discard all queued messages in mailbox
        (handle on top of stack)
    03h discard all queued messages in current
        task's default mailbox
    04h discard all input queued to KEYBOARD
        (handle on top of stack)
    05h discard all input queued to task's default
        KEYBOARD
    06h remove all objects from OBJECTQ (task's
        handle on top of stack)
    07h remove all objects from current task's
        OBJECTQ
    0Ch (DV 2.26+) clear window of task owning
        handle on top of stack
    0Dh (DV 2.26+) clear default window of parent
        of current task

Restrictions: TopView or compatible must be running.

Return Registers: n/a

Details: When an OBJECTQ is erased, each object in the OBJECTQ is also erased.
Conflicts: MultiDOS Plus (chapter 16), VMiX (chapter 17).
See Also: Function 12h Subfunction 02h

INTERRUPT 15h - Function 12h, Subfunction 0Fh
SEND MESSAGE "STATUS" - GET OBJECT STATUS

Purpose: Determine the current state of the specified object.

Available on: All machines.

Registers at call:
AH = 12h
BH = 0Fh
BL = object
    00h handle is DWORD on top of stack
        timer: is it running?
        pointer: return status of last message

Restrictions: TopView or compatible must be running.

Return Registers:
DWORD on top of stack is status

      panel: verify success of last OPEN or
        APPLY
02h return status of last msg READ from
      mailbox (handle on stack)
03h return status of last msg READ from task's
      default mailbox
04h get status of last msg from task's
      KEYBOARD (task handle on stk)
05h get status of last msg from task's default
      KEYBOARD
06h return whether OBJECTQ is open or not
      (handle on top of stack)
07h return whether task's default OBJECTQ is
      open or not

Details: If object is a panel object, the status indicates the error code:
      00h successful
      14h panel name not in panel directory
      15h not enough memory to apply panel
      16h invalid panel format
      17h panel file already open
      81h-92h DOS error codes+80h   \ codes > 80h indicate
      95h not enough memory to open panel file > that the panel was
      98h null panel file name   / not opened

If object is a timer, the status is:
      00000000h open but not running
      40000000h open and running
      80000000h closed

If object is an OBJECTQ, the status is:
      00000000h open
      80000000h closed

If object is a keyboard in keystroke mode, the status is the extended character code (scan code) of the last keystroke

If object is a keyboard in field mode, the status indicates the reason for the last return from the field manager:
      00h Enter key pressed
      01h Button 1 or keystroke selection
      02h Button 2
      03h validation
      04h auto Enter on field
      1Bh Escape pressed
      46h ^Break pressed
      other: extended code for key terminating input

The status of mailbox messages sent by the window manager is always 80h. The status of a pointer message is the same as the status field in the message.

Conflicts: MultiDOS Plus (chapter 16), VMiX (chapter 17).
See Also: Function 12h Subfunction 04h

INTERRUPT 15h - Function 12h, Subfunction 10h
SEND MESSAGE "EOF" - GET OBJECT EOF STATUS

Purpose: Determine whether the end of the specified object's contents has been reached.

Available on: All machines.

Restrictions: TopView or compatible must be running.

Registers at call:
AH = 12h
BH = 10h

Return Registers:
DWORD on top of stack is status

BL = object
  00h handle is DWORD on top of stack
        window: return TRUE if logical cursor past
              end of window
        mailbox: *unknown*
  01h returns TRUE if logical cursor past end of
        task's def window
  02h return EOF for task's mailbox (task's handle
        on top of stack)
  03h return EOF for current task's mailbox
  0Ch (DV 2.26+) check logical cursor of window
        owning handle on top of stack
  0Dh (DV 2.26+) check logical cursor of window
        of parent task
Conflicts: MultiDOS Plus (chapter 16), VMiX (chapter 17).

INTERRUPT 15h - Function 12h, Subfunction 11h
SEND MESSAGE "AT" - POSITION OBJECT CURSOR

Purpose: Specify the logical cursor position for the indicated window.

Available on: All machines.

Restrictions: TopView or compatible must be running.

Registers at call:
AH = 12h
BH = 11h
BL = window for which to move cursor
  00h window's handle is DWORD on top of
        stack
  01h task's default window
  0Ch (DV 2.26+) default window of task owning
        handle on top of stack
  0Dh (DV 2.26+) default window of parent of
        current task
STACK: DWORD column
     DWORD row
Conflicts: MultiDOS Plus (chapter 16), VMiX (chapter 17).

Return Registers:
STACK arguments popped

INTERRUPT 15h - Function 12h, Subfunction 11h
SEND MESSAGE "SETNAME" - ASSIGN NAME TO MAILBOX

Purpose: Specify a globally-visible string with which the indicated mailbox object may be found by tasks who do not know the mailbox's object handle.

Available on: All machines.

Restrictions: TopView or compatible must be running.

Registers at call:
  AH = 12h
  BH = 11h
  BL = mailbox to name
    00h DWORD on top of stack is mailbox
        handle
    02h use given task's mailbox (task's handle
        on top of the stack)
    03h use current task's default mailbox

Return Registers:
STACK arguments popped

STACK: DWORD object handle if passed on top of
the stack
DWORD length of name
DWORD address of name
Conflicts: MultiDOS Plus (chapter 16), VMiX (chapter 17).
See Also: Function DEh Subfunction 0Eh

INTERRUPT 15h - Function 12h, Subfunction 11h
SEND MESSAGE "SETSCALE" - SET POINTER SCALE FACTOR
Purpose: Specify the correspondence between positions in a window and the positions reported by or written to pointer objects.
Available on: All machines.

Registers at call:
AH = 12h
BX = 1100h
STACK: DWORD object handle for pointer
object
DWORD number of colums to scale pointer
position to
DWORD number of rows to scale pointer
position to

Restrictions: TopView or compatible must be running.
Return Registers:
STACK arguments popped

Details: Pointer positions will be scaled as if the window had the specified number of rows and columns; thus, reported positions may not be contiguous or multiple rows/columns may report the same value, depending on the scaling factors.
Conflicts: MultiDOS Plus (chapter 16), VMiX (chapter 17).
See Also: Function 12h Subfunction 12h

INTERRUPT 15h - Function 12h, Subfunction 12h
SEND MESSAGE "READN" - GET NEXT N OBJECT BYTES
Purpose: Retrieve the specified number of characters or display attributes from the indicated window.
Available on: All machines.

Registers at call:
AH = 12h
BH = 12h
BL = window to read from
00h handle is DWORD on top of stack
01h read next N chars or attributes on task's
default window
0Ch (DV 2.26+) read window of task owning
handle on top of stack
0Dh (DV 2.26+) read default window of parent
of current task
STACK: DWORD count

Restrictions: TopView or compatible must be running.
Return Registers:
STACK: DWORD width of screen line
DWORD address
DWORD count actually read

Details: Reading starts at the current logical cursor position; the cursor is updated to point at the character following the last one read. Any translucent blanks (FFh) which are visible on screen are changed to the character which is seen through them. The string produced by the read is placed in an input buffer which may be reused by the next READ or READN of a window. Window stream opcodes D8h and D9h determine whether the read returns characters or attributes.
Conflicts: MultiDOS Plus (chapter 16), VMiX (chapter 17).
See Also: Function 12h Subfunctions 04h and 05h for windows

INTERRUPT 15h - Function 12h, Subfunction 12h
SEND MESSAGE "GETSCALE" - GET POINTER SCALE FACTOR

Purpose: Determine the correspondence between positions in a window and the positions reported by or written to pointer objects.

Available on: All machines.

Registers at call:
AH = 12h
BX = 1200h
STACK: DWORD object handle for pointer

Restrictions: TopView or compatible must be running.

Return Registers:
STACK: DWORD pointer pos scaled as if window were this many colums wide
DWORD pointer pos scaled as if window were this many rows high

Conflicts: MultiDOS Plus (chapter 16), VMiX (chapter 17).
See Also: Function 12h Subfunction 11h

INTERRUPT 15h - Function 12h, Subfunction 13h
SEND MESSAGE "REDRAW" - REDRAW WINDOW

Purpose: Force an immediate update of the physical screen to reflect any changes made to the specified window. Most modifications to a window do not become visible until the window is redrawn.

Available on: All machines.

Registers at call:
AH = 12h
BH = 13h
BL = window object
    00h DWORD on top of stack is handle for
       window to redraw
    01h redraw task's default window
    0Ch (DV 2.26+) redraw window of task owning
       handle on top of stack
    0Dh (DV 2.26+) redraw default window of
       parent of current task

Restrictions: TopView or compatible must be running.

Return Registers: n/a

Conflicts: MultiDOS Plus (chapter 16), VMiX (chapter 17).
See Also: Function 12h Subfunction 0Eh

INTERRUPT 15h - Function 12h, Subfunction 13h
SEND MESSAGE "SETICON" - SPECIFY POINTER ICON

Purpose: Specify the character which should be used to indicate the current position of the mouse pointer.

Available on: All machines.

Registers at call:
AH = 12h
BX = 1300h
STACK: DWORD object handle for pointer
    DWORD character to use for pointer

Restrictions: TopView or compatible must be running.

Return Registers:
STACK arguments popped

Details: DESQview accepts but ignores this call; its pointer icon is always a diamond (screen character 4).
Conflicts: MultiDOS Plus (chapter 16), VMiX (chapter 17).

INTERRUPT 15h - Function 12h, Subfunction 14h
SEND MESSAGE "SETESC" - SET ESCAPE ROUTINE ADDRESS

Purpose: Specify a handler for intercepting keyboard input or user stream output.

Available on: All machines.

Restrictions: TopView or compatible must be running.

Registers at call:
AH = 12h
BH = 14h
BL = message modifier
    00h handle is DWORD on top of stack
    01h define user stream
    04h intercept keystrokes from KEYBOARD to
      a window (handle on stack)
    05h intercept keystrokes from task's default
      KEYBOARD to a window
STACK:
(if window)
    DWORD user stream number (14h-1Fh)
    DWORD address of FAR user stream handler
(if keyboard)
    DWORD address of FAR filter function

Return Registers:
STACK arguments popped

Details: The filter function is not allowed to make INT 15h, DOS, or BIOS calls.
    The keyboard filter function is called with the following when the keyboard is in field mode:
        AL = character
        AH = 00h or extended ASCII code if AL = 00h
        BL = field number
        CH = cursor column
        CL = cursor row
        DL = field type modifier (sixth item in field table entry)
        DH = seventh item in field table entry
        ES:SI = window's handle
        DS:DI -> field table entry for field containing the cursor
    The filter function should return
        AH = 00h use keystroke
                01h ignore keystroke
                FFh beep and ignore keystroke
Conflicts: MultiDOS Plus (chapter 16), VMiX (chapter 17).
See Also: Function 12h Subfunction 05h

INTERRUPT 15h - Function 12h, Subfunction 14h
SEND MESSAGE "LOCK" - REQUEST EXCLUSIVE ACCESS TO RESOURCE

Purpose: Attempt to become the sole task allowed to use a resource which may not be accessed by multiple tasks simultaneously.
Available on: All machines.

Restrictions: TopView or compatible must be running.

Registers at call:
AH = 12h
BH = 14h
BL = object
    00h mailbox handle is DWORD on top of stack
    02h use given task's mailbox (task's handle on
      top of stack)
    03h use current task's default mailbox

Return Registers: n/a

Details: If some other task has already locked the mailbox, the caller is suspended until the mailbox becomes unlocked. Release exclusive access by sending a CLOSE message to the mailbox. A single task may request a lock multiple times, which then requires multiple CLOSEs.
Conflicts: MultiDOS Plus (chapter 16), VMiX (chapter 17).
See Also: Function 12h Subfunction 0Dh

INTERRUPT 15h - Function 12h, Subfunction 15h
SEND MESSAGE "SETFLAGS" - SET OBJECT FLAGS

Purpose: Specify new values for an object's attributes; the meaning of the flag bits depends on the type of the object.

Available on: All machines.

Restrictions: DESQview version 2.20 or higher must be running.

Registers at call:
AH = 12h
BH = 15h
BL = object
    00h DWORD on top of stack (mailbox,
       keyboard, or pointer only)
    02h mailbox for task whose handle is on top of
       stack
    03h mailbox for current task
    04h keyboard for task whose handle is on top of
       stack
    05h keyboard for current task
STACK: DWORD flags
    if mailbox:
       bit 0: all mail messages stored in common
          memory
       bit 1: allow write even if closed
       bit 2: don't erase messages when mailbox is
          closed
    if keyboard:
       bit 5: exclusive input when keyboard is in
          use for input

Return Registers:
STACK arguments popped

Details: This function is only available if the API level has been set to at least 2.20. It is equivalent to performing SUBFROM and ADDTO calls on the object.

Conflicts: MultiDOS Plus (chapter 16), VMiX (chapter 17).

See Also: Function 12h Subfunctions 0Ah, 0Bh, and 16h

INTERRUPT 15h - Function 12h, Subfunction 16h
SEND MESSAGE "GETFLAGS" - GET OBJECT FLAGS

Purpose: Determine the current attributes of the specified object; the meaning of the flag bits depends on the type of the object.

Available on: All machines.

Restrictions: DESQview version 2.20 or higher must be running.

Registers at call:
AH = 12h
BH = 16h
BL = object
    00h DWORD on top of stack (mailbox, keyboard,
       or pointer only)
    02h mailbox for task whose handle is on top of
       stack
    03h mailbox for current task
    04h keyboard for task whose handle is on top of
       stack
    05h keyboard for current task

Return Registers:
STACK: DWORD current control flags

Details: This function is only available if the API level has been set to at least 2.20.

Conflicts: MultiDOS Plus (chapter 16), VMiX (chapter 17).

See Also: Function 12h Subfunctions 0Ah, 0Bh, and 15h

DESQview

As mentioned at the beginning of the chapter, the DESQview API is for the most part a superset of the TopView API. Subfunctions 00h through 0Ah of INT 15h Function DEh correspond exactly to the TopView subfunctions of INT 15h Function 11h. Some additional DESQview-specific calls are listed above in the TopView section because they fit in more logically there.

INTERRUPT 15h - Function 11h, Subfunction DEh
XDV.COM INSTALLATION CHECK

Purpose: Determine whether DESQview was loaded using XDV.

Available on: All machines.

Registers at call:
AX = 11DEh

Restrictions: DESQview must be running and must have been loaded with XDV.

Return Registers:
CF clear if installed
   AX = segment at which XDV is located

Conflicts: MultiDOS Plus (chapter 16), VMiX (chapter 17).

INTERRUPT 15h - Function DEh, Subfunction 00h
GET PROGRAM NAME

Purpose: Determine the offset of the calling program's name within the DESQview program list file.

Available on: All machines.

Registers at call:
AX = DE00h

Restrictions: DESQview must be running.

Return Registers:
AX = offset into DESQVIEW.DVO of current
   program's record (see below)

Conflicts: None known.
See Also: Function DEh Subfunction 07h

Table 15-7. Format of Program Entry in DESQVIEW.DVO:

Offset	Size	Description
00h	BYTE	length of name
01h	N BYTEs	name
	2 BYTEs	keys to invoke program (second = 00h if only one key used)
	WORD	*apparently always 0000h*
	BYTE	end flag: 00h for all but last entry, which is FFh

INTERRUPT 15h - Function DEh, Subfunction 01h
UPDATE "OPEN WINDOW" MENU

Purpose: Force DESQview to reread its program list file and rebuild the menu of available programs.

Available on: All machines.

Registers at call:
AX = DE01h

Restrictions: DESQview must be running.

Return Registers: n/a

Details: This function attempts to read DESQVIEW.DVO, and disables the Open Window menu if the file is not in the current directory.

Conflicts: None known.

INTERRUPT 15h - Function DEh, Subfunction 02h
SET Unknown FLAG FOR CURRENT WINDOW

Purpose: unknown.

Available on: All machines.

Registers at call:
AX = DE02h

Restrictions: DESQview version 1.x must be running.

Return Registers: n/a

Details: This call is a NOP in DV 2.x; it may correspond to a TopView function which is no longer necessary.
Conflicts: None known.
See Also: Function DEh Subfunction 03h

INTERRUPT 15h - Function DEh, Subfunction 03h
GET Unknown Values FOR CURRENT WINDOW

Purpose: unknown.
Available on: All machines.
Registers at call:
AX = DE03h

Restrictions: DESQview version 1.x must be running.
Return Registers:
AX = *unknown value* for current window
BX = *unknown value* for current window

Details: This call is a NOP in DESQview 2.x; it may correspond to a TopView function which is no longer necessary.
Conflicts: None known.
See Also: Function DEh Subfunction 02h

INTERRUPT 15h - Function DEh, Subfunction 04h
GET AVAILABLE COMMON MEMORY

Purpose: Determine the total and available amounts of memory reserved by DESQview for storing objects, messages, and other items.
Available on: All machines.
Registers at call:
AX = DE04h

Restrictions: DESQview must be running.
Return Registers:
BX = bytes of common memory available
CX = largest block available
DX = total common memory in bytes

Conflicts: None known.
See Also: Function DEh Subfunctions 05h and 06h

INTERRUPT 15h - Function DEh, Subfunction 05h
GET AVAILABLE CONVENTIONAL MEMORY

Purpose: Determine the total and available amounts of non-expanded, non-extended memory available for running programs.
Available on: All machines.
Registers at call:
AX = DE05h

Restrictions: DESQview must be running.
Return Registers:
BX = K of memory available
CX = largest block available
DX = total conventional memory in K

Conflicts: None known.
See Also: Function DEh Subfunctions 04h and 06h

INTERRUPT 15h - Function DEh, Subfunction 06h
GET AVAILABLE EXPANDED MEMORY

Purpose: Determine the total and available amounts of expanded memory available for allocation or running programs.
Available on: All machines.
Registers at call:
AX = DE06h

Restrictions: DESQview must be running.
Return Registers:
BX = K of expanded memory available
CX = largest block available
DX = total expanded memory in K

Conflicts: None known.
See Also: Function DEh Subfunctions 04h and 05h

INTERRUPT 15h - Function DEh, Subfunction 07h
"APPNUM" - GET CURRENT PROGRAM'S NUMBER

Purpose: Determine the caller's position in the "Switch Windows" menu.

Available on: All machines.

Registers at call:
AX = DE07h

Restrictions: DESQview must be running.

Return Registers:
AX = number of program as it appears on the "Switch Windows" menu

Details: this API call may be made from a hardware interrupt handler

Conflicts: None known.

See Also: Function DEh Subfunction 00h

INTERRUPT 15h - Function DEh, Subfunction 08h
CHECK Unknown Value

Purpose: *unknown.*

Available on: All machines.

Registers at call:
AX = DE08h

Restrictions: DESQview must be running.

Return Registers:
AX = 0000h if *unknown value* is not set to the current task
0001h if *unknown value* is set to the current task

Conflicts: None known.

INTERRUPT 15h - Function DEh, Subfunction 09h
UNIMPLEMENTED

Purpose: This call presumably corresponds to a TopView function which is no longer necessary or meaningful under DESQview.

Available on: All machines.

Registers at call:
AX = DE09h

Restrictions: DESQview must be running.

Return Registers: n/a (NOP in DESQview)

Conflicts: None known.

INTERRUPT 15h - Function DEh, Subfunction 0Ah
"DBGPOKE" - DISPLAY CHARACTER ON STATUS LINE

Purpose: The specified character is displayed on the 25th line of the screen; the next call will display in the next position (which wraps back to the start of the line if off the right edge of screen).

Available on: All machines.

Registers at call:
AX = DE0Ah
BL = character

Restrictions: DESQview version 2.00 or higher must be running.

Return Registers:
Character displayed, next call will display in next position (which wraps back to the start of the line if off the right edge of screen)

Details: Displays character on bottom line of **physical** screen, regardless of current size of window (even entirely hidden). Does not know about graphics display modes, just pokes the characters into display memory. This API call may be made from a hardware interrupt handler.

Conflicts: None known.

See Also: TopView Function 10h Subfunction 03h

INTERRUPT 15h - Function DEh, Subfunction 0Bh
"APILEVEL" - DEFINE MINIMUM API LEVEL REQUIRED

Purpose: Since some calls have slightly different semantics in different versions of DESQview, this call allows an older program to use the semantics of the version for which it was written. Conversely, a program can ensure that it is not run on older versions of DESQview which may not have all of the API calls the program uses.

Available on: All machines.

Registers at call:
AX = DE0Bh
BL = API level major version number
BH = API level minor version number

Restrictions: DESQview version 2.00 or higher must be running.
Return Registers:
AX = maximum API level (AL = major, AH = minor)

Details: If the requested API level is greater than the version of DESQview, a "You need a newer version" error window is popped up. The API level defaults to 1.00, and is inherited by child tasks.
Some early copies of DV 2.00 return AX=0200h instead of 0002h.
Conflicts: None known.

INTERRUPT 15h - Function DEh, Subfunction 0Ch
"GETMEM" - ALLOCATE "SYSTEM" MEMORY

Purpose: Request a portion of the per-process pool of reserved memory.
Available on: All machines.

Registers at call:
AX = DE0Ch
BX = number of bytes

Restrictions: DESQview version 2.00 or higher must be running.
Return Registers:
ES:DI -> allocated block or 0000h:0000h (DV 2.26+)

Details: Use SETERROR (Function DEh Subfunction 15h) to avoid a user prompt if there is insufficient system memory.
Conflicts: None known.
See Also: Function DEh Subfunctions 0Dh and 15h, TopView Function 10h Subfunction 01h

INTERRUPT 15h - Function DEh, Subfunction 0Dh
"PUTMEM" - DEALLOCATE "SYSTEM" MEMORY

Purpose: Free a previously allocated block of the per-process pool of reserved memory.
Available on: All machines.

Registers at call:
AX = DE0Dh
ES:DI -> previously allocated block

Restrictions: DESQview version 2.00 or higher must be running.
Return Registers: n/a

Conflicts: None known.
See Also: Function DEh Subfunction 0Ch, TopView Function 10h Subfunction 02h

INTERRUPT 15h - Function DEh, Subfunction 0Eh
"FINDMAIL" - FIND MAILBOX BY NAME

Purpose: Determine the handle of the mailbox (if any) which has been given the specified string as a name.
Available on: All machines.

Registers at call:
AX = DE0Eh
ES:DI -> name to find
CX = length of name

Restrictions: DESQview version 2.00 or higher must be running.
Return Registers:
BX = 0000h not found
     0001h found
     DS:SI = object handle

Conflicts: None known.
See Also: Function 12h Subfunction 11h

INTERRUPT 15h - Function DEh, Subfunction 0Fh
ENABLE DESQview EXTENSIONS

Purpose: Permit the use of certain extensions to the TopView API provided by DESQview.
Available on: All machines.

Restrictions: DESQview version 2.00 or higher must be running.

Registers at call:	Return Registers:
AX = DE0Fh	AX and BX destroyed (seems to be bug, weren't saved & restored)

Details: This function sends a manager stream with opcodes AEh, BDh, and BFh (see Function 12h Subfunction 05h) to the task's window. It also enables an additional mouse mode.
Conflicts: None known.

INTERRUPT 15h - Function DEh, Subfunction 10h
"PUSHKEY" - PUT KEY INTO KEYBOARD INPUT STREAM

Purpose: Store a keystroke such that it will later be read as actual keyboard input by the same process that stored the keystroke.

Available on: All machines.	**Restrictions:** DESQview version 2.00 or higher must be running.

Registers at call:	Return Registers:
AX = DE10h	Early copies of DESQview 2.00 destroy
BH = scan code	AX, BX, ES, and DI.
BL = character	

Details: A later read will get the keystroke as if it had been typed by the user. Multiple pushes are read last-in first-out. If a script exists for the pushed key in the current application, the script will be executed.
Conflicts: None known.
See Also: INT 16h Function 05h (chapter 3)

INTERRUPT 15h - Function DEh, Subfunction 11h
"JUSTIFY" - ENABLE/DISABLE AUTOMATIC JUSTIFICATION OF WINDOW

Purpose: Specify whether a window smaller than its virtual screen should automatically shift the origin of its viewport whenever the cursor is moved outside the visible area.

Available on: All machines.	**Restrictions:** DESQview version 2.00 or higher must be running.

Registers at call:	Return Registers: n/a
AX = DE11h	
BL = 00h viewport will not move automatically	
nonzero viewport will move to keep cursor visible (default)	

Conflicts: None known.

INTERRUPT 15h - Function DEh, Subfunction 12h
"CSTYLE" - SET "C"-COMPATIBLE CONTROL CHAR INTERPRETATION

Purpose: Specify whether line-ends consist of a carriage return and line feed or a lone linefeed.

Available on: All machines.	**Restrictions:** DESQview version 2.01 or higher must be running.

Registers at call:	Return Registers: n/a
AX = DE12h	
BX = 0000h select normal style (linefeed only moves down)	
nonzero select C style (linefeed moves to start of next line)	

Details: Set on a per-task basis, and inherited from the parent task.
Conflicts: None known.

INTERRUPT 15h - Function DEh, Subfunction 13h
"GETCRIT" - GET CRITICAL NESTING COUNT

Purpose: Determine how many critical regions are currently in effect.

Available on: All machines.

Registers at call:
AX = DE13h

Restrictions: DESQview version 2.20 or higher must
be running.
Return Registers:
BX = number of calls to BEGINC or ENTERC (see
Function 10h Subfunction 1Bh and Function DEh
Subfunction 1Ch) without matching ENDC (see
TopView Function 10h Subfunction 1Ch)

Details: This API call may be made from within a hardware interrupt handler.
Conflicts: None known.
See Also: Function DEh Subfunctions 1Bh and 1Ch, TopView Function 10h Subfunctions 1Bh and 1Ch

INTERRUPT 15h - Function DEh, Subfunction 14h
GET OBJECT TYPE

Purpose: Determine the type of an object given its handle.
Available on: All machines.

Registers at call:
AX = DE14h
ES:DI -> object

Restrictions: DESQview version 2.20 or higher must
be running.
Return Registers:
BL = 00h not an object
08h window or task
09h mailbox
0Ah keyboard
0Bh timer
0Ch objectq
0Fh pointer
10h panel

Conflicts: None known.
See Also: TopView Function 10h Subfunction 16h

INTERRUPT 15h - Function DEh, Subfunction 15h
"SETERROR" - SET ERROR HANDLING

Purpose: Specify how DESQview should handle a number of common errors which were always fatal in early
versions of DESQview.
Available on: All machines.

Registers at call:
AX = DE15h
BL = 00h post system error on all error
conditions.
= 01h return carry flag set on calls to ADDTO,
SUBFROM, and WRITE messages sent
to mailboxes which fail due to lack of
system or common memory.
= 02h (v2.26+) same as 01h, but return null
pointer for GETMEM calls which fail
due to lack of system memory.
Conflicts: None known.
See Also: Function DEh Subfunction 16h

Restrictions: DESQview version 2.20 or higher must
be running.
Return Registers: n/a

INTERRUPT 15h - Function DEh, Subfunction 16h
"GETERROR" - GET ERROR HANDLING

Purpose: Determine how DESQview will handle a number of common errors.
Available on: All machines.

Restrictions: DESQview version 2.20 or higher must
be running.

Registers at call:
AX = DE16h

Return Registers:
BL = 00h always post system error
  01h return carry flag set on failed mailbox writes
  02h return CF set on failed mailbox writes and
  NULL on failed GETMEM calls

Conflicts: None known.
See Also: Function DEh Subfunction 15h

INTERRUPT 15h - Function DEh, Subfunction 17h
Reserved Function

Purpose: Not available, perhaps due to an oversight.
Available on: All machines.

Restrictions: DESQview version 2.20 through 2.25
  must be running.

Registers at call:
AX = DE17h

Return Registers:
pops up "Programming error" window

Details: AX = 1117h is NOT identical to this call under DESQview 2.20 thru 2.25
Conflicts: None known.
See Also: Function 11h Subfunction 17h

INTERRUPT 15h - Function DEh, Subfunction 17h
"ASSERTMAP" - GET/SET MAPPING CONTEXT

Purpose: Force a specified EMS mapping register set into activity, to ensure addressability of a particular program's code or data.
Available on: All machines.

Restrictions: DESQview version 2.26 or higher must
  be running.

Registers at call:
AX = DE17h
BX = 0000h   get current mapping context without
                setting
   nonzero   set new mapping context

Return Registers:
BX = mapping context in effect before call

Details: Mapping contexts determine conventional-memory addressability; setting a mapping context ensures that the associated program and data areas are in memory for access. Usable by drivers, TSRs and shared programs. Caller need not be running under DESQview. This API call may be made from a hardware interrupt handler.
Conflicts: None known.
See Also: Function 11h Subfunction 17h, MS Windows INT 2Fh Function 16h Subfunction 85h (chapter 14)

INTERRUPT 15h - Function DEh, Subfunction 18h
internal - Unknown Function

Purpose: *unknown.*
Available on: All machines.

Restrictions: DESQview version 2.20 or higher must
  be running.

Registers at call:
AX = DE18h
BP = function number; high byte must be 10h, low
      byte is function:
   00h set *unknown value*
      BL = *unknown* (00h-10h, *video mode*)
      BH = value to store
   03h set *unknown value*
      BL = *unknown* (stored in driver)
   0Ah get *unknown value*
ES:DI -> 18-byte buffer to hold *unknown values*.

Return Registers: *unknown.*

Details: Calls video driver (NOP for Hercules driver, probably CGA and MCGA also).

Conflicts: None known.

INTERRUPT 15h - Function DEh, Subfunction 19h
"GETCOMMON" - ALLOCATE "COMMON" MEMORY

Purpose: Request a portion of the global pool of reserved memory, which is also used by DESQview to store objects, messages, and other items.

Available on: All machines.

Restrictions: DESQview version 2.23 or higher must be running.

Registers at call:
AX = DE19h
BX = number of bytes to allocate

Return Registers:
AX = 0000h   successful
    ES:DI -> allocated block
    nonzero   insufficient memory

Details: This API call may be made from within a hardware interrupt handler.
Conflicts: None known.
See Also: Function DEh Subfunctions 0Ch, 15h, and 1Ah

INTERRUPT 15h - Function DEh, Subfunction 1Ah
"PUTCOMMON" - DEALLOCATE "COMMON" MEMORY

Purpose: Free a previously allocated block of the global pool of reserved memory.

Available on: All machines.

Restrictions: DESQview version 2.23 or higher must be running.

Registers at call:
AX = DE1Ah
DS:SI -> previously allocated block

Return Registers: n/a

Details: This function may be called from within a hardware interrupt handler.
Conflicts: None known.
See Also: Function DEh Subfunctions 0Dh and 19h

INTERRUPT 15h - Function DEh, Subfunction 1Bh
internal - DECREMENT CRITICAL NESTING COUNT

Purpose: Low-level routine to indicate that it is now permissible for DESQview to resume task-switching.

Available on: All machines.

Restrictions: DESQview version 2.23 or higher must be running.

Registers at call:
AX = DE1Bh

Return Registers: n/a

Conflicts: None known.
See Also: Function DEh Subfunctions 13h and 1Ch, TopView Function 10h Subfunction 1Ch

INTERRUPT 15h - Function DEh, Subfunction 1Ch
"ENTERC" - INCREMENT CRITICAL NESTING COUNT

Purpose: Indicate to DESQview that the calling program is about to enter an uninterruptible section of code, and DESQview should temporarily stop task-switching.

Available on: All machines.

Restrictions: DESQview version 2.23 or higher must be running.

Registers at call:
AX = DE1Ch

Return Registers: n/a

Details: This call is similar to TopView Function 10h Subfunction 1Bh, but begins the critical region without ensuring that DOS is free. The official documentation states that this call should be paired with "ENDC" (Function 10h Subfunction 1Ch); no mention is made of Function DEh Subfunction 1Bh. This API call may be made from within a hardware interrupt handler.
Conflicts: None known.
See Also: Function DEh Subfunctions 13h and 1Bh, TopView Function 10h Subfunctions 1Bh and 1Ch

INTERRUPT 15h - Function DEh, Subfunction 1Dh
"PUTKEY" - FAKE USER KEYSTROKES

Purpose: Control another process by sending it keypresses.

Available on: All machines.

Registers at call:
AX = DE1Dh
DX = segment of handle for task to receive
   keystroke
BL = character
BH = scan code

Restrictions: DESQview version 2.23 or higher must be running.

Return Registers:
AX = 0000h if successful
   nonzero if receiver's keyboard buffer was full

Details: The key is treated as though the user had pressed it, ignoring any script which may be bound to the key, and using the current field table if the keyboard object is in field processing mode. Multiple PUTKEYs are seen in the order in which they are executed.

Conflicts: None known.

See Also: Function DEh Subfunction 10h

INTERRUPT 15h - Function DEh, Subfunction 1Eh
"SCRNINFO" - GET TRUE VIDEO PARAMETERS

Purpose: Determine the actual video mode and screen size rather than the values presented by the standard BIOS functions.

Available on: All machines.

Registers at call:
AX = DE1Eh

Restrictions: DESQview version 2.23 or higher must be running.

Return Registers:
CL = actual number of rows on screen
CH = actual number of columns on screen
BL = actual video mode (may differ from INT 10h
   Function 0Fh return) (v2.26+)

Details: This API call may be made from a hardware interrupt handler.

Conflicts: None known.

See Also: INT 10h Function 0Fh (chapter 5)

INTERRUPT 15h - Function DEh, Subfunction 1Fh
"DOSUSER" - GET HANDLE OF TASK CURRENTLY USING DOS

Purpose: Determine which task, if any, is currently executing a DOS functoin call.

Available on: All machines.

Registers at call:
AX = DE1Fh

Restrictions: DESQview version 2.23 or higher must be running.

Return Registers:
BX = segment of task handle or 0000h if no tasks are
   using DOS

Details: This API call may be made from within a hardware interrupt handler.

Conflicts: None known.

See Also: Function DEh Subfunction 13h

INTERRUPT 15h - Function DEh, Subfunction 20h
"DISPATCHINT" - INTERRUPT ANOTHER TASK

Purpose: Force a task to execute the specified subroutine, regardless of what it is currently executing.

Available on: All machines.

Restrictions: DESQview version 2.26 or higher must be running.

Registers at call:
AX = DE20h
BX = segment of handle of task to interupt
DX:CX -> FAR interrupt routine

Return Registers: n/a

Details: Unlike PGMINT (Function 10h Subfunction 21h), DISPATCHINT may be applied to the task making the DISPATCHINT call. Multiple DISPATCHINT calls are processed in the order in which they were executed. The FAR routine is entered with the current ES, DS, SI, DI, and BP values, using the task's internal stack (see Function 10h Subfunction 1Ah); only SS:SP needs to be preserved. This API call may be made from within a hardware interrupt handler.
Conflicts: None known.
See Also: TopView Function 10h Subfunction 21h

INTERRUPT 15h - Function DEh, Subfunction 21h
"ASSERTVIR" - CONTROL 386 SCREEN VIRTUALIZATION

Purpose: Specify whether DESQview-386 should virtualize the display.
Available on: All machines.

Restrictions: DESQview version 2.26 or higher must be running.

Registers at call:
AX = DE21h
BX = 0000h   turn off
     nonzero   turn on

Return Registers:
BX = old state of virtualization

Details: this API call may be made from within a hardware interrupt handler
Conflicts: None known.

INTERRUPT 15h - Function DEh, Subfunction 22h
"PROCESSMEM" - GET TASK MEMORY STATUS

Purpose: Determine how much memory as task is using, and whether it is currently loaded into memory.
Available on: All machines.

Restrictions: DESQview version 2.26 or higher must be running.

Registers at call:
AX = DE22h
DX = segment of task handle

Return Registers:
DX = total amount of memory in paragraphs
BX = amount of system memory in paragraphs
CX = largest block of system memory available in paragraphs
AX = flags
     bit 0: system memory resides in shared memory
     1: process's memory is swapped out
     2: process's system memory is swapped out

Details: If the task handle is a child task, the returned values will be for the process containing the task, rather than the task itself. If the process's system memory is swapped out, BX,CX,DX remain unchanged, because the memory usage cannot be determined.
Conflicts: None known.
See Also: Function DEh Subfunctions 04h, 05h, and 06h

INTERRUPT 15h - Function DEh, Subfunction 23h
Unknown Function

Purpose: *unknown.*
Available on: All machines.

Restrictions: DESQview version 2.31 or higher must be running.
Return Registers: *unknown.*

Registers at call:
AX = DE23h
BX = *unknown.*
CX = *unknown.*

Conflicts: None known.

INTERRUPT 21h - Function 2Bh
INSTALLATION CHECK

Purpose: Determine whether DESQview is installed.

Available on: All machines.

Registers at call:
AH = 2Bh
AL = subfunction (DV v2.00+):
    01h get version

    02h get shadow buffer info, and start
       shadowing

    04h get shadow buffer info

    05h stop shadowing
       CX = 4445h ('DE')
       DX = 5351h ('SQ')

Restrictions: none.

Return Registers:
AL = FFh if DESQview not installed

BX = version
BH = major, BL = minor
Note: early copies of v2.00 return 0002h
BH = rows in shadow buffer
BL = columns in shadow buffer
DX = segment of shadow buffer
BH = rows in shadow buffer
BL = columns in shadow buffer
DX = segment of shadow buffer

Details: In DESQview v1.x, there were no subfunctions; this call only identified whether or not DESQview was loaded.

Conflicts: DOS Set System Date (chapter 8), PC Tools v5.1 PC-CACHE (chapter 6), pcANYWHERE IV (chapter 28), ELRES v1.1 (chapter 36), TAME (chapter 36).

See Also: INT 10h Functions FEh and FFh

DESQview 2.26 External Device Interface

The functions in this section are called by DESQview itself, and should not be called by applications (except subfunctions 00h and 01h). The XDI permits programs (usually TSRs loaded before DESQview) to keep track of the state of the system under DESQview.

INTERRUPT 2Fh - Function DEh, Subfunction 00h
INSTALLATION CHECK

Purpose: Determine whether any External Device Interface drivers are installed.

Available on: All machines.

Registers at call:
AX = DE00h
BX = 4445h ("DE")
CX = 5844h ("XD")
DX = 4931h ("I1")

Restrictions: none.

Return Registers:
AL = FFh if installed (even if other registers do not
    match)
if BX,CX, and DX were as specified on entry,
    BX = 4845h ("HE")
    CX = 5245h ("RE")
    DX = 4456h ("DV")

Details: AH=DEh is the default XDI multiplex number, but may range from C0h-FFh. Programs should check for XDI starting at DEh to FFh, then C0h to DDh. The XDI handler should not issue any DOS or BIOS calls, nor should it issue DESQview API calls other than those allowed from hardware interrupts.

INTERRUPT 2Fh - Function DEh, Subfunction 01h
DRIVER CUSTOM SUBFUNCTION

Purpose: Allow communication with resident XDI drivers.

Available on: All machines.

Restrictions: XDI driver must be installed.

Registers at call:
AX = DE01h
BX = driver ID (5242h "RB" will be used by future
    programs by Ralf Brown)
other registers as needed by driver
Details: XDI drivers should pass this call through to the previous handler if the ID does not match. DESQview never calls this function.
Conflicts: None known.

INTERRUPT 2Fh - Function DEh, Subfunction 01h
DVTXDI.COM API

Purpose: Allow communication between DVTree or DVTMAN and the resident DVTXDI driver.
Available on: All machines.
Registers at call:
AX = DE01h
BX = 7474h
CL = function
    00h installation check
    01h get process handle
        DX = keys on Open Window menu
            (DL = first, DH = second)
    02h (v1.3+) set TMAN handle
        DX = TMAN process handle
    03h (v1.3+) set set open keys to ignore on
    next subfunc 01h call
        DX = keys on Open Window menu

Return Registers: varies with driver and inputs

Restrictions: DVTXDI must be resident.
Return Registers:
BX = 4F4Bh ("OK")
DL = DL destroyed

AL = FFh
AX = process handle or 0000h if not running

Details: DVTXDI is distributed as part of the shareware products DVTree (DOS shell/DESQview process manager) and DVTMAN by Mike Weaver.
Conflicts: None known.

INTERRUPT 2Fh - Function DEh, Subfunction 01h
DESQview 2.26 XMS XDI driver - Possible INSTALLATION CHECK

Purpose: *Determine whether the DVXMS.DVR driver is loaded.*
Available on: All machines.
Registers at call:
AX = DE01h
BX = FFFEh
CX = 4D47h
DX = 0052h
Conflicts: None known.

Restrictions: none.
Return Registers:
AL = FFh
DX = 584Dh ("XM")

INTERRUPT 2Fh - Function DEh, Subfunction 02h
DESQview INITIALIZATION COMPLETE

Purpose: Called by DESQview to indicate to any interested programs that it is now executing, allowing those programs to make any necessary preparations for operation with DESQview.
Available on: All machines.

Restrictions: DESQview version 2.26 or higher must be running.

Registers at call:
AX = DE02h
BX = mapping context of DESQview
DX = handle of DESQview system task

Return Registers: n/a

Details: The driver should pass this call to the previous handler after doing its work.

Conflicts: None known.
See Also: Function DEh Subfunction 03h

INTERRUPT 2Fh - Function DEh, Subfunction 03h
DESQview TERMINATION

Purpose: Called by DESQview to indicate that it is exiting, allowing any interested programs to perform whatever cleanup is necessary to resume normal DOS operation.

Available on: All machines.

Restrictions: DESQview version 2.26 or higher must be running.

Registers at call:
AX = DE03h
BX = mapping context of DESQview
DX = handle of DESQview system task

Return Registers: n/a

Details: The driver should pass this call to the previous handler before doing its work. DESQview makes this call when it is exiting, but before unhooking any interrupt vectors.
Conflicts: None known.
See Also: Function DEh Subfunction 02h

INTERRUPT 2Fh - Function DEh, Subfunction 04h
ADD PROCESS

Purpose: Called by DESQview to indicate to any interested programs that it is creating a new process.

Available on: All machines.

Restrictions: DESQview 2.26 or higher must be running.

Registers at call:
AX = DE04h
BX = mapping context of new process
DX = handle of process

Return Registers: n/a

Details: The XMS XDI handler (installed by default) allocates a 22-byte record (see below) from "common" memory to control access to XMS memory. All DOS, BIOS, and DV API calls are valid in handler. The driver should pass this call to the previous handler after processing it.
Conflicts: None known.
See Also: Function DEh Subfunction 05h

Table 15-8. Format of XMS XDI structure:

Offset	Size	Description
00h	DWORD	pointer to *10-byte record*
04h	DWORD	pointer to next XMS XDI structure
08h	WORD	mapping context
0Ah	BYTE	*unknown.*
0Bh	5 BYTEs	XMS entry point to return for INT 2Fh Function 43h Subfunction 10h (chapter 10) (FAR jump to next field)
10h	6 BYTEs	FAR handler for XMS driver entry point (consists of a FAR CALL followed by RETF)

INTERRUPT 2Fh - Function DEh, Subfunction 05h
REMOVE PROCESS

Purpose: Called by DESQview to indicate to any interested programs that it is terminating a process.

Available on: All machines.

Restrictions: DESQview 2.26 or higher must be running.

Registers at call:
AX = DE05h
BX = mapping context of process
DX = handle of last task in process

Return Registers: n/a

Details: XMS XDI handler releases the structure allocated by Function DEh Subfunction 04h. The driver should pass this call to the previous handler before processing it. All DOS, BIOS, and DV API calls except those generating a task switch are valid in handler.
Conflicts: None known.
See Also: Function DEh Subfunction 04h

INTERRUPT 2Fh - Function DEh, Subfunction 06h
CREATE TASK

Purpose: Called by DESQview to indicate to any interested programs that it is creating a new thread of execution within a process.
Available on: All machines.

Restrictions: DESQview 2.26 or higher must be running.

Registers at call:
AX = DE06h
BX = mapping context of the process containing
   task
DX = handle of new task

Return Registers: n/a

Details: The driver should pass this call to the previous handler after processing it. All DOS, BIOS, and DV API calls are valid in handler.
Conflicts: None known.

INTERRUPT 2Fh - Function DEh, Subfunction 07h
TERMINATE TASK

Purpose: Called by DESQview to indicate to any interested programs that it is terminating a thread of execution.
Available on: All machines.

Restrictions: DESQview 2.26 or higher must be running.

Registers at call:
AX = DE07h
BX = mapping context of the process containing
   task
DX = handle of task

Return Registers: n/a

Details: The driver should pass this call to the previous handler before processing it. All DOS, BIOS, and DV API calls except those generating a task switch are valid in handler.
Conflicts: None known.

INTERRUPT 2Fh - Function DEh, Subfunction 08h
SAVE STATE

Purpose: Called by DESQview to permit interested programs to save their current state in preparation for a context switch.
Available on: All machines.

Restrictions: DESQview 2.26 or higher must be running.

Registers at call:
AX = DE08h
BX = mapping context of task being switched from
DX = handle of task being switched from

Return Registers: n/a

Details: Invoked prior to task swap, interrupts, etc. The driver should pass this call to the previous handler after processing it.
Conflicts: None known.

INTERRUPT 2Fh - Function DEh, Subfunction 09h
RESTORE STATE

Purpose: Called by DESQview to permit interested programs to restore a previously saved state after a context switch.

Available on: All machines.

Registers at call:
AX = DE09h
BX = mapping context of task being switched to
DX = handle of task being switched to
Details: State is restored except for interrupts. The driver should pass this call to the previous handler before processing it.
Conflicts: None known.

Restrictions: DESQview 2.26 or higher must be running.
Return Registers: n/a

INTERRUPT 2Fh - Function DEh, Subfunction 0Ah
CHANGE KEYBOARD FOCUS

Purpose: Called by DESQview to indicate to interested programs that the user has made a different window the foreground window.

Available on: All machines.

Registers at call:
AX = DE0Ah
BX = mapping context of task receiving focus
DX = handle of running task
Details: The driver should pass this call to the previous handler before processing it. This call often occurs inside a keyboard interrupt.
Conflicts: None known.

Restrictions: DESQview 2.26 or higher must be running.
Return Registers: n/a

INTERRUPT 2Fh - Function DEh, Subfunction 0Bh
DVP PROCESSING COMPLETE

Purpose: Called by DESQview to permit indicated programs to examine or modify the program information file for a program which is being started up.

Available on: All machines.

Registers at call:
AX = DE0Bh
BX = mapping context of DESQview system task
CX = number of system memory paragraphs
    required for the use of all XDI drivers (DV will
    add this to system memory in DVP buffer)
DX = handle of DESQview system task
SI = mapping context of new process if it starts
ES:DI -> DVP buffer
Details: Once DV invokes this function, the DVP buffer contents may be changed. The driver should pass this call to the previous handler before processing it.
Conflicts: None known.

Restrictions: DESQview 2.26 or higher must be running.
Return Registers:
CX incremented as needed

INTERRUPT 2Fh - Function DEh, Subfunction 0Ch
SWAP OUT PROCESS

Purpose: Called by DESQview to indicate to interested programs that a process is about to be written to disk and suspended.

Available on: All machines.

Registers at call:
AX = DE0Ch

Restrictions: DESQview 2.26 or higher must be running.
Return Registers: n/a

BX = mapping context of task being swapped out
DX = handle of DESQview system task
Details: The driver should pass this call to the previous handler after processing it.
Conflicts: None known.

INTERRUPT 2Fh - Function DEh, Subfunction 0Dh
SWAP IN PROCESS

Purpose: Called by DESQview to indicate to interested programs that a process is being placed back in memory from disk.

Available on: All machines.   **Restrictions:** DESQview 2.26 or higher must be running.

Registers at call: **Return Registers:** n/a
AX = DE0Dh
BX = mapping context of process just swapped in
DX = handle of DESQview system task
Details: The driver should pass this call to the previous handler before processing it.
Conflicts: None known.

INTERRUPT 2Fh - Function DEh, Subfunction 0Eh
DVP START FAILED

Purpose: Called by DESQview to indicated to interested programs that the attempted startup of a program was unsuccessful.

Available on: All machines.   **Restrictions:** DESQview 2.26 or higher must be running.

Registers at call: **Return Registers:** n/a
AX = DE0Eh
BX = mapping context of DESQview system task
DX = handle of DESQview system task
SI = mapping context of failed process (same as for
     call to Function DEh Subfunction 0Bh)
Details: The driver should pass this call to the previous handler after processing it.
Conflicts: None known.

Quarterdeck Programs
In addition to DESQview, Quarterdeck Office Systems produces a number of other programs, some of which are either resident or optionally resident. Among those, QEMM-386, QRAM (pronounced "cram"), MANIFEST, and VIDRAM provide function calls on the Multiplex interrupt. There is one general installation check to determine whether any of the above are installed, permitting all of the programs to share a single multiplex number, and specific installation checks for each of the programs.

INTERRUPT 2Fh - Function D2h, Subfunction 00h
INSTALLATION CHECK

Purpose: Determine whether any Quarterdeck programs are loaded.
Available on: All machines.   **Restrictions:** none.
Registers at call: **Return Registers:**
AX = D200h   AL = FFh if any Quarterdeck resident programs
BX = 5144h ("QD")   installed
CX = 4D45h ("ME")   if BX,CX,DX were specified on entry:
DX = 4D30h ("M0")   BX = 4D45h ("ME")
                                                    CX = 4D44h ("MD")
                                                    DX = 5652h ("VR")

Details: QEMM/QRAM/VIDRAM/MANIFEST will search for a free AH value from D2h through FFh, then C0h through D1h. Once one of the programs has been installed, all others will use the same multiplex number.

Conflicts: None known.
See Also: MANIFEST Function D2h, QEMM/QRAM Function D2h, VIDRAM Function D2h

Quarterdeck MANIFEST

INTERRUPT 2Fh - Function D2h, Subfunction 01h
INSTALLATION CHECK

Purpose: Determine whether MANIFEST has been loaded as a TSR.

Available on: All machines.

Restrictions: none.

Registers at call:
AX = D201h
BX = 4D41h ("MA")
CX = 4E49h ("NI")
DX = 4645h ("FE")

Return Registers:
BX = 5354h ("ST")

Details: QEMM/QRAM/VIDRAM/MANIFEST will search for a free AH value from D2h through FFh, then C0h through D1h.

MANIFEST chains to the previous INT 2Fh handler if BX/CX/DX are not as specified.

Conflicts: None known.
See Also: QEMM/QRAM Function D2h Subfunction 01h, VIDRAM Function D2h Subfunction 01h

Quarterdeck QEMM/QRAM 5.0

INTERRUPT 2Fh - Function D2h, Subfunction 01h
GET HIRAM MEMORY CHAIN

Purpose: Determine the address of the first block of high memory.

Available on: All machines.

Restrictions: QEMM version 5.0 or higher, or QRAM, must be running.

Registers at call:
AX = D201h
BX = 4849h ("HI")
CX = 5241h ("RA")
DX = 4D30h ("M0")

Return Registers:
BX = 4F4Bh ("OK")
CX = segment of start of HIRAM chain
DX = QEMM/QRAM code segment

Details: QEMM, QRAM, VIDRAM, and MANIFEST will search for a free AH value from D2h through FFh, then C0h through D1h. QEMM and QRAM both responded the same. The HIRAM memory chain has the same format as the regular DOS 4.0 memory chain (see INT 21h Function 52h in chapter 8), except that XMS Upper Memory Blocks have the block header program name field set to "UMB".

QEMM and QRAM chain to the previous INT 2Fh handler if BX/CX/DX are not as specified.

Conflicts: None known.
See Also: MANIFEST Function D2h Subfunction 01h, VIDRAM Function D2h Subfunction 01h

INTERRUPT 2Fh - Function D2h, Subfunction 01h
INSTALLATION CHECK

Purpose: Determine whether QEMM-386 version 5.0 or higher, is installed.

Available on: All machines.

Restrictions: none.

Registers at call:
AX = D201h
BX = 5145h ("QE")
CX = 4D4Dh ("MM")
DX = 3432h ("42")

Return Registers:
BX = 4F4Bh ("OK")
ES:DI -> QEMM/QRAM *entry point*

Details: QEMM/QRAM/VIDRAM/MANIFEST will search for a free AH value from D2h through FFh, then C0h through D1h. QEMM and QRAM both respond the same.

QEMM and QRAM chain to the previous INT 2Fh handler if BX/CX/DX are not as specified.

Conflicts: None known.

See Also: VIDRAM Function D2h Subfunction 01h, MANIFEST Function D2h Subfunction 01h

Quarterdeck VIDRAM 5.0

INTERRUPT 2Fh - Function D2h, Subfunction 01h
Quarterdeck VIDRAM 5.0 - INSTALLATION CHECK

Purpose: Determine whether VIDRAM is installed, and if so, the address to call to make requests of VIDRAM.

Available on: All machines.   **Restrictions:** none.

Registers at call: **Return Registers:**

AX = D201h   BX = 4F4Bh ("OK") if installed

BX = 5649h ("VI")   ES:DI -> VIDRAM entry point

CX = 4452h ("DR")

DX = 414dh ("AM")

Details: QEMM/QRAM/VIDRAM/MANIFEST will search for a free AH value from D2h through FFh, then C0h through D1h.

VIDRAM chains to the previous INT 2Fh handler if BX/CX/DX are not as specified.

Conflicts: None known.

See Also: QEMM/QRAM Function D2h Subfunction 01h, MANIFEST Function D2h Subfunction 01h

    Call VIDRAM entry point with:

        AH = 00h get status

    VIDRAM returns:

        AL = VIDRAM state (00h off, 01h no EGA graphics, 02h no graphics)

        BL = flags

          bit 0: *unknown.*

          bits 1-7 not used

        BH = *unknown.*

        CL = current monitor (01h = mono, 80h = color)

        SI = *current top of memory (paragraph)*

        DI = segment of *unknown.*

    Call VIDRAM entry point with:

        AH = 01h setup

        AL = VIDRAM state (as returned by function 00h)

        BL = flags (as returned by function 00h)

        BH = *unknown.*

        CL = monitor (as returned by function 00h)

        SI = *new top of memory (paragraph)*

    VIDRAM returns:

        unknown

    Call VIDRAM entry point with:

        AH = 02h get *unknown pointer.*

        ES:DI -> *unknown* data

    VIDRAM returns:

        CF set on error

        CF clear if successful

Chapter 16

MultiDOS Plus

MultiDOS Plus is a multitasker by Nanosoft, Inc. The description of the API and a full-featured, but time-limited, demonstration version of MultiDOS are available for free on the Nanosoft BBS.

INTERRUPT 14h - Function 04h
INITIALIZE PORT

Purpose: Establish operating conditions for the specified serial port.

Available on: All machines.

Restrictions: MultiDOS Plus IODRV software must be installed.

Registers at call:
AH = 04h

Return Registers: n/a

Details: The desired serial port is initialized; if a Hayes-compatible modem is attached, a connection has been established on return. The port number is stored at offset BEh in the Task Control Block (see INT 15h Function 13h).

Conflicts: SERIAL I/O (chapter 7), FOSSIL (chapter 7).

See Also: Functions 05h and 20h, INT 15h Function 13h, Serial I/O Function 00h (chapter 7)

INTERRUPT 14h - Function 05h
READ CHARACTER FROM PORT

Purpose: Read one character from the specified port, waiting if necessary.

Available on: All machines.

Restrictions: MultiDOS Plus IODRV software must be installed.

Registers at call:
AH = 05h
AL = timeout in seconds (00h = never)

Return Registers:
AL = status:
    00h successful
AH = character read
    01h read error
    02h timed out
other modem status (CTS, DSR) changed

Details: The port number is stored at offset BEh in the Task Control Block (see INT 15h Function 13h).

Conflicts: SERIAL I/O (chapter 7), FOSSIL (chapter 7).

See Also: Functions 04h, 06h, and 22h, Serial I/O Function 02h (chapter 7)

INTERRUPT 14h - Function 06h
WRITE CHARACTER TO PORT

Purpose: Output one character to the specified serial port.

Available on: All machines.

Restrictions: MultiDOS Plus IODRV software must be installed.

Registers at call:
AH = 06h
AL = character

Return Registers:
AL = status
    00h successful

Details: The port number is stored at offset BEh in the Task Control Block (See INT 15h Function 13h). If output queue is full, the calling task is blocked until the character can be stored.

Conflicts: FOSSIL (chapter 7).

See Also: Functions 04h, 05h, and 21h, Serial I/O Function 01h (chapter 7)

INTERRUPT 14h - Function 07h
GET PORT STATUS

Purpose: Determine conditions at the specified serial port.

Available on: All machines.

Registers at call:
AH = 07h

Restrictions: MultiDOS Plus IODRV software must be installed.

Return Registers:
CL = modem status (see Function 23h)
CH = character at head of input queue (if any)
DX = number of characters in input queue

Details: The port number is stored at offset BEh in the Task Control Block (See INT 15h Function 13h).
Conflicts: FOSSIL (chapter 7).

INTERRUPT 14h - Function 08h
GET AND RESET PORT LINE STATUS

Purpose: Determine line status for the specified port.

Available on: All machines.

Registers at call:
AH = 08h

Restrictions: MultiDOS Plus 4.0 or higher IODRV software must be installed.

Return Registers:
AL = line status (see Function 23h)
AH destroyed

Details: The port number is stored at offset BEh in the Task Control Block (See INT 15h Function 13h). On every line status change, the line status is ORed with the line status accumulator; this function returns the accumulator and clears it.
Conflicts: FOSSIL (chapter 7).
See Also: Functions 04h and 07h, Serial I/O Function 03h (chapter 7)

INTERRUPT 14h - Function 09h
RESET PORT STATUS

Purpose: Resets the status byte of the specified port.

Available on: All machines.

Registers at call:
AH = 09h

Restrictions: MultiDOS Plus IODRV software must be installed.

Return Registers:
Modem status byte cleared.

Details: The port number is stored at offset BEh in the Task Control Block (see INT 15h Function 13h).
Conflicts: FOSSIL (chapter 7).
See Also: Functions 04h and 07h.

INTERRUPT 14h - Function 20h
INITIALIZE PORT

Purpose: Establish operating conditions for the specified serial port.

Available on: All machines.

Registers at call:
AH = 20h
AL = port parameters (see Serial I/O Function 00h in chapter 7)
DX = port number (0-3)

Restrictions: MultiDOS Plus must be installed.

Return Registers:
AH = status:
 00h successful
 41h no such port
 64h monitor mode already active

Conflicts: X00 FOSSIL (chapter 7), Alloy MW386 (chapter 18).
See Also: Functions 04h, 21h, and 23h, Serial I/O Function 00h (chapter 7)

INTERRUPT 14h - Function 21h
TRANSMIT CHARACTER

Purpose: Transmit one character out the specified port.

Available on: All machines.

Registers at call:
AH = 21h
AL = character to send
DX = port number

Restrictions: MultiDOS Plus must be installed.

Return Registers:
AH = status:
    00h successful
    39h no DSR or CTS
    3Ch no DSR
    3Bh no CTS
    41h no such port
    42h monitor mode not active
    97h timed out

Details: Monitor mode must have been turned on with Function 24h before calling.

Conflicts: X00 FOSSIL (chapter 7), Alloy MW386 (chapter 18).

See Also: Functions 20h, 22h and 24h

INTERRUPT 14h - Function 22h
RECEIVE CHARACTER

Purpose: Receive one character from the specified port. If no character is available, this function waits until a character arrives or an implementation-dependent timeout elapses.

Available on: All machines.

Registers at call:
AH = 22h
DX = port number

Restrictions: MultiDOS Plus must be installed.

Return Registers:
AH = status (see also Function 21h):
    00h successful
        AL = character
    3Dh framing and parity error
    3Eh overrun error
    3Fh framing error
    40h parity error
    96h ring buffer overflow

Conflicts: None known.

See Also: Functions 20h, 21h, and 27h

INTERRUPT 14h - Function 23h
GET PORT STATUS

Purpose: Determine the status of the specified serial port.

Available on: All machines.

Registers at call:
AH = 23h
DX = port number

Restrictions: MultiDOS Plus must be installed.

Return Registers:
AH = line status:
  bit 7: timeout
           6: transmit shift register empty
     5: transmit holding register empty
     4: break detected
     3: framing error
     2: parity error
     1: overrun error
     0: receive data ready
AL = modem status:
  bit 7: carrier detect
     6: ring indicator
     5: data set ready

4: clear to send
3: delta carrier detect
2: trailing edge of ring indicator
1: delta data set ready
0: delta clear to send

Details: The returned status flags are identical to those returned by Serial I/O Function 03h (chapter 7).
Conflicts: Alloy MW386 (chapter 18).
See Also: Functions 07h and 20h, Serial I/O Function 03h (chapter 7)

INTERRUPT 14h - Function 24h
SET MONITOR MODE

Purpose: Control status reporting for the specified port.

Available on: All machines.	**Restrictions:** MultiDOS Plus must be installed.
Registers at call:	**Return Registers:**
AH = 24h	AH = status:
AL = port status storage:	00h successful
00h single status for entire receive buffer	3Ah invalid status storage specified
01h separate status kept for each byte in receive	41h no such port
buffer	64h monitor mode already active
DX = port number	

Details: In monitor mode, MultiDOS redirects all BIOS video output to a serial port.
Conflicts: Alloy MW386 (chapter 18).
See Also: Functions 20h and 25h

INTERRUPT 14h - Function 25h
CLEAR BUFFERS

Purpose: Flush the buffers for the specified port and optionally deactivate the port.

Available on: All machines.	**Restrictions:** MultiDOS Plus must be installed.
Registers at call:	**Return Registers:**
AH = 25h	AH = status:
AL = function:	00h successful
00h only clear buffers	3Ah invalid function
01h clear buffers and deactivate	41h no such port
DX = port number	42h monitor mode not active

Conflicts: None known.
See Also: Functions 20h and 24h

INTERRUPT 14h - Function 27h
GET BUFFER CHARACTER COUNT

Purpose: Determine how many characters are available for reading from the serial port.

Available on: All machines.	**Restrictions:** MultiDOS Plus must be installed.
Registers at call:	**Return Registers:**
AH = 27h	AH = status
DX = port number	00h successful
	41h no such port
	42h monitor mode not active
	AL = number of characters in receive buffer

Conflicts: None known.

INTERRUPT 15h - Function 00h
GIVE UP TIME SLICE

Purpose: Indicate that the caller is idle and that MultiDOS may give the rest of its time slice to other programs.

Available on: All machines.	**Restrictions:** MultiDOS Plus must be running.

Registers at call: **Return Registers:** n/a
AH = 00h

Details: If this call is issued by the highest-priority task while MultiDOS is using priority-based rather than round-robin scheduling, control will be returned to the caller immediately.

Conflicts: Cassette (chapter 3), Amstrad PC1512 (chapter 4), VMiX (chapter 17).

See Also: Function 03h, TopView Function 10h Subfunction 00h (chapter 15)

INTERRUPT 15h - Function 01h
REQUEST RESOURCE SEMAPHORE

Purpose: Gain exclusive access to a resource, suspending the caller if necessary.

Available on: All machines.   **Restrictions:** MultiDOS Plus must be running.

Registers at call: **Return Registers:**
AH = 01h   AH = status
AL = semaphore number (00h-3Fh)   00h successful
                                                       02h invalid semaphore number

Details: If the semaphore is not owned, ownership is assigned to the calling task and the call returns immediately. If the semaphore is already owned by another task, the calling task is placed on a queue for the semaphore and suspended until it can become owner of the semaphore. Semaphore 0 is used internally by MultiDOS to synchronize DOS access.

Conflicts: Cassette (chapter 3), Amstrad PC1512 (chapter 4), VMiX (chapter 17).

See Also: Functions 02h, 10h, and 1Bh

INTERRUPT 15h - Function 02h
RELEASE RESOURCE SEMAPHORE

Purpose: Indicate that other tasks may now access the resource controlled by the specified semaphore.

Available on: All machines.   **Restrictions:** MultiDOS Plus must be running.

Registers at call: **Return Registers:**
AH = 02h   AH = status
AL = semaphore number (00h-3Fh)   00h successful
                                                       01h not semaphore owner
                                                       02h invalid semaphore number

Details: If any tasks are waiting for the semaphore, the first task on the wait queue will become the new owner and be reawakened. Do not use within an interrupt handler.

Conflicts: Cassette (chapter 3), Amstrad PC1512 (chapter 4), VMiX (chapter 17).

See Also: Functions 01h, 10h, and 1Ch

INTERRUPT 15h - Function 03h
SUSPEND TASK FOR INTERVAL

Purpose: Request that the caller not receive control of the CPU for the indicated period.

Available on: All machines.   **Restrictions:** MultiDOS Plus must be running.

Registers at call: **Return Registers:**
AH = 03h   after specified interval has elapsed
DX = number of time slices to remain suspended

Details: When priority-based scheduling is in use, high-priority tasks should use this function to yield the processor.

Conflicts: Cassette (chapter 3), Amstrad PC1512 (chapter 4), VMiX (chapter 17).

See Also: Functions 00h and 0Ah

INTERRUPT 15h - Function 04h
SEND MESSAGE TO ANOTHER TASK

Purpose: Append data to the specified mailbox.

Available on: All machines.   **Restrictions:** MultiDOS Plus must be running.

Registers at call:
AH = 04h
AL = mailbox number (00h-3Fh)
CX = message length in bytes
DS:SI -> message

Return Registers:
AH = status
   00h successful
   01h out of message memory
   02h invalid mailbox number

Details: The message is copied into a system buffer; the caller may immediately reuse its buffer.
See Also: Function 05h

INTERRUPT 15h - Function 05h
CHECK MAILBOX

Purpose: Determine whether any messages have been received.
Available on: All machines.   **Restrictions:** MultiDOS Plus must be running.
Registers at call:
AH = 05h
AL = mailbox number (00h-3Fh)

Return Registers:
AH = status
   00h successful
      DX = length of first message in queue,
         0000h if no message
   02h invalid mailbox number

Conflicts: System - Build ABIOS Initialisation Table (chapter 3), Amstrad PC1512 (chapter 4), VMiX (chapter 17).
See Also: Functions 04h and 06h

INTERRUPT 15h - Function 06h
READ MAILBOX

Purpose: Retrieve the next message in the indicated mailbox.
Available on: All machines.   **Restrictions:** MultiDOS Plus must be running.
Registers at call:
AH = 06h
AL = mailbox number (00h-3Fh)
CX = size of buffer in bytes
ES:DI -> buffer for message

Return Registers:
AH = status
   00h successful
      CX = number of bytes copied
      DX = actual length of message
   02h invalid mailbox number

Details: If the caller's buffer is not large enough, the message is truncated and the remainder is lost.
Conflicts: Amstrad PC1512 (chapter 4), VMiX (chapter 17).
See Also: Functions 04h and 05h

INTERRUPT 15h - Function 07h
SPAWN INTERNAL TASK (CREATE NEW THREAD)

Purpose: Start a new thread of execution which will perform subroutines independent of the existing thread of execution.
Available on: All machines.   **Restrictions:** MultiDOS Plus must be running.
Registers at call:
AH = 07h
BX:CX = entry point of new task
DX = stack size in paragraphs

Return Registers:
AH = status
   00h successful
   01h no free task control blocks
   02h no free memory for task's stack

Details: Execution returns immediately to calling task.
Conflicts: VMiX (chapter 17).
See Also: Functions 08h, 09h, and 13h

INTERRUPT 15h - Function 08h
TERMINATE INTERNAL TASK (KILL THREAD)

Purpose: Stop an independent thread of execution.
Available on: All machines.   **Restrictions:** MultiDOS Plus must be running.

Registers at call:
AH = 08h

Return Registers:
calling task terminated, so execution never returns to
caller

Details: An internal task must be terminated with this function rather than a DOS termination function. Task's stack space is returned to parent task's memory pool.
Conflicts: VMiX (chapter 17).
See Also: Function 07h

INTERRUPT 15h - Function 09h
CHANGE TASK'S PRIORITY

Purpose: Specify the relative importance of the calling task.
Available on: All machines.
Registers at call:
AH = 09h
AL = new priority
Details: The priority has different meanings depending on whether priority-based or round-robin scheduling is used.
Conflicts: VMiX (chapter 17).
See Also: Function 07h

Restrictions: MultiDOS Plus must be running.
Return Registers: n/a

INTERRUPT 15h - Function 0Ah
CHANGE TIME SLICE INTERVAL

Purpose: Specify the desired granularity of time slices.
Available on: All machines.
Registers at call:
AH = 0Ah
AL = new interval
   00h = 55.0 ms (default)
   80h = 27.5 ms
   40h = 13.75 ms
   20h = 6.88 ms
   10h = 3.44 ms
   08h = 1.72 ms
Conflicts: VMiX (chapter 17).
See Also: Function 03h

Restrictions: MultiDOS Plus must be running.
Return Registers: n/a

INTERRUPT 15h - Function 0Bh
FORCE DISPLAY OUTPUT TO PHYSICAL SCREEN MEMORY

Purpose: Request that video output be sent directly to the display rather than to a virtual screen.
Available on: All machines.
Registers at call:
AH = 0Bh
Details: Sets calling task's screen pointer to actual screen memory; the pointer may be restored with Function 0Ch. Caller's video mode must be same as foreground task's video mode. Any text written while in the background will be saved to the foreground task's virtual screen when it switches to the background. Useful if a background task wants to display a message on the foreground screen.
Conflicts: VMiX (chapter 17).
See Also: Function 0Ch

Restrictions: MultiDOS Plus must be running.
Return Registers: n/a

INTERRUPT 15h - Function 0Ch
RESTORE OLD VIDEO DISPLAY MEMORY

Purpose: Request that video output be sent to a virtual screen rather than the actual display.
Available on: All machines.

Restrictions: MultiDOS Plus must be running.

Registers at call: **Return Registers:** n/a
AH = 0Ch
Details: Restores task's screen pointer saved by Function 0Bh; must not be called unless Function 0Bh has been called first.
Conflicts: VMiX (chapter 17).
See Also: Function 0Bh

INTERRUPT 15h - Function 0Dh
DISABLE MULTITASKING

Purpose: Temporarily suspend time-slicing to allow the caller to process time-ciritcal events or nonreentrant code.
Available on: All machines.   **Restrictions:** MultiDOS Plus must be running.
Registers at call: **Return Registers:** n/a
AH = 0Dh
Details: Calling task receives all time slices until Function 0Eh is called.
Conflicts: VMiX (chapter 17).
See Also: Functions 0Eh, 10h, and 20h, TopView Function 10h Subfunction 1Bh (chapter 15)

INTERRUPT 15h - Function 0Eh
ENABLE MULTITASKING

Purpose: Restart time-slicing after the caller has processed a time-critical event or nonreentrant code.
Available on: All machines.   **Restrictions:** MultiDOS Plus must be running.
Registers at call: **Return Registers:** n/a
AH = 0Eh
Conflicts: VMiX (chapter 17).
See Also: Functions 0Dh and 20h, TopView Function 10h Subfunction 1Ch

INTERRUPT 15h - Function 0Fh
EXECUTE A MULTIDOS PLUS COMMAND

Purpose: Request that the specified string be executed as if it had been typed at the MultiDOS command prompt by the user.
Available on: All machines.   **Restrictions:** MultiDOS Plus must be running.
Registers at call: **Return Registers:**
AH = 0Fh   after command has been processed
DS:BX -> ASCIZ command
Details: The task is placed on a queue which MultiDOS examines periodically and is suspended until MultiDOS has processed the command. All lowercase characters up to the first blank are converted to upper case within the given buffer.
Conflicts: System - Format Unit Periodic Interrupt (chapter 6), VMiX (chapter 17).

INTERRUPT 15h - Function 10h
TEST RESOURCE SEMAPHORE

Purpose: Determine whether a non-shareable resource is currently in use.
Available on: All machines.   **Restrictions:** MultiDOS Plus must be running.
Registers at call: **Return Registers:**
AH = 10h   AH = status
AL = semaphore number (00h-3Fh)   00h semaphore not in use
                                                     01h semaphore owned by another task
                                                     02h invalid semaphore number
                                                     03h semaphore owned by caller

Conflicts: VMiX (chapter 17).
See Also: Functions 02h, 0Dh, and 1Dh

INTERRUPT 15h - Function 11h
TURN OFF AltZ TOGGLE

Purpose: Disable the Alt-Z command/program-selection hotkey which allows the user to switch between programs and the MultiDOS command prompt.

Available on: All machines.   **Restrictions:** MultiDOS Plus must be running.

Registers at call: **Return Registers:** n/a

AH = 11h

Conflicts: Topview commands (chapter 15), VMiX (chapter 17).

See Also: Function 12h

INTERRUPT 15h - Function 12h
TURN ON AltZ TOGGLE

Purpose: Enable the Alt-Z command/program-selection hotkey which allows the user to switch between programs and the MultiDOS command prompt.

Available on: All machines.   **Restrictions:** MultiDOS Plus must be running.

Registers at call: **Return Registers:** n/a

AH = 12h

Details: Enables the Alt-Z MultiDOS command/program-selection hotkey.

Conflicts: VMiX (chapter 17).

See Also: Function 11h

INTERRUPT 15h - Function 13h
GET TASK CONTROL BLOCK

Purpose: Determine address of data block for the calling task.

Available on: All machines.   **Restrictions:** MultiDOS Plus must be running.

Registers at call: **Return Registers:**

AH = 13h   BX:AX -> task control block (Table 16-1)

Conflicts: VMiX (chapter 17).

See Also: Function 15h

Table 16-1. Format of MultiDOS Plus v4.0 Task Control Block:

Offset	Size	Description
00h	DWORD	pointer to next TCB
04h	8 BYTEs	ASCIZ task name
0Ch	2 BYTEs	*unknown*.
0Eh	WORD	task PSP segment
10h	WORD	abort/suspend flags
12h	WORD	current screen segment (see Functions 0Bh,0Ch)
14h	WORD	priority level (0000h-FFFEh)
16h	WORD	time slice counter
18h	2 BYTEs	*unknown*.
1Ah	WORD	suspend timer value
1Ch	WORD	stack segment
1Eh	WORD	stack pointer
20h	WORD	display type
22h	WORD	display memory
24h	2 BYTEs	*unknown*.
26h	WORD	termination count
28h	WORD	equipment flag for BIO10 driver
2Ah	BYTE	background CRT mode
2Bh	WORD	screen width in columns
2Dh	WORD	screen size in bytes
2Fh	WORD	segment of physical screen memory

Table 16-1. Format of MultiDOS Plus v4.0 task control block (continued)

Offset	Size	Description
31h	16 BYTEs	eight cursor positions
41h	WORD	current cursor shape
43h	BYTE	active display page
44h	WORD	CRT controller I/O port base
46h	2 BYTEs	*unknown.*
48h	WORD	foreground task flag
4Ah	6 BYTEs	*unknown.*
50h	WORD	saved video segment (see Functions 0Bh,0Ch)
52h	DWORD	old INT 22
56h	DWORD	old INT 23
5Ah	DWORD	old INT 24
5Eh	WORD	top of memory for task
60h	4 BYTEs	*unknown.*
64h	WORD	DTA segment (see INT 21h Function 1Ah in chapter 8)
66h	WORD	DTA offset
68	4 BYTEs	*unknown.*
6Ch	BYTE	current ANSI.SYS attribute
6Dh	BYTE	current ANSI.SYS column
6Eh	BYTE	current ANSI.SYS row
6Fh	BYTE	current ANSI.SYS display state
70h	BYTE	maximum ANSI.SYS columns
71h	BYTE	current ANSI.SYS page
72h	WORD	saved ANSI.SYS cursor position
74h	BYTE	ANSI.SYS parameter buffer index
75h	BYTE	current ANSI.SYS screen mode
76h	BYTE	ANSI.SYS wrap flag
77h	6 BYTEs	ANSI.SYS parameter buffer
7Dh	BYTE	ANSI.SYS keyboard DSR state
7Eh	7 BYTEs	ANSI.SYS keyboard DSR buffer
85h	3 BYTEs	*unknown.*
88h	16 BYTEs	request header for DOS driver calls
98h	14 BYTEs	*unknown.*
A6h	WORD	segment of EMS map if EMS task
A8h	WORD	flag: task makes EMS calls
AAh	WORD	EMS handle for task
ACh	WORD	keyboard shift state
AEh	12 BYTEs	*unknown.*
BAh	WORD	TCB of parent if child task
BCh	WORD	termination code
BEh	WORD	COM port number
C0h	4 BYTEs	*unknown.*
C4h	WORD	current IRQ number
C6h	2 BYTEs	*unknown.*
C8h	WORD	miscellaneous flag word
CAh	2 BYTEs	*unknown.*
CCh	DWORD	old INT 10
D0h	WORD	EMS alternate map set number
D2h	414 BYTEs	DOS current disk and directory context (optional)

INTERRUPT 15h - Function 14h
CHECK IF MultiDOS FOREGROUND OR BACKGROUND

Purpose: Determine whether the user is at the command prompt or in an application.

Available on: All machines.   **Restrictions:** MultiDOS Plus must be running.

Registers at call:
AH = 14h

Return Registers:
AX = current state
    0000h MultiDOS Plus command prompt is
        background task
    0001h command prompt is foreground task

Conflicts: VMiX (chapter 17).
See Also: Function 0Bh

INTERRUPT 15h - Function 15h
GET SYSTEM BLOCK

Purpose: Determine address of control record containing system-wide data.
Available on: All machines.   **Restrictions:** MultiDOS Plus must be running.
Registers at call: **Return Registers:**
AH = 15h   BX:AX -> system block (Table 16-2)
Conflicts: VMiX (chapter 17).
See Also: Function 13h

Table 16-2. Format of MultiDOS Plus 4.0 System Block:

Offset	Size	Description
00h	WORD	segment of system control block
02h	WORD	redirection flag set by /NOREDIRECT
04h	WORD	no-INT 10 flag set by /NO10
06h	DWORD	old INT 10
0Ah	DWORD	new INT 10
0Eh	DWORD	pointer to WORD with current TCB offset (see Function 13h)
12h	DWORD	pointer to WORD with idle task TCB offset
16h	DWORD	pointer to WORD with foreground TCB offset
1Ah	DWORD	pointer to WORD with MultiDOS TCB offset
1Eh	WORD	Task Control Block size
20h	WORD	number of TCBs
22h	WORD	flag: EMS present
24h	WORD	EMS page frame base segment
26h	WORD	16K pages in EMS page frame
28h	WORD	base segment for conventional memory tasks
2Ah	WORD	conventional memory size in paragraphs
2Ch	DWORD	pointer to list of queue pointers

INTERRUPT 15h - Function 16h
INITIALIZATION

Purpose: Used internally during initialization; any other calls will cause unpredicatable results.
Available on: All machines.   **Restrictions:** MultiDOS Plus must be running.
Registers at call: **Return Registers:** n/a
AH = 16h
Conflicts: VMiX (chapter 17).

INTERRUPT 15h - Function 17h
MAP IRQ

Purpose: Associate the EMS memory map of the specified task control block with the indicated hardware interrupt. The interrupt handler will gain control with the given memory map in effect.
Available on: All machines.   **Restrictions:** MultiDOS Plus must be running.

Registers at call:
AH = 17h
AL = IRQ to map (01h-0Fh)
BX = offset of task control block (see Function 13h)
    to associate with the IRQ
Conflicts: VMiX (chapter 17).
See Also: Functions 18h and 19h

Return Registers:
AX = status
    0000h successful
    other invalid IRQ

INTERRUPT 15h - Function 18h
UNMAP IRQ

Purpose: Remove a previously-specified association between the indicated hardware interrupt an an EMS memory map.
Available on: All machines.
Registers at call:
AH = 18h
AL = IRQ to unmap (01h-0Fh)

Restrictions: MultiDOS Plus must be running.
Return Registers:
AX = status
    0000h successful
    0001h invalid IRQ

Details: Results are unpredictable if the IRQ has not been mapped.
Conflicts: VMiX (chapter 17).
See Also: Functions 17h and 19h

INTERRUPT 15h - Function 19h
UNMAP ALL IRQs

Purpose: Remove all previously-specified associations between hardware interrupts and EMS memory maps.
Available on: All machines.
Registers at call:
AH = 19h
Details: For MultiDOS internal use only.
Conflicts: VMiX (chapter 17).
See Also: Functions 17h and 18h

Restrictions: MultiDOS Plus must be running.
Return Registers:
AX destroyed

INTERRUPT 15h - Function 1Ah
MAP SEMAPHORE NAME TO NUMBER

Purpose: Create a new semaphore name and associate it with an available semaphore.
Available on: All machines.
Registers at call:
AH = 1Ah
DS:SI -> 8-byte name

Restrictions: MultiDOS Plus must be running.
Return Registers:
AL = status
    00h successful
        AH = semaphore number (20h-3Fh)
    04h out of string space

Details: All eight bytes of the name are significant. If the name does not already exist, it is added to the name table and associated with a free semaphore number. Names cannot be destroyed.
Conflicts: VMiX (chapter 17).
See Also: Functions 1Bh, 1Ch, and 1Dh

INTERRUPT 15h - Function 1Bh
REQUEST RESOURCE SEMAPHORE BY NAME

Purpose: Gain exclusive access to the resource with the specified name, suspending caller if necessary.
Available on: All machines.

Restrictions: MultiDOS Plus must be running.

Registers at call:
AH = 1Bh
DS:SI -> 8-byte name

Return Registers:
AH = status
    00h successful
    02h invalid semaphore number
    03h caller already owns semaphore
    04h out of string space

Details: Equivalent to Function 1Ah followed by Function 01h (see notes for Function 01h).
Conflicts: VMiX (chapter 17).
See Also: Functions 01h, 1Ah, 1Ch, and 1Dh

INTERRUPT 15h - Function 1Ch
RELEASE RESOURCE SEMAPHORE BY NAME

Purpose: Indicate that other tasks may access the non-shareable resource corresponding to the given name.
Available on: All machines.   **Restrictions:** MultiDOS Plus must be running.
Registers at call: **Return Registers:**
AH = 1Ch   AH = status
DS:SI -> 8-byte name   00h successful
    01h not semaphore owner
    02h invalid semaphore number
    04h out of string space

Details: Equivalent to Function 1Ah followed by Function 02h (see notes for Function 02h).
Conflicts: VMiX (chapter 17).
See Also: Functions 02h, 1Ah, 1Bh, and 1Dh

INTERRUPT 15h - Function 1Dh
TEST RESOURCE SEMAPHORE BY NAME

Purpose: Determine whether the resource corresponding to the specified name is in use.
Available on: All machines.   **Restrictions:** MultiDOS Plus must be running.
Registers at call: **Return Registers:**
AH = 1Dh   AH = status
DS:SI -> 8-byte name   00h semaphore not in use
    01h semaphore owned by another task
    02h invalid semaphore number
    03h caller owns semaphore
    04h out of string space

Details: Equivalent to Function 1Ah followed by Function 10h. (see notes for Function 10h)
Conflicts: VMiX (chapter 17).
See Also: Functions 10h, 1Ah, 1Bh, and 1Ch

INTERRUPT 15h - Function 1Eh, Subfunction 00h
CLEAR EVENT COUNTER

Purpose: Discard any pending events on the specified counter.
Available on: All machines.   **Restrictions:** MultiDOS Plus must be running.
Registers at call: **Return Registers:**
AX = 1E00h   AH = status
DX = event/trigger number (00h-3Fh)   00h successful
Conflicts: VMiX (chapter 17).
See Also: Function 1Eh Subfunctions 01h and 02h

INTERRUPT 15h - Function 1Eh, Subfunction 01h
TRIGGER EVENT

Purpose: Restart any task waiting for the specified event; if no task is waiting, the event counter is incremented (and will roll over if it was 65535).

Available on: All machines.
Registers at call:
AX = 1E01h
DX = event/trigger number (00h-3Fh)

Restrictions: MultiDOS Plus must be running.
Return Registers:
AH = status
    00h successful
    01h invalid event/trigger number

Details: This function may be invoked by an interrupt handler.
Conflicts: None known.
See Also: Function 1Eh Subfunctions 00h and 02h

INTERRUPT 15h - Function 1Eh, Subfunction 02h
WAIT FOR EVENT

Purpose: Suspend until the specified event is triggered; if the event had already been triggered, return immediately.
Available on: All machines.
Registers at call:
AX = 1E02h
DX = event/trigger number (00h-3Fh)

Restrictions: MultiDOS Plus must be running.
Return Registers:
AH = status
    00h successful
    01h invalid event/trigger number

Details: If the event counter is zero, the task is suspended until the event is triggered with Function 1Eh Subfunction 01h; else, the counter is decremented and the call returns immediately.
Conflicts: None known.
See Also: Function 1Eh Subfunctions 00h and 01h

INTERRUPT 15h - Function 1Fh
GET MEMORY PARAMETERS

Purpose: Determine the starting addresses of conventional and EMS memory.
Available on: All machines.

Registers at call:
AH = 1Fh

Restrictions: MultiDOS Plus version 4.01 or higher must be running.
Return Registers:
BX = first segment of conventional memory
DX = first segment of EMS swap frame into which MultiDOS will load programs

Conflicts: None known.

INTERRUPT 15h - Function 20h
CHECK IF MULTITASKING ENABLED

Purpose: Determine whether MultiDOS is currently time-slicing, and if not, who disabled the time-slicing.
Available on: All machines.

Registers at call:
AH = 20h

Restrictions: MultiDOS Plus version 4.01 or higher must be running.
Return Registers:
AX = current state
    0000h multitasking enabled
    other TCB of task that disabled multitasking

Conflicts: SYSREQ Routine (chapter 3).
See Also: Functions 0Dh and 13h

Chapter ▪ 17

Other Multitaskers and Task Switchers

Microsoft Windows, TopView, DESQview, and MultiDOS were covered in chapters 14 through 16; Alloy 386/Multi-Ware is in chapter 18 because it includes both multitasking and networking. This chapter contains the remainder of the multitaskers and task switchers on which we have information: Back&Forth, Cswitch, CTask, DoubleDOS, Multi-Link, Omniview, and VMiX.

Back&Forth is a task switcher by Progressive Solutions (Sandi and Shane Stump).

CTask and Cswitch are primarily designed to provide multitasking within single programs. CTask is public domain software by Thomas Wagner, while Cswitch was written by Herb Rose.

DoubleDOS by Softlogic Solutions, Inc. permits two programs to run concurrently.

Omniview by Sunny Hill Software is a TopView-compatible multitasker; see chapter 15 for the TopView calls.

VMiX is a shareware multiuser multitasker by Commercial Software Associates (ComSoft). Recent versions are able to run an 80386 in Virtual-86 mode; all versions have been able to make use of 80286 protected mode for much of VMiX's operation.

INTERRUPT 11h - Function FFh, Subfunction FEh
Back&Forth API

Purpose: Determine whether Back&Forth is running; if so, permit communication with it.

Available on: All machines.

Restrictions: Back&Forth prior to version 1.62 must be installed for functions other than the installation check.

Registers at call:
AX = FFFEh
CX = FFFEh
BX = function
  00h installation check
  01h *unknown.*
  02h *unknown.*
  03h *unknown.*
  04h *unknown.*
  05h *unknown.* switches current PSP segment and stack if BNFLOW has not yet announced itself installed**.**
  06h *unknown.*

Return Registers:
AX = 0001h BNFHIGH and BNFLOW both loaded
   = 0003h only BNFHIGH loaded
   else neither loaded

DX:AX - > *unknown.*
n/a

AX = *unknown.*

Conflicts: BIOS interface (chapter 3).
See Also: INT 12h Function FFh Subfunction FEh

INTERRUPT 12h - Function FFh, Subfunction FEh
Back&Forth API

Purpose: Determine whether Back&Forth is running, and if so, permit communication with it.

Available on: All machines.

Restrictions: Back&Forth version 1.62 or higher must be installed for functions other than the installation check.

Registers at call:
AX = FFFEh
CX = FFFEh
BX = function
   00h installation check
   02h build program ID list
      ES:DI -> buffer of at least 100 bytes, to be
        filled with words
   03h switch to specified task (task need not be
      open yet)
      DX = two-letter program ID
Conflicts: BIOS Get Memory Size (chapter 3).
See Also: INT 11h Function FFh Subfunction FEh

Return Registers:
AX = 0001h installed
   else not loaded

AX = number of programs defined
ES:DI buffer filled with AX words

AX = 0000h if task undefined

INTERRUPT 15h - Function 00h
INSTALLATION CHECK

Purpose: Determine whether VMiX version 2.0 or higher is running.
Available on: All machines.
Registers at call:
AH = 00h
Conflicts: Cassette (chapter 3), Amstrad PC1512 (chapter 4), Multidos Plus (chapter 16).

Restrictions: none.
Return Registers:
DX = 0798h

INTERRUPT 15h - Function 01h
I/O CHANNEL OBJECT MANAGER

Purpose: Manipulate I/O channel objects.
Available on: All machines.
Registers at call:
AH = 01h
STACK: WORD object ID of requestor
   DWORD pointer to name of requested method
   WORD arg1
   WORD arg2
   WORD arg3
   WORD arg4
Conflicts: Cassette (chapter 3), Amstrad PC1512 (chapter 4), MultiDOS Plus (chapter 16).

Restrictions: VMiX must be running.
Return Registers:
DX:AX -> IRP structure or 0000h:0000h

INTERRUPT 15h - Function 02h
MEMORY OBJECT MANAGER

Purpose: Manipulate memory objects.
Available on: All machines.
Registers at call:
AH = 02h
STACK: WORD object ID of requestor DWORD
pointer to name of requested method
   WORD arg1
   WORD arg2
   WORD arg3
   WORD arg4
   WORD arg5
Conflicts: Cassette (chapter 2), Amstrad PC1512 (chapter 4), MultiDOS Plus (chapter 16).

Restrictions: VMiX must be running.
Return Registers:
DX:AX = pointer to memory block

INTERRUPT 15h - Function 03h
PROMPTED CONSOLE INPUT

Purpose: Request input from the user.

Available on: All machines.

Registers at call:

AH = 03h

STACK: DWORD   pointer to ASCII prompt
      WORD   field outline character
      WORD   length of input field
      DWORD   address of pointer to input
                  buffer
      WORD   number of characters input

Restrictions: VMiX must be running.

Return Registers:

AX = length of input (input buffer is padded with blanks)

Conflicts: Cassette (chapter 3), Amstrad PC1512 (chapter 4), MultiDOS Plus (chapter 16).

INTERRUPT 15h - Function 04h
VPRINTF

Purpose: Display a string with varying arguments.

Available on: All machines.

Registers at call:

AH = 04h

STACK: DWORD control string
     DWORD array of arguments

Restrictions: VMiX must be running.

Return Registers: n/a

Conflicts: System (PS) Build ABIOS System Parameter Table (chapter 3), Amstrad PC1512 (chapter 4).

INTERRUPT 15h - Function 05h
GET PROCESS ID OF CURRENT PROCESS

Purpose: Determine calling program's process identifier.

Available on: All machines.

Registers at call:

AH = 05h

Restrictions: VMiX must be running.

Return Registers:

AX = process ID

Conflicts: MultiDOS Plus (chapter 16), System - Build ABIOS Initialisation Table (chapter 3), Amstrad PC1512 (chapter 4).

See Also: Functions 06h and 0Bh

INTERRUPT 15h - Function 06h
GET POINTER TO PROCESS CONTROL BLOCK

Purpose: Determine the address of the control block for calling program.

Available on: All machines.

Registers at call:

AH = 06h

STACK: WORD process ID

Restrictions: VMiX must be running.

Return Registers:

DX:AX -> process control block

Conflicts: Amstrad PC1512 (chapter 4), MultiDOS Plus (chapter 16).

See Also: Functions 07h and 08h

INTERRUPT 15h - Function 07h
GET POINTER TO OBJECT CONTROL BLOCK

Purpose: Determine the address of the control block for a specified object type.

Available on: All machines.

Registers at call:

AH = 07h

STACK: WORD object type

Restrictions: VMiX must be running.

Return Registers:

DX:AX -> object control block

Conflicts: MultiDOS Plus (chapter 16).

See Also: Functions 06h and 08h

INTERRUPT 15h - Function 08h
GET CHANNEL CONTROL BLOCK

Purpose: Determine the address of the control block for a specified I/O channel.

Available on: All machines.

Registers at call:
AH = 08h
STACK: WORD channel ID

Conflicts: MultiDOS Plus (chapter 16).

See Also: Functions 06h and 07h

Restrictions: VMiX must be running.

Return Registers:
DX:AX -> channel control block

INTERRUPT 15h - Function 09h
GET ID OF QUEUED ELEMENT

Purpose: Determine the identifier of the first item in the specified queue.

Available on: All machines.

Registers at call:
AH = 09h
STACK: WORD queue ID (0 = process queue, 1 =
      object, 3 = type)
     WORD subqueue ID

Conflicts: MultiDOS Plus (chapter 16).

See Also: Function 0Ah

Restrictions: VMiX must be running.

Return Registers:
AX = ID

INTERRUPT 15h - Function 0Ah
GET ID OF NEXT QUEUED ELEMENT

Purpose: Determine the identifier of the next item in the specified queue.

Available on: All machines.

Registers at call:
AH = 0Ah
STACK: WORD queue ID (0 = process queue, 1 =
     object, 3 = type)
   WORD ID of current element in queue chain

Conflicts: MultiDOS Plus (chapter 16).

See Also: Functions 09h and 0Fh

Restrictions: VMiX must be running.

Return Registers:
AX = ID of next element

INTERRUPT 15h - Function 0Bh
GET TOTAL NUMBER OF ACTIVE PROCESSES

Purpose: Determine how many processes are currently active in the system.

Available on: All machines.

Registers at call:
AH = 0Bh

Conflicts: MultiDOS Plus (chapter 16).

See Also: Functions 05h and 0Eh

Restrictions: VMiX must be running.

Return Registers:
AX = number of active processes

INTERRUPT 15h - Function 0Ch
GET POINTER TO PROCESS TSS STACK

Purpose: Determine the address of the hardware task-switching stack for the specified process.

Available on: All machines.

Registers at call:
AH = 0Ch
STACK: WORD process ID

Conflicts: MultiDOS Plus (chapter 16).

Restrictions: VMiX must be running.

Return Registers:
DX:AX -> TSS stack store

INTERRUPT 15h - Function 0Dh
START A CHILD PROCESS JOB SHELL

Purpose: Initiate a new shell with its own process.
Available on: All machines.
Registers at call:
AH = 0Dh
STACK: DWORD ASCIZ string starting with
    requested I/O channel and followed by standard
    VMiX shell command string
Conflicts: MultiDOS Plus (chapter 16).
See Also: Function 0Eh

Restrictions: VMiX must be running.
Return Registers:
AX = status

INTERRUPT 15h - Function 0Eh
TERMINATE PROCESS

Purpose: Permanently stop a process and deallocate its resources.
Available on: All machines.
Registers at call:
AH = 0Eh
STACK: WORD process ID
Conflicts: MultiDOS Plus (chapter 16).
See Also: Functions 0Bh and 0Dh

Restrictions: VMiX must be running.
Return Registers:
AX = status

INTERRUPT 15h - Function 0Fh
GET KEY FIELD OF QUEUED ELEMENT

Purpose: Determine the key value of the specified element in the indicated queue.
Available on: All machines.
Registers at call:
AH = 0Fh
STACK: WORD queue ID
      (0 = process queue, 1 = object q, 3 = type q)
    WORD ID of element in queue chain
Conflicts: System - Format Unit Periodic Interrupt (chapter 3), MultiDOS Plus (chapter 16).
See Also: Function 0Ah

Restrictions: VMiX must be running.
Return Registers:
AX = key

INTERRUPT 15h - Function 10h
EXECUTE FUNCTION IN PROTECTED MODE

Purpose: Call a subroutine running in protected mode.
Available on: All machines.
Registers at call:
AH = 10h
STACK: DWORD pointer to function
    N WORDs function args
Conflicts: DESQview (chapter 15), TopView (chapter 15), MultiDOS Plus (chapter 16).

Restrictions: VMiX must be running.
Return Registers: *unknown.*

INTERRUPT 15h - Function 11h
EXECUTE SHELL SYSTEM COMMANDS

Purpose: Perform the command contained in a string as though the user had entered it at the VMiX prompt
Available on: All machines.

Restrictions: VMiX must be running.

Registers at call:
AH = 11h
STACK: DWORD pointer to an ASCIZ string
   containing a VMiX shell request (max length =
   127)

Return Registers:
AX = status

Conflicts: DESQview (chapter 15), Topview (chapter 15), MultiDOS Plus (chapter 16).

INTERRUPT 15h - Function 12h
PUT PROCESS TO SLEEP

Purpose: Suspend the specified process until it is explicitly restarted.

Available on: All machines.
Restrictions: VMiX must be running.

Registers at call:
AH = 12h
STACK: WORD process ID

Return Registers:
AX = status

Conflicts: DESQview (chapter 15), TopView (chapter 15), MultiDOS Plus (chapter 16).
See Also: Function 13h, MultiDOS Function 03h (chapter 16), TopView Function 10h Subfunction 1Dh (chapter 15)

INTERRUPT 15h - Function 13h
WAKE PROCESS

Purpose: Restart a previously-suspended process.

Available on: All machines.
Restrictions: VMiX must be running.

Registers at call:
AH = 13h
STACK: WORD process ID

Return Registers:
AX = status

Conflicts: MultiDOS Plus (chapter 16).
See Also: Function 12h

INTERRUPT 15h - Function 14h
CLEAR WINDOW

Purpose: Fill the specified portion of the display with blanks.

Available on: All machines.
Restrictions: VMiX must be running.

Registers at call:
AH = 14h
STACK: WORD top left corner of window
WORD bottom right corner of window

Return Registers:
AX = status

Conflicts: MultiDOS Plus (chapter 16).
See Also: Function 15h

INTERRUPT 15h - Function 15h
SET BANNER WINDOW MESSAGE

Purpose: Specify the message to be displayed in the banner window.

Available on: All machines.
Restrictions: VMiX must be running.

Registers at call:
AH = 15h
STACK: DWORD pointer to ASCIZ banner
   message

Return Registers:
AX = status

Conflicts: MultiDOS Plus (chapter 16).
See Also: Function 14h

INTERRUPT 15h - Function 16h
SET ROOT WINDOW SIZE AND HOME CURSOR

Purpose: Specify the size of the root window and move the cursor to its new upper left corner.

Available on: All machines.
Restrictions: VMiX must be running.

Registers at call:
AH = 16h
STACK: DWORD pointer to I/O Request Packet
WORD top left corner of window
WORD bottom right corner of window
Conflicts: MultiDOS Plus (chapter 16).
See Also: Function 17h

Return Registers:
AX = status

INTERRUPT 15h - Function 17h
GET CONSOLE WINDOW COLORS

Purpose: Determine the colors used by the console window.
Available on: All machines.
Registers at call:
AH = 17h

Restrictions: VMiX must be running.
Return Registers:
AH = foreground color
AL = background color

Conflicts: MultiDOS Plus (chapter 16).
See Also: Functions 16h and 18h

INTERRUPT 15h - Function 18h
SET CONSOLE COLORS

Purpose: Specify the colors to be used by the console window.
Available on: All machines.
Registers at call:
AH = 18h
STACK: WORD new background/foreground
    colors
Conflicts: MultiDOS Plus (chapter 16).
See Also: Function 17h

Restrictions: VMiX must be running.
Return Registers:
AX = color

INTERRUPT 15h - Function 19h
Unknown Function

Purpose: *unknown.*
Available on: All machines.

Registers at call:
AH = 19h
STACK: WORD *unknown.*
Conflicts: MultiDOS Plus (chapter 16).

Restrictions: VMiX version 2.0 or higher must be
    running.
Return Registers: *unknown.*

INTERRUPT 15h - Function 1Ah
Unknown Function

Purpose: *unknown.*
Available on: All machines.

Registers at call:
AH = 1Ah
STACK: 3 WORDs *unknown.*
Conflicts: MultiDOS Plus (chapter 16).

Restrictions: VMiX version 2.0 or higher must be
    running.
Return Registers: *unknown.*

INTERRUPT 15h - Functions 1Bh and 1Ch
Unknown Functions

Purpose: *unknown.*

Available on: All machines.

Registers at call:
AH = 1Bh or 1Ch
STACK: 5 WORDs *unknown*.
Conflicts: MultiDOS Plus (chapter 16).

Restrictions: VMiX version 2.0 or higher must be running.
Return Registers: *unknown*.

INTERRUPT 15h - Function 1Dh
Unknown Function

Purpose: *unknown*.
Available on: All machines.

Registers at call:
AH = 1Dh
other *unknown*.
Conflicts: MultiDOS Plus (chapter 16).

Restrictions: VMiX version 2.0 or higher must be running.
Return Registers: *unknown*.

INTERRUPT 15h - Function 1Eh
Unknown Function

Purpose: *unknown*.
Available on: All machines.

Registers at call:
AH = 1Eh
STACK: WORD *unknown*.
Conflicts: MultiDOS Plus (chapter 16).

Restrictions: VMiX version 2.0 or higher must be running.
Return Registers: *unknown*.

INTERRUPT 15h - Function 54h, Subfunction 00h
Omniview INSTALLATION NOTIFICATION

Purpose: Called by Omniview on startup to allow any interested programs loaded before Omniview to perform whatever preparations are needed for operation under Omniview.
Available on: All machines.
Registers at call:
AX = 5400h
ES:BX -> device information tables
DI:DX -> dispatcher entry point
Conflicts: None known.
See Also: Function 54h Subfunction 07h

Restrictions: none.
Return Registers: *unknown*.

INTERRUPT 15h - Function 54h, Subfunction 01h
PROCESS CREATION

Purpose: Called by Omniview on creating a new, independent process.
Available on: All machines.
Registers at call:
AX = 5401h
ES:BX = process handle
Conflicts: None known.
See Also: Function 54h Subfunction 02h

Restrictions: Omniview must be running.
Return Registers: *unknown*.

INTERRUPT 15h - Function 54h, Subfunction 02h
PROCESS DESTRUCTION

Purpose: Called by Omniview when it terminates a process and deallocate its resources.
Available on: All machines.

Restrictions: Omniview must be running.

Registers at call:
AX = 5402h
ES:DX = process handle
Conflicts: None known.
See Also: Function 54h Subfunction 01h

Return Registers: *unknown.*

INTERRUPT 15h - Function 54h, Subfunction 03h
SAVE STATE

Purpose: Called by Omniview to inform interested programs that they should save their current state in preparation for a task switch.

Available on: All machines.
Registers at call:
AX = 5403h
ES:DX = process swapping out
Conflicts: None known.
See Also: Function 54h Subfunction 04h

Restrictions: Omniview must be running.
Return Registers: *unknown.*

INTERRUPT 15h - Function 54h, Subfunction 04h
RESTORE STATE

Purpose: Called by Omniview to inform interested programs that they should restore a previously saved state after a task switch.

Available on: All machines.
Registers at call:
AX = 5404h
ES:DX = process swapping in
Conflicts: None known.
See Also: Function 54h Subfunction 03h

Restrictions: Omniview must be running.
Return Registers: *unknown.*

INTERRUPT 15h - Function 54h, Subfunction 05h
SWITCHING TO BACKGROUND

Purpose: Called by Omniview to inform interested programs that it is placing itself in the background.

Available on: All machines.
Registers at call:
AX = 5405h
ES:DX = process swapping in
Conflicts: None known.
See Also: Function 54h Subfunction 06h

Restrictions: Omniview must be running.
Return Registers: *unknown.*

INTERRUPT 15h - Function 54h, Subfunction 06h
SWITCHING TO FOREGROUND

Purpose: Called by Omniview to inform interested programs that it is placing itself in the foreground.

Available on: All machines.
Registers at call:
AX = 5406h
ES:DX = process swapping in
Conflicts: None known.
See Also: Function 54h Subfunction 05h

Restrictions: Omniview must be running.
Return Registers: *unknown.*

INTERRUPT 15h - Function 54h, Subfunction 07h
EXIT NOTIFICATION

Purpose: Called by Omniview to allow any interested programs to perform whatever cleanup is necessary for resuming normal DOS operation.

Available on: All machines.

Restrictions: Omniview must be running.

Registers at call:
AX = 5407h
Conflicts: None known.
See Also: Function 54h Subfunction 00h

Return Registers: *unknown.*

INTERRUPT 21h - Function 30h, Subfunction 00h
CTask INSTALLATION CHECK

Purpose: Determine whether CTask multitasker version 2.0 or higher is installed.
Available on: All machines.
Registers at call:
AX = 3000h
BX = 1234h
DS:DX -> 8-byte version string (DX < FFF0h)
    "CTask21", 00h for v2.1-2.2

Restrictions: none.

Return Registers:
AL = DOS major version
AH = DOS minor version
CX:BX -> Ctask global data block

Details: If the first eight bytes of returned data block equal the eight bytes passed in, CTask is resident. CTask is a multitasking kernel for C written by Thomas Wagner.
Conflicts: DOS 2+ Get DOS Version (chapter 8), Phar Lap 386/DOS-Extender (chapter 9), "Dutch-555" virus (chapter 34).

INTERRUPT 21h - Function E0h
MENU CONTROL

Purpose: Perform actions which a user is able to request at the DoubleDOS menu.
Available on: All machines.
Registers at call:
AH = E0h
AL = subfunction
    01h exchange tasks
    73h resume invisible job if suspended
    74h kill other job
    75h suspend invisible job

Restrictions: DoubleDOS must be running.
Return Registers: n/a

Details: This function is identical to Function F0h.
Conflicts: OS/286, OS/386 (chapter 1), Alloy NTNX (chapter 18), Novell NetWare (chapter 20), "Jerusalem", "Armagedon", and "8-tunes" viruses (chapter 34).
See Also: Function F0h

INTERRUPT 21h - Function E1h
CLEAR KEYBOARD BUFFER FOR CURRENT JOB

Purpose: Discard any pending keystrokes.
Available on: All machines.
Registers at call:
AH = E1h

Restrictions: DoubleDOS must be running.
Return Registers: n/a

Details: This function is identical to Function F1h.
Conflicts: OS/286, OS/386 (chapter 1), Novell NetWare (chapter 20), "Mendoza", "Fu Manchu" viruses (chapter 34).
See Also: Functions E2h, E3h, and E8h

INTERRUPT 21h - Function E2h
SEND CHARACTER TO KEYBOARD BUFFER OF OTHER JOB

Purpose: Supply fake keyboard input to the other program running under DoubleDOS.

Available on: All machines.
Registers at call:
AH = E2h
AL = character
Conflicts: OS/286, OS/386 (chapter 1), Alloy NTNX (chapter 18), Novell NetWare (chapter 20).
See Also: Functions E1h, E3h, E8h, and F2h

Restrictions: DoubleDOS must be running.
Return Registers:
AL = 00h successful
    01h buffer full (128 characters)

INTERRUPT 21h - Function E3h
ADD CHARACTER TO KEYBOARD BUFFER OF CURRENT JOB

Purpose: Store a keystroke for later retrieval as if the user had pressed it.
Available on: All machines.
Registers at call:
AH = E3h
AL = character
Conflicts: Alloy NTNX (chapter 18), Novell NetWare (chapter 20).
See Also: Functions E1h, E2h, E8h, and F3h

Restrictions: DoubleDOS must be running.
Return Registers:
AL = 00h successful
    01h buffer full (128 characters)

INTERRUPT 21h - Function E4h, Subfunction 00h
INSTALLATION CHECK/PROGRAM STATUS

Purpose: Determine whether DoubleDOS is running, and if so, which partition the caller is in.
Available on: All machines.
Registers at call:
AX = E400h

Restrictions: none.
Return Registers:
AL = 00h if DoubleDOS not present
   = 01h if running in visible DoubleDOS partition
   = 02h if running in invisible DoubleDOS partition

Conflicts: Novell NetWare (chapter 20), "Anarkia" virus (chapter 34).
See Also: Functions E5h and F4h

INTERRUPT 21h - Function E5h
OTHER PROGRAM STATUS

Purpose: Determine whether there is another program loaded under DoubleDOS, and if so, whether it is current running.
Available on: All machines.
Registers at call:
AH = E5h

Restrictions: DoubleDOS must be running.
Return Registers:
AL = 00h no program in other partition
   = 01h program in other partition is running
   = 02h program in other partition is suspended

Conflicts: Novell NetWare (chapter 20).
See Also: Function E4h Subfunction 00h, Function F5h

INTERRUPT 21h - Function E8h
SET/RESET KEYBOARD CONTROL FLAGS

Purpose: Specify which keyboard actions the user is allowed to perform.
Available on: All machines.
Registers at call:
AH = E8h
AL = 00h set flags for this program
   = 01h set flags for other program
DX = keyboard control flags (bit set enables,
   cleared disables)
     bit 0: menu
     bit 1: exchange
     bit 2: entire keyboard enable/disable

Restrictions: DoubleDOS must be running.
Return Registers:
DX = previous flags

bit 3: Ctrl-C
bit 4: Ctrl-PrtSc
bit 5: Alt/Erase
bit 6: Ctrl-Break
bit 7: Ctrl-NumLock
bit 8: shift-PrtSc
bit 9-13: undefined
bit 14: cancel key (clear keyboard buffer)
bit 15: suspend key

Details: Disabling Ctrl-PrtSc will allow the program to intercept the keystroke; disabling any of the other keystrokes disables them completely.

Conflicts: Alloy NTNX (chapter 18), Novell NetWare (chapter 20).

See Also: Functions E1h, E2h, E3h, and F8h.

INTERRUPT 21h - Function E9h
SET TIMESHARING PRIORITY

Purpose: Specify the percentage of CPU time each program gets.

Available on: All machines.   **Restrictions:** DoubleDOS must be running.

Registers at call: **Return Registers:**
AH = E9h   AL = priority setting (function 05h)
AL = 00h visible program gets 70
        invisible gets 30 (default)
   = 01h visible program gets 50
        invisible gets 50
   = 02h visible program gets 30
        invisible gets 70
   = 03h Top program gets 70
        bottom program gets 30
   = 04h Top program gets 30
        bottom program gets 70
   = 05h get current priority

Conflicts: Alloy NTNX (chapter 18), Novell NetWare (chapter 20).

See Also: Functions EAh, EBh, and F9h

INTERRUPT 21h - Function EAh
TURN OFF TASK SWITCHING

Purpose: Temporarily suspend multitasking so that the calling program may execute time-critical or nonreentrant code.

Available on: All machines.   **Restrictions:** DoubleDOS must be running.

Registers at call: **Return Registers:**
AH = EAh   task switching turned off

Conflicts: Alloy NTNX (chapter 18), Novell NetWare (chapter 20).

See Also: Functions E9h, EBh, and FAh, INT FAh

INTERRUPT 21h - Function EBh
TURN ON TASK SWITCHING

Purpose: Reenable multitasking after the calling program completes time-critical or nonreentrant code.

Available on: All machines.   **Restrictions:** DoubleDOS must be running.

Registers at call: **Return Registers:**
AH = EBh   task switching turned on

Conflicts: Alloy NTNX (chapter 18), Novell NetWare (chapter 20).

See Also: Functions E9h, EAh, and FBh, INT FBh

INTERRUPT 21h - Function ECh
GET VIRTUAL SCREEN ADDRESS

Purpose: Determine the address of the memory to use instead of the physical display memory.

Available on: All machines.   **Restrictions:** DoubleDOS must be running.

Registers at call: **Return Registers:**

AH = ECh   ES = segment of virtual screen

Details: The screen address can change if task-switching is on.

Conflicts: Alloy NTNX (chapter 18), Novell NetWare (chapter 20), "Terror" virus (chapter 34).

See Also: Function FCh, INT FCh

INTERRUPT 21h - Function EEh
GIVE AWAY TIME TO OTHER TASKS

Purpose: Indicate to DoubleDOS that the program is idle and that the CPU time it would normally receive may be given to the other program.

Available on: All machines.   **Restrictions:** DoubleDOS must be running.

Registers at call: **Return Registers:**

AH = EEh   returns after giving away time slices

AL = number of 55ms time slices to give away

Conflicts: Alloy NTNX (chapter 18), Novell NetWare (chapter 20), "Jerusalem-G" virus (chapter 34).

See Also: Function FEh, INT FEh

INTERRUPT 21h - Functions F0h through FEh
DoubleDOS

Purpose: These functions are identical to DoubleDOS functions E0h through EEh (see above).

Available on: All machines.   **Restrictions:** DoubleDOS must be running.

Registers at call: **Return Registers:**

varies by function   varies by function

Conflicts: Novell NetWare (chapter 20), "Frere Jacques", "Flip", "2468", and "Black Monday" viruses (chapter 34), PC Magazine PCMANAGE/DCOMPRES (chapter 36).

See Also: Functions E0h through EEh

INTERRUPT 62h - Function 01h
GIVE UP REST OF TIME SLICE

Purpose: Indicate to Cswitch that the caller is idle and the remainder of its time slice may be given to other programs.

Available on: All machines.   **Restrictions:** Cswitch must be installed.

Registers at call: **Return Registers:** n/a

AH = 01h

Details: Cswitch is a set of multitasking functions by Herb Rose.

Conflicts: MS SQL Server/Sybase DBLIBRARY (chapter 27), PC Tools 7 COMMUTE (chapter 33).

See Also: Functions 05h and 06h

INTERRUPT 62h - Function 02h
WAIT FOR SEMAPHORE

Purpose: Suspend calling task until the specified resource is available.

Available on: All machines.   **Restrictions:** Cswitch must be installed.

Registers at call: **Return Registers:**

AH = 02h   AX = FFFFh bad semaphore number

DX = semaphore number (0-63)   else success

Conflicts: MS SQL Server/Sybase DBLIBRARY (chapter 27), PC Tools 7 COMMUTE (chapter 33).

See Also: Functions 03h and 04h

INTERRUPT 62h - Function 03h
CHECK SEMAPHORE

Purpose: Determine whether the specified resource is in use.

Available on: All machines.

Registers at call:
AH = 03h
DX = semaphore number (0-63)

Restrictions: Cswitch must be installed.

Return Registers:
AX = FFFFh not owned
    else owned

Conflicts: MS SQL Server/Sybase DBLIBRARY (chapter 27), PC Tools 7 COMMUTE (chapter 33).
See Also: Functions 02h and 04h

INTERRUPT 62h - Function 04h
TRIGGER SEMAPHORE

Purpose: Indicate that the specified resource is now available for use.

Available on: All machines.

Registers at call:
AH = 04h
DX = semaphore number (0-63)

Restrictions: Cswitch must be installed.

Return Registers:
AX = FFFFh bad semaphore number
    else success

Conflicts: MS SQL Server/Sybase DBLIBRARY (chapter 27), PC Tools 7 COMMUTE (chapter 33).
See Also: Functions 02h and 03h

INTERRUPT 62h - Function 05h
SLEEP

Purpose: Suspend the calling task for the indicated period of time.

Available on: All machines.

Registers at call:
AH = 05h
BX = seconds to sleep

Restrictions: Cswitch must be installed.

Return Registers: n/a

Conflicts: MS SQL Server/Sybase DBLIBRARY (chapter 27), PC Tools 7 COMMUTE (chapter 33).
See Also: Functions 01h, 06h, and 08h

INTERRUPT 62h - Function 06h
SUSPEND

Purpose: Suspend the calling task until it is explicitly restarted.

Available on: All machines.

Registers at call:
AH = 06h

Restrictions: Cswitch must be installed.

Return Registers: n/a

Conflicts: MS SQL Server/Sybase DBLIBRARY (chapter 27), PC Tools 7 COMMUTE (chapter 33).
See Also: Functions 05h and 08h

INTERRUPT 62h - Function 07h
SPAWN

Purpose: Create a new thread of execution.

Available on: All machines.

Registers at call:
AH = 07h
ES:BX -> function address to start executing at
CX = priority (1-10)

Restrictions: Cswitch must be installed.

Return Registers:
AX = FFFDh no free memory control blocks
   = FFFEh no free task control blocks
   = FFFFh not enough memory to create new task
                stack
   = >0   the tcb number of the new task,
                indicating no error

Conflicts: MS SQL Server/Sybase DBLIBRARY (chapter 27), PC Tools 7 COMMUTE (chapter 33).
See Also: Functions 0Fh and 10h

INTERRUPT 62h - Function 08h
WAKE UP TASK

Purpose: Restart a task which previously suspended itself.

Available on: All machines.

Registers at call:
AH = 08h
BX = tcb identifier

Restrictions: Cswitch must be installed.

Return Registers: n/a

Conflicts: MS SQL Server/Sybase DBLIBRARY (chapter 27), PC Tools 7 COMMUTE (chapter 33).
See Also: Functions 05h and 06h

INTERRUPT 62h - Function 09h
SET PRIORITY

Purpose: Specify the relative importance of the calling task.

Available on: All machines.

Registers at call:
AH = 09h
BX = new base priority (1-10)

Restrictions: Cswitch must be installed.

Return Registers: n/a

Details: The lower the priority is numerically, the more often the task will run.
Conflicts: MS SQL Server/Sybase DBLIBRARY (chapter 27), PC Tools 7 COMMUTE (chapter 33).

INTERRUPT 62h - Function 0Ah
TEST MESSAGE QUEUE

Purpose: Determine whether any messages are available in the specified queue.

Available on: All machines.

Registers at call:
AH = 0Ah
DX = queue number (0-63)

Restrictions: Cswitch must be installed.

Return Registers:
AX = FFFFh bad queue number
= 0000h nothing on queue
else number of bytes in first message in
queue

Conflicts: MS SQL Server/Sybase DBLIBRARY (chapter 27), PC Tools 7 COMMUTE (chapter 33).
See Also: Functions 0Bh and 0Ch

INTERRUPT 62h - Function 0Bh
SEND MESSAGE

Purpose: Append data to the specified queue.

Available on: All machines.

Registers at call:
AH = 0Bh
CX = number of bytes to write
DS:SI -> buffer
DX = queue number (0-63)

Restrictions: Cswitch must be installed.

Return Registers:
AX = FFFEh triggered by something arriving, redo the
call
= FFFFh bad queue number
= 0000h no message was on queue
else number of bytes in message

Conflicts: MS SQL Server/Sybase DBLIBRARY (chapter 27), PC Tools 7 COMMUTE (chapter 33).
See Also: Functions 0Ah and 0Ch

INTERRUPT 62h - Function 0Ch
READ MESSAGE

Purpose: Retrieve the next message in the specified queue.

Available on: All machines.

Restrictions: Cswitch must be installed.

Registers at call:
AH = 0Ch
CX = number of bytes to read
DS:SI -> buffer
DX = queue number (0-63)

Return Registers:
AX = FFFFh bad queue number
   else number of bytes transferred

Conflicts: MS SQL Server/Sybase DBLIBRARY (chapter 27), PC Tools 7 COMMUTE (chapter 33).
See Also: Functions 0Ah and 0Bh

INTERRUPT 62h - Function 0Dh
DON'T ALLOW TASK TO BE SWAPPED OUT

Purpose: Specify that the calling task must remain in main memory.
Available on: All machines.
Registers at call:
AH = 0Dh

Restrictions: Cswitch must be installed.
Return Registers: n/a

Conflicts: MS SQL Server/Sybase DBLIBRARY (chapter 27), PC Tools 7 COMMUTE (chapter 33).
See Also: Function 0Eh

INTERRUPT 62h - Function 0Eh
ALLOW TASK TO BE SWAPPED OUT

Purpose: Specify that the calling task need not remain in main memory, and may be swapped to disk if memory becomes scarce.
Available on: All machines.
Registers at call:
AH = 0Eh

Restrictions: Cswitch must be installed.
Return Registers: n/a

Conflicts: MS SQL Server/Sybase DBLIBRARY (chapter 27), PC Tools 7 COMMUTE (chapter 33).
See Also: Function 0Dh

INTERRUPT 62h - Function 0Fh
LOAD AND RUN PROGRAM FROM DISK

Purpose: Start a new program.
Available on: All machines.
Registers at call:
AH = 0Fh
ES:BX -> command line
CX = priority (1-10)
DX = background flag
   nonzero allows loading to EMS

Restrictions: Cswitch must be installed.
Return Registers:
AX = 0000h task loader queue is full
   = 0001h no error

Conflicts: MS SQL Server/Sybase DBLIBRARY (chapter 27), PC Tools 7 COMMUTE (chapter 33).
See Also: Functions 07h, 10h, and 13h

INTERRUPT 62h - Function 10h
TERMINATE SPAWNED PROGRAM

Purpose: End the execution of the calling program.
Available on: All machines.
Registers at call:
AH = 10h

Restrictions: Cswitch must be installed.
Return Registers: n/a

Conflicts: MS SQL Server/Sybase DBLIBRARY (chapter 27), PC Tools 7 COMMUTE (chapter 33).
See Also: Functions 07h and 0Fh

INTERRUPT 62h - Function 11h
GET TCB INFORMATION

Purpose: Determine information about the caller's task control block.
Available on: All machines.

Restrictions: Cswitch must be installed.

Registers at call:
AH = 11h
ES:BX -> a pointer which will be set to the TCB
   address

Return Registers:
AX = TCB indentifier

Conflicts: MS SQL Server/Sybase DBLIBRARY (chapter 27), PC Tools 7 COMMUTE (chapter 33).
See Also: Function 12h

INTERRUPT 62h - Function 12h
GET TCB ADDRESS

Purpose: Determine the address of the caller's task control block.
Available on: All machines.   **Restrictions:** Cswitch must be installed.
Registers at call: **Return Registers:**
AH = 12h   AX = tcb indentifier
ES:BX -> a pointer which will be
   set to the tcb table address
Conflicts: MS SQL Server/Sybase DBLIBRARY (chapter 27), PC Tools 7 COMMUTE (chapter 33).
See Also: Function 11h

INTERRUPT 62h - Function 13h
CHECK STATUS OF PREVIOUS LOAD_TASK

Purpose: Determine whether a request to start a new task was successful.
Available on: All machines.   **Restrictions:** Cswitch must be installed.
Registers at call: **Return Registers:**
AH = 13h   AX = FFFCh no Memory Control Blocks available
                              = FFFDh no TCBs available
                              = FFFEh insufficient memory
                              = FFFFh cannot open file
                              = 0000h load in progress (not done yet)
                              else TCB indentifier
Conflicts: MS SQL Server/Sybase DBLIBRARY (chapter 27), PC Tools 7 COMMUTE (chapter 33).
See Also: Function 0Fh

INTERRUPT 7Fh - Function 09h
SET TASK PRIORITY

Purpose: Specify the relative importance of the calling task.
Available on: All machines.   **Restrictions:** MultiLink Advanced must be running.
Registers at call: **Return Registers:** n/a
AH = 09h
AL = priority (0-7)
Details: The MultiLink installation check consists of ensuring that the interrupt vector is not pointing at segment 0000h, then checking whether the byte at offset 0000h in the interrupt handler's segment is E9h.
Conflicts: Alloy NTNX and MW386 (chapter 18).

INTERRUPT F4h
GIVE UP REST OF CURRENT CLOCK TICK AND ALL OF NEXT TICK

Purpose: This call is the same as INT 21h Function EEh and INT FEh.
Available on: All machines.   **Restrictions:** DoubleDOS must be running.
Conflicts: None known.
See Also: INT 21h Function EEh, INT FEh

INTERRUPTS F5h through F9h
Unknown Functions

Purpose: *unknown.*

Available on: All machines.
Registers at call: *unknown.*
Conflicts: None known.

Restrictions: DoubleDOS must be running.
Return Registers: *unknown.*

INTERRUPT FAh
TURN OFF TIMESHARING

Purpose: Temporarily disable time-slicing while the caller processes time-critical or nonreentrant code.
Available on: All machines.
Registers at call: n/a
Details: This call is the same as INT 21h Function EAh.
Conflicts: None known.
See Also: INT 21h Function EAh, INT FBh

Restrictions: DoubleDOS must be running.
Return Registers: n/a

INTERRUPT FBh
TURN ON TIMESHARING

Purpose: Resume time-slicing after the caller completes the processing of time-critical or nonreentrant code.
Available on: All machines.
Registers at call: n/a
Details: This call is the same as INT 21h Function EBh.
Conflicts: None known.
See Also: INT 21h Function EBh, INT FAh

Restrictions: DoubleDOS must be running.
Return Registers: n/a

INTERRUPT FCh
GET CURRENT SCREEN BUFFER ADDRESS

Purpose: Determine the address of the memory to use instead of the physical display memory.
Available on: All machines.
Registers at call: n/a

Restrictions: DoubleDOS must be running.
Return Registers:
ES = segment of display buffer

Details: The display buffer may be moved if multitasking is enabled. This call is the same as INT 21h Function ECh.
Conflicts: None known.
See Also: INT 21h Function ECh, INT FBh

INTERRUPT FDh
Unknown Function

Purpose: *unknown.*
Available on: All machines.
Registers at call: *unknown.*
Conflicts: None known.

Restrictions: DoubleDOS must be running.
Return Registers: *unknown.*

INTERRUPT FEh
GIVE UP TIME

Purpose: Indicate to DoubleDOS that the program is idle and that the CPU time it would normally receive may be given to the other program.
Available on: All machines.
Registers at call:
AL = number of 55ms time
    slices to give away
Details: This call is the same as INT 21h Function EEh.
Conflicts: 80286+ return from protected mode (chapter 1)
See Also: INT 21h Function EEh, INT F4h

Restrictions: DoubleDOS must be installed.
Return Registers: n/a

Chapter ▪ 18

Alloy Multiuser/Network Systems

One of the first mini-network solutions for small office use was the Alloy network system, which originally made it possible to add a "dumb terminal" to a PC as an additional, independently operating, console. From this beginning, the system has evolved into a true networking solution based on a host-slave relationship rather than peer-to-peer or server-oriented operation. The three Alloy Computuer Products systems described here are the Alloy NetWare Support Kit (ANSK), Novell-Type Network Executive (NTNX), and 386/MultiWare (MW386).

In this chapter, all interrupt functions that are unique to the Alloy systems are described, in sequence of interrupt number and function number within each interrupt. However, Alloy also shares a number of functions with Novell networks, which are described in Chapter 20, and it shares three functions with PC-Net, which are described in chapter 27.

INTERRUPT 10h - Function 8Bh
FORCE WORKSTATION SCREEN UPDATE

Purpose: Indicate that the calling program's display should be brought up-to-date immediately.
Available on: All machines.   **Restrictions:** Alloy MW386 must be installed.
Registers at call: **Return Registers:** n/a
AH = 8Bh
Conflicts: None known.
See Also: Functions 92h and 93h

INTERRUPT 10h - Function 90h
GET PHYSICAL WORKSTATION DISPLAY MODE

Purpose: Determine the true video mode for the workstation on which the calling program is running.
Available on: All machines.   **Restrictions:** Alloy MW386 must be installed.
Registers at call: **Return Registers:**
AH = 90h   AL = current video mode (see Function 00h in chapter 5)

Conflicts: None known.
See Also: Function 91h

INTERRUPT 10h - Function 91h
GET PHYSICAL WORKSTATION ADAPTER TYPE

Purpose: Determine type of video card installed in the workstation on which the calling program is running.
Available on: All machines.   **Restrictions:** Alloy MW386 must be installed.
Registers at call: **Return Registers:**
AH = 91h   AL = video adapter type
                                                  00h monochrome
                                                  01h Hercules monochrome graphics
                                                  02h CGA
                                                  03h EGA
                                                  04h VGA
                                                  80h monochrome text terminal

81h Hercules graphics terminal
82h color graphics terminal

Details: Types less than 80h do not imply that the current user is on the host.
Conflicts: None known.
See Also: Function 90h

INTERRUPT 10h - Function 92h
INHIBIT WORKSTATION SCREEN UPDATES

Purpose: Indicate that the calling program's physical display should not be updated until explicitly enabled.

Available on: All machines.	**Restrictions:** Alloy MW386 must be installed.
Registers at call:	**Return Registers:** n/a

AH = 92h

Details: The terminal will be updated even when screen updates are inhibited if TTY output is used.
Conflicts: None known.
See Also: Function 8Bh

INTERRUPT 10h - Function 93h
REDRAW SCREEN

Purpose: Indicate that the calling program's physical display should be completely repainted, in case the screen has been corrupted (as might be the case after data operations on the console port).

Available on: All machines.	**Restrictions:** Alloy MW386 must be installed.
Registers at call:	**Return Registers:** n/a

AH = 93h

Conflicts: None known.
See Also: Function 8Bh

INTERRUPT 14h - Function 20h
ATTACH LOGICAL COMMUNICATIONS PORT TO PHYSICAL PORT

Purpose: Map a logical port to a physical communications port address.

Available on: All machines.	**Restrictions:** Alloy MW386 must be installed.
Registers at call:	**Return Registers:**
AH = 20h	AX = status:
AL = logical port	0000h successful
(01h COM1, 02h COM2)	FFFFh failed
DX = physical port number	

Conflicts: X00 FOSSIL (chapter 7), MultiDOS Plus (chapter 16).
See Also: Functions 21h, 22h, and 23h, INT 17h Function 8Bh

INTERRUPT 14h - Function 21h
RELEASE PHYSICAL COMMUNICATIONS PORT

Purpose: Make the specified physical port available for other users of network.

Available on: All machines.	**Restrictions:** Alloy MW386 version 1.x must be installed.
Registers at call:	**Return Registers:**
AH = 21h	AX = status:
DX = physical port number	0000h successful
	FFFFh failed

Conflicts: X00 FOSSIL (chapter 7), MultiDOS Plus (chapter 16).
See Also: Functions 20h and 22h

INTERRUPT 14h - Function 22h
RELEASE LOGICAL COMMUNICATIONS PORT

Purpose: Detach the specified logical port from the physical port it was previously associated with.

Available on: All machines.

Registers at call:
AH = 22h
AL = logical port
    (01h COM1, 02h COM2)
Conflicts: MultiDOS Plus (chapter 16).
See Also: Functions 20h and 21h

Restrictions: Alloy MW386 version 2.0 or higher must be installed.
Return Registers:
AX = status (0000h successful)

INTERRUPT 14h - Function 23h
GET PORT NUMBER FROM LOGICAL PORT ID

Purpose: Determine physical port number and mode of the specified logical COMx port.
Available on: All machines.

Registers at call:
AH = 23h
AL = logical port (01h COM1, 02h COM2)
DH = user ID
DL = process ID (DH, DL both FFh for current task)

Restrictions: Alloy MW386 version 2.0 or higher must be installed.
Return Registers:
AL = MW386 port mode:
    bit 0: port is shared (spooler only)
    1: port is spooled instead of direct (spooler only)
    2: port is assigned as logical COM device, not in spooler
    3: port is free
CX = MW386 port number
DH = owner's user ID
DL = owner's task ID

Conflicts: MultiDOS Plus (chapter 16).
See Also: Function 20h, INT 17h Function 8Bh

INTERRUPT 14h - Function 24h
CHANGE PHYSICAL PORT PARAMETERS

Purpose: Establish operating conditions for the specified serial port.
Available on: All machines.

Registers at call:
AH = 24h
CX = physical I/O port number
DS:DX -> configuration table
    (Table 18-1)
Details: Invalid port numbers are merely ignored.
Conflicts: MultiDOS Plus (chapter 16).
See Also: INT 17h Function 96h

Restrictions: Alloy MW386 version 2.0 or higher must be installed.
Return Registers:
AH = 00h

Table 18-1. Format of Configuration Table:

Offset	Size	Description
00h	BYTE	baud rate:
		00h 38400
		01h 19200
		02h 9600
		03h 7200
		04h 4800
		05h 3600
		06h 2400
		07h 2000
		08h 1200

Table 18-1. Format of Configuration Table (continued)

Offset	Size	Description
		09h 600
		0Ah 300
		0Bh 150
		0Ch 134.5
01h	BYTE	data bits:
		00h=5
		01h=6
		02h=7
		03h=8
02h	BYTE	parity:
		00h none
		01h odd
		02h even
03h	BYTE	stop bits:
		00h=1
		01h=2
04h	BYTE	receive flow control:
		00h none
		01h XON/XOFF
		02h DTR/DSR
		03h XPC
		04h RTS/CTS
05h	BYTE	transmit flow control (as for receive)

INTERRUPT 17h - Function 81h
CANCEL JOBS FOR CURRENT USER

Purpose: Cancel the specified number of print jobs most recently submitted by the caller.

Available on: All machines.

Restrictions: Alloy NTNX or MW386 must be installed.

Registers at call:
AH = 81h
AL = 00h (NTNX compatibility mode)
CL = number of jobs to cancel

Return Registers:
AL = status
    00h success
    01h..7Fh warning
    80h general failure
    81h host overloaded (NTNX only)
    82h module busy (NTNX only)
    83h host busy (NTNX only)
    84h re-entry flag set
    85h invalid request
    86h invalid printer
    87h invalid process ID
    89h access denied
    8Ah option not available for given port type
    8Bh option not available for given task type
    91h printer busy
    C2h file not found
    C3h path not found
    C4h file access failure

Details: This fucntion cancels the last CL printouts for the current task.

Conflicts: None known.

See Also: Function 82h

INTERRUPT 17h - Function 82h
CANCEL ALL JOBS FOR CURRENT USER

Purpose: Cancel all outstanding print jobs for the calling task.

Available on: All machines.

Registers at call:
AH = 82h
AL = 00h (NTNX compatibility mode)
Conflicts: None known.
See Also: Function 81h

Restrictions: Alloy NTNX or MW386 must be installed.

Return Registers:
AL = status (see Function 81h)

INTERRUPT 17h - Function 83h
SET NUMBER OF COPIES

Purpose: Establish the number of copies to be printed.

Available on: All machines.

Registers at call:
AH = 83h
AL = mode
    00h NTNX compatibility
        CL = number of copies (max 99, default 1)
    02h MW386 v2.0+
        BX = logical device
            number
            00h-03h = LPT1-LPT4
            04h-07h = COM1- COM4
        CX = number of copies
Details: In NTNX compatibility mode, this function only affects LPT1.
Conflicts: None known.

Restrictions: Alloy NTNX or MW386 must be installed.

Return Registers:
AL = status (see Function 81h)

INTERRUPT 17h - Function 84h
GENERATE PRINT BREAK

Purpose: Release spooled data for printing.

Available on: All machines.

Registers at call:
AH = 84h
AL = mode
    00h NTNX compatibility
    02h MW386 v2.0+
        BX = logical device number
        00h-03h = LPT1-LPT4
        04h-07h = COM1-COM4
Details: This call closes the spool file and tells the spooler to queue the print job (LPT1 only under MW386 in NTNX compatibility mode).
Conflicts: None known.

Restrictions: Alloy NTNX or MW386 must be installed.

Return Registers: n/a

INTERRUPT 17h - Function 87h
SET INDOS POINTER

Purpose: Permit a transient program to provide a pointer for flushing print buffers on user-written printer drivers.

Available on: All machines.

Restrictions: Alloy NTNX must be installed.

Registers at call:
AH = 87h
AL = 00h
CX:BX -> buffer for user-written printer drivers
Details: This function must be executed before the printer is enabled.
Conflicts: None known.
See Also: Function 8Ah

Return Registers:
BX,CX destroyed

INTERRUPT 17h - Function 88h
REMOVE PRINTER FROM SPOOLER

Purpose: Make the specified printer unavailable to the spooler by removing it from the spooler's list of available printers.

Available on: All machines.

Restrictions: Alloy NTNX or MW386 must be installed.

Registers at call:
AH = 88h
AL = mode
   00h NTNX compatibility
     DX = NTNX printer number
      00h host LPT1
      01h host LPT2
      02h host LPT3
      03h host LPT4
      04h host COM1
      05h host COM2
      06h user's logical COM2
      07h user's terminal AUX port
      08h user's logical COM1 (MW386 only)
   01h MW386
     DX = MW386 printer number
Conflicts: None known.
See Also: Functions 89h and 8Bh

Return Registers:
AH = status (see Function 81h)

INTERRUPT 17h - Function 89h
ADD PRINTER TO SPOOLER

Purpose: Make the specified printer available to the spooler by adding it to the spooler's list of available printers.

Available on: All machines.

Restrictions: Alloy NTNX or MW386 must be installed.

Registers at call:
AH = 89h
AL = mode
   00h NTNX compatibility
     DX = NTNX printer number (see Function
       88h)
   01h MW386
     DX = MW386 printer number
Conflicts: None known.
See Also: Functions 88h and 8Bh

Return Registers:
AL = status (see Function 81h)

INTERRUPT 17h - Function 8Ah
ACTIVATE USER-WRITTEN PRINTER DRIVER

Purpose: Make a user-written printer driver active.
Available on: All machines.

Restrictions: Alloy NTNX must be installed.

Registers at call:
AH = 8Ah
others, if any, unknown.
Conflicts: None known.
See Also: Function 92h

Return Registers: *unknown.*

INTERRUPT 17h - Function 8Bh
GET PHYSICAL DEVICE NUMBER FROM NAME

Purpose: Determine the physical device number corresponding to the given name string.
Available on: All machines.
Registers at call:
AH = 8Bh
DS:DX -> ASCIZ printer name

Restrictions: Alloy MW386 must be installed.
Return Registers:
AL = status (see also Function 81h)
   00h successful
      DX = physical device number

Conflicts: None known.
See Also: Functions 89h and 8Ch, INT 14h Function 20h

INTERRUPT 17h - Function 8Ch
GET DEVICE NAME FROM PHYSICAL DEVICE NUMBER

Purpose: Determine the name string corresponding to the given device number.
Available on: All machines.
Registers at call:
AH = 8Ch
DX = physical device number
ES:DI -> 17-byte buffer for ASCIZ device name
Conflicts: None known.
See Also: Functions 88h and 8Bh

Restrictions: Alloy MW386 must be installed.
Return Registers:
AL = status (see also Function 81h)
   00h successful
      ES:DI buffer filled

INTERRUPT 17h - Function 8Dh
RESET SPOOLER

Purpose: Initialize the spooler software to boot-up values and clear all buffers.
Available on: All machines.

Restrictions: Alloy NTNX or MW386 must be installed.

Registers at call:
AH = 8Dh
AL = 00h
Details: MW386 accepts this call for NTNX compatibility, but does nothing.
Conflicts: None known.

Return Registers:
AL = status (see Function 81h)

INTERRUPT 17h - Function 8Eh
GET INT 28h ENTRY POINT

Purpose: Determine the current INT 28h entry point.
Available on: All machines.
Registers at call:
AH = 8Eh
AL = 00h
Conflicts: None known.
See Also: Function 8Fh

Restrictions: Alloy NTNX must be installed.
Return Registers:
CX:BX -> INT 28h entry point

INTERRUPT 17h - Function 8Fh
GET DOS INTERCEPT ENTRY POINT

Purpose: Determine the current DOS intercept routine.
Available on: All machines.

Restrictions: Alloy NTNX must be installed.

Registers at call:
AH = 8Fh
AL = 00h
Conflicts: None known.
See Also: Function 8Eh

Return Registers:
CX:BX -> DOS intercept routine

INTERRUPT 17h - Function 90h
SPOOL FILE BY NAME

Purpose: Specify a file to be queued for printing.
Available on: All machines.

Restrictions: Alloy NTNX or MW386 must be installed.

Registers at call:
AH = 90h
AL = mode
  00h NTNX compatibility
    DL = printer code (FFh=current) (NTNX, MW386 v1.x only)
    DH = number of copies (FFh=current) (NTNX, MW386 v1.x only)
  02h MW386 v2.0+
    BX = logical device number
      00h-03h = LPT1-LPT4
      04h-07h = COM1- COM4
    CX:SI -> ASCIZ pathname
Details: In mode 00h, the file is always sent to logical LPT1.
Conflicts: None known.
See Also: Function A0h

Return Registers:
AL = status (see Function 81h)

INTERRUPT 17h - Function 91h
GET USER NUMBER AND CURRENT PRINTER

Purpose: Determine the caller's user number and current printer assignment for LPT1 (or other device if MW386).
Available on: All machines.

Restrictions: Alloy NTNX or MW386 must be installed.

Registers at call:
AH = 91h
AL = mode
  00h NTNX compatibility
  01h MW386

  02h MW386 v2.0+
    BX = logical device number
      00h-03h = LPT1- LPT4
      04h-07h = COM1- COM4
Conflicts: None known.
See Also: Function 8Ch

Return Registers:
AL = status (see Function 81h)
CX = user number (00h = host)
DX = currently selected printer number (00h-08h)
CX = user number
DX = physical device number of currently selected printer
CX = user number
DX = physical device number

INTERRUPT 17h - Function 92h, Subfunction 00h
CHECK PRINTER DRIVER

Purpose: Determine whether a printer driver is installed.
Available on: All machines.

Restrictions: Alloy NTNX must be installed.

Registers at call:
AH = 92h
AL = 00h
CL = 00h

Return Registers:
CL = driver state
    01h initialized
    80h not initialized
AX = status (see Function 81h)

Conflicts: None known.
See Also: Function 8Ah

INTERRUPT 17h - Function 94h
SELECT PRINTER

Purpose: Specify which physical device will be associated with LPT1 (or other logical device for MW386).

Available on: All machines.

Restrictions: Alloy NTNX or MW386 must be installed.

Registers at call:
AH = 94h
AL = mode
    00h NTNX compatibility
        DX = NTNX printer number (see Function 88h)
    01h MW386
        DX = MW386 printer number
    02h MW386 v2.0+
        BX = logical printer number
        DX = MW386 printer number

Return Registers:
AL = status (see Function 81h)

Details: Modes 00h and 01h affect only logical LPT1.
Conflicts: None known.
See Also: Functions 8Bh and 95h

INTERRUPT 17h - Function 95h
GET CURRENT PRINTER

Purpose: Determine the physical device assigned to LPT1 (or other logical device for MW386).

Available on: all machines.

Restrictions: Alloy NTNX or MW386 must be installed.

Registers at call:
AH = 95h
AL = mode
    00h NTNX compatibility

    01h MW386
    02h MW386 v2.0+
        BX = logical device number
            00h-03h = LPT1-LPT4
            04h-07h = COM1- COM4

Return Registers:
AL = status (see Function 81h)
DX = NTNX printer number (see Function 88h)
    (FFFFh if current printer is not compatible with NTNX)
DX = MW386 printer number
DX = MW386 printer number (FFFFh = none)

Details: Modes 00h and 01h return the printer number of logical LPT1 only.
Conflicts: None known.
See Also: Function 94h

INTERRUPT 17h - Function 96h
SET SERIAL PORT PARAMETERS

Purpose: The documentation states that this is a NOP, doing only XOR AX,AX before returning.

Available on: All machines.

Restrictions: Alloy NTNX must be installed.

Registers at call:
AH = 96h
AL = 00h
Conflicts: None known.
See Also: INT 14h Function 24h

Return Registers: n/a

INTERRUPT 17h - Function 97h
SET DATA DRIVEN PRINT BREAK

Purpose: Specify the embedded character sequence which will be used to indicate that the current job is ready for printing.

Available on: All machines.

Restrictions: Alloy NTNX or MW386 must be installed.

Registers at call:
AH = 97h
AL = mode
    00h NTNX compatibility
    02h MW386 v2.0+
        BX = logical device number
            00h-03h = LPT1-LPT4
            04h-07h = COM1- COM4
        CH,CL,DH = three character break
            sequence
        DL = subfunction
            00h set break string
            else reset break

Return Registers:
AL = status (see Function 81h)

Details: Mode 00h affects only logical LPT1. When the break string is encountered, the spool file will be closed and queued for printing automatically. The break string is not permanently saved, and will be reset each time MW386 or the user is rebooted.
Conflicts: None known.
See Also: Function 9Bh

INTERRUPT 17h - Function 98h
RESTART PRINTER

Purpose: Continue printing after a printer error.

Available on: All machines.

Restrictions: Alloy NTNX or MW386 must be installed.

Registers at call:
AH = 98h
AL = 00h
DL = printer number (FFh = current)

Return Registers:
AL = status
    00h successful
    01h incorrect printer
    02h task not found

Details: This call is a null function in MW386 because MW386 automatically continues after printer errors; it is included solely for NTNX compatibility.
Conflicts: None known.

INTERRUPT 17h - Function 99h
GET/SET PRINTER MODE

Purpose: Specify or determine the ownership and mode of a printer.

Available on: All machines.

Restrictions: Alloy NTNX or MW386 must be installed.

Registers at call:
AH = 99h
AL = mode

Return Registers:
AL = status (see Function 81h)
DH = mode (bits 1 and 2 set as left)

00h NTNX compatibility
    DL = NTNX printer number (see Function
        88h) (FFh = task's current logical LPT1)
    DH = mode
        bit 0: get mode if 1, set mode if 0
        1: private ("attached")
        2: direct instead of spooled
        3-7 reserved (0)
01h MW386
    DX = MW386 printer number
    CL = mode (as for DH above)

Conflicts: None known.

DL = printer owner's user number if not spooled

INTERRUPT 17h - Function 9Ah
SET TAB EXPANSION

Purpose: Control printer expansion of tab characters.
Available on: All machines.

Registers at call:
AH = 9Ah
AL = mode
    00h NTNX compatibility
        DX = NTNX printer number (see Function
            88h) (FFFFh = current logical LPT1)
    01h MW386
        DX = MW386 printer number
        CL = tab length (00h = no expansion, 01h-
            63h = spaces per tab)

Restrictions: Alloy NTNX or MW386 must be installed.
Return Registers:
AL = status (see Function 81h)

Details: Beginning with MW386 v2.0, tab expansion is set on a per-printer basis rather than a per-user basis; NTNX and MW386 v1.x ignore DX.
Conflicts: None known.
See Also: Function A4h

INTERRUPT 17h - Function 9Bh
SET PRINT BREAK TIMEOUT

Purpose: Specify the interval of idleness after which the current print job will automatically be closed and queued for printing.
Available on: All machines.

Registers at call:
AH = 9Bh
AL = mode
    00h NTNX compatibility
        CX = timeout value in clock ticks (1/18 sec)
            (00h = never)
    01h MW386
        CX = timeout value in seconds (00h =
            never)
    02h MW386 v2.0+
        BX = logical device number
            00h-03h = LPT1-LPT4
            04h-07h = COM1- COM4

Restrictions: Alloy NTNX or MW386 must be installed.
Return Registers:
AL = status (see Function 81h)

CX = timeout value in seconds (00h =
　　never)

Details: Modes 00h and 01h affect only the current logical LPT1.
Conflicts: None known.
See Also: Function 97h

INTERRUPT 17h - Function A0h
SPOOL COPY OF FILE

Purpose: Make a copy of the specified file in the spooler's directory and queue the copy for printing, allowing the original file to be modified or deleted while the copy is printed.

Available on: All machines.　　　　　　**Restrictions:** Alloy MW386 must be installed.
Registers at call:　　　　　　　　　　**Return Registers:**
AH = A0h　　　　　　　　　　　　　　　　AL = status (see Function 81h)
AL = mode
　　00h NTNX compatibility
　　　　DX = *unknown* (NTNX, MW386 v1.x only)
　　　　CX:SI -> ASCIZ pathname
　　02h MW386 v2.0+
　　　　BX = logical device number
　　　　　　00h-03h = LPT1-LPT4
　　　　　　04h-07h = COM1- COM4
　　　　CX:SI -> ASCIZ pathname

Details: In mode 00h, the file is printed on logical LPT1.
Conflicts: None known.
See Also: Function 90h

INTERRUPT 17h - Function A4h
ENABLE/DISABLE FORM FEED

Purpose: Control the spooler's use of formfeeds after print jobs.

Available on: All machines.　　　　　　**Restrictions:** Alloy MW386 must be installed.
Registers at call:　　　　　　　　　　**Return Registers:**
AH = A4h　　　　　　　　　　　　　　　　AL = status (see Function 81h)
AL = new state
　　00h form feed after end of print job disabled
　　01h form feed enabled

Details: This function only affects the current logical LPT1.
Conflicts: None known.
See Also: Functions 9Ah and A6h, NTNX Host INT 7Fh Function 05h

INTERRUPT 17h - Function A6h
ENABLE/DISABLE BANNER PAGE

Purpose: Control the generation of a banner page by the spooler.

Available on: All machines.　　　　　　**Restrictions:** Alloy MW386 must be installed.
Registers at call:　　　　　　　　　　**Return Registers:**
AH = A6h　　　　　　　　　　　　　　　　AL = status (see Function 81h)
AL = new state
　　00h banner page before print job disabled
　　01h banner page enabled

Details: This function only affects the current logical LPT1.
Conflicts: None known.
See Also: Function A4h

INTERRUPT 17h - Function A7h
GET/SET SPOOL FLAGS

Purpose: Control the spooler flags with a single command.

Available on: All machines.

Registers at call:
AH = A7h
AL = spool flags
    bit 0: banner page enabled (see Function A4h)
    1: form feed enabled (see Function A6h)
    2-6: reserved (0)
    7: set flags if 1, get flags if 0
BX = logical device number
    00h-03h = LPT1-LPT4
    04h-07h = COM1-COM4

Restrictions: Alloy MW386 version 2.0 or higher must be installed.

Return Registers:
AL = status (see Function 81h)

Details: The Alloy documentation does not state which register contains the result of a GET.
Conflicts: None known.
See Also: Functions A4h and A6h

INTERRUPT 17h - Function A8h
DEFINE TEMPORARY FILENAME

Purpose: Specify the filename printed on the banner page for spool files collected from the application's printer output.

Available on: All machines.

Registers at call:
AH = A8h
CX:SI -> ASCIZ filename without extension (max 8 chars)

Restrictions: Alloy MW386 must be installed.

Return Registers:
AL = status (see Function 81h)

Conflicts: None known.
See Also: Function A9h

INTERRUPT 17h - Function A9h
CHANGE TEMPORARY SPOOL DRIVE

Purpose: Specify the drive on which the spooler stores temporary files.

Available on: All machines.

Registers at call:
AH = A9h
AL = new spool drive (2=C:,3=D:,etc)

Restrictions: Alloy MW386 must be installed.

Return Registers:
AL = status (see Function 81h)

Details: This function does not remove the previous spooling directory since jobs may be pending.
Conflicts: None known.
See Also: Function A8h

INTERRUPT 17h - Function AAh
GET REAL-TIME PRINTER STATUS

Purpose: Determine the actual current status of the specified printer.

Available on: All machines.

Registers at call:
AH = AAh
AL = mode
    00h NTNX

Restrictions: Alloy MW386 version 2.0 or higher must be installed.

Return Registers:
AH = instantaneous printer status
    00h printer ready
    01h not ready

DX = NTNX printer number (see Function 88h)
01h MW386
DX = MW386 printer number

12h off line
13h out of paper
14h general device failure
15h device timeout
16h bad device number

Conflicts: None known.

INTERRUPT 17h - Function AFh
CHECK SPOOLER

Purpose: Determine whether the spooler is loaded and available for use.
Available on: All machines.   **Restrictions:** Alloy MW386 must be installed.
Registers at call: **Return Registers:**
AH = AFh   AX = 55AAh if spooler is available
Conflicts: None known.

INTERRUPT 5Bh
Used by Alloy NTNX

Purpose: *unknown.*
Available on: All machines.   **Restrictions:** Alloy NTNX must be installed.
Registers at call: *unknown.*   **Return Registers:** *unknown.*
Conflicts: Microsoft Network Transport Layer (chapter 27), AT&T Starlan Extended NetBIOS (chapter 27), Cluster adapter (chapter 27).

INTERRUPT 7Fh
INSTALLATION CHECK

Purpose: Determine whether Alloy NTNX (Novell-Type Network Executive) or 386/MultiWare multitasking system is installed.
Available on: All machines.   **Restrictions:** none.
Details: The words at C800h:0000h and C800h:0002h will both be 584Eh if this multitasking system is present. NTNX allows its API to be placed on a different interrupt than 7Fh at load time.

To determine the actual vector used, open the device "SPOOLER" with INT 21h Function 3Dh Subfunction 02h, place it in RAW mode with INT 21h Function 44h Subfunctions 00h and 01h, then read one byte which will be the actual interrupt number being used; the other interrupts may be found with INT 7Fh Function 09h Subfunction 03h.

INTERRUPT 7Fh
INSTALLATION CHECK

Purpose: Determine whether running under the ANSK (Alloy NetWare Support Kit) system, version 2.2 or higher.
Available on: All machines.   **Restrictions:** This check will not work on Slaves with less than 1MB of RAM, or those using the SLIM.SYS device driver.

Details: A program may determine that it is running on an ANSK Slave by checking the five bytes at F000h:0000h for the ASCIZ signature "ANSK"; this address is RAM, and should not be written.

INTERRUPT 7Fh - Function 00h
SEMAPHORE LOCK AND WAIT

Purpose: Attempt to gain exclusive access to a resource, waiting until the resource is available.
Available on: All machines.   **Restrictions:** Alloy NTNX or MW386 must be installed.

Registers at call: **Return Registers:**
AH = 00h   AL = status
DS:DX -> ASCIZ semaphore name (max 64 bytes)   00h successful
                                                     01h invalid function
                                                     02h semaphore already locked

03h unable to lock semaphore
04h semaphore space exhausted
05h host/target PC did not respond (NTNX)
AH = semaphore owner if status=02h

Conflicts: Halo88 API (chapter 5), ClusterShare access (chapter 27).
See Also: Functions 01h, 02h, and 41h, PC-Net INT 67h Function 00h (chapter 27)

INTERRUPT 7Fh - Function 01h
SEMAPHORE LOCK

Purpose: Attempt to gain exclusive access to a resource, but return immediately if the resource is not available.

Available on: All machines. **Restrictions:** Alloy NTNX or MW386 must be installed.

Registers at call: **Return Registers:**
AH = 01h AL = status (see Function 00h)
DS:DX -> ASCIZ semaphore name (max 64 bytes) AH = semaphore owner if status=02h
Conflicts: Halo88 API (chapter 5), ClusterShare access (chapter 27).
See Also: Functions 00h, 02h, and 41h

INTERRUPT 7Fh - Function 02h
RELEASE SEMAPHORE

Purpose: Indicate that the specified resource is now available for other tasks to use.

Available on: All machines. **Restrictions:** Alloy NTNX or MW386 must be installed.

Registers at call: **Return Registers:**
AH = 02h AL = status
DS:DX -> ASCIZ semaphore name (max 64 bytes)   00h successful
    01h invalid function
    02h semaphore locked by other user
  AH = semaphore owner
    03h unable to unlock semaphore
    05h target PC did not respond

Conflicts: Halo88 API (chapter 5), ClusterShare access (chapter 27).
See Also: Functions 00h, 01h, and 42h

INTERRUPT 7Fh - Function 03h
GET USER NUMBER

Purpose: Determine the caller's user number, and (for MW386) on which machine the caller is running.

Available on: All machines. **Restrictions:** Alloy ANSK, NTNX, or MW386 must be installed.

Registers at call: **Return Registers:**
AH = 03h AL = user number
  AH = machine number (MW386)

Details: This function call is the recommended method for a CPU-bound process to prevent its priority from being lowered.
Conflicts: Halo88 API (chapter 5), ClusterShare access (chapter 27).
See Also: Functions 04h, 05h, and A1h

INTERRUPT 7Fh - Function 04h
GET NUMBER OF USERS

Purpose: Determine the total number of users on the current machine.

Available on: All machines. **Restrictions:** Alloy NTNX or MW386 must be installed.

Registers at call:
AH = 04h

Return Registers:
AL = total number of users on currrent machine
    (MW386)
AL = number of slaves on system (NTNX)

Conflicts: Halo88 API (chapter 5), ClusterShare access (chapter 27), HLLAPI (IBM 3270 High-Level Language API).
See Also: Function 03h

INTERRUPT 7Fh - Function 05h
LOCK/UNLOCK SYSTEM, SPOOLER CONTROL

Purpose: Control user activity, the print spooler, and slave timers.
Available on: All machines.

Restrictions: Must be running on an Alloy NTNX host.
Return Registers: n/a

Registers at call:
AH = 05h
AL = function
    00h lock system (disable slave services)
    01h unlock system
    02h enable spooler
    03h disable spooler
    04h enable slave timer update
    05h disable slave timer update
    06h enable form feeds
    07h disable form feeds

Conflicts: Halo88 API (chapter 5), ClusterShare access (chapter 27), HDILOAD.EXE - 8514/A Video Controller Interface (chapter).
See Also: INT 17h Function A4h

INTERRUPT 7Fh - Function 05h
GET USER PARAMETERS

Purpose: Retrieve operating environment and parameters for the calling task.
Available on: All machines.

Restrictions: Must be running under Alloy MW386 or on an Alloy NTNX slave.
Return Registers:
buffer filled

Registers at call:
AH = 05h
DX:DI -> buffer for user information record
    (Table 18-2)
Details: MW386 provides this function for backward compatibility only, and sets many of the fields to zero because they are meaningless under MW386. This function has no effect when called by the host (user 0).
Conflicts: Halo88 API (chapter 5), ClusterShare access (chapter 27), HDILOAD.EXE - 8514/A Video Controller Interface (chapter).
See Also: Function 03h

Table 18-2. Format of user information record:

Offset	Size	Description
00h	WORD	segment of video RAM
02h	WORD	segment of secondary copy of video RAM
04h	WORD	offset of screen update flag (see INT 10h Function 8Bh) flag nonzero if update needed
06h	WORD	video NMI enable port (not used by MW386, set to 0000h)
08h	WORD	video NMI disable port (not used by MW386, set to 0000h)
0Ah	BYTE	processor type
		00h 8088
		01h V20

Table 18-2. Format of User Information Record (continued)

Offset	Size	Description
		02h 8086
		03h V30
		06h 80386
0Bh	WORD	multitasking flag (00h = single tasking, 01h = multitasking) (not used by MW386, set to 0000h)
0Dh	WORD	offset of terminal driver (not used by MW386, set to 0000h)
0Fh	BYTE	port for console I/O (not used by MW386, set to 0000h)
10h	WORD	offset of processor communication busy flag; bit 7 set when slave communicating with host
12h	WORD	pointer to FAR NX system call (not used by MW386, set to 0000h)
14h	WORD	offset of 16-byte user configuration record (see Function 38h)
16h	WORD	offset of command/status word
18h	WORD	offset of screen valid flag (see INT 10h Function 93h) nonzero if screen must be repainted
1Ah	WORD	offset of screen repaint flag
1Ch	WORD	pointer to NEAR NX system call (not used by MW386, set to 0000h)
1Eh	WORD	offset for intercept flags (not used by MW386, set to 0000h) intercept flag = FFh if MSDOS intercepts should be disabled
20h	WORD	offset of terminal lock flag (see INT 10h Function 92h) lock flag = FFh if backgrnd screen updates should be suspended
22h	26 BYTEs	reserved

INTERRUPT 7Fh - Function 06h
GET SHARED DRIVE INFO

Purpose: Determine information about the specified drive shared with the network.

Available on: All machines.

Restrictions: Must be running on an Alloy NTNX host.

Registers at call:
AH = 06h
AL = drive number (1=A:, 2=B:, etc)
ES:DI -> drive info record (Table 18-3)

Return Registers:
AX = status
    0000h successful
        ES:DI buffer filled
    0001h not shared drive

Conflicts: None known.

Table 18-3. Format of Drive Info Record:

Offset	Size	Description
00h	WORD	segment of drive IO-REQUEST structure (MSDOS DPB)
02h	WORD	segment of allocation map (owner table) one byte per FAT entry, containing user ID owning that entry
04h	WORD	segment of master FAT for drive (copy of FAT on disk)
06h	WORD	pointer to configuration file
08h	WORD	total number of clusters
0Ah	WORD	bytes per sector
0Ch	WORD	sectors per cluster
0Eh	BYTE	FAT type (0Ch = 12-bit, 10h = 16-bit)

INTERRUPT 7Fh - Function 06h
ALLOCATE FREE CLUSTER ON SHARED DRIVE

Purpose: Dynamically reallocate space on the specified shared drive.

Available on: All machines.

Restrictions: Must be running on an Alloy NTNX slave.

Registers at call:
AH = 06h

Return Registers:
AH = status

DL = drive number (1=A:,2=B:,etc)
CX = number of clusters to allocate

00h successful
CX = number of clusters still free
10h invalid shared drive request
CL = first and second shared drives
11h invalid cluster count
(must be 01h-FFh)

Conflicts: None known.

INTERRUPT 7Fh - Function 07h
GET LIST OF SHARED DRIVES

Purpose: Determine which disks are shared with other machines on the network.
Available on: All machines.
Restrictions: Alloy NTNX or MW386 must be installed.

Registers at call:
AH = 07h
Return Registers:
ES:DI -> shared drive list (Table 18-4)
Details: MW386 considers all fixed disks to be shared drives; only C and D will be returned as shared.
Conflicts: None known.

Table 18-4. Format of shared drive list:

Offset	Size	Description
00h	BYTE	string length
01h	BYTE	number of shared drives
02h	N BYTEs	one byte per shared drive

INTERRUPT 7Fh - Function 08h, Subfunctions 00h and 01h
GET INTERRUPT VECTORS

Purpose: Determine the entry point the specified interrupt used by the system software.
Available on: All machines.
Restrictions: Must be running on an Alloy NTNX host.

Registers at call:
AH = 08h
CL = function
  00h get original interrupt vector
  01h get Network Executive interrrupt
AL = interrupt number
DX:SI -> DWORD to hold interrupt vector
Return Registers:
AL = status
  00h successful
  01h interrupt vector not used by network executive
  02h invalid subfunction

Details: The network executive uses interrupts 02h, 08h, 09h, 0Fh, 10h, 13h, 16h-19h, 1Ch, 20h, 28h, 2Ah, 2Fh, 5Bh, 67h, 7Fh, ECh, and F0h-FFh.
Conflicts: Halo88 API (chapter 5), ClusterShare access (chapter 27).
See Also: Function 09h Subfunction 03h, DOS INT 21h Function 35h (chapter 8)

INTERRUPT 7Fh - Function 08h, Subfunction 02h
SET MESSAGE DISPLAY TIMEOUT

Purpose: Specify how long messages will be displayed.
Available on: All machines.
Restrictions: Alloy NTNX must be installed.
Registers at call:
AH = 08h
CL = 02h
DX = timeout in seconds
Return Registers:
AL = status
  00h successful
  02h invalid subfunction
Conflicts: None known.

INTERRUPT 7Fh - Function 09h, Subfunctions 00h and 01h
ENABLE/DISABLE MUD FILE CHECKING

Purpose: Specify whether the RTNX.MUD file will be checked.
Available on: All machines.   **Restrictions:** Alloy NTNX must be installed.
Registers at call: **Return Registers:** n/a
AH = 09h
CL = function
   00h enable checking of RTNX.MUD file
   01h disable RTNX.MUD checking
Conflicts: MultiLink Advanced (chapter 17).

INTERRUPT 7Fh - Function 09h, Subfunction 02h
SWITCH HOST TO DEDICATED MODE

Purpose: Specify that the host cease to provide workstation services, and only poll for I/O requests from the slave processors.
Available on: All machines.   **Restrictions:** Alloy NTNX must be installed.
Registers at call: **Return Registers:** n/a
AH = 09h
CL = 02h
Conflicts: MultiLink Advanced (chapter 17).

INTERRUPT 7Fh - Function 09h, Subfunction 03h
GET ALTERNATE INTERRUPT

Purpose: Determine the actual interrupt number used to provide a particular service.
Available on: All machines.   **Restrictions:** Alloy NTNX or MW386 must be installed.

Registers at call: **Return Registers:**
AH = 09h   CL = actual interrupt which handles the specified
CL = 03h   interrupt's calls
AL = default interrupt number (67h,7Fh,etc)
Conflicts: MultiLink Advanced (chapter 17).
See Also: Function 08h

INTERRUPT 7Fh - Function 0Ah, Subfunction 00h
GET SYSTEM FLAGS

Purpose: Determine the addresses of important system flags.
Available on: All machines.   **Restrictions:** Alloy NTNX must be installed.
Registers at call: **Return Registers:**
AH = 0Ah   ES:DI buffer filled
CL = 00h
ES:DI -> buffer for system flags (Table 18-5)
Details: On a slave, only the NX_Busy flag is returned. All three flags are at fixed positions, so this function only needs to be called once. An interrupt handler should only perform DOS or device accesses when all three flags are 00h.

Table 18-5. Format of System Flags:

Offset	Size	Description
00h	DWORD	pointer to NX_Busy flag (nonzero when communicating with users)
04h	DWORD	pointer to device driver busy flag
08h	DWORD	pointer to InTimer flag

INTERRUPT 7Fh - Function 0Bh, Subfunction 02h
SET/RESET GRAPHICS DOS ON SLAVE

Purpose: Specify whether or not graphics will be available on the indicated slave processor.

Available on: All machines.

Restrictions: Must be running on an Alloy NTNX host.

Registers at call:
AH = 0Bh
CL = 02h
AL = slave ID number
CH = DOS to activate
    00h graphics DOS
    01h character DOS

Return Registers:
AL = status
    00h successful
    01h nothing done, proper DOS type already loaded

Conflicts: None known.

INTERRUPT 7Fh - Function 10h, Subfunction 00h
CHANNEL CONTROL - OPEN CHANNEL

Purpose: Prepare a channel for reception.

Available on: All machines.

Restrictions: Alloy NTNX or MW386 must be installed.

Registers at call:
AH = 10h
CL = 00h
AL = channel number
DX:DI -> channel buffer

Return Registers:
AL = status
    00h successful
    01h busy
    02h channel range error (not 00h-3Fh)
    03h invalid subfunction
    0Dh unable to open

Details: This function may not be invoked from within a hardware interrupt handler.

Conflicts: Halo88 API (chapter 5), ClusterShare access (chapter 27).

See Also: Function 10h Subfunctions 01h and 04h, Function 14h Subfunction 02h

INTERRUPT 7Fh - Function 10h, Subfunction 01h
CHANNEL CONTROL - CLOSE CHANNEL

Purpose: Disable reception on the specified channel and clear its buffer pointer.

Available on: All machines.

Restrictions: Alloy NTNX or MW386 must be installed.

Registers at call:
AH = 10h
CL = 01h
AL = channel number

Return Registers:
AL = status
    00h successful
    01h busy
    02h channel range error (not 00h-3Fh)
    03h invalid subfunction
    0Ah channel not open

Details: This function may not be invoked from within a hardware interrupt handler.

Conflicts: Halo88 API (chapter 5), ClusterShare access (chapter 27).

See Also: Function 10h Subfunctions 00h and 05h

INTERRUPT 7Fh - Function 10h, Subfunction 02h
CHANNEL CONTROL - LOCK CHANNEL

Purpose: Temporarily stop reception on the specified channel.

Available on: All machines.

Restrictions: Alloy NTNX or MW386 must be installed.

Registers at call:
AH = 10h
CL = 02h
AL = channel number

Return Registers:
AL = status
    00h successful
    01h busy
    02h channel range error (not 00h-3Fh)
    03h invalid subfunction
    0Ah channel not open
    0Ch channel already locked

Details: This function may not be invoked from within a hardware interrupt handler.
Conflicts: Halo88 API (chapter 5), ClusterShare access (chapter 27).
See Also: Function 10h Subfunctions 03h, 06h, and 08h

INTERRUPT 7Fh - Function 10h, Subfunction 03h
CHANNEL CONTROL - UNLOCK CHANNEL

Purpose: Resume reception on the specified channel.
Available on: All machines.

Restrictions: Alloy NTNX or MW386 must be installed.

Registers at call:
AH = 10h
CL = 03h
AL = channel number

Return Registers:
AL = status (see Function 10h Subfunction 02h)

Details: This function should only be used on channels locked with Function 10h Subfunction 02h, not on those locked by receipt of a datagram. It may not be invoked from within a hardware interrupt handler.
Conflicts: Halo88 API (chapter 5), ClusterShare access (chapter 27).
See Also: Function 10h Subfunctions 02h, 04h, and 09h

INTERRUPT 7Fh - Function 10h, Subfunction 04h
CHANNEL CONTROL - RELEASE BUFFER

Purpose: Indicate that the datagrame in the channel buffer has been processed.
Available on: All machines.

Restrictions: Alloy NTNX or MW386 must be installed.

Registers at call:
AH = 10h
CL = 04h
AL = channel number

Return Registers:
AL = status
    00h successful
    01h busy
    02h channel range error (not 00h-3Fh)
    03h invalid subfunction

Details: This function unlocks buffer after received datagram has been processed. It may not be invoked from within a hardware interrupt handler.
Conflicts: Halo88 API (chapter 5), ClusterShare access (chapter 27).
See Also: Function 10h Subfunction 00h

INTERRUPT 7Fh - Function 10h, Subfunction 05h
CHANNEL CONTROL - CLOSE ALL CHANNELS

Purpose: Clear all pending datagrams and close every open channel.
Available on: All machines.

Restrictions: Alloy NTNX or MW386 must be installed.

Registers at call:
AH = 10h
CL = 05h

Return Registers:
AL = status
    00h successful
    01h busy
    02h channel range error (not 00h-3Fh)
    03h invalid subfunction

Details: This call clears all pending datagrams and clears buffer pointers before closing the channels. It may not be invoked from within a hardware interrupt handler.
Conflicts: Halo88 API (chapter 5), ClusterShare access (chapter 27).
See Also: Function 10h Subfunction 01h

INTERRUPT 7Fh - Function 10h, Subfunction 06h
CHANNEL CONTROL - LOCK ALL OPEN CHANNELS

Purpose: Temporarily stop reception on all open channels.

Available on: All machines.

Restrictions: Alloy NTNX or MW386 must be installed.

Registers at call:
AH = 10h
CL = 06h

Return Registers:
AL = status
  00h successful
  01h busy
  02h channel range error (not 00h-3Fh)
  03h invalid subfunction

Details: This functio may not be invoked from within a hardware interrupt handler.
Conflicts: Halo88 API (chapter 5), ClusterShare access (chapter 27).
See Also: Function 10h Subfunctions 02h and 08h

INTERRUPT 7Fh - Function 10h, Subfunction 07h
CHANNEL CONTROL - UNLOCK ALL LOCKED IDLE CHANNELS

Purpose: Restart reception on all open channels which have no datagrams.

Available on: All machines.

Restrictions: Alloy NTNX or MW386 must be installed.

Registers at call:
AH = 10h
CL = 07h

Return Registers:
AL = status
  00h successful
  01h busy
  02h channel range error (not 00h-3Fh)
  03h invalid subfunction

Details: This call unlocks all locked channels which have no pending datagrams. It may not be invoked from within a hardware interrupt handler.
Conflicts: Halo88 API (chapter 5), ClusterShare access (chapter 27).
See Also: Function 10h Subfunctions 03h and 09h

INTERRUPT 7Fh - Function 10h, Subfunction 08h
CHANNEL CONTROL - LOCK MULTIPLE CHANNELS

Purpose: Temporarily stop reception on the specified set of channels.

Available on: All machines.

Restrictions: Alloy NTNX or MW386 must be installed.

Registers at call:
AH = 10h
CL = 08h
DX = maximum channel number to lock

Return Registers:
AL = status
  00h successful
  01h busy
  02h channel range error (not 00h-3Fh)
  03h invalid subfunction

Details: This call locks channels numbered 00h through the value in DX. It may not be invoked from within a hardware interrupt handler.
Conflicts: Halo88 API (chapter 5), ClusterShare access (chapter 27).
See Also: Function 10h Subfunctions 02h, 06h, and 09h

INTERRUPT 7Fh - Function 10h, Subfunction 09h
CHANNEL CONTROL - UNLOCK MULTIPLE CHANNELS

Purpose: Resume reception on the specified set of channels.

Available on: All machines.

Registers at call:
AH = 10h
CL = 09h
DX = maximum channel number to unlock

Restrictions: Alloy NTNX or MW386 must be installed.

Return Registers:
AL = status
    00h successful
    01h busy
    02h channel range error (not 00h-3Fh)
    03h invalid subfunction

Details: This functio unlocks channels numbered 00h through the value in DX. It may not be invoked from within a hardware interrupt handler.

Conflicts: Halo88 API (chapter 5), ClusterShare access (chapter 27).

See Also: Function 10h Subfunctions 03h, 07h, and 08h

INTERRUPT 7Fh - Function 11h
SEND DATAGRAM

Purpose: Transmit a datagram to the specified user(s).

Available on: All machines.

Registers at call:
AH = 11h
DX:SI -> request block (Table 18-6)

Restrictions: Alloy NTNX or MW386 must be installed.

Return Registers:
AL = status
    00h successful
    01h busy
    02h channel range error (not 00h-3Fh)
    03h invalid subfunction
    0Ah packet too large (or <2 bytes if NTNX)
    0Bh can't send packet to itself
    0Ch invalid number of destinations
    0Dh destination channel number out of range
    0Eh destination user is busy
    0Fh destination user has locked channel
    10h channel not open
    11h no datagram server on destination (NTNX)

Details: If the wildcard channel FFh used, the actual channel number will be filled in.

Conflicts: Halo88 API (chapter 5), ClusterShare access (chapter 27).

See Also: Function 12h

Table 18-6. Format of Request Block:

Offset	Size	Description
00h	DWORD	pointer to packet to send
04h	WORD	packet size in bytes (1-4096)
06h	BYTE	number of destinations for packet (max 1Fh)
07h	31 BYTEs	destination user IDs (FFh = broadcast to all except sender)
26h	31 BYTEs	destination channels (FFh = first available channel)
45h	31 BYTEs	return destination statuses

INTERRUPT 7Fh - Function 12h
ACKNOWLEDGE DATAGRAM

Purpose: Send an acknowledgement of the receipt of a datagram back to its sender.

Available on: All machines.

Registers at call:
AH = 12h
AL = channel number being acknowledged
DI:DX = 32-bit status to return to sender

Restrictions: Alloy NTNX or MW386 must be installed.

Return Registers:
AL = status
    00h successful
    01h busy
    02h channel range error (not 00h-3Fh)
    03h invalid subfunction
    0Ah channel not open
    0Bh no message in channel
    0Ch destination slave busy--retry (NTNX)
    0Dh destination user not active
    0Eh destination slave not active (NTNX)
    0Fh destination disabled datagram service

Details: This call also unlocks the channel, allowing the next datagram to be received.
Conflicts: Halo88 API (chapter 5), ClusterShare access (chapter 27).
See Also: Function 11h, Function 15h Subfunction 04h

INTERRUPT 7Fh - Function 13h, Subfunction 00h
RESET USER DATAGRAMS

Purpose: Clear all pending datagrams and remove all channels which are open in NTNX-compatible mode and belong to the current task, in preparation for the termination of the task.

Available on: All machines.

Registers at call:
AH = 13h
CL = 00h
Conflicts: None known.

Restrictions: Alloy NTNX or MW386 must be installed.

Return Registers: n/a

INTERRUPT 7Fh - Function 14h, Subfunction 00h
SET RECEIVE ISR

Purpose: Specify a handler to be called upon the receipt of a datagram.

Available on: All machines.

Registers at call:
AH = 14h
CL = 00h
DX:DI -> application FAR receive service routine
    (see below)

Restrictions: Alloy NTNX or MW386 must be installed.

Return Registers:
AL = status
    00h successful
    01h busy
    02h channel range error (not 00h-3Fh)
    03h invalid subfunction

Conflicts: Halo88 API (chapter 5), ClusterShare access (chapter 27).
See Also: Function 14h Subfunctions 01h and 03h

    Service routine called with:
        DH = sender ID
        DL = channel with datagram
        interrupts disabled

    Return Registers:
        AL = response code
               00h leave buffer locked, set channel status, and repeat call later
               01h release channel buffer
               02h change buffer pointer to DX:DI
        AH, CX, DX, DI, SI may be destroyed

INTERRUPT 7Fh - Function 14h, Subfunction 01h
SET ACKNOWLEDGE ISR

Purpose: Specify a handler to be called upon the receipt of an acknowledgement.

Available on: All machines.

Restrictions: Alloy NTNX or MW386 must be installed.

Registers at call:
AH = 14h
CL = 01h
DX:DI -> application FAR acknowledge service
    routine (see below)

Return Registers:
AL = status
    00h successful
    01h busy
    02h channel range error (not 00h-3Fh)
    03h invalid subfunction

Conflicts: Halo88 API (chapter 5), ClusterShare access (chapter 27).
See Also: Function 12h, Function 14h Subfunctions 00h and 04h, Function 15 Subfunction 04h

Service routine called with:
DS:SI -> acknowledge structure (see Function 15h Subfunction 04h)

Return Registers:
AL = response code
        00h application busy, network executive should call again later
        01h acknowledge accepted
AH, DX, SI may be destroyed

INTERRUPT 7Fh - Function 14h, Subfunction 02h
SET CHANNEL BUFFER POINTER

Purpose: Specify the data buffer to be used by the indicated channel.

Available on: All machines.

Restrictions: Alloy NTNX or MW386 must be installed.

Registers at call:
AH = 14h
CL = 02h
AL = channel number
DX:DI -> receive buffer

Return Registers:
AL = status
    00h successful
    01h busy
    02h channel range error (not 00h-3Fh)
    03h invalid subfunction

Details: This function may be called from within a receive ISR or when a datagram is pending.
Conflicts: Halo88 API (chapter 5), ClusterShare access (chapter 27).
See Also: Function 10h Subfunction 00h, Function 14h Subfunction 00h

INTERRUPT 7Fh - Function 14h, Subfunction 03h
GET RECEIVE ISR

Purpose: Determine which handler is called upon the receipt of a datagram.

Available on: All machines.

Restrictions: Alloy NTNX or MW386 must be installed.

Registers at call:
AH = 14h
CL = 03h

Return Registers:
DX:DI -> current receive ISR

Conflicts: Halo88 API (chapter 5), ClusterShare access (chapter 27).
See Also: Function 14h Subfunctions 00h and 04h

INTERRUPT 7Fh - Function 14h, Subfunction 04h
GET ACKNOWLEDGE ISR

Purpose: Determine which handler is called upon the receipt of an acknowledgement.

Available on: All machines.

Registers at call:
AH = 14h
CL = 04h
Conflicts: Halo88 API (chapter 5), ClusterShare access (chapter 27).
See Also: Function 14h Subfunctions 01h and 03h

Restrictions: Alloy NTNX or MW386 must be installed.

Return Registers:
DX:DI -> current acknowledge ISR

INTERRUPT 7Fh - Function 14h, Subfunction 05h
GET BUSY POINTER

Purpose: Determine the address of a flag which indicates whether the system software is busy.

Available on: All machines.

Restrictions: Must be running under Alloy MW386 or on an Alloy NTNX host.

Registers at call:
AH = 14h
CL = 05h
DX:DI -> buffer for busy structure (Table 18-7)
Conflicts: None known.

Return Registers:
DX:DI buffer filled

Table 18-7. Format of Busy Structure:

Offset	Size	Description
00h	DWORD	pointer to busy flag byte
04h	WORD	fixed port address (FF00h)

INTERRUPT 7Fh - Function 15h, Subfunction 00h
GET CHANNEL STATUS

Purpose: Determine the status of the specified channel.

Available on: All machines.

Restrictions: Alloy NTNX or MW386 must be installed.

Registers at call:
AH = 15h
CL = 00h
AL = channel number
DX:DI -> status structure (Table 18-8)

Return Registers:
AL = status
  00h successful
  01h busy
  02h channel range error (not 00h-3Fh)
  03h invalid subfunction

Conflicts: Halo88 API (chapter 5), ClusterShare access (chapter 27).
See Also: Function 15h Subfunction 01h

Table 18-8. Format of Status Structure:

Offset	Size	Description
00h	BYTE	channel status
		bit 0: channel open
		1: channel buffer contains received data
		7: channel locked
01h	BYTE	sender ID

INTERRUPT 7Fh - Function 15h, Subfunction 01h
GET NEXT FULL CHANNEL

Purpose: Determine the next channel which requires servicing.

Available on: All machines.

Restrictions: Alloy NTNX or MW386 must be installed.

Registers at call:
AH = 15h
CL = 01h
DX:DI -> full-channel structure (Table 18-9)

Return Registers:
AL = status
  00h successful
  01h busy
  0Ah no datagrams available

Details: MW386 v1.0 returns the lowest channel with a datagram; newer versions and NTNX return the oldest datagram.
Conflicts: Halo88 API (chapter 5), ClusterShare access (chapter 27).
See Also: Function 15h Subfunction 00h

Table 18-9. Format of full-channel structure:

Offset	Size	Description
00h	BYTE	number of channel with oldest datagram
01h	BYTE	sender ID

INTERRUPT 7Fh - Function 15h, Subfunction 02h
GET MAXIMUM NUMBER OF CHANNELS

Purpose: Determine the maximum number of channels available on the network.
Available on: All machines.   **Restrictions:** Alloy NTNX or MW386 must be installed.

Registers at call:
AH = 15h
CL = 02h

Return Registers:
AH = number of channels available (40h for MW386)

Details: The application may always assume at least 32 channels available.
Conflicts: Halo88 API (chapter 5), ClusterShare access (chapter 27).
See Also: Function 15h Subfunction 03h

INTERRUPT 7Fh - Function 15h, Subfunction 03h
GET MAXIMUM PACKET SIZE

Purpose: Determine the maximum size of a packet permitted on the network.
Available on: All machines.   **Restrictions:** Alloy NTNX or MW386 must be installed.

Registers at call:
AH = 15h
CL = 03h
DX:DI -> WORD for return value

Return Registers:
buffer WORD filled with maximum packet size (4096 for MW386)

Conflicts: Halo88 API (chapter 5), ClusterShare access (chapter 27).
See Also: Function 15h Subfunction 02h

INTERRUPT 7Fh - Function 15h, Subfunction 04h
GET AND CLEAR ACKNOWLEDGE STATUS

Purpose: Determine whether a new acknowledgement has been received.
Available on: All machines.   **Restrictions:** Alloy NTNX or MW386 must be installed.

Registers at call:
AH = 15h
CL = 04h
DX:DI -> status structure (Table 18-10)

Return Registers:
AL = status
  00h successful
    DX:DI structure filled
  01h busy
  0Ah no acknowledgement has arrived

Conflicts: Halo88 API (chapter 5), ClusterShare access (chapter 27).
See Also: Function 12h, Function 14h Subfunction 01h

Table 18-10. Format of Status Structure:

Offset	Size	Description
00h	BYTE	sender ID
01h	BYTE	channel number
02h	4 BYTEs	receiver status (see Function 12h)

INTERRUPT 7Fh - Function 16h
DIRECT MEMORY TRANSFER

Purpose: Peform a direct memory-to-memory transfer between two users.

Available on: All machines. **Restrictions:** Alloy NTNX or MW386 must be installed.

Registers at call:
AH = 16h
DX:SI -> transfer structure (Table 18-11)

Return Registers:
AL = status
  00h successful
  0Ah source or destination out of range
  0Bh transfer kernal busy--try again

Details: This call transfers memory contents directly between users; both source and destination user IDs may differ from the caller's ID. No segment wrap is allowed.

Table 18-11. Format of Transfer Structure:

Offset	Size	Description
00h	WORD	bytes to transfer
02h	BYTE	source ID
		FEh = caller
03h	DWORD	source address
07h	BYTE	destination ID
		FFh = all slaves except caller
		FEh = caller
08h	DWORD	destination address

INTERRUPT 7Fh - Function 21h
SEND MESSAGE OR COMMAND TO USER(S)

Purpose: Transmit a message or command to the specified user or to all users.

Available on: All machines. **Restrictions:** Alloy NTNX or MW386 must be installed.

Registers at call:
AH = 21h
AL = sender's user ID
DS:DX -> control packet (Table 18-12)

Return Registers: n/a

Details: Messages or commands are ignored if disabled by the destination user.

Conflicts: Halo88 API (chapter 5), ClusterShare access (chapter 27).

See Also: Function 22h

Table 18-12. Format of Control Packet:

Offset	Size	Description	
00h	BYTE	packet type:	00h message
			01h NTNX command
			02h MW386 command
01h	BYTE	destination user ID or 'A' for all users	
02h	62 BYTEs	ASCIZ message (packet type 00h) BIOS keycodes terminated by NUL byte (type 01h) or word (02h)	

A maximum of 16 keycodes will be processed for NTNX and MW386 commands.

INTERRUPT 7Fh - Function 22h
GET MESSAGE

Purpose: Display pending messages on the user's screen.

Available on: All machines.

Restrictions: Alloy NTNX must be installed.

Registers at call:

AH = 22h

Return Registers:

pending messages displayed on user's screen

Conflicts: Halo88 API (chapter 5), ClusterShare access (chapter 27).

See Also: Function 21h

INTERRUPT 7Fh - Function 24h, Subfunctions 00h and 01h
ATTACH OR RELEASE DRIVE FOR LOW-LEVEL WRITE ACCESS

Purpose: Request control of a floppy drive for writing or a hard disk for low-level writes.

Available on: All machines.

Restrictions: Alloy NTNX or MW386 must be installed.

Registers at call:

AH = 24h

CL = function

   00h attach

   01h release

CH = drive (0=A:,1=B:,etc)

Return Registers:

AX = status

   00h successful

   01h invalid request

   02h already attached

   03h not attached

   04h lock table full

Details: Only drives on the current machine may be attached.

Conflicts: None known.

INTERRUPT 7Fh - Function 24h, Subfunctions 02h and 03h
ATTACH/RELEASE HOST PROCESSOR

Purpose: Temporarily take control of the host processor to perform I/O on the host system.

Available on: All machines.

Restrictions: Alloy NTNX must be installed.

Registers at call:

AH = 24h

CL = function

   02h attach host

   03h release host

Return Registers:

AX = status

   00h successful

   01h invalid request

   02h already attached

   03h not attached

   04h lock table full

Conflicts: None known.

INTERRUPT 7Fh - Function 25h, Subfunctions 00h and 01h
GET NETWORK EXECUTIVE TYPE AND VERSION

Purpose: Determine the type and version of the network executive.

Available on: All machines.

Restrictions: Alloy ANSK, NTNX, or MW386 must be installed.

Registers at call:

AH = 25h

CL = function

   00h get version

   01h get type

Return Registers:

Function 00h:

   AH = version suffix letter

   CH = major version number

   CL = minor version number

Function 01h:

   CL = type

      00h RTNX

      01h ATNX

02h NTNX
03h BTNX
04h MW386
05h ANSK

Conflicts: None known.

INTERRUPT 7Fh - Function 26h, Subfunction 00h
GET NTNX FILE MODE

Purpose: Determine the type of file access checking and disk buffer flushing to perform.

Available on: All machines.

Restrictions: Alloy NTNX or MW386 must be installed.

Registers at call:
AH = 26h
CL = 00h

Return Registers:
AX = file mode bits
    bit 0: directory protection enabled
        1: extended open enabled
        2: flush on every disk write
        3: flush on every disk write in locked interval
        4: flush on reads from simultaneously opened file

Details: MW386 does not support file modes, and always returns AX=001Fh.

Conflicts: Halo88 API (chapter 5), ClusterShare access (chapter 27).

See Also: Function 26h, Function 26h Subfunction 06h

INTERRUPT 7Fh - Function 26h, Subfunctions 01h thru 05h
SET FILE I/O CHECKING LEVEL

Purpose: Specify the types of file access checking and disk buffer flushing to perform.

Available on: All machines.

Restrictions: Alloy NTNX must be installed.

Registers at call:

Return Registers: n/a

AH = 26h
CL = check type to set/reset
    01h directory protection
    02h extended open
    03h flush on every disk write
    04h flush on disk write if any lock set during
        write
    05h flush on all reads if file written
AL = new state (00h off, 01h on)

Conflicts: Halo88 API (chapter 5), ClusterShare access (chapter 27).

See Also: Function 26h Subfunctions 00h and 06h

INTERRUPT 7Fh - Function 26h, Subfunction 06h
CANCEL FLUSH ON WRITE

Purpose: Stop flushing buffers on disk writes.

Available on: All machines.

Restrictions: Alloy NTNX must be installed.

Registers at call:

Return Registers: n/a

AH = 26h
CL = 06h

Details: This function cancels the flags set by Function 26h Subfunctions 03h and 04h

Conflicts: Halo88 API (chapter 5), ClusterShare access (chapter 27).

See Also: Function 26h Subfunction 00h

INTERRUPT 7Fh - Function 30h
GET PORT INFORMATION

Purpose: Determine whether a port is in use and where it is physically located.

Available on: All machines.
Registers at call:
AH = 30h
CX = MW386 port number

Restrictions: Alloy MW386 must be installed.
Return Registers:
AL = FFh if port not found
   else driver unit number
BL = port mode
BH = port type
  02h remote
      DH = owner's machine ID
      DL = owner's user ID

Conflicts: Halo88 API (chapter 5), ClusterShare access (chapter 27).
See Also: INT 17h Function 8Bh

INTERRUPT 7Fh - Function 31h
CHECK PORT ASSIGNMENT

Purpose: *unknown*. This function is not described in the MW386 v2.0 documentation.
Available on: All machines.

Registers at call:
AH = 31h
unknown.
Conflicts: None known.

Restrictions: Alloy MW386 version 1.x must be installed.
Return Registers: *unknown*.

INTERRUPT 7Fh - Function 37h
GET SEMAPHORE TABLE

Purpose: Determine the adderss of the semaphore table.
Available on: All machines.
Registers at call:
AH = 37h
Conflicts: None known.

Restrictions: Alloy NTNX host must be installed.
Return Registers:
ES:AX -> semaphore table

INTERRUPT 7Fh - Function 37h
DUMP STRING TO TERMINAL

Purpose: Display the specified string on the terminal.
Available on: All machines.

Restrictions: Must be running under Alloy ANSK or on an NTNX slave.
Return Registers: n/a

Registers at call:
AH = 37h
DS:DX -> ASCIZ string to display
Details: If the string is empty, a terminal update will be forced.
Conflicts: None known.

INTERRUPT 7Fh - Function 38h
SET NEW TERMINAL DRIVER

Purpose: Specify the terminal driver to use for the current user.
Available on: All machines.

Restrictions: Must be running under MW386 or on an Alloy NTNX slave.
Return Registers: n/a

Registers at call:
AH = 38h
AL = new terminal driver number
  FFh dummy driver
  FEh current driver
  FDh load new driver
DS:SI -> new driver

Conflicts: Halo88 API (chapter 5), ClusterShare access (chapter 27).
See Also: Function 39h

INTERRUPT 7Fh - Function 39h
SET TERMINAL DRIVER FOR ANOTHER USER

Purpose: Specify which terminal driver to install on the next reboot of the indicated user.

Available on: All machines.	**Restrictions:** Alloy MW386 must be installed.
Registers at call:	**Return Registers:**
AH = 39h	CF set if invalid user number
AL = new terminal driver number	CF clear if successful
DL = user number (FFh = caller)	
DH = machine number if DL <> FFh	

Details: This call is only available to supervisors.
Conflicts: Halo88 API (chapter 5), ClusterShare access (chapter 27).
See Also: Function 38h

INTERRUPT 7Fh - Function 3Ah
GET TERMINAL PARAMETERS

Purpose: Obtain the current terminal parameters for the specified user.

Available on: All machines.	**Restrictions:** Alloy MW386 must be installed.
Registers at call:	**Return Registers:**
AH = 3Ah	CF clear if successful
DL = user number (FFh = caller)	AH = terminal driver number
DH = machine number	AL = baud rate (00h = 38400, 01h = 19200, etc)
	CL = parity (00h none, 01h even, 02h odd)
	CH = handshaking (00h none, 01h XON/XOFF,
	02h DTR/DSR, 03h XPC)
	CF set if invalid user number

Conflicts: Halo88 API (chapter 5), ClusterShare access (chapter 27).
See Also: Function 3Bh

INTERRUPT 7Fh - Function 3Bh
SET TERMINAL PARAMETERS

Purpose: Modify the terminal parameters for the specified user.

Available on: All machines.	**Restrictions:** Alloy MW386 must be installed.
Registers at call:	**Return Registers:**
AH = 3Bh	CF set if invalid user number
AL = baud rate (00h = 38400, 01h = 19200, etc)	
CL = parity (00h none, 01h even, 02h odd)	
CH = handshaking (00h none, 01h XON/XOFF, 02h	
DTR/DSR, 03h XPC)	
DL = user number (FFh = caller)	
DH = machine number for user	

Details: This call is only available to supervisors. The new parameters will take effect immediately if the user's terminal has not been started, else Function 3Dh must be called to post the changes.
Conflicts: Halo88 API (chapter 5), ClusterShare access (chapter 27).
See Also: Functions 3Ah and 3Dh

INTERRUPT 7Fh - Function 3Ch
ENABLE/DISABLE AUTOBAUD DETECT

Purpose: Specify whether MW386 should attempt the autobaud detection sequence for the specified user's terminal.

Available on: All machines.	**Restrictions:** Alloy MW386 must be installed.

Registers at call:
AH = 3Ch
AL = new state 00h disabled, 01h enabled
DL = user number (FFh = caller)
DH = machine number for user

Return Registers:
CF set if invalid user number

Details: This function is only available to supervisors.
Conflicts: Halo88 API (chapter 5), ClusterShare access (chapter 27).
See Also: Function 3Dh

INTERRUPT 7Fh - Function 3Dh
POST TERMINAL CONFIGURATION CHANGES

Purpose: Permanently store changes in terminal type or parameters.
Available on: All machines.
Restrictions: Alloy MW386 must be installed.
Registers at call:
Return Registers: n/a
AH = 3Dh
Details: This function should be called whenever a program changes the terminal type or its parameters.
Conflicts: Halo88 API (chapter 5), ClusterShare access (chapter 27).
See Also: Function 3Bh

INTERRUPT 7Fh - Function 41h
LOCK FILE FOR USER

Purpose: Request exclusive read/write access to the specified file.
Available on: All machines.
Restrictions: Alloy NTNX must be installed.
Registers at call:
AH = 41h
AL = user ID
DS:DX -> ASCIZ filename

Return Registers:
AL = status
    00h successful
    01h invalid function
    02h already locked
    03h unable to lock
    04h lock table full

Conflicts: Halo88 API (chapter 5), ClusterShare access (chapter 27).
See Also: Functions 00h and 42h, 386/MultiWare Functoin 41h

INTERRUPT 7Fh - Function 41h
LOCK SEMAPHORE FOR USER

Purpose: Request per-user exclusive access to a resource.
Available on: All machines.
Restrictions: Alloy MW386 must be installed.
Registers at call:
AH = 41h
AL = user ID
DS:DX -> ASCIZ semaphore name

Return Registers:
AL = status
    00h successful
    01h invalid function
    02h semaphore already locked
    03h unable to lock semaphore
    04h semaphore space exhausted

Conflicts: Halo88 API (chapter 5), ClusterShare access (chapter 27).
See Also: Functions 00h and 42h

INTERRUPT 7Fh - Function 42h
UNLOCK FILE FOR USER

Purpose: Permit others access to the specified file.
Available on: All machines.
Restrictions: Alloy NTNX must be installed.
Registers at call:
Return Registers:
AH = 42h
AL = status

AL = user ID

DS:DX -> ASCIZ filename

00h successful

01h invalid function

02h already locked

03h unable to lock

04h lock table full

Conflicts: Halo88 API (chapter 5), ClusterShare access (chapter 27).

See Also: Functions 00h and 41h, 386/MultiWare Function 42h

INTERRUPT 7Fh - Function 42h
UNLOCK SEMAPHORE FOR USER

Purpose: Indicate the the specified resource is once again available for use by the given user.

Available on: All machines.   **Restrictions:** Alloy MW386 must be installed.

Registers at call: **Return Registers:**

AH = 42h   AL = status

AL = user ID   00h successful

DS:DX -> ASCIZ semaphore name   01h invalid function

                                                   03h unable to unlock semaphore

Conflicts: Halo88 API (chapter 5), ClusterShare access (chapter 27).

See Also: Functions 02h and 41h, NTNX Function 42h

INTERRUPT 7Fh - Function 4Eh
SET ERROR MODE

Purpose: Control the display of critical (Abort, Retry, Fail) error messages.

Available on: All machines.   **Restrictions:** Alloy MW386 version 2.0 or higher must be installed.

Registers at call: **Return Registers:**

AH = 4Eh   AL = status

AL = error mode flags   00h successful

    bit 0: display critical disk errors

       1: display sharing errors

DX = 4E58h ("NX")

Conflicts: Halo88 API (chapter 5), ClusterShare access (chapter 27).

See Also: Function 4Fh

INTERRUPT 7Fh - Function 4Fh
SET FCB MODE

Purpose: Specify the sharing mode with which FCBs will be opened.

Available on: All machines.   **Restrictions:** Alloy MW386 version 2.0 or higher must be installed.

Registers at call: **Return Registers:**

AH = 4Fh   AL = status

AL = FCB mode   00h successful

    02h read/write compatibility

    42h read/write shared

DX = 4E58h ("NX")

Conflicts: None known.

INTERRUPT 7Fh - Function 81h
ATTACH DEVICE FOR USER

Purpose: Request exclusive access to the specified device.

Available on: All machines.   **Restrictions:** Alloy NTNX must be installed.

Registers at call: **Return Registers:** n/a

AH = 81h

AL = user ID
DS:DX -> ASCIZ device name
Conflicts: Halo88 API (chapter 5), ClusterShare access (chapter 27).
See Also: Function 82h

INTERRUPT 7Fh - Function 82h
RELEASE DEVICE FOR USER

Purpose: Permit others access to the specified device.
Available on: All machines.   **Restrictions:** Alloy NTNX must be installed.
Registers at call: **Return Registers:** n/a
AH = 82h
AL = user ID
DS:DX -> ASCIZ device name
Conflicts: Halo88 API (chapter 5), ClusterShare access (chapter 27).
See Also: Function 81h

INTERRUPT 7Fh - Function A0h
GET USER NAME

Purpose: Determine the name corresponding to the given user number.
Available on: All machines.   **Restrictions:** Alloy MW386 must be installed.
Registers at call: **Return Registers:**
AH = A0h   CF set if invalid user number
DL = user number (FFh = caller)
DH = machine number for user
ES:DI -> 17-byte buffer for ASCIZ user name
Conflicts: Halo88 API (chapter 5), ClusterShare access (chapter 27).
See Also: Functions 03h and A1h

INTERRUPT 7Fh - Function A1h
GET MACHINE, USER, AND PROCESS NUMBER

Purpose: Determine the machine on which the caller is running, which user is running the calling program, and the program's process number.
Available on: All machines.   **Restrictions:** Alloy MW386 must be installed.
Registers at call: **Return Registers:**
AH = A1h   AL = process number
                                                   DL = user number
                                                   DH = machine number
Conflicts: Halo88 API (chapter 5), ClusterShare access (chapter 27).
See Also: Functions 03h, A0h, and A2h

INTERRUPT 7Fh - Function A2h
GET USER PRIVILEGE LEVEL

Purpose: Determine the specified user's operating privileges.
Available on: All machines.   **Restrictions:** Alloy MW386 must be installed.
Registers at call: **Return Registers:**
AH = A2h   CF clear if successful
DL = user number (FFh = caller)   AL = privilege level
DH = machine number for user   00h supervisor
                                                           01h high
                                                           02h medium
                                                           03h low
                                                   CF set if invalid user number
Conflicts: Halo88 API (chapter 5), ClusterShare access (chapter 27).

See Also: Functions A1h and A3h

INTERRUPT 7Fh - Function A3h
GET USER LOGIN STATE

Purpose: Determine whether the specified user is currently logged onto the indicated machine.

Available on: All machines.

Registers at call:
AH = A3h
DL = user number
DH = machine number for user

Restrictions: Alloy MW386 must be installed.

Return Registers:
CF clear if successful
   AL = login state
      00h never logged in
      01h currently logged out
      03h currently logged in
CF set if invalid user number or user not
      active

Conflicts: Halo88 API (chapter 5), ClusterShare access (chapter 27).

See Also: Function A2h

INTERRUPT 7Fh - Function A4h
VERIFY USER PASSWORD

Purpose: Determine whether the specified string is the password for the user running the calling program.

Available on: All machines.

Registers at call:
AH = A4h
DS:DX -> ASCIZ password (null-padded to 16
   bytes)

Restrictions: Alloy MW386 must be installed.

Return Registers:
AL = 00h if accepted
   else invalid password

Conflicts: None known.

INTERRUPT 7Fh - Function A5h
GET/SET USER STATUS

Purpose: Read or write user status information.

Available on: All machines.

Registers at call:
AH = A5h
DI = machine number and user number
AL = function
   00h get status

Restrictions: Alloy MW386 must be installed.

Return Registers:
CF set if invalid user number

BX = user flags
   bit 5: allow messages
CL = scan code for task manager hotkey
CH = scan code for spooler hotkey
DL = scan code for task swapper hotkey
DH = modifier key status

   01h set status
      BX = user flags (see above)
      CL = scan code for task manager hotkey
      CH = scan code for spooler hotkey
      DL = scan code for task swapper hotkey
      DH = modifier key status

Details: The caller must have supervisor privilege to set another user's status.

Conflicts: None known.

INTERRUPT 7Fh - Function B0h
RELEASE ALL SEMAPHORES FOR USER

Purpose: Free locks on all resources used by the indicated user.

Available on: All machines.

Registers at call:
AH = B0h
AL = user number
DS = code segment
Details: MW386 ignores AL and DS; it releases all semaphores locked using the INT 67h or INT 7Fh locking functions.
Conflicts: Halo88 API (chapter 5), ClusterShare access (chapter 27).
See Also: Functions B1h, B2h, B3h, and B4h

Restrictions: Alloy NTNX or MW386 must be installed.
Return Registers: n/a

INTERRUPT 7Fh - Function B1h
RELEASE NORMAL SEMAPHORES FOR USER

Purpose: Free locks on the resources used by the indicated user.
Available on: All machines.

Restrictions: Alloy NTNX or MW386 must be installed.
Return Registers: n/a

Registers at call:
AH = B1h
AL = (bits 7-5) 000
  (bits 4-0) user ID
Details: MW386 ignores AL; it releases all semaphores locked using the INT 67h or INT 7Fh locking functions.
Conflicts: Halo88 API (chapter 5), ClusterShare access (chapter 27).
See Also: Functions B0h, B2h, B3h, and B4h

INTERRUPT 7Fh - Function B2h
RELEASE MESSAGES FOR USER

Purpose: *Not specified in documentation; presumably discards all pending messages.*
Available on: All machines.
Registers at call:
AH = B2h
AL = (bits 7-5) 001
  (bits 4-0) user ID
Conflicts: Halo88 API (chapter 5), ClusterShare access (chapter 27).
See Also: Functions B0h, B1h, B3h, and B4h

Restrictions: Alloy NTNX must be installed.
Return Registers: n/a

INTERRUPT 7Fh - Function B3h
RELEASE FILES FOR USER

Purpose: *Not specified in documentation; presumably removes all locks requested with Function 41h.*
Available on: All machines.
Registers at call:
AH = B3h
AL = (bits 7-5) 010
  (bits 4-0) user ID
Conflicts: Halo88 API (chapter 5), ClusterShare access (chapter 27).
See Also: Functions B0h, B1h, B2h, and B4h

Restrictions: Alloy NTNX must be installed.
Return Registers: n/a

INTERRUPT 7Fh - Function B4h
RELEASE DEVICES FOR USER

Purpose: *Not specified in documentation; presumably removes all attachments made with Function 81h.*
Available on: All machines.
Registers at call:
AH = B4h
AL = user ID

Restrictions: Alloy NTNX must be installed.
Return Registers: n/a

Conflicts: Halo88 API (chapter 5), ClusterShare access (chapter 27).
See Also: Functions B0h, B1h, B2h, and B3h

INTERRUPT 7Fh - Function C3h
WRITE BYTE TO TERMINAL AUX PORT

Purpose: Output a character directly to the caller's terminal port.
Available on: All machines.   **Restrictions:** Alloy MW386 must be installed.
Registers at call: **Return Registers:**
AH = C3h   CF clear if successful
AL = byte to write   CF set on error
Conflicts: Halo88 API (chapter 5), ClusterShare access (chapter 27).
See Also: Function C6h

INTERRUPT 7Fh - Function C5h
CHANGE CONSOLE MODE

Purpose: Switch into or out of data communications mode.
Available on: All machines.   **Restrictions:** Alloy MW386 must be installed.
Registers at call: **Return Registers:**
AH = C5h   CF clear if successful
AL = new console mode   AL = prior console mode
   00h keyboard indirect   CF set on error (caller is not remote user)
   01h keyboard direct
   02h data handshake enforced
   03h no data handshake
Details: Modes 2 and 3 may be used for input through the console port; no video output should be performed in these modes.
Conflicts: None known.

INTERRUPT 7Fh - Function C6h
WRITE BYTE TO CONSOLE PORT

Purpose: Output a character directly to the console port without any translations by the terminal driver.
Available on: All machines.   **Restrictions:** Alloy MW386 must be installed.
Registers at call: **Return Registers:**
AH = C6h   CF clear if successful
AL = byte to write   CF set on error (caller is not remote user)
Conflicts: Halo88 API (chapter 5), ClusterShare access (chapter 27).
See Also: Functions C3h and C7h

INTERRUPT 7Fh - Function C7h
READ CONSOLE DATA BYTE

Purpose: Get input from the console while in data mode.
Available on: All machines.   **Restrictions:** Alloy MW386 must be installed.
Registers at call: **Return Registers:**
AH = C7h   CF clear if successful
                                                        AL = byte read
                                                    CF set on error (no data available or caller is
                                                        not remote user)
Details: This function may be used to read data after placing the console in mode 2 or 3 (see Function C5h).
Conflicts: Halo88 API (chapter 5), ClusterShare access (chapter 27).
See Also: Functions C5h, C6h, and C8h

INTERRUPT 7Fh - Function C8h
READ CONSOLE DATA INTO BUFFER

Purpose: Input multiple bytes directly from the console port while in data mode.
Available on: All machines.
Registers at call:
AH = C8h
AL = maximum bytes to read
ES:DI -> buffer for console data
Conflicts: Halo88 API (chapter 5), ClusterShare access (chapter 27).
See Also: Function C7h

Restrictions: Alloy MW386 must be installed.
Return Registers:
CF clear if successful
  CX = number of bytes read
CF set on error (caller is not remote user)

INTERRUPT 7Fh - Function CFh
REBOOT USER PROCESSOR

Purpose: Reset the specified user processor.
Available on: All machines.
Registers at call:
AH = CFh
DS:DX -> ASCIZ string containing user number to
  be reset
Conflicts: Halo88 API (chapter 5), ClusterShare access (chapter 27).
See Also: Function D6h

Restrictions: Alloy NTNX must be installed.
Return Registers: n/a

INTERRUPT 7Fh - Function D6h
RESET NETWORK EXECUTIVE

Purpose: Flush all disk buffers and reinitialize the network operation.
Available on: All machines.
Registers at call:
AH = D6h
DS:DX -> reset packet (Table 18-13)
Details: All users will be shut down immediately if this function is successful.
Conflicts: Halo88 API (chapter 5), ClusterShare access (chapter 27).
See Also: Function CFh

Restrictions: Alloy MW386 must be installed.
Return Registers:
never if succesful

Table 18-13. Format of reset packet:

Offset	Size	Description
00h	DWORD	reset code (60606060h)
04h	16 BYTEs	ASCIZ supervisor password padded with nulls

INTERRUPT 7Fh - Function D7h
POST EVENT

Purpose: Post an event for the specified user.
Available on: All machines.
Registers at call:
AH = D7h
AL = user number (if local event)
DX = event number
Conflicts: None known.

Restrictions: Alloy MW386 must be installed.
Return Registers: n/a

INTERRUPT 7Fh - Function D8h
FLUSH DISK BUFFERS

Purpose: Force all disk buffers to be written out immediately.

Available on: All machines.
Registers at call:
AH = D8h
Conflicts: Halo88 API (chapter 5), ClusterShare access (chapter 27).

Restrictions: Alloy MW386 must be installed.
Return Registers:
CF set on error

See Also: DOS INT 21h Function 0Dh (chapter 8), DOS INT 21h Function 5Dh Subfunction 01h (chapter 8), Network Redirector INT 2Fh Function 11h Subfunction 20h (chapter 19)

INTERRUPT 7Fh - Function DBh
GET MW386 INVOCATION DRIVE

Purpose: Determine the drive from which MW386 was started, in order to find system data files.
Available on: All machines.

Restrictions: Alloy MW386 version 2.0 or higher must be installed.

Registers at call:
AH = DBh

Return Registers:
AL = drive from which MW386 was started
     (2=C:,3=D:,etc)

Conflicts: None known.

INTERRUPT 7Fh - Function E0h
CREATE DOS TASK

Purpose: Initiate a new task with the specified amount of memory.
Available on: All machines.
Registers at call:
AH = E0h
AL = memory size (00h=128K, 01h=256K,
     02h=384K, 03h=512K, 04h=640K)
DS:DX -> ASCIZ task name (max 16 bytes)

Restrictions: Alloy MW386 must be installed.
Return Registers:
CF clear if successful
     AL = task create ID
CF set on error

Details: Only foreground DOS tasks can use this function.
Conflicts: Halo88 API (chapter 5), ClusterShare access (chapter 27).
See Also: Functions E1h, E2h, E3h, E6h, and E7h

INTERRUPT 7Fh - Function E1h
GET DOS TASK PID FROM CREATE ID

Purpose: Determine the actual process number of a recently-created task.
Available on: All machines.
Registers at call:
AH = E1h
AL = create ID (from Function E0h)

Restrictions: Alloy MW386 must be installed.
Return Registers:
AL = DOS process number
CL = memory size (00h=128K, 01h=256K, 02h=384K,
     03h=512K, 04h=640K)

Details: This function should not be called immediately after creating a new DOS task, since the new task is being initialized by a concurrent process.
Conflicts: Halo88 API (chapter 5), ClusterShare access (chapter 27).
See Also: Functions E0h and E2h

INTERRUPT 7Fh - Function E2h
SWITCH TO NEW DOS TASK

Purpose: Place the current task in the background and move the specified task to the foreground.
Available on: All machines.
Registers at call:
AH = E2h
AL = DOS process number (from Function E1h)

Restrictions: Alloy MW386 must be installed.
Return Registers:
CF set on error (invalid process number or caller not
     foreground task)

Details: This function may only be called by a foreground task.
Conflicts: Halo88 API (chapter 5), ClusterShare access (chapter 27).
See Also: Functions E0h and E1h

INTERRUPT 7Fh - Function E3h
CHANGE NAME OF DOS TASK

Purpose: Rename a running DOS task.

Available on: All machines.

Registers at call:

AH = E3h

---v1.x

AL = user number

---v2.0+

BH = user number

BL = task number

DS:DX -> ASCIZ task name

Restrictions: Alloy MW386 must be installed.

Return Registers:

CF set on error (invalid process number)

Conflicts: Halo88 API (chapter 5), ClusterShare access (chapter 27).

See Also: Functions E0h, E4h, and E5h

INTERRUPT 7Fh - Function E4h
GET TASK NAME FROM PROCESS NUMBER

Purpose: Determine the name corresponding to the given process number.

Available on: All machines.

Registers at call:

AH = E4h

---v1.x

AL = user number

---v2.0+

BH = user number

BL = task number

ES:DI -> buffer for task name

Restrictions: Alloy MW386 must be installed.

Return Registers:

CF clear if successful

    CL = memory size (00h=128K, 01h=256K,
02h=384K, 03h=512K, 04h=640K)

    DX = task flags bit 7: MSDOS process

    ES:DI buffer filled

CF set on error (invalid process number)

Conflicts: Halo88 API (chapter 5), ClusterShare access (chapter 27).

See Also: Functions E3h and E5h

INTERRUPT 7Fh - Function E5h
GET PROCESS NUMBER FROM TASK NAME

Purpose: Determine the process number corresponding to the given name.

Available on: All machines.

Registers at call:

AH = E5h

DS:DX -> ASCIZ task name

BH = user number

Restrictions: Alloy MW386 must be installed.

Return Registers:

CF clear if successful

    AL = DOS process number

    CL = memory size (00h=128K, 01h=256K,
02h=384K, 03h=512K, 04h=640K)

CF set on error (no match for name)

Conflicts: Halo88 API (chapter 5), ClusterShare access (chapter 27).

See Also: Functions E3h and E4h

INTERRUPT 7Fh - Function E6h
GET NUMBER OF AVAILABLE USER TASKS

Purpose: Determine the total number of DOS tasks for the current user.

Available on: All machines.

Registers at call:

AH = E6h

Restrictions: Alloy MW386 must be installed.

Return Registers:

AX = number of processes available to current user

Conflicts: Halo88 API (chapter 5), ClusterShare access (chapter 27).

See Also: Function E0h

INTERRUPT 7Fh - Function E7h
REMOVE DOS TASK

Purpose: Terminate the specified task.

Available on: All machines.

Registers at call:
AH = E7h
AL = DOS process number

Details: This function can only be called by a foreground task.

Conflicts: Halo88 API (chapter 5), ClusterShare access (chapter 27).

See Also: Function E0h

Restrictions: Alloy MW386 must be installed.

Return Registers:
CF set on error (invalid process number or first process)

INTERRUPT 7Fh - Function E8h
DOS TASK DELAY

Purpose: Suspend the calling task for the specified interval.

Available on: All machines.

Registers at call:
AH = E8h
CX = delay time in milliseconds

Details: A delay of 0 may be used to surrender the current time slice.

Conflicts: Halo88 API (chapter 5), ClusterShare access (chapter 27).

See Also: TopView INT 15h Function 10h Subfunction 00h (chapter 15), DoubleDOS INT 21h Function EEh (chapter 17), MS Windows INT 2Fh Function 16h Subfunction 80h (chapter 14)

Restrictions: Alloy MW386 must be installed.

Return Registers: n/a

INTERRUPT 7Fh - Function F0h
RESTRICT DIRECTORY TO GROUP

Purpose: Permit only a specified group of users to access the given directory.

Available on: All machines.

Registers at call:
AH = F0h
AL = group number
DS:DX -> ASCIZ directory name

Restrictions: Alloy MW386 must be installed.

Return Registers:
CF clear if successful
    AX = status
        0002h directory not found
        0003h directory not found
        0005h directory in use, cannot be restricted
        02xxh restricted to group xxh
CF set on error

Details: The restriction on the directory may be removed by calling this function with group 0, then using Function F1h to assign the directory to group 0.

See Also: Functions F1h, F2h, and F3h

INTERRUPT 7Fh - Function F1h
ASSIGN DIRECTORY TO GROUP

Purpose: Permanently mark the given directory as owned by the specified group.

Available on: All machines.

Registers at call:
AH = F1h
AL = group number
DS:DX -> ASCIZ directory name

Details: This call performs permanent assignment to a group; no immediate action is taken unless the directory has been restricted with Function F0h. It may be used to restrict a nonexistent directory.

Conflicts: Halo88 API (chapter 5), ClusterShare access (chapter 27).

See Also: Function F0h

Restrictions: Alloy MW386 must be installed.

Return Registers: n/a

INTERRUPT 7Fh - Function F2h
READ RESTRICTED DIRECTORY ENTRY

Purpose: Retrieve an entry from the list of restricted directories.

Available on: All machines.

Registers at call:
AH = F2h
CX = entry number
ES:DI -> 64-byte buffer

Restrictions: Alloy MW386 must be installed.

Return Registers:
CF clear if successful
    buffer filled with 63-byte directory info and 1-byte
      group number
CF set on error (invalid entry)

Conflicts: Halo88 API (chapter 5), ClusterShare access (chapter 27).

See Also: Functions F0h and F3h

INTERRUPT 7Fh - Function F3h
READ RESTRICTED DIRECTORY ENTRY FOR GROUP

Purpose: Retrieve an entry from the list of restricted directories belonging to the specified group.

Available on: All machines.

Registers at call:
AH = F3h
AL = group number
CX = entry number
ES:DI -> 64-byte buffer

Restrictions: Alloy MW386 must be installed.

Return Registers:
CF clear if successful
    CX = next entry number
    buffer filled with 63-byte directory info and 1-byte
      group number
CF set on error (no more matching entries)

Details: This call is like Function F2h, but only returns directories belonging to the specified group.

Conflicts: Halo88 API (chapter 5), ClusterShare Access (chapter 27).

See Also: Function F2h

INTERRUPT 7Fh - Function F8h
ASSIGN USER TO GROUP

Purpose: Make the specified user a member of the indicated group.

Available on: All machines.

Registers at call:
AH = F8h
AL = group number
DL = user number
DH = machine number (currently 00h)

Restrictions: Alloy MW386 must be installed.

Return Registers:
CF clear if successful
CF set on error (user already in maximum number of groups)

Details: Each user is allowed eight group assignments.

Conflicts: Halo88 API (chapter 5), ClusterShare Access (chapter 27).

See Also: Functions F9h and FAh

INTERRUPT 7Fh - Function F9h
REMOVE USER FROM GROUP

Purpose: End the specified user's membership in the indicated group.

Available on: All machines.

Registers at call:
AH = F9h
AL = group number
DL = user number
DH = machine number (currently 00h)

Restrictions: Alloy MW386 must be installed.

Return Registers:
CF set if failed

Conflicts: Halo88 API (chapter 5), ClusterShare access (chapter 27).

See Also: Functions F8h and FAh

INTERRUPT 7Fh - Function FAh
GET USER GROUP LIST

Purpose: Determine to which groups the specified user belongs.

Available on: All machines.

Registers at call:

AH = FAh

DL = user number

DH = machine number (currently 00h)

ES:DI -> 16-byte buffer for group list

Conflicts: Halo88 API (chapter 5), ClusterShare access (chapter 27).

See Also: Functions F8h and F9h

Restrictions: Alloy MW386 must be installed.

Return Registers:

CX = number of groups

ES:DI buffer filled with group numbers

INTERRUPT 7Fh - Function FBh
ASSIGN GROUP NAME

Purpose: Specify a name for the indicated group.

Available on: All machines.

Registers at call:

AH = FBh

CL = group number

ES:DI -> ASCIZ group name (max 17 bytes)

Conflicts: Halo88 API (chapter 5), ClusterShare access (chapter 27).

See Also: Function FCh

Restrictions: Alloy MW386 must be installed.

Return Registers: n/a

INTERRUPT 7Fh - Function FCh
GET GROUP NAME

Purpose: Determine the name of the indicated group.

Available on: All machines.

Registers at call:

AH = FCh

CL = group number

ES:DI -> 17-byte buffer for ASCIZ name

Details: If the group has not been named, "(unnamed)" is returned.

Conflicts: Halo88 API (chapter 5), ClusterShare access (chapter 27).

See Also: Function FBh

Restrictions: Alloy MW386 must be installed.

Return Registers:

ES:DI buffer filled

INTERRUPT ECh
Used by Alloy NTNX

Purpose: *unknown.*

Available on: All machines.

Registers at call: *unknown.*

Conflicts: Exact (chapter 36).

Restrictions: Alloy NTNX must be installed.

Return Registers: *unknown.*

Chapter 19

Network Redirector and CD-ROM Extensions

This chapter describes the interrupt functions used by the network redirector (including the IFSFUNC driver supplied as part of DOS versions 4.0x), the CD-ROM extensions to MS-DOS, and certain additional network redirection services. The CD-ROM extensions (MSCDEX) include a network redirector, so the redirector calls apply to the extensions even though the CD-ROM extensions are not explicitly mentioned on each redirector call.

The functions are all included in the Multiplex Interrupt, 2Fh; they are described in sequence by function and subfunction. In the case of the REDIR/REDIRIFS functions, this splits the application since it uses both the lowest and the highest functions covered in this chapter.

INTERRUPT 2Fh - Function 02h, Subfunction 00h
internal - INSTALLATION CHECK

Purpose: Determine whether the PC LAN Program REDIR or REDIRIFS is installed.

Available on: All machines.	**Restrictions:** none.
Registers at call:	**Return Registers:**
AX = 0200h	AL = FFh if installed
Conflicts: None known.	

INTERRUPT 2Fh - Function 02h, Subfunctions 01h through FFh
internal - Unknown Functions

Purpose: *unknown.*
Available on: All machines.

Restrictions: PC LAN Program REDIR or REDIRIFS must be installed.

Registers at call:	**Return Registers:**
AX = 0201h	*nothing*
AX = 0202h	*nothing*
other *unknown.*	
AX = 0203h	*nothing*
AX = 0204h	*nothing*
other unknown.	
AX = 02xxh	*unknown.*
other *unknown.*	

Details: Subfunctions 01h and 02h appear to be paired opposites, as do Subfunctions 03h and 04h. These four subfunctions are called by DOS 3.3+ PRINT.COM.
Conflicts: None known.

INTERRUPT 2Fh - Function 11h, Subfunction 00h
MSCDEX INSTALLATION CHECK

Purpose: Determine whether the Microsoft CD-ROM Extensions are installed.

Available on: All machines.	**Restrictions: none.**
Registers at call:	**Return Registers:**
AX = 1100h	AL = 00h not installed, OK to install
STACK: WORD DADAh	STACK unchanged

= 01h not installed, not OK to install
    STACK unchanged
= FFh installed
    STACK: WORD ADADh

Conflicts: Network Redirector.

INTERRUPT 2Fh - Function 11h, Subfunction 00h
NETWORK REDIRECTOR INSTALLATION CHECK

Purpose: Determine whether a Network Redirector is installed.
Available on: All machines.
Registers at call:
AX = 1100h

Restrictions: none.
Return Registers:
AL = 00h not installed, OK to install
= 01h not installed, not OK to install
= FFh installed

Details: This function is called by the DOS 3.1+ kernel. In DOS 4.0x only, the 11xxh calls are all in IFSFUNC.EXE rather than in the PC LAN Program redirector.
Conflicts: MSCDEX (MS CD-ROM Extensions).

INTERRUPT 2Fh - Function 11h, Subfunction 01h
REMOVE REMOTE DIRECTORY

Purpose: Remove the specified directory on the network or installable file system drive.
Available on: DOS 3.1 or higher.

Restrictions: Network redirector or IFS driver must be installed.

Registers at call:
AX = 1101h
SS = DOS DS
SDA first filename pointer -> fully-qualified
    directory name
SDA CDS pointer -> current directory structure for
    drive with directory

Return Registers:
CF set on error
    AX = DOS error code (see INT 21h Function 59h,
       chapter 8)
CF clear if successful

Details: This function is called by the DOS 3.1+ kernel.
Conflicts: None known.
See Also: Function 11h Subfunctions 03h and 05h, INT 21h Functions 3Ah and 60h (chapter 8)

INTERRUPT 2Fh - Function 11h, Subfunction 02h
REMOVE REMOTE DIRECTORY

Purpose: Remove the specified directory on the network or installable file system drive.
Available on: DOS 4.x only.
Registers at call:
AX = 1102h
SS = DOS DS
SDA first filename pointer -> fully- qualified
    directory name
SDA CDS pointer -> current directory structure for
    drive with directory

Restrictions: IFSFUNC.EXE must be installed.
Return Registers:
CF set on error
    AX = DOS error code (see INT 21h Function 59h,
       chapter 8)
CF clear if successful

Details: This call appears to be identical to Function 11h Subfunction 01h.
Conflicts: None known.
See Also: Function 11h Subfunction 01h

INTERRUPT 2Fh - Function 11h, Subfunction 03h
MAKE REMOTE DIRECTORY

Purpose: Create the specified directory on the network or installable file system drive if it does not already exist.

Available on: DOS 3.1 or higher.

Registers at call:
AX = 1103h
SS = DOS DS
SDA first filename pointer -> fully-qualified
    directory name
SDA CDS pointer -> current directory structure for
    drive with directory
Details: This function is called by the DOS 3.1+ kernel.
Conflicts: None known.
See Also: Function 11h Subfunctions 01h and 05h, INT 21h Functions 39h and 60h (chapter 8)

Restrictions: Network redirector or IFS driver must be
    installed.
Return Registers:
CF set on error
    AX = DOS error code (see INT 21h Function 59h,
    chapter 8)
CF clear if successful

INTERRUPT 2Fh - Function 11h, Subfunction 04h
MAKE REMOTE DIRECTORY

Purpose: Create the specified directory on the network or installable file system drive if it does not already exist.
Available on: DOS 4.x only.
Registers at call:
AX = 1104h
SS = DOS DS
SDA first filename pointer -> fully- qualified
    directory name
SDA CDS pointer -> current directory structure for
    drive with directory
Details: This call appears to be identical to Function 11h Subfunction 03h.
Conflicts: None known.
See Also: Function 11h Subfunction 03h

Restrictions: IFSFUNC.EXE must be installed.
Return Registers:
CF set on error
    AX = DOS error code (see INT 21h Function 59h,
    chapter 8)
CF clear if successful

INTERRUPT 2Fh - Function 11h, Subfunction 05h
CHDIR

Purpose: Specify the current directory on the indicated network or installable file system drive.
Available on: DOS 3.1 or higher.

Restrictions: Network redirector or IFS driver must be
    installed.

Registers at call:
AX = 1105h
SS = DOS DS
SDA first filename pointer -> fully-qualified
    directory name
SDA CDS pointer -> current directory structure for
    drive with directory

Return Registers:
CF set on error
    AX = DOS error code (see INT 21h Function 59h,
    chapter 8)
CF clear if successful
    CDS updated with new path

Details: This function is called by the DOS 3.1+ kernel. The directory string in the CDS should not have a terminating backslash unless the current directory is the root.
Conflicts: None known.
See Also: Function 11h Subfunction 01h, Function 11h Subfunction 03h, INT 21h Functions 3Bh and 60h (chapter 8)

INTERRUPT 2Fh - Function 11h, Subfunction 06h
CLOSE REMOTE FILE

Purpose: Close the specifed file on the network or installable file system drive.
Available on: DOS 3.1 or higher.

Restrictions: Network redirector or IFS driver must be
    installed.

Registers at call:
AX = 1106h

Return Registers:
CF set on error

ES:DI -> SFT
SFT DPB field -> DPB of drive containing file

AX = DOS error code (see INT 21h Function 59h, chapter 8)
CF clear if successful
SFT updated (except handle count, which DOS manages itself)

Details: This function is called by the DOS 3.1+ kernel.
Conflicts: None known.
See Also: Function 12h Subfunctions 01h and 27h, DOS INT 21h Function 3Eh (chapter 8)

INTERRUPT 2Fh - Function 11h, Subfunction 07h
COMMIT REMOTE FILE

Purpose: Force all buffered data for the specified file to be written to the disk and the directory entry to be updated.
Available on: DOS 3.1 or higher.

Restrictions: Network redirector or IFS driver must be installed.

Registers at call:
AX = 1107h
ES:DI -> SFT
SFT DPB field -> DPB of drive containing file

Return Registers:
CF set on error
AX = DOS error code (see INT 21h Function 59h, chapter 8)
CF clear if successful
all buffers for file flushed
directory entry updated

Details: This function is called by the DOS 3.1+ kernel.
Conflicts: None known.
See Also: INT 21h Function 68h (chapter 8), INT 21h Function 5Dh Subfunction 01h (chapter 8)

INTERRUPT 2Fh - Function 11h, Subfunction 08h
READ FROM REMOTE FILE

Purpose: Retrieve data from the specified file on the network or installable file system drive.
Available on: DOS 3.1 or higher.

Restrictions: Network redirector or IFS driver must be installed.

Registers at call:
AX = 1108h
ES:DI -> SFT
SFT DPB field -> DPB of drive containing file
CX = number of bytes
SS = DOS DS
SDA DTA field -> user buffer

Return Registers:
CF set on error
AX = DOS error code (see INT 21h Function 59h, chapter 8)
CF clear if successful
CX = number of bytes read (0000h = end of file)
SFT updated

Details: This function is called by the DOS 3.1+ kernel.
Conflicts: None known.
See Also: Function 11h Subfunction 09h, Function 12h Subfunction 29h, INT 21h Function 3Fh (chapter 8), INT 21h Function 5Dh Subfunction 06h (chapter 8)

INTERRUPT 2Fh - Function 11h, Subfunction 09h
WRITE TO REMOTE FILE

Purpose: Write data to the specified file on the network or installable file system drive.
Available on: DOS 3.1 or higher.

Restrictions: Network redirector or IFS driver must be installed.

Registers at call:
AX = 1109h
ES:DI -> SFT
SFT DPB field -> DPB of drive containing file

Return Registers:
CF set on error
AX = DOS error code (see INT 21h Function 59h, chapter 8)

CX = number of bytes
SS = DOS DS
SDA DTA field -> user buffer

CF clear if successful
CX = number of bytes written
SFT updated

Details: This function is called by the DOS 3.1+ kernel.
Conflicts: None known.
See Also: Function 11h Subfunction 07h, Function 11h Subfunction 08h, INT 21h Function 40h (chapter 8), INT 21h Function 5Dh Subfunction 06h (chapter 8)

INTERRUPT 2Fh - Function 11h, Subfunction 0Ah
LOCK REGION OF FILE

Purpose: Temporarily prohibit others from accessing the specified portion of the file.
Available on: DOS 3.1 or higher.   **Restrictions:** Network redirector or IFS driver must be installed.

Registers at call: **Return Registers:**
AX = 110Ah   CF set on error
BX = file handle   AL = DOS error code (see INT 21h Function 59h,
CX:DX = starting offset   chapter 8)
SI = high word of size   STACK unchanged
STACK: WORD low word of size
ES:DI -> SFT
SFT DPB field -> DPB of drive containing file
SS = DOS DS

Details: This function is called by the DOS 3.1+ kernel; the redirector is expected to resolve lock conflicts. DOS 4.0 and higher also call this function to unlock the region, and do not use subfunction 0Bh.
Conflicts: None known.
See Also: Function 11h Subfunction 0Bh, INT 21h Function 5Ch (chapter 8)

INTERRUPT 2Fh - Function 11h, Subfunction 0Bh
UNLOCK REGION OF FILE

Purpose: Permit others to access the specified portion of the indicated file.
Available on: DOS 3.1 through 3.31 only.   **Restrictions:** Network redirector or IFS driver must be installed.

Registers at call: **Return Registers:**
AX = 110Bh   CF set on error
BX = file handle   AL = DOS error code (see INT 21h Function 59h,
CX:DX = starting offset   chapter 8)
SI = high word of size   STACK unchanged
STACK: WORD low word of size
ES:DI -> SFT for file
SFT DPB field -> DPB of drive containing file

Details: This function is called by the DOS 3.x+ kernel. DOS 4.0 and higher call Function 0Ah instead to unlock the file.
Conflicts: None known.
See Also: Function 11h Subfunction 0Ah, INT 21h Function 5Ch (chapter 8)

INTERRUPT 2Fh - Function 11h, Subfunction 0Ch
GET DISK SPACE

Purpose: Determine the allocations units of the network or installable file system drive and how many clusters are free.
Available on: DOS 3.1 or higher.   **Restrictions:** Network redirector or IFS driver must be installed.

Registers at call: **Return Registers:**
AX = 110Ch   AL = sectors per cluster

ES:DI -> current directory structure for desired
    drive

AH = media ID byte
BX = total clusters
CX = bytes per sector
DX = number of available clusters

Details: This function is called by the DOS 3.1+ kernel.
Conflicts: None known.
See Also: INT 21h Function 36h (chapter 8)

INTERRUPT 2Fh - Function 11h, Subfunction 0Dh
Unknown Function

Purpose: unknown.
Available on: DOS 4.x only.
Registers at call:
AX = 110Dh
SDA first filename pointer -> name of file
other *unknown*.

Restrictions: IFSFUNC.EXE must be installed.
Return Registers: *unknown*.

Details: This call appears to be similar to Function 11h Subfunction 0Fh.
Conflicts: None known.
See Also: Function 11h Subfunction 0Fh

INTERRUPT 2Fh - Function 11h, Subfunction 0Eh
SET REMOTE FILE'S ATTRIBUTES

Purpose: Specify new attribute bits for the given file on the network or installable file system drive.
Available on: DOS 3.1 or higher.

Restrictions: Network redirector or IFS driver must be
    installed.

Registers at call:
AX = 110Eh
SS = DOS DS
SDA first filename pointer -> fully-qualified name
    of file
SDA CDS pointer -> current directory structure for
    drive with file
STACK: WORD new file attributes

Return Registers:
CF set on error
    AX = DOS error code (see INT 21h Function 59h,
      chapter 8)
CF clear if successful
STACK unchanged

Details: This function is called by the DOS 3.1+ kernel.
Conflicts: None known.
See Also: Function 11h Subfunction 0Fh, INT 21h Function 43h Subfunction 01h (chapter 8), INT 21h Function 60h
(chapter 8)

INTERRUPT 2Fh - Function 11h, Subfunction 0Fh
GET REMOTE FILE'S ATTRIBUTES AND SIZE

Purpose: Determine the current attribute bits for the given file on the network or installable file system drive.
Available on: DOS 3.1 or higher.

Restrictions: Network redirector or IFS driver must be
    installed.

Registers at call:
AX = 110Fh
SS = DOS DS

SDA first filename pointer -> fully-qualified name
    of file
SDA CDS pointer -> current directory structure for
    drive with file

Return Registers:
CF set on error
    AX = DOS error code (see INT 21h Function 59h,
      chapter 8)
CF clear if successful
    AX = file attributes
    BX:DI = file size

Details: This function is called by the DOS 3.1+ kernel.
Conflicts: None known.

See Also: Function 11h Subfunction 0Eh, INT 21h Function 43h Subfunction 00h (chapter 8), INT 21h Function 60h (chapter 8)

INTERRUPT 2Fh - Function 11h, Subfunction 10h
Unknown Function

Purpose: *unknown.*
Available on: DOS 4.x only.
Registers at call:
AX = 1110h
SDA first filename pointer -> name of file
other *unknown.*
Details: This call appears to be similar to Function 11h Subfunction 0Eh.
Conflicts: None known.
See Also: Function 11h Subfunction 0Eh

Restrictions: IFSFUNC.EXE must be installed.
Return Registers: *unknown.*

INTERRUPT 2Fh - Function 11h, Subfunction 11h
RENAME REMOTE FILE

Purpose: Change the name of the specified file to the given new name.
Available on: DOS 3.1 or higher.

Registers at call:
AX = 1111h
SS = DS = DOS DS
SDA first filename pointer = offset of fully-
    qualified old name
SDA second filename pointer = offset of fully-
    qualified new name
SDA CDS pointer -> current directory structure for
    drive with file
Details: This function is called by the DOS 3.1+ kernel.
Conflicts: None known.
See Also: INT 21h Functions 56h and 60h (chapter 8)

Restrictions: Network redirector or IFS driver must be
    installed.
Return Registers:
CF set on error
    AX = DOS error code (see INT 21h Function 59h,
        chapter 8)
CF clear if successful

INTERRUPT 2Fh - Function 11h, Subfunction 12h
Unknown Function

Purpose: *unknown.*
Available on: DOS 4.x only.
Registers at call:
AX = 1112h
SS = DS = DOS DS
SDA first filename pointer -> name of file
other *unknown.*
Conflicts: None known.
See Also: Function 11h Subfunction 11h (chapter 19)

Restrictions: IFSFUNC.EXE must be installed.
Return Registers: *unknown.*

INTERRUPT 2Fh - Function 11h, Subfunction 13h
DELETE REMOTE FILE

Purpose: Erase the indicated file on the network or installable file system drive.
Available on: DOS 3.1 or higher.

Registers at call:
AX = 1113h

Restrictions: Network redirector or IFS driver must be
    installed.
Return Registers:
CF set on error

SS = DS = DOS DS
SDA first filename pointer -> fully-qualified
   filename in DOS DS
SDA CDS pointer -> current directory structure for
   drive with file

AX = DOS error code (see INT 21h Function 59h,
   chapter 8)
CF clear if successful

Details: This function is called by the DOS 3.1+ kernel. The filespec may contain wildcards.
Conflicts: None known.
See Also: INT 21h Functions 41h and 60h (chapter 8)

INTERRUPT 2Fh - Function 11h, Subfunction 14h
Unknown Function

Purpose: *unknown.*
Available on: DOS 4.x only.
Registers at call:
AX = 1114h
SDA first filename pointer -> name of file
other *unknown.*

Restrictions: IFSFUNC.EXE must be installed.
Return Registers: *unknown.*

Conflicts: None known.
See Also: Function 11h Subfunction 13h (chapter 19)

INTERRUPT 2Fh - Function 11h, Subfunction 15h
Unknown Function

Purpose: *unknown.*
Available on: DOS 4.x only.
Registers at call:
AX = 1115h
SS = DOS DS
ES:DI -> *SFT*
other *unknown.*

Restrictions: IFSFUNC.EXE must be installed.
Return Registers: *unknown.*

Conflicts: None known.
See Also: Function 11h Subfunction 2Eh

INTERRUPT 2Fh - Function 11h, Subfunction 16h
OPEN EXISTING REMOTE FILE

Purpose: Prepare for operations on the specified file on the network or installable file system drive.
Available on: DOS 3.1 or higher.

Restrictions: Network redirector or IFS driver must be
   installed.

Registers at call:
AX = 1116h
ES:DI -> uninitialized SFT
SS = DOS DS
SDA first filename pointer -> fully-qualified name
   of file to open
STACK: WORD file open mode (see INT 21h
   Function 3Dh, chapter 8)

Return Registers:
CF set on error
   AX = DOS error code (see INT 21h Function 59h,
      chapter 8)
CF clear if successful
   SFT filled (except handle count, which DOS
      manages itself)
STACK unchanged

Details: This function is called by the DOS 3.1+ kernel.
Conflicts: None known.
See Also: Function 11h Subfunctions 06h, 17h, 18h, and 2Eh, INT 21h Functions 3Dh and 60h (chapter 8)

INTERRUPT 2Fh - Function 11h, Subfunction 17h
CREATE/TRUNCATE REMOTE FILE

Purpose: Create the specified file if it does not already exist, or truncate it to zero bytes if it does exist.

Available on: DOS 3.1 or higher.

Registers at call:
AX = 1117h
ES:DI -> uninitialized SFT
SS = DOS DS
SDA first filename pointer -> fully-qualified name
    of file to open
SDA CDS pointer -> current directory structure for
    drive with file
creation mode
      STACK at call: WORD file
        low byte = file attributes
        high byte = 00h normal create, 01h create
          new file

Restrictions: Network redirector or IFS driver must be
          installed.
Return Registers:
CF set on error
    AX = DOS error code (see INT 21h Function 59h,
      chapter 8)
CF clear if successful
    SFT filled (except handle count, which DOS
      manages itself)
STACK unchanged

Details: This function is called by the DOS 3.1+ kernel.
Conflicts: None known.
See Also: Function 11h Subfunctions 06h, 16h, 18h, and 2Eh, INT 21h Functions 3Ch and 60h (chapter 8)

INTERRUPT 2Fh - Function 11h, Subfunction 18h
CREATE/TRUNCATE FILE WITHOUT CDS

Purpose: Create or truncate to zero bytes the specified file on a network or installable file system drive which does not have a current directory structure.
Available on: DOS 3.1 or higher.

Registers at call:
AX = 1118h
ES:DI -> uninitialized SFT
SS = DOS DS
SDA first filename pointer -> fully-qualified name
    of file

Restrictions: Network redirector or IFS driver must be
          installed.
Return Registers:
unknown.
STACK unchanged

Details: This function is called by the DOS 3.1+ kernel when creating a file on a drive for which the SDA CDS pointer has offset FFFFh.
      STACK at call: WORD file creation mode
              low byte = file attributes
              high byte = 00h normal create, 01h create new file
Conflicts: None known.
See Also: Function 11h Subfunctions 06h, 16h, 17h, and 2Eh, INT 21h Function 60h (chapter 8)

INTERRUPT 2Fh - Function 11h, Subfunction 19h
FINDFIRST WITHOUT CDS

Purpose: Find the first file matching the given specification on a network or installable file system drive which does not have a current directory structure.
Available on: DOS 3.1 or higher.

Registers at call:
AX = 1119h
SS = DS = DOS DS
[DTA] = uninitialized 21-byte findfirst search data
    (see INT 21 Function 4Eh, chapter 8)
SDA first filename pointer -> fully-qualified search
    template
SDA search attribute = attribute mask for search

Restrictions: Network redirector or IFS driver must be
          installed.
Return Registers:
CF set on error
    AX = DOS error code (see INT 21h Function 59h,
      chapter 8)
CF clear if successful
    [DTA] = updated findfirst search data (bit 7 of first
      byte must be set)
    [DTA+15h] = standard directory entry for file

Details: This function is called by the DOS 3.1+ kernel. DOS 4.0 IFSFUNC returns CF set, AX=0003h.
Conflicts: None known.
See Also: Function 11h Subfunction 1Bh

INTERRUPT 2Fh - Function 11h, Subfunction 1Ah
Unknown Function

Purpose: *unknown*.
Available on: DOS 4.x only.
Registers at call:
AX = 111Ah
other *unknown*.
Conflicts: None known.

Restrictions: IFSFUNC.EXE must be installed.
Return Registers:
CF set
    AX = error code (03h for DOS 4.01 IFSFUNC)

INTERRUPT 2Fh - Function 11h, Subfunction 1Bh
FINDFIRST

Purpose: Find the first file matching the indicated specification in the specified directory on the network or installable file system drive.
Available on: DOS 3.1 or higher.

Restrictions: Network redirector or IFS driver must be installed.

Registers at call:
AX = 111Bh
SS = DS = DOS DS
[DTA] = uninitialized 21-byte findfirst search data
    (see INT 21 Function 4Eh, chapter 8)
SDA first filename pointer -> fully-qualified search template
SDA CDS pointer -> current directory structure for drive with file
SDA search attribute = attribute mask for search
Details: This function is called by the DOS 3.1+ kernel.
Conflicts: None known.
See Also: Function 11h Subfunctions 19h and 1Ch, INT 21h Functions 4Eh and 60h (chapter 8)

Return Registers:
CF set on error
    AX = DOS error code (see INT 21h Function 59h, chapter 8)
CF clear if successful
    [DTA] = updated findfirst search data (bit 7 of first byte must be set)
    [DTA+15h] = standard directory entry for file

INTERRUPT 2Fh - Function 11h, Subfunction 1Ch
FINDNEXT

Purpose: Find subsequent files matching a file specification on the network or installable file system drive.
Available on: DOS 3.1 or higher.

Restrictions: Network redirector or IFS driver must be installed.

Registers at call:
AX = 111Ch
SS = DS = DOS DS
[DTA] = 21-byte findfirst search data (see INT 21h Function 4Eh, chapter 8)

Return Registers:
CF set on error
    AX = DOS error code (see INT 21h Function 59h, chapter 8)
CF clear if successful
    [DTA] = updated findfirst search data (bit 7 of first byte must be set)
    [DTA+15h] = standard directory entry for file

Details: This function is called by the DOS 3.1+ kernel.
Conflicts: None known.
See Also: Function 11h Subfunction 1Bh, INT 21h Function 4Fh (chapter 8).

INTERRUPT 2Fh - Function 11h, Subfunction 1Dh
CLOSE ALL REMOTE FILES FOR PROCESS

Purpose: Close all files owned by the calling process which were opened using FCBs.

Available on: DOS 3.1 or higher.

Registers at call:
AX = 111Dh
DS *unknown.*
SS = DOS DS
Details: This function is called by the DOS 3.1+ kernel.
Conflicts: None known.

Restrictions: Network redirector or IFS driver must be installed.
Return Registers: *unknown.*

INTERRUPT 2Fh - Function 11h, Subfunction 1Eh
DO REDIRECTION

Purpose: Control the redirector.
Available on: DOS 3.1 or higher.

Restrictions: Network redirector or IFS driver must be installed.

Registers at call:
AX = 111Eh
SS = DOS DS
WORD on top of STACK is function to execute:

Return Registers:
CF set on error
    AX = error code (see INT 21h Function 59h, chapter 8)
STACK unchanged
BH = state (00h off, 01h on)

    5F00h get redirection mode
        BL = type (03h printer, 04h disk)
    5F01h set redirection mode
        BL = type (03h printer, 04h disk)
        BH = state (00h off, 01h on)
    5F02h get redirection list entry
        BX = redirection list index
        DS:SI -> 16-byte local device name buffer
        ES:DI -> 128-byte network name buffer
    5F03h redirect device
        BL = device type (see INT 21h Function
            5Fh Subfunction 03h, chapter 8)
        CX = stored parameter value
        DS:SI -> ASCIZ source device name
        ES:DI -> destination ASCIZ network path +
            ASCIZ passwd
    5F04h cancel redirection
        DS:SI -> ASCIZ device name or network
            path
    5F05h get redirection list extended entry
        BX = redirection list index
        DS:SI -> buffer for ASCIZ source device
            name
        ES:DI -> buffer for destination ASCIZ
            network path
    5F06h *apparently similar to 5F05h*

BH = status flag
BL = type (03h printer, 04h disk)
CX = stored parameter value
BP = NETBIOS local session number

Details: This function is called by the DOS 3.1+ kernel.
Conflicts: None known.
See Also: INT 21h Function 5Fh Subfunctions 00h through 06h (chapter 8)

INTERRUPT 2Fh - Function 11h, Subfunction 1Fh
PRINTER SETUP

Purpose: Get or set the printer mode or the printer setup string.

Available on: DOS 3.1 or higher.

Registers at call:
AX = 111Fh
STACK: WORD function
   5E02h set printer setup
   5E03h get printer setup
   5E04h set printer mode
   5E05h get printer mode

Details: This function is called by the DOS 3.1+ kernel.
Conflicts: None known.
See Also: INT 21h Function 5Eh Subfunctions 02h through 05h (chapter 8)

Restrictions: Network redirector or IFS driver must be installed.

Return Registers:
CF set on error
   AX = error code (see INT 21h Function 59h, chapter 8)
STACK unchanged

INTERRUPT 2Fh - Function 11h, Subfunction 20h
FLUSH ALL DISK BUFFERS

Purpose: Force all pending writes to be performed immediately.
Available on: DOS 3.1 or higher.

Registers at call:
AX = 1120h
DS = DOS DS
unknown.

Details: This function is called by the DOS 3.1+ kernel; it uses the CDS array pointer and LASTDRIVE= entries in the DOS list of lists.
Conflicts: None known.
See Also: INT 21h Function 0Dh (chapter 8), INT 21h Function 5Dh Subfunction 01h (chapter 8)

Restrictions: Network redirector or IFS driver must be installed.

Return Registers:
CF clear (successful)

INTERRUPT 2Fh - Function 11h, Subfunction 21h
SEEK FROM END OF REMOTE FILE

Purpose: Set the file pointer to the specified offset from the current end of the given file.
Available on: DOS 3.1 or higher.

Registers at call:
AX = 1121h
CX:DX = offset (in bytes) from end
ES:DI -> SFT
SFT DPB field -> DPB of drive with file
SS = DOS DS

Details: This function is called by the DOS 3.1+ kernel.
Conflicts: None known.
See Also: Function 12h Subfunction 28h, INT 21h Function 42h (chapter 8)

Restrictions: Network redirector or IFS driver must be installed.

Return Registers:
CF set on error
   AL = DOS error code (see INT 21h Function 59h, chapter 8)
CF clear if successful
   DX:AX = new file position

INTERRUPT 2Fh - Function 11h, Subfunction 22h
PROCESS TERMINATION HOOK

Purpose: Perform any necessary cleanup when a program exits.
Available on: DOS 3.1 or higher.

Registers at call:
AX = 1122h
SS = DOS DS
unknown.

Details: This function is called by the DOS 3.1+ kernel.
Conflicts: None known.

Restrictions: Network redirector or IFS driver must be installed.

Return Registers: *unknown.*

INTERRUPT 2Fh - Function 11h, Subfunction 23h
QUALIFY REMOTE FILENAME

Purpose: Determine the canonical name for the specified file.

Available on: DOS 3.1 or higher.

Restrictions: Network redirector or IFS driver must be installed.

Registers at call:
AX = 1123h
DS:SI -> ASCIZ filename to canonicalize
ES:DI -> 128-byte buffer for qualified name

Return Registers:
CF set if not resolved

Details: This function is called first by the DOS 3.1+ kernel when DOS attempts to resolve a filename (unless inside a Function 5Dh Subfunction 00h server call); if this fails, DOS resolves the name locally.

Conflicts: None known.

See Also: Function 12h Subfunction 21h, INT 21h Function 60h (chapter 8)

INTERRUPT 2Fh - Function 11h, Subfunction 24h
CANCEL PRINT ECHOING

Purpose: *Tell the redirector to disable print echoing.*

Available on: DOS 3.1 or higher.

Restrictions: Network redirector or IFS driver must be installed.

Registers at call:
AX = 1124h
ES:DI -> SFT
SS = DOS DS
unknown.

Return Registers:
CX = *unknown.*

Details: This function is called by the DOS 3.1+ kernel if Subfunction 26h returns with CF set.

Conflicts: None known.

See Also: Function 11h Subfunction 26h

INTERRUPT 2Fh - Function 11h, Subfunction 25h
REDIRECTED PRINTER MODE

Purpose: Specify or determine whether redirected printer output is combined into a single job, or start a new job immediately.

Available on: DOS 3.1 or higher.

Restrictions: Network redirector or IFS driver must be installed.

Registers at call:
AX = 1125h

Return Registers:
CF set on error
    AX = error code
        (see INT 21h Function 59h, chapter 8)

STACK: WORD subfunction
    5D07h get print stream state
    5D08h set print stream state
        DL = new state
    5D09h finish print job

STACK unchanged
DL = current state

Details: This function is called by the DOS 3.1+ kernel.

Conflicts: None known.

See Also: DOS INT 21h Function 5Dh Subfunctions 07h, 08h, and 09h

INTERRUPT 2Fh - Function 11h, Subfunction 26h
TOGGLE PRINT ECHOING

Purpose: Indicate to the redirector that the printer echo of console output has been toggled.

Available on: DOS 3.1 or higher.

Restrictions: Network redirector or IFS driver must be installed.

Registers at call:
AX = 1126h
unknown.
Details: This function is called by the DOS 3.1+ kernel when print echoing (^P, ^PrtSc) changes state.
Conflicts: None known.
See Also: Function 11h Subfunction 24h

Return Registers:
CF set on error

INTERRUPT 2Fh - Function 11h, Subfunctions 27h through 29h
UNUSED

Purpose: None.
Available on: DOS 4.x only.
Registers at call:
AX = 1127h through 1129h

Restrictions: IFSFUNC.EXE must be installed.
Return Registers:
CF set
    AX = 0001h (invalid function) (see INT 21h
        Function 59h, chapter 8)

Conflicts: None known.

INTERRUPT 2Fh - Function 11h, Subfunction 2Ah
Unknown Function

Purpose: Perform an unknown action on each IFS driver.
Available on: DOS 4.x only.
Registers at call:
AX = 112Ah
DS = DOS DS
other *unknown.*
Conflicts: None known.

Restrictions: IFSFUNC.EXE must be installed.
Return Registers: *unknown.*

INTERRUPT 2Fh - Function 11h, Subfunction 2Bh
GENERIC IOCTL

Purpose: *Perform an IOCTL operation on a network drive.*
Available on: DOS 4.x only.
Registers at call:
AX = 112Bh
SS = DOS DS
CX = function/category
DS:DX -> parameter block
STACK: WORD value of AX on entry to INT 21h
    Function 44h (Subfunctions 0Ch or 0Dh)
other inputs, if any, unknown.
Details: This function is called by the DOS 4.0 kernel.
Conflicts: None known.

Restrictions: IFSFUNC.EXE must be installed.
Return Registers:
CF set on error
    AX = DOS error code
        (see INT 21h Function 59h, chapter 8)
CF clear if successful

INTERRUPT 2Fh - Function 11h, Subfunction 2Ch
Unknown Function

Purpose: unknown.
Available on: DOS 4.x only.
Registers at call:
AX = 112Ch
SS = DOS DS
SDA current SFT pointer -> SFT for file
other inputs, if any, unknown.
Conflicts: None known.

Restrictions: IFSFUNC.EXE must be installed.
Return Registers:
CF set on error

INTERRUPT 2Fh - Function 11h, Subfunction 2Dh
Unknown Function

Purpose: unknown.
Available on: DOS 4.x only.
Registers at call:
AX = 112Dh
BL = subfunction (value of AL on INT 21h)
  04h *unknown.*
  else *unknown.*
ES:DI -> SFT
SS = DOS DS

Restrictions: IFSFUNC.EXE must be installed.
Return Registers:
DS = DOS DS
CF clear

CX = *unknown.* (00h or 02h for DOS 4.01)

Details: This function is called by the DOS 4.0 kernel on INT 21h Function 57h Subfunctions 02h through 04h.
Conflicts: None known.

INTERRUPT 2Fh - Function 11h, Subfunction 2Eh
EXTENDED OPEN/CREATE FILE

Purpose: Same as INT 21h Function 6Ch for IFS.
Available on: DOS 4.0 or higher.

Restrictions: Network redirector or IFSFUNC.EXE must be installed.

Registers at call:
AX = 112Eh
SS = DS = DOS DS
ES:DI -> uninitialized SFT for file
STACK: WORD file attribute for created/truncated
      file:
     low byte = file attributes
     high byte = 00h normal create/open,
       01h create new file
SDA first filename pointer -> fully-qualified
   filename
SDA extended file open action -> action code (see
   INT 21h Function 6Ch Subfunction 00h)

Return Registers:
CF set on error
   AX = error code
CF clear if successful
   CX = result code:
     01h file opened
     02h file created
     03h file replaced (truncated)
   SFT initialized (except handle count, which DOS
     manages itself)

SDA extended file open mode -> open mode for file
   (see INT 21h Function 6Ch Subfunction 00h)
Details: This function is called by the DOS 4.0 kernel.
Conflicts: None known.
See Also: Function 11h Subfunction 15h, Function 11h Subfunction 16h, Function 11h Subfunction 17h, INT 21h Function 6Ch Subfunction 00h

INTERRUPT 2Fh - Function 11h, Subfunction 2Fh
Unknown Function

Purpose: unknown.
Available on: DOS 4.x only.
Registers at call:
AX = 112Fh
SS = DOS DS
STACK: WORD function in low byte

Restrictions: IFSFUNC.EXE must be installed.
Return Registers:
CF set on error
   AX = DOS error code (see INT 21h Function 59h,
    chapter 8)

00h unknown.
    DS:SI -> *Current Directory Structure*
    CL = drive (1=A:)
01h unknown.
    DS:SI -> unknown.
    CL = *file handle*
02h unknown.
    DS:SI -> *Current Directory Structure*
    DI = unknown.
    CX = drive (1=A:)
other *unknown*.

CF clear if successful

Details: This function is called by the DOS 4.0 kernel.
Conflicts: None known.
See Also: INT 21h Function 6Bh (chapter 8)

INTERRUPT 2Fh - Function 11h, Subfunction 30h
GET IFSFUNC SEGMENT

Purpose: Locate IFSFUNC routine.
Available on: DOS 4.x only.
Registers at call:
AX = 1130h
Conflicts: None known.

Restrictions: IFSFUNC.EXE must be installed.
Return Registers:
ES = CS of resident IFSFUNC

INTERRUPT 2Fh - Function 15h, Subfunction 00h
INSTALLATION CHECK

Purpose: Determine whether the CDROM extensions are installed, and how many drives are CDROMs.
Available on: All machines.
Registers at call:
AX = 1500h
BX = 0000h

Restrictions: none.
Return Registers:
BX = number of CDROM drive letters used
CX = starting drive letter (0=A:)

Details: This installation check DOES NOT follow the format used by other software. It conflicts with the DOS 4.00 GRAPHICS.COM installation check.
Conflicts: DOS 4.00 GRAPHICS.COM (chapter 8).

INTERRUPT 2Fh - Function 15h, Subfunction 01h
GET DRIVE DEVICE LIST

Purpose: Determine which logical drives are controlled by which device drivers.
Available on: All machines.
Registers at call:
AX = 1501h
ES:BX -> buffer to hold drive letter list (5 bytes per
    drive letter, see Table 19-1)
Conflicts: DOS 4.00 GRAPHICS.COM (chapter 8).

Restrictions: CDROM extensions must be installed.
Return Registers:
buffer filled, for each drive letter

Table 19-1. Format of Buffer layout:

Offset	Size	Description
00h	BYTE	subunit number in driver
01h	DWORD	address of device driver header

INTERRUPT 2Fh - Function 15h, Subfunction 02h
GET COPYRIGHT FILE NAME

Purpose: Determine the name of the file in the CDROM's volume table of contents containing the copyright notice.

Available on: All machines.
Registers at call:
AX = 1502h
ES:BX -> 38-byte buffer for name of copyright file
CX = drive number (0=A:)
Conflicts: DOS 4.00 GRAPHICS.COM (chapter 8).
See Also: Function 15h Subfunction 03h

Restrictions: CDROM extensions must be installed.
Return Registers:
CF set if drive is not a CDROM drive
   AX = 15 (invalid drive)
CF clear if successful

INTERRUPT 2Fh - Function 15h, Subfunction 03h
GET ABSTRACT FILE NAME

Purpose: Determine the name of the file in the CDROM's volume table of contents which contains the abstract describing the disk.
Available on: All machines.
Registers at call:
AX = 1503h
ES:BX -> 38-byte buffer for name of abstract file
CX = drive number (0=A:)
Conflicts: DOS 4.00 GRAPHICS.COM (chapter 8).
See Also: Function 15h Subfunction 02h

Restrictions: CDROM extensions must be installed.
Return Registers:
CF set if drive is not a CDROM drive
   AX = 15 (invalid drive)
CF clear if successful

INTERRUPT 2Fh - Function 15h, Subfunction 04h
GET BIBLIOGRAPHIC DOC FILE NAME

Purpose: Determine the name of the file on the CDROM which contains the bibliography.
Available on: All machines.
Registers at call:
AX = 1504h
ES:BX -> 38-byte buffer for name of bibliographic
   documentation file
CX = drive number (0=A:)
Conflicts: DOS 4.00 GRAPHICS.COM (chapter 8).

Restrictions: CDROM extensions must be installed.
Return Registers:
CF set if drive is not a CDROM drive
   AX = 15 (invalid drive)
CF clear if successful

INTERRUPT 2Fh - Function 15h, Subfunction 05h
READ VTOC

Purpose: Retrieve the CDROM's volume table of contents to scan the volume descriptors on the disk.
Available on: All machines.
Registers at call:
AX = 1505h
ES:BX -> 2048-byte buffer
CX = drive number (0=A:)
DX = sector index (0=first volume descriptor,
   1=second,...)
Conflicts: DOS 4.00 GRAPHICS.COM (chapter 8).

Restrictions: CDROM extensions must be installed.
Return Registers:
CF set on error
   AX = error code (15=invalid drive, 21=not ready)
CF clear if successful
   AX = volume descriptor type (1=standard,
      FFh=terminator, 0=other)

INTERRUPT 2Fh - Function 15h, Subfunction 06h
TURN DEBUGGING ON

Purpose: Enable debugging during development; only available in development versions.
Available on: All machines.
Registers at call:
AX = 1506h
BX = debugging function to enable
Conflicts: DOS 4.00 GRAPHICS.COM (chapter 8).
See Also: Function 15h Subfunction 07h

Restrictions: CDROM extensions must be installed.
Return Registers: n/a

INTERRUPT 2Fh - Function 15h, Subfunction 07h
TURN DEBUGGING OFF

Purpose: Disable debugging; only available in development versions.

Available on: All machines.

Registers at call:
AX = 1507h
BX = debugging function to disable
Conflicts: DOS 4.00 GRAPHICS.COM (chapter 8).
See Also: Function 15h Subfunction 06h

Restrictions: CDROM extensions must be installed.
Return Registers: n/a

INTERRUPT 2Fh - Function 15h, Subfunction 08h
ABSOLUTE DISK READ

Purpose: Retrieve one or more sectors from the CDROM by physical sector number.

Available on: All machines.

Registers at call:
AX = 1508h
ES:BX -> buffer
CX = drive number (0=A:)
SI:DI = starting sector number
DX = number of sectors to read
Conflicts: DOS 4.00 GRAPHICS.COM (chapter 8).
See Also: Function 15h Subfunction 09h

Restrictions: CDROM extensions must be installed.
Return Registers:
CF set on error
    AL = error code (15=invalid drive, 21=not ready)
CF clear if successful

INTERRUPT 2Fh - Function 15h, Subfunction 09h
ABSOLUTE DISK WRITE

Purpose: Reserved for storing sectors on an erasable CDROM authoring system by physical sector number.

Available on: All machines.

Registers at call:
AX = 1509h
ES:BX -> buffer
CX = drive number (0=A:)
SI:DI = starting sector number
DX = number of sectors to write
Details: This call corresponds to INT 26h and is currently reserved and nonfunctional.
Conflicts: DOS 4.00 GRAPHICS.COM (chapter 8).
See Also: Function 15h Subfunction 08h

Restrictions: CDROM extensions must be installed.
Return Registers:
unspecified

INTERRUPT 2Fh - Function 15h, Subfunction 0Ah
RESERVED

Purpose: This function is reserved and should not be called.

Available on: All machines.

Registers at call:
AX = 150Ah
Conflicts: DOS 4.00 GRAPHICS.COM (chapter 8).

Restrictions: CDROM extensions must be installed.
Return Registers: n/a

INTERRUPT 2Fh - Function 15h, Subfunction 0Bh
DRIVE CHECK

Purpose: Determine whether or not a drive letter is an MSCDEX CDROM drive.

Available on: All machines.

Restrictions: CDROM extensions version 2.00 or higher must be installed.

Registers at call:
AX = 150Bh
CX = drive number (0=A:)

Return Registers:
BX = ADADh if MSCDEX.EXE installed
AX = 0000h if drive not supported
　　　nonzero if supported

Conflicts: DOS 4.00 GRAPHICS.COM (chapter 8).
See Also: Function 15h Subfunction 0Dh

INTERRUPT 2Fh - Function 15h, Subfunction 0Ch
GET MSCDEX.EXE VERSION

Purpose: Determine which version of MSCDEX is loaded.
Available on: All machines.

Restrictions: Only valid if CDROM extensions version 2.00 or higher is installed.

Registers at call:
AX = 150Ch

Return Registers:
BH = major version
BL = minor version

Details: MSCDEX.EXE versions prior to 2.00 return BX=0000h.
Conflicts: DOS 4.00 GRAPHICS.COM (chapter 8).

INTERRUPT 2Fh - Function 15h, Subfunction 0Dh
GET CDROM DRIVE LETTERS

Purpose: Determine which logical drives correspond to CDROM drives.
Available on: All machines.

Restrictions: CDROM extensions version 2.00 or higher must be installed.

Registers at call:
AX = 150Dh
ES:BX -> buffer for drive letter list (1 byte per
　　drive)

Return Registers:
buffer filled with drive numbers (0=A:).

Details: Each byte corresponds to the drive in the same position as for function subfunction 01h.
Conflicts: DOS 4.00 GRAPHICS.COM (chapter 8).
See Also: Function 15h Subfunction 0Bh

INTERRUPT 2Fh - Function 15h, Subfunction 0Eh
GET/SET VOLUME DESCRIPTOR PREFERENCE

Purpose: Control whether MSCDEX scans for the primary or secondary volume descriptor when initializing a CDROM.
Available on: All machines.

Restrictions: CDROM extensions version 2.00 or higher must be installed.

Registers at call:
AX = 150Eh

BX = subfunction
　　00h get preference
　　　　DX = 0000h
　　01h set preference
　　　　DH = volume descriptor preference
　　　　　　01h = primary volume descriptor
　　　　　　02h = supplementary volume descriptor
　　　　DL = supplementary volume descriptor
　　　　　　preference
　　　　　　01h = shift-Kanji
　　　　CX = drive number (0=A:)

Return Registers:
CF set on error
　　AX = error code
　　　　(15=invalid drive, 1=invalid function)
CF clear if successful

DX = preference settings

Conflicts: DOS 4.00 GRAPHICS.COM (chapter 8).

INTERRUPT 2Fh - Function 15h, Subfunction 0Fh
GET DIRECTORY ENTRY

Purpose: Retrieve the directory entry for a file on the CDROM.

Available on: All machines.

Restrictions: CDROM extensions version 2.00 or higher must be installed.

Registers at call:
AX = 150Fh
CL = drive number (0=A:)
CH bit 0 = copy type (0 = direct, 1 = canonicalize)
ES:BX -> ASCIZ path name
SI:DI -> 255-
    byte/285-byte buffer for directory entry
    (Tables 19-2 and 19-3)

Return Registers:
CF set on error
    AX = error code
CF clear if succesful
    AX = disk format (0=High Sierra, 1=ISO 9660)

Conflicts: DOS 4.00 GRAPHICS.COM (chapter 8).

Table 19-2. Format of Directory Entry:

Offset	Size	Description
00h	BYTE	length of directory entry
01h	BYTE	length of XAR in Logical Block Numbers
02h	DWORD	LBN of data, Intel (little-endian) format
06h	DWORD	LBN of data, Motorola (big-endian) format
0Ah	DWORD	length of file, Intel format
0Eh	DWORD	length of file, Motorola format
---High Sierra		
12h	6 BYTEs	date and time
18h	BYTE	bit flags
19h	BYTE	reserved
---ISO 9660		
12h	7 BYTEs	date and time
19h	BYTE	bit flags
---both formats		
1Ah	BYTE	interleave size
1Bh	BYTE	interleave skip factor
1Ch	WORD	volume set sequence number, Intel format
1Eh	WORD	volume set sequence number, Motorola format
20h	BYTE	length of file name
21h	N BYTEs	file name
	BYTE	(optional) padding if filename is odd length
	N BYTEs	system data

Table 19-3. Format of Canonicalized Directory Entry:

Offset	Size	Description
00h	BYTE	length of XAR in Logical Block Numbers
01h	DWORD	Logical Block Number of file start
05h	WORD	size of disk in logical blocks
07h	DWORD	file length in bytes
0Bh	7 BYTEs	date and time
12h	BYTE	bit flags
13h	BYTE	interleave size
14h	BYTE	interleave skip factor
15h	WORD	volume set sequence number
17h	BYTE	length of file name

18h   38 BYTEs ASCIZ filename

Table 19-3. Format of Canonicalized Directory Entry (continued)

Offset	Size	Description
3Eh	WORD	file version number
40h	BYTE	number of bytes of system use data
41h	220 bytes	system use data

INTERRUPT 2Fh - Function 15h, Subfunction 10h
SEND DEVICE DRIVER REQUEST

Purpose: Communicate with CDROM device drivers.

Available on: All machines.

Registers at call:
AX = 1510h
CX = CD-ROM drive letter (0 = A, 1 = B, etc)
ES:BX -> CD-ROM device driver request header
    (see Function 08h Subfunction 02h, chapter 8)
Conflicts: DOS 4.00 GRAPHICS.COM (chapter 8).

Restrictions: CDROM extensions version 2.10 or higher must be installed.

Return Registers: n/a

INTERRUPT 2Fh - Function B9h, Subfunction 00h
PC Network RECEIVER.COM - INSTALLATION CHECK

Purpose: Determine whether RECEIVER.COM is installed.

Available on: All machines.

Registers at call:
AX = B900h

Restrictions: none.

Return Registers:
AL = 00h if not installed
     FFh if installed

Conflicts: None known.

INTERRUPT 2Fh - Function B9h, Subfunction 01h
GET RECEIVER.COM INT 2Fh HANDLER ADDRESS

Purpose: Determine RECEIVER.COM entry point.

Available on: All machines.

Registers at call:
AX = B901h

Restrictions: PC Network RECEIVER.COM must be installed.

Return Registers:
AL = *unknown.*
ES:BX -> RECEIVER.COM INT 2Fh handler

Details: This function allows more efficient execution by letting the caller bypass any other INT 2Fh handlers which have been added since RECEIVER.COM was installed.
Conflicts: None known.

INTERRUPT 2Fh - Function B9h, Subfunction 03h
GET RECEIVER.COM POST ADDRESS

Purpose: Determine address RECEIVER.COM calls on network events.

Available on: All machines.

Registers at call:
AX = B903h
Conflicts: None known.
See Also: Function B8h Subfunction 03h, Function B9h Subfunction 04h

Restrictions: PC Network RECEIVER.COM must be installed.

Return Registers:
ES:BX -> POST handler

INTERRUPT 2Fh - Function B9h, Subfunction 04h
SET RECEIVER.COM POST ADDRESS

Purpose: Specify which routine RECEIVER.COM invokes on network events.

Available on: All machines.

Restrictions: PC Network RECEIVER.COM must be installed.

Registers at call:
AX = B904h
ES:BX -> new POST handler

Return Registers: n/a

Conflicts: None known.

See Also: Function B8h Subfunction 04h, Function B9h Subfunction 03h

INTERRUPT 2Fh - Function B9h, Subfunction 05h
GET FILENAME

Purpose: Determine the names of files used by the PC Network RECEIVER.COM module.

Available on: All machines.

Restrictions: PC Network RECEIVER.COM must be installed.

Registers at call:
AX = B905h
DS:BX -> 128-byte buffer for filename 1
DS:DX -> 128-byte buffer for filename 2

Return Registers:
buffers filled from RECEIVER.COM internal buffers

Details: The use of the filenames is unknown, but one appears to be for storing messages.

Conflicts: None known.

See Also: Function B9h Subfunction 06h

INTERRUPT 2Fh - Function B9h, Subfunction 06h
SET FILENAME

Purpose: Specify the names of files used by the PC Network RECEIVER.COM module.

Available on: All machines.

Restrictions: PC Network RECEIVER.COM must be installed.

Registers at call:
AX = B906h
DS:BX -> 128-byte buffer for filename 1
DS:DX -> 128-byte buffer for filename 2

Return Registers:
RECEIVER.COM internal buffers filled from user buffers

Details: The use of the filenames is unknown, but one appears to be for storing messages.

Conflicts: None known.

See Also: Function B9h Subfunction 05h

INTERRUPT 2Fh - Function B9h, Subfunction 08h
UNLINK KEYBOARD HANDLER

Purpose: Remove the last keyboard handler loaded before RECEIVER.COM.

Available on: All machines.

Restrictions: PC Network RECEIVER.COM must be installed.

Registers at call:
AX = B908h
ES:BX -> INT 09 handler RECEIVER should call
     after it finishes INT 09

Return Registers: n/a

Details: This call replaces the address to which RECEIVER.COM chains on an INT 09h without preserving the original value. This allows a prior handler to unlink, but does not allow a new handler to be added such that RECEIVER gets the INT 09h first.

Conflicts: None known.

INTERRUPT 2Fh - Function BFh, Subfunction 00h
internal - INSTALLATION CHECK

Purpose: Determine whether the PC LAN Program REDIRIFS.EXE module is installed.

Available on: All machines.

Registers at call:
AX = BF00h

Conflicts: None known.

Restrictions: none.

Return Registers:
AL = FFh if installed

INTERRUPT 2Fh - Function BFh, Subfunction 01h
internal - Unknown Function

Purpose: *unknown.*

Available on: All machines.

Registers at call:
AX = BF01h
unknown.

Conflicts: None known.

Restrictions: PC LAN Program REDIRIFS.EXE must
be installed.

Return Registers: *unknown.*

INTERRUPT 2Fh - Function BFh, Subfunction 80h
internal - SET REDIRIFS ENTRY POINT

Purpose: Specify a handler which is to be invoked on all future IFS calls to REDIR.SYS.

Available on: All machines.

Registers at call:
AX = BF80h
ES:DI -> FAR entry point to IFS handler in
    REDIRIFS

Conflicts: None known.

Restrictions: PC LAN Program REDIR.SYS must be
installed.

Return Registers:
AL = FFh if installed
ES:DI -> internal workspace

Chapter 20

Novell NetWare

In the world of network operation, Novell NetWare appears to hold a position similar to that held by MS-DOS with respect to operating systems. While NetWare is by no means the only networking system available, it is the accepted standard to which all others are compared.

It should come as no surprise, then, to find that the interrupt functions used by NetWare provide a multitude of services, or that some other networking systems have also adopted certain NetWare interrupt functions. This chapter lists the functions used by NetWare, including those calls provided by other networking systems. The functions are listed in sequence by interrupt number, function, and subfunction.

A note about version numbers: NetWare 4.0 and 4.6 are old versions that predate the current Advanced Netware, which is commonly called just "NetWare". Thus, functions for "NetWare 4.0 or higher" also apply to Advanced NetWare.

INTERRUPT 21h - Function B5h, Subfunction 03h
TASK MODE CONTROL

Purpose: Determine the current value of the task mode byte.

Available on: All machines.

Restrictions: NetWare shell version 3.01 or higher must be installed.

Registers at call:
AX = B503h

Return Registers:
AH = 00h
AL = current task mode byte (Table 20-1)

Details: The task mode byte specifies how task cleanup should be performed, but is declared to be version-dependent.

Conflicts: None known.

See Also: Function B5h Subfunction 04h.

Table 20-1. VaLues For Task Mode Byte In Version 3.01:

Value	Meaning
00h-03h	reserved
04h	no task cleanup

INTERRUPT 21h - Function B5h, Subfunction 04h
TASK MODE CONTROL

Purpose: Get a pointer to the task mode byte.

Available on: All machines.

Restrictions: NetWare shell version 3.01 or higher must be installed.

Registers at call:
AX = B504h

Return Registers:
ES:BX - >task mode byte

Details: The task mode byte specifies how task cleanup should be performed, but is declared to be version-dependent. The mode byte allows a programs managing task swapping, etc. to disable the automatic cleanup.

Conflicts: None known.

See Also: Function B5h Subfunction 03h.

INTERRUPT 21h - Function B6h, Subfunctions 00h and 01h
EXTENDED FILE ATTRIBUTES

Purpose: Determine or modify the extended attributes for the specified file.

Available on: All machines.

Restrictions: NetWare SFT Level II software must be installed.

Registers at call:
AH = B6h
AL = subfunction
   00h get extended file attributes
   01h set extended file attributes
CL = attributes
   bits 2-0: search mode (executables only)
      000 none (use shell's default search)
      001 search on all opens without path
      010 do not search
      011 search on read-only opens without path
      100 reserved
      101 search on all opens
      110 reserved
      111 search on all read- only opens
   3: reserved
   4: transaction tracking file
   5: indexing file
   6: read audit (to be implemented)
   7: write audit (to be implemented)
DS:DX -> ASCIZ pathname

Return Registers:
CF set on error
AL = error code
   8Ch caller lacks privileges
   FFh file not found
CL = current extended file attributes

Conflicts: None known.

See Also: DOS Function 43h Subfunction 00h (chapter 8)

INTERRUPT 21h - Function B8h, Subfunctions 00h thru 09h
PRINT JOBS

Purpose: Determine or modify various print spooler options.

Available on: All machines.

Restrictions: Advanced NetWare version 2.0 or higher must be installed.

Registers at call:
AH = B8h
AL = subfunction
   00h get default print job flags
   01h set default capture flags (Table 20-2)
   02h get specific capture flags
   03h set specific print job flags
   04h get default local printer
   05h set default local printer
   06h set capture print queue
   07h set capture print job
   08h get banner user name
   09h set banner user name
CX = buffer size
ES:BX -> buffer

Return Registers: none

Conflicts: Attachmate Extra (chapter 26).

Table 20-2. Format of Capture Flags Table:

Offset	Size	Description
00h	BYTE	status (used internally, should be set to 00h)
01h	BYTE	print flags
		bit 2: print capture file if interrupted by loss of connection
		3: no automatic form feed after print job
		6: printing control sequences interpreted by print service
		7: print banner page before capture file
02h	BYTE	printer number on server
03h	BYTE	number of copies to print
04h	BYTE	form type required in printer (default 00h)
05h	13 BYTEs	text to be placed on banner page
12h	BYTE	reserved
13h	BYTE	default local printer (00h = LPT1)
14h	BYTE	flush capture file on LPT close if nonzero
15h	WORD	timeout in clock ticks for flushing capture file on inactivity (high byte first) 0000h = never timeout
17h	WORD	maximum lines per page (high byte first)
19h	WORD	maximum characters per line (high byte first)
1Bh	13 BYTEs	name of form required in printer
28h	BYTE	LPT capture flag: 00h inactive, FFh LPT device is being captured
29h	BYTE	file capture flag: 00h if no file specified, FFh if capturing to file
2Ah	BYTE	timing out (00h if no timeout in effect, FFh if timeout counter running)
2Bh	WORD	offset of printer setup string (high byte first)
2Dh	WORD	offset of printer reset string (high byte first)
2Fh	BYTE	target connection ID
30h	BYTE	capture in progress if FFh
31h	BYTE	print job number assigned to capture if FFh
32h	WORD	bindery object ID of print queue if previous byte FFh
34h	WORD	print job number (high byte first)

INTERRUPT 21h - Function BBh
SET END OF JOB STATUS

Purpose: Specify whether an End of Job call will automatically be made on process termination.

Available on: All machines.

Restrictions: NetWare 4.0 or higher, or Alloy network software, must be installed.

Registers at call:
AH = BBh
AL = new EOJ flag
   00h disable EOJs
   otherwise enable EOJs
Conflicts: None known.
See Also: Function D6h

Return Registers:
AL = old EOJ flag

INTERRUPT 21h - Function BCh
LOG/LOCK PHYSICAL RECORD

Purpose: Prevent other processes from accessing the specified record, and add the record to the log table.

Available on: All machines.

Restrictions: NetWare 4.6 or higher, or Alloy network software, must be installed.

Registers at call:
AH = BCh
AL = flags
   bit 0: lock as well as log record
   1: non-exclusive lock

Return Registers:
AL = error code
   00h successful
   96h no dynamic memory for file
   FEh timed out

BX = file handle
CX:DX = offset
BP = timeout in timer ticks (1/18 sec)
SI:DI = length of region to lock
Conflicts: None known.
See Also: Functions BDh and BFh

FFh failed

INTERRUPT 21h - Function BDh
RELEASE PHYSICAL RECORD

Purpose: Unlock the specified record but do not remove it from the log table.
Available on: All machines.

Restrictions: NetWare 4.6 or higher, or Alloy network software, must be installed.

Registers at call:
AH = BDh
BX = file handle
CX:DX = offset
Conflicts: None known.
See Also: Functions BCh, BEh, and C0h

Return Registers:
AL = error code (see Function BCh)

INTERRUPT 21h - Function BEh
CLEAR PHYSICAL RECORD

Purpose: Unlock the specified record and remove it from the log table.
Available on: All machines.

Restrictions: NetWare 4.6 or higher, or Alloy network software, must be installed.

Registers at call:
AH = BEh
BX = file handle
CX:DX = offset
Conflicts: "Datalock" and "1049" viruses (chapter 34).
See Also: Functions BCh, BDh, and C1h

Return Registers:
AL = error code (see Function BCh)

INTERRUPT 21h - Function BFh
LOG/LOCK RECORD (FCB)

Purpose: Prevent other processes from accessing the specified record, and add the record to the log table.
Available on: All machines.

Restrictions: NetWare 4.6 or higher, or Alloy network software, must be installed.

Registers at call:
AH = BFh
AL = flags
    bit 0: lock as well as log record
    1: non-exclusive lock
DS:DX -> opened FCB (see DOS Function 0Fh,
    chapter 8)
BX:CX = offset
BP = lock timeout in timer ticks (1/18 sec)
SI:DI = length
Conflicts: None known.
See Also: Functions BCh, C0h, and C2h

Return Registers:
AL = error code (see Function BCh)

INTERRUPT 21h - Function C0h
RELEASE RECORD (FCB)

Purpose: Unlock the specified record but do not remove it from the log table.

Available on: All machines.

Registers at call:
AH = C0h
DS:DX -> FCB (see DOS Function 0Fh, chapter 8)
BX:CX = offset
Conflicts: "Slow" virus, "Solano" virus (both in chapter 34).
See Also: Functions BDh, BFh, C1h, and C3h

Restrictions: NetWare 4.6 or higher, or Alloy network software, must be installed.
Return Registers:
AL = error code (see Function BCh)

INTERRUPT 21h - Function C1h
CLEAR RECORD (FCB)

Purpose: Unlock the specied record and remove it from the log table.
Available on: All machines.

Registers at call:
AH = C1h
DS:DX -> opened FCB (see DOS Function 0Fh, chapter 8)
BX:CX = offset
Conflicts: "Solano" virus (chapter 34).
See Also: Functions BEh, C0h, and C4h

Restrictions: NetWare 4.6 or higher, or Alloy network software, must be installed.
Return Registers:
AL = error code (see Function BCh)

INTERRUPT 21h - Function C2h
LOCK PHYSICAL RECORD SET

Purpose: Prevent other processes from accessing the specified records, and add them to the log table.
Available on: All machines.

Registers at call:
AH = C2h
AL = flags
    bit 1: non-exclusive lock
BP = lock timeout in timer ticks (1/18 sec)
Conflicts: "Scott's Valley" virus (chapter 34).
See Also: Functions BFh and C3h

Restrictions: NetWare 4.6 or higher, or Alloy network software, must be installed.
Return Registers:
AL = error code
    00h successful
    FEh timed out
    FFh failed

INTERRUPT 21h - Function C3h
RELEASE PHYSICAL RECORD SET

Purpose: Unlock the specified records but do not remove any of them from the log table.
Available on: All machines.

Registers at call:
AH = C3h
Conflicts: "905" virus (chapter 34).
See Also: Functions C0h, C2h, and C4h

Restrictions: NetWare 4.6 or higher, or Alloy network software, must be installed.
Return Registers:
AL = error code

INTERRUPT 21h - Function C4h
CLEAR PHYSICAL RECORD SET

Purpose: Both unlock and remove from the log table the specified set of records.
Available on: All machines.

Registers at call:
AH = C4h
Conflicts: None known.

Restrictions: NetWare 4.6 or higher, or Alloy network software, must be installed.
Return Registers:
AL = error code

See Also: Function C1h

INTERRUPT 21h - Function C5h, Subfunctions 00h thru 04h
SEMAPHORES

Purpose: Control access to resources which are not shareable or can only be accessed by a limited number of processes at once.

Available on: All machines.

Restrictions: NetWare 4.6 or higher, or Alloy network software, must be installed.

Registers at call:
AH = C5h
AL = subfunction

Return Registers:
AL = error code
    00h successful
    01h semaphore value overflow
    96h out of string space on server
    FEh invalid string length (AL=00h) or timeout
    FFh invalid initial value (AL=00h) or invalid
        handle

    00h open semaphore
        DS:DX -> semaphore name (counted string)
        CL = initial value
    01h examine semaphore
        CX:DX = semaphore handle
    02h wait on semaphore
        CX:DX = semaphore handle
        BP = timeout in timer ticks (1/18 sec)
            (0000h = no wait)
    03h signal semaphore
        CX:DX = semaphore handle
    04h close semaphore
        CX:DX = semaphore handle

CX:DX = semaphore handle
BL = open count

CX = semaphore value (sign extended)
DL = open count

Conflicts: "Sverdlov" virus (chapter 34).

INTERRUPT 21h - Function C6h, Subfunctions 00h thru 02h
GET OR SET LOCK MODE

Purpose: Determine or specify the file locking mode.

Available on: All machines.

Restrictions: NetWare 4.6 or higher, or Alloy network software, must be installed.

Registers at call:
AH = C6h
AL = subfunction
    00h set old "compatibility" mode
    01h set new extended locks mode
    02h get lock mode

Return Registers:
AL = current lock mode

Conflicts: "Yankee" or "MLTI" virus (chapter 34).

INTERRUPT 21h - Function C7h, Subfunctions 00h thru 08h
TRANSACTION TRACKING SYSTEM

Purpose: Allow multiple stations to protect their concurrent database updates by permitting the server to back out of interrupted transactions.

Available on: All machines.

Registers at call:
AH = C7h
AL = subfunction
    00h begin transaction (NetWare SFT level II)

Restrictions: NetWare 4.0 or higher must be installed.

Return Registers:
Subfunction 00h:
    AL = error code

01h end transaction (NetWare SFT level II)

02h TTS available (NetWare SFT level II)

03h abort transaction (NetWare SFT level II)

04h transaction status
05h get application thresholds
06h set application thresholds
07h get workstation thresholds
08h set workstation thresholds
Conflicts: None known.

Subfunction 01h:
    AL = error code
    CX:DX = transaction reference number
Subfunction 02h:
    AL = completion code
        00h TTS not available
        01h TTS available
        FDh TTS available but disabled
Subfunction 03h:
    AL = error code
others: *unknown*

INTERRUPT 21h - Function C8h
BEGIN LOGICAL FILE LOCKING

Purpose: Enable file locking.
Available on: All machines.
Registers at call:
AH = C8h
if function C6h lock mode 00h:
    DL = mode: 00h no wait, 01h wait
if function C6h lock mode 01h:
    BP = timeout in timer ticks (1/18 sec)
Conflicts: None known.
See Also: Function C9h

Restrictions: NetWare 4.0 or higher must be installed.
Return Registers:
AL = error code

INTERRUPT 21h - Function C9h
END LOGICAL FILE LOCKING

Purpose: Disable file locking.
Available on: All machines.
Registers at call:
AH = C9h
Conflicts: None known.
See Also: Function C8h

Restrictions: NetWare 4.0 or higher must be installed.
Return Registers:
AL = error code

INTERRUPT 21h - Function CAh
LOG/LOCK PERSONAL FILE (FCB)

Purpose: Prohibit others from accessing the file corresponding to the specified File Control Block.
Available on: All machines.

Registers at call:
AH = CAh
DS:DX -> FCB (see DOS Function 0Fh, chapter 8)
if function C6h lock mode 01h:
    AL = log and lock flag
        00h log file only
        01h lock as well as log file
    BP = lock timeout in timer ticks (1/18 sec)
Conflicts: "Piter" virus (chapter 34).

Restrictions: NetWare 4.0 or higher, or Alloy network software, must be installed.
Return Registers:
AL = error code
    00h successful
    96h no dynamic memory for file
    FEh timeout
    FFh failed

See Also: Function CBh

INTERRUPT 21h - Function CBh
LOCK FILE SET

Purpose: Attempt to place locks on all logged personal files.
Available on: All machines.

Restrictions: NetWare 4.0 or higher, or Alloy network software, must be installed.

Registers at call:
AH = CBh
if function C6h lock mode 00h:
    DL = mode
        00h no wait
        01h wait
if function C6h lock mode 01h:
    BP = lock timeout in timer ticks (1/18 sec)
Conflicts: None known.
See Also: Function CAh

Return Registers:
AL = error code
    00h successful
    FEh timed out
    FFh failed

INTERRUPT 21h - Function CCh
RELEASE FILE (FCB)

Purpose: Unlock the specified file, but do not remove it from the log table or close it.
Available on: All machines.

Restrictions: NetWare 4.0 or higher, or Alloy network software, must be installed.

Registers at call:
AH = CCh
DS:DX -> FCB (see DOS Function 0Fh, chapter 8)
Conflicts: "Westwood" virus (chapter 34).
See Also: Functions CAh and CDh

Return Registers: none

INTERRUPT 21h - Function CDh
RELEASE FILE SET

Purpose: Unlock all personal files, but do not remove any of them from the log table.
Available on: All machines.

Restrictions: NetWare 4.0 or higher, or Alloy network software, must be installed.

Registers at call:
AH = CDh
Conflicts: "Westwood" virus (chapter 34).
See Also: Functions CAh and CCh

Return Registers: none

INTERRUPT 21h - Function CEh
CLEAR FILE (FCB)

Purpose: Unlock the specified file and remove it from the log table, then close all opened and logged occurrences of the file.
Available on: All machines.

Restrictions: NetWare 4.0 or higher, or Alloy network software, must be installed.

Registers at call:
AH = CEh
DS:DX -> FCB (see DOS Function 0Fh, chapter 8)
Conflicts: None known.
See Also: Functions CAh, CFh, and EDh

Return Registers:
AL = error code

INTERRUPT 21h - Function CFh
CLEAR FILE SET

Purpose: Unlock and remove all entries in the personal file log table.

Available on: All machines.

Restrictions: NetWare 4.0 or higher, or Alloy network software, must be installed.

Registers at call:
AH = CFh
Conflicts: None known.
See Also: Functions CAh and CEh

Return Registers:
AL = 00h

INTERRUPT 21h - Function D0h
LOCK LOGICAL RECORD

Purpose: Prevent other processes from accessing the specified record, and add the record to the log table.

Available on: All machines.

Restrictions: NetWare 4.6 or higher, Banyan VINES, or Alloy network software must be installed.

Registers at call:
AH = D0h
DS:DX -> record string (counted string, max 100 data bytes)
if function C6h lock mode 01h: (Novell, Alloy NTNX only)
    AL = flags
        bit 0: lock as well as log the record
        bit 1: non-exclusive lock
    BP = lock timeout in timer ticks (1/18 sec)
Conflicts: "Fellowship" virus (chapter 34).
See Also: Functions D1h and D2h

Return Registers:
AL = error code
    00h successful
    96h no dynamic memory for file
    FEh timed out
    FFh unsuccessful

INTERRUPT 21h - Function D1h
LOCK LOGICAL RECORD SET

Purpose: Prevent other processes from accessing the specified records, and add them to the log table.

Available on: All machines.

Restrictions: NetWare 4.6 or higher, Banyan VINES, or Alloy network software must be installed.

Registers at call:
AH = D1h
if function C6h lock mode 00h:
    DL = mode
        00h no wait
        01h wait
if function C6h lock mode 01h: (Novell only)
    BP = lock timeout in timer ticks (1/18 sec)
        0000h no wait
Conflicts: None known.
See Also: Functions D0h and D3h

Return Registers:
AL = error code (see Function D0h)

INTERRUPT 21h - Function D2h
UNLOCK LOGICAL RECORD

Purpose: Unlock the specified record but do not remove it from the log table.

Available on: All machines.

Registers at call:
AH = D2h
DS:DX -> semaphore identifier (counted string up
   to 100 chars long)
Conflicts: None known.
See Also: Functions D0h and D3h

Restrictions: NetWare 4.0 or higher, Banyan VINES,
   or Alloy network software must be
   installed.
Return Registers:
AL = error code (see Function D0h)

INTERRUPT 21h - Function D3h
UNLOCK LOGICAL RECORD SET

Purpose: Unlock all semaphores logged in the requesting PC's semaphore set.
Available on: All machines.

Restrictions: NetWare 4.0 or higher, Banyan VINES,
   or Alloy network software must be
   installed.

Registers at call:
AH = D3h
Conflicts: None known.
See Also: Functions D1h and D2h

Return Registers:
AL = error code (see Function D0h)

INTERRUPT 21h - Function D4h
CLEAR LOGICAL RECORD

Purpose: Unlock the specified record and remove it from the log table.
Available on: All machines.

Restrictions: NetWare 4.0 or higher, Banyan VINES,
   or Alloy network software must be
   installed.

Registers at call:
AH = D4h
DS:DX -> semaphore identifier (counted string up
   to 100 chars long)
Conflicts: None known.
See Also: Function D5h

Return Registers:
AL = error code
   00h successful
   FFh not successful

INTERRUPT 21h - Function D5h
CLEAR LOGICAL RECORD SET

Purpose: Unlock and clear all semaphores associated with the requesting PC's semaphore set.
Available on: All machines.

Restrictions: NetWare 4.0 or higher, Banyan VINES,
   or Alloy network software must be
   installed.

Registers at call:
AH = D5h
Conflicts: "Dir", "Diamond-A", and "Diamond-B" viruses (chapter 34).
See Also: Function D4h

Return Registers:
AL = error code (see Function D4h)

INTERRUPT 21h - Function D6h
END OF JOB

Purpose: Clean up on program termination by unlocking and clearing all locked or logged files and records held by the terminating process, then closing all files, resetting error and lock modes, and releasing all network resources held by the process.
Available on: All machines.

Restrictions: NetWare 4.0 or higher, or Alloy network
   software, must be installed.

Registers at call:
AH = D6h
Conflicts: None known.
See Also: Function BBh

Return Registers:
AL = error code

INTERRUPT 21h - Function D7h
SYSTEM LOGOUT

Purpose: Log the user out of the system.
Available on: All machines.

Registers at call:
AH = D7h
Conflicts: None known.

Restrictions: NetWare 4.0 or higher, or Alloy network
software, must be installed.
Return Registers:
AL = error code

INTERRUPT 21h - Function D8h
ALLOCATE RESOURCE

Purpose: Request the use of a specified resource.
Available on: All machines.

Registers at call:
AH = D8h
DL = resource number

Conflicts: None known.
See Also: Function D9h

Restrictions: NetWare or Banyan VINES must be
installed.
Return Registers:
AL = status
00h successful
FFh unsucessful

INTERRUPT 21h - Function D9h
DEALLOCATE RESOURCE

Purpose: Return the specified resource to the system.
Available on: All machines.

Registers at call:
AH = D9h
DL = resource number
Conflicts: None known.
See Also: Function D8h

Restrictions: NetWare or Banyan VINES must be
installed.
Return Registers:
AL = status (see Function D8h)

INTERRUPT 21h - Function DAh
GET VOLUME STATISTICS

Purpose: Determine available space on the specified disk volume.
Available on: All machines.
Registers at call:
AH = DAh
DL = volume number
ES:DI -> reply buffer (Table 20-3)
Conflicts: None known.
See Also: DOS Function 36h (chapter 8)

Restrictions: NetWare 4.0 or higher must be installed.
Return Registers:
AL = 00h

Table 20-3. Format of Reply Buffer:

Offset	Size	Description
00h	WORD	sectors/block
02h	WORD	total blocks

Table 20-3. Format of Reply Buffer (continued)

Offset	Size	Description
04h	WORD	unused blocks
06h	WORD	total directory entries
08h	WORD	unused directory entries
0Ah	16 BYTEs	volume name, null padded
1Ah	WORD	removable flag, 0000h = not removable

INTERRUPT 21h - Function DBh
GET NUMBER OF LOCAL DRIVES

Purpose: Determine how many disk drives are local to the caller's machine.

Available on: All machines.

Restrictions: NetWare 4.0 or higher, or Alloy network software, must be installed.

Registers at call:
AH = DBh

Return Registers:
AL = number of local disks

Conflicts: None known.

See Also: DOS Function 0Eh (chapter 8)

INTERRUPT 21h - Function DCh
GET STATION NUMBER

Purpose: Determine the network station number of the caller's machine.

Available on: All machines.

Restrictions: NetWare 4.0 or higher, Banyan VINES, or Alloy network software must be installed.

Registers at call:
AH = DCh

Return Registers:
AL = station number:
    00h if NetWare not loaded or this machine is a non-dedicated server
CX = station number in ASCII

Details: The station number is only unique for those PCs connected to the same semaphore service.

Conflicts: PC Magazine PCMANAGE/DCOMPRES (chapter 36).

INTERRUPT 21h - Function DDh
SET ERROR MODE

Purpose: Control critical error handling.

Available on: All machines.

Restrictions: NetWare 4.0 or higher, or Alloy network software, must be installed.

Registers at call:
AH = DDh
DL = error mode
    00h invoke INT 24h on critical I/O errors
    01h return NetWare extended error code in AL
    02h return error code in AL, mapped to standard
        DOS error codes

Return Registers:
AL = previous error mode

Conflicts: None known.

INTERRUPT 21h - Function DEh
SET BROADCAST MODE

Purpose: Specify how incoming broadcast messages are to be handled.

Available on: All machines.

Registers at call:
AH = DEh

Restrictions: NetWare 4.0 or higher must be installed.

Return Registers:
AL = old broadcast mode

AL = broadcast mode:

    00h receive console and workstation broadcasts

    01h receive console broadcasts only

    02h receive no broadcasts

    03h store all broadcasts for retrieval

    04h get broadcast mode

    05h disable shell timer interrupt checks

    06h enable shell timer interrupt checks

Conflicts: "Durban" virus (chapter 34).

INTERRUPT 21h - Function DFh, Subfunctions 00h thru 07h
CAPTURE

Purpose: Control printer output capturing.

Available on: All machines.

Restrictions: NetWare 4.0 or higher, or Alloy network software, must be installed.

Registers at call:

AH = DFh

AL = subfunction

    00h start LPT capture

    01h end LPT capture

    02h cancel LPT capture

    03h flush LPT capture

    04h start specific capture

    05h end specific capture

    06h cancel specific capture

    07h flush specific capture

Return Registers:

AL = error code

Details: Under NTNX, only Subfunctions 00h-03h are supported, and all four send a print break (see INT 17h Function 84h in chapter 18).

Conflicts: None known.

INTERRUPT 21h - Function E0h, Subfunctions 00h thru 06h and 09h
PRINT SPOOLING

Purpose: Control the print spooler.

Available on: All machines.

Restrictions: NetWare 4.0 or higher, or Alloy network software, must be installed.

Registers at call:

AH = E0h

DS:SI -> request buffer

ES:DI -> reply buffer

    subfunction in third byte of request buffer:

    00h spool data to a capture file

    01h close and queue capture file

    02h set spool flags

    03h spool existing file

    04h get spool queue entry

    05h remove entry from spool queue

    06h get printer status

    09h create a disk capture file

Return Registers:

AL = error code

Conflicts: OS/286 and OS/386 (chapter 9), DoubleDOS (chapter 17), "Jerusalem", "Armagedon" and "8-tunes" viruses (chapter 34).

INTERRUPT 21h - Function E1h, Subfunctions 00h thru 09h
BROADCAST MESSAGES

Purpose: Send or receive messages.

Available on: All machines.

Registers at call:
AH = E1h
DS:SI -> request buffer
ES:DI -> reply buffer
   subfunction in third byte of request buffer:
   00h send broadcast message
   01h get broadcast message
   02h disable station broadcasts
   03h enable station broadcasts
   04h send personal message
   05h get personal message
   06h open message pipe
   07h close message pipe
   08h check pipe status
   09h broadcast to console

Restrictions: NetWare 4.0 or higher must be installed.

Return Registers:
AL = error code

Conflicts: OS/286 and OS/386 (chapter 9), DoubleDOS (chapter 17), "Mendoza" and "Fu Manchu" viruses (chapter 34).

INTERRUPT 21h - Function E2h, Subfunctions 00h thru 19h
DIRECTORY FUNCTIONS

Purpose: Perform manipulations on the specified directory.

Available on: All machines.

Restrictions: NetWare 4.0 or higher, or Alloy network software, must be installed.

Registers at call:
AH = E2h
DS:SI -> request buffer
ES:DI -> reply buffer
   subfunction in third byte of request buffer
   00h set directory handle
   01h get directory path
   02h scan directory information
   03h get effective directory rights
   04h modify maximum rights mask
   05h get volume number
   06h get volume name
   0Ah create directory
   0Bh delete directory
   0Ch scan directory for trustees
   0Dh add trustee to directory
   0Eh delete trustee from directory
   0Fh rename directory
   10h purge erased files
   11h restore erased file
   12h allocate permanent directory handle
   13h allocate temporary directory handle
   14h deallocate directory handle
   15h get volume info with handle
   16h allocate special temporary directory handle

Return Registers:
AL = error code

17h retrieve a short base handle (Advanced
  NetWare 2.0)
18h restore a short base handle (Advanced
  NetWare 2.0)
19h set directory information
Conflicts: OS/286 and OS/386 (chapter 9), DoubleDOS (chapter 17).

INTERRUPT 21h - Function E3h
CONNECTION CONTROL

Purpose: Establish a new connection or modify an existing one; also provides file and object manipulation functions.

Available on: All machines.

Restrictions: NetWare 4.0 or higher, or Alloy network software, must be installed.

Registers at call:
AH = E3h
DS:SI -> request buffer
ES:DI -> reply buffer
  subfunction in third byte of request buffer
  (Table 20-4)
Conflicts: DoubleDOS (chapter 17).

Return Registers:
AL = error code

Table 20-4. Connection Control Subfunctions:

Value	Function
00h	login
01h	change password
02h	map user to station set
03h	map object to number
04h	map number to object
05h	get station's logged information
06h	get station's root mask (obsolete)
07h	map group name to number
08h	map number to group name
09h	get memberset M of group G
0Ah	enter login area
0Bh	unknown.
0Ch	unknown.
0Dh	log network message
0Eh	get disk utilization (Advanced NetWare 1.0)
0Fh	scan file information (Advanced NetWare 1.0)
10h	set file information (Advanced NetWare 1.0)
11h	get file server information (Advanced NetWare 1.0)
12h	unknown.
13h	get internet address (Advanced NetWare 1.02)
14h	login to file server (Advanced NetWare 2.0)
15h	get object connection numbers (Advanced NetWare 2.0)
16h	get connection information (Advanced NetWare 1.0)
32h	create object (Advanced NetWare 1.0)
33h	delete object (Advanced NetWare 1.0)
34h	rename object (Advanced NetWare 1.0)
35h	get object ID (Advanced NetWare 1.0)
36h	get object name (Advanced NetWare 1.0)
37h	scan object (Advanced NetWare 1.0)
38h	change object security (Advanced NetWare 1.0)
39h	create property (Advanced NetWare 1.0)
3Ah	delete property (Advanced NetWare 1.0)
3Bh	change property security (Advanced NetWare 1.0)

Table 20-4. Connection Control Subfunctions (continued)

Value	Function
3Ch	scan property (Advanced NetWare 1.0)
3Dh	read property value (Advanced NetWare 1.0)
	request buffer contains the property name in all caps
	property "IDENTIFICATION" returns the user's name
3Eh	write property value (Advanced NetWare 1.0)
3Fh	verify object password (Advanced NetWare 1.0)
40h	change object password (Advanced NetWare 1.0)
41h	add object to set (Advanced NetWare 1.0)
42h	delete object from set (Advanced NetWare 1.0)
43h	is object in set? (Advanced NetWare 1.0)
44h	close bindery (Advanced NetWare 1.0)
45h	open bindery (Advanced NetWare 1.0)
46h	get bindery access level (Advanced NetWare 1.0)
47h	scan object trustee paths (Advanced NetWare 1.0)
C8h	check console priviledges
C9h	get file server description strings
CAh	set file server date and time
CBh	disable file server login
CCh	enable file server login
CDh	get file server login status
CEh	purge all erased files
CFh	disable transaction tracking
D0h	enable transaction tracking
D1h	send console broadcast
D2h	clear connection number
D3h	down file server
D4h	get file system statistics
D5h	get transaction tracking statistics
D6h	read disk cache statistics
D7h	get drive mapping table
D8h	read physical disk statistics
D9h	get disk channel statistics
DAh	get connection's task information
DBh	get list of connections open files
DCh	get list of connections using a file
DDh	get physical record locks by connection and file
DEh	get physical record locks by file
DFh	get logical records by connection
E0h	get logical record information
E1h	get connection's semaphores
E2h	get semaphore information
E3h	get LAN driver's configuration information
E5h	get connection's usage statistics
E6h	get object's remaining disk space
E7h	get server LAN I/O statistics
E8h	get server miscellaneous information
E9h	get volume information

Table 20-5. Format of Object Property:

Offset	Size	Description
00h	1-16 BYTEs	property name
N	BYTE	flags: bit 0: propertyis dynamic
		4: property belongs to set rather than item
N+1	BYTE	security levels (Table 20-6)

Table 20-6. Values for security levels:

Value	Security Level
00h	everyone may access
01h	only logged-in clients may access
02h	only clients logged-in with object's name, type, and password
03h	only clients logged-in with supervisor privileges
04h	only NetWare may access

The above values are stored in a nybble; the high half-byte is write access and the low half-byte is read access.

Table 20-7. Values for object type:

Value	Object Type
00h	unknown
01h	user
02h	user group
03h	print queue
04h	file server
05h	job server
06h	gateway
07h	print server
08h	archive queue
09h	archive server
0Ah	job queue
0Bh	administration
24h	remote bridge server
47h	advertising print server
FFh	wild (used only for finding objects)

INTERRUPT 21h - Function E4h
SET FILE ATTRIBUTES (FCB)

Purpose: Specify new file attributes for the file corresponding to the specified file control block.

Available on: All machines.　　　　**Restrictions:** NetWare 4.0 or higher must be installed.

Registers at call:　　　　**Return Registers:**

AH = E4h　　　　AL = error code

CL = file attributes
   bit 0: read only
   1: hidden
   2: system
   7: shareable

DX:DX -> FCB (see DOS Function 0Fh, chapter 8)

Conflicts: DoubleDOS (chapter 17), "Anarkia" virus (chapter 34).

See Also: DOS Function 43h Subfunction 01h (chapter 8)

INTERRUPT 21h - Function E5h
UPDATE FILE SIZE (FCB)

Purpose: Force the file size field of the specified File Control Block to reflect the current size of the file, which may have been modified by other processes.

Available on: All machines.　　　　**Restrictions:** NetWare 4.0 or higher must be installed.

Registers at call:　　　　**Return Registers:**

AH = E5h　　　　AL = error code

DS:DX -> FCB (see DOS Function 0Fh, chapter 8)

Conflicts: DoubleDOS (chapter 17).

INTERRUPT 21h - Function E6h
COPY FILE TO FILE (FCB)

Purpose: Copy the contents of one file into another, where both files are specified using File Control Blocks.

Available on: All machines.

Registers at call:
AH = E6h
CX:DX = number of bytes to copy
DS:SI -> source FCB
ES:DI -> destination FCB

Conflicts: None known.

Restrictions: NetWare 4.0 or higher must be installed.

Return Registers:
AL = error code

INTERRUPT 21h - Function E7h
GET FILE SERVER DATE AND TIME

Purpose: Determine the current date and time as known to the network server.

Available on: All machines.

Registers at call:
AH = E7h
DS:DX -> date/time buffer (Table 20-8)

Conflicts: None known.
See Also: DOS Functions 2Ah and 2Ch (chapter 8)

Restrictions: NetWare 4.0 or higher, Banyan VINES, or Alloy network software must be installed.

Return Registers:
AL = error code
   00h successful
   FFh unsuccessful

Table 20-8. Format of Date/Time Buffer:

Offset	Size	Description
00h	BYTE	year - 1900
01h	BYTE	month (1=Jan)
02h	BYTE	day
03h	BYTE	hours
04h	BYTE	minutes
05h	BYTE	seconds
06h	BYTE	day of week (0 = Sunday) (Novell and NTNX only)

INTERRUPT 21h - Function E8h
SET FCB RE-OPEN MODE

Purpose: Specify whether File Control Blocks will be re-opened automatically.

Available on: All machines.

Registers at call:
AH = E8h
DL = mode
   00h no automatic re-open
   01h auto re-open

Conflicts: DoubleDOS (chapter 16).

Restrictions: NetWare 4.6 or higher, or Alloy network software, must be installed.

Return Registers:
AL = error code

INTERRUPT 21h - Function E9h, Subfunction 00h
SHELL'S "GET BASE STATUS"

Purpose: Determine whether the specified drive is mapped to a base.

Available on: All machines.

Restrictions: NetWare 4.6 or higher, or Alloy network software, must be installed.

Registers at call:
AX = E900h
DX = drive number to check (0 = A:)

Return Registers:
AL = network pathbase
AH = base flags
    00h drive not currently mapped to a base
    01h drive is mapped to a permanent base
    02h drive is mapped to a temporary base
    03h drive exists locally

Conflicts: None known.

INTERRUPT 21h - Function E9h, Subfunction 05h
MAP A FAKE ROOT DIRECTORY

Purpose: Specify a directory which will henceforth appear to be the root directory of the specified drive.
Available on: All machines.

Restrictions: NetWare shell 3.01 or higher must be installed.

Registers at call:
AX = E905h
BL = drive number (0=default, 1=A:, ...)
DS:DX -> ASCIZ path for fake root (may include
    server name or be empty)

Return Registers:
CF set on error
    AL = error code (03h, 0Fh, 11h) (see DOS
        Function 59h, chapter 8)
CF clear if successful

Details: If the drive is not currently mapped, a drive mapping will be created.
Conflicts: None known.
See Also: Function E9h Subfunction 06h

INTERRUPT 21h - Function E9h, Subfunction 06h
DELETE FAKE ROOT DIRECTORY

Purpose: Stop pretending that a subdirectory is the root directory of the specified drive.
Available on: All machines.

Restrictions: NetWare shell 3.01 or higher must be installed.

Registers at call:
AX = E906h
BL = drive number (0=default, 1=A:, ...)

Return Registers: *unknown.*

Details: The drive remains mapped.
Conflicts: None known.
See Also: Function E9h Subfunction 05h

INTERRUPT 21h - Function E9h, Subfunction 07h
GET RELATIVE DRIVE DEPTH

Purpose: Determine how deep the directory tree extends below the directory which currently appears to be the root directory.
Available on: All machines.

Restrictions: NetWare shell 3.01 or higher must be installed.

Registers at call:
AX = E907h
BL = drive number (0=default, 1=A:, ...)

Return Registers:
AL = number of directories below the fake root
    FFh if no fake root assigned

Conflicts: None known.
See Also: Function E9h Subfunction 05h

INTERRUPT 21h - Function E9h, Subfunction 08h
SET SHOW DOTS

Purpose: Specify whether directory searches will return the "." and ".." entries.
Available on: All machines.

Restrictions: NetWare shell 3.01 or higher must be installed.

Registers at call:
AX = E908h
BL = 00h: don't return '.' or '..' during directory
      scans
   = nonzero: directory scans will return '.' or '..'
      entries
Conflicts: None known.

Return Registers:
BL = previous show-dots setting

INTERRUPT 21h - Function EAh
RETURN SHELL VERSION

Purpose: Determine which version of the NetWare shell is running, and which hardware and operating system it is running under.

Available on: All machines.

Restrictions: NetWare 4.6 or higher, or Alloy network software, must be installed.

Registers at call:
AH = EAh
AL = return version environment string
   00h: don't return string
   nonzero: return string in 40-byte buffer pointed
      to by ES:DI

Return Registers:
AH = operating system (00h = MSDOS)
AL = hardware type
   00h IBM PC
   01h Victor 9000
BH = major shell version
BL = minor shell version
CH = (v3.01+) shell type
   00h conventional memory
   01h expanded memory
   02h extended memory
CL = shell revision number
if AL nonzero on entry, the ES:DI buffer is filled with
   three null-terminated entries:
      major operating system
      version
      hardware type

Conflicts: DoubleDOS (chapter 16).

INTERRUPT 21h - Function EBh
LOG FILE

Purpose: Add the specified file to the log table and optionally prohibit other processes access to the file.

Available on: All machines.

Restrictions: NetWare 4.6 or higher, or Alloy network software, must be installed.

Registers at call:
AH = EBh
DS:DX -> ASCIZ filename
if function C6h lock mode 01h:
   AL = flags
      00h log file only
      01h lock as well as log file
   BP = lock timeout in timer ticks (1/18 second)
Conflicts: DoubleDOS (chapter 16).
See Also: Functions CAh and ECh

Return Registers:
AL = error code
   00h successful
   96h no dynamic memory for file
   FEh timed out
   FFh failed

INTERRUPT 21h - Function ECh
RELEASE FILE

Purpose: Unlock the specified file, permitting other processes access.

Available on: All machines.

Registers at call:
AH = ECh
DS:DX -> ASCIZ filename
Conflicts: DoubleDOS (chapter 16), "Terror" virus (chapter 34).
See Also: Function EBh

Restrictions: NetWare 4.6 or higher, or Alloy network software, must be installed.
Return Registers: none

INTERRUPT 21h - Function EDh
CLEAR FILE

Purpose: Unlock the specified file and remove it from the log table.
Available on: All machines.

Registers at call:
AH = EDh
DS:DX -> ASCIZ filename
Conflicts: None known.
See Also: Functions CEh and EBh

Restrictions: NetWare or Alloy network software must be installed.
Return Registers:
AL = error code

INTERRUPT 21h - Function EEh
GET PHYSICAL STATION NUMBER

Purpose: Determine the physical network address of the caller's machine.
Available on: All machines.

Registers at call:
AH = EEh
Conflicts: DoubleDOS (chapter 16), "Jerusalem-G" virus (chapter 34).

Restrictions: NetWare 4.6 or higher, or Alloy network software, must be installed.
Return Registers:
CX:BX:AX = six-byte address

INTERRUPT 21h - Function EFh
GET DRIVE INFO

Purpose: Determine information about the attached drives.
Available on: All machines.

Registers at call:
AH = EFh
AL = subfunction
    00h get drive handle table
    01h get drive flag table (Table 20-9)
    02h get drive connection ID table
    03h get connection ID table (Table 20-10)
    04h get file server name table
Details: The drive handle, flag, and connection ID tables each contain 32 entries

Restrictions: Advanced NetWare 1.0 or higher must be installed.
Return Registers:
ES:DI -> shell status table

Table 20-9. Values in drive flag table:

Value	Meaning
00h	drive is not mapped
01h	permanent network drive
02h	temporary network drive
80h	mapped to local drive
81h	local drive used as permanent network drive
82h	local drive used as temporary network drive

Table 20-10. Format of Connection ID Table:

Offset	Size	Description
00h	BYTE	in use flag:
		E0h AES temporary
		F8h IPX in critical section
		FAh processing
		FBh holding
		FCh AES waiting
		FDh waiting
		FEh receiving
		FFh sending
01h	BYTE	order number
02h	DWORD	file server's network address (high byte first)
06h	6 BYTEs	file server's node address (high byte first)
0Ch	WORD	socket number (high byte first)
0Eh	WORD	base receive timeout in clock ticks (high byte first)
10h	6 BYTEs	preferred routing node (high byte first)
16h	BYTE	packet sequence number
17h	BYTE	connection number
18h	BYTE	connection status (FFh if active)
19h	WORD	maximum receive timeout in clock ticks (high byte first)
1Bh	5 BYTEs	reserved

INTERRUPT 21h - Function F0h, Subfunctions 00h thru 05h
CONNECTION ID

Purpose: Determine or specify the identifier for the current connection.

Available on: All machines.

Restrictions: Advanced NetWare 1.0 or higher must be installed.

Registers at call:
AH = F0h
AL = subfunction
   00h set preferred connection ID
   01h get preferred connection ID
   02h get default connection ID
   03h LPT capture active
   04h set primary connection ID
   05h get primary connection ID
DL = preferred file server

Return Registers:
AL = selected file server

Conflicts: DoubleDOS (chapter 16), "Frere Jacques" virus (chapter 34).

INTERRUPT 21h - Function F1h, Subfunctions 00h thru 02h
FILE SERVER CONNECTION

Purpose: Control communication with the file server.

Available on: All machines.

Restrictions: Advanced NetWare 1.0 or higher must be installed.

Registers at call:
AH = F1h
AL = subfunction
   00h attach to file server
      DL = preferred file server
   01h detach from file server
   02h logout from file server

Return Registers:
AL = completion code

Conflicts: DoubleDOS (chapter 16).

INTERRUPT 21h - Function F2h
SHELL INTERFACE MULTIPLEXOR

Purpose: Access other net interface functions which were accessed via a separate AH function in older versions.

Available on: All machines.

Restrictions: NetWare shell version 3.01 or higher must be installed.

Registers at call:
AH = F2h
AL = function
    15h broadcast services (see Function E1h)
    17h connection control (see Function E3h)
DS:SI -> request buffer
ES:DI -> reply buffer

Return Registers: *unknown.*

Details: The function number in AL is added to CCh to get the old function number which is desired.
Conflicts: DoubleDOS (chapter 16).

INTERRUPT 21h - Function F3h
FILE SERVER FILE COPY

Purpose: Copy data from one file to another without involving the workstation in the copy.

Available on: All machines.

Restrictions: Advanced NetWare version 2.0 or higher must be installed.

Registers at call:
AH = F3h
ES:DI -> request string (Table 20-11)
Conflicts: DoubleDOS (chapter 16).

Return Registers:
AL = status/error code
CX:DX = number of bytes copied

Table 20-11. Format of Request String:

Offset	Size	Description
00h	WORD	source file handle
02h	WORD	destination file handle
04h	DWORD	starting offset in source
08h	DWORD	starting offset in destination
0Ch	DWORD	number of bytes to copy

INTERRUPT 2Fh - Function 7Ah, Subfunction 00h
LOW-LEVEL API (IPX) INSTALLATION CHECK

Purpose: Determine whether Novell IPX software is installed.

Available on: All machines.
Registers at call:
AX = 7A00h

Restrictions: none.
Return Registers:
AL = 00h not installed
   = FFh installed
ES:DI -> FAR entry point for routines accessed exclusively through INT 7Ah in NetWare versions through 2.0a. Call this entry point with the same values as INT 7Ah.

Conflicts: None known.
See Also: INT 64h, INT 7Ah

INTERRUPT 2Fh - Function 7Ah, Subfunction 80h
Unknown Function

Purpose: *unknown.*

Available on: All machines.

Registers at call:
AX = 7A80h
Details: This function is apparently called on abnormal exit of the shell.

Restrictions: NetWare shell version 3.01d must be installed.
Return Registers: nothing

INTERRUPT 2Fh - Function 7Ah, Subfunction 81h
Unknown Function

Purpose: *unknown.*
Available on: All machines.

Registers at call:
AX = 7A81h
CX:DX -> *unknown* in shell's CS (may be callback
   address or data structure)
Conflicts: None known.

Restrictions: NetWare shell version 3.01d must be installed.
Return Registers: *apparently nothing*

INTERRUPT 2Fh - Function 7Ah, Subfunction 85h
BROADCAST INFORM

Purpose: Called by the NetWare shell to inform any interested programs that a broadcast message has been received.
Available on: All machines.

Registers at call:
AX = 7A85h
CX = broadcast server number

Conflicts: None known.

Restrictions: NetWare shell version 3.01 must be installed.
Return Registers:
CX = 0000h if broadcast message handled by another
   program
CX unchanged if broadcast not handled

INTERRUPT 2Fh - Function 7Ah, Subfunction FEh
Unknown Function

Purpose: *unknown.*
Available on: All machines.

Registers at call:
AX = 7AFEh

Conflicts: None known.

Restrictions: NetWare shell version 3.01d must be installed.
Return Registers:
AL = FFh ???
other *unknown.*

INTERRUPT 2Fh - Function 7Ah, Subfunction FFh
Unknown Function

Purpose: *unknown.*
Available on: All machines.

Registers at call:
AX = 7AFFh
BX = 0001h
CX = offset of *unknown data or function*
DX = offset of *unknown data or function*
Conflicts: None known.

Restrictions: NetWare shell version 3.01d must be installed.
Return Registers:
CX unchanged if *unknown conditions*

INTERRUPT 2Fh - Function C0h, Subfunction 00h
Novell ODI Link Support Layer (LSL.COM) INSTALLATION CHECK

Purpose: Determine if LSL.COM is present.

Available on: All machines.　　　　　　　　**Restrictions:** none.

Registers at call:　　　　　　　　　　　　**Return Registers:**
AX = C000h　　　　　　　　　　　　　　　　AL = FFh
　　　　　　　　　　　　　　　　　　　　　ES:BX -> call entry point
　　　　　　　　　　　　　　　　　　　　　ES:SI -> signature string "LINKSUP$"

Details: LSL.COM may use any multiplex number between C0h and FFh; it searches for itself in that range, and installs using the first free multiplex number in the range if it is not already loaded.

Conflicts: None known.

INTERRUPT 44h
Novell NetWare - HIGH-LEVEL LANGUAGE API

Purpose: Communication between applications and NetWare.

Available on: Novell networks.　　　　　　**Restrictions:** none.

Registers at call: *unknown.*　　　　　　　**Return Registers:** n/a.

Conflicts: PCjr character font vector (chapter 5), IBM 3270-PC API (chapter 26), Z100 master 8259 (chapter 2).

INTERRUPT 64h
LOW-LEVEL API

Purpose: Provide direct packet-level access to the network.

Available on: All machines.　　　　　　　　**Restrictions:** Advanced NetWare version 2.0a or earlier must be installed.

Details: This interrupt is equivalent to INT 7Ah for NetWare versions through 2.0a only; later versions do not use this interrupt for IPX/SPX access, instead getting an entry point from INT 2Fh Function 7Ah Subfunction 00h.

Conflicts: None known.

See Also: INT 2Fh Function 7Ah Subfunction 00h, INT 7Ah

INTERRUPT 6Bh
Novell NASI/NACS

Purpose: Emulate a serial port over the network. The calls for this interrupt are described in chapter 7.

INTERRUPT 6Fh
Novell NetWare - PCOX API (3270 PC terminal interface)

Purpose: IBM 3270 emulation.

Available on: All machines.　　　　　　　　**Restrictions:** Applicable network software must be installed.

Registers at call: *unknown.*　　　　　　　**Return Registers:** *unknown.*

Conflicts: None known.

INTERRUPT 7Ah
LOW-LEVEL API - Notes

Purpose: The functions of this interrupt provide direct packet-level IPX/SPX access to the network.

Available on: All machines.　　　　　　　　**Restrictions:** NetWare IPX and/or SPX driver must be installed.

Details: This interrupt is used for IPX/SPX access in NetWare versions through 2.0a; in later versions, you should use INT 2Fh Function 7Ah Subfunction 00h to get an entry point. For both INT 7Ah and the FAR entry point, BX contains the function number; IPX is sometimes called internally with BX bit 15 set.

Conflicts: IBM3270 Emulation (chapter 26), Topware Network Operating System (chapter 27), AutoCAD Device Interface (chapter 36).

See Also: INT 2Fh Function 7Ah Subfunction 00h, INT 64h

INTERRUPT 7Ah - Function 0000h
OPEN SOCKET

Purpose: Establish a connection over the network.
Available on: All machines.

Registers at call:
BX = 0000h
AL = mode
   00h open until close or terminate
   FFh open until close
DX = socket number (high byte in DL)
   0000h dynamic allocation
   else socket to open

Restrictions: NetWare low-level (IPX) driver must be installed.
Return Registers:
AL = return code
   00h success
DX = socket number
   FEh socket table full
   FFh socket already open

Conflicts: IBM3270 Emulation (chapter 26), Topware Network Operating System (chapter 27), AutoCAD Device Interface (chapter 36).
See Also: Function 0001h

INTERRUPT 7Ah - Function 0001h
CLOSE SOCKET

Purpose: Terminate a connection over the network.
Available on: All machines.

Registers at call:
BX = 0001h
DX = socket (high byte in DL)

Restrictions: NetWare low-level (IPX) driver must be installed.
Return Registers: n/a.

Conflicts: IBM3270 Emulation (chapter 26), Topware Network Operating System (chapter 27), AutoCAD Device Interface (chapter 36).
See Also: Function 0000h

INTERRUPT 7Ah - Function 0002h
GET LOCAL TARGET

Purpose: Determine the address in the caller's own network to which to transmit in order to reach the specified machine.
Available on: All machines.

Registers at call:
BX = 0002h
ES:SI -> target internetwork address
ES:DI -> 6-byte buffer for local target

Restrictions: NetWare low-level (IPX) driver must be installed.
Return Registers:
AL = return code
   00h success
      CX = expected one-way transfer time (clock ticks)
      ES:DI -> local target
   FAh unsuccessful

Details: The internetwork address consists of a 4-byte network address followed by a 6-byte node address. The local target is only a 6-byte node address. If the target is in the same network, the local target is just the node address of target; otherwise, the local target is the node address of the bridge that leads to the target.
Conflicts: IBM3270 Emulation (chapter 26), Topware Network Operating System (chapter 27), AutoCAD Device Interface (chapter 36).
See Also: Function 0009h

INTERRUPT 7Ah - Function 0003h
SEND PACKET

Purpose: Transmit data over the network.
Available on: All machines.

Restrictions: NetWare low-level (IPX) driver must be installed.

Registers at call:
BX = 0003h
ES:SI -> Event Control Block (Table 20-12)
Conflicts: IBM3270 Emulation (chapter 26), Topware Network Operating System (chapter 27), AutoCAD Device Interface (chapter 36).
See Also: Functions 0004h and 000Fh

Return Registers: *n/a.*

Table 20-12. Format of Event Control Block:

Offset	Size	Description
00h	DWORD	Link
04h	DWORD	-> Event Service Routine (00000000h if none)
08h	BYTE	in use flag
09h	BYTE	completion code
0Ah	WORD	socket (high byte first [big-endian])
0Ch	4 BYTEs	IPX workspace
10h	12 BYTEs	driver workspace
1Ch	6 BYTEs	immediate local node address
22h	WORD	fragment count
26h	varies	fragment descriptors:

Offset	Size	Description
00h	DWORD	-> fragment data
04h	WORD	size of fragment in bytes.

Details: The Event Service Routine (ESR) is a far procedure that is called when the ECB has been handled. On call, the in use flag is zero if the ECB has been handled, non-zero otherwise. If the flag is zero, the completion code holds the result of the event:

Table 20-13. Values of ESR Completion Codes:

Value	Meaning
00h	success
F9h	event should not be cancelled
FCh	cancelled
FDh	malformed packet
FEh	packet undeliverable
FFh	physical error

The first fragment should start with an IPX header (see below). All fragments are concatenated and sent in one piece. Node address FF FF FF FF FF FF broadcasts to all nodes.

Event Service Routine called with:
AL = caller's identity (00h = AES, FFh = IPX)
ES:SI -> event control block
interrupts disabled

Table 20-14. Format of IPX Header:

Offset	Size	Description
00h	WORD	checksum (high byte first [big-endian])
02h	WORD	length in bytes (high byte first) of total packet
04h	BYTE	transport control

Table 20-14. Format of IPX Header (continued)

Offset	Size	Description
05h	BYTE	packet type

           00h unknown packet type
           01h routing information packet
           02h echo packet
           03h error packet
           04h packet exchange packet (always use this one)
           05h SPX packet
           11h (used internally)

Offset	Size	Description
06h	10 BYTES	destination internetwork address
10h	WORD	destination socket (high byte first)
12h	10 BYTES	source internetwork address
1Ch	WORD	source socket

INTERRUPT 7Ah - Function 0004h
LISTEN FOR PACKET

Purpose: Await data arriving over the network.

Available on: All machines.

Restrictions: NetWare low-level (IPX) driver must be installed.

Registers at call:
BX = 0004h
ES:SI -> Event Control Block (Table 20-12)

Return Registers: *n/a.*

Conflicts: IBM3270 Emulation (chapter 26), Topware Network Operating System (chapter 27), AutoCAD Device Interface (chapter 36).

See Also: Function 0003h

INTERRUPT 7Ah - Function 0005h
SCHEDULE IPX EVENT

Purpose: Add an event to the IPX scheduler.

Available on: All machines.

Restrictions: NetWare low-level (IPX) driver must be installed.

Registers at call:
BX = 0005h
AX = delay time
ES:SI -> Event Control Block (Table 20-12)

Return Registers: *n/a.*

Conflicts: IBM3270 Emulation (chapter 26), Topware Network Operating System (chapter 27), AutoCAD Device Interface (chapter 36).

See Also: Functions 0006h and 0007h

INTERRUPT 7Ah - Function 0006h
CANCEL EVENT

Purpose: Remove a previously-added event.

Available on: All machines.

Restrictions: NetWare low-level (IPX) driver must be installed.

Registers at call:
BX = 0006h
ES:SI -> Event Control Block (Table 20-12)

Return Registers:
AL = return code
    00h success
    F9h event in use
    FFh unsuccessful, event not in use

Conflicts: IBM3270 Emulation (chapter 26), Topware Network Operating System (chapter 27), AutoCAD Device Interface (chapter 36).

See Also: Function 0005h

INTERRUPT 7Ah - Function 0007h
SCHEDULE SPECIAL EVENT

Purpose: Add a non-IPX event to the scheduler.
Available on: All machines.

Restrictions: NetWare low-level (IPX) driver must be installed.
Return Registers: *n/a.*

Registers at call:
BX = 0007h
AX = delay time
ES:SI -> Event Control Block (Table 20-12)
Conflicts: IBM3270 Emulation (chapter 26), Topware Network Operating System (chapter 27), AutoCAD Device Interface (chapter 36).
See Also: Function 0006h

INTERRUPT 7Ah - Function 0008h
GET INTERVAL MARKER

Purpose: Network action timing.
Available on: All machines.

Restrictions: NetWare low-level (IPX) driver must be installed.
Return Registers:
AX = interval marker in clock ticks

Registers at call:
BX = 0008h
Conflicts: IBM3270 Emulation (chapter 26), Topware Network Operating System (chapter 27), AutoCAD Device Interface (chapter 36).

INTERRUPT 7Ah - Function 0009h
GET INTERNETWORK ADDRESS

Purpose: Determine the caller's full address in a set of interconnected networks.
Available on: All machines.

Restrictions: NetWare low-level (IPX) driver must be installed.
Return Registers:
ES:SI -> own internetwork address

Registers at call:
BX = 0009h
ES:SI -> 10-byte buffer
Conflicts: IBM3270 Emulation (chapter 26), Topware Network Operating System (chapter 27), AutoCAD Device Interface (chapter 36).
See Also: Functions 0002h and 000Bh

INTERRUPT 7Ah - Function 000Ah
RELINQUISH CONTROL

Purpose: Indicate to NetWare that the caller is idle.
Available on: All machines.

Restrictions: NetWare low-level (IPX) driver must be installed.
Return Registers: *n/a.*

Registers at call:
BX = 000Ah
Details: This call permits the IPX driver to do some work.
Conflicts: IBM3270 Emulation (chapter 26), Topware Network Operating System (chapter 27), AutoCAD Device Interface (chapter 36).

INTERRUPT 7Ah - Function 000Bh
DISCONNECT FROM TARGET

Purpose: Terminate a network connection.
Available on: All machines.

Restrictions: NetWare low-level (IPX) driver must be installed.

Registers at call:
BX = 000Bh
ES:SI -> internetwork address
Details: This function is only of use in point-to-point networks.
Conflicts: IBM3270 Emulation (chapter 26), Topware Network Operating System (chapter 27), AutoCAD Device Interface (chapter 36).
See Also: Functions 0002h and 0009h

Return Registers: *n/a.*

INTERRUPT 7Ah - Function 000Ch to 000Eh
Unknown Internal Functions

Purpose: *unknown.*
Available on: All machines.

Restrictions: NetWare low-level (IPX) driver must be installed.

Registers at call:
BX = 000Ch to 000Eh
others, if any, unknown.
Conflicts: IBM3270 Emulation (chapter 26), Topware Network Operating System (chapter 27), AutoCAD Device Interface (chapter 36).

Return Registers: *unknown.*

INTERRUPT 7Ah - Function 000Fh
internal - SEND PACKET

Purpose: Transmit data over the network.
Available on: All machines.

Restrictions: NetWare low-level (IPX) driver must be installed.

Registers at call:
BX = 000Fh
ES:SI -> Event Control Block (Table 20-12)
Details: This call is similar to function 0003h, but apparently does not allow multiple fragments.
Conflicts: IBM3270 Emulation (chapter 26), Topware Network Operating System (chapter 27), AutoCAD Device Interface (chapter 36).
See Also: Function 0003h

Return Registers: *n/a.*

INTERRUPT 7Ah - Function 0010h
SPX INSTALLATION CHECK

Purpose: Determine whether NetWare's SPX module is installed.
Available on: All machines.

Restrictions: NetWare low-level (IPX) driver must be installed.

Registers at call:
BX = 0010h
AL = 00h
Conflicts: IBM3270 Emulation (chapter 26), Topware Network Operating System (chapter 27), AutoCAD Device Interface (chapter 36).
See Also: Function 0015h

Return Registers:
AL = FFh if SPX loaded

INTERRUPT 7Ah - Function 0011h
ESTABLISH SPX CONNECTION

Purpose: Create a new network connection using the SPX reliable sequenced packet service.
Available on: All machines.

Restrictions: NetWare low-level (IPX) driver must be installed.

Registers at call:
BX = 0011h
AL = retry count

Return Registers:
DX = assigned connection number

AH = watchdog flag
ES:SI -> Event Control Block (Table 20-12)
Details: There should always be at least two SPX ECB's listening to a socket, so that NetWare can perform its internal packet exchanges. The first fragment should start with an SPX header (Table 20-15).
All destination addresses should be filled in.
Conflicts: IBM3270 Emulation (chapter 26), Topware Network Operating System (chapter 27), AutoCAD Device Interface (chapter 36).
See Also: Functions 0000h, 0012h, 0013h, and 0014h

Table 20-15. Format of SPX Header:

Offset	Size	Description
00h	WORD	checksum (high byte first [big-endian])
02h	WORD	length in bytes of total packet (high byte first)
04h	BYTE	transport control
05h	BYTE	packet type
06h	10 BYTEs	destination internet address
10h	WORD	destination socket (high byte first)
12h	10 BYTEs	source internet address
1Ch	WORD	source socket (high byte first)
1Eh	BYTE	connection control
1Fh	BYTE	datastreamtype
20h	WORD	source connection ID
22h	WORD	destination connection ID
24h	WORD	sequence number
26h	WORD	acknowledge number
28h	WORD	allocation number

INTERRUPT 7Ah - Function 0012h
LISTEN FOR SPX CONNECTION

Purpose: Await a request to establish a network connection using the SPX service.
Available on: All machines.   **Restrictions:** NetWare low-level (IPX) driver must be installed.

Return Registers: *n/a.*

Registers at call:
BX = 0012h
AL = retry count
AH = watchdog flag
ES:SI -> Event Control Block (Table 20-12)
Details: There should always be at least two SPX ECB's listening to a socket, so that NetWare can perform its internal packet exchanges.
Conflicts: IBM3270 Emulation (chapter 26), Topware Network Operating System (chapter 27), AutoCAD Device Interface (chapter 36).
See Also: Functions 0011h, 0013h, and 0014h

INTERRUPT 7Ah - Function 0013h
TERMINATE SPX CONNECTION

Purpose: Close the specified network connection using the SPX service.
Available on: All machines.   **Restrictions:** NetWare low-level (IPX) driver must be installed.

Return Registers: *n/a.*

Registers at call:
BX = 0013h
DX = connection ID to terminate
ES:SI -> Event Control Block (Table 20-12)
Conflicts: IBM3270 Emulation (chapter 26), Topware Network Operating System (chapter 27), AutoCAD Device Interface (chapter 36).

See Also: Functions 0011h, 0012h, and 0014h

INTERRUPT 7Ah - Function 0014h
ABORT SPX CONNECTION

Purpose: Shut down the specified network connection immediately.

Available on: All machines.

Restrictions: NetWare low-level (IPX) driver must be installed.

Registers at call:
BX = 0014h
DX = connection ID to terminate

Return Registers: *unknown.*

Details: This function does not tell the other side that the connection has been terminated.

Conflicts: IBM3270 Emulation (chapter 26), Topware Network Operating System (chapter 27), AutoCAD Device Interface (chapter 36).

See Also: Functions 0011h and 0013h

INTERRUPT 7Ah - Function 0015h
GET SPX STATUS

Purpose: Determine the current status of the SPX driver for the specified connection.

Available on: All machines.

Restrictions: NetWare low-level (IPX) driver must be installed.

Registers at call:
BX = 0015h
DX = connection ID
ES:SI -> status buffer (Table 20-16)

Return Registers:
AL = return code
   00h connection still valid
     ES:SI -> status buffer filled

Conflicts: IBM3270 Emulation (chapter 26), Topware Network Operating System (chapter 27), AutoCAD Device Interface (chapter 36).

See Also: Functions 0010h

Table 20-16. Format of Status Buffer:

Offset	Size	Description
00h	BYTE	status
01h	BYTE	flag
02h	WORD	source connection (high byte first [big-endian])
04h	WORD	destination connection (high byte first)
06h	WORD	sequence number (high byte first)
08h	WORD	acknowledge number (high byte first)
0Ah	WORD	allocation number (high byte first)
0Ch	WORD	remote acknowledge number (high byte first)
0Eh	WORD	remote allocation number (high byte first)
10h	WORD	connection socket (high byte first)
12h	6 BYTEs	immediate node address
18h	10 BYTEs	destination internet address
22h	WORD	retransmit count (high byte first)
24h	WORD	estimated roundtrip delay
26h	WORD	retransmitted packets
28h	WORD	suppressed packets

INTERRUPT 7Ah - Function 0016h
SEND SPX PACKET

Purpose: Transmit data over an SPX network connection.

Available on: All machines.

Restrictions: NetWare low-level (IPX) driver must be installed.

Registers at call:
BX = 0016h

Return Registers: *n/a.*

DX = connection ID
ES:SI -> Event Control Block (Table 20-12)
Details: CX may need to be 0001h.
Conflicts: IBM3270 Emulation (chapter 26), Topware Network Operating System (chapter 27), AutoCAD Device Interface (chapter 36).
See Also: Functions 0011h and 0017h

INTERRUPT 7Ah - Function 0017h
LISTEN FOR SPX PACKET

Purpose: Await data arriving over the specified SPX network connection.
Available on: All machines.

Restrictions: NetWare low-level (IPX) driver must be installed.
Return Registers: *n/a.*

Registers at call:
BX = 0017h
DX = connection ID
ES:SI -> Event Control Block (Table 20-12)
Details: CX may need to be 0001h.
Conflicts: IBM3270 Emulation (chapter 26), Topware Network Operating System (chapter 27), AutoCAD Device Interface (chapter 36).
See Also: Functions 0011h and 0016h

INTERRUPT 7Ah - Functions 0018h to 001Bh
Unknown Internal Functions

Purpose: *unknown.*
Available on: All machines.

Restrictions: NetWare low-level (IPX) driver must be installed.
Return Registers: *unknown.*

Registers at call:
BX = 0018h to 001Bh
others, if any, unknown.
Conflicts: IBM3270 Emulation (chapter 26), Topware Network Operating System (chapter 27), AutoCAD Device Interface (chapter 36).

Chapter 21

LANtastic Network Operating System

LANtastic is a low-cost network by Artisoft, Inc. for a small to medium number of machines.

INTERRUPT 21h - Function 5Dh, Subfunctions 07h through 09h
Printer Redirection

These functions are identical to the MSDOS implementation, and are described in chapter 8.

INTERRUPT 21h - Function 5Eh, Subfunctions 00h and 01h
Network Machine Name

These functions are identical to the MSDOS implementation, and are described in chapter 8.

INTERRUPT 21h - Function 5Fh, Subfunctions 02h through 04h
Redirection

These functions are identical to the MSDOS implementation, and are described in chapter 8.

INTERRUPT 21h - Function 5Fh, Subfunction 80h
GET LOGIN ENTRY

Purpose: Determine the name of the machine on which the user is logged in.

Available on: All machines.

Registers at call:
AX = 5F80h
BX = login entry index (0-based)
ES:DI - > 16-byte buffer for machine name

Restrictions: LANtastic network software must be installed.

Return Registers:
CF clear if successful
    buffer filled with machine name ("\" prefix removed)
    DL = adapter number (v3+)
CF set on error
    AX = error code
    BX = next login entry index (BX-1 is current index)

Conflicts: None known.

INTERRUPT 21h - Function 5Fh, Subfunction 81h
LOGIN TO SERVER

Purpose: Authenticate user to remote machine.

Available on: All machines.

Registers at call:
AX = 5F81h
ES:DI - > ASCIZ login path followed immediately
    by ASCIZ password
BL = adapter number
    FFh try all valid adapters
    00h-03h try only specified adapter

Restrictions: LANtastic network software must be installed.

Return Registers:
CF clear if successful
CF set on error
    AX = error code

Details: The login path is of the form "\machine".
Conflicts: None known.
See Also: Function 5Fh Subfunctions 82h and 84h

INTERRUPT 21h - Function 5Fh, Subfunction 82h
LOGOUT FROM SERVER

Purpose: Terminate the current session with the indicated remote machine.

Available on: All machines.

Restrictions: LANtastic network software must be installed.

Registers at call:
AX = 5F82h
ES:DI -> ASCIZ server name (in form "\machine")

Return Registers:
CF clear if successful
CF set on error
    AX = error code

Conflicts: None known.
See Also: Function 5Fh Subfunction 81h

INTERRUPT 21h - Function 5Fh, Subfunction 83h
GET USERNAME ENTRY

Purpose: Determine name under which the user is logged into the specified remote machine.

Available on: All machines.

Restrictions: LANtastic network software must be installed.

Registers at call:
AX = 5F83h
BX = login entry index (0-based)
ES:DI -> 16-byte buffer for username currently
    logged into

Return Registers:
CF clear if successful
    DL = adapter number (v3+)
CF set on error
    AX = error code
    BX = next login entry index (BX-1 is current
        index)

Conflicts: None known.

INTERRUPT 21h - Function 5Fh, Subfunction 84h
GET INACTIVE SERVER ENTRY

Purpose: Determine the name of an available server which the user is not currently logged into.

Available on: All machines.

Restrictions: LANtastic network software must be installed.

Registers at call:
AX = 5F84h
BX = server index not currently logged into
ES:DI -> 16-byte buffer for server name which is
    available for logging in to ('\' prefix omitted)

Return Registers:
CF clear if successful
    DL = adapter number to non-logged in server is on
CF set on error
    AX = error code

Conflicts: None known.
See Also: Function 5Fh Subfunction 81h

INTERRUPT 21h - Function 5Fh, Subfunction 85h
CHANGE PASSWORD

Purpose: Specify a new password for the user on the specified remote machine.

Available on: All machines.

Restrictions: LANtastic network software must be installed.

Registers at call:
AX = 5F85h
ES:DI -> buffer containing "\machine" 00h
    "newpassword" 00h

Return Registers:
CF clear if successful
CF set on error
    AX = error code

Details: The caller must be logged into the named machine.

Conflicts: None known.

INTERRUPT 21h - Function 5Fh, Subfunction 86h
DISABLE ACCOUNT

Purpose: Prevent further use of an account until it is manually re-enabled.

Available on: All machines.

Restrictions: LANtastic network software must be installed.

Registers at call:
AX = 5F86h
ES:DI -> ASCIZ machine name and password in
   form "\machine"

Return Registers:
CF clear if successful
CF set on error
   AX = error code

Details: The caller must be logged into the named machine and concurrent logins must be set to 1 by NET_MGR. Re-enabling the account requires the system manager.

Conflicts: None known.

INTERRUPT 21h - Function 5Fh, Subfunction 87h
GET ACCOUNT

Purpose: Determine information about the currently active account on the specified machine.

Available on: All machines.

Restrictions: LANtastic network software version 3.0 or higher must be installed.

Registers at call:
AX = 5F87h
DS:SI -> 128-byte buffer for account information
   (Table 21-1)
ES:DI -> ASCIZ machine name in form "\machine"

Return Registers:
CF clear if successful
CF set on error
   AX = error code
BX destroyed

Details: The caller must be logged into the specified machine.

Conflicts: None known.

Table 21-1. Format of User Account Structure:

Offset	Size	Description
00h	16 BYTEs	blank-padded username
10h	16 BYTEs	reserved (00h)
20h	32 BYTEs	user description
40h	BYTE	privilege bits:
		bit 7: bypass access control lists
		bit 6: bypass queue protection
		bit 5: treat as local process
		bit 4: bypass mail protection
		bit 3: allow audit entry creation
		bit 2: system manager
41h	BYTE	maximum concurrent users
42h	42 BYTEs	bit map for disallowed half hours, beginning on Sunday (bit set if half-hour not an allowed time)
6Ch	WORD	internal (0002h)
6Eh	2 WORDs	last login time
72h	2 WORDs	account expiration date (MSDOS-format year/month:day)
76h	2 WORDs	password expiration date (0 = none)
7Ah	BYTE	number of days to extend password after change (1-31)
7Bh	5 BYTEs	reserved

INTERRUPT 21h - Function 5Fh, Subfunction 97h
COPY FILE

Purpose: Copy data from one file into another.

Available on: All machines.

Registers at call:
AX = 5F97h
CX:DX = number of bytes to copy (FFFFFFFFh =
    entire file)
SI = source file handle
DI = destination file handle
Details: The file copy is performed by the server.
Conflicts: None known.

Restrictions: LANtastic network software must be
    installed.
Return Registers:
CF clear if successful
    AX:DX = number of bytes copied
CF set on error
    AX = error code

INTERRUPT 21h - Function 5Fh, Subfunction 98h
SEND UNSOLICITED MESSAGE

Purpose: Queue a message for another user, possibly on another machine.
Available on: All machines.

Registers at call:
AX = 5F98h
DS:SI -> message buffer (Table 21-2)

Conflicts: None known.
See Also: Function 5Fh Subfunction 99h

Restrictions: LANtastic network software must be
    installed.
Return Registers:
CF clear if successful
CF set on error
    AX = error code

Table 21-2. Format of Message Buffer:

Offset	Size	Description
00h	BYTE	reserved
01h	BYTE	message type:
		00h general
		01h server warning
		02h-7Fh reserved
		80h-FFh user-defined
02h	16 BYTEs	ASCIZ destination machine name
12h	16 BYTEs	ASCIZ server name which user must be logged into
22h	16 BYTEs	ASCIZ user name
32h	16 BYTEs	ASCIZ originating machine name (filled in when received)
42h	80 BYTEs	message text

INTERRUPT 21h - Function 5Fh, Subfunction 99h
GET LAST RECEIVED UNSOLICITED MESSAGE

Purpose: Retrieve a message from another user.
Available on: All machines.

Registers at call:
AX = 5F99h
ES:DI -> messsage buffer (Table 21-2)

Conflicts: None known.
See Also: Function 5Fh Subfunction 98h

Restrictions: LANtastic network software must be
    installed.
Return Registers:
CF clear if successful
CF set on error
    AX = error code

INTERRUPT 21h - Function 5Fh, Subfunction 9Ah
GET MESSAGE PROCESSING FLAGS

Purpose: Determine what processing is performed when an unsolicited message is received.

Available on: All machines.

Registers at call:
AX = 5F9Ah

Restrictions: LANtastic network software must be installed.
Return Registers:
CF clear if successful
    DL = bits describing processing for received
        unsolicited messages
      bit 0: beep before message is delivered
        1: deliver message to message service
        2: pop up message automatically (v3+)
CF set on error
    AX = error code

Conflicts: None known.
See Also: Function 5Fh Subfunctions 9Bh and 9Ch

INTERRUPT 21h - Function 5Fh, Subfunction 9Bh
SET MESSAGE PROCESSING FLAG

Purpose: Specify what processing is to be performed when an unsolicited message is received.
Available on: All machines.

Registers at call:
AX = 5F9Bh
DL = bits describing processing for received
    unsolicited messages (see Function 5Fh
    Subfunction 9Ah)
Conflicts: None known.
See Also: Function 5Fh Subfunction 9Ah

Restrictions: LANtastic network software must be installed.
Return Registers:
CF clear if successful
CF set on error
    AX = error code

INTERRUPT 21h - Function 5Fh, Subfunction 9Ch
POP UP LAST RECEIVED MESSAGE

Purpose: Display a message from another user.
Available on: All machines.

Registers at call:
AX = 5F9Ch
CX = time to leave on screen in clock ticks
DH = 0-based screen line on which to place
    message
Details: The original screen contents are restored when the message is removed.
Conflicts: None known.
See Also: Function 5Fh Subfunction 9Ah

Restrictions: LANtastic version 3.0 or higher must be installed.
Return Registers:
CF clear if successful
CF set on error
    AX = error code (0Bh)

INTERRUPT 21h - Function 5Fh, Subfunction A0h
GET QUEUE ENTRY

Purpose: Determine the type of, and other information about, an entry in the specified server's queue.
Available on: All machines.

Registers at call:
AX = 5FA0h
BX = queue entry index (0000h is first entry)
DS:SI -> buffer for queue entry (Table 21-3)
ES:DI -> ASCIZ server name in form "\name"

Conflicts: None known.

Restrictions: LANtastic network software must be installed.
Return Registers:
CF clear if successful
CF set on error
    AX = error code
BX = entry index for next queue entry
    (BX-1 is current index)

See Also: Function 5Fh Subfunctions A1h and A2h

Table 21-3. Format of Queue Entry:

Offset	Size	Description
00h	BYTE	status of entry:
		00h empty
		01h being updated
		02h being held
		03h waiting for despool
		04h being despooled
		05h canceled
		06h spooled file could not be accessed
		07h destination could not be accessed
		08h rush job
01h	DWORD	size of spooled file
05h	BYTE	type of entry:
		00h printer queue file
		01h message
		02h local file
		03h remote file
		04h to remote modem
		05h batch processor file
06h	BYTE	output control
		bit 6: don't delete (for mail)
		bit 5: mail file contains voice mail (v3+)
07h	WORD	number of copies
09h	DWORD	sequence number of queue entry
0Dh	48 BYTEs	pathname of spooled file
3Dh	16 BYTEs	user who spooled file
4Dh	16 BYTEs	name of machine from which file was spooled
5Dh	WORD	date file was spooled (see Function 57h Subfunction 00h, chapter 8)
5Fh	WORD	time file was spooled (see Function 57h Subfunction 00h, chapter 8)
61h	17 BYTEs	ASCIZ destination device or user name
72h	48 BYTEs	comment field

INTERRUPT 21h - Function 5Fh, Subfunction A1h
SET QUEUE ENTRY

Purpose: Modify an entry in a server's queue.

Available on: All machines.

Restrictions: LANtastic network software must be installed.

Registers at call:
AX = 5FA1h
BX = handle of opened queue entry
DS:SI -> queue entry (Table 21-3)

Return Registers:
CF clear if successful
CF set on error
    AX = error code

Details: The only queue entry fields which may be changed are output control, number of copies, destination device, and comment.

Conflicts: None known.

See Also: Function 5Fh Subfunctions A0h and A2h

INTERRUPT 21h - Function 5Fh, Subfunction A2h
CONTROL QUEUE

Purpose: Alter print jobs and manipulate the despooling of entries in the specified server's queue.

Available on: All machines.

Restrictions: LANtastic network software must be installed.

Registers at call:
AX = 5FA2h
BL = control command
    00h start despooling (privileged)
    01h halt despooling (privileged)
    02h halt despooling at end of job (privileged)
    03h pause despooler at end of job (privileged)
    04h print single job (privileged)
    05h restart current job (privileged)
    06h cancel the current job
    07h hold queue entry
    08h release a held queue entry
    09h make queue entry a rushed job (privileged)
CX:DX = sequence number to control (commands
    06h-09h)
DX = physical printer number (commands 00h-05h)
    00h-02h LPT1-LPT3
    03h,04h COM1,COM2
    other   all printers
ES:DI -> ASCIZ computer name
Conflicts: None known.

Return Registers:
CF clear if successful
CF set on error
    AX = error code

INTERRUPT 21h - Function 5Fh, Subfunction A3h
GET PRINTER STATUS

Purpose: Determine the state of the printer and which print job (if any) it is executing.
Available on: All machines.

Restrictions: LANtastic version 3.0 or higher must be installed.

Registers at call:
AX = 5FA3h
BX = physical printer number (00h-02h = LPT1-
    LPT3, 03h-04h = COM1-COM2)
DS:SI -> buffer for printer status (Table 21-4)
ES:DI -> ASCIZ server name in form "\machine"
Conflicts: None known.

Return Registers:
CF clear if successful
CF set on error
    AX = error code
BX = next physical printer number

Table 21-4. Format of printer status:

Offset	Size	Description
00h	BYTE	printer state
		bit 7: printer paused
		bits 0-6: 0 printer disabled
		1 will stop at end of job
		2 print multiple jobs
01h	WORD	queue index of print job being despooled; FFFFh if not despooling--ignore all following fields
03h	WORD	actual characters per second being output
05h	DWORD	number of characters actually output so far
09h	DWORD	number of bytes read from spooled file so far
0Dh	WORD	copies remaining to print

INTERRUPT 21h - Function 5Fh, Subfunction A4h
GET STREAM INFO

Purpose: Determine the state of a stream.

Available on: All machines.

Registers at call:
AX = 5FA4h
BX = 0-based stream index number DS:SI -> buffer
    for stream information (Table 21-5)
ES:DI -> ASCIZ machine name in form "\machine"
Conflicts: None known.
See Also: Function 5Fh Subfunction A5h

Restrictions: LANtastic version 3.0 or higher must be
    installed.
Return Registers:
CF clear if successful
CF set on error
    AX = error code
BX = next stream number

Table 21-5. Format of Stream Information:

Offset	Size	Description
00h	BYTE	queueing of jobs for logical printer (0=disabled,other=enabled)
01h	11 BYTEs	logical printer resource template (may contain ? wildcards)

INTERRUPT 21h - Function 5Fh, Subfunction A5h
SET STREAM INFO

Purpose: Specify the state of a stream.
Available on: All machines.

Registers at call:
AX = 5FA5h
BX = 0-based stream index number
DS:SI -> buffer containing stream information (see
    Function 5Fh Subfunction A4h)
ES:DI -> ASCIZ machine name in form "\machine"
Conflicts: None known.
See Also: Function 5Fh Subfunction A4h

Restrictions: LANtastic version 3.0 or higher must be
    installed.
Return Registers:
CF clear if successful
CF set on error
    AX = error code

INTERRUPT 21h - Function 5Fh, Subfunction A7h
CREATE USER AUDIT ENTRY

Purpose: Add an entry to the audit file.
Available on: All machines.

Registers at call:
AX = 5FA7h
DS:DX -> ASCIZ reason code (max 8 bytes)
DS:SI -> ASCIZ variable reason code (max 128
    bytes)
ES:DI -> ASCIZ machine name in form "\machine"
Conflicts: None known.

Restrictions: LANtastic network software must be
    installed.
Return Registers:
CF clear if successful
CF set on error
    AX = error code

INTERRUPT 21h - Function 5Fh, Subfunction B0h
GET ACTIVE USER INFORMATION

Purpose: Determine name and last action of a user logged into the specified machine.
Available on: All machines.

Registers at call:
AX = 5FB0h
BX = server login entry index
DS:SI -> buffer for active user entry (Table 21-6)
ES:DI -> ASCIZ machine name in form "\server"

Restrictions: LANtastic network software must be
    installed.
Return Registers:
CF clear if successful
CF set on error
    AX = error code
BX = next login index

Conflicts: None known.

Table 21-6. Format of Active User Entry:

Offset	Size	Description
00h	WORD	virtual circuit number
02h	BYTE	login state
		bit 0: fully logged in
		1: remote program load login
		3: user can create audit entries
		4: bypass mail protection
		5: treat as local process
		6: bypass queue protection
		7: bypass access control lists
03h	BYTE	last command issued (Table 21-7)
04h	5 BYTEs	number of I/O bytes (40-bit unsigned number)
09h	3 BYTEs	number of server requests (24-bit unsigned)
0Ch	16 BYTEs	name of user who is logged in
1Ch	16 BYTEs	name of remote logged in machine

Table 21-7. Values for Last Command:

Value	Command	Value	Command
00h	login	15h	set a queue entry
01h	process termination	16h	control the queue
02h	open file	17h	return login information
03h	close file	18h	return link description
04h	create file	19h	seek on file
05h	create new file	1Ah	get server's time
06h	create unique file	1Bh	create audit entry
07h	commit data to disk	1Ch	open file in multitude of modes
08h	read file	1Dh	change password
09h	write file	1Eh	disable account
0Ah	delete file	1Fh	local server file copy
0Bh	set file attributes	---v3.0+	
0Ch	lock byte range	20h	get username from account file
0Dh	unlock byte range	21h	translate server's logical path
0Eh	create subdirectory	22h	make indirect file
0Fh	remove subdirectory	23h	get indirect file contents
10h	rename file	24h	get physical printer status
11h	find first matching file	25h	get logical print stream info
12h	find next matching file	26h	set logical print stream info
13h	get disk free space	27h	get user's account record
14h	get a queue entry		

INTERRUPT 21h - Function 5Fh, Subfunction B1h
GET SHARED DIRECTORY INFORMATION

Purpose: Determine information about a directory which may be shared with other users.

Available on: All machines.

Restrictions: LANtastic network software must be installed.

Registers at call:
AX = 5FB1h
DS:SI -> 64-byte buffer for link description
ES:DI -> ASCIZ machine and shared directory
name in form "\machine"

Return Registers:
CF clear if successful
CX = access control list privilege bits for

requesting user
bit 5: allow attribute changing
6: allow physical access to device

    7: allow program execution
    8: allow file renaming
    9: allow directory deletion
    10: allow file deletion
    11: allow file/directory lookups
    12: allow directory creation
    13: allow file creation
    14: allow open for write and writing
    15: allow open for read and reading
CF set on error
    AX = error code

Conflicts: None known.

INTERRUPT 21h - Function 5Fh, Subfunction B2h
GET USERNAME FROM ACCOUNT FILE

Purpose: Determine the permanently-stored name for the calling user.

Available on: All machines.

Restrictions: LANtastic version 3.0 or higher must be installed.

Registers at call:
AX = 5FB2h
BX = username entry index (0 for first)
DS:SI -> 16-byte buffer for username
ES:DI -> ASCIZ server name in form "\machine"
Conflicts: None known.

Return Registers:
CF clear if successful
CF set on error
    AX = error code
    BX = next queue entry index

INTERRUPT 21h - Function 5Fh, Subfunction B3h
TRANSLATE PATH

Purpose: Determine the true directory for a pathname in the presence of indirect files.

Available on: All machines.

Restrictions: LANtastic version 3.0 or higher must be installed.

Registers at call:
AX = 5FB3h
DS:SI -> 128-byte buffer for ASCIZ result
ES:DI -> full ASCIZ path, including server name
DX = types of translation to be performed
    bit 0: expand last component as indirect file
    bit 1: return actual path relative to server's
          physical disk

Return Registers:
CF clear if successful
CF set on error
    AX = error code

Details: This call always expands any indirect files along the path.
Conflicts: None known.
See Also: Function 5Fh Subfunction B4h

INTERRUPT 21h - Function 5Fh, Subfunction B4h
CREATE INDIRECT FILE

Purpose: Make a link from one part of the network filespace to another, possibly on a different machine; this is equivalent to symbolic links under Unix.

Available on: All machines.

Restrictions: LANtastic version 3.0 or higher must be installed.

Registers at call:
AX = 5FB4h
DS:SI -> 128-byte buffer containing ASCIZ
    contents of indirect file

Return Registers:
CF clear if successful
CF set on error
    AX = error code

ES:DI -> full ASCIZ path of indirect file to create,
including machine name
Details: The contents of the indirect file may be any valid server-relative path.
Conflicts: None known.

INTERRUPT 21h - Function 5Fh, Subfunction B5h
GET INDIRECT FILE CONTENTS

Purpose: Determine the destination of a link from one part of the network filespace to another.

Available on: All machines.

Registers at call:
AX = 5FB5h
DS:SI -> 128-byte buffer for ASCIZ indirect file
contents
ES:DI -> full ASCIZ path of indirect file
Conflicts: None known.

Restrictions: LANtastic version 3.0 or higher must be installed.

Return Registers:
CF clear if successful
CF set on error
AX = error code

INTERRUPT 21h - Function 5Fh, Subfunction C0h
GET TIME FROM SERVER

Purpose: Determine the system date and time as known to the specified server.

Available on: All machines.

Registers at call:
AX = 5FC0h
DS:SI -> time block (Table 21-8)
ES:DI -> ASCIZ server name to get time from
Conflicts: None known.

Restrictions: LANtastic network software must be installed.

Return Registers:
CF clear if successful
CF set on error
AX = error code

Table 21-8. Format of time block:

Offset	Size	Description
00h	WORD	year
02h	BYTE	day
03h	BYTE	month
04h	BYTE	minutes
05h	BYTE	hour
06h	BYTE	hundredths of second
07h	BYTE	second

INTERRUPT 21h - Function 5Fh, Subfunction D0h
GET REDIRECTED PRINTER TIMEOUT

Purpose: Determine the duration of idleness before the printer times out.

Available on: All machines.

Registers at call:
AX = 5FD0h

Restrictions: LANtastic network software must be installed.

Return Registers:
CF clear if successful
CX = redirected printer timeout in clock ticks of
55ms
0000h if timeout disabled
CF set on error
AX = error code

Conflicts: None known.
See Also: Function 5Fh Subfunction D1h

INTERRUPT 21h - Function 5Fh, Subfunction D1h
SET REDIRECTED PRINTER TIMEOUT

Purpose: Specify the duration of idleness before the printer times out.

Available on: All machines.

Restrictions: LANtastic network software must be installed.

Registers at call:
AX = 5FD1h
CX = printer timeout in clock ticks of 55ms,
   0000h to disable timeouts

Return Registers:
CF clear if successful
CF set on error
   AX = error code

Conflicts: None known.
See Also: Function 5Fh Subfunction D0h

INTERRUPT 21h - Function 5Fh, Subfunction E0h
GET DOS SERVICE VECTOR

Purpose: Determine address of function handling DOS calls for LANtastic.

Available on: All machines.

Restrictions: LANtastic network software must be installed.

Registers at call:
AX = 5FE0h

Return Registers:
CF clear if successful
   ES:BX -> current FAR service routine
CF set on error
   AX = error code

Conflicts: None known.
See Also: Function 5Fh Subfunction E1h

INTERRUPT 21h - Function 5Fh, Subfunction E1h
SET DOS SERVICE VECTOR

Purpose: Specify a new function which is to handle DOS calls.

Available on: All machines.

Restrictions: LANtastic network software must be installed.

Registers at call:
AX = 5FE1h
ES:BX -> FAR routine to call for DOS service

Return Registers:
CF clear if successful
CF set on error
   AX = error code

Details: The new handler must chain to the previous handler as its first action.
Conflicts: None known.
See Also: Function 5Fh Subfunction E0h

INTERRUPT 21h - Function 5Fh, Subfunction E2h
GET MESSAGE SERVICE VECTOR

Purpose: Determine the subroutine currently called on receipt of a message.

Available on: All machines.

Restrictions: LANtastic network software must be installed.

Registers at call:
AX = 5FE2h

Return Registers:
CF clear if successful
   ES:BX -> current FAR message service routine
CF set on error
   AX = error code

Conflicts: None known.
See Also: Function 5Fh Subfunction E3h

INTERRUPT 21h - Function 5Fh, Subfunction E3h
SET MESSAGE SERVICE VECTOR

Purpose: Specify the subroutine to be called when a message is received.

Available on: All machines.

Restrictions: LANtastic network software must be installed.

Registers at call:
AX = 5FE3h
ES:BX -> FAR routine for processing network
   messages

Return Registers:
CF clear if successful
CF set on error
   AX = error code

Details: The new handler must chain to the previous handler as its first action; on invocation, ES:BX points at the just-received message.

Conflicts: None known.

See Also: Function 5Fh Subfunction E2h

INTERRUPT 2Ah
Microsoft-compatible Functions

Purpose: LANtastic supports subfunctions 00h, 01h, 04h, 05h, and 06h of the Microsoft Networks INT 2Ah alternate NetBIOS interface. These functions are described in chapter 27.

INTERRUPT 2Fh - Function B8h, Subfunction 09h
VERSION CHECK

Purpose: Determine which version of the LANtastic software is installed.

Available on: All machines.

Restrictions: LANtastic network software must be installed.

Registers at call:
AX = B809h

Return Registers:
AH = major version
AL = minor version

Conflicts: None known.

Chapter 22

Banyan VINES

The **VI**rtual **NE**twork Software package from Banyan Systems, Inc. is one of the major players in the large-network competition. This system was one of the first to offer full interconnection between such diverse operating systems as MS-DOS and UNIX, and because of this, found early acceptance by large corporations.

For compatibility, VINES provides a number of functions from other networking software; those are merely pointed out here and are described in full in other chapters.

Although the majority of the API is listed under INT 61h, the actual interrupt number used may range from 60h through 66h depending on system configuration. The VINES entry point is identified by the signature "BANV" immediately preceding the handler.

INTERRUPT 21h - Functions D0h through D5h
LOGICAL RECORD LOCKING AND UNLOCKING
These functions are identical to Novell NetWare's implementation and are described in chapter 20.

INTERRUPT 21h - Functions D8h and D9h
RESOURCE ALLOCATION
This function is identical to Novell NetWare's implementation and is described in chapter 20.

INTERRUPT 21h - Function DCh
GET STATION NUMBER
This function is identical to Novell NetWare's implementation and is described in chapter 20.

INTERRUPT 21h - Function E7h
GET FILE SERVER DATE AND TIME
This function is identical to Novell NetWare's implementation and is described in chapter 20.

INTERRUPT 2Fh - Function D7h, Subfunction 01h
GET BANV INTERRUPT NUMBER
Purpose: Determine whether Banyan VINES version 4.0 or higher is installed, and which interrupt the API is using.

Available on: All machines.   **Restrictions: none.**

Registers at call: **Return Registers:**

AX = D701h   AX = 0000h installed

                          BX = interrupt number (60h to 66h)

                nonzero not present

Details: If AX is nonzero, VINES 3.x or earlier may be installed, in which case it is necessary to examine the four bytes preceding the handlers for INT 60h through INT 66h for the string "BANV".

Conflicts: None known.

INTERRUPT 60h - Function 0Ch
GET STATION ADDRESS

This function is identical to the 3com implementation, and is described in chapter 27.

INTERRUPT 60h - Functions 11h through 13h
SEMAPHORE LOCKING AND UNLOCKING

Purpose: Arbitrate access to resources. These functions are identical to the 3com implementation, and are described in chapter 27.

INTERRUPT 61h - Function 0001h, Subfunction 0001h
"Sosock" - OPEN COMMUNICATIONS SOCKET

Purpose: Establish a connection to a protocol service.
Available on: All machines.
Registers at call:
AX = 0001h
DS:DX -> communications control block
   (Table 22-1)

Restrictions: Banyan VINES must be installed.
Return Registers:
AX = status
   0000h successful
   0001h service not installed
   0002h invalid service ID
   0098h resource already in use
   009Eh address family does not exist
   009Fh socket type does not exist
   00A0h protocol does not exist
   00A1h no more sockets available
   00A2h no more buffer space available

Details: BANYAN can use any interrupt from 60h through 66h. The Banyan interrupt handler is identified by the string "BANV" in the four bytes immediately preceding the interrupt handler.
Conflicts: See Chapter 1.

Table 22-1. Format of Control Block:

Offset	Size	Description
00h	WORD	0001h
02h	WORD	pointer to argument block (Table 22-2)
04h	WORD	error return code
06h	4 BYTEs	reserved

Table 22-2. Format of Argument Block:

Offset	Size	Description
00h	WORD	pointer to 2-byte buffer for socket identifier
02h	WORD	address family
		0003h Banyan
04h	WORD	socket type
		in address family 0003h
		0001h IPC socket
		0002h SPP socket
06h	WORD	protocol number
		FFFFh default
08h	WORD	pointer to 16-byte buffer for socket address (Table 22-3)
0Ah	WORD	local port number
		0000h if service should assign transient port number
		0001h to 01FFh well-known port number (assigned by Banyan)

Table 22-3. Format of IPC Port:

Offset	Size	Description
00h	WORD	address family (always 0003h for Banyan ports)
04h	4 BYTEs	network number (server's serial number)

Table 22-3. Format of IPC port (continued)

Offset	Size	Description
06h	WORD	subnet number (0001h = server, 8000h-FFFEh = PC)
08h	WORD	port ID (0001h-01FFh for "well-known" ports)
0Ah	BYTE	hop count
0Bh	5 BYTEs	filler

INTERRUPT 61h - Function 0001h, Subfunction 0002h
"Sosend" - INITIATE OUTPUT EVENT

Purpose: Request data transmission or the establishment or termination of a virtual connection.

Available on: All machines.

Registers at call:
AX = 0001h
DS:DX -> communications control block
   (Table 22-4)

Restrictions: Banyan VINES must be installed.

Return Registers:
AX = status
   0000h successful
   0001h service not installed
   0002h invalid service ID
   0003h-000Ah reserved for BANV interface errors
   0097h invalid socket identifier
   009Bh destination node unreachable
   009Ch message overflow
   009Dh destination socket nonexistent
   00A2h no more buffer space
   00A3h timeout
   00B1h resource disconnect

Conflicts: See Chapter 1.

Table 22-4. Format of Control Block:

Offset	Size	Description
00h	WORD	0002h
02h	WORD	pointer to argument block (Table 22-5)
04h	WORD	error return code
		0000h successful
		0097h invalid socket ID
		00A2h no more buffer space
		00A3h timeout event
		00A5h resource not available
		00A6h internal communication failure
		00B1h resource disconnect
06h	4 BYTEs	reserved

Table 22-5. Format of Argument Block:

Offset	Size	Description
00h	WORD	routine metric
02h	WORD	error return code
04h	WORD	socket identifier
06h	WORD	pointer to send buffer (Table 22-6)
08h	WORD	length of send buffer
0Ah	WORD	flags
		bit 0: async request
		1: reliable message
		3: end of user message received
		4: vectored request (if set, send buffer contains buffer
		descriptors)

Table 22-5. Format of Argument Block (continued)

Offset	Size	Description
		5: connection-specific receive
		6: change to connection-specific receive mode
0Ch	16 BYTEs	socket address (Table 22-7)
1Ch	WORD	timeout value in multiples of 200ms
1Eh	WORD	connection identifier
20h	WORD	type of request
		0001h send message
		0002h establish a virtual connection
		0003h terminate a virtual connection

Table 22-6. Format of Buffer Descriptor:

Offset	Size	Description
00h	WORD	data segment
02h	WORD	buffer pointer
04h	WORD	buffer length
06h	WORD	character count

Table 22-7. Format of Socket Address for Unreliable Datagrams:

Offset	Size	Description	
00h	WORD	0003h	address family
02h	DWORD	FFFFFFFFh	network number
06h	WORD	FFFFh	subnet number
08h	WORD		local port number
0Ah	BYTE	00h-0Fh	hop count
0Bh	5 BYTEs	0000h	filler

INTERRUPT 61h - Function 0001h, Subfunction 0003h
"Sorec" - RECEIVE INPUT EVENT NOTIFICATION

Purpose: Request notification on the reception of data or the establishment or termination of a virtual connection.

Available on: All machines.   **Restrictions:** Banyan VINES must be installed.

Registers at call: **Return Registers:**

AX = 0001h   AX = status

DS:DX -> communications control block   0000h successful
   (Table 22-8)   0001h service not installed
                                                       0002h invalid service ID
                                                       0003h-000Ah reserved for BANV interface errors
                                                       0097h invalid socket identifier
                                                       00A2h no more buffer space
                                                       00A3h timeout

Conflicts: See Chapter 1.

Table 22-8. Format of control block:

Offset	Size	Description
00h	WORD	0003h
02h	WORD	pointer to argument block (Table 22-9)

Table 22-8. Format of Control Block (continued)

Offset	Size	Description
04h	WORD	error return code
		0000h successful
		0097h invalid socket ID
		00A2h no more buffer space
		00A3h timeout event
		00A5h resource not available
		00A6h internal communication failure
		00B1h resource disconnect
06h	4 Bytes	reserved

Table 22-9. Format of Argument Block:

Offset	Size	Description
00h	WORD	character count
02h	WORD	error return code
04h	WORD	socket identifier
06h	WORD	pointer to receive buffer (Table 22-10)
08h	WORD	length of receive buffer
0Ah	WORD	flags
		bit 0: async request
		2: flush receive buffer on overflow
		3: end of user message received
		4: vectored request (if set, receive buffer contains buffer descriptors)
		5: connection-specific receive
		6: change to connection-specific receive mode
0Ch	16 Bytes	socket address
1Ch	WORD	timeout value in multiples of 200ms
1Eh	WORD	connection identifier
20h	WORD	type of response
		0001h message received
		0002h virtual connection established
		0003h virtual connection terminated

Table 22-10. Format of Buffer Descriptor:

Offset	Size	Description
00h	WORD	data segment
02h	WORD	buffer pointer
04h	WORD	buffer length
06h	WORD	character count

INTERRUPT 61h - Function 0001h, Subfunction 0004h
"Soclose" - CLOSE A SOCKET

Purpose: Terminate the specified connection to a protocol service and all virtual connections established through that socket.

Available on: All machines.

Registers at call:
AX = 0001h
DS:DX -> communications control block
   (Table 22-11)

Restrictions: Banyan VINES must be installed.

Return Registers:
AX = status
   0000h successful
   0001h service not installed
   0002h invalid service ID
   0003h-000Ah reserved for BANV interface errors
   0097h invalid socket identifier

Conflicts: See Chapter 1.

Table 22-11. Format of Control Block:

Offset	Size	Description
00h	WORD	0004h
02h	WORD	pointer to argument block (Table 22-12)
04h	WORD	error return code
06h	4 BYTEs	reserved

Table 22-12. Format of Argument Block:

Offset	Size	Description
00h	WORD	socket identifier

INTERRUPT 61h - Function 0001h, Subfunction 0005h
"Sowait" - WAIT FOR ASYNCHRONOUS EVENT COMPLETION

Purpose: Receive notification on the completion of outstanding send or receive requests.

Available on: All machines.　　　　　　　　**Restrictions:** Banyan VINES must be installed.

Registers at call:　　　　　　　　　　　　**Return Registers:**
AX = 0001h　　　　　　　　　　　　　　　　AX = status
DS:DX -> communications control block　　　　　0000h successful
　(Table 22-13)　　　　　　　　　　　　　　0001h service not installed
　　　　　　　　　　　　　　　　　　　　　0002h invalid service ID
　　　　　　　　　　　　　　　　　　　　　0003h-000Ah reserved for BANV interface errors
　　　　　　　　　　　　　　　　　　　　　00A2h no more buffer space available
　　　　　　　　　　　　　　　　　　　　　00A3h timeout event

Details: This function returns the results for all asynchronous operations invoked from the data segment used for this call.

Conflicts: See Chapter 1.

Table 22-13. Format of Control Block:

Offset	Size	Description
00h	WORD	0005h
02h	WORD	pointer to argument block (Table 22-14)
04h	WORD	error return code
06h	4 BYTEs	reserved

Table 22-14. Format of Argument Block:

Offset	Size	Description
00h	WORD	pointer to WORD event pointer
02h	WORD	timeout in multiples of 200ms, FFFFh = infinite

INTERRUPT 61h - Function 0001h, Subfunction 0008h
"Sosession" - REGISTER APPLICATION WITH COMM SERVICE

Purpose: Called by the application at startup to allow the communications service layer to perform initializations and release any resources which may have inadvertently been left in an active state.

Available on: All machines.　　　　　　　　**Restrictions:** Banyan VINES must be installed.

Registers at call:　　　　　　　　　　　　**Return Registers:**
AX = 0001h　　　　　　　　　　　　　　　　AX = status
DS:DX -> communications control block　　　　　0000h successful
　(Table 22-15)　　　　　　　　　　　　　　00A2h no more buffer space available

Conflicts: See Chapter 1.

Table 22-15. Format of Control Block:

Offset	Size	Description
00h	WORD	0008h
02h	WORD	process type
		0001h transient process
		0002h resident process
04h	WORD	error return code
06h	4 BYTEs	reserved

INTERRUPT 61h - Function 0001h, Subfunction 000Bh
"Soint" - SET USER COMPLETION FUNCTION

Purpose: Specify a handler to be invoked on the completion of an asynchronous send or receive operation.

Available on: All machines.

Restrictions: Banyan VINES must be installed.

Registers at call:
AX = 0001h
DS:DX -> communications control block
   (Table 22-16)

Return Registers:
AX = status
   0000h successful
   0001h service not installed
   0002h invalid service ID
   0003h-000Ah reserved for BANV interface errors
   00A2h no more buffer space available

Details: The FAR user function is invoked with SS,DS, and ES set to the segment of the control block, and with the stack containing:
     DWORD return address
     WORD   argument pointer (sosend or sorec argument block)
     WORD   error return code
            0000h argument pointer is valid
            00A3h timeout

Conflicts: See Chapter 1.

Table 22-16. Format of Control Block:

Offset	Size	Description
00h	WORD	000Bh
02h	WORD	pointer to argument block (Table 22-17)
04h	WORD	error return code
06h	2 BYTEs	reserved
08h	WORD	user CS register

Table 22-17. Format of Argument Block:

Offset	Size	Description
00h	WORD	pointer to user interrupt function
02h	WORD	pointer to user stack
04h	WORD	initial timeout value in multiples of 200ms, FFFFh = infinite

INTERRUPT 61h - Function 0002h
3270 INTERFACE

Purpose: Provide mainframe access. The 3270/SNA and 3270/BSC options emulate a 3270 terminal on the PC and a 3274 controller in the server node.

Available on: All machines.

Restrictions: Banyan VINES must be installed.

Registers at call:
AX = 0002h

Return Registers:
AX = status

BH = function

00h "pi2reset" reset 3270/SNA or 3270/BSC driver

02h "pi2bsc" (3270/BSC only)

03h "pi2get" get information stored in 3270 resident driver

04h "pi2put" store information in 3270 resident driver

05h "pi2gcur" get current screen position

07h "pi2sdat" send data keystroke

08h "pi2scom" send command keystroke

0Ah "pi2field" get field info for arbitrary screen positions

0Fh "pi2stat" get logical unit/device status

12h "pi2nlus" determine logical unit/device assignment

13h "pi2gate" specifies comm port address to gateway service

14h "pi2attach" attach a logical unit/device

15h "pi2sdev" save logical unit/device info in resident driver (not supported in >3.0)

16h "pi2gdev" get device information (not supported in >3.0)

17h "pi2luinfo" get info about specific logical unit/device

18h "pi2gerr" get finer error detail

19h "pi2dhold" (3270/SNA only) holds a 3270 device

1Ah "pi2shut" release memory-resident module

1Ch "pi2sprof" save profile info in res driver (not supported in >3.0)

1Dh "pi2gprof" get prevsly stored profile info (not supported in >3.0)

DS:CX -> argument block (except BH=00h,1Ah) (Tables 22-18 thru 22-31)

0000h successful

000Bh invalid parameter or data does not fit data area

000Ch another code path currently active in resident driver

000Dh operation currently not allowed

0032h encountered connection disconnect error

0033h encountered "sosend" completion error

0034h encountered "sosend" communication error

0035h attach request refused. extended error info via "pi2gerr":

01h resource unavailable

02h invalid type

03h version mismatch

04h invalid logical unit number

05h error during ARL processing

06h no access for user

0071h encountered "sosock" error

0072h encountered unrecognizable error

0073h encountered "sowait" error (extended info via "pi2gerr")

0074h encountered invalid type-of-request on "sowait"

0075h encountered "sorec" error (extended info via "pi2gerr")

0076h encountered "sorec" completion error (ext info via "pi2gerr")

0077h encountered connection request

0078h encountered unrecognizable data

0079h encountered unknown connection ID (ext info via "pi2gerr")

Details: Either 3270/SNA or 3270/BSC interface may use Function 0002h, depending on which is loaded first. The other interface will then use Function 000Ah. Status codes greater than 63h indicate an inconsistency in the 3270/SNA or 3270/BSC resident driver, which must be reloaded by the user.

Conflicts: See Chapter 1.

Table 22-18. Format of Argument Block for BH=03h,04h:

Offset	Size	Description
00h	WORD	size of data area (max 256)
02h	N BYTEs	data area

Table 22-19. Format of Argument Block for BH=05h:

Offset	Size	Description
00h	WORD	logical unit/device number
02h	WORD	pointer to WORD buffer for cursor index
04h	WORD	pointer to BYTE buffer for current field attribute

Table 22-20. Format of Argument Block for BH=07h:

Offset	Size	Description
00h	WORD	logical unit/device number
02h	WORD	ASCII data byte
04h	WORD	pointer to WORD count of characters which will need updating

Table 22-21. Format of Argument Block for BH=08h:

Offset	Size	Description
00h	WORD	logical unit/device number
02h	WORD	keystroke

        0000h Enter
        0001h Clear
        0002h PA1
        0003h PA2
        0004h PA3
        0005h PF1

        ...
        001Ch PF26
        001Dh CSELECT (cursor select)
        001Eh Insert
        001Fh Delete
        0020h EOField
        0021h EINPUT (erase input)
        0022h Reset
        0023h Attention
        0024h SysReq
        0025h Duplicate
        0026h Fieldmark
        0027h Home
        0028h NextLine
        0029h Tab
        002Ah BackTab
        002Bh cursor up
        002Ch cursor down
        002Dh cursor right
        002Eh cursor left
        002Fh double cursor right
        0030h double cursor left
        0031h PRINT
        0032h CANCEL
        0033h Backspace

Table 22-22. Format of Argument Block for BH=0Ah:

Offset	Size	Description
00h	WORD	logical unit/device number
02h	WORD	screen index
04h	WORD	pointer to WORD buffer for field length
06h	WORD	pointer to WORD buffer for offset in screen of field start

Table 22-23. Format of Argument Block for BH=0Fh:

Offset	Size	Description
00h	WORD	logical unit/device number
02h	WORD	clear mask (clear these bits of status after returning status)
04h	WORD	pointer to WORD buffer for status
		bit 10: status modified

Table 22-23. Format of Argument Block for BH=0Fh (continued)

Offset	Size	Description

        bit 9: buffer modified
        bit 8: set cursor
        bit 5: sound alarm
        bits 0,1: size of print line for printer logical units
            00 unformatted line
            01 40-character line
            10 64-character line
            11 80-character line

Table 22-24. Format of Argument Block for BH=12h:

Offset	Size	Description
00h	WORD	pointer to WORD buffer for number of logical units or devices
02h	WORD	pointer to WORD buffer for version number
04h	WORD	pointer to 64-byte buffer for logical unit/device list

Table 22-25. Format of Argument Block for BH=13h:

Offset	Size	Description
00h	16 BYTEs	communications port address (see Function 0001h Subfunction 0001h)

Table 22-26. Format of Argument Block for BH=14h:

Offset	Size	Description
00h	WORD	logical unit/device number
		0000h attach any free device of the specified type
02h	WORD	logical unit/device type
		(3270/SNA) 01h, 02h, or 03h
		(3270/BSC) 02h display
		(3270/BSC) 03h printer
04h	WORD	pointer to WORD buffer for attached logical unit/device number

Table 22-27. Format of Argument Block for BH=16h:

Offset	Size	Description
00h	WORD	pointer to 18-byte buffer for device block (see below).
		first WORD must be set to desired logical unit/device number

Table 22-28. Format of Argument Block for BH=17h:

Offset	Size	Description
00h	WORD	logical unit/device number
02h	WORD	pointer to information block in caller's DS (Table 22-33)

Table 22-29. Format of Argument Block for BH=18h:

Offset	Size	Description
00h	WORD	pointer to WORD buffer for major error code
02h	WORD	pointer to WORD buffer for minor error code

Table 22-30. Format of Argument block for BH=19h:

Offset	Size	Description
00h	WORD	logical unit/device number

Table 22-31. Format of Argument Block for BH=1Ch,1Dh:

Offset	Size	Description
00h	WORD	pointer to profile block in caller's DS (Table 22-35)

Table 22-32. Format of Device Block, Argument Block for BH=15h:

Offset	Size	Description
00h	WORD	logical unit/device number
02h	WORD	logical unit/device type
04h	WORD	display model number
06h	WORD	numeric checking
08h	WORD	status line
0Ah	BYTE	unprotected normal field attribute
0Bh	BYTE	unprotected intensified field attribute
0Ch	BYTE	protected normal field attribute
0Dh	BYTE	protected intensified field attribute
0Eh	WORD	reserved
10h	WORD	printer port number

Table 22-33. Format of Information Block:

Offset	Size	Description
00h	WORD	device model number
02h	DWORD	screen buffer pointer
06h	DWORD	status line pointer (Table 22-34)
0Ah	DWORD	reserved

Table 22-34. Format of Status Line:

Offset	Size	Description
00h	BYTE	comm line status
		00h inactive
		01h active
01h	BYTE	activation level
		01h physical unit activated
		02h logical unit also activated
		03h session is bound
02h	BYTE	data traffic state
		00h inactive
		01h active
03h	BYTE	screen ownership
		00h SLU->PLU sessoin owns screen
		01h SLU->SSCP session owns screen
04h	BYTE	keyboard status
		00h UNLOCK - ready to accept data
		01h TIME - aid was struck
		02h SYSTEM - received response no restore
		03h FUNCTION - unavailable keyboard function
		04h INPUT - not currently used
		05h ENDFIELD - field filled in insert mode
		06h PROTECTED - attempt to enter in protected field
		07h NUMERIC - attempt to enter in numeric field
		08h PROGRAM - error in outbound data stream
05h	BYTE	insert mode: 01h if in insert mode
06h	BYTE	numeric: 01h if current screen buffer is numeric only
07h	BYTE	printer status:
		00h printer not assigned
		01h printer is inactive

Table 22-34. Format of Status Line (continued)

Offset	Size	Description
		02h printer error
		03h currently printing
		04h printer is busy
		05h printer is very busy
08h	BYTE	printer assignment
09h	BYTE	maximum size of network name
0Ah	N BYTEs	ASCIZ network name
	BYTE	maximum size of message window
	M BYTEs	null-terminated message window
	BYTE	code set:
		00h EBCDIC
		01h ASCII
	M BYTEs	extended attributes:
		01h extended attributes are in effect (stored at screen+1920).
		Each extended attribute specifies bits 0,1: 00=normal, 01=blink, 10=reverse, 11=underscore bits 2-4: 000=default, 001=blue, 010=red, 011=pink, 100=green, 101=turquoise, 110=yellow, 111=white
	BYTE	extended color: 01h other than base color is in effect

Table 22-35. Format of Profile Block:

Offset	Size	Description
00h	64 BYTEs	gateway service name
40h	16 BYTEs	gateway comm port address
50h	WORD	primary logical unit number
52h	WORD	secondary logical unit type
54h	WORD	secondary logical unit number
56h	WORD	printer assignment
58h	50 BYTEs	keyboard definitions filename

INTERRUPT 61h - Function 0003h
ASYNCHRONOUS TERMINAL EMULATION

Purpose: Provide terminal emulation functions to allow communications with a remote host.

Available on: All machines.

Registers at call:
AX = 0003h
DS:BX -> argument block with function number
    (Table 22-36)

Restrictions: Banyan VINES must be installed.

Return Registers:
AX = status
   0000h successful
   000Bh invalid session ID
   000Ch session not active
   000Dh invalid request type
   000Eh invalid parameters
   000Fh out of heap space
   0010h timeout on send
   0011h Banyan communications error
   0012h session not waiting for host
   0013h session is active
   0014h duplicate suspend session request
   0015h no session suspended
   0016h ring data buffer full
   0017h printer error encountered
   0018h Banyan communications error
   0019h unable to make connection
   001Ah no ring buffer specified at startup

001Bh service is down
001Ch invalid service name
001Dh service is closed
001Eh invalid connection name
001Fh max session limit reached for service
0020h access rights list for connection/dialout does
    not include this user
0021h service not responding
0022h missing telephone number

Conflicts: See chapter 1.

Table 22-36. Format of Argument Block:

Offset	Size	Description
00h	BYTE	session ID (00h)
01h	BYTE	asynchronous interface request number

    00h initialize user buffer pointer information area
    01h send to host
    02h "control monitor"
    03h "flow control data": freeze/unfreeze display, ring buffer
    04h end active session
    05h set session parameter
    06h get session parameter
    07h set tab settings
    08h get tab settings
    09h refresh emulation screen
    0Ah suspend session temporarily
    0Bh restore previously suspended session
    0Ch set state of scroll lock checking
    0Dh exit emulation
    0Eh interrupt on character from host
    0Fh start a session
    10h start/stop printing of data received from host
    11h get file transfer parameters
    12h get connection information
    13h start/stop tracing data traffic in session
    14h interrupt on message from host
    15h reset error

---request=00h

02h	WORD	pointer to info area in caller's current DS:

Offset	Size	Description
00h	WORD	flags

    0000h don't read interface's data buffer
    0001h read data buffer

02h	DWORD	pointer to ring buffer
06h	WORD	length of ring buffer
08h	WORD	ring buffer offset to last byte read by caller
0Ah	DWORD	pointer to WORD containing offset of last byte in ring buffer filled
0Eh	DWORD	pointer to screen buffer
12h	DWORD	pointer to field containing cursor position
16h	DWORD	pointer to terminal status area (Table 22-37)

---request=01h

02h	BYTE	type

    00h ASCII byte
    01h ASCII string

Table 22-36. Format of Argument Block (continued)

Offset	Size	Description
		02h terminal function code
		03h up arrow
		04h down arrow
		05h left arrow
		06h right arrow
		07h break
03h	N BYTEs	type-specific info:

Offset	Size	Description
---ASCII byte		
03h	BYTE	byte to send to host
---ASCII string		
03h	WORD	length of string
05h	WORD	pointer to string
---terminal function code (VT52/VT100)		
03h	BYTE	function code
		00h keypad 0
		01h keypad 1
		...
		09h keypad 9
		0Ah keypad -
		0Bh keypad ,
		0Ch keypad .
		0Dh keypad ENTER
		0Eh PF1
		0Fh PF2
		10h PF3
		11h PF4
---terminal function code (IBM3101)		
03h	BYTE	function code
		00h PF1
		...
		07h PF8
		08h Home

---request=02h

02h	BYTE	display flag
		00h don't display data received from host
		01h display data

---request=03h

02h	BYTE	flow control flag
		00h allow characters to be put into display or ring buffer
		01h don't place any more characters into display or ring buffer

---request=05h,06h

02h	BYTE	parameter number
		00h line speed (00h=any, 01h=50, 02h=110, 03h=134.5, 04h=150, 05h=300, 06h=600, 07h=1200, 08h=2400, 09h=4800, 0Ah=9600)
		01h parity (00h=none, 01h=odd, 02h=even)
		02h duplex (00h=full, 01h=half)
		03h character size (00h=7 bits, 01h=8 bits)
		04h stop bits (00h=1, 01h=2)
		05h XON/XOFF flow control (00h=no, 01h=yes)

Table 22-36. Format of Argument Block (continued)

Offset	Size	Description
		07h intercharacter delay in tenths of a second
		08h interline delay in tenths of a second
		09h auto linefeed (00h=no, 01h=yes)
		0Ah filter control characters (00h=no, 01h=yes)
		0Bh terminal type (00h=VT100,01h=glassTTY,02h=VT52,03h=IBM3101)
		0Ch auto wrap (00h=no, 01h=yes)
		0Dh cursor shape (00h=underscore, 01h=block)
		0Eh character set (00h=UK, 01h=US ASCII)
		0Fh printer port (00h=LPT1, 01h=LPT2, 02h=LPT3)
03h	BYTE	parameter value (returned for 06h)

---request=07h,08h

Offset	Size	Description
02h	WORD	pointer to 80-byte buffer in caller's current DS: each byte = 00h if no tab, 01h if tab at that position

---request=0Ah

Offset	Size	Description
02h	WORD	size of session information to be saved
04h	WORD	pointer to buffer in caller's DS

---request=0Bh

Offset	Size	Description
02h	WORD	size of buffer into which session info is restored
04h	WORD	pointer to buffer in caller's DS

---request=0Ch

Offset	Size	Description
02h	BYTE	check_scroll_lock flag
		00h off
		01h on (display of host data stopped while ScrollLock on)

---request=0Eh,14h

Offset	Size	Description
02h	DWORD	pointer to routine to be called (0000h:0000h = don't call)
06h	DWORD	stack pointer to use when call is made

---request=0Fh

Offset	Size	Description
02h	WORD	pointer to information area in caller's current DS:

Offset	Size	Description
00h	WORD	length of service name
02h	WORD	pointer to service name in caller's DS
04h	BYTE	type of connection
		(00h=connection name, 01h=dialout)
05h	WORD	length of connection name/telephone number
07h	WORD	pointer to connection name/telephone number

---request=10h

Offset	Size	Description
02h	WORD	print capture flag (00h=off, 01h=on)

---request=11h

Offset	Size	Description
02h	WORD	pointer to info area in caller's current DS:

Offset	Size	Description
00h	BYTE	protocol flag (00h none, 01h Kermit)
01h	BYTE	direction flag (00h send, 01h receive)
02h	BYTE	length of null-terminated PC filename
03h	DWORD	pointer to null-terminated PC filename
07h	BYTE	length of null-terminated host filename
08h	DWORD	pointer to null-terminated host filename

---request=12h

Offset	Size	Description
02h	WORD	pointer to info area in caller's current DS:
Offset	Size	Description
00h	WORD	length of service name (returned)
02h	WORD	pointer to 64-byte buffer for service name

Table 22-36. Format of argument block (continued)

Offset	Size	Description	
	04h	BYTE	type of connection
			00h connection name
			01h dialout
	05h	WORD	length of connection name/telephone number
	07h	WORD	pointer to 64-byte buffer for name/telno
	09h	BYTE	server line number being used (returned)

---request=13h
02h	BYTE	trace flag (00h=off, 01h=on)

Table 22-37. Format of Terminal Status Area:

Offset	Size	Description	
00h	BYTE	status of session: 4Eh=oNline, 46h=oFfline, 57h=Waiting	
01h	BYTE	terminal type (00h=VT100, 01h=TTY, 02h=VT52, 03h=IBM3101)	
02h	BYTE	current keypad mode (VT100,VT52 only)	
		4Eh ("N") numeric mode	
		41h ("A") application mode	
03h	4 BYTEs	current state of LEDs (VT100 only)	
		00h off	
		01h on	
07h	WORD	line error count	
09h	WORD	primary error code	
		0000h no error
		0001h unable to make connection
		0002h communications error, restart session
		0003h async terminal emulation service unavailable
		0004h lost carrier
		0005h all matching lines busy
		0006h no lines defined for connection name
		0007h no dial lines available on server
		0008h no matching dial lines available
		0009h out of heap space
		000Ah service error encountered
		000Bh timed out waiting to connect
		000Ch communications error
		000Dh communications error
		000Eh host wants file transferred to/from PC
		000Fh host software changed session parameter
		0010h host software changed tap settings
		0011h host software changed LED indicator
		0012h host software changed display background (secondary error code 00h for white on black, 01h for black on white)
		0013h host software changed display option (secondary error code 00h for off, 01h for on)
		0014h communications error
		0015h communications error
		0016h unable to make connection
		0017h unable to make connection
0Bh	WORD	secondary error code	

INTERRUPT 61h - Function 0004h
GET SERVER SERIAL NUMBER

Purpose: Determine the serial number of the server providing a particular network drive.
Available on: All machines.   **Restrictions:** Banyan VINES must be installed.

Registers at call:
AX = 0004h
DS:DX -> request block (Table 22-38)

Return Registers:
AX = status
    0000h server ID returned in request block
    000Fh invalid drive
    0015h drive not ready

Conflicts: See chapter 1.

Table 22-38. Format of request block:

Offset	Size	Description
00h	WORD	0008h
02h	WORD	drive number (0=default, 1=A, ...)
04h	6 BYTEs	buffer for server ID

INTERRUPT 61h - Function 0005h
PRINTER CONTROL

Purpose: Determine the current printer port or schedule a print job.
Available on: All machines.
Registers at call:
AX = 0005h
DS:DX -> request block (Table 22-39)

Restrictions: Banyan VINES must be installed.
Return Registers:
AX = status
    0000h successful
    0001h network software not installed or
        incompatible

Conflicts: See Chapter 1.

Table 22-39. Format of request block:

Offset	Size	Description
00h	WORD	function
		0201h "endspool" all data for a print job has been sent
		0205h "getactive" get currently active printer port
02h	WORD	number of active port (1-3)
04h	WORD	*unknown.* (0 for func 0201h, 3 for func 0205h)
06h	WORD	0000h

INTERRUPT 61h - Function 0007h, Subfunction 0002h
GET PORTS FOR A SERVICE

Purpose: Determine which ports may be used to communicate with the specified service.
Available on: All machines.
Registers at call:
AX = 0007h
BX = 0002h
DS:DX -> StreetTalk service name
DS:DI -> port record block (Table 22-40)

Restrictions: Banyan VINES must be installed.
Return Registers:
AX = status
    0000h successful
    0001h PC network software not installed or
        incompatible
    03E9h incorrect name syntax
    03EAh organization name too long
    03EBh group name too long
    03ECh item name too long
    03EDh StreetTalk name too long
    03F3h organization not found
    03F4h group not found
    03F5h StreetTalk name not found
    03F8h not a StreetTalk name
    040Dh appropriate StreetTalk name unavailable

Conflicts: See chapter 1.

Table 22-40. Format of Port Record Block:

Offset	Size	Description
00h	WORD	number of 17-byte elements
02h	17 BYTEs	element (byte 00h = input port type, bytes 01h-10h = port)
		(see Function 0001h Subfunction 0001h for port format)

INTERRUPT 61h - Function 0007h, Subfunction 0004h
SET PORTS FOR SERVICE

Purpose: Specify which ports may be used to communicate with the specified service. This call is used only by the PC-based services.

Available on: All machines.

Registers at call:
AX = 0007h
BX = 0004h
DS:DX -> StreetTalk name of service

DS:DI -> port record block (Table 22-41)

Restrictions: Banyan VINES must be installed.

Return Registers:
AX = status
    0000h successful
    0001h PC network software not installed or
        incompatible
    03E9h incorrect name syntax
    03EAh organization name too long
    03EBh group name too long
    03ECh item name too long
    03EDh StreetTalk name too long
    03F3h organization not found
    03F4h group not found
    03F5h StreetTalk name not found
    03F8h not a StreetTalk name
    0409h modify access denied
    040Dh appropriate StreetTalk name unavailable

Conflicts: See chapter 1.

Table 22-41. Format of Port Record Block:

Offset	Size	Description
00h	WORD	number of 17-byte elements
02h	17 BYTEs	element: byte 00h = input port type, 01h-10h = port (see Function 0001h Subfunction 0001h for port format)

INTERRUPT 61h - Function 0007h, Subfunction 0005h
GET USER NAME

Purpose: Determine the StreetTalk name of the user logged into the caller's machine.

Available on: All machines.

Registers at call:
AX = 0007h
BX = 0005h
DS:DX -> 64-byte buffer for user's StreetTalk name

Restrictions: Banyan VINES must be installed.

Return Registers:
AX = status
    0000h successful
    0001h network software not installed or
        incompatible

Details: If no user logged in, the first byte of the returned name will be 00h.

Conflicts: See Chapter 1.

INTERRUPT 61h - Function 0007h, Subfunction 0006h
TRANSLATE ERROR INTO ASCII STRING

Purpose: Retrieve a printable string corresponding to the specified error code.

Available on: All machines.
Registers at call:
AX = 0007h
BX = 0006h
SI = error code (>100)
DS:DX -> 80-byte buffer for error text
Conflicts: See chapter 1.

Restrictions: Banyan VINES must be installed.
Return Registers:
AX = status
    0000h successful
    0001h network software not installed or
        incompatible

INTERRUPT 61h - Function 0007h, Subfunction 0007h
VERIFY EXISTENCE OF NAME AND RETURN CANONICAL FORM

Purpose: Determine whether the specified name exists, and if so, its full form with the correct case.
Available on: All machines.
Registers at call:
AX = 0007h
BX = 0007h
DS:DX -> NiceName block (Table 22-42)

Restrictions: Banyan VINES must be installed.
Return Registers:
AX = status
    0000h successful
    0001h PC network software not installed or
        incompatible
    03E9h incorrect name syntax
    03EAh organization name too long
    03EBh group name too long
    03ECh item name too long
    03EDh StreetTalk name too long
    03F3h organization not found
    03F4h group not found
    03F5h StreetTalk name not found
    03F8h not a StreetTalk name
    040Dh appropriate StreetTalk name unavailable

Conflicts: See Chapter 1.
See Also: Function 0007h Subfunction 0008h

Table 22-42. Format of NiceName block:

Offset	Size	Description
00h	WORD	type of name
		0064h organization
		00C8h group
		012Ch item
02h	WORD	pointer to ASCIZ input name
04h	WORD	pointer to 64-byte buffer for output name

INTERRUPT 61h - Function 0007h, Subfunction 0008h
ENUMERATE StreetTalk NAMES

Purpose: Retrieve a list of all names matching the specified criteria.
Available on: All machines.
Registers at call:
AX = 0007h
BX = 0008h
DS:DX -> enumerate block (Table 22-43)

Restrictions: Banyan VINES must be installed.
Return Registers:
AX = status
    0000h successful
    0411h all matching names have been returned
    0412h some groups unavailable, all available
        matches returned

Details: Each program using this call should continue until a nonzero status is returned; otherwise, some resources will not be freed for several hours.
Conflicts: See Chapter 1.
See Also: Function 0007h Subfunction 0007h

Table 22-43. Format of Enumerate Block:

Offset	Size	Description
00h	WORD	return code
02h	WORD	pointer to pattern string
04h	WORD	enumerate type
		0064h organization
		00C8h group
		012Ch item
06h	WORD	enumerate class
		0000h unspecified (return all matching items)
		0001h user names
		0002h service names
		0003h list names
		0004h nicknames
08h	WORD	pointer to category criteria block (Table 22-44) or 0
0Ah	WORD	pointer to array of 64-byte returned names
0Ch	WORD	number of names returned
0Eh	6 BYTEs	reserved for subsequent enumerated calls (set to zeros on first call)

Table 22-44. Format of Category Criteria Block:

Offset	Size	Description
00h	WORD	exclude flag
		0000h return only items with the specified categories
		0001h return all items except those with the given categories
02h	WORD	number of categories
04h	WORD	category 1 value (Table 22-45)
06h	WORD	category 2 value
		...

Table 22-45. Values for Common Service Categories:

Value	Service Category
0002h	file service
0003h	print service
0004h	mail service
0005h	StreetTalk
0006h	time service
0008h	semaphore service
0009h	3270/SNA service
000Ah	asynchronous terminal emulation service
000Ch	NETBIOS service
000Dh	PC-based service

INTERRUPT 61h - Function 0008h, Subfunction 0002h
POST MESSAGE ON LOCAL DISPLAY

Purpose: Display a message on the 25th line of the PC's display until a timeout or the user presses ^X.

Available on: All machines.　　　　　　　　　　**Restrictions:** Banyan VINES must be installed.

Registers at call:
AX = 0008h
BX = 0002h
CX = flags
    bit 0: message will remain on screen until user
        presses ^X
    bit 1: ring bell after displaying message
    bit 2: blink
DS:DX -> ASCIZ string to display (only the first 80
    characters are used)

Return Registers:
AX = status
    0000h successful
    000Bh message display function currently busy
    000Ch message queue full

Details: This function queues up to three messages to be displayed on the bottom line.
Conflicts: See Chapter 1.

INTERRUPT 61h - Function 0008h, Subfunction 0003h
INTERCEPT VINES 25th-LINE MESSAGES AT LOCAL PC

Purpose: Specify a routine to process messages sent to the 25th line by VINES.
Available on: All machines.
Registers at call:
AX = 0008h
BX = 0003h
DS:DX -> request block (Table 22-46)

Restrictions: Banyan VINES must be installed.
Return Registers:
AX = status
    0000h successful
    0001h network software not installed or
        incompatible

Details: The message handler should not call BIOS or DOS functions, and should either call the next handler or simply return. To stop intercepting messages, the routine should set the previous and next request blocks to point at each other.
Conflicts: See chapter 1.

Table 22-46. Format of Request Block:

Offset	Size	Description
00h	DWORD	pointer to user-written message handler
04h	DWORD	pointer to next request block (filled in by VINES)
08h	DWORD	pointer to previous request block (filled in by VINES)
0Ch	DWORD	pointer to message storage area (Table 22-47) (filled by VINES)

Table 22-47. Format of Message Storage Area:

Offset	Size	Description
00h	16 BYTEs	IPC port of message sender (see Function 0001h Subfunction 0001h)
10h	BYTE	message flags
11h	WORD	reserved
13h	BYTE	length of message
14h	80 BYTEs	message text

INTERRUPT 61h - Function 000Ah
SECONDARY 3270 INTERFACE

Purpose: Provide mainframe access. The 3270/SNA and 3270/BSC options emulate a 3270 terminal on the PC and a 3274 controller in the server node.
Available on: All machines.
Registers at call:
AX = 000Ah

Restrictions: Banyan VINES must be installed.
Return Registers:
Same as for Function 0002h

Details: Either 3270/SNA or 3270/BSC interface will use Function 000Ah, depending on which is loaded second. The first interface loaded will use Function 0002h.
Conflicts: See Chapter 1.

See Also: Function 0002h

INTERRUPT 61h - Function 01h
CHECK SERVICE

Purpose: Determine whether the specified service is installed and available.

Available on: All machines.

Registers at call:

AH = 01h

AL = service ID

    01h communications
    02h primary 3270 emulation
    03h asynchronous terminal emulation
    04h file deflection
    07h StreetTalk
    08h environment
    0Ah secondary 3270 emulation
    0Bh semaphore service
    0Ch 3270 emulation active status
    0Dh 3270 keyboard interrupt simulator

Conflicts: See chapter 1.

Restrictions: Banyan VINES must be installed.

Return Registers:

AX = status

    0000h installed
    0001h not installed
    0002h invalid ID

INTERRUPT 61h - Function 02h
GET REVISION NUMBER

Purpose: Determine the current revision of the Banyan software which is installed.

Available on: All machines.

Registers at call:

AH = 02h

DS:DX -> 2-byte buffer for result

Conflicts: See Chapter 1.

Restrictions: Banyan VINES must be installed.

Return Registers:

AX = 0000h installed

DS:DX buffer contains revision number as 10000d * major_ver + 100d * minor_ver + patch_revision

Chapter 23

10Net

The 10NetPlus LAN Operating System from Digital Communications Associates, Inc. (the Crosstalk and IRMA folks) is, like Lantastic, an MS-DOS-based network rather than a DOS emulator. It uses SMB protocols, and interfaces to NetBIOS and OSDI transport software to communicate between stations.

INTERRUPT 60h - Functions 11h through 13h
SEMAPHORE LOCKING AND UNLOCKING
Purpose: Arbitrate access to resources. These functions are identical to the 3com implementation, and are described in chapter 27.

INTERRUPT 6Fh - Function 00h
LOGIN
Purpose: Authenticate user to network server.
Available on: All machines.
Registers at call:
AH = 00h
DS:DX - > login record (Table 23-1)
Conflicts: HP ES-12 Extended BIOS (chapter 4).
See Also: Function 01h

Restrictions: 10Net software must be installed.
Return Registers:
CL = security level
AX = status (see Table 23-2)

Table 23-1. Format of Login Record:

Offset	Size	Description
00h	8 BYTEs	user name
08h	8 BYTEs	password
10h	12 BYTEs	name of SuperStation

Table 23-2. 10Net Status Codes

Note: One of our sources indicates that the error codes are FFxxh, another that they are xxFFh. We are unsure which source is correct.

Code	Status	Code	Status
0000h	*successful*	*17FFh*	*record lock time out error*
01FFh	*time out on response*	*18FFh*	*currently spooling to named device*
02FFh	*network (hardware) error*	*19FFh*	*dropped receive message (throttle)*
03FFh	*invalid password*	*1AFFh*	*open sharing violation*
04FFh	*local resource not available*	*1BFFh*	*no more tuf entries left*
05FFh	*server resource not available*	*1CFFh*	*not file owner on open*
06FFh	*already logged in under different name*	*1DFFh*	*read security not passed*
07FFh	*login security failure (node)*	*1EFFh*	*write security not passed*
08FFh	*not logged in*	*1FFFh*	*group security not passed*
09FFh	*position calc error*	*20FFh*	*security file failure*
0AFFh	*receive subfunction not = send*	*21FFh*	*activity file failure*
	subfunction (i.e. read, write)	*22FFh*	*spool control file failure*
0BFFh	*request function not in range*	*23FFh*	*device not mounted (spooling)*
0CFFh	*no more server file handle entries left*	*24FFh*	*spool file has not been terminated*

Table 23-2. 10Net Status Codes (continued)

Code	Status	Code	Status
0DFFh	no more shared file table entries left	25FFh	device not mounted or is not being shared
0EFFh	no more user file handle entries left	26FFh	duplicate node ID
0FFFh	chat permit not on	27FFh	file not found error
10FFh	not a server on request	28FFh	no more files
11FFh	no transporter board error	29FFh	unknown internal system error
12FFh	time out on send	2AFFh	print queue is full or corrupted
13FFh	item not found (spool item not on queue)	2BFFh	invalid function
		2CFFh	invalid handle
14FFh	DOS access incompatible	2DFFh	too many files opened
15FFh	record already locked	2EFFh	path not found
16FFh	invalid parameter	2FFFh	named file is active

INTERRUPT 6Fh - Function 01h
LOGOFF

Purpose: Terminate a login session with the specified server.
Available on: All machines.
Registers at call:
AH = 01h
DS:DX -> superstation ID or nulls (12 bytes)

Restrictions: 10Net software must be installed.
Return Registers:
CX = number of files closed
AX = status (see Table 23-2)
      FF08h superstation ID not already logged in

Conflicts: HP ES-12 Extended BIOS (chapter 4).
See Also: Function 00h

INTERRUPT 6Fh - Function 02h
STATUS OF NODE

Purpose: Determine the type and state of a machine on the network.
Available on: All machines.
Registers at call:
AH = 02h
DS:DX -> 512-byte status record (Table 23-3)

Restrictions: 10Net software must be installed.
Return Registers:
CF clear if successful
CF set on error
      AX = error code (see Table 23-2)

Table 23-3. Format of Node Status Record:

Offset	Size	Description
00h	8 BYTEs	user name (0 if none)
08h	BYTE	station type
		00h workstation
		01h superstation
		02h gateway station
		03h gateway active
		04h logged into multiple superstations
		05h reserved
09h	24 BYTEs	list of superstations logged into more than one superstation
21h	12 BYTEs	node ID
2Dh	WORD	message count for this station (send for user node, receive for superstations)

---for superstations only

Offset	Size	Description
2Fh	WORD	drives allocated (bit 0=A:, bit 1=B:,...)
31h	BYTE	user service flag
		bit 7: gate
		bit 6: print permit on
		bit 4: SUBMIT is on
		bit 3: mail waiting for node
		bit 2: calendar waiting for you

Table 23-3. Format of Node Status Record (continued)

Offset	Size	Description
		bit 1: news waiting for you
		bit 0: mail waiting for you
32h	BYTE	printers allocated (bit 0=LPT1,...)
33h	BYTE	number of unprinted spool files
34h	BYTE	number of opened files
35h	BYTE	number of logged on nodes
36h	BYTE	primary drive (1=A:)
37h	BYTE	reserved
38h	N BYTEs	list of logged on node IDs (each 12 bytes, max 37 IDs)
1F4h	3 BYTEs	time: sec/min/hrs
1F7h	3 BYTEs	date: day/mon/year-1980

INTERRUPT 6Fh - Function 03h
GET ADDRESS OF CONFIGURATION TABLE

Purpose: Determine the location of a table specifying the network configuration and statistics.

Available on: All machines.

Registers at call:
AH = 03h
DS:DI -> node ID (optional)
Conflicts: HP ES-12 Extended BIOS (chapter 4).
See Also: Function 13h

Restrictions: 10Net software must be installed.
Return Registers:
ES:BX -> configuration table (Table 23-4)

Table 23-4. Format of Configuration Table:

Offset	Size	Description
-41	WORD	local device table address
-39	WORD	extended network error mapping table address
-37	WORD	shared device table address
-35	WORD	mounted device table address
-33	BYTE	receive buffer counter
-32	BYTE	collect buffer counter
-31	WORD	TUF address
-29	BYTE	enable flag
-28	BYTE	FCB keep flag
-27	WORD	reserved
---up to here, 10Net v3.3+		
-25	WORD	count of dropped Send6F
-23	WORD	buffer start address
-21	WORD	comm driver base address
-19	WORD	send/receive retry count
-17	BYTE	number of 550ms loops before timeout
-16	WORD	UFH address
-14	WORD	CDIR address
-12	WORD	LTAB address
-10	WORD	SFH address
-8	WORD	FTAB address
-6	WORD	RLTAB address
-4	WORD	SMI address
-2	WORD	NTAB address
00h	WORD	address of first CT_DRV
02h	BYTE	number of DRV entries
03h	8 BYTEs	login name
0Bh	12 BYTEs	node ID (blank-padded)
17h	6 BYTEs	node address
1Dh	BYTE	flag

Table 23-4. Format of Configuration Table (continued)

Offset	Size	Description
1Eh	BYTE	CT_CFLG (chat permit)
		bit 1: sound bell
		bit 0: CHAT permit
1Fh	BYTE	CT_PSFLG
		bit 5: PRINT permit
		bit 4: KB initiated
		bit 3: CHAT called FOXPTRM
		bit 2: SUBMIT active
		bit 1: SUBMIT received
		bit 0: SUBMIT permit
20h	BYTE	in 10Net flag
21h	WORD	receive message count
23h	WORD	send message count
25h	WORD	retry count
27h	WORD	failed count
29h	WORD	driver errors
2Bh	WORD	dropped responses/CHATs
2Dh	9 BYTEs	LIST ID/NTAB address (3 entries--LPT1-3)
36h	6 BYTEs	AUX ID/NTAB address (2 entries--COM1-2)
3Ch	BYTE	active CB channel
3Dh	BYTE	received INT 6Fh messages on queue
3Eh	9 BYTEs	activity counters for channels 1-9

---beyond here, 10Net v3.3+

Offset	Size	Description
47h	BYTE	bit 0 = RS232 gate, 1 = Send6F gate (user set)
48h	DWORD	pointer into gate (user set)
4Ch	DWORD	pointer into 10Net send
50h	N WORDs	addresses of timer blocks

INTERRUPT 6Fh - Function 04h
SEND

Purpose: Transmit data over the network.
Available on: All machines.
Registers at call:
AH = 04h
DS:BX -> send data description record (Table 23-5)
DS:DX -> data (max 1024 bytes)
Conflicts: HP ES-12 Extended BIOS (chapter 4).
See Also: Function 05h

Restrictions: 10Net software must be installed.
Return Registers:
CF set on error
    AX = error code (see Table 23-2)
CF clear if successful

Table 23-5. Format of Send Data Description Record:

Offset	Size	Description
00h	12 BYTEs	receiving node's ID:
		if the first byte has its high-order bit set, the message is directed to the CT_RGATE vector at the receiver
		if the second byte is 00h, the first byte is taken as a CB channel number and the message is delivered to all nodes on the same channel
0Ch	WORD	length of data at DX

INTERRUPT 6Fh - Function 05h
RECEIVE

Purpose: Await data from the network.
Available on: All machines.

Restrictions: 10Net software must be installed.

Registers at call:
AH = 05h
CX = number of seconds before timeout
DS:DX -> receive buffer (Table 23-6)

Conflicts: HP ES-12 Extended BIOS (chapter 4).
See Also: Function 04h

Return Registers:
CF set on error
    AX = error code (see Table 23-2)
CF clear if successful
    AH = FEh if dequeued message is a CB message

Table 23-6. Format of Receive Buffer:

Offset	Size	Description
00h	12 BYTEs	sending node's ID
0Ch	WORD	length of message
0Eh	N BYTEs	message (maximum 1024 bytes)

INTERRUPT 6Fh - Function 07h
LOCK HANDLE

Purpose: Request exclusive access to a portion of the file corresponding to the indicated file handle.
Available on: All machines.   **Restrictions:** 10Net software must be installed.
Registers at call: **Return Registers:**
AH = 07h   CF set on error
BX = file handle   AX = error code (see also Table 23-2)
CX:DX = starting offset in file   0002h file not found
SI = record length   CF clear if successful
Conflicts: HP ES-12 Extended BIOS (chapter 4).
See Also: Function 08h, DOS INT 21h Function 5Ch (chapter 8)

INTERRUPT 6Fh - Function 08h
UNLOCK HANDLE

Purpose: Allow others to access the file corresponding to the indicated file handle.
Available on: All machines.   **Restrictions:** 10Net software must be installed.
Registers at call: **Return Registers:**
AH = 08h   CF set on error
BX = file handle   AX = error code (see also Table 23-2)
AL = mode   0002h file not found
    00h unlock all   CF clear if successful
    01h unlock record at CX:DX
Conflicts: HP ES-12 Extended BIOS (chapter 4).
See Also: Function 07h, DOS INT 21h Function 5Ch (chapter 8)

INTERRUPT 6Fh - Function 09h
SUBMIT

Purpose: Specify a command to be executed on another machine.
Available on: All machines.   **Restrictions:** 10Net software must be installed.
Registers at call: **Return Registers:** n/a
AH = 09h
DS:BX -> submit record (Table 23-7)

Table 23-7. Format of Submit Record:

Offset	Size	Description
00h	12 BYTEs	destination node ID (must be logged in)
0Ch	WORD	length+2 of following 'command line' text
0Eh	N BYTEs	command line text (<=100 bytes), system adds CR

INTERRUPT 6Fh - Function 0Ah
CHAT

Purpose: Send a message to another user or all users on the network.

Available on: All machines.

Restrictions: 10Net software must be installed.

Registers at call: AH = 0Ah

Return Registers: n/a

DS:BX -> control parameters (Table 23-8)
DS:DX -> chat message (Table 23-9)

Table 23-8. Format of Chat Control Parameters:

Offset	Size	Description
00h	8 BYTEs	sender ID, defaults to node's userID if nulls
08h	8 BYTEs	destination user ID, 'EVERYONE' may be used
10h	12 BYTEs	destination node ID

Table 23-9. Format of Chat Message:

Offset	Size	Description
00h	WORD	length+2 of following text
02h	N BYTEs	text, max 101 bytes

INTERRUPT 6Fh - Function 0Bh
LOCK SEMAPHORE, RETURN IMMEDIATELY

Purpose: Attempt to gain exclusive access to the specified resource.

Available on: All machines.

Restrictions: 10Net software must be installed.

Registers at call:

AH = 0Bh

AL = drive number or 0

ES:SI = Ethernet address or 0

DS:BX -> 31-byte ASCIZ semaphore name

Return Registers:

AL = status
   00h successful
   01h semaphore currently locked
   02h server not responding
   03h invalid semaphore name
   04h semaphore list is full
   05h invalid drive ID
   06h invalid Ethernet address
   07h not logged in
   08h write to network failed
   09h semaphore already logged in this CPU

Details: This call is the same as INT 60h Function 12h.

Conflicts: HP ES-12 Extended BIOS (chapter 4).

See Also: Function 0Ch, INT 60h Function 12h

INTERRUPT 6Fh - Function 0Ch
UNLOCK SEMAPHORE

Purpose: Indicate that the specified resource is once again available.

Available on: All machines.

Restrictions: 10Net software must be installed.

Registers at call:

AH = 0Ch

AL = drive number or 0

ES:SI = Ethernet address or 0

DS:BX -> 31-byte ASCIZ semaphore name

Return Registers:

AL = status (see also Function 0Bh)
   01h semaphore not locked

Details: This call is the same as INT 60h Function 13h.

Conflicts: HP ES-12 Extended BIOS (chapter 4).

See Also: Function 0Bh, INT 60h Function 13h

INTERRUPT 6Fh - Function 0Dh
WHO

Purpose: Determine the names of the machines on the network and the users currently logged into them.

Available on: All machines.   **Restrictions:** 10Net software must be installed.

Registers at call: **Return Registers:**

AH = 0Dh   CL = number of records returned (responding stations)

AL = type code
    01h return superstations only
    02h return non-superstations only
    otherwise return all

CX = length of data

DS:DX -> array of records to be filled (Table 23-10)

Conflicts: HP ES-12 Extended BIOS (chapter 4).

Table 23-10. Format of Station Record:

Offset	Size	Description
00h	12 BYTEs	node ID
0Ch	BYTE	flags
		bit 1 = workstation
		bit 2 = superstation
		bit 3 = xgate
		bit 4 = active gate

---if AL = 01h

Offset	Size	Description
0Dh	BYTE	version number
	WORD	level number of 10Net software in responding node

---if AL = 02h

Offset	Size	Description
0Dh	8 BYTEs	user ID
15h	BYTE	version number
16h	WORD	level number

INTERRUPT 6Fh - Function 0Eh
SPOOL/PRINT

Purpose: Control the print spooler.

Available on: All machines.   **Restrictions:** 10Net software must be installed.

Registers at call: **Return Registers:**

AH = 0Eh   CF set on error

DS:DX -> spool/print record (Table 23-11)
    AX = error code (see also Table 23-2)
        FF17h device not mounted
        FF18h already spooling to named device

CF clear if successful

Conflicts: HP ES-12 Extended BIOS (chapter 4).

Table 23-11. Format of Spool/Print Record:

Offset	Size	Description
00h	WORD	operation code
		00h initiate spool
		01h abort print
		02h close spool
		03h delete spool
		04h print
		05h get report info

Table 23-11. Format of Spool/Print Record (continued)

Offset	Size	Description
		06h set chat template
		07h queue
		08h return queue
		09h queue non-spooled file for printing
02h	11 BYTEs	file name in FCB format

---if operation code = 00h or 06h

Offset	Size	Description
0Dh	BYTE	notification
		bit 7: queue to top
		bit 6: do ID page
		bit 5: no form feed
		bit 4: reserved
		bit 3: explicity queuing only
		bit 2: notify at print completion
		bit 1: notify server operator/reply
		bit 0: notify at print start
0Eh	BYTE	days to keep (FFh=forever)
0Fh	BYTE	bits 0,1: device (1=LPT1)
		bits 4-7: remote drive to store spool file (1=A,...)
10h	WORD	length of following data area
12h	N BYTEs	up to 64 bytes of description

---if operation code = 03h

Offset	Size	Description
0Dh	8 BYTEs	user ID to associate with filename

---if operation code = 04h

Offset	Size	Description
0Dh	WORD	block number
0Fh	8 BYTEs	user ID to associate with filename

---if operation code = 05h

Offset	Size	Description
0Dh	BYTE	RRN to start retrieve
0Eh	BYTE	bits 0,1: local print device (LPTx)
		bit 3: if set, return entries for all users
0Fh	WORD	length of following area
11h	N BYTEs	up to 1500 bytes to receive $SCNTL records returned

---if operation code = 07h

Offset	Size	Description
0Dh	BYTE	queue number
0Eh	BYTE	bits 0,1: local print device (LPTx)
0Fh	WORD	number of bytes of test print to be done
11h	BYTE	code: 01h print device
		02h test print count
		03h prn

---if operation code = 08h

Offset	Size	Description
0Dh	BYTE	queue location or $SCNTL location to start access
		returns next item for access:
		00h-7Fh queued items
		80h-FEh non-queued, non-printed items
		FFh no more items
0Eh	WORD	unused
10h	WORD	length of following area
12h	N BYTEs	up to 64 bytes to receive $SCNTL records (Table 23-12)

---if operation code = 09h

Offset	Size	Description
0Dh	3 BYTEs	unused
10h	N BYTEs	path to non-spooled file to be queued for printing

Table 23-12. Format of $SCNTL Record:

Offset	Size	Description
00h	8 BYTEs	user ID
08h	11 BYTEs	filename in FCB format
13h	6 BYTEs	node ID
19h	3 BYTEs	creation date
1Ch	BYTE	flags

bit 7: queue to top
bit 6: do ID page
bit 5: no form feed at end
bit 4: reserved
bit 3: explicit queueing only
bit 2: notify at completion
bit 1: notify server operator/reply
bit 0: notify at start

1Dh	BYTE	retention time in days
1Eh	BYTE	printing device (LPTx)
1Fh	3 BYTEs	date last printed (0 = never)
22h	BYTE	device containing spoolfile
23h	WORD	bytes to print for test print
25h	WORD	block number to start print
27h	BYTE	reserved

INTERRUPT 6Fh - Function 10h
ATTACH/DETACH PRINTER

Purpose: Specify whether to spool data to the printer.

Available on: All machines.

Restrictions: 10Net software must be installed.

Registers at call:

Return Registers: n/a

AH = 10h

AL = subfunction

    00h initiate spooling if LPT1 is mounted

    01h terminate spooling if LPT1 is mounted

Conflicts: HP ES-12 Extended BIOS (chapter 4).

See Also: DOS INT 21h Function 5Dh Subfunction 08h (chapter 8)

INTERRUPT 6Fh - Function 11h
LOCK FCB

Purpose: Request exclusive access to a portion of the file corresponding to the specified File Control Block.

Available on: All machines.

Restrictions: 10Net software must be installed.

Registers at call:

Return Registers:

AH = 11h

CF set on error

AL = mode

    AX = error code (see also Table 23-2)

    01h sequential

        0002h file not found

    02h random

CF clear if successful

    03h random block

CX = number of records

DS:DX -> FCB (see DOS INT 21h Function 0Fh,

    chapter 8)

Conflicts: HP ES-12 Extended BIOS (chapter 4).

See Also: Function 12h

INTERRUPT 6Fh - Function 12h
UNLOCK FCB

Purpose: Allow others to access the indicated portion of the file corresponding to the File Control Block.

Available on: All machines.   **Restrictions:** 10Net software must be installed.

Registers at call: **Return Registers:**
AH = 12h   CF set on error
AL = mode   AX = error code (see also Table 23-2)
   00h sequential   0002h file not found
   01h random   CF clear if successful
   02h random block
CX = number of records
DS:DX -> FCB (see DOS INT 21h Function 0Fh,
   chapter 8)
Conflicts: HP ES-12 Extended BIOS (chapter 4).
See Also: Function 11h

INTERRUPT 6Fh - Function 13h
GET REMOTE CONFIGURATION TABLE ADDRESS

Purpose: Determine the address of the configuration table for another machine on the network.

Available on: All machines.   **Restrictions:** 10Net version 3.3 or higher must be
                                                           installed.

Registers at call: **Return Registers:**
AH = 13h   CF set on error
DS:DX -> node ID, 12 bytes blank-padded   AX = error code (see Table 23-2)
                                                CF clear if successful
                                                ES:BX = configuration table address on the given
                                                       machine

Conflicts: HP ES-12 Extended BIOS (chapter 4).
See Also: Function 03h

INTERRUPT 6Fh - Function 14h
GET REMOTE MEMORY

Purpose: Make a copy of a portion of another machine's memory.

Available on: All machines.   **Restrictions:** 10Net version 3.3 or higher must be
                                                           installed.

Registers at call: **Return Registers:**
AH = 14h   CF set on error
BX:SI = address of remote memory   AX = error code (see Table 23-2)
CX = length (<=1024 bytes)   CF clear if successful
DS:DX -> node ID, 12 bytes blank-padded   CX = amount of memory copied to DS:SI
DS:DI -> area to receive remote memory image

INTERRUPT 6Fh - Function 15h, Subfunction 01h
GET SHARED DEVICE ENTRY

Purpose: Determine the name and attributes of a device shared with other machines on the network.

Available on: All machines.   **Restrictions:** 10Net version 3.3 or higher must be
                                                           installed.

Registers at call: **Return Registers:**
AX = 1501h   CF set on error
BX = zero-based index   AX = error code (see Table 23-2)
DS:SI -> node ID, 12 bytes blank-padded   CF clear if successful

ES:DI -> 85-byte buffer for shared device table
    entry (Table 23-13)
Conflicts: HP ES-12 Extended BIOS (chapter 4).
See Also: Function 15h Subfunctions 02h and 03h

ES:DI buffer contains shared device table entry of
    BXth device:

Table 23-13. Format of Shared Device Table Entry:

Offset	Size	Description
00h	8 BYTEs	device
08h	8 BYTEs	alias
10h	64 BYTEs	path
50h	8 BYTEs	password
58h	BYTE	access
59h	4 BYTEs	mask

INTERRUPT 6Fh - Function 15h, Subfunction 02h
SET SHARED DEVICE ENTRY

Purpose: Modify the attributes of a device shared with other machines on the network.
Available on: All machines.

Restrictions: 10Net version 3.3 or higher must be
    installed.

Registers at call:
AX = 1502h
DS:SI -> node ID, 12 bytes blank-padded
ES:DI -> valid shared device table entry (see
    Table 23-13)
Conflicts: HP ES-12 Extended BIOS (chapter 4).
See Also: Function 15h Subfunctions 01h and 03h

Return Registers:
CF set on error
    AX = error code (see Table 23-2)
CF clear if successful

INTERRUPT 6Fh - Function 15h, Subfunction 03h
DELETE SHARED DEVICE ENTRY

Purpose: Stop sharing a device with other machines on the network.
Available on: All machines.

Restrictions: 10Net version 3.3 or higher must be
    installed.

Registers at call:
AX = 1503h
BX = zero-based index
DS:SI -> node ID, 12 bytes blank-padded
Conflicts: HP ES-12 Extended BIOS (chapter 4).
See Also: Function 15h Subfunctions 01h and 02h

Return Registers:
CF set on error
    AX = error code (see Table 23-2)
CF clear if successful

INTERRUPT 6Fh - Function 17h
MOUNT

Purpose: Associate a remote drive or device with a local drive number.
Available on: All machines.

Restrictions: 10Net version 3.3 or higher must be
    installed.

Registers at call:
AH = 17h
AL = local drive number (0=A:)
BL = remote drive letter
    or '1'..'3' for LPTn
    or '4' or '5' for COMx
DS:DX -> node ID, 12 bytes blank-padded
Conflicts: HP ES-12 Extended BIOS (chapter 4).
See Also: Function 18h

Return Registers:
CF set on error
    AX = error code (see Table 23-2)
CF clear if successful

INTERRUPT 6Fh - Function 18h
UNMOUNT

Purpose: Terminate the association between a local drive number and a remote drive or device.

Available on: All machines.

Restrictions: 10Net version 3.3 or higher must be installed.

Registers at call:
AH = 18h
AL = local drive number (0=A:)
BL = type
    00h disk
    01h-03h   LPTn
    04h,05h   COMx

Return Registers:
CF set on error
    AX = error code (see Table 23-2)
CF clear if successful

Conflicts: HP ES-12 Extended BIOS (chapter 4).

See Also: Function 17h

Chapter 24

DECnet DOS

DECnet is Digital Equipment Corporation's trademark for their communications protocol and line of networking products that are compatible with Ethernet. Originally introduced with the VAX 11/780, DECnet became the basis for all of Digital's networking products. When the company actively entered the MS-DOS arena in mid-1989, it moved to integrate DECnet with existing standards, and the result was DECnet DOS.

INTERRUPT 69h - Function 01h, Subfunction 00h
INSTALLATION CHECK

Purpose: Determine whether the DECnet DOS CTERM module is installed.

Available on: All machines.   **Restrictions:** none.

Registers at call: **Return Registers:**

AX = 0100h   AL = FFh if present

Conflicts: Zenith AT BIOS (chapter 4).

See Also: Function 01h Subfunction 0Fh

INTERRUPT 69h - Function 01h, Subfunction 01h
SEND BYTE

Purpose: Transmit a character over the network on the specified connection.

Available on: All machines.   **Restrictions:** DECnet DOS CTERM must be installed.

Registers at call: **Return Registers:**

AX = 0101h   AH >= 80h on error

BL = character

DX = session handle

Conflicts: Zenith AT BIOS (chapter 4).

See Also: Function 01h Subfunction 02h

INTERRUPT 69h - Function 01h, Subfunction 02h
READ BYTE

Purpose: Await a character on the specified network connection.

Available on: All machines.   **Restrictions:** DECnet DOS CTERM must be installed.

Registers at call: **Return Registers:**

AX = 0102h   AH >= 80h on error

DX = session handle   AH< 80h if successful

     AL = character

Conflicts: Zenith AT BIOS (chapter 4).

See Also: Function 01h Subfunction 01h

INTERRUPT 69h - Function 01h, Subfunction 03h
STATUS

Purpose: Determine the status of the specified connection.

Available on: All machines.   **Restrictions:** DECnet DOS CTERM must be installed.

Registers at call:
AX = 0103h
DX = session handle

Return Registers:
AH status flags
    bit 7: session has been aborted
    bit 6: DECnet error
    bit 1: trace data available
    bit 0: receive data available
AL = reason code if DECnet error
    00h normal disconnect
    01h unknown message from host
    02h protocol violation from host
    03h could not process the initiate message
    04h error receiving message from host
    05h error sending message to host
    06h error checking for message from host
    07h remote system does not support CTERM
    08h remote system does not support correct
        protocol version
    09h did not receive BIND message from host
    0Ah could not send BIND message to host
    0Bh no more sessions available
    0Ch session does not exist
    0Dh not enough memory to complete operation
    0Eh connection has broken

Conflicts: Zenith AT BIOS (chapter 4).
See Also: Function 01h Subfunction 04h

INTERRUPT 69h - Function 01h, Subfunction 04h
DECnet STATUS

Purpose: Determine the reason for the last DECnet error.
Available on: All machines.
Restrictions: DECnet DOS CTERM must be installed.
Registers at call:
Return Registers:
AX = 0104h
AX = reason code (see Function 01h Subfunction 03h)
DX = session handle
Details: Use this call when Function 01h Subfunction 03h returns a DECnet error.
Conflicts: Zenith AT BIOS (chapter 4).
See Also: Function 01h Subfunction 03h

INTERRUPT 69h - Function 01h, Subfunction 05h
OPEN SESSION

Purpose: Establish a network connection.
Available on: All machines.
Restrictions: DECnet DOS CTERM must be installed.
Registers at call:
Return Registers:
AX = 0105h
AX <= θ on error
DS:BX -> ASCIZ node name
AX > 0 session handle
ES:DX -> buffer for session control block
    (Table 24-1)
Conflicts: Zenith AT BIOS (chapter 4).
See Also: Function 01h Subfunctions 03h, 06h, and 0Ah

Table 24-1. Format of LAT Session Control Block

Offset	Size	Description
00h	18 BYTEs	service name
12h	18 BYTEs	node name (future use)

Table 24-1. Format of LAT Session Control Block (continued)

Offset	Size	Description
24h	18 BYTEs	port name (future use)
36h	DWORD	-> session stopped post routine
3Ah	DWORD	-> service table overflow post routine
3Eh	DWORD	-> transmit post routine
42h	DWORD	-> receive post routine
46h	WORD	session status:
		04h circuit failure
		08h stop slot received
48h	WORD	slot state (LAT driver use)
4Ah	WORD	local credits (LAT driver use)
4Ch	DWORD	-> VCB (LAT driver use)
50h	WORD	backward slot (LAT driver use)
52h	WORD	forward slot (LAT driver use)
54h	WORD	remote slot ID (LAT driver use)
56h	WORD	local slot ID (LAT driver use)
58h	WORD	slot byte count (LAT driver use)
5Ah	BYTE	remote credits (LAT driver use)
5Bh	255 BYTEs	transmitted data slot
15Ah	BYTE	number of receive data slots (4 recommended)
15Bh	BYTE	number of occupied slots
15Ch	BYTE	index of next receive slot to use
15Dh	BYTE	index of current receive slot
15Eh	WORD	pointer to first received character
160h	N WORDs	pointers to receive slots (buffers); each is 259 bytes

INTERRUPT 69h - Function 01h, Subfunction 06h
CLOSE SESSION

Purpose: Terminate the specified network connection.

Available on: All machines.

Registers at call:
AX = 0106h
DX = session handle

Restrictions: DECnet DOS CTERM must be installed.

Return Registers:
AH = 00h good close
    other error code (see Function 01h Subfunction 03h)

Conflicts: Zenith AT BIOS (chapter 4).
See Also: Function 01h Subfunctions 03h and 05h

INTERRUPT 69h - Function 01h, Subfunction 0Ah
GET SESSION CONTROL BLOCK SIZE

Purpose: Determine how much space is required to store a session control block.

Available on: All machines.

Registers at call:
AX = 010Ah

Restrictions: DECnet DOS CTERM must be installed.

Return Registers:
AX = length of session control block in bytes

Conflicts: Zenith AT BIOS (chapter 4).
See Also: Function 01h Subfunction 05h

INTERRUPT 69h - Function 01h, Subfunction 0Bh
GET DECnet SOCKET

Purpose: Determine the network socket corresponding to a network connection.

Available on: All machines.

Registers at call:
AX = 010Bh
DX = session handle

Restrictions: DECnet DOS CTERM must be installed.

Return Registers:
AX > 0 DECnet socket for the session
   = 0 no match for handle

Conflicts: Zenith AT BIOS (chapter 4).

INTERRUPT 69h - Function 01h, Subfunction 0Fh
DEINSTALL CTERM

Purpose: Remove CTERM from memory.
Available on: All machines.   **Restrictions:** DECnet DOS CTERM must be installed.
Registers at call: **Return Registers:**
AX = 010Fh   AH = 00h   succesful uninstall
                                                         other   error code (see Function 01h Subfunction
                                                                 03h)

Details: CTERM must have been the last TSR loaded in order to deinstall it.
Conflicts: Zenith AT BIOS (chapter 4).
See Also: Function 01h Subfunction 00h

INTERRUPT 6Ah
LOCAL AREA TRANSPORT PROGRAM

Purpose: Determine whether the DECnet DOS Local Area Transport program is installed.
Available on: All machines.   **Restrictions:** none.
Details: The 3 bytes preceding the interrupt handler are "LAT"; this serves as the installation check.
Conflicts: OPTHELP.COM (chapter 36).

INTERRUPT 6Ah - Function 01h
SEND BYTE

Purpose: Transmit a character over the specified network connection.
Available on: All machines.   **Restrictions:** DECnet DOS Local Area Transport
                                                                 program must be installed.
Registers at call: **Return Registers:**
AH = 01h   AH >= 80h on error
AL = character
DH = FFh
DL = handle
Conflicts: OPTHELP.COM (chapter 36).
See Also: Function 02h

INTERRUPT 6Ah - Function 02h
READ BYTE

Purpose: Await a character on the specified network connection.
Available on: All machines.   **Restrictions:** DECnet DOS Local Area Transport
                                                                 program must be installed.
Registers at call: **Return Registers:**
AH = 02h   AH < 80h if successful
DH = FFh   AL = character
DL = handle   AH >= 80h on error
Conflicts: OPTHELP.COM (chapter 36).
See Also: Function 01h

INTERRUPT 6Ah - Function 03h
STATUS

Purpose: Determine the status of the specified network connection.
Available on: All machines.   **Restrictions:** DECnet DOS Local Area Transport
                                                                 program must be installed.
Registers at call: **Return Registers:**
AH = 03h   AH = status flags
DH = FFh   bit 5: transmit buffer empty

DL = handle

bit 3: session in start state
bit 2: session not active
bit 1: unable to queue transmit data
bit 0: receive data available

Conflicts: OPTHELP.COM (chapter 36).

INTERRUPT 6Ah - Function D0h
OPEN SESSION

Purpose: Establish a network connection.
Available on: All machines.

Restrictions: DECnet DOS Local Area Transport program must be installed.

Registers at call:
AH = D0h
AL = FFh no password
  = 0Fh password at ES:DI
DH = FFh
DS:BX -> LAT session control block (Table 24-1)
ES:DI -> 16-byte blank-padded password

Return Registers:
AH = 00h success
DL = handle

Details: The caller should set post routines to 0000h:0000h if polled operation will be used.
Conflicts: OPTHELP.COM (chapter 36).
See Also: Function D0h Subfunction 00h

INTERRUPT 6Ah - Function D0h, Subfunction 00h
CLOSE SESSION

Purpose: Terminate the specified network connection.
Available on: All machines.

Restrictions: DECnet DOS Local Area Transport program must be installed.

Registers at call:
AX = D000h
DH = FFh
DL = handle
Conflicts: OPTHELP.COM (chapter 36).
See Also: Function D0h

Return Registers:
AX = 0000h successful
  = 0001h no such session
  = 0002h session not running, try again later

INTERRUPT 6Ah - Function D1h, Subfunction 00h
SEND BREAK

Purpose: Send a signal on the specified connection requesting an interruption in the normal flow of data on that connection.
Available on: All machines.

Restrictions: DECnet DOS Local Area Transport program must be installed.

Registers at call:
AX = D100h
DH = FFh
DL = handle

Return Registers:
AX = 0000h if successful
AH bit 7 set if unable to send break

INTERRUPT 6Ah - Function D3h, Subfunction 00h
RESET LAT COUNTERS

Purpose: Zero the data transfer statistics for the Local Area Transport program.
Available on: All machines.

Restrictions: DECnet DOS Local Area Transport program must be installed.

Registers at call:
AX = D300h
DH = FFh

Return Registers: n/a

rConflicts: OPTHELP.COM (chapter 36).
See Also: Function D4h Subfunction 00h

INTERRUPT 6Ah - Function D4h, Subfunction 00h
COPY LAT COUNTERS

Purpose: Retrieve the transfer statistics for the Local Area Transport program.
Available on: All machines.   **Restrictions:** DECnet DOS Local Area Transport program must be installed.

Registers at call: **Return Registers:**
AX = D400h   AX = 0000h counters copied into buffer
DH = FFh   = FFFFh buffer too small
CX = buffer size
ES:BX -> buffer for LAT counters
Conflicts: OPTHELP.COM (chapter 36).
See Also: Function D3h Subfunction 00h

INTERRUPT 6Ah - Function D5h, Subfunction 00h
GET NEXT LAT SERVICE NAME

Purpose: Retrieve the names of the hosts on the network, one name per call.
Available on: All machines.   **Restrictions:** DECnet DOS Local Area Transport program must be installed.

Registers at call: **Return Registers:**
AX = D500h   AH = 00h if successful
DH = FFh   ES:BX buffer filled
ES:BX -> 17-byte buffer for name   AX = FFFFh if end of table or no name available
Conflicts: OPTHELP.COM (chapter 36).
See Also: Function D6h Subfunction 00h

INTERRUPT 6Ah - Function D6h, Subfunction 00h
LAT SERVICE TABLE RESET

Purpose: Set pointer to next name to retrieve back to beginning of table, and determine number of entries in the table.
Available on: All machines.   **Restrictions:** DECnet DOS Local Area Transport program must be installed.

Registers at call: **Return Registers:**
AX = D600h   AX = number of service table entries
DH = FFh   BX = 0000h service table has not overflowed
                                                             = FFFFh service table has overflowed

Conflicts: OPTHELP.COM (chapter 36).
See Also: Function D5h Subfunction 00h

INTERRUPT 6Dh
DATA LINK LAYER PROGRAM API

Purpose: Access the Data Link Layer program.
Available on: All machines.   **Restrictions:** DECnet DOS must be installed.
Conflicts: VGA (chapter 5), ATI VGA Wonder (chapter 5).

INTERRUPT 6Eh
DECnet NETWORK PROCESS API

Purpose: Access the network process.
Available on: All machines.   **Restrictions:** DECnet DOS Network must be installed.

Details: This is the main DECnet DOS access, and is described in Digital manual AA-EB46B-TV ("DECnet-DOS Programmer's Reference Manual"). There is a signature/data area (Table 24-2) immediately prior to the interrupt handler which may be used as an installation check.
Conflicts: None known.

Table 24-2. Format of Signature Area:

Offset	Size	Description
-5	BYTE	major version number
-4	BYTE	minor version number
-3	3 BYTEs	signature (ASCII "DNP")

Chapter · *25*

APPC/PC

IBM's Advanced Program-to-Program Communication is one protocol within the Systems Network Architecture; it is roughly equivalent to the OSI's "session layer" and according to company press releases, is the communications basis for all future applications and system products. APPC/PC is the software package for personal computers that implements one end of the APPC protocol; the mainframe end of the link is handled by LU 6.2.

APPC/PC has yet to establish itself in the PC world despite its official blessing, but its interface will be of interest to all programmers faced with a need to communicate with IBM mainframes.

INTERRUPT 68h - Function 01h
APPC/PC - NETWORK DEVICE CONTROL
Purpose: Attach or detach physical or logical units.
Available on: All machines.
Registers at call:
AH = 01h
DS:DX -> control block (Table 25-1)
Conflicts: Sangoma CCPOP 3270 resident module (chapter 26).

Restrictions: APPC/PC software must be installed.
Return Registers: n/a

Table 25-1. ForMat Of Control Block:

Offset	Size	Description
00h	12 BYTEs	reserved
0Ch	WORD	verb (action)
0Eh	6 BYTEs	00h
14h	DWORD	(high byte first) return code (Table 25-2)
---if verb = 1B00h (DISPLAY)		
18h	WORD	00h
1Ah	8 BYTEs	(high byte first) logical unit ID
22h	8 BYTEs	(high byte first) partner logical unit name
2Ah	8 BYTEs	(high byte first) mode name
32h	BYTE	logical unit session limit
33h	BYTE	partner logical unit session limit
34h	BYTE	node maximum negotiable session limit
35h	BYTE	current session limit
36h	BYTE	minimum negotiated winner limit
37h	BYTE	maximum negotiated loser limit
38h	BYTE	active session count
39h	BYTE	active CONWINNER session count
3Ah	BYTE	active CONLOSER session count
3Bh	BYTE	session termination count
3Ch	BYTE	bit 7: SESSION_TERMINATION_TARGET_DRAIN
		bit 6: SESSION_TERMINATION_SOURCE_DRAIN
---if verb=2000h (Attach Physical Unit)		
18h	WORD	00h
1Ah	BYTE	version
1Bh	BYTE	release

Table 25-1. Format of Control Block (continued)

Offset	Size	Description
1Ch	8 BYTEs	(high byte first) net name
24h	8 BYTEs	(high byte first) physical unit name
2Ch	8 BYTEs	00h
34h	DWORD	pointer to SYSTEM_LOG_EXIT routine, FFFFFFFFh=don't log errors
38h	DWORD	00h
3Ch	BYTE	00h RETURN_CONTROL: COMPLETE
		01h RETURN_CONTROL: INCOMPLETE

---*if verb=2100h (Attach Logical Unit)*

Offset	Size	Description
18h	WORD	70 offset to partner logical unit record
1Ah	8 BYTEs	(high byte first) logical unit name
22h	8 BYTEs	(high byte first) logical unit ID
2Ah	BYTE	logical unit local address
2Bh	BYTE	logical unit session limit
2Ch	DWORD	pointer to CREATE_TP_EXIT routine,
		FFFFFFFFh = reject incoming ALLOCATEs
		00000000h = queue ALLOCATEs
30h	DWORD	00h
34h	DWORD	pointer to SYSTEM_LOG_EXIT routine, FFFFFFFFh=don't log errors
38h	DWORD	00h
3Ch	BYTE	maximum TPs
3Dh	BYTE	queue depth
3Eh	DWORD	pointer to LU_LU_PASSWORD_EXIT routine, FFFFFFFFh=no pswd exit
42h	DWORD	00h
46h	WORD	total length of partner records
		for each partner logical unit:
	WORD	length of this partner logical unit record
	WORD	42 offset to mode records
	8 BYTEs	(high byte first) partner logical unit name
	BYTE	partner logical unit security capabilities
		bit 7: already verified
		bit 6: conversation level security
		bit 5: session level security
	BYTE	partner logical unit session limit
	WORD	partner logical unit maximum MC_SEND_LL
	8 BYTEs	(high byte first) partner logical unit DLC name
	BYTE	partner logical unit adapter number
	17 BYTEs	(counted string) partner logical unit adapter address
	WORD	total length of mode records
		for each mode:
	WORD	16 length of this mode record
	8 BYTEs	(high byte first) mode name
	WORD	RU_SIZE high bound
	WORD	RU_SIZE low bound
	BYTE	mode maximum negotiable session limit
	BYTE	pacing size for receive

---*if verb=2200h (Detach Logical Unit)*

Offset	Size	Description
18h	8 BYTEs	(high byte first) logical unit ID
20h	BYTE	00h

---*if verb=2700h (Detach Physical Unit)*

Offset	Size	Description
18h	BYTE	00h type: hard
		01h type: soft

---*if verb=2B00h (Activate DLC)*

Offset	Size	Description
18h	8 BYTEs	(high byte first) DLC name
20h	BYTE	adapter number

Table 25-2. Values for Return Code:

Value	Meaning
0000h	successful
0001h	BAD_TP_ID
0002h	BAD_CONV_ID
0003h	bad logical unit ID
0008h	no physical unit attached
0110h	bad state
01B1h	BAD_PART_LUNAME
01B2h	bad mode name
0201h	physical unit already active
0211h	logical unit already active
0212h	BAD_PART_SESS
0213h	BAD_RU_SIZES
0214h	BAD_MODE_SESS
0216h	BAD_PACING_CNT
0219h	EXTREME_RUS
021Ah	SNASVCMG_1
0223h	SSCP_CONNECTED_LU
0230h	invalid change
0243h	too many TPs
0272h	adapter close failure
0281h	GET_ALLOC_BAD_TYPE
0282h	unsuccessful
0283h	DLC failure
0284h	unrecognized DLC
0286h	duplicate DLC
0301h	SSCP_PU_SESSION_NOT_ACTIVE
0302h	data exceeds RU size
0401h	invalid direction
0402h	invalid type
0403h	segment overlap
0404h	invalid first character
0405h	table error
0406h	conversion error
F0010000h	APPC disabled
F0020000h	APPC busy
F0030000h	APPC abended
F0040000h	incomplete

Routines defined by LU_LU_PASSWORD_EXIT, CREATE_TP_EXIT, and SYSTEM_LOG_EXIT pointers are called by pushing the DWORD pointer to the verb on the stack and then performing a FAR call.

Table 25-3. Format of ACCESS_LU_LU_PW verb:

Offset	Size	Description
00h	12 BYTEs	reserved
0Ch	WORD	1900h
0Eh	8 BYTEs	(high byte first) logical unit ID
16h	8 BYTEs	(high byte first) logical unit name
1Eh	8 BYTEs	(high byte first) partner logical unit name
26h	17 BYTEs	(counted string) partner fully qualified logical unit name
37h	BYTE	password available (0=no, 1=yes)
38h	8 BYTEs	password

Table 25-4. Format of CREATE_TP Verb:

Offset	Size	Description
00h	12 BYTEs	reserved
0Ch	WORD	2300h
0Eh	6 BYTEs	00h
14h	DWORD	(high byte first) sense code
		00000000h	Ok
		080F6051h	SECURITY_NOT_VALID
		084B6031h	TP_NOT_AVAIL_RETRY
		084C0000h	TP_NOT_AVAIL_NO_RETRY
		10086021h	TP_NAME_NOT_RECOGNIZED
		10086034h	CONVERSATION_TYPE_MISMATCH
		10086041h	SYNC_LEVEL_NOT_SUPPORTED
18h	8 BYTEs	(high byte first) TP ID
20h	8 BYTEs	(high byte first) logical unit ID
28h	DWORD	(high byte first) conversation ID
2Ch	BYTE	0 basic conversation, 1 mapped conversation
2Dh	BYTE	0 no sync level, 1 confirm
2Eh	BYTE	reserved
2Fh	65 BYTEs	(counted string) transaction program name
70h	6 BYTEs	00h
76h	WORD	length of ERROR_LOG_DATA to return
78h	DWORD	pointer to ERROR_LOG_DATA buffer
7Ch	8 BYTEs	(high byte first) partner logical unit name
84h	18 BYTEs	(counted string) partner fully qualified logical unit name
96h	8 BYTEs	(high byte first) mode name
9Eh	12 BYTEs	00h
AAh	11 BYTEs	(counted string) password
B5h	11 BYTEs	(counted string) user ID
C0h	BYTE	0 verification should be performed
		1 already verified

Table 25-5. Format of SYSLOG Verb:

Offset	Size	Description
00h	12 BYTEs	reserved
0Ch	WORD	2600h
0Eh	10 BYTEs	00h
18h	WORD	(high byte first) type
1Ah	DWORD	(high byte first) subtype
1Eh	DWORD	pointer to ADDITIONAL_INFO
22h	DWORD	(high byte first) conversation ID
26h	8 BYTEs	(high byte first) TP ID
2Eh	8 BYTEs	(high byte first) physical unit or logical unit name
36h	WORD	length of data
38h	DWORD	pointer to data
3Ch	BYTE	00h

INTERRUPT 68h - Function 02h
APPC/PC - CONNECTION CONTROL

Purpose: Establish or terminate network connections, or send or receive data over an established connection.

Available on: All machines.　　　　**Restrictions:** APPC/PC software must be installed.

Registers at call:　　　　**Return Registers:** n/a

AH = 02h

DS:DX -> control block (Table 25-6)

Conflicts: Sangoma CCPOP 3270 resident module (chapter 26).

Table 25-6. Format of Control Block:

Offset	Size	Description
00h	12 BYTEs	reserved
0Ch	WORD	verb (action)
0Eh	BYTE	1 if MC_ (mapped conversation) form of verb
		0 if basic verb
0Fh	5 BYTEs	reserved (0)
14h	WORD	(high byte first) primary return code (Table 25-7)
16h	DWORD	(high byte first) error code (Table 25-8)
1Ah	8 BYTEs	(high byte first) TP_ID
22h	DWORD	(high byte first) conversation ID

---if verb=0100h (Allocate or MC_Allocate)

26h	BYTE	(MC_Allocate only) 0 basic conversation
		1 mapped conversation
27h	BYTE	00h SYNC_LEVEL = none
		01h SYNC_LEVEL = confirm
28h	WORD	0000h
2Ah	BYTE	00h RETURN_CONTROL: when session allocated
		01h RETURN_CONTROL: immediate
		02h RETURN_CONTROL: when session free
2Bh	8 BYTEs	00h
33h	8 BYTEs	(high byte first) partner logical unit name
3Bh	8 BYTEs	(high byte first) mode name
43h	65 BYTEs	(counted string) TP name
84h	BYTE	00h security: none
		01h security: same
		02h security: pgm
85h	11 BYTEs	00h
90h	11 BYTEs	(counted string) password
9Bh	11 BYTEs	(counted string) user ID
A6h	WORD	PIP_DATA length
A8h	DWORD	pointer to PIP_DATA

---if verb=0300h (Confirm or MC_Confirm)

26h	BYTE	request to send received (0=no, 1=yes)

---if verb=0400h (Confirmed or MC_Confirmed), no additional fields

---if verb=0500h (Deallocate or MC_Deallocate)

26h	BYTE	00h
27h	BYTE	type 0 SYNC_LEVEL
		1 FLUSH
		2 ABEND_PROC
		3 ABEND_SVC
		4 ABEND_TIMER
		5 ABEND
28h	WORD	(MC_Deallocate only) length of error log data
2Ah	DWORD	(MC_Deallocate only) pointer to error log data

---if verb=0600h (Flush or MC_Flush), no additional fields

---if verb=0700h (Get_Attributes or MC_Get_Attributes)

26h	8 BYTEs	(high byte first) logical unit ID
2Eh	BYTE	00h
2Fh	BYTE	SYNC_LEVEL (0=none, 1=confirm)
30h	8 BYTEs	(high byte first) mode name
38h	8 BYTEs	(high byte first) own net name
40h	8 BYTEs	(high byte first) own logical unit name
48h	8 BYTEs	(high byte first) partner logical unit name
50h	18 BYTEs	(counted string) partner's fully qualified logical unit name

Table 25-6. Format of Control Block (continued)

Offset	Size	Description
62h	BYTE	00h
63h	11 BYTEs	(counted string) user ID

---if verb=0800h (Get_Type)

26h	BYTE	type (0=basic conversation, 1=mapped conversation)

---if verb=0900h (Post_on_Receipt)

26h	WORD	maximum length
28h	BYTE	fill (0=buffer, 1=LL)

---if verb=0A00h (Prepare_to_Receive or MC_Prepare_to_Receive)

26h	BYTE	type (0=SYNC_LEVEL, 1=FLUSH)
27h	BYTE	locks (0=short, 1=long)

---if verb=0B00h (Receive_and_Wait or MC_Receive_and_Wait)

26h	BYTE	what received
		00h data
		01h data complete
		02h data incomplete
		03h confirm
		04h confirm send
		05h confirm deallocate
		06h send
27h	BYTE	(MC_Receive_and_Wait only) fill (0=buffer, 1=LL)
28h	BYTE	Request_to_Send_Received (0=no, 1=yes)
29h	WORD	maximum length
2Bh	WORD	data length
2Dh	DWORD	pointer to data

---if verb=0C00h (Receive_Immediate or MC_Receive_Immediate)

26h	BYTE	what received
		00h data
		01h data complete
		02h data incomplete
		03h confirm
		04h confirm send
		05h confirm deallocate
		06h send
27h	BYTE	(MC_Receive_Immediate only) fill (0=buffer, 1=LL)
28h	BYTE	Request_to_Send_Received (0=no, 1=yes)
29h	WORD	maximum length
2Bh	WORD	data length
2Dh	DWORD	pointer to data

---if verb=0E00h (Request_to_Send or MC_Request_to_Send), no other fields

---if verb=0F00h (Send_Data or MC_Send_Data)

26h	BYTE	request to send received (0=no, 1=yes)
27h	BYTE	00h
28h	WORD	data length
2Ah	DWORD	pointer to data

---if verb=1000h (Send_Error or MC_Send_Error)

26h	BYTE	request to send received (0=no, 1=yes)
27h	BYTE	type (0=program, 1=SVC)
28h	DWORD	00h
2Ch	WORD	(MC_Send_Error only) LOG_DATA length
2Eh	DWORD	(MC_Send_Error only) pointer to LOG_DATA

Table 25-6. Format of Control Block (continued)

Offset	Size	Description

---if verb=1200h (Test or MC_Test)

| 26h | BYTE | (MC_Test only) test (0=posted, 1=request_to_send received) |

Note: error code has different interpretations for:
  0 posted data
  1 posted not data (primary return code = 0)
  1 bad TP_ID (primary return code = 1)

---if verb=1300h (Wait)

| 26h | BYTE | number of conversations to wait on |

Note: error codes have interpretations as for 1200h above

Table 25-7. Values for primary return code:

Value	Meaning	Value	Meaning
0000h	successful	000Eh	PROG_ERROR_PURGING
0001h	parameter check	000Fh	CONV_FAILURE_RETRY
0002h	state check	0010h	CONV_FAILURE_NO_RETRY
0003h	allocation error	0011h	SVC_ERROR_NO_TRUNC
0005h	deallocate abended	0012h	SVC_ERROR_TRUNC
0006h	deallocate abended program	0013h	SVC_ERROR_PURGING
0007h	deallocate abended SVC	0014h	unsuccessful
0008h	deallocate abended timer	0018h	CNOS partner logical unit reject
0009h	deallocate normal return	0019h	conversation type mixed
000Ah	data posting blocked	F001h	APPC disabled
000Bh	posting not active	F002h	APPC busy
000Ch	PROG_ERROR_NO_TRUNC	F003h	APPC abended
000Dh	PROG_ERROR_TRUNC	F004h	incomplete

Table 25-8. Values for error code:

Value	Meaning	Value	Meaning
0001h	bad TP ID	0055h	deallocate: NOT_LL_BDY
0002h	bad conversation ID	0057h	deallocate: log LL_WRONG
0004h	allocation error, no retry	0061h	flush: not send state
0005h	allocation error, retry	0091h	post on receipt: invalid length
0006h	data area crosses segment boundary	0092h	post on receipt: not in receive state
0010h	bad TPN length	0093h	post on receipt: bad fill
0011h	bad CONV length	00A1h	prepare to receive:invalid type
0012h	bad SYNC level	00A2h	prepare to receive: unfinished LL
0013h	bad security selection	00A3h	prepare to receive: not in send state
0014h	bad return control	00B1h	receive and wait: bad state
0015h	SEC_TOKENS too big	00B2h	receive and wait: NOT_LL_BDY
0016h	PIP_LEN incorrect	00B5h	receive and wait: bad fill
0017h	no use of SNASVCMG	00C1h	receive immediate: not in receive state
0018h	unknown partner mode	00C4h	receive immediate: bad fill
0031h	confirm: SYNC_NONE	00E1h	request to send: not in receive state
0032h	confirm: bad state	00F1h	send data: bad LL
0033h	confirm: NOT_LL_BDY	00F2h	send data: not in send state
0041h	confirmed: bad state	0102h	send error: log LL wrong
0051h	deallocate: bad type	0103h	send error: bad type
0052h	deallocate: flush bad stat	0121h	test: invalid type
0053h	deallocate: confirm bad state	0122h	test: not in receive state

INTERRUPT 68h - Function 03h
APPC/PC

Purpose: Miscellaneous network control.

Available on: All machines.
Registers at call:
AH = 03h
DS:DX -> control block (Table 25-9)
Conflicts: Sangoma CCPOP 3270 resident module (chapter 26).

Restrictions: APPC/PC software must be installed.
Return Registers: n/a

Table 25-9. Format of Control Block:

Offset	Size	Description
00h	12 BYTEs	reserved
0Ch	WORD	verb (action)
0Eh	6 BYTEs	0
14h	DWORD	(high byte first) return code (see Function 01h)
18h	WORD	0
1Ah	8 BYTEs	(high byte first) logical unit ID

---if verb=2400h (TP Started), control block continues

22h	8 BYTEs	(high byte first) TP ID

---if verb=2800h (Get ALLOCATE), control block continues

22h	BYTE	type: 00h dequeue
		01h test
23h	DWORD	pointer to CREATE_TP record

---if verb=2A00h (Change Logical Unit). control block continues

22h	DWORD	pointer to CREATE_TP_EXIT routine
		FFFFFFFFh reject incoming ALLOCATEs
		00000000h queue ALLOCATEs
26h	DWORD	00000000h
2Ah	DWORD	pointer to SYSTEM_LOG_EXIT routine, FFFFFFFFh= don't log errors
2Eh	DWORD	00000000h
32h	BYTE	maximum TPs
33h	BYTE	00h stop QUEUE_ALLOCATEs
		01h resume QUEUE_ALLOCATEs
34h	DWORD	pointer to LU_LU_PASSWORD_EXIT routine, FFFFFFFFh = no exit
38h	DWORD	00000000h

INTERRUPT 68h - Function 04h
APPC/PC - TRANSACTION PROCESSING

Purpose: Start or end transaction processing.
Available on: All machines.
Registers at call:
AH = 04h
DS:DX -> control block (Table 25-10)
Conflicts: Sangoma CCPOP 3270 resident module (chapter 26).

Restrictions: APPC/PC software must be installed.
Return Registers: n/a

Table 25-10. Format of Control Block:

Offset	Size	Description
00h	12 BYTEs	reserved
0Ch	WORD	verb (action)
		2500h TP_ENDED
		2900h TP_VALID
0Eh	6 BYTEs	0
14h	DWORD	(high byte first) return code (see Function 01h)
18h	WORD	0
1Ah	8 BYTEs	(high byte first) TP_ID
22h	DWORD	-> CREATE_TP record (only if verb = 2900h)

INTERRUPT 68h - Function 05h
TRANSFER MESSAGE DATA

Purpose: Send a message of user-defined format.
Available on: All machines.
Registers at call:
AH = 05h
DS:DX -> control block (Table 25-11)
Conflicts: Sangoma CCPOP 3270 resident module (chapter 26).

Restrictions: APPC/PC software must be installed.
Return Registers:
n/a

Table 25-11. Format of Control Block:

Offset	Size	Description
00h	12 BYTEs	reserved
0Ch	WORD	1C00h
0Eh	BYTE	00h user defined
		01h NMVT
		02h alert subvectors
		03h PDSTATS subvectors
0Fh	5 BYTEs	0
14h	DWORD	(high byte first) return code (see Function 01h)
18h	12 BYTEs	0
24h	BYTE	if bit 0 clear, add correlation subvector
		if bit 1 clear, add product set ID subvector
		if bit 2 clear, do SYSLOG
		if bit 3 clear, send SSCP_PU_SESSION
25h	BYTE	0
26h	WORD	length of data
28h	N BYTEs	data

INTERRUPT 68h - Function 06h
CHANGE NUMBER OF SESSIONS

Purpose: Specify the number of concurrent network connections allowed.
Available on: All machines.
Registers at call:
AH = 06h
DS:DX -> control block (Table 25-12)
Conflicts: Sangoma CCPOP 3270 resident module (chapter 26).

Restrictions: APPC/PC software must be installed.
Return Registers: n/a

Table 25-12. Format of Control Block:

Offset	Size	Description
00h	12 BYTEs	reserved
0Ch	WORD	1500h
0Eh	6 BYTEs	0
14h	WORD	(high byte first) primary return code (see Function 02h)
16h	DWORD	(high byte first) secondary return code (see Table 25-13, Function 01h)
1Ah	8 BYTEs	(high byte first) logical unit ID
22h	8 BYTEs	blanks
2Ah	8 BYTEs	(high byte first) partner logical unit name
32h	8 BYTEs	(high byte first) mode name
3Ah	BYTE	bit 7: use MODE_NAME_SELECT_ALL rather than MODE_NAME
		bit 6: set negotiable values
3Bh	BYTE	partner logical unit mode session limit
3Ch	BYTE	minimum CONWINNERS_SOURCE
3Dh	BYTE	maximum CONWINNERS_TARGET
3Eh	BYTE	automatic activation

Table 25-12. Format of Control Block (continued)

Offset	Size	Description
3Fh	BYTE	0
40h	BYTE	bit 7: drain target
		bit 6: drain source
		bit 5: target responsible, not source

Table 25-13. Values for Secondary Return Code (see also Function 01h):

Value	Meaning	Value	Meaning
0000h	accepted	0156h	mode closed (prim return code = 1)
0001h	negotiated		CNOS mode closed (prim return code = 18h)
0003h	bad logical unit ID	0157h	bad mode name (prim return code = 1)
0004h	allocation failure, no retry		CNOS bad mode name (prim return code = 18h)
0005h	allocation failure, retry	0159h	reset SNA drains
0151h	can't raise limits	015Ah	single not SRC response
0153h	all modes must reset	015Bh	bad partner logical unit
0154h	bad SNASVCMG limits	015Ch	exceeds maximum allowed
0155h	minimum greater than total	015Dh	change SRC drains
		015Eh	logical unit detached
		015Fh	CNOS command race reject

INTERRUPT 68h - Function 07h
PASSTHROUGH

Purpose: Invoke an installable application subsystem.

Available on: All machines.   **Restrictions:** APPC/PC software must be installed.

Registers at call: **Return Registers:** n/a

AH = 07h

DS:DX -> control block (format depends on
    application subsystem)

Conflicts: Sangoma CCPOP 3270 resident module (chapter 26).

See Also: Function FFh

INTERRUPT 68h - Function FAh
ENABLE/DISABLE APPC

Purpose: Specify whether APPC should respond to function calls.

Available on: All machines.   **Restrictions:** APPC/PC software must be installed.

Registers at call: **Return Registers:** n/a

AH = FAh

AL bit 0 = 0 enable
       1 disable

Conflicts: Sangoma CCPOP 3270 resident module (chapter 26).

INTERRUPT 68h - Function FBh
CONVERT DATA

Purpose: Translate text between ASCII and EBCDIC formats.

Available on: All machines.   **Restrictions:** APPC/PC software must be installed.

Registers at call: **Return Registers:** n/a

AH = FBh

DS:DX -> control block (Table 25-14)

Conflicts: Sangoma CCPOP 3270 resident module (chapter 26).

Table 25-14. Format of Control Block:

Offset	Size	Description
00h	12 BYTEs	reserved
0Ch	WORD	1A00h
0Eh	6 BYTEs	0
14h	DWORD	(high byte first) return code
18h	BYTE	conversion: 00h ASCII to EBCDIC
		01h EBCDIC to ASCII
19h	BYTE	character set: 00h AE
		01h A
		02h G
1Ah	WORD	length of string to convert
1Ch	DWORD	pointer to source
20h	DWORD	pointer to target

INTERRUPT 68h - Function FCh
ENABLE/DISABLE MESSAGE TRACING

Purpose: Specify whether message traffic should be traced.

Available on: All machines.

Registers at call:

AH = FCh

AL = 00h disable tracing

  = 01h enable tracing

DX = number of bytes to keep (0=all)

Restrictions: APPC/PC software must be installed.

Return Registers: n/a

Conflicts: Sangoma CCPOP 3270 resident module (chapter 26).

See Also: Function FDh

INTERRUPT 68h - Function FDh
ENABLE/DISABLE API VERB TRACING

Purpose: Specify whether API calls should be traced.

Available on: All machines.

Registers at call:

AH = FDh

AL = 00h disable tracing

  = 01h enable tracing

Restrictions: APPC/PC software must be installed.

Return Registers: n/a

Conflicts: Sangoma CCPOP 3270 resident module (chapter 26).

See Also: Functions FCh and FEh

INTERRUPT 68h - Function FEh
SET TRACE DESTINATION

Purpose: Determine where trace messages will be output.

Available on: All machines.

Registers at call:

AH = FEh

AL = trace destinations

   bit 0 storage (DS:DX -> trace stats record,

       Table 25-15)

   bit 1 display

   bit 2 file (trace written to file OUTPUT.PC)

   bit 3 printer

Restrictions: APPC/PC software must be installed.

Return Registers: n/a

Details: The statistics record may not be moved while the trace is active.

Conflicts: Sangoma CCPOP 3270 resident module (chapter 26).

See Also: Function FDh

Table 25-15. Format of Trace Statistics Record:

Offset	Size	Description
00h	DWORD	pointer to storage trace buffer
04h	WORD	max number of 80-byte records in trace
06h	WORD	(high-order byte first!) current record number (must init to 0)
08h	DWORD	(high-order byte first!) number of records written (init to 0)
0Ch	DWORD	reserved

INTERRUPT 68h - Function FFh
SET PASSTHROUGH

Purpose: Specify the function which is to handle passthrough requests; this allows a subsystem to install itself into APPC/PC.

Available on: All machines.

Registers at call:
AH = FFh
DS:DX -> passthrough exit routine

Restrictions: APPC/PC software must be installed.

Return Registers: n/a

Conflicts: Sangoma CCPOP 3270 resident module (chapter 26).
See Also: Function 07h

IBM Mainframe Connectivity

A number of products that provide connectivity between PC's and IBM mainframe systems exist, but we have specific information on only two groups that make special use of the PC interrupt structure (most operate simply as terminal emulators and leave it to the mainframe software to handle terminal communications). These are the IBM System 36/38 Workstation emulator (a single program), and those programs which emulate the IBM3270 terminal.

IBM System 36/38

The IBM System 36/38 Workstation emulator makes the PC appear, to a System 36/38, to be nothing more than another workstation. While the emulator program is running, no other DOS applications can be active; for this reason, conflicts between this emulator and other programs are of little consequence.

INTERRUPT 0Ch
IBM SYSTEM 36/38 WORKSTATION EMULATION - API POINTER

Purpose: Provides pointer to API. Call offset 100h in the interrupt handler's segment.

Available on: All machines.

Registers at call:
AH = function
    03h update screen
    05h select next session
AL = session number (00h-03h)

Restrictions: Emulator software must be installed.

Return Registers:
AL = session type code
    00h not active
    01h display session
    02h printer session
    FEh invalid session number
DS = requested sessi's data segment (0 if not active)

Conflicts: COM1 (chapter 2).

Table 26-1. Format of Emulator's Data Area (offsets into interrupt handler's segment):

Offset	Size	Description
13Eh	BYTE	bit flags for status line indicators turned on since this byte was last zeroed
13Fh	BYTE	bit flags for status line indicators turned off since this byte was last set to FFh
140h	WORD	offset of EBCDIC to ASCII translation
146h	WORD	offset of EBCDIC screen buffer
148h	WORD	offset of EC (engineering change) level signature
150h	BYTE	"KEYI"
151h	BYTE	5250 key scan code to be sent to remote
15Bh	BYTE	"SYSAV"
15Dh	BYTE	5250 cursor column
15Eh	BYTE	5250 cursor row
167h	BYTE	"DVCTAD"
178h	BYTE	"FLAGS"
184h	BYTE	"SESSNOAD"
193h	BYTE	"STNAD"
198h	BYTE	"NSDS"

INTERRUPT 21h - Function 44h, Subfunction 02h
VDI.SYS - GET Unknown Data

Purpose: *unknown.*

Available on: All machines.

Registers at call:
AX = 4402h
BX = handle for character device "GDMS"
CX = number of bytes to read (>= 4)
DS:DX -> buffer (see below)
Conflicts: DOS 2+ IOCTL Read Control (chapter 8), Network Driver Interface Spec 2.0.1 (chapter 27), HIGHUMM.SYS - IOCTL - Get API Address (chapter 36).

Restrictions: IBM   System   36/38   Workstation Emulation software must be installed.

Return Registers:
CF set on error
    AX = error code (see Function 59h)
CF clear if successful
    AX = number of bytes read

Table 26-2. Format of returned data:

Offset	Size	Description
00h	4 BYTEs	unknown.
04h	DWORD	pointer to unknown.
08h	4 BYTEs	unknown.

IBM 3270 Emulation
At least six different packages for the PC provide emulation of the IBM 3270 terminal for mainframe connectivity. They are Attachmate Extra; IBM's PC3270 emulator; Tangram Arbiter, which makes a PC disk look like a slow mainframe disk over an SNA link to the mainframe; Sangoma's CCIP Interface; the IBM 3270 Workstation Program (which is not the same as the PC3270 emulator); and Eicon Access.

INTERRUPT 21h - Function A0h
GET 3270 DISPLAY STATE

Purpose: Determine which windows on the emulated 3270 terminal are available and/or displayed, and which is currently active.

Available on: All machines.

Registers at call:
AH = A0h

Restrictions: Attachmate Extra must be installed.

Return Registers:
AL = display status:
    bit 7 : 0=windowed, 1=enlarged
    bits 6-3: current screen profile number
        0-9
        bits 2-0: active window number: 0=PC,
            1-4=host B-E, 5-6=notepad F-G
BX = host window status:
    bit 15: reserved
    bit 14: 0=host E window installed,
        1=not
    bit 13: 0=host E terminal on,
        1=off
    bit 12: 0=host E window displayed,
        1=not
    bit 11: reserved
    bit 10: 0=host D window installed,
        1=not
    bit 9: 0=host D terminal on,
        1=off
    bit 8: 0=host D window displayed,
        1=not

bit 7: reserved
bit 6: 0=host C window installed,
        1=not
bit 5: 0=host C terminal on,
        1=off
bit 4: 0=host C window displayed,
        1=not
bit 3: reserved
bit 2: 0=host B window installed,
        1=not
bit 1: 0=host B terminal on,
        1=off
bit 0: 0=host B window displayed,
        1=not

Details: Attachmate Extra is a 3270 emulator by Attachmate Corporation.
Conflicts: None known.
See Also: Function A1h

INTERRUPT 21h - Function A1h
SET 3270 DISPLAY STATE

Purpose: Specify which window of the emulated 3270 terminal will be active.
Available on: All machines.
Registers at call:
AH = A1h
AL = set status byte:
    bit 7 : 0=windowed, 1=enlarged
    bits 6-3: current screen profile number 0-9
    bits 2-0: active window number: 0=PC,
        1-4=host B-E, 5-6=notepad F-G
Conflicts: "789" virus (chapter 34).
See Also: Functions A0h and A2h

Restrictions: Attachmate Extra must be installed.
Return Registers: n/a

INTERRUPT 21h - Function A2h
SET HOST WINDOW STATE

Purpose: Specify the state of the specified window as known to the host.
Available on: All machines.
Registers at call:
AH = A2h
AL = set status byte:
    bit 7 : 0=power off, 1=power on
    bit 6 : 0=not installed, 1=installed
    bits 5-3: reserved
    bits 2-0: window number: 1-4=host B-E
Conflicts: None known.
See Also: Function A1h

Restrictions: Attachmate Extra must be installed.
Return Registers: n/a

INTERRUPT 21h - Function A3h
SEND KEYSTROKES TO HOST WINDOW

Purpose: Fake user input.
Available on: All machines.
Registers at call:
AH = A3h
AL = window number (1-4=host B-E)

Restrictions: Attachmate Extra must be installed.
Return Registers:
CX = zero if character sent, non-zero if not
BX incremented if CX=0

CX = 0001h
DS:BX -> keystroke buffer
DL = zero if keystroke buffer contains host function
        code,
   non-zero if keystroke buffer contains ASCII
        character
Conflicts: None known.

Table 26-3. Values for Host Function Code:

00h=reserved	10h=PF16	20h=Clear	30h=SysRq
01h=PF1	11h=PF17	21h=Print	31h=ErInp
02h=PF2	12h=PF18	22h=Left	32h=ErEof
03h=PF3	13h=PF19	23h=Right	33h=Ident
04h=PF4	14h=PF20	24h=Up	34h=Test
05h=PF5	15h=PF21	25h=Down	35h=Reset
06h=PF6	16h=PF22	26h=Home	36h=DevCncl
07h=PF7	17h=PF23	27h=Fast Left	37h=Dup
08h=PF8	18h=PF26	28h=Fast Right	38h=FldMark
09h=PF9	19h=Alt on	29h=Bksp	39h=Enter
0Ah=PF10	1Ah=Alt off	2Ah=Insert	3Ah=CrSel
0Bh=PF11	1Bh=Shift on	2Bh=Delete	
0Ch=PF12	1Ch=Shift off	2Ch=Backtab	
0Dh=PF13	1Dh=PA1	2Dh=Tab	
0Eh=PF14	1Eh=PA2	2Eh=Newline	
0Fh=PF15	1Fh=PA3	2Fh=Attn	

INTERRUPT 21h - Function A4h
GET HOST WINDOW BUFFER ADDRESS

Purpose: Determine the address of the virtual screen for the specified window.

Available on: All machines.   **Restrictions:** Attachmate Extra must be installed.

Registers at call: **Return Registers:**

AH = A4h   DS:BX -> 3270 display buffer

AL = window number (1-4=host B-E)

Conflicts: None known.

See Also: Functions A5h and B8h

INTERRUPT 21h - Function A5h
GET HOST WINDOW CURSOR POSITION

Purpose: Determine the current cursor position in the specified window.

Available on: All machines.   **Restrictions:** Attachmate Extra must be installed.

Registers at call: **Return Registers:**

AH = A5h   BX = cursor position

AL = window number (1-4=host B-E)   (80 * row + column, where 0:0 is upper left)

Details: If the host window is configured with the Extended Attribute (EAB) feature, multiply the cursor position by 2 to obtain the byte offset into the display buffer.

Conflicts: "Eddie-2" virus (chapter 34).

See Also: Function A4h

INTERRUPT 21h - Function AFh
GET TRANSLATE TABLE ADDRESS

Purpose: Determine the address of a table for translating between ASCII, EBCDIC, and 3270 buffer codes.

Available on: All machines.   **Restrictions:** Attachmate Extra must be installed.

Registers at call: **Return Registers:**

AH = AFh   DS:BX -> translate tables

Conflicts: None known.

Table 26-4. Format of Translate Tables:

Offset	Size	Description
00h	256 BYTEs	ASCII to 3270 buffer code translate table
100h	256 BYTEs	3270 buffer code to ASCII translate table
200h	256 BYTEs	3270 buffer code to EBCDIC translate table
300h	256 BYTEs	EBCDIC to 3270 buffer code translate table

INTERRUPT 21h - Function B8h
Attachmate Extra - DISABLE HOST BUFFER UPDATES

Purpose: Temporarily halt screen updates from the host to avoid changes while manipulating the screen memory.

Available on: All machines.

Registers at call:
AH = B8h
AL = window number (1-4=host B-E)
DL = 01h

Restrictions: Attachmate Extra must be installed.

Return Registers: n/a

Details: Only valid in CUT mode. Next AID keystroke (e.g., Enter) enables host buffer updates.

Conflicts: Novell Advanced NetWare (chapter 20).

See Also: Function A4h

INTERRUPT 2Ah - Function 90h
Unknown Function

Purpose: *unknown.*

Available on: All machines.

Registers at call:
AH = 90h
Others, if any, unknown.

Conflicts: None known.

Restrictions: IBM PC3270 Emulation program must be installed.

Return Registers: *unknown.*

INTERRUPT 2Fh - Function B4h, Subfunction 00h
INSTALLATION CHECK

Purpose: Determine whether version 3.0 or higher of the IBM PC3270 Emulation Program is installed.

Available on: All machines.

Registers at call:
AX = B400h

Conflicts: None known.

Restrictions: none.

Return Registers:
AL = FFh if installed

INTERRUPT 2Fh - Function B4h, Subfunction 01h
GET HOST BUFFER ADDRESS

Purpose: Determine the address of the screen memory used by the 3270 emulator.

Available on: All machines.

Registers at call:
AX = B401h

Conflicts: None known.

Restrictions: IBM PC3270 Emulation program version 3.0 or higher must be installed.

Return Registers:
ES -> host screen buffer (PC ASCII format)
ES unchanged if communications not started

INTERRUPT 2Fh - Function B4h, Subfunction 02h
Unknown Function

Purpose: *unknown.*

Available on: All machines.

Registers at call:
AX = B402h
BX = *unknown*.
Conflicts: None known.

Restrictions: IBM PC3270 Emulation program version 3.0 or higher must be installed.
Return Registers: *unknown*.

INTERRUPT 2Fh - Function B4h, Subfunctions 03h to 05h
Unknown Functions

Purpose: *unknown*.
Available on: All machines.

Registers at call:
AX = B403h to B405h
Others, if any, unknown.
Conflicts: None known.

Restrictions: IBM PC3270 Emulation program version 3.0 or higher must be installed.
Return Registers: *unknown*.

INTERRUPT 44h
IBM 3270-PC High Level Language API

Purpose: Provides an interface to the IBM 3270-PC emulator.
Available on: All machines.

Registers at call:
DS:SI -> parameter control block
Conflicts: PCjr character font vector(chapter 5), Novell Netware HLL API (chapter 20), Z100 master 8259 (chapter 2).

Restrictions: IBM PC3270 Emulation program must be installed.
Return Registers: n/a

INTERRUPT 60h
Tangram Arbiter - API

Purpose: Provides interface to Arbiter functions.
Available on: All machines.
Details: Arbiter may use any interrupt from 60h to 66h (parameterized). The actual interrupt used is identified by the string "@ARB_API" immediately following a short jump at the interrupt handler's address. Arbiter makes a PC disk look like a slow mainframe disk over an SNA link to an IBM mainframe.
Conflicts: See chapter 1.

Restrictions: Arbiter software must be installed.

INTERRUPT 61h
Sangoma CCIP INTERFACE

Purpose: Provide access to the CCPOP module's functions.
Available on: All machines.

Registers at call:
BX:DX -> control block
Conflicts: See chapter 1.

Restrictions: Sangoma CCPOP 3270 resident module must be installed.
Return Registers: n/a

INTERRUPT 67h
Sangoma CCPOP 3270 resident module

Purpose: *unknown*.
Available on: All machines.

Conflicts: EMS (chapter 10), Alloy NTNX (chapter 18), PC-NET (chapter 27).

Restrictions: Sangoma CCPOP 3270 resident module must be installed.

INTERRUPT 68h
Sangoma CCPOP 3270 resident module

Purpose: *unknown.*
Available on: All machines.

Conflicts: APPC/PC (chapter 25).

Restrictions: Sangoma CCPOP 3270 resident module must be installed.

INTERRUPT 7Ah - Function 04h
IBM 3270 Workstation Program API - CREATE A QUEUE

Purpose: Initiate a new queue for *unknown* uses.
Available on: All machines.

Registers at call:
AH = 04h
others, if any, unknown.
Conflicts: Novell NetWare Low-level API (chapter 20), Topware Network Operating System (chapter 27), AutoCAD Device Interface (chapter 36).
See Also: Function 06h

Restrictions: IBM 3270 Workstation Program must be installed.
Return Registers: *unknown.*

INTERRUPT 7Ah - Function 06h
IBM 3270 Workstation Program API - DELETE A QUEUE

Purpose: Erase a previously-created queue and return its resources to the system.
Available on: All machines.

Registers at call:
AH = 06h
others, if any, unknown.
Conflicts: Novell NetWare Low-level API (chapter 20), Topware Network Operating System (chapter 27), AutoCAD Device Interface (chapter 36).
See Also: Function 04h

Restrictions: IBM 3270 Workstation Program must be installed.
Return Registers: *unknown.*

INTERRUPT 7Ah - Function 09h
IBM 3270 Workstation Program API - SESSION SERVICES

Purpose: Manipulate a connection with the mainframe host.
Available on: All machines.

Registers at call:
AH = 09h
BX = 8020h (synchronous request)
CX = 0000h
DX = ID of session manager (SESSMGR)
AL = service
    01h get session ID
    02h get session info
    04h dettach from session
    05h attach to session
    06h get list of windows available
    07h get environment of window
    08h get 'PIF' (program information file) info
    0Ah get base window ID
    0Bh get cursor info
ES:DI -> control block

Restrictions: IBM 3270 Workstation Program must be installed.
Return Registers: *unknown.*

Conflicts: Novell NetWare Low-level API (chapter 20), Topware Network Operating System (chapter 27), AutoCAD Device Interface (chapter 36).

INTERRUPT 7Ah - Function 09h
KEYBOARD SERVICES

Purpose: Manipulate the state of the keyboard as seen by the host mainframe.

Available on: All machines.

Registers at call:
AH = 09h
BX = 8020h (synchronous request)
CX = 0000h
DX = ID of keyboard manager
AL = service
    01h connect to keyboard
    02h disconnect from keyboard
    03h read from keyboard
    04h send keystroke to session
    05h disable input
    06h enable input
    07h update status code
ES:DI -> control block

Restrictions: IBM 3270 Workstation Program must be installed.

Return Registers: *unknown.*

Conflicts: Novell NetWare Low-level API (chapter 20), Topware Network Operating System (chapter 27), AutoCAD Device Interface (chapter 36).

INTERRUPT 7Ah - Function 09h
WINDOW SERVICES

Purpose: Manipulate windows on the screen.

Available on: All machines.

Registers at call:
AH = 09h
AL = service (see Table 26-5)
BX = 8020h (synchronous request)
CX = 00FFh
DX = ID of window service controller (WSCTRL)
ES:DI -> control block

Restrictions: IBM 3270 Workstation Program must be installed.

Return Registers: *unknown.*

Conflicts: Novell NetWare Low-level API (chapter 20), Topware Network Operating System (chapter 27), AutoCAD Device Interface (chapter 36).

Table 26-5. 3270 Workstation API Service Codes

Code	Meaning	Code	Meaning
01h	connect to WS control	0Ah	change screen background color
02h	disconnect from WS control		
03h	add a window	0Bh	get window's position on screen
04h	change window's position on screen		
		0Ch	get window's size
05h	change window's size	0Dh	get window's color
06h	change window's color	0Eh	get window's position in the presentation space
07h	change window's position in the presentation space		
		0Fh	determine whether hidden
08h	hide/unhide toggle	10h	determine whether enlarged
09h	enlarge/reduce toggle	11h	get background color

Table 26-5. 3270 Workstation API Service Codes (continued)

Code	Meaning	Code	Meaning
12h	get window names	17h	delete a window from profile
13h	delete all windows from profile	18h	get active window
14h	pick active window	19h	get active screen
15h	redraw screen	1Ah	get window data
16h	redraw window	1Bh	change window data
		1Ch	select active screen

INTERRUPT 7Ah - Function 09h
PRESENTATION SPACE SERVICES

Purpose: Manipulate presentation spaces.
Available on: All machines.

Restrictions: IBM 3270 Workstation Program must be installed.
Return Registers: *unknown.*

Registers at call:
AH = 09h
BX = 8020h
CX = 00FFh
DX = ID of PCPSM
AL = service
    01h define presentation space
    02h delete presentation space
    03h display presentation space
    04h position cursor in presentation space
    05h change default presentation space
ES:DI -> control block
Conflicts: Novell NetWare Low-level API (chapter 20), Topware Network Operating System (chapter 27), AutoCAD Device Interface (chapter 36).

INTERRUPT 7Ah - Function 09h
3270 EMULATION

Purpose: Specify whether to connect or disconnect from the mainframe host.
Available on: All machines.

Restrictions: IBM 3270 Workstation Program must be installed.
Return Registers: *unknown.*

Registers at call:
AH = 09h
BX = 8020h
CX = 00FFh
DX = ID of 3270EML
AL = service:
    01h connect
    02h disconnect
ES:DI -> control block
Conflicts: Novell NetWare Low-level API (chapter 20), Topware Network Operating System (chapter 27), AutoCAD Device Interface (chapter 36).

INTERRUPT 7Ah - Function 09h
OPERATOR INFORMATION AREA

Purpose: Determine the contents of the 25th line on the Host session.
Available on: All machines.

Restrictions: IBM 3270 Workstation Program must be installed.
Return Registers: *unknown.*

Registers at call:
AH = 09h

BX = 8020h
CX = 00FFh
DX = ID of OIAM
AL = service
    01h read Operator Information Area
    02h read OIA subset
ES:DI -> control block
Conflicts: Novell NetWare Low-level API (chapter 20), Topware Network Operating System (chapter 27), AutoCAD Device Interface (chapter 36).

INTERRUPT 7Ah - Function 09h
TRANSLATE DATA

Purpose: Convert data between ASCII and the host mainframe's character set.

Available on: All machines.

Registers at call:
AH = 09h
BX = 8020h
CX = 00FFh
DX = ID of XLATE
AL = service
    01h translate from host characters to ASCII and
        vice versa (determined by control block
        byte 11)
ES:DI -> control block

Restrictions: IBM 3270 Workstation Program must be installed.

Return Registers: *unknown.*

Conflicts: Novell NetWare Low-level API (chapter 20), Topware Network Operating System (chapter 27), AutoCAD Device Interface (chapter 36).

INTERRUPT 7Ah - Function 09h
COPY SERVICE

Purpose: Copy data between presentation spaces.

Available on: All machines.

Registers at call:
AH = 09h
BX = 8020h
CX = 00FFh
DX = ID of copy service
AL = service
    01h copy string from one presentation space to
        another
    02h copy block from one presentation space to
        another
    03h connect to PC session for copy
    04h disconnect PC session from copy
ES:DI -> control block

Restrictions: IBM 3270 Workstation Program must be installed.

Return Registers: *unknown.*

Conflicts: Novell NetWare Low-level API (chapter 20), Topware Network Operating System (chapter 27), AutoCAD Device Interface (chapter 36).

INTERRUPT 7Ah - Function 09h
Multi-DOS

Purpose: Get environment size or perform DOS memory allocation functions.

Available on: All machines.

Registers at call:
AH = 09h
BX = 8020h
CX = 00FFh
ES:DI -> control block
DX = ID of INDJQRY (get environment size)
  = ID of INDJASY (request DOS functions from
      workstation)
  = ID of MEMORY
AL = function
    01h allocate memory
    02h deallocate memory
    03h modify allocated size

Restrictions: IBM 3270 Workstation Program must be
  installed.
Return Registers: *unknown.*

Conflicts: Novell NetWare Low-level API (chapter 20), Topware Network Operating System (chapter 27), AutoCAD Device Interface (chapter 36).

INTERRUPT 7Ah - Function 09h
HOST SERVICES

Purpose: Control connection to host mainframe or transfer data between PC and host.

Available on: All machines.

Registers at call:
AH = 09h
BX = 4000h for async request, 8028h for
    synchronous request
CX = 0000h
DX = ID of MFIC
AL = service
    01h connect to host
    02h disconnect from host
    03h read DFT structured data from host
    04h write DFT structured data to host
    05h create a host buffer
ES:DI -> control block

Restrictions: IBM 3270 Workstation Program must be
  installed.
Return Registers: n/a

Conflicts: Novell NetWare Low-level API (chapter 20), Topware Network Operating System (chapter 27), AutoCAD Device Interface (chapter 36).

INTERRUPT 7Ah - Function 13h
GET DATA FROM A QUEUE

Purpose: Determine the contents of a queue.

Available on: All machines.

Registers at call:
AH = 13h
others, if any, unknown.

Restrictions: IBM 3270 Workstation Program must be
  installed.
Return Registers: *unknown.*

Conflicts: Novell NetWare Low-level API (chapter 20), Topware Network Operating System (chapter 27), AutoCAD Device Interface (chapter 36).

INTERRUPT 7Ah - Function 81h
RESOLVE A GATE NAME

Purpose: Determine the identifier corresponding to the name of a service.

Available on: All machines.

Registers at call:
AH = 81h
ES:DI -> 8-char blank-padded gate name:
    "SESSMGR ", "KEYBOARD", "WSCTRL ",
    "MFIC   ", "PCPSM   ", "3270EML ",
    "COPY   ", "XLATE   ", "OIAM   ",
    "MEMORY ", "INDJQRY ", or "INDJASY "

Restrictions: IBM 3270 Workstation Program must be installed.
Return Registers:
DX = gate ID

Conflicts: Novell NetWare Low-level API (chapter 20), Topware Network Operating System (chapter 27), AutoCAD Device Interface (chapter 36).

INTERRUPT 7Ah - Function 83h
GET COMPLETION RESULTS

Purpose: Determine the status of an operation.
Available on: All machines.

Registers at call:
AH = 83h
others, if any, unknown.

Restrictions: IBM 3270 Workstation Program must be installed.
Return Registers: *unknown.*

Conflicts: Novell NetWare Low-level API (chapter 20), Topware Network Operating System (chapter 27), AutoCAD Device Interface (chapter 36).

INTERRUPT 7Ah - Function FDh, Subfunction CBh
INSTALLATION CHECK

Purpose: Determine whether the IBM Personal Communications/3270 (PC3270) program is installed.
Available on: All machines.
Registers at call:
AX = FDCBh

Restrictions: none.
Return Registers:
DX:AX -> PCS/3270 signature block if loaded
    (Table 26-6)

Conflicts: Novell NetWare Low-level API (chapter 20), Topware Network Operating System (chapter 27), AutoCAD Device Interface (chapter 36).

Table 26-6. Format of signature block:

Offset	Size	Description
04h	WORD	PCS/3270 signature (5741h)
06h	WORD	version (0501h = PCS/3270 v1.0)

INTERRUPT 7Ah - Function FEh, Subfunction 01h
INTERNAL SEND/RECEIVE FUNCTION

Purpose: Called internally for data transfer.
Available on: All machines.

Registers at call:
AX = FE01h
others, if any, unknown.

Restrictions: IBM PC3270 Emulator Program version 3.0 or higher must be installed.
Return Registers: *unknown.*

Conflicts: Novell NetWare Low-level API (chapter 20), Topware Network Operating System (chapter 27), AutoCAD Device Interface (chapter 36).
See Also: Function FEh Subfunction 02h

INTERRUPT 7Ah - Function FEh, Subfunction 02h
INTERNAL SEND/RECEIVE FUNCTION

Purpose: Called internally for data transfer.
Available on: All machines.

Restrictions: IBM PC3270 Emulator Program version 3.0 or higher must be installed.
Return Registers: *unknown.*

Registers at call:
AX = FE02h
others, if any, unknown.
Conflicts: Novell NetWare Low-level API (chapter 20), Topware Network Operating System (chapter 27), AutoCAD Device Interface (chapter 36).
See Also: Function FEh Subfunction 01h

INTERRUPT 7Ah - Function FFh, Subfunction 01h
INTERNAL API INITIALIZATION

Purpose: Called internally at startup.
Available on: All machines.

Restrictions: IBM PC3270 Emulator Program version 3.0 or higher must be installed.
Return Registers:
CX = 1200h

Registers at call:
AX = FF01h
ES:DI -> API function handler routine
Conflicts: Novell NetWare Low-level API (chapter 20), Topware Network Operating System (chapter 27), AutoCAD Device Interface (chapter 36).
See Also: Function FFh Subfunctions 02h and 03h

INTERRUPT 7Ah - Function FFh, Subfunction 02h
INTERNAL API TERMINATION

Purpose: Called internally when the PC3270 emulator is shut down.
Available on: All machines.

Restrictions: IBM PC3270 Emulator Program version 3.0 or higher must be installed.
Return Registers:
CX = 1200h

Registers at call:
AX = FF02h
Conflicts: Novell NetWare Low-level API (chapter 20), Topware Network Operating System (chapter 27), AutoCAD Device Interface (chapter 36).
See Also: Function FFh Subfunction 01h

INTERRUPT 7Ah - Function FFh, Subfunction 03h
INTERNAL API INITIALIZATION

Purpose: Called internally at startup.
Available on: All machines.

Restrictions: IBM PC3270 Emulator Program version 3.0 or higher must be installed.
Return Registers:
CX = 1200h

Registers at call:
AX = FF03h
ES:DI -> send/receive function handler routine
Conflicts: Novell NetWare Low-level API (chapter 20), Topware Network Operating System (chapter 27), AutoCAD Device Interface (chapter 36).
See Also: Function FFh Subfunction 01h

INTERRUPT 7Ah - Function FFh, Subfunction 04h
Unknown Internal Function

Purpose: *unknown.*
Available on: All machines.

Restrictions: IBM PC3270 Emulator Program version 3.0 or higher must be installed.

Registers at call:
AX = FF04h
ES:DI -> *unknown*.
Conflicts: Novell NetWare Low-level API (chapter 20), Topware Network Operating System (chapter 27), AutoCAD Device Interface (chapter 36).

Return Registers:
CX = 1200h

INTERRUPT 7Bh
Eicon Access API (3270/5250 gateways)

Purpose: Communicate with the Access program.
Available on: All machines.
Conflicts: Btrieve API (chapter 36).

Restrictions: Eicon Access program must be installed.

INTERRUPT 7Fh - Function 01h, Subfunction 04h
HLLAPI (IBM 3270 High-Level Language API)

Purpose: Provide access to 3270 emulator services.
Available on: All machines.
Registers at call:
AX = 0104h (HLLAPI gate ID)
BX = 0000h
DS:SI -> parameter control block (Table 26-7)
Conflicts: Halo88 API (chapter 5), Alloy NTNX, MW386 (chapter 18), ClusterShare access (chapter 25).

Restrictions: HLLAPI function must be installed.
Return Registers:
parameter control block updated

Table 26-7. Format of Parameter Control Block:

Offset	Size	Description
00h	3 BYTEs	signature = 'PCB'
03h	BYTE	function number (Table 26-8)
04h	WORD	segment of control string
06h	WORD	offset of control string
08h	WORD	length of control string, unless explicit end-of-str char set
0Ah	BYTE	unused
0Bh	WORD	return code
0Dh	WORD	maximum length of control string

Table 26-8. Values for Function Number:

Value	Significance	Value	Significance
00h	Query system (Attachmate implementation only)	0Bh	Lock current presentation space
01h	Connect presentation space	0Ch	Unlock previously locked presentation space
02h	Disconnect presentation space	0Dh	Return copy of operator info area (OIA) of current presentation space
03h	Send string of keystrokes as if typed from keyboard	0Eh	get attribute byte for given position in the current presentation space
04h	Wait ~60s, returns status of presentation space	0Fh	copy string of characters to the current presentation space
05h	Copy current presentation space into a user-defined buffer	10h	workstation control functions
06h	Search presentation space for first occurrence of a specified string	11h	storage manager functions, intended primarily for BASIC applications
07h	Query cursor location in current presentation space	12h	set delay period in half-second intervals
08h	Copy part or all of current presentation space into user buffer	14h	get info on level of workstation support used
09h	Set session parameters; parameters vary by vendor	15h	reset session parameters to default values
0Ah	Get info on sessions currently connected	16h	get detailed info on the current session

Table 26-8. Values for Function Number (continued)

Value	Significance	Value	Significance
17h	start host notification to application on presentation sp or OIA update	25h	display cursor in specified area (IBM only), don't use with BASIC
18h	check host update when host notification enabled	26h	display alternate presentation space (IBM only), don't use with BASIC
19h	stop host notification	27h	delete alternate presentation space (IBM only), don't use with BASIC
1Eh	search field within current presentation space for string	32h	start intercepting keystrokes to allow filtering
1Fh	get first positionof a selected field in the current presentation space	33h	get keystrokes after turning on interception
20h	get length of specified field	34h	notify operator when keystroke rejected by filter subroutine
21h	copy string into a specified field	35h	stop intercepting keystrokes
22h	copy specified field into a user-defined buffer	5Ah	send file
23h	create alternate presentation space (IBM only), don't use with BASIC	5Bh	receive file
		5Ch	run a program
24h	switch to alternate presentation space (IBM only), not with BASIC	5Dh	execute DOS command
		63h	change presentation space position to PC display row/col or vice versa
		FFh	Get info on DCA implementation

Table 26-9. Values of Session Parameters for function 09h:

Value	Significance	Value	Significance
ATTRIB	return attributes in hex	SRCHBKWD	search backward from last position in presentation space
NOATTRIB	return attributes as blanks		
CONPHYS	make physical connection	TWAIT	wait specified time for keyboard ready
CONLOG	only make logical connection	LWAIT	wait until keyboard ready
EAB	copy extended attribute bytes along with data	NWAIT	no wait
		TRON	enable tracing
NOEAB	copy data only	TROFF	disable tracing
ESC=n	set escape character to "n" (default '@')	AUTORESE	send reset before sending keys with function 03h
EOT=n	set end of string character (default 00h)	NORESET	don't send reset
		QUIET	don't display messages sent with INT 21/AH=9
FPAUSE	full-duration pause		
IPAUSE	interruptible pause	NOQUIET	allow messages to be displayed
STRLEN	use explicit string lengths	TIMEOUT=	set timeout in 30-second intervals, 0 = wait until ^Break
STREOT	use terminated strings		
SRCHALL	search entire presentation space	XLATE	translate extended attribute bytes
SRCHFRO	search from specified offset	NOXLATE	don't translate
SRCHFRW	search forward from position 1	NEWRET	use HLLAPI v3.0 return code conventions
		OLDRET	use HLLAPI v2.0 return code conventions

Chapter 27

Miscellaneous Networking Calls

This chapter contains all those network-related functions which do not have their own chapter. Such diverse products as Shamrock Software's EMAIL and NET.24, NetBIOS, LAN Manager, and the IBM Token Ring are covered here.

INTERRUPT 16h - Function 45h, Subfunction 00h
GET STATUS

Purpose: Determine EMAIL version and the current user's name and privileges.

Available on: All machines.

Registers at call:
AX = 4500h
DL = port number (01h = COM1)
ES:BX - > 13-byte buffer for ASCIZ name

Restrictions: Shamrock Software EMAIL must be installed.

Return Registers:
AX = 4D00h if EMAIL installed on specified port
ES:BX -> "" if no connection
         -> "*" if connection but caller has not identified name
         - > name otherwise
CX = version (CH = major, CL = minor)
DL = privilege level of user (00h = guest)
DH = chosen language (00h German, 01h English)

Conflicts: None known.
See Also: Function 45h Subfunctions 01h and 02h

INTERRUPT 16h - Function 45h, Subfunction 01h
GET ELAPSED ONLINE TIME AND MAXIMUM TIME

Purpose: Determine how long the current user has been connected and the maximum length of time he is allowed.

Available on: All machines.

Registers at call:
AX = 4501h
DL = port number (01h = COM1)

Restrictions: Shamrock Software EMAIL must be installed.

Return Registers:
AX = 4D00h if EMAIL installed on specified port
BX = maximum connect time in clock ticks
CX = maximum connect time for guests (without name) in clock ticks
DX = elapsed connect time of current user in clock ticks

Conflicts: None known.
See Also: Function 45h Subfunction 00h

INTERRUPT 16h - Function 45h, Subfunction 02h
GET CURRENT COMMUNICATIONS PARAMETERS

Purpose: Determine the current serial port parameters and communications options.

Available on: All machines.

Restrictions: Shamrock Software EMAIL must be installed.

Registers at call:
AX = 4502h
DL = port number (01h = COM1)

Return Registers:
AX = 4D00h if EMAIL installed on specified port
BL = current value of serial port's Line Control
     Register (see chapter 7)
BH = flags
     bit 0: ISO code
         1: pause
         2: linefeed
         3: ANSI sequences
CX = selected country code (33 = France, 49 =
     Germany, etc)
DX = baudrate divisor (115200/DX = baudrate)

Conflicts: None known.
See Also: Function 45h Subfunction 00h

INTERRUPT 16h - Function 45h, Subfunction 03h
SPECIFY COMMAND-WORD FOR USER FUNCTION

Purpose: Store a keyword which may be used to invoke a user function extending the standard command set.
Available on: All machines.

Restrictions: Shamrock Software EMAIL must be
             installed.

Registers at call:
AX = 4503h
DL = port number (01h = COM1)
DH = maximum execution time in clock ticks
     (00h = 5 seconds)
ES:BX -> ASCIZ string with new user command-
     word

Return Registers:
AX = 4D00h if EMAIL installed on specified port

Details: A single user command (consisting of only uppercase letters and digits) may be defined, and remains valid until it is overwritten or the EMAIL program terminates; the user command must be activated by calling Function 45h Subfunction 04h at least once. This function may be used to redefine an existing command word.
Conflicts: None known.
See Also: Function 45h Subfunctions 04h and 05h

INTERRUPT 16h - Function 45h, Subfunction 04h
CHECK FOR USER FUNCTION COMMAND-WORD

Purpose: Determine whether the user has entered a command beginning with the previously stored keyword.
Available on: All machines.

Restrictions: Shamrock Software EMAIL must be
             installed.

Registers at call:
AX = 4504h
DL = port number (01h = COM1)
ES:BX -> 80-byte buffer for ASCIZ user input line

Return Registers:
AX = 4D00h if EMAIL installed on specified port
DL = flags
     bit 0: user function supported (always set)
         1: user entered user-function command word
     if DL bit 1 set, ES:BX buffer contains line entered
         by user which begins with the defined
         command word and has been converted to all
         caps

Details: The caller must process the returned commandline and invoke Function 45h Subfunction 05h within five seconds with the result of that processing, or the user function will be timed out.
Conflicts: None known.
See Also: Function 45h Subfunctions 03h and 05h

INTERRUPT 16h - Function 45h, Subfunction 05h
SEND RESULT OF USER FUNCTION

Purpose: Inform EMAIL of the result of the command set extension function.

Available on: All machines.

Restrictions: Shamrock Software EMAIL must be installed.

Registers at call:
AX = 4505h
DL = port number (01h = COM1)
DH = error flag
    bit 3: set on error
ES:BX -> ASCIZ text to return to user, max 1024
    bytes

Return Registers:
AH = 4Dh if EMAIL installed on specified port
AL = status
    00h successful
    02h unable to perform function (timeout, prev call
        not complete)
    other: error

Details: If the error flag in DH is set, the string is not sent and an error message is generated instead; if this function is not called within five seconds of Function 45h Subfunction 04h, EMAIL automatically generates an error message.

    The string is copied into an internal buffer, allowing this function's caller to continue immediately.

Conflicts: None known.

See Also: Function 45h Subfunctions 03h and 04h, INT 17h Function 24h Subfunction 00h

INTERRUPT 16h - Function 45h, Subfunction 06h
MONITOR XMODEM DOWNLOAD

Purpose: Determine whether an XMODEM download is in progress or whether one has successfully completed.

Available on: All machines.

Restrictions: Shamrock Software EMAIL must be installed.

Registers at call:
AX = 4506h
DL = port number (01h = COM1)
ES:BX -> 13-byte buffer for ASCIZ filename

Return Registers:
AX = 4D00h if EMAIL installed on specified port
DH = Xmodem status
    00h no XGET command given
    01h XGET in progress
    02h XGET completed successfully
ES:BX buffer filled with last filename given to XGET
    command (without path)

Details: DH=02h will only be returned once per XGET; subsequent calls will return DH=00h.

Conflicts: None known.

See Also: Function 45h Subfunction 00h, INT 17h Function 24h Subfunction 08h

INTERRUPT 17h - Function 24h, Subfunction 00h
ENABLE/DISABLE API FUNCTIONS

Purpose: Specify whether the other NET.24 functions should be accessible, and return the current status.

Available on: All machines.

Restrictions: Shamrock Software NET.24 version 3.11 or higher must be installed.

Registers at call:
AX = 2400h
DL = new state
    00h disabled
    01h enabled

Return Registers:
DL = 24h if installed
DH = minor version number
CX = network address of this machine
AL = status
    00h successful
    01h timeout
    02h header error
    03h data error
    04h busy
    05h invalid parameters

Conflicts: None known.
See Also: Function 24h Subfunction 03h, INT 16h Function 45h Subfunction 00h

INTERRUPT 17h - Function 24h, Subfunction 01h
RECEIVE BLOCK, NO HANDSHAKE

Purpose: Attempt to read a block of data without performing any handshaking.
Available on: All machines.

Restrictions: Shamrock Software NET.24 version 3.11 or higher must be installed.

Registers at call:
AX = 2401h
BL = timeout in clock ticks

Return Registers:
AL = status (see Function 24h Subfunction 00h)
DX:BX -> receive buffer

Conflicts: None known.
See Also: Function 24h Subfunctions 02h, 04h, and 08h

INTERRUPT 17h - Function 24h, Subfunction 02h
TRANSMIT BLOCK, NO HANDSHAKE

Purpose: Attempt to transmit a block of data without performing any handshaking.
Available on: All machines.

Restrictions: Shamrock Software NET.24 version 3.11 or higher must be installed.

Registers at call:
AX = 2402h
transmit buffer filled (see Function 24h Subfunction 03h)

Return Registers:
AL = status (see Function 24h Subfunction 00h)

Conflicts: None known.
See Also: Function 24h Subfunctions 01h, 03h, 04h, and 09h

INTERRUPT 17h - Function 24h, Subfunction 03h
GET STATUS AND TRANSMISSION BUFFER

Purpose: Determine the current status and the address of the buffer to use for transmitting data.
Available on: All machines.

Restrictions: Shamrock Software NET.24 version 3.11 or higher must be installed.

Registers at call:
AX = 2403h

Return Registers:
AL = status (see Function 24h Subfunction 00h)
CX = number of characters in receive ring buffer
DX:BX -> transmit buffer

Conflicts: None known.
See Also: Function 24h Subfunctions 00h and 02h

INTERRUPT 17h - Function 24h, Subfunction 04h
SEND ACK BLOCK

Purpose: Acknowledge the successful receipt of a data block.
Available on: All machines.

Restrictions: Shamrock Software NET.24 version 3.11 or higher must be installed.

Registers at call:
AX = 2404h
BX = target address

Return Registers:
AL = status (see Function 24h Subfunction 00h)

Conflicts: None known.
See Also: Function 24h Subfunctions 02h and 05h

INTERRUPT 17h - Function 24h, Subfunction 05h
SEND NAK BLOCK

Purpose: Indicate to the sender of a data block that it was received in error.

Available on: All machines.

Registers at call:
AX = 2405h
BX = target address
Conflicts: None known.
See Also: Function 24h Subfunctions 02h and 04h

Restrictions: Shamrock Software NET.24 version 3.11 or higher must be installed.
Return Registers:
AL = status (see Function 24h Subfunction 00h)

INTERRUPT 17h - Function 24h, Subfunction 06h
PREPARE CHARACTER-ORIENTED RECEIVE

Purpose: Indicate to NET.24 that the caller will be performing character-by-character input over the network.
Available on: All machines.

Registers at call:
AX = 2406h
Conflicts: None known.
See Also: Function 24h Subfunctions 07h and 0Ah

Restrictions: Shamrock Software NET.24 version 3.11 or higher must be installed.
Return Registers:
AL = status (see Function 24h Subfunction 00h)

INTERRUPT 17h - Function 24h, Subfunction 07h
RECEIVE CHARACTER FROM REMOTE

Purpose: Retrieve the next character, if any, from another machine.
Available on: All machines.

Registers at call:
AX = 2407h

Restrictions: Shamrock Software NET.24 version 3.11 or higher must be installed.
Return Registers:
AL = status (see also Function 24h Subfunction 00h)
  06h end of data
DL = received character

Conflicts: None known.
See Also: Function 24h Subfunction 06h

INTERRUPT 17h - Function 24h, Subfunction 08h
RECEIVE BLOCK, WITH HANDSHAKE

Purpose: Retrieve a block of data from a remote system using handshaking to ensure correct reception.
Available on: All machines.

Registers at call:
AX = 2408h

Restrictions: Shamrock Software NET.24 version 3.11 or higher must be installed.
Return Registers:
AL = status (see also Function 24h Subfunction 00h)
  06h end of data
CX = number of bytes in receive buffer
DX:SI -> receive buffer

Conflicts: None known.
See Also: Function 24h Subfunctions 01h, 05h, and 09h

INTERRUPT 17h - Function 24h, Subfunction 09h
TRANSMIT COMMAND, WITH HANDSHAKE

Purpose: Send a command to another system, using handshaking to ensure correct reception.
Available on: All machines.

Registers at call:
AX = 2409h
BX = target address
CX = number of data bytes

Restrictions: Shamrock Software NET.24 version 3.11 or higher must be installed.
Return Registers:
AL = status (see also Function 24h Subfunction 00h)
  03h no response
  06h remote currently unable to perform command

DL = command code to send
DS:SI -> data bytes for command
Conflicts: None known.
See Also: Function 24h Subfunctions 05h and 08h

INTERRUPT 17h - Function 24h, Subfunction 0Ah
PREPARE CHARACTER-ORIENTED TRANSMIT

Purpose: Indicate to NET.24 that the caller will be performing character-by-character output over the network.

Available on: All machines.

Restrictions: Shamrock Software NET.24 version 3.11 or higher must be installed.

Registers at call:
AX = 240Ah
Conflicts: None known.
See Also: Function 24h Subfunctions 06h, 0Bh, and 0Ch

Return Registers:
AL = status (see Function 24h Subfunction 00h)

INTERRUPT 17h - Function 24h, Subfunction 0Bh
TRANSMIT SINGLE CHARACTER TO REMOTE

Purpose: Output a single byte over the network.

Available on: All machines.

Restrictions: Shamrock Software NET.24 version 3.11 or higher must be installed.

Registers at call:
AX = 240Bh
DL = character to send

Return Registers:
AL = status (see also Function 24h Subfunction 00h)
  03h transmission error
  06h write error

Conflicts: None known.
See Also: Function 24h Subfunctions 07h, 0Ah, and 0Ch

INTERRUPT 17h - Function 24h, Subfunction 0Ch
END CHARACTER-ORIENTED TRANSMIT

Purpose: Indicate to NET.24 that the caller will no longer perform character-by-character network output.

Available on: All machines.

Restrictions: Shamrock Software NET.24 version 3.11 or higher must be installed.

Registers at call:
AX = 240Ch

Return Registers:
AL = status (see also Function 24h Subfunction 00h)
  03h transmission error
  06h remote breaks connection

Conflicts: None known.
See Also: Function 24h Subfunctions 0Ah and 0Bh

INTERRUPT 21h - Function 44h, Subfunction 02h
PROTOCOL MANAGER

Purpose: Communicate with the Microsoft LAN Manager or compatible network software. The Network Driver Interface specification (currently at version 2.0.1) was developed by Microsoft and 3com.

Available on: All machines.

Restrictions: NDIS 2.0.1-conformant network driver must be installed.

Registers at call:
AX = 4402h
BX = file handle for device "PROTMAN$"
CX = 000Eh (size of request block)
DS:DX -> request block (see Tables 27-2 thru 27-11)

Return Registers: n/a

Conflicts: DOS IOCTL Read (chapter 8), IBM System 36/38 Workstation Emulation - VDI.SYS (chapter 26), HIGHUMM.SYS (chapter 36).

Table 27-1. Values of Status Codes for NDIS:

Value	Meaning	Value	Meaning
0000h	success	0022h	driver not initialized
0001h	wait for release--protocol has retained control of the data buffer	0023h	hardware not found
		0024h	hardware failure
0002h	request queued	0025h	configuration failure
0003h	frame not recognized	0026h	interrupt conflict
0004h	frame rejected	0027h	MAC incompatible
0005h	frame should be forwarded	0028h	initialization failed
0006h	out of resource	0029h	no binding
0007h	invalid parameter	002Ah	network may be disconnected
0008h	invalid function	002Bh	incompatible OS version
0009h	not supported	002Ch	already registered
000Ah	hardware error	002Dh	path not found
000Bh	transmit error	002Eh	insufficient memory
000Ch	unrecognized destination	002Fh	info not found
000Dh	buffer too small	00FFh	general failure
0020h	already started	F000h-FFFFh	reserved for vendor-specific codes, treated as general failure
0021h	binding incomplete		

Table 27-2. Format of Request Block for GetProtocolManagerInfo:

Offset	Size	Description
00h	WORD	01h
02h	WORD	returned status (see Table 27-1)
04h	DWORD	returned pointer to structure representing parsed user config
08h	DWORD	unused
0Ch	WORD	returned BCD version of NDIS on which Protocol Manager is based

Table 27-3. Format of Request Block for RegisterModule:

Offset	Size	Description
00h	WORD	02h
02h	WORD	returned status (see Table 27-1)
04h	DWORD	pointer to module's common characteristics table (see below)
08h	DWORD	pointer to list of modules to which the module is to be bound
0Ch	WORD	unused

Table 27-4. Format of Request Block for BindAndStart:

Offset	Size	Description
00h	WORD	03h
02h	WORD	returned status (see Table 27-1)
04h	DWORD	caller's virtual address in FailingModules structure
08h	DWORD	unused
0Ch	WORD	unused

Table 27-5. Format of Request Block for GetProtocolManagerLinkage:

Offset	Size	Description
00h	WORD	04h
02h	WORD	returned status (see Table 27-1)
04h	DWORD	returned dispatch point
08h	DWORD	unused
0Ch	WORD	returned protocol manager DS

Details: The dispatch point may be called as follows instead of using this IOCTL:
STACK: WORD   protocol manager DS
             DWORD   pointer to request block
Return: AX = returned status
             STACK popped

Table 27-6. Format of Request Block for GetProtocolIniPath:

Offset	Size	Description
00h	WORD	05h
02h	WORD	returned status (see Table 27-1)
04h	DWORD	pointer to a buffer for the ASCIZ pathname of PROTOCOL.INI
08h	DWORD	unused
0Ch	WORD	buffer length

Table 27-7. Format of Request Block for RegisterProtocolManagerInfo:

Offset	Size	Description
00h	WORD	06h
02h	WORD	returned status (see Table 27-1)
04h	DWORD	pointer to structure containing parsed user config file
08h	DWORD	unused
0Ch	WORD	length of structure

Table 27-8. Format of Request Block for InitAndRegister:

Offset	Size	Description
00h	WORD	07h
02h	WORD	returned status (see Table 27-1)
04h	DWORD	unused
08h	DWORD	poitner to ASCIZ name of the module to be prebind initialized
0Ch	WORD	unused

Table 27-9. Format of Request Block for UnbindAndStop:

Offset	Size	Description
00h	WORD	08h
02h	WORD	returned status (see Table 27-1)
04h	DWORD	failing modules as for BindAndStart
08h	DWORD	if not 0000h:0000h, pointer to ASCIZ name of module to unbind
		if 0000h:0000h, terminate a set of previously dynamically bound protocol modules
0Ch	WORD	unused

Table 27-10. Format of Request Block for BindStatus:

Offset	Size	Description
00h	WORD	09h
02h	WORD	returned status (see Table 27-1)
04h	DWORD	must be 0000h:0000h
		on return, points to root tree
08h	DWORD	0000h:0000h
0Ch	WORD	unused under DOS

Table 27-11. Format of Request Block for RegisterStatus:

Offset	Size	Description
00h	WORD	0Ah
02h	WORD	returned status (0000h, 0008h, 002Ch) (see Table 27-1)

Table 27-11. Format of Request Block for RegisterStatus (continued)

Offset	Size	Description
04h	DWORD	0000h:0000h
08h	DWORD	pointer to 16-byte ASCIZ module name
0Ch	WORD	0000h

Table 27-12. Format of Common Characteristics Table:

Offset	Size	Description
00h	WORD	size of table in bytes
02h	BYTE	NDIS major version
03h	BYTE	NDIS minor version
04h	WORD	reserved
06h	BYTE	module major version
07h	BYTE	module minor version
08h	DWORD	module function flag bits: bit 0: binding at upper boundary supported bit 1: binding at lower boundary supported bit 2: dynamically bound bits 3-31 reserved, must be 0
0Ch	16 Bytes	ASCIZ module name
1Ch	BYTE	upper boundary protocol level: 01h Media Access Control 02h Data link 03h network 04h transport 05h session FFh not specified
1Dh	BYTE	upper boundary interface type: for MACs: 1 = MAC for data links and transports: to be defined for session: 1 = NCB any level: 0 = private (ISV-defined)
1Eh	BYTE	lower boundary protocol level: 00h physical 01h Media Access Control 02h Data link 03h network 04h transport 05h session FFh not specified
1Fh	BYTE	lower boundary interface type, same as offset 1Dh
20h	WORD	module ID filled in by protocol manager
22h	WORD	module DS
24h	DWORD	system request entry point
28h	DWORD	pointer to service-specific characteristics, 0000h:0000h if none
2Ch	DWORD	pointer to service-specific status, 0000h:0000h if none
30h	DWORD	pointer to upper dispatch table (see below), 0000h:0000h if none
34h	DWORD	pointer to lower dispatch table (see below), 0000h:0000h if none
38h	DWORD	reserved, must be 0
3Ch	DWORD	reserved, must be 0

Details: For compatibility with NDIS 1.x.x, a major version of 00h is interpreted as 01h.

Table 27-13. Format of MAC Service-Specific Characteristics Table:

Offset	Size	Description
00h	WORD	length of table in bytes
02h	16 BYTEs	ASCIZ MAC type name, "802.3", "802.4", "802.5", "802.6", "DIX", "DIX+802.3", "APPLETALK", "ARCNET", "FDDI", "SDLC", "BSC", "HDLC", or "ISDN"
12h	WORD	length of station addresses in bytes
14h	16 BYTEs	permanent station address
24h	16 BYTEs	current station address
34h	DWORD	current functional adapter address (00000000h if none)
38h	DWORD	pointer to multicast address list
3Ch	DWORD	link speed in bits/sec
40h	DWORD	service flags:

> bit 0: supports broadcast
> 1: supports multicast
> 2: supports functional/group addressing
> 3: supports promiscuous mode
> 4: station address software settable
> 5: statistics always current
> 6: supports InitiateDiagnostics
> 7: supports loopback
> 8: MAC does primarily ReceiveChain indications instead of ReceiveLookahead indications
> 9: supports IBM source routing
> 10: supports MAC reset
> 11: supports Open/Close adapter
> 12: supports interrupt request
> 13: supports source routing bridge
> 14: supports GDT virtual addresses (OS/2 version)
> 15: multiple TransferDatas allowed durign a single indication
> 16: MAC normally sets FrameSize = 0 in ReceiveLookahead
> 17-31: reserved, must be 0

Offset	Size	Description
44h	WORD	maximum frame size which may be both sent and received
46h	DWORD	total transmit buffer capacity in bytes
4Ah	WORD	transmit buffer allocation block size in bytes
4Ch	DWORD	total receive buffer capacity in bytes
50h	WORD	receive buffer allocation block size in bytes
52h	3 BYTEs	IEEE vendor code
55h	BYTE	vendor adapter code
56h	DWORD	pointer to ASCIZ vendor adapter description
5Ah	WORD	IRQ used by adapter
5Ch	WORD	transmit queue depth
5Eh	WORD	maximum supported number of data blocks in buffer descriptors
60h	N BYTEs	vendor-specific info

Table 27-14. Format of NetBIOS Service-Specific Characteristics Table:

Offset	Size	Description
00h	WORD	length of table in bytes
02h	16 BYTEs	ASCIZ type name of NetBIOS module
12h	WORD	NetBIOS module code
14h	N BYTEs	vendor-specific info

Table 27-15. Format of MAC Service-Specific Status Table:

Offset	Size	Description
00h	WORD	length of table in bytes
02h	DWORD	seconds since 0:00 1/1/70 when diagnostics last run (FFFFFFFFh = never)

Table 27-15. Format of MAC Service-Specific Status Table (continued)

Offset	Size	Description
06h	DWORD	MAC status bits:

                              bits 0-2:   000 hardware not installed
                                                    001 hardware failed startup diagnostics
                                                    010 hardware configuration problem
    011 hardware fault
    100 operating marginally due to soft faults
    101 reserved
    110 reserved
    111 hardware fully operational

    bit 3:   MAC bound
    4:    MAC open
    5:    diagnostics in progress
    6-31:   reserved

| 0Ah | WORD | current packet filter flags: |

    bit 0:   directed/multicast or group/functional
    1:    broadcast
    2:    promiscuous
    3:    all source routing
    4-15:   reserved, must be zero

Offset	Size	Description
0Ch	DWORD	pointer to media-specific status table or 0000h:0000h
10h	DWORD	seconds past 0:00 1/1/70 of last ClearStatistics
14h	DWORD	total frames received (FFFFFFFFh = not counted)
18h	DWORD	frames with CRC error (FFFFFFFFh = not counted)
1Ch	DWORD	total bytes received (FFFFFFFFh = not counted)
20h	DWORD	frames discarded--no buffer space (FFFFFFFFh = not counted)
24h	DWORD	multicast frames received (FFFFFFFFh = not counted)
28h	DWORD	broadcast frames received (FFFFFFFFh = not counted)
2Ch	DWORD	frames with errors (FFFFFFFFh = not counted)
30h	DWORD	overly large frames (FFFFFFFFh = not counted)
34h	DWORD	frames less than minimum size (FFFFFFFFh = not counted)
38h	DWORD	multicast bytes received (FFFFFFFFh = not counted)
3Ch	DWORD	broadcast bytes received (FFFFFFFFh = not counted)
40h	DWORD	frames discarded--hardware error (FFFFFFFFh = not counted)
44h	DWORD	total frames transmitted (FFFFFFFFh = not counted)
48h	DWORD	total bytes transmitted (FFFFFFFFh = not counted)
4Ch	DWORD	multicast frames transmitted (FFFFFFFFh = not counted)
50h	DWORD	broadcast frames transmitted (FFFFFFFFh = not counted)
54h	DWORD	broadcast bytes transmitted (FFFFFFFFh = not counted)
58h	DWORD	multicast bytes transmitted (FFFFFFFFh = not counted)
5Ch	DWORD	frames not transmitted--timeout (FFFFFFFFh = not counted)
60h	DWORD	frames not transmitted--hardware error (FFFFFFFFh = not counted)
64h	N BYTEs	vendor-specific info

INTERRUPT 21h - Function 5Fh, Subfunctions 32h through 53h
LOCAL INTERFACE

Purpose: Request LAN Manager enhanced services.

Available on: All machines.

Restrictions: LAN Manager Enhanced DOS must be installed.

Registers at call:
AH = 5Fh
AL = function
    32h DosQNmPipeInfo
    33h DosQNmPHandState
    34h DosSetNmPHandState
    35h DosPeekNmPipe

Return Registers:
not known at the time of writing.

36h DosTransactNmPipe
37h DosCallNmPipe
38h DosWaitNmPipe
39h DosRawReadNmPipe
3Ah DosRawWriteNmPipe
3Bh NetHandleSetInfo
3Ch NetHandleGetInfo
40h NetMessageBufferSend
42h NetServiceControl
44h NetWkstaGetInfo
45h NetWkstaSetInfo
46h NetUseEnum
47h NetUseAdd
48h NetUseDel
49h NetUseGetInfo
4Ah NetRemoteCopy
4Bh NetRemoteMove
4Ch NetServerEnum
4Dh DosMakeMailslot
4Eh DosDeleteMailslot
4Fh DosMailslotInfo
50h DosReadMailslot
51h DosPeekMailslot
52h DosWriteMailslot
53h NetServerEnum2

Other registers vary by function,
but *were not known at the time of writing.*
Conflicts: None known.

INTERRUPT 21h - Function CFh
LANstep

Purpose: Control LANstep.
Available on: All machines.
Registers at call:
AH = CFh
other *unknown.*

Restrictions: LANstep must be installed.
Return Registers: *unknown.*

Details: LANstep is a redesign of the Waterloo Microsystems PORT network.
Conflicts: Novell NetWare (chapter 20).

INTERRUPT 21h - Function FFh
Unknown Function

Purpose: *unknown.*
Available on: All machines.

Registers at call:
AH = FFh
other *unknown.*

Restrictions: Topware Network Operating System must be installed.
Return Registers: *unknown.*

Conflicts: "Sunday" virus, "PSQR/1720" virus, and "Ontario" virus (all in chapter 34); DJ GO32.EXE 80386+ DOS extender (chapter 9); and DOSED and CED (chapter 36).

INTERRUPT 2Ah - Function 00h, Subfunction 00h
INSTALLATION CHECK

Purpose: Determine whether AT&T Starlan Extended NetBIOS (supporting variable-length names) is installed.

Available on: All machines.
Registers at call:
AX = 0000h
Conflicts: Microsoft/LANtastic NETWORK Installation Check.
See Also: INT 5Bh

Restrictions: none.
Return Registers:
AH = DDh if installed

INTERRUPT 2Ah - Function 00h
INSTALLATION CHECK

Purpose: Determine whether the alternate NetBIOS interface is present. This function is supported by Microsoft and LANtastic network software.
Available on: All machines.
Registers at call:
AH = 00h
Conflicts: AT&T Starlan Extended NetBIOS Installation Check.
See Also: INT 5Ch

Restrictions: none.
Return Registers:
AH <> 00h if installed

INTERRUPT 2Ah - Function 01h
EXECUTE NetBIOS REQUEST, NO ERROR RETRY

Purpose: Perform a NetBIOS command, reporting whether it was successful.
Available on: All machines.

Registers at call:
AH = 01h
ES:BX -> NCB (see INT 5Ch)

Restrictions: Microsoft or LANtastic network software must be installed.
Return Registers:
AL = NetBIOS error code
AH = 00h if no error
   = 01h on error

Conflicts: None known.
See Also: Function 04h, INT 5Ch

INTERRUPT 2Ah - Function 02h
SET NET PRINTER MODE

Purpose: Specify the mode of the redirected network printer.
Available on: All machines.

Registers at call:
AH = 02h
unknown.
Conflicts: None known.

Restrictions: Microsoft network software must be installed.
Return Registers: *unknown.*

INTERRUPT 2Ah - Function 03h, Subfunction 00h
CHECK DIRECT I/O

Purpose: Determine whether direct disk accesses (INT 13h, INT 25h, or INT 26h) are allowed on the specified drive.
Available on: All machines.

Registers at call:
AX = 0300h
DS:SI -> ASCIZ disk device name (may be full path
   or only drive specifier--must include the colon)

Restrictions: Microsoft or LANtastic network software must be installed.
Return Registers:
CF clear if absolute disk access allowed

Details: Do not use direct disk accesses if this function returns CF set or the device is redirected (INT 21h Function 5Fh Subfunction 02h, chapter 8). The call may take some time to execute.
Conflicts: None known.
See Also: INT 13h, INT 25h, INT 26h, INT 21h Function 5Fh Subfunction 02h (chapter 8)

INTERRUPT 2Ah - Function 04h
EXECUTE NetBIOS REQUEST

Purpose: Perform a NetBIOS command, optionally retrying the command on errors 09h, 12h, and 21h.

Available on: All machines.

Registers at call:
AH = 04h
AL = 00h for error retry, 01h for no retry
ES:BX -> NCB (see INT 5Ch)
Conflicts: None known.
See Also: Function 01h, INT 5Ch

Restrictions: Microsoft or LANtastic network software must be installed.

Return Registers:
AX = 0000h for no error
AH = 01h, AL = error code

INTERRUPT 2Ah - Function 05h, Subfunction 00h
GET NETWORK RESOURCE INFORMATION

Purpose: Determine the number of names, commands, and sessions still available.

Available on: All machines.

Registers at call:
AX = 0500h

Restrictions: Microsoft or LANtastic network software must be installed.

Return Registers:
AX = reserved
BX = number of network names available
CX = number of commands (NCBs) available
DX = number of sessions available

Conflicts: None known.

INTERRUPT 2Ah - Function 06h
NETWORK PRINT-STREAM CONTROL

Purpose: Specify when to queue the current printer output and start a new print job.

Available on: All machines.
Registers at call:
AH = 06h
AL = 01h set concatenation mode (all printer output
        put in one job)
   = 02h set truncation mode (default; printer
        open/close starts new print job)
   = 03h flush printer output and start new print
        job

Restrictions: NetBIOS software must be installed.
Return Registers:
CF set on error
   AX = error code
CF clear if successful

Details: Subfunction 03h is equivalent to Ctrl/Alt/keypad-*.
Conflicts: None known.
See Also: INT 21h Function 5Dh Subfunctions 08h and 09h (chapter 8), INT 2Fh Function 11h Subfunction 25h (chapter 19)

INTERRUPT 2Ah - Function 20h, Subfunctions 01h through 03h
Unknown Functions

Purpose: *unknown.*
Available on: All machines.

Registers at call:
AX = 2001h to 2003h
other *unknown.*

Restrictions: MS Networks or NetBIOS software must be installed.
Return Registers: *unknown.*

Details: Subfunction 01h is intercepted by DESQview 2.x; Subfunctions 02h and 03h are called by MSDOS 3.30 APPEND.
Conflicts: None known.

INTERRUPT 2Ah - Function 80h
BEGIN DOS CRITICAL SECTION

Purpose: Called by DOS or DOS programs to indicate the beginning of uninterruptible or nonreentrant code.

Available on: All machines.

Restrictions: Microsoft-compatible network software must be installed.

Return Registers: n/a

Registers at call:
AH = 80h
AL = critical section number (00h-0Fh)
    01h DOS kernel (SHARE.EXE) apparently for
        maintaining the integrity of
        DOS/SHARE/NET data structures
    02h DOS kernel, ensures that no multitasking
        occurs while DOS is calling an installable
        device driver
    05h DOS 4 IFSFUNC
    06h DOS 4 IFSFUNC
    08h ASSIGN.COM

Details: This function is normally hooked to avoid interrupting a critical section, rather than called. The handler should ensure that none of the critical sections are reentered, usually by suspending a task which attempts to reenter an active critical section.

The DOS kernel does not invoke critical sections 01h and 02h unless it is patched by the network software. DOS 3.1 through 3.31 contain a zero-terminated list of words beginning at offset 02C3h in the IBMDOS segment; each word contains the offset within the IBMDOS segment of a byte which must be changed from C3h to 50h to enable the use of critical sections.

Conflicts: None known.

See Also: Functions 81h, 82h, and 87h; INT 21h Function 5Dh Subfunctions 06h and 0Bh (chapter 8)

INTERRUPT 2Ah - Function 81h
END DOS CRITICAL SECTION

Purpose: Called by DOS or DOS programs to indicate the end of a section of uninterruptible or nonreentrant code.

Available on: All machines.

Restrictions: Microsoft-compatible network software must be installed.

Return Registers: n/a

Registers at call:
AH = 81h
AL = critical section number (00h-0Fh) (see
Function 80h)

Details: Normally hooked rather than called. The handler should reawaken any tasks which were suspended due to an attempt to enter the specified critical section.

Conflicts: None known.

See Also: Functions 80h, 82h, and 87h

INTERRUPT 2Ah - Function 82h
END DOS CRITICAL SECTIONS 0 THROUGH 7

Purpose: Called by DOS to clear any critical sections which may have been left active by an aborted system call.

Available on: All machines.

Restrictions: Microsoft-compatible network software must be installed.

Return Registers: n/a

Registers at call:
AH = 82h

Details: This function is called by the INT 21h function dispatcher for function 0 and functions greater than 0Ch except 59h, and on process termination. The handler should reawaken any tasks which were suspended due to an attempt to enter one of the critical sections 0 through 7.

Conflicts: None known.

See Also: Function 81h

INTERRUPT 2Ah - Function 84h
KEYBOARD BUSY LOOP

Purpose: Called by DOS when waiting for keyboard input in order to allow the network to process requests from remote machines.

Available on: All machines.

Restrictions: Microsoft-compatible network software must be installed.

Return Registers: n/a

Registers at call:
AH = 84h
Details: This call is similar to DOS's INT 28h.
Conflicts: None known.
See Also: INT 28h

INTERRUPT 2Ah - Function 87h
CRITICAL SECTION

Purpose: Called by PRINT.COM to indicate the beginning and end of uninterruptible or nonreentrant code.

Available on: All machines.

Restrictions: Network software must be installed.

Registers at call:

Return Registers: n/a

AH = 87h
AL = start/end: 00h start
                01h end
Conflicts: None known.
See Also: Functions 80h and 81h

INTERRUPT 2Ah - Function 89h
Unknown Function

Purpose: *unknown.*
Available on: All machines.

Restrictions: Network software must be installed.

Registers at call:

Return Registers: *unknown.*

AH = 89h
AL = *unknown.*(ASSIGN uses 08h)
unknown.
Conflicts: None known.

INTERRUPT 2Ah - Function C2h
Unknown Function

Purpose: *unknown.*
Available on: All machines.

Restrictions: Network software must be installed.

Registers at call:

Return Registers: *unknown.*

AH = C2h
AL = subfunction
    07h *unknown.*
    08h *unknown.*
BX = 0001h
unknown.
Details: This function is called by DOS 3.30 APPEND.
Conflicts: None known.

INTERRUPT 2Fh - Function 11h, Subfunctions 86h, 8Ah, and 8Fh
LAN Manager ENHANCED SERVICES

Purpose: Request enhanced functions such as encryption or named pipes.

Available on: All machines.

Registers at call:
AH = 11h
AL = function
    86h DosReadAsynchNmPipe
    8Ah (ENCRYPT.EXE) stream encryption
    8Fh DOSwriteAsynchNmPipe
other registers vary according to function, *but were not known at the time of writing.*

Restrictions: LAN Manager DOS Enhanced version 2.0 must be installed.

Return Registers: *unknown.*

Details: LAN Manager enhanced mode adds features beyond the standard redirector file/printer services.
See Also: Functions 41h, 42h, and 4Bh, INT 21h Function 5Fh Subfunctions 39h and 3Ah

INTERRUPT 2Fh - Function 41h
NETWORK POP-UP SERVICE

Purpose: Communicate with the pop-up interface.
Available on: All machines.

Restrictions: LAN Manager DOS Enhanced version 2.0 NETPOPUP.EXE module must be installed.

Return Registers: *unknown.*

Registers at call:
AH = 41h
other *unknown.*

Details: LAN Manager enhanced mode adds features beyond the standard redirector file/printer services.
Conflicts: None known.
See Also: Function 11h Subfunction 8Ah, Functions 42h and 4Bh

INTERRUPT 2Fh - Function 42h
MESSENGER SERVICE

Purpose: Communicate with the messenger module.
Available on: All machines.

Restrictions: LAN Manager DOS Enhanced version 2.0 MSRV.EXE module must be installed.

Return Registers: *unknown.*

Registers at call:
AH = 42h
other *unknown.*

Details: LAN Manager enhanced mode adds features beyond the standard redirector file/printer services.
Conflicts: None known.
See Also: Function 11h Subfunction 8Ah, Functions 41h and 4Bh

INTERRUPT 2Fh - Function 4Bh
NETWORK WORKSTATION REDIRECTOR

Purpose: Communicate with the enhanced workstation redirector.
Available on: All machines.

Restrictions: LAN Manager DOS Enhanced version 2.0 NETWKSTA.EXE module must be installed.

Return Registers: *unknown.*

Registers at call:
AH = 4Bh
other *unknown.*

Details: LAN Manager enhanced mode adds features beyond the standard redirector file/printer services.
Conflicts: DOS 5 task switcher (chapter 8).
See Also: Function 11h Subfunction 8Ah, Functions 41h and 42h

INTERRUPT 2Fh - Function 80h, Subfunction 00h
INSTALLATION CHECK

Purpose: Determine whether EASY-NET is installed.

Available on: All machines.

Registers at call:

AX = 8000h

Restrictions: none.

Return Registers:

AL = 00h not installed

FFh installed

Details: EASY-NET is a shareware two-machine serial-port network by EasyNet Systems, Inc.

INTERRUPT 2Fh - Function B8h, Subfunction 00h
INSTALLATION CHECK

Purpose: Determine whether network software is installed.

Available on: All machines.

Registers at call:

AX = B800h

Restrictions: none.

Return Registers:

AL = status

    00h   not installed

    nonzero installed

BX = installed component flags (test in this order!)

    bit 6   server

    bit 2   messenger

    bit 7   receiver

    bit 3   redirector

Conflicts: None known.

INTERRUPT 2Fh - Function B8h, Subfunction 03h
GET NETWORK EVENT POST HANDLER

Purpose: Determine which routine the network software invokes on network events.

Available on: All machines.

Registers at call:

AX = B803h

Restrictions: Network software must be installed.

Return Registers:

ES:BX -> event post handler (see Function B8h Subfunction 04h)

Conflicts: None known.

See Also: Function B8h Subfunction 04h, Function B9h Subfunction 03h (chapter 19)

INTERRUPT 2Fh - Function B8h, Subfunction 04h
SET NETWORK EVENT POST HANDLER

Purpose: Specify which routine the network software should invoke on network events.

Available on: All machines.

Registers at call:

AX = B804h

ES:BX -> new event post handler

Restrictions: Network software must be installed.

Return Registers: *unknown*.

Details: This call is used in conjunction with Function B8h Subfunction 03h to hook into the network event post routine. The specified handler is called on any network event. Two events are defined: message received and critical network error.

Conflicts: None known.

See Also: Function B8h Subfunction 03h, Function B9h Subfunction 04h (chapter 19)

Post routine is called with:

AX = 0000h single block message

    DS:SI -> ASCIZ originator name

    DS:DI -> ASCIZ destination name

    ES:BX -> text header (Table 27-16)

AX = 0001h start multiple message block

Returns with:

AX = response code

    0000h user post routine processed message

    0001h PC LAN will process message, but message

        window not displayed

    FFFFh PC LAN will process message

CX = block group ID
DS:SI -> ASCIZ originator name
DS:DI -> ASCIZ destination name
AX = 0002h multiple block text
   CX = block group ID
   ES:BX -> text header (Table 27-16)
AX = 0003h end multiple block message
   CX = block group ID
AX = 0004h message aborted due to error
   CX = block group ID
AX = 0101h server received badly formatted
     network request
AX = 0102h unexpected network error
   ES:BX -> NCB (see INT 5Ch)
AX = 0103h server received INT 24h error
   other registers as for INT 24h, except AH is in
     BH

Note: Function 0101h always returns FFFFh, and
Function 0103h may only return 0000h or FFFFh

Table 27-16. Format of Text Header:

Offset	Size	Description
00h	WORD	length of text (maximum 512 bytes)
02h	N BYTEs	text of message

Details: All CRLF sequences in the message text are replaced by character 14h (control-T).

INTERRUPT 2Fh - Function B8h, Subfunction 07h
GET NetBIOS NAME NUMBER OF MACHINE NAME

Purpose: Determine the NetBIOS number corresponding to the caller's machine's name.
Available on: All machines.
Registers at call:
AX = B807h
Conflicts: None known.
See Also: INT 21h Function 5Eh Subfunction 00h (chapter 8)

Restrictions: Network software must be installed.
Return Registers:
CH = NetBIOS name number of the machine name

INTERRUPT 2Fh - Function B8h, Subfunction 08h
Unknown Function

Purpose: *unknown.*
Available on: All machines.
Registers at call:
AX = B808h
other *unknown.*
Conflicts: None known.

Restrictions: Network software must be installed.
Return Registers: *unknown.*

INTERRUPT 2Fh - Function FFh, Subfunction 00h
INSTALLATION CHECK

Purpose: Determine whether the Topware Network Operating System is installed.
Available on: All machines.
Registers at call:
AX = FF00h

Restrictions: none.
Return Registers:
AL = 00h not installed, OK to install
    = 01h not installed, not OK to install
    = FFh installed

Conflicts: None known.

INTERRUPT 2Fh - Function FFh, Subfunction 01h
GET VERSION

Purpose: Determine which version of the Topware Network Operating System is installed.

Available on: All machines.

Registers at call:
AX = FF01h
Conflicts: None known.

Restrictions: Topware Network Operating System must be installed.

Return Registers:
AX = version

INTERRUPT 50h
TIL Xpert AIM (X.25)

Purpose: Communicate with the TIL X.25 networking software.

Available on: All machines.

Registers at call:
AH = function
Conflicts: None known.

Restrictions: TIL Xpert AIM must be installed.

Return Registers: *unknown.*

INTERRUPT 5Ah
Cluster Adapter BIOS entry address

Purpose: Communicate with the Cluster Adapter BIOS.

Available on: All machines.

Registers at call: *unknown.*

Conflicts: DESQview 2.26+ IRQ10, DoubleDOS IRQ2 (Chapter 2).

Restrictions: Cluster Adapter BIOS must be installed.

Return Registers: *unknown.*

INTERRUPT 5Bh
AT&T Starlan Extended NetBIOS (variable length names)

Purpose: Perform NetBIOS commands using variable-length names rather than the standard fixed-length names.

Available on: All machines.

Registers at call:
ES:BX -> Network Control Block (Table 27-17)

Conflicts: Microsoft Network Transport Layer Interface; Cluster Adapter; IRQ3 relocated by DoubleDOS and IRQ11 relocated by DESQview 2.26+ (chapter 2).

See Also: INT 5Ch

Restrictions: AT&T Starlan Extended NetBIOS (supporting variable-length names) must be installed.

Return Registers:
AL = status (see INT 5Ch)

Table 27-17. Format of Network Control Block

Offset	Size	Description	
00h	BYTE	ncb_command (see below)	
01h	BYTE	ncb_retcode	
02h	BYTE	ncb_lsn	
03h	BYTE	ncb_num	
04h	DWORD	-> ncb_buffer	
08h	WORD	ncb_length	
0Ah	16 BYTEs	ncb_callname	
1Ah	16 BYTEs	ncb_name	
2Ah	BYTE	ncb_rto	
2Bh	BYTE	ncb_sto	
2Ch	DWORD	-> ncb_post	/* int (far *ncb_post)(); */
30h	BYTE	ncb_lana_num	
31h	BYTE	ncb_cmd_cplt	
32h	DWORD	-> ncb_vname	

Table 27-17. Format of Network Control Block (continued)

Offset	Size	Description
36h	BYTE	ncb_vnamelen
37h	9 BYTEs	ncb_reserve

Details: Fields 00h-31h are the same as for a standard NetBIOS NCB (see INT 5Ch). Values for the ncb_command field are the same as for INT 5Ch, except:

    70h   send net Break

INTERRUPT 5Bh
Microsoft Network Transport Layer Interface

Purpose: Communicate with the Network Transport Layer module.

Available on: All machines.　　　　　　　　　**Restrictions:** Microsoft Network Transport Layer must be installed.

Registers at call: *unknown.*　　　　　　　　**Return Registers:** *unknown.*

Conflicts: Cluster Adapter; AT&T Starlan Extended NetBIOS; IRQ3 relocated by DoubleDOS and IRQ11 relocated by DESQview 2.26+ (chapter 2)

INTERRUPT 5Bh
Used by cluster adapter

Purpose: *unknown.*

Available on: All machines.　　　　　　　　　**Restrictions:** Cluster adapter must be installed.

Conflicts: AT&T Starlan Extended NetBIOS; Microsoft Network Transport Layer Interface; IRQ3 relocated by DoubleDOS and IRQ11 relocated by DESQview 2.26+ (chapter 2).

INTERRUPT 5Ch
INSTALLATION CHECK

Purpose: Determine whether the $25 LAN by Information Modes is installed.

Available on: All machines.　　　　　　　　　**Restrictions:** none.

Details: Current versions only check whether the vector is 0000h:0000h or not. Future versions are supposed to have the signature "NET" in the three bytes preceding the INT 5C handler.

Conflicts: IRQ4 relocated by DoubleDOS and IRQ12 relocated by DESQview 2.26+ (chapter 2); $25 LAN, ATALK.SYS, IBM 802.2 interface (LLC), NetBIOS interface, and TOPS interface (chapter 27).

INTERRUPT 5Ch - Function 04h
CHECK IF CONNECTION ALIVE

Purpose: Determine whether the connection to the remote machine has been established and is valid.

Available on: All machines.　　　　　　　　　**Restrictions:** $25 LAN must be installed.

Registers at call:　　　　　　　　　　　　　**Return Registers:**
AH = 04h　　　　　　　　　　　　　　　　　　ZF set if link alive
AL = COM port (0 = default)
CX = wait count in character times (should be at
　　least 100)

Details: The $25 LAN is a network which connects two machines via their serial ports; up to three machines may be connected by dedicating both ports on one machine to the network.

Conflicts: IRQ4 relocated by DoubleDOS and IRQ12 relocated by DESQview 2.26+ (chapter 2); $25 LAN, ATALK.SYS, IBM 802.2 interface (LLC), NetBIOS interface, and TOPS interface (chapter 27).

INTERRUPT 5Ch
ATALK.SYS - AppleTalk INTERFACE

Purpose: Communicate with the AppleTalk module.

Available on: All machines.　　　　　　　　　**Restrictions:** ATALK.SYS must be installed.

Registers at call: **Return Registers:** n/a

DX:BX -> control block (Table 27-18)

Details: This driver can use any interrupt from 5Ch to 70h. The signature 'AppleTalk' appears 16 bytes prior to the interrupt handler; this serves as the installation check.

Conflicts: IRQ4 relocated by DoubleDOS and IRQ12 relocated by DESQview 2.26+ (chapter 2); $25 LAN, ATALK.SYS, IBM 802.2 interface (LLC), NetBIOS interface, and TOPS interface (chapter 27).

Table 27-18. Format of AppleTalk Control Block:

Offset	Size	Description
00h	WORD	command code
		01h "AT_INIT" initialize the driver
		02h "AT_KILL"
		03h "AT_GETNETINFO" get current network info incl init status
		04h "AT_GETCLOCKTICKS"
		05h "AT_STARTTIMER"
		06h "AT_RESETTIMER"
		07h "AT_CANCELTIMER"
		10h "LAP_INSTALL"
		11h "LAP_REMOVE"
		12h "LAP_WRITE"
		13h "LAP_READ"
		14h "LAP_CANCEL"
		20h "DDP_OPENSOCKET"
		21h "DDP_CLOSESOCKET"
		22h "DDP_WRITE"
		23h "DDP_READ"
		24h "DDP_CANCEL"
		30h "NBP_REGISTER"
		31h "NBP_REMOVE"
		32h "NBP_LOOKUP"
		33h "NBP_CONFIRM"
		34h "NBP_CANCEL"
		35h "ZIP_GETZONELIST"
		36h "ZIP_GETMYZONE"
		37h "ZIP_TAKEDOWN"
		38h "ZIP_BRINGUP"
		40h "ATP_OPENSOCKET"
		41h "ATP_CLOSESOCKET"
		42h "ATP_SENDREQUEST"
		43h "ATP_GETREQUEST"
		44h "ATP_SENDRESPONSE"
		45h "ATP_ADDRESPONSE"
		46h "ATP_CANCELTRANS"
		47h "ATP_CANCELRESPONSE"
		48h "ATP_CANCELREQUEST"
		50h "ASP_GETPARMS"
		51h "ASP_CLOSESESSION"
		52h "ASP_CANCEL"
		53h "ASP_INIT"
		54h "ASP_KILL"
		55h "ASP_GETSESSION"
		56h "ASP_GETREQUEST"
		57h "ASP_CMDREPLY"
		58h "ASP_WRTCONTINUE"
		59h "ASP_WRTREPLY"
		5Ah "ASP_CLOSEREPLY"
		5Bh "ASP_NEWSTATUS"
		5Ch "ASP_ATTENTION"

Table 27-18. Format of AppleTalk control block (continued)

Offset	Size	Description
		5Dh "ASP_GETSTATUS"
		5Eh "ASP_OPENSESSION"
		5Fh "ASP_COMMAND"
		60h "ASP_WRITE"
		61h "ASP_GETATTENTION"
		70h "PAP_OPEN"
		71h "PAP_CLOSE"
		72h "PAP_READ"
		73h "PAP_WRITE"
		74h "PAP_STATUS"
		75h "PAP_REGNAME"
		76h "PAP_REMNAME"
		77h "PAP_INIT"
		78h "PAP_NEWSTATUS"
		79h "PAP_GETNEXTJOB"
		7Ah "PAP_KILL"
		7Bh "PAP_CANCEL" OR with the following flags:
		8000h start command then return
		4000h wait for interrupt service to complete
02h	WORD	returned status:
		0000h success (already initialized if func 01h)
04h	DWORD	pointer to completion function
08h	WORD	network number
0Ah	BYTE	node ID

---if general function (01h,03h)

Offset	Size	Description
0Bh	BYTE	"inf_abridge"
0Ch	WORD	"inf_config"
0Eh	DWORD	pointer to buffer
12h	WORD	buffer size

---if DDP function (20h-24h)

Offset	Size	Description
0Bh	BYTE	"ddp_addr_socket"
0Ch	BYTE	"ddp_socket"
0Dh	BYTE	"ddp_type"
0Eh	DWORD	pointer to buffer
12h	WORD	buffer size
14h	BYTE	"ddp_chksum"

---if Name Binding Protocol (30h-34h)

Offset	Size	Description
0Bh	BYTE	"nbp_addr_socket"
0Ch	WORD	"nbp_toget"
0Eh	DWORD	pointer to buffer (Table 27-19)
12h	WORD	buffer size
14h	BYTE	"nbp_interval"
15h	BYTE	"nbp_retry"
16h	DWORD	"nbp_entptr"

---if AppleTalk Transaction Protocol (42h)

Offset	Size	Description
0Bh	BYTE	"atp_addr_socket"
0Ch	WORD	"atp_socket"
0Eh	DWORD	pointer to buffer
12h	WORD	buffer size
14h	BYTE	"atp_interval"
15h	BYTE	"atp_retry"
16h	BYTE	ATP flags
		bit 5: exactly one transaction
17h	BYTE	"atp_seqbit"
18h	BYTE	transaction ID

Table 27-18. Format of AppleTalk Control Block (continued)

Offset	Size	Description
19h	4 BYTEs	ATP user bytes
1Dh	BYTE	number of BDS buffers
1Eh	BYTE	number of BDS responses
1Fh	DWORD	pointer to BDS buffers (Table 27-20)

Table 27-19. Format of Name Binding Protocol Name-to-Address Binding Entries for NBP_LOOKUP:

Offset	Size	Description
00h	WORD	"tup_address_network"
02h	BYTE	"tup_address_notid"
03h	BYTE	"tup_address_socket"
04h	BYTE	"tup_enum"
05h	99 BYTEs	name

Table 27-20. Format of BDS Entries:

Offset	Size	Description
00h	DWORD	pointer to buffer
04h	WORD	size of buffer
06h	WORD	BDS data size
08h	4 BYTEs	"bds_userbytes"

INTERRUPT 5Ch
IBM 802.2 INTERFACE (LLC)

Purpose: Communicate with the LLC module.
Available on: All machines.
Registers at call:
ES:BX -> CCB (Table 27-21)

Restrictions: IBM 802.2 Interface must be installed.
Return Registers: n/a

Conflicts: IRQ4 relocated by DoubleDOS and IRQ12 relocated by DESQview (chapter 2); $25 LAN, ATALK.SYS, IBM 802.2 interface (LLC), NetBIOS interface, and TOPS interface (chapter 27).

Table 27-21. Format of CCB:

Offset	Size	Description
00h	BYTE	adapter
01h	BYTE	command code
02h	BYTE	return code
03h	BYTE	work
04h	DWORD	pointer to *unknown code or data*
08h	DWORD	pointer to *completion function*
0Ch	DWORD	pointer to *parameters*

INTERRUPT 5Ch
NetBIOS INTERFACE

Purpose: Perform NetBIOS network commands.
Available on: All machines.
Registers at call:
ES:BX -> network control block
    (NCB) (Table 27-23)

Restrictions: NetBIOS must be installed.
Return Registers:
AL = status (Table 27-22)

Details: The Sytek PCnet card uses DMA channel 3.
Conflicts: $25 LAN, ATALK.SYS, IBM 802.2 interface, TOPS interface, and NetBIOS; IRQ4 relocated by DoubleDOS and IRQ12 relocated by DESQview (chapter 2).
See Also: INT 5Bh

Table 27-22. Values of NetBIOS Status Codes:

Value	Meaning	Value	Meaning
00h	successful	17h	bad delete
01h	bad buffer size	18h	abnormal end
03h	invalid NETBIOS command	19h	name error, multiple identical names in use
05h	timeout	1Ah	bad packet
06h	receive buffer too small	21h	network card busy
07h	No-ACK command failed	22h	too many commands queued
08h	bad session number	23h	bad LAN card number
09h	LAN card out of memory	24h	command finished while cancelling
0Ah	session closed	26h	command can't be cancelled
0Bh	command has been cancelled	30h	name defined by another process (OS/2)
0Dh	name already exists	34h	NetBIOS environment not defined, must issue reset (OS/2)
0Eh	local name table full		
0Fh	name still in use, can't delete	35h	required operating system resources exhausted (OS/2)
11h	local session table full		
12h	remote PC not listening	36h	maximum applications exceeded (OS/2)
13h	bad NCB_NUM field	37h	no SAPs available for NetBIOS (OS/2)
14h	no answer to CALL or no such remote	38h	requested resources not available (OS/2)
15h	name not in local name table	FFh	NetBIOS busy (command pending)
16h	duplicate name		

Table 27-23. Format of Network Control Block:

Offset	Size	Description
00h	BYTE	command code (Table 27-24)
01h	BYTE	return code
02h	BYTE	local session number (LSN)
03h	BYTE	"ncb_num" datagram table entry from ADD NAME
04h	DWORD	-> I/O buffer
08h	WORD	length of data in buffer
0Ah	16 BYTEs	remote system to call
1Ah	16 BYTEs	network name of local machine
2Ah	BYTE	receive timeout in 1/2 seconds
2Bh	BYTE	send timeout in 1/2 seconds
2Ch	DWORD	-> FAR post handler /* int (far *ncb_post)(); */
30h	BYTE	network adapter number on which to execute command
		00h-03h IBM NetBIOS specs
		F0h-FFh Eicon NABios interface
31h	BYTE	command completion code (see returned status above)
32h	14 BYTEs	reserved for network card

Table 27-24. Values for command code field in NCB (or with 80h for non-waiting call):

Value	Meaning	Value	Meaning
10h	start session with NCB_NAME name (call)	20h	send unACKed message (datagram)
		21h	receive datagram
11h	listen for call	22h	send broadcast datagram
12h	end session with NCB_NAME name (hangup)	23h	receive broadcast datagram
		30h	add name to name table (Table 27-25)
14h	send data via NCB_LSN	31h	delete name from name table
15h	receive data from a session	32h	reset adapter card and tables
16h	receive data from any session	33h	get adapter status (Table 27-26)
17h	send multiple data buffers	*34h*	*status of all sessions for name (Table 27-27)*

Table 27-24. Values for command code field in NCB (continued)

Value	Meaning	Value	Meaning
35h	cancel	71h	send data without ACK
36h	add group name to name table	72h	send multiple buffers without ACK
70h	unlink from IBM remote program (no F0h function)	78h	find name
		79h	token-ring protocol trace

Table 27-25. Format of Structure "name":

Offset	Size	Description
00h	16 BYTEs	"nm_name" symbolic name
10h	BYTE	"nm_num" number associated with name
11h	BYTE	nm_status

Table 27-26. Format of Structure "astatus":

Offset	Size	Description
00h	6 BYTEs	as_id
06h	BYTE	as_jumpers
07h	BYTE	as_post
08h	BYTE	as_major
09h	BYTE	as_minor
0Ah	WORD	as_interval
0Ch	WORD	as_crcerr
0Eh	WORD	as_algerr
10h	WORD	as_colerr
12h	WORD	as_abterr
14h	DWORD	as_tcount
18h	DWORD	as_rcount
1Ch	WORD	as_retran
1Eh	WORD	as_xresrc
20h	8 BYTEs	as_res0
28h	WORD	as_ncbfree
2Ah	WORD	as_ncbmax
2Ch	WORD	as_ncbx
2Eh	4 BYTEs	as_res1
32h	WORD	as_sespend
34h	WORD	as_msp
36h	WORD	as_sesmax
38h	WORD	as_bufsize
3Ah	WORD	as_names
3Ch	16 name structures	as_name

Table 27-27. Format of Structure "sstatus":

Offset	Size	Description
00h	BYTE	number of sessions being reported
01h	BYTE	number of sessions with this name
02h	BYTE	number of outstanding receive datagrams
03h	BYTE	number of outstanding ReceiveAnys
04h	var	session structures (Table 27-28)

Table 27-28. Format of Structure "session":

Offset	Size	Description
00h	BYTE	local session number
01h	BYTE	state:
		01h listen pending
		02h call pending
		03h session established
		04h hangup pending
		05h hangup done
		06h session aborted
02h	16 BYTEs	local name
12h	16 BYTEs	remote name
22h	BYTE	number of outstanding receives
23h	BYTE	number of outstanding sends/chainsends

INTERRUPT 5Ch
TOPS INTERFACE

Purpose: Communicate with the TOPS network program.

Available on: All machines.

Restrictions: TOPS software must be installed.

Registers at call:

Return Registers: n/a

ES:BX -> Network Control Block (Table 27-23)

Details: The TOPS card uses DMA channels 1 or 3, or non-DMA operation.

Conflicts: IRQ4 relocated by DoubleDOS and IRQ12 relocated by DESQview 2.26+ (chapter 2); $25 LAN, ATALK.SYS, IBM 802.2 interface (LLC), NetBIOS interface, and TOPS interface (chapter 27).

INTERRUPT 60h
FTP Packet Driver - PC/TCP Packet Driver Specification

Purpose: Provide portable access to a wide variety of network hardware.

Available on: All machines.

Restrictions: FTP Packet Driver must be installed.

Details: The handler for the interrupt will start with a 3-byte jump instruction, followed by the ASCIZ string "PKT DRVR". To find the interrupt being used by the driver, an application should scan through interrupt vectors 60h to 80h until it finds one with the "PKT DRVR" string.

Conflicts: See chapter 1.

INTERRUPT 60h - Function 01h, Subfunction FFh
GET DRIVER INFORMATION

Purpose: Determine the version and type of the packet driver which is installed.

Available on: All machines.

Restrictions: FTP Packet Driver must be installed.

Registers at call:

Return Registers:

AX = 01FFh

BX = handle returned by function 02h

CF set on error
    DH = error code (Table 27-29)
CF clear if successful
    BX = version
    CH = network interface class (see below)
    DX = interface type (Table 27-30)
    CL = number
    DS:SI -> name
    AL = driver functions supported
        01h basic
        02h basic and extended
        05h basic and high-performance

06h basic, high-performance, and extended
FFh not installed

Details: The handle in BX is optional for drivers written to version 1.07 or later of the packet driver specification.
Conflicts: See chapter 1.

Table 27-29. Values for Error Code:

01h	invalid handle number	07h	this packet driver cannot terminate
02h	no interfaces of the specified class found	08h	invalid receiver mode
		09h	insufficient space
03h	no interfaces of the specified type found	0Ah	type accessed but never released
		0Bh	bad command
04h	no interfaces of the specified number found	0Ch	packet could not be sent
		0Dh	hardware address could not be changed
05h	bad packet type	0Eh	hardware address has a bad length or format
06h	interface does not support multicast messages	0Fh	could not reset interface

Table 27-30. Values for Network Interface classes/types:

Class 01h	Ethernet/IEEE 802.3	25h	Vestra LANMASTER 8-bit
01h	3COM 3C500/3C501	26h	Allied Telesis PC/XT/AT
02h	3COM 3C505	27h	Allied Telesis NEC PC-98
03h	MICOM-Interlan NI5010	28h	Allied Telesis Fujitsu FMR
04h	BICC Data Networks 4110	29h	Ungermann-Bass NIC/PS2
05h	BICC Data Networks 4117	2Ah	Tiara LANCard/E AT
06h	MICOM-Interlan NP600	2Bh	Tiara LANCard/E MC
08h	Ungermann-Bass PC-NIC	2Ch	Tiara LANCard/E TP
09h	Univation NC-516	2Dh	Spider Communications SpiderComm 8
0Ah	TRW PC-2000	2Eh	Spider Communications SpiderComm 16
0Bh	MICOM-Interlan NI5210	2Fh	AT&T Starlan NAU
0Ch	3COM 3C503	30h	AT&T Starlan-10 NAU
0Dh	3COM 3C523	31h	AT&T Ethernet NAU
0Eh	Western Digital WD8003	32h	Intel smart card
0Fh	Spider Systems S4		
10h	Torus Frame Level	Class 02h	ProNET-10
11h	10Net Communications	01h	Proteon p1300
12h	Gateway PC-bus	02h	Proteon p1800
13h	Gateway AT-bus	Class 03h	IEEE 802.5/ProNet-4
14h	Gateway MCA-bus	01h	IBM Token-Ring Adapter
15h	IMC PCnic	02h	Proteon p1340
16h	IMC PCnic II	03h	Proteon p1344
17h	IMC PCnic 8-bit	04h	Gateway PC-bus
18h	Tigan Communications	05h	Gateway AT-bus
19h	Micromatic Research	06h	Gateway MCA-bus
1Ah	Clarkson "Multiplexor"	Class 04h	Omninet
1Bh	D-Link 8-bit	Class 05h	Appletalk
1Ch	D-Link 16-bit	Class 06h	Serial Line
1Dh	D-Link PS/2	01h	Clarkson 8250-SLIP
1Eh	Research Machines 8	02h	Clarkson "Multiplexor"
1Fh	Research Machines 16	Class 07h	StarLAN (subsumed by Ethernet class)
20h	Research Machines MCA	Class 08h	ARCnet
21h	Radix Microsystems EXM1 16-bit	01h	Datapoint RIM
22h	Interlan Ni9210	Class 09h	AX.25
23h	Interlan Ni6510	Class 0Ah	KISS
24h	Vestra LANMASTER 16-bit	Class 0Bh	IEEE 802.3 with 802.2 headers
			types same as for class 01h

Table 27-30. Values for Network Interface Classes/Types (continued)

Class 0Ch	FDDI with 802.2 headers	Class 0Eh	N.T. LANSTAR (encapsulating DIX Ethernet)
Class 0Dh	Internet X.25		
01h	Western Digital	01h	NT LANSTAR/8
02h	Frontier Technology	02h	NT LANSTAR/MC

Note: The class and type numbers are cleared through FTP Software.

INTERRUPT 60h - Function 02h
ACCESS TYPE

Purpose: Prepare to use the specified interface type; informs the packet driver that it should perform whatever initialization is necessary.

Available on: All machines.

Registers at call:
AH = 02h
AL = interface class
BX = interface type
DL = interface number
DS:SI -> type
CX = length of type
ES:DI -> receiver

Conflicts: See chapter 1.

See Also: Function 03h

Restrictions: FTP Packet Driver must be installed.

Return Registers:
CF set on error
    DH = error code   (see Function 01h
Subfunction FFh)
CF clear if successful
    AX = handle

    Receiver is called with:
        AX = subfunction:
                00h application to return pointer to buffer in ES:DI
                    returned ES:DI = 0000h:0000h means throw away packet
            01h copy completed
                DS:SI -> buffer
        BX = handle
        CX = buffer length
when a packet is received

INTERRUPT 60h - Function 03h
RELEASE TYPE

Purpose: Indicate that the specified interface will no longer be needed; the packet driver may perform any necessary cleanup.

Available on: All machines.

Registers at call:
AH = 03h
BX = handle

Restrictions: FTP Packet Driver must be installed.

Return Registers:
CF set on error
    DH = error code (see Function 01h
Subfunction FFh)
CF clear if successful

Conflicts: See chapter 1.
See Also: Function 02h

INTERRUPT 60h - Function 04h
SEND PACKET

Purpose: Transmit data over the network.

Available on: All machines.

Restrictions: FTP Packet Driver must be installed.

Registers at call:
AH = 04h
DS:SI -> buffer
CX = length

Return Registers:
CF set on error
    DH = error code (see Function 01h
Subfunction FFh)
CF clear if successful

Details: The buffer may be modified immediately upon return from this call.
Conflicts: See chapter 1.
See Also: Function 0Bh

INTERRUPT 60h - Function 05h
TERMINATE DRIVER FOR HANDLE

Purpose: Stop providing network services for the specified connection.
Available on: All machines.

Restrictions: FTP Packet Driver must be installed.

Registers at call:
AH = 05h
BX = handle

Return Registers:
CF set on error
    DH = error code (see Function 01h
Subfunction FFh)
CF clear if successful

Conflicts: See chapter 1.

INTERRUPT 60h - Function 06h
GET ADDRESS

Purpose: Determine the caller's network address.
Available on: All machines.

Restrictions: FTP Packet Driver must be installed.

Registers at call:
AH = 06h
BX = handle
ES:DI -> buffer
CX = length

Return Registers:
CF set on error
    DH = error code (see Function 01h
Subfunction FFh)
CF clear if successful
    CX = length of returned address

Details: This function copies the local net address associated with the handle into the buffer.
Conflicts: See chapter 1.

INTERRUPT 60h - Function 07h
RESET INTERFACE

Purpose: Place the network adapter hardware into a known initial state.
Available on: All machines.

Restrictions: FTP Packet Driver must be installed.

Registers at call:
AH = 07h
BX = handle

Return Registers:
CF set on error
    DH = error code (see Function 01h
Subfunction FFh)
CF clear if successful

Conflicts: See chapter 1.

INTERRUPT 60h - Function 0Ah
GET PARAMETERS

Purpose: Determine the sizes and addresses of various data structures used by the packet driver, as well as the version of the packet driver specification supported by the driver.
Available on: All machines.

Restrictions: FTP Packet Driver supporting the version 1.09 high-performance function set must be installed.

Registers at call:
AH = 0Ah

Return Registers:
CF set on error
    DH = error code (0Bh) (see Function 01h
Subfunction FFh)
CF clear if successful
    ES:DI -> parameter table (Table 27-31)

Conflicts: See chapter 1.

Table 27-31. Format of Packet Driver Parameter Table:

Offset	Size	Description
00h	BYTE	major revision of packet driver spec to which the driver conforms
01h	BYTE	minor revision of packet driver spec
02h	BYTE	length of this structure in bytes
03h	BYTE	length of a MAC-layer address
04h	WORD	maximum transfer unit, including MAC headers
06h	WORD	buffer size for multicast address
08h	WORD	number of receive buffers (one less than back-to-back MTU receives)
0Ah	WORD	number of transmit buffers
0Ch	WORD	interrupt number to hook for post-EOI processing, 00h=none

INTERRUPT 60h - Function 0Bh
ASYNCHRONOUS SEND PACKET

Purpose: Transmit a block of data without waiting for the transmission to complete.

Available on: All machines.

Restrictions: FTP Packet Driver supporting the version 1.09 high-performance function set must be installed.

Registers at call:
AH = 0Bh
DS:SI -> buffer
CX = length of buffer
ES:DI -> FAR function to call when buffer becomes
    available

Return Registers:
CF set on error
    DH = error code (0Bh,0Ch) (see Function 01h
Subfunction FFh)
CF clear if successful

Details: Unlike function 04h, the buffer for this call is not available for modification as soon as the call returns; the buffer may be queued by the driver and not processed until later.

Conflicts: See chapter 1.

See Also: Function 04h

    Completion function called with:
        AX = result
                00h copy OK
                nonzero error
        ES:DI -> buffer passed to Function 0Bh call

INTERRUPT 60h - Function 0Ch
GET STATION ADDRESS

Purpose: Determine the network address of the caller's machine.

Available on: All machines.

Restrictions: 3com or Banyan VINES must be installed.

Registers at call:
AH = 0Ch

Return Registers:
AL = status
    00h successful
        ES:SI -> 6-byte station address
    02h semaphore service is unavailable

Conflicts: See chapter 1.

INTERRUPT 60h - Function 11h
LOCK AND WAIT

Purpose: Request exclusive access to the specified resource, waiting until it becomes available or a timeout elapses.

Available on: All machines.

Restrictions: 3com, 10-NET or Banyan VINES must be installed.

Registers at call:
AH = 11h
AL = drive number or 0
DX = number of seconds to wait
ES:SI = Ethernet address or 0
DS:BX -> 31-byte ASCIZ semaphore name

Return Registers:
AL = status
    00h successful
    01h timeout
    02h server not responding
    03h invalid semaphore name
    04h semaphore list is full
    05h invalid drive ID
    06h invalid Ethernet address
    07h not logged in
    08h write to network failed
    09h semaphore already logged for this CPU

Conflicts: See Chapter 1.
See Also: Functions 12h and 13h

INTERRUPT 60h - Function 12h
LOCK

Purpose: Attempt to gain exclusive access to a resource.

Available on: All machines.

Restrictions: 3com, 10-NET or Banyan VINES must be installed.

Registers at call:
AH = 12h
AL = drive number or 00h
ES:SI = Ethernet address or 0000h:0000h
DS:BX -> 31-byte ASCIZ semaphore name
Details: Unlike Function 11h, this function returns immediately.
Conflicts: See Chapter 1.
See Also: Functions 11h and 13h

Return Registers:
AL = status (see also Function 11h)
    01h semaphore currently locked by another PC

INTERRUPT 60h - Function 13h
UNLOCK

Purpose: Indicate that the specified resource is now available to others.

Available on: All machines.

Restrictions: 3com, 10-NET or Banyan VINES must be installed.

Registers at call:
AH = 13h
AL = drive number or 00h
ES:SI = Ethernet address or 0000h:0000h
DS:BX -> 31-byte ASCIZ semaphore name
Conflicts: See Chapter 1.
See Also: Functions 11h and 12h

Return Registers:
AL = status (see also Function 11h)
    01h semaphore not locked

INTERRUPT 60h - Function 14h
SET RECEIVE MODE

Purpose: Specify which types of packets will be received from the network.

Available on: All machines.

Restrictions: FTP Packet Driver supporting the extended function set must be installed.

Registers at call:
AH = 14h
BX = handle
CX = mode
    01h turn off receiver
    02h receive only packets sent to this interface
    03h mode 2 plus broadcast packets
    04h mode 3 plus limited multicast packets
    05h mode 3 plus all multicast packets
    06h all packets
Conflicts: See chapter 1.
See Also: Function 15h

Return Registers:
CF set on error
    DH = error code (01h,08h) (see Function 01h
Subfunction FFh)
CF clear if successful

INTERRUPT 60h - Function 15h
GET RECEIVE MODE

Purpose: Determine which types of network packets are currently accepted by the packet driver.
Available on: All machines.

Restrictions: FTP Packet Driver supporting the extended function set must be installed.

Registers at call:
AH = 15h
BX = handle

Return Registers:
CF set on error
    DH = error code (01h) (see Function 01h
Subfunction FFh)
CF clear if successful
    AX = mode

Conflicts: See chapter 1.
See Also: Function 14h

INTERRUPT 60h - Function 16h
SET MULTICAST LIST

Purpose: Specify the destinations of a multicast.
Available on: All machines.

Restrictions: FTP Packet Driver supporting the extended function set must be installed.

Registers at call:
AH = 16h
ES:DI -> multicast list
CX = length of list in bytes

Return Registers:
CF set on error
    DH = error code (06h,09h,0Eh) (see Function 01h
Subfunction FFh)
CF clear if successful

Conflicts: See chapter 1.
See Also: Function 17h

INTERRUPT 60h - Function 17h
GET MULTICAST LIST

Purpose: Determine the destinations of a multicast.
Available on: All machines.

Restrictions: FTP Packet Driver supporting the extended function set must be installed.

Registers at call:
AH = 17h

Return Registers:
CF set on error
    DH = error code (06h,09h) (see Function 01h
Subfunction FFh)
CF clear if successful
    ES:DI -> multicast addresses (do not modify)
    CX = bytes of multicast addresses currently in use

Conflicts: See chapter 1.

See Also: Function 16h

INTERRUPT 60h - Function 18h
GET STATISTICS

Purpose: Determine how much data has been transferred over the network and how many errors occurred.

Available on: All machines.

Restrictions: FTP Packet Driver supporting the extended function set must be installed.

Registers at call:
AH = 18h
BX = handle

Return Registers:
CF set on error
    DH = error code (01h) (see Function 01h Subfunction FFh)
CF clear if successful
    DS:SI -> statistics (Table 27-32)

Conflicts: See chapter 1.

Table 27-32. Format of Statistics:

Offset	Size	Description
00h	DWORD	packets in
04h	DWORD	packets out
08h	DWORD	bytes in
0Ch	DWORD	bytes out
10h	DWORD	errors in
14h	DWORD	errors out
18h	DWORD	packets dropped

INTERRUPT 60h - Function 19h
SET NETWORK ADDRESS

Purpose: Specify the network address to be used by the packet driver.

Available on: All machines.

Restrictions: FTP Packet Driver supporting the extended function set must be installed.

Registers at call:
AH = 19h
ES:DI -> address
CX = length of address

Return Registers:
CF set on error
    DH = error code (0Dh,0Eh) (see Function 01h Subfunction FFh)
CF clear if successful
    CX = length

Conflicts: See chapter 1.

INTERRUPT 61h
FTP Software PC/TCP - TCP/IP TSR System Call interface

Purpose: Communicate with the resident module providing Internet TCP/IP (Transmission Control Protocol/Internet Protocol) functionality.

Available on: All machines.

Registers at call:
AH = system call number

Restrictions: FTP TCP/IP TSR must be installed.

Return Registers:
AL = basic error
AH = suberror number

Conflicts: See chapter 1.

INTERRUPT 65h
POST PROCESSING INTERRUPT

Purpose: Called by the packet driver after processing is complete.

Available on: All machines.

Restrictions: FTP Software NDIS-Packet Driver must be installed.

Registers at call: *unknown.*
Conflicts: See chapter 1.

Return Registers: *unknown.*

INTERRUPT 67h - Function 00h
LOCK SEMAPHORE AND WAIT

Purpose: Request exclusive access to the specified resource, waiting until it becomes available.
Available on: All machines.

Restrictions: PC-Net or Alloy networking software must be installed.

Registers at call:
AH = 00h
DS:DX -> ASCIZ semaphore name (max 64 bytes)

Return Registers:
AL = status
  00h successful
  01h invalid function
  02h semaphore already locked
  03h unable to lock semaphore
  04h semaphore space exhausted
AH = semaphore owner if status=02h

Conflicts: None known.
See Also: Functions 01h and 02h, INT 7Fh Function 00h (chapter 18)

INTERRUPT 67h - Function 01h
LOCK SEMAPHORE

Purpose: Attempt to gain exclusive access to the specified resource.
Available on: All machines.

Restrictions: PC-Net or Alloy networking software must be installed.

Registers at call:
AH = 01h
DS:DX -> ASCIZ semaphore name (max 64 bytes)
Conflicts: None known.
See Also: Functions 00h and 02h, INT 7Fh Function 01h (chapter 18)

Return Registers:
AL = status (see Function 00h)
AH = semaphore owner if status=02h

INTERRUPT 67h - Function 02h
UNLOCK SEMAPHORE

Purpose: Indicate that the specified resource is now available for use by others.
Available on: All machines.

Restrictions: PC-Net or Alloy networking software must be installed.

Registers at call:
AH = 02h
DS:DX -> ASCIZ semaphore name (max 64 bytes)
Conflicts: None known.
See Also: Functions 00h and 01h, INT 7Fh Function 02h (chapter 18)

Return Registers:
AL = status (see Function 00h)
AH = semaphore owner if status=02h

INTERRUPT 7Ah
Unknown Function

Purpose: *unknown.*
Available on: All machines.

Restrictions: Topware Network Operating System must be installed.

Registers at call:
AL = *unknown.*
others, if any, unknown.
Conflicts: Novell NetWare Low-level API (chapter 20), IBM 3270 Workstation Program API (chapter 26), AutoCAD Device Interface (chapter 36).

Return Registers: *unknown.*

INTERRUPT 7Fh - Function 43h, Subfunction 54h
CONVERGENT TECHNOLOGIES ClusterShare CTOS ACCESS VECTOR

Purpose: Communicate with the ClusterShare software.

Available on: All machines.

Registers at call:
CX = 4354h ('CT')
AL = request ID
   01h "Request"/"RequestDirect"
      ES:BX -> pRq
      DX ignored
   04h "Wait"
      ES:BX -> ppMsgRet
      DX = exchange
   05h "AllocExch"
      ES:BX -> pExchRet
   06h "DeAllocExch"
      DX = exchange
   07h "Check"
      ES:BX -> ppMsgRet
      DX = exchange

Restrictions: Convergent Technologies ClusterShare software must be installed.

Return Registers:
AX = status
   0000h successful

Conflicts: Halo88 API (chapter 2), Alloy NTNX and MW386 (chapter 18).

INTERRUPT 80h - Function 01h
INITIALIZE

Purpose: Prepare the PKTINT software for operation.

Available on: All machines.

Registers at call:
AH = 01h

Restrictions: QPC Software's PKTINT.COM must be installed.

Return Registers:
AX = 0000h
CX = FFFFh
DX = FFFFh

Details: This interrupt is the WinQVTNet protected mode interface to Windows 3.0. As part of the initialization, all buffer pointers are reset back to 0.

Conflicts: Q-PRO4 (chapter 36), SoundBlaster SBFM (chapter 36).

INTERRUPT 80h - Function 02h
GET BUFFER ADDRESSES

Purpose: Determine the addresses of the buffers used for sending and receiving data.

Available on: All machines.

Registers at call:
AH = 02h
BX = extra bytes to allocate per packet

Restrictions: QPC Software's PKTINT.COM must be installed.

Return Registers:
AX = segment address of 10K buffer (*for receives*)
BX = segment address of 2K buffer (*for sends*)

Conflicts: Q-PRO4 (chapter 36), SoundBlaster SBFM (chapter 36).

See Also: Function 05h

INTERRUPT 80h - Function 03h
GET ENTRY POINT

Purpose: Determine address to be called on receipt of a packet from the network.

Available on: All machines.

Restrictions: QPC Software's PKTINT.COM must be installed.

Registers at call:
AH = 03h

Return Registers:
CX:DX -> receive call address

Details: The returned address can be used in the packet driver calls since it will be a valid address in all DOS boxes.
Conflicts: Q-PRO4 (chapter 36), SoundBlaster SBFM (chapter 36).
See Also: Function 06h

INTERRUPT 80h - Function 04h
ENABLE

Purpose: Turn on PKTINT's functionality.
Available on: All machines.

Restrictions: QPC Software's PKTINT.COM must be installed.

Registers at call:
AH = 04h
BX = *unknown.*

Return Registers: *unknown.*

Conflicts: Q-PRO4 (chapter 36), SoundBlaster SBFM (chapter 36).

INTERRUPT 80h - Function 05h
GET RECEIVE STATISTICS

Purpose: Determine how much data has been received.
Available on: All machines.

Restrictions: QPC Software's PKTINT.COM must be installed.

Registers at call:
AH = 05h

Return Registers:
AX = amount of buffer currently in use
BX = current offset in buffer
CX = number of times receive has been called

Conflicts: Q-PRO4 (chapter 36), SoundBlaster SBFM (chapter 36).
See Also: Function 02h

INTERRUPT 80h - Function 06h
REMOVE RECEIVED PACKET

Purpose: Indicate that the current packet has been processed, and that the caller is ready for the next.
Available on: All machines.

Restrictions: QPC Software's PKTINT.COM must be installed.

Registers at call:
AH = 06h

Return Registers:
BX = next packet offset
CX = number of bytes still buffered
DX = size of packet released back into buffer pool

Conflicts: Q-PRO4 (chapter 36), SoundBlaster SBFM (chapter 36).
See Also: Function 03h

INTERRUPT 81h
Unknown Function

Purpose: *unknown.*
Available on: All machines.

Restrictions: IBM Token Ring Adapter software must be installed.

Registers at call: *unknown.*
Conflicts: Basic interpreter (chapter 1).

Return Registers: *unknown.*

INTERRUPT 82h
Unknown Function

Purpose: *unknown.*
Available on: All machines.

Restrictions: IBM Token Ring Adapter software must be installed.

Registers at call:
AH = function
  00h *display message*
    DS:BX -> string
others, if any, unknown.
Conflicts: Basic interpreter (chapter 1).

Return Registers: *unknown.*

INTERRUPT 86h
ORIGINAL INT 18h

Purpose: Some implementations of NetBIOS use this vector to store the original value of INT 18h.
Available on: All machines.   **Restrictions:** NetBIOS must be installed.
Conflicts: Basic interpreter (chapter 1), APL*PLUS/PC (chapter 31).

INTERRUPT 91h
Unknown Function

Purpose: *unknown.*
Available on: All machines.

Registers at call: *unknown.*
Conflicts: Basic interpreter (chapter 1).

Restrictions: IBM Token Ring Adapter software must be installed.
Return Registers: *unknown.*

INTERRUPT 92h
Sangoma X.25 INTERFACE PROGRAM

Purpose: *unknown.*
Available on: All machines.

Registers at call:
BX:DX -> control block
Conflicts: BASIC interpreter (chapter 1).

Restrictions: Sangoma X.25 interface program must be installed.
Return Registers: *unknown.*

INTERRUPT 93h
Unknown Function

Purpose: *unknown.*
Available on: All machines.

Registers at call: *unknown.*
Conflicts: BASIC interpreter (chapter 1).

Restrictions: IBM Token Ring Adapter software must be installed.
Return Registers: *unknown.*

INTERRUPT E1h
Unknown Function

Purpose: *unknown.*
Available on: All machines.

Registers at call: *unknown.*
Conflicts: BASIC interpreter (chapter 1).

Restrictions: PC Cluster Disk Server must be installed.
Return Registers: *unknown.*

INTERRUPT E2h
Unknown Function

Purpose: *unknown.*
Available on: All machines.
Registers at call: *unknown.*
Conflicts: BASIC interpreter (chapter 1).

Restrictions: PC Cluster Program must be installed.
Return Registers: *unknown.*

Chapter 28

Remote Control Software

One class of software that has become invaluable to consultants and others who must troubleshoot systems from a distance is that which permits one computer to take full control of another at a remote location. By using such systems, the troubleshooter can make a "house call" by telephone without having to travel anywhere.

The two best known such systems are Carbon Copy and pcAnywhere. The interrupts used by these to provide remote control are described in this chapter, together with that of a third less widely known system, TeleReplica, and the new PC Tools version 7 COMMUTE. In addition, LapLink's Quick Connect and DeskConnect are covered in this chapter even though they are file transfer utilities more than remote control software.

Carbon Copy

Carbon Copy is produced by Meridian Technology, Inc.

INTERRUPT 10h - Function FFh, Subfunction 00h
CHECK IF CC CONNECTED TO CCHELP

Purpose: Determine whether a connection has been established to the remote machine.
Available on: All machines.
Registers at call:
AX = FF00h

Restrictions: Carbon Copy Plus 5.0 must be installed.
Return Registers:
BL = 00h not connected
    = 01h connected

Conflicts: None known.

INTERRUPT 10h - Function FFh, Subfunction 01h
DISCONNECT AND RESET LINE

Purpose: Terminate the current connection.
Available on: All machines.
Registers at call:
AX = FF01h
Conflicts: None known.

Restrictions: Carbon Copy Plus 5.0 must be installed.
Return Registers: n/a

INTERRUPT 10h - Function FFh, Subfunction 02h
GET LAST PHONE NUMBER DIALED

Purpose: Determine with which machine a connection was last established or attempted.
Available on: All machines.
Registers at call:
AX = FF02h
Conflicts: None known.

Restrictions: Carbon Copy Plus 5.0 must be installed.
Return Registers:
ES:DI - > ASCIZ phone number

COMMUTE

One of the additions in PC Tools version 7 is a remote control program called COMMUTE. COMMUTE allows the machine it is run on to control another PC or be controlled by another PC. Features of COMMUTE include scripts, security control, and file transfers in addition to interactive remote control.

INTERRUPT 62h - Function 47h
Unknown Function

Purpose: *unknown.*
Available on: All machines.

Registers at call:
AH = 47h
AL = subfunction (00h-31h)
CF set
other *unknown.*
Conflicts: See chapter 1.

Restrictions: PC Tools 7 COMMUTE must be installed.
Return Registers: *unknown.*

INTERRUPT 62h - Function 48h
Unknown Function

Purpose: *unknown.*
Available on: All machines.

Registers at call:
AH = 48h
AL = *unknown.*
CF set
other *unknown.*
Conflicts: See chapter 1.

Restrictions: PC Tools 7 COMMUTE must be installed.
Return Registers: *unknown.*

INTERRUPT 62h - Function 49h
Unknown Function

Purpose: *unknown.*
Available on: All machines.

Registers at call:
AH = 49h
CF set
other *unknown.*
Conflicts: See chapter 1.

Restrictions: PC Tools 7 COMMUTE must be installed.
Return Registers: *unknown.*

INTERRUPT 62h - Function 4Ah
Unknown Function

Purpose: *unknown.*
Available on: All machines.

Registers at call:
AH = 4Ah
AL = subfunction (00h-46h)
CF set
other *unknown.*
Conflicts: See chapter 1.

Restrictions: PC Tools 7 COMMUTE must be installed.
Return Registers: *unknown.*

INTERRUPT 62h - Function 4Bh
Unknown Function

Purpose: *unknown.*
Available on: All machines.

Restrictions: PC Tools 7 COMMUTE must be installed.

Registers at call:
AH = 4Bh
BX = 1234h
CX = 1234h
ES = *unknown.*
CF set
Conflicts: See chapter 1.

Return Registers: *unknown.*

INTERRUPT 62h - Function 4Ch
Unknown Function

Purpose: *unknown.*
Available on: All machines.

Restrictions: PC Tools 7 COMMUTE must be
installed.

Registers at call:
AH = 4Ch
BL = subfunction (00h,02h,probably others)
CF set
other *unknown.*
Conflicts: See chapter 1.

Return Registers:
CF set on error
other *unknown.*

INTERRUPT 62h - Function 62h, Subfunction 62h
INSTALLATION CHECK

Purpose: Determine whether PC Tools 7 COMMUTE is installed.
Available on: All machines.

Restrictions: none.

Registers at call:
AX = 6262h
CF set
Conflicts: See chapter 1.

Return Registers:
AX = 0000h
BX = segment of resident code

LapLink
LapLink was one of the first to provide high-speed file transfers between PCs with incompatible floppy disk drives
using a direct connection. Quick Connect is distributed as part of PC Tools version 6; DeskConnect is distributed as
part of PC Tools version 7.

INTERRUPT 2Fh - Function D3h, Subfunction CBh
LapLink API

Purpose: Communicate with the LapLink file transfer programs.
Available on: All machines.

Restrictions: LapLink Quick Connect or DeskConnect
must be installed.

Registers at call:
AX = D3CBh
CX = function
   0002h get *configuration.*

  0003h *initialization*
  0004h *unknown.*
  0005h *initialization*
  0006h reset/clear *unknown flag/data*

  0007h *initialization*

Return Registers:
BX:AX -> *unknown code or data.*
CL = *unknown.*
CH = *unknown.*
DX = *unknown.*
DI = *COM1 I/O port*
SI = *COM2 I/O port*
CX = 534Bh

AX = 0000h
CX = 534Bh
ES:DI -> next byte after value cleared by this call
CX = 534Bh

0008h uninstall

BX = status
  0000h successful
  FFFFh incomplete, stub remains in
    memory
CX = 534Bh

pcANYWHERE

pcANYWHERE is a remote-control program by Dynamic Microprocessor Associates.

INTERRUPT 16h - Function 75h
SET TICK COUNT FOR SCANNING

Purpose: Specify how often pcANYWHERE transmits screen changes to the controlling PC.
Available on: All machines.
Registers at call:
AH = 75h
AL = number of ticks between checks for new
    screen changes
Conflicts: None known.

Restrictions: pcANYWHERE III must be installed.
Return Registers: n/a

INTERRUPT 16h - Function 76h
SET ERROR CHECKING TYPE

Purpose: Specify the error correction to be used on the connection between the two PCs.
Available on: All machines.
Registers at call:
AH = 76h
AL = error checking type
    00h none
    01h fast
    02h slow
Conflicts: None known.

Restrictions: pcANYWHERE III must be installed.
Return Registers: n/a

INTERRUPT 16h - Function 77h
LOG OFF

Purpose: Terminate the connection with a remote machine.
Available on: All machines.
Registers at call:
AH = 77h
AL = mode
    00h wait for another call
    01h leave in Memory Resident Mode
    02h leave in Automatic Mode
    FFh leave in current operating mode
Conflicts: WATCH.COM Installation Check (chapter 36), PC Magazine PUSHDIR.COM INSTALLATION
CHECK (chapter 36).

Restrictions: pcANYWHERE III must be installed.
Return Registers: n/a

INTERRUPT 16h - Function 79h
CHECK STATUS

Purpose: Determine whether pcANYWHERE III is loaded, and if so, how it was loaded.
Available on: All machines.
Registers at call:
AH = 79h

Restrictions: none.
Return Registers:
AX = status
    FFFFh if resident and active
    FFFEh if resident but not active

FFFDh if in Memory Resident mode
FFFCh if in Automatic mode
other value if not resident

Conflicts: None known.
See Also: Function 7Bh Subfunction 00h, INT 21h Function 2Bh Subfunction 44h

INTERRUPT 16h - Function 7Ah
CANCEL SESSION

Purpose: Abort the current connection.
Available on: All machines.   **Restrictions:** pcANYWHERE III must be installed.
Registers at call: **Return Registers:** n/a
AH = 7Ah
Conflicts: None known.

INTERRUPT 16h - Function 7Bh, Subfunction 00h
SUSPEND

Purpose: Temporarily disable pcANYWHERE to allow other uses of the serial port such as file transfers.
Available on: All machines.   **Restrictions:** pcANYWHERE III must be installed.
Registers at call: **Return Registers:** n/a
AX = 7B00h
Conflicts: None known.
See Also: Function 79h, Function 7Bh Subfunction 01h

INTERRUPT 16h - Function 7Bh, Subfunction 01h
RESUME

Purpose: Enable pcANYWHERE after other use of the serial port is complete.
Available on: All machines.   **Restrictions:** pcANYWHERE III must be installed.
Registers at call: **Return Registers:** n/a
AX = 7B01h
Conflicts: None known.
See Also: Function 79h, Function 7Bh Subfunction 00h

INTERRUPT 16h - Function 7Ch
GET PORT CONFIGURATION

Purpose: Determine which serial port and what speed pcANYWHERE is using.
Available on: All machines.   **Restrictions:** pcANYWHERE III must be installed.
Registers at call: **Return Registers:**
AH = 7Ch   AH = port number
AL = baud rate
     00h = 50
     01h = 75
     02h = 110
     03h = 134.5
     04h = 150
     05h = 300
     06h = 600
     07h = 1200
     08h = 1800
     09h = 2000
     0Ah = 2400
     0Bh = 4800
     0Ch = 7200

                                           0Dh = 9600
                                           0Eh = 19200

INTERRUPT 16h - Function 7Dh
GET/SET TERMINAL PARAMETERS

Purpose: Determine or specify the parameters to be used by the terminal emulation.

Available on: All machines.   **Restrictions:** pcANYWHERE III must be installed.

Registers at call: **Return Registers:** n/a

AH = 7Dh

AL = subfunction

    00h set terminal parameters

    01h get terminal parameters

    02h get configuration header and terminal
        parameters

DS:CX -> terminal parameter block

Conflicts: None known.

INTERRUPT 16h - Function 7Eh
COMMUNICATIONS I/O THROUGH PORT

Purpose: Permit data transfer over the same serial port being used for remote control.

Available on: All machines.   **Restrictions:** pcANYWHERE III must be installed.

Registers at call: **Return Registers:** n/a

AH = 7Eh

AL = subfunction

    01h port input status

        Return AX = 0 if no character ready,

            AX = 1 if character ready

    02h port input character

        Return AL = received character

    03h port output character in CX

    11h hang up phone

Conflicts: None known.

INTERRUPT 16h - Function 7Fh
SET KEYBOARD/SCREEN MODE

Purpose: Specify which machine's keyboard is to be active, which portion of the screen to display, and what type of hardware is being used for the remote control connection.

Available on: All machines.   **Restrictions:** pcANYWHERE III must be installed.

Registers at call: **Return Registers:** n/a

AH = 7Fh

AL = subfunction

    00h enable remote keyboard only

    01h enable host keyboard only

    02h enable both keyboards

    08h display top 24 lines

    09h display bottom 24 lines

    10h Hayes modem

    11h other modem

    12h direct connect

Conflicts: None known.

INTERRUPT 21h - Function 2Bh, Subfunction 44h
pcANYWHERE IV - INSTALLATION CHECK

Purpose: Determine whether pcANYWHERE IV is installed, and if so, the address to call in order to request services.

Available on: All machines.

Registers at call:
AX = 2B44h ('D')
BX = 4D41h ('MA')
CX = 7063h ('pc')
DX = 4157h ('AW')

Restrictions: none.

Return Registers:
AX = 4F4Bh ('OK') if loaded and *unknown condition*
  = 6F6Bh ('ok') if loaded and *unknown condition*
CX:DX -> API entry point

Details: Call the API entry point with:
        AX = 0000h *unknown*
          = 0003h *suspend*
          = 0004h *resume*

Conflicts: PC Tools v5.1 PC-CACHE (chapter 6), DOS Set System Date (chapter 8), DESQview Installation Check (chapter 15), ELRES v1.1 (chapter 36), TAME (chapter 36).

See Also: INT 16h Function 79h

TeleReplica

TeleReplica is a shareware remote control program by Douglas Thomson.

INTERRUPT 2Fh - Function D3h, Subfunction 00h
INSTALLATION CHECK

Purpose: Determine whether TeleReplica is installed.

Available on: All machines.

Registers at call:
AX = D300h
BX = 4562h
CX = 2745h
DX = *unknown*. (03F8h for v3.9)

Restrictions: none.

Return Registers:
SI = segment of resident code
AX = 251Dh
BX = DF21h
CX = F321h
DX = *unknown*.

Conflicts: None known.

Chapter 29

Communicating Applications Specification

The DCA/Intel Communicating Applications Specification was developed as a joint effort by Digital Communications Associates, Inc., and Intel Corporation. It was originally intended to define a standard, high-level programming interface for data communications applications, that would be independent of the hardware and software involved. It is rapidly becoming a *de facto* standard for fax modem applications; a recent industry survey showed that nearly half the fax-card vendors who responded claimed to use CAS-compliant software, while the remaining vendors were all using unique proprietary formats.

To be CAS-compliant, a system must provide a "Resident Manager" (which may be either a conventional TSR, a device driver, or a Windows DLL) that supports the functions listed in this chapter. Applications then use these functions to communicate with the Resident Manager, which provides the actual hardware interfacing.

INTERRUPT 2Fh - Function CBh, Subfunction 00h
INSTALLATION CHECK

Purpose: Determine whether a CAS-compliant driver is present.

Available on: All machines.

Registers at call:
AX = CB00h

Restrictions: none.

Return Registers:
AL = 00h not installed, OK to install
01h not installed, not OK to install
FFh installed

Details: CBh is the default multiplex number, but it may be reconfigured.
Conflicts: None known.
See Also: Function CBh Subfunction 0Eh

INTERRUPT 2Fh - Function CBh, Subfunction 01h
SUBMIT A TASK

Purpose: Request that some action be performed at a later time.

Available on: All machines.

Registers at call:
AX = CB01h
DS:DX -> ASCIZ name of task control file

Restrictions: CAS-compliant driver must be installed.

Return Registers:
AX > = 0: event handle
<0: error code (Table 29-1)

Details: The files needed for an event must be kept until the task is complete or an error occurs.
Conflicts: None known.
See Also: Function CBh Subfunctions 0Bh and 15h

Table 29-1. Values of Error Codes (AH = class, AL = subcode, value passed back is 2's complement):

Class	Subcode	Meaning
00h		--- FAX warnings
	00h	no error
	02h	bad scanline count
	03h	page sent with errors, could not retransmit
	04h	received data lost
	05h	invalid or missing logo file

Table 29-1. Values of Error Codes (continued)

Class	Subcode	Meaning
	06h	filename does not match nonstandard format (NSF) header
	07h	file size does not match NSF header
01h		--- *DOS warnings (data was sent)*
	01h	invalid function
	05h	access denied
	06h	invalid handle
	others	see DOS INT 21h Function 59h (chapter 8)
02h		--- *fatal errors (data not sent)*
	00h	multiplex handler failed
	01h	unknown command
	02h	bad event handle
	03h	FIND NEXT attempted before FIND FIRST
	04h	no more events
	07h	invalid queue type
	08h	bad control file
	09h	communication board busy
	0Ah	invalid command parameter
	0Bh	can't uninstall resident code
	0Ch	file exists
	80h	unknown task type
	81h	bad phone number
	82h	bad .PCX file header
	83h	unexpected EOF
	84h	unexpected disconnect
	85h	too many dialing retries
	86h	no file specified for send
	87h	communication board timeout
	88h	received too many pages (>1023) of data
	89h	manual connect initiated too long ago
	8Ah	hardware command set error
	8Bh	bad NonStandard Format (NSF) header file
03h		--- *fatal DOS errors*
	02h	file not found
	03h	path not found
	others	see INT 21h Function 59h (chapter 8)
04h		--- *FAX errors*
	01h	remote unit not Group 3 compatible
	02h	remote unit did not send capabilities
	03h	other FAX machine incompatible
	04h	other FAX incapable of file transfers
	05h	exceeded retrain or FAX resend limit
	06h	line noise or failure to agree on bit rate
	07h	remote disconnected after receiving data
	08h	no response from remote after sending data
	09h	remote's capabilities incompatible
	0Ah	no dial tone (v1.2+)
	0Bh	invalid response from remote unit after sending data
	0Dh	phone line dead or remote unit disconnected
	0Eh	timeout while waiting for secondary dial tone (v1.2+)
	11h	invalid command from remote after receiving data
	15h	tried to receive from incompatible hardware
	5Ch	received data overflowed input buffer
	5Dh	remote unexpectedly stopped sending data
	5Eh	other FAX machine jammed (no data sent)
	5Fh	remote took too long to send fax scan line

Table 29-1. Values of Error Codes (continued)

Class	Subcode	Meaning
	63h	can't get through to remote unit
	64h	user canceled event
05h		--- application-specific (v1.2+)
	---Intel FAXPOP.EXE	
	00h	tried to send while in graphics mode
	01h	insufficient disk space
	02h	internal buffer overflow
06h		--- CAS implementation-specific (v1.2+)

INTERRUPT 2Fh - Function CBh, Subfunction 02h
ABORT CURRENT EVENT

Purpose: Terminate the event currently in progress.
Available on: All machines.
Registers at call:
AX = CB02h

Restrictions: CAS-compliant driver must be installed.
Return Registers:
AX >= 0: event handle of aborted event
    < 0: error code (see Table 29-1)

Details: Termination could take up to 30 seconds.
Conflicts: None known.
See Also: Function CBh Subfunctions 08h and 10h

INTERRUPT 2Fh - Function CBh, Subfunction 05h
FIND FIRST QUEUE ENTRY

Purpose: Retrieve the first event matching the specified criteria.
Available on: All machines.
Registers at call:
AX = CB05h
CX = status of events to find
    0000h successful completion
    0001h waiting to be processed
    0002h number has been dialed
    0003h connection established, sending
    0004h connection established, receiving
    0005h event aborted
    FFFFh find any event, regardless of status
    other negative values, match error code
DH = direction
    00h chronological order, earliest to latest
    01h reverse chronological order, latest to
        earliest
DL = queue to search
    00h task queue
    01h receive queue
    02h log queue

Restrictions: CAS-compliant driver must be installed.
Return Registers:
AX = 0000h successful
BX = event handle for found event
    < 0 error code (see Table 29-1)

Conflicts: None known.
See Also: Function CBh Subfunctions 06h and 07h

INTERRUPT 2Fh - Function CBh, Subfunction 06h
FIND NEXT QUEUE ENTRY

Purpose: Retrieve the next event matching previously specified criteria.
Available on: All machines.

Restrictions: CAS-compliant driver must be installed.

Registers at call:
AX = CB06h
DL = queue to search
  00h task queue
  01h receive queue
  02h log queue

Return Registers:
AX = 0000h successful
BX = event handle for found event
  < 0   error code (see Table 29-1)

Details: The direction of search is the same as for the preceding FIND FIRST call.
Conflicts: None known.
See Also: Function CBh Subfunction 05h

INTERRUPT 2Fh - Function CBh, Subfunction 07h
OPEN FILE

Purpose: Prepare to read a received file or a control file.
Available on: All machines.
Registers at call:
AX = CB07h
BX = event handle from find (Subfunctions 05h or
  06h) or submit task (Subfunction 01h)
CX = receive file number (ignored for task queue
  and log queue)
  0000h open receive control file
  N   open Nth received data file
DL = queue
  00h task queue
  01h receive queue control file or received file,
    as given by CX
  02h log queue
  03h group file in task queue (v1.2+)
  04h group file in log queue (v1.2+)

Restrictions: CAS-compliant driver must be installed.
Return Registers:
AX = 0000h successful
BX = DOS file handle for requested file
  < 0   error code (see Table 29-1)

Details: The returned file handle has been opened in read-only mode and should be closed with DOS INT 21h Function 3Eh (chapter 8) after use.
Conflicts: None known.
See Also: Function CBh Subfunctions 01h, 05h, and 14h

INTERRUPT 2Fh - Function CBh, Subfunction 08h
DELETE FILE

Purpose: Erase a control file or received data file which is no longer needed.
Available on: All machines.
Registers at call:
AX = CB08h
BX = event handle
CX = receive file number
  0000h delete ALL received files and receive
    control file
  N   delete Nth received file
DL = queue
  00h delete control file in task queue and
    corresponding group file if it exists
  01h delete file in receive queue, as given by CX
  02h delete control file in log queue (individual
    deletions not recommended, to maintain
    integrity of log) and corresponding group
    file if it exists

Restrictions: CAS-compliant driver must be installed.
Return Registers:
AX = 0000h successful
  < 0   error code (see Table 29-1)

Conflicts: None known.
See Also: Function CBh Subfunctions 02h and 09h

INTERRUPT 2Fh - Function CBh, Subfunction 09h
DELETE ALL FILES IN QUEUE

Purpose: Erase all files of a particular type.
Available on: All machines.

Restrictions: CAS-compliant driver must be installed.

Registers at call:
AX = CB09h
DL = queue
    00h delete all control files in task queue,
        including all group files
    01h delete all files in receive queue
    02h delete all control files in log queue,
        including all group files

Return Registers:
AX = 0000h successful
    < 0 error code (see Table 29-1)

Conflicts: None known.
See Also: Function CBh Subfunction 08h

INTERRUPT 2Fh - Function CBh, Subfunction 0Ah
GET EVENT DATE

Purpose: Determine the day on which the specified event will occur.
Available on: All machines.

Restrictions: CAS-compliant driver must be installed.

Registers at call:
AX = CB0Ah
BX = event handle
DL = queue
    00h task queue
    01h receive queue
    02h log queue

Return Registers:
AX = 0000h successful
    CX = year
    DH = month
    DL = day
AX < 0 error code (see Table 29-1)

Conflicts: None known.
See Also: Function CBh Subfunctions 0Bh and 0Ch

INTERRUPT 2Fh - Function CBh, Subfunction 0Bh
SET TASK DATE

Purpose: Specify the date on which the indicated task should be performed.
Available on: All machines.

Restrictions: CAS-compliant driver must be installed.

Registers at call:
AX = CB0Bh
BX = event handle (task event only)
CX = year
DH = month
DL = day

Return Registers:
AX = 0000h successful
AX < 0 error code (see Table 29-1)

Details: Setting a task's date and time to before the current date and time causes it to execute immediately.
Conflicts: None known.
See Also: Function CBh Subfunctions 01h, 0Ah, and 0Dh

INTERRUPT 2Fh - Function CBh, Subfunction 0Ch
GET EVENT TIME

Purpose: Determine the time of day at which the specified event will occur.
Available on: All machines.

Restrictions: CAS-compliant driver must be installed.

Registers at call:
AX = CB0Ch
BX = event handle

Return Registers:
AX = 0000h successful
    CH = hour

DL = queue
  00h task queue
  01h receive queue
  02h log queue
Conflicts: None known.
See Also: Function CBh Subfunctions 0Ah and 0Dh

CL = minute
DH = second
DL = 00h
AX < 0 error code (see Table 29-1)

INTERRUPT 2Fh - Function CBh, Subfunction 0Dh
SET TASK TIME

Purpose: Specify the time of day at which the indicated task should be performed.
Available on: All machines.
Registers at call:
AX = CB0Dh
BX = event handle (task events only)
CH = hour
CL = minute
DH = second
DL unused

Restrictions: CAS-compliant driver must be installed.
Return Registers:
AX = 0000h successful
AX < 0 error code (see Table 29-1)

Details: Setting a task's date and time to before the current date and time causes it to execute immediately.
Conflicts: None known.
See Also: Function CBh Subfunctions 0Bh, 0Ch, and 10h

INTERRUPT 2Fh - Function CBh, Subfunction 0Eh
GET EXTERNAL DATA BLOCK

Purpose: Retrieve the CAS version, the names of various data files, and the identification of the attached FAX device.
Available on: All machines.
Registers at call:
AX = CB0Eh
DS:DX -> 256-byte buffer (Table 29-2)

Restrictions: CAS-compliant driver must be installed.
Return Registers:
AX = 0000h successful
  buffer filled
AX < 0 error code (see Table 29-1)

Conflicts: None known.

Table 29-2. Format of External Data Block:

Offset	Size	Description
00h	BYTE	CAS major version
01h	BYTE	CAS minor version
02h	68 BYTEs	ASCIZ path to directory containing CAS software, ends in slash
46h	13 BYTEs	ASCIZ name of current phonebook (in CAS directory)
53h	13 BYTEs	ASCIZ name of current logo file (in CAS directory)
60h	32 BYTEs	ASCIZ default sender name
80h	21 BYTEs	ASCIZ CCITT identification of fax device
95h	107 BYTEs	reserved

INTERRUPT 2Fh - Function CBh, Subfunction 0Fh
GET/SET AUTORECEIVE

Purpose: Specify or determine whether the FAX will automatically answer incoming calls.
Available on: All machines.
Registers at call:
AX = CB0Fh
DL = subfunction
  00h get current autoreceive state

Restrictions: CAS-compliant driver must be installed.
Return Registers:
AX = 0000h autoreceive disabled
  = N number of rings before answer
  < 0 error code (see Table 29-1)

01h set autoreceive state
DH = number of rings before answer, 00h = never
Conflicts: None known.

INTERRUPT 2Fh - Function CBh, Subfunction 10h
GET CURRENT EVENT STATUS

Purpose: Determine which event is currently executing and what its status is.

Available on: All machines.

Registers at call:
AX = CB10h
DS:DX -> 512-byte buffer (Table 29-3)

Restrictions: CAS-compliant driver must be installed.

Return Registers:
AX = 0000h successful
  BX = event handle of current event or negative
    error code if no current event
  buffer filled
AX < 0 error code (see Table 29-1)

Conflicts: None known.
See Also: Function CBh Subfunctions 02h and 0Dh

Table 29-3. Format of Status Area:

Offset	Size	Description
00h	BYTE	event type:
		00h send
		01h receive
		02h polled send
		03h polled receive
		04h to 7Fh reserved
		FFh serious hardware error
01h	BYTE	transfer type:
		00h 200x200 dpi, FAX mode
		01h 100x200 dpi, FAX mode
		02h file transfer mode
		03h to 7Fh reserved
02h	WORD	event status:
		0000h completed successfully
		0001h waiting
		0002h number dialed
		0003h connected, sending
		0004h connected, receiving
		0005h aborted
		0006h to 007Fh reserved
		0080h to 7FFFh application-specific events
		8000h to FFFFh error codes
04h	WORD	event time (packed DOS time format, see INT 21h Function 57h Subfunction 00h, chapter 8)
06h	WORD	event date (packed DOS date format, see INT 21h Function 57h Subfunction 00h, chapter 8)
08h	WORD	number of files to transfer, max 7FFFh
0Ah	WORD	offset of file transfer record
0Ch	47 BYTEs	ASCIZ phone number to call
3Bh	64 BYTEs	ASCIZ application-specific tag string
7Bh	BYTE	reserved (00h)
7Ch	BYTE	connect time, seconds
7Dh	BYTE	connect time, minutes

Table 29-3. Format of Status Area (continued)

Offset	Size	Description
7Eh	BYTE	connect time, hours
7Fh	DWORD	total number of pages in all files
83h	DWORD	pages already transmitted
87h	WORD	number of files already transmitted
89h	BYTE	cover page flag:
		00h don't transmit cover page
		01h transmit cover page
		02h to 7Fh reserved
8Ah	WORD	total number of transmission errors
8Ch	78 BYTEs	reserved (zeros)
DAh	21 BYTEs	ASCIZ remote FAX's CCITT identification
EFH	32 BYTEs	ASCIZ destination name
10Fh	32 BYTEs	ASCIZ sender name
12Fh	80 BYTEs	filename of PCX logo file (max 1780x800 pixels)
17Fh	128 BYTEs	file transfer record for current event (Table 29-4)

Table 29-4. Format of File Transfer Record:

Offset	Size	Description
00h	BYTE	file type (ignored unless FAX):
		00h ASCII
		01h PCX
		02h DCX
		03h to 7Fh reserved
01h	BYTE	text size for ASCII FAX file:
		00h = 80 columns by 66 lines (11 inches)
		01h = 132 columns by 88 lines (11 inches)
		02h to 7Fh reserved
02h	BYTE	status of file:
		00h untouched
		01h opened
		02h moved
		03h deleted
		04h not yet received
		05h to 7Fh reserved
03h	DWORD	bytes already transmitted
07h	DWORD	file size in bytes
0Bh	WORD	pages alread transmitted
0Dh	WORD	number of pages in file
0Fh	80 BYTEs	ASCIZ filename
5Fh	BYTE	1/8 inch page length. If page length below set to 01h through 7Fh, this value specifies additional 1/8 inch increments to page length
60h	BYTE	page length:
		00h = 11 inches
		01h to 7Fh = page length is this number of inches plus value of 1/8 inch field above
		80h to FEh reserved
		FFh = ASCII pages ending with formfeed
61h	31 BYTEs	reserved (zeros)

INTERRUPT 2Fh - Function CBh, Subfunction 11h
GET QUEUE STATUS

Purpose: Determine the state of the specified queue.

Available on: All machines.   **Restrictions:** CAS-compliant driver must be installed.

Registers at call:
AX = CB11h
DL = queue to get status of
  00h task queue
  01h receive queue
  02h log queue

Return Registers:
AX >= 0   total number of changes made to queue,
       modulo 32768
  BX = number of control files currently in queue
  CX = number of received files (zero for task and
log   queues)
AX < 0 error code (see Table 29-1)

Conflicts: None known.
See Also: Function CBh Subfunction 12h

INTERRUPT 2Fh - Function CBh, Subfunction 11h
GET NUMBER OF SEND EVENTS

Purpose: Determine how many times transmissions were attempted and how many were successful.
Available on: All machines.

Restrictions: CAS 1.2-compliant driver must be installed.

Registers at call:
AX = CB11h
DL = 03h

Return Registers:
AX = number of successful sends since resident
    manager started
BX = number of unsuccessful sends, including
    warnings

Conflicts: None known.
See Also: Function CBh Subfunction 11h/DL=04h

INTERRUPT 2Fh - Function CBh, Subfunction 11h
GET NUMBER OF RECEIVE EVENTS

Purpose: Determine how many files and faxes have been received.
Available on: All machines.

Restrictions: CAS 1.2-compliant driver must be installed.

Registers at call:
AX = CB11h
DL = 04h

Return Registers:
AX = number of received file events since resident
    manager started
BX = number of received FAX events

Conflicts: None known.
See Also: Function CBh Subfunction 11h/DL=03h

INTERRUPT 2Fh - Function CBh, Subfunction 12h
GET HARDWARE STATUS

Purpose: Determine the current state of the FAX hardware.
Available on: All machines.
Registers at call:
AX = CB12h
DS:DX -> 128-byte status buffer (Tables 29-5, 29-6)

Restrictions: CAS-compliant driver must be installed.
Return Registers:
AX = 0000h successful
    buffer filled with hardware-dependent status
      information
AX < 0 error code (see Table 29-1)

Conflicts: None known.
See Also: Function CBh Subfunctions 10h and 11h

Table 29-5. Format of Status Buffer for Intel Connection CoProcessor:

Offset	Size	Description
00h	BYTE	bit flags:
		bit 7: hardware busy sending or receiving
		bit 6: last page of data
		bit 5: no data on current page

Table 29-5. Format of Status Buffer for Intel Connection CoProcessor (continued)

Offset	Size	Description
		bit 4: retransmit request for current page being transmitted
		bit 3: NSF mode active
		bits 2-0: reserved
01h	BYTE	number of kilobytes of free buffer space
02h	BYTE	page buffer status:
		bit 7: Connection CoProcessor has documents to send
		bits 6-0: number of pages in buffer
03h	BYTE	number of retries left for dialing number
04h	BYTE	page number to retransmit
05h	BYTE	communications status
		bit 7: originating call
		bit 6: FAX message to be sent
		bit 5: on line
		bit 4: ring detected and receive enabled
		bit 3: buffer dumped on receive
		bits 2-0: hardware sequence state
		000 idle
		001 dial
		010 answer
		011 transmit
		100 receive
		101 pre-message
		110 post-message
		111 disconnect
06h	BYTE	baud rate
		bit 7: reserved
		bits 6-4: baud rate
		000 = 300 baud (V.21 SDLC or HDLC mode)
		100 = 2400 baud (V.27 ter)
		101 = 4800 baud (V.27 ter)
		110 = 7200 baud (V.29)
		111 = 9600 baud (V.29)
		bits 3-0: reserved, should be 0110
07h	3 BYTEs	reserved
0Ah	BYTE	hardware status
		bit 7: modem option installed
		bit 6: Connection CoProcessor has control of DAA (not latched)
		bit 5: on line (not latched)
		bit 4: ring detected (not latched)
		bit 3: data in command buffer (not latched)
		bit 2: set if using DMA channel 1, clear if using DMA channel 3
		bit 1: line length compensation bit 1 set (not latched)
		bit 0: line length compensation bit 0 set (not latched)
0Bh	BYTE	switch states
		bit 7: reserved
		bit 6: unused
		bit 5: spare switch open
		bit 4: FAX ADR1 switch open
		bit 3: FAX ADR0 switch open
		bit 2: alternate interrupt switch open
		bit 1: COM SEL 1 switch open
		bit 0: COM SEL 0 switch open
		Note: valid combinations of bits 0-2 are
		000 COM2 IRQ3 IObase 2F8h
		001 COM1 IRQ4 IObase 3F8h
		010 COM4 IRQ3 IObase 2E8h
		011 COM3 IRQ4 IObase 3E8h

Table 29-5. Format of status buffer for Intel Connection CoProcessor (continued)

Offset	Size	Description
		110 COM4 IRQ2 IObase 2E8h
		111 COM3 IRQ5 IObase 3E8h
0Ch	BYTE	bit flags
		bit 7: reserved
		bit 6: auxiliary relay forced ON
		bit 5: modem select relay forced ON
		bit 4: offhook relay forced ON
		bit 3: 9600 bps enabled
		bit 2: 7200 bps enabled
		bit 1: 4800 bps enabled
		bit 0: 2400 bps enabled
0Dh	BYTE	reserved
0Eh	WORD	error count (only valid while busy, reset when idle)
10h	DWORD	size of nonstandard format (NSF) file in bytes
14h	BYTE	'A' if Connection CoProcessor board present
15h	9 BYTEs	reserved
1Eh	21 BYTEs	ASCIZ CCITT identification
33h	77 BYTEs	reserved

Table 29-6. Format of status buffer for Intel SatisFAXion board:

Offset	Size	Description
00h	BYTE	connection status flags
		bit 7: busy in T.30 CCITT fax protocol
		bit 6: data on current page/file (only used for block xfers)
		bit 5: retransmission of last page requested
		bit 4: in file transfer mode
		bit 3: data in buffer
		bit 2: data buffer dumped on receive
		bit 1: 200x100 dpi resolution instead of 200x200 dpi
		bit 0: data modem in use, FAX image modem not available
01h	BYTE	board state
		bit 7: reserved
		bit 6: handset jack active, data and FAX modems not available
		bits 5-3: current bit rate
		000 300 bps (V.21 HDLC)
		100 2400 bps (V.27 ter)
		101 4800 bps (V.27 ter)
		110 7200 bps (V.29)
		111 9600 bps (V.29)
		bits 2-0: T.30 CCITT protocol state
		000 idle
		001 dialing
		010 answering
		011 transmitting
		100 receiving
		101 pre-message
		110 post-message
		111 disconnect
02h	BYTE	number of KB free in buffer
03h	BYTE	number of pages or files in buffer
04h	BYTE	number of redials remaining on current number
05h	BYTE	FAX page number to retransmit
06h	BYTE	current page/file in block transfer
07h	BYTE	number of rings received (only if auto-answer enabled)
08h	WORD	error count

Table 29-6. Format of Status Buffer for Intel SatisFAXion board (continued)

Offset	Size	Description
0Ah	DWORD	length of file being transferred
0Eh	6 BYTEs	reserved
14h	BYTE	'B' if SatisFAXtion board present
15h	13 BYTEs	ASCIZ transfer agent name
22h	5 BYTEs	ASCIZ transfer agent version number
27h	13 BYTEs	ASCIZ resident loader name
34h	5 BYTEs	ASCIZ resident loader version number
39h	21 BYTEs	ASCIZ remote CSID
4Eh	13 BYTEs	ASCIZ resident manager name
5Bh	5 BYTEs	ASCIZ resident manager version number
60h	32 BYTEs	reserved

Details: The Intel Connection CoProcessor and SatisFAXtion may be distinguished by examining the byte at offset 14h.

INTERRUPT 2Fh - Function CBh, Subfunction 13h
GET DIAGNOSTICS RESULTS

Purpose: Determine whether the hardware passed its diagnostics.

Available on: All machines.

Restrictions: CAS-compliant driver must be installed.

Registers at call:
AX = CB13h
DL = 00h

Return Registers:
AX = 0040h in progress
>= 0   passed
< 0   hardware-dependent failure code
(Tables 29-7, 29-8)

Conflicts: None known.

See Also: Function CBh Subfunction 13h/DL=01h

Table 29-7.   Values of Intel Connection CoProcessor failure codes:

bit 3:   9600 bps FAX modem module failed
bit 2:   SDLC chip failed
bit 1:   RAM failed
bit 0:   ROM checksum failed
.i.Intel SatisFAXtion:failure codes;
.i.CAS:error codes;
.i.error codes:CAS;
.i.error codes:Intel SatisFAXtion;

Table 29-8. Values of Intel SatisFAXion failure codes:

bit 1:   2400 bps data modem failed
bit 0:   9600 bps FAX modem failed
.i.CAS:diagnostics;
.i.INT 2Fh:Function CBh;
.i.Multiplex function CBh:subfunction 13h;

INTERRUPT 2Fh - Function CBh, Subfunction 13h
START DIAGNOSTICS

Purpose: Request that diagnostics be performed on the FAX hardware.

Available on: All machines.

Restrictions: CAS-compliant driver must be installed.

Registers at call:
AX = CB13h
DL = 01h

Return Registers:
AX = 0000h successfully started
< 0 error code (see Table 29-1)

Conflicts: None known.

See Also: Function CBh Subfunction 13h/DL=00h

INTERRUPT 2Fh - Function CBh, Subfunction 14h
MOVE RECEIVED FILE

Purpose: Specify a new name for a file received from another system.

Available on: All machines.

Registers at call:

AX = CB14h

BX = event handle

CX = receive file number

    0001h first received file

    N   Nth received file

DS:DX -> ASCIZ string specifying new name for
file (must not exist)

Restrictions: CAS-compliant driver must be installed.

Return Registers:

AX = 0000h successful

    < 0 error code (see Table 29-1)

INTERRUPT 2Fh - Function CBh, Subfunction 15h
SUBMIT FILE TO SEND

Purpose: Request that the specified file be sent at the indicated time to the given destination.

Available on: All machines.

Registers at call:

AX = CB15h

DS:DX -> variable-length data area (Table 29-9)

Conflicts: None known.

See Also: Function CBh Subfunction 01h

Restrictions: CAS-compliant driver must be installed.

Return Registers:

AX >= 0 event handle

    < 0 error code (see Table 29-1)

Table 29-9. Format of Data Area:

Offset	Size	Description
00h	BYTE	transfer type:
		00h = 200x200 dpi, fax mode
		01h = 100x200 dpi, fax mode
		02h = file transfer mode
		03h to 7Fh reserved
01h	BYTE	text size:
		00h = 80 columns
		01h = 132 columns
		02h to 7Fh reserved
02h	WORD	time to send (DOS packed time format, see INT 21h Function 57h Subfunction 00h, chapter 8)
04h	WORD	date to send (DOS packed date format, see INT 21h Function 57h Subfunction 00h, chapter 8)
06h	32 BYTEs	ASCIZ destination name
26h	80 BYTEs	ASCIZ name of file to send
76h	47 BYTEs	ASCIZ phone number to dial
A5h	64 BYTEs	ASCIZ application-specific tag string
E5h	BYTE	reserved (00h)
E6h	BYTE	cover page:
		00h don't send cover page
		01h send cover page
		02h to 7Fh reserved
E7h	23 BYTEs	reserved (zeros)
FEh	variable	ASCIZ string containing text of cover page (if cover page flag set to 01h)

INTERRUPT 2Fh - Function CBh, Subfunction 16h
UNLOAD RESIDENT MANAGER

Purpose: Attempt to remove the CAS driver from memory.

Available on: All machines.

Registers at call:
AX = CB16h
BX = 1234h
CX = 5678h
DX = 9ABCh
Conflicts: None known.
See Also: Function CBh Subfunction 00h

Restrictions: CAS 1.2-compliant driver must be installed.
Return Registers:
AX = 0000h successful
   < 0 error code

INTERRUPT 2Fh - Function CBh, Subfunction 17h
SET COVER PAGE STATUS

Purpose: Specify whether a cover page should be sent ahead of the indicated transmission.

Available on: All machines.

Registers at call:
AX = CB17h
BX = event handle
CL = cover page status
   00h not read
   01h read by user
Conflicts: None known.

Restrictions: CAS 1.2-compliant driver must be installed.
Return Registers:
AX = 0000h successful
   < 0 error code

Chapter 30

Intel Image Processing Interface

The Image Processing Interface permits communication with Intel's printer controller products such as the Visual Edge.

INTERRUPT 2Fh - Function CDh, Subfunction 00h
INSTALLATION CHECK
Purpose: Determine whether Image Processing Interface is installed.

Available on: All machines.	**Restrictions:** none.
Registers at call:	**Return Registers:**
AX = CD00h	AL = 00h not installed, OK to install
	01h not installed, not OK to install
	FFh installed

Conflicts: SWELL.EXE (chapter 36).

INTERRUPT 2Fh - Function CDh, Subfunction 01h
SET DEVICE NAME
Purpose: Specify which device is to receive the printed output.

Available on: All machines.	**Restrictions:** Image Processing Interface must be installed.
Registers at call:	**Return Registewrs:**
AX = CD01h	AL = 00h successful
CX:BX - > ASCIZ character device name ("LPTn", "COMn", "PRN")	CX:BX -> internal character device name
	= 80h error

Conflicts: SWELL.EXE (chapter 36).

INTERRUPT 2Fh - Function CDh, Subfunction 02h
GET VERSION NUMBER
Purpose: Determine which version of the Image Processing Interface is present.

Available on: All machines.	**Restrictions:** Image Processing Interface must be installed.
Registers at call:	**Return Registers:**
AX = CD02h	AL = 00h/01h successful
	BH = major version number (BCD)
	BL = minor version number (BCD)
	= 80h error

Details: If AL = 01h on return, the IPI supports network redirection.
Conflicts: SWELL.EXE (chapter 36).

INTERRUPT 2Fh - Function CDh, Subfunction 03h
SELECT SCAN LINE
Purpose: Specify which scan line following function calls should manipulate.

Available on: All machines.	**Restrictions:** Image Processing Interface must be installed.

Registers at call:
AX = CD03h
BX = scan line
CX = requested density in dots per inch (300, 600, or 1200)

Return Registers:
AL = 00h successful
    CX = density at which scan line was mapped
    ES:DI -> start of scan line
AL = 80h unsuccessful
    = 81h scan line out of range
    = 82h unsupported scan line density
    = 83h out of memory

Conflicts: SWELL.EXE (chapter 36).

INTERRUPT 2Fh - Function CDh, Subfunction 04h
MOVE BITMAP TO SCANLINE

Purpose: Copy a portion of a graphic to the in-memory image of the current page.
Available on: All machines.

Restrictions: Image Processing Interface must be installed.

Registers at call:
AX = CD04h
CX:BX -> bitmap structure (Table 30-1)

Return Registers:
AL = 00h successful
    = 80h unsuccessful
    = 81h scan line out of range
    = 82h unsupported scan line density
    = 83h out of memory
    = 84h unrecognized source
    = 85h initialization error

Conflicts: SWELL.EXE (chapter 36).

Table 30-1. Format of Bitmap Structure:

Offset	Size	Description
00h	WORD	image source (0 = conventional memory, 1 = expanded memory)
02h	DWORD	pointer to image data
06h	WORD	scan line on which to place
08h	WORD	bit offset from start of scan line at which to place
0Ah	WORD	density of bitmap data (300, 600, or 1200 dpi)
0Ch	WORD	width in bits of data
0Eh	WORD	source logical page number
10h	WORD	source handle (only if source in expanded memory)
12h	WORD	source offset (only if source in expanded memory)

INTERRUPT 2Fh - Function CDh, Subfunction 05h
PRINT PAGE

Purpose: Output the final image of a page to the printer.
Available on: All machines.

Restrictions: Image Processing Interface must be installed.

Registers at call:
AX = CD05h

Return Registers:
AL = 00h successful
    = 80h unsuccessful

Details: Page image is retained, so multiple calls will print multiple copies of the page.
Conflicts: SWELL.EXE (chapter 36).

INTERRUPT 2Fh - Function CDh, Subfunction 06h
CLEAR PAGE

Purpose: Erase the in-memory image of the current page.
Available on: All machines.

Restrictions: Image Processing Interface must be installed.

Registers at call:
AX = CD06h

Return Registers:
AL = 00h successful
= 80h unsuccessful

Details: Palette is reset to default.
Conflicts: SWELL.EXE (chapter 36).

INTERRUPT 2Fh - Function CDh, Subfunction 07h
Reserved Function

Purpose: This function has been reserved by Intel and should not be called.
Available on: All machines.

Restrictions: Image Processing Interface must be installed.
Return Registers: *unknown.*

Registers at call:
AX = CD07h
Conflicts: SWELL.EXE (chapter 36).

INTERRUPT 2Fh - Function CDh, Subfunction 08h
SCREEN IMAGE

Purpose: Display a preview of the current page image.
Available on: All machines.

Restrictions: Image Processing Interface must be installed.

Registers at call:
AX = CD08h
CX:BX -> image structure (Table 30-2)

Return Registers:
AL = 00h successful
= 80h unsuccessful
= 81h scan line out of range
= 82h unsupported scan line density
= 83h out of memory
= 84h unrecognized source
= 85h initialization error

Conflicts: SWELL.EXE (chapter 36).

Table 30-2. Format of Image Structure:

Offset	Size	Description
00h	WORD	image source (0 = conventional memory, 1 = expanded memory)
02h	DWORD	pointer to image data
06h	WORD	horizontal position on paper of left edge (in 1200 dpi units)
08h	WORD	vertical position on paper of top edge (in 1200 dpi units)
0Ah	WORD	left cropping (currently must be zero)
0Ch	WORD	top cropping (currently must be zero)
0Eh	WORD	width (currently must be 8000h)
10h	WORD	height (currently must be 8000h)
12h	WORD	horizontal size of image in 1200 dpi units
14h	WORD	vertical size of image in 1200 dpi units
16h	WORD	aspect ratio (currently reserved)
18h	WORD	initialization flag (if 01h, initialization is performed)
1Ah	WORD	pixels per line of source data
1Ch	WORD	number of scan lines in source data
1Eh	WORD	number of scan lines in packet
20h	WORD	bits per pixel (1,2,4,6, or 8)
22h	WORD	pixels per byte (1,2,4, or 8)
24h	WORD	compression type (currently only 00h [uncompressed] supported)
26h	WORD	source page number (if in expanded memory)
28h	WORD	source handle (if in expanded memory)
2Ah	WORD	source offset (if in expanded memory)

INTERRUPT 2Fh - Function CDh, Subfunction 09h
LOAD SCREEN

Purpose: Specify the style, size, and angle of the half-toning screen to be used when printing.

Available on: All machines.

Restrictions: Image Processing Interface must be installed.

Registers at call:
AX = CD09h
CX:BX -> half-toning screen structure (Table 30-3)
Conflicts: SWELL.EXE (chapter 36).
See Also: Function CDh Subfunction 0Ah

Return Registers:
AL = 00h successful
  = 80h unsuccessful

Table 30-3. Format of Half-toning Screen Structure:

Offset	Size	Description
00h	BYTE	style: 44h ('D') diamond style
		4Ch ('L') line style
01h	BYTE	reserved (00h)
02h	WORD	frequency in lines per inch, Currently coerced to nearest of 50, 60, 68, 70, 75, 85, or 100
04h	WORD	screen angle in degrees (-360 to 360)
		currently coerced to nearest of -45, 0, 45, or 90

INTERRUPT 2Fh - Function CDh, Subfunction 0Ah
LOAD PALETTE

Purpose: Specify the correspondence between pixel values and colors.

Available on: All machines.

Restrictions: Image Processing Interface must be installed.

Registers at call:
AX = CD0Ah
CX:BX -> palette structure (Table 30-4)
Conflicts: SWELL.EXE (chapter 36).
See Also: Function CDh Subfunction 09h

Return Registers:
AL = 00h successful
  = 80h unsuccessful

Table 30-4. Format of Palette Structure:

Offset	Size	Description
00h	BYTE	bits per pixel for which palette is to be used (1,2,4,6, or 8)
01h	2**N	palette translation values, one per possible pixel value

Chapter 31

STSC APL*Plus/PC

APL is a mathematically-oriented programming language well-suited to manipulating vectors and matrices. In its original incarnation, it used the Greek alphabet and numerous special symbols as commands and operators. Such use of special symbols leads to compact but difficult-to-read code, and resulted in APL's reputation as a "write-only" language.

STSC, Inc. has been the major vendor of APL products on the IBM PC family, and has produced a number of interpreters over the years. Some include special display fonts to provide the original symbol set, while others allow the use of keywords rather than symbols. In addition to interpreters, STSC provides such varied products based on APL as programming tools and a spreadsheet manager for interfacing with Lotus 1-2-3.

INTERRUPT 86h
TERMINATE APL SESSION AND RETURN TO DOS
Purpose: Exit the APL interpreter.

Available on: All machines.

Registers at call: n/a

Conflicts: Basic interpreter (chapter 1), Relocated (by NETBIOS) INT 18 (chapter 27).

Restrictions: APL*Plus/PC must be running.

Return Registers: n/a

INTERRUPT 87h
Unknown Function
Purpose: *unknown.*

Available on: All machines.

Registers at call: *unknown*

Conflicts: BASIC interpreter (chapter 1).

Restrictions: APL*Plus/PC must be running.

Return Registers: *unknown.*

INTERRUPT 88h - Function 00h
CREATE OBJECT OF ARBITRARY RANK OR SHAPE
Purpose: Assign a new variable of the specified type and dimensions.

Available on: All machines.

Registers at call:
AL = 00h
BX = STPTR of the variable to be assigned
ES:SI - > model of type, rank, and shape (Table 31-1)

Conflicts: BASIC interpreter (chapter 1).
See Also: INT C8h

Restrictions: APL*Plus/PC must be running.

Return Registers:
ES:DI - > first data byte of object
DX:CX = number of elements in the object

Table 31-1. Format of Shape Model:

Offset	Size	Description
00h	BYTE	type: 01h character (2-byte dimension sizes)
		02h integer (2-byte dimension sizes)
		08h floating point (2-byte dimension sizes)
		11h character (4-byte dimension sizes)

Table 31-1. Format of Shape Model (continued)

Offset	Size	Description
		12h integer (4-byte dimension sizes)
		18h floating point (4-byte dimension sizes)
01h	BYTE	rank
02h	(note)	first dimension of shape
N	(note)	second dimension of shape

Note: May be WORD/DWORD as indicated by "type" value.

...

INTERRUPT 88h - Function 01h
CREATE CHARACTER SCALAR/VECTOR/MATRIX <64K IN SIZE

Purpose: Reserve storage for a character or a one- or two-dimensional array of characters.

Available on: All machines.   **Restrictions:** APL*Plus/PC must be running.

Registers at call: **Return Registers:**

AL = 01h   ES:DI -> object

AH = rank   CX = number of elements in the object

BX = STPTR of the variable to be assigned

CX = first dimension (if any)

DX = second dimension (if any)

Details: Each dimension must be 32767 or smaller.

Conflicts: BASIC interpreter (chapter 1).

See Also: Functions 02h and 08h, INT C8h

INTERRUPT 88h - Function 02h
CREATE INTEGER SCALAR/VECTOR/MATRIX <64K IN SIZE

Purpose: Reserve storage for an integer or a one- or two-dimensional array of integers.

Available on: All machines.   **Restrictions:** APL*Plus/PC must be running.

Registers at call: **Return Registers:**

AL = 02h   ES:DI -> object

AH = rank   CX = number of elements in the object

BX = STPTR of the variable to be assigned

CX = first dimension (if any)

DX = second dimension (if any)

Details: Each dimension must be 32767 or smaller.

Conflicts: BASIC interpreter (chapter 1).

See Also: Functions 01h and 08h, INT C8h

INTERRUPT 88h - Function 08h
CREATE FLOATING POINT SCALAR/VECTOR/MATRIX <64K IN SIZE

Purpose: Reserve storage for a floating point number or a one- or two-dimensional array of floating point numbers.

Available on: All machines.   **Restrictions:** APL*Plus/PC must be running.

Registers at call: **Return Registers:**

AL = 08h   ES:DI -> object

AH = rank   CX = number of elements in the object

BX = STPTR of the variable to be assigned

CX = first dimension (if any)

DX = second dimension (if any)

Details: Each dimension must be 32767 or smaller.

Conflicts: BASIC interpreter (chapter 1).

See Also: Functions 01h and 02h, INT C8h

INTERRUPT 88h - Function F5h
FORCE OBJECT INTO REAL WORKSPACE FROM VIRTUAL

Purpose: Copy the specified object into main memory if it is not currently there.

Available on: All machines.

Registers at call:

AL = F5h

BX = STPTR of object

Conflicts: BASIC interpreter (chapter 1).

See Also: INT C8h

Restrictions: APL*Plus/PC must be running.

Return Registers: n/a

INTERRUPT 88h - Function F6h
MAKE NAME IMMUNE FROM OUTSWAPPING

Purpose: Specify that the indicated object must remain in main memory.

Available on: All machines.

Registers at call:

AL = F6h

BX = STPTR of object

Conflicts: BASIC interpreter (chapter 1).

See Also: Functions F7h and F8h, INT C8h

Restrictions: APL*Plus/PC must be running.

Return Registers: n/a

INTERRUPT 88h - Function F7h
MAKE NAME ELIGIBLE FOR OUTSWAPPING

Purpose: Specify that the indicated object may be moved out of main memory if memory becomes scarce.

Available on: All machines.

Registers at call:

AL = F7h

BX = STPTR of object

Conflicts: BASIC interpreter (chapter 1).

See Also: Functions F6h and F8h, INT C8h

Restrictions: APL*Plus/PC must be running.

Return Registers: n/a

INTERRUPT 88h - Function F8h
REPORT WHETHER NAME IS ELIGIBLE FOR OUTSWAPPING

Purpose: Determine whether the indicated object may be moved out of main memory.

Available on: All machines.

Registers at call:

AL = F8h

BX = STPTR of object

Conflicts: BASIC interpreter (chapter 1).

See Also: Functions F6h and F7h, INT C8h

Restrictions: APL*Plus/PC must be running.

Return Registers:

BX = 0000h eligible

    0001h not eligible

INTERRUPT 88h - Function F9h
DETERMINE NAME STATUS

Purpose: Determine whether the indicated object name is available for use.

Available on: All machines.

Registers at call:

AL = F9h

ES:SI -> name

CX = length of name

Details: Does not force the name into the workspace.

Conflicts: BASIC interpreter (chapter 1).

See Also: Functions FEh and FFh, INT C8h

Restrictions: APL*Plus/PC must be running.

Return Registers:

CF set if name ill-formed or already in use

    BX = STPTR if already in symbol table

CF clear if name is available for use

    BX = 0000h

INTERRUPT 88h - Function FCh
DETERMINE IF MEMORY AVAIL WITHOUT GARBAGE COLLECTION

Purpose: Determine whether there is currently a block of free memory large enough to hold the specified memory request.

Available on: All machines.

Registers at call:
AL = FCh
BX = amount of memory needed (paragraphs)

Conflicts: BASIC interpreter (chapter 1).

See Also: Function FDh, INT C8h

Restrictions: APL*Plus/PC must be running.

Return Registers:
CF clear if memory available
CF set if a workspace compaction is required

INTERRUPT 88h - Function FDh
PERFORM GARBAGE COLLECTION AND RETURN AVAILABLE MEMORY

Purpose: Determine the free space after compacting all allocated memory in the workspace.

Available on: All machines.

Registers at call:
AL = FDh

Conflicts: BASIC interpreter (chapter 1).

See Also: Function FCh, INT C8h

Restrictions: APL*Plus/PC must be running.

Return Registers:
BX = number of paragraphs available in workspace

INTERRUPT 88h - Function FEh
CREATE NAME

Purpose: Store the specified name which will later be associated with an object.

Available on: All machines.

Registers at call:
AL = FEh
ES:SI -> name
CX = length of name

Conflicts: BASIC interpreter (chapter 1).

See Also: Functions F9h and FFh, INT C8h

Restrictions: APL*Plus/PC must be running.

Return Registers:
BX = STPTR of name
DX = interpreter's data segment

INTERRUPT 88h - Function FFh
DETERMINE NAME STATUS

Purpose: Determine whether the specified name is available for use, and create it if it did not already exist.

Available on: All machines.

Registers at call:
AL = FFh
ES:SI -> name
CX = length of name

Restrictions: APL*Plus/PC must be running.

Return Registers:
CF set if name ill-formed or already in use
    BX = STPTR if already in symbol table
CF clear if name is available for use
    BX = 0000h

Details: Forces the name into the workspace and makes it immune from outswapping.

Conflicts: BASIC interpreter (chapter 1).

See Also: Functions F9h and FEh, INT C8h

INTERRUPT 8Ah
PRINT SCREEN

Purpose: Dump the current contents of the screen to the printer.

Available on: All machines.

Details: This call is the same as INT 05h.

Conflicts: BASIC interpreter (chapter 1).

See Also: INT 05h (chapter 3), INT CAh

Restrictions: APL*Plus/PC must be running.

INTERRUPT 8Bh
BEEP

Purpose: Sound a beep.
Available on: All machines.
Registers at call: n/a
Details: This call is the same as printing a ^G via INT 21h Function 02h.
Conflicts: BASIC interpreter (chapter 1).
See Also: INT CBh, DOS INT 21h Function 02h (chapter 8)

Restrictions: APL*Plus/PC must be running.
Return Registers: n/a

INTERRUPT 8Ch
CLEAR SCREEN MEMORY

Purpose: Erase the display to blanks.
Available on: All machines.
Registers at call:
AX = flag
   0000h do not save display attributes
   0001h save attributes
Conflicts: BASIC interpreter (chapter 1).
See Also: INT CCh

Restrictions: APL*Plus/PC must be running.
Return Registers: n/a

INTERRUPT 90h
USED BY PORT 10 PRINTER DRIVER

Purpose: *unknown.*
Available on: All machines.
Registers at call: *unknown.*
Conflicts: BASIC interpreter (chapter 1).

Restrictions: APL*Plus/PC must be running.
Return Registers: *unknown.*

INTERRUPT 95h
DETERMINE R= SPACE

Purpose: *unknown.*
Available on: All machines.
Registers at call: *unknown.*
Details: Use only when the R= option is invoked on entering APL.
Conflicts: BASIC interpreter (chapter 1).

Restrictions: APL*Plus/PC must be running.
Return Registers: *unknown.*

INTERRUPT A0h
*USED BY APL/GSS*CGI GRAPHICS INTERFACE*

Purpose: Support the display of graphics.
Available on: All machines.
Registers at call: *unknown.*
Conflicts: BASIC interpreter (chapter 1).
See Also: INT 59h (chapter 5)

Restrictions: APL*Plus/PC must be running.
Return Registers: *unknown.*

INTERRUPT C6h through INT CCh
IDENTICAL TO INT 86h through INT 8Ch

Purpose: STSC moved its interrupts from 86h-8Ch to C6h-CCh, but did not delete the older interrupts.
Available on: All machines.
Registers at call: *unknown.*
Conflicts: BASIC interpreter (chapter 1).

Restrictions: APL*Plus/PC must be running.
Return Registers: *unknown.*

INTERRUPTS CDh and CEh
MAY BE USED IN FUTURE RELEASES

Purpose: STSC has indicated that it may use these interrupts in future releases of APL*Plus/PC.
Available on: All machines.   **Restrictions:** APL*Plus/PC must be running.
Registers at call: *unknown.*   **Return Registers:** *unknown.*
Conflicts: BASIC interpreter (chapter 1).

INTERRUPT CFh
DEFAULT LOW-RESOLUTION TIMER FOR QUAD MF FUNCTION

Purpose: *Time function execution.*
Available on: All machines.   **Restrictions:** APL*Plus/PC must be running.
Registers at call: *unknown.*   **Return Registers:** *unknown.*
Conflicts: BASIC interpreter (chapter 1).

INTERRUPTS D0h through DBh
MAY BE USED IN FUTURE RELEASES

Purpose: STSC has indicated that it may use these interrupts in future releases of APL*Plus/PC.
Available on: All machines.   **Restrictions:** APL*Plus/PC must be running.
Conflicts: BASIC interpreter (chapter 1), PC-MOS API on INT D4h (chapter 1).

INTERRUPT DCh
MAY BE USED IN FUTURE RELEASES

Purpose: STSC has indicated that it may use this interrupt in future releases of APL*Plus/PC.
Available on: All machines.   **Restrictions:** APL*Plus/PC must be running.
Registers at call: *unknown.*   **Return Registers:** *unknown.*
Conflicts: BASIC interpreter (chapter 1), PC/370 v4.1- - API (chapter 36).

INTERRUPT DDh
MAY BE USED IN FUTURE RELEASES

Purpose: STSC has indicated that it may use this interrupt in future releases of APL*Plus/PC.
Available on: All machines.   **Restrictions:** APL*Plus/PC must be running.
Registers at call: *unknown.*   **Return Registers:** *unknown.*
Conflicts: BASIC interpreter (chapter 1).

INTERRUPT DEh
Unknown Function

Purpose: *This interrupt appears to be the same as INT 16h.*
Available on: All machines.   **Restrictions:** APL*Plus/PC must be running.
Registers at call: *unknown.*   **Return Registers:** *unknown.*
Conflicts: BASIC interpreter (chapter 1).

INTERRUPT DFh
SAME AS INT 10h

Purpose: Alternate entry point for video services.
Available on: All machines.   **Restrictions:** APL*Plus/PC must be running.
Registers at call: **Return Registers:**
see INT 10h in chapter 5.   see INT 10h in chapter 5.
Conflicts: BASIC interpreter (chapter 1), Victor 9000 - SuperBIOS (chapter 4).
See Also: INT 10h

INTERRUPT E0h
RESTIME HIGH-RESOLUTION TIMER FOR QUAD MF FUNCTION

Purpose: *Time function execution.*
Available on: All machines.
Registers at call: *unknown.*
Conflicts: CP/M-86 function calls, BASIC interpreter (chapter 1), "Micro-128" virus (chapter 34).

Restrictions: APL*Plus/PC must be running.
Return Registers: *unknown.*

Chapter 32

ZIPKEY

ZIPKEY is a shareware resident ZIP code and area code database by Eric Isaacson.

INTERRUPT B3h - Function 70h
GET VERSION
Purpose: Determine whether ZIPKEY is present and if so, get its version.
Available on: All machines.
Restrictions: none.
Registers at call:
AH = 70h
Return Registers:
AH = major version
AL = minor version
CL = number of states and territories in the current
    database
DH = year of current database - 1900
DL = month of current database's file date

Details: If installed, the string "ZIPKEY" is present at offset 75h in the interrupt handler's segment, and the byte at 7Bh contains the API version number (00h for versions 1.x and 01h for version 2.0).
Conflicts: BASIC interpreter (chapter 1).

INTERRUPT B3h - Function 71h
CONVERT TWO-LETTER ABBREVIATION TO STATE CODE
Purpose: Determine the internal code number corresponding to the postal state code.
Available on: All machines.
Restrictions: ZIPKEY must be installed.
Registers at call:
AH = 71h
BX = abbreviation, in upper or lower case; BL is the
    first letter
Return Registers:
CF set on error
    AL = FFh
CF clear if successful
    AL = ZIPKEY state code

Conflicts: BASIC interpreter (chapter 1).
See Also: Function 72h

INTERRUPT B3h - Function 72h
CONVERT STATE CODE TO TWO-LETTER ABBREVIATION
Purpose: Determine the postal state code corresponding to the specified ZIPKEY internal code number.
Available on: All machines.
Restrictions: ZIPKEY must be installed.
Registers at call:
AH = 72h
BL = ZIPKEY state code
Return Registers:
CF clear if successful
    AX = abbreviation, in upper case; AL is the first
        letter
CF set on error
    AX destroyed

Conflicts: BASIC interpreter (chapter 1).
See Also: Functions 71h and 73h

INTERRUPT B3h - Function 73h
CONVERT STATE CODE TO STATE NAME

Purpose: Determine the name of the state for the indicated ZIPKEY internal code number.

Available on: All machines.

Registers at call:
AH = 73h
BL = ZIPKEY state code
ES:DI -> buffer for name

Restrictions: ZIPKEY must be installed.

Return Registers:
AX destroyed
CF clear if successful
    ES:DI points one byte beyond end of name
CF set on error

Conflicts: BASIC interpreter (chapter 1).
See Also: Function 72h

INTERRUPT B3h - Function 74h
CONVERT ZIPCODE TO ASCII DIGITS

Purpose: Generate a printable ZIP code into a user-specified buffer.

Available on: All machines.

Registers at call:
AH = 74h
DX = zipcode region (0-999)
CH = last two digits of zipcode (0-99)
ES:DI -> buffer

Restrictions: ZIPKEY must be installed.

Return Registers:
AX destroyed
CF clear if successful
    ES:DI points one byte beyond end of digit string
CF set on error

Conflicts: BASIC interpreter (chapter 1).

INTERRUPT B3h - Function 75h
LOOK UP STATE CODE FOR ZIPCODE

Purpose: Determine in which state the specified ZIP code is located.

Available on: All machines.

Registers at call:
AH = 75h
DX = zipcode region (0-999)
CH = last two digits of zipcode (0-99)

Restrictions: ZIPKEY must be installed.

Return Registers:
CF clear if successful
    AL = ZIPKEY state code
    BX = (version 2.0+) telephone area code
CF set on error (zipcode not found)
    AL = suggested state code, FFh if none

Details: This function does not check whether the individual ZIP code actually exists, only the region. The validity of a ZIP code may be checked with Function 76h.
Conflicts: BASIC interpreter (chapter 1).
See Also: Functions 76h and 79h

INTERRUPT B3h - Function 76h
LOOK UP CITY AND STATE FOR ZIPCODE

Purpose: Determine the exact location of the indicated ZIP code.

Available on: All machines.

Registers at call:
AH = 76h
DX = zipcode region (0-999)
CH = last two digits of zipcode (0-99)
ES:DI -> buffer for name

Restrictions: ZIPKEY must be installed.

Return Registers:
CF clear if successful
    AL = ZIPKEY state code
    BX = (version 2.0+) telephone area code
    ES:DI points one byte beyond end of the name
CF set on error
    AL = suggested state code, FFh if none
    ES:DI buffer filled with suggested city name

Conflicts: BASIC interpreter (chapter 1).
See Also: Functions 75h and 78h

INTERRUPT B3h - Function 77h
PLAY BACK EXIT KEY FOR ENTRY WITH GIVEN ZIPCODE

Purpose: Trigger stuffing of the keyboard buffer with a found entry as if the user had requested the action.

Available on: All machines.

Registers at call:
AH = 77h
DX = zipcode region (0-999)
CH = last two digits of zipcode (0-99)
BX = 16-bit BIOS keycode for a defined ZIPKEY
    alternate exit key

Restrictions: ZIPKEY must be installed.

Return Registers:
AX destroyed
CF clear if successful
    zipcode specification as defined by the BX
    keystroke is placed in keyboard buffer, as if the
    user had popped up ZIPKEY and exited by
    pressing the key specified by BX
CF set on error

Conflicts: BASIC interpreter (chapter 1).

INTERRUPT B3h - Function 78h
LOOK UP ZIPCODES FOR A GIVEN STATE AND CITY

Purpose: Determine the ZIP codes located in a specific city.

Available on: All machines.

Registers at call:
AH = 78h
BL = ZIPKEY state code
DS:SI -> city name, terminated with 0Dh if
    complete name, 00h if prefix

Restrictions: ZIPKEY must be installed.

Return Registers:
AX destroyed
BH = number of matching entries (set to 51 if more
    than 50)
DX = zipcode region of first match (0-999)
CL = last two digits of first zipcode in the range (0-99)
CH = last two digits of last zipcode in the range (0-99)

Conflicts: BASIC interpreter (chapter 1).
See Also: Functions 79h and 7Ah

INTERRUPT B3h - Function 79h
LOOK UP ZIPCODES FOR A GIVEN CITY

Purpose: Determine the states for all cities with the given name, and the ZIP codes located in those cities.

Available on: All machines.

Registers at call:
AH = 79h
BL = ZIPKEY state code of first state to search
DS:SI -> city name, terminated with 0Dh if
    complete name, 00h if prefix

Restrictions: ZIPKEY must be installed.

Return Registers:
AL = ZIPKEY state code of first matching state
BH = number of matching entries (set to 51 if more
    than 50)
DX = zipcode region of first match (0-999)
CL = last two digits of first zipcode in first range
    (0-99)
CH = last two digits of last zipcode in first range
    (0-99)

Details: To find all matching cities, repeat search with BL set to one more than the returned AL.
Conflicts: BASIC interpreter (chapter 1).
See Also: Functions 78h and 7Ah

INTERRUPT B3h - Function 7Ah
FETCH AN ENTRY FROM A PREVIOUS LOOKUP

Purpose: Retrieve one of the matches from the last search.

Available on: All machines.

Restrictions: ZIPKEY must be installed.

Registers at call:
AH = 7Ah
BL = case number (0 to one less than value returned
   in BH by lookup)

Conflicts: BASIC interpreter (chapter 1).
See Also: Functions 78h and 79h

Return Registers:
AL = ZIPKEY state code
DX = zipcode region (0-999)
CL = last two digits of first zipcode in the range (0-99)
CH = last two digits of last zipcode in the range (0-99)

INTERRUPT B3h - Function 7Bh
GET VALUES NEEDED TO SAVE ZIPKEY CONTEXT

Purpose: Determine the current state of a search for later restoration.
Available on: All machines.
Registers at call:
AH = 7Bh

Restrictions: ZIPKEY must be installed.
Return Registers:
AX destroyed
BL = maximum number of characters for a city name
BH = ZIPKEY state code for last city-name search
   FFh if none
CX:DX = internal code identifying last city search

Conflicts: BASIC interpreter (chapter 1).
See Also: Function 7Ch

INTERRUPT B3h - Function 7Ch
RESTORE ZIPKEY CONTEXT

Purpose: Reset searching to a previous state.
Available on: All machines.
Registers at call:
AH = 7Ch
BL = maximum number of characters for a city
   name
BH = ZIPKEY state code for last city-name search
   FFh if none
CX:DX = internal code returned by Function 7Bh
Conflicts: BASIC interpreter (chapter 1).
See Also: Function 7Bh

Restrictions: ZIPKEY must be installed.
Return Registers:
AX destroyed
CF clear if successful
CF set on error

INTERRUPT B3h - Function 7Dh
REQUEST POP UP

Purpose: Trigger the TSR pop-up sequence as though the user had pressed the hotkey.
Available on: All machines.
Registers at call:
AH = 7Dh
BL = index number to simulate pressing a hotkey
   FFh for immediate popup with no playback on
      return

Conflicts: BASIC interpreter (chapter 1).

Restrictions: ZIPKEY must be installed.
Return Registers:
CF clear if successful
   AX destroyed
   window popped up and was closed by the user
CF set on error
   AL = FDh already busy with another request
      = FEh illegal function

INTERRUPT B3h - Function 7Eh
GET NAME OF PRIMARY CITY FOR A ZIPCODE REGION

Purpose: Translate ZIP code to primary city name.
Available on: All machines.

Restrictions: ZIPKEY must be installed.

Registers at call:
AH = 7Eh
DX = zipcode region (0-999)
ES:DI -> buffer for name

Return Registers:
CF clear if successful
    AL = ZIPKEY state code
    BX = (version 2.0+) telephone area code
    ES:DI points one byte beyond end of the name
CF set on error
    AL = FFh region does not exist

Conflicts: BASIC interpreter (chapter 1).

INTERRUPT B3h - Function 7Fh
ENABLE/DISABLE HOTKEYS

Purpose: Control hotkey actions.
Available on: All machines.
Registers at call:
AH = 7Fh
BL = function
    00h turn off hotkeys
    01h turn on hotkeys
    02h return hotkey status
    03h toggle hotkey status
Conflicts: BASIC interpreter (chapter 1).

Restrictions: ZIPKEY must be installed.
Return Registers:
AL = hotkey status
    00h off
    01h on

INTERRUPT B3h - Function 80h
DETERMINE STATE FOR AREA CODE

Purpose: Given a telephone area code, determine which state contains that area code and the range of ZIP codes for the state.
Available on: All machines.

Registers at call:
AH = 80h
BX = telephone area code (decimal)

Restrictions: ZIPKEY version 2.0 or higher must be installed.
Return Registers:
CF clear if successful
    AL = ZIPKEY state code
    DX = first zip region for state, 03E8h (1000) if Canada
    CX = number of zip regions in state
CF set if error (no such area code)
    AL = FFh
    DX = 03E9h (1001)

Conflicts: BASIC interpreter (chapter 1).

Chapter 33

PC Tools

PC Tools by Central Point Software has been described as the "Swiss Army knife of software." While many software packages perform individual functions more quickly or more efficiently, few contain the sheer functionality of PC Tools. In addition to a DOS shell; desktop utilities such as calculators, notepads, data base retrieval, appointment calendar, and communications; hard disk backup; and data recovery utilities, PC Tools contains numerous other programs.

PC Tools version 7 was released as this book was written. Thus, the version 7 information presented here is quite preliminary and even sketchier than the remainder of the API (which is entirely undocumented). Calls which do not explicitly mention version 7 may have changed between versions 6 and 7; further, many of the calls marked "version 5.1 or higher" may have been present in earlier versions, although we do not have any information on versions prior to 5.1.

INTERRUPT 16h - Function 6969h, Subfunction 6968h
UNHOOK BACKTALK

Purpose: Restore the interrupt vectors which were hooked by BACKTALK in preparation for unloading.

Available on: All machines.

Restrictions: PC Tools version 5.1 or higher
BACKTALK must be installed.

Registers at call:
AX = 6969h
BX = 6968h
Conflicts: None known.

Return Registers:
resident code unhooked, but not removed from
memory

INTERRUPT 16h - Function 6969h, Subfunction 6969h
BACKTALK INSTALLATION CHECK

Purpose: Determine whether PC Tools version 5.1 or higher BACKTALK is installed.

Available on: All machines.

Restrictions: none.

Registers at call:
AX = 6969h
BX = 6969h
DX = 0000h

Return Registers:
DX nonzero if installed
BX = CS of resident code
DX = PSP segment of resident code
DS:SI - > ASCIZ identification string "CPoint Talk"

Conflicts: None known.

INTERRUPT 16h - Function FEh, Subfunction A4h
Unknown Function

Purpose: The purpose of this function had not been determined at the time of writing.

Available on: All machines.

Restrictions: PC Tools version 7.0 CPSCHED or
DESKTOP must be installed.

Registers at call:
AX = FEA4h
other *unknown.*
Conflicts: None known.

Return Registers: *unknown.*

INTERRUPT 16h - Function FEh, Subfunction C6h
Unknown Function

Purpose: The purpose of this function had not been determined at the time of writing.
Available on: All machines.

Restrictions: PC Tools version 7.0 CPSCHED must be installed.
Return Registers: *unknown.*

Registers at call:
AX = FEC6h
DL = *unknown.*
Conflicts: None known.

INTERRUPT 16h - Function FEh, Subfunction D3h
Unknown Function

Purpose: The purpose of this function had not been determined at the time of writing.
Available on: All machines.

Restrictions: PC Tools version 7.0 CPSCHED or DESKTOP must be installed.
Return Registers: *unknown.*

Registers at call:
AX = FED3h
other *unknown.*
Conflicts: None known.

INTERRUPT 16h - Function FEh, Subfunction DCh
Unknown Function

Purpose: The purpose of this function had not been determined at the time of writing.
Available on: All machines.

Restrictions: PC Tools version 7.0 CPSCHED must be installed.
Return Registers: *unknown.*

Registers at call:
AX = FEDCh
other *unknown.*
Conflicts: None known.

INTERRUPT 16h - Function FEh, Subfunction EFh
INSTALLATION CHECK

Purpose: Determine whether the PC Tools scheduler is installed.
Available on: All machines.

Restrictions: PC Tools version 7.0 CPSCHED or DESKTOP must be installed.

Registers at call:
AX = FEEFh
CX = 0000h

Return Registers:
CX = ABCDh if PC Tools scheduler is installed
BX = segment of resident portion

Details: This call is identical to Function FFh Subfunction EFh for DESKTOP.
Conflicts: None known.

INTERRUPT 16h - Function FEh, Subfunction F1h
Unknown Function

Purpose: The purpose of this function had not been determined at the time of writing.
Available on: All machines.

Restrictions: PC Tools version 7.0 CPSCHED or DESKTOP must be installed.

Registers at call:
AX = FEF1h
other *unknown*.
Conflicts: None known.

Return Registers: *unknown*.

INTERRUPT 16h - Function FFh, Subfunctions 91h to 99h
Unknown Functions

Purpose: The purpose of these functions had not been determined at the time of writing.
Available on: All machines.

Restrictions: PC Tools version 7.0 DESKTOP must be installed.
Return Registers: *unknown*.

Registers at call:
AX = FF91h to FF9Bh
other *unknown*.
Conflicts: None known.

INTERRUPT 16h - Function FFh, Subfunction 9Ah
GET COLOR SCHEME

Purpose: Retrieve the name of the color scheme currently in use.
Available on: All machines.

Restrictions: PC Tools version 7.0 DESKTOP must be installed.

Registers at call:
AX = FF9Ah
Conflicts: None known.

Return Registers:
ES:BX -> ASCIZ name of current color scheme

INTERRUPT 16h - Function FFh, Subfunction 9Eh
Unknown Function

Purpose: The purpose of this function had not been determined at the time of writing.
Available on: All machines.

Restrictions: PC Tools version 7.0 DESKTOP must be installed.
Return Registers: *unknown*.

Registers at call:
AX = FF9Eh
other *unknown*.
Conflicts: None known.

INTERRUPT 16h - Function FFh, Subfunction A1h
Unknown Function

Purpose: The purpose of this function had not been determined at the time of writing.
Available on: All machines.

Restrictions: PC Tools version 7.0 DESKTOP must be installed.
Return Registers: *unknown*.

Registers at call:
AX = FFA1h
other *unknown*.
Conflicts: None known.

INTERRUPT 16h - Function FFh, Subfunction A2h
Unknown Function

Purpose: The purpose of this function had not been determined at the time of writing.
Available on: All machines.

Restrictions: PC Tools version 7.0 DESKTOP must be installed.
Return Registers: *unknown*.

Registers at call:
AX = FFA2h
other *unknown*.
Conflicts: None known.

INTERRUPT 16h - Function FFh, Subfunction A3h
DATAMON

Purpose: Control the operation of the DATAMON file protection program.

Available on: All machines.

Restrictions: PC Tools version 7.0 DATAMON must be installed.

Registers at call:
AX = FFA3h
BX = CX = function
    0000h installation check

Return Registers:

    AX = resident code segment
    BX = 5555h
    CX = 5555h

    0001h *unknown*

    AX:BX -> *unknown*.
    CX = BX

    0002h *unknown*

    AX = *unknown* (0000h or 0001h)
    CX = BX = AX

    0003h *unknown*

    AX = *unknown* (0000h or 0001h)
    CX = BX = AX

    0004h set *unknown* flag

    n/a

    0005h clear *unknown* flag

    n/a

    0006h *set current PSP*
DX = *current PSP as known to DOS*, or 0000h

    n/a

Conflicts: None known.

INTERRUPT 16h - Function FFh, Subfunction A4h
Unknown Function

Purpose: The purpose of this function had not been determined at the time of writing.

Available on: All machines.

Restrictions: PC Tools version 7.0 DESKTOP must be installed.

Registers at call:
AX = FFA4h
other *unknown*.

Return Registers: *unknown*.

Conflicts: None known.

INTERRUPT 16h - Function FFh, Subfunction A5h
PC-Cache

This function is described in chapter 6.

INTERRUPT 16h - Function FFh, Subfunction A6h
GET Unknown Pointer

Purpose: *unknown*.

Available on: All machines.

Restrictions: PC Tools version 6.0 or higher DESKTOP must be installed.

Registers at call:
AX = FFA6h

Return Registers:
DS:SI -> *unknown code or data*.

Conflicts: None known.

INTERRUPT 16h - Function FFh, Subfunction A7h
GET Unknown PATH

Purpose: *Apparently returns the location of the desktop's executable.*
Available on: All machines.

Registers at call:
AX = FFA7h

Conflicts: None known.

Restrictions: PC Tools version 6.0 or higher DESKTOP must be installed.

Return Registers:
DS:SI -> ASCIZ path (*directory from which PCTools was run*)

INTERRUPT 16h - Function FFh, Subfunction A8h
Unknown Function

Purpose: *unknown.*
Available on: All machines.

Registers at call:
AX = FFA8h
DS:SI -> three consecutive *unknown*
    ASCIZ strings (max 256 bytes
    total)
other *unknown.*

Restrictions: PC Tools version 6.0 or higher DESKTOP must be installed.
Return Registers: *unknown.*

Details: This function is only available when popped up. The specified strings are copied into internal buffer, among other actions.
Conflicts: None known.

INTERRUPT 16h - Function FFh, Subfunction A9h
GET VERSION STRING

Purpose: Retrieve a printable string identifying the version of PC Tools DESKTOP installed.
Available on: All machines.

Registers at call:
AX = FFA9h
Conflicts: None known.

Restrictions: PC Tools version 6.0 or higher DESKTOP must be installed.

Return Registers:
DS:SI -> version string

INTERRUPT 16h - Function FFh, Subfunction AAh
Unknown Function

Purpose: *unknown.*
Available on: All machines.

Registers at call:
AX = FFAAh
unknown.
Details: This function is only available when popped up.
Conflicts: None known.

Restrictions: PC Tools version 6.0 or higher DESKTOP must be installed.
Return Registers: *unknown.*

INTERRUPT 16h - Function FFh, Subfunction ABh
GET EDITOR SETTINGS

Purpose: *Determine the settings used by the desktop's editor.*
Available on: All machines.

Registers at call:
AX = FFABh

Restrictions: PC Tools version 6.0 or higher DESKTOP must be installed.

Return Registers:
DS:SI -> *editor setting strings*

Conflicts: None known.

INTERRUPT 16h - Function FFh, Subfunction ACh
SET Unknown Value

Purpose: *unknown.*
Available on: All machines.

Registers at call:
AX = FFACh
DL = *unknown.*
Details: This function is only available when popped up.
Conflicts: None known.

Restrictions: PC Tools version 6.0 or higher DESKTOP must be installed.
Return Registers: n/a

INTERRUPT 16h - Function FFh, Subfunction ADh
SET Unknown Value

Purpose: *unknown.*
Available on: All machines.

Registers at call:
AX = FFADh
DL = *unknown.*
Conflicts: None known.

Restrictions: PC Tools version 6.0 or higher DESKTOP must be installed.
Return Registers: n/a

INTERRUPT 16h - Function FFh, Subfunction AEh
GET Unknown Value

Purpose: Determine the value of an unknown flag or counter.
Available on: All machines.

Registers at call:
AX = FFAEh
Conflicts: None known.

Restrictions: PC Tools version 6.0 or higher DESKTOP must be installed.
Return Registers:
AL = *unknown.*

INTERRUPT 16h - Function FFh, Subfunction AFh
SET Unknown Value

Purpose: *unknown.*
Available on: All machines.

Registers at call:
AX = FFAFh
DL = *unknown.*
Conflicts: None known.

Restrictions: PC Tools version 6.0 or higher DESKTOP must be installed.
Return Registers: n/a

INTERRUPT 16h - Function FFh, Subfunction B0h
SET Unknown Value

Purpose: *unknown.*
Available on: All machines.

Registers at call:
AX = FFB0h
BL = *unknown.*
Conflicts: None known.

Restrictions: PC Tools version 6.0 or higher DESKTOP must be installed.
Return Registers: n/a

INTERRUPT 16h - Function FFh, Subfunction B1h
Unknown Function

Purpose: *unknown.*
Available on: All machines.

Registers at call:
AX = FFB1h
unknown.
Conflicts: None known.

Restrictions: PC Tools version 6.0 or higher DESKTOP must be installed.
Return Registers: *unknown.*

INTERRUPT 16h - Function FFh, Subfunction B2h
GET Unknown Pointer

Purpose: *unknown.*
Available on: All machines.

Registers at call:
AX = FFB2h
Conflicts: None known.

Restrictions: PC Tools version 5.5 or higher DESKTOP must be installed.
Return Registers:
DS:SI -> *unknown.*

INTERRUPT 16h - Function FFh, Subfunction B3h
Unknown Function

Purpose: *unknown.*
Available on: All machines.

Registers at call:
AX = FFB3h
unknown.
Details: This function is only available when popped up.
Conflicts: None known.

Restrictions: PC Tools version 5.5 or higher DESKTOP must be installed.
Return Registers: *unknown.*

INTERRUPT 16h - Function FFh, Subfunction B4h
SET Unknown FLAG

Purpose: *unknown.*
Available on: All machines.

Registers at call:
AX = FFB4h
Details: This function is available only when popped up.
Conflicts: None known.
See Also: Function FFh Subfunction BBh

Restrictions: PC Tools version 5.5 or higher DESKTOP must be installed.
Return Registers: n/a

INTERRUPT 16h - Function FFh, Subfunction B5h
GET/SET WINDOW PARAMETERS

Purpose: Determine or specify the window parameters for the indicated desktop application.
Available on: All machines.

Registers at call:
AX = FFB5h
BX = window specifier (000Fh to 0019h)
(Table 33-1)
DX = 0000h get, nonzero = set
ES:DI -> window parameter buffer (Table 33-2)

Restrictions: PC Tools version 5.5 or higher DESKTOP must be installed.
Return Registers: n/a

Details: If running in monochrome mode, character attributes at offsets 04h to 06h are stored unchanged, but attributes other than 07h, 0Fh, or 70h are changed to 07h on reading.
Conflicts: None known.
See Also: Function FFh Subfunction CBh

Table 33-1. Values for Window Specifier:

Value	Meaning
000Fh	comm/FAX
0014h	hotkey selection
0015h	ASCII table
0016h	system colors menu

Table 33-2. Format of Window Parameters:

Offset	Size	Description
00h	BYTE	rows in window, not counting frame
01h	BYTE	columns in window, not counting frame
02h	BYTE	row number of top of window
03h	BYTE	2*column number of left of window
04h	BYTE	character attribute for *unknown text*
05h	BYTE	character attribute for background/border
06h	BYTE	character attribute for *unknown text*
07h	DWORD	pointer to *unknown location* on screen
0Bh	4 BYTEs	*unknown.*
0Fh	BYTE	nonzero if window may be resized

INTERRUPT 16h - Function FFh, Subfunction B6h
GET Unknown Values

Purpose: *unknown.*
Available on: All machines.

Restrictions: PC Tools version 5.5 or higher DESKTOP must be installed.

Registers at call:
AX = FFB6h

Return Registers:
AH = *unknown.*
AL = *unknown.*

Conflicts: None known.

INTERRUPT 16h - Function FFh, Subfunction B7h
GET/SET Unknown Buffer

Purpose: *unknown.*
Available on: All machines.

Restrictions: PC Tools version 5.5 or higher DESKTOP must be installed.

Registers at call:
AX = FFB7h
BX = direction
  0000h copy to buffer
  else copy from buffer
DS:SI -> 70-byte buffer with *unknown data*

Return Registers:
data copied

Details: This function is available only when popped up under version 6.0 or higher.
Conflicts: None known.

INTERRUPT 16h - Function FFh, Subfunction B8h
GET/SET Unknown Values

Purpose: *unknown.*

Available on: All machines.

Registers at call:
AX = FFB8h
BH = subfunction
  00h get

  nonzero set
    BL = new value for *unknown*
    CL = new value for *unknown* (v6.0+)
    CH = new value for *unknown* (v6.0+)
    DH = *unknown*.
Conflicts: None known.

Restrictions: PC Tools version 5.1 or higher DESKTOP must be installed.
Return Registers:

BL = old value of *unknown*
CL = old value of *unknown* (v6.0+)
CH = old value of *unknown* (v6.0+)

AL = old value replaced by CL (v6.0+)
AH = old value replaced by CH (v6.0+)

INTERRUPT 16h - Function FFh, Subfunction B9h
Unknown Function

Purpose: *unknown*.
Available on: All machines.

Registers at call:
AX = FFB9h
unknown.

Conflicts: None known.

Restrictions: PC Tools version 5.1 or higher DESKTOP must be installed.
Return Registers:
AX = *unknown*.
CX = *unknown*.
DS:SI -> *unknown*.
ES:DI -> *unknown*.

INTERRUPT 16h - Function FFh, Subfunction BAh
Unknown Function

Purpose: *unknown*.
Available on: All machines.

Registers at call:
AX = FFBAh
unknown.
Details: This function is only available when popped up.
Conflicts: None known.

Restrictions: PC Tools version 5.1 or higher DESKTOP must be installed.
Return Registers:
AX = *unknown*.

INTERRUPT 16h - Function FFh, Subfunction BBh
CLEAR Unknown FLAG

Purpose: *unknown*.
Available on: All machines.

Registers at call:
AX = FFBBh
Details: This function is only available when popped up.
Conflicts: None known.
See Also: Function FFh Subfunction B4h

Restrictions: PC Tools version 5.1 or higher DESKTOP must be installed.
Return Registers: n/a

INTERRUPT 16h - Function FFh, Subfunction BCh
RESTORE ORIGINAL SCREEN

Purpose: *Restore the display to its state at the time the desktop was started or popped up.*

Available on: All machines.

Registers at call:
AX = FFBCh
Conflicts: None known.

Restrictions: PC Tools version 5.1 or higher DESKTOP must be installed.
Return Registers: n/a

INTERRUPT 16h - Function FFh, Subfunction BDh
DATABASE INDEXING MESSAGES

Purpose: *unknown.*
Available on: All machines.

Registers at call:
AX = FFBDh
unknown.
Conflicts: None known.

Restrictions: PC Tools version 5.1 or higher DESKTOP must be installed.
Return Registers: *unknown.*

INTERRUPT 16h - Function FFh, Subfunction BEh
Unknown Function

Purpose: *unknown.*
Available on: All machines.

Registers at call:
AX = FFBEh
unknown.
Details: This function is only available when popped up.
Conflicts: None known.

Restrictions: PC Tools version 5.1 or higher DESKTOP must be installed.
Return Registers: *unknown.*

INTERRUPT 16h - Function FFh, Subfunction BFh
Unknown Function

Purpose: *unknown.*
Available on: All machines.

Registers at call:
AX = FFBFh
BX = DOS file handle to write on
other *unknown.*
Details: This function is only available when popped up.
Conflicts: None known.

Restrictions: PC Tools version 5.1 or higher DESKTOP must be installed.
Return Registers: *unknown.*

INTERRUPT 16h - Function FFh, Subfunction C0h
Unknown Function

Purpose: *unknown.*
Available on: All machines.

Registers at call:
AX = FFC0h
unknown.
Details: This function is only available when popped up.
Conflicts: None known.

Restrictions: PC Tools version 5.1 or higher DESKTOP must be installed.
Return Registers:
AX = 0000h if successful
AX = FFFFh on error

INTERRUPT 16h - Function FFh, Subfunction C1h
Unknown Function

Purpose: *unknown.*

Available on: All machines.

Registers at call:
AX = FFC1h
BL = *unknown.*
ES:DI -> data structure (Table 33-3)
other registers, if any, unknown.
Details: This function is only available when popped up.
Conflicts: None known.

Table 33-3. Format of Data Structure:

Offset	Size	Description
00h	WORD	*unknown.*
02h	WORD	*unknown.*
04h	WORD	*unknown.*
06h	WORD	*unknown.*
08h	WORD	*unknown.*
0Ah	BYTE	*unknown.*
0Bh	BYTE	*unknown.*
further		*unknown.*

Restrictions: PC Tools version 5.1 or higher DESKTOP must be installed.
Return Registers:
AX = *unknown.*

INTERRUPT 16h - Function FFh, Subfunction C2h
Unknown Function

Purpose: *unknown.*
Available on: All machines.

Registers at call:
AX = FFC2h
unknown.

Details: This function is only available when popped up.
Conflicts: None known.
See Also: Function FFh Subfunction C3h

Restrictions: PC Tools version 5.1 or higher DESKTOP must be installed.
Return Registers:
AH = *unknown.*
CX = *unknown.*
DH = *unknown.*
DL = *unknown.*

INTERRUPT 16h - Function FFh, Subfunction C3h
Unknown Function

Purpose: *unknown.*
Available on: All machines.

Registers at call:
AX = FFC3h
unknown.

Details: This function is only available when popped up.
Conflicts: None known.
See Also: Function FFh Subfunction C2h

Restrictions: PC Tools version 5.1 or higher DESKTOP must be installed.
Return Registers:
AH = *unknown.*
CX = *unknown.*
DH = *unknown.*
DL = *unknown.*

INTERRUPT 16h - Function FFh, Subfunction C4h
GET Unknown DATA POINTERS

Purpose: Determine the addresses of a number of internal data structures.

Available on: All machines.

Registers at call:
AX = FFC4h

Restrictions: PC Tools version 5.1 or higher DESKTOP must be installed.

Return Registers:
AL = *unknown*.
BX = segment of *scratch space*
CX = segment of stored screen data (*section covered by window*)
DX = segment of window parameters for *unknown window*
ES:BP -> *unknown*.

Details: This function is only available when popped up in versions prior to 6.0.
Conflicts: None known.

INTERRUPT 16h - Function FFh, Subfunction C5h
CHECK WHETHER DESKTOP LOADED RESIDENT

Purpose: Determine whether the PC Tools version 5.1 or higher DESKTOP is loaded as a TSR.
Available on: All machines.
Registers at call:
AX = FFC5h

Restrictions: none.
Return Registers:
BL = nonzero if loaded resident
= 00h if nonresident

Details: This function is only available when popped up. Call Subfunction EFh first to ensure that DESKTOP is actually present.
Conflicts: None known.
See Also: Function FFh Subfunctions EFh and F3h

INTERRUPT 16h - Function FFh, Subfunction C6h
SET Unknown Value

Purpose: *unknown*.
Available on: All machines.

Registers at call:
AX = FFC6h
BL = new value for *unknown*.
Conflicts: None known.

Restrictions: PC Tools version 5.1 or higher DESKTOP must be installed.

Return Registers: n/a

INTERRUPT 16h - Function FFh, Subfunction C7h
REMOVE WINDOW

Purpose: Remove the specified (*or possibly the current*) window and restore the portion of the screen it covered.
Available on: All machines.

Registers at call:
AX = FFC7h
unknown.
Conflicts: None known.

Restrictions: PC Tools version 5.1 or higher DESKTOP must be installed.

Return Registers: *unknown*.

INTERRUPT 16h - Function FFh, Subfunction C8h
GET Unknown Pointer

Purpose: *unknown*.
Available on: All machines.

Registers at call:
AX = FFC8h
Details: Valid only while popped up.

Restrictions: PC Tools version 5.1 or higher DESKTOP must be installed.

Return Registers:
DS:SI -> *unknown*.

Conflicts: None known.

INTERRUPT 16h - Function FFh, Subfunction C9h
COPY DATA TO CLIPBOARD

Purpose: Place text into the clipboard for later pasting.
Available on: All machines.

Restrictions: PC Tools version 5.1 or higher DESKTOP must be installed.

Registers at call:
AX = FFC9h
DS:SI -> characters to store in clipboard
CX = size in bytes

Return Registers:
CF set on error

Details: This function is only available when popped up. While copying, bytes of 00h and 0Ah are skipped.
Conflicts: None known.

INTERRUPT 16h - Function FFh, Subfunction CAh
SET Unknown Value

Purpose: *unknown.*
Available on: All machines.

Restrictions: PC Tools version 5.1 or higher DESKTOP must be installed.

Registers at call:
AX = FFCAh
DX = *unknown.*

Return Registers:
AX destroyed

Details: available only when popped up.
Conflicts: None known.

INTERRUPT 16h - Function FFh, Subfunction CBh
SELECT WINDOW PARAMETERS

Purpose: *Specify the set of window parameters (size, color, etc.) to use.*
Available on: All machines.

Restrictions: PC Tools version 5.i or higher DESKTOP must be installed.

Registers at call:
AX = FFCBh
DX = *window specifier*

Return Registers:
AX destroyed

Details: This function is only available when popped up.
Conflicts: None known.
See Also: Function FFh Subfunction B5h

INTERRUPT 16h - Function FFh, Subfunction CCh
DISPLAY ASCIZ STRING CENTERED IN WINDOW

Purpose: Display the specified string centered within the current window.
Available on: All machines.

Restrictions: PC Tools version 5.1 or higher DESKTOP must be installed.

Registers at call:
AX = FFCCh
DS:SI -> ASCIZ string

Return Registers:
AX = *unknown.*
CX = *unknown.*
ES:DI -> address past last character displayed
      (v5.1/5.5 only)
       -> *unknown.* on menu bar (v6.0)

Conflicts: None known.

INTERRUPT 16h - Function FFh, Subfunction CDh
Unknown Function

Purpose: *unknown.*

Available on: All machines.

Registers at call:
AX = FFCDh
DS:DX -> *unknown*.
Details: This function is only available when popped up.
Conflicts: None known.

Restrictions: PC Tools version 5.1 or higher DESKTOP must be installed.
Return Registers: *unknown*.

INTERRUPT 16h - Function FFh, Subfunction CEh
SET Unknown DELAYS

Purpose: Specify the delays used in *unknown situations*.
Available on: All machines.

Registers at call:
AX = FFCEh
CX = *unknown*.
Conflicts: None known.

Restrictions: PC Tools version 5.1 or higher DESKTOP must be installed.
Return Registers: *apparently nothing*

INTERRUPT 16h - Function FFh, Subfunction CFh
CLOSE PRINTER/PRINT FILE

Purpose: Terminate printing.
Available on: All machines.

Registers at call:
AX = FFCFh
Details: available only when popped up
Conflicts: None known.

Restrictions: PC Tools version 5.1 or higher DESKTOP must be installed.
Return Registers: n/a

INTERRUPT 16h - Function FFh, Subfunction D0h
PREPARE TO PRINT

Purpose: *Perform any necessary initializations before printing data.*
Available on: All machines.

Registers at call:
AX = FFD0h
unknown.
Details: This function is only available when popped up.
Conflicts: None known.

Restrictions: PC Tools version 5.1 or higher DESKTOP must be installed.
Return Registers: *unknown*.

INTERRUPT 16h - Function FFh, Subfunction D1h
DISPLAY PRINT OPTIONS MENU

Purpose: Allow the user to select the number of copies to be printed and where to print them.
Available on: All machines.

Registers at call:
AX = FFD1h

Restrictions: PC Tools version 5.1 or higher DESKTOP must be installed.
Return Registers:
BX = number of copies
DX = destination
00h cancel
01h LPT1
02h LPT2
03h LPT3
04h COM1

05h COM2
06h disk file

Details: This function is only available when popped up.
Conflicts: None known.

INTERRUPT 16h - Function FFh, Subfunction D2h
Unknown Function

Purpose: *unknown.*
Available on: All machines.

Registers at call:
AX = FFD2h
BX = *unknown.*
Details: This function is only available when popped up.
Conflicts: None known.

Restrictions: PC Tools version 5.1 or higher DESKTOP must be installed.
Return Registers:
BL = *unknown.*

INTERRUPT 16h - Function FFh, Subfunction D3h
Unknown Function

Purpose: *unknown.*
Available on: All machines.

Registers at call:
AX = FFD3h
DS:SI -> 92-byte data record for *unknown.*
Conflicts: None known.

Restrictions: PC Tools version 5.1 or higher DESKTOP must be installed.
Return Registers: *unknown.*

INTERRUPT 16h - Function FFh, Subfunction D4h
CREATE/OPEN/DELETE FILE

Purpose: Access or delete the specified data file.
Available on: All machines.

Registers at call:
AX = FFD4h
BH = 3Ch create file (with no attributes)
    3Dh open file
    41h delete file
BL = access mode
    00h read only
    01h write only
    02h read/write
DS:SI -> ASCIZ filename
Details: Operation is attempted in (in order) the directory from which the desktop was *started/run*, the directory specified with the filename, X:\PCTOOLS\ and X:\.
Conflicts: None known.

Restrictions: PC Tools version 5.1 or higher DESKTOP must be installed.
Return Registers:
BX = file handle
    0000h on error

INTERRUPT 16h - Function FFh, Subfunction D5h
Unknown Function

Purpose: *unknown.*
Available on: All machines.

Registers at call:
AX = FFD5h
unknown.

Restrictions: PC Tools version 5.1 or higher DESKTOP must be installed.
Return Registers: *unknown.*

Details: This function is only available when popped up.
Conflicts: None known.

INTERRUPT 16h - Function FFh, Subfunction D6h
Unknown Function

Purpose: *unknown.*
Available on: All machines.

Registers at call:
AX = FFD6h
BX = *unknown.*
CX = *unknown.*
DX = offset in *unknown.*
other *unknown.*

Restrictions: PC Tools version 5.1 or higher DESKTOP must be installed.
Return Registers: *unknown.*

Details: This function is only available when popped up.
Conflicts: None known.

INTERRUPT 16h - Function FFh, Subfunction D7h
Unknown Function

Purpose: *unknown.*
Available on: All machines.

Registers at call:
AX = FFD7h
other *unknown.*

Restrictions: PC Tools version 5.1 or higher DESKTOP must be installed.
Return Registers:
BL = *unknown.*

Details: This function is only available when popped up.
Conflicts: None known.

INTERRUPT 16h - Function FFh, Subfunction D8h
SAFE CREATE FILE

Purpose: Create a new file, prompting the user for confirmation before overwriting an existing file.
Available on: All machines.

Registers at call:
AX = FFD8h
DS:BX -> ASCIZ filename

Restrictions: PC Tools version 5.1 or higher DESKTOP must be installed.
Return Registers:
BX = file handle
0000h on error

Details: This function is probably only available when the desktop is popped up.
Conflicts: None known.

INTERRUPT 16h - Function FFh, Subfunction D9h
GET Unknown Value

Purpose: *unknown.*
Available on: All machines.

Registers at call:
AX = FFD9h

Restrictions: PC Tools version 5.1 or higher DESKTOP must be installed.
Return Registers:
AX = *unknown.*

Details: This function is only available when popped up.
Conflicts: None known.

INTERRUPT 16h - Function FFh, Subfunction DAh
GET NAME OF LAST FILE OPENED

Purpose: Determine the full name of the last file opened via the DESKTOP API.

Available on: All machines.

Registers at call:
AX = FFDAh
DS:SI -> *unknown.* (v5.1/5.5 only)
Conflicts: None known.

Restrictions: PC Tools version 5.1 or higher DESKTOP must be installed.
Return Registers:
DS:SI -> filename

INTERRUPT 16h - Function FFh, Subfunction DBh
SET Unknown Value

Purpose: *unknown.*
Available on: All machines.

Registers at call:
AX = FFDBh
BL = *unknown.*
Details: This function is only available when popped up.
Conflicts: None known.

Restrictions: PC Tools version 5.1 or higher DESKTOP must be installed.
Return Registers: n/a

INTERRUPT 16h - Function FFh, Subfunction DCh
UNHOOK DESKTOP

Purpose: Restore the interrupt vectors hooked by the desktop in preparation for unloading it from memory.
Available on: All machines.

Registers at call:
AX = FFDCh

Conflicts: None known.

Restrictions: PC Tools version 5.1 or higher DESKTOP must be installed.
Return Registers:
interrupt vectors 09h, 10h (v6.0+), 16h, 1Ch, and 21h restored to original values

INTERRUPT 16h - Function FFDDh, Subfunction 0000h
PCShell INSTALLATION CHECK

Purpose: Determine whether the PC Tools version 5.1 or higher PCShell is installed.
Available on: All machines.
Registers at call:
AX = FFDDh
BX = 0000h
Conflicts: None known.

Restrictions: none.
Return Registers:
CX = 5555h
DX = 5555h if PCShell installed in resident mode

INTERRUPT 16h - Function FFDDh, Subfunction 0001h
REQUEST POP-UP

Purpose: Force PCShell to pop up as soon as possible.
Available on: All machines.

Registers at call:
AX = FFDDh
BX = 0001h
Conflicts: None known.
See Also: Function FFDDh Subfunction 0003h

Restrictions: PC Tools version 5.1 or higher PCShell must be installed.
Return Registers: n/a

INTERRUPT 16h - Function FFDDh, Subfunction 0002h
GET Unknown Value

Purpose: *unknown.*
Available on: All machines.

Restrictions: PC Tools version 5.1 through 5.5 PCShell must be installed.

Registers at call:
AX = FFDDh
BX = 0002h
Details: PCShell versions 6.0 and higher display the error message "Incorrect PCRUN version", await a keystroke, and abort the current process.
Conflicts: None known.

Return Registers:
AL = 00h *unknown.*
    01h *unknown.*

INTERRUPT 16h - Function FFDDh, Subfunction 0003h
REQUEST POP-UP

Purpose: Force PCShell to pop up as soon as possible.
Available on: All machines.

Restrictions: PC Tools version 5.1 or higher PCShell must be installed.
Return Registers: n/a

Registers at call:
AX = FFDDh
BX = 0003h
Conflicts: None known.
See Also: Function FFDDh Subfunction 0001h

INTERRUPT 16h - Function FFDDh, Subfunction 0004h
GET Unknown Pointer

Purpose: *unknown.*
Available on: All machines.

Restrictions: PC Tools version 5.1 or higher PCShell must be installed.

Registers at call:
AX = FFDDh
BX = 0004h
Conflicts: None known.

Return Registers:
CF clear if successful
    DS:SI -> *unknown.*

INTERRUPT 16h - Function FFDDh, Subfunction 0005h
Unknown Function

Purpose: *unknown.*
Available on: All machines.

Restrictions: PC Tools version 5.1 or higher PCShell must be installed.
Return Registers: *unknown.*

Registers at call:
AX = FFDDh
BX = 0005h
other *unknown.*
Conflicts: None known.

INTERRUPT 16h - Function FFDDh, Subfunction 0006h
Unknown Function

Purpose: *unknown.*
Available on: All machines.

Restrictions: PC Tools version 5.1 or higher PCShell must be installed.
Return Registers: *unknown.*

Registers at call:
AX = FFDDh
BX = 0006h
other *unknown.*
Conflicts: None known.

INTERRUPT 16h - Function FFDDh, Subfunction 0007h
SET Unknown FLAG

Purpose: *unknown.*

Available on: All machines.

Registers at call:
AX = FFDDh
BX = 0007h
Conflicts: None known.
See Also: Function FFDDh Subfunction 0008h

Restrictions: PC Tools version 5.1 or higher PCShell must be installed.
Return Registers:
CF clear if successful
CF set on error

INTERRUPT 16h - Function FFDDh, Subfunction 0008h
CLEAR Unknown FLAG

Purpose: *unknown.*
Available on: All machines.

Registers at call:
AX = FFDDh
BX = 0008h
Conflicts: None known.
See Also: Function FFDDh Subfunction 0007h

Restrictions: PC Tools version 5.1 or higher PCShell must be installed.
Return Registers: *unknown.*

INTERRUPT 16h - Function FFDDh, Subfunction 0009h
GET PCRUN PARAMETERS

Purpose: Determine the parameters with which PCRUN was invoked.
Available on: All machines.

Registers at call:
AX = FFDDh
BX = 0009h

Restrictions: PC Tools version 6.0 or higher PCShell must be installed.
Return Registers:
CF clear if successful
    DS:SI -> parameter pointers (Table 33-4)
CF set on error

Conflicts: None known.

Table 33-4. Format of PCRUN Parameter List:

Offset	Size	Description
00h	WORD	offset of WORD containing *unknown.*
02h	WORD	offset of name of program to execute
04h	WORD	offset of 80-byte buffer for *unknown.*
06h	WORD	offset of buffer for *unknown.* (length in WORD preceding buffer)
08h	WORD	offset of buffer for *unknown.* (length in WORD preceding buffer)

INTERRUPT 16h - Function FFDDh, Subfunction 000Ah
PCRUN INSTALLATION CHECK

Purpose: Determine whether PC Tools version 6.0 or higher PCRUN is installed.
Available on: All machines.
Registers at call:
AX = FFDDh
BX = 000Ah
Details: This call also sets an unknown flag.
Conflicts: None known.

Restrictions: none.
Return Registers:
CX = 5555h if running
DX = 5555h

INTERRUPT 16h - Function FFDDh, Subfunction 000Bh
Unknown Function

Purpose: *unknown.*

Available on: All machines.

Registers at call:
AX = FFDDh
BX = 000Bh
other *unknown*.
Details: This function also clears the flag set by Function FFDDh Subfunction 000Ah
Conflicts: None known.

INTERRUPT 16h - Function FFh, Subfunction DEh
DISPLAY POPUP MENU

Purpose: Popup the specified dialog box.
Available on: All machines.

Registers at call:
AX = FFDEh
DS:DX -> menu description, must be on a
    paragraph boundary (see Function FFh
    Subfunction EEh)
Details: This function is only available when popped up.
Conflicts: None known.

INTERRUPT 16h - Function FFh, Subfunction DFh
Unknown Function

Purpose: *unknown*.
Available on: All machines.

Registers at call:
AX = FFDFh
other *unknown*.
Conflicts: None known.

INTERRUPT 16h - Function FFh, Subfunction E0h
Unknown Function

Purpose: *unknown*.
Available on: All machines.

Registers at call:
AX = FFE0h
CX = *unknown*.
DX = *unknown*.
Details: This function is only available when popped up.
Conflicts: None known.

INTERRUPT 16h - Function FFh, Subfunction E1h
BEEP

Purpose: Sound a beep.
Available on: All machines.

Registers at call:
AX = FFE1h
Conflicts: None known.

Restrictions: PC Tools version 6.0 or higher PCRUN
    must be installed.
Return Registers:
CX = 5555h if PCRUN active
DX = 5555h

Restrictions: PC Tools version 5.1 or higher
    DESKTOP must be installed.
Return Registers:
AX = *unknown*.
AL appears to be the number of the selected button

Restrictions: PC Tools version 5.1 or higher
    DESKTOP must be installed.
Return Registers: *unknown*.

Restrictions: PC Tools version 5.1 or higher
    DESKTOP must be installed.
Return Registers: n/a

Restrictions: PC Tools version 5.1 or higher
    DESKTOP must be installed.
Return Registers: n/a

INTERRUPT 16h - Function FFh, Subfunction E2h
Unknown Function

Purpose: *unknown.*
Available on: All machines.

Registers at call:
AX = FFE2h
DX = *unknown.*
Details: This function is only available when popped up.
Conflicts: None known.

Restrictions: PC Tools version 5.1 or higher DESKTOP must be installed.
Return Registers: *unknown.*

INTERRUPT 16h - Function FFh, Subfunction E3h
PRINT CHARACTER

Purpose: Send a byte to the current printer or print file.
Available on: All machines.

Registers at call:
AX = FFE3h
BL = character to print to currently open printer or print file
Details: This function is only available when popped up.
Conflicts: None known.

Restrictions: PC Tools version 5.1 or higher DESKTOP must be installed.
Return Registers:
CF clear if successful
CF set on error

INTERRUPT 16h - Function FFh, Subfunction E4h
Unknown Function

Purpose: *unknown.*
Available on: All machines.

Registers at call:
AX = FFE4h
DX = segment of *unknown.*
Details: This function is only available when popped up.
Conflicts: None known.

Restrictions: PC Tools version 5.1 or higher DESKTOP must be installed.
Return Registers: *unknown.*

INTERRUPT 16h - Function FFh, Subfunction E5h
POP UP FILE SELECTION MENU

Purpose: Allow the user to select a file.
Available on: All machines.

Registers at call:
AX = FFE5h
DS:SI -> ASCIZ wildcard filespec followed by ASCIZ menu title
DX = *segment of window parameters*
Details: This function is only available when popped up.
Conflicts: None known.
See Also: Function FFh Subfunction DAh

Restrictions: PC Tools version 5.1 or higher DESKTOP must be installed.
Return Registers:
AX = DOS file handle for file
    DS:DX -> *filename*
    = FFFFh if cancelled by user

INTERRUPT 16h - Function FFh, Subfunction E6h
CHECK FOR AND GET KEYSTROKE

Purpose: Determine whether any keystrokes are available and read the next keystroke if so.

Available on: All machines.

Registers at call:
AX = FFE6h

Restrictions: PC Tools version 5.1 or higher DESKTOP must be installed.
Return Registers:
AX = 0000h if no key available
else BIOS keycode

Details: This function is only available when popped up. Invokes INT 28h idle interrupt before checking for key.
Conflicts: None known.

INTERRUPT 16h - Function FFh, Subfunction E7h
Unknown Function

Purpose: *unknown.*
Available on: All machines.

Registers at call:
AX = FFE7h
BX = segment of *unknown.*
Details: This function is only available when popped up.
Conflicts: None known.

Restrictions: PC Tools version 5.1 or higher DESKTOP must be installed.
Return Registers: *unknown.*

INTERRUPT 16h - Function FFh, Subfunction E8h
DISPLAY NUMBER

Purpose: Convert a number to a string of characters and attributes suitable for direct display on the screen.
Available on: All machines.

Registers at call:
AX = FFE8h
CX = number
DH = attribute
DS:SI -> destination for ASCII number
Conflicts: None known.

Restrictions: PC Tools version 5.1 or higher DESKTOP must be installed.
Return Registers:
DS:SI buffer filled in with alternating characters and attributes

INTERRUPT 16h - Function FFh, Subfunction E9h
GET FILE LIST

Purpose: Determine the files matching a previous wildcard search.
Available on: All machines.

Registers at call:
AX = FFE9h

Details: This function is only available when popped up.
Conflicts: None known.

Restrictions: PC Tools version 5.1 or higher DESKTOP must be installed.
Return Registers:
BX = segment of file/directory list (14 bytes per file, NUL-padded)

INTERRUPT 16h - Function FFh, Subfunction EAh
DISPLAY COUNTED STRING

Purpose: Output a counted string to the current window.
Available on: All machines.

Registers at call:
AX = FFEAh
DS:SI -> counted string (count byte followed by string)
Details: This function is only available when popped up.
Conflicts: None known.

Restrictions: PC Tools version 5.1 or higher DESKTOP must be installed.
Return Registers: *unknown.*

INTERRUPT 16h - Function FFh, Subfunction EBh
Unknown Function

Purpose: *unknown.*
Available on: All machines.

Registers at call:
AX = FFEBh
other *unknown.*
Conflicts: None known.

Restrictions: PC Tools version 5.1 or higher DESKTOP must be installed.
Return Registers: *unknown.*

INTERRUPT 16h - Function FFh, Subfunction ECh
GET KEY

Purpose: Wait for the next keystroke.
Available on: All machines.

Registers at call:
AX = FFECh
DS:SI -> FAR routine to *unknown.*
BX = *unknown.*
unknown.

Restrictions: PC Tools version 5.1 or higher DESKTOP must be installed.
Return Registers:
AX = keystroke
   FFFFh if F10 pressed to go to menu

Details: This function is only available when popped up. Invokes INT 28h while waiting for keystroke. F10 is hotkey to Desktop menu.
Conflicts: None known.

INTERRUPT 16h - Function FFh, Subfunction EDh
GET Unknown Value

Purpose: *unknown.*
Available on: All machines.

Registers at call:
AX = FFEDh
Details: This function is only available when popped up.
Conflicts: None known.

Restrictions: PC Tools version 5.1 or higher DESKTOP must be installed.
Return Registers:
AX = *unknown.*

INTERRUPT 16h - Function FFh, Subfunction EEh
DEFINE PULLDOWN MENUS

Purpose: Specify the contents of the pulldown menus at the top of the screen.
Available on: All machines.

Registers at call:
AX = FFEEh
DS:SI -> pulldown menu system description
   (Table 33-5)

Restrictions: PC Tools version 5.1 or higher DESKTOP must be installed.
Return Registers:
AX destroyed

Details: This function is only available when popped up. If the accessory does not need any menu items of its own, it should call Function FFh Subfunction FAh instead.
Conflicts: None known.
See Also: Function FFh Subfunctions F7h and FAh

Table 33-5. Format of Pulldown Menu System Description:

Offset	Size	Description
00h	WORD	offset of menu bar contents (counted string)
02h	WORD	number of items on menu bar
04h	10 BYTEs	scan codes for hotkeying to each of up to ten menu items
0Eh	10 BYTEs	which character to highlight in each menu item (01h=first)
18h	WORD	offset of first menu definition (Table 33-6)
1Ah	WORD	offset of second menu definition
	...	

Table 33-6. Format of Menu Definition:

Offset	Size	Description
00h	WORD	offset of menu contents (Table 33-7)
02h	WORD	number of entries in menu
04h		for each entry:

Offset	Size	Description
00h	BYTE	scancode of Alt-key to invoke entry
01h	BYTE	character to highlight (01h=first, etc)
02h	WORD	offset of FAR routine to handle selection

Table 33-7. Format of Menu Contents:

Offset	Size	Description
00h	BYTE	number of lines in menu
01h	BYTE	width of menu
02h	N BYTEs	counted strings, one for each line in menu

INTERRUPT 16h - Function FFh, Subfunction EFh
DESKTOP INSTALLATION CHECK

Purpose: Determine whether the PC Tools version 5.1 or higher DESKTOP is running or installed resident.

Available on: All machines.

Restrictions: none.

Registers at call:
AX = FFEFh
CX = 0000h

Return Registers:
CX = ABCDh if PC Tools DESKTOP.EXE is installed
BX = segment of resident portion
AX = *unknown*. (v5.1/5.5 only)

Conflicts: None known.
See Also: Function FFh Subfunctions C5h and F3h

INTERRUPT 16h - Function FFh, Subfunction F0h
SET Unknown Value

Purpose: *unknown*.

Available on: All machines.

Restrictions: PC Tools version 5.1 or higher DESKTOP must be installed.

Registers at call:
AX = FFF0h
DX = *unknown*.

Return Registers:
AX destroyed

Details: This function is only available when popped up.
Conflicts: None known.

INTERRUPT 16h - Function FFh, Subfunction F1h
ALTERNATE INSTALLATION CHECK

Purpose: Determine whether the PC Toolvs version 5.1 or higher DESKTOP is running or installed resident.

Available on: All machines.
Registers at call:
AX = FFF1h
BX = 0000h leave *unknown* flag as is
    nonzero set the flag
Conflicts: None known.

Restrictions: none.
Return Registers:
CX = 5555h if installed
DX = 5555h

INTERRUPT 16h - Function FFh, Subfunction F2h
DISPLAY HELP LINE

Purpose: Display a line of help or function key labels on the last line of the screen.
Available on: All machines.

Restrictions: PC Tools version 5.1 or higher
    DESKTOP must be installed.

Registers at call:
AX = FFF2h
DS:SI -> ASCIZ function key label string (each
    label preceded by '[') or help text

Return Registers:
AX destroyed

Details: This function is only available when popped up. If the specified string does not start with '[', it is displayed centered on the bottom line, else the function key labels are shown.
Conflicts: None known.

INTERRUPT 16h - Function FFh, Subfunction F3h
PREPARE TO UNLOAD RESIDENT DESKTOP

Purpose: Indicate to the resident portion that DESKTOP is about to be removed from memory and should release any EMS being used; restore the video mode, page, and cursor shape; and restore all modified interrupt vectors.
Available on: All machines.

Restrictions: PC Tools version 5.1 or higher
    DESKTOP must be installed as a TSR.

Return Registers: n/a

Registers at call:
AX = FFF3h
Conflicts: None known.
See Also: Function FFh Subfunctions C5h and EFh

INTERRUPT 16h - Function FFh, Subfunction F4h
Unknown Function

Purpose: *unknown.*
Available on: All machines.

Restrictions: PC Tools version 5.1 or higher
    DESKTOP must be installed.

Return Registers: *unknown.*

Registers at call:
AX = FFF4h
unknown.
Details: This function is only available when popped up.
Conflicts: None known.
See Also: Function FFh Subfunction F6h

INTERRUPT 16h - Function FFh, Subfunction F5h
GET SCREEN ATTRIBUTE ARRAY

Purpose: Determine the attributes used by various portions of the PC Tools desktop.
Available on: All machines.

Restrictions: PC Tools version 5.1 or higher
    DESKTOP must be installed.

Registers at call:
AX = FFF5h

Return Registers:
ES:BX -> screen attributes data structure (Table 33-8)
AL = *unknown.* (v6.0+)

Conflicts: None known.

Table 33-8. Format of Attribute Data Structure:

Offset	Size	Description
-1	BYTE	attribute for desktop background
00h	BYTE	attribute for normal characters on desktop menu
01h	BYTE	attribute for highlighted characters on desktop menu
02h	5 BYTEs	*unknown.*
07h	BYTE	attribute for dialog boxes
08h	15 BYTEs	*unknown.*
17h	BYTE	attribute for message boxes

INTERRUPT 16h - Function FFh, Subfunction F6h
INVOKE NOTEPAD EDITOR

Purpose: Start the editor on the specified file.

Available on: All machines.

Restrictions: PC Tools version 5.1 or higher DESKTOP must be installed.

Registers at call:
AX = FFF6h
DS = segment of editor buffer structure (Table 33-9)
BX = *unknown.*
DX = segment of window parameters structure (see Function FFh Subfunction B5h)

Return Registers: *unknown.*

Details: This function is only available when popped up.
Conflicts: None known.
See Also: Function FFh Subfunction F4h

Table 33-9. Format of Editor Buffer Structure:

Offset	Size	Description
00h	WORD	offset of current cursor position in buffer segment
02h	2 BYTEs	*unknown.*
04h	WORD	offset of beginning of file data in buffer segment
06h	10 BYTEs	*unknown.*
10h	N BYTEs	ASCIZ name of file being edited

INTERRUPT 16h - Function FFh, Subfunction F7h
PROCESS MENU BAR ENTRY

Purpose: Perform input processing on the menu bar set up with Function FFh Subfunction EEh.

Available on: All machines.

Restrictions: PC Tools version 5.1 or higher DESKTOP must be installed.

Registers at call:
AX = FFF7h
DS:SI -> *unknown.*
unknown.

Return Registers: *unknown.*

Details: This function is only available when popped up.
Conflicts: None known.
See Also: Function FFh Subfunctions EEh and FBh

INTERRUPT 16h - Function FFh, Subfunction F8h
DRAW EMPTY WINDOW

Purpose: Place an empty window on the screen with the size, position, and colors specified by the indicated window parameters.

Available on: All machines.

Registers at call:
AX = FFF8h
DS:0000h -> window parameters structure (see Function FFh Subfunction B5h)
DS:BX -> DWORD to store address of *unknown location* on screen
Conflicts: None known.

Restrictions: PC Tools version 5.1 or higher DESKTOP must be installed.
Return Registers: n/a

INTERRUPT 16h - Function FFh, Subfunction F9h
DEFINE SCREEN REFRESH ROUTINE

Purpose: Specify the subroutine to be invoked whenever the caller's window needs to be redrawn after another application has overwritten it.
Available on: All machines.

Registers at call:
AX = FFF9h
ES:BX -> FAR routine to redisplay the utility's window
Details: This function is only available when popped up.
Conflicts: None known.

Restrictions: PC Tools version 5.1 or higher DESKTOP must be installed.
Return Registers: n/a

INTERRUPT 16h - Function FFh, Subfunction FAh
DEFINE STANDARD PULLDOWN MENUS

Purpose: Specify that the calling accessory will not add any pulldown menus to the standard "Desktop" and "Window" menus.
Available on: All machines.

Registers at call:
AX = FFFAh
Details: This function is only available when popped up. Unlike Function FFh Subfunction EEh, no additional menu items are added between "Desktop" and "Window".
Conflicts: None known.
See Also: Function FFh Subfunctions EEh and FBh

Restrictions: PC Tools version 5.1 or higher DESKTOP must be installed.
Return Registers: n/a

INTERRUPT 16h - Function FFh, Subfunction FBh
PROCESS STANDARD MENU BAR

Purpose: Allow the user to make a selection from the pulldown menus when no accessory-specific menus are defined.
Available on: All machines.

Registers at call:
AX = FFFBh
Details: This function is only available when popped up. Performs input processing on the standard menu bar set up with Function FFh Subfunction FAh.
Conflicts: None known.
See Also: Function FFh Subfunction F7h

Restrictions: PC Tools version 5.1 or higher DESKTOP must be installed.
Return Registers:
unknown.

INTERRUPT 16h - Function FFh, Subfunction FCh
GET HOTKEYS AND KEYBOARD VECTOR

Purpose: Determine the hotkeys used by the desktop and the original vector for INT 09h.

Available on: All machines.

Registers at call:
AX = FFFCh

Conflicts: None known.

Restrictions: PC Tools version 5.1 or higher DESKTOP must be installed.

Return Registers:
ES:BX -> hotkey table (Table 33-10)
DS:DX = original INT 9 vector

Table 33-10. Format of hotkey table:

Offset	Size	Description
00h	2 BYTEs	scancode/shift state for desktop hotkey
02h	2 BYTEs	scancode/shift state for clipboard paste key
04h	2 BYTEs	scancode/shift state for clipboard copy key
06h	2 BYTEs	scancode/shift state for screen autodial key

INTERRUPT 16h - Function FFh, Subfunction FDh
COPY SCREEN IMAGE

Purpose: Copies 4000 bytes (probably a screen image) from one *unknown* location to another under certain circumstances.

Available on: All machines.

Registers at call:
AX = FFFDh
Conflicts: None known.

Restrictions: PC Tools version 5.1 or higher DESKTOP must be installed.

Return Registers:
AX destroyed

INTERRUPT 16h - Function FFh, Subfunction FEh
SHOW MOUSE CURSOR

Purpose: Unhide the mouse cursor after updating the screen.

Available on: All machines.

Registers at call:
AX = FFFEh
Conflicts: None known.
See Also: Function FFh Subfunction FFh, INT 33h Function 0001h

Restrictions: PC Tools version 5.1 or higher DESKTOP must be installed.

Return Registers: n/a

INTERRUPT 16h - Function FFh, Subfunction FFh
HIDE MOUSE CURSOR

Purpose: Make the mouse cursor invisible in preparation for updating the screen.

Available on: All machines.

Registers at call:
AX = FFFFh
Conflicts: None known.
See Also: Function FFh Subfunction FEh, INT 33h Function 0002h

Restrictions: PC Tools version 5.1 or higher DESKTOP must be installed.

Return Registers: n/a

INTERRUPT 21h - Function FAh
VDEFEND API

Purpose: Control the operation of the VDEFEND virus scanner.

Available on: All machines.

Registers at call:
AH = FAh
DX = 5945h

Restrictions: PC Tools version 7.0 VDEFEND must be installed.

Return Registers:
vary with subfunction:

AL = subfunction
    00h null function
    01h uninstall

n/a

CF set on error
DI = *unknown* (apparently 4559h)

    02h set *unknown* value
        BL = *unknown*.

CF clear
CL = old value of byte set to BL

INTERRUPT 2Fh - Function 62h, Subfunction 82h
FILE PROTECTION

Purpose: Specify an *unknown* address, which may be a callback.
Available on: All machines.

Restrictions: PC Tools version 7.0 DATAMON or
                  VDEFEND must be installed.

Registers at call:
AX = 6282h
CX:DX -> *unknown*.
DI = segment of *unknown* or FFFFh (or 0000h,
    VDEFEND only)

Return Registers:
BX = 0062h

Details: If CX:DX = 0000h:0000h on entry, no action is taken beyond setting BX to 0062h; this serves as an installation check.
Conflicts: None known.
See Also: Function 62h Subfunction 84h, INT 16h Function FFh Subfunction A3h

INTERRUPT 2Fh - Function 62h, Subfunction 84h
DATAMON

Purpose: Control the operation of the DATAMON file protection program.
Available on: All machines.

Restrictions: PC Tools version 7.0 DATAMON must
                  be installed.

Registers at call:
AX = 6284h
BX = function

Return Registers:

    0000h installation check
        CX = 0000h

AX = resident code segment
BX = 5555h
CX = 5555h

    0001h *unknown*
        CX = 0001h

AX:BX -> *unknown*.
CX = BX

    0002h *unknown*
        CX = 0002h

AX = CX = *unknown*.
BX = DX = *unknown*.

    0003h set *unknown* flags
        CX = flags
            bit 12: *unknown*.
            bit 10: *unknown*.
            bit 5: *unknown*.
            bit 3: *unknown*.
        DX = flags
            bit 15: *unknown*.

n/a

Conflicts: None known.
See Also: Function 62h Subfunction 82h, INT 16h Function FFh Subfunction A3h

Chapter 34

Viruses and Anti-Viral Tools

One of the less attractive features accompanying the free sharing of data files and programs within the microcomputer community has been the appearance of "virus" programs. While the term "virus" is validly applied to any program that infiltrates a system and reproduces itself, most of the publicized viruses have been characterized by wanton vandalism and destruction of data.

From a class of programs so rare that many active participants in on-line data exchange considered them to be mythical only a few years ago, the virus phenomenen has now become so commonplace that it has given birth to an industry devoted to anti-viral programs.

In this chapter we describe both the disease and some of the cures. This listing is necessarily incomplete; new viruses are being created continually, and several of the leading producers of anti-viral programs insist on complete secrecy about their programs' methods of operation (a not entirely paranoid viewpoint, considering that not too long ago, one virus checker was, itself, clandestinely infected and distributed!).

Viruses Themselves

We have mixed feelings about providing publicity to the virus programs themselves; however, in the interests of providing as complete coverage as possible of the PC's interrupt usage, we've included all those about which we have information. Almost all of them hook into the DOS service interrupt 21h; in the following pages they are listed by interrupt, function, and subfunction sequence.

INTERRUPT 21h - Function 0Bh, Subfunction 56h
"G" virus - INSTALLATION CHECK

Purpose: Determine whether the "G" virus is resident.
Available on: All machines.
Registers at call:
AX = 0B56h
Conflicts: DOS 1+ Get STDIN Status (chapter 8).

Restrictions: none.
Return Registers:
AX = 4952h if resident

.INTERRUPT 21h - Function 30h, Subfunction F1h
"Dutch-555" virus - INSTALLATION CHECK

Purpose: Determine whether virus is already present.
Available on: All machines.
Registers at call:
AX = 30F1h
AL = 00h if resident
Conflicts: DOS 2+ Get DOS Version (chapter 8), Phar Lap 386/DOS-Extender (chapter 9), CTask 2.0+ (chapter 17).

Restrictions: none.
Return Registers:

INTERRUPT 21h - Function 33h, Subfunction E0h
"Oropax" virus - INSTALLATION CHECK

Purpose: Determine whether virus is already present.
Available on: All machines.
Registers at call:
AX = 33E0h
Conflicts: None known.

Restrictions: none.
Return Registers:
AL = FFh if resident

INTERRUPT 21h - Function 35h, Subfunction 7Fh
"Agiplan" virus - INSTALLATION CHECK

Purpose: Determine whether virus is already present.
Available on: All machines.
Registers at call:
AX = 357Fh
Conflicts: DOS 2+ Get Interrupt Vector (chapter 8).

Restrictions: none.
Return Registers:
DX = FFFFh if installed

INTERRUPT 21h - Function 42h, Subfunction 03h
"Shake" virus - INSTALLATION CHECK

Purpose: Determine whether virus is already present.
Available on: All machines.
Registers at call:
AX = 4203h "Shake"
Conflicts: DOS 2+ Set Current File Position (chapter 8)

Restrictions: none.
Return Registers:
AX = 1234h if resident

INTERRUPT 21h - Function 42h, Subfunction 43h
"Invader" virus - INSTALLATION CHECK

Purpose: Determine whether virus is already present.
Available on: All machines.
Registers at call:
AX = 4243h "Invader"
Conflicts: DOS 2+ Set Current File Position (chapter 8)

Restrictions: none.
Return Registers:
AX = 5678h if resident

INTERRUPT 21h - Function 4Bh, various Subfunctions
VIRUS INSTALLATION CHECKS

Purpose: Determine whether a virus is already present.
Available on: All machines.
Registers at call:
AX = 4B04h "MG" and "699"

Restrictions: none.
Return Registers:
CF clear if "MG" resident
AX = 044Bh if "699" resident

AX = 4B40h "Plastique"

AX = 5678h if resident
See also Function 4Bh Subfunction 41h

AX = 4B4Dh "Murphy-2"

CF clear if resident

AX = 4B50h "Plastique-2576"

AX = 1234h if resident
See also Function 4Bh Subfunction 60h

AX = 4B59h "Murphy-1"

CF clear if resident

AX = 4BAAh "Nomenklatura"

CF clear if resident

AX = 4BAFh "948", "Magnitogorsk"

AL = FAh if "948" resident
AL = AFh if "Magnitogorsk" resident

AX = 4BDDh "Lozinsky"

AX = 1234h

AX = 4BFFh "707", "Justice"

BL = FFh if "707" resident
DI = 55AAh if "Justice" resident

INTERRUPT 21h - Function 4Bh, Subfunction 41h
Unknown Function

Purpose: *unknown.*
Available on: All machines.
Registers at call:
AX = 4B41h
others, if any, unknown.
See Also: Function 4Bh Subfunction 40h
Conflicts: None known.

Restrictions: "Plastique" virus must be resident.
Return Registers: *unknown.*

INTERRUPT 21h - Function 4Bh, Subfunction 60h
Unknown Function

Purpose: *unknown.*
Available on: All machines.
Registers at call:
AX = 4B60h
others, if any, unknown.
See Also: Function 4Bh Subfunction 50h
Conflicts: None known.

Restrictions: "Plastique-2576" virus must be resident.
Return Registers: *unknown.*

INTERRUPT 21h - Function 52h, Subfunction 52h
"516" virus - INSTALLATION CHECK

Purpose: Determine whether virus is already present.
Available on: All machines.
Registers at call:
AX = 5252h
Conflicts: DOS 2+ internal Get List of Lists (chapter 8).

Restrictions: none.
Return Registers:
BX = FFEEh if resident

INTERRUPT 21h - Function 58h, Subfunction CCh
"1067" virus - INSTALLATION CHECK

Purpose: Determine whether virus is already present.
Available on: All machines.
Registers at call:
AX = 58CCh
Conflicts: None known.

Restrictions: none.
Return Registers:
CF clear if resident

INTERRUPT 21h - Function 76h
"Klaeren" virus - INSTALLATION CHECK

Purpose: Determine whether virus is already present.
Available on: All machines.
Registers at call:
AH = 76h
Conflicts: None known.

Restrictions: none.
Return Registers:
AL = 48h if resident

INTERRUPT 21h - Function 83h
"SVC" virus - INSTALLATION CHECK

Purpose: Determine whether virus is already present.
Available on: All machines.
Registers at call:
AH = 83h
Conflicts: None known.

Restrictions: none.
Return Registers:
DX = 1990h if resident

INTERRUPT 21h - Function 89h
"Vriest" virus - INSTALLATION CHECK

Purpose: Determine whether virus is already present.
Available on: All machines.
Registers at call:
AH = 89h
Conflicts: None known.

Restrictions: none.
Return Registers:
AX = 0123h if resident

INTERRUPT 21h - Function 90h
"Carioca" virus - INSTALLATION CHECK

Purpose: Determine whether virus is already present.
Available on: All machines.
Registers at call:
AH = 90h
Conflicts: None known.

Restrictions: none.
Return Registers:
AH = 01h if resident

INTERRUPT 21h - Function 97h, Subfunction 53h
"Nina" virus - INSTALLATION CHECK

Purpose: Determine whether virus is already present.
Available on: All machines.
Registers at call:
AX = 9753h
Conflicts: None known.

Restrictions: none.
Return Registers:
never (executes original program)

INTERRUPT 21h - Function A1h, Subfunction D5h
"789" virus - INSTALLATION CHECK

Purpose: Determine whether virus is already present.
Available on: All machines.
Registers at call:
AX = A1D5h
Conflicts: Attachmate Extra (chapter 26).

Restrictions: none.
Return Registers:
AX = 900Dh if resident

INTERRUPT 21h - Function A5h, Subfunction 5Ah
"Eddie-2" virus - INSTALLATION CHECK

Purpose: Determine whether virus is already present.
Available on: All machines.
Registers at call:
AX = A55Ah
Conflicts: Attachmate Extra (chapter 26).

Restrictions: none.
Return Registers:
AX = 5AA5h if resident

INTERRUPT 21h - Function ABh
"600" or "Voronezh" virus - INSTALLATION CHECK

Purpose: Determine whether virus is already present.
Available on: All machines.
Registers at call:
AH = ABh
Conflicts: None known.

Restrictions: none.
Return Registers:
AX = 5555h

INTERRUPT 21h - Function BEh
"Datalock" virus - INSTALLATION CHECK

Purpose: Determine whether virus is already present.

Available on: All machines.
Registers at call:
AH = BEh
Conflicts: Novell NetWare 4.6/Alloy NTNX (both in chapter 20), "1049" virus (chapter 34).

Restrictions: none.
Return Registers:
AX = 1234h if resident

INTERRUPT 21h - Function BEh, Subfunction 00h
"1049" virus - INSTALLATION CHECK

Purpose: Determine whether virus is already present.
Available on: All machines.
Registers at call:
AX = BE00h
CF set
Conflicts: Novell NetWare 4.6/Alloy NTNX (both in chapter 20), "Datalock" virus (chapter 34).

Restrictions: none.
Return Registers:
CF clear if resident

INTERRUPT 21h - Function C0h
"Slow" virus, "Solano" virus - INSTALLATION CHECK

Purpose: Determine whether virus is already present.
Available on: All machines.
Registers at call:
AH = C0h

Restrictions: none.
Return Registers:
AX = 0300h if "Slow" resident
AX = 1234h if "Solano" resident

Conflicts: Novell NetWare 4.6/Alloy NTNX (both in chapter 20).
See Also: Function C1h

INTERRUPT 21h - Function C1h
"Solano" virus - Unknown Function

Purpose: *unknown.*
Available on: All machines.
Registers at call:
AH = C1h
other *unknown.*
Conflicts: Novell NetWare 4.6/Alloy NTNX (both in chapter 20).
See Also: Function C0h

Restrictions: "Solano" virus must be resident.
Return Registers: *unknown.*

INTERRUPT 21h - Function C2h
"Scott's Valley" virus - Unknown Function

Purpose: *unknown.*
Available on: All machines.
Registers at call:
AH = C2h
other *unknown.*
Conflicts: Novell NetWare/Alloy NTNX (both in chapter 20).

Restrictions: "Scott's Valley" virus must be resident.
Return Registers: *unknown.*

INTERRUPT 21h - Function C3h, Subfunction 01h
"905" virus - INSTALLATION CHECK

Purpose: Determine whether virus is already present.
Available on: All machines.
Registers at call:
AX = C301h
DX = F1F1h
Conflicts: Novell NetWare/Alloy NTNX (both in chapter 20).

Restrictions: none.
Return Registers:
DX = 0E0Eh if resident

INTERRUPT 21h - Function C5h, Subfunction 00h
"Sverdlov" virus - INSTALLATION CHECK

Purpose: Determine whether virus is already present.
Available on: All machines.   **Restrictions:** none.
Registers at call: **Return Registers:**
AX = C500h   AX = 6731h if resident
Conflicts: Novell NetWare 4.6/Alloy NTNX (both in chapter 20).

INTERRUPT 21h - Function C6h, Subfunction 03h
"Yankee" or "MLTI" virus - INSTALLATION CHECK

Purpose: Determine whether virus is already present.
Available on: All machines.   **Restrictions:** none.
Registers at call: **Return Registers:**
AX = C603h   CF clear if resident
CF set
Conflicts: Novell NetWare/Alloy NTNX (both in chapter 20).

INTERRUPT 21h - Function CAh, Subfunction 15h
"Piter" virus - Unknown Function

Purpose: *unknown.*
Available on: All machines.   **Restrictions:** "Piter" virus must be resident
Registers at call: **Return Registers:** *unknown.*
AX = CA15h
unknown.
Conflicts: Novell NetWare/Alloy NTNX (both in chapter 20).
See Also: Function CCh

INTERRUPT 21h - Function CCh
"Westwood" virus - INSTALLATION CHECK

Purpose: Determine whether virus is already present.
Available on: All machines.   **Restrictions:** none.
Registers at call: **Return Registers:**
AH = CCh   AX = 0700h if resident
Conflicts: Novell NetWare/Alloy NTNX (both in chapter 20).
See Also: Function CDh

INTERRUPT 21h - Function CDh
"Westwood" virus - Unknown Function

Purpose: *unknown.*
Available on: All machines.   **Restrictions:** "Westwood" virus must be resident.
Registers at call: **Return Registers:** *unknown.*
AH = CDh
other, if any, unknown.
Conflicts: Alloy NTNX (chapter 18), Novell NetWare 4.0 (chapter 20).
See Also: Function CCh

INTERRUPT 21h - Function D0h, Subfunction 00h
"Fellowship" virus - INSTALLATION CHECK

Purpose: Determine whether virus is already present.
Available on: All machines.   **Restrictions:** none.

Registers at call:
AX = D000h

Return Registers:
BX = 1234h if resident

Conflicts: Alloy NTNX (chapter 18), Novell NetWare 4.6 (chapter 20), Banyan VINES (chapter 22).

INTERRUPT 21h - Function D5h, Subfunction AAh
"Diamond-A", "Diamond-B" viruses - INSTALLATION CHECK

Purpose: Determine whether virus is already present.
Available on: All machines.
Registers at call:
AX = D5AAh

Restrictions: none.
Return Registers:
AX = 2A55h if "Diamond-A" resident
AX = 2A03h if "Diamond-B" resident

Conflicts: Alloy NTNX (chapter 18), Novell NetWare 4.0 (chapter 20), Banyan VINES (chapter 22), "Dir" virus (chapter 34).

INTERRUPT 21h - Function D5h, Subfunction AAh
"Dir" virus - INSTALLATION CHECK

Purpose: Determine whether virus is already present.
Available on: All machines.
Registers at call:
AX = D5AAh
BP = DEAAh

Restrictions: none.
Return Registers:
SI = 4321h if resident

Conflicts: Alloy NTNX (chapter 18), Novell NetWare 4.0 (chapter 20), Banyan VINES (chapter 22), "Diamond-A", "Diamond-B" viruses (chapter 34).

INTERRUPT 21h - Function DDh
"Jerusalem"-family viruses - Unknown Function

Purpose: *unknown.*
Available on: All machines.

Registers at call:
AH = DDh
others, if any, unknown.
Conflicts: Novell NetWare/Alloy NTNX (chapter 20).
See Also: Fuctions E0h and EEh

Restrictions: A "Jerusalem"-family virus must be resident.
Return Registers: *unknown.*

INTERRUPT 21h - Function DEh
"April 1st EXE" virus - Unknown Function

Purpose: *unknown.*
Available on: All machines.
Registers at call:
AH = DEh
others, if any, unknown.
Conflicts: "Durban" virus, Novell NetWare (chapter 20).

Restrictions: "April 1st EXE" virus must be resident.
Return Registers: *unknown.*

INTERRUPT 21h - Function DEh
"Durban" virus - INSTALLATION CHECK

Purpose: Determine whether virus is already present.
Available on: All machines.
Registers at call:
AH = DEh
Conflicts: "April 1st EXE" virus, Novell NetWare (chapter 20).

Restrictions: none.
Return Registers:
AH = DFh if resident

INTERRUPT 21h - Function E0h
"Jerusalem", "Armagedon" viruses - INSTALLATION CHECK

Purpose: Determine whether virus is already present.
Available on: All machines.
Registers at call:
AH = E0h

Restrictions: none.
Return Registers:
AX = 0300h if "Jerusalem" resident
AX = DADAh if "Armagedon" resident

Conflicts: OS/286 and OS/386 (chapter 1), DoubleDOS (chapter 17), Alloy NTNX (chapter 18), Novell NetWare (chapter 20), "8-tunes" virus.
See Also: Functions DDh and DEh

INTERRUPT 21h - Function E0h, Subfunction 0Fh
"8-tunes" virus - INSTALLATION CHECK

Purpose: Determine whether virus is already present.
Available on: All machines.
Registers at call:
AX = E00Fh

Restrictions: none.
Return Registers:
AX = 4C31h if resident

Conflicts: OS/286 and OS/386 (chapter 1), DoubleDOS (chapter 17), Alloy NTNX (chapter 18), Novell NetWare (chapter 20), "Jerusalem", "Armagedon" viruses.

INTERRUPT 21h - Function E1h
"Mendoza", "Fu Manchu" viruses - INSTALLATION CHECK

Purpose: Determine whether virus is already present.
Available on: All machines.
Registers at call:
AH = E1h

Restrictions: none.
Return Registers:
AX = 0300h if "Mendoza" resident
AX = 0400h if "Fu Manchu" resident

Conflicts: OS/286 and OS/386 (chapter 1), DoubleDOS (chapter 17), Novell NetWare (chapter 20).

INTERRUPT 21h - Function E4h
"Anarkia" virus - INSTALLATION CHECK

Purpose: Determine whether virus is already present.
Available on: All machines.
Registers at call:
AH = E4h

Restrictions: none.
Return Registers:
AH = 04h if resident

Conflicts: DoubleDOS (chapter 17), Novell NetWare (chapter 20).

INTERRUPT 21h - Function E7h
"Spyer" virus - INSTALLATION CHECK

Purpose: Determine whether virus is already present.
Available on: All machines.
Registers at call:
AH = E7h

Restrictions: none.
Return Registers:
AH = 78h if resident

Conflicts: OS/286 and OS/386 (chapter 9), Novell NetWare (chapter 20).

INTERRUPT 21h - Function ECh, Subfunction 59h
"Terror" virus - INSTALLATION CHECK

Purpose: Determine whether virus is already present.
Available on: All machines.
Registers at call:
AX = EC59h

Restrictions: none.
Return Registers:
BP = EC59h if resident

Conflicts: DoubleDOS (chapter 16), Alloy NTNX (chapter 18), Novell NetWare 4.6 (chapter 20).

INTERRUPT 21h - Function EEh
"Jerusalem-G" virus - INSTALLATION CHECK

Purpose: Determine whether virus is already present.
Available on: All machines.   **Restrictions:** none.
Registers at call: **Return Registers:**
AH = EEh   AX = 0300h if resident
Conflicts: DoubleDOS (chapter 16), Alloy NTNX (chapter 18), Novell NetWare 4.6 (chapter 20).
See Also: Functions DDh and DEh

INTERRUPT 21h - Function F0h
"Frere Jacques" virus - INSTALLATION CHECK

Purpose: Determine whether virus is already present.
Available on: All machines.   **Restrictions:** none.
Registers at call: **Return Registers:**
AH = F0h   AX = 0300h if resident
Conflicts: None known.

INTERRUPT 21h - Function F7h
"GP1" virus - INSTALLATION CHECK

Purpose: Determine whether virus is already present.
Available on: All machines.   **Restrictions:** none.
Registers at call: **Return Registers:**
AH = F7h   AX = 0300h if resident
Conflicts: None known.

INTERRUPT 21h - Function FBh, Subfunction 0Ah
"dBASE" virus - INSTALLATION CHECK

Purpose: Determine whether virus is already present.
Available on: All machines.   **Restrictions:** none.
Registers at call: **Return Registers:**
AX = FB0Ah   AX = 0AFBh if resident
Conflicts: DoubleDOS (chapter 16).

INTERRUPT 21h - Function FEh, Subfunction 01h
"Flip" virus - INSTALLATION CHECK

Purpose: Determine whether virus is already present.
Available on: All machines.   **Restrictions:** none.
Registers at call: **Return Registers:**
AX = FE01h   AX = 01FEh if resident
Conflicts: DoubleDOS (chapter 16).

INTERRUPT 21h - Function FEh, Subfunction 02h
"2468" virus - INSTALLATION CHECK

Purpose: Determine whether virus is already present.
Available on: All machines.   **Restrictions:** none.
Registers at call: **Return Registers:**
AX = FE02h   AX = 01FDh if resident
Conflicts: DoubleDOS (chapter 16).

INTERRUPT 21h - Function FEh, Subfunction DCh
"Black Monday" virus - INSTALLATION CHECK

Purpose: Determine whether virus is already present.
Available on: All machines.   **Restrictions:** none.
Registers at call: **Return Registers:**
AX = FEDCh   AL = DCh if resident
Conflicts: PCMANAGE/DCOMPRES (chapter 6), DoubleDOS (chapter 16).

INTERRUPT 21h - Function FFh
"Sunday" virus - INSTALLATION CHECK

Purpose: Determine whether virus is already present.
Available on: All machines.   **Restrictions:** none.
Registers at call: **Return Registers:**
AH = FFh   AX = 0400h if resident
Conflicts: "PSQR/1720" and "Ontario" viruses, DJ GO32.EXE (chapter 9), Topware Network Operating System (chapter 27), CED and DOSED (chapter 36).

INTERRUPT 21h - Function FFh, Subfunction 0Fh
"PSQR/1720" virus - INSTALLATION CHECK

Purpose: Determine whether virus is already present.
Available on: All machines.   **Restrictions:** none.
Registers at call: **Return Registers:**
AX = FF0Fh   AX = 0101h if resident
Conflicts: "Sunday" virus, DJ GO32.EXE (chapter 9), Topware Network Operating System (chapter 27), CED and DOSED (chapter 36).

INTERRUPT 21h - Function FFh, Subfunction FFh
"Ontario" virus - INSTALLATION CHECK

Purpose: Determine whether virus is already present.
Available on: All machines.   **Restrictions:** none.
Registers at call: **Return Registers:**
AX = FFFFh   AX = 0000h if resident
Conflicts: "Sunday" virus, DJ GO32.EXE (chapter 9), Topware Network Operating System (chapter 27), CED and DOSED (chapter 36).

INTERRUPT 32h
Reportedly used by "Tiny" Viruses

Purpose: *unknown.*
Available on: All machines.   **Restrictions:** A "Tiny"-family virus must be resident.
Registers at call: **Return Registers:**
unknown.   *unknown.*
Conflicts: None known.

INTERRUPT 60h
Zero Bug Virus

Purpose: The "Zero Bug" virus hooks this vector to provide an installation check.

Available on: All machines.   **Restrictions:** The Zero Bug virus must be resident.
Details: The Zero Bug virus considers itself already installed if the two bytes at offset 103h in the handler's segment are "ZE".
Conflicts: See chapter 1.

INTERRUPT 6Bh
Unknown Function

Purpose: *unknown.*
Available on: All machines.
Registers at call: *unknown.*
Conflicts: Novell NASI/NACS (chapter 7), Tandy SCHOOLMATE (chapter 36).

Restrictions: "Saddam" virus must be resident.
Return Registers: *unknown.*

INTERRUPT 70h
Unknown Function

Purpose: *unknown.*
Available on: All machines.
Registers at call: *unknown.*
Conflicts: IRQ8 (chapter 2).

Restrictions: "Stupid" virus must be resident.
Return Registers: *unknown.*

INTERRUPT E0h
Unknown Function

Purpose: *unknown.*
Available on: All machines.
Registers at call: *unknown.*
Conflicts: BASIC interpreter (chapter 1), CP/M-86 function calls (chapter 36).

Restrictions: "Micro-128" virus must be resident.
Return Registers: *unknown.*

Anti-Virals

Only a few of the anti-viral programs are described here. Those which are covered appear in alphabetic sequence by program name.

INTERRUPT 21h - Function 4Bh, Subfunction EEh
F-DRIVER.SYS - GRAB INT 21h

Purpose: When called the first time, this function moves the INT 21h monitoring code from its original location in the INT 21h chain to be the first thing called by INT 21h. This is the mechanism used by F-NET.
Available on: All machines.

Restrictions: F-DRIVER.SYS version 1.14 or higher must be installed.

Registers at call:
AX = 4BEEh

Return Registers:
AX = 1234h if grab successful
   = 2345h if it failed (INT 21h grabbed previously)

Details: F-DRIVER.SYS and F-NET are parts of the shareware F-PROT virus/trojan protection package by Fridrik Skulason.
Conflicts: various viruses (see above), ELRES V1.0 (chapter 36).
See Also: INT 2Fh Function 46h Subfunction 53h

INTERRUPT 2Fh - Function 46h, Subfunction 53h
F-DLOCK.EXE

Purpose: Control F-DLOCK, a hard disk access restrictor.
Available on: All machines.

Restrictions: F-DLOCK must be installed for all calls except the installation check.

Registers at call:
AX = 4653h
CX = 0005h
BX =   0000h   installation check
        0001h uninstall

Return Registers:
installation check:
   AX = FFFFh
uninstall:
   AX,BX,ES destroyed

Details: F-DLOCK is part of the shareware F-PROT virus/trojan protection package by Fridrik Skulason.
Conflicts: None known.
See Also: Function 46h Subfunction 53h/CX=0004h

INTERRUPT 2Fh - Function 46h, Subfunction 53h
F-LOCK.EXE

Purpose: Control the operation of the F-LOCK operating system restrictor which attempts to detect suspicious activity.

Available on: All machines.

Restrictions: F-LOCK must be installed for all calls except the installation check.

Registers at call:
AX = 4653h
CX = 0002h
BX = subfunction
    0000h installation check
    0001h uninstall
    0002h disable (v1.08 and below only)
    0003h enable (v1.08 and below only)

Return Registers:
Subfunction 0000h:
    AX = FFFFh
Subfunction 0001h:
    AX, BX, ES destroyed

Details: F-LOCK is part of the shareware F-PROT virus/trojan protection package by Fridrik Skulason.
Conflicts: None known.
See Also: Function 46h Subfunction 53h/CX=0003h, INT 21h Function 4Bh Subfunction EEh

INTERRUPT 2Fh - Function 46h, Subfunction 53h
F-POPUP.EXE

Purpose: Control F-POPUP, the popup menu system for F-PROT.

Available on: All machines.

Restrictions: F-POPUP must be installed for all calls except the installation check.

Registers at call:
AX = 4653h
CX = 0004h
BX = subfunction
    0000h installation check
    0001h uninstall
    0002h disable (v1.08 and below only)
        display message (v1.14+)
        other registers: *unknown.*
    0003h enable (v1.08 and below only)
        display message (v1.14+)
        other registers: *unknown.*

Return Registers:
Subfunction 0000h:
    AX = FFFFh
Subfunction 0001h:
    AX, BX, ES destroyed
Subfunction 0003h:
    AX = key pressed by user

Details: F-POPUP is part of the shareware F-PROT virus/trojan protection package by Fridrik Skulason. It is called by the F-LOCK and F-DLOCK programs.
Conflicts: None known.
See Also: Function 46h Subfunction 53h/CX=0003h,0005h

INTERRUPT 2Fh - Function 46h, Subfunction 53h
F-XCHK.EXE

Purpose: Control the operation of F-XCHK, which prevents the execution of any programs which have not had self-checking code added by F-XLOCK.

Available on: All machines.

Restrictions: F-XCHK must be installed for all calls except the installation check.

Registers at call:
AX = 4653h
CX = 0003h
BX = subfunction
    0000h installation check
    0001h uninstall

Return Registers:
Subfunction 0000h:
    AX = FFFFh
Subfunction 0001h:
    AX, BX, ES destroyed

Details: F-XCHK is part of the shareware F-PROT virus/trojan protection package by Fridrik Skulason.
Conflicts: None known.
See Also: Function 46h Subfunction 53h/CX=0002h,0004h

INTERRUPT 2Fh - Function CAh, Subfunction 00h
TBSCANX - INSTALLATION CHECK

Purpose: Determine whether TBSCANX is installed.

Available on: All machines.

Registers at call:
AX = CA00h
BX = 5442h ('TB')

Restrictions: none.

Return Registers:
AL = 00h not installed
 = FFh installed
BX = 7462h ('tb') if BX was 5442h on entry

Details: TBSCANX is a resident virus scanning module by Frans Veldman. Programs may perform virus checks on themselves, other program files, or their data files by invoking the TBSCANX API.
Conflicts: None known.

INTERRUPT 2Fh - Function CAh, Subfunction 01h
TBSCANX - GET STATUS

Purpose: Determine whether TBSCANX is active, how many virus signatures it contains, and where it has stored itself.

Available on: All machines.

Registers at call:
AX = CA01h

Restrictions: TBSCANX must be installed.

Return Registers:
AH = BCD version number (v2.2+)
 = CAh for versions before 2.2
AL = state (00h = disabled, 01h = enabled)
CX = number of signatures which will be searched
---v2.0---
BX = EMS handle, 0000h if not using EMS
---v2.3+---
BX = segment of swap area, 0000h if not swapped
DX = EMS handle, FFFFh if not using EMS

Conflicts: None known.
See Also: Function CAh Subfunction 02h

INTERRUPT 2Fh - Function CAh, Subfunction 02h
TBSCANX - SET STATE

Purpose: Specify whether TBSCANX should be active.

Available on: All machines.

Registers at call:
AX = CA02h
BL = new state (00h = disabled, 01h = enabled)
Conflicts: None known.
See Also: Function CAh Subfunction 01h

Restrictions: TBSCANX must be installed.
Return Registers: n/a

INTERRUPT 2Fh - Function CAh, Subfunction 03h
TBSCANX - SCAN BUFFER

Purpose: Request that TBSCANX scan the supplied buffer for virus signatures.

Available on: All machines.

Registers at call:
AX = CA03h

Restrictions: TBSCANX must be installed.
Return Registers:
CF clear if no virus signatures found
 BX,ES destroyed

CX = size of buffer
DS:DX -> buffer containing data to scan

CF set if signature found
    ES:BX -> ASCIZ virus name (v2.3+)
    DS:DX -> ASCIZ virus name (v2.0)
    AX,CX,DX destroyed (v2.3+)
    all other registers except CS:IP and SS:SP
      destroyed (v2.0)

Conflicts: None known.
See Also: Function CAh Subfunction 04h

INTERRUPT 2Fh - Function CAh, Subfunction 04h
TBSCANX - SCAN FILE

Purpose: Request that TBSCANX scan the specified file for virus signatures.
Available on: All machines.
Registers at call:
AX = CA04h
DS:DX -> filename

Restrictions: TBSCANX must be installed.
Return Registers:
CF clear if no virus signatures found
    BX,ES destroyed
CF set if signature found
    ES:BX -> ASCIZ virus name
    AX,CX,DX destroyed

Details: This function requires at least 4K free memory.
Conflicts: None known.
See Also: Function CAh Subfunction 03h

INTERRUPT 2Fh - Function C9h, Subfunction 00h
ThunderByte - INSTALLATION CHECK

Purpose: *Determine whether ThunderByte is installed.*
Available on: All machines.
Registers at call:
AX = C900h
BP = 0000h

Restrictions: none.
Return Registers:
AL = FFh if installed
    BP >= 0014h

Details: This function is called by TBSCANX.
See Also: Function C9h Subfunction 87h, Function CAh Subfunction 00h

INTERRUPT 2Fh - Function C9h, Subfunction 87h
ThunderByte - DISINFECT FILE

Purpose: Called by TBSCANX, apparently to disinfect an executable.
Available on: All machines.
Registers at call:
AX = C987h
BX:DX -> filename
BX:CX -> virus name
See Also: Function CAh Subfunction 00h

Restrictions: *ThunderByte* must be installed.
Return Registers:
AX = status
    0000h *successful*

INTERRUPT 21h - Function FAh
VDEFEND

This function is described in chapter 33 (PC Tools).

INTERRUPT 2Fh - Function 62h
VDEFEND

This function is described in chapter 33 (PC Tools).

Chapter ■ 35

Programming Language Runtime Support

Most high-level languages include a sizable runtime library of useful (and even essential) subroutines. A number of them use interrupts rather than direct calls to invoke or control functions in the runtime library. In this chapter, we cover floating-point emulation, overlays, JPI TopSPEED Modula-2, Logitech Modula-2, Exact, and BASIC.

Both Borland International and Microsoft Corporation use the same group of interrupts to emulate numeric coprocessor floating-point operations. Each interrupt emulates a specific coprocessor opcode. Typically, the compiler outputs either an FWAIT or a NOP instruction followed by the desired coprocessor instruction and a special linker fixup record. When linked with a coprocessor-only math library, the fixup records have no effect, but when linked with the emulator library, the FWAIT/NOP and opcode of each coprocessor instruction become the appropriate INT instructions.

These interrupts use registers on entry and exit only to the extent that the emulated instructions use them; in most cases, registers are either not used at all or used only to specify the memory operand of an instruction.

INTERRUPT 34h
Borland/Microsoft languages - Floating Point emulation

Purpose: Emulate coprocessor instructions with opcode D8h.
Available on: All machines.   **Restrictions:** Program using the floating point emulator must be running.

Conflicts: None known.

INTERRUPT 35h
Borland/Microsoft languages - Floating Point emulation

Purpose: Emulate coprocessor instructions with opcode D9h.
Available on: All machines.   **Restrictions:** Program using the floating point emulator must be running.

Conflicts: None known.

INTERRUPT 36h
Borland/Microsoft languages - Floating Point emulation

Purpose: Emulate coprocessor instructions with opcode DAh.
Available on: All machines.   **Restrictions:** Program using the floating point emulator must be running.

Conflicts: None known.

INTERRUPT 37h
Borland/Microsoft languages - Floating Point emulation

Purpose: Emulate coprocessor instructions with opcode DBh.
Available on: All machines.   **Restrictions:** Program using the floating point emulator must be running.

Conflicts: None known.

INTERRUPT 38h
Borland/Microsoft languages - Floating Point emulation

Purpose: Emulate coprocessor instructions with opcode DCh.

Available on: All machines.

Restrictions: Program using the floating point emulator must be running.

Conflicts: None known.

INTERRUPT 39h
Borland/Microsoft languages - Floating Point emulation

Purpose: Emulate coprocessor instructions with opcode DDh.

Available on: All machines.

Restrictions: Program using the floating point emulator must be running.

Conflicts: None known.

INTERRUPT 3Ah
Borland/Microsoft languages - Floating Point emulation

Purpose: Emulate coprocessor instructions with opcode DEh.

Available on: All machines.

Restrictions: Program using the floating point emulator must be running.

Conflicts: None known.

INTERRUPT 3Bh
Borland/Microsoft languages - Floating Point emulation

Purpose: Emulate coprocessor instructions with opcode DFh.

Available on: All machines.

Restrictions: Program using the floating point emulator must be running.

Conflicts: None known.

INTERRUPT 3Ch
Borland/Microsoft languages - Floating Point emulation

Purpose: Emulate coprocessor instructions with a segment override.

Available on: All machines.

Restrictions: Program using the floating point emulator must be running.

Details: The generated code is CDh 3Ch xy mm .... where xy is a modified ESC instruction and mm is the modR/M byte. The xy byte is encoded as either

$$s\,s\,0\,1\,1\,x\,x\,x$$
or
$$s\,s\,0\,0\,0\,x\,x\,x$$

(depending on the implementation), where "ss" specifies the segment override:

$$00 \to DS:$$
$$01 \to SS:$$
$$10 \to CS:$$
$$11 \to ES:$$

Conflicts: None known.

INTERRUPT 3Dh
Borland/Microsoft languages - Floating Point emulation

Purpose: Emulate a standalone FWAIT instruction.

Available on: All machines.

Restrictions: Program using the floating point emulator must be running.

Conflicts: None known.

INTERRUPT 3Eh
Borland languages - Floating Point emulation "shortcut" call

Purpose: Provide a number of common functions which do not necessarily correspond to a single floating point instruction.

Available on: All machines.

Restrictions: Program using the Borland floating point emulator (Turbo Pascal, Turbo C, Turbo BASIC, Quattro Pro) must be running.

Details: The two bytes following the INT 3Eh instruction are the subcode (Table 35-1) and a NOP (90h). The shortcut call has been changed for Borland C++ version 2; it now supports only subcodes E6h through FEh, and at the time of writing it was not yet known whether those subcodes correspond to the subcodes in earlier products.

Conflicts: None known.

Table 35-1. Values of Shortcut Subcodes:

Subcode	Description
DCh	load 8086 stack with 8087 registers
DEh	load 8087 registers from 8086 stack
E0h	round TOS and R1 to single precision, compare, pop twice
E2h	round TOS and R1 to double precision, compare, pop twice; **Note:** apparently buggy in Turbo Pascal 5.5, actually rounding to single precision.
E4h	compare TOS/R1 with two POP's
E6h	compare TOS/R1 with POP
E8h	FTST (check TOS value)
EAh	FXAM (check TOS value)
ECh	sine
EEh	cosine
F0h	tangent
F2h	arctangent
F4h	Ln (FLDLN2 to TOS)
F6h	Log2 (FLDLG2 to TOS)
F8h	Log10 (FLDLG10 to TOS)
FAh	Exp (FLDL2E to TOS)
FCh	TOS = 2**TOS
FEh	TOS = 10**TOS

Overlay Managers

When using overlays, a mechanism is needed to permit calling functions which may not be in memory, and loading them if necessary. Microsoft chose to do so using a software interrupt; loading a 16-bit register and calling an interrupt requires a total of five bytes, the same as a far CALL. This allows the overlay linker to perform the necessary fixups to create the overlaid executable.

INTERRUPT 3Fh
Microsoft Dynamic Link Library manager

Purpose: Provide DLL services such as loading libraries on the first access.

Available on: All machines.

Restrictions: Dynamic Link Library manager must be active.

Conflicts: None known.

INTERRUPT 3Fh
Overlay manager interrupt (Microsoft LINK.EXE, Borland TLINK VROOMM)

Purpose: Invoke the specified overlay, loading it into memory if not presently there.

Available on: All machines.

Restrictions: Must be running a program using an internal overlay manager.

Registers at call: *unknown.*

Return Registers: *unknown.*

Details: INT 3Fh is the default, and may be overridden while linking.
Conflicts: None known.

JPI TopSPEED Modula-2

INTERRUPT 60h
Procedure Entry Trap

Purpose: Call a debugging or profiling routine on entry to a procedure, in order to determine which procedure is active or how much time is spent in each procedure.
Available on: All machines.

Restrictions: A program written using JPI TopSPEED Modula-2 version must be running.
Return Registers: n/a

Registers at call:
unknown
Conflicts: See Table 1-3 (chapter 1).
See Also: INT 61h

INTERRUPT 61h
Procedure Exit Trap

Purpose: Call a debugging or profiling routine when leaving a procedure, in order to determine which procedure is active or how much time is spent in each procedure.
Available on: All machines.

Restrictions: A program written using JPI TopSPEED Modula-2 version must be running.
Return Registers: n/a

Registers at call:
unknown
Conflicts: See Table 1-3 (chapter 1).
See Also: INT 60h

Logitech Modula-2

INTERRUPT E4h - Function 00h, Subfunction 05h
Monitor Entry

Purpose: *unknown.*
Available on: All machines.

Restrictions: A program written using Logitech Modula-2 version 2 must be running.
Return Registers: n/a

Registers at call:
AX = 0005h
BX = priority
Conflicts: BASIC interpreter (chapter 1).
See Also: Function 00h Subfunction 06h

INTERRUPT E4h - Function 00h, Subfunction 06h
Monitor Exit

Purpose: *unknown.*
Available on: All machines.

Restrictions: A program written using Logitech Modula-2 version 2 must be running.
Return Registers: n/a

Registers at call:
AX = 0006h
Conflicts: BASIC interpreter (chapter 1).
See Also: Function 00h Subfunction 05h

EXACT

The following interrupt is the interface from applications to the runtime system by Exact Automatisering B.V. of the Netherlands. By using this interrupt, it can provide DLL-style capabilities under MSDOS.

INTERRUPT ECh
Exact - RUNTIME INTERFACE MULTIPLEXOR

Purpose: Invoke the Exact runtime system.
Available on: All machines.

Restrictions: The Exact runtime system must be installed.

Registers at call:
AX = function number (0000h to 0140h)
STACK: DWORD   address to return to
     any arguments required by function

Return Registers:
STACK: return address popped, but otherwise unchanged

Details: The interrupt handler removes the return address and flags placed on the stack by the INT ECh, then jumps to the appropriate function.
Conflicts: BASIC interpreter (chapter 1).

BASIC

In addition to the two below, the IBM ROM BASIC interpreter uses interrupts 86h through EEh to allow extensions and execution tracing; those interrupts are mentioned briefly in chapter 1.

INTERRUPT EFh
ORIGINAL INT 09h VECTOR

Purpose: Stores the address of the handler for INT 09h that was current before BASIC was started.
Available on: All machines.

Restrictions: Valid only while BASIC (interpreted or compiled) is running.

Registers at call: n/a

Return Registers: n/a

Details: IBM BASIC.COM/BASICA.COM do not restore this vector on termination.
Conflicts: GEM interface (chapter 36)

INTERRUPT F0h
ORIGINAL INT 08h VECTOR

Purpose: Stores the address of the handler for INT 08h that was current before BASIC was started.
Available on: All machines.

Restrictions: Valid only while BASIC (interpreted or compiled) is running.

Registers at call: n/a

Return Registers: n/a

Details: IBM BASIC.COM/BASICA.COM do not restore this vector on termination.
Conflicts: None known.

Chapter ■ 36

Miscellaneous APIs

The preceding 35 chapters of this volume have grouped the various services that use the interrupt structure such that similar services are described in the same chapters. Now, however, we've reached the end of the book, so this chapter describes "everything else" (ranging from alternative command interpreters through sound interfaces, with varied stops in between).

In this chapter, the descriptions are arranged in alphabetic sequence by service/program/library name, and within each such group, by numeric sequence of interrupt, function, and subfunction.

4DOS

4DOS, from JP Software, is an alternative command interpreter that replaces COMMAND.COM in all versions of MS-DOS from 2.1 through 5.0, and also works with DOS-compatible alternative operating systems such as DR-DOS. In addition to the calls listed here, the KEYSTACK.SYS driver included with 4DOS supports INT 21h Function 44h Subfunction 03h (see chapter 8).

INTERRUPT 2Eh - Function E22Eh
SHELL2E.COM - UNINSTALL

Purpose: Causes SHELL2E to uninstall itself. SHELL2E.COM is a utility that emulates some actions of COM-MAND.COM's undocumented "backdoor" entry to permit use of programs (notably NetWare) that require these actions when the 4DOS command interpreter is installed.

Available on: All machines.

Registers at call:
BX = E22Eh
DS:SI -> zero byte

Conflicts: None known.

Restrictions: none.

Return Registers:
If successful, SHELL2E terminates itself with INT 21h
   Function 4Ch

INTERRUPT 2Fh - Function D44Dh, Subfunction 00h
INSTALLATION CHECK

Purpose: Determine whether 4DOS version 2.1 or higher is installed.

Available on: All machines.

Registers at call:
AX = D44Dh
BH = 00h

Restrictions: none.

Return Registers:
AX = 44DDh
BL = minor version number
BH = major version number
CX = PSP segment address for current invocation
DL = 4DOS shell number (0 for the first (root) shell,
          updated each time a new copy is loaded)

Details: A bug in version 3.00 will crash the system if BH contains an unrecognized subfunction number on entry.

Conflicts: None known.

INTERRUPT 2Fh - Function D44Dh, Subfunction 01h
internal - TERMINATE CURRENT COPY OF 4DOS

Purpose: Exit the current invocation of 4DOS.COM when the 4DOS.EXE it loaded terminates.

Available on: All machines.

Registers at call:
AX = D44Dh
BH = 01h
Details: A bug in version 3.00 will crash the system if BH contains an unrecognized subfunction number on entry.
Conflicts: None known.

Restrictions: 4DOS version 2.1 or higher must be installed.
Return Registers: n/a

INTERRUPT 2Fh - Function D44Dh, Subfunction 02h
Unknown Function

Purpose: *unknown*.
Available on: All machines.

Registers at call:
AX = D44Dh
BH = 02h
DX = *unknown*.
Details: A bug in version 3.00 will crash the system if BH contains an unrecognized subfunction number on entry.
Conflicts: None known.

Restrictions: 4DOS version 2.1 or higher must be installed.
Return Registers: *unknown*.

INTERRUPT 2Fh - Function D44Dh, Subfunction 03h
EXEC PROGRAM

Purpose: Execute a child program.
Available on: All machines.

Registers at call:
AX = D44Dh
BH = 03h
CX:DX -> EXEC record (Table 36-1)
Details: A bug in version 3.00 will crash the system if BH contains an unrecognized subfunction number on entry.
Conflicts: None known.
See Also: INT 21h Function 4Bh (chapter 8)

Restrictions: 4DOS version 2.1 or higher must be installed.
Return Registers: *unknown*.

Table 36-1. Format of EXEC Record:

Offset	Size	Description
00h	WORD	offset of ASCIZ program name in same segment as EXEC record
02h	WORD	offset of DOS commandline in same segment as EXEC record
04h	WORD	segment of environment for child process (see INT 21h Function 26h, chapter 8)

INTERRUPT 2Fh - Function D44Dh, Subfunction FEh
DEALLOCATE SHELL NUMBER

Purpose: Release the shell number allocated to the calling invocation of 4DOS.
Available on: All machines.

Registers at call:
AX = D44Dh
BH = FEh deallocate shell number (passed through
    to root shell)
Details: A bug in version 3.00 will crash the system if BH contains an unrecognized subfunction number on entry.
Conflicts: None known.

Restrictions: 4DOS version 2.1 or higher must be installed.
Return Registers: n/a

INTERRUPT 2Fh - Function D44Dh, Subfunction FFh
ALLOCATE SHELL NUMBER

Purpose: Request a shell number for use in creating unique swap files.

Available on: All machines.

Restrictions: 4DOS version 2.1 or higher must be installed.

Registers at call:

AX = D44Dh

BH = FFh allocate shell number (passed through to
  root shell)

Return Registers: *unknown.*

Details: A bug in version 3.00 will crash the system if BH contains an unrecognized subfunction number on entry.

Conflicts: None known.

INTERRUPT 2Fh - Function D4h, Subfunction 4Eh
AWAITING USER INPUT

Purpose: Provides hooks for user programs to know when command interpreter is at prompting leve.

Available on: All machines.

Restrictions: 4DOS version 3.0 or higher must be running.

Registers at call:

AX = D44Eh

--4DOS v3.01+

BX = 0000h 4DOS is ready to display prompt
 = 0001h 4DOS has displayed the prompt, and is
      about to accept user input

Return Registers:

Handler must preserve SI, DI, BP, SP, DS, ES, and SS

Details: Version 3.00 only makes the call corresponding to BX=0001h, and does not set BX.

Conflicts: None known.

Ad Lib SOUND.COM

INTERRUPT 65h
SOUND.COM INTERFACE

Purpose: Control the Ad Lib sound board's driver.

Available on: All machines.

Restrictions: SOUND.COM must be installed.

Registers at call:

SI = function number (see the separate entries
      below for details on several)

  = 0000h Init
  = 0002h RelTimeStart
  = 0003h SetState
  = 0004h GetState
  = 0005h Flush
  = 0006h SetMode
  = 0007h GetMode
  = 0008h SetRelVolume
  = 0009h SetTempo
  = 000Ah SetTranspose
  = 000Bh GetTranspose
  = 000Ch SetActVoice
  = 000Dh GetActVoice
  = 000Eh PlayNoteDel
  = 000Fh PlayNote
  = 0010h SetTimbre
  = 0011h SetPitch

Return Registers:

varies by function

= 0012h SetTickBeat
= 0013h NoteOn
= 0014h NoteOff
= 0015h Timbre
= 0016h SetPitchBend
= 0017h WaveForm

ES:BX -> arguments

Details: The installation check consists of checking for the signature block immediately preceding the interrupt handler (Table 36-2).

Conflicts: See chapter 1.

Table 36-2. Format of Signature Block:

Offset	Size	Description
00h	WORD	version number
02h	19 BYTEs	"SOUND-DRIVER-AD-LIB"
15h	BYTE	01h
16h	BYTE	01h
17h	BYTE	00h

INTERRUPT 65h - Function 0000h
INITIALIZE (RESET)

Purpose: Return the sound board and driver to a known initial state.

Available on: Systems equipped with an Ad Lib sound board.

Restrictions: SOUND.COM must be installed.

Registers at call:
SI = 0000h

Return Registers: n/a

Conflicts: See chapter 1.

INTERRUPT 65h - Function 0003h
SET STATE

Purpose: Specify whether the sound board should be active.

Available on: Systems equipped with an Ad Lib sound board.

Restrictions: SOUND.COM must be installed.

Registers at call:
SI = 0003h
ES:BX -> WORD state
  = 0000h disabled
  = 0001h enabled

Return Registers: n/a

Conflicts: See chapter 1.
See Also: Function 0004h

INTERRUPT 65h - Function 0004h
GET STATE

Purpose: Determine whether the sound board is currently active.

Available on: Systems equipped with an Ad Lib sound board.

Restrictions: SOUND.COM must be installed.

Registers at call:
SI = 0004h

Return Registers:
AX = 0000h all done playing sounds
     else still playing sounds

Conflicts: See chapter 1.
See Also: Function 0003h

INTERRUPT 65h - Function 0006h
SET MODE

Purpose: Specify the type of sound to be played by the sound board.

Available on: Systems equipped with an Ad Lib sound board.

Restrictions: SOUND.COM must be installed.

Registers at call:
SI = 0006h
ES:BX -> WORD mode
   = 0000h melodic
   = 0001h percussive

Return Registers: n/a

Conflicts: See chapter 1.
See Also: Function 0007h

INTERRUPT 65h - Function 0007h
GET MODE

Purpose: Determine the type of sound the board is supposed to be playing.

Available on: Systems equipped with an Ad Lib sound board.

Restrictions: SOUND.COM must be installed.

Registers at call:
SI = 0007h

Return Registers:
AX = 0000h melodic
     0001h percussive

Conflicts: See chapter 1.
See Also: Function 0006h

INTERRUPT 65h - Function 000Ch
SET ACTIVE VOICE

Purpose: Specify which of the sound board's voices is to be active.

Available on: Systems equipped with an Ad Lib sound board.

Restrictions: SOUND.COM must be installed.

Registers at call:
SI = 000Ch
ES:BX -> WORD voice (0000h to 0008h)

Return Registers:
n/a

Conflicts: See chapter 1.
See Also: Function 000Dh

INTERRUPT 65h - Function 000Dh
GET ACTIVE VOICE

Purpose: Determine which of the sound board's voices is currently active.

Available on: Systems equipped with an Ad Lib sound board.

Restrictions: SOUND.COM must be installed.

Registers at call:
SI = 000Dh

Return Registers:
AX = voice (0000h to 0008h)

Conflicts: See chapter 1.
See Also: Function 000Ch

ANARKEY

ANARKEY.COM is a commandline recall program by Steven Calwas.

INTERRUPT 2Fh - Function E3h, Subfunction 00h
INSTALLATION CHECK

Purpose: Determine whether ANARKEY is installed.

Available on: All machines.

Restrictions: none.

Registers at call:
AX = E300h

Return Registers:
AL = 00h not installed
     FEh if installed but suspended (v3.0+)
     FFh installed

Details: The default multiplex number is E3h, but it can be set to any value from C0h to FFh.
Conflicts: See chapter 1.

INTERRUPT 2Fh - Function E3h, Subfunction 01h
GET Unknown Data

Purpose: *unknown.*
Available on: All machines.

Restrictions: ANARKEY.COM version 2.0 or higher
     must be installed.

Registers at call:
AX = E301h
Conflicts: See chapter 1.

Return Registers:
DX:BX -> *unknown.*

Table 36-3. Format of Returned Data Structure for ANARKEY v2.0:

Offset	Size	Description
-7	7 BYTEs	signature ('ANARKEY')
00h	WORD	*unknown* (0001h in v2.0)
02h	WORD	*unknown* (0001h in v2.0)
04h	WORD	*unknown* (0000h in v2.0)
06h	WORD	PSP segment of next program loaded

Table 36-4. Format of Returned Data Structure for ANARKEY v3.0:

Offset	Size	Description
-1	BYTE	multiplex number
00h	WORD	*unknown* (0001h in v3.0)
02h	WORD	*unknown* (0001h in v3.0)
04h	BYTE	*unknown* (0000h in v3.0)
05h	WORD	PSP segment of next program loaded

INTERRUPT 2Fh - Function E3h, Subfunction 02h
Unknown Function

Purpose: *unknown.*
Available on: All machines.

Restrictions: ANARKEY.COM version 3.0 or higher
     must be installed.
Return Registers: *unknown.*

Registers at call:
AX = E302h
BL = *unknown.*
Conflicts: See chapter 1.

INTERRUPT 2Fh - Function E3h, Subfunction 03h
ANARKMD API

Purpose: Perform the functions available to the user through the ANARKMD program.
Available on: All machines.

Restrictions: ANARKEY.COM version 3.0 or higher
     must be installed.
Return Registers: *unknown.*

Registers at call:
AX = E303h
BL = function
   01h toggle insert mode
   02h display contents of history buffer

03h write history buffer to file
    ES:DX -> file name
04h clear history buffer
05h undefine all aliases
06h show aliases
07h list programs using Unix switchar
08h jump to bottom of history buffer
---v4.0
09h add string to history buffer
    ES:DI -> ASCIZ string
0Ah   *unknown.*
    ES:DI -> unknown code or data.
0Bh   copy string to edit buffer for use as
            next input line.
    ES:DI -> ASCIZ string
0Ch   *unknown.*
0Dh   *unknown copying operation*
0Eh   *unknown.*
0Fh*unknown.*
10h set *unknown* flag
11h display error message about running in
        EMS under MS Windows.
Conflicts: See chapter 1.

INTERRUPT 2Fh - Function E3h, Subfunction 04h
Unknown Function

Purpose: *unknown.*
Available on: All machines.

Registers at call:
AX = E304h
BL = *unknown.*
Conflicts: See chapter 1.

Restrictions: ANARKEY.COM version 2.0 or higher
                must be installed.
Return Registers: *unknown.*

INTERRUPT 2Fh - Function E3h, Subfunction 05h
SUSPEND/ENABLE ANARKEY

Purpose: Specify whether ANARKEY is to be active and provide commandline recall/editing.
Available on: All machines.

Registers at call:
AX = E305h
BL = 01h suspend
    00h enable
Conflicts: See chapter 1.
See Also: Function E3h Subfunction 00h

Restrictions: ANARKEY.COM version 3.0 or higher
                must be installed.
Return Registers: n/a

INTERRUPT 2Fh - Function E3h, Subfunction 06h
Unknown Function

Purpose: *unknown.*
Available on: All machines.

Registers at call:
AX = E306h

Restrictions: ANARKEY.COM version 4.0 must be
                installed.
Return Registers: *unknown.*

Conflicts: See chapter 1.
See Also: Function E3h Subfunction 00h

INTERRUPT 2Fh - Function E3h, Subfunction 07h
Unknown Function

Purpose: *unknown.*
Available on: All machines.

Restrictions: ANARKEY.COM version 4.0 must be installed.

Registers at call:
AX = E307h

Return Registers:
AX = *unknown.*
BL = *unknown.*

Conflicts: See chapter 1.
See Also: Function E3h Subfunction 00h

AutoCAD

INTERRUPT 7Ah
AutoCAD Device Interface

Purpose: Communication between AutoCAD and its device drivers.
Available on: All machines.
Registers at call: *unknown.*

Restrictions: Must be running AutoCAD.
Return Registers: *unknown.*

Conflicts: Novell NetWare Low-level API (chapter 20), IBM 3270 Workstation Program API (chapter 26), Topware Network Operating System (chapter 27).

AVATAR.SYS
AVATAR.SYS is a CON replacement by George Adam Stanislav which interprets AVATAR command codes in the same way that ANSI.SYS interprets ANSI command codes.

INTERRUPT 2Fh - Function 1Ah, Subfunction 00h
INSTALLATION CHECK

Purpose: Determine whether AVATAR.SYS is installed.
Available on: All machines.
Registers at call:
AX = 1A00h
BX = 4156h ('AV')
CX = 4154h ('AT')
DX = 4152h ('AR')

Restrictions: none.
Return Registers:
AL = FFh if installed
CF clear
BX = AVATAR protocol level supported
CX = driver type:
    0000h AVATAR.SYS
    4456h DVAVATAR.COM inside a DESQview
        window
DX = 0016h

Details: AVATAR also identifies itself as ANSI.SYS if BX, CX, or DX differ from the magic values.
Conflicts: DOS 4+ ANSI.SYS (chapter 8).

INTERRUPT 2Fh - Function 1Ah, Subfunction 21h
SET DRIVER STATE

Purpose: Specify whether AVATAR.SYS is to be active, what type of screen output to perform, and whether to translate the gray plus and minus keys.
Available on: All machines.

Restrictions: AVATAR.SYS must be installed.

Registers at call:
AX = 1A21h (AL='!')
DS:SI -> command string with one or more state
    characters (Table 36-5)
CX = length of command string
Details: The characters in the state string are interpreted left to right, and need not be in any particular order.
Conflicts: None known.
See Also: Function 1Ah Subfunction 3Fh

Return Registers:
CF set on error (invalid subfunction)
CF clear if successful

Table 36-5. Values of State Characters:

Value	Meaning
'a'	activate driver
'd'	disable driver
'f'	use fast screen output
'g'	always convert gray keys (+ and -) to function keys
'G'	never convert gray keys
'l'	convert gray keys only when ScrollLock active
's'	use slow screen output
't'	Tandy 1000 keyboard (not yet implemented)

INTERRUPT 2Fh - Function 1Ah, Subfunction 3Ch
Unknown Function

Purpose: *unknown.*
Available on: All machines.

Restrictions: AVATAR.SYS version 0.11 must be installed.

Registers at call:
AX = 1A3Ch
unknown.
Conflicts: None known.

Return Registers:
CX = 0000h

INTERRUPT 2Fh - Function 1Ah, Subfunction 3Eh
Unknown Function

Purpose: *unknown.*
Available on: All machines.

Restrictions: AVATAR.SYS version 0.11 must be installed.

Registers at call:
AX = 1A3Eh
CL = *unknown.*
CH = *unknown.*
DL = *unknown.*
DH = *unknown.*
Conflicts: None known.

Return Registers:
CL = *unknown.*
CH = *unknown.*
DL = *unknown.*
DH = *unknown.*

INTERRUPT 2Fh - Function 1Ah, Subfunction 3Fh
QUERY DRIVER STATE

Purpose: Determine whether AVATAR.SYS is active, which type of screen output it is performing, and whether it is translating the gray plus and minus keys.
Available on: All machines.
Registers at call:
AX = 1A3Fh (AL='?')
ES:DI -> buffer
CX = length of buffer in bytes

Restrictions: AVATAR.SYS must be installed.
Return Registers:
CF clear
        CX = actual size of returned info

Details: The returned information consists of multiple letters whose meanings are described under Function 1Ah Subfunction 21h.
Conflicts: None known.
See Also: Function 1Ah Subfunction 21h

INTERRUPT 2Fh - Function 1Ah, Subfunction 44h
GET DATA SEGMENT

Purpose: Called by AVATAR.SYS whenever it is invoked in order to determine where to store its data.
Available on: All machines.
Restrictions: AVATAR.SYS version 0.11 or higher must be installed.

Registers at call:
AX = 1A44h
BX = 4156h ('AV')

Return Registers:
AX = 0000h
DS = data segment
CX = size of data segment

Details: If each process under a multitasker hooks this function and provides a separate data segment, AVATAR.SYS becomes fully reentrant.
Conflicts: None known.
See Also: Function 1Ah Subfunctions 21h and 3Fh

INTERRUPT 2Fh - Function 1Ah, Subfunction 52h
GET Unknown Data

Purpose: *unknown.*
Available on: All machines.
Restrictions: AVATAR.SYS version 0.11 must be installed.

Registers at call:
AX = 1A52h
CX = size of buffer
ES:DI -> buffer

Return Registers:
unknown data copied into user buffer

Details: The maximum size of the data which may be copied is returned by Function 1Ah Subfunction 72h.
Conflicts: None known.
See Also: Function 1Ah Subfunction 72h

INTERRUPT 2Fh - Function 1Ah, Subfunction 53h
Unknown Function

Purpose: *unknown.*
Available on: All machines.
Restrictions: AVATAR.SYS version 0.11 must be installed.

Registers at call:
AX = 1A53h
CL = *unknown.* (00h-05h)
unknown.

Return Registers: *unknown.*

Conflicts: None known.

INTERRUPT 2Fh - Function 1Ah, Subfunction 72h
GET Unknown SIZE

Purpose: Determine the maximum size of the data which may be returned by Subfunction 52h.
Available on: All machines.
Restrictions: AVATAR.SYS version 0.11 must be installed.

Registers at call:
AX = 1A72h
Conflicts: None known.
See Also: Function 1Ah Subfunction 52h

Return Registers:
CX = maximum size of *unknown data*

INTERRUPT 2Fh - Function 1Ah, Subfunction 7Bh
Unknown Function

Purpose: *unknown.*
Available on: All machines.

Registers at call:
AX = 1A7Bh

Conflicts: None known.

Restrictions: AVATAR.SYS version 0.11 must be installed.
Return Registers:
AX = 0000h
CX = 0000h

INTERRUPT 2Fh - Function 1Ah, Subfunction 7Dh
Unknown Function

Purpose: *unknown.*
Available on: All machines.

Registers at call:
AX = 1A7Dh

Restrictions: AVATAR.SYS version 0.11 must be installed.
Return Registers:
AX = *unknown.*

INTERRUPT 2Fh - Function 1Ah, Subfunction ADh
Unknown Function

Purpose: *unknown.*
Available on: All machines.

Registers at call:
AX = 1AADh
DX = 0000h
CX = subfunction (00h-0Ch)
unknown.
Conflicts: None known.

Restrictions: AVATAR.SYS version 0.11 must be installed.
Return Registers:
AX = 0000h if DX was nonzero
unknown.

INTERRUPT 79h
FAST GET KEYSTROKE

Purpose: Retrieve the next keystroke from the keyboard buffer, if available.
Available on: All machines.
Registers at call: n/a

Restrictions: AVATAR.SYS must be installed.
Return Registers:
CF set if no keystroke available
    AX = FFFFh
CF clear if key pressed
    AX = keystroke

Details: If a keystroke is available, it is removed from the keyboard buffer before being returned.
Conflicts: None known.
See Also: INT 29h

BMB Compuscience Canada Utilities
BMB Compuscience Canada produces a number of utilities which all use the common installation check described here.

INTERRUPT 2Fh
INSTALLATION CHECK

Purpose: Determine whether one of the BMB Compuscience Canada utilities or another program using the same interface is installed.
Available on: All machines.

Restrictions: none.

Registers at call:
AH = xx (dynamically assigned based upon a search
    for a multiplex number which doesn't answer
    installed)
AL = 00h install check
ES:DI = EBEBh:BEBEh

Return Registers:
AL = 00h not installed
    01h not installed, not OK to install
    FFh installed

Details: If ES:DI was EBEBh:BEBEh on entry, ES:DI will point to a string of the form 'MMMMPPPPPPPPvNNNN' where MMMM is a short form of the manufacturer's name, PPPPPPPP is a product name and NNNN is the product's version number.

Btrieve

Btrieve is a record management system originally produced by SoftCraft but now published and maintained by Novell. One of the most widely used record managers, it offers automatic record locking for network support, and pre- and post-imaging to preserve data integrity in case of power failure. Though often called a database manager, Btrieve does not maintain field information within the data files as do most database management systems, nor does it even distinguish between "fields" within a record. Thus the same records may be viewed in quite different ways by different programs.

In single-user environments, Btrieve requires that its TSR be loaded; in network environments, the TSR may be loaded at each workstation, or a special BREQUEST server may be invoked.

INTERRUPT 7Bh
Btrieve API

Purpose: Open, access, modify, and close data files using Btrieve record manager.
Available on: All machines.

Restrictions: BTRIEVE's TSR, or network BREQUEST, must be active.

Registers at call:
DS:DX -> 38-byte parameter record (Table 36-6)

Return Registers:
return code field set

Details: Btrieve sets low byte of vector to 33h; this serves as the installation check.
Conflicts: Eicon Access API (chapter 26).

Table 36-6. Format of Btrieve Parameter Record:

Offset	Size	Description
00h	DWORD	pointer to data buffer
04h	WORD	data buffer length
06h	DWORD	pointer to 90-byte record containing positioning info (should be the same for all calls for the same file)
0Ah	DWORD	pointer to 38-byte FCB info buffer (should be same for all calls for same file)
0Eh	WORD	function code (Table 36-7)
10h	DWORD	pointer to file name/key buffer
14h	BYTE	key length
15h	BYTE	key number
16h	DWORD	pointer to status code (Table 36-8)
1Ah	WORD	interface code (version specific)

Table 36-7. Values for Btrieve function code:

Value	Function	Value	Function
00h	open	08h	get_greater
01h	close	09h	get_gr_eql
02h	insert	0Ah	get_less
03h	update	0Bh	get_less_eq
04h	delete	0Ch	get_first
05h	get_equal	0Dh	get_last
06h	get_next	0Eh	create
07h	get_prev	0Fh	stat

Table 36-7. Values for Btrieve function code (continued)

Value	Function	Value	Function
10h	extend	1Eh	clear owner
11h	set_dir: set directory information	1Fh	create supplemental index
12h	get_dir: get directory information	20h	drop supplemental index
13h	begin_trans	21h	step first
14h	end_trans	22h	step last
15h	abort_trans	23h	step next
16h	get_pos: get record position number	31h	*unknown.*
17h	get_direct: get data by sending record position	37h	*unknown.*
		38h	*unknown.*
18h	step_direct	39h	*unknown.*
19h	stop	3Ah	*unknown.*
1Ah	version	3Bh	*unknown.*
1Bh	unlock	3Ch	*unknown.*
1Ch	reset	3Dh	*unknown.*
1Dh	set owner	3Eh	*unknown.*
		3Fh	*unknown.*

Add 100 (64h) for a single-record wait lock (automatically released on next get)
Add 200 (C8h) for a single-record nowait lock (returns error 54h or 55h if the record is already locked)
Add 300 (12Ch) for a multiple-record wait lock (not released until unlock called)
Add 400 (190h) for a multiple-record nowait lock (returns error 54h or 55h if the record is already locked)

Table 36-8. Values for Status Code:

Value	Function	Value	Function
00h	successful	20h	extended I/O error
01h	invalid operation	22h	invalid extension name
02h	I/O error	23h	directory error
03h	file not open	24h	transaction error
04h	key value not found	25h	transaction is active
05h	duplicate key value	26h	transaction control file I/O error
06h	invalid key number	27h	end/abort transaction error
07h	different key number	28h	transaction max files
08h	invalid positioning	29h	operation not allowed
09h	end of file	2Ah	incomplete accelerated access
0Ah	modifiable key value error	2Bh	invalid record address
0Bh	invalid file name	2Ch	null key path
0Ch	file not found	2Dh	inconsistent key flags
0Dh	extended file error	2Eh	access to file denied
0Eh	pre-image open error	2Fh	maximum open files
0Fh	pre-image I/O error	30h	invalid alternate sequence definition
10h	expansion error		
11h	close error	31h	key type error
12h	disk full	32h	owner already set
13h	unrecoverable error	33h	invalid owner
14h	record manager inactive	34h	error writing cache
15h	key buffer too short	35h	invalid interface
16h	data buffer lengthoverrun	36h	variable page error
17h	position block length	37h	autoincrement error
18h	page size error	38h	incomplete index
19h	create I/O error	39h	expanded memory error
1Ah	number of keys	3Ah	compression buffer too short
1Bh	invalid key position	3Bh	file already exists
1Ch	invalid record length	50h	conflict
1Dh	invalid key length	51h	lock error
1Eh	not a Btrieve file	52h	lost position
1Fh	file already extended	53h	read outside transaction

Table 36-8. Values for Status Code (continued)

Value	Function		Value	Function
54h	record in use		57h	handle table full
55h	file in use		58h	incompatible open mode
56h	file table full		5Dh	incompatible lock type
			5Eh	permission error

CED (Command Editor)

CED is a shareware DOS command-line enhancer by Christopher J. Dunford; its follow-on is the commercial product PCED. One feature which CED adds is the ability to install user-provided commands, which will be treated as "internal commands" by CED. DOS 3.3 and higher provide an equivalent capability in COMMAND.COM; see INT 2Fh Function AEh in chapter 8.

INTERRUPT 21h - Function FFh, subfunction 00h
ADD INSTALLABLE COMMAND

Purpose: Store the name and handler for a new CED command.

Available on: All machines.

Registers at call:
AH = FFH
AL = 00h
BL = mode
   bit 0 = 1 callable from DOS prompt
   bit 1 = 1 callable from application
DS:SI -> CR-terminated command name
ES:DI -> FAR routine entry point

Conflicts: None known.

See Also: WCED Function 0Ah Subfunction 00h (below)

Restrictions: CED must be installed.

Return Registers:
CF clear if successful
CF set on error
   AX = 01h invalid function
      08h insufficient memory
      0Eh bad data
   AH = FFh if CED not installed

INTERRUPT 21h - Function FFh, subfunction 01h
REMOVE INSTALLABLE COMMAND

Purpose: Erase the name and handler for the specified installed CED command.

Available on: All machines.

Registers at call:
AH = FFH
AL = 01h
DS:SI -> CR-terminated command name

Restrictions: CED must be installed.

Return Registers:
CF clear if successful
CF set on error
   AX = 01h invalid function
      02h command not found
   AH = FFh if CED not installed

Conflicts: None known.

See Also: WCED Function 0Ah Subfunction 00h (below)

INTERRUPT 21h - Function FFh, subfunction 02h
RESERVED, MAY BE USED TO TEST FOR CED INSTALLATION

Purpose: Determine whether CED is installed.

Available on: All machines.

Registers at call:
AH = FFH
AL = 02h

Restrictions: none.

Return Registers:
CF clear if successful
CF set on error
   AX = 01h invalid function
   AH = FFh if CED not installed

Conflicts: None known.

See Also: WCED Function 0Ah Subfunction 00h (below)

CP/M-86

Digital Research's CP/M-86 was one of the three operating systems originally offered by IBM for its PC. Although it never gained much popularity, its descendant DR-DOS is currently selling fairly successfully. Unlike DR-DOS, however, CP/M-86 is entirely incompatible with MS-DOS.

INTERRUPT E0h
CP/M-86 function calls

Purpose: Request operating system functions.
Available on: Machines running CP/M-86.   **Restrictions:** none.
Conflicts: BASIC interpreter (chapter 1), APL*PLUS/PC (chapter 31), "Micro-128" virus (chapter 34).

Disk Spool II

Disk Spool II by Budget Software Company is a disk-based print spooler. When an application produces printer output, that output is captured and stored on disk; as the printer becomes ready for more output, previously-stored data is retrieved from the disk and sent to the printer.

INTERRUPT 1Ah - Function A0h
INSTALLATION CHECK

Purpose: Determine whether Disk Spool II (*version unknown*) is installed.
Available on: All machines.
Registers at call:
AH = A0h

Restrictions: none.
Return Registers:
AH = B0h
ES = code segment
BX -> name of current spool file
SI -> current despool file
CL = 00h despooler is disabled
    41h despooler is enabled
CH = 00h spooler is disabled
    41h spooler is enabled
DL = 00h despooler is currently active printing a file
    41h despooler is standing by

Conflicts: None known.
See Also: Function D0h

INTERRUPT 1Ah - Function ABh
INSTALLATION CHECK

Purpose: Determine whether Disk Spool II version 1.83 is installed.
Available on: All machines.
Registers at call:
AH = ABh

Restrictions: none.
Return Registers:
ES = code segment
BX -> name of current spool file
SI -> current despool file
CL = *unknown.*
CH = *unknown.*
DL = *unknown.*
DH = 00h *unknown.*
  = 41h *unknown.*
AL = *unknown.*
AH = BAh
DI = 0000h *unknown.*
    0001h *unknown.*

Conflicts: None known.

See Also: Functions ACh and ADh

INTERRUPT 1Ah - Function ACh
INSTALLATION CHECK

Purpose: Determine whether Disk Spool II version 1.83 is installed.

Available on: All machines.

Registers at call:
AH = ACh

Details: This function is identical to Function ABh.

Conflicts: None known.

See Also: Functions ABh and ADh

Restrictions: none.

Return Registers:
(see Function ABh)

INTERRUPT 1Ah - Function ADh
Disk Spool FUNCTION CALLS

Purpose: Control the print spooler.

Available on: All machines.

Registers at call:
AH = ADh
AL = function code
   02h enable spooler only
   03h enable the despooler
   04h disable the despooler
   08h inhibit popup menu
   09h enable popup menu
   0Ah *unknown.*
   0Bh disable the spooler
   0Ch *unknown.*
   0Dh *unknown.*
   0Eh pop up the menu
   0Fh *unknown.*
   11h *unknown.*
   14h *unknown.*
   15h *unknown.*
   16h *unknown.*
   17h *unknown.*
   18h *unknown.*
   19h *unknown.*
   20h *unknown.*
   21h *unknown.*
   22h *unknown.*
   23h *unknown.*
   30h *unknown.*

Conflicts: None known.

See Also: Function ABh

Restrictions: Disk Spool II version 1.83 must be installed.

Return Registers:
AH = 00h if successful

INTERRUPT 1Ah - Function D0h
Disk Spool FUNCTION CALLS

Purpose: Control the print spooler.

Available on: All machines.

Registers at call:
AH = D0h

Restrictions: Disk Spool II (*unknown version*) must be installed.

Return Registers: n/a

AL = function code
    01h enable spooler and despooler
    02h enable spooler only
    03h enable despooler at beginning of file
    04h disable the despooler
    05h disable the despooler and spooler
    06h clear the spool file
    08h inhibit the popup menu
    09h enable the popup menu
    0Bh disable the spooler
    0Ch start despooler after last successfully
        printed document
    0Dh start despooler at the exact point where it
        last left off
    0Eh pop up the menu
    20h clear file pointed to by the despooler
Conflicts: None known.
See Also: Function A0h

DOSED

DOSED is a free DOS commandline editor/history buffer by Sverre H. Huseby.

INTERRUPT 21h - Function FFh
INSTALLATION CHECK

Purpose: Determine whether DOSED is present.
Available on: All machines.
Registers at call:
AH = FFh
DS:SI -> "DOSED"
ES = 0000h

Restrictions: none.
Return Registers:
ES:DI -> "DOSED" if installed

Conflicts: CED (see above), DJ GO32.EXE DOS extender (chapter 9), Topware Network Operating System (chapter 27), "Sunday", "PSQR/1720", and "Ontario" viruses (chapter 34).

ELRES

ELRES is an MSDOS return code (errorlevel) recorder by David H. Bennett which stores recent errorlevel values, allows them to be retrieved for use in batch files, and can place them in an environment variable.

INTERRUPT 21h - Function 2Bh
INSTALLATION CHECK

Purpose: Determine whether ELRES version 1.1 or higher is present.
Available on: All machines.
Registers at call:
AH = 2Bh
CX = 454Ch ('EL')
DX = 5253h ('RS')

Restrictions: none.
Return Registers:
ES:BX -> ELRES history structure (Table 36-9)
DX = DABEh (signature, DAve BEnnett)

Conflicts: PC Tools v5.1 PC-CACHE (chapter 6), DOS 1+ Set System Date (chapter 8), DESQview (chapter 15), pcANYWHERE IV (chapter 28), TAME (chapter 36).
See Also: Function 4Bh, DOS Function 4Dh (chapter 8)

Table 36-9. Format of ELRES History Structure:

Offset	Size	Description
00h	WORD	number of return codes which can be stored by following buffer
02h	WORD	current position in buffer (treated as a ring)

Table 36-9. Format of ELRES History Structure (continued)

Offset	Size	Description
04h	N BYTEs	ELRES buffer

INTERRUPT 21h - Function 4Bh
INSTALLATION CHECK

Purpose: Determine whether ELRES version 1.0 is present.

Available on: All machines.

Registers at call:
AH = 4Bh
DS:DX = 0000h:0000h

Restrictions: none.

Return Registers:
ES:BX -> ELRES history structure (see Function 2Bh above)
DX = DABEh (signature, DAve BEnnett)

Conflicts: DOS 2+ "EXEC" (chapter 8), various viruses (chapter 34), F-DRIVER.SYS (chapter 34).

See Also: Function 2Bh (above)

Extended Batch Language

Extended Batch Language is a batch-file enhancer by Seaware.

INTERRUPT 64h - Functions 00h to 6Ch
UNUSED

Purpose: These functions are not used by EBL.

Available on: All machines.

Registers at call:
AH = function
    00h to 5Fh chained to previous handler
    60h to 6Ch reserved, return immediately

Restrictions: EBL must be installed.

Return Registers:
unchanged for functions 60h to 6Ch
as returned by previous handler otherwise

Details: The chaining code does not check whether the interrupt had been hooked before, so attempting to chain when the previous vector was 0000h:0000h will crash the system.

Conflicts: None known.

INTERRUPT 64h - Function 6Dh
INSERT TONE IN QUEUE

Purpose: Specify a sound to be played as soon as the currently-stored notes have been played.

Available on: All machines.

Restrictions: EBL version 4.01 or higher must be installed.

Registers at call:
AH = 6Dh
AL = *unknown*.
CX = frequency in Hertz
DL = duration in clock ticks

Return Registers:
AL = 00h if note stored
    01h if no room to store

Conflicts: See Table 1-3 in chapter 1.

INTERRUPT 64h - Function 6Eh
CLEAR Unknown COUNTER/FLAG

Purpose: Reset an *unknown* state.

Available on: All machines.

Restrictions: EBL version 3.14 or higher must be installed.

Registers at call:
AH = 6Eh

Return Registers: n/a

Conflicts: See Table 1-3 in chapter 1.

INTERRUPT 64h - Function 6Fh
RETURN COUNTER/FLAG Function 6Eh CLEARS

Purpose: Determine *unknown* state.
Available on: All machines.
Registers at call:
AH = 6Fh
Conflicts: See Table 1-3 in chapter 1.

Restrictions: EBL must be installed.
Return Registers:
unknown. -> counter/flag

INTERRUPT 64h - Function 70h
Unknown Function

Purpose: *unknown.*
Available on: All machines.
Registers at call:
AH = 70h
AL = *unknown.*
Conflicts: See Table 1-3 in chapter 1.

Restrictions: EBL must be installed.
Return Registers: *unknown.*

INTERRUPT 64h - Function 71h
Unknown Function

Purpose: *unknown.*
Available on: All machines.
Registers at call:
AH = 71h
AL = *unknown.*
Conflicts: See Table 1-3 in chapter 1.

Restrictions: EBL must be installed.
Return Registers: *unknown.*

INTERRUPT 64h - Function 72h
Unknown Function

Purpose: *unknown.*
Available on: All machines.
Registers at call:
AH = 72h

Restrictions: EBL must be installed.
Return Registers: *unknown.*

Details: Functions 72h and 7Ah-7Dh appear to be interfaces to the optional floating-point and extended function packages.
Conflicts: See Table 1-3 in chapter 1.

INTERRUPT 64h - Function 73h
INSERT BYTE AT END OF KEYBOARD BUFFER

Purpose: Store a character which will be retrieved when reading the keyboard at a later time.
Available on: All machines.
Registers at call:
AH = 73h
AL = byte to insert
Conflicts: See Table 1-3 in chapter 1.

Restrictions: EBL must be installed.
Return Registers:
AL = 00h if byte inserted
01h if no room to store

INTERRUPT 64h - Function 74h
INSERT BYTE AT FRONT OF KEYBOARD BUFFER

Purpose: Store a character which will be retrieved the next time the keyboard is read.
Available on: All machines.

Restrictions: EBL must be installed.

Registers at call:
AH = 74h
AL = byte to insert
Conflicts: See Table 1-3 in chapter 1.

Return Registers:
AL = 00h if byte inserted
    01h if no room to store

INTERRUPT 64h - Function 75h
Unknown Function

Purpose: *unknown.*
Available on: All machines.
Registers at call:
AH = 75h
Conflicts: See Table 1-3 in chapter 1.

Restrictions: EBL must be installed.
Return Registers: *unknown.*

INTERRUPT 64h - Function 76h
GET KEYBOARD "STACK" STATUS

Purpose: Determine whether the next keyboard read will actually read the keyboard or the internal EBL buffer.
Available on: All machines.
Registers at call:
AH = 76h

Restrictions: EBL must be installed.
Return Registers:
AL = 'K' if kbd read will read physical keyboard
    'S' if it will read EBL internal keyboard buffer
AH = *unknown.*

Conflicts: See Table 1-3 in chapter 1.

INTERRUPT 64h - Function 77h
CLEAR INTERNAL KEYBOARD BUFFER

Purpose: Discard all stored keystrokes which have not yet been read by an application.
Available on: All machines.
Registers at call:
AH = 77h
Conflicts: See Table 1-3 in chapter 1.

Restrictions: EBL must be installed.
Return Registers: n/a

INTERRUPT 64h - Function 78h
Unknown Function

Purpose: *unknown.*
Available on: All machines.
Registers at call:
AH = 78h
AL = *unknown.*
Conflicts: See Table 1-3 in chapter 1.

Restrictions: EBL must be installed.
Return Registers: *unknown.*

INTERRUPT 64h - Function 79h
Unknown Function

Purpose: *unknown.*
Available on: All machines.
Registers at call:
AH = 79h
Conflicts: See Table 1-3 in chapter 1.

Restrictions: EBL must be installed.
Return Registers: *unknown.*

INTERRUPT 64h - Function 7Ah through 7Dh
Unknown Function

Purpose: *unknown.*
Available on: All machines.

Restrictions: EBL must be installed.

Registers at call:
AH = 7Ah through 7Dh
AL = *unknown*.
Details: Functions 72h and 7Ah-7Dh appear to be interfaces to the optional floating-point and extended function packages.
Conflicts: See Table 1-3 in chapter 1.

Return Registers: *unknown*.

INTERRUPT 64h - Function 7Eh
CLEAR Unknown BUFFER

Purpose: *unknown*.
Available on: All machines.

Restrictions: EBL version 3.14 or higher must be installed.
Return Registers: n/a

Registers at call:
AH = 7Eh
Conflicts: See Table 1-3 in chapter 1.

INTERRUPT 64h - Function 7Fh
INSTALLATION CHECK

Purpose: Determine whether EBL is installed.
Available on: All machines.
Registers at call:
AH = 7Fh

Restrictions: none.
Return Registers:
CX = version in BCD
DI = segment of *unknown*.
BX = segment of *next program's PSP*

Conflicts: See Table 1-3 in chapter 1.

INTERRUPT 64h - Functions 80h to FFh
UNUSED

Purpose: These functions are not used by EBL and are chained to the previous handler.
Available on: All machines.
Registers at call:
AH = 80h to FFh

Restrictions: none.
Return Registers:
as returned by previous handler

Details: The chaining code does not check whether the interrupt had been hooked before, so attempting to chain when the previous vector was 0000h:0000h will crash the system.
Conflicts: None known.

FAKEY.COM
FAKEY is a keystroke faking utility by System Enhancement Associates.

INTERRUPT 16h - Function 70h
INSTALLATION CHECK

Purpose: Determine whether FAKEY.COM is installed.
Available on: All machines.
Registers at call:
AH = 70h
Conflicts: None known.

Restrictions: none.
Return Registers:
AX = 1954h if installed

INTERRUPT 16h - Function 71h
PUSH KEYSTROKES

Purpose: Place keystrokes into the keyboard buffer as if the user had pressed the keys.
Available on: All machines.

Restrictions: FAKEY.COM must be installed.

Registers at call:
AH = 71h
CX = number of keystrokes
DS:SI -> array of words containing keystrokes to be
    returned by INT 16h Function 00h (chapter 3)
Conflicts: None known.
See Also: Functions 05h and 72h

Return Registers: n/a

INTERRUPT 16h - Function 72h
CLEAR FAKED KEYSTROKES

Purpose: Forget all keystrokes which were pushed but have not yet been read by the application.
Available on: All machines.
Restrictions: FAKEY.COM must be installed.
Registers at call:
Return Registers: n/a
AH = 72h
Conflicts: None known.
See Also: Function 71h

INTERRUPT 16h - Function 73h
PLAY TONES

Purpose: Specify a series of musical notes to play on the system's speaker.
Available on: All machines.
Restrictions: FAKEY.COM must be installed.
Registers at call:
Return Registers: n/a
AH = 73h
CX = number of tones to play
DS:SI -> array of tones (Table 36-10)
Conflicts: None known.
See Also: TopView INT 15h Function 10h Subfunction 19h (chapter 15)

Table 36-10. Format of Tone Array Entries:

Offset	Size	Description
00h	WORD	divisor for timer channel 2
02h	WORD	duration in clock ticks

FASTBUFF.COM
FASTBUFF.COM is a keyboard speedup/screen blanking utility by David Steiner.

INTERRUPT 10h - Function FAh
INSTALLATION CHECK

Purpose: Determine whether FASTBUFF.COM is installed.
Available on: All machines.
Restrictions: none.
Registers at call:
Return Registers:
AH = FAh
AX = 00FAh if installed
ES = segment of resident code
Conflicts: EGA Register Interface Library (chapter 5).

FLASHUP.COM
FLASHUP.COM is part of Flash-Up Windows by The Software Bottling Co. FLASHUP also hooks INT 10h and receives commands via INT 10h Functions 09h and 0Ah consisting of an 80h followed by the actual command.

INTERRUPT 17h - Function 60h
INSTALLATION CHECK
Purpose: Determine whether FLASHUP.COM is installed.

Available on: All machines.
Registers at call:
AH = 60h

Restrictions: none.
Return Registers:
AL = 60h
DX = CS of resident code

Conflicts: None known.
See Also: INT 10h Functions 09h and 0Ah

GEM

Digital Research's GEM (Graphics Environment Manager) was one of the earliest graphical interfaces for the IBM PC, available long before the current craze began. While it was never a bestseller like Microsoft Windows 3.0 has been, particularly as an operating environment, it has enjoyed continuing success in vertical applications where it provides the user interface primitives. Ventura Publisher is one example of such a combination.

INTERRUPT EFh - Function 0473h
GEM INTERFACE

Purpose: Communicate with the GEM environment.
Available on: All machines.

Restrictions: Must be running Digital Research's GEM.

Registers at call:
CX = 0473h
DS:DX -> GEM parameter block
Conflicts: BASIC Interpreter (chapter 1).

Return Registers:
varies by function

GOLD.COM

GOLD is a TSR by Bob Eager which makes the NumLock key return the code for F1; the purpose is to improve Kermit's VTxxx emulation.

INTERRUPT 2Fh - Function DCh, Subfunction 00h
INSTALLATION CHECK

Purpose: Determine whether GOLD is installed.
Available on: All machines.
Registers at call:
AX = DC00h

Restrictions: none.
Return Registers:
AL = 00h not installed
    FFh installed

Conflicts: None known.

INTERRUPT 2Fh - Function DCh, Subfunction 01h
GET STATE

Purpose: Determine whether GOLD is currently translating the NumLock key.
Available on: All machines.
Registers at call:
AX = DC01h

Restrictions: GOLD must be installed.
Return Registers:
AL = status
    00h off
    01h on

Conflicts: None known.
See Also: Function DCh Subfunctions 00h and 02h

INTERRUPT 2Fh - Function DCh, Subfunction 02h
SET STATE

Purpose: Specify whether GOLD should translate the NumLock key into F1.
Available on: All machines.

Restrictions: GOLD must be installed.

Registers at call:
AX = DC02h
DL = new state
00h off
01h on
Conflicts: None known.
See Also: Function DCh Subfunction 01h

Return Registers:
AL = 00h (OK)

The IBM Digitized Sound Package
The IBM Digitized Sound Package was written by John W. Ratcliff.

INTERRUPT 66h - Function 06h, Subfunctions 88h and 89h
Unknown Functions

Purpose: *unknown.*
Available on: All machines.

Restrictions: The IBM Digitized Sound Package must be installed.
Return Registers: *unknown.*

Registers at call:
AX = 0688h or 0689h
unknown.
Conflicts: Data General DG10 (chapter 1), MicroHelp Stay-Res Plus.

InnerMission
InnerMission is a shareware graphical screen blanker by Kevin Stokes.

INTERRUPT 2Fh - Function 93h
INSTALLATION CHECK

Purpose: Determine whether InnerMission version 1.7 or higher is installed.
Available on: All machines.
Registers at call:
AH = 93h
BX = CX = AX

Restrictions: none.
Return Registers:
AL = FFh if installed and BX=CX=AX on entry
BX = segment of resident code
01h if installed but BX or CX differ from AX

Conflicts: None known.

INSET
INSET is a text/graphics integration program for printers.

INTERRUPT 17h - Function 02h, Subfunction 07C3h
INSTALLATION CHECK

Purpose: Determine whether INSET is installed.
Available on: All machines.
Registers at call:
AH = 02h
DX = 0000h
CX = 07C3h (1987d)
Conflicts: None known.

Restrictions: none.
Return Registers:
CX = 07C2h (1986d) if installed

INTERRUPT 17h - Function CDh, Subfunction 00h
EXECUTE COMMAND STRING

Purpose: Perform one or more commands as though typed by the user.
Available on: All machines.

Restrictions: INSET must be installed.

Registers at call:
AX = CD00h
DS:DX -> ASCIZ command string (max 80 bytes)
Details: The user interface menus pop up after the last command unless that command exits INSET.
Conflicts: None known.

Return Registers:
CX = 07C2h (1986d)

INTERRUPT 17h - Function CDh, Subfunction 01h
GET IMAGE SIZE

Purpose: Determine the width and height of the specified image.
Available on: All machines.
Registers at call:
AX = CD01h
DS:DX -> ASCIZ name of image file

Conflicts: None known.

Restrictions: INSET must be installed.
Return Registers:
AX = height in 1/720th inch
BX = width in 1/720th inch
CX = 07C2h (1986d)

INTERRUPT 17h - Function CDh, Subfunction 02h
INITIALIZE

Purpose: Prepare INSET for operation.
Available on: All machines.
Registers at call:
AX = CD02h
Details: This call closes all open files and resets the printer.
Conflicts: None known.
See Also: Function CDh Subfunction 04h

Restrictions: INSET must be installed.
Return Registers:
CX = 07C2h (1986d)

INTERRUPT 17h - Function CDh, Subfunction 03h
EXECUTE INSET MENU WITHIN OVERRIDE MODE

Purpose: Perform the menu function in OVERRIDE entry mode.
Available on: All machines.
Registers at call:
AX = CD03h
Conflicts: None known.

Restrictions: INSET must be installed.
Return Registers:
CX = 07C2h (1986d)

INTERRUPT 17h - Function CDh, Subfunction 04h
INITIALIZE LINKED MODE

Purpose: Begin using an application function for the graphics output stream rather than INT 17h Functions 00h through 02h.
Available on: All machines.
Registers at call:
AX = CD04h
ES:SI -> FAR routine for linked mode
Details: Use the linked-mode routine as follows:
Calling Sequence:
AL = 00h   send character in BL to printer
AL = 01h   send CX bytes from DS:DX to printer
AL = 02h   move print head to horizontal starting
                 position of image
Conflicts: None known.
See Also: Function CDh Subfunctions 02h and 08h

Restrictions: INSET must be installed.
Return Registers:
CX = 07C2h

Return Code for Linked-mode Routine:
AX = 0000h success
        0001h failure

INTERRUPT 17h - Function CDh, Subfunction 05h
START MERGING IMAGE INTO TEXT

Purpose: Prepare to include an image into the textual output to the printer.

Available on: All machines.

Registers at call:
AX = CD05h
DS:DX -> ASCIZ name of PIX file
CX = left margin of text in 1/720th inch

Restrictions: INSET must be installed.

Return Registers:
AH = printer type
    00h page-oriented (multiple images may be placed
       side-by-side)
    01h line-oriented (use Function CDh Subfunction
       06h for vertical paper movement)
CX = 07C2h (1986d)

Conflicts: None known.
See Also: Function CDh Subfunction 07h

INTERRUPT 17h - Function CDh, Subfunction 06h
GRAPHICS LINE FEED

Purpose: Advance the paper sufficiently to make the next line of graphics abut the bottom of the current line; should be used instead of a line feed on line-oriented printers while merging in graphics.

Available on: All machines.

Registers at call:
AX = CD06h

Restrictions: INSET must be installed.

Return Registers:
AH = completion status
    00h image complete
    01h image incomplete
CX = 07C2h (1986d)

Conflicts: None known.
See Also: Function CDh Subfunction 09h

INTERRUPT 17h - Function CDh, Subfunction 07h
FLUSH GRAPHICS FROM MERGE BUFFER

Purpose: Clear the contents of the merge buffer.

Available on: All machines.

Registers at call:
AX = CD07h

Conflicts: None known.
See Also: Function CDh Subfunction 05h

Restrictions: INSET must be installed.

Return Registers:
CX = 07C2h

INTERRUPT 17h - Function CDh, Subfunction 08h
CANCEL LINK MODE

Purpose: Return to normal output via INT 17h Functions 00h through 02h rather than the application's link function.

Available on: All machines.

Registers at call:
AX = CD08h

Conflicts: None known.
See Also: Function CDh Subfunction 04h

Restrictions: INSET must be installed.

Return Registers:
CX = 07C2h

INTERRUPT 17h - Function CDh, Subfunction 09h
ALTER TEXT LINE SPACING

Purpose: Specify the amount to advance the printer after the end of a line of text.

Available on: All machines.

Registers at call:
AX = CD09h
CX = line spacing in 1/720th inch

Restrictions: INSET must be installed.

Return Registers:
CX = 07C2h

Details: This function was not yet implemented as of late 1988; line spacing is fixed at 1/6 inch for versions which do not implement this call.
Conflicts: None known.
See Also: Function CDh Subfunction 06h

INTERRUPT 17h - Function CDh, Subfunction 0Ah
GET SETUP

Purpose: Determine current configuration.
Available on: All machines.
Registers at call:
AX = CD0Ah
DS:DX -> buffer for IN.SET data
Conflicts: None known.

Restrictions: INSET must be installed.
Return Registers:
CX = 07C2h

INTERRUPT 17h - Function CDh, Subfunction 0Bh
START GETTING SCALED IMAGE

Purpose: Prepare to retrieve a graphical image for inclusion in the printer output.
Available on: All machines.
Registers at call:
AX = CD0Bh
DS:SI -> ASCIZ pathname of .PIX file
BX = number of bitplanes
CX = number of rows in output bitmap
DX = number of columns in output bitmap

Restrictions: INSET must be installed.
Return Registers:
AX = status
  0000h OK
  FFFFh error

Details: The entire image is returned in strips by repeated calls to Function CDh Subfunction 0Ch.
Conflicts: None known.

INTERRUPT 17h - Function CDh, Subfunction 0Ch
GET NEXT IMAGE STRIP

Purpose: Retrieve the portion of the image corresponding to the next line on the printer.
Available on: All machines.
Registers at call:
AX = CD0Ch

Restrictions: INSET must be installed.
Return Registers:
AX = status
  0000h OK but not complete
  0001h OK and image complete
  FFFFh error
DS:SI -> buffer (max 4K) for bit map strip
CX = start row
DX = number of rows
BX = offset in bytes between bit planes

Details: The returned buffer may be overwritten by subsequent calls.
Conflicts: None known.
See Also: Function CDh Subfunction 0Bh

INTRSPY

INTRSPY is a script-driven debugger included with the book *Undocumented_DOS*. It will hook the first available interrupt in the range 60h through 67h.

INTERRUPT 60h
INTRSPY/CMDSPY API

Purpose: Determine whether INTRSPY is installed, and if so, retrieve the address of the routine to call for communicating with INTRSPY.
Available on: All machines.

Restrictions: none.

Registers at call: n/a

Return Registers: preserved.

Details: The installation check is to (a) determine that the handler is an IRET instruction, then (b) determine that the signature 0Dh "INTRSPY vN.NN" immediately precedes the handler. If INTRSPY is installed, the DWORD immediately after the IRET stores its entry point.

Call INTRSPY entry point with:
AH = function:

Return Registers:
AH = 00h
AL = status
    00h successful
    01h invalid function
    02h *unknown.*
    03h *unknown.*
    04h *unknown.*
    05h *unknown.*

00h *unknown.*
01h set current directory (for use in reporting)
    ES:DI -> counted string containing directory
            name (max 79 char)
02h set name of script file
    ES:DI -> counted string containing file name
            (max 79 chars)
03h set script arguments
    ES:DI -> counted string containing arguments
            (max 79 chars)
04h get directory set with function 01h
    ES:DI -> 80-byte buffer for directory name
05h get name of script file
    ES:DI -> 80-byte buffer for script filename
06h get script arguments
    ES:DI -> 80-byte buffer for script arguments
07h get *unknown.*
    CL = 00h-15h specifies what to get
    ES:DI -> WORD to be set with desired value
            on return
08h get *unknown.*
    ES:DI -> WORD to be set with returned value
09h get *unknown.*
    ES:DI -> WORD to be set with returned value
0Bh *store code for interrupt handler*
    ES:DI -> data
    CX = number of bytes
0Ch *unknown.*
    ES:DI -> *unknown.*
0Dh get *unknown.*
    ES:DI -> BYTE to be set with returned value
0Eh set *unknown* flag
0Fh clear *unknown* flag
10h *unknown.*

11h *unknown.*

12h get *unknown.*
    ES:DI -> buffer
13h *unknown.*

Conflicts: See chapter 1.

AL = 04h or 05h if failed

AL = 05h if failed

CX = number of bytes returned in buffer

Jetstream

The NorthNet Jetstream is a high-performance DMA-driven parallel card able to drive printers at up to 80000 characters per second

INTERRUPT 17h - Function F0h
INSTALLATION CHECK

Purpose: Determine whether Jetstream is installed.

Available on: All machines.

Registers at call:

AH = F0h

DX = printer port (0-3)

Conflicts: None known.

Restrictions: none.

Return Registers:

AX = 0001h   Jetstream present

     else   non-Jetstream port

INTERRUPT 17h - Function F1h
PRINT DATA BUFFER

Purpose: Transmit the contents of the specified buffer to the printer.

Available on: All machines.

Registers at call:

AH = F1h

CX = data buffer length

DX = printer port (0-3)

DS:SI -> data buffer

Conflicts: None known.

See Also: Functions F2h, F3h, and F5h

Restrictions: NorthNet Jetstream must be installed.

Return Registers:

AX = status

    0000h printer not ready (see also INT 17h

                Function 02h, chapter 3)

    other printing started

INTERRUPT 17h - Function F2h
GET PRINT PROGRESS STATUS

Purpose: Determine how much data remains to be printed.

Available on: All machines.

Registers at call:

AH = F2h

DX = printer port (0-3)

Conflicts: None known.

See Also: Functions F1h and F3h

Restrictions: NorthNet Jetstream must be installed.

Return Registers:

AX = status

    0000h prior print request finished

    other number of characters left to print

INTERRUPT 17h - Function F3h
ABORT PRINT OPERATION

Purpose: Immediately terminate the printing currently in progress.

Available on: All machines.

Registers at call:

AH = F3h

DX = printer port (0-3)

Conflicts: None known.

See Also: Functions F1h and F4h

Restrictions: NorthNet Jetstream must be installed.

Return Registers:

AX = number of unprinted characters due to abort

INTERRUPT 17h - Function F4h
SET COMPLETION (POST) ADDRESS

Purpose: Specify the subroutine to invoke at the end of a print job.

Available on: All machines.

Restrictions: NorthNet Jetstream must be installed.

Registers at call:
AH = F4h
DX = printer port (0-3)
DS:DS -> FAR post address (called with interrupts
    on)
Conflicts: None known.
See Also: Functions F1h and F3h

Return Registers: n/a

INTERRUPT 17h - Function F5h
PRINT DATA BUFFER FROM EXTENDED MEMORY

Purpose: Transmit the specified data stored in extended memory to the printer.
Available on: All machines.
Registers at call:
AH = F5h
CX = data buffer length
DX = printer port (0-3)
DS:SI -> data buffer (32-bit physical address)
Conflicts: None known.
See Also: Function F1h

Restrictions: NorthNet Jetstream must be installed.
Return Registers:
AX = status
    0000h printer not ready (see also INT 17h Function
        02h in chapter 3)
    other printing started

KBUF

INTERRUPT 16h - Function FFh
ADD KEY TO TAIL OF KEYBOARD BUFFER

Purpose: Store a keystroke which will be retrieved by a later keyboard read.
Available on: All machines.
Registers at call:
AH = FFh
DX = scan code

Conflicts: PC Tools (chapter 33)
See Also: Function 05h (chapter 3)

Restrictions: KBUF must be installed.
Return Registers:
AX = status
    0000h success
    0001h failure

The Last Byte
The Last Byte by Key Software Products is a shareware high-memory manager designed to create upper memory blocks from shadow RAM on various chip sets. The two drivers from The Last Byte covered here are LASTBYTE.SYS, which directs the system's chip set to convert shadow RAM into directly usable memory, and HIGHUMM.SYS, which manages the converted memory.

INTERRUPT 21h - Function 44h, Subfunction 02h
GET Unknown TABLE

Purpose: *unknown.*
Available on: All systems.

Registers at call:
AX = 4402h
BX = handle for device "LA$TBYTE"
CX = 0004h
DS:DX -> DWORD to hold address of 39-byte
    table of *unknown.*
See Also: HIGHUMM.SYS Function 44h Subfunction 02h (below)

Restrictions: LASTBYTE.SYS version 1.19 or higher
                must be installed.
Return Registers:
CF set on error
    AX = error code (see Function 59h, chapter 8)
CF clear if successful
    AX = number of bytes read

INTERRUPT 21h - Function 44h, Subfunction 02h
GET HIGHUMM API ADDRESS

Purpose: Determine the routine to call for communicating with the HIGHUMM memory manager.

Available on: All systems.   **Restrictions:** HIGHUMM.SYS must be installed.

Registers at call:
AX = 4402h
BX = handle for device "KSP$UMM"
CX = 0004h
DS:DX -> DWORD to hold entry point

Return Registers:
CF set on error
   AX = error code (see Function 59h, chapter 8)
CF clear if successful
   AX = number of bytes read

Details: HIGHUMM.SYS is used by calling its entry point as described in the following pages.

Conflicts: DOS 2+ IOCTL (chapter 8), Network Driver Interface Specification (chapter 27), IBM System 36/38 Workstation Emulation (chapter 26).

Call entry point with:
AH = 00h allocate UMB (same as XMS function
   10h) (see INT 2Fh Function 43h Subfunction
   10h, chapter 10)
DX = size in paragraphs

Return Registers:
AX = status code:
   0001h successful
      BX = segment number
      DX = size of requested block
   0000h failed
      BL = error code:
         80h not implemented
         B0h insufficient memory, smaller block
            available
         B1h insufficient memory, no blocks
            available
         B2h invalid segment number
      DX = size of largest available block

Call entry point with:
AH = 01h deallocate UMB (same as XMS func
   11h) (see INT 2Fh Function 43h
   Subfunction 10h, chapter 10)
DX = segment number of UMB

Return Registers:
AX = status code:
   0001h successful
   0000h failed
      BL = error code (see Function 00h)

Call entry point with:
AH = 02h request a bank-switched memory block
DX = size in paragraphs

Return Registers:
AX = status code:
   0001h successful
      BX = segment number
      DX = size of requested block
   0000h failed
      BL = error code (see Function 00h)
      DX = size of largest available block

Call entry point with:
AH = 03h release a bank-switched memory block
DX = segment number

Return Registers:
AX = status code:
   0001h successful
   0000h failed
      BL = error code (see Function 00h)

Call entry point with:
AH = 04h transfer data to/from high memory
DS:SI -> source
ES:DI -> destination
CX = length in bytes

Return Registers:
AX = status code:
   0001h successful
   0000h failed
      BL = error code (see Function 00h)

Note: enables bank-switched memory, does the copy, then disables bank-switched memory.

Call entry point with:
AH = 05h get a word from bank-switched memory
ES:DI -> word to read

Return Registers:
AX = status code:
    0001h successful
        DX = word
    0000h failed
        BL = error code (see Function 00h)

Call entry point with:
AH = 06h put a word to bank-switched memory
ES:DI -> word to write
DX = word

Return Registers:
AX = status code:
    0001h successful
    0000h failed
        BL = error code (see Function 00h)

Call entry point with:
AH = 07h put a byte to bank-switched memory
ES:DI -> byte to write
DL = byte

Return Registers:
AX = status code:
    0001h successful
    0000h failed
        BL = error code (see Function 00h)

Call entry point with:
AH = 08h enable bank-switched memory
DS:SI -> 6-byte status save area

Return Registers:
AX = status code:
    0001h successful
    0000h failed
        BL = error code (see Function 00h)

Call entry point with:
AH = 09h disable bank-switched memory
DS:SI -> 6-byte save area from enable call
      (Function 08h)

Return Registers:
AX = status code:
    0001h successful
    0000h failed
        BL = error code (see Function 00h)

Call entry point with:
AH = 0Ah assign name to UMB or bank-switched
      block
DX = segment number
DS:SI -> 8-byte blank-padded name

Return Registers:
AX = status code:
    0001h successful
    0000h failed
        BL = error code (see Function 00h)

Call entry point with:
AH = 0Bh locate UMB block by name
DS:SI -> 8-byte blank-padded name

Return Registers:
AX = status code:
    0001h successful
        BX = segment number
        DX = size of block
    0000h failed
        BL = error code (see Function 00h)

Call entry point with:
AH = 0Ch locate bank-switched block by name
DS:SI -> 8-byte blank-padded name

Return Registers:
AX = status code:
    0001h successful
        BX = segment number
        DX = size of block
    0000h failed
        BL = error code (see Function 00h)

LPTx

LPTx by Mark DiVecchio and Kepa Zubeldia is a printer output capturing program which stores the captured printer output in a disk file. The various versions use differing algorithms for capturing the printer output; as a result, for some versions of DOS, an older version of LPTx may work more reliably than a newer version.

INTERRUPT 17h - Function 0ABCh
v5.x INSTALLATION CHECK

Purpose: Determine whether LPTx version 5.x is installed.
Available on: All machines.
Registers at call:
DX = 0ABCh

Restrictions: none.
Return Registers:
AX = AAAAh
DX = BAAAh
ES = code segment of resident portion

Conflicts: None known.

INTERRUPT 17h - Function 0B90h
v6.x INSTALLATION CHECK

Purpose: Determine whether LPTx version 6.x is installed.
Available on: All machines.
Registers at call:
DX = 0B90h

Restrictions: none.
Return Registers:
DX = ABBBh
ES = code segment of resident portion

Conflicts: None known.

INTERRUPT 17h - Function 0B91h
v7.x INSTALLATION CHECK

Purpose: Determine whether LPTx version 7.x is installed.
Available on: All machines.
Registers at call:
DX = 0B91h

Restrictions: none.
Return Registers:
DX = ABCBh
ES = code segment of resident portion

Conflicts: None known.

INTERRUPT 17h - Function 0F5Fh
v4.x INSTALLATION CHECK

Purpose: Determine whether LPTx version 4.x is installed.
Available on: All machines.
Registers at call:
DX = 0F5Fh

Restrictions: none.
Return Registers:
AX = AAAAh
DX = F555h
ES = code segment of resident portion

Conflicts: None known.

MAGic

MAGic (MAGnification In Color) is a TSR by Microsystems Software, Inc. providing 2x2 text and graphics magnification on VGA, XGA, and SVGA systems. It uses INT 49h by default, but the interrupt number may be overridden on the commandline. The actual interrupt in use may be found by searching for the signature "MAGic" immediately preceding the interrupt handler (this is also the installation check). MAGic uses CodeRunneR, which places the signature "RT" at offset 0000h in the interrupt handler's segment, followed by MAGic's TSR ID of "VMAG".

INTERRUPT 49h - Function 0001h
TURN ON MAGNIFICATION

Purpose: Begin displaying the screen contents with both height and width doubled.
Available on: Systems equipped with VGA, SuperVGA, or XGA displays.
Restrictions: MAGic version 1.16 or higher must be installed.

Registers at call:
AX = 0001h

Return Registers:
AX = status
   0000h cannot magnify current video mode
   0002h magnified (text mode)
   0003h magnified (graphics mode)
   FFFDh function works only in magnified mode
   FFFFh MAGic busy, retry later
BX,CX,DX destroyed

See Also: Functions 0001h, 0003h, and 0004h

INTERRUPT 49h - Function 0002h
TURN OFF MAGNIFICATION

Purpose: Display the screen at its normal size.

Available on: Systems equipped with VGA, SuperVGA, or XGA displays.

Restrictions: MAGic version 1.16 or higher must be installed.

Registers at call:
AX = 0002h

Return Registers:
AX = status (see Function 0001h)
BX,CX,DX destroyed

See Also: Function 0001h

INTERRUPT 49h - Function 0003h
SHIFT MAGNIFIED WINDOW TO INCLUDE SPECIFIED LOCATION

Purpose: Ensure that the specified location is visible on the magnified screen.

Available on: Systems equipped with VGA, SuperVGA, or XGA displays.

Restrictions: MAGic version 1.16 or higher must be installed.

Registers at call:
AX = 0003h
BX = vertical position (character row [text] or pixel row [graphics])
DX = horizontal position (char column [text] or 8-pixel units [graphics])

Return Registers:
AX = status
   0000h successful
   FFFFh MAGic busy, retry later
BX,CX,DX destroyed

Details: The window is not moved if the specified position is already inside the current window.

See Also: Functions 0001h, 0004h, and 0005h

INTERRUPT 49h - Function 0004h
REPOSITION MAGNIFIED WINDOW

Purpose: Specify a new location for the window into the magnified screen.

Available on: Systems equipped with VGA, SuperVGA, or XGA displays.

Restrictions: MAGic version 1.16 or higher must be installed.

Registers at call:
AX = 0004h
BX = vertical position of upper left corner
DX = horizontal position

Return Registers:
AX = status (see Function 0003h)
BX,CX,DX destroyed

See Also: Functions 0001h, 0003h, and 0005h

INTERRUPT 49h - Function 0005h
GET POSITION OF MAGNIFIED WINDOW

Purpose: Determine which portion of the screen is currently visible with magnification.

Available on: Systems equipped with VGA, SuperVGA, or XGA displays.

Restrictions: MAGic version 1.16 or higher must be installed.

Registers at call:
AX = 0005h

Return Registers:
AX = status
   0000h successful
      BX = vertical position (character or pixel row)
      DX = horizontal position (character column
        or 8-pixel units)
   FFFFh MAGic busy, retry later
      BX,DX destroyed
CX destroyed

See Also: Functions 0001h, 0003h, 0004h, 0006h, and 0007h

INTERRUPT 49h - Function 0006h
GET SIZE OF FULL SCREEN

Purpose: Determine the actual size of the full display area.

Available on: Systems equipped with VGA, SuperVGA, or XGA displays.

Registers at call:
AX = 0006h

Restrictions: MAGic version 1.16 or higher must be installed.

Return Registers:
AX = status
   0000h successful
      BX = vertical size (character or pixel rows)
      DX = horizontal size (character columns or
        8-pixel units)
   FFFFh MAGic busy, retry later
      BX,DX destroyed
CX destroyed

See Also: Functions 0001h, 0005h, and 0007h

INTERRUPT 49h - Function 0007h
GET SIZE OF MAGNIFICATION WINDOW

Purpose: Determine the size of the visible portion of the screen when magnified.

Available on: Systems equipped with VGA, SuperVGA, or XGA displays.

Registers at call:
AX = 0007h

Restrictions: MAGic version 1.16 or higher must be installed.

Return Registers:
AX = status
   0000h successful
      BX = vertical size (character or pixel rows)
      DX = horizontal size (character columns or
        8-pixel units)
   FFFEh invalid function
   FFFFh MAGic busy, retry later
      BX,DX destroyed
CX destroyed

BUG: In versions 1.16 and 1.17, this function is not recognized as valid, but Function 0000h is accepted and will branch to an invalid address.

See Also: Functions 0001h and 0006h

MAKEY

MAKEY is a utility by System Enhancement Associates.

INTERRUPT 16h - Function 80h
INSTALLATION CHECK

Purpose: Determine whether MAKEY.COM has been loaded.

Available on: All machines.

Restrictions: none.

Registers at call:
AH = 80h
Conflicts: None known.

Return Registers:
AX = 1954h if installed

MDEBUG

MDEBUG is a shareware memory-resident debugger by Bernd Schemmer. It consists of a main program, a command driver and a display driver; the interfaces used by the main program to call the two drivers are described here, followed by the API of the main program.

MDEBUG can use any two consecutive multiplex numbers between C0h and FFh; the default is D0h for the display driver and D1h for the command driver.

INTERRUPT 2Fh - Function D0h, Subfunction 00h
GET DISPLAY DRIVER STATUS

Purpose: Called by MDEBUG to determine the version, location, and current state of the display driver.

Available on: All machines.

Restrictions: MDEBUG display driver must be installed.

Registers at call:
AX = D000h

Return Registers:
CF set on error
    (all other registers must be unchanged)
CF clear if successful
    AL = FFh
    AH = driver semaphore
        00h driver is not active
        01h driver is active
    BX = code segment of the driver
    CX = driver version (CH = major, CL = minor, must be >= 0151h)
    DL = buffer semaphore
        00h driver is not pending
        01h driver is pending between functions 02h and 03h
    DH = show semaphore
        00h driver is not pending
        01h driver is pending between functions 04h and 05h

Details: This function MUST be reentrant, as MDEBUG calls it after every popup before any other actions. The handler should not change any registers if the display is in an unsupported mode or in a mode MDEBUG supports itself, e.g. a normal text mode like 80x25. In this case MDEBUG will not call any of the other functions for this popup session.

MDEBUG will not call the other functions if the returned version is less than the actual version of MDEBUG.

If the driver is reentrant, DL and DH should be 00h.

Conflicts: None known.

See Also: Function D0h Subfunctions 01h, 02h, 03h, 04h, and 05h

INTERRUPT 2Fh - Function D0h, Subfunction 01h
INITIALIZE DISPLAY DRIVER

Purpose: Prepare the display driver for operation in an MDEBUG popup session.

Available on: All machines.

Restrictions: MDEBUG display driver must be installed.

Registers at call:
AX = D001h

Return Registers:
CF set on error
    AL = driver semaphore
    AH = buffer semaphore

Details: MDEBUG calls this function after every succesful call of Function 00h. The handler should reset all internal data and the status of the driver. If this function returns an error, MDEBUG will not call the other functions in this popup session.
Conflicts: None known.
See Also: Function D0h Subfunction 00h

INTERRUPT 2Fh - Function D0h, Subfunction 02h
SAVE GRAPHIC DATA

Purpose: Store the current contents of the screen for restoration when MDEBUG pops down.
Available on: All machines.

Restrictions: MDEBUG display driver must be installed.

Registers at call:
AX = D002h

Return Registers:
CF set on error
CF clear if successful
    display memory saved and display switched to one
        of the text modes 02h, 03h or 07h.

Details: MDEBUG calls this function only once every popup session before displaying its windows.
Conflicts: None known.
See Also: Function D0h Subfunctions 00h and 03h

INTERRUPT 2Fh - Function D0h, Subfunction 03h
RESTORE GRAPHIC DATA

Purpose: Restore the screen contents to the state they were in prior to MDEBUG popping up.
Available on: All machines.

Restrictions: MDEBUG display driver must be installed.

Registers at call:
AX = D003h

Return Registers:
CF set on error
CF clear if successful
    display restored to the mode it was in before
        calling Function D0h Subfunction 02h and the
        display memory is restored

Details: MDEBUG calls this function only once every popup session just before it exits to normal DOS.
Conflicts: None known.
See Also: Function D0h Subfunctions 00h and 02h

INTERRUPT 2Fh - Function D0h, Subfunction 04h
MDEBUG display driver - SHOW SAVED DATA

Purpose: Temporarily restore the screen to the state it was in when MDEBUG popped up.
Available on: All machines.

Restrictions: MDEBUG display driver must be installed.

Registers at call:
AX = D004h

Return Registers:
CF set on error
CF clear if successful
    display switched to mode it was in before calling
        Function D0h Subfunction 02h and the display
        memory is restored

Details: This function need not save the display memory before changing it.
Conflicts: None known.
See Also: Function D0h Subfunctions 00h and 05h

INTERRUPT 2Fh - Function D0h, Subfunction 05h
MDEBUG display driver - SWITCH BACK TO TEXT SCREEN

Purpose: Return to MDEBUG's screen display after showing the saved screen.

Available on: All machines.

Registers at call:
AX = D005h

Restrictions: MDEBUG display driver must be installed.

Return Registers:
CF set on error
CF clear if successful
   display restored to mode it was in before calling
      Function D0h Subfunction 04h

Details: This function need not save or change the display memory.
Conflicts: None known.
See Also: Function D0h Subfunctions 00h and 04h

INTERRUPT 2Fh - Function D0h, Subfunctions 06h-7Fh
RESERVED FUNCTIONS

Purpose: These functions are reserved for future use.

Available on: All machines.

Registers at call:
AH = D0h
AL = 06h-7Fh
Conflicts: None known.

Restrictions: MDEBUG display driver must be installed.

Return Registers: *unknown.*

INTERRUPT 2Fh - Function D0h, Subfunctions 80h-FFh
USER DEFINED FUNCTIONS

Purpose: These functions numbers are reserved for user defined features (e.g. communication between the transient und resident parts of the driver).

Available on: All machines.

Registers at call:
AH = D0h
AL = 80h-FFh
Conflicts: None known.

Restrictions: MDEBUG display driver must be installed.

Return Registers: user-defined

INTERRUPT 2Fh - Function D1h, Subfunction 00h
GET COMMAND DRIVER STATUS

Purpose: Determine the version and state of the command driver.

Available on: All machines.

Registers at call:
AX = D100h
BX = version of MDEBUG (BH = major, BL = minor)
CX = command driver counter

Restrictions: MDEBUG command driver must be installed.

Return Registers:
DL = FFh
BX = version number of the driver if it is less than the version in BX, else unchanged
CX incremented
---v1.60+
DS:SI -> MDEBUG identification table (Table 36-11)
ES = segment of display memory used by MDEBUG
DI = size of video mode used by MDEBUG (high byte = lines, low byte = columns)

Details: This function must end with a far call to the old INT 2Fh handler after changing the registers. This function MUST be reentrant. If the version number returned in BX is less than the version of MDEBUG, MDEBUG will not call any of the other functions during this popup session.

    Command drivers must also declare the data listed in Table 36-12 at the given offsets in the code segment.

    MDEBUG will pass every key and command to the command driver(s) before checking for a valid internal command.

Conflicts: None known.
See Also: Function D0h Subfunction 00h, Function D1h Subfunction 01h

Table 36-11. Format of MDEBUG Identification Table:

Offset	Size	Description
-2	WORD	entry offset
00h	WORD	CS of MDEBUG
02h	DWORD	old INT 08h vector
06h	DWORD	old INT 09h vector
0Ah	DWORD	address INT 16h routine used by MDEBUG
0Eh	BYTE	length of version string
0Fh	N BYTEs	version string

Table 36-12. Format of MDEBUG Command Driver Data:

Offset	Size	Description
100h	3 BYTEs	JMP-command in .COM-files
103h	BYTE	NOP-command (90h)
104h	26 BYTEs	signature "Kommandotreiber für MDEBUG"
11Eh	12 BYTEs	name of driver, e.g. "MDHISDRV.COM". Each driver must have a unique name

INTERRUPT 2Fh - Function D1h, Subfunction 01h
INITIALIZE COMMAND DRIVER

Purpose: Prepare the command driver for operation.
Available on: All machines.

Restrictions: MDEBUG command driver must be installed.

Registers at call:
AX = D101h
CX = command driver counter

Return Registers:
DL = FFh if successful
    CX incremented
    else error: all registers unchanged

Details: This function must be reentrant and must end with a far call to the old INT 2Fh handler after changing the registers.
Conflicts: None known.

INTERRUPT 2Fh - Function D1h, Subfunction 02h
EXECUTE DEBUGGER COMMAND

Purpose: Perform an action specified by the given string.
Available on: All machines.

Restrictions: MDEBUG command driver must be installed.

Registers at call:
AX = D102h
BL = first character of the debugger command
BH = last character of the debugger command (or blank)
DS:SI -> parameter for the debugger command as ASCIZ string
DS:DI -> MDEBUG data structure (Table 36-13)

Return Registers:
AL = FFh
CF set on error
    AH = error number
        01h syntax error
        02h first shell of COMMAND.COM is active
        03h Esc pressed
        04h Break pressed
        05h dos-busy-flag not zero
        06h command ended
        07h division by zero
        08h invalid display driver
        09h invalid command driver
        0Ah both errors 8 and 9
        0Bh unknown error

0Ch new error
    DS:SI -> ASCIZ error message (max 30
        characters)
    else unknown error
CF clear if successful
    AH = return code
        00h continue processing the command line
        01h leave MDEBUG popup session
        02h leave MDEBUG popup session and
            automatically popup again if the InDOS
            flag is zero
        03h put new command line into the input
            buffer, DS:SI -> new command line
            (ASCIZ string, max 66 chars)
        04h process new command line, DS:SI -> new
            command line (ASCIZ string, max 66
            chars)
        else unknown status, but continue processing
            commmand line

Details: This function must end with a far call to the old INT 2Fh handler (with registers unchanged) if the driver does not support the debugger command in BX. Otherwise, the driver must not chain to the old INT 2Fh.

Table 36-13. Format of MDEBUG Data Structure:

Offset	Size	Description
00h	WORD	register SE (segment)
02h	WORD	register OF (offset)
04h	WORD	register FS
06h	WORD	register FO
08h	WORD	register AX
0Ah	WORD	register BX
0Ch	WORD	register CX
0Eh	WORD	register DX
10h	WORD	register SI
12h	WORD	register DI
14h	WORD	register DS
16h	WORD	register ES
18h	WORD	register BP
1Ah	WORD	register SS
1Ch	WORD	register SP
1Eh	WORD	register FL (flags)
20h	WORD	register R0
22h	WORD	register R1
24h	WORD	register R2
26h	WORD	register R3
28h	WORD	register R4
2Ah	WORD	register R5
2Ch	WORD	register R6
2Eh	WORD	register R7
30h	WORD	register R8
32h	WORD	register CS, return-address
34h	WORD	register IP, return-address
36h	WORD	saved data for key \<F6\>, segment
38h	WORD	saved data for key \<F6\>, offset
3Ah	12 WORDs	saved registers for the key \<F8\> (original register values at popup entry of MDEBUG) AX, BX, CX, DX, SI, DI, DS, ES, BP, SS, SP, flags

Table 36-13. Format of MDEBUG Data Structure (continued)

Offset	Size	Description
52h	12 WORDs	saved registers for the key <SHIFT-F8> AX, BX, CX, DX, SI, DI, DS, ES, BP, SS, SP, flags
6Ah	DWORD	address of the DOS-invars-table
6Eh	DWORD	address of the InDOS flag
72h	WORD	offset of the register which is used for the segment of the first monitor window
74h	WORD	offset of the register which is used for the offset of the first monitor window
76h	WORD	name of the register which is used for the segment of the first monitor segment
78h	WORD	name of the register which is used for the offset of the first monitor window
7Ah	WORD	pseudo register 1
7Ch	WORD	pseudo register 2

INTERRUPT 2Fh - Function D1h, Subfunction 03h
EXECUTE KEY IN THE MONITOR

Purpose: Perform the monitor action corresponding to the indicated key.

Available on: All machines.

Restrictions: MDEBUG command driver must be installed.

Registers at call:
AX = D103h
BX = key code (like result of an interrupt 16h call)
CX = 0 if the cursor is in the ASCII column of the monitor
CX = 1 if the cursor is in one of the hex fields of the monitor
DS:SI -> MDEBUG data structure (Table 36-13)
ES:DI -> actual byte in the monitor

Return Registers:
AL = FFh
AH = return code
   00h key processed, read next key
   01h leave MDEBUG popup session
   02h leave MDEBUG popup session and automatically popup again if the InDOS flag is zero
   03h signal an error (beep)
   04h driver has redefined the key, proceed with the new key: BX = new key code. MDEBUG will not pass the new key to the command driver
   else treat like code 00h

Details: This function must end with a far call to the old INT 2Fh handler (with registers unchanged) if the driver does not support the key in BX. Otherwise, the driver must not chain to the old INT 2Fh.

Conflicts: None known.

See Also: Function D1h Subfunction 04h

INTERRUPT 2Fh - Function D1h, Subfunction 04h
EXECUTE KEY IN THE DEBUGGER

Purpose: Perform the debugger action corresponding to the indicated key.

Available on: All machines.

Restrictions: MDEBUG command driver must be installed.

Registers at call:
AX = D104h
DS:SI -> MDEBUG data structure (see Function D1h Subfunction 02h)

Return Registers:
AL = FFh
AH = return code
   00h key processed, read next key
   01h leave MDEBUG popup session
   02h leave MDEBUG popup session and automatically popup again if the DOS-busy flag is zero
   03h signal an error (beep)
   04h driver has redefined the key, proceed with the new key: BX = new key code. MDEBUG won't pass the new key to the command driver

05h put new command line into the input buffer
> DS:SI -> new command line (ASCIZ string,
> max 66 chars)

06h process new command line
> DS:SI -> new command line (ASCIZ string,
> max 66 chars)

else treat like code 00h

Details: This function must end with a far call to the old INT 2Fh handler if the driver does not support the key in BX. Otherwise, the driver must not chain to the old INT 2Fh.

Conflicts: None known.

See Also: Function D1h Subfunction 03h

INTERRUPT 2Fh - Function D1h, Subfunctions 05h-0Ah
RESERVED FUNCTIONS

Purpose: These functions are reserved for future use.

Available on: All machines.

Restrictions: MDEBUG command driver must be installed.

Registers at call:
AH = D1h
AL = 05h-0Ah

Return Registers: n/a

Conflicts: None known.

INTERRUPT 2Fh - Function D1h, Subfunction 10h
GET ADDRESS OF THE OLD INT 2Fh HANDLER

Purpose: Determine which handler received control on an INT 2Fh before MDEBUG was loaded.

Available on: All machines.

Restrictions: MDEBUG command driver must be installed.

Registers at call:
AX = D110h

Return Registers:
DL = FFh
ES:BX -> next program in the chain for INT 2Fh
CX = code segment of this driver

Details: This function is only called by the transient part of the driver. It must be reentrant and the driver must not chain this function to the old INT 2Fh vector.

Conflicts: None known.

INTERRUPT 2Fh - Function D1h, Subfunction 11h
START COMMAND DRIVER

Purpose: Called by the transient part of the command driver to inform the resident part that it has begun execution.

Available on: All machines.

Restrictions: MDEBUG command driver must be installed.

Registers at call:
AX = D111h

Return Registers:
DL = FFh

Details: The function must be reentrant and the driver must not chain this function to the old INT 2Fh.

Conflicts: None known.

See Also: Function D1h Subfunctions 01h and 12h

INTERRUPT 2Fh - Function D1h, Subfunction 12h
END COMMAND DRIVER

Purpose: Called by the transient part of the dirver to inform the resident part that it will be released after the call.

Available on: All machines.

Restrictions: MDEBUG command driver must be installed.

Registers at call:
AX = D112h

Return Registers:
DL = FFh

Details: The function must be reentrant and the driver must not chain this function to the old INT 2Fh.
Conflicts: None known.
See Also: Function D1h Subfunctions 01h and 11h

INTERRUPT 2Fh - Function D1h, Subfunctions 13h-7Fh
RESERVED FUNCTIONS

Purpose: These functions are reserved for future use.
Available on: All machines.

Registers at call:
AH = D1h
AL = 13h-7Fh
Conflicts: None known.

Restrictions: MDEBUG command driver must be installed.
Return Registers: n/a

INTERRUPT 2Fh - Function D1h, Subfunctions 80h-FFhh
USER DEFINED FUNCTIONS

Purpose: These functions are reserved for user defined features (e.g. communication between the transient und resident parts of the driver).
Available on: All machines.

Registers at call:
AH = D1h
AL = 80h-FFh
Conflicts: None known.

Restrictions: MDEBUG command driver must be installed.
Return Registers: user-defined

INTERRUPT 60h - Function 00h
GET STATUS

Purpose: Determine MDEBUG's current status, including its colors, hotkey, and multiplex number.
Available on: All machines.

Registers at call:
AH = 00h
DS:SI -> password or a null byte

Restrictions: MDEBUG display driver must be installed.
Return Registers:
AX = return code
    FFFEh password is invalid
    FFFDh display mode is invalid
    else successful
        ES = value of monitor register SE
        DI = value of monitor register OF
        CH = monitor color
        CL = debugger color
        BH = monitor start line
        BL = debugger start line
        AH = makecode of the hotkey
        AL = ASCII code of the hotkey
        DL = status of special keys (only SHIFT, ALT, CTRL) for the hotkey, coded as for the keyboard flag at 0040h:0017h
        DH = basic process number for the communication with drivers; DH = multiplex number for the display driver, DH+1 = multiplex number for the command driver(s)
        DS:SI -> MDEBUG identification table (Table 36-14)

Details: MDEBUG uses INT 60h by default, but may be directed to any of INT 60h through INT 67h; the interrupt is not chained. If DS:SI points at a null byte, MDEBUG will prompt for a password if passwords are active; enough stack space must be provided for an INT 10h call.

Conflicts: See chapter 1.

See Also: Function 02h

Table 36-14. Format of MDEBUG Identification Table:

Offset	Size	Description
-2	WORD	entry offset
00h	WORD	CS of MDEBUG
02h	DWORD	old INT 08h vector
06h	DWORD	old INT 09h vector
0Ah	DWORD	address INT 16h routine used by MDEBUG
0Eh	BYTE	length of version string
0Fh	N BYTEs	version string

INTERRUPT 60h - Function 01h
GET ADDRESS OF THE HELP REGISTERS

Purpose: Determine the location of the debugger's help registers.

Available on: All machines.

Registers at call:
AH = 01h
DS:SI -> password or a null byte

Restrictions: MDEBUG must be installed.

Return Registers:
AX = return code
    FFFEh password is invalid
    FFFDh display mode is invalid
    else successful
        ES:DI point to the help registers of MDEBUG
        ES:DI-02h -> R0
        ES:DI   -> R1
        ES:DI+02h -> R2
        ...
        ES:DI+0Eh -> R8

Conflicts: See chapter 1.

INTERRUPT 60h - Function 02h
SET STATUS

Purpose: Specify new colors, location on screen, hotkey, and multiplex number for the debugger.

Available on: All machines.

Registers at call:
AH = 02h
DS:SI -> password or a null byte
ES = new value for the register SE
DI = new value for the register OF
CH = new monitor color if nonzero
CL = new debugger color if nonzero
BH = new monitor start line if nonzero
BL = new debugger start line if nonzero
AL = new ASCII code for the hotkey ('A'..'Z', 'a'..'z')
    if nonzero
DL = new status of the special keys (SHIFT, ALT,
    CTRL) for the hotkey if nonzero

Restrictions: MDEBUG must be installed.

Return Registers:
AX = return code
    FFFFh call not allowed
    FFFEh password is invalid
    FFFDh display mode is invalid
    0000h successful, status changed
    else AL = error code
        bit 0 invalid monitor start line
        1 invalid debugger start line
        2 invalid hotkey
        3 invalid process number
        4-7 reserved

DH = if nonzero, new basic process number for
      communication with the drivers;
   DH = multiplex number for the display driver
   DH+1 = multiplex number for command driver
Details: The values of the debugger registers SE (segment) and OF (offset) are always changed; the other values are only changed if they are nonzero and valid.
Conflicts: See chapter 1.
See Also: Function 00h

INTERRUPT 60h - Function 03h
POP UP

Purpose: Request that the debugger pop up with the specified debugging address.
Available on: All machines.
Registers at call:
AH = 03h
DS:SI -> the password or a null byte
ES -> new value for register SE
DI -> new value for register OF

Restrictions: MDEBUG must be installed.
Return Registers:
AX = return code
   FFFFh call not allowed
   FFFEh password is invalid
   FFFDh display mode is invalid
   else successful

Conflicts: See chapter 1.
See Also: Function 04h

INTERRUPT 60h - Function 04h
POP UP

Purpose: Request that the debugger pop up with the current debugging address.
Available on: All machines.
Registers at call:
AH = 04h
DS:SI -> password or a null byte

Restrictions: MDEBUG must be installed.
Return Registers:
AX = return code
   FFFFh call not allowed
   FFFEh password is invalid
   FFFDh display mode is invalid
   else successful

Conflicts: See chapter 1.
See Also: Function 03h

INTERRUPT 60h - Function 05h
GET AND SET MDEBUG FLAGS

Purpose: Determine the current values of the popup enable and INT 08h flags, then adjust the popup enable flag.
Available on: All machines.
Registers at call:
AH = 05h
DS:SI -> password or a null byte
BL = new value for the MDEBUG semaphore
   00h enable popup of MDEBUG
   else disable popup of MDEBUG

Restrictions: MDEBUG must be installed.
Return Registers:
AX = return code
   FFFEh password is invalid
   FFFDh display mode is invalid
   else successful
      BL = old value of the MDEBUG
         semaphore
      BH = old value of the INT 08h
         semaphore (this semaphore is
         always reset after this function)

Conflicts: See chapter 1.

INTERRUPT 60h - Function 06h
GET PASSWORD STATUS

Purpose: Determine whether a password is being used.

Available on: All machines.

Registers at call:

AH = 06h

Restrictions: MDEBUG must be installed.

Return Registers:

AL = status

    00h password inactive

    01h password active

Conflicts: See chapter 1.

Microsoft Word

INTERRUPT 16h - Function 55h, Subfunction 00h
internal - MICROSOFT WORD COOPERATION WITH TSR

Purpose: Called by MS Word to determine whether it should install its own INT 09h and INT 16h handlers.

Available on: All machines.

Registers at call:

AX = 5500h

Restrictions: none.

Return Registers:

AX = 4D53h if keyboard TSR present

Details: During startup, Microsoft Word tries to communicate with any TSRs that are present using this call. If the return is not 4D53h, Word installs its own INT 09h and INT 16h handlers; otherwise it assumes that the TSR will handle the keyboard.

Conflicts: None known.

Minix

Minix is an AT&T Unix Version 7-compatible operating system by Andrew Tanenbaum which includes complete source code.

INTERRUPT 20h
Minix - SEND/RECEIVE MESSAGE

Purpose: Request services of the Minix kernel.

Available on: All machines.

Registers at call:

AX = process ID of other process

BX -> message:

CX = 1 send

    2 receive

    3 send&receive

Restrictions: Minix operating system must be installed.

Return Registers:

various

Details: The message contains the system call number (numbered as in V7 Unix(tm)) and the call parameters.

Conflicts: DOS Terminate Program (chapter 8).

NDOS

Symantec has licensed 4DOS version 3.03 for inclusion with the Norton Utilities. The API is identical to that for 4DOS (see above) with the following exceptions:

    1. INT 2Fh calls use AH=E4h rather than AH=D4h.

    2. The installation check returns AX=44EEh rather than AX=44DDh.

    3. The character device for KEYSTACK.SYS is called NDOSSTAK rather than 4DOSSTAK.

Norton Utilities

The Norton Utilities (now owned by Symantec) are a series of programs for data recovery, hard disk management, batch file enhancement, etc. A number of the programs in the package are TSRs, and use the multiplex interrupt for communication.

INTERRUPT 2Fh - Function FEh, Subfunction 00h
INSTALLATION CHECK/STATUS REPORT

Purpose: Determine whether specific Norton Utilities 5.0 TSRs are installed, and whether they are enabled.

Available on: All machines.

Restrictions: none.

Registers at call:
AX = FE00h
DI = 4E55h ("NU")
SI = TSR identifier
    4346h ("CF") NCACHE-F
    4353h ("CS") NCACHE-S
    4443h ("DC") DISKREET
    444Dh ("DM") DISKMON
    4653h ("FS") FILESAVE

Return Registers:
SI = TSR reply (lowercase version of SI on entry)
AH = state
    00h installed but internally disabled
    01h installed and enabled
AL = status
    00h NCACHE or DISKREET installed
    01h FILESAVE installed
    45h DISKMON installed
BX = length of *.INI file (DISKMON and FILESAVE only)
CX = segment of resident portion
DL = *unknown* (FILESAVE only)
DX = *unknown* (DISKMON only)

Conflicts: See chapter 1.

OPTHELP.COM

OPTHELP is an optionally-resident help system for SLR Systems's OPTASM assembler.

INTERRUPT 6Ah
OPTHELP.COM

Purpose: Communicate with the resident OPTHELP program.

Available on: All machines.

Registers at call: *unknown.*

Restrictions: OPTHELP must be installed.

Return Registers: *unknown.*

Details: OPTHELP may be configured to use any interrupt from 60h to 7Fh (the default is 6Ah).

Conflicts: DECnet DOS Local Area Transport Program (chapter 24).

PC Magazine PCSpool

PC Magazine's PCSpool is a print spooler which can store captured printer output either in RAM or on disk. It can control up to three printers at once, and allows control of the print queue.

INTERRUPT 17h - Function C0h
GET CONTROL BLOCK ADDRESS

Purpose: Determine the current status of the specified by retrieving the printer's control block.

Available on: All machines.

Registers at call:
AH = C0h
DX = printer port (0-3)

Restrictions: PC Magazine PCSpool must be installed.

Return Registers:
ES:BX -> control block (Table 36-15)

Conflicts: None known.

See Also: Function C1h

Table 36-15. Format of PCSpool Control Block:

Offset	Size	Description
00h	WORD	printer number
02h	WORD	address of printer status port
04h	WORD	number of first record in queue
06h	WORD	number of last record in queue

Table 36-15. Format of PCSpool Control Block (continued)

Offset	Size	Description
08h	DWORD	characters already printed
0Ch	DWORD	number of characters remaining
10h	DWORD	pointer to dequeue buffer
14h	DWORD	previous count of characters printed
18h	DWORD	number of clock ticks taken to print them
1Ch	WORD	offset of next character to output
1Eh	WORD	offset of next character to print
20h	WORD	pointer to spooling queue record
22h	BYTE	current spooling status
23h	BYTE	current printer status:
		00h OK
		01h not ready
		02h paused with message
		03h paused
		04h initializing
		FEh non-existent port
		FFh not spooled
24h	BYTE	current control record type
25h	WORD	observed printer speed
27h	WORD	characters to print per service
29h	BYTE	01h if disk write needed
2Ah	BYTE	01h if queued data should be flushed
2Bh	BYTE	01h to update cps status

INTERRUPT 17h - Function C1h
BUILD PAUSE CONTROL RECORD

Purpose: Insert a pause record into the specified printer's queue.

Available on: All machines.

Registers at call:

AH = C1h

DX = printer port (0-3)

DS:SI -> ASCIIZ string to save for display

Details: This call flushes any pending writes.

Conflicts: None known.

See Also: Functions C0h and C2h

Restrictions: PC Magazine PCSpool must be installed.

Return Registers: n/a

INTERRUPT 17h - Function C2h
FLUSH PENDING WRITES

Purpose: Force all buffered data to be written to the queue or sent to the printer.

Available on: All machines.

Registers at call:

AH = C2h

DX = printer port (0-3)

Conflicts: None known.

See Also: Function C3h

Restrictions: PC Magazine PCSpool must be installed.

Return Registers: n/a

INTERRUPT 17h - Function C3h
CANCEL PRINTER QUEUE (DISCARD ALL QUEUED OUTPUT)

Purpose: Discard all pending output for the specified printer.

Available on: All machines.

Registers at call:

AH = C3h

DX = printer port (0-3)

Restrictions: PC Magazine PCSpool must be installed.

Return Registers: n/a

Conflicts: None known.
See Also: Functions C2h and C7h

INTERRUPT 17h - Function C4h
QUERY SPOOLER ACTIVE (INSTALLATION CHECK)

Purpose: Determine whether the spooler is present.
Available on: All machines.
Registers at call:
AH = C4h

Restrictions: none.
Return Registers:
DI = B0BFh
SI = spooler segment

Conflicts: None known.

INTERRUPT 17h - Function C5h
JOB SKIP PRINTER QUEUE

Purpose: Discard one or more print jobs.
Available on: All machines.
Registers at call:
AH = C5h
DX = printer port (0-3)
Details: This call cancels all print jobs up to the pause record.
Conflicts: None known.

Restrictions: PC Magazine PCSpool must be installed.
Return Registers: n/a

INTERRUPT 17h - Function C6h
CHECK PRINTER QUEUE STATUS

Purpose: Determine whether the printer is currently busy.
Available on: All machines.
Registers at call:
AH = C6h
DX = printer port (0-3)
Conflicts: None known.

Restrictions: PC Magazine PCSpool must be installed.
Return Registers:
AX = 0 printer not active or at pause
   = 1 printer busy

INTERRUPT 17h - Function C7h
CLOSE QUEUE

Purpose: Close the disk file containing the printer queue.
Available on: All machines.
Registers at call:
AH = C7h
DX = printer port (0-3)
Conflicts: None known.
See Also: Function C3h

Restrictions: PC Magazine PCSpool must be installed.
Return Registers: n/a

PC Magazine PUSHDIR.COM

PC Magazine's PUSHDIR.COM and POPDIR.COM provide the ability to remember the current directory and return to it at a later time, with up to six levels of nesting. The first time it is run, PUSHDIR becomes resident, providing the storage for the current directories for that and all subsequent invocations.

INTERRUPT 16h - Function 77h, Subfunction 88h
PUSHDIR INSTALLATION CHECK

Purpose: Determine whether PUSHDIR.COM is installed.
Available on: All machines.
Registers at call:
AX = 7788h

Restrictions: none.
Return Registers:
AX = 7789h

BX = 7789h
DS:SI -> signature string
    "PUSHDIR VERSION 1.0"

BX = 7788h
SI destroyed

Conflicts: WATCH.COM, PcAnywhere III (chapter 28).

PC-IPC

PC-IPC is a shareware TSR by Donnelly Software Engineering which allows communication between independent programs.

INTERRUPT 60h
PC-IPC API

Purpose: Communicate with PC-IPC.
Available on: All machines.
Registers at call:
STACK: DWORD   pointer to parameter block
                           (Table 36-16)

Restrictions: PC-IPC must be installed.
Return Registers:
STACK: unchanged

Details: INT 60h is the default, but any interrupt vector may be used by specifying the vector on the commandline.
Conflicts: See chapter 1.

Table 36-16. Format of PC-IPC Parameter Block:

Offset	Size	Description
00h	WORD	caller's ID
02h	WORD	to ID
04h	WORD	command code (Table 36-17)
06h	WORD	returned status
		bit 0: unused
		bit 1: IPC enabled
		bit 2: IPC installed
		bit 3: error
		bit 4: message(s) available
08h	WORD	returned error code (Table 36-18)
0Ah	WORD	size of data
0Ch	DWORD	pointer to data buffer

Table 36-17. Values of PC-IPC command codes:

Value	Mnemonic	Command Action
01h	"IPC_CMND_INQUIRE"	inquire current status: Set status field, writes WORD to data buffer containing free message space in bytes, and sets the "size" field to the number of messages waiting.
02h	"IPC_CMND_ENABLE"	reenable PC-IPC: Ignored unless called with the same ID that disabled PC-IPC.
03h	"IPC_CMND_DISABLE"	disable PC-IPC
04h	"IPC_CMND_INSTALL"	reset PC-IPC
06h	"IPC_CMND_RDATA"	read data: Returns first message in data buffer, sets "size" to message length and "to ID" field to sender's ID. If no messages available, bit 4 of status is cleared and "size" is set to zero.
07h	"IPC_CMND_SDATA"	send data
08h	"IPC_CMND_REQID"	require user ID: Create a new recognized ID and return in "caller's ID" field.
09h	"IPC_CMND_DELID"	cancel user ID: Delete caller's ID from pool of recognized IDs.
0Ah	"IPC_CMND_RDATAW"	read data, wait if no messages available
0Bh	"IPC_CMND_VERS"	get PC-IPC version: String representing version returned in data buffer, "size" field set to length of string.

Table 36-18. Values for PC-IPC error codes:

Value	Meaning	Value	Meaning
00h	no error	06h	invalid destination process ID
01h	invalid command or parameter	07h	invalid sending process ID
02h	only process 0 can install/reset IPC	08h	invalid data destination
03h	process can not install/reset IPC	09h	no more process IDs available
04h	IPC is not enabled	0Ah	can not relinquish that process ID
05h	process can not disable IPC	0Bh	message space is full
		0Ch	IPC is not installed

PC/370
PC/370 is an IBM 370 emulator by Donald S. Higgins.

INTERRUPT 2Fh - Function 7Fh, Subfunction 24h
Unknown Function

Purpose: *unknown* function called by PC/370.
Available on: All machines.

Registers at call:
AX = 7F24h
other *unknown*.
Conflicts: None known.

Restrictions: PC/370 version 4.2 or higher must be running.
Return Registers: *unknown*.

INTERRUPT 2Fh - Function 7Fh, Subfunction 24h
Unknown Function

Purpose: *unknown* function called by PC/370.
Available on: All machines.

Registers at call:
AX = 7F26h
other *unknown*.
Conflicts: None known.

Restrictions: PC/370 version 4.2 or higher must be running.
Return Registers: *unknown*.

INTERRUPT 60h
Unknown Function

Purpose: *unknown*.
Available on: All machines.

Registers at call: *unknown*.
Details: This is the default interrupt, however the documentation includes instructions for patching the system for another interrupt.
Conflicts: See chapter 1.
See Also: INT 2Fh Function 7Fh Subfunction 24h, INT DCh

Restrictions: PC/370 version 4.2 or higher must be running.
Return Registers: *unknown*.

INTERRUPT DCh
PC/370 v4.1 - API

Purpose: Control the operation of PC/370.
Available on: All machines.

Registers at call: *unknown*.
Conflicts: BASIC interpreter (chapter 1), STSC APL*PLUS/PC (chapter 31).
See Also: INT 60h

Restrictions: PC/370 version 4.1 or earlier must be running.
Return Registers: *unknown*.

Q-PRO4

INTERRUPT 80h
Unknown Function

Purpose: *unknown.*
Available on: All machines.
Registers at call: *unknown.*
Conflicts: BASIC interpreter (chapter 1), SoundBlaster SBFM driver, QPC Software PKTINT.COM (chapter 27).

Restrictions: Q-PRO4 must be installed.
Return Registers: *unknown.*

RAID

RAID (Resident AID) is a TSR utility program by Ross Neilson Wentworth that resides mostly in EMS. It provides a clock/calendar, ASCII table, memory dump, file finder, and keyboard scan code display.

INTERRUPT 2Fh - Function 90h, Subfunction 00h
INSTALLATION CHECK

Purpose: Determine whether RAID is installed.
Available on: All machines.
Registers at call:
AX = 9000h
Conflicts: None known.

Restrictions: none.
Return Registers:
AL = FFh if installed.

INTERRUPT 2Fh - Function 90h, Subfunction 01h
GET Unknown Data

Purpose: *unknown.*
Available on: All machines.
Registers at call:
AX = 9001h
Conflicts: None known.

Restrictions: RAID must be installed.
Return Registers:
DX:AX -> *unknown.*

INTERRUPT 2Fh - Function 90h, Subfunction 02h
GET RESIDENT SEGMENT

Purpose: Determine the address at which RAID was loaded into memory.
Available on: All machines.
Registers at call:
AX = 9002h
Conflicts: None known.

Restrictions: RAID must be installed.
Return Registers:
AX = segment of resident code.

INTERRUPT 2Fh - Function 90h, Subfunction 03h
UNINSTALL

Purpose: Remove RAID from memory.
Available on: All machines.
Registers at call:
AX = 9003h
unknown.
Conflicts: None known.

Restrictions: RAID must be installed.
Return Registers: *unknown.*

INTERRUPT 2Fh - Function 90h, Subfunction 04h
GET NEXT AVAILABLE MEMORY

Purpose: Determine the address of the first paragraph of memory beyond the end of RAID's resident portion.
Available on: All machines.

Restrictions: RAID must be installed.

Registers at call:
AX = 9004h

Return Registers:
AX = segment of first available memory after resident portion
CX destroyed

Conflicts: None known.

RESPLAY
RESPLAY is a freeware sound sampling/playback utility by Mark J. Cox.

INTERRUPT 2Fh - Function 82h, Subfunction 00h
SAMPLE/PLAYBACK

Purpose: Begin sampling sound or playing back previously recorded sound.

Available on: All machines.

Registers at call:
AX = 8200h
DX:DI -> start of sample space
CX:BX = length in bytes

Restrictions: RESPLAY must be installed.

Return Registers:
AX = status
    1000h successful
    2000h not initialized (see Function 82h Subfunction 10h)
    other RESPLAY not installed

Conflicts: None known.
See Also: Function 82h Subfunctions 01h and 10h

INTERRUPT 2Fh - Function 82h, Subfunction 01h
INSTALLATION CHECK

Purpose: Determine whether RESPLAY has been installed.

Available on: All machines.

Registers at call:
AX = 8201h

Conflicts: None known.
See Also: Function 82h Subfunction 02h

Restrictions: none.
Return Registers:
AX = 7746h if installed

INTERRUPT 2Fh - Function 82h, Subfunction 02h
UNINSTALL

Purpose: Remove RESPLAY from memory.

Available on: All machines.

Registers at call:
AX = 8202h

Restrictions: RESPLAY must be installed.
Return Registers:
AX = status
    1000h successful

Conflicts: None known.
See Also: Function 82h Subfunction 01h

INTERRUPT 2Fh - Function 82h, Subfunction 10h
INITIALIZE

Purpose: Specify sample rate, sound device, and whether to sample or replay.

Available on: All machines.

Registers at call:
AX = 8210h
BL = sound device
    00h printer port LPT1
    01h printer port LPT2
    02h prototype board at I/O address 0300h
    03h printer port (alternative LPT1)
    04h internal speaker

Restrictions: RESPLAY must be installed.
Return Registers:
AX = status
    1000h successful
    2000h parameter out of range
    other RESPLAY not installed

BH = sample rate in multiples of 250 Hz (14h to
   A0h)
CL = direction
   00h playback
   01h sample
Conflicts: None known.
See Also: Function 82h Subfunction 00h

Right-Hand Man

Right-Hand Man is a TSR desk-top utility by Red E Products, Inc.

INTERRUPT A4h
Right Hand Man API

Purpose: Called by desktop accessories to request services from the resident kernel.
Available on: All machines.   **Restrictions:** Right Hand Man v3.3 must be installed
          and popped up.
Registers at call: function number in AH   **Return Registers:** *unknown*.
Details: Right-Hand Man only hooks this interrupt while popped up.
Conflicts: None known.

SCROLOCK

SCROLOCK is a utility supplied with System Enhancement Associates' ARC.

INTERRUPT 10h - Function 50h
INSTALLATION CHECK

Purpose: Determine whether SCROLOCK is installed.
Available on: All machines.   **Restrictions:** none.
Registers at call: **Return Registers:**
AH = 50h   BX = 1954h if installed
                          AL = 00h if inactive, nonzero if active
Conflicts: None known.
See Also: Function 51h

INTERRUPT 10h - Function 51h
ENABLE/DISABLE

Purpose: Specify whether SCROLOCK should be active.
Available on: All machines.   **Restrictions:** SCROLOCK must be installed.
Registers at call: **Return Registers:** n/a
AH = 51h
AL = state (00h disable, nonzero enable)
Conflicts: None known.
See Also: Function 50h

SD.COM

SD.COM is a shareware sorted directory lister by John F. Stetson.

INTERRUPT 65h
SD.COM version 6.2

Purpose: Maintain a count of the number of uses.
Available on: All machines.   **Restrictions:** none.
Details: The unregistered version of SD62.COM uses the low byte of this vector to count the number of invocations, displaying a registration reminder each time after the 20th use.
Conflicts: See chapter 1.

Soft-ICE

Nu-Mega Technologies's Soft-ICE is an 80386 systems debugger which runs the debugger in protected mode, permitting recovery from otherwise fatal program crashes.

INTERRUPT 03h - Function 4647h
Soft-ICE BACK DOOR COMMANDS

Purpose: Control the Soft-ICE debugging system.
Available on: All machines.
Registers at call:
AH = 09h
SI = 4647h ('FG')
DI = 4A4Dh ('JM')
AL = function
    10h display string in Soft-ICE window
        DS:DX -> ASCIZ string to display (max
            100 bytes, 0Dh OK)
    11h execute Soft-ICE command
        DS:DX -> ASCIZ command string (max
            100 bytes, 0Dh OK)
    12h get breakpoint information

Restrictions: Soft-ICE must be installed.
Return Registers:

n/a

n/a

BH = entry number of last breakpoint set
BL = type of last breakpoint set
    00h BPM (breakpoint register types)
    01h I/O
    02h INTerrupt
    03h BPX (INT 03h-style breakpoint)
    04h reserved
    05h range
DH = entry number of last breakpoint to be triggered
DL = type of last triggered breakpoint (see above)

Conflicts: None known.

SoundBlaster SBFM Driver

INTERRUPT 80h - Function 0000h
GET VERSION

Purpose: Determine which version of the SBFM driver is installed.
Available on: All machines.

Registers at call:
BX = 0000h
Details: SBFM installs at the first free interrupt in the range 80h through BFh.
Conflicts: Q-PRO4, BASIC interpreter (chapter 1), QPC Software PKTINT.COM (chapter 27).
See Also: Function 0008h

Restrictions: SoundBlaster SBFM driver must be installed.
Return Registers: *unknown.*

INTERRUPT 80h - Function 0001h
SET MUSIC STATUS BYTE ADDRESS

Purpose: Specify the location to update whenever the music status changes.
Available on: All machines.

Registers at call:
BX = 0001h
DX:AX -> music status byte

Restrictions: SoundBlaster SBFM driver must be installed.
Return Registers: n/a

Conflicts: Q-PRO4, BASIC interpreter (chapter 1), QPC Software PKTINT.COM (chapter 27).
See Also: Functions 0000h, 0002h, and 0003h

INTERRUPT 80h - Function 0002h
SET INSTRUMENT TABLE

Purpose: Specify the instrument setup of the sound board.
Available on: All machines.

Restrictions: SoundBlaster SBFM driver must be installed.

Registers at call:
BX = 0002h
CX = number of instruments
DX:AX -> instrument table

Return Registers: n/a

Conflicts: Q-PRO4, BASIC interpreter (chapter 1), QPC Software PKTINT.COM (chapter 27).
See Also: Functions 0000h, 0001h, and 0005h

INTERRUPT 80h - Function 0003h
SET SYSTEM CLOCK RATE

Purpose: Specify the rate of the system clock, used to time sounds.
Available on: All machines.

Restrictions: SoundBlaster SBFM driver must be installed.

Registers at call:
BX = 0003h
AX = clock rate divisor (1193180 / desired
        frequency in Hertz)
   FFFFh to restore to 18.2 Hz

Return Registers: n/a

Conflicts: Q-PRO4, BASIC interpreter (chapter 1), QPC Software PKTINT.COM (chapter 27).
See Also: Functions 0000h, 0001h, and 0004h

INTERRUPT 80h - Function 0004h
SET DRIVER CLOCK RATE

Purpose: Specify the rate of the driver's clock.
Available on: All machines.

Restrictions: SoundBlaster SBFM driver must be installed.

Registers at call:
BX = 0004h
AX = driver clock rate divisor (1193180 / frequency
    in Hertz)

Return Registers: n/a

Details: The default frequency is 96 Hz.
Conflicts: Q-PRO4, BASIC interpreter (chapter 1), QPC Software PKTINT.COM (chapter 27).
See Also: Functions 0000h and 0003h

INTERRUPT 80h - Function 0005h
TRANSPOSE MUSIC

Purpose: Change the overall pitch of the music being played.
Available on: All machines.

Restrictions: SoundBlaster SBFM driver must be installed.

Registers at call:
BX = 0005h
AX = semi-tone offset

Return Registers: n/a

Conflicts: Q-PRO4, BASIC interpreter (chapter 1), QPC Software PKTINT.COM (chapter 27).
See Also: Functions 0000h, 0002h, and 0006h

INTERRUPT 80h - Function 0006h
PLAY MUSIC

Purpose: Begin playing the specified music.
Available on: All machines.

Registers at call:
BX = 0006h
DX:AX -> music block

Restrictions: SoundBlaster SBFM driver must be installed.

Return Registers:
AX = status
    0000h successful
    0001h music already active

Conflicts: Q-PRO4, BASIC interpreter (chapter 1), QPC Software PKTINT.COM (chapter 27).
See Also: Functions 0000h, 0007h, and 000Ah

INTERRUPT 80h - Function 0007h
STOP MUSIC

Purpose: Halt the currently-playing music and discard any remaining notes.
Available on: All machines.

Registers at call:
BX = 0007h

Restrictions: SoundBlaster SBFM driver must be installed.

Return Registers:
AX = status
    0000h successful
    0001h music not active

Conflicts: Q-PRO4, BASIC interpreter (chapter 1), QPC Software PKTINT.COM (chapter 27).
See Also: Functions 0000h, 0006h, and 0009h

INTERRUPT 80h - Function 0008h
RESET DRIVER

Purpose: Place the driver into a known initial state.
Available on: All machines.

Registers at call:
BX = 0008h

Restrictions: SoundBlaster SBFM driver must be installed.

Return Registers:
AX = status
    0000h successful
    0001h music is active

Conflicts: Q-PRO4, BASIC interpreter (chapter 1), QPC Software PKTINT.COM (chapter 27).
See Also: Function 0000h

INTERRUPT 80h - Function 0009h
PAUSE MUSIC

Purpose: Temporarily stop playing the current music.
Available on: All machines.

Registers at call:
BX = 0009h

Restrictions: SoundBlaster SBFM driver must be installed.

Return Registers:
AX = status
    0000h successful
    0001h no music active

Conflicts: Q-PRO4, BASIC interpreter (chapter 1), QPC Software PKTINT.COM (chapter 27).
See Also: Functions 0000h, 0007h, and 000Ah

INTERRUPT 80h - Function 000Ah
RESUME MUSIC

Purpose: Restart the music after a temporary stop.

Available on: All machines.

Registers at call:
BX = 000Ah

Restrictions: SoundBlaster SBFM driver must be installed.

Return Registers:
AX = status
  0000h successful
  0001h no music paused

Conflicts: Q-PRO4, BASIC interpreter (chapter 1), QPC Software PKTINT.COM (chapter 27).
See Also: Functions 0000h, 0006h, and 0009h

INTERRUPT 80h - Function 000Bh
SET USER-DEFINED TRAP FOR SYSTEM-EXCLUSIVE COMMANDS

Purpose: Specify the handler to be invoked on system-exclusive commands.
Available on: All machines.

Restrictions: SoundBlaster SBFM driver must be installed.

Registers at call:
BX = 000Bh
DX:AX -> trap routine

Return Registers: n/a

Conflicts: Q-PRO4, BASIC interpreter (chapter 1), QPC Software PKTINT.COM (chapter 27).
See Also: Function 0000h

SPEECH.COM
There are two different resident text-to-speech converters available under the name SPEECH.COM. The first is by Andy C. McGuire (SPEECH.COM and SAY.COM), the other is by Douglas Sisco.

INTERRUPT F1h
CONVERT TEXT STRING TO SPEECH

Purpose: Output the supplied string through the system's speaker as speech.
Available on: All machines.

Restrictions: Douglas Sisco's SPEECH.COM must be installed.

Registers at call:
DS:BX -> '$'-terminated text string

Return Registers: *unknown.*

Conflicts: McGuire's SPEECH.COM.

INTERRUPT F1h
Unknown Function

Purpose: *unknown.*
Available on: All machines.

Restrictions: Andy C. McGuire's SPEECH.COM/SAY.COM must be installed.

Registers at call: *unknown.*
Conflicts: Sisco's SPEECH.COM.

Return Registers: *unknown.*

INTERRUPT F2h
Unknown Function

Purpose: *unknown.*
Available on: All machines.

Restrictions: Andy C. McGuire's SPEECH.COM/SAY.COM must be installed.

Registers at call: *unknown.*
Conflicts: None known.

Return Registers: *unknown.*

SPEEDSCR.COM
SPEEDSCR.COM is a video speedup utility by The Software Bottling Co.

INTERRUPT 17h - Function 61h
INSTALLATION CHECK

Purpose: Determine whether SPEEDSCR.COM is present.
Available on: All machines.
Registers at call:
AH = 61h

Restrictions: none.
Return Registers:
AL = 61h
DX = CS of resident code

Conflicts: None known.

SQL Base
SQL Base is a network-oriented database engine by Gupta Technologies.

INTERRUPT 47h - Function 80h, Subfunction 00h
DATABASE ENGINE API

Purpose: Invoke the SQL Base database engine.
Available on: All machines.
Registers at call:
AX = 8000h
DS:BX -> parameter block, first word is function
    number (Table 36-19)

Restrictions: SQL Base must be installed.
Return Registers: n/a

Conflicts: None known.

Table 36-19. Values for SQL Base Function Number:

Value	Name	Meaning
01h	"SQLFINI"	initialize application's use of the database
02h	"SQLFDON"	application is done using the database
03h	"SQLFCON"	connect to a cursor/database
04h	"SQLFDIS"	disconnect from a cursor/database
05h	"SQLFCOM"	compile a SQL command
06h	"SQLFEXE"	execute a SQL command
07h	"SQLFCEX"	compile and execute a SQL command
08h	"SQLFCMT"	commit a transaction to the database
09h	"SQLFDES"	describe the items of a SELECT statement
0Ah	"SQLFGFI"	get fetch information
0Bh	"SQLFFBK"	fetch previous result row from SELECT statement
0Ch	"SQLFFET"	etch next result row from SELECT statement
0Dh	"SQLFEFB"	enable fetch backwards
0Eh	"SQLFPRS"	position in result set
0Fh	"SQLFURS"	undo result set
10h	"SQLFNBV"	get number of bind variables
11h	"SQLFBND"	bind data variables
12h	"SQLFBNN"	bind numerics
13h	"SQLFBLN"	bind long number
14h	"SQLFBLD"	bind long data variables
15h	"SQLFSRS"	start restriction set processing
16h	"SQLFRRS"	restart restriction set processing
17h	"SQLFCRS"	close restriction set
18h	"SQLFDRS"	drop restriction set
19h	"SQLFARF"	apply Roll Forward journal
1Ah	"SQLFERF"	end Roll Forward journal
1Bh	"SQLFSRF"	start Roll Forward journal

Table 36-19. Values for SQL Base Function Number (continued)

Value	Name	Meaning
1Ch	"SQLFSTO"	store a compiled SQL command
1Dh	"SQLFRET"	retrieve a compiled SQL command
1Eh	"SQLFDST"	drop a stored command
1Fh	"SQLFCTY"	get command type
20h	"SQLFEPO"	get error position
21h	"SQLFGNR"	get number of rows
22h	"SQLFNSI"	get number of select items
23h	"SQLFRBF"	get Roll Back flag
24h	"SQLFRCD"	get return code
25h	"SQLFROW"	get number of ROWs
26h	"SQLFSCN"	set cursor name
27h	"SQLFSIL" set isolation level	
28h	"SQLFSLP"set log parameters	
29h	"SQLFSSB"set select buffer	
2Ah	"SQLFSSS" set sort space	
2Bh	"SQLFRLO"	read long
2Ch	"SQLFWLO"	rite long
2Dh	"SQLFLSK"	long seek
2Eh	"SQLFGLS"	get long size
2Fh	"SQLFELO"	end long operation
30h	"SQLFRBK"	roll back a transaction from the database
31h	"SQLFERR"	error message
32h	"SQLFCPY"	copy
33h	"SQLFR01" reserved	
34h	"SQLFSYS"	system
35h	"SQLFSTA"	statistics
36h	"SQLFR02" reserved	
37h	"SQLFXAD"	extra add
38h	"SQLFXCN"	extra character to number
39h	"SQLFXDA"	extra date add
3Ah	"SQLFXDP"	extra date picture
3Bh	"SQLFXDV"	extra divide
3Ch	"SQLFXML"	extra multiply
3Dh	"SQLFXNP"	extra number picture
3Eh	"SQLFXPD"	extra picture date
3Fh	"SQLFXSB"	extra subtract
40h	"SQLFINS" install database	
41h	"SQLFDIN"	deinstall database
42h	"SQLFDIR"directory of databases	
43h	"SQLFTIO" timeout	
44h	"SQLFFQN"	get fully qualified column name
45h	"SQLFEXP"	explain execution plan
46h	"SQLFFER"	get full error
47h	"SQLFBKP"	begin online backup
48h	"SQLFRDC"	read backup data chunk
49h	"SQLFEBK"	end backup
4Ah	"SQLFRES"	begin restore from backup
4Bh	"SQLFWDC"	write backup data chunk for restore
4Ch	"SQLFRRD"	recover restored database to consistent state
4Dh	"SQLFERS"	end restore
4Eh	"SQLFNRR"	return number of result set rows
4Fh	"SQLFSTR"	start restriction mode
50h	"SQLFSPR"	stop restriction mode
51h	"SQLFCNC"	connect 2
52h	"SQLFCNR"	connect with no recovery
53h	"SQLFOMS"	set output message size
54h	"SQLFIMS"	set input message size

Table 36-19. Values for SQL Base Function Number (continued)

Value	Name	Meaning
55h	"SQLFSCP"	set cache pages
56h	"SQLFDSC"	describe items of a SELECT statement (external)
57h	"SQLFLAB"	get label info for items in SELECT statement
58h	"SQLFCBV"	clear bind variables
59h	"SQLFGET"	get database information
5Ah	"SQLFSET"	set database information
5Bh	"SQLFTEC"	translate error code

INTERRUPT 47h - Function 80h, Subfunction 01h
GET VERSION NUMBER

Purpose: Determine which version of SQL Base is installed.

Available on: All machines.

Registers at call:

AX = 8001h

Conflicts: None known.

Restrictions: SQL Base must be installed.

Return Registers: *unknown.*

Microsoft SQL Server/Sybase DBLIBRARY interface

These two products use INT 62h; no further information was available at the time of writing.

MicroHelp Stay-Res Plus

MicroHelp's Stay-Res and Stay-Res Plus are wrappers which allow an ordinary non-resident program to be converted into a TSR with minimal changes.

Programs which use Stay-Res include ThesPlus (internal program identifier "THESPLUS") and Personal Calendar (internal program identifier "CAL") by Paul Muñoz-Colman.

INTERRUPT 66h - Function FFh, Subfunction FBh
Unknown Function

Purpose: *unknown.*

Available on: All machines.

Registers at call:

AX = FFFBh

BX = FFFBh

others, if any, unknown.

Restrictions: Program built with MicroHelp Stay-Res Plus must be installed.

Return Registers: *unknown.*

Conflicts: Data General DG10 MicroECLIPSE coprocessor interface (chapter 1), The IBM Digitized Sound Package; see also chapter 1.

See Also: Function FFh Subfunction FEh

INTERRUPT 66h - Function FFh, Subfunction FEh
UNINSTALL

Purpose: Remove the program created with Stay-Res from memory.

Available on: All machines.

Registers at call:

AX = FFFEh

BX = FFFEh

Restrictions: Program built with MicroHelp Stay-Res or Stay-Res Plus must be installed.

Return Registers:

only returns if unsuccessful

Details: The installation check is for the interrupt handler to begin with the bytes FBh 9Ch or 9Ch FAh, and the program name (not case-sensitive) to appear at offset 0005h (older versions) or the offset returned by Function FFh Subfunction FFh/BX=FFF0h in the interrupt handler segment.

onflicts: Data General DG10 (Chapter 1), The IBM Digitized Sound Package; see also chapter 1.

See Also: Function FFh Subfunctions FBh and FFh

INTERRUPT 66h - Function FFh, Subfunction FFh
FIND PROGRAM NAME

Purpose: Determine the address of the program identifier within the program created using Stay-Res Plus.

Available on: All machines.

Restrictions: Program built with MicroHelp Stay-Res Plus must be installed.

Registers at call:
AX = FFFFh
BX = FFF0h

Return Registers:
DI = offset of program name in interrupt handler segment

Conflicts: Data General DG10 MicroECLIPSE coprocessor interface (chapter 1), The IBM Digitized Sound Package; see also chapter 1.

See Also: Function FFh Subfunctions FBh and FEh

SWAP Utilities

The SWAP Utilities by Innovative Data Concepts are a series of shareware programs which significantly reduce the amount of memory taken by a number of popular but large TSR programs (SideKick, Tornado Notes, Lotus Metro, PC Tools Shell and Desktop, The Norton Guides, etc.). These programs can be swapped to disk, EMS, or XMS rather than taking up main memory. In addition, the SWAP utilities allow the hotkey to be changed on all of the supported programs, even those which normally have fixed hotkeys.

Central Point Software has licenced SWAPDT.COM and SWAPSH.COM (version 1.77j) for inclusion with PC Tools version 7.0.

INTERRUPT 16h - Function 55h, Subfunction FFh
Unknown Function

Purpose: *unknown.*

Available on: All machines.

Restrictions: SWAPDT.COM or SWAPSH.COM version 1.77j must be installed.

Registers at call:
AX = 55FFh
BX >= 0004h
CX = subfunction
   0000h set *unknown* flag
   other clear *unknown* flag

Return Registers: n/a

Conflicts: None known.

SWELL (SWapping shELL)

SWELL.EXE is a shareware TSR by Peter Fitzsimmons which swaps programs to disk when they EXEC a child process with INT 21h Function 4Bh (chapter 8).

INTERRUPT 2Fh - Function CDh, Subfunction 00h
INSTALLATION CHECK

Purpose: Determine whether SWELL.EXE is installed.

Available on: All machines.

Registers at call:
AX = CD00h

Restrictions: none.

Return Registers:
AX = 00FFh installed
   BH = major version
   BL = minor version

Conflicts: Intel Image Processing Interface (chapter 30).

INTERRUPT 2Fh - Function CDh, Subfunction 01h
SUSPEND ONCE

Purpose: Specify that the next DOS EXEC function call should be ignored.

Available on: All machines.

Restrictions: SWELL.EXE must be installed.

Registers at call:
AX = CD01h
Conflicts: Intel Image Processing Interface (chapter 30).
See Also: Function CDh Subfunction 02h

Return Registers:
AX = 0000h

INTERRUPT 2Fh - Function CDh, Subfunction 02h
SUSPEND

Purpose: Specify that SWELL should not swap out programs calling the DOS EXEC function.
Available on: All machines.   **Restrictions:** SWELL.EXE must be installed.
Registers at call: **Return Registers:**
AX = CD02h   AX = 0000h
Conflicts: Intel Image Processing Interface (chapter 30).
See Also: Function CDh Subfunction 03h

INTERRUPT 2Fh - Function CDh, Subfunction 03h
ACTIVATE

Purpose: Allow SWELL to swap out programs calling the DOS EXEC function.
Available on: All machines.   **Restrictions:** SWELL.EXE must be installed.
Registers at call: **Return Registers:**
AX = CD03h   AX = 0000h
Conflicts: Intel Image Processing Interface (chapter 30).
See Also: Function CDh Subfunction 02h

INTERRUPT 2Fh - Function CDh, Subfunction 04h
TURN OFF VERBOSE MODE

Purpose: Specify that SWELL should be silent when swapping programs out of memory.
Available on: All machines.   **Restrictions:** SWELL.EXE must be installed.
Registers at call: **Return Registers:**
AX = CD04h   AX = 0000h
Conflicts: Intel Image Processing Interface (chapter 30).
See Also: Function CDh Subfunction 05h

INTERRUPT 2Fh - Function CDh, Subfunction 05h
TURN ON VERBOSE MODE

Purpose: Allow SWELL to report on the programs it swaps out of memory.
Available on: All machines.   **Restrictions:** SWELL.EXE must be installed.
Registers at call: **Return Registers:**
AX = CD05h   AX = 0000h
Conflicts: Intel Image Processing Interface (chapter 30).
See Also: Function CDh Subfunction 04h

INTERRUPT 2Fh - Function CDh, Subfunction 06h
UNINSTALL

Purpose: Remove SWELL.EXE from memory.
Available on: All machines.   **Restrictions:** SWELL.EXE must be installed.
Registers at call: **Return Registers:**
AX = CD06h   AX = 0000h uninstalled
                                                       8002h programs still swapped, not uninstalled
Conflicts: Intel Image Processing Interface (chapter 30).

INTERRUPT 2Fh - Function CDh, Subfunction 07h
GET INFO

Purpose: Determine the current settings for SWELL.

Available on: All machines.

Registers at call:

AX = CD07h

ES:BX -> 32-byte buffer for info (Table 36-20)

Restrictions: SWELL.EXE must be installed.

Return Registers:

AX = 0000h successful

    ES:BX buffer filled

    8001h buffer wrong size

Conflicts: Intel Image Processing Interface (chapter 30).

Table 36-20. Format of Info Buffer:

Offset	Size	Description
00h	WORD	20h (total size of buffer)
02h	BYTE	suspend-once mode active if nonzero
03h	BYTE	00h active, 01h suspended
04h	BYTE	00h quiet, 01h verbose
05h	BYTE	"Borland support" (allowing INT 21h Function 4Bh Subfunction 01h) on if nonzero
06h	26 BYTEs	*apparently unused*

INTERRUPT 2Fh - Function CDh, Subfunction 08h
UNUSED

Purpose: This function is not used and should not be called.

Available on: All machines.

Registers at call:

AX = CD08h

Restrictions: SWELL.EXE must be installed.

Return Registers:

AX = FFFFh (error)

Conflicts: Intel Image Processing Interface (chapter 30).

INTERRUPT 2Fh - Function CDh, Subfunction 09h
SWELL.EXE - TURN OFF "BORLAND SUPPORT"

Purpose: Disable SWELL from responding to INT 21h Function 4Bh Subfunction 01h, an undocumented DOS call used by several Borland products. This is the default state.

Available on: All machines.

Registers at call:

AX = CD09h

Restrictions: SWELL.EXE must be installed.

Return Registers:

AX = 0000h

Conflicts: Intel Image Processing Interface (chapter 30).

See Also: Function CDh Subfunction 0Ah

INTERRUPT 2Fh - Function CDh, Subfunction 0Ah
SWELL.EXE - TURN ON "BORLAND SUPPORT"

Purpose: Permit SWELL to respond to INT 21h Function 4Bh Subfunction 01h, an undocumented DOS call used by several Borland products.

Available on: All machines.

Registers at call:

AX = CD0Ah

Restrictions: SWELL.EXE must be installed.

Return Registers:

AX = 0000h

Conflicts: Intel Image Processing Interface (chapter 30).

See Also: Function CDh Subfunction 09h

SYS_PROF

SYS_PROF.EXE is the TSR portion of a system profiler from Micro Cornucopia magazine, issue #47.

INTERRUPT 60h - Function 00h
PROFILER STATUS

Purpose: Determine whether profiling is currently turned on.

Available on: All machines.

Registers at call:

AH = 00h

Restrictions: SYS_PROF.EXE must be installed.

Return Registers:

AX = 0000h   profiling is off
           otherwise profiling is on

Conflicts: See chapter 1.

See Also: Functions 01h and 02h

INTERRUPT 60h - Function 01h
TURN PROFILING OFF

Purpose: Stop recording the time spent in various interrupt calls.

Available on: All machines.

Registers at call:

AH = 01h

Conflicts: See chapter 1.

See Also: Functions 00h and 02h

Restrictions: SYS_PROF.EXE must be installed.

Return Registers: n/a

INTERRUPT 60h - Function 02h
TURN PROFILING ON

Purpose: Begin recording the number of calls to various interrupt functions and the total times spent in each.

Available on: All machines.

Registers at call:

AH = 02h

Conflicts: See chapter 1.

See Also: Functions 00h, and 01h

Restrictions: SYS_PROF.EXE must be installed.

Return Registers: n/a

INTERRUPT 60h - Function 03h
GET ADDRESS OF PROFILING TABLE

Purpose: Determine the address of the profiling results.

Available on: All machines.

Registers at call:

AH = 03h

Restrictions: SYS_PROF.EXE must be installed.

Return Registers:

ES:BX -> profiling table

Details: The format of the profiling table depends on how many functions of each interrupt are being profiled; this varies in different tweaked versions which are available.

Conflicts: See chapter 1.

See Also: Function 04h

INTERRUPT 60h - Function 04h
CLEAR PROFILING TABLE

Purpose: Reset all counts of interrupt calls and times to zero.

Available on: All machines.

Registers at call:

AH = 04h

Conflicts: See chapter 1.

See Also: Function 03h

Restrictions: SYS_PROF.EXE must be installed.

Return Registers: n/a

TAME

TAME is a shareware program by David G. Thomas which gives up CPU time to other partitions under a multitasker when the current partition's program incessantly polls the keyboard or system time.

INTERRUPT 21h - Function 2Bh, Subfunction 01h
INSTALLATION CHECK

Purpose: Determine whether TAME version 2.10 or higher is installed.

Available on: All machines.   **Restrictions:** none.

Registers at call: **Return Registers:**

AX = 2B01h   AL = 02h if installed

CX = 5441h ('TA')   ES:DX -> data area in TAME-RES (Tables 36-21

DX = 4D45h ('ME')   thru 36-23)

---v2.60---

BH = 00h skip *unknown*,

   else do *unknown*.

Conflicts: PC Tools v5.1 PC-CACHE (chapter 6), DOS 1+ Set System Date (chapter 8), DESQview (chapter 15), pcANYWHERE IV (chapter 28), ELRES v1.1.

Table 36-21. Format of TAME 2.10-2.20 Data Area:

Offset	Size	Description
00h	BYTE	data structure minor version number (01h in TAME 2.20)
01h	BYTE	data structure major version number (07h in TAME 2.20)
02h	DWORD	number of task switches
06h	DWORD	number of keyboard polls
0Ah	DWORD	number of time polls
0Eh	DWORD	number of times DESQview told program runs only in foreground
12h	DWORD	original INT 10h
16h	DWORD	original INT 14h
1Ah	DWORD	original INT 15h
1Eh	DWORD	original INT 16h
22h	DWORD	original INT 17h
26h	DWORD	original INT 21h
2Ah	DWORD	original INT 28h
2Eh	WORD	offset of TAME INT 10h handler
30h	WORD	offset of TAME INT 14h handler
32h	WORD	offset of TAME INT 15h handler
34h	WORD	offset of TAME INT 16h handler
36h	WORD	offset of TAME INT 17h handler
38h	WORD	offset of TAME INT 21h handler
3Ah	WORD	offset of TAME INT 28h handler
3Ch	WORD	X in /max:X,Y or /freq:X,Y
3Eh	WORD	Y in /max:X,Y or /freq:X,Y
40h	WORD	number of polls remaining before next task switch
42h	WORD	/KEYIDLE value
44h	BYTE	flags for interrupts already grabbed by TAME:
		bit 0: INT 10h
		1: INT 14h
		2: INT 15h
		3: INT 16h
		4: INT 17h
		5: INT 21h
		6: INT 28h
45h	BYTE	flags for interrupts which may be acted on (same bits as above)
46h	BYTE	TAME enabled (01h) or disabled (00h)
47h	BYTE	/TIMEPOLL (01h) or /NOTIMEPOLL (00h)
48h	BYTE	/NOTIMER (01h) or /TIMER (00h)
49h	BYTE	window or task number for this task

Table 36-21. Format of TAME 2.10-2.20 Data Area (continued)

Offset	Size	Description
4Ah	BYTE	multitasker type
		01h DESQview
		02h DoubleDOS
		03h TopView
		unknown.
4Bh	BYTE	type of task switching selected:
		bit 0: *DESQview*
		1: *DoubleDOS*
		2: *TopView*
		3: KeySwitch
		4: HLT instruction
4Ch	BYTE	unknown.
4Dh	BYTE	flags: bit 1: /FREQ instead of /MAX
4Eh	BYTE	/FG: value
4Fh	BYTE	task switches left until next FGONLY DESQview API call
50h	BYTE	unknown.

Table 36-22. Format of TAME 2.30 data area:

Offset	Size	Description
00h	BYTE	data structure minor version number (02h in TAME 2.30)
01h	BYTE	data structure major version number (0Ah in TAME 2.30)
02h	DWORD	number of task switches
06h	DWORD	number of keyboard polls
0Ah	DWORD	number of time polls
0Eh	DWORD	number of times DESQview told program runs only in foreground
12h	DWORD	time of last /CLEAR or TAME-RES load
16h	DWORD	time yielded
1Ah	DWORD	time spent polling
1Eh	DWORD	time spent waiting on key input with INT 16h Functions 01h,11h (chapter 3)
22h	DWORD	original INT 10h
26h	DWORD	original INT 14h
2Ah	DWORD	original INT 15h
2Eh	DWORD	original INT 16h
32h	DWORD	original INT 17h
36h	DWORD	original INT 21h
3Ah	DWORD	original INT 28h
3Eh	WORD	offset of TAME INT 10h handler
40h	WORD	offset of TAME INT 14h handler
42h	WORD	offset of TAME INT 15h handler
44h	WORD	offset of TAME INT 16h handler
46h	WORD	offset of TAME INT 17h handler
48h	WORD	offset of TAME INT 21h handler
4Ah	WORD	offset of TAME INT 28h handler
4Ch	WORD	X in /max:X,Y or /freq:X,Y
4Eh	WORD	Y in /max:X,Y or /freq:X,Y
50h	WORD	number of polls remaining before next task switch
52h	WORD	/KEYIDLE value
54h	WORD	/FG: value
56h	WORD	task switches left until next FGONLY DESQview API call
58h	WORD	multitasker version
5Ah	WORD	virtual screen segment

Table 36-22. Format of TAME 2.30 data area (continued)

Offset	Size	Description

5Ch	BYTE	flags for interrupts already grabbed by TAME:
		    bit 0: INT 10h
		      1: INT 14h
		      2: INT 15h
		      3: INT 16h
		      4: INT 17h
		      5: INT 21h
		      6: INT 28h

5Dh	BYTE	flags for interrupts which may be acted on (same bits as above)
5Eh	BYTE	window or task number for this task

5Fh	BYTE	multitasker type:
		    01h DESQview
		    02h DoubleDOS
		    03h TopView
		    04h OmniView
		    05h VM/386

60h	BYTE	type of task switching selected (bit flags):
		    bit 0: DESQview
		      1: DoubleDOS
		      2: TopView
		      3: OmniView
		      4: KeySwitch
		      5: HLT instruction

61h	BYTE	watch_DOS

62h	BYTE	bit flags:
		    bit 0: TAME enabled
		      1: /FREQ instead of /MAX (counts in 3Ch and 3Eh per tick)
		      2: /TIMEPOLL
		      3: /KEYPOLL
		      4: inhibit timer
		      5: enable status monitoring

63h	BYTE	old status
64h	WORD	signature DA34h

Table 36-23. Format of TAME 2.60 data area:

Offset	Size	Description
00h	BYTE	data structure minor version number (02h in TAME 2.60)
01h	BYTE	data structure major version number (0Bh in TAME 2.60)
02h	DWORD	number of task switches
06h	DWORD	number of keyboard polls
0Ah	DWORD	number of time polls
0Eh	DWORD	number of times DESQview told program runs only in foreground
12h	DWORD	time of last /CLEAR or TAME-RES load
16h	DWORD	time yielded
1Ah	DWORD	time spent polling
1Eh	DWORD	time spent waiting on key input with INT 16h Function 01h,11h (chapter 3)
22h	4 BYTEs	unknown.
26h	DWORD	original INT 10h
2Ah	DWORD	original INT 14h
2Eh	DWORD	original INT 15h
32h	DWORD	original INT 16h
36h	DWORD	original INT 17h
3Ah	DWORD	original INT 21h
3Eh	DWORD	original INT 28h
42h	WORD	offset of TAME INT 10h handler

Table 36-23. Format of TAME 2.60 Data Area (continued)

Offset	Size	Description
44h	WORD	offset of TAME INT 14h handler
46h	WORD	offset of TAME INT 15h handler
48h	WORD	offset of TAME INT 16h handler
4Ah	WORD	offset of TAME INT 17h handler
4Ch	WORD	offset of TAME INT 21h handler
4Eh	WORD	offset of TAME INT 28h handler
50h	WORD	X in /max:X,Y or /freq:X,Y
52h	WORD	Y in /max:X,Y or /freq:X,Y
54h	WORD	number of polls remaining before next task switch
56h	WORD	/KEYIDLE value
58h	4 BYTEs	unknown.
5Ch	WORD	X in /boost:X,Y
5Eh	WORD	Y in /boost:X,Y
60h	WORD	/FG: value
62h	WORD	task switches left until next FGONLY DESQview API call
64h	WORD	*multitasker version*
66h	WORD	virtual screen segment
68h	BYTE	flags for interrupts already grabbed by TAME:
		bit 0: INT 10h
		1: INT 14h
		2: INT 15h
		3: INT 16h
		4: INT 17h
		5: INT 21h
		6: INT 28h
69h	BYTE	flags for interrupts which may be acted on (same bits as above)
6Ah	BYTE	window or task number for this task
6Bh	BYTE	multitasker type:
		01h DESQview
		02h DoubleDOS
		03h TopView
		04h OmniView
		05h VM/386
6Ch	BYTE	type of task switching selected (bit flags):
		bit 0: DESQview
		1: DoubleDOS
		2: TopView
		3: OmniView
		4: KeySwitch
		5: HLT instruction
6Dh	BYTE	watch_DOS
6Eh	BYTE	bit flags:
		bit 0: TAME enabled
		1: /FREQ instead of /MAX (counts in 50h and 52h per tick)
		2: /TIMEPOLL
		3: /KEYPOLL
		4: inhibit timer
		5: enable status monitoring
6Fh	BYTE	old status
70h	WORD	signature DA34h

Tandy SCHOOLMATE Plus

INTERRUPT 6Bh - Function 6Bh
SCHOOLMATE API

Purpose: Communicate with the SCHOOLMATE Plus program.

Available on: Tandy systems.
Registers at call:
AH = 6Bh
AL = E0h to FFh
Conflicts: None known.

Restrictions: SCHOOLMATE Plus must be present.
Return Registers: varies

TesSeRact RAM-RESIDENT PROGRAM INTERFACE

The TesSeRact RAM-resident program interface is a standardized method for assuring compatibility between TSRs. The standard was created by a group of independent TSR developers (which included one of the authors of this volume) and is freely distributed; any TSR designer is encouraged to comply with the standard in order to maximize compatibility with other programs. The leader of the TesSeRact Development Team, Innovative Data Concepts, publishes a shareware development library which implements the standard, but use of this library is not necessary for a program to qualify as TesSeRact-compliant.

INTERRUPT 2Fh - Function 5453h, Subfunction 00h
INSTALLATION CHECK

Purpose: Determine whether the specified TesSeRact-compliant TSR is present in the system.
Available on: All machines.
Registers at call:
AX = 5453h
BX = 00h
DS:SI -> 8-char blank-padded name

Restrictions: none.
Return Registers:
AX = FFFFh installed
    CX = ID number of already-installed copy
anything else, not installed
    CX = ID number for TSR when installed

Details: Borland's THELP.COM popup help system for Turbo Pascal, Turbo C, and Turbo Assembler fully supports the TesSeRact API, as do the SWAP?? programs by Innovative Data Concepts.

AVATAR.SYS supports functions 00h and 01h (only the first three fields of the user parameter block) using the name "AVATAR " (note the two trailing blanks, which are required).
Conflicts: None known.

INTERRUPT 2Fh - Function 5453h, Subfunction 01h
GET USER PARAMETERS

Purpose: Retrieve a data block indicating which functions are supported, which hotkeys are being used, and other TSR data.
Available on: All machines.

Restrictions: TesSeRact-compliant TSR must be present in system for return to be valid; else error code will be returned.

Registers at call:
AX = 5453h
BX = 01h
CX = TSR ID number
Conflicts: None known.

Return Registers:
AX = 0000h successful
    ES:BX -> user parameter block (Table 36-24)
nonzero failed

Table 36-24. Format of TesSeRact User Parameter Block:

Offset	Size	Description
00h	8 BYTEs	blank-padded TSR name; all 8 bytes must be used
08h	WORD	TSR ID number
0Ah	DWORD	bitmap of supported functions
0Eh	BYTE	scan code of primary hotkey:
		00h = pop up when shift states match
		FFh = no popup (if shift state also FFh)
0Fh	BYTE	shift state of primary hotkey, FFh = no popup (if scan code also FFh)
10h	BYTE	number of secondary hotkeys
11h	DWORD	pointer to extra hotkeys set by func 05h

Table 36-24. Format of TesSeRact User Parameter Block (continued)

Offset	Size	Description
15h	WORD	current TSR status flags
17h	WORD	PSP segment of TSR
19h	DWORD	DTA for TSR
1Dh	WORD	default DS for TSR
1Fh	DWORD	stack at popup
23h	DWORD	stack at background invocation

INTERRUPT 2Fh - Function 5453h, Subfunction 02h
CHECK IF HOTKEY IN USE

Purpose: Determine whether another TesSeRact-compliant program is already using the indicated hotkey.

Available on: All machines.

Restrictions: TesSeRact-compliant TSR must be present in system for return to be valid; else error code will be returned.

Registers at call:
AX = 5453h
BX = 02h
CL = scan code of hot key
Conflicts: None known.

Return Registers:
AX = FFFFh hot key conflicts with another TSR
otherwise safe to use the hotkey

INTERRUPT 2Fh - Function 5453h, Subfunction 03h
REPLACE CRITICAL ERROR HANDLER

Purpose: Specify a new handler for the DOS critical error interrupt.

Available on: All machines.

Restrictions: TesSeRact-compliant TSR must be present in system for return to be valid; else error code will be returned.

Registers at call:
AX = 5453h
BX = 03h
CX = TSR ID number
DS:SI -> new routine for INT 24h
Conflicts: None known.

Return Registers:
AX = nonzero if unable to install new handler

INTERRUPT 2Fh - Function 5453h, Subfunction 04h
GET INTERNAL DATA AREA

Purpose: Determine the address of the specified TSR's internal data.

Available on: All machines.

Restrictions: TesSeRact-compliant TSR must be present in system for return to be valid; else error code will be returned.

Registers at call:
AX = 5453h
BX = 04h
CX = TSR ID number

Return Registers:
AX = 0000h
ES:BX -> TSR's internal data area
(Table 36-25)
nonzero, TSR not found

Conflicts: None known.

Table 36-25. Format of TesSeRact Internal Data Area:

Offset	Size	Description
00h	BYTE	revision level of TesSeRact library
01h	BYTE	type of popup in effect
02h	BYTE	INT 08 occurred since last invocation
03h	BYTE	INT 13 occurred since last invocation

Table 36-25. Format of TesSeRact Internal Data Area (continued)

Offset	Size	Description
04h	BYTE	active interrupts
05h	BYTE	active soft interrupts
06h	BYTE	DOS major version
07h	BYTE	how long to wait before popping up
08h	DWORD	pointer to INDOS flag
0CH	DWORD	pointer to DOS critical error flag
10h	WORD	PSP segment of interrupted program
12h	WORD	PSP segment of prog interrupted by INT 28
14h	DWORD	DTA of interrupted program
18h	DWORD	DTA of program interrupted by INT 28
1Ch	WORD	SS of interrupted program
1Eh	WORD	SP of interrupted program
20h	WORD	SS of program interrupted by INT 28
22h	WORD	SP of program interrupted by INT 28
24h	DWORD	INT 24 of interrupted program
28h	3 WORDs	DOS 3+ extended error info
2Eh	BYTE	old BREAK setting
2Fh	BYTE	old VERIFY setting
30h	BYTE	were running MS WORD 4.0 before popup
31h	BYTE	MS WORD 4.0 special popup flag
32h	BYTE	enhanced keyboard call in use
33h	BYTE	delay for MS WORD 4.0
34h	table	Interrupt vector data, repeated 11 times (for INTs 08h, 09h, 13h, 16h, 1Ch, 21h, 28h, 2Fh, 1Bh, 23h, and 24h):
	DWORD	old interrupt vector
	BYTE	interrupt number
	WORD	offset in TesSeRact code segment of new interrupt handler

INTERRUPT 2Fh - Function 5453h, Subfunction 05h
SET MULTIPLE HOT KEYS

Purpose: Request one or more secondary hotkeys.

Available on: All machines.

Restrictions: TesSeRact-compliant TSR must be present in system for return to be valid; else error code will be returned.

Registers at call:
AX = 5453h
BX = 05h
CX = TSR ID number
DL = number of additional hot keys to allocate
DS:SI -> table of hot keys
    BYTE hotkey scan code
    BYTE hotkey shift state
    BYTE flag value to pass to TSR (nonzero)

Return Registers:
AX = nonzero, unable to install hot keys

Conflicts: None known.

INTERRUPT 2Fh - Function 5453h, Subfunctions 06h-0Fh
RESERVED

Purpose: These functions are reserved for future enhancements to the standard.

Available on: All machines.

Restrictions: TesSeRact-compliant TSR must be present in system for return to be valid; else error code will be returned.

Registers at call:
AX = 5453h
BX = 06h - 0Fh
Conflicts: None known.

Return Registers: unchanged.

INTERRUPT 2Fh - Function 5453h, Subfunction 10h
ENABLE TSR

Purpose: Turn on the specified TSR which was previously installed.
Available on: All machines.

Restrictions: TesSeRact-compliant TSR must be present in system for return to be valid; else error code will be returned.

Registers at call:
AX = 5453h
BX = 10h
CX = TSR ID number
Conflicts: None known.

Return Registers:
AX = nonzero if unable to enable

INTERRUPT 2Fh - Function 5453h, Subfunction 11h
DISABLE TSR

Purpose: Temporarily turn off the specified TSR.
Available on: All machines.

Restrictions: TesSeRact-compliant TSR must be present in system for return to be valid; else error code will be returned.

Registers at call:
AX = 5453h
BX = 11h
CX = TSR ID number
Conflicts: None known.

Return Registers:
AX = nonzero if unable to disable

INTERRUPT 2Fh - Function 5453h, Subfunction 12h
UNLOAD TSR

Purpose: Attempt to remove the specified TSR from memory.
Available on: All machines.

Restrictions: TesSeRact-compliant TSR must be present in system for return to be valid; else error code will be returned.

Registers at call:
AX = 5453h
BX = 12h
CX = TSR ID number

Return Registers:
AX = nonzero if invalid TSR number

Details: If any interrupts used by the TSR have been grabbed by another TSR, the TesSeRact routines will wait until it is safe to remove the indicated TSR from memory. This may never happen, as the grabbed interrupts must be restored before a "safe" condition exists.
Conflicts: None known.

INTERRUPT 2Fh - Function 5453h, Subfunction 13h
RESTART TSR

Purpose: Attempt to restore a partially-unloaded TSR to operation.
Available on: All machines.

Restrictions: TesSeRact-compliant TSR must be present in system for return to be valid; else error code will be returned.

Registers at call:
AX = 5453h
BX = 13h

Return Registers:
AX = nonzero, unable to restart TSR

CX = TSR ID number of TSR which was unloaded
    but is still in memory
Conflicts: None known.

INTERRUPT 2Fh - Function 5453h, Subfunction 14h
GET STATUS WORD

Purpose: Determine the current values of application-dependent bit flags.

Available on: All machines.

Restrictions: TesSeRact-compliant TSR must be present in system for return to be valid; else error code will be returned.

Registers at call:
AX = 5453h
BX = 14h
CX = TSR ID number
Conflicts: None known.

Return Registers:
AX = FFFFh invalid ID number
    other, successful
    BX = bit flags

INTERRUPT 2Fh - Function 5453h, Subfunction 15h
SET STATUS WORD

Purpose: Specify a new state for application-dependent bit flags.

Available on: All machines.

Restrictions: TesSeRact-compliant TSR must be present in system for return to be valid; else error code will be returned.

Registers at call:
AX = 5453h
BX = 15h
CX = TSR ID number
DX = new bit flags
Conflicts: None known.

Return Registers:
AX = nonzero if unable to set status word

INTERRUPT 2Fh - Function 5453h, Subfunction 16h
GET INDOS STATE AT POPUP

Purpose: Determine whether the TSR was popped up while a DOS call was in progress.

Available on: All machines.

Restrictions: TesSeRact-compliant TSR must be present in system for return to be valid; else error code will be returned.

Registers at call:
AX = 5453h
BX = 16h
CX = TSR ID number
Conflicts: None known.

Return Registers:
AX = 0000h successful
    BX = value of INDOS flag

INTERRUPT 2Fh - Function 5453h, Subfunctions 17h-1Fh
RESERVED

Purpose: These functions are reserved for future enhancements to the standard.

Available on: All machines.

Restrictions: TesSeRact-compliant TSR must be present in system for return to be valid; else error code will be returned.

Registers at call:
AX = 5453h
BX = 17h - 1Fh
Conflicts: None known.

Return Registers: unchanged.

INTERRUPT 2Fh - Function 5453h, Subfunction 20h
CALL USER PROCEDURE

Purpose: Invoke the specified TSR's user function.
Available on: All machines.

Restrictions: TesSeRact-compliant TSR must be present in system for return to be valid; else error code will be returned.

Registers at call:
AX = 5453h
BX = 20h
CX = TSR ID number
ES:DI -> user-defined data
Conflicts: None known.

Return Registers:
AX = 0000h successful

INTERRUPT 2Fh - Function 5453h, Subfunction 21h
STUFF KEYBOARD BUFFER

Purpose: Request that the specified keystrokes be placed in the keyboard buffer after the TSR pops down.
Available on: All machines.

Restrictions: TesSeRact-compliant TSR must be present in system for return to be valid; else error code will be returned.

Registers at call:
AX = 5453h
BX = 21h
CX = TSR ID number
DL = speed
   00h stuff keystrokes only when buffer is empty
   01h stuff up to four keystrokes per clock tick
   02h stuff up to 15 keystrokes per clock tick
DH = scan code flag
   if zero, buffer contains alternating ASCII and
      scan codes
   if nonzero, buffer contains only ASCII codes
SI = number of keystrokes
ES:DI -> buffer of keystrokes to stuff
Conflicts: None known.

Return Registers:
AX = 0000h success
   F0F0h user aborted with ^C or ^Break
   other unable to stuff keystrokes

INTERRUPT 2Fh - Function 5453h, Subfunction 22h
TRIGGER POPUP

Purpose: Request that the specified TSR pop up if possible.
Available on: All machines.

Restrictions: TesSeRact v1.10-compliant TSR must be present in system for return to be valid; else error code will be returned.

Registers at call:
AX = 5453h
BX = 22h (v1.10)
CX = TSR ID number

Conflicts: None known.

Return Registers:
AX = 0000h success
   TSR will either pop up or beep to indicate that
      it is unable to pop up
   nonzero invalid ID number

INTERRUPT 2Fh - Function 5453h, Subfunction 23h
INVOKE TSR'S BACKGROUND FUNCTION

Purpose: Permit the specified TSR to perform actions in the background.

Available on: All machines.

Registers at call:
AX = 5453h
BX = 23h (v1.10)
CX = TSR ID number
Conflicts: None known.

Restrictions: TesSeRact v1.10-compliant TSR must be present in system for return to be valid; else error code will be returned.
Return Registers:
AX = 0000h success
    FFFFh not safe to call background function
    else invalid ID number

INTERRUPT 2Fh - Function 5453h, Subfunctions 24h-2Fh
RESERVED

Purpose: These functions are reserved for future enhancements to the standard.
Available on: All machines.

Restrictions: TesSeRact-compliant TSR must be present in system for return to be valid; else error code will be returned.

Registers at call:
AX = 5453h
BX = 24h - 2Fh
Conflicts: None known.

Return Registers: unchanged.

TRAP.COM
TRAP is an interrupt call tracer by Patrick Phillipot and Udo Chrosziel.

INTERRUPT 2Fh - Function DAh, Subfunction 55h
INSTALLATION CHECK

Purpose: Determine whether TRAP.COM has been installed.
Available on: All machines.
Registers at call:
AX = DA55h
DL = interrupt number
DH = *unknown.*

Restrictions: none.
Return Registers:
if installed
    AH = interrupt number
    AL = *unknown.*
    ES:BX -> *unknown.*

Details: A separate copy of TRAP is loaded for each interrupt to be traced; thus the interrupt number is part of the installation check.
Conflicts: None known.

TurboPower TSRs
TurboPower Software's Turbo Professional and Object Professional libraries for Turbo Pascal provide standardized methods for creating TSR programs.

INTERRUPT 16h - Function E0h, Subfunction E0h
ALTERNATE INSTALLATION CHECK

Purpose: Check for the presence of TurboPower TSRs.
Available on: All machines.
Registers at call:
AX = E0E0h

Restrictions: none.
Return Registers:
AX = 1F1Fh if installed
    DWORD 0040h:00F0h -> last data block in TSR
        list (see Function F0h Subfunction F0h)

Details: The returned TSR list provides support for communication among TSRs built with TurboPower's Turbo Professional and Object Professional libraries for Turbo Pascal.
Conflicts: None known.
See Also: Function F0h Subfunction F0h

INTERRUPT 16h - Function F0h, Subfunction F0h
INSTALLATION CHECK

Purpose: Check for the presence of TurboPower TSRs.
Available on: All machines.
Registers at call:
AX = F0F0h

Restrictions: none.
Return Registers:
AX = 0F0Fh if installed
ES:DI -> last data block (Table 36-26) in TSR list

Details: The returned TSR list provides support for communication among TSRs built with TurboPower's Turbo Professional and Object Professional libraries for Turbo Pascal.
Conflicts: Compaq 386 Set CPU Speed (chapter 4).
See Also: Function E0h Subfunction E0h

Table 36-26. Format of TurboPower TSR Data Block:

Offset	Size	Description
00h	DWORD	pointer to program tag (counted ASCII string)
04h	WORD	interface version number (0400h)
06h	DWORD	pointer to command entry point
0Ah	DWORD	pointer to previous data block (0000h:0000h if none)
0Eh	DWORD	pointer to next data block (0000h:0000h if none)

---swappable TSRs only---

12h	DWORD	pointer to swapping data
16h	DWORD	pointer to user data
		possibly additional fields

VIDCLOCK.COM
VIDCLOCK.COM is a memory-resident clock by Thomas G. Hanlin III.

INTERRUPT 2Fh - Function AAh, Subfunction 00h
INSTALLATION CHECK

Purpose: Determine whether VIDCLOCK.COM has been installed.
Available on: All machines.
Registers at call:
AX = AA00h

Restrictions: none.
Return Registers:
AL = 00h not installed
FFh installed

Conflicts: None known.

WATCH.COM
WATCH.COM is part of the "TSR" package by Kim Kokkonen (TurboPower Software), which also includes MARK and RELEASE.

INTERRUPT 16h - Function 77h, Subfunction 61h
INSTALLATION CHECK

Purpose: Determine whether WATCH.COM has been installed.
Available on: All machines.
Registers at call:
AX = 7761h ('wa')

Restrictions: none.
Return Registers:
AX = 5741h ('WA') if installed

Conflicts: PcAnywhere III (chapter 28), PC Magazine PUSHDIR.COM.

WCED
WCED is a free command-line editor and history utility by Stuart Russell.

INTERRUPT 21h - Function 0Ah, Subfunction 00h
INSTALLATION CHECK

Purpose: Determine whether WCED version 1.6 or higher has been installed.

Available on: All machines.

Registers at call:

AX = 0A00h

DS:DX -> 6-byte buffer whose first two bytes must
   be 00h

Conflicts: DOS 1+ Buffered Input (chapter 8).

See Also: CED Function FFh

Restrictions: none.

Return Registers:

buffer offset 02h-05h filled with "Wced" if installed

WHOA!.COM

WHOA!.COM is a system slow-down utility by Brad D. Crandall.

INTERRUPT 2Fh - Function 89h, Subfunction 00h
INSTALLATION CHECK

Purpose: Determine whether WHOA!.COM is installed.

Available on: All machines.

Registers at call:

AX = 8900h

Conflicts: None known.

See Also: Function 89h Subfunctions 01h and 02h

Restrictions: none.

Return Registers:

AL = 00h not installed
    FFh installed

INTERRUPT 2Fh - Function 89h, Subfunction 01h
UNINSTALL

Purpose: Attempt to remove WHOA! from memory.

Available on: All machines.

Registers at call:

AX = 8901h

Conflicts: None known.

See Also: Function 89h Subfunction 00h

Restrictions: WHOA!.COM must be installed.

Return Registers:

AL = FDh successful
    FEh error

INTERRUPT 2Fh - Function 89h, Subfunction 02h
SET DELAY COUNT

Purpose: Specify how much to slow down the system.

Available on: All machines.

Registers at call:

AX = 8902h

BX = delay count (larger values slow system down
   more)

Conflicts: None known.

See Also: Function 89h Subfunction 00h

Restrictions: WHOA!.COM must be installed.

Return Registers:

AL = FDh successful
    FEh error

WILDUNIX.COM

WILDUNIX.COM is a resident UNIX-style wildcard expander by Steve Hosgood and Terry Barnaby.

INTERRUPT 21h - Function 4Eh
INSTALLATION CHECK

Purpose: Determine whether WILDUNIX.COM is installed.

Available on: All machines.

Restrictions: none.

Registers at call:
AH = 4Eh
DS:DX = 0000h:0000h
Conflicts: DOS 2+ Find First Matching File (chapter 8).

Return Registers:
AH = 99h if installed

WORD PERFECT 5.0 Third Party Interface

INTERRUPT 1Ah - Function 36h, Subfunction 01h
WORD PERFECT 5.0 Third Party Interface - INSTALLATION CHECK

Purpose: Called by Word Perfect 5.0 at startup to determine whether a third-party product wishes to monitor Word Perfect's keyboard input.

Available on: All machines.

Registers at call:
AX = 3601h

Restrictions: none.

Return Registers:
DS:SI = routine to monitor keyboard input,
        immediately preceded by the ASCIZ string
        "WPCORP\0"

Details: Before checking for keyboard input, and after every key entered by the user, Word Perfect will call the routine whose address was provided in DS:SI, with the following parameters:

Entry:	AX = key code or 0	
	BX = WordPerfect state flag	
Exit:	AX = 0 or key code	
	BX = 0 or segment address of buffer with key codes	

See the "WordPerfect 5.0 Developer's Toolkit" for further information.

Conflicts: None known.

Bibliography

Julie Anderson, "Irresistible DOS 3.0", *PC Tech Journal*, volume 3 number 12, December 1984, p. 74-87.

Steven Armbrust and Ted Forgeron, ".OBJ Lessons", *PC Tech Journal*, volume 4 number 10, October 1985, p. 62-81.

Penn Brumm and Don Brumm, *80386: A Programming and Design Handbook* (2nd ed). TAB Books, 1989. ISBN 0-8306-3237-9.

Banyan Systems, Inc., *VINES Programmer's Interface (DOS)*. Banyan Systems, Inc. 2 June 1988.

Btrieve Reference Manual, Rev. 2.00, for Btrieve Version 5.0 and above. Novell Development Products Division, 6034 W. Courtyard Suite 220, Austin TX 78370, October 1988. Novell P/N 100-410000-410.

Byte Magazine, Volume 1 number 12 (1987 Extra Edition).

Ken W. Christopher, Jr., Barry A. Feigenbaum, and Shon O. Saliga, *Developing Applications Using DOS*, John Wiley and Sons 1990, 573pp. ISBN 0-471-52231-7.

Computer Language Magazine, March 1990 (special issue on Windows).

Ralph Davis, "Developing for NetWare", *PC Tech Journal*, volume 6 number 8, August 1988, p. 108-129.

DECnet DOS Programmer's Reference Manual, Digital Equipment Corp., AA-EB46C-TV.

Digital Communications Associates, Inc. and Intel Corporation, *DCA/Intel Communicating Applications Specification, version 1.2*, 27 September 1990. Intel Corporation, part number 301812-004 (supercedes DCA/Intel Communicating Applications Specification, Version 1.0A, September 1988).

The DPMI Committee, *DOS Protected Mode Interface (DPMI) Specification, Version 0.9*. Intel Corporation, 15 May 1990, order number 240763-001.

The DPMI Committee, *DOS Protected Mode Interface (DPMI) Specification, Version 1.0*. Intel Corporation, 12 March 1991, order number 240977-001.

Ray Duncan, *Advanced MS-DOS* (1st ed), Microsoft Press, 1986, 468pp. ISBN 0-914845-77-2.

Ray Duncan, *Advanced MS-DOS Programming: The Microsoft Guide for Assembly Language and C Programmers* (2nd ed), Microsoft Press, 1988.

Ray Duncan, "DOS Extenders Old and New: Protected-Mode Programming in DOS", *PC*, volume 10 number 4, 26 February 1991, p. 385-391.

Ray Duncan (editor), *Extending DOS*, Addison-Wesley 1990, 432pp. ISBN 0-201-55053-9.

Ray Duncan, *IBM ROM BIOS*, Microsoft Press, 1988, 126pp. ISBN 1-55615-135-7.

Ray Duncan (editor), *The MS-DOS Encyclopedia*, Microsoft Press, 1988, 1570pp. ISBN 1-55615-174-8.

Bo Ericsson, "VESA VGA BIOS Extensions", *Dr. Dobb's Journal* #163, April 1990, p. 65H-70.

Ted Forgeron, "We Interrupt This Program", *PC Tech Journal*, volume 4 number 4, April 1985, p. 42.
Tech Notebook on trapping control-break.

Susan Glinert-Cole, "A Network for All Reasons", *PC Tech Journal*, volume 3 number 12, December 1984, p. 90-106.
Discussion of the IBM PC Network, and brief looks at INT 2Ah and INT 5Ch.

Augie Hansen, "Detecting Display Systems", *PC Tech Journal*, volume 5 number 7, July 1987, p. 174-182.

J. Axorr Haugdahl, "The DOS-LAN Juncture", *PC Tech Journal*, volume 5 number 7, July 1987, p 78-90.
Includes a detailed description of file-sharing modes.

Thomas V. Hoffmann, "Graphic Enhancement", *PC Tech Journal*, volume 4 number 4, April 1985, p. 58-71.

Michael Holmes and Bob Flanders, "PCSPOOL Lets You Get Back to Work While You Print", *PC*, volume 10 number 1, 15 January 1991, p. 419-433.

Intel Corporation, 80286 and 80287 Programmer's Reference Manual. Intel Corporation 1987, order number 210498-004. ISBN 1-55512-055-5.

Intel Corporation, *i486 Microprocessor Programmer's Reference Manual.* McGraw-Hill 1990. ISBN 0-07-881674-2.

Stephen E. Jones, *General Software Project STARLITE: Architecture Specification*, 1 October 1990.

Art Krumrey, "NetWare in Control", *PC Tech Journal*, volume 4 number 11, November 1985, p. 102-119.
Briefly covers NetWare interrupt calls.

John A. Lefor and Karen Lund, "Reaching into Expanded Memory", *PC Tech Journal*, volume 5 number 5, May 1987, p. 100-124.

Pete Maclean, "1STCLASS and COURIERS Make Binary MCI Transfers Easy", *PC*, volume 8 number 19, 14 November 1989, p. 399-408.

Microsoft MS-DOS CD-ROM Extensions Function Requests, Microsoft Corporation, 28 May 1988. MSCDEX v2.00 documentation.

Microsoft MS-DOS CD-ROM Extensions Function Requests Specification, Microsoft Corporation, 29 March 1989. MSCDEX v2.10 documentation.

Microsoft MS-DOS CD-ROM Extensions Hardware-Dependent Device Driver Specification, Microsoft Corporation, 17 March 1989. Document number 000080010-100-O00-1186.

Stan Mitchell, "Building Device Drivers", *PC Tech Journal*, volume 4 number 5, May 1985, p. 76-87.

Rick Moore, "Fundamentals of FOSSIL Implementation and Use, Version 5", *Fidonet document FSC-0015*, 11 February 1988.

Rick Moore, "VFOSSIL - An OS/2-Subset Video FOSSIL Appendage, Version 1.00", *Fidonet document FSC-0021*, 23 May 1988.

Novell, Inc., *NetWare System Calls, Rev. 1.00*. Novell Development Products Division, #917, P.O.Box 9802, Austin TX 78766, April 1989. Novell P/N 100-000571-001.
supercedes Advanced NetWare 2.0 Reference, Novell, and NetWare Function Call Reference.

Novell, Inc., *NetWare System Interface Technical Overview*. Addison-Wesley 1990, 346+xvi pp. ISBN 0-201-57027-0.

Vincent E. Perriello, "Fundamentals of FOSSIL Implementation and Use, Draft Version 4", *Fidonet document FSC-0008*, 10 August 1987.

Phoenix Technologies, *System BIOS for IBM PC/XT/AT Computers and Compatibles*, Addison-Wesley, 1989, 524pp. ISBN 0-201-51806-6.

Paul Pierce, "The Dashed Cursor", *PC Tech Journal*, volume 4 number 12, December 1985, p. 47.
Discusses a bug in the EGA BIOS which turns underline cursor into dash.

Jeff Prosise, "Mouse Software: See How They Run", *PC*, volume 6 number 13, July 1987, p. 411-428.

Quarterdeck Office Systems, *DESQview API Reference Guide*, 232pp.

Que Corporation, *DOS and BIOS Functions Quick Reference*. Que Corporation, 1989, 154pp. ISBN 0-88022-426-6.

Guy Quedens and Gary Webb, "Switching Modes", *PC Tech Journal*, volume 4 number 8, August 1985, p. 163-173.
Switching the 286 into and out of protected mode.

Glen F. Roberts, "Finding Disk Parameters", *PC Tech Journal,* volume 4 number 5, May 1986, p. 112-150.

Robin Rodabaugh, "Accelerating 2.1", *PC Tech Journal*, volume 5 number 4, April 1986, p. 43.
Reducing floppy head-settling time for faster throughput.

Leo J. Scanlon, "An Alarm for the AT", *PC Tech Journal*, volume 5 number 4, April 1986, p. 179-182.
Introduces the real-time clock's alarm and INT 4Ah.

Andrew Schulman, Raymond J. Michels, Jim Kyle, Tim Paterson, David Maxey, and Ralf Brown, *Undocumented DOS: A Programmer's Guide to Reserved MS-DOS Functions and Data Structures*. Addison-Wesley, 1990, 694+xviii pp. ISBN 0-201-57064-5.

W. David Schwaderer, "Exploiting NetBIOS", *Programmer's Journal*, volume 8.1, January/February 1990, p. 39-45.

W. David Schwaderer, *C Programmer's Guide to NetBIOS*. Howard Sams 1988. ISBN 0-672-22638-3.

Paul Somerson, "DOS Lives", *PC*, volume 6 number 13, July 1987, p. 175-188. Overview of DOS 3.3.

Robert B. Stam, "Environmental Excavations", *PC Tech Journal*, volume 4 number 2, February 1985, p. 90-98.
Getting at the DOS environment from Turbo Pascal.

George Adam Stanislav, "AVATAR: Advanced Video Attribute Terminal Assembler and Recreator", *Fidonet document FSC-0025*, 23 August 1988.
Describes AVATAR level 0 codes as used in the Opus BBS software.

George Adam Stanislav, "AVATAR: Advanced Video Attribute Terminal Assembler and Recreator", *Fidonet document FSC-0037*, 1 May 1989 (revised 25 November 1989).
Describes the additional codes made available in AVATAR level 0+.

Michael Triner, "The High Road to Host Connectivity", *PC Tech Journal*, volume 7 number 1, January 1989, p. 85-94.

Video Electronics Standards Association, *Super VGA BIOS Extension*, Standard #VS900602, 2 June 1990.

Virtual Control Program Interface, Version 1.0. Phar Lap Software, 12 June 1989.

Richard Wilton, "DOS Marches On", *PC Tech Journal*, volume 7 number 1, January 1989, p. 99-108.
Description of new DOS 4.0 features.

Additional References

Many of the reference materials from which information in the interrupt list were extracted have been lost in the mists of time, or were never indicated by contributors in the first place. The following is a list of the materials for which we have only partial references.

10-Net Reference Manual v2.0.
Advanced Program-to-Program Communication for the IBM Personal Computer, Programming Guide (2nd ed), December 1986.
Carbon Copy Plus user's manual.
Compaq DeskPro 386 Technical Reference Guide .
Dr. Dobbs' Journal, May 1986 (BIOS Window Ext.).
ET4000 Graphics Controller Data Book, Tseng Labs.
Everex Viewpoint Owner's Manual and Reference Guide, version 1.0, Everex Corp.
Hercules GraphX manual, edition 2.1, August 1986.
IBM 3270 Workstation Program Version 1.10, Programming Guide, December 1987.
Inset Systems, *Inset Extended Specification*, 23 November 1988.
Intel Image Processing Interface Specification, Version 1.0, 1989.
LAN-Magazine, issue #1.
LANtastic (tm) Network Operating System Technical Reference Manual .
LANtastic (tm) Network Operating System Technical Reference Manual, version 3.0, 13 June 1990.
MS-DOS Extensions Quick Reference, *Ray Duncan Microsoft Systems Journal*, September 1987.
Microsoft Windows 3.0 Device Driver Kit.
Novell Network Driver Interface Specification 2.01, 18 May 1990
Networking Software, ed. Colin B. Ungaro, McGraw Hill, p265.
PC Mouse Reference Manual v4.00.
PC/TCP Packet Driver Specification, version 1.09.
FTP Software Professional Development Series Bulletins, v2n5, June 1990.
Video Seven VGA Technical Reference Manual.
pcANYWHERE v2.10 User's Guide .

Index